Legal B2

Internet Law and Regulation

AUSTRALIA
Law Book Co.
Sydney

CANADA and USA
Carswell
Toronto

HONG KONG
Sweet & Maxwell Asia

NEW ZEALAND
Brookers
Wellington

SINGAPORE and MALAYSIA
Sweet & Maxwell Asia
Singapore and Kuala Lumpur

Internet Law and Regulation

www.internetlawbook.com

FOURTH EDITION

by

Graham J H Smith

Partner, Bird & Bird

with UK contributors from Bird & Bird

Ruth Boardman, Partner

Lorna Brazell, Partner

Richard Eccles, Partner

Peter Fisher, Consultant

Graeme Maguire, Partner

Hilary Pearson, Consultant

Simon Phillips, Partner

Felicity Reeve, Partner

Trystan Tether, Partner

Sweet & Maxwell
London

First edition 1996
Second edition 1997
Third edition 2002
Fourth edition 2007

Published by
Sweet & Maxwell
100 Avenue Road
London NW3 3PF
(**http://www.sweetandmaxwell.co.uk**)

Typeset by YHT Ltd, London
Printed in Great Britain by William Clowes Ltd, Beccles, Suffolk

No natural forests were destroyed to make this product: only farmed timber was
used and replanted

A CIP catalogue record for this book is available from the British Library

ISBN 978-0-421-909908

Non-UK Contributors

Australia
Corrs Chambers Westgarth
Melbourne

Stephen Stern
Matthew Swinn
Nicholas Blackmore

Belgium
Bird & Bird
Bruxelles

Rosane Stas de Richelle
Serge Flecijn

Canada
Cameron MacKendrick LLP
Toronto

Donald M Cameron

China
Bird & Bird
Hong Kong

Claire Robley

Finland
Roschier Holmberg
Helsinki

Rainer Hilli

France
Bird & Bird
Paris

Stéphane Lemarchand
Stéphane Leriche

Germany
Bird & Bird
München

Alexander Duisberg

and Ingo Gehring (formerly of
Bird & Bird)

Frankfurt

Henning Krieg

Hong Kong
Bird & Bird
Hong Kong

Claire Robley

and Edward Alder, barrister

Israel
Eitan Mehulal Law Group
Herzlia

Sally Gillis
Yael Rozenman

v

Italy
Bird & Bird
Milano

Maria Francesca Quattrone

Japan
The Chambers of Mr Ikuo
  Takahashi
Fukushima

Ikuo Takahashi

The Netherlands
Bird & Bird
Den Haag

Wouter Pors

New Zealand
M G F Webb
Auckland

Malcolm Webb
Ken Ginn

Singapore
Rodyk & Davidson
Singapore

Gilbert Leong
Lee Ai Ming

Spain
Bird & Bird
Madrid

Manuel Lobato
Beatriz Diaz de Escauriaza

Sweden
Bird & Bird
Stockholm

Jim Runsten
Henrik Nilsson

Switzerland
Dr. Widmer & Partners
Berne

Dr. Ursula Widmer
Konrad Bähler

USA
Brown Rudnick Berlack Israels LLP
New York City

Dov H Scherzer

Preface to the Fourth Edition

Over a decade has passed since April 1996, when the first edition of *Internet Law and Regulation* appeared. During that period on-line business has boomed and crashed, then bounced back with renewed vigour. Today attention is centred on internet video, user-generated content and social networking. While the hyperbole surrounding Web 2.0 may be reminiscent of the dotcom era, this time the consumer on-line business is for real. Internet shopping in the UK alone has now reached a cumulative total of £100 billion since April 1995.[1]

Despite some pruning of historic material, this fourth edition is nearly 50% longer than the last edition. Some of this increase is due to new subject matter and broader geographic coverage. The bulk of the growth, however, reflects the increasing output of legislators and judges in their efforts to come to grips with the internet.

Notwithstanding the industry of these lawmakers, many of the problems that lawyers have grappled with since the early days remain unanswered or poorly analysed. Foremost amongst these is cross-border liability, a field in which there is precious little consensus about what policy goals the legal rules should embody, let alone how the law should be crafted to achieve them. These issues are discussed in Chapters 6 and 12.

While extensive updating for this edition has been necessary in most fields, copyright deserves special mention. This area has seen significant judicial activity, albeit mainly outside the UK. Examples include the US Supreme Court decision in *Grokster* and the Australian *Cooper* and *Sharman* decisions. There have also been important legislative changes, such as the implementation of the Copyright in the Information Society Directive.

Chapter 8 has required a very substantial rewrite with the enactment of the Communications Act 2003 and the introduction of a new European electronic communications regime. We have also taken the opportunity to

---

[1] Interactive Media in Retail Group, Press Release May 18, 2007. The IMRG suggests that the first secure on-line purchase in the UK was a book purchased in April 1995 from W.H. Smith's CompuServe on-line bookstore, which was at the time a dial-up rather than an internet service. Internet shopping rapidly overtook proprietary dial-up services.

add China, Italy and Spain to the countries with specific coverage of domain name and cross-border issues in Chapters 3 and 6.

The last few years have seen many more cases in which judges have had to grapple with the details of internet technologies. Some decisions that, regardless of the merits of the legal outcome, stand out for quality of technical exposition are: for pop-up advertisements, the US decisions in *Wells Fargo & Co v WhenU.com, Inc*[2] and *1-800 Contacts, Inc. v WhenU.com, Inc.*[3]; for hyperlinks, the German Federal Court decision in *Paperboy*[4] and the first instance Australian decision in *Universal v Cooper*[5]; and for search engines, the US first instance decision in *Perfect 10 v Google, Inc.*[6].

As with previous editions, I will attempt as far possible to attribute the authorship of each section of the book, taking due account of previous authors' surviving contributions. For this edition the authorship is as follows:

Chapter 1	Graham Smith
Chapter 2	Updated for this edition by Hilary Pearson (Patents) and Graham Smith; previously also Morag Macdonald
Chapter 3	UK section updated for this edition by Graham Smith; previously also Morag Macdonald; and non-UK contributors
Chapter 4	Graham Smith
Chapter 5	Graham Smith
Chapter 6	Graham Smith and non-UK contributors
Chapter 7	Updated for this edition by Ruth Boardman with the assistance of Elizabeth Brownsdon; previously Simon Chalton
Chapter 8	Substantially rewritten for this edition by Graeme Maguire; previously Graham Defries and (for the third edition) Sally Trebble
Chapter 9	Updated for this edition by Graham Smith; previously Rory Graham
Chapter 10	Updated for this edition by Simon Phillips (assisted by Ian Williamson) and Graham Smith; previously also Rory Graham
Chapter 11	Trystan Tether, with the assistance of Andrew Hallgarth
Chapter 12	Cross-border content, Computer misuse: Graham Smith Gambling: updated for this edition by Felicity Reeve and Paul O'Dowd; previously Graham Smith and Hilary Pearson Pornography, Contempt, Advertising: updated for this edition by Graham Smith; previously also Hilary Pearson

---

[2] 293 F. Supp. 2d 734 (E.D. Mich. 2003).

[3] 2005 US App. Lexis 12711 (2d Cir. 2005); and first instance decision at 309 F. Supp. 2d 467 (S.D.N.Y. 2003).

[4] *Verlagsgruppe Handelsblatt GmbH v Paperboy Bundesgerichtshof*, No. I ZR 259/00, July 17, 2003 [2005] E.C.D.R. 7.

[5] *Universal Music Australia Pty Ltd v Cooper* [2005] FCA 9.

[6] U.S.D.C. C.D. Cal. February 17, 2006.

Financial services: Trystan Tether and Charles Proctor
Encryption: Lorna Brazell
Pharmaceuticals: Jane Mutimear

Chapter 13   Substantially rewritten for this edition by Peter Fisher, assisted by Caroline Brown with the help of Sarah Timms; previously Richard Ward

Chapter 14   Updated for this edition by Richard Eccles, assisted by Louise Baner and Karen Nightingale; previously Simon Topping

The domestic law is that of England and Wales. The law is stated as at December 1, 2006, although it has been possible to incorporate some more recent developments.

Thanks are due to the States of Guernsey for permission to adapt, as part of Chapter 10, extracts from a report prepared by Bird & Bird in connection with their electronic transactions legislation.

At Bird & Bird I particularly thank Cecilia Cheung for assistance in tracking down and checking references and Rachel Fetches for proof-reading and liaising with contributors. At Sweet & Maxwell thanks go to Julian Chase for nurturing this latest edition though its long gestation and to Alison Harley for checking numerous web references. Any errors, however, remain attributable to the authors.

We have taken the opportunity in this edition to review the book's format and layout. Some changes have ensued, including altering the paper size and moving from chapter endnotes to page footnotes. We have endeavoured to retain the clarity of the layout and to improve the readability of the text.

From time to time updates to accommodate significant developments will be available on a dedicated website at *www.internetlawbook.com*.

Graham J H Smith
Hammersmith
May 2007

Preface to the First Edition

In 1973 an enterprising American publisher released a book entitled *Essential Government Economic Controls, Regulations and Guidelines*, consisting entirely of blank pages. The reader's first reaction to a book on Internet Law and Regulation might be that the content would be equally insubstantial. However, the suggestion that the Internet has no law is born of wishful thinking more than of cogitation. Local laws of each jurisdiction do apply to activities conducted using the Internet. While enforcing such laws presents new challenges, the pan-political nature of the Internet may in fact render it vulnerable rather than immune to the laws of jurisdictions around the world.

The purpose of this book is to draw together the most relevant law and legislation in England and Wales and analyse how it applies to activities carried on by means of the Internet. This exercise is unavoidably selective. We have tried to include issues that have arisen in practice, have caused concern or should be giving pause for thought. Although some international aspects are discussed, the focus is primarily English law. We have not set out to write a textbook of comparative law.

The Internet and the uses to which it is put change by the day. The law is stated as at 31 December 1995, although it has been possible to take account of some more recent developments. Until case law develops, the task of applying the law to the Internet is to some extent speculative. We hope that readers will bear that in mind when using the book.

The individual authorship of the chapters is as follows: Graham J H Smith: 'What is the Internet?', 'Defamation' and 'Content Liability and Protection'; Rory Graham: 'Contracts between Hosts, Content Providers and Others' and 'Making Contracts over the Internet'; Hilary Pearson: 'Intellectual Property' (co-author) and 'Prohibited and Regulated Activities'; Morag Macdonald: 'Intellectual Property' (co-author); Simon Chalton: 'Data Protection'; David Kerr and Graham Defries: 'Telecommunications and Broadcast Regulation'; Trystan Tether: 'Payment Mechanisms over the Internet'; and Richard Ward: 'Tax'.

The seeds of this book were sown during a series of seminars given by some of the authors during the summer of 1995. Out of those seminars grew the idea of a book. To convert the idea into text was a daunting prospect, and thanks are due to all those who made it happen: to my fellow authors who produced their contributions with only light touches of the whip (administered in part by Jane Gunter); to those who assisted with some of the chapters, Mark O'Conor, Gaynor Clements, Ravinder Chahil, Nicholas Perry and Dominic Cook; and to John Lambert, who reviewed a draft of Chapter 1 for technical accuracy. Joanna Hicks of FT Law & Tax fostered the idea and remained enthusiastic and firm in equal measure. Any errors remain those of the authors.

It is sometimes suggested that the Internet should be regulated. I hope this book shows that the Internet does not exist in a legal vacuum. Unless and until the existing law is found wanting there should be a presumption against further legislation. As to the form of any legislation that may be required, let there be a presumption against regulation of a discretionary nature, in favour of known, certain laws capable of general application.

Graham J.H. Smith
Hammersmith
February 1996

Contents

Table of Cases

Table of Statutes

Table of Statutory Instruments

Table of European Legislation and International Conventions

Table of Foreign Legislation

CHAPTER 1

Overview of the Internet

1.1 THE INTERNET: WHAT IS IT?

A search of UK primary legislation in January 2007 reveals that although **1–001** 12 current statutes[1] now contain the word "internet", none attempts to define it. The internet is undoubtedly easier to describe than it is to define. A full description has to encompass the internet's physical parts, its functions and the players who create and use it.

Physically, the internet is a collection of packet computer networks (see Figure 1.1 below). The core of the internet was originally a set of high capacity backbone networks in the USA. Over the years many thousands of other networks around the world have linked into the internet, so that today it is virtually impossible to identify its physical boundaries.[2] A "network of networks" conveys an impression of the internet, but is inadequate of itself to describe the internet.

A technical definition of the internet would focus not on physical devices, but on the suite of internet network transmission and addressing protocols that glues them together. These protocols allow the networks and the computers attached to them to communicate and (using a common address system) to find other computers attached to the internet. The collection of protocols is known as TCP/IP,[3] after the two most important protocols in the suite: TCP (Transmission Control Protocol) and IP (Internet Protocol).

---

[1] The Adoption and Children Act 2002, the Copyright, Designs and Patents Act 1988, the Gambling Act 2005, the Government of Wales Act 2006, the Horserace Betting and Olympic Lottery Act 2004, the Legal Deposit Libraries Act 2003, the London Olympic Games and Paralympic Games Act 2006, the Northern Ireland Act 1998, the Scotland Act 1998, the Terrorism Act 2006 (section heading only), the Tobacco Advertising and Promotion Act 2002 and the Violent Crime Reduction Act 2006 (section heading only). Secondary legislation contains many more references to "internet". The word "website" (or "web site") also appears with increasing frequency.

[2] For a collection of visualisations of the structure of the internet, see *www.cybergeography.org* (especially the topology and geography sections).

[3] For a simplified diagram showing how the various components of TCP/IP relate to each other, see *http://csrc.nist.gov/publications/nistpubs/800–10/node15.html*.

The most characteristic, omnipresent, indicator of the internet is the IP address. This is the unique 32 bit[4] number (e.g. 194.72.244.100) permanently or temporarily allocated to every device on the internet. IP addressing alone, however, is not enough to distinguish the internet. The internet is a public network. IP addresses are used on both public and private networks, certain ranges of addresses being reserved for private use. Private internet networks are often known as intranets. These are internal company networks which make use of internet protocols and internet-compliant software such as web browsers. Intranets are hidden from the public internet by a protective firewall, configured so that the intranet cannot (or should not) be accessed from outside. An extranet is semi-public, available only to selected outsiders such as suppliers and customers.

Links to the internet can now be made from personal organisers, telephones, pagers, set-top boxes, television sets and other devices beyond the bounds of the traditional business and personal computer markets. The internet now can really be described only in terms of the features that bind its components together—common software protocols and addressing systems—and its public accessibility.

For many on-line legal issues, an understanding of the technical aspects of the internet is necessary in order to conduct an adequate legal analysis. How, for instance, can one decide whether someone using the internet has infringed the copyright reproduction right without knowing what copies are created, in which devices and by whom? It is dangerous, however, to frame policies or legislation around detailed technical features, which are liable to be superseded more rapidly than law can be made and unmade. Legislators may indeed be wise to avoid attempting a definition of the internet.

1–002   From the point of view of the domestic end-user the feature of the internet, now taken for granted, that differentiates it from its predecessors is the ability, during one telephone connection to a local internet access provider, to browse around the world from one internet site to another using one piece of internet-compliant software. The precursors of the internet—bulletin boards and on-line services—often required dedicated user software; and the user had to terminate the telephone connection and redial to access a new service.

---

[4] The 32 bit form consisting of four 8 bit blocks (in decimal xxx.xxx.xxx.xxx, where $0 \leq$ xxx ≤ 255) is used by IPv4, the current version of the Internet Protocol. IPv4 addresses are running short and are predicted to become scarce in about 2008. They will be superseded by IPv6 addresses, which have a 128 bit form consisting of eight hexadecimal 16 bit blocks with colon separators. An example of an IPv6 address would be 3ffe:ffff:0100:-f101:0210:a4ff:fee3:9566. See *www.ipv6.org* for further information.

Figure 1.1 The Internet—a typical arrangement

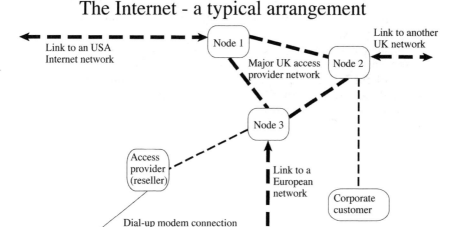

For many years dial-up connections were the norm on the internet for home users. The user dialed into the telephone network and paid a per-minute charge for the telephone call in addition to the flatrate monthly fee to the internet service provider. The connection was low bandwidth and the user would, for cost reasons, only connect to the internet for limited periods. For as long as the typical home user still accessed the internet via a modem and a copper wire connection, the ability to provide high-bandwidth content such as graphics, audio and (especially) video remained limited.

1–003

Dial-up is now rapidly giving way to broadband, "always-on" connections, typically provided over an ADSL-enabled telephone line which squeezes compressed data down existing copper wire. Cable television and video on demand companies are also offering broadband internet connections. Third generation (3G) mobile telephone networks, providing broadband mobile data connectivity, have come on stream. The advent of home wireless networking (Wi-Fi) with reasonable bandwidth has now opened up the prospect of streaming sound and video around the home. Wide area wireless networking such as WiMAX is starting to make an impact.

In the 1990s there was much talk of something variously described as the information superhighway, the Global Information Infrastructure or the infobahn. It was, however, a purely political vision of a broadband future. It never did exist. In its place we now have the reality of broadband internet. So far the main feature that distinguishes broadband internet from dial-up is the vastly increased capacity in the last link to the home, bringing with it the ability to sustain continuous high quality data streams such as voice, audio and video.

However, a more fundamental change is under way. Traditional telephone trunk networks are now being converted to IP backbones. BT's 21CN project is an example. These backbones will carry voice, data (including television-quality video) and internet services over a single internet-based network.

While an underlying collection of networks makes up the internet, various applications designed to work with internet protocols provide facilities to users of the internet. The most significant applications are the World Wide Web, electronic mail, file downloading (using file transfer protocol (ftp)), Usenet newsgroups, instant messaging, streaming audio and video, and voice telephony (Voice over IP, or VoIP).

1–004   Internet email is the oldest application of the internet. The internet form of email address is now universal. On the internet, mail is addressed using the form "joebloggs@yourco.com", where "joebloggs" is the name of the individual and "yourco.com" is the domain name of the host at which Joe Bloggs has his internet account. The host (a computer accessible from the internet which stores data) might be a commercial internet access provider, or the company or institution for which Joe Bloggs works. The domain name is the plain language address of a computer or network on the internet.

Ftp is the application protocol used to download a software program or other file from an internet site to the user's own computer. Ftp is normally invoked automatically when a user selects a file to download from, say, a website to his computer.

1–005   Usenet newsgroups are public discussion forums, to which users can post "articles" (i.e. public messages) and contribute to a continuing thread of messages on a particular topic. Newsgroups are organised into thousands of separate subject areas, ranging from the serious and the frivolous to the dubious.

The World Wide Web, which uses the HTTP application protocol, is the system of joining documents to each other across the internet by hypertext links devised by Tim Berners-Lee at CERN. The Web, on which the rapid growth of the internet since 1994 has been built, is described in more detail in section 1.2.2 below.

Internet Relay Chat (IRC) and more recent proprietary real time messaging technologies allow participants to converse in real time on their screens, the conversation scrolling up the screen as the discussion continues. This is a much more ephemeral medium than newsgroups, where users can read and reply to posted messages days or weeks later.

1.2 THE INTERNET: WHO'S WHO AND WHAT DO THEY DO?

1–006   As important as understanding the technicalities of the internet is to analyse correctly the roles of internet actors. The technical framework of the internet both constrains and enables the activities of a whole cast of players to which it has given rise.

A player on the internet often performs more than one role. When determining the legal consequences of activities on the internet, it is important to identify which roles the person is performing. For instance, what is generically known as an internet service provider may perform some or all of the roles of network provider, host and access provider. It is necessary to look behind the outward description of the player, identify each of its actual roles and apply the relevant law to that activity.

1.2.1 Infrastructure and network providers

The core infrastructure of the internet consists largely of routers or switches   1–007
(computers designed to receive and forward packets of data), hosts (which store programs and data) and pipes (telecommunications connections which link the hosts and routers together). Hosts, routers and switches are owned by various government and private organisations whose computers are fully connected into the internet. Many of the pipes tend to be owned by telecommunications companies, who typically either provide internet-compliant routing and switching facilities themselves or lease capacity to network providers who add those facilities to create sections of the internet. The telecommunications companies are of great importance to the internet and are intimately involved in it. Many telecommunications companies have expanded from infrastructure into network and internet service provision.

Network providers have both physical links to and contractual relations   1–008
with other networks and their providers. The physical connection (which may be a bilateral link to the other network, or at a special purpose multilateral traffic exchange centre such as MAE-East in Washington DC, or LINX in London) enables traffic to flow direct from one network to the next. The contractual arrangement (often known as a "peering agreement") governs the exchange of traffic between the networks. Considerable problems were originally posed by Appropriate Use Policies, whereby certain networks (typically government-funded ones) prohibited commercial traffic. These problems are now a thing of the distant past as the internet infrastructure has become privately funded.

The pricing aspects of peering arrangements are noteworthy. The internet   1–009
model has been mutual exchange or a flat-rate charge for connection to a network, irrespective of the amount of traffic passed across the connection. This model extends to the typical flat rate end-user charge. Concerns have been expressed that if access providers were asked to pay for their connections on a per-packet basis, they would have to abandon the flat rate for the end-user. In any event, access providers are increasingly adopting differing charging structures in order to differentiate themselves. Concerns have also been expressed at suggestions that the international settlements system applicable to traditional voice telecommunications traffic might be applied to internet traffic in place of a free market.

If there is no direct physical connection and peering agreement in place between two networks, the traffic has to find another route. Messages use the internet protocols to route around gaps or blockages. So a user in London accessing a site down the road could find that the message is routed via America.

1–010 This can happen if the user's internet access provider is, say, a US company with an international network but no peering arrangement with another English network. The user connects to an English node of the access provider's network, but the network's gateway to the rest of the internet is in the US. The message has to go from the user to the London node, across the access provider's network to America, transfer to another internet-compliant US network, travel back across the Atlantic to another English network and thence to the target English site.

The route, however, is unpredictable. So not only is responsibility for ensuring safe delivery of a message diffused among various networks, but the identity of those networks cannot necessarily be predicted in advance. This poses obvious problems if the sender wishes to have one person take legal responsibility for end-to-end delivery of the message. This has led some global corporations or alliances to build international networks offering, at a premium price, end-to-end transport of internet traffic within their networks.

1–011 The capacity, or "bandwidth", of the pipes which carry internet traffic affects the amount of data which can be carried and the speed at which it is delivered to the user. The backbones of the internet are typically high bandwidth. Academic institutions are often connected directly into high bandwidth elements of the internet such as JANET (the UK academic network). A commercial user may have a higher capacity leased line, ISDN (Integrated Services Digital Network) or other high capacity connection. Home users, who have until quite recently had low bandwidth dial-up connections, are increasingly switching over to always-on broadband connections.

1.2.2 Content providers

1–012 Content providers are among the most important people on the internet. They range from multinational companies to individuals. The internet may have approximated more closely than anything to Marshall McLuhan's adage that the medium is the message but, even on the internet, content is king.

Content comes in many forms. It divides generally into real-time and downloadable content. Real-time content is that which can be viewed or heard as the user accesses it, either delivered in batches or by maintaining a continuous stream of data. A page of text or graphics on the World Wide Web is, in a sense, an example of real-time content. It appears on screen as the data, sent in batches, reaches the PC from the internet site. However, real-time content is more usually taken to mean streaming voice, audio and video.

6

Downloadable content takes the form of a file which can be copied from the internet site to the user's own computer. The user, once off-line from the internet, uses his own applications to read, view or play the file. The internet protocol ftp is typically used to download files from the internet. Content can range from simple text files, graphics and video to computer programs, updates and patches. Content may be free or paid for.

Many developments in internet applications have aimed at expanding the range of real-time applications and overcoming constraints imposed by lack of bandwidth. Real-time applications also tend to make greater demands on internet capacity generally, because of the need to maintain a more or less continuous flow of data across the networks. None of this is a problem with downloadable content, which can be transmitted in bursts with no effect other than on the speed of download.   1–013

Audio (speech and music), video, animation, video-conferencing and voice telephony are examples of real-time applications in which great progress has been made. The paucity of bandwidth in the last connection to the home was until recently a real hindrance to such applications, especially to streaming video. The advent of broadband to the home has brought with it a revolution in available content, illustrated by the offering from BT (nominally a telephone company) of IPTV (television over IP), launched in December 2006.

The internet application that made content accessible and interesting to the average user is the World Wide Web. The web is a hypertext internet application which allows the user, during the course of one telephone connection and using familiar graphical software interfaces, to point click and jump across the internet, leaping from one website to the next. Before the web, reading and downloading files from the internet required expert ability with arcane software.   1–014

The web creates a mesh of software links between documents. Clicking on a hypertext link in a web document can take the user to another part of the same document, to another document on the same computer, or to a document on another computer on the other side of the world. This is made possible by the IP address scheme of the internet (which enables each computer to be uniquely identified) and the HTTP (HyperText Transmission Protocol), HTML (HyperText Mark-up Language) and other protocols and document formats which underlie the web. By means of these a unique Uniform Resource Locator (URL) is created for each document on the web.

Creating a link is simply a matter of coding selected text in the document so that it points at the target URL. The user sees the text as highlighted and clicking on it takes the user to the document represented by the target URL. A link may be created to the home page of the target site, or to a page or file within it (a practice known as deep-linking which, while extremely common, has sometimes led to litigation—see Ch. 2).

Frames added further sophistication to the web. A site using frames can be designed so that when the user clicks on a link to an external site, he sees the contents of the external site within a border generated by the original site. So frames provide an opportunity to encase someone else's site in advertising generated by the linking site. This use of frames is occasionally controversial and has led to litigation in the US (see Ch. 2).

The web achieved a Holy Grail of computing: the ability to use a web browser to browse not just through one document, but a world-wide collection of documents. More recent developments (known as the "semantic web") involve devising a common syntax not just for the look of documents on the web, but for the meaning of their content. Innovations have also taken place in the area of collaborative computing, such as the Wikipedia project (a collaborative set of documents) and the SETI@home project (collaborative use via the web of distributed processing resources).

1–015 The growth in commercial activity on the internet is built around the web. Any self-respecting company has a website. While many of these are essentially still promotional, an ever-increasing number of sites offer electronic commerce facilities. In the retail (business to consumer "B2C") sector these typically use payment by credit card or dedicated payment systems such as PayPal. Sites offering digital products (information, music, software etc), physical goods (PCs, DVDs, CDs, books, cars etc) and services (travel, holidays, tickets etc) abound on the net. Almost anything can be found on auction sites such as eBay.

In the wake of the dot-com boom and bust at the turn of the century, a few "pure-play" B2C internet companies survived to face a challenging future. At the time of writing retail on-line spending is on the increase and for the first time appears to be threatening high street sales. This time, it seems, the on-line boom is for real.

1–016 The legal consequences of the web can be subtle. Boundaries of ownership and responsibility are blurred. The traditional paper document or book exists as a self-contained unit, easily distinguishable from the next one on the shelf. The web takes the covers off the books and stitches the pages together. So new boundary markers have to be put in place if the user is not to be confused about whose document he is looking at. Strong branding of sites, entry pages, exit pages and ownership notices are common on the web.

Questions also arise as to whether linking to other sites can generate legal liabilities in respect of content on the target site, such as for defamation or copyright infringement. These questions have to be considered separately in the context of each right and liability.

Lawyers also need to appreciate that the site proprietor has limited control over the appearance of the website to the user. Browsers may interpret the HTML tags in numerous different ways, so that for instance point sizes of text may differ. These may also be affected by, for instance, the screen resolution at which the user is accessing the site. At the extreme, the user may not "see" the text at all. Some software translates the text of a website into audio, for the benefit of blind users. All these issues can assume especial importance where laws or regulations require matters to be brought to the notice of the user in a particular way, or specify the appearance of forms which the user has to complete.

1.2.3 Hosts

A host is a digital storage place accessible via the internet. The type of data 1–017
stored on the host can vary from computer programs to text documents to
graphics, audio or video or any other kind of data. Classically a host stored
the actual content. However, in peer-to-peer (P2P) arrangements the content is distributed among individual users' own computers. P2P search or
tracking sites host not the content itself, but only files that enable users to
download and upload content among themselves.

The way in which the files are stored can also vary, the internet protocol
used to store them dictating the software needed to access it, such as ftp or
the World Wide Web. A host may also act as a storage place for Usenet
newsgroups, or for holding internet email in subscribers' mailboxes. Hosts
are often also referred to as servers, thus mail server or news server.

The owner of a host has a spectrum of possible relationships to the data
stored on the host. It may own and actively control all of the data, as in the
case of a company that self-hosts an ftp resource. At the other end of the
range the host owner may have only the most tenuous connection with the
stored content. A Usenet news server is a good example. Usenet is a system
of thousands of discussion groups on a huge variety of topics, to which
anyone can post a public message. The Usenet host receives automatic
updating newsgroup feeds from other Usenet hosts. It receives postings
direct from its own subscribers, sending out its own updates to other Usenet
hosts.

The Usenet host in practice has only two main potential areas of control: 1–018
selecting the newsgroups for which it takes feeds and monitoring postings
from its own subscribers. The other main choice it has is over how long to
retain postings on the server. Some servers "scroll off" postings after a few
days. Until the advent of domain name disputes (see Ch. 3) and then peer-
to-peer filesharing (see Ch. 2) Usenet discussion groups and traditional
proprietary on-line discussion groups gave rise to more litigation activity,
mostly concerned with defamation, than any other area of the internet.

Between the ends of the spectrum are numerous variations. A host may
store its own material or material held on behalf of other parties, for free or
for reward as a commercial service. The material may be ephemeral or it
may be permanent. The host owner may be actively involved in the process
of placing the material on the host, for instance if it provides web design
and HTML coding services; or it may do nothing more than provide a
storage area, bandwidth and a URL, taking no part in the selection and
design of the materials.

The host may promote itself as a desirable area to visit such as an
interactive shopping mall, an on-line magazine, a social networking site, or
some other form of umbrella site with a unifying identity; or promotion
may be left entirely up to individual content providers, so that each collection of resources on the host appears to the world at large entirely
separate and unconnected with any other.

The legal responsibilities of the host will vary according to the exact 1–019 nature of the role that it has assumed. It has, to date, been impossible to generalise about those responsibilities. They have had to be analysed separately for each type of right and liability, in the light of the actual role that the host owner plays. Liability for defamation has had its own set of rules, liability for copyright infringement another set, trade mark infringement another and so on. The determining factors for one species of liability do not necessarily map on to another species.

However, this is starting to change. In 2002 the EU Electronic Commerce Directive created, at least for damages and criminal offences, uniform liability thresholds for hosts and conduits (i.e. network and access providers) across a wide range of liabilities.

One specialised variety of host plays an important role in the functioning of the internet: the domain name server. The domain name is the plain language address of an entity on the internet. The domain name has the form "yourinc.com", "yourltd.co.uk", "youruni.ac.uk", etc. Computers accessing the internet have to have a way of finding which computer corresponds to which domain name. So there is a distributed system of domain name servers, or simply name servers, which hold frequently updated databases of domain names. There are many thousands of name servers, ultimately taking their cue from "source of authority" name servers which hold, or can identify, authoritative lists of domain names. Domain names are allocated by a variety of organisations.

1–020　　As well as the list of domain names, a name server holds the IP addresses that correspond to the domain names. So when a computer is asked to access "yourco.com", it looks up the domain name in its local name server, finds out the IP address and uses that to send its query out over the internet.

IP addresses are understood by routers and switches, the computer waystations around the internet that receive and forward messages. Each router contains routing tables which store the locations of the networks connected to the internet and thus enable the router to know where to send the message. For instance, if a router receives a message and discerns from the destination IP address that the destination network is directly connected to the router's local network, it will send the message to that network. If there is no direct connection it will forward the message on to a network closer to the destination network. Routers may contain instructions to bar traffic to or from particular networks, or to carry only traffic received from certain networks.

Inclusion on databases of domain names and on routing tables is vital to maintaining a presence on the internet. These addressing systems are of particular interest to those seeking to enforce intellectual property rights, who may want to explore ways of trying to isolate or close down a pirate site. National authorities bent on compelling access providers to block access to objectionable sites also take a keen interest in internet addressing systems.

1.2.4 Administrators

The glue that holds the internet together, and ultimately the only feature   1–021
common to all its disparate parts, is the set of internet protocols. These
evolved and developed over time under the guidance of various bodies
associated with the Internet Society, who promulgated internet protocols
and guided other aspects of internet evolution. The effectiveness of these
protocols depended on the accepted legitimacy of these bodies, and the
people associated with them, within the internet community.

In new and fast-developing fields such as the World Wide Web the
committee method of promulgating protocols came under strain as software vendors, especially in the "browser wars" between Netscape and
Microsoft, adopted extensions to existing standards before they were promulgated. The increasing pace of commercialisation of the internet has
continued to cause *de facto* standards to evolve continuously out of competitive activity, in tandem with the standards activities of bodies such as
the World Wide Web Consortium (W3C).

Until late 1998 or early 1999 one influential body, IANA (the Internet   1–022
Assigned Numbers Authority, largely synonymous with the late Dr Jon
Postel) performed two especially important co-ordinating functions. These
related to identifying computers connected to the internet and giving them
unique names and addresses. The domain name system and IP address
system, for the co-ordination of which IANA was mainly responsible until
the transition to ICANN (the Internet Corporation for Assigned Names and
Numbers), are described in Ch. 3. These systems are both crucial to the
operation of the internet.

There have been concerns that in the foreseeable future the internet will
run out of domain names and numerical addresses. New domain spaces
started to be introduced in 2001. A new version of IP addressing (IPv6)
which provides many more IP addresses and more facilities than the current
IPv4 is available though not yet widely used.

The actual allocation of blocks of IP addresses to individual organisations
is carried out by the American Registry for Internet Numbers (ARIN) for
North America, African Network Information Centre (AFRINIC) for
Africa, Regional Latin-American and Caribbean IP Address Registry
(LACNIC) for South America and some of the Caribbean, Réseaux IP
Européens Network Coordination Centre (RIPE) for Europe, the Middle
East and Central Asia and by Asia-Pacific Network Information Center
(APNIC) for the Asia Pacific region.

1.2.5 Access providers

The first access providers were academic institutions and government   1–023
bodies, with high capacity internet-compliant links to other such bodies.
They provided internet access to staff, faculty and students who had access
to the institution's own network.

The typical access provider is now a commercial organisation selling internet access to home and commercial users. Commercial access providers are commonly known as internet service providers, or ISPs. ISPs range from large organisations (sometimes telephone companies) with their own geographically dispersed networks, local broadband connection points and dial-up numbers (POPs, or Points of Presence) around the country and numerous connections to other internet-compliant networks, to small providers with a single connection into someone else's network. These small providers are often in effect local re-sellers of capacity on a large ISP's network.

1-024   ISPs have traditionally provided a variety of services, ranging from a cheap dial-up account suitable for the home user, to broadband home services using ADSL, to a permanent leased-line connection aimed at commercial use. The typical narrowband dial-up account-holder will pay a fixed monthly access fee and will pay the local call charges on top. The leased-line account-holder has no usage-based charges at all, as the leased line provides capacity at a fixed rental. Leased lines are expensive, so are attractive only to high-volume users such as businesses. However, broadband home services now offer a flat fee rate affordable by home users. Other variations such as ISDN connections are also possible.

Internet connections are also provided by others such as cable companies and video on demand operators. In their role as ISPs they provide internet access and may also provide hosting services.

ISPs often provide additional services, such as website hosting and design. This is an example of someone on the internet playing more than one role. The access provider role is to provide facilities to communicate with the internet. The access provider who stores web pages for its customers, or maintains a collection of Usenet newsgroups, is adding the role of host to that of access provider.

Similarly, an access provider generally maintains its own domain name server (DNS). This is, in theory, not a necessary part of providing internet access, as a customer can configure its internet client software to access a domain name server elsewhere if the access provider does not maintain its own DNS. In practice, an access provider will provide client software to its customer, pre-set to use the access provider's domain name servers.

The multi-role internet service provider

Access provider ReadyNet Ltd is an internet service provider. As an access provider (or conduit), it leases a telecommunications link from a network provider. This connects to a larger backbone provider, which in turn has a transatlantic link to the US internet and links to other European networks. ReadyNet offers a service whereby for a flat monthly fee, users can dial-up its computers, access the internet and send and receive email. It also provides broadband ADSL services.

Software distributor ReadyNet provides software for its users to install on their PCs to enable them to connect to the service, browse the web and send and receive email.

Host ReadyNet provides free web space for its dial-up and home broadband customers and offers to design, host and maintain websites for its business customers. It also stores email sent and received by its customers. It acts as a domain name system server for its customers and hosts a selection of Usenet newgroups. It also hosts discussion forums on its own website.

Cache ReadyNet eases the load on its bandwidth by storing on its own servers temporary copies of frequently accessed pages from third party websites. User requests are diverted to those pages instead of being routed across further telecommunications links to the third party website.

Content Provider ReadyNet has created its own content-rich website for its users, offering news, opinions and many other content items. Most of these are bought in from third parties.

The Californian case of *Religious Technology Center v Netcom On-line* **1–025**
Communication Services Inc[5] provides a good example of the differing roles often performed by internet service providers. In the judgment Netcom is introduced as a large internet access provider. But the question of its liability for alleged copyright infringement in fact turned around a detailed analysis of its role not as a provider of internet access, but as a Usenet host. This case is discussed in more detail in Ch. 2.

Although the terms internet service provider and ISP are in universal usage, they are potentially confusing because they do not distinguish between the underlying roles of access provider, host and others. In this book we will, therefore, where appropriate, eschew the use of "internet service provider" and "ISP" in favour of the terminology introduced in this chapter. Where those terms are used, the reader should be alert to understand which role or roles are under discussion.

---

[5] November 21, 1995, ND Cal.

1.2.6 Navigation providers

1–026 A common complaint about the internet is that the content is distinguished by quantity rather than quality; or if there is quality content out there, there is no easy way either of finding it or of knowing the quality of what you have found when you get there.

Navigation providers, close relations of content providers and hosts, act as signposts to quality information. They may take many forms. Umbrella sites such as on-line shopping malls are effectively navigation providers, attracting customers to their collection of selected retailers who pay for space on the mall. So are content aggregators and customisers. These range from relatively conventional on-line newspapers, to the now common sites which allow the user to select categories of news or other content, or which watch the user's reading habits and display selected content based on that. Such sites may produce some of their own content, but are more likely to have done deals with content providers enabling them to select from a pool of quality-assured information.

1–027 Currently, some of the most important navigation providers are search engines and directories. These catalogue resources across the internet, so that the user can either perform a keyword search for relevant sites, or consult a structured directory for sites of interest. Many of these have become "portals", designed to be the user's permanent gateway to the web.

As navigation providers compete and gain reputations for effective sifting of wheat from chaff, so they have become some of the strongest brands on the internet. As such they can command higher prices for third party advertising and sponsorship on their sites. Search engines and directories are probably the best known sites on the internet at present, and among the most successful in attracting advertising-related revenue. Content sifted by navigation providers may be stored on hosts owned and operated by someone else. Thus navigation providers will tend to be at the centre of some of the more complex sets of contractual relationships to be found on the internet.

1.2.7 Transaction facilitators

1–028 The advent of commerce on the internet has stimulated investment in ways and means of overcoming perceived shortcomings: mainly lack of security and inability to identify with certainty with whom you are communicating. As these problems are addressed, so vendors are proposing and licensing various security and digital signature products. For financial transactions trusted intermediaries have emerged who verify identities and credit standing and process credit card transactions. As these systems develop, a role has emerged for the transaction facilitator who, whether by licensing security software or active involvement at the time of the transaction, helps reduce the transaction risk to an acceptable level.

1.3 CONVERGENCE

Whilst the internet grew up, until the mid–1990s, almost unnoticed by   **1–029**
regulatory authorities, broadband was in their sights even before it existed.
Once real-time video is contemplated, interactive networks start to
resemble and impinge upon the highly regulated mass-market of television
to the living room. That being of more interest to the regulators than the
hobbyist in the back room, the scene is set for regulatory confusion as the
two worlds collide and merge.

That confusion is epitomised by the continued unwillingness of many
policy-makers to understand that content on the internet is most akin to
personal speech, and should be subject only to the laws applicable to personal speech rather than the more restrictive content rules and discretionary
regulation historically applied to broadcast content. The European Commission's proposed revision of the Television Without Frontiers Directive,
discussed in Ch. 12, is the latest manifestation of this misconceived desire to
regulate anything in which the pictures move.

Two other worlds are also in collision: the computer industry and the   **1–030**
consumer electronics industry. The consumer electronics industry has tended to produce dumb but reliable equipment: televisions, video and DVD
recorders and so on. The computer industry produces dumb but reliable
hardware, intelligent but relatively unreliable software, and has tended to
sell it to customers who regard trying to get it all to work as a stimulating
and satisfying challenge.

Now that broadband and Wi-Fi have moved the focus of interactive
applications from the back room to the living room, the living room consumer is demanding the simplicity and reliability of consumer electronics
equipment. Already we see equipment such as Personal Video Recorders
that are in essence PCs equipped with massive hard disks and some specialised software, encased in a consumer electronics box. The distinction
between the PC and consumer electronics will continue to blur.

CHAPTER 2

Copyright, Patents and Confidential Information

2.1 INTRODUCTION

2–001 Intellectual property laws govern the subsistence and scope of property rights in the intangible fruits of human creativity and labour: writing, drama, music and art; craft, inventions and knowledge. Those products, formerly confined to physical media, can now be transformed into bits of information, stored electronically, set free and routed around networks.

The law has had to adapt to cope with this new digital form of subject matter. In this and the next chapter we address the areas of intellectual property law most relevant to the internet.

Copyright and its neighbouring rights are probably the first intellectual property rights that spring to mind, copyright being the nearest thing to a "bit right". However, patent law cannot be ignored in the increasingly technical environment of the internet. Confidential information also has to be considered. Trade marks and branding, considered in Ch.3, are a vital aspect of trading on the internet and are key to resolving disputes over domain names.

2.2 COPYRIGHT—RECENT HISTORY

2.2.1 Digitisation and dematerialisation of information

Digitisation

2–002 The digitisation of information has perhaps been the most far-reaching aspect of the computer revolution. Traditionally, most information was conveyed by graphic means, such as letters or drawings, or in analogue form, such as sound waves or electro-magnetic signals.

Computers can only operate on binary numbers, so analogue information must be reduced to such digital form if it is to be manipulated by a computer. The development of inexpensive computing power and bandwidth has made it advantageous to transform many kinds of information from analogue to digital form for transmission.

The digital CD has replaced the vinyl record and is now itself under threat from downloaded digital music. Telephone conversations are increasingly transmitted digitally. As more information is converted to bits, so previously distinct forms of transmitted content—radio, TV, telephone— become varieties of digital data, capable of being carried simultaneously over the same networks.

Increases in bandwidth have allowed the use of the internet to advance progressively from text, to graphics, to sound and music and now to video. Broadband connections have sufficient capacity that it has become feasible to download full-length movies.

There are two main advantages of digitisation: copying and transmission can take place without degradation, so that every copy is perfect; and copies can be made very quickly and cheaply. So a document can be sent via the internet to potentially millions of people for only the relatively low transmission costs. While this has obvious benefits for mankind, it also makes copyright infringement possible on a scale previously unknown.

Dematerialisation

The older aspects of copyright law based on tangible media are difficult to apply to the internet because of dematerialisation, the separation of information from a tangible substrate.

The copyright legislators have had in the past to develop copyright laws to take account of yesterday's new media: the film, broadcast television, radio and cable television industries. These were in some respects precursors to networks such as the internet. But they lacked both interactivity and the plummeting costs of electronic document creation which render every individual user of the internet potentially both a reader and a publisher.

Even newer provisions fashioned for broadcast and cable transmission, having been formulated with particular communication technologies and distribution models in mind, have had to be radically altered to take account of the internet.

Digital manipulation

Information in digital form is much more easily manipulated and adapted than traditional forms of information, and the changes are harder to detect. In the days of typewriters if the typist made a mistake it could only be corrected by painting over the incorrect characters with correcting fluid or something similar and then typing in the correct characters. As this correction was easily detected with the naked eye, the only way to produce a "clean" copy was to retype the whole page. Now, with word processing software, mistakes can be banished for ever with a few keystrokes.

Hollywood provides much more sophisticated examples of manipulation

2–003

of digital information. In an early example, the dinosaurs in *Jurassic Park* were images created in a computer and combined with film images of human actors in such a way that the viewer is unable to detect the difference. Indeed, the technology has reached such a level that even human actors can be recreated by computer. When the star was accidentally killed half way through shooting the film *The Crow*, the film was completed using images of the actor created by digital manipulation of existing footage.

More recently, *The Polar Express* was the first film made entirely by using advanced motion capture techniques to recreate its actors digitally and merge them with computer generated characters and scenery.

2–004 Digital manipulation in skilled hands can make it very difficult to detect, or to prove, infringement of the copyright in the work which has been used as the starting point.[1] Would we recognise the Mona Lisa if all the colours were altered and the face changed by "morphing" to that of the sitter as a child, albeit still with that mysterious smile? If the use of the original work is detected, the mere fact that the original has been changed does not prevent copyright infringement, as one of the rights given to the author is the right to distribute modified copies of the work.

Under-protection of digital works

Of greater concern to rights owners than digital manipulation is the practical difficulty of identifying and pursuing those who obtain and share unauthorised perfect digital copies of copyright works, in particular music and video. But problems of identification can be over-emphasised. It is, in fact, remarkably difficult to engage in activities on the internet without leaving behind some kind of digital trail. We discuss in Ch.6 methods of using that trail to identify wrongdoers.

Effective pursuit of remedies, however, is an entirely different matter. A far greater challenge to the rights owners and their existing business models is posed by the sheer scale on which the citizens of the world have thumbed their collective nose at copyright by engaging in the sharing of unlicensed music and video.

Over-protection of digital works

It should not be thought, however, that the only effect of digitisation, dematerialisation and the internet is to reduce the practical level of protection of copyright works.

Paradoxically, applying old copyright laws to the internet and other forms of electronic transmission can have the unexpected consequence of increasing the reach of copyright, compared with its application to physical works, resulting in concerns about over-protection.

Two ways in which applying traditional copyright laws to the internet

---

[1] Digital manipulation is not necessarily impossible to detect. See, for an early discussion of techniques for detecting manipulation, "When Is Seeing Believing?" *Scientific American*, February 1994 p.44.

can result in over-protection are through the convergence of primary and secondary infringement and by the very way in which electronic works are used in computers.

Convergence of primary and secondary infringement

The application of traditional copyright law to open public global networks such as the internet is bedevilled by the roots of copyright being in the protection of information contained in tangible media such as books.   **2–005**

Distribution of the information contained in those media required two separate, slow and costly steps: copying from one tangible medium to another, followed by physical transport of the new copy to a distant location. The acts of copying and distribution were clearly distinct and formed the basis of the division in copyright law between acts of primary infringement (such as copying), for which the defendant is strictly liable irrespective of knowledge, and acts of secondary infringement (such as distribution) for which the defendant is liable only if he is fixed with some degree of guilty knowledge.

The advent of digital technology has overturned the underlying economic assumptions of the original law. Digitisation has caused the cost of copying to fall to virtually zero. Digital communications networks such as the internet have reduced the cost of distribution to zero and the speed of distribution has become instantaneous.

What is more, the technical distinction between copying and distribution has blurred. In the attempt to apply copyright law to the age of computers, and in particular to infringement of copyright by running computer programs, the notion was formed that infringement could occur through the creation of a transient copy in the RAM (random access memory) of a computer.   **2–006**

In the UK this is reflected in s.17(2) and (6) of the Copyright, Designs and Patents Act 1988 (the "1998 Act"). However, any distribution of a copyright work over an electronic network inevitably results in the creation at least of a transient copy at the receiving end, and possibly further transient copies at points in between. Here the distinction between primary and secondary infringement starts to break down. Every act of electronic distribution is also an act of copying if a transient copy counts as infringement.

This problem has now gained some statutory recognition. The Copyright in the Information Society Directive (2001/29/EC), implemented on October 31, 2003 in the UK by the Copyright and Related Rights Regulations 2003 (SI 2003/2498), exempts from the reproduction right the making of certain transient or incidental copies for the sole purpose of transmission in a network (see discussion at para. 2–014 below).

Use of electronic works

A further consequence of characterising the making of a transient copy as a restricted act is that reading the copyright work becomes an act potentially controllable by the copyright owner. Someone who reads a book does not   **2–007** commit any restricted act. A person who reads an electronic work necessarily creates a transient copy in the course of so doing and therefore potentially falls under the control of the copyright owner.

This has been recognised to some extent in the Copyright and Related Rights Regulations 2003, which exempt from infringement certain transient or incidental copies the sole purpose of which is a lawful use of the work.[2] As discussed below (para. 2–014), however, the requirement that the use of the work be lawful leaves the control of reading an electronic work firmly in the hands of the copyright owner.

These concerns—both lack of protection and over-protection—have led to changes in copyright law[3] stimulated by the 1996 World Intellectual Property Organisation (WIPO) Treaties, which we discuss now.

2.2.2 The WIPO Treaties

2–008   It is no surprise that the challenge of seeking to apply traditional copyright laws to the internet has provoked international activity. This culminated in a diplomatic conference held under the auspices of the World Intellectual Property Organisation in December 1996, out of which came agreed texts for two treaties (on copyright and on performances and phonograms) intended to adapt copyright law to the challenges of the digital age. A third treaty on establishing a *sui generis* database right failed to achieve consensus.

2–009   Some of the main features of the treaty on copyright are:

- The establishment of a digital transmission right, described in the treaty as the exclusive right of the authors of literary and artistic works to authorise any communication to the public of their works, by wire or wireless means, including the making available to the public of their works in such a way that members of the public may access these works from a place and at a time individually chosen by them.
- Contracting Parties are at liberty to provide for limitations of, or exceptions to, rights in certain special cases that do not conflict with a normal exploitation of the work and do not unreasonably prejudice the legitimate interests of the author.
- Contracting Parties shall provide adequate legal protection and effective legal remedies against circumvention of copy-protection technology.

No consensus was reached on an article concerning whether temporary and

---

[2] Copyright, Designs and Patents Act 1988 s.28A, added by the Copyright and Related Rights Regulations 2003.

[3] In the UK these changes were introduced as from October 31, 2003 by the Copyright and Related Rights Regulations 2003 (SI 2003/2498).

incidental reproduction should be included in the reproduction right. No such article was therefore included in the treaty. After debate a substantial majority agreed the following statement to be included in the records of the conference:

> "...that it is understood that the storage of a protected work in digital form in an electronic medium constitutes a reproduction within the meaning of Article 9 of the Berne Convention."

It was recorded that the question of what constitutes storage was left open.

2.2.3 Europe—the Copyright in the Information Society Directive and its UK implementation

History

In July 1995 the European Commission published a Green Paper entitled 2–010
"Copyright and Related Rights in the Information Society". In the introduction the Commission stated that full development of the information society in Europe would require harmonisation of laws, including intellectual property, to ensure that right holders would make material available while balancing the interests of users. The "information society" is a piece of Commission jargon which has not only invaded the copyright field, but also (with the concept of "information society services") underpins the EU Electronic Commerce Directive.

The Green Paper identified certain issues key to the application of 2–011
copyright to the new technology. These were the new services, in particular the effects of digitisation and the interactive nature of such services, the new market structures and the importance of cross-border services. These raised a number of legal issues, including the identification of the "author", the applicability of the traditional concept of "originality" as a condition for protection, the concept of "first publication" when a work can be simultaneously disseminated world-wide, the concept of "fair use", and the scope of exclusive rights giving the right to prohibit exploitation of the work. The paper then went on to examine the existing law in certain key areas and to pose a series of questions relating to each of those areas.

A Communication from the European Commission in November 1996 2–012
following the consultation process on the Green Paper concluded that rights in "on-demand" services should be protected by a further harmonised right of "communication to the public".

The Commission noted that the question of "private use" exceptions to such a right was controversial, with right holders suggesting that such an exception would put new services at risk and user groups taking an opposite view. Limitations and exceptions would have to be harmonised across Europe, along the lines also proposed for further harmonisation of the reproduction right. In this case the Commission proposed widening the right holder's exclusive right of reproduction in cases where certain acts of reproduction would risk unreasonably prejudicing the right holder's interests or would conflict with normal exploitation of his intellectual property.

In some cases a licence combined with a right to remuneration might suffice, and in others closely defined fair use exceptions would be appropriate. The Commission also proposed that the harmonised right should make clear that digitisation, scanning, uploading and downloading of protected material were covered by the right, as would be transient and other ephemeral acts of reproduction.

Lastly, the distribution right should be harmonised so that only the first sale within the Community by or with the consent of the right holder exhausts the right; and exhaustion should not apply to services, including on-line services.

The Commission then published a draft "Directive on the Harmonisation of Certain Aspects of Copyright and Related Rights in the Information Society" in November 1997. After much further debate and lobbying a Parliament and Council Directive[4] was adopted on May 22, 2001. This was supposed to be implemented by Member States before December 22, 2002. Only two Member States met the deadline. In the UK it was implemented on October 31, 2003 by the Copyright and Related Rights Regulations 2003.

General

2–013　The Directive is intended to harmonise, to a degree, the reproduction right, a right of communication to the public by wire or wireless means (including on-demand services), the distribution right and legal protection of anti-copying systems and information for managing rights. It includes implementation of some aspects of the WIPO treaties of 1996.

The Directive does not, however, directly address the question of who is liable for copyright infringement in a network environment. This is largely dealt with, at least as far as the activities of on-line intermediaries are concerned, in the liability provisions of the Electronic Commerce Directive,[5] to which the Copyright Directive is stated to be without prejudice. Those provisions are discussed in Ch.5. However, in one respect the Directive is directly relevant to certain acts by users and service providers. That is the exception to the right of reproduction in Art.5(1) for temporary acts of reproduction (discussed below).

The main provisions of the Directive deal with definitions of the rights of reproduction, communication with the public and distribution, as well as

---

[4] Directive 2001/29 [2001] O.J. L167/10
[5] Directive 2001/31 [2000] O.J. L178/1.

protection of the use of technical measures to prevent unauthorised copying. These provisions and their UK implementation are discussed in detail below.[6]

We have mentioned the liability provisions of the E-Commerce Directive. The mechanism adopted in the UK for the implementation of this Directive has resulted in an undesirably complex interaction with other legislation such as the Copyright, Designs and Patents Act 1988.

The intermediary liability aspects of the Electronic Commerce Directive were implemented by regs.17–22 of the Electronic Commerce (EC Directive) Regulations 2002 (SI 2002/2013), which provisions came into force on August 21, 2002.

However, the Electronic Commerce Regulations were stated not to have prospective effect. This means that they have to be applied individually to every new and amended piece of legislation to which they are relevant. When the Copyright, Designs and Patents Act 1988 was amended by the Copyright and Related Rights Regulations 2003 it was therefore necessary to apply the Electronic Commerce Regulations to the amended version of the 1988 Act. That was done by the Electronic Commerce (EC Directive) (Extension) (No. 2) Regulations 2003 (SI 2003/2500).

Right of reproduction—temporary acts

The reproduction right provided in Art.2 of the Copyright Directive **2–014** includes permanent and temporary, direct and indirect reproductions of the whole or part of the copyright work by any means and in any form. This must be taken to include non-visible temporary copies of a work in the working memory of a computer. However, there is an exception to this right under Art.5(1). This exception covers "temporary acts of reproduction ... which are transient or incidental and an integral and essential part of a technological process and whose sole purpose is to enable: (a) a transmission in a network between third parties by an intermediary, or (b) a lawful use of a work or other subject matter to be made, and which have no independent economic significance".

Recital (33) states that to the extent that they meet these conditions, this exception should include acts which enable browsing as well as acts of caching to take place, including those which enable transmission systems to function efficiently, provided that the intermediary "does not modify the information and does not interfere with the lawful use of technology, widely recognised and used by industry, to obtain data on the use of the information". This wording echoes, but does not fully replicate, that of Art.13 of the Electronic Commerce Directive concerning caching. Recital (33)

---

[6] The Copyright and Related Rights Regulations 2003 extend to some 53 pages. While we comment on relevant aspects of the implementation at the most convenient point in the text, we do not attempt a comprehensive description. In particular, we do not address the implementation of the bulk of the Directive's optional exceptions. A full Transposition Note prepared by the Patent Office may be found at *http://web.archive.org/web/20041023054323/http://www.patent.gov.uk/copy/notices/2003/copy_direct3a.htm*.

goes on to say that a use should be considered lawful where it is authorised by the rightholder or not restricted by law.

The wording of Art.5(1) represents a compromise between providing protection for technology designed to ensure the efficient operation of networks, yet at the same time ensuring that networks do not operate as vectors for the transmission of pirated content. It is to be observed that this Article is broader than the WIPO treaties, because there was no agreement at the diplomatic conference on temporary reproductions.

The Copyright and Related Rights Regulations 2003 implement the "temporary acts of reproduction" exception provided for in Art.5(1) by inserting a new s.28A into the 1988 Act:

> "Copyright in a literary work, other than a computer program or a database, or in a dramatic, musical or artistic work, the typographical arrangement of a published edition, a sound recording or a film, is not infringed by the making of a temporary copy which is transient or incidental, which is an integral and essential part of a technological process and the sole purpose of which is to enable–
>
> (a) a transmission of the work in a network between third parties by an intermediary; or
> (b) a lawful use of the work;
>
> and which has no independent economic significance.".

2–015   Although the Directive exempts such acts only from the reproduction right, the Copyright and Related Rights Regulations 2003 purport to apply the exception to all aspects of copyright.[7]

The exclusion of computer programs and databases, while lacking in any obvious logic, necessarily follows from the fact that the Copyright Directive does not apply to these types of copyright work. This is significant, since much website content may constitute a computer program or a database.

As to computer programs, the 1988 Act does not define "computer program". But even in its simplest (HTML) form, a web page could be regarded as a computer program. An HTML page consists of text, marked up with instructions upon which the browsing computer will act to format the page on the screen, fetch components from other computers and so on in order to assemble the page at the viewer's computer. The raw HTML text is commonly known as "source code" (a term used in connection with computer programs).

More complex pages making use of Java applets (mini-programs delivered to the user's computer when the website is accessed), or with sections written in languages such as JavaScript, are effectively indistinguishable

---

[7] For the most recent judicial analysis of the extent to which implementing regulations made under the European Communities Act 1972 can validly go further than the underlying Directive, see *Oakley Inc v Animal Ltd.* [2005] EWCA Civ 1191.

from traditional program source code. As to websites as databases, see para. 2–110 below.

The exceptions for temporary copies are narrowly defined. As can be seen from s.28A quoted above, the copy must be an "integral and essential" part of a technological process and the sole purpose must be to "enable" (not merely, for example, facilitate) the permitted purpose (either network transmission or a lawful use of the work).

While the network transmission exception should be read in the light of Recital (33) of the Directive, which states that the relevant purpose is "efficient" transmission, there is no such qualification for the "lawful use of the work" exception. So a browser cache would probably not be within the exception, since its purpose is not to enable browsing but only to speed it up (a browser still works with its caching switched off).

In contrast transient copies of the work stored in the RAM of the user's computer would be within the exception, since browsing cannot function without them. To that extent, it would no longer be necessary to construct an "implied licence to browse" to legitimise the transient copies made by a user who accesses a website (see para 2–007, 2–081, 2–083, 2–097 and 2–174).

However, the exception does not significantly affect the rights of the **2–016** copyright owner since if the copyright owner withdraws permission to access a work there will be no "lawful use of the work" to which the exception can apply unless the act can be justified under another exception to copyright. This is confirmed by Recital (33) of the Directive, which as we have mentioned states that a use should be considered lawful where it is authorised by the rightholder or not restricted by law.

The transmission exception goes further in one respect than the similarly worded provisions of the conduit defence under Art.12 of the Electronic Commerce Directive. The Electronic Commerce Directive provides a defence for a defined type of online actor and leaves the status of the underlying copies untouched. The Copyright Directive, on the other hand, exempts the relevant acts from infringement for all purposes.

Injunctions against on-line intermediaries

While the transmission exception would not affect acts of infringement by **2–017** hosting, it could create a situation in which no underlying cause of action could be established in respect of a conduit, since all the conduit's relevant activities were exempted from infringement. That could render it impossible to obtain an injunction against a conduit, notwithstanding that the Electronic Commerce Directive does not prevent such injunctions. Even without the transmission exception a conduit could argue that it was at the most an involuntary copyist and so not an infringer (see paras 2–104, 2–169 below).

Article 8.3 of the Copyright Directive now requires that rights owners be able to apply for injunctions against intermediaries whose services are used by third parties to infringe rights. Recital (59) makes clear that this must be available even where the acts carried out by the intermediary are exempted under Art.5.

The Copyright and Related Rights Regulations 2003 therefore introduce a specific power to grant injunctions against service providers, irrespective of the existence or otherwise of any underlying act of infringement by the service provider. This is contained in a new s.97A of the 1988 Act:

> "(1) The High Court (in Scotland, the Court of Session) shall have power to grant an injunction against a service provider, where that service provider has actual knowledge of another person using their service to infringe copyright.
>
> (2) In determining whether a service provider has actual knowledge for the purpose of this section, a court shall take into account all matters which appear to it in the particular circumstances to be relevant and, amongst other things, shall have regard to–
>
> > (a) whether a service provider has received a notice through a means of contact made available in accordance with regulation 6(1)(c) of the Electronic Commerce (EC Directive) Regulations 2002 (SI 2002/2013); and
> > (b) the extent to which any notice includes–
> >
> > > (i) the full name and address of the sender of the notice;
> > > (ii) details of the infringement in question.
>
> (3) In this section 'service provider' has the meaning given to it by regulation 2 of the Electronic Commerce (EC Directive) Regulations 2002.".

2–018   All that is required for the power to grant an injunction to be available is actual knowledge on the part of the service provider of another person using the service to infringe copyright. It is unnecessary to prove that the service provider was itself directly or indirectly liable for infringement.

Article 8.3 of the Directive makes no mention of actual knowledge as a condition of the availability of an injunction. Recital (59) states that the "conditions and modalities" relating to such injunctions should be left to the national law of the Member States.

The notice provisions of s.97A(2) are broadly similar to those of the reg.22 of the Electronic Commerce (EC Directive) Regulations 2002 (see para 5–043 to 5–044).

Section 97A does not entitle the copyright owner to an injunction. It only vests power in the court to grant one. The circumstances in which it would be appropriate to grant an injunction against a conduit are likely to be unusual. At any event a court would be expected to approach with circumspection the prospect of granting an injunction against a conduit.

The terms of any injunction against a service provider engaged in conduit activities would raise difficult issues, since in order to comply with an injunction framed by reference to specific infringing material the service provider would have to find a means of filtering out the offending material. That raises issues of practicality and also of the extent to which the terms of such an injunction might offend against Art.15 of the Electronic Commerce Directive, which prohibits Member States from imposing on information society service providers who provide conduit, caching or hosting services a general obligation to monitor the information which they transmit or store.

It could be argued that even though the obligation under an injunction framed by reference only to certain identified material is specific in the sense that it relates to identified material, it is general in the sense that it requires the service provider to monitor all its traffic, rather than (for instance) traffic originating from one user.

A Belgian court, in *SABAM v Tiscali*,[8] has held that it has standing to grant an injunction against a service provider acting as a conduit, requiring it to block or filter out certain types of material. In that case SABAM, the Belgian music rights collecting society, took action against Tiscali, an internet service provider, seeking an injunction to prevent it carrying infringing peer-to-peer (P2P) traffic. By their very nature P2P files are stored only on end users' computers. They are not stored anywhere in the service provider's network, but only transmitted across it.

The court held that it had the power to grant an injunction against Tiscali and found that that would be consistent with Art.8.3 of the Copyright Directive and not in conflict with the Electronic Commerce Directive. While SABAM contended that the blocking or filtering of infringing P2P fileshares was technically feasible, Tiscali contested this. As a result, before giving a final decision, the court appointed an expert to investigate the feasibility and costs of technical measures to block or filter infringing file exchanges.

2–019 The Danish Supreme Court, in a case brought by the International Federation of the Phonographic Industry, held in February 2006 that an ISP given notice of illegal filesharing can be required, if necessary by injunction, to disconnect the service of the customer in question.[9] The court relied heavily on Art.8 of the Copyright Directive.

In another Danish case brought by IFPI, the Copenhagen City Court in October 2006 ordered the Danish ISP Tele2 to block access to the Russian AllofMP3 site.[10]

For further discussion of the terms of injunctions against internet service providers, see Ch.5 para.5–057.

Broadcasts and the right of communication to the public

2–020 The "communication to the public" right for authors provided in Art.3 of the Copyright Directive covers electronic communication of a work to the public "by wire or wireless means, including ... in such a way that mem-

---

[8] *SABAM v Tiscali*, Court of First Instance, Brussels, June 24, 2004.
[9] E.C.L.R. Vol. 11, No. 9 p.243; IFPI press release: *www.ifpi.org/content/section_news/ 20060215.html*.
[10] IFPI press release: *www.ifpi.org/content/section_news/20061026.html*.

bers of the public may access them from a place and at a time individually chosen by them". Recital (23) makes clear that this is intended to include broadcasting.

A narrower right is granted to performers, phonogram producers, film producers and broadcasters, applying only to "making available to the public, by wire or wireless means, in such a way that members of the public may access them from a place and at a time individually chosen by them". Neither right is exhausted by communication or making available to the public. Recital (27) states that the mere provision of physical communications facilities does not of itself amount to communication.

The implementation of this new right has resulted in some of the most significant changes made to the UK copyright legislation by the Copyright and Related Rights Regulations 2003.

Cable programme services have been abolished as a separate type of work in which copyright may subsist. Inclusion in a cable programme service has also been abolished as a separate species of restricted act. A new definition of 'broadcast', replacing the existing s.6(1) of the 1988 Act, is adopted:

> "6(1) In this Part a 'broadcast' means an electronic transmission of visual images, sounds or other information which–
>
> > (a) is transmitted for simultaneous reception by members of the public and is capable of being lawfully received by them, or
> > (b) is transmitted at a time determined solely by the person making the transmission for presentation to members of the public,
>
> and which is not excepted by subsection (1A); and references to broadcasting shall be construed accordingly.
>
> (1A) Excepted from the definition of 'broadcast' is any internet transmission unless it is–
>
> > (a) a transmission taking place simultaneously on the internet and by other means,
> > (b) a concurrent transmission of a live event, or
> > (c) a transmission of recorded moving images or sounds forming part of a programme service offered by the person responsible for making the transmission, being a service in which programmes are transmitted at scheduled times determined by that person".

2–021   The new definition of broadcast focuses not, like traditional definitions, on whether transmission is made via a wireless medium, but on the simultaneity of the reception.[11]

---

[11] The approach based on simultaneity of reception is similar in concept to that of the Communications Act 2003, which seeks to exclude from broadcast-style content regulation by OFCOM most internet content (see Ch.8). However, the definitional structures of the amendments to the 1988 Act are completely different.

The exclusion of most internet transmissions from the definition of broadcast affects the applicability of certain exceptions from infringement. The time-shifting exception under s.70 of the 1988 Act, for instance, which previously applied to broadcasts and cable programme services, now applies only to broadcasts. Even though the new definition of broadcast is broader than formerly, the overall effect of the changes is to restrict the applicability of the time-shifting exception to traditional broadcasts and to quasi-broadcasts via the internet.[12]

The phrases "internet transmission" and "internet" are not defined. The use of such technology-specific terms may cause difficulties, especially when considering network technologies that do not employ internet protocols, or that employ internet protocols in part only of the network.

The separate restricted acts relating to broadcasting and inclusion in a cable programme service under the old 1988 Act are abolished. In their place is a new restricted act of communication of a work to the public:

> "20(1) The communication to the public of the work is an act restricted by the copyright in–
>
> (a) a literary, dramatic, musical or artistic work,
> (b) a sound recording or film, or
> (c) a broadcast.
>
> (2) References in this Part to communication to the public are to communication to the public by electronic transmission, and in relation to a work include–
>
> (a) the broadcasting of the work;
> (b) the making available to the public of the work by electronic transmission in such a way that members of the public may access it from a place and at a time individually chosen by them".

Section 20(2)(b) is the "making available" right required by the WIPO Treaties. A similar right is introduced for performers in respect of recordings of their performances.[13]

Distribution right

The distribution right, which relates to the original work and physical copies, is limited to authors. Article 4(2) provides that this right will only be exhausted by a first sale by, or with the consent of, the right holder in the Community. No amendments to the 1988 Act were considered necessary. **2–022**

---

[12] Section 70 has also been modified in other ways, in particular to restrict its application to domestic premises and to prevent subsequent dealing with copies made under the protection of the section.

[13] 1988 Act, s.182CA.

Exceptions to copyright

2–023 The stated aim of the Copyright Directive is harmonisation of the law of copyright and related rights (Recital (1) *etc.*). The exceptions to copyright infringement historically have differed significantly between Member States and therefore would seem to be an area where harmonisation is required. However, apart from the exception for incidental technological copying referred to above, all the exceptions dealt with in Art.5 are made optional; so there is no guaranteed harmonisation of copyright law as a result of the Directive.

Exceptions to copyright is the area that has attracted the most debate and criticism, and Art.5 was extensively amended by the European Parliament. All exceptions in Art.5 are to be applied "only in certain special cases which do not conflict with a normal exploitation of the work or other subject-matter and do not unreasonably prejudice the legitimate interests of the rightholder" (Art.5(5)).

The optional exceptions are contained in Art.5(2) (limitations to the exclusive right of reproduction provided in Art.2) and Art.5(3) (limitations to both the Art.2 right of reproduction and the Art.3 right of communication to the public); Art.5(4) provides that where Member States may provide for an exception to the reproduction right pursuant to these exceptions, they may also apply these exceptions to the Art.4 right of distribution, "to the extent justified by the purpose of the authorised act of reproduction".

The 2003 Regulations introduced no new exceptions. They made some amendments to existing exceptions in order to conform with the Directive. Such amendments are noted in the following list of the optional exceptions provided for in the Directive.

2–024 **Article 5(2)(a)—photocopying** This is subject to fair compensation to the right holder.

2–025 **Article 5(2)(b)—copying for private use** This allows copying on any medium for private and non-commercial use. This is subject to a requirement that the rightholders should receive fair compensation, which takes account of the application (or not) of technological copy protection measures. The UK has not implemented a general private copying right.[14]

The existing private study exception (s.29 of the 1988 Act) has been amended so as to exclude study which is directly or indirectly for a commercial purpose. The private study exception is not considered to require compensation and none is provided for in the 1998 Act.

---

[14] Notwithstanding this, some types of private copying (such as "ripping" commercial music CDs on to MP3 players) are commonplace in the UK. In June 2006 the BPI, which represents the British recording industry, gave evidence to a House of Commons Select Committee that it would not pursue consumers who copied their own purchased CDs from one format to another (BPI Press Release "BPI outlines vision for recording industry to Select Committee" June 6, 2006). The Gowers Review of Intellectual Property published on December 6, 2006 recommended that a limited private copying exception for format-shifting, without compensation to rightsholders, should be introduced.

Amendments to s.61 (and the regulations made thereunder) concerning recordings of folksongs have been made as a consequence of Art.5(2)(b) and (c), and Art.5(3)(a).

The time shifting provisions of s.70 and the photographs of broadcasts provisions of s.71 have also been amended to render them more limited. In particular, the recording or photograph must be made in domestic premises, the rights now only apply to broadcasts (following the abolition of cable programme services) and copies made within the protection of the sections become infringing if dealt with subsequently.

Article 5(2)(c)—libraries This is an exception for organisations such as libraries and archives to make copies for non-commercial purposes. However, the exception must be for specific acts of reproduction which must not be for direct or indirect economic or commercial advantage. Recital (40) states that the exception should not cover on-line delivery. The regulations made under s.41 and 42 of the 1988 Act have been amended to reflect the requirement that there be no economic or commercial advantage. **2–026**

Article 5(2)(d)—ephemeral fixations made by broadcasters This allows ephemeral recordings by broadcasters for their own broadcasts, and extends to official archival preservation of these recordings on grounds of exceptional documentary character. **2–027**

Article 5(2)(e)—hospitals, prisons, etc. This exception relates to reproduction of broadcasts made by social institutions pursuing non-commercial purposes, subject to the rightholder receiving fair compensation. **2–028**

Article 5(3)(a)—teaching and scientific research This relates to use for the sole purpose of illustration for teaching or scientific research. The source, including the author's name, must be indicated unless this is impossible. The exception applies to the extent justified by the non-commercial purpose to be achieved. Section 29 of the 1988 Act has been amended to conform with this exception, by limiting it to non-commercial research and adding a requirement that the source be acknowledged. **2–029**

Similar amendments have been made to ss.38, 39 and 43 concerning copying by librarians. Section 32(1) and (2) have been amended to limit the teaching exception to the extent justified by the non-commercial purpose to be achieved and to add a requirement of source acknowledgment. Similar amendments have been made to s.35 concerning recordings by educational establishments of broadcasts and to s.36 concerning reprographic copying by educational establishments.

Article 5(3)(b)—disability This covers non-commercial use for disabled people, where the use is directly related to the disability and of a non-commercial nature. Talking books for the blind would be an example. **2–030**

Article 5(3)(c)—reporting of current events, etc. This relates to published **2–031**

articles on current economic, political or religious topics, in cases where such use is not expressly reserved, subject to indicating the source including the author's name, and to reporting of current events to the extent justified by the informatory purpose and as long as the source (including the author's name) is indicated, unless that is impossible. Section 30 of the 1988 Act has been amended to comply with these requirements.

2–032   **Article 5(3)(d)—criticism and review**   This has to relate to a work already lawfully made available to the public. It is subject to conditions including naming the source, including the author, unless that it impossible. Amendments have been made to s.30 and Sch. 2 para.2(1) of the 1988 Act to comply with these requirements. A separate exception for fair dealing in the course of instruction has been provided in a new s.32(2A) and (for rights in performances) in Sch.2 para.4.

2–033   **Article 5(3)(e)—public interest**   This covers use for public security, or the reporting of an administrative, parliamentary or judicial procedure.

2–034   **Article 5(3)(f)—political speeches**   Use of political speeches, extracts of public lectures or similar to the extent justified by the informatory purpose and provided that the source, including the author's name, is indicated, except where this turns out to be impossible.

2–035   **Article 5(3)(g)—official and religious celebrations**   Use during religious celebrations or official celebrations organised by a public authority.

2–036   **Article 5(3)(h)—sculptures in public places**   Use of works, such as works of architecture or sculpture, made to be located permanently in public places.

2–037   **Article 5(3)(i)—incidental inclusion**   Incidental inclusion of a work or other subject-matter in other material.

2–038   **Article 5(3)(j)—art exhibitions and sales**   Use for the purpose of advertising the public exhibition or sale of artistic works, to the extent necessary to promote the event, excluding any other commercial use.

2–039   **Article 5(3)(k)—caricature, etc.**   Use for the purpose of caricature, parody or pastiche.

2–040   **Article 5(3)(l)—equipment**   Use in connection with the demonstration or repair of equipment.

2–041   **Article 5(3)(m)—reconstruction of buildings**   Use of an artistic work in the form of a building or a drawing or plan of a building for the purposes of reconstructing the building.

Article 5(3)(n)—on-line research and private study in public libraries Use 2–042 (by communication or making available) for the purpose of research or private study, to individual members of the public by dedicated terminals on the premises of establishments referred to in Art.5(2)(c) of works not subject to purchase or licensing terms which are contained in their collections.

Article 5(3)(o)—Miscellaneous Use in certain other cases of minor 2–043 importance where exceptions or limitations already exist under national law, provided that they only concern analogue uses and do not affect the free circulation of goods and services within the Community, without prejudice to the other exceptions and limitations contained in Art.5.

Prevention of circumvention of technical protection measures

Article 6 of the Copyright Directive requires Member States to prohibit the 2–044 circumvention of technical protection measures (TPMs) designed to protect copyright works, which the person concerned carries out in the knowledge, or with reasonable grounds to know, that he or she is pursuing that objective. The knowledge test has particular relevance in the case of dual use technology, which can be used to crack copy protection but which also has other uses.[15] Such technology is within the Article, but subject to the knowledge requirement.

New ss.296ZA to ZF of the 1998 Act have been introduced to implement Art.6. A recast S.296 is limited to apply only to computer programs.

The implementation of these aspects of the Directive was one of the most controversial aspects of the pre-legislation consultation carried out by the Department of Trade and Industry. The controversy focused in particular on the balance between protection of TPMs and maintenance of exceptions to copyright protection, the concern being that the practical effect of TPMs could be to prevent access to the work even if the person concerned was intending to do something permitted under a statutory exception.

UK law has in fact provided some protection for TPMs for some time, in the old s.296 of the 1988 Act (see below, para.2–070). The existing protection (providing civil remedies) is substantially continued for computer programs in a revised s.296. But for other works a different regime applies, providing civil remedies for the act of circumvention and both civil and criminal sanctions for making and dealing in circumvention devices and the provision of circumvention services.

The provisions for computer programs apply to "technical devices", i.e. "any device intended to prevent or restrict acts that are not authorised by the copyright owner of that computer program and are restricted by copyright".

---

[15] See, for instance, "Jail Time in the Digital Age", Lawrence Lessig, *New York Times* July 30, 2001.

2–045   The provisions for works other than computer programs apply to "technological measures". These are defined in s.296 ZF:

> "(1) In sections 296ZA to 296ZE, "technological measures" are any technology, device or component which is designed, in the normal course of its operation, to protect a copyright work other than a computer program.
>
> (2) Such measures are 'effective' if the use of the work is controlled by the copyright owner through–
>
> (a) an access control or protection process such as encryption, scrambling or other transformation of the work, or
>
> (b) a copy control mechanism,
>
> which achieves the intended protection.
>
> (3) In this section, the reference to–
>
> (a) protection of a work is to the prevention or restriction of acts that are not authorised by the copyright owner of that work and are restricted by copyright; and
>
> (b) use of a work does not extend to any use of the work that is outside the scope of the acts restricted by copyright."

A specific exception is introduced protecting cryptography research unless, in so doing, or in issuing information derived from the research, the person affects prejudicially the rights of the copyright owner. This exception does not apply to the provisions of s.296 regarding computer programs.

Where an effective technological measure applied to a work prevents a person from carrying out a permitted act (as defined), a procedure for applying to the Secretary of State is established, which may result in the Secretary of State issuing directions to the copyright owner or exclusive licensee to ensure that the copyright owner or exclusive licensee makes available to the complainant the means of carrying out the permitted act to the extent necessary to so benefit from that permitted act.

Electronic rights management information

2–046   Article 7 of the Copyright Directive prohibits the removal or alteration of electronic rights management (ERM) information and makes ancillary provisions.

A new s.296ZG of the 1988 Act has been introduced to implement Art.7. This introduces new civil remedies where a person knowingly and without authority, removes or alters electronic rights management information which is associated with a copy of a copyright work or appears in connection with the communication to the public of a copyright work where the person knows, or has reason to believe, that by so doing he is inducing, enabling, facilitating or concealing an infringement of copyright. There are also remedies for knowing distribution, import for distribution or communication to the public of works from which ERM information has been removed.

"Rights management information" means any information provided by the copyright owner or the holder of any right under copyright which identifies the work, the author, the copyright owner or the holder of any intellectual property rights, or information about the terms and conditions of use of the work, and any numbers or codes that represent such information.

2.2.4 USA—the Digital Millennium Copyright Act 1998

The US administration in 1994 set up an Information Infrastructure Task Force to plan for and implement the National Information Infrastructure (NII). The task force included the Information Policy Committee, dealing with issues relating to the use of information on the NII. As part of the Information Policy Committee's work, a working group on Intellectual Property Rights was set up, chaired by the US Commissioner of Patents and Trademarks. After issuing a preliminary draft report in July 1994 and taking both oral and written evidence from a large number of interested organisations and individuals, the working group issued its final report in September 1995.

2–047

After examining the existing state of the US law, and the arguments for and against intellectual property protection for various kinds of information on the NII, the working group proposed to deal with the main problems that it perceived arising from dealings with works in cyberspace by amending the US Copyright Act.

At least some of these amendments were made by the Digital Millennium Copyright Act 1998 ("DMCA"). Title I of the DMCA implements the WIPO treaties by prohibiting the circumvention of copyright protection systems and protecting the integrity of copyright management information. The former provisions caused a great deal of controversy while the legislation was going through Congress, as they provide a sweeping prohibition on the circumvention of "technological protection measures", regardless of whether infringement occurs as a result. Also prohibited is the manufacture, importation and distribution of devices primarily intended for such circumvention.

2–048

Groups which had benefited from the fair use exemption from copyright infringement, such as librarians, teachers and software developers pointed out that such a broad prohibition would effectively remove the fair use provisions and leave them at the mercy of the copyright owners, thus tilting the current balance heavily in favour of the content provider against the users. As a result, Congress added a long list of exemptions for non-profit libraries, archives and educational establishments, for law enforcement and intelligence activities and reverse engineering provisions for software developers which adopt the language of the European Software Protection Directive.[16]

---

[16] Directive 91/250 [1991] O.J. L122/42.

The *Felten* case

2–049 The enforcement of the DMCA copyright protection circumvention provisions has proved controversial. The threat of action under the Digital Millennium Copyright Act deterred an academic from presenting a paper about weaknesses in music access-control technologies. This gave rise to a First Amendment lawsuit by the academic, Dr Edward Felten, aimed at establishing his right to present the paper.[17] The lawsuit was dismissed by the New Jersey District Court in November 2001. This followed a filing by the Recording Industry Association of America stating that it had not intended to interfere with the presentation and therefore no dispute existed. Dr Felten's paper was subsequently presented at a technology conference in August 2001, having been previously withdrawn from a conference in April 2001.

The *Sklyarov* case

2–050 In July 2001 a Russian programmer, Dmitry Sklyarov, the author of a program that disabled restrictions on Adobe eBooks, who had presented at the Las Vegas Defcon–9 hacker conference, was arrested and charged with an offence under the DMCA of trafficking in a product designed to circumvent copyright protection for electronic books (Adobe eBooks).[18] Adobe subsequently recommended his release and withdrew support for the criminal complaint.[19] The complaint, which was also brought against Mr Sklyarov's employer Elcomsoft, survived a challenge to the constitutionality of the circumvention provisions of the DMCA. Sklyarov himself had previously been released from custody and permitted to return to Russia pending trial, on the basis of an agreement with the prosecutor that he would testify at trial and having made certain admissions as to his conduct. On the basis of the agreement the charges against him were deferred for one year. The case went to trial in December 2002 against Elcomsoft and resulted in a jury acquittal.

Other DMCA cases

The DMCA has given rise to commercial lawsuits in which its provisions have been deployed in attempts to deny interoperability to competing products. In one example the printer manufacturer Lexmark sued Static Control Components, Inc. Lexmark sold print toner cartridges on a "prebate" basis, i.e. with a discount in exchange for the customer promising to return the cartridge to Lexmark for refilling. Lexmark's printers include software that would normally reject a cartridge refilled by a third party. SCC manufacture a chip that enables cartridges refilled by third parties to work with the Lexmark printers. Lexmark alleged (*inter alia*) that the chip

---

[17] Electronic Frontier Foundation, *http://www.eff.org/IP/DMCA/Felten_v_RIAA/20010606_eff_felten_pr.html*.

[18] See Lessig, n.15 above; also E.C.L.R. July 25, 2001 p.776.

[19] *www.adobe.com/aboutadobe/pressroom/pressreleases/200107/20010723dcma.html*.

violated the circumvention provisions of the DMCA. In October 2004 the Court of Appeals for the 6th Circuit discharged a preliminary injunction previously granted against SCC.[20]

In another case, *Chamberlain Group v Skylink Technologies Inc.*,[21] The US Court of Appeals for the Federal Circuit upheld summary judgment in favour of the defendant, which had developed a universal remote control that would work with garage door opener systems manufactured by the plaintiff.

2.3 THE ELEMENTS OF COPYRIGHT AND DATABASE RIGHT

2.3.1 The historical development of copyright

Copyright developed to deal with the analogue world. Historically, our present system of copyright grew out of attempts by the government to control the information revolution brought about by the development of printing. The right to print books was given exclusively to members of the guild of stationers, which was a recognised body with privileges that made it susceptible to government influence. When unlicensed publishing began to flourish, the guild members sought a law to prevent this. The Copyright Act 1709 gave the author and his assigns the exclusive right to print a book. The exclusive rights and the types of work protected gradually increased through a series of statutes, culminating in the present legislation, the Copyright, Designs and Patents Act 1988.

2–051

2.3.2 What is protected?

Categories of protected works

Because of this historical development, the 1988 Act contains a list of the types of work protected, in three categories. These are:

2–052

- original literary, dramatic, musical or artistic works
- sound recordings, films or broadcasts; and
- the typographical arrangement of a published edition.

Before October 31, 2003, when they were abolished by the Copyright and Related Rights Regulations 2003,[22] cable programme services were a spe-

---

[20] *Lexmark International, Inc. v Static Control Components, Inc.*, 6th Cir., No. 03–5400, October 26, 2004.
[21] Fed. Cir., No. 04–1118, August 31, 2004.
[22] See para.2–020 above.

cies of copyright work. The 2003 Regulations redefined broadcasts to include some internet transmissions such as simultaneous webcasts.

Compilations (defined to exclude databases), computer programs and databases are included as literary works, while films include video recordings and any moving image.

Originality

2–053 In order to be protected a literary, dramatic, musical or artistic work must be original. There is no definition of "originality" in the 1988 Act. Case law in the UK has required only that the work is not copied and has a minimal amount of creativity, reflecting the approach of the UK courts to copyright as an economic, rather than a personal, right.

The position regarding originality of databases protected by copyright is modified as a consequence of the introduction of database right (discussed below). Section 3A of the 1988 Act provides that a literary work consisting of a database is original if, and only if, by reason of the selection or arrangement of the contents of the database the database constitutes the author's own intellectual creation. Generally, mere facts are regarded as non-copyright.

Similarly, European Council Directive 91/250/EEC on the legal protection of computer programs ("the Software Directive") provides (Art.1(3)) that a computer program shall be protected "if it is original in the sense that it is the author's own intellectual creation" and states that no other criteria shall be applied to determine its eligibility for protection. But unlike with databases, this requirement is not written into the 1988 Act.

Recordal

2–054 Copyright in a literary, dramatic or musical work comes into existence only when the work is recorded, in writing or otherwise.[23] The 1988 Act[24] defines a "writing" to include "any form of notation or code, whether by hand or otherwise and regardless of the method by which, or medium in or on which, it is recorded".

This means that the contents of a screen ought to be capable of copyright protection (subject to its meeting the other criteria, such as originality), regardless of whether an underlying design for that screen has been recorded. This conclusion is arrived at not because displaying the contents on the screen constitutes a recordal—it may not[25]—but because the screen

---

[23] 1988 Act, s.3(2). For an example of denial of copyright in a literary work on the ground, *inter alia*, of lack of recordal within software source code, see *Navitaire, Inc. v Easyjet Airline Company* [2004] EWHC 1725 (Ch).
[24] s.178.
[25] *Cf.* fn.45 below.

contents are stored, even if only transiently, in the memory of the computer.[26]

On the internet, material and information is accessed and (temporarily at least) resides in the computer's RAM (random access memory). In order for the user to see that information, it must be copied into the computer's memory. As well as being potentially relevant to the question of recordal, the creation of such temporary or transient copies can amount to infringement of the rights of a copyright owner.

Ideas and expression

It is a truism that copyright protects the expression of ideas but not ideas   **2–055**
themselves. The European Software Directive provides that "Ideas and principles which underlie any element of the computer program, including those which underlie its interfaces, are not protected by copyright under this Directive".[27] This provision was not expressly incorporated in the UK regulations implementing the Directive on the ground that it was already part of judge-made copyright law in the UK.

2.3.3 Authorship and ownership

Who is the author?

The author of a work is the person who creates it. A work of joint   **2–056**
authorship is produced by the collaboration of two or more authors in which the contribution of each author is not distinct from that of the other author or authors. In the case of a literary work which is computer-generated, the author is by statute the person by whom the arrangements necessary for the creation of the work are undertaken. The term "computer-generated" means that "the work is generated by computer in circumstances such that there is no human author of the work".[28]

Who is the first owner?

In general, the author of a work is the first owner of any copyright in it.   **2–057**
However, where the work is made by an employee in the course of his employment, his employer is the first owner of any copyright in the work subject to any agreement to the contrary.

---

[26] The question of whether temporary or transient storage in RAM is sufficient to constitute "recordal" has similarities to the question of whether loading a copy into RAM is sufficient to render the loaded RAM chip an article constituting an infringing copy for the purpose of s.27 of the 1988 Act. This question was answered in the affirmative in *Kabushiki Kaisha Sony Computer Entertainment Inc v Ball* [2004] EWHC 1738 (Ch).

[27] Art.1.2, Council Directive 91/250/EEC of May 14, 1991 on the legal protection of computer programs. For an application of this provision see *Navitaire v Easyjet*, fn.23 above.

[28] 1988 Act, s.9(3). In *Nova Productions Ltd v Mazooma Games Ltd* [2006] EWHC 24 (Ch) Kitchin J. held that composite frames generated by a computer game program from various bitmap files were either a creation of the author of the software or were a computer generated work for which he had made the arrangements.

This only applies to employees, not to contractors, so the mere fact that a work has been commissioned and paid for does not give the ownership of the copyright to the commissioning party. It is important, therefore, to ensure that appropriate mechanisms are in place to deal with the ownership of the rights in content. For example, an organisation may wish to put up information onto a website. That information may have come from a number of sources, external developers and consultants, internal employees, etc. The organisation in question will therefore need to be certain that it secures assignments of rights from any third parties, and be sure that any employees created the content during the course of their employment.

Qualifying author

2–058 Copyright does not subsist in a work unless the author is a qualifying person or the work was first published in a qualifying country. A qualifying person includes a British citizen, an individual domiciled or resident in the UK or another country to which the Act has been extended (including the Member States of the Berne Convention and the Universal Copyright Convention), or a body incorporated under the law of the UK or another country to which the Act has been extended. A qualifying country includes the UK or another country to which the Act has been extended (including the Member States of the Berne Convention and the Universal Copyright Convention).

2.3.4 Period of copyright

2–059 Copyright in original literary, dramatic, musical or artistic works of European origin now lasts for 70 years beyond the year in which the author died. If there are joint authors then copyright duration is linked to the last death of any identifiable author.

Computer generated works are protected for 50 years from the end of the year of creation. Copyright in sound recordings lasts for 50 years from the end of the year in which the work was made, first published or made available to the public by playing in public or communication to the public. Copyright in broadcasts lasts for 50 years from the end of the year in which the broadcast was first made. Copyright in films expires 70 years from the end of the year in which the last of the director, screenplay author, dialogue author or composer of music written specially for the film dies. Copyright in the typographical arrangement of a published edition lasts for 25 years from the year of first publication. Works originating outside the European Economic Area are given the same period of protection as in their native country.

This different treatment of types of works will cause problems with digital products containing a variety of content, e.g. a multimedia product containing film, photographs, text and sound. The copyright in the individual elements of the product will expire at different times.

2.4 MORAL RIGHTS

The rights pertaining to copyright discussed above are economic rights. The **2–060** Continental systems of copyright have long recognised another set of rights, which belong to the creator of the work even if he or she does not own the economic rights. These are known as the moral rights. A system of moral rights was introduced into English law for the first time by the 1988 Act. There are four elements to moral rights which subsist alongside copyright:

- The paternity right: which is the right to be identified as author (or director of a film). This right does not exist unless it is asserted by the author or film maker.
- The integrity right: the right to object to the derogatory treatment of a work.
- False attribution: the right not to suffer false attribution of a work. This lasts for life plus 20 years only.
- Privacy of photographs: this is the right of a person commissioning photographs not to have copies issued to the public.

Moral rights cannot be assigned, but they may be waived. Infringement of the above rights is actionable as a breach of a statutory duty. The moral rights of paternity and integrity do not apply to computer programs or computer-generated works.

2.5 DATABASE RIGHT

The Database Directive

In 1992 the European Commission issued a draft Directive to harmonise **2–061** the protection of databases in the EU. Comments from interested parties revealed many deficiencies, and the draft was extensively amended by the European Parliament. Extensive negotiations between the Member States resulted in a Directive being adopted on March 11, 1996, to be implemented by January 1, 1998.

Under the Directive "database" is defined as: "a collection of works, data or other independent materials arranged in a systematic or methodical way and capable of being individually accessed by electronic or other means". This includes non-computer databases, on-line databases, CD-ROMs and DVD.

The content materials may be protected by their own individual copyrights, which are not affected by the Directive. A database as a whole qualifies for copyright protection if there is creativity in the selection or arrangement of its contents. This test is wider than the test previously applied by most European countries, but narrower than the test formerly used by the UK and the Republic of Ireland. However, under transitional provisions, existing databases protected by copyright retain that protection for the full copyright term.

2–062 A *sui generis* right is given to database proprietors for any database whether or not it and/or its contents are protected by copyright. This is the right to prevent the unauthorised extraction and/or re-utilisation of all or a substantial part of the database.

This right lasts for 15 years from the first public availability of the database, and can be renewed if there has been a substantial change which would result in the database being considered a "substantial new investment". This means that databases which are subject to regular significant updating could in theory be protected forever.

This right, however, is only given to proprietors who are EU nationals or residents, although it may be extended to nationals of third countries who give equivalent protection to databases of EU origin—which currently excludes the US.

This Directive was implemented in the UK by the Copyright and Rights in Databases Regulations 1997, which came into force on January 1, 1998. These regulations amended the 1998 Act so as to bring the standard of originality for subsistence of copyright in databases into line with that required by the Directive, to specify what constitutes adaptation and fair dealing in relation to a database, and to specify the permitted acts by a person who has a right to use a database.

The Regulations also created the new database right, giving the maker of a database in which there has been a substantial investment in obtaining, verifying or presenting the contents the right to prevent extraction or re-utilisation of all or a substantial part of the contents.

The *William Hill* case

2–063 The first case on the scope of database right to reach the English courts culminated in a decision of the European Court of Justice, *British Horseracing Board Ltd v William Hill Organisation Ltd*,[29] which significantly restricts the scope of database right.

The facts were that the main claimant (BHB) is the governing authority for the British horseracing industry. In 1985 the claimant, Weatherbys, on behalf of the claimant, the Jockey Club, started to compile an electronic database of (among other things) registered horses, their owners and trainers, their handicap ratings, details of jockeys, and fixture list information (venues, dates, times, race conditions and entries and runners). After June 1993 Weatherbys maintained and developed the database on behalf of BHB.

The database was constantly updated. The cost of continuing to obtain, verify and present the contents of the database was approximately £4,000,000 per annum, involving about 80 staff and extensive computer

---

[29] ECJ Case C–203/02 [2005] 1 C.M.L.R. 15; and subsequently in the Court of Appeal [2005] EWCA Civ 863.

software and hardware. The database contained details of over one million horses. An estimated total of 800,000 new records or changes to existing records were made each year.

Information from the database, in particular information about forth- **2–064** coming races, was made available in various ways. This included circulation of essential extracts to the racing industry, including publication in BHB's journal *The Racing Calendar*. There were also electronic feeds, the Declaration Feed and Raw Data Feed (RDF). The Declaration Feed contained a list of races, declared runners and jockeys, distances and names of races, race times and numbers of runners in each race and other infor- mation. It was made available to subscribers by Racing Pages Ltd, a joint venture between Weatherbys and the Press Association. Satellite Informa- tion Services (SIS) was allowed to use information from the database to provide services to its own subscribers. One such service was the RDF, consisting of details of meetings, races and the list of runners and other related information. SIS also supplied FACTS, comprising television cov- erage, audio and captions for race meetings.

William Hill, a large bookmaker, provided internet betting on horse- **2–065** racing from a website. It had formal licences for the Declarations Feed and for the FACTS service. It also received the RDF from SIS. This was supplied with no formal contract. However SIS had no right, and had not purported to sublicense William Hill to use the RDF on its website.

William Hill made use of certain information from the RDF on its website: the identity of the horses in a race, the date and time of the race and the identity of the racecourse. BHB objected to this use. It claimed that the use made each day was an extraction or reutilisation of a substantial part of the database (contrary to Art.7(1) of the Directive); or that, if each day's use was an insubstantial part, the use amounted to a repeated and systematic extraction and reutilisation of insubstantial parts of the database (contrary to Art.7(5)).

On Art.7(1) William Hill argued (1) that it had not used a part, in a **2–066** relevant sense, of BHB's database; (2) even if it had used a part, it was not a substantial part; (3) the use did not amount to an extraction from the database; (4) it was not a reutilisation of the database. Laddie J. at first instance found in favour of BHB on all points.

On appeal to the Court of Appeal William Hill contended that the judge had given a wide meaning to the database right and that the effect was that information that might have been thought to have entered the public domain and to be freely usable might prove to be derived from a database, the right in which was protected, even though the user was unaware of that ultimate source and right. The Court of Appeal referred a number of questions to the European Court of Justice, which held that:

— the relevant investment was in (a) the resources used to seek out existing independent materials and collect them in the database, not the resources used for the creation of such independent materials; or (b) the resources used to monitor the accuracy of the

    materials collected when the database was created and during its
operation, not for verification during the stage of creation of data
or other materials subsequently collected in a database.

— the resources used to draw up a list of horses in a race and to carry
out checks in that connection did not constitute investment in the
obtaining and verification of the contents of the database in which
that list appeared.

— the concepts of extraction and re-utilisation referred to any
unauthorised act of appropriation and distribution to the public of
the whole or part of the contents of a database and do not imply
direct access to the database concerned.

— the fact that the contents of a database were made accessible to the
public by its maker or with his consent does not affect the right of
the maker to prevent acts of extraction and/or reutilisation of the
whole or a substantial part of the contents of a database.

— "substantial part, evaluated ... quantitatively" refers to the
volume of data extracted and/or reutilised compared with the total
volume of the contents of the database; and "substantial part,
evaluated ... qualitatively" refers to the scale of investment in the
obtaining, verification or presentation of the part of the database
extracted and/or reutilised, regardless of whether that represents a
quantitatively substantial part of the general contents of the protected database.

— the prohibition on repeated and systematic extraction or reutilisation of insubstantial parts of a database refers to acts the
cumulative effect of which is to reconstitute and/or make available
to the public the whole or a substantial part of the database and
thereby seriously prejudice the investment by the maker.

2–067   On the facts the ECJ was of the view that the resources invested by BHB in
selecting horses related to the creation of the data and therefore could not
be taken into account; and that William Hill had not taken a quantitatively
or qualitatively substantial part of the database, because the data taken had
not been the subject of relevant investment. As to repeated acts, the ECJ
thought there was no possibility that William Hill's acts would result in the
reconstitution of the whole or a substantial part of the database.

When the case returned to the Court of Appeal the court confirmed the
ECJ's views on the facts[30] and found in favour of William Hill.

In the *Fixtures Marketing*[31] cases, in which the ECJ issued judgments
simultaneously with the *William Hill* case, the issue was database right in
football fixtures lists. The ECJ came to similar conclusions in relation to
those lists.

---

[30] BHB failed in an argument that the ECJ had misunderstood the facts and that in fact the
BHB did put independent investment into compiling the final database of runners and
riders.

[31] ECJ Cases C–46/02, C–338/02 and C–444/02.

2.6 INFRINGEMENT OF COPYRIGHT AND DATABASE RIGHT

2.6.1 Introduction

Copyright is infringed by doing any of the prohibited acts (as to which, see **2–068** section 2.6.2 below) in relation to the whole or a substantial part of the work. It can be very difficult to determine whether a "substantial part of the work" has been copied. A single word or a single note of music cannot be the subject of copyright, even when the word is an invented word such as "Exxon".[32] The courts have held that copyright in a work is infringed by taking a "substantial" part of it, and the test of substantiality is quality rather than quantity. Thus, were Beethoven's 5th Symphony still in copyright, few would doubt that the copying of those instantly recognisable first four notes would be actionable infringement. Similarly, "Reader, I married him" would likely be held to be a substantial part of *Jane Eyre*. The test seems to be whether the part taken has itself some originality and merit; or, put another way, whether a substantial part of the author's relevant skill and labour has been taken.[33]

There are a number of statutory limitations on the scope of the exclusive **2–069** rights, which provide a defence to a charge of copyright infringement. Fair dealing with some classes of copyright work for research or private study, or for criticism or review, or reporting of current events; or the incidental inclusion in another work (e.g. a statue in the background of a photograph of a city square) is not an infringement.

There are detailed provisions dealing with those educational uses and those activities of libraries which are exempt from infringement liability. The time-shifting exceptions, although primarily aimed at recording from television, may be of some relevance to digital activities.

Copyright infringement may also be a criminal offence, although there must be either a commercial motive or distribution to such an extent as to seriously affect the copyright owner before there is criminal liability for copyright infringement.

Copy-protection

The 1988 Act introduced protection for copies of a work issued to the **2–070** public in an electronic form which is copy-protected. References to copy-protection include "any device or means intended to prevent or restrict copying of a work or to impair the quality of copies made".

Under the original s.296 a person issuing copy-protected electronic copies to the public had the same rights as a copyright owner had against an

---

[32] *Exxon Corporation v Exxon Insurance Consultants International Ltd* [1982] Ch. 119.
[33] The principles governing the taking of a substantial part, particularly of artistic works, are authoritatively set out in the speech of Lord Hoffmann in *Designers Guild Ltd v Russell Williams (Textiles) Ltd* [2001] F.S.R. 11.

infringer, against a person who made or distributed a device specifically designed or adapted to circumvent the form of copy-protection employed, knowing or having reason to believe that it would be used to make infringing copies, or who published information intended to enable or assist persons to circumvent the copy-protection.[34]

As from October 31, 2003 the original s. 296 was replaced by a new s.296, restricted to computer programs and still providing only for civil liability. The new s.296 applies where a "technical device" has been applied to a computer program. A technical device is "any device intended to prevent or restrict acts that are not authorised by the copyright owner of that computer program and are restricted by copyright".

2–071 The categories of person who may take action under the section are:

(a) a person issuing to the public copies of, or communicating to the public, the computer program to which the technical device has been applied;
(b) the copyright owner or his exclusive licensee;
(c) the owner or exclusive licensee of any intellectual property right in the technical device applied to the computer program.

Action may be taken under the section against a person who knowing or having reason to believe that it will be used to make infringing copies—

(a) manufactures for sale or hire, imports, distributes, sells or lets for hire, offers or exposes for sale or hire, advertises for sale or hire or has in his possession for commercial purposes any means the sole intended purpose of which is to facilitate the unauthorised removal or circumvention of the technical device; or
(b) publishes information intended to enable or assist persons to remove or circumvent the technical device.

New anti-circumvention provisions contained in ss.296ZA–296ZF, which include criminal offences, apply to works other than computer programs. (See para.2–044 above.)

---

[34] See *Sony Computer Entertainment v Paul Owen* [2002] EWHC 45 (Ch) for an example of the application of the original s.296. The claimant applied for summary judgment against the defendant in an action based on importation and sale of chips enabling the copy-protection and region-control technology of the Playstation 2 console to be circumvented, contrary to s.296 of the 1988 Act. The judge found that there was no doubt that the codes used by Sony for these purposes fell within the legislation. The copying prevented by them was the loading of the game into the computer. The defendant argued that there were lawful purposes to which the chips could be put, namely running independent software devised by people with no connection with Sony. Section 296 applied to "any device or means specifically designed or adapted to circumvent the form of copy-protection employed" imported etc by a person "knowing or having reason to believe that it will be used to make infringing copies". The judge found that it did not matter if there were some lawful uses, given that there were some that were not.

Exclusive rights of copyright owners

The copyright owner's exclusive rights are generally[35] the rights to copy, issue copies of the work to the public, rent or lend the work to the public perform, show or play in public, to communicate the work to the public and to make adaptations. Copyright is infringed by doing any of those acts without the consent of the copyright owner. These acts constitute primary infringement. **2–072**

Authorising infringement

It is also a primary infringement of copyright, for which the person authorising is strictly liable, to authorise another to do an act of primary infringement. "Authorise" is not defined in the 1988 Act. **2–073**

The meaning of authorisation is a significant issue when rights owners, as they do from time to time, go on the offensive against technology industries for producing devices that the rights owners think make it too easy for customers to infringe copyright. By arguing for a broad meaning of authorisation the rights owners seek to hold the technology manufacturers and sellers responsible for what their customers do with the products. The technology industries in turn naturally resist any attempt by the rights owners to dictate what devices they can produce and how they should be designed.

Authorisation was considered in just such a case by the House of Lords in *C.B.S. Songs v Amstrad Consumer Electronics*,[36] which concerned the marketing by the defendant of a high speed twin-headed cassette recorder. The House of Lords held that authorisation means the grant or purported grant, which may be express or implied, of the right to do the act complained of, whether the intention is that the grantee should do the act on his own account or only on account of the grantor. Merely enabling someone else to infringe copyright does not suffice.

Although this case was decided under the Copyright Act 1956, the principles hold good for the 1988 Act. The House of Lords considered both the sale of the machines themselves and the manner of advertising them. In relation to the sale of the machines, their Lordships stated: **2–074**

> "No manufacturer and no machine confers on the purchaser authority to copy unlawfully. The purchaser or other operator of the recorder determines whether he shall copy and what he shall copy. By selling the recorder Amstrad may facilitate copying in breach of copyright, but do not authorise it."

This finding was against the factual background that, notwithstanding that it was statistically certain that most, but not all consoles were used for the

---

[35] The exclusive rights may vary according to the type of copyright work. Reference should be made to the specific provisions of the 1988 Act defining each exclusive right.

[36] [1988] A.C. 1013.

purpose of home copying in breach of copyright, the machine was capable of being used for lawful purposes and the decision whether to use it for lawful or unlawful purposes was entirely that of the purchaser.

2–075 A lawful purpose could arise either because the material being copied was not the subject of copyright protection at all, or because the user had permission to copy copyright content, or because the user fell within limited rights to copy granted by the Copyright Act.

The separate allegation was made that by their advertisement Amstrad had authorised the infringement. Amstrad had advertised the advantages of its high-speed twin-head tape recorder with an asterisked footnote to the effect that the recording and the playback of certain material might only be possible by permission.

Although commenting somewhat negatively on the advertising, the House of Lords stated that: "the advertisement did not authorise the unlawful copying of records; on the contrary, the footnote warned that some copying required permission and made it clear that Amstrad had not authority to grant that permission".

Therefore, neither the sale of the machine, nor the particular advertising was found to constitute authorisation.

Joint tortfeasorship

2–076 Allegations of authorising infringement often go hand in hand with allegations of joint tortfeasorship, either as the result of a common design, or as a result of the defendant procuring the infringement by a third party. In *Amstrad* all three grounds of liability were pursued. All three failed.

Liability for a common design can accrue where two or more persons act in concert with one another pursuant to a common design in the infringement.[37] There must be a concerted action to a common end.[38] Mere facilitation or assistance is not sufficient. However, tacit agreement will suffice.[39] There does not have to be a common design to infringe, but only to do acts that in the event prove to be infringements.[40]

In *Amstrad* liability based on common design was rejected, on grounds of dual-use of the equipment and Amstrad's lack of control over the user after purchase.

Procuring infringement

2–077 A further head of liability exists for procuring copyright infringement which, although closely related to common design, is probably separate from it.[41] It is unclear whether common design is a necessary component of

---

[37] *CBS v Amstrad*, fn.36.
[38] *The Koursk* [1924] All ER 168, C.A.
[39] *Unilever Plc v Gillette (UK) Ltd* [1989] RPC 583, C.A.
[40] *ibid.*
[41] *ibid.*; the point is undecided, *per* the Court of Appeal in *MCA Records v Charly Records Ltd* [2001] EWCA Civ 1441, at para.36.

this head, but in any event procurement may lead to a common design, rather than there being a common design at the outset.[42]

In *Amstrad* the claim based on procurement failed. Lord Templeman said:

> "My Lords, I accept that a defendant who procures a breach of copyright is liable jointly and severally with the infringer for the damages suffered by the plaintiff as a result of the infringement. The defendant is a joint infringer; he intends and procures and shares a common design that infringement shall take place.
>
> A defendant may procure an infringement by inducement, incitement or persuasion. But in the present case Amstrad does not procure infringement by offering for sale a machine which may be used for lawful or unlawful copying and it does not procure infringement by advertising the attractions of its machine to any purchaser who may decide to copy unlawfully. Amstrad is not concerned to procure and cannot procure unlawful copying. The purchaser will not make unlawful copies because he has been induced or incited or persuaded to do so by Amstrad. The purchaser will make unlawful copies for his own use because he chooses to do so. Amstrad's advertisements may persuade the purchaser to buy an Amstrad machine but will not influence the purchaser's later decision to infringe copyright.
>
> Buckley L.J. observed in *Belegging- en Exploitatiemaatschappij Lavender BV v Witten Industrial Diamonds Ltd* (at 65): 'Facilitating the doing of an act is obviously different from procuring the doing of an act'. Sales and advertisements to the public generally of a machine which may be used for lawful or unlawful purposes, including infringement of copyright, cannot be said to 'procure' all breaches of copyright thereafter by members of the public who use the machine."

It might be thought, on the basis of this passage, that it is a complete answer 2–078 to an allegation of procurement or common design that the means of infringing have passed out of the control of the supplier and into the hands of the purchaser. However, that would not be consistent with the "supplier cases".

These cases established that mere supply of materials, in the knowledge that they could be used for infringement of a patent, did not make the supplier a joint tortfeasor. However, doing more (such as giving instructions on how to use powdered zinc in a way that infringed a process patent[43]; or selling a compost bin kit with assembly instructions[44]) was sufficient for there to be liability.

---

[42] *ibid.*
[43] *Innes v Short and Beal* (1898) 15 R.P.C. 449.
[44] *Rotocrop International Ltd v Glenbourne Ltd* [1982] F.S.R. 241.

If lack of control over the purchaser were a complete answer, then the supplier in the powdered zinc case could not have been liable, since notwithstanding the supplier's provision of instructions it was still the customer's choice how to use the product. Bingham J. in that case said:

> "There is no reason whatever why Mr. Short should not sell powdered zinc, and he will not be in the wrong, though he may know or expect that the people who buy it from him are going to use it in such a way it will amount to an infringement of Mr. Innes' patent rights. But he must not ask the people to use it in that way, and he must not ask the people to use it in that way in order to induce them to buy his powdered zinc from him."

In *Amstrad* Lord Templeman commented on that passage:

> "Assuming that decision to be correct, it does not assist BPI because in the present case Amstrad did not ask anyone to use an Amstrad model in a way which would amount to an infringement."

He concluded, as regards liability for procurement:

> "Sales and advertisements to the public generally of a machine which may be used for lawful or unlawful purposes, including infringement of copyright, cannot be said to 'procure' all breaches of copyright thereafter by members of the public who use the machine. Generally speaking, inducement, incitement or persuasion to infringe must be by a defendant to an individual infringer and must identifiably procure a particular infringement in order to make the defendant liable as a joint infringer."

2–079 That passage distinguishes the general advertising to the public in *Amstrad* from the individual instructions in the powdered zinc case. It suggests that if the inducement, incitement or persuasion is sufficiently focused on an individual infringer and an identifiable particular infringement, then joint liability will accrue for actual infringements that ensue even if, after the inducement has taken place, the means of infringing leave the defendant's control and the ultimate infringer retains the ability to choose whether or not to infringe.

Authorisation and joint tortfeasorship are discussed further in relation to the distribution of peer-to-peer software (para.2–151 below). They are also relevant to the discussion of the legality of creating hypertext links to other people's copyright works without permission (para.2–093) and of liability for creating hypertext links to infringing material (para.2–143).

Secondary infringement

The importation, sale, distribution, possession in the course of business or public distribution of an infringing article is also infringement, as is permitting a place of public entertainment to be used to perform an infringing work in public. This is "secondary infringement". Acts of secondary infringement require an element of knowledge or reason to believe that the article was an infringing copy. **2–080**

There is a specific secondary infringement provision of the 1998 Act applicable to remote copying by means of networks (s.24(2)). According to this provision a person who transmits the work over a telecommunications system (otherwise than by communication to the public) knowing or having reason to believe that infringing copies of the work will be made by means of the reception of the transmission in the UK or elsewhere is himself an infringer. A "telecommunications system" is broadly defined by s.178 of the 1988 Act as "a system for conveying visual images, sounds or other information by electronic means".

Infringement involving the use of electronic media

The 1988 Act made provision for infringement involving the use of electronic media. Under the Act copying includes storing the work in any medium by electronic means, and translation of a computer program includes conversion from source to object code or translation into a different source code. The term "electronic" means "actuated by electric, magnetic, electro-magnetic, electro-chemical or electro-mechanical energy". **2–081**

The 1988 Act provides that copying includes the making of a copy which is transient or incidental to some other use of the work, so that an unauthorised copy made temporarily in RAM while accessing a copyright work on the internet would *prima facie* render the person viewing the work an infringer.

However, the potential for the mere viewing of a work other than a computer program or database to result in infringement is now somewhat reduced as a result of the "temporary acts of reproduction" exception introduced by the Copyright and Related Rights Regulations 2003 (see para.2–014 above).

2.6.2 Applying copyright infringement to the internet

Activities on the internet potentially fall within a variety of infringement provisions. Some activities throw into clear relief the problems of classification caused by the historic roots of copyright being in tangible media. Some examples of these will be considered individually. First, we will examine the potentially relevant acts of primary infringement in turn. **2–082**

Infringement by copying—section 17 of the 1988 Act

2–083   It is a restricted act to copy a work. Copying includes storing the work in any medium by electronic means. Copying in relation to any description of work includes the making of copies which are transient or are incidental to some other use of the work. The proliferation of transient, temporary and permanent copies which arises on a network means that there will almost certainly be a copy somewhere on the basis of which a wronged copyright owner could potentially base his complaint. It may also be arguable that the user's screen display itself amounts to a copy.[45]

Usually the target defendant will have created a copy of the work on his own computer system. However, on a public network that is not always the case. The copies may be created on some other person's system.

Further, persons on whose equipment the copies are created as a result of the target defendant's activities may be relatively innocent intermediaries or end-users, who may (depending on the circumstances) seek to invoke the protection of fair dealing, implied licence or other defences such as the "temporary acts of reproduction" exception introduced on October 31, 2003 by the Copyright and Related Rights Regulations 2003 (see para.2–014 above), or argue that they are mere involuntary copyists (see paras 2–104, 2–169 below).

The copyright owner who wishes to rely on copying may sometimes have to argue that the defendant has in some way copied remotely (e.g. by causing the copy to be stored on someone else's computer), or resort to alleging authorisation or procurement of primary infringement by someone else. These difficulties are compounded if the activities are carried on cross-border.

Infringement by issue of copies to the public—section 18 of the 1988 Act

2–084   It is a restricted act to issue to the public copies of a work. These provisions were amended by the Copyright and Related Rights Regulations 1996, which came into force on December 1, 1996. The amended provisions create a regime of exhaustion of rights within the EEA, but not internationally. The section, as amended, gives the copyright owner the right to control the act of putting into circulation copies not previously put into circulation in the EEA, but not any subsequent distribution, sale, hiring or loan of those copies or any subsequent importation of those copies into the EEA.

This section is aimed at what can loosely be described as publishing. Its obvious application is to permanent copies issued on tangible media such as books or disks.

---

[45] In *Bookmakers' Afternoon Greyhound Services Ltd v Wilf Gilbert (Staffordshire) Ltd* [1994] F.S.R. 723, a case under the 1956 Act, Aldous J. (as he then was) held that a race card transmitted by satellite link to a bookmaker's shop was reproduced in a material form when the bookmaker turned on the monitor and the race card materialised on the screen. However, it is arguable that such an interpretation does not conform with the scheme of the 1988 Act (see Laddie, Prescott and Victoria *"The Modern Law of Copyright and Designs"* (3rd edn., para.14.11)).

However, on the face of it the section may apply equally to copies issued in intangible and even transient form, such as when a person makes a work available for viewing and/or download from a website. There may be contrary arguments to the effect that the stream of bits from the website to the viewer's computer does not constitute a copy at any one time, so that no new copy comes into existence until the bits are assembled at the recipient computer; and if that is so, how can the website proprietor have issued the copy?

Another related argument could be that the website proprietor has not actively issued copies. He has only passively made the site available and it is the act of a third party visiting the site which causes the copy to be made. Such arguments may be unconvincing to a court seeking to ensure that the legislation retains its effectiveness in a digital context.[46] However, now that the "making available" right has been introduced (see para.2–087 below) there is less need to adopt a stretched interpretation of s.18.

It is also noteworthy that "publication" (which is now relevant only to subsistence of copyright) in relation to a work is defined in s.175 of the 1998 Act, which states that it "means the issue of copies to the public" and "includes ... making it available to the public by means of an electronic retrieval system".

Section 18A provides for infringement by rental or lending to the public   2–085
of copies of a literary, dramatic or musical work, most types of artistic work, and films and sound recordings. These provisions give rise to no particular issues arise in the context of the internet.

Infringement by performance—section 19 of the 1988 Act

It is a restricted act to perform in public a literary, dramatic or musical   2–086
work, or to play or show in public a sound recording, film, or broadcast. Performance includes any mode of visual or acoustic presentation, including presentation by means of a sound recording, film, or broadcast. Where copyright in a work is infringed by its being performed, played or shown in public by means of apparatus for receiving visual images or sounds conveyed by electronic means, the person by whom the visual images or sounds are sent, and in the case of a performance the performers, are not to be regarded as responsible for the infringement.

It is not clear whether public performance is restricted to what happens at the receiving screen, or whether making material available on a website for public consumption could in itself constitute public performance. The former probably fits better with the scheme of the 1998 Act, given that there is now a separate category of infringement by communication to the

---

[46] In the different context of a prosecution under the Obscene Publications Act 1959, the Court of Appeal, while conceding for the sake of argument that active steps were necessary, was unimpressed with an argument that a defendant's giving certain others passwords access did not amount to "showing" the pictures as contended by the prosecution. Although the defendant in that case did more than merely make the archive available because he had taken steps to issue passwords and so on, it would be surprising if a defendant who had to take fewer active steps because he gave unrestricted access would thereby have escaped liability. See *R v Fellows, R v Arnold* [1997] 2 All ER 548 (also discussed in Ch.6 para.6–050).

public by electronic transmission, which includes broadcasting and making available to the public (see para.2–087). Infringement by performance does not appear to be restricted to a performance of a theatrical or declamatory nature. It has been held in a case under the 1956 Act[47] that a greyhound racecard was performed when it was transmitted by satellite to a television monitor in a bookmaker's shop.

Infringement by communication to the public—section 20 of the 1988 Act

2–087   Under the predecessor of the current s.20, in force until October 31, 2003, it was a restricted act to broadcast a work or to include it in a cable programme service. This applied to literary, dramatic, musical or artistic works and also to sound recordings and films or a broadcast or cable programme.

These provisions were difficult to apply to the internet and had the curious result that much (but not all) of the information provided on websites probably fell within the definition of cable programme services.[48] These provisions have now been swept away and replaced by the right of communication to the public introduced by the Copyright and Related Rights Regulations 2003, implementing the EU Copyright in the Information Society Directive (see para.2–020 above).

2–088   Under the new s.20 the communication to the public of the work is an act restricted by the copyright in a literary, dramatic, musical or artistic work, a sound recording or film, or a broadcast. References to communication to the public are to communication to the public by electronic transmission, and include—

(a) the broadcasting of the work;
(b) the making available to the public of the work by electronic transmission in such a way that members of the public may access it from a place and at a time individually chosen by them.

The "making available" right is clearly formulated to cover publication on the internet. Under s.6 a "broadcast" means an electronic transmission of visual images, sounds or other information which—

(a) is transmitted for simultaneous reception by members of the public and is capable of being lawfully received by them, or
(b) is transmitted at a time determined solely by the person making the transmission for presentation to members of the public,

---

[47] *Bookmakers' Afternoon Greyhound Services Ltd v Wilf Gilbert (Staffordshire) Ltd* [1994] F.S.R. 723.

[48] See the discussion at paras 2–068 to 2–070 and 2–078 to 2–079 of the Third Edition of this work. See also *Sony Music Entertainment (UK) Ltd v Easyinternetcafe Ltd* [2003] EWHC 62 (Ch), in which the judge expressed the *obiter* view that the transmission of material via the internet was a cable programme service and that the decision in *Shetland Times Ltd v Wills* [1997] F.S.R. 604 was correct on that point.

and which is not excepted by subs.(1A).

Section 6(1A) excepts from the definition of "broadcast" any internet 2–089
transmission unless it is—

(a) a transmission taking place simultaneously on the internet and by other means,
(b) a concurrent transmission of a live event, or
(c) a transmission of recorded moving images or sounds forming part of a programme service offered by the person responsible for making the transmission, being a service in which programmes are transmitted at scheduled times determined by that person.

The 1998 Act does not attempt a definition of "internet transmission".

Infringement by making adaptation or act done in relation to adaptation— section 21 of the 1988 Act

It is a restricted act to make an adaptation of a literary, dramatic or musical 2–090
work. Adaptation includes translation. In relation to computer programs
(which may have wide ranging effect on the web—see para.2–015 above)
an adaptation means an arrangement or altered version of the program or a
translation of it. A translation of a computer program includes a version of
the program in which it is converted into or out of a computer language or
code or into a different computer language or code.

It should be noted that under s.50C of the 1988 Act, it is not an
infringement of copyright for a lawful user of a copy of a computer program to copy or adapt it, provided that the copying or adapting (a) is
necessary for his lawful use; and (b) is not prohibited under any term or
condition of an agreement regulating the circumstances in which his use is
lawful. There are also separate provisions relating to back-up copies and
reverse engineering under ss.50A and 50B of the 1988 Act.

In *Sony Computer Entertainment v Paul Owen*[49] Jacob J. (as he then
was) commented on the meaning of "necessary" in s. 50A in relation to
back-up copies. He suggested that the provision was aimed at cases in
which there was separate express licence other than the implied licence to
use the article itself as embodied on a disc. For certain types of software,
such as computer games, where there might not be a separate licence, back-
ups were not necessary at all and if the CD was spoiled the customer would
have to purchase a new one.

Pumfrey J. in *Navitaire, Inc v Easyjet Airline Co Ltd*[50] held that 2–091
"necessary" in s.50D (things necessary for the purposes of access to and use
of the contents of the database) excluded the merely desirable or convenient, but did not require the merely absurd.

While on the subject of computer programs we should note that on

---

[49] [2002] EWHC 45 (Ch).
[50] [2004] EWHC 1725 (Ch), [2005] E.C.D.R. 17.

October 31, 2003 the Copyright and Related Rights Regulations 2003 introduced a new s.50BA of the 1988 Act, to ensure compliance with Art.5.3 of the Software Directive. The new section provides that it is not an infringement of copyright for a lawful user of a copy of a computer program to observe, study or test the functioning of the program in order to determine the ideas and principles which underlie any element of the program, if he does so while performing any of the acts of loading, displaying, running, transmitting or storing the program which he is entitled to do. Section 296A renders void any term or condition in an agreement which purports to prohibit or restrict the act.

Secondary infringement

2–092 Sections 22–26 of the 1988 Act set out various categories of secondary infringement: importing an infringing copy, possessing or dealing with an infringing copy, providing means for making infringing copies, permitting the use of premises for an infringing performance and provision of apparatus for an infringing performance.

The common factor in all of these categories is a requirement of knowledge: for instance, in the case of importation, possession or dealing, that the person knew or had reason to believe that the article was an infringing copy of the work.[51]

In general, given the convergence of copying and distribution in the on-line environment and the consequent likelihood of primary infringement, secondary infringement will be of lesser importance.

We now turn to some examples of scenarios peculiar to the internet which have posed particular problems for analysis of copyright and database right infringement.

2.6.3 Web linking

Can the website owner prevent linking to his site?

2–093 The web, we have observed, is a system of hypertext links which enables the browser to skip from one document to another by clicking on a highlighted part of the document. The web is no respecter of boundaries or ownership. The web has flourished precisely because a web page author can create links which point to documents on any other site, whether or not he has any connection with it.

In the light of this the question is sometimes asked whether the proprietor of a site has any right to control who links to his site. This is not necessarily

---

[51] Note *Universal Music Australia Pty Ltd v Cooper* [2005] Federal Court of Australia 972 (July 14, 2005), in which Tamberlin J. decided that providing hypertext links to infringing MP3 files did not amount to sale or exposure for sale of an "article". Compare with Laddie J's comments on the meaning of "article" for the purpose of s. 27 of the 1988 Act in *Kabushiki Kaisha Sony Computer Entertainment, Inc v Ball* [2004] EWHC 1738 (Ch).

just a question of copyright. Database right is also important. There could be trade mark or passing off questions, or in some countries moral rights or unfair competition aspects. Here we will review some aspects of the copyright and database right position.

How an ordinary hypertext link works

The technical aspects of web linking are important to the copyright ana-   2–094
lysis. An HTML link is a pointer to the address of a page (or sometimes to a place within a page) stored on a host. The author of a web page can create a link to another part of the same page, to another document on his own site, or to a document on any other internet host whose address he knows or can find out. So if a web page author wanted to create a link to the home page of Bird & Bird's website he would use the following HTML text:

<A HREF="http://www.twobirds.com"> Bird & Bird</A>.

When read by a typically configured web browser that code would appear on the user's screen as:

Bird & Bird

Looking at the constituent parts of the HTML text making up the link, "http:// www.twobirds.com" is the address (or "URL"—Uniform Resource Locator) of the target website, in this case Bird & Bird. The <A HREF ... > code instructs the computer to fetch the home page directly from the target site when the user clicks on the Bird & Bird link. The author can target a particular page inside the site by noting the URL of that page and using that in the link. The URL, it should be noted, is copied from the target website. For a "deep link" (see para.2–095 below) the URL may be a reasonably lengthy string of words and characters.

It should be stressed that using the link on the linking website does not cause any copy of the target page to come into existence, at any stage, on the linking website's web server. Nothing happens on the target site until the link is clicked by the user. When the link is clicked the user's browser establishes a connection direct to the target site and fetches the target page directly from it, just as if the user had typed in the URL on his browser to go to the site. The user receives the target page directly from the target site, not via the linking site. This can be shown graphically as follows:

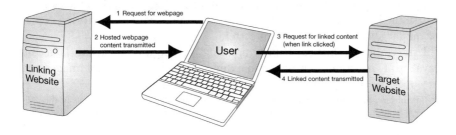

This basic form of link is the defining feature of the web.

Deep linking

2–095   Where a link is created not to the home page of the target site, but to a subsidiary page, this is known as "deep linking". The web is full of deep links which provoke no objection. Some deep links, however, threaten the business model and revenues of the target site. For instance, if the target site depends on advertising revenues those may be reduced if users are directed straight to a subsidiary page, by-passing pages containing advertising.

Inline linking—the virtual document

2–096   Another form of HTML link, the "inline" link, may also be encountered. A web page is built up of text and images. But the images are stored separately on the server. The HTML text document includes a code which not only tells the user's browser the URL of the image, but also instructs the browser to load the image automatically as part of the document if the user has not disabled images. The code to achieve that is:

    <IMG SRC ... >

Using this code to instruct the user's browser to assemble documents from the web host's own collection of data is unexceptional. However, the <IMG SRC ... > code can also be used to fetch images from other sites. These links work in the same way as an ordinary link except that the user's computer fetches and loads the target images automatically when the web page is loaded, rather than waiting for the user to click on the link. In the same way as with the ordinary link, no copy of the target image comes into existence at any time on the linking host's server. The images are sent directly from the target server to the user's computer.

    <IMG SRC ... > links could be used to build up a complete "virtual document" consisting of images sourced from other hosts—but which on the home host consists of nothing but a few lines of text with pointers to the URLs of the target images. The version of the document including the images is automatically assembled only when the user fetches the page from the home host, and comes into existence only on the user's screen and in his computer. The effect for the user is almost the same as if the home host had copied the images on to his own host.[52] But by using pointers to the genuine works the linking host avoids the clearly infringing activity of storing copies of the target images on his own system.

    Using more sophisticated programming techniques (e.g. using Java and JavaScript) it would be possible to extend the principle beyond images and

---

[52] The observant user might notice the browser status bar indicating that elements of the page were being fetched from the target site. However, that is nothing unusual in an environment where, for instance, banner advertisements are often supplied from locations other than the website's own servers.

create sophisticated virtual documents drawing on other hosts' content. As with <IMG SRC ... > links, these would not involve the home host in creating, or causing to be created, any copies other than those in the user's computer, which would also come into existence if the user were to access the target host direct.

Linking and implied licence

Does either of these examples of linking (user-activated links and in-line links) constitute copyright infringement if done without permission, and if so why?[53]   2–097

Whichever route to infringement is examined, the answer seems to boil down (at least for the virtual document created by in-line linking) either to a question of fair dealing or to a question of the scope of the implied licence granted by the target host to the public to access and browse its site.

It might be thought that there is no longer any need to imply a permission to browse in the light of the "temporary reproductions" exception in Art.5 of the Copyright in the Information Society Directive. However, as discussed in para.2–014 above, the exception only applies in relation to a lawful use of the work, and Recital (33) of the Directive states that a use is to be considered lawful where it is authorised by the rightholder or not restricted by law. Since the applicability of the exception, therefore, itself turns on the extent of the implied licence to browse, the exception changes nothing.

The fundamental challenge to any allegation of infringement by linking, whatever kind of restricted act the infringement argument may be based upon, is that no more copies are created in the user's computer or anywhere else when the user accesses a website by a link than when he accesses it directly by typing or pasting the URL into the address bar of his browser. So no extra or different copies of the target content are created that might require a separate permission. If, then, a user has permission to browse a site, why does he not have permission to do so regardless of whether he initiates the browsing directly from the address bar of his browser or from a link?

The point that a link is functionally equivalent to the user typing in the URL to his browser was heavily relied upon by the German Federal Court in *Verlagsgruppe Handelsblatt GmbH v Paperboy*,[54] holding that deep linking by an aggregator who compiled an email list of links to articles on the plaintiff's site was unobjectionable so long as it did not evade technical protection mechanisms and did not provide content access that the rightholder had not authorised.

Even if it were possible to draw a convincing distinction between direct browsing and browsing originating from a link, it would normally be   2–098

---

[53] The possibility that manual and automatic links could lead to different consequences in copyright law was mentioned in *SOCAN v Canadian Association of Internet Providers* [2004] 2 S.C.R. 427, 2004 SCC 45, at para. 25.

[54] Bundesgerichtshof, No. I ZR 259/00, July 17, 2003 [2005] E.C.D.R. 7. For more linking cases see para.2–107 below.

fanciful to suggest that a public website forbids any links to it at all. It would be a very strange website indeed that could seriously suggest that it forbade all links to it including, for instance, links in directories such as Yahoo!, links in search engine results lists, links contained in private emails, or links in private browser home pages or favourites and history lists. Linking is so embedded at the heart of the operation of the web that it would be absurd to take that position.

A website seeking to prevent certain types of linking would have enormous difficulty in suggesting, as a starting point, that no-one is entitled to link to it at all without express permission. The site is almost certain to be taken to have impliedly permitted users to load its pages via at least some types of link. The question then turns to the extent of the implied permission to browse—does it extend to browsing from all types of link, or is it restricted to some types of link and to some types or combinations of content?

One might think that an implied licence would be bound to cover user-activated links. However, the scenario does raise two possibilities: first, that a court in the factual circumstances of an extreme case may be persuaded to find that what the defendant has done is so beyond the pale as to be outside the scope of any implied licence; and second, that a claimant could gain the right to control (and charge for) linking to his site by seeking to assert an express prohibition on unauthorised linking, or linking of particular types, to the site, overriding any implied licence.

These considerations may lead on to questions of whether there is a minimum use of material on its website from which a claimant may not derogate, either by virtue of fair dealing considerations, or by invocation of the doctrine of derogation from grant, or on some other public interest ground.[55]

Copyright in a URL?

2–099 We have noted that creating a deep link to a target page entails copying the URL of the page and incorporating it into the link code. If it is asserted that this amounts to infringement of copyright in the URL, the subsistence of copyright in the URL is likely to be disputed.

In the US case of *Ticketmaster v Tickets.com*[56] the court granted the defendant's motion to dismiss Ticketmaster's copyright claims, which included a deep linking claim. Among other things the claimant alleged that

---

[55] The Court of Appeal has confirmed, in *Ashdown v Telegraph Group Ltd* [2001] EWCA Civ 1142, that rare cases could arise where the right of freedom of expression under Art. 10 of the European Convention on Human Rights comes into conflict with the protection afforded by the 1988 Act. This could give rise to a public interest defence under s.171(3) of the 1988 Act. Further, the circumstances in which the public interest might override copyright are not capable of precise categorisation or definition. They are not limited to cases in which enforcement of copyright would offend against the policy of the law. Nor need the circumstances derive from the work in question, as opposed to the ownership of the copyright. See also the comments of Buxton L.J. in *Musical Fidelity Ltd v David Vickers* [2002] EWCA Civ 1989.

[56] 2003 U.S. Dist. LEXIS 6483.

reproduction of the claimant's URLs on the defendant's site amounted to copyright infringement. The court dismissed this claim on the basis that a URL lacked sufficient originality to constitute a copyright work:

> "A URL is simply an address, open to the public, like the street address of a building, which, if known, can enable the user to reach the building. There is nothing sufficiently original to make the URL a copyrightable item, especially the way it is used (*Feist Publications ('91)*, 499 U.S. 340, 113 L. Ed. 2d 358 at 369, 111 S. Ct. 1282). There appear to be no cases holding the URLs to be subject to copyright. On principle, they should not be."

This was a decision under US law which, at least since the *Feist* decision   **2–100**
referred to in the extract from the judgment, has set arguably a higher threshold for originality than has English law. By way of contrast, in *Navitaire, Inc. v Easyjet Airline Co Ltd*[57] Pumfrey J. appears to have contemplated that a complex keyboard command such as A13JUNLT-NAMS could have been sufficiently original for copyright to subsist if it had been recorded and if it had not, as he found, formed part of a computer language and was therefore denied protection by the terms of the EU Software Directive.[58]

If Pumfrey J. was correct that the keyboard commands in *Navitaire* were part of a computer language and therefore should be denied copyright protection, could the same be said of a URL? A URL exhibits some characteristics in common with the keyboard commands. The URL has to be written with a certain (albeit simple) four part structure: [http://][www].[string/string/string]. [htm] (http, www and htm may be substituted with a number of other permitted codes.)

The URL, when transmitted, is effectively an instruction to the server to   **2–101**
return the corresponding web pages. In that sense it is as much a "defined user command interface" to the web server and part of a computer program as the keyboard commands were in *Navitaire*. A URL, however, can also be seen as nothing more than a document file name conforming to a particular convention. The idea that document file names can be regarded as part of a programming language would strike many as absurd.

There are, in any event, certain aspects of the reasoning in *Navitaire* which may give a future court pause for thought. First, the Recitals to the EU Software Directive do not in terms state that they deny protection to computer languages. Recital (14) states that:

---

[57] [2004] EWHC 1725 (Ch), [2005] E.C.D.R. 17.
[58] Paras 83 and 85 of the judgment suggest that if the command had been recorded it could have been the subject of copyright. The judge's conclusions based on the EU Software Directive are set out at paras 86 to 89 and 93 to 94.

> "to the extent that logic, algorithms and programming languages comprise ideas and principles those ideas and principles are not protected under this Directive".

Programming languages *per se* are not denied protection—only to the extent that they comprise ideas and principles.

The Recital refers to algorithms as well as programming languages. We doubt if it could be suggested that the effect of the Recital is to deny copyright protection to algorithms as such. It is difficult to see why programming languages should be different.

It is also notable that the Recital does not use the term "computer language" at all. It uses "programming language". It is surely open to question whether a set of keyboard commands for operating an existing computer program, as opposed to a defined syntax for commands destined to form part of a computer program, can properly be regarded as a programming language.[59]

So although on the basis of *Navitaire* it might be possible to regard a URL as being denied protection under the Software Directive, it is also possible that *Navitaire* will prove to be a flimsy foundation on which to build such a case. It should also be noted that Pumfrey J. observed that the question whether computer languages are included in the protection afforded to computer programs is not entirely clear and would require referral to the European Court of Justice.

2–102   If (which we doubt) a URL is to be regarded as a computer program, then regardless of whether it constitutes a programming language, that could affect the degree of originality required to attract copyright. Article 1(3) of the Software Directive provides that a computer program shall be protected "if it is original in the sense that it is the author's own intellectual creation" and states that no other criteria shall be applied to determine its eligibility for protection. Unlike with databases, this requirement is not written into the 1988 Act. However, the 1988 Act should be interpreted so as to conform with the Directive. That could have the effect of raising the originality threshold for computer programs to something akin to the *Feist* level discussed above.

As for implied permission, for a URL no extra copy is made when including the URL in a link than when typing it into a browser. However, it might be argued that a different type of copy is made, since the URL pasted into the browser exists only for a short time whereas that in a link is permanent. However, that distinction is less easy to sustain if the comparison is made with links created in an on-line directory page, or in a user's favourites or history list.

---

[59] So, for instance, an Applications Programming Interface (API) could properly be regarded as a programming language, since it provides a set of functions designed to be incorporated into another computer program enabling it to interoperate with the first program. While many of those functions might achieve exactly the same result as certain user keyboard commands, we suggest that that does not mean that the equivalent user keyboard commands necessarily constitute a *programming* language.

Did *Shetland Times* find that linking to a site without its permission amounted to infringement?

The issue of linking as infringement has been touched on in the Scottish case   **2–103**
of *Shetland Times Ltd v Wills* (see note to para.2–087 above). The case, in
which the pursuer (plaintiff) was granted an interim interdict (i.e. injunction) against the defender (defendant) over aspects of its "Shetland News"
website, attracted considerable publicity, being interpreted as holding that
linking to another website can infringe copyright. However, the judgment
was given at an interim interdict stage before a full trial. Further, any
linking issues were somewhat overshadowed by the allegation that the
defender had included actual copies of headlines from the plaintiff's site on
its website.[60]

The judgment was notable for holding that the pursuer had a *prima facie*
case that its website constituted a cable programme service under the then
version of the 1988 Act and that the defender was infringing under both
s.17 (copying) and the then version of s.20 (inclusion in a cable programme
service).

Although the question of links from the defender's allegedly copied
headlines to the equivalent news stories within the pursuer's site featured in
the judgment, and the judge found in considering the balance of convenience that "it was fundamental to the setting up by the pursuers of their
website that access to their material should be gained only by accessing
their web directly" (as opposed to by-passing the front page by links from
the defender's site directly to the pursuer's news stories), it is certainly not
clear that the judge held there was a *prima facie* case that the links (as
opposed to the headlines) constituted infringement.

The case ought not to be regarded as authority for the proposition that
linking to a site without its permission can constitute infringement. The
case was settled before full trial, on terms permitting the Shetland News to
link to *Shetland Times* stories under certain conditions. These required the
Shetland News to acknowledge, using a specified legend, the *Shetland
Times* as the source of the linked story and to provide links and adjacent
logo button links to the *Shetland Times* online headline page.

Linking to a site without permission—causation, authorisation and joint tortfeasorship

In the case of in-line links the user, when he loads the web page, inevitably   **2–104**
loads the target site content and creates at least a transient copy of the
target content in his computer's RAM in the course of automatically
assembling the virtual document as directed by the defendant's website.

It is quite possible that a court would regard the assembly of a virtual

---

[60] The legality of including copies of newspaper headlines in the Google News service was
addressed in the judgment of the Brussels Court of First Instance in *Copiepresse v Google,
Inc*, dated February 15, 2007. The court found that some headlines were sufficiently original to be capable of constituting copyright works.

document by means of automatic links to selected content on a target website as being outside the scope of any implied licence to browse and therefore as infringing. If so, there would be a strong argument that the person who created the links had authorised or procured the infringement[61] and also quite possibly that he had directly caused the infringing copies to come into existence.

Conversely, the user might escape any theoretical[62] liability, on the basis that his role was purely passive. The argument would be that the user's computer was no more than a machine on which the copies of the third party content were created automatically by the proprietor of the linking web page; and that as with the owner of a fax machine to whom a third party sent an infringing document it could not be said that the owner of the machine had caused the infringing copy to be created.[63] However, it could also persuasively be argued that the user's role in accessing and loading the linking site was sufficient take him outside the scope of purely passive involvement.[64]

For a user-activated link it may be argued that the causal connection between actions of the proprietor of the linking website and the loading of the target content is broken by the intervention of the user of the website in clicking on the link.

If so, the questions are then whether the proprietor of the linking website has authorised the user's acts by including the links on his page, and, what is the scope of the implied licence to copy attaching to the target website.

2–105   As to authorisation, in *C.B.S. Songs v Amstrad Consumer Electronics*[65] the House of Lords held that for a person to be liable for authorisation there should have been a grant or purported grant, which might be express or implied, of the right to do the act complained of. Providing a user-activated link to a third party website could (in the appropriate context and

---

[61] To create a collection of links that automatically load content from a third party site, giving the impression that the imported content is the website's own content, must surely satisfy the condition laid down by the House of Lords in *C.B.S. Songs v Amstrad Consumer Electronics* [1988] A.C. 1013 that for a person to be liable for authorisation there should have been a grant or purported grant, which might be express or implied, of the right to do the act complained of (see para.2–073 above). In a different context, for instance a search engine, creating in-line links to (say) third party streaming video in a search result would not necessarily carry the same implication or amount to authorisation.

[62] We say "theoretical" because it is hardly likely that a potential claimant would have any interest in pursuing a user.

[63] *Sony Music Entertainment (UK) Ltd v Easyinternetcafe Ltd* [2003] EWHC 62 (Ch).

[64] If successful, the argument that the user's role was passive as regards the third party linked content would illustrate the tension between the principle that knowledge is not a component of primary copyright infringement and the notion that there can be such a thing as involvement in copying so passive as to be non-causative. If the user returned to the website knowing, as a result of the first visit, that it contained in-line links to third party content, it would be hard to avoid the conclusion that on the return visit the user caused the target content to be loaded onto his computer. However, the only difference between the first and second visits would be the degree of the user's knowledge.

[65] [1988] A.C. 1013 (see para.2–073 above).

in the absence of a suitable disclaimer[66]) be regarded as authorising the user to load the third party content by activating the link.[67]

The context is likely to be critical in determining whether providing the link amounts to authorisation. It is most unlikely that a user would regard a search engine, whose object is to index the whole or a substantial part of the internet, as impliedly granting the right to use the content to which it creates links in its search results. However, a user would probably view a proprietary content site differently, and expect the site owner to have a sufficient right in the content made available on the site through links. As the search sites start to move into content provision in their own right, and users become less sure what type of site they are looking at, so this line may become blurred.

There is a suggestion in the Canadian Supreme Court case of *SOCAN v Canadian Association of Internet Providers*[68] that although ordinarily the activities of an internet service provider would not amount to authorising infringement, that could change if it failed to take action after receiving notice of infringing activity:

> "123 The operation of the internet is obviously a good deal more complicated than the operation of a photocopier, but it is true here, as it was in the *CCH* case, that when massive amounts of non-copyrighted material are accessible to the end user, it is not possible to impute to the internet service provider, based solely on the provision of internet facilities, an authority to download copyrighted material as opposed to non-copyrighted material.
>
> 124 On this point the Board concluded as follows (at p. 458):
>
> > "Even knowledge by an ISP that its facilities may be employed for infringing purposes does not make the ISP liable for authorizing the infringement if it does not purport to grant to the person committing the infringement a license or permission to infringe. An intermediary would have to sanction, approve or countenance more than the mere use of equipment that may be used for infringement. Moreover, an ISP is entitled to presume that its facilities will be used in accordance with law."
>
> This conclusion is generally consistent with the decision of this Court in the *CCH* case, although I would point out that copyright liability may well attach if the activities of the internet service provider cease to be content neutral, e.g. if it has notice that a content provider has posted infringing material on its system and fails to take remedial action.

---

[66] The efficacy of a disclaimer may be doubtful where, unlike in *Amstrad*, the technology is not dual-use. So if clicking on a particular link inevitably results in infringement the presence of a disclaimer may not be determinative.

[67] See also the discussion at para.2–143 below of liability for authorisation when a link is established that points to infringing material.

[68] [2004] 2 S.C.R. 427, 2004 SCC 45.

...

127 ... I agree that notice of infringing content, and a failure to respond by "taking it down" may in some circumstances lead to a finding of "authorization". However, that is not the issue before us. Much would depend on the specific circumstances. An overly quick inference of 'authorization' would put the internet service provider in the difficult position of judging whether the copyright objection is well founded, and to choose between contesting a copyright action or potentially breaching its contract with the content provider. A more effective remedy to address this potential issue would be the enactment by Parliament of a statutory 'notice and take down' procedure as has been done in the European Community and the United States.

128 In sum, I agree with the Court of Appeal that 'authorization' could be inferred in a proper case but all would depend on the facts."

2–106 Context, including statements made on the website, is also likely to be important in determining whether there has been common design or inducement. The richer and more personalised the user experience offered by the website, the more likely it is that the *Amstrad* test that the "inducement, incitement or persuasion to infringe must be by a defendant to an individual infringer and must identifiably procure a particular infringement"[69] will be satisfied.

Linking and communication to the public

2–107 Section 20 of the 1988 Act now provides for a restricted act of communication to the public, introduced as from October 31, 2003 by the Copyright and Related Rights Regulations 2003 (see para.2–020 above). Communication to the public includes broadcasting and a new "making available" right. Broadcasting is redefined to include some internet transmissions such as simultaneous webcasts. "Making available" is a broadly defined act that covers internet and other user-selectable electronic transmissions available to members of the public.

In *Polydor v Brown*[70] it was held that as soon as a copy of a music file is placed without licence in a peer-to-peer (P2P) fileshare directory on a user's computer running P2P software and connected to the internet, that infringes the "communication to the public" right.

The question arises whether creating a link to a work on a target website constitutes the making available to the public of the work by electronic transmission in such a way that members of the public may access it from a place and at a time individually chosen by them (CDPA 1988 s.20(2)(b)); and if not, whether it constitutes authorisation of such an act.

---

[69] See para.2–078 above.
[70] [2005] EWHC 3191.

The first problem for a claimant is that he has himself already made the content available by putting it on his site. It is difficult to see how creating a link to the content could be regarded as authorising an infringing act of making available, since the target content is already legitimately available.

The claimant could resort to the argument that creating a publicly available link is itself a new and separate act of "making available". If that argument were correct, there would be a basis for a website owner to argue that he had not authorised that act, and that it was distinguishable from his own act of putting his content on his site and creating his own publicly available links to it.

That argument probably ought not to succeed, since creating a link is no 2–108 more than a method (functionally indistinguishable from typing a URL into a browser[71]) by which a member of the public may access the content that has been made available. The making available right is directed not to protecting the method of access, but to protecting the making available of the content in such a way that members of the public can exercise that type of access. Creating a link ought not to amount to a separate act of making available.

That view is supported by cases in Europe and Australia (in particular *Bruvik* and *Cooper*). These are discussed in para.2–143 below, since on their facts they concerned liability for linking to infringing material.

A claimant might consider invoking the secondary infringement provision of s.24(2) of the 1988 Act (transmitting a work over a telecommunications system knowing or having reason to believe that infringing copies of the work will be made by means of the reception of the transmission in the UK or elsewhere). However, given the exclusion from this provision of communication to the public, the likelihood of its applying to the situations discussed appears to be remote.

In a US case, *Ticketmaster Corp., et al v Tickets.com, Inc.*[72], the plaintiff alleged copyright infringement based (among other things) on deep linking to pages of the plaintiff's website. The judge, on a motion for an interlocutory injunction, observed:

> "Hyperlinking does not itself involve a violation of the Copyright Act ... since no copying is involved. The customer is automatically transferred to the particular genuine web page of the original author. There is no deception in what is happening. This is analogous to using a library's card index to get a reference to particular items, albeit faster and more efficiently".

Some European decisions based on database right are discussed below. More recently, the US District Court for the Northern District of Texas,

---

[71] *Cf. Paperboy*, para.2–097 above.
[72] US Dist. Ct., C.D. Cal March 27, 2000 (2000 US Dist. LEXIS 4553). In March 2003 the court granted the defendant's motion to dismiss Ticketmaster's copyright claims (2003 US Dist. LEXIS 6483), including the deep linking claim. Claims alleging breach of the claimant's website terms of use were allowed to go forward.

in *Live Nation Motor Sports Inc v Davis*[73], considered the argument that an unauthorised link on the defendant's website to the claimant's webcast of a live sporting event qualified as a copied display or performance. The court found the argument sufficiently strong to justify granting an interim injunction.

Deep linking and database right

2–109 The advent of a database right, created in UK law by the implementation of the EU Database Directive (discussed in para.2–061 above), may provide a further basis on which a qualifying website owner may seek to assert control over those linking to its site. The Directive is implemented by the Copyright and Rights in Databases Regulations 1997.

Websites as databases

2–110 The definition of "database"—a collection of independent works, data or other materials which are arranged in a systematic or methodical way and are individually accessible by electronic or other means (reg.6)—is sufficiently wide to include a collection of materials on a website. The owner of the database right has, under reg.16, the right to prevent the extraction or re-utilisation of all or a substantial part of the contents of his database without his consent.

"Extraction" means the permanent or temporary transfer of contents to another medium by any means and in any form. "Re-utilisation" means making the contents available to the public by any means. "Substantial" means substantial in terms or quality or quantity or a combination of both

Under reg.19, the lawful user of a database which has been made available to the public in any manner is entitled to extract or re-use insubstantial parts of the contents of the database for any purpose. We have discussed at para.2–063 above the interpretation placed by the European Court of Justice on the scope of database right.

It is likely that the contents of at least some websites would constitute a database for the purpose of the Regulations and that, if the database has been made by a qualified person, database right would subsist in the website. We will assume in this discussion for simplicity that one website may constitute one database. However, especially given the seamlessly linked nature of the web, it is quite likely that one database may not be coterminous with one website.

The question whether any particular website would qualify as a database depends on how widely "systematic or methodical" is to be interpreted. A simple website typically consists of a number of static pages of text and graphics, linked by hypertext links. The result has a structure of a sort, and typically considerable thought goes into the arrangement of the contents. However, the structure is essentially free-form rather than comprised of

---

[73] "Unauthorized link to Webcast Likely Infringes Webcaster's Copyrights" E.C.L.R. Vol.11, No. 48 p.1204, December 20, 2006.

information organised into pre-defined records and fields in the manner of a traditional structured database. In short, in a simple website the systematic and methodical aspects are more in the means of access to the information (the links) than in the data itself.

Many websites show more systematic and methodical characteristics in the underlying data. At the simplest level the text and graphics files are organised in hierarchical directory structures—not necessary for the operation of a site, but useful for ease of maintenance. Often the web page seen by the user contains selected data, perhaps in the form of a table, generated dynamically from a traditional database engine driving the website. **2–111**

In considering this issue, the terms of the Directive itself need to be borne in mind. Recital (21) states that, although the materials have to be arranged systematically or methodically, it is not necessary for those materials to have been physically stored in an organised manner. Recital (40) stresses that the object of the database right is to ensure protection of any investment in obtaining, verifying or presenting the contents of a database for the limited duration of the right. These recitals suggest that a wide interpretation of "systematic or methodical" arrangement may be appropriate.

Linking to a site without permission as infringement of database right

Turning to infringement, it appears that the person who accesses a website may extract content from the site to his own computer, within the definition in the Regulations, at least if temporary transfer includes transfer to the relatively transient medium of RAM. That is the equivalent for copyright purposes of making a copy. The person who creates a link provides a pointer to the target site, thereby assisting the user to extract from the target site, but does not himself extract data from that site. **2–112**

It is possibly arguable that the person creating the link makes the target content available to the public, and thereby re-utilises the target content within the meaning of the Regulations. Whether that would constitute re-utilising a substantial part of the database would depend on the circumstances, but where the link brings up the contents of an entire page that could very well be a substantial part, particularly when the quality test is applied.

Under reg.16(2), repeated and systematic extraction or re-utilisation of insubstantial parts of the contents of a database may amount to extraction or re-utilisation of a substantial part of those contents. That suggests that creating a collection of links to content on the same website may constitute re-utilisation of a substantial part, even if each individual link re-utilises only an insubstantial part. Arguably, even repeated use of the link by different users amounts to repeated re-utilisation for the purposes of reg.16(2).

A real life example to which this could apply occurred in the US, where a fan of the *Dilbert* comic strip created a series of links to comic strips on the *Dilbert* web page of the owner of the copyright in the strips, United Media Services. In this way he created a new (and, he asserted, improved) *Dilbert* website, in which the comic strips were displayed in a new and different context and manner. While each individual drawing and strip is the subject of copyright, and it was with copyright infringement that United Media Services threatened the fan, in the EU the assertion of database right would have been an alternative way of dealing with the re-utilisation of substantially all of the comic strips on the official *Dilbert* site.

European and Asian caselaw on deep linking

2–113   A number of decisions on database right and deep linking have been issued in different European countries. Although all of these were before the ECJ decisions in *William Hill* and *Fixtures Marketing*, they are still of interest from the point of view of their approach to deep linking. Some of these cases include elements of spidering, which is discussed further in para.2–119 below.

In *Stepstone v Ofir*,[74] a German decision, the plaintiff and defendant were both on-line job agencies, competing with each other. The defendant created deep links to a substantial number of vacancies on the plaintiff's site. The plaintiff claimed that the defendant automatically searched its database and copied and disseminated substantial parts of it. It claimed that this, as well as the deep links, infringed its database right. The defendant claimed that copying only took place when the user accessed the database, and that there was an implied licence to create the links.

The court granted an injunction against the defendant. The court held (1) that Stepstone's collection of job advertisements was a database; (2) that enabling users to have direct access to Stepstone's job vacancies, by-passing the main pages, infringed the exclusive right of copying, distribution and representation, in particular distribution which included making parts of the database available; and that the defendant had made repeated and systematic use of insubstantial parts; (3) That what the defendant had done was prejudicial to Stepstone, since it undermined its business concept and deprived it of advertising revenue; (4) that the question of implied consent did not arise where such prejudice existed. This case was before the decision of the German Federal Court in *Paperboy* considered below, which found deep linking to be unobjectionable.

Stepstone also sued Ofir in France. In a decision of the Nanterre Tribunal of Commerce,[75] the court held that the deep links to Stepstone's job vacancies did not infringe any intellectual property right.

2–114   In the Dutch case of *PCM v Kranten.com*,[76] the plaintiffs were news-

---

[74] Landgericht Köln, February 28, 2001, Electronic Business Law June 2001 p.13; [2000] E.B.L.R. 87; E-Commerce Law Reports Vol.1 Issue 2, p.14. See also "The Database Right Revolution Begins", G. Taylor, *Managing Intellectual Property* May 2001 p.18.

[75] *Sarl Stepstone France v Sarl Ofir France*, Commercial Court of Nanterre, November 8, 2000 (*www.legalis.net/breves-article.php3?id_article=83*).

[76] Sub. nom. *Algemeen Dagblad B.V. v Eureka Internetdiensten* District Court of Rotterdam August 22, 2000, [2002] E.C.D.R. 1. See also "Applying the Database Act to On Line Information Services" S.J.H. Gijrath and B.J.E. Gorissen *Copyright World* Dec 2000/Jan 2001 p.14.

papers who operated websites containing selections of news reports and articles from their newspapers. The home pages contained indexes to the contents. The defendants placed equivalent indexes on a page of their website entitled "National Newspapers", with deep links to the relevant articles and news items. The plaintiffs alleged copyright and database right infringement and sought an interim injunction.

The court held (1) that the argument that the home page was by-passed, causing loss of advertising revenue, was of little importance because there was nothing preventing the user from going to the home page; (2) the links were likely to have a promotional effect and it was unlikely that the plaintiffs were suffering real damage; (3) deep linking was not a reproduction of the linked work, so there was no copyright infringement; (4) while there had been a reproduction of the list of articles and news items, this was saved from copyright infringement by specific provisions of the Dutch Copyright Act 1912 permitting reproduction of work by a press medium provided the source is indicated; (5) it could not be said that the plaintiffs had invested substantially in the contents of the lists of titles of news items and articles. These were, therefore, not protected by database right. An interim injunction was refused.

In *NVM v De Telegraaf*[77] the plaintiff was the Dutch Association of Real Estate Agents. It operated a database of properties for sale. The defendant, a national newspaper, operated a search engine called "El Cheapo". It searched other sites, including that of the plaintiff, for properties and presented the results to the user as links. **2–115**

The first instance judge ruled in favour of the claimants on database right, also holding that there was no copyright infringement. On appeal, the Court of Appeals of the Hague overturned the finding on database right. The defendant argued that the plaintiff's database was not protectable, since it was only a fusion of the individual databases of NVM agents. The appeals court held that there was no protection where the database could be regarded as a "spin-off" of the main activity of the database owner.

On further appeal in March 2002 the Dutch Supreme Court reversed the Hague Court of Appeals judgment, holding that the investment in the original database was sufficient to qualify the "spin-off" database for database right protection. The case would now have to be considered in the light of the European Court of Justice decision in *William Hill* (para.2–063 above).

In *Havas Numerique, SNC and Cadres On Line S.A. v Keljob*,[78] the plaintiff was a leading French jobs website. The defendant operated a jobs search engine which had established deep links to specific jobs advertised on the plaintiff's site. The plaintiff sued under articles of the Intellectual Property Code implementing the database right and prohibiting the act of representing a work without the consent of its author. **2–116**

---

[77] See "El Cheapo comes out on top" D. Oosterbaan, World eBusiness Law Report July 17, 2001; also G. Taylor, *op. cit.* And S.J.H. Gijrath/B.J.E. Gorissen *op. cit.*
[78] E-commerce Law Reports Vol.1 Issue 2 p.16 (first instance); on appeal, World Internet Law Report August 2001 p.15.

The Paris Commercial Court, in an interim ruling at first instance, distinguished between the implicit authorisation for simple hypertext links and deep links, for which there was no such authorisation and which had a variety of damaging consequences, including amounting to an appropriation of the work and financial efforts of others. This was so, even though the defendant stated that it was not in competition with the plaintiff.

On appeal, the Paris Court of Appeal found that Keljob operated a search engine which presented the results of the search to users and openly redirected them the target site. Keljob merely queried the database from time to time and did not download it. The court, reversing the decision at first instance, found that this did not infringe the database right, nor was there passing off. In a later decision on the merits, the Paris Civil Court found that Keljob, by use of its search engine crawler, had extracted data from the plaintiff's website in contravention of the database right.

2–117   In the *Paperboy* decision, *Verlagsgruppe Handelsblatt GmbH v Paperboy*,[79] the German Federal Court (Germany's highest court) held that deep linking by an aggregator who compiled an email list of links to articles on the plaintiff's newspaper site was unobjectionable so long as it did not evade technical protection mechanisms and did not provide content access that the rightholder had not authorised. The court observed that without the use of hypertext links and search engines reasonable use of the internet would not be possible.

The Danish courts in *Danish Newspaper Publishers' Association v Newsbooster.com ApS*,[80] have held that crawling newspaper websites to compile lists of headlines deep linked to individual news articles violated the newspapers' rights under the Danish implementation of the Database Directive.

The Austrian Supreme Court in December 2002 held, in *Meteodata v Bernegger Bau*;[81] in favour of a defendant whose site linked to weather charts from the plaintiff's site and displayed them within frames on the defendant's pages.

2–118   A Norwegian court has held, in *Finn Eiendom AS v Notar AS*,[82] that so-called surface hyperlinks returned by a property search engine pointing to properties in a rival real estate website did not infringe copyright. Clicking on these hypertext links opened up a new window displaying the property from the target website. The court found that links to information willingly published on the internet are a normal practice on the internet.

In India, it is reported[83] that in December 2005 the Delhi High Court granted a temporary injunction restraining Bixee.com, a jobs aggregator,

---

[79] Bundesgerichtshof, No. I ZR 259/00, July 17, 2003, [2005] E.C.D.R. 7.
[80] Denmark Bailiff's Court May 7, 2002; grant of interim injunction upheld by Copenhagen City Court July 5, 2002 [2003] E.C.D.R. 5; injunction affirmed at trial by Copenhagen Maritime and Commercial Court in the absence of the defendant, which by then was in administration, 2003 (World eBusiness Law Report, May 12, 2003).
[81] Austrian Supreme Court December 17, 2002.
[82] Trondheim District Court January 29, 2004, E.C.L.R. Vol.9, No.7 February 18, 2004.
[83] *www.efytimes.com/fullnews.asp?edid=9018.*

from "deeplinking into, copying, downloading and reproducing content" from Naukri.com, an advertising-driven jobs site. The evidence was that Bixee were continuously spidering Naukri's website database of jobs in order to maintain an up-to-date set of deep links into Naukri's site, by-passing Naukri's advertising. It is unclear from the public reports what cause of action Naukri relied upon.

2.6.4 Spidering

Can a site owner prevent spidering?

We have mentioned spidering as an issue that arises in connection with deep linking. Spidering (also known as crawling) is the automated searching of a target site with a view to creating links to elements of the site. Some of the activities in issue in the deep linking cases discussed above amount to spidering, particularly in the search engine cases where the site makes automated searches of the target site in order to create the deep links to the target site.

2–119

In the *US Ticketmaster v Tickets.com* case discussed above one of the allegations made by the plaintiffs was that in the course of searching the target site to extract (unprotectable) factual information for use on the defendant's site, the defendants made temporary copies of copyright material from the target site. The plaintiffs argued that this was copyright infringement, even if only factual information and not the copies themselves were used on the defendant's site.

The court held[84] that it was arguable, in the context of an application for an interim injunction, that this would be protected by the US fair use doctrine (analogous to copying for the purpose of reverse engineering a computer program to obtain non-protectable information). In March 2003 the court[85] granted the defendant's motion to dismiss Ticketmaster's copyright claims, including the claim that the temporary copies made in the course of the spidering of the plaintiff's site amounted to copyright infringement. The finding as regards temporary copies was that the copying amounted to fair use, where the purpose of the copying was to enable the defendant to extract mere facts (which were not copyright) from the plaintiff's website. The copies came into existence for some 10–15 seconds in the defendant's computers.

A similar conclusion was reached in a Florida case concerning website listings of yachts for sale.[86]

---

[84] Hearing August 10, 2000 (*http://web.archive.org/web/20060530094425/http://www.giga-law.com/library/ticketmaster-tickets–2000–08–10-p1.html*).

[85] 2003 US Dist. LEXIS 6483.

[86] *Nautical Solutions Marketing, Inc., v Boats.com*, M.D. Fla, No. 8:02-CV–760-T–23TGW, April 1, 2004. NSM's spidering activities for the purpose of extracting and reposting factual information were held not to infringe Boats.com's copyright.

Spidering as trespass to chattels

2-120   The plaintiffs in *Ticketmaster v Tickets.com* also sought to rely on the doctrine of trespass to chattels, following the decision in *eBay Inc. v Bidder's Edge*.[87] The *eBay* case was another spidering case. In this case the defendants had created an auction consolidation site, which used spiders to aggregate auction items from other sites. The parties had tried, but failed, to come to a licensing arrangement permitting Bidder's Edge to spider the eBay site. eBay made available on its servers a "robots.txt" file in accordance with the Robot Exclusion Standard.[88] When the defendants continued to spider the eBay site, the plaintiffs attempted to prevent access from Bidder's Edge by blocking IP addresses that the defendants were believed to be using. The defendants countered by using proxy servers to rotate IP addresses.

2-121   The evidence was that the defendant's spider would make about 100,000 accesses per day to the plaintiff's site, which eBay assessed at between 1.11 per cent and 1.53 per cent of the total load on its listing servers. An average 10 million searches per day were made by users on the eBay site.

Trespass arguments had already successfully been invoked by ISPs against bulk emailers,[89] where there was clear evidence that the volume of email was affecting the operation of the plaintiff's system. In the *eBay* case, the court relied upon the potential harm that would ensue should aggregators generally be allowed free rein to spider the plaintiff's site and granted a preliminary injunction against the defendant.

The court found that eBay was likely to be able to demonstrate at trial that the defendant's activities diminished the quality or value of eBay's computer systems, in that it was depriving eBay of the ability to use the portion of its personal property for its own purposes that was occupied in processing the defendant's searches. If the preliminary injunction were denied, and other aggregators began to crawl the eBay site, there would be little doubt that the load on eBay's computer system would qualify as a substantial impairment of condition or value.

In *Ticketmaster*, the court on the preliminary injunction hearing found that there was no evidence of either physical harm to the chattel or obstruction to its basic function and declined to grant a preliminary injunction. On the later hearing for summary judgment the court dismissed the plaintiff's case based on trespass to chattels, on the basis that the

---

[87] NDCA 2000 100 F Supp 2d 1058. See "Protecting Web Site Databases through Intentional Tort or Contract: eBay meets UCITA" K.M. McDermott, Journal of Internet Law Sept. 2000, 15; and "Virtual Trespass in Cyberspace?" D.A. Guberman, World Internet Law Report 12/00, 27.

[88] The Robot Exclusion Standard can be found at *www.robotstxt.org/wc/norobots.html*. It enables websites to promulgate, in the robots.txt file, its policies for visiting robots (i.e. webcrawlers and spiders). Search engine programmers and other robot users can program their robots to respect the guidelines that they encounter. Websites can also set certain metatags to exclude or affect the behaviour of search robots. Both types of exclusionary protocols featured heavily in *Field v Google, Inc.*, U.S.D.C Nevada, January 19, 2006 (see fn.92 below).

[89] e.g., *CompuServe, Inc. v Cyber Promotions, Inc.*, 962 F. Supp. 1015 (S.D. Ohio 1997).

plaintiff had shown no adverse effect to the use or utility of the plaintiff's computers.

That finding foreshadowed a decision of the California Supreme Court in *Intel Corporation v Hamidi*.[90] The case concerned en ex-employee of Intel who sent thousands of emails to Intel employees. Intel sued for trespass. The California Supreme Court, by a majority of 4–3, held that unwelcome content was insufficient to constitute trespass. Time spent by Intel's staff attempting to block the messages did not constitute relevant damage. There had to be some actual or threatened impairment of the functioning of the system.
2–122

Some of the US cases invoking trespass can be viewed as an attempt to fill a gap resulting from the lack of a database right in the USA. There may at first sight, therefore, be less need for the development of a similar doctrine in Europe where database protection exists. However, it should not be forgotten that there are so far very few countries outside the European Economic Area to which database right protection within the EU has been granted. In cases where that protection is not available, it may be possible to resort to trespass theories in the UK. Trespass is discussed in more detail in Chapter 5, in connection with liability for the dissemination of viruses.

2.6.5 Framing

Can a site owner prevent his site being framed?

An issue related to web linking is the use of frames on a website. Frames are an HTML enhancement which enable the website designer to split the screen into a number of separate areas, or frames. Each frame can be made to act independently, so that while one frame accesses new pages the others (which will typically contain menu buttons and advertising banners) remain in place.
2–123

The use of frames as a way of navigating content on one site is uncontroversial. However, frames can be used to access other sites. So when the user clicks on a link to another site from within a frame, instead of the target site's content completely replacing the pointing site's content, it appears surrounded by the material in the frames remaining from the pointing site. This arrangement has potential to undermine the assumptions on which advertising and sponsorship deals are done. For example, if RedBurger agree to sponsor a site, they are unlikely to be amused when the site contents appear to the user surrounded by frames of advertising from YellowBurger.

However, the question whether the practice is unlawful is far from clear. As far as copyright is concerned, the arguments will be similar to those applicable to ordinary linking. Other intellectual property rights may also be relevant.
2–124

---

[90] Ct.App. 3 C033076 June 30, 2003.

In the USA a group of on-line news providers commenced litigation against Total News Inc, complaining of its framing practices at its Total News website. The Total News site consisted of lists of links to on-line news sites, identified by the names of the plaintiffs. The plaintiffs complained that when their sites appeared in the Total News frame their content was partially obscured to fit the frame, reduced in size and placed alongside the Total News logo, menus, URL and advertisements.

The plaintiffs particularly complained that advertisers might buy space on a website based on the expectation that their advertisement would appear in a certain location or slot, be of a certain size or duration, or be free of the "clutter" of competing advertisements, particularly advertisements for competing products; and that the framing activities of the defendants might defeat any of those expectations.

This claim, based on misappropriation, trade mark dilution, trade mark infringement, false designations of origin, false representations and false advertising, deceptive acts and practices, copyright infringement and tortious interference with advertising contracts, was settled before trial. Under the settlement, Total News could continue linking, but could not display the target content within a frame or (in effect), purposefully using an intermediate site as a conduit to frame one of the plaintiffs' pages.

2.6.6 Search engines

Can text search engines infringe?

2–125   Other internet activities can give rise to the sometimes novel application of existing laws to new situations. The position of text search engines is generally well accepted on the internet, assisted by the fact that they are rightly regarded as providing a service of great public benefit. However, the fact that a search engine may temporarily store on its servers not just links or abstracts but the entire text contents of other people's websites, might cause a copyright lawyer (other than a US lawyer equipped with a sympathetic view of fair use) to raise an eyebrow.[91]

It could plausibly be suggested that, by copying first and answering questions later, the search industry has successfully bootstrapped its way from a possibly questionable starting point into a position of legality based (if fair use or similar exceptions do not suffice) on implied licence, thus supporting the typical search engine policy of opt-out (i.e. including material unless the owners object). It is also notable that the search industry started in the US, which has a flexible doctrine of fair use capable of accommodating new technologies. That is, however, not true in Europe where exceptions to copyright infringement are more closely prescribed.

It can already be seen from the European cases discussed above that when

---

[91] See for instance "Google Cache Raises Copyright Concerns" *http://news.com.com/2100–1032–1024234.html*.

a search engine enters into activity that competes with sites that it is indexing, operations that are acceptable in a wider context are likely to come under close legal scrutiny. Similarly, when a general search engine extends its activities from text into new types of content it may find that it is challenged and that the bootstrapping process is now less easy than in the earlier days of the internet. Difficult questions may arise as to the extent to which the search engine can rely upon acquired legitimacy in its existing general search activities to support an opt-out policy in new types of search.

Cases addressing the question of implied licence and search engines have started to reach the courts. In the US a copyright suit based on Google's temporary (14 to 20 days) storage of web pages and making them available to users through its "Cached" link failed in *Field v Google, Inc.*[92] The judge held (1) that Google's delivery of cached content to users when they clicked on the Cached link was, following *Netcom* (see paras 2–164, 2–169) non-volitional and therefore not an act of direct infringement (2) the Plaintiff had impliedly licensed inclusion in Google's cache by not setting exclusion parameters in his site's metatags or robots.txt file, when he was familiar with those processes (3) for similar reasons he was estopped from complaining about Google's conduct (4) Google's caching activities and provision of the Cached link amounted to fair use (5) Google was protected by the system cache safe harbour provided by the Digital Millennium Copyright Act 1998, ss. 512(a), (c) and (d). The judge paid particular attention to the steps taken by Google to educate users as to how to prevent Google's robot from indexing their site or providing a Cached link, and the fact that Google removed the Cached links to the plaintiff's site as soon as they heard about the lawsuit. 2–126

In the Belgian case of *Copiepresse v Google, Inc.*, decided in February 2007, the court took a different view. In that case Copiepresse, an association of Belgian newspaper publishers, objected to the inclusion of headlines and extracts from newspaper articles in the Google News service and to the provision of links to cached copies of the articles in the Google search service. Copiepresse argued that because Google News provided the headlines and extracts on its home page prior to any search by the user, it was a news portal and not a mere search facility.

Google argued before the Brussels Court of First Instance that it was open to the publishers to use technical means (robots.txt files and metatags) to exclude their publications from being indexed by search engines. These were standard methods known worldwide. Insofar as the publishers did not use them they were explicitly or implicitly agreeing to have their pages indexed and accessible via the cached links. 2–127

The court rejected this argument. It held that copyright is not a right of opposition but a right for prior authorisation. This meant that the authorisation had to be obtained in a certain way, prior to the intended use. It could not be maintained that "the use on the sites of robot files implies a

[92] USDC Nevada, January 19, 2006. *Netcom* and *Field* were also followed in *Parker v Google, Inc.* No. 04–3918 (E.D. Pa., March 10, 2006).

certain and explicit agreement of the site publishers to the use of works included on the site as concretely used by Google News …". In the same way an unconditional authorisation for referencing could not be deduced from the absence of technical protection. That appeared to be all the more the case here, as Google News did not merely reference the articles but reproduced the title and an extract.

The *Copiepresse* decision is understood to be under appeal.

2–128   A potential problem with relying on implied licence is that the licence can be withdrawn. That ought not to be an issue since the opt-out policy generally adopted by search engines should mean that copyright material is excluded once the copyright owner notifies his objection. For instance Google states "if a content owner asks us to remove his or her content from our web search results, we do. If a newspaper does not want to be part of Google News, we take the paper's stories out".[93]

In the *Copiepresse* case the issues were complicated by the fact that, for whatever reason, Google apparently did not respond to various communications from Copiepresse or the court, and did not remove the publishers' content until the first court order was made against it. So even if the court had accepted the implied licence argument, on the basis of the facts found by the court the period for which it would have applied would have been relatively short.

This illustrates the importance, if an online intermediary is relying upon implied licence, of having good procedures to respond to licence withdrawals in whatever form they are received. Clearly it is most convenient for search engines if website owners use standard technical means to do this such as the Robots Exclusion Standard (robots.txt) and metatags. However, it is difficult to see how the beneficiary of a bare implied licence could validly stipulate that that is the only mechanism by which the licence may be revoked.

A more sophisticated variation on the robots.txt theme is the Automated Content Access Protocol (ACAP), which at the time of writing is in pilot.[94] This project, backed by a group of newspaper and publishing trade associations, aims to provide in a website file a set of technical parameters, understandable by automated spiders, which will express licensing terms applicable to the content on the site.

Can image search engines infringe?

2–129   A challenge to non-text search occurred in the US case of *Kelly v Arriba Soft Corp*,[95] which concerned a "visual" search engine. This operated in the same way as a traditional text search engine, save that it indexed images that its spider or crawler software found on the web. The captured images were copied onto Arriba's server and briefly retained in order to reduce them to a thumbnail form. The full size images were then deleted from

---

[93] *http://googleblog.blogspot.com/2006/09/our-approach-to-content.html.*
[94] *www.the-acap.org/press_releases/googlerel-feb_07with%20logo.pdf.*
[95] [2000] Ent. L.R. 11(3), N–38.

Arriba's server and the thumbnails indexed and stored. Clicking on the thumbnail would load the full-size image from the target website, together with the URL for the website where it originated. In a later version, clicking on the thumbnail opened two windows: one containing the full-size image, the other containing the full target web page. The Plaintiff was a photographer who complained about the use of images obtained from his website in this way.

The District Court found that the reproduction and display of the images were protected by the US fair use provisions. Although the display of the full-size image in a window out of context from the target web page was a factor that told against fair use, on the whole the purpose and character of the defendant's use was transformative rather than exploitative and was a fair use. The fact that the thumbnail deep linked to the image on the plaintiff's site did not produce harm or adverse impact that would detract from that.

In July 2003 the US Court of Appeals for the Ninth Circuit[96] affirmed the lower court decision that the creation and use of the thumbnails amounted to fair use.[97] The question whether the display of the full-size images also amounted to fair use was remitted to the district court.

Two and a half years later a US court in *Perfect 10 v Google, Inc.*[98]   **2–130** reached the opposite conclusion on whether creating thumbnails was a fair use, having received evidence that the plaintiff had a commercial market for thumbnail versions of its adult images for download to mobile telephones. The decision is under appeal.

In a German case in September 2003 an interim injunction was granted against incorporating thumbnails in search engine results.[99]

New types of search activity

The extension of the Google search engine's activities into new areas of   **2–131** search has given rise to litigation. In March 2005 Agence France Presse started US proceedings against Google complaining that the automated Google News service had included AFP's photos, news headlines and stories without permission.

We have mentioned the Belgian *Copiepresse* decision. In September 2006 Copiepresse, obtained an injunction preventing Google from including its members' French and German language newspaper content in its index and cache.[1] The injunction was confirmed by the decision of the Brussels Court of First Instance on February 13, 2007. The decision is understood to be under appeal.

---

[96] *Kelly v Arriba Soft Corp.*, 9th Cir., No. 00–55521.
[97] The US concept of fair use tends to be broader and is more flexible than the UK statutory provisions permitting fair dealing for certain specified purposes.
[98] U.S.D.C. C.D. Cal. February 17, 2006.
[99] BNA's World Internet Law Report July 2004, p.11; Electronic Business Law May 2004, p.1; decision (in German) at *http://www.jurpc.de/rechtspr/20040146.htm*.
[1] *www.twobirds.com/english/publications/articles/ Belgian_press_association_sued_Google_News.cfm.*

The *Copiepresse* litigation is of particular interest because the rights-owners' case directly challenges Google's opt-out policy. The rightsowners maintain that Google was obliged to obtain permission before including their content in Google News, and is therefore liable for the period before the rightsowners objected and Google removed their material. So far the Belgian courts have agreed. The case illustrates the point that we have discussed regarding the extent to which search engines, when extending their activities into arguably new areas, can rely upon existing acquired legitimacy to justify an opt-out policy. Or put another way, does the acquired legitimacy of search engines justify the inference in new areas of activity that, to the extent that they might otherwise infringe, they have the benefit of an implied licence until such time as a rightsowner objects?

The *Copiepresse* decision

2–132   In January 2006 Google, Inc. launched its Google News service in Belgium. On February 9, 2006 Copiepresse, an association of Belgian newspaper publishers, petitioned the Brussels court for an order for "saisie description". The court granted this on March 27, 2006 and appointed an expert to investigate. The court order was served on Google on April 27, 2006. The expert submitted his report on July 6, 2006. By letter of July 13, 2006 counsel for Copipresse formally requested Google to remove its members' newspaper articles from Google News and the Google cache. Google did not respond to this letter.

Copiepresse started proceedings in Belgium on August 3, 2006 and obtained a default judgment against Google on September 5, 2006. Google applied to set aside the order, but it was confirmed by the summary judge on September 22, 2006. Google then made a further application to have the claim dismissed, resulting in the judgment of February 15, 2007.

2–133   **The rival contentions**   Google described Google News as a specialised search engine based on indexing press articles published on the internet. Copiepresse, however, considered that the Google News service went beyond a simple search engine service and acted as a "portal to the written press".

Google's principal activity is providing its well-known general search engine, described in the judgment thus:

> "Google stipulates that its search engine is made up of indexation software or 'robots' ... that trawl through websites moving through page after page, at regular intervals and in an entirely automatic way in order to list these in an index of all the web pages accessible to the public and the corresponding web address for each (called the URL address); internet users can consult the index by means of keywords entered in the search bar, the search engine then displays the reference lists of pages available including the keywords searched and proceeds to an automated classification by relevance."

Google's general search engine displays a blank screen and search box to   2–134
the user. Google News displayed on its home page, in addition to a search
box, a series of article titles, each accompanied by a short extract from the
article itself, automatically selected and organised by topic. The titles
constituted hyperlinks to the original articles on the newspaper publishers'
websites. In support of its argument that Google News was more than a
simple search facility Copiepresse relied heavily on the fact that Google
News presented these items to the user on the Google News home page
before any search was carried out.

Google's general search results also include links (labelled "Cached")
enabling the user to call up the HTML text copy of an article stored for a
period in Google's own caching servers. However, "Cached" links were not
provided in Google News.

Copiepresse's complaints   Although Copiepresse did not object to the   2–135
provision of hyperlinks to the newspaper publishers' sites, it did object to
the following:

1. The display on Google News of the titles and first few lines of the
   newspaper articles.
2. The "Cached" links into Google's cached version of the articles.
   Although not available from Google News, the "Cached" link was
   provided as part of Google's general search facility on Google.be.

Google News   In response to the complaints about Google News, Google   2–136
made a number of arguments. It made the general point that the same
material was in any event available to users searching though its general
search service. The Google News service was based on indexation similar to
that carried out for Google's general search service and was therefore a search
engine, not a site distributing news. It then argued several specific legal points:

– Google was not reproducing and communicating protected works
  to the public, the user being referred by a hyperlink to the publisher's site. Google, therefore, only made the article more
  accessible by means of the hyperlink.

The court concluded that this point was irrelevant since Copiepresse's
objection was based not on linking to the publishers' sites but on the
reproduction of the titles and extracts from the press articles. It was
unambiguously apparent that Google News reproduced and communicated
to the public on the homepage of its site (these elements being accessible on
the Google News site itself by the simple consultation of this site), the press
article titles and extracts from some of these articles.

– The titles of the newspaper articles and the displayed first sentence
  or sentences of the articles were not original elements benefiting
  from the protection of copyright law.

The court found that some of the titles appeared to be sufficiently original to qualify for copyright protection, while others did not.

The articles themselves were copyright works, so the question was whether reproducing the opening lines could amount to substantial reproduction. The court concluded that at least in some cases it would.

2–137   Google therefore reproduced and communicated to the public works protected by copyright.

> – That in any event Google could rely on the citation and news reporting exceptions to copyright infringement under Belgian copyright law.

As to the citation exception, the court found that this did not apply since Google limits itself to listing the articles and classifying them in an automatic way. Google News did not carry out any analysis, comparison or critique of the articles, which were not commented on in any way.

As to news reporting, the court commented that Google's reliance on this exception was contradictory to Google's position that it was only a search engine, not an information portal. There was no commentary on the news, only extracts from articles grouped by topic. The exception did not apply where reproduction of the protected works was the principal object rather than secondary to the reporting. Google could not, therefore, rely on the news reporting exception.

2–138   **"Cached" link**   In response to the complaint about the Cached link in its general search results, Google argued that it only copies the HTML code of websites into its cache, containing text elements and links but no images. Google maintained that it is the user, not Google, who creates a copy of the work so that the user is the author of any reproduction or communication to the public, the only involvement of Google being the supply of the installations intended to make it possible or to realise a communication to the public by internet users.

The court rejected this analysis as inaccurate. Google stored copies of web pages in its memory and the fact that it only stored HTML code was irrelevant. There was a digital reproduction from the moment that the material was stored and Google was the author of that reproduction. Google made that reproduction available on its own website via the "Cached" link. Unlike with hyperlinks that referred to the site of origin, by consulting the "Cached" link the user was consulting the document on the Google website. Google's role was consequently not limited simply to providing facilities. Google had reproduced and made available to the public a copy of the original documents stored in its own memory.

2–139   **Implied licence**   Finally, Google argued generally that if it were found to make copies of works protected by copyright and/or to communicate them to the public, the newspaper publishers had explicitly or implicitly consented to that.

The court rejected this argument, for the reasons set out above.

Electronic Commerce Directive   The court also held that the hosting and 2–140
caching provisions of the Electronic Commerce Directive (see Ch.5) did not
assist Google. Neither protection applied since it was Google's own behaviour that was in question, not the content of sites to which it permitted
access. Further, the caching protection did not apply because it was not the
temporary storage required for indexation that was in dispute, but making
it available by means of the "Cached" link.

The complaint based on the "Cached" link was, as can be seen from the
account of the judgment above, separate from the complaint about Google
News. The "Cached" link was available on Google's general search results,
but not on Google News. Again, the court reached a different conclusion
from that in the US *Field v Google* case. There the court found, among
other reasons for holding in Google's favour, that Google's delivery of
cached content to users when they clicked on the "Cached" link was non-
volitional and therefore not an act of direct infringement. The provision of
the cached link was additionally found to be fair use and also protected
under the Digital Millennium Copyright Act.

Lastly, the territorial aspect of the order in the *Copiepresse* case is of
interest. Like the French judge in *LICRA v Yahoo!* (the Nazi memorabilia
case) the judge in this case appears to have been little concerned by the
possible extra-territorial effects of his judgment either as a result of
declining to limit his order to the Belgian sites, or due to the practical effect
of his order on Google. It is reminiscent of one of the earliest cases involving internet content, when CompuServe in December 1995 removed
several hundred newsgroups from their systems worldwide as a result of the
actions of a prosecutor in Bavaria.

Searchable hard copy

The Authors Guild and several publishing companies have launched US 2–141
proceedings in respect of Google Print, a US project designed to make print
books searchable on the Web by digitising library collections in collaboration with five US libraries.

The technological principle underlying this project is very little different
from an ordinary text search engine. In both cases the whole text must be
copied and stored in the search engine's servers; and in both cases small
extracts are made available in search results. The main technical difference
is that the Google Print project requires Google to scan and OCR hard copy
books, rather than copy them from existing digital form. Google operates
an opt-out policy for publishers in Google Print, effectively mirroring the
way in which search engines have gone about indexing web content.[2]

---

[2] See *http://googleblog.blogspot.com/2005/09/google-print-and-authors-guild.html* for a
response by Google to news of the Authors Guild lawsuit.

Linking into search engines

2–142 Search engines are themselves vulnerable to a particular form of linking, whereby a third party web page includes a query box that transmits the user's search query back to the search engine. The third party site then displays the results page generated by the search engine. The question can arise whether this "front-end" can be created without permission. Again, and depending on exactly how the unauthorised "front-end" has been built and presented, the various forms of intellectual property right that we have discussed, and perhaps trespass, may be relevant. In this type of case attention may need to be paid to whether the unauthorised front-end incorporates any source code derived from the search engine site in order to construct and transmit the search query to the target search engine.

2.6.7 Liability for linking to infringing material

2–143 Liability for authorising or procuring infringement[3] may arise when a website owner provides users of the site with access to infringing material on another site by means of hypertext links.

There has been an increasing number of cases in which linking to unlawful material has been enjoined, although none (other than possibly the Nottinghamshire County Council JET Report case discussed in Ch.6) in the UK.

The Australian case of *Universal Music Pty Ltd v Cooper*[4] concerned a website consisting of links to third party sites which contained infringing MP3 music files, and sometimes links directly to the files themselves. Cooper's site did not itself store any infringing files. The court found that the creation of links to infringing MP3 files on other websites, and to websites containing such files, did not directly infringe the "making available" right under the Australian Copyright Act 1968,[5] but did amount to authorising infringement. Tamberlin, J. said:

> "65 The Cooper website contains hyperlinks to thousands of sound recordings which are located on remote websites and are downloaded directly from those websites to the computer of the internet user. When a visitor to the Cooper website clicked on a link on the website to an MP3 file hosted on another server, this caused the user's browser to send a 'GET' request to that server, resulting in the MP3 file being transmitted directly across the internet from the host server to the user's computer. The MP3 file

---

[3] See discussion, para.2–073 above.

[4] [2005] FCA 972, Federal Court of Australia, July 14, 2005; on appeal [2006] FCAFC 187, Federal Court of Australia—Full Court, December 18, 2006.

[5] Section 85 of the Act provided that it was a restricted act to communicate a sound recording to the public. By s.10(1) "communicate" included "to make available on-line or electronically transmit ... a work or other subject matter".

does not pass through or via or across the Cooper website. The Cooper website facilitates the easier location and selection of digital music files and specification to the remote website, from which the user can then download the files by clicking on the hyperlink on the Cooper website. However, the downloaded subject matter is not transmitted or made available from the Cooper website and nor does the downloading take place through the Cooper website. While the request that triggers the downloading is made from the Cooper website, it is the remote website which makes the music file available and not the Cooper website.

66 The applicants also submitted that Cooper, by establishing and operating the website, has 'electronically transmitted' the sound recordings. I am of the view that Cooper cannot be said to have transmitted the sound recordings. In my view, the actual transmission of the music sound recording begins with the commencement of the downloading of the recording from the remote website on which the recording is located to the end user. I accept that the electronic transmission of the sound recording to a user who triggers the hyperlink on the Cooper website is a communication to a member of the public from the remote website, however, it is not a transmission from the Cooper website.

67 Accordingly, for these reasons, I do not consider that Cooper has 'communicated' the sound recording to the public. That is, Cooper has not made the sound recording available to the public or electronically transmitted it to the public."

However, the judge found that the links did amount to authorisation[6] of **2–144** infringement, both of infringement by users who downloaded MP3 files from target sites and by the operators of those sites. The liability for authorisation covered both links created by the defendant himself, and those submitted by users of his website which his website automatically accepted. The judge said:

"84 The Cooper website is carefully structured and highly organised and many of its pages contain numerous references to linking and downloading. The website also provides the hyperlinks that enable the user to directly access the files on, and activate the downloading from, the remote websites. The website is clearly designed to, and does, facilitate and enable this infringing downloading. I am of the view that there is a reasonable inference available that Cooper, who sought advice as to the establishment and operation of his website, knowingly permitted or approved the use of his website in this manner and designed and organised it to achieve this result. In view of the absence of Cooper from the

---

[6] See para.2–157 below for the Australian provisions on authorisation, which differ significantly from those of the 1988 Act.

witness box, without any reasonable explanation apart from a tactical forensic suggestion that he was not a necessary or appropriate witness to be called in his own case, I am satisfied that the available inference of permission or approval by Cooper can more safely and confidently be drawn. Accordingly, I infer that Cooper has permitted or approved, and thereby authorized, the copyright infringement by internet users who access his website and also by the owners or operators of the remote websites from which the infringing recordings were downloaded.

85 The words 'sanction' and 'approve' are expressions of wide import. Cooper, in my view, could have prevented the infringements by removing the hyperlinks from his website or by structuring the website in such a way that the operators of the remote websites from which MP3 files were downloaded could not automatically add hyperlinks to the website without some supervision or control by Cooper. The evidence of Professor Sterling, who was called on behalf of the applicants, is unchallenged to the effect that a website operator is always able to control the hyperlinks on his or her website, either by removal of the links or by requiring measures to be taken by the remote website operator prior to adding a hyperlink. A person cannot create a hyperlink between a music file and a website without the permission of the operator of the website because access to the code that is required to create the link must occur at level of the website. The Cooper website employed a 'CGI-BIN' script to accept hyperlink suggestions from visitors to the website. By virtue of this script, such suggestions were automatically added to the website without the intervention of Cooper. The evidence is that alternative software was in existence that would have enabled a third party to add a hyperlink to a website but which required the consent or approval of the website operator before such hyperlinks were added."

2–145   A disclaimer on Cooper's website warning users that MP3s could be both legal and illegal and that the downloading of MP3s would be legal only with permission of the copyright owner was held ineffective to counter a finding of authorisation. On the contrary, the disclaimer was held to indicate Cooper's knowledge of the existence of illegal MP3s on the internet and the likelihood that at least some of the MP3s to which the website provided hyperlinks were infringing copies.

On appeal by Cooper against the finding of authorisation, the judge's conclusions were upheld for similar reasons.

In the US *DeCCS* case,[7] concerning the publication on a website of software alleged to allow users to decode DVD discs, part of the judgment

---

[7] *Universal City Studios, Inc and ors v Corley* SD Cal August 17, 2000. Affirmed on appeal to the US Court of Appeals for the Second Circuit No 00–9185, November 28, 2001.

concerned the defendant's links to other sites carrying the software. The judge had to decide whether creating such links amounted to "offering DeCSS to the public" or "providing or otherwise trafficking in it", within the DMCA.

The defendants' links were of three types: (1) links to a web page on an outside site that does not itself contain a link to DeCCS, but links either directly or indirectly via a series of other pages to another page on the same site that posts the software; (2) links to a web page on an outside site that does contain a link to DeCCS, with or without other text and links; (3) links to a DeCSS file on an outside site that automatically starts to download without further user intervention. **2–146**

As to the third type, the judge held that there was no serious question that this fell within the anti-trafficking provisions of DeCSS. The defendants were engaged in the functional equivalent of transferring the DeCSS code to the user themselves.

As to the second type, substantially the same was held to be true of the defendants' hyperlinks to web pages that displayed nothing more than the DeCSS code or presented the user only with the choice of commencing a download of DeCSS and no other content. The only distinction was that the entity extending to the user the option of downloading the program was the transferee site rather than defendants, which the court held to be "a distinction without a difference".

The judge also considered links to pages that offered "a good deal of content other than DeCSS but that offer a hyperlink for downloading, or transferring to a page for downloading, DeCSS". He regarded these as potentially more troublesome. He said: **2–147**

> "If one assumed, for the purposes of argument, that the *Los Angeles Times* website somewhere contained the DeCSS code, it would be wrong to say that anyone who linked to the *Los Angeles Times* website, regardless of purpose or the manner in which the link was described, thereby offered, provided or otherwise trafficked in DeCSS merely because DeCSS happened to be available on a site to which one linked."

However, he went on to distinguish that situation from the one under consideration, in which:

> "Defendants urged others to post DeCSS in an effort to disseminate DeCSS and to inform defendants that they were doing so. Defendants then linked their site to those 'mirror' sites, after first checking to ensure that the mirror sites in fact were posting DeCSS or something that looked like it, and proclaimed on their own site that DeCSS could be had by clicking on the hyperlinks on defendants' site. By doing so, they offered, provided or otherwise trafficked in DeCSS, and they continue to do so to this day".

2-148   The court observed that anything that would impose strict liability on a website operator for the entire contents of any website to which the operator linked would raise grave constitutional concerns, as website operators would be inhibited from linking for fear of exposure to liability.

The judge for this and other constitutional reasons held that there should be:

> "no injunction against, nor liability for, linking to a site containing circumvention technology, the offering of which is unlawful under the DMCA, absent clear and convincing evidence that those responsible for the link (a) know at the relevant time that the offending material is on the linked-to site, (b) know that it is circumvention technology that may not lawfully be offered, and (c) create or maintain the link for the purpose of disseminating that technology".

He enjoined the defendants, Eric Corley and 2600 Enterprises, Inc., (other defendants having previously settled with the plaintiffs) from (*inter alia*): "knowingly linking any internet website operated by them to any other website containing DeCSS, or knowingly maintaining any such link, for the purpose of disseminating DeCSS".

After this judgment the defendants removed the links to other DeCCS sites, but continued to publish the web addresses and URLs of those sites.

In another US case the Mormon Church obtained a preliminary injunction restraining the publication of web addresses of sites containing material alleged to infringe copyright. The court found that it was likely that the defendants knew, or should have known, that the websites contained the copies and so were likely to be liable for contributory infringement.[8]

2-149   Courts in Denmark[9] and France[10] have held that web links to infringing music files on the internet constitute infringement. A German appeals court has held that on-line news agency may publish a review of software used to make infringing copies of DVDs, but may not link to a website where the software can be downloaded.[11]

A Dutch court has held[12] that if a search engine provides links to infringing MP3 files that does not amount to copyright infringement. The

---

[8] *New York Times CyberLaw Journal* "Copyright Decision Threatens Freedom to Link" C.S. Kaplan December 10, 1999.

[9] *Koda and ors v Lauritzen*, Vestre Landset [2002] E.C.D.R. 25, 259.

[10] *SCPP v Conraud* District Court of Epinal, October 24, 2000.

[11] *BMG Records GmbH v Heise Zeitschriften Verlag GmbH & Co KG* Oberlandesgericht Munchen, No 29 U 2887/05 July 28, 2005; E.C.L.R. Vol.10, No.31, p.792. cf the decision of the German Federal Supreme Court of April 1, 2004, holding that it was not unfair competition for an online newspaper to provide a link to an Austrian gambling site (BGH, April 1, 2004–I ZR 317/01).

[12] *Techno Design v Brein*, District Court of Haarlem, May 12, 2004. English translation of judgment: *www.solv.nl/rechtspraak_docs/District%20Court%20Haarlem%20120504.pdf*. The decision is reported to have been appealed.

court in part relied upon the Copyright in the Information Society Directive in reaching this conclusion, holding that a website enabling users to search a database of MP3 files, so making finding MP3 files on the internet easier, was merely providing physical facilities for enabling or making a publication, which does not constitute publication.[13]

The court's reasoning was very similar to that of the Australian *Cooper* decision in finding that links did not amount to "making available" (para.2–143 above). However, Dutch law appears to have no equivalent of liability for authorisation, which may explain the divergence in ultimate conclusions. The Dutch court did find, on the basis of a "standard of due care to be observed in society" theory of liability, that the search engine would be under a duty to render assistance and take adequate measures in respect of any link that it was notified was pointing at infringing material. That would include, in a clear case, removing the link.

In *Public Prosecutor v Tommy Olsson*,[14] a case before the Copyright in   **2–150**
the Information Society Directive came into force, the Swedish Supreme Court held that linking to MP3 files did constitute "making available to the public" under domestic Swedish legislation on the narrow basis that it amounted to public performance.

The Norwegian Supreme Court in *TONO v Bruvik*[15] has held that providing links to infringing MP3 files caused no separate infringement of the copyright owner's "making available" right. The court observed that the meaning of the right was the same, whether the links were to legitimate or illegitimate content. The parties had agreed that merely a publishing a web address did not make the underlying work available to the public. It made no difference whether that was in a newspaper or on the internet. If on the internet, the user could easily convert a web address to a link by copying and pasting it in the browser window, thus giving the same access to the music files.[16] Software was now available that recognises a web address and creates a link to it. It would be very problematic if such a transformation amounted to making available to the public. Linking did not breach the making available right. However, on the facts, the defendant's activities did amount to abetting unlawful communication of the works to the public.

In the *Perfect 10 v Google* case (see para.2–130 above), as well as objecting to Google's creation of thumbnail images the plaintiffs complained about Google's search result links. Their allegation that the links constituted a "display" of infringing material was rejected. The court held,

---

[13] The relevant part of the Copyright in the Information Society Directive is Recital (27).

[14] [2001] E.C.D.R. 22.

[15] Norwegian Supreme Court, January 27, 2005; English summary at *www.lessig.org/blog/ archives/Napster-case.pdf*.

[16] The court distinguished the Swedish *Olsson* decision on the ground that the Swedish Supreme Court did not consider the problem whether the music-files could have been reached through Olsson's website simply by providing the web addresses in writing on the website and not as links.

applying what it dubbed the "server" test,[17] that the display was by the target website and that creating links to it was not a direct infringement. The judge commented that:

> "the server test maintains, however uneasily, the delicate balance for which copyright law strives—i.e. between encouraging the creation of creative works and encouraging the dissemination of information. Merely to index the web so that users can more readily find the information they seek should not constitute direct infringement, but to *host* and *serve* infringing content may directly violate the rights of copyright owners."

Although the plaintiff had also alleged contributory and vicarious infringement, there was no evidence of direct infringement by users of the links that would enable the court to determine the likelihood of the plaintiff succeeding at trial on those issues.

The UK Department of Trade and Industry issued a consultation paper in June 2005 to explore whether the UK should extend the intermediary liability protections of the Electronic Commerce Directive (as to which, see Chapter 5) to hyperlinkers, location tool services and content aggregators. It concluded in December 2006[18] that there was currently insufficient evidence to justify any extension to these limitations. The DTI observed that the second review of the Electronic Commerce Directive by the European Commission is due in 2007 and said that it would encourage the Commission to take on board the important issues raised during the consultation.

2.6.8 Peer-to-peer

2–151   We discuss below (section 2.7) the liability of hosts for third party material stored by them. From about 1999 new, decentralised, file-sharing technologies started to appear, which reduced or eliminated the function of a central host, but still enabled users to search for and share files. This technology, which comes in many different variations, is known as peer-to-peer, often abbreviated to P2P.

---

[17] As formulated by the court, according to the "server" test the act of display is the act of serving content over the web, i.e. physically sending ones and zeroes over the internet to the user's browser. According to the rival "incorporation" test the act of display is the act of incorporating content in the webpage pulled up by the browser. The judge commented that to adopt the incorporation test would "cause a tremendous chilling effect on the core functionality of the web—its capacity to link, a vital feature of the internet that makes it accessible, creative, and valuable".

[18] "Government Response and Summary of Responses to Consultation Document on the Electronic Commerce Directive: the Liability of Hyperlinkers, Location Tool Services and Content Aggregators" (*www.dti.gov.uk/consultations/page13985.html*).

The *Napster* case

The first litigation about peer-to-peer was the US *Napster* case.[19] Napster   **2–152**
distributed peer-to-peer software from its website. The software enabled
users to store MP3 compressed music files on their individual hard drives,
to make the files available to other Napster users, to search for MP3 music
files stored on other users' computers and to transfer copies of MP3 files
between individual users. Napster's own central servers provided facilities
for indexing and searching MP3 files available from users logged on to the
Napster system and other functions such as a chat room.

The plaintiffs, seeking a preliminary injunction against Napster, claimed
that the Napster users were engaged in the wholesale reproduction of
copyright works, all constituting direct infringement.

The court found that this was likely and that the plaintiffs would likely
succeed at trial in establishing that Napster users did not have a fair use
defence. The court went on to consider liability for contributory infringement. This did not follow merely because peer-to-peer file sharing
technology may be used for infringing purposes. However, the evidence was
sufficient to show that the plaintiffs would likely establish at trial that
Napster knew or had reason to know of its users' infringements of their
copyrights. The evidence was also sufficient to show that the plaintiffs
would likely succeed at trial in holding Napster vicariously liable for their
users' infringements. This arose from a combination of Napster's failure to
police the system and the financial benefit that accrued to it from the
continuing presence of infringing files on the system. A preliminary
injunction was granted, which was substantially upheld on appeal in February 2001.

The *Grokster* case

Following *Napster* a second generation of P2P software appeared, this time   **2–153**
eliminating the central indexing server by distributing the indexing and
searching function to users.[20] This gave rise to the *Grokster*[21] litigation, in
which the US Supreme Court held on the specific facts that the two
defendants, Grokster and Streamcast, who were both suppliers of free peer-
to-peer filesharing software, could be held liable for copyright infringements perpetrated by the users of the software in sharing proprietary music
and movie files.

The case was expected in advance to be an opportunity to revisit the
Sony/Betamax[22] decision, in which the Supreme Court had previously held
that distribution of a product capable of substantial non-infringing uses did

---

[19] *A & M Records Inc. v Napster, Inc.*, U.S.D.C. N.D. Cal, 114 F.Supp.2d 896 August 10,
2000; substantially affirmed on appeal to the US Court of Appeals for the Ninth Circuit, No
00–16401, February 12, 2001.
[20] Some systems, such as Gnutella, treat all users equally. Others, such as KaZaA, allow some
users to be designated as supernodes which provide extra services to other users.
[21] *MGM Studios, Inc. v Grokster Ltd* 125 S. Ct 2764 (2005).
[22] *Sony Corporation of America v Universal City Studios* 464 US 417 (Supreme Court, 1984).

not give rise to liability for infringement by purchasers of the product, at least absent knowledge of specific instances of infringement on which the distributor failed to act.

However, in *Grokster* the Supreme Court sidestepped *Sony/Betamax*.[23] It held that on the specific evidence in this case Grokster and Streamcast were both capable of being held liable on a different basis, namely that they had induced the infringements perpetrated by the users. The court below had been wrong to find that the *Sony/Betamax* decision precluded a finding of inducement. The *Sony/Betamax* decision precluded the presumption or imputation of fault from mere distribution of the product where the product was capable of substantial non-infringing uses, but did not bar the introduction of evidence of statements and actions from which a patently illegal objective could be inferred. In *Sony/Betamax* there had been no evidence of stated or indicated intent to promote infringing uses.

The Supreme Court remitted the Grokster and Streamcast cases back to the District Court to proceed with determinations on the merits. The Supreme Court pronounced that:

> "one who distributes a device with the object of promoting its use to infringe copyright, as shown by clear expression or other affirmative steps taken to foster infringement, is liable for the resulting acts of infringement by third parties".

Grokster subsequently agreed to settle the proceedings and to stop distributing its software. Streamcast were found liable in September 2006 following a subsequent District Court summary judgment hearing.

How would *Grokster* play out in the UK?

2–154   The US approach, in the light of the inducement theory adopted by the US Supreme Court in *Grokster*, may be compared with the UK approach to procurement of copyright infringement set out in *Amstrad* (above, para.2–077).

The evidence on which the court relied in *Grokster* included advertising or promotional materials produced and published by both companies, evidence that in response to specific user requests for help in locating and playing copyrighted materials both had responded affirmatively, and internal documents demonstrating that they had specifically aimed to pick up users of the then defunct Napster file-sharing service. The court also pointed to other internal documents indicating an unlawful purpose. The court also pointed to evidence of the companies' business models, whereby the suppliers' advertising revenue was dependent on volume of usage of the software. It also relied as reinforcing evidence on the fact that neither company attempted to develop filtering tools. The court stressed, however,

---

[23] Some of the Justices went on to discuss the *Sony/Betamax* test. Two conflicting opinions were expressed: the Ginsburg concurring opinion (in which Rehnquist and Kennedy joined) and the Breyer concurring opinion (in which Stevens and O'Connor joined).

that such failure would not, in the absence other evidence of intent, be sufficient to find liability if the device was capable of substantial non-infringing uses.

The Supreme Court took a broad view of inducement, holding that although evidence of advertising was the classic way of showing unlawful purpose, there could be inducement without any communication to the end user. Justice Souter, giving the judgment of the Court, said:

> "Whether the messages were communicated is not to the point ... The function of the message in the theory of inducement is to prove by a defendant's own statements that his unlawful purpose disqualifies him from claiming protection ... Proving that a message was sent out, then, is the pre-eminent but not the exclusive way of showing that active steps were taken with the purpose of bringing about infringing acts, and of showing that infringing acts took place by using the device distributed."

The court also rejected any requirement to show a causal link between the encouragement of the consumer and a resulting specific act of infringement: **2–155**

> "...the distribution of a product can itself give rise to liability where evidence shows that the distributor intended and encouraged the product to be used to infringe. In such a case the culpable act is not merely the encouragement of infringement but also the distribution of the tool intended for infringing use."

As discussed above (para.2–078), in *Amstrad* Lord Templeman held that generally speaking, inducement, incitement or persuasion to infringe must be by a defendant to an individual infringer and must identifiably procure a particular infringement in order to make the defendant liable as a joint infringer.

So procurement of copyright infringement already exists in the UK as a basis of claim, but appears to have a narrower compass than the inducement theory promulgated by the US Supreme Court in *Grokster*. The differences are first, that the UK version appears to require communication between the distributor and the end user, such as by advertising. That differs from the *Grokster* requirements of unlawful purpose plus distribution plus end-user infringement. Second, there is a suggestion in *Amstrad* that general inducement by advertising will not suffice, without proof of a specific infringement as a result of the communication to an individual infringer. Whether a House of Lords faced with the *Grokster* facts would hold to that position, or move in the direction of more general inducement, is an open question.

Peer-to-peer software—Australia

2–156   The question of authorising infringement by distributing peer-to-peer software has come before an Australian court in a case concerning KaZaA file sharing software, *Universal Music Australia Pty. Ltd v Sharman License Holdings Ltd*[24]. On the facts Wilcox J. held that certain of the defendants had authorised KaZaA users to make copies of sound recordings and to communicate those recordings to the public. The court reached that conclusion in reliance on a combination of positive conduct and failure to implement filtering. The court found that filtering was in the power of the defendants and would prevent, or at least substantially reduce, the incidence of copyright file-sharing.

The positive conduct relied upon by the court included e.g. Sharman Network Ltd's website promotion of KaZaA as a file-sharing facility, exhortations to users to use this facility and share their files, and promotion of the "Join the Revolution" movement, which "is based on file-sharing, especially of music, and which scorns the attitude of record and movie companies in relation to their copyright works ... especially to a young audience, the 'Join the Revolution' website material would have conveyed the idea that it was 'cool' to defy the record companies and their stuffy reliance on their copyrights".

The court added that "importantly, these acts took place in the context that Sharman knew the files shared by KaZaA users were largely copyright works". A disclaimer on every page of the website that Sharman did not "condone activities and actions that breach the rights of copyright owners" was held insufficient to counteract the positive conduct, especially since any belief in the effectiveness of the disclaimer on the users of KaZaA could not have survived after receiving a market research report showing that, in May 2003, KaZaA was being predominantly used for music file sharing:

> "A reader who had even a general understanding of copyright law would also have realised this necessarily involved copyright infringement on a massive scale."

2–157   It is noteworthy that the Australian provisions on authorisation differ from the UK provisions. First, the Australian concept of authorisation has been expressed in broader terms ("sanction, approve or countenance") than the English version. Further, s.101A of the Australian Copyright Act, introduced in 2000, specifies matters that the court should take into account, including:

(a) the extent (if any) of the person's power to prevent the doing of the act concerned;

(b) the nature of any relationship existing between the person and the person who did the act concerned;

---

[24] Federal Court of Australia, No FCA 1242, September 5, 2005, Wilcox, J.

(c) whether the person took any other reasonable steps to prevent or avoid the doing of the act, including whether the person complied with any relevant industry codes of practice.

Peer-to-peer software—The Netherlands

The *Grokster* and *Sharman* decisions in the US and Australia contrast with the *KaZaA* decision in The Netherlands. The Dutch Supreme Court dismissed an appeal by BUMA/Stemra against the decision of the Amsterdam Court of Appeal that KaZaA B.V. (the then distributor of KaZaA file sharing software in The Netherlands) could not be held liable for infringing activity of users of the software and affirmed the reasons of the Court of Appeal.[25]   **2–158**

The Court of Appeal had concluded that KaZaA could not prevent the use of its software to copy files that are copyright protected. The Court also took into account that the only option KaZaA had to comply with the injunction imposed by the court below, was to completely shut down its website.

The Court of Appeal ruled that KaZaA itself did not commit any copyright infringement. In as far as committing any acts which were relevant under copyright law, this was done by KaZaA users and not by KaZaA itself. Providing the means to publish or multiply works that are copyright protected was not itself an act of publication or multiplication. Nor was it true that the KaZaA software was exclusively used for illegally downloading copyright protected works. Therefore, the Court of Appeal concluded, supplying KaZaA software was not unlawful.

Peer-to-peer software—Japan

In Japan the developer of the Winny filesharing program was, in December 2006, found guilty in the Kyoto District Court of criminal copyright infringement, even though the court found that he had no intention of actively causing infringement. He was fined about £6,000. The decision is under appeal.[26]   **2–159**

Peer-to-peer—going forward

Peer-to-peer services still flourish and are reported to consume the bulk of bandwidth on broadband networks.[27] The latest peer-to-peer technology has moved on from swapping whole files. Current software such as Bit-Torrent splits up the files, so that the user's software simultaneously downloads and assembles file fragments from a "swarm" made up of many   **2–160**

---

[25] *Vereniging BUMA, Stichting STEMRA v KaZaA B.V.* [2004] E.C.D.R. 16.

[26] "Developer of P2P Software Deemed Criminally Liable for Copyright Infringement" E.C.L.R. Vol. 11 No. 48, p.1204, December 20, 2006.

[27] Press release from Sandvine, Inc., September 13, 2005 (*www.sandvine.com/news/pr_detail.asp?ID=88*).

other users' computers. This process is especially suited to downloading large files.

As well as pursuing lawsuits against the distributors of some peer-to-peer software, rightsholders have also taken action against some of the P2P tracker and/or index sites that show what files are available for sharing at any given time. Some of these have been subject to criminal prosecution.[28] The Motion Picture Association of America started at the end of 2004 to issue lawsuits against websites that used the BitTorrent protocol to distribute unauthorised movie material.[29] In November 2005 the MPAA announced that BitTorrent, Inc would collaborate with the MPAA in removing links from its search engine to infringing copies of material owned by the MPAA.[30]

A US civil lawsuit against the operators of a BitTorrent search site, alleging inducement of copyright infringement, was met with an application to dismiss based partly on an argument that they were only providing links to third party content, which was doing nothing different from Google. The district court judge held that the allegation that by providing an index of links they were encouraging infringement was sufficient to defeat the dismissal application.[31]

2.7 LIABILITY OF HOSTS AND ACCESS PROVIDERS FOR THIRD PARTY MATERIAL

2–161　　The potential liability of on-line intermediaries for storing and making available material provided by others has always been a contentious issue. With the growth of social networking sites and user-generated content, a number of events since 2006 have served to bring the possible liabilities associated with user-generated content into sharp relief. These have included:

---

[28] For example in October 2006 Grant Stanley was sentenced in the US to five months imprisonment having pleaded guilty to criminal copyright infringement as a result of his part in running the EliteTorrents P2P site. At the same time, in Finland, 21 operators of the Finreactor BitTorrent network were convicted of copyright offences and have also been found liable for civil damages for active encouragement of copyright infringement (E.C.L.R. Vol. 11, No. 44 Nov 15, 2006).

[29] Such lawsuits would have to be founded on the websites' liability for storing and making available collections of the files that co-ordinate the peer-to-peer downloads and the related links to infringing files on users' computers, since the websites themselves do not store infringing files. After *Grokster*, plaintiffs are likely to found such cases on theories of inducing copyright infringement. For a discussion of such liability see para.2–053 above. An injunction granted in Germany against a website listing eDonkey P2P links to over 900 television shows, and against the website's Swiss hosting service, as a result of an MPAA lawsuit is reported at E.C.L.R. Vol. 10, No. 38 p. 950 (October 5, 2005).

[30] MPAA press release November 22, 2005 (*www.mpaa.org/press_releases/2005_11_22.pdf*).

[31] *Columbia Pictures Inc v Bunnell*, C.D. Cal., No. CV 06–01093, May, 2006; E.C.L.R. Vol. 11, No. 17 p.481 and Vol. 11, No. 20 p.567.

- Google's purchase of YouTube, a video-sharing social networking site, for $1.65bn and its subsequent scramble to purge the site of infringing videos
- Universal's decision to sue the social networking sites MySpace, Grouper and Bolt for copyright infringement in respect of user-uploaded content
- A French lawsuit against Google alleging that it "distributed" a copy of the documentary "The World according to Bush". Google responded to the complaint by removing the link to the material
- Separate UK lawsuits by Viacom and the FA Premier League against YouTube (and Google as it parent company) alleging copyright infringement in respect of user-uploaded content.

The typical response of defendants in such cases is likely to be that they are protected by the hosting provisions of (in the USA) the Digital Millennium Copyright Act or (in Europe) the Electronic Commerce Directive. We now turn to these.

2.7.1 The Electronic Commerce Directive

Can the internet host or access provider be liable for copyright infringe- **2–162** ment? The following discussion addresses the position according to the copyright legislation. However, any consideration of the liability of intermediaries such as internet service providers now has also to take account of Arts 12 to 14 of the Electronic Commerce Directive, which were implemented on August 21, 2002 by regs 17–22 of the Electronic Commerce (EC Directive) Regulations 2002.[32] These are enacted as a horizontal overlay on other legislation, including copyright.

Under the Directive "information society service providers" who act as conduits or hosts, or engage in caching, will be able to invoke the protection of Arts 12–14, at least in relation to damages. Although the matter is not free from doubt, the Directive may confer the benefit of these liability provisions only on on-line intermediaries established in the European Economic Area. However, the Regulations apply them to all intermediary service providers.[33] The liability provisions are discussed more fully in Chapter 5.

Internet service providers and telecommunications companies will be among those who are able to invoke these provisions for some of these activities. However, the provisions are without prejudice to the ability of a court or administrative authority, in accordance with a Member State's legal system, to require the service provider to terminate or prevent an infringement.

---

[32] SI 2002/2013.

[33] For the most recent judicial analysis of the extent to which implementing regulations made under the European Communities Act 1972 can validly go further than the underlying Directive, see *Oakley, Inc. v Animal Ltd* [2005] EWCA Civ 1191.

Moreover, the Copyright and Related Rights Regulations 2003 introduced, for copyright, both specific exemptions from infringement for the making of certain transient or incidental copies for the sole purpose of transmission in a network, and specific provision for the granting of injunctions against service providers where a service provider has actual knowledge of another person using its service to infringe copyright (see para.2–017 above). The latter provision is remarkable since it enables an injunction to be granted against a service provider regardless of whether there is a cause of action against it.

It should be appreciated that the 2002 Regulations are implemented as a broad overlay on existing law. The Regulations specify conditions which, if fulfilled, will exempt a service provider from liability for damages. It does not follow that if the conditions are not fulfilled, the service provider will automatically be liable. Certainly the service provider will not be able to rely upon the exemption, but it will still be necessary to prove that the service provider is liable for damages in accordance with the relevant underlying law. In most cases the grant of injunctions will have to be considered almost entirely under the underlying law,[34] since the intermediary exemptions do not extend to injunctions.

2.7.2 US and other cases

2–163 It is clear from the scope of the exclusive rights of the copyright owner that any internet host or access provider who uses or knowingly permits others to use his internet service to disseminate unauthorised copies of copyright works is in danger of a civil action for infringement. There is also a risk of infringement even if the host or access provider does this unknowingly.

A number of early cases in the US involved bulletin boards containing copyright material which could be downloaded by those accessing the board. In *Playboy Enterprises Inc v Frena*[35], the defendant's bulletin board had distributed unauthorised copies of photographs from the *Playboy* magazine. The defendant was held to have infringed *Playboy's* copyright, even though he claimed that he did not himself put such material on his board and was unaware that some of his subscribers were doing so. The mere fact that he was making copies available was an infringement. Also, the fact that subscribers were able to view the photographs on their computer screen constituted an infringement of the public display right. Such a case would now have to be considered in the light of the Digital Millennium Copyright Act.

2–164 An early decision from California, *Religious Technology Center v Netcom Online Communications Services*[36], dealt with the liability of a Usenet

---

[34] The scope of an injunction could still be affected by Art.15 of the Electronic Commerce Directive, which prohibits the imposition of general monitoring obligations on conduit, caching and hosting intermediaries.

[35] 839 F Supp 1552 (MD Fla 1993).

[36] 907 F. Supp. 1361 (ND Cal. 1995). Followed in *CoStar Group, Inc. v LoopNet, Inc.*, 373 F.3d 544, 555 (4th Cir. 2004) and *Field v Google, Inc.*, U.S.D.C. Nevada, January 19, 2006.

host. Although overtaken by subsequent US legislation, the case is still interesting for the analysis of who causes an infringement to occur. The case involved postings to a Usenet newsgroup on a bulletin board (BBS) connected to the internet by Netcom, a large internet service provider. A former scientologist posted portions of scientology works to the alt.religion.scientologynewsgroup, resulting in an action for copyright infringement. The suit was brought against the former scientologist, the BBS and Netcom.

Usenet newsgroups are automatically copied from one computer to the next across the internet. The plaintiffs argued that copies of the newsgroup postings were made and held on Netcom's computers for up to 11 days after they were posted, and that Netcom were thus direct infringers and strictly liable irrespective of their knowledge of the contents of the posting.

The court had to consider whether "possessors of computers are liable for incidental copies automatically made on their computers using their software as part of a process initiated by a third party". Neither Netcom nor the BBS initiated the copying, which resulted from the former scientologist posting the articles to the alt.religion.scientology newsgroup. The copying then followed from the automatic process of replicating newsgroups across the Usenet system.

Netcom was held not to be a direct infringer. Any copies on its machines were made automatically and the court did not find workable "a theory of infringement that would hold the entire internet liable for activities that cannot reasonably be deterred". The court said that although copyright is a strict liability statute, there should still be some element of volition or causation which is lacking where a system is merely used to create a copy by a third party. The court made a similar finding in respect of alleged infringement of the plaintiff's right of public distribution and display.

The plaintiff also argued that distribution of these postings after Netcom had been given notice of infringement constituted contributory infringement (which requires knowledge of the infringing activity). That question was left to go to trial.

At para.2–169 below we discuss the similar concept of involuntary copying in English law.

In *Sega Enterprises v Maphia*[37] the Northern District Court of California followed *Netcom* and declined to hold a BBS operator liable for direct copyright infringement, notwithstanding that the activities of the BBS operator was more participatory than were those of the *Netcom* defendants. The plaintiff had not shown that the defendant personally uploaded or downloaded files or caused that to occur. The most it had shown was that when the defendant operated his BBS, he knew infringing activity was occurring and solicited others to upload games. However, the court went on to hold the defendant liable for contributory infringement. **2–165**

For US cases on peer-to-peer file sharing, see para.2–152 above. **2–166**

---

[37] EIPLR Jan. 10, 1997, p.63.

In a Dutch case on liability of hosts, *Scientology v XS 4ALL cs*,[38] the Court of Appeal in The Hague held that internet providers only provide the technical facilities to make possible publication of information by others, and that it would, therefore, not be correct to equate them with publishers.

A well-publicised US criminal case involved a student at MIT who operated a bulletin board which invited the free exchange of commercial software. He made no personal gain from these activities, which allegedly cost software publishers over $1 million in lost sales, so the criminal provisions of the US Copyright Act did not apply. Instead he was prosecuted under the US Computer Fraud and Abuse Act 1986.

Although the court characterised his behaviour as "heedlessly irresponsible, and at worst as nihilistic, self-indulgent and lacking in any fundamental sense of values", it dismissed the indictment on the grounds the Copyright Act provided exclusively for criminal copyright infringement, so a "back-door" prosecution under the 1986 Act was not permitted (see *United States v LaMaccia*[39]).

2.7.3 US Digital Millennium Copyright Act

2–167   There are now statutory provisions in the US dealing with copyright liability of internet service providers, Title II of the DMCA (see section 2.2.4 above). This provides a number of "safe harbours"; if the service provider's activities come within one of these safe harbours it will not be liable for any monetary relief (including damages, court costs and attorney's fees) for any claims of infringement based on these activities, and also the types of injunctions that can be issued are limited.

The wording of the legislation is very complicated, but basically there are four safe harbours. The first is "conduit" activities, transmission, routing or providing connections; provided the ISP is a mere conduit and does not modify the content, it qualifies for protection. The same is true for automatic caching.

The other two safe harbours, for hosting content provided by users and for linking, will only apply if the ISP does not have actual knowledge of the infringement and is not aware of facts or circumstances from which infringing activity would be apparent, and the ISP must not receive a direct financial benefit from the infringing activity.

In order to qualify for any of the safe harbours the ISP must have a termination policy for repeat offenders, and must comply with certain technical measures. The first of these is that the ISP must accommodate and not interfere with "standard technical measures", which are those that have been developed pursuant to a broad consensus of copyright owners and service providers in an open standards process, available to anyone to use on non-discriminatory terms and which do not place an undue burden on the ISP.

---

[38] [2004] E.C.D.R. 25, September 4, 2003.
[39] 871 F Supp 535 (D Mass 1994).

Individual safe harbours have their own additional requirements. For caching, hosting and linking, the ISP must be able to expeditiously remove or disable access to material claimed to be infringing upon notification of a claim of infringement and must provide a method for communicating such notifications, such as a designated agent listed in a directory compiled by the Copyright Office.

2.7.4 UK analysis

Leaving on one side the defences created by the Electronic Commerce Directive and the exception created by Art.5 of the Copyright in the Information Society Directive (see above, para.2–014), an internet host could in principle be found liable for copyright infringement by copying, by issuing unauthorised copies of the work to the public, by making them available to the public, or by showing or playing the work in public in cases of works such as photographs and video games.

2–168

In the Australian case of *Universal Music Pty Ltd v Cooper*[40] an ISP was found to have authorised infringement. In this case an internet service provider provided free hosting in return for advertising on a site named *mp3s4free.net*. The site consisted of links to third party MP3 websites and to MP3 files on those sites. The ISP's customer was held liable for authorising infringement by creating the links (see para.2–143 below).

On the particular facts of the case the ISP was also held liable for authorising infringement. At first instance the judge found on the facts that the ISP's personnel were aware of the copyright problems with the site, but took no steps to address them. He said that under the specific provisions of s.101(1A) of the Australian Copyright Act 1968 (as amended):

> "in determining whether a person has authorised an infringement of copyright, the Court must take into account the extent of that person's power to prevent the doing of the act concerned and whether that person took any other reasonable steps to prevent or avoid the doing of the act. E-Talk/Com-Cen were responsible for hosting the website and providing the necessary connection to the internet and therefore had the power to prevent the doing of the infringing acts. They could have taken the step of taking down the website. Instead, they took no steps to prevent the acts of infringement."

The judge's decision was upheld on an appeal by E-Talk, for similar reasons.[41]

---

[40] [2005] FCA 972, Federal Court of Australia, July 14, 2005; [2006] FCAFC 187, Federal Court of Australia—Full Court, December 18, 2006.

[41] Judgments of Branson J. at para.64 and Kenny J at paras 157 and 170.

2–169   It should however be borne in mind that the 1988 Act contains no equivalent to the provisions of s.101(1A) of the Australian Act.

As in the US *Netcom* case (above, para.2–164), the question arises whether an internet host can be regarded as making unauthorised copies, or whether its role is sufficiently passive that it does not cause the copies to come into existence.

In *Sony Music Entertainment (UK) Ltd v Easyinternetcafé Ltd*[42] the judge made *obiter* comments about the position of an ISP closely echoing the approach of the court in *Netcom*. In that US decision, it will be recalled, the court refused to find an ISP guilty of direct infringement in respect of automatic copying occurring during storage and onward transmission of infringing material resulting from a third party's actions in posting to Usenet newsgroups.

In the *Sony* case the defendants were the proprietors of a chain of internet cafés. The defendants offered a CD burning service at each café. Upon payment of a fee, a customer was provided with access to the internet via a PC. Those PCs were connected to a central server. There were no copying or other facilities that could be used by the customer at the screen. Upon payment of the fee the customer was given a user ID. Files downloaded by the customer could be stored by the customer on a private directory on the café's server identified by reference to the personal ID.

2–170   After the termination of a session the customer could ask staff to download on to a recordable CD the material in his private file area. That could include sound recordings downloaded from the internet. If the option were taken up, the customer would present his user ID to the staff member, who had access to the relevant customer's allocated area, and download the relevant files on to the CD using a CD writer program. The customer paid £5 for this, comprising £2.50 for the CD and £2.50 for the service.

The defendant's evidence was that members of staff were prohibited from looking at the contents of any files unless the customer agreed. In the logon process a significant number of warnings were given to customers in respect of copyright infringement.

The claimants were the owners of copyright in five sound recordings. They alleged that the defendants were liable for copyright infringement. The defendant did not dispute that if there had been a downloading and copying in the way described, the customer would (subject to a statutory defence) infringe copyright in the sound recordings. The defendant denied that it was liable itself by virtue of that process. The claimants applied for summary judgment.

The defendants argued that the defendant was an involuntary copier, similar to the owner of a fax machine who receives infringing material sent by someone else; and that intervention of the human operator made no difference, as the operator had no knowledge of what was being copied.

The judge found that in this case the copying was voluntary, not involuntary. The lack of knowledge arose only because of the terms on which

---

[42] [2003] EWHC 62 (Ch).

the defendant chose to permit customers to copy information. Further, the defendant was doing this for a profit. The judge rejected this and other defences and granted summary judgment.

The judge did comment, however, that an internet service provider would be an involuntary copyist since it could not stop material being sent to it.

Does the specific provision in the 1988 Act that copying includes storing **2–171** the work in any medium by electronic means affect the passive copying analysis? It might be thought that since the continuing storage is undoubtedly carried out by the internet host, even though a third party may have put the material there in the first place, the internet host could be regarded as volitionally storing the work.

However, the reference to storage in the 1988 Act was intended to clarify the types of copying that would count for the purposes of infringement, not to introduce a new species of infringement. In *Ocular Sciences Ltd v Aspect Vision Care Ltd*[43] Laddie J. held that the activity of putting something into computer storage involved making a copy, in digital form, of that thing. The purpose of specifying storage in the 1988 Act was to avoid arguments that making a copy in a series of magnetic locations was not reproduction in a material form. That did not affect the general requirement that for a defendant to infringe he must have performed some activity. Being in possession of a medium on which a copyright work was recorded, for example, a floppy disk, was not of itself an act of infringement.[44] On the other hand, making the recording or lifting data into and out of storage could be.

Even if the acts associated with an ISP's receipt of information are involuntary, it does not necessarily follow that acts associated with sending out the information are also involuntary. A claimant could try to argue that a service provider who hosts a website is engaged in a volitional act of communicating the work to the public (see para.2–087 above), even if the work was received and stored by him involuntarily, and thus is liable subject only to any hosting defence that might be available under the Electronic Commerce Directive.

The service provider could argue, with some force, that since it has no participation in any decision as to what information to make available from its servers, and the information is sent out automatically in response to requests from third parties, any making available by it of information posted by its customers is no more volitional than the receipt and storage of the information.[45]

In the Canadian case of *SOCAN v Canadian Association of Internet* **2–172** *Providers*[46] it was held that the person who makes a work available for

---

[43] [1997] R.P.C. 289.

[44] This refers to acts of primary infringement. Possession in the course of business, coupled with relevant knowledge, is an act of secondary infringement under s.23 of the 1988 Act.

[45] In *Field v Google, Inc.* U.S.D.C Nevada, January 19, 2006, Google's transmission of cached web pages to users who clicked on the cached link on a search results page was held to be non-volitional and therefore not a direct infringement of copyright (see fn.92 above).

[46] [2004] 2 S.C.R. 427, 2004 S.C.C. 45.

communication is the content provider, not the host server. Although this was in the context of a specific exception from the communication right in the Canadian Copyright Act for those who only provide means of communication, it was also observed (at paras 94 to 103) to be consistent with the Agreed Statements accompanying the WIPO Copyright Treaty, which included the statement: "It is understood that the mere provision of physical facilities for enabling or making a communication does not in itself amount to a communication within the meaning of this Treaty or the Berne Convention".

Establishing that copying is involuntary and thus that the host has committed no act of copyright infringement will not prevent an injunction being granted against an internet service provider, since that would still be permissible by virtue of the Copyright and Related Rights Regulations 2003 (see para.2–017 above) and in principle would not offend against the Electronic Commerce Directive.

2–173   Difficult questions of split responsibility may arise where infringing material is placed on a website. Arrangements for control of content may diverge widely from the simple example of the site where the host owner is responsible for the content. The host may rent space on the site to an intermediary who themes and promotes the space as an attractive site on which content providers can place their wares. If a content provider places infringing material on the site, the question of the liability of each of the host and the intermediary fall to be considered within the framework that we have described.

2.7.5 Caches and mirrors

2–174   Another thorny issue on the internet is caching and mirroring. A cache is an electronic store of material, usually in the context of the internet web pages or their components, copied from somewhere else. Different types of cache have varying characteristics, but they all have the common purpose of enabling the internet to function more efficiently by reducing the load on communications link.

The idea of a cache is to store content locally, so that if the content has not changed since the last access the browser will load up the locally stored copy instead of accessing the original remote site. The most familiar type of cache to end users of the internet is that created by popular web browsers. These create caches on the hard disk of the user's computer. Like most caches the contents are temporary, in the sense that they change dynamically as the user accesses further websites and the browser decides what to add to and delete from the cache. However, they are certainly not transient and are stored on the disk between browser sessions like any other electronic file.

Other caches may be created by companies with intranets. Some firewalls create an intermediate cache of pages between the internal and external network. Or a company may wish to reduce traffic on its external communications links by creating a cache of commonly accessed pages for internal access.

Internet service providers often create caches for the use of their subscribers. Lastly, it has been known for bodies to create special local cache sites containing collections of websites, which people can access in preference to the original, remote sites. This type of cache is closer to a mirror site (see below) than a normal cache.

What is common to all these varieties of cache is that they involve storing electronic copies of copyright works, which is clearly a restricted act and therefore potentially infringing.

Although caches are generally understood to be beneficial to the efficient working of the internet, there are parties who can be prejudiced by their use and who could have reason to object.   **2–175**

Many websites are free to access, generating revenue from advertising based on the number of visitors to the site. Such a site needs to have accurate visitor statistics to support its advertising rates. If the visitor accesses a cached version of the page bearing the advertisement, then unless some technical means can be found to transmit the "hit" to the original site, the visitor will be lost to the statistics.

Many sites have real-time elements: stock prices perhaps, or advertisements that change every few seconds. The timely operation of such features may be prejudiced if the visitor is accessing through a cache.

Caching may prejudice charging systems based on recording visits to the original site.

Although caching is *prima facie* an infringing act, it does not follow that all types of caching are necessarily so. Much network caching is likely to be covered by the "temporary acts of reproduction" exception introduced by the Copyright and Related Rights Regulations 2003. This is discussed in para.2–014 above. However, as explained in that discussion the exception does not apply to all types of caching nor to all types of content.

There may be an implied licence to cache if the practice is widespread and generally accepted, or possibly if the person creating the cache can demonstrate that the internet could not function effectively without it so that the person putting the material on the public internet must be taken to have consented to it. That would be a matter for expert technical evidence if the issue were litigated. Browser caches are so common that there is likely to be an implied licence for that.

To the extent that web pages are computer programs (see above), the provisions of ss.50A and 50C of the 1988 Act may be relevant—at least to browser caching.

Section 50A legitimises the making of a back-up copy of a program by a lawful user, which it is necessary for him to have for the purposes of his lawful use. It might be arguable that a browser cache is the equivalent of a back-up copy of a traditional program. However, there are at least two problems with this. First, it will be difficult to argue necessity. The user can turn off his browser cache and the browser will continue to function, albeit more slowly. Second, the browser will often cache discrete elements of the website (especially graphic elements), which do not constitute a computer program. Similar problems would be encountered in seeking to apply s.50C, which legitimises (subject to contrary agreement) the copying or adapting by a lawful user of a computer program if it is necessary for his lawful use.

2–176   It is difficult to see how caching could be brought within any of the fair dealing provisions of the 1988 Act.

What is really required to enable copyright law to adapt to changing technology and practices is a more flexible fair use provision, such as exists in the US, the advantage of fair use compared with implied licence being that the copyright owner cannot reverse its effect by express prohibition. Even then, the problem with a fair use doctrine in relation to an activity such as caching is that it is not possible to assess fairness only as a function of the activity of caching. What may be fair in relation to one type of website may be unfair in relation to another, so that a person creating a dynamic, changing, cache for efficiency purposes would still need some means of distinguishing between individual websites and (at least in some circumstances) for excluding from the cache those who did not want their material to be cached.[47] Some websites have in fact included anti-caching clauses in their copyright licences or site use agreements.

A mirror site, while created like a cache to lessen the load on communications links, is a more permanent collection of data, typically containing files (such as software programs) for the user to download to disk. So a software company may create a number of mirror sites around the world from which local users can download programs, upgrades, patches and so on. Someone who created an unauthorised mirror site would not be able to argue for the existence of an implied licence, unless he could demonstrate a custom permitting it.

Some kinds of caching are covered by the Copyright Directive (discussed above) and by the Electronic Commerce Directive (discussed in Chapter 5). The Copyright Directive was implemented on October 31, 2003 by the Copyright and Related Rights Regulations 2003. The intermediary liability aspects of the Electronic Commerce Directive were implemented in the UK by regs 17–22 of the Electronic Commerce (EC Directive) Regulations 2002 (SI 2002/2013), which provisions came into force on August 21, 2002.

2.7.6 Remedies for infringement

2–177   In a civil action for infringement of copyright the successful claimant may be awarded an injunction to prevent further infringement, damages or an

---

[47] See *Field v Google, Inc* above, fn.45 for a detailed description of the steps taken by Google in respect of its search engine cache. The judge held, among other things that Google's caching activities and provision of a cached link to users amounted to fair use. The judge paid particular attention to the steps taken by Google to educate users as to how to prevent Google's robot from indexing their site or providing a cached link, and the fact that Google removed the cached links to the plaintiff's site as soon as they heard about the lawsuit.

account of profits, an order for delivery up or destruction of infringing copies in the defendant's possession or control, and costs. There is also a right to seize infringing copies found on sale, but this remedy is subject to a number of conditions.

The owner of copyright in published literary works (including computer programs) may in certain circumstances be able to prevent importation of infringing copies by giving notice to HM Customs & Excise requesting them to treat infringing copies of the work as prohibited goods, in which case importation of such copies will be prohibited for up to five years and any found by Customs will be liable to forfeiture.

The claimant may be able to seize infringing goods and evidence relating **2–178** to the infringement by a seizure order, previously known as an *Anton Piller* order. This originated in *Anton Piller KG v Manufacturing Processes Ltd*,[48] where the Court of Appeal approved the grant of an *ex parte* order authorising the claimant's solicitor to enter the defendant's premises and remove evidence of copyright infringement. The claimant must show that:

(a) the claimant has a strong *prima facie* case;
(b) the actual or potential damage to the claimant's interest is very serious;
(c) the defendant is likely to have infringing copies of the work in his possession; and
(d) there is a real possibility that if the defendant is forewarned he might destroy the evidence.

Conviction for criminal copyright infringement carries, in some cases, a maximum of ten years imprisonment and/or a fine.

EU Member States were required to implement the Directive on Enforcement of Intellectual Property Rights (2004/48/EC) by April 29, 2006. This (and certain other EU requirements) were implemented by the Intellectual Property (Enforcement, etc) Regulations 2006,[49] which came into force on April 29, 2006. The main changes were to the assessment of damages where the defendant has knowingly infringed.

The European Commission has published a proposal for a Directive on criminal measures aimed at ensuring the enforcement of intellectual property rights (2005/0127(COD)) and a proposal for a Council Framework Decision to strengthen the criminal law framework to combat intellectual property offences. These are under consideration by the Council and the European Parliament.

---

[48] [1976] Ch 55.
[49] SI 2006/1028.

2.8 ELECTRONIC PUBLISHING ON THE INTERNET— COPYRIGHT LICENSING ISSUES

2–179   Distributing copyright material electronically via the internet is becoming increasingly common. At first it was mainly software that was distributed this way, but now most newspapers publish an on-line version and technical book publishers find it a convenient way to provide updates (as is the case with this book). Distribution of music over the internet is now massively successful, video clips have been available for some time, and at the time of writing full length TV and films are on the point of becoming mainstream content not just on the internet, but via mobile devices (which will typically have internet technology sitting at some point behind them).

The first copyright question that arises when it is proposed to deliver content over the internet or similar networks is whether the publisher has the right to distribute the work in this way. There have been two reported cases, one in the US and one in France, where journalists objected to having their copy, originally submitted for print, reproduced in an on-line publication.

2–180   In the US case, *Tasini v New York Times*, a number of freelance journalists sued a number of publishers to whom they had submitted articles for print and who had then reused the articles in various electronic publications. Their contracts with the publishers had not assigned copyright, so the issue was whether what the publishers had done came within the scope of rights given to the owner of the copyright in a collective work, which is how the original print publications are classed for US copyright purposes. The owner of the collective work can use a contribution owned by another for the purpose of reproducing the collective work, any revision of that collective work and any later collective work in the same series.[50]

The US Supreme Court held that the revision right did not include rights to republish individually copyrighted articles from the collective work in electronic media. The databases on which the articles are stored reproduce articles separately, not as part of the collective work. Unlike conversion of newsprint to microfilm, the transfer to a database is not a mere transfer of the collective work from one medium to another, because it allows users to access individual articles.[51]

2–181   The French case, *Union Syndicale des Journalistes Français CFDT v Societé Plurimédia*[52] also found in favour of the authors. The court decided that publication on-line was not the same as print publications, and, as it was a form of exploitation unforeseen when, in 1983, the Union had negotiated the collective contract for its members with the publishers, it was not covered by the contract, so that the publishers had not acquired the right to reproduce the articles in this new medium.

---

[50] 17 U.S.C. s.201(c).
[51] Electronic Commerce and Law Report, Vol. 6 No. 7, July 4, 2001, p.700.
[52] Tribunal de Grande Instance de Strasbourg, November 16, 2001 [2002] E.C.D.R. 33.

It is interesting that the defendant Plurimedia was not a publisher but an ISP which carried certain on-line news services. The court held that it should have verified with the publishers whether they had the right to publish these materials on the internet, and it was enjoined from making these news services available so long as the newspapers and the journalists did not have a contract permitting on-line publication.

In Germany a photographer sued the publisher of *Der Spiegel*, claiming that a licence agreement allowing the magazine to use photographs in print editions did not extend to CD-ROM. In July 2001 the Federal Supreme Court upheld the photographer's claim.[53] The District Court of Munich is reported to have reached a similar decision over a film distribution agreement entered into in 1980, which it found did not extend to DVD.[54]

A Norwegian decision, involving columns submitted to a newspaper by a freelance in 1997 and 1998, went in favour of the newspaper on appeal.[55]

Outside the field of journalism, questions can similarly arise whether the rights granted by an author to a publisher did or did not include electronic publishing. A well known example of such a dispute was the US litigation between Random House and Rosetta Books. Random House had been granted rights at various times by three authors, including Kurt Vonnegut. The rights were in the form "print, publish and sell the work in book form". Rosetta contracted directly with the authors in about 2000 to publish the same works in electronic format. Random House sued Rosetta and were denied a preliminary injunction both at first instance and on appeal. Finally, in December 2002, the parties reached a settlement under which Rosetta were able to continue publishing.

Distribution of works electronically via the internet has commercial 2–182 attractions for publishers. The considerable costs of printing books or making CDs (in both cases from material which is already in digital form) and of storing and distributing the resulting physical objects are almost completely avoided. Innovative ways of buying works are possible. For example, the number of times or the length of time for which you could play a piece of music could be limited, so you would pay less for access to a pop song that you only wanted to listen to a few times than with physical recordings for which you pay the same however few or many times you listen to them.

However, the ease with which digital works can be copied provides the publishers with the nightmare of widespread copying with no financial return. Although all unauthorised copies would be infringing, it would be unrealistic to catch and sue all the of individuals world wide who end up with these copies—although in the last few years the music industry, in particular, has embarked on a campaign of lawsuits against thousands of individuals in a number of countries engaged in peer-to-peer filesharing of

---

[53] [2002] C.T.L.R. Issue 5, p.84.
[54] World eBusiness Law Report, April 17, 2002.
[55] World eBusiness Law Report, January 14, 2003.

music files. This has coincided with the growth of legitimate music download services such as, most famously, Apple's iTunes.

Technological methods of protection are increasingly relied upon, now usually known as Digital Rights Management (DRM). These are methods of "digital watermarking", the inclusion in the work of digital signals which identify, *inter alia*, whether the copy is authorised or not and enable the rights owner to trace and control the numbers of copies made. As discussed above, the 1996 WIPO treaties and the legislation enacted following on from the treaties include protection for anti-copying and rights management systems.

DRM systems are not universally popular, even among legitimate users. In France DVD vendors were successfully sued by a consumer organisation over the restrictions imposed by copy-protection, after a consumer found that he could not make a copy on video-cassette for personal use. The court found that this was a breach of privacy and also of consumer protection laws due to insufficient notice of the restrictions. In the US, Sony found itself on the receiving end of a class action, which it settled in January 2006, over a so-called "rootkit" copy protection system on some Sony music CDs which would prevent them running on Windows PCs.

2.9 PROTECTION OF CONFIDENTIAL INFORMATION

2–183 UK law provides legal protection for various types of confidential information. In general, this is a body of law which has developed through case law, although there is some legislation, mainly dealing with personal information (data protection) and things such as telephone tapping. Most recently, following the introduction of the Human Rights Act 1998, the courts have developed the law of confidential information to embrace the concept of privacy.[56]

However, we are here concerned with the confidential information of commercial entities, which is mainly protected through case law development. This case law has developed over the last 200 years, and has shown itself capable of adapting to new circumstances and technologies. While there are, as yet, few cases dealing with modern information technology, there is no reason why the case law should not continue to develop to cover it. This flexibility makes the law of confidential information useful in the fast changing world of IT.

---

[56] *Wainwright and an or v Home Office* [2003] UKHL 53; *Campbell v MGN Ltd* [2004] UKHL 22; see also *Von Hannover v Germany* (2005) 40 E.H.R.R. 1, *McKennitt v Ash* [2006] EWCA Civ 1714 and *HRH Prince of Wales v Associated Newspapers Ltd* [2006] EWCA Civ 1776.

2.9.1 What is protectable confidential information?

The primary requirement for protection is that the person seeking protection has kept the information secret. The definition frequently quoted is that of Lord Greene M.R. in *Saltman Engineering v Campbell*,[57] that confidential information is something which is not "public property or public knowledge". This secrecy need not be absolute in that it may be known by more than one person, provided that that person is not free to make the information public. It is a less stringent test than the test for novelty under patent law.

2–184

There are no defined limits on the type of confidential information that will be protected. The main categories involved in decided cases are technical information (sometimes referred to as "trade secrets" or "know how"), commercial information such as customer lists, personal information such as confidences between spouses or private photographs, ideas for plays, TV shows and the like and government information (e.g. the *Spycatcher* case). It may very well be that the confidential information is comprised of public information and the confidentiality attaches to the selection; for example, the names and addresses on a customer list may be published in directories but the protectable information is the fact that those particular names and addresses represent this company's customer base. Such information is clearly of value, both to the company and potentially to its competitors, and will be kept secret.

There is no specific requirement that confidential information must be of value in order to be protected, but in practice most of the remedies which could be granted by a court which has found that there has been a breach of confidence require that this breach has in some way damaged the person whose information it is.

2.9.2 What is an obligation of confidence?

Although cases discuss confidentiality in terms of being a property right, like the other forms of intellectual property, the preferred view is that confidential information law is an exercise of the court's equitable jurisdiction,[58] a law of obligations rather than of property rights. Therefore, once confidentiality of the information is established, the next requirement for protection is that the confidential information was disclosed in circumstances which imposed an obligation on the confidant to respect the confidentiality of the information.[59]

2–185

---

[57] [1948] 65 R.P.C. 203.
[58] *Kitechnology BV v Unicor GmbH Plastmachinen C.A.* [1995] F.S.R. 765, at 777–8.
[59] The requirement of receipt in circumstances importing an obligation of confidence has now been removed for privacy cases (*Douglas v Hello!*, above).

2.9.3 How does an obligation of confidence arise?

2-186 There are a number of "circumstances which impose an obligation to respect the confidentiality of the information" recognised in the case law. The most common are legally enforceable contractual obligations and the obligations imposed by the law on employees. However, the courts have also developed an equitable jurisdiction to restrain breaches of confidence where there is no legal relationship between the parties. As it is important to understand the basis on which an obligation of confidence may be imposed, each of these is considered in more detail below.

Contract

2-187 **Contractual obligations of confidentiality may be either express or implied.** The best way of ensuring that a recipient of confidential information is bound by an obligation of confidence is to impose it by an express, written agreement. Such agreements may be very short, dealing only with the obligation of confidence, or the obligation may form part of a much longer agreement, for example, a know-how licence or development agreement. It is also a good idea to provide expressly that the contract may be terminated immediately if there is a breach of the obligation of confidence.

An obligation of confidentiality will be implied in a contract under the same rules as other implied terms, namely to give the transaction the effect the parties clearly intended. However, there are obvious dangers in having to rely upon an implied term, as it will only be enforced if a court believes that there was such need for the term and that both parties would have agreed to its inclusion at the time the contract was entered into if they had thought about the matter. The best practice is always to include an express obligation of confidentiality.

Employees and contractors

2-188 A well drafted employment contract will contain express obligations of confidence, as well as dealing with post-employment issues such as a non-compete provision. Similarly, when an independent contractor is hired, that contract should contain an express obligation of confidence whenever there is any chance that the contractor will learn company confidential information. When the contractor is likely to help to develop confidential information or any other intellectual property, there should be an obligation to protect the confidentiality and to assign all rights to the employer.

Even in the absence of an employment contract, certain obligations of confidentiality are imposed by law on employees. A distinction must be drawn between the situation where the employment is continuing and that where is has ended. However, there are general principles which apply to both, and these were discussed fully in the leading case *Faccenda Chicken*

Ltd v Fowler,[60] which involved an ex-employee starting a competing business selling chickens by home delivery. These principles are as follows:

(1) The obligations of confidence of the employee are governed by his contract of employment.
(2) Where there is no express obligation, there are obligations implied by law into this contract.
(3) While the employee remains employed, there is an implied term imposing a duty of good faith and fidelity, which encompasses an obligation of confidence. The extent of this duty depends upon the nature of the employment—a senior manager is held to a higher standard than the caretaker.
(4) To determine whether any particular item is covered by the obligation, all circumstances must be considered, particularly the nature of the employment, the nature of the information, whether the employee was made aware by the employer of the confidentiality of the information and whether the relevant information can be isolated from the general knowledge that the employee is free to use in another employment or disclose.

Once the employment ends, the implied duty of good faith continues but becomes narrower in scope. There is now a potential conflict between an obligation of confidentiality and the rule against restraint of trade. Anyone must be free to use their general stock of knowledge and skill in a subsequent employment, even if that knowledge and skill has been gained during the previous employment.   **2–189**

The problem is distinguishing between what the employee must be free to use and what is information belonging to his former employer which is the subject of a continuing obligation of confidence. The courts tend to find in favour of mobility of labour unless the former employer has taken express steps to indicate what information he considers to be proprietary and confidential. For the application of these principles to computer programmers see *FSS Travel and Leisure Systems Ltd v Johnson*.[61]

Obligations arising from specific relationships

Certain professions are obliged to maintain the confidentiality of disclosures made by their clients, in particular doctors, lawyers, bankers and priests. These obligations are in general imposed by professional rules, and are enforced both by the governing body of the relevant profession and by the courts. Certain private relationships carry implied obligations of confidentiality, in particular marriage. Fiduciary relationships, such as between a company and its directors, a partnership and its individual partners,   **2–190**

---

[60] C.A. [1987] Ch. 117.
[61] C.A. [1998] I.R.L.R. 382. For a more recent application of *FSS Travel* to a claim brought against ex-employee software engineers, see *BCT Software Solutions Ltd v Jones* [2002] 12 E.I.P.R. N–196.

trustee and beneficiary and principal and agent, carry within the general duty of loyalty and good faith implied by such relationships an obligation of confidentiality.

Equity

2–191   There are cases where there is no contractual relationship of any kind between the parties, but it would be shocking if the recipient of clearly confidential information were therefore under no obligation to keep it secret and not to use it other than for the purpose for which it was disclosed. The courts have used their general equitable jurisdiction to deal with such circumstances. Indeed, the equitable concepts of good faith and fair dealing may be applied even when the parties have an express contractual confidentiality agreement. The advantage of the equitable jurisdiction is that it is flexible, and can be adapted to the particular circumstances of the case. The main requirement for the imposition of an equitable obligation of confidence on the recipient of information is that the recipient knew or, from the circumstances should have known, that the information was confidential and was being imparted for a limited purpose.

The equitable jurisdiction is particularly useful in the case where there has been a disclosure in breach of an obligation of confidence to a third party. Provided that the circumstances were such that the third party knew or should have known that the disclosure should not have been made, he can be restrained from further disclosing or misusing the information.

2.9.4 How long does an obligation of confidence last?

2–192   The general rule is that, unless the parties agree to the contrary, the obligation of confidence lasts as long as the information remains confidential.

Where there is an express contractual obligation of confidence, then the contract may specify the term of this obligation. This can be for a specified period or may be expressed to last as long as the information retains its confidential nature. Where no period is specified, the obligation is in effect of perpetual duration, although once the information becomes fully disclosed to the public other than through a breach of the obligation of confidence there would be no damage to the confider if the confidant itself disclosed the information.

Where the person under the obligation of confidence has in breach of that obligation made the information public, or has continued to use the information after termination of an agreement permitting him to do so and the information has become public in some other way, the courts acknowledge that making that person subject to a continuing obligation when the rest of the world is free to use the information can be a somewhat draconian remedy. In such cases they may apply what is called the "springboard" doctrine. Inherently, this "special disability" must be of limited duration; it is usually an injunction for the period which it would take a competitor without the special knowledge to get up and running, or it may take the form of royalties for such period.

2.9.5 How is confidential information protected?

The main way of protecting confidential information is through a civil **2–193** action for breach of an obligation of confidentiality. Provisional remedies, particularly an interim injunction, can be of great value in cases of breach of confidentiality where the full disclosure of the secret lets the "cat out of the bag" and where damages either cannot be readily calculated or are an inadequate remedy.

Many breach of confidentiality cases are, in fact, decided by the outcome of the hearing for an interim injunction. Cases where the person under an obligation has acted in an underhand way, which particularly occurs in cases where a departing employee makes secret preparations by smuggling out confidential documents (increasingly these days by email) before giving in his notice and departing to his own or another's competing business, are particularly suitable for a search order).

An injunction may also be granted as a final remedy. In light of the springboard doctrine, this may be limited in duration. In suitable cases the defendant may also be ordered to destroy or deliver up the items which contain the confidential material; for example, customer lists or drawings in the case of a departing employee. The claimant in a case involving a breach of a contractual obligation of confidence will be awarded damages on the normal compensatory basis that applies to any breach of contract.

In theory, a court of equity cannot grant damages (a legal remedy) but only an account of profits. An account of profits is difficult to carry out, and in many cases the wrongdoer has made no, or only very small, profits compared to the loss to the wronged person. By statute the court can grant damages in lieu of an injunction, but in some cases where the breach was of an equitable injunction the court has nevertheless awarded both an injunction and damages without further explanation.

A special defence is that the disclosure was in the public interest. This **2–194** most often applies either to government information (e.g. the *Spycatcher* case) or to information about people in public life, but it could apply to commercial information. For example, the defendant may have been given information in confidence that shows that a product is dangerous. The cases show the courts trying to balance the general public interest in maintaining confidentiality with specific public interests which may be considered to override this general public interest, but it is very hard to derive any black and white rules from the case law. In general, the more egregious the information that is disclosed, and the purer the motives of the defendant in making the disclosure, the more likely it is that a court will find that this defence has been made out.

2.9.6 Theft and industrial espionage

2–195   Under English law, pure information is not subject matter capable of being stolen under the Theft Act. This was decided in *Oxford v. Moss*,[62] in which a student "borrowed" the papers for the exam he was about to sit, copied and returned them. As the university had not been "permanently deprived" of the papers, this did not come within the statutory definition of theft. In 1997 the Law Commission issued a consultation paper examining the issues and recommending the creation of an offence of the unauthorised disclosure or misuse of confidential information. This suggestion has so far not been taken up.

2–196   Other criminal statutes which may provide some assistance in the case of espionage are the Wireless Telegraphy Act 1949 and the Regulation of Investigatory Powers Act 2000 (RIPA), which deal with unauthorised interception of communications.

The 1949 Act covers use of wireless telegraphy to obtain the contents of a message, however sent, while RIPA covers interception by any means of communications made by post or on telecommunications networks. Unlike its predecessor, the Interception of Communications Act 1985, RIPA applies to both private and public networks. The provisions of RIPA prohibiting interception are discussed in more detail in Chapter 5.

The Computer Misuse Act 1990, introduced to deal with hacking, which the previous criminal law could not cope with, requires unauthorised access to a computer. Although this does not cover employees making an authorised access for an unauthorised purpose, the lack of authority relates to the actual data involved. So, an employee with password access to the system, but who was authorised to access only certain accounts, would commit an offence in accessing other accounts[63]; whereas an employee who was authorised to access and copy confidential information but who copied that information for his own use would appear not to commit an offence.

The specific offences cover unauthorised modification of the contents, so cover introduction of viruses and the like, or access in order to commit another serious offence. (For a detailed discussion of these offences, see Chapter 12.) As we have seen, copying information is not theft, so this provision does not help in most espionage situations. Government information is generally covered by the Official Secrets Act. At present the only viable approaches are often to use the civil law of confidentiality or, where personal data is involved, to invoke the provisions of the Data Protection Act 1998 (see Chapter 7).

---

[62] [1979] 68 Cr.Law Rep.119.
[63] *R v Bow Street Metropolitan Stipendiary Magistrate, Ex p. Government of the United States of America* [1999] 4 All ER 1.

2.9.7 Transmitting confidential information by the internet

The nature of the internet means that transmissions on it are not, in general, **2–197** secure. Therefore, use of the internet to transmit confidential information could endanger the secrecy needed for legal protection. Ideally, such information should be sent encrypted. Where encryption is impossible or impracticable and the internet must be used, clear notices that the information is confidential, should not be disclosed or copied and is only intended for the named recipient should be attached to each item of data. This will help to establish a basis for an equitable obligation of confidence in the event of deliberate or accidental interception of the data by a third party.

2.9.8 Misuse of confidential information on the internet

Some internet users are the same kind of people who tend to carry out **2–198** computer hacking, "phone phreaking" or similar activities. This group of people tend to believe that any kind of property right in information is basically wrong, particularly if that information is owned by the government or big business, and take great pride in discovering and making available such confidential information.

It is, therefore, not surprising that there have been a number of cases in the US which involve the publication of stolen proprietary information. For example, in *United States v Riggs and Neidorf*,[64] the defendants had between them hacked into a Bell Telephone Company computer, obtained highly confidential information about that computer company's emergency telephone number system, and had published it in a magazine. This was the first case which addressed whether electronic transfer of confidential information from one computer to another across state lines constituted interstate transfer of stolen property. The court held that there should be no distinction between transferring electronic information on a floppy disk and actually transferring it by electronic impulses from one computer's magnetic storage to another's.

The position in the UK is somewhat different, as there is no legislation **2–199** specifically directed to dishonest appropriation of pure information. The current law is that information is not property capable of being stolen; this was the holding in *Oxford v Moss*,[65] in which a university student broke into the examination committee's premises, studied and made a copy of the exam paper and departed, leaving the original exam paper behind. These activities were held not to be theft.

---

[64] 741 F Supp 556 (ND Il 1990). Other US cases involve Defence Department information (*United States v Morrison*, 859 F 2d 151 (4th Circuit 1988)), law enforcement records (*United States v Girard*, 601 F 2d 69 (2nd Circuit 1979)), banking information (*United States v Cherif*, 943 F 2d 692 (7th Circuit 1991)) and stock market information (*Carpenter v United States*, 484 US 19 (1987)).

[65] (1978) 68 Cr App R. 183.

As regards civil remedies, the internet service provider is unlikely to be under an express contractual obligation of secrecy with the owner of the confidential information. It is possible that the equitable obligation will apply. However, it is obvious that there would be considerable difficulties for the claimant in proving that such an obligation existed, particularly in the case of a defendant service provider who claimed ignorance of what was on its service. It may be that specific legislation covering misappropriation of confidential information will be required as electronic networks grow in importance in this country.

2–200 However, subject to defences available to conduit, caching and hosting intermediaries under the Electronic Commerce Directive (as to which, see Chapter 5) there may be the potential for criminal liability in some of the more serious cases.

For example, where an internet service is used to publish passwords to allow unauthorised entry into a computer system, the service provider may be liable for any offence under the Computer Misuse Act 1990 that is then committed. The exact liability will depend on the circumstances. If it is actually advertised to a community of people who are likely to carry out computer hacking that passwords are available from this host, this would amount to incitement to commit an offence under the Computer Misuse Act. In a case involving police radar detectors, it was held that advertising an article for sale, representing its virtue to be that it may be used to do an act which is an offence, is an incitement to commit that offence—even if the advertisement is accompanied by a warning that the act is an offence.

To establish incitement, it must be proved that the defendant knew or believed that the person incited has the necessary *mens rea* to commit the offence, but as the *mens rea* for an offence under s.1 of the Computer Misuse Act is merely that the defendant intends to secure access to a program and knows that such access is unauthorised, this will probably not be too difficult to establish.

An alternative approach is to charge the internet host with aiding, abetting, counselling or procuring commission of an offence. In each case, the defendant must have the intention to do the acts which he knows to be capable of assisting or encouraging the commission of a crime, but does not actually need to have the intent that such crime be committed. Which type of participation is most applicable will depend on circumstances: the distinction given by a leading textbook on criminal law is that there must be a causal link for it to be procurement; aiding requires assistance but not consensus nor causation; while abetting and counselling require consensus but not causation.

There is also the possibility of a charge of conspiracy, if the necessary agreement between the service provider and subscriber could be demonstrated.

2–201 There have also been cases where improperly obtained credit card numbers have been placed on computer bulletin boards, thus facilitating the making of fraudulent purchases using that card number. Here again, if the host knew or ought to have known this was going on, he may have liability as a secondary participant in the crime that is then committed.

In the case of defence information, it should be noted that, in a case in California, a hacker who obtained information from a Defence computer was charged with espionage, even though there was no evidence that he ever passed the information on or intended to supply it to an enemy of the US. In the UK, placing stolen government confidential information onto the internet is likely to fall foul of the Official Secrets Acts.

2.10 PATENTS

2.10.1 Patents and protecting ideas

While copyright protects the expression of ideas, the patent system is **2–202** intended to protect the ideas themselves.

Patents are "available for any inventions, whether products or processes, in all fields of technology, provided that they are new, involve an inventive step, and are capable of industrial application",[66] subject to some possible exceptions (exceptions relevant to the internet are discussed below).

The basis for the patent system is that, in exchange for the inventor publishing details of an invention and how to put it into effect he will obtain from the State a limited monopoly over his invention, but that after the expiry of the patent the invention will be available for the public to use freely.

Patents thus contrast with confidential information, and a choice must be made between these methods of protection. Most countries publish patent applications approximately 18 months after filing, unless the application is previously withdrawn (which will maintain trade secret protection if the applicant believes that a patent will not be granted).

A patent is essentially national in nature and is granted by the individual patent offices of various countries in the world. A patent gives its owner a monopoly for a fixed period of time (generally 20 years from filing) in the use of the inventive idea described in the section of the patent known as the "claims".

To be patentable an invention must be "new", i.e. not have been made available to the public before the "priority date"—the date of the earliest patent application for the invention in any country of the world. The applicant for a patent can only rely on a priority date where either the subsequent national filings in those countries where protection is sought or an international Patent Co-operation Treaty application (discussed below) are made within one year of the priority date and the priority is claimed.

There must also be an inventive advance over what was previously known, also expressed by saying that the invention must not be "obvious".

Although patent protection is currently national, there are international **2–203** conventions which can reduce the number of patent applications that have

---

[66] TRIPs Art.27(1).

to be prosecuted to grant. The Patent Co-operation Treaty ("PCT"), to which most countries belong, permits a single application to be filed and to undergo a single prior art search, and provides an option of a single initial examination, before the national phase in which the remainder of the prosecution process must be carried out in each of the selected countries. Making a PCT application has the advantage of delaying the time at which a decision must be made as to whether filings in other countries, with the associated expense, should be made.

The European Patent Convention ("EPC"), which covers all the members of the European Community, Switzerland, Iceland, Liechtenstein, Monaco and Turkey, goes further in providing a single route to the grant of a European Patent, which then operates in the member countries designated by the patentee as a bundle of national patent rights, governed by the domestic laws of each of the designated countries, except for the availability for nine months after grant of a central challenge to validity by means of the opposition procedure. The European Patent Convention also effected a significant harmonisation of substantive patent law throughout Europe.

2.10.2 Patenting the internet

2–204   As far as the internet is concerned, the patent system applies particularly to those unseen but vital technical aspects which make the internet and the traffic on it possible. These "unseen" aspects include such things as the hardware, software and communications interfaces and protocols used not only to interface across equipment but to allow improved and more user-friendly access for humans to the internet. They also include the ingenious compression and encryption algorithms used to improve speed of transfer of information and the amount of information which can be transmitted.

An interesting recent example of a patent for just such an "unseen" component is the compression technique at the centre of the controversy surrounding Unisys and CompuServe. An aspect of the public domain graphics compression software produced by CompuServe incorporates a compression technique which Unisys claimed it owned, namely the .GIF graphics file format. When CompuServe started to charge for this software in order to pay a royalty to Unisys, not unsurprisingly, there was an outcry largely, one suspects, because Unisys had been so late in coming forward with its rights claim. The basis for the claim was a patent owned by Unisys claiming the compression algorithm in question.

Such patents cover technical inventions, which are indisputably the kind of thing the patent system is designed to protect. A much more controversial type of patent originating from the US, that covering business methods, has potentially a similarly wide effect on internet applications.

2.10.3 Business method patents—US

For most of the twentieth century it was accepted that there was a judicially created so-called "business methods exception" to statutory subject matter, relying on the *Hotel Security* case decided by the 2nd Circuit in 1908.[67]

2–205

Almost as soon as it became accepted that software could be a patentable invention, patents for achieving various methods of doing business using software were applied for. Merrill Lynch were pioneers in filing patents on computerised methods of doing financial transactions.

Many people questioned whether the patent system should ever be used to protect business methods which were only "technical" in that a computer was being used to carry them out, and the USPTO were rejecting many such applications on the basis of the "business methods exception".

However, in 1998 the US appeal court for patent matters, the Court of Appeals for the Federal Circuit (CAFC), reversed a lower court's ruling in the *State Street Bank* case that a method of managing mutual funds was not patentable subject matter.[68] The CAFC ruled that the so-called "business methods exception" was in fact a myth, and that the same tests for patentability (new and non-obvious, useful) applied to business methods as had always applied to industrial methods.

This same court confirmed this approach in *AT&T Corp v Excel Communications Inc.*,[69] going even further to make it clear that the fact that the claims in issue were pure method claims with no recital of use of a computer was irrelevant to the question of their patentability. The Court strictly limited the mathematical algorithms exception to algorithms in the abstract, any process applying the algorithm to a new and useful purpose is potentially patentable, and also said that there was no invariable rule that this useful end must involve a "physical transformation" to be patentable. This seems to confirm that non-statutory exclusions from patentability, however venerable, would no longer automatically be applied.

Following these decisions, the USPTO was inundated with applications for business method inventions, many of which were not computer-related and which did not refer to any technological means for carrying out the claimed method.

In determining whether such claims were patentable, the examiners applied three criteria, (1) did the claimed method produce a useful, concrete and tangible result, (2) was it directed to a law of nature, physical phenomena and abstract ideas and (3) was it within the "technological arts".

However, in November 2005 the Board of Patent Appeals and Interferences held that the third criterion should not be applied as there was no separate "technological arts" test (*Ex p. Lundgren* Bd. Pat. App. & Int., No. 2003–2088, 10/05). As a result, the USPTO has issued interim guide-

---

[67] *Hotel Security Checking Co. v Lorraine Co.*, 160 F. 467.
[68] *State Street Bank & Trust Co. v Signature Financial Group. Inc.*, 47 U.S.P.Q. 2d 1596.
[69] 172 F.3d 1352 (Fed. Cir. 1999).

lines to assist examiners in their determination whether an invention is within statutory subject matter.

2–206   For many new internet and e-commerce companies, the ownership of a patent or at least patent applications is a vital part of their assets in persuading investors to pour large sums of money into the company. It is not surprising, therefore, to find that there are already a large number of US patents relating to internet business methods, and that litigation has already started.

For example Priceline.com, which has obtained US Patent No. 5,794,207 on its method of "buyer-driven pricing", sued Microsoft alleging that its "Expedia" website was infringing this patent. In a case which has caused a lot of controversy, Amazon.com, the on-line bookstore, sued its main competitor, Barnes & Noble, for infringement of its "one-click purchasing" patent, US No. 5,960,411. Although Amazon won the first round by obtaining a preliminary injunction just before the Christmas season forcing its rival to change the way customers on its site transact purchases, this was reversed on appeal, with the CAFC casting doubt on the validity of the patent.

Two MIT professors sued the "Ask Jeeves" site for allegedly using their patents on natural language searching. Other patents which could cover a lot of e-commerce activities are Cybergold's patent on a method of paying web surfers for paying attention to on-line adverts, DoubleClick's patent on a method of keeping track of internet advertisements and who is looking at them and Sightsound.com's patent on downloading music online.

2–207   The internet business bonanza led to a number of lawsuits by companies that had older patents which did not refer to the internet but which they alleged had claims broad enough to cover internet activities.

Trying to enforce such patents can be hazardous; when Compton's newMedia, the owners of *Encyclopedia Britannica*, announced that they had been granted a patent covering a computer-based multimedia searching system and that it would be seeking royalties from the multimedia industry, there was an outcry. As a result, the US Patent Office initiated a re-examination of the validity of the patent on the basis of the prior art turned up by the protestors, and rejected all the claims.

Undeterred, E-Data has launched extensive litigation over its patent covering downloading music or books to special terminals in shops against companies delivering music and other information on-line to users' computers; although the claims were narrowly construed by a District Court so as not to cover on-line delivery, the Federal Circuit reversed this in November 2000, holding that the claims could cover real time delivery to a home personal computer. Most companies who had been sued by E-Data then settled by taking a licence, but in June 2005 the UK Patents Court held that the British equivalent of the E-Data patent was invalid because it had been anticipated by an earlier US patent.

However, most attempts to assert pre-internet patents against internet businesses seem to be failing, unless both the claims and the description were very widely worded—thus making them more vulnerable to being found invalid. This happened to British Telecom when it dusted off an old teletext patent and sued in the US, asserting that the patent covered hypertext linking.

This activity has led to a great deal of very vocal criticism of some of the business method patents issuing from the USPTO, which in turn has led to attempts by that Office to improve both the quality of the examination process and the examiners carrying it out. The databases searched for applications in Class 705, into which most business method applications fall, have been considerably expanded to include numerous non-patent literature databases. A number of examiners with business qualifications and experience have been recruited for this group. All applications in this class have to have a second review before a notice of grant is issued.

The US Congress has also acted. A new "prior user" defence to patent infringement was added to the patent statute in 1999. This applies only to patents for "a method of doing or conducting business". The defendant must prove that, acting in good faith, he "actually reduced the subject matter to practice at least one year before the effective filing date of such patent, and commercially used the subject matter before the effective filing date of such patent".   **2–208**

It remains to be seen if this defence will be much used in practice; there are uncertainties as to how broadly a court would interpret the definition of a "business method" and, in proving his case the defendant will be admitting literal infringement—fatal if his prior use defence fails unless he can successfully challenge the patent's validity.

A more extensive bill dealing with business method patents was introduced into the House on April 3, 2001. This proposed that all business method applications should be published at 18 months, there would be a presumption of obviousness if the patent merely disclosed the computer implementation of a known business method, there would be the ability for members of the public to submit prior art to the USPTO in respect of published, pending patents and there would be a post-grant opposition procedure. In litigation the issue of validity would be decided on the normal civil burden of proof, rather than the heavier burden currently borne by the challenger, and the patentee would have to disclose whether a validity search had been carried out. This bill was referred to the Subcommittee on Courts, the Internet, and Intellectual Property, but has made no further progress.

While some argue that these type of patents go far beyond what the patent system is meant to protect, a great deal of investment is today being poured into these areas. Unless that investment is given some reward, opportunities will be missed and pioneers can find themselves pushed by those with more financial muscle out of markets their innovation has established. It is often the case that innovation, far from being stifled by the patent system as is sometimes thought to be the case, is actually a direct result of an attempt to "design around" a patent which is particularly dominant in a field.   **2–209**

One of the real problems with patent protection in this area is that many people do not realise that it is available. There is a wide-spread belief that software is not patentable in Europe. Stated this broadly, the belief is not correct, as is discussed below. However, there is still considerable uncertainty as to what kinds of innovations in this field are patentable. In particular, as between the European-wide patenting system operating through the European Patent Office and the UK national system (which run in parallel to each other), there has recently been considerable divergence over what is and is not patentable *vis-à-vis* what are generically termed "software" patents. This is discussed below.

2.10.4 Internet Publications as Prior Art under the EPC

2–210   Prior art, for which the EPC uses the term "state of the art", is defined in Art.54(2):

> "The state of the art shall be held to comprise everything made available to the public by means of a written or oral description, by use, or in any other way, before the date of filing of the European patent application."

The "date of filing" in the case of an application entitled to priority under an international convention is that priority date (Art.89). US entities should note, however, that there is no grace period equivalent to the one year period of 35 U.S.C. §102(b).

In addition, Art.54(3) provides that the state of the art (for novelty but not for obviousness) also includes "the content of European patent applications as filed", which were filed before the priority date of the patent in issue but which were published after that filing date.

The EPC itself does not provide any definition of what is encompassed by "made available to the public". For the purposes of examination the EPO Guidelines apply, which define the term as follows:

> "A written description ... should be regarded as made available to the public if, at the relevant date, it was possible for members of the public to gain knowledge of the content of the document and there was no bar of confidentiality restricting the use or dissemination of such knowledge."[70]

The validity of a granted patent is decided by the courts of the country where that particular patent is registered. This means that the question of what is meant by "made available to the public" will be decided under national law in most cases where the issue arises, although the national court may give some weight to the EPO Guidelines.

2–211   In theory, anything placed in plain text on the World Wide Web is

---

[70] Guidelines C IV 5.2.

available to any member of the public anywhere in the world who manages to find it through luck or a suitable search. This may not be true of material which is in encrypted form, or which is only available by use of a password.

However, a number of questions are raised; the first, and least troublesome, is whether this information in electronic form is a "written" description, even if it is never downloaded and printed out. Unlike the equivalent US provision[71] which refers to "a printed publication", the EPC wording is sufficiently broad that web pages and other electronic documents clearly will come within it.

A second, and more difficult question, is the status as prior art of a disclosure made on an obscure website, perhaps only appearing for a short time. Previous case law dealing with traditional paper publications have indicated that the presence of only a single copy, anywhere in the world, will constitute prior art provided that copy is available to any member of the public who chose to read it. The issue is probably the practical one of proof of the public availability of the information, rather than the legal status as prior art of such information.

Another question which relates to proof results from the ease with which electronic information can be altered. Typically, such prior art is put forward several years after it became available by an accused infringer seeking to invalidate the patent. He must prove that the information was publicly available before the patent's priority date. In the case of printed publications with a publication date on the cover page this is not usually a problem (unless the publication date is very close to the priority date, when it is also necessary to prove when the document became available), because forging such a date would be very difficult. Forging the date of an electronic document would be easy; it will be necessary to provide an audit trail of the document to ensure that has not happened.

Finally, information posted to a corporate intranet could be held to be publicly available if enough people are able to read it, particularly those outside the group of those who need to know about the invention.

This shows that companies must take care that they do not lose patent **2-212** rights by publishing information about new products or developments on the internet (or even their intranet) before they have filed a patent application to obtain a priority date. Even a confidential publication has risks. Although a hacker breaking into the confidential file would probably be under an equitable obligation of confidence, if that hacker then posted the information openly on the internet those accessing that information without knowledge of the way it was obtained would be free to use it, and so there would have been a public disclosure. In Europe there would still be a six month period from the first date of such unauthorised public disclosure in which a patent application could be filed,[72] but that may not be true in other countries.

---

[71] (35 USC § 102).
[72] (EPC Art. 55).

2.10.5 Patentability of software—Europe

2–213   The European Patent Convention provides that certain types of things will not be regarded as patents and will consequently not be patentable.

Article 52 of the European Patent Convention (implemented now by 32 European countries) states that:

> "(1) European patents shall be granted for any inventions which are susceptible of industrial application, which are new, and which involve an inventive step.
>
> (2) The following in particular shall not be regarded as inventions within the meaning of paragraph 1:
>
> (a) discoveries, scientific theories and mathematical methods;
> (b) aesthetic creations;
> (c) schemes, rules and methods for performing mental acts, playing games or doing business, and programs for computers;
> (d) presentations of information.
>
> (3) The provisions of paragraph 2 shall exclude patentability of the subject-matter or activities referred to in that provision only to the extent to which a European patent relates to such subject-matter or activities as such.
>
> (4) ..."

2–214   Possibly because it saw how many software patents were being granted by the US Patent Office, or possibly due to pressure from the computer industry, the European Patent Office (EPO) has, in its decisions concerning patentability of this type of patent, tried to circumscribe as closely as possible the above exclusion as it relates to programs for computers.

To do this, it has relied upon the limitation placed on the exclusions to patentability by Art. 52(3) and has pinned its colours to the mast of the final two words, "as such". In essence, it has said that the exclusion from patentability for programs for computers will only apply where the invention claimed consists solely of a computer program running on a "known" computer.

2–215   In the 1980s the EPO developed the doctrine of "technical effect". The doctrine was first developed in the case of *Re Vicom* (T208/84) which essentially concerned a new method of handling the images for a CAD (computer aided design) system. In this case, the Board of Appeal decided that:

> "the method described in the patent was susceptible of industrial application since it could be used (for example) in investigating the properties of a real or simulated object or in designing an industrial article."

The Board also decided that:

> "...a mathematical method as such is an abstract concept prescribing how to operate on numbers, without producing any direct technical result. By contrast, where a mathematical method is used in a technical process, the process is carried out on a physical entity (for example, an image stored as an electrical signal) by some technical means which produces a change in that entity."

To a computer programmer, the distinction made in this latter paragraph may appear baffling but this has been the basis for most subsequent decisions of the EPO in this area.

Following the *Re Vicom* decision, the technical effect doctrine was developed by the EPO Board of Appeal in *Koch & Sterzel/X-ray Apparatus* (T26/86). This involved a patent for a data processing device which was used to adjust certain parameters of X-ray apparatus where the prior art used the same apparatus and the same known computer but a different computer program.

It was held that the patent was valid as the invention has to be assessed as a whole and the use of non-technical means did not detract from the overall technical teaching. The Board commented that the rule followed by the original German court dealing with this matter, i.e. that since the only new element for the invention was excluded from patentability the whole apparatus was not patentable, was "impractical".

Since these two decisions, there have been several cases decided by the EPO Board of Appeal in this area although none of these matters have gone to the extended Board of Appeal. Six of the cases concerned IBM text handling patents which were all held to be invalid. These decisions all seem to have been based on the idea that text processing is not a "technical" activity and, therefore, the effect of the program on the displayed text was not a technical one. Interestingly, the same six IBM text processing patents have been granted in the US by the US Patent Office.

2–216

1994 seemed to be the turning point in the EPO's approach to software patents, with two important cases. In the first, *Sohei/Yamamoto's Application* (T769/92), the applicant claimed a computer system for plural types of independent management including at least financial and inventory management and a method for operating said system. Data for the various types of management which could be performed independently from each other with this system could be inputted using a single "transfer slip", in the form of an image displayed on the screen of the display unit of the computer system, for example. This would seem to be a "method of doing business", and thus excluded from patentability under Art.52(2)(c) even if it did not fall at the first hurdle because it involved software.

The Technical Board of Appeal held that an invention comprising functional features implemented by software is not excluded from patentability under Arts.52(2)(c) and (3), if technical considerations concerning particulars of the solution of the problem the invention solves are required in order to carry out that same invention. Such technical considerations lend a technical nature to the invention in that they imply a technical problem to be solved by implicit technical features. An invention of this kind does not pertain to a computer program as such under Art.52(3).

They also found that non-exclusion from patentability cannot be destroyed by an additional feature which as such would itself be excluded, as in the present case features referring to management systems and methods which may fall under the "methods for doing business" exclusion from patentability (Art.52(2)(c)).

2–217   The second decision, *Petterson's Application* (T1002/92), related to a system for determining the queue sequence for serving customers at a plurality of service points. The system gave the customer the possibility of selecting one particular service point; it comprised, in particular, a turn-allocating unit, terminals for each service point, an information unit which indicated the particular turn-number and the particular free service point to the customer. The corresponding Swedish application had been rejected by the Swedish patent office and the rejection upheld through the Swedish courts.

The EPO Board of Appeal took the view that the claim was directed to an apparatus which comprised, *inter alia*, computer hardware operated by a particular computer program. The program determined output signal of the hardware was used for an automatic control of the operation of another system component (the information unit) and thus solved a problem which was of a technical nature. Further, the fact that one of the practical applications of the system concerned the service of customers of "a business" did not mean that the claimed subject matter must be equated with a method for doing business.

Other 1994 decisions which show this more liberal approach of the Board of Appeals include two IBM cases, T59/93 relating to a method for the interactive rotation of displayed graphic objects (overturning rejections that this was a mathematical method, a method of doing business, a computer program and presentation of information on the basis that the entirety of the claimed method was not excluded under any of these heads) and T453/91, a method for VLSI-chip design and manufacture (rejection of design method claims upheld as having no tangible result, manufacturing claims allowed as having a technical effect).

2–218   A startling demonstration of how far the Board of Appeal is prepared to go in giving Art.52(2)(c) a liberal interpretation was given in two IBM cases, T0935/97 and T1173/97. In both cases IBM had included claims for a computer program product which had the effect of making a computer carry out certain actions, as well as the more conventional claims to a programmed computer capable of carrying out these actions and to the method. T0935/97 relates to a technique of displaying information in the obscured portion of an overlapped window in another part of the screen. T1173/97 relates to a method of resource recovery in a computer system. The Examining Division had allowed the method and apparatus claims, but unsurprisingly (in view of existing case law) had rejected claims to the program product as software "as such" and therefore not saved from the exclusion of Art.52(2)(c) by Art.52(3).

The Board considered that the exclusion only related to software with no technical character. Technical character would be found when the execution of the software instructions resulted in some "further technical effect", such as the solution of a technical problem (e.g. *Viacom*) or where technical considerations are required to arrive at the invention (e.g. *Sohei*). The Board stated that it would be illogical to grant a patent for a method and for a programmed computer carrying out the method, but not for the software that in fact produces the technical effect. This approach is in line with the current US approach to patentability of the programs themselves.

Following the decision of the Board of Appeals in the *Pension benefits* case (see below), in 2003 the EPO issued new Guidelines. On examination of patentability, after setting out the general principles (including the requirement that the invention must be of "technical character"), the various exclusions are considered. In relation to programs for computers, the Guidelines say:

> "Programs for computers are a form a of "computer-implemented invention", an expression intended to cover claims which involve computers, computer networks or other conventional programmable apparatus whereby *prima facie* the novel features of the invention are realised by means of a program or programs...
>
> When considering whether a claimed computer-implemented invention is patentable, the following is to be borne in mind. In the case of a method, specifying technical means for a purely non-technical purpose and/or for processing purely non-technical information does not necessarily confer technical character on any such individual step of use or on the method as a whole. On the other hand, a computer system suitably programmed for use in a particular field, even if that is, for example, the field of business and economy, has the character of a concrete apparatus, in the sense of a physical entity or product, and thus is an invention within the meaning of Art. 52(1).
>
> If a claimed invention does not have a *prima facie* technical character, it should be rejected under Art. 52(2) and (3). In the practice of examining computer-implemented inventions, however, it may be more appropriate for the examiner to proceed directly to the questions of novelty and inventive step, without considering beforehand the question of technical character. In assessing whether there is an inventive step the examiner must establish an objective technical problem which has been overcome ... The solution of that problem constitutes the inventor's technical contribution to the art ... If no such technical problem is found, the claimed subject matter does not satisfy at least the requirement of an inventive step..."

Draft directive on the patentability of computer implemented inventions

3–219   The European Commission decided that there was a need for harmonisation of law of the Member States on the controversial topic of the patentability of computer programs and software-related inventions. Following a Green Paper, a consultation process showed general agreement that the present legal position on the patentability of software was unclear and therefore unsatisfactory. However, a majority of the responses to a further consultation were from people hostile to both software and business method patents.

As a result, in February 2002, the Commission produced a draft Directive on the patentability of computer-implemented inventions, attempting to maintain the current position on software patents while trying to clarify where the boundary between technical and non-technical software innovations lay, but excluding business method patents.

The European Parliament was very heavily lobbied by both sides during its consideration of the proposed Directive. The amendments to the Commission's draft approved in the vote on September 24, 2003 show it was clearly influenced by those who were opposing patents for software and business methods. In particular, the Parliament added detailed and very limiting definitions of "technical contribution", "technical field" and "industry", added "data processing" to the list of unpatentable subject matter and expanded the scope of the rights under the decompilation and interoperability provisions of the 1991 Software Directive.

Many of the amendments made by the Parliament were highly controversial and were opposed by a number of Member States and the Commission. Industry groups challenged the amendments as dangerous to the competitiveness of European industry, not least because they were so broad as to exclude much more than pure software and business methods from patentability.

The Council of Ministers finally reached a common position in March 2005, rejecting most of these amendments, although this was delayed by the addition of the new members to the EU in May 2004. The European Parliament in July 2005 rejected this common position and voted by an overwhelming majority to reject the entire Directive. The European Commission then said that it would not prepare a new version of the Directive. This means that the current situation, where patentability of software and business method inventions is left to be decided by the EPO and national patent offices and courts, will remain.

2.10.6 Business method patents—Europe

2–220   On the face of it, business method patents do not appear to be available in Europe, as Art.52(2), discussed above, also excludes methods of doing business from patentability. However, as we have seen in the case of software, this is not an absolute bar. Indeed, the key 1995 *Sohei* case involved a business method, a financial trading system. The technical effect test applied equally to this as to a purely technological system.

Other patents for computer systems which carry out business methods have been granted; for example, in 1997 Citibank obtained EP 0 762 304 for a computer system for an automated warrant trading system. However, the claims tended to concentrate on the system itself, rather than the method it carries out.

However, recent decisions of the Appeal Board of the EPO have taken a somewhat different approach to assessing patentability of business method inventions to the decisions discussed above. The first of these involved an application for an "Improved Pension Benefits System" EP-A 0 332 770 was rejected in September 2000 (Decision T0931/95). Claim 1 of this application reads: **2–221**

"A method of controlling a pension benefits program by administering at least one subscriber employee account on behalf of each of subscriber employer's enrolled employees, each of whom is to receive periodic benefits payments, said method comprising:

providing to a data processing means information from each said subscriber employee defining the number, earnings and ages of all enrolled employees of the said subscriber employer; determining the average age of all enrolled employees by average age computing means; determining the periodic cost of life insurance for all enrolled employees of said subscriber employer by life insurance cost computing means; and estimating all administrative, legal, trustee and government premium yearly expenses for said subscriber employer by administrative cost computing means;

the method producing, in use, information defining each subscriber employer's periodic monetary contribution to a master trust, the face amount of a life insurance policy on each enrolled employee's life to be purchased from a life insurer and assigned to the master trust and to be maintained in full force and effect until the death of the said employee, and the periodic benefits to be received by each enrolled employee upon death, disability or retirement."

There were also claims to apparatus to carry out the method.

The Examining Division rejected the application on the grounds that the invention was excluded under Art. 52(2) as a method for doing business and lacking any technical character. One of the grounds on which the applicant challenged this decision was that there was no requirement of "technical character" in the EPC. This ground was rejected on the basis of the consistent case law of the EPO Appeals Board, concluding that there is an implicit requirement in Art.52(1) EPC that an invention must have "technical character" in order to be patentable.

2–222 The Board also considered the issue as to whether the invention here had "technical character". They considered that the method claims were claims only to a method of doing business, the fact that it used "technical means" for a "purely non-technical purpose and/or for processing purely non-technical information" "does not necessarily confer a technical character to such a method." However, they did consider that "a computer system suitably programmed for use in a particular field, even if that is the field of business and economy, has the character of a concrete apparatus in the sense of a physical entity, man-made for a utilitarian purpose and is thus an invention within the meaning of Article 52(1) EPC." They justified this rather artificial distinction by reference to the wording of Art. 52(2), which does not refer to "apparatus" but only to "schemes, rules and methods".

However, the applicant's victory was short-lived, as the Board then, at its own initiative (this was not an issue on appeal), considered whether the apparatus claims were patentable over the prior art identified in the application itself and held that they were not, for lack of inventive step. Unfortunately, in doing so they ignored the case law that requires that the claimed invention must be looked at as a whole when considering whether there is an inventive step (e.g. *Koch & Sterzel*), stating "... the improvement envisaged by the invention according to the application is an essentially economic one ... which, therefore, cannot contribute to inventive step." On this basis they had no difficulty in finding there was no inventive step so the application should be rejected.

If this approach is followed in other cases, turning the clock back 20 years, then there seems little chance that even apparatus claims for business methods will be granted unless there is clearly something clever technically involved in the implementation of the method.

2–223 In April 2004 the Appeals Board returned to the question of how to examine the patentability of inventions which appear to fall within subject matter excluded under Arts.52(2) and (3) in the *Auction method/HITACHI* case.[73]. This involved a patent application for a system for conducting an on-line Dutch auction. This had been rejected by the examiner as being a business method excluded by Arts.52(2) and (3), also as lacking inventive step.

The Board of Appeal took the opportunity to review the general approach to examination for patentability. They rejected the "contribution" approach adopted by earlier Appeal Board decisions, which involved some consideration of the prior art in order to determine the contribution to the art made by the claimed invention, instead approving the view of some recent decisions that it was inappropriate to make a comparison with prior art when examining for the presence of an invention. An invention may consist of a mix of technical and non-technical features, which may be difficult to separate prior to examination for inventive step. The invention

---

[73] T0258/03—3.5.1.

in this case included clearly technical features to make it an invention within Art.52(1). Indeed, Art.52(1) is sufficiently broad to include as technical activities such as writing using a pen and paper. However:

"...this does not imply that all methods involving the use of technical means are patentable. They still have to be new, involve a non-obvious technical solution to a technical problem and be susceptible of industrial application."

In this case, although there was a technical problem with the prior art method of conducting an on-line auction caused by delay issues, the solution to the problem was non-technical, namely making changes to the auction method. This was purely a method of doing business.

Those drafting patent applications for methods of doing business must   2–224
primarily ensure that their claims include technical elements. Claims drafted for the US, where there is no technical requirement (see above) will be rejected immediately under Art.52(2) and (3). However, even if that hurdle is overcome, there remains the considerable difficulty of demonstrating both a technical problem and a novel and inventive technical solution to this problem

In conclusion, it can be seen that even those who are of the school of thought that this sort of idea should not be patentable should be aware that patents are being obtained in this field and be wary of infringing them. Even if something is considered not to be patentable in Europe it may well, nevertheless, be given patent protection in the US where a similar battle over what is and is not patentable in this area has been raging for some time now.

Whatever the outcome of that battle, it can be said that more of this type of patent is granted by the US Patent Office and since anyone trading on the internet cannot fail at least to offer access in the US this is something worth bearing in mind from both sides of the fence. On the one hand, a potential patenteè should consider obtaining patent protection in the US even if it is not available elsewhere; and on the other hand, in considering copying the techniques of others on the internet, the existence of patent protection, if nowhere else than in the US, should be considered.

2.10.7 Patentability of computer-implemented inventions—UK

There were five cases in the UK court between 1989 and 1997 considering   2–225
the issue of patentability of software patents, but only in relation to the grant of patents rather than in full blown infringement actions. The first such case, *Merrill Lynch Inc's Application*[74] which reached the Court of

---

[74] [1989] R.P.C. 561 (first instance reported at [1988] R.P.C. 1).

Appeal, the court found that the trading system claimed in the patent application was not patentable as it was a means of performing a business method. The interesting thing to note in this instance is that the claims for this application were subsequently amended essentially to link the method claimed to the relevant apparatus and communications means and the patent was then granted.

The next case after this, *Gale's Application*,[75] involved an application for a patent for a read-only memory (ROM) chip on which was stored a novel method for calculating a square root. This was found not to be a patentable invention as not having a technical effect. Then there was *Wang's Application*[76] which involved a computer system operable as an expert system and which was also found not to be patentable.

2–226   Then the UK High Court considered the matter in *Raytheon's Application*[77] which involved a pattern recognition system. Both the Patent Office and the Patents High Court on appeal agreed in this instance that this patent application related to no more than a conventional computer processing information. Bearing in mind the nature of this invention and the nature of the invention in the case of *Re Vicom*, it is difficult to see how one can reconcile these two decisions, as they would both appear to achieve what the EPO thinks of as a technical effect. Possibly the judge in this instance did not appreciate the incredibly complex procedure that the human brain must go through in order to achieve the pattern recognition which it does.

In *Re Patent Application No. 9204959.2 by Fujitsu Ltd*,[78] Laddie J. made a detailed review of the cases. He referred in particular to the leading cases in the European Patent Office of *Re Vicom* and *IBM/Text Processing* and the two cases of this type which had been looked at by the UK Court of Appeal, *Merrill Lynch* and *Gale's Application*. Having done so his conclusion on the issue of patentability for software is best summarised by saying that the UK court considers that the issue of patentability is an issue of substance and not form. Thus, where it is clear that a computer program printed out on paper will not be patentable, similarly a computer program sitting on the hard disk of a computer will not be patentable. The issue is whether when the computer program is actually run on that computer it causes the computer to operate in a novel way and/or produce a novel result which in itself is not excluded from patentability under s.1(2) of the Patents Act. Although he decided that the claims were not to a computer program "as such", they were still excluded from patentability as being a method of performing a mental act.

On appeal,[79] Aldous L.J., after referring to the need to construe the UK Patents Act in the light of EPO decisions, decided that this invention was not analogous to that in *Viacom*, and disagreed with Laddie J. in holding

[75] [1991] R.P.C. 305.
[76] [1991] R.P.C. 463.
[77] [1993] R.P.C. 427.
[78] [1996] R.P.C. 511.
[79] [1997] R.P.C. 608.

that the claims were to a computer program as such, but stating that it was "doubtful" that this was a method of performing a mental act.

After *Fujitsu*, there was a long gap before the High Court again con- **2–227** sidered the scope of the exclusion under s.1(2) of the Patents Act 1977. Then, on the same day in July 2005, two decisions were handed down which considered the application of s.1(2) to computer-related inventions, *In re Patent Applications GB 0226884.3 and 0419317.3 by CFPH L.L.C*[80] and *Halliburton Energy Services, Inc v Smith International (North Sea) Ltd.*[81]

The former, an appeal from the Patent Office, was given by Peter Prescott, QC, sitting as a deputy judge. The *Halliburton* case was a patent infringement action, heard by Pumfrey J. In *CFPH* the deputy judge reviewed the nature of the exclusions from patentability under Art. 52(2) of the EPC and the differing public policy reasons for such exclusions. He then looked at the English case law on software and business method patents, which he found to follow the earlier EPO approach, which has now been superseded (see para.2–223 above), concluding that the current EPO approach is preferable and that the UK Patent Office should follow that approach.

Pumfrey J. also looked at the reasons for the exclusions and the case law, concluding that it was not easy to reconcile the cases on the various exclusions. However, he concluded that part of the difficulty was an unspoken belief that all the excluded matters had something in common. Like Prescott QC, Pumfrey J. concluded they did not, there were different rationales for exclusion. He also adopted the current EPO approach.

Shortly after these decisions, the UK Patent Office issued a notice on examination for patentability,[82] stating that it would follow the approach taken in the *CFPH* and *Halliburton* decisions. This approach had the following four steps:

- In identifying the advance in the art, the examiners will look at the claim as a whole, including aspects that might fall within s.1(2).
- It may not always be necessary to carry out a search before concluding the application fails the second step.
- In applying the tests, examiners will continue to look at the substance of the invention rather than the form of the claim.
- An invention will be unpatentable if the new and non-obvious aspect falls under the description of something excluded by s.1(2).

On October 27, 2006 the Court of Appeal handed down a judgment in the conjoined *Macrossan* and *Aerotel* appeals.[83] The judgment addressed patentability of software and business methods. The Court of Appeal

---

[80] [2005] EWHC 1589 (Pat).
[81] [2005] EWHC 1623 (Pat).
[82] Patent Office Notice, "Patents Act 1977: Examining for Patentability", July 29, 2005
[83] *Aerotel Ltd v Telco Holdings* [2006] EWCA Civ 1371.

carried out a thorough review of the existing law in the UK, the European Patent Office Boards of Appeal and elsewhere. It found recent decisions of the EPO Boards of Appeal to be flawed and contradictory.

The Court of Appeal found that it was bound by its own precedent and therefore was constrained to adopt the "technical effect" approach with the rider that any "technical contribution" could not reside in novel or inventive purely excluded matter.

In doing so, the Court of Appeal followed its decision in *Merrill Lynch* (see above). In so holding, the Court of Appeal followed the decision of the EPO Board of Appeal in *Viacom*, but added the rider referred to above. Applying this test, the Court of Appeal held that the new technical result in *Merrill Lynch* was simply a method of doing business and was excluded subject matter. Thus, the application failed.

2–228   The Court of Appeal reformulated its previous approach in English decisions as a practical four-step test. The four steps are:

1. to construe the claim properly;
2. to identify the actual contribution;
3. to ask whether it falls solely within the excluded subject matter;
4. to check whether the actual or alleged contribution is actually technical in nature.

The Court of Appeal acknowledged that, in particular, the second step could in some circumstances be difficult and would require an investigation into what the invention involved, how it worked and the problems that it solved. Thus the requirement was to look at the substance of the claim, not its form.

Applying the four-step test, the court upheld the validity of the Aerotel patent and dismissed Macrossan's application.

The court suggested that in due course a reference to the EPO Enlarged Board of Appeal was inevitable and suggested the questions that the Enlarged Board of Appeal should consider. The questions the Court of Appeal suggested the EPO Enlarged Board of Appeal ought to consider are as follows:

1. What is the correct approach to adopt in determining whether an invention relates to subject matter that is excluded under Art.52?
2. How should those elements of a claim that relate to excluded subject matter be treated when assessing whether an invention is novel and inventive under Arts. 54 and 56? and specifically:

    (a) Is an operative computer program loaded onto a medium such as a chip or hard drive of a computer excluded by Art.52(2) unless it produces a technical effect, if so what is meant by "technical effect"?
    (b) What are the key characteristics of the method of doing business exclusion?

Following the publication of the *Aerotel/Macrossan* appeal judgment, the **2–229** Patent Office issued a new practice notice taking account of the four step approach promulgated by the Court of Appeal.[84]

2.10.8 Patent Infringement and the internet

Infringing acts

Under UK law infringement is defined by s.60 of the 1977 Patents Act. **2–230** Section 60(1) deals with direct infringement. For a product, the infringing acts are making, disposing of, offering to dispose of, use, importation and keeping the product for any reason. Process patents are infringed by a person who uses or offers for use in the UK when he knows or it is obvious to a reasonable person in the circumstances that its unauthorised use would be an infringement. It is also an infringement of a process patent to dispose of, offer to dispose of, use, import or keep any product "obtained directly by means of that process".

Indirect infringement is covered by s.60(2), which makes it an infringement to supply or offer to supply someone not entitled to work the invention "with any of the means, relating to an essential element of the invention, for putting the invention into effect", provided that there is actual or deemed knowledge that "those means are suitable for putting, and are intended to put, the invention into effect in the United Kingdom." However, under s.60(3), this provision does not apply to staple commercial products unless the supply or offer of supply is made for the purpose of inducing the person to whom the supply is made or is offered to infringe the patent.

Except for use of a patented process relating to the internet itself (such as **2–231** the Lycos search engine patent), or the electronic transfer (disposal or import) of software which forms an essential part of a patented invention, the only possible infringing act that could be carried out over the internet is an offer to dispose. While an offer for sale is clearly covered, it is doubtful whether a mere advertisement, which is normally classed as an invitation to treat rather than an offer, is an "offer to dispose". In the US it has been held that merely listing products on a website did not qualify as an "offer to sell" under US patent law.[85] However, it may be possible to persuade a court that such an advertisement is a threat to dispose and that it should give injunctive relief on a *quia timet* basis. Obviously, where the website is set up to actually accept orders then there is no problem in finding an offer to dispose.

There has been an English case relating to an allegation of infringement under s.60(2) of a patented process carried out using the internet, *Menashe*

---

[84] *www.patent.gov.uk/patent/p-decisionmaking/p-law/p-law-notice/p-law-notice-subjectmatter.htm.*

[85] *ESAB Group Inc. v Centricut LLC*, DSC No. 4:98–1654–22, 1/15/99.

Business Mercantile Ltd v William Hill Organization Ltd.[86] The patent related to an interactive, computerised gaming system. The parties agreed to try as a preliminary issue the question whether it was a defence that the host computer and part of the communication means, both elements of claim 1 of the patent, were not located in the UK. The agreed facts were that the William Hill system was available to punters in the UK William Hill would supply them with software which turned their computers into a terminal communicating with the host computer via the internet. The host computer had the properties and carries out the functions of the host computer in the patent claims, but was located outside the UK.

2-232   At first instance Jacob J. (as he then was) decided the question should be answered in the negative. The Court of Appeal, in a decision given by Aldous L.J., upheld this decision although for somewhat different reasons. Aldous L.J. approached the question from the point of view of the punter who obtains a CD in the UK and then uses the invention in the UK. The punter neither knows nor cares where the host computer is located, it is the input and output of that computer at the punter's terminal computer that is of importance. Thus it was the supply of the CD in the UK which was intended to put the invention into effect in the UK.

A similar answer was given in the US in the "BlackBerry" litigation, *NTP, Inc. v Research in Motion, Ltd.*[87] The patents in suit related to an electronic mail system integrated with RF wireless communications networks. The defendant's BlackBerry system as used in the US used a relay server based in Canada. RIM argued that it could not be liable as a direct infringer because s.271(a) of the patent statute should be construed to require that all steps of the infringing activity to take place within the US The Federal Circuit appeals court disagreed, saying:

> "Even though one of the accused components in RIM's Black-Berry system may not be physically located in the United States, it is beyond dispute that the location of the beneficial use and function of the whole operable system assembly is the United States."

It seems likely that other courts will follow this lead, so patent infringement for systems and methods using communication with a server cannot be avoided by locating the server in a different country.

Liability for infringement

2-233   The Patents Act sets out the acts that constitute infringement, but does not expressly deal with who is liable for such acts. The UK courts apply the tort rules, in particular in determining the liability for acts by servants and agents and whether persons are joint tortfeasors.

---

[86] [2002] EWCA Civ 1702.
[87] 418 F.3d. 1282, 1326 (Fed. Cir. 2005).

The latter is relevant when determining whether a parent company can be liable for the infringing acts of a subsidiary. The case law is clear that ownership by the parent of an infringing subsidiary is not enough on its own to make the parent also liable. There must be some evidence of "common design" (also referred to as "concerted action" or "agreed on common action" in some cases) to carry out the infringing acts. A finding that there has been such a common design will in each case depend upon the facts, but examples of parent company activities that could lead to a finding of common design are manufacture and supply to the subsidiary of the infringing article, control of worldwide marketing by its subsidiaries, acting in such a way as to lead customers for the infringement to believe that they are dealing with the parent (e.g., calling the subsidiary a "sales office" in its marketing literature).

Corporate websites may provide ammunition for a patentee seeking to   **2–234**
join the parent of an infringing subsidiary in an infringement action, particularly where that parent is located in a different jurisdiction. Very often the parent's website will have a generic rather than country specific domain name (e.g. "Bigco.com", rather than "Bigco.co.uk"), and potential customers are likely to look for generic domain names first. The parent company's website will usually provide information about world-wide operations, and may tend to give a picture of a single global organisation, with the national subsidiaries integrated rather than independent. For example, national subsidiaries may not have independent websites but merely their own pages within the parent site. Similarly, listing of national subsidiaries as "sales offices", particularly when combined with some kind of offer of the infringing goods, is evidence of a common design to dispose of the goods in the UK between a foreign parent and UK subsidiary.

Jurisdiction

The issue of jurisdiction is a tricky one in relation to the internet. The UK   **2–235**
case law is that the offer to dispose must be an offer *within the jurisdiction* to dispose of infringing products *in* the jurisdiction: *Kalman v PCL Packaging (U.K.).*[88] In that case the offer involved transfer of title in the US to a UK company, so the court held that the US defendant had not made an offer which involved disposal in the UK of infringing products. It did not make any finding on whether the offer itself, made in the US but communicated by telex to the UK, was an offer "within the jurisdiction". There has not yet been any UK case law on whether an offer made on a foreign based website accessible in the UK is an offer within the jurisdiction.

---

[88] [1982] FSR 406.

CHAPTER 3

Trade Marks and Domain Names

3.1 TRADE MARKS AND BRANDING

3.1.1 Trade marks

Introduction

3–001   The internet, in particular the World Wide Web, is from a commercial point of view a combination of a shop window and an advertising hoarding. Branding and, therefore, trade marks are consequently vital aspects of trading on the internet. However, unlike traditional advertising campaigns an "advertisement" placed on the internet will by default be a global campaign, in the sense that it is available worldwide. This makes the legal position more than usually troublesome. (We discuss in detail in Chapter 6 whether the mere availability in the UK of a non-UKwebsite, without more directed targeting, amounts to use of a trade mark in the UK under the Trade Marks Act 1994.)

National trade marks and the international internet

3–002   First and foremost, trade marks are national by nature. They can be registered or unregistered. The protection offered to unregistered trade marks varies considerably from country to country, both as to extent (ranging from none to strong) and as to the legal basis on which they are protected (such as unfair competition in some countries, or passing off in the UK). The laws relating to registered trade marks are far more uniform across the globe. Therefore it is such registered rights which should be of most interest to those who wish to entrench their ability to use their brands on the internet.[1]

---

[1] This is not to downplay the usefulness of rights other than registered trade marks in pursuing internet infringers. In the UK, passing off has proved to be a particularly flexible and potent weapon against infringers such as domain name pirates (see the discussion of domain name disputes at para.3–063 *et seq*). Also, Community registered and unregistered design rights may also form part of a cross-border branding strategy. However, their specific relevance to the internet is at best peripheral and we do not address them, or their domestic UK counterparts, in this book.

When a trade mark is registered, it is designated as covering certain goods   3–003
or services only. A registered trade mark gives the owner the exclusive right
to use that mark on the goods or services for which it is registered in the
countries in which it is registered. Anyone else who then uses that mark
without the authority or licence of the trade mark owner in any of those
countries on the relevant goods or services will be infringing the registered
trade mark. They may then be subject to injunctions preventing them from
continuing to use the mark and awards of damages to compensate the trade
mark owner.

Although registered trade mark regimes are relatively uniform from
country to country, there still exist significant differences. For example, in
some countries it is the first person to use the trade mark in relation to the
relevant goods or services who has the priority right over others to claim
ownership of the mark. However, in other countries it is the first person to
register the mark who obtains such priority ownership rights, regardless of
what use others have previously made of the mark. This is one major reason
why ownership of registered trade marks tends to be fragmented around the
world.

Indeed, it is not unusual for a trade mark to be owned by different,   3–004
unrelated companies in different countries. Very few companies will have
any trade marks which they have registered in all countries of the world. So
an advertisement put on the internet in one country by the owner of that
mark in that country may infringe the registered trade mark of another
company which has it registered in a country in which the advertisement in
question is accessed and read.

This is not an entirely new problem. It has previously been encountered
with, for example, the cross-border nature of satellite broadcasting—particularly when, as is so often still the case in Europe, trade mark ownership
is split between countries. The direct sales advertising on such satellite
broadcasts necessarily reaches the whole footprint of the satellite (or, for
encrypted broadcasts, at least those countries in which transmission deco-
ders are legitimately supplied). Such advertising, although legal in the
country at which it is directed, may infringe a trade mark in another
country into which the satellite footprint spills over. Spillover problems can
also occur in the physical world of print media, where the advertiser does
not control the ultimate destination of copies of the newspaper or magazine
in which he advertises.[2]

Nevertheless, advertising on the internet raises spillover concerns to a   3–005
vastly different degree than does advertising in print media such as newspapers and magazines. These have to be physically distributed, while the
World Wide Web is constantly available in any country in the world to
anyone who has the equipment capable of accessing it. Advertising on the
web does not depend on any form of physical distribution which might
limit its availability in certain countries. The issue of spillover advertising

---

[2] See discussion in Ch.6, contrasting the effect of UK spillover circulation in defamation
(liability) and trade mark infringement (no liability) respectively.

has thus become especially vexed with information flowing all around the globe on the internet.

However, as discussed in detail in Chapter 6, mere availability in the UK may not be sufficient to amount to infringement. Even in the physical world the mere availability of an advertisement in a magazine circulating in the UK (even primarily in the UK) has been held not necessarily to amount to an infringement of a UK registered trade mark.[3] This likely to be all the more true of the mere availability of a website.[4]

While registered trade marks are national in nature, there are some international trade mark registration systems either in place or currently being created which may help to give trade mark owners an easier means of broadening their ownership. But even these by no means give global coverage and certainly do not deal with existing clashing registered rights.

3–006   For example, the Community Trade Mark is a unitary right effective for the whole of the EU. There are also two systems, the Madrid Arrangement and the Madrid Protocol, which make it easier to extend trade mark registrations in certain countries to any of the other countries who are part of this system. The US and the EU both joined the Madrid Protocol, in 2003 and 2004 respectively. A US federal trade mark registration will cover a very large and commercially worthwhile market even though, strictly speaking, it is only a registration in one country.

It is likely that only large companies will be financially able to register their brands as trade marks throughout the world. It will only be the well-established brands or those relating to new types of goods which will not experience some sort of clash somewhere in the world. Therefore, a brand owner will have to be realistic as to what sort of coverage it requires and what level of risk in terms of infringement is acceptable. One way to look at this is to draw up a list of major markets for the goods in question together with those countries where infringement is most likely to occur and ensure that trade mark registration has been secured at least in those.

3.1.2 Branding—choice and use

3–007   One interesting aspect of using brands on the internet is the difference, compared with print media, of the interface with the viewer or prospective purchaser. The on-line interface will generally be very limited. There may be little opportunity to give a large amount of information about the product, or the information may have to be split up into numerous small, separately accessible, chunks. In this context the brand itself may convey a comparatively large amount of information.

Brands are often thought of as badges of origin and quality. Skilful advertising campaigns can augment this with more inchoate values such as

---

[3] *Euromarket Designs, Inc. v Peters, a.k.a. "Crate & Barrel"* [2001] FSR 288; and *800 FLOWERS Trade Mark* [2001] E.W.C.A. Civ. 721.
[4] *ibid.*

service, innovation, value or market leadership. Products may be sold in a catalogue type fashion where the purchaser never sees the item until after it has been purchased. The nature of the web means that not only is it interactive, but also visual. Usually distinctive brands are now scattered all over web pages cheek by jowl with each other, reinforcing the need to have a strong visual identity—one, incidentally, capable of achieving impact at the low graphic resolutions typical of the web.

The interactive and visual nature of the World Wide Web has also meant   3–008 that a wider variety of types of trade marks have been and will in the future be used. Word and logo marks are the most popular and widely used, but as audio becomes more prevalent on the web, tunes and distinctive jingles could well become popular.[5] Under the Trade Marks Act 1994 registration of sounds became possible, enabling registration of marks such as the Direct Line jingle. Other examples of sound marks could include the Intel note-series or the Windows startup chimes. Animated trade marks may also become popular and are registrable.

In Europe any distinctive[6] non-descriptive sign is registrable as a trade mark. This is also the case in the majority of countries in the world. Trade marks simply consisting of a word are the most common, followed closely by logos. But even single colours can be registered as trade marks provided they constitute a sign, are capable of graphical representation and have become distinctive of the particular goods or services sold or offered by the company claiming exclusive rights to the colour.[7]

The range and number of disputes which have arisen over domain names also demonstrates how important internet branding has become. This specific area is discussed in more detail below.

3.1.3 Proper use

The traditional need to ensure proper use of trade marks so as to maintain   3–009 their strength and value still applies to the internet. If a company does find itself enjoying the benefit of that extraordinarily valuable asset (particularly for the internet), a global trade mark, it should pay more attention than ever to ensuring that it is not put in jeopardy by misuse.

It is important, for example, that a mark is not used in such a way as to allow it to lose its distinctiveness and become generic. The mark should always be depicted as registered and in consistent colours and styles. Trade mark notices and the like are as appropriate, if not more so, for trade marks

---

[5] It is possible, for instance, to associate a tune with the home page of a website. This plays through the user's computer loudspeakers as the page is loaded. While it may be debatable whether such practices attract or deter users, such tunes would certainly be candidates for registration as trade marks.

[6] For European Court of Justice decisions on distinctiveness see *Procter & Gamble v O.H.I.M.* (E.C.J. Case No C–383/99 (September 20, 2001), *O.H.I.M. v Wm. Wrigley Jr. Co.* E.C.J. Case No C–191/01 (October 23, 2003).

[7] *Libertel v Benelux Trade Mark Office* E.C.J. Case No C–104/01 (May 6, 2003); *Heidelberger Bauchemie* E.C.J. Case No C–49/02 (June 24, 2004).

used on a website as for those used on paper. They should state who the trade mark owner is.

Since there is a widely, but mistakenly, held belief that any material (including a trade mark or distinctive logo) on a web page can freely be copied on to other web pages, it is advisable (although strictly speaking not legally necessary) to make clear in any trade mark notice that copying and use of the mark may only be done under licence from the proprietor.

Some companies for a variety of different reasons are only too happy to promote such use of their trade marks since, amongst other things, it is a useful form of advertising. However, if this is the case they would still want such use to be subject to an appropriate licence so that the mark is not put in jeopardy by misuse. A trade mark notice can easily point to a place on the web page giving details of the relevant licence. The licence should extend to any other relevant rights, such as copyright.

3–010   Most companies with valuable brands will have proper use handbooks and these should be updated to refer to use of their marks on the web. In appropriate circumstances, sections of such a proper use handbook can be put on the company's web page if it is prepared to license others to use its marks in certain circumstances. A company might also want to consider making this proper use information available through their web pages for reference by, for example, journalists.

One major use to which trade marks are put on the internet is in sponsorship arrangements, often where web pages are sponsored by a particular brand owner and a branded link to the brand owner's website is placed on the sponsored page. In such circumstances, the way in which the brand is used is entirely in the hands of the sponsored website proprietor. Therefore, the sponsor will want to ensure by way of appropriate contract that such use is, for example, proper, as well as dealing with issues of liability dealt with elsewhere in this book. Similar considerations will also apply to contracts with publishers and advertisers on the internet.

3.2 TRADE MARK CLASHES ON THE INTERNET

3–011   Inevitably, clashes between competing trade mark owners, and between trade mark owners and infringers, have occurred on the internet. These can generally be divided into genuine disputes and cybersquatting (or domain name piracy).

3.2.1 Genuine disputes

3–012   "Genuine" disputes include:

- the same mark owned and used by different persons (whether in the same country or different countries) in respect of different goods or services;

144

- the same mark owned and used by different persons in different countries in relation to the same goods or services (the "split mark").

Both of these types of disputes may be regarded as genuine disputes, since both parties have a legitimate claim to some rights in the mark and the dispute is over the boundaries between them. The advent with the internet of cheap cross-border on-line commerce has exposed such latent clashes between the owners of the same marks in different countries, or even in different regions of the same country.[8] These owners may have traded in ignorance of each other for years, the internet providing the first market-place in which they have been brought into conflict. Or they may have clashed previously, but the internet has provided a new commercial context in which the old dispute is re-opened.[9]

Same mark, different goods or services

The first type of genuine dispute (same mark, different goods or services) is often only a problem in relation to domain names, since only the desire to register the identical domain name brings the parties into conflict at all.[10] This, of course, assumes that it is clear that the trade mark is being used by the different individuals in relation to different goods or services. However, where, for some reason this is not clear, it should be possible to clarify this by way of notice or disclaimer on the relevant web page. Domain names are dealt with in detail below.   **3–013**

Same mark, same goods or services

As to the second type of genuine dispute, the "split mark" where the same mark in respect of the same goods and services is owned by different companies in different countries, it might be acceptable simply to state in a notice that the goods in question are not available for sale to that country. Arguably, this would mean that the mark was not being used as a trade mark in that country since the company is not engaging in trade there. It may also be advisable to identify the other owner of the mark and the territory in which it owns the mark.[11]   **3–014**

In the UK some support for this approach—at least where the notice is a

---

[8] For an early example see *Bensusan Restaurant Corporation v King* (126 F. 3d 25, 1997 US App. LEXIS 23742).

[9] See *e.g. Playboy Enterprises Inc. v Chuckleberry Publishing, Inc* 939 F. Supp. 1032 (SDNY 1996), a cross-border US/Italian dispute in which the court had to interpret a previous settlement agreement between the protagonists.

[10] See *e.g. Prince Plc v Prince Sports Group, Inc* [1998] F.S.R. 21, discussed at para.3–083 below. In the case of a well-known trade mark, the trade mark owner may be in a position to assert rights in respect of goods or services different from those for which the mark is registered. See the discussion of s.10(3) of the Trade Marks Act 1994 at para.3–043 below.

[11] See *www.scrabble.com* for an example of a split mark web entry page.

true reflection of the facts—can be gained from *Euromarket Designs Inc. v Peters*[12] (the *"Crate & Barrel"* case). However, the efficacy of this approach will depend very much on the laws of the individual countries involved and the facts of any particular case, since the use of a trade mark that amounts to trade mark infringement may differ between countries.

It is also unlikely that a notice would be considered in isolation, without considering other evidence of the practice of the website owner. In *Dearlove v Combs*[13] the provision on a web page of links to separate websites for UK and US users was insufficient to prevent there being use of a trade mark in the UK, where there was other material containing the mark on the same and associated pages that, the judge found, were directed to UK users.

Hopefully, in many instances, it will be possible for the relevant companies to come to mutually beneficial trade mark co-operation agreements allowing them to continue to use the trade mark with suitable disclaimers or in a certain fashion on their web pages even though those web pages will inevitably be accessible in each other's territories.[14] Whatever the solution, the key will be pragmatism since as the global marketplace gets even smaller, the potential for trade mark clashes is bound to increase.

Reducing the potential for unnecessary cross-border internet trade mark clashes

3–015 As to the future, common sense suggests that if the objective is to encourage peaceful co-existence of potentially clashing websites across national borders, then there should be a threshold requirement that a claimant trade mark owner establish that the defendant has targeted or directed his website at the jurisdiction in question. That would tend to restrict disputes to those where there is real prospect of damage through competition under a similar mark. This approach has found favour in the UK caselaw (see discussion in Ch.6).

In June 2000 the WIPO Standing Committee on the Law of Trade Marks published a discussion paper[15] addressing this question. It suggested that only use of a sign on the internet which has a "commercial effect" in a Member State should constitute use of a sign for the purposes of determining infringement of industrial property rights in a mark or other sign.

As to commercial effect, the Committee suggested a non-cumulative, non-exhaustive list of factors to be taken into account. Generally, these go to the question whether the user of the sign is doing business with customers and others in the Member State, or directing the internet activity towards it, taking into account factors such as language, currency, territory

---

[12] Above, fn 3. And see discussion in Ch.6.

[13] [2007] EWHC 375 (Ch), at paras 30 to 35.

[14] Any such agreement, and indeed, notices concerning the non-availability of goods and services in particular countries, would need to be prepared with due to regard to any constraints imposed by competition law.

[15] *Protection of Industrial Property Rights in Relation to the Use of Signs on the Internet* SCT/5/2, WIPO Standing Committee on the Law of Trademarks, Industrial Designs and Geographical Indications, June 21, 2000.

disclaimers, degree of interactivity, provision of contact details and use of a ccTLD (country code Top Level Domain—see discussion of domain names below).

3.2.2 Cybersquatting

A rather different type of clash is the phenomenon of cybersquatting. This is a reincarnation of the old practice of registering company names in advance of their registration by the "true" owner of the name (for instance, where a company has announced an intention to expand its activities to other countries) with the intention of exacting a substantial price from the company to transfer the new company to it. Such practices were looked upon with disfavour by the English courts.[16]   **3–016**

Cybersquatters, similarly, register domain names before the trade mark owners have done so, with a view to exacting a price for transferring the domain name to the trade mark owner. Cybersquatters have also been known as domain name pirates and domain name hijackers. The terms are interchangeable. Occasionally, cybersquatters go further and create fake websites, sometimes for the purpose of perpetrating frauds upon the public.[17] Domain names and cybersquatting are discussed in detail below.

3.3 DOMAIN NAMES

The major new trade mark issue that has arisen with the internet relates to domain names. Thanks to the proliferation of cybersquatting, domain names have acted as a lightning rod, stimulating heated debate and polarising opinions over the appropriate relationship of intellectual property rights to domain names, the ease of registration of domain names, how to prevent abusive domain name registrations and many other related topics. The debate has also become entangled with disputes about appropriate institutional structures for managing the technical features of the internet, so that questions such as whether new classes of domain name   **3–017**

---

[16] *Glaxo Plc v Glaxowellcome Ltd* [1996] F.S.R. 388. The defendant company, Glaxowellcome Ltd, was registered at the time of the merger of Glaxo and Wellcome. The court found that the defendants were engaged in a "dishonest scheme to appropriate the plaintiffs' goodwill in the names Glaxo and Wellcome, and to extort a substantial sum for not damaging it". The court ordered the defendants to change the name of their company from Glaxowellcome Ltd to enable the merged company to take the name. In *Direct Line Group Ltd v Direct Line Estate Agency* [1997] F.S.R. 374, Laddie J. also granted an interlocutory injunction restraining passing off against defendants with a track record of incorporating companies with famous names, stating that the court would "view with extreme displeasure any attempt by traders to embark upon a scam designed to make illegitimate use of other companies' trade marks".

[17] See *e.g. Marks & Spencer Plc v Cottrell* Ch.D., Lightman J., February 26, 2001 (unreported).

should be made available have been discussed in parallel with the question of who should be empowered to make that decision.

3.3.1 What are domain names and how do they work?

3–018 What is a domain name? A word of technical explanation is appropriate.

IP addresses

Computers on the internet recognise each other by IP addresses. Each computer attached to the internet has a unique IP address, which may be allocated to it permanently or temporarily.[18] An IP address has a form such as 194.72.244.100.[19]

The DNS

3–019 While fine for computers, the IP address is not user-friendly for human beings. So in 1984/85[20] the domain name system (DNS) was introduced. This overlays the IP address system, allowing alphanumeric identifiers to be used such as "twobirds.co.uk". When the user types into a browser, for instance, "www.twobirds.co.uk", the browser sends a request to look up a database table in its local DNS name server,[21] receives the corresponding IP address (either from the local server or through a series of queries to locate an authoritative name server[22]) and uses that IP address to contact the target internet computer (e.g. a website host).[23] The process of finding out the IP address that corresponds to a domain name is known as "resolving" the domain name.

The DNS database is, like most aspects of the internet, distributed across

---

[18] As with most technical explanations of the internet, this is a simplification. For instance, a company with many individual computers on its network may appear to the outside world to have one IP address (that of its firewall). The individual computers behind the firewall may have a set of private IP addresses allocated internally, which are invisible to computers on the outside of the firewall. The effect, therefore, as seen from the public internet, is that the whole of the company's network has only one IP address.

[19] This is the form of IP version 4. This will change if and when IP version 6 supersedes it (See Ch.1, fn 4).

[20] See e.g. RFC 921 *www.rfc-editor.org/rfc/rfc921.txt*.

[21] The identity of the name server, or DNS server, is set in the browser preferences. Usually, the name server will be provided by the ISP from whom the user obtains his internet access services.

[22] If the local name server is authoritative for the requested domain name, or has cached a recent request for the name, then that server will return the corresponding IP address. If not, the browser will send a query out to the most general server (e.g. that responsible for ".uk". If that server does not have the corresponding IP address it will return the name of the authoritative name server for the next level down (e.g. ".co"). The process repeats until the browser finds the authoritative name server for the requested domain name, which will return the corresponding IP address.

[23] A practical way of demonstrating that the domain name system sits on top of the IP address system is to find out the IP address of a website and to type that into the browser instead of the normal URL. The browser will connect to the site in the normal way, if anything a little more quickly since it does not have to translate the URL into the IP address before making the connection.

many computers. They co-ordinate with each other, and utilise technical methods to determine which of the many thousands of DNS servers holds authoritative information about which groups of domain names.

The DNS root

There is, however, a hierarchical element to the DNS. Certain "root" ser- **3–020** vers are ultimately authoritative in that they hold (in the "root zone file") the definitive information about which other name servers are authoritative for which domains.[24] Among the 13 root servers[25] the "A" root server was originally first among equals, the other 12 servers taking their cue from it. In a process started in February 2002 and completed in November 2002 the authoritative root zone file was moved to a hidden distribution master server, which updates all 13 public root servers.

Authority over the DNS root

The master server is operated by Verisign, Inc (formerly Network Solutions **3–021** Inc.), although subject to oversight by the Internet Corporation for Assigned Names and Numbers (ICANN) (see para 3–025) and, ultimately by the US Department of Commerce who, under its contract with Verisign, has the right to approve any changes to the authoritative root zone file.[26]

---

[24] There have been occasional attempts to create "alternative roots", which would recognise a different or larger set of domains than those recognised by the root servers operated by Verisign. However, an alternative root will not succeed unless it gains wide acceptance among ISPs, who have to configure their domain name servers to recognise the alternative root if their users are to be able to see domain names registered with it. An early attempt to do this can be seen at *www.alternic.org*. A later attempt (see *www.new.net*) involved two strategies: creation of an alternative root and provision of a browser plug-in that offers users the appearance of extra gTLDs. Such attempts excite great controversy in the internet community. See, for instance, *www.icann.org/icp/icp–3-background/lynn-statement–09jul01.htm* for views on this topic.

[25] The organisation of the root server system continues to be under review by ICANN (see Memorandum of Understanding dated November 25, 1998 between US Department of Commerce and ICANN and Amendment 2 through 6 thereto (Amendment 6 is dated September 16, 2003 and extends the Memorandum of Understanding to September 30, 2006); The MoU and its Amendments are available at *www.icann.org/general/agreements.htm*.

[26] See Amendments 11 and 19 to the Cooperative Agreement between NSI (now Verisign) and the US Department of Commerce dated October 7, 1998 and November 10, 1999 respectively. The Agreement and both amendments are accessible at *www.icann.org/nsi*. The various agreements are well summarised, albeit from a critical perspective, in Political Oversight of ICANN: A Briefing for the WSIS Summit, Internet Governance Project November 1, 2005 (*www.internetgovernance.org*). The former importance of the "A" root server (and now of the hidden authoritative server) was illustrated by the controversy that erupted in February 1998 when the late Jon Postel conducted what was afterwards described as a "test", in which he asked the operators of the subsidiary root servers to redirect them to point to the "B" root server at his university, the University of Southern California, instead of to the "A" root server on the NSI computer in Herndon, Virginia. For an account of the incident see "US Government Counters Claims that DNS Root-Servers were 'Hijacked'" E.C.L.R. February 11, 1998 p. 179. In a separate incident Eugene Kashpureff, proprietor of the "alternative root" AlterNIC, pleaded guilty in March 1998 to computer fraud charges after diverting traffic from NSI to AlterNIC (see *http://www.usdoj.gov/criminal/cybercrime/kashpurepr.htm*).

The current procedure is that root zone change requests from TLD operators are received by ICANN (performing its IANA function), which if it considers them appropriate forwards them to the Department of Commerce for approval. The Department of Commerce then transmits the approved requests to Verisign, which edits and generates the new root zone file.[27]

In June 2005 the US Government made a clear assertion of its continued authority over the root zone file.[28] Whether all the operators of the various root servers around the world[29] would accept that authority in a controversial situation has, thankfully, never had to be put to the test.

gTLDs and ccTLDs

3–022 The domain name system is organised into various classes of domain types, known as domain spaces or just domains. Until mid-2001 there were seven non-localised, or generic domains: .com, .org, .net, .gov, .edu, .mil, .int. These (or at least the three available for general use, .com, .org and .net and the new generic domains introduced from 2001 onwards) are now known as gTLDs (generic top level domains). Additionally there are nearly 250 country-specific domains, now known as ccTLDs (country code top level domains).[30] The ccTLD for the UK is ".uk", for Spain ".es", for Malaysia ".my", for Poland ".pl", etc.

3.3.2 Who controls the domain name system?

Historical overview

3–023 Until the late 1990s overall responsibility for deciding what top level domains could be created and who should manage the country code top

---

[27] Public Summary of Reports provided Under Co-operative Research and Development Agreement Between ICANN and US Department of Commerce March 14, 2003 (*www.icann.org/general/crada-report-summary–14mar03.htm*). This report contains a comprehensive description of the root server system.

[28] US Principles on the Internet's Domain Name and Addressing System (June 30, 2005) *www.ntia.doc.gov/ntiahome/domainname/USDNSprinciples_06302005.htm*. This position survives following the World Summit on the Information Society (WSIS) meeting in November 2005 (Tunis Commitment, November 18, 2005, *http://www.itu.int/wsis/docs2/tunis/off/7.html*).

[29] Although it is convenient to refer to 13 root servers, many root server operators (C, F, I, J, K and M) have implemented an "anycast" scheme, whereby the root server is itself replicated in a number of "instances" in different locations, all behind the same root server IP address. As a result root server instances in over 100 physical locations now hold copies of the authoritative root zone file. Most of these physical locations are now outside the US (See the list of root servers and locations at *www.root-servers.org.*).

[30] For a full list of ccTLDs and the persons responsible for managing them see *www.iana.org/cctld/cctld-whois.htm*.

level domains was vested, in a somewhat informal fashion,[31] in a loosely formed group or project called IANA (the Internet Assigned Numbers Authority). IANA, which was the central co-ordinator for the assignment of unique parameter values for internet protocols generally,[32] was run by and synonymous with[33] the late Dr Jon Postel,[34] one of the original founders of the internet, based in the University of Southern California's Information Sciences Institute.

IANA's legitimacy to discharge this responsibility derived partly from the respect in which Jon Postel was held within the internet community.[35] However, the US internet was funded to a degree by US Government contracts (e.g. from the National Science Foundation which ran NSFNet, which became the internet backbone, and from the Defence Advanced Projects Research Agency (DARPA)), so that an element of legitimacy of the early internet institutions such as IANA also derived from the sanction of the US funding bodies.

Indeed, the US Government, when it came to consider these matters closely in 1997/98, made clear that it regarded IANA's functions as being carried out on behalf of the US Government, and the transfer of functions to a private sector body as representing the privatisation of domain name management functions.[36] The 1999 contract between the University of Southern California and ICANN, providing for the transition (subject to US Government approval) of IANA's functions from USC to ICANN, recites that USC had been operating IANA as a research project pursuant to a Teranode Network Technology contract awarded by DARPA to USC.[37]

Identifying a conventional legal source of authority over, and responsibility for, the domain system during the period before the introduction of ICANN was a somewhat elusive quest, especially since in practice the degree of involvement of the US government was less obvious to outside observers

3–024

---

[31] "IANA has functioned as a government contractor, albeit with considerable latitude, for some time now. Moreover, IANA is not formally organised or constituted. It describes a function more than an entity ..." (US Department of Commerce White Paper, Management of Internet Names and Addresses, June 5, 1998). See also, especially regarding IANA's process of delegation of responsibility for country code domains, interview with Dr. Willie Black, *Computers and Law* 1999, 10(3), 25–29.

[32] Thus IANA was also responsible for allocating blocks of IP addresses. IANA delegated this to various three regional registries: see Ch.1, para.1–022).

[33] See Vint Cerf's remembrance of Jon Postel, RFC–2468 "I remember IANA", October 17, 1998, at *http://ftp.isi.edu/in-notes/rfc2468.txt*.

[34] *www.postel.org/postel.html*.

[35] IANA was, for instance, "chartered" by the Internet Society to act as "the clearinghouse to assign and co-ordinate the use of numerous internet protocol parameters" (*www.ietf.org/overview.html*).

[36] See *www.ntia.doc.gov/ntiahome/domainname/icann.htm* for a collection of US government press releases and papers on the management of the internet numbering and domain name systems from 1997 onwards. As early as November 1995 a claim had been made that the Federal Networking Council (comprising representatives of 18 US Federal administrative agencies) owned the domain name number space and held policy control over the .com, .org and .net name spaces—see M. St. Johns, "FNC's Role in the DNS Issue" Harvard University DNS Workshop November 20, 1995 (*http://web.archive.org/web/20030515065559/http://ksgwww.harvard.edu/iip/GIIconf/fnc.html*).

[37] See *www.icann.org/general/usc-icann-transition-agreement.htm*.

than it became subsequently.[38] The pursuit of an "authority trail" was, rather like seeking the source of a great river, liable to lead the explorer only to a muddy field.[39]

Although the authority of IANA may have been largely derived from consensus and legitimacy within the internet community, it was none the less valid or real for that. The tradition of "bottom-up" processes for validating decisions about the internet was so strong that it was recognised in the 1998 US Government Green and White Papers on management of the domain name system, and has been translated into an elaborate, formalised consensus structure for ICANN.[40]

As funding of the internet and ownership of the US internet backbone was moved into private hands in the mid-1990s, as government contracts expired and as the internet came to be used by commerce and the public at large, so wider communities and interest groups came to have an interest in the future of the internet. This created immense tensions, with academia, commerce, the internet community, intellectual property proponents, the US Government, the European Commission, existing domain name registration managers, country code domain space managers and others all promoting their own perceptions of how the internet should be run.

3–025 The resulting, extraordinarily painful, worldwide consensus-building process culminated (or so one might have thought at the time) in the acceptance in November 1998 of an application from ICANN, a not-for-profit body incorporated in California, as the body to take responsibility for future policy for the technical operation of the internet—effectively to be the "new IANA".

ICANN is a consensus-based body intended to represent a broad church of constituencies with interests in the effective operation of the internet. Jon Postel would almost certainly, but for his untimely death on October 16, 1998, have been the first head of ICANN.

Provision was made for the transfer of most of the functions of IANA to ICANN.[41] Indeed, the IANA name lives on under the ICANN umbrella, and within the context of ICANN, IANA continues to make decisions on

---

[38] See e.g. David W. Maher "Trademarks on the Internet: Who's in Charge?" (1996) (*www.isoc.org/inet96/proceedings/f4/f4_2.htm*). A comprehensive, although sceptical, account of internet governance at this time is contained in a paper by Robert Shaw of the International Telecommunications Union, "Internet Domain Names: Whose Domain is This?" (*http://web.archive.org/web/20030127215804/http://people.itu.int/~shaw/docs/dns.html*). In addition to IANA, a number of other bodies, many associated with the internet Society (ISOC), had (and still have) roles in the technical management and evolution of the internet. These include the Internet Engineering Task Force (IETF), the Internet Architecture Board (IAB), InterNIC (run by Verisign Inc (formerly Network Solutions Inc) on behalf of the US Department of Commerce) and the Internet Engineering Steering Group (IESG).

[39] See the section "Climbing the Domain Space Authority Trail" in Shaw, *op. cit.*

[40] For a review of ICANN's progress in seeking to achieve consensus and legitimacy, see "The consensus machine", *The Economist* June 10, 2000.

[41] ICANN/USC transition agreement (fn. 37 above). This was followed by agreements directly between the US Department of Commerce and ICANN on February 8, 2000, March 21, 2001, March 13, 2003 and August 14, 2006 (see ICANN press release August 15, 2006 (*www.icann.org/announcements/announcement-15aug06.htm*).

matters such as delegation of ccTLDs.[42] ICANN has direct policy control over the gTLDs. It does not exercise operational control over the ccTLDs, although one of its tasks is to pursue contractual arrangements with the operators of ccTLDs.

ccTLDs

A wide variety of organisations, some state, some private, have responsibility delegated by IANA for managing country code domains.[43] The reasons for this variety are mainly historical, reflecting differing political perspectives around the world as to whether such control should be in state or private hands.

3–026

Each ccTLD is able to organise and sub-divide its own domain space as it wishes within general policy laid down by IANA.[44] This leads to local differences in domain structures. So for instance, the most commonly used commercial sub-domain in the UK name space is named ".co.uk", whereas in Hong Kong it is named ".com.hk".

Each ccTLD tends to have its own local requirements for registration, which vary widely. Some are extremely restrictive, for instance permitting registrations only by locally registered companies.

gTLDs

IANA had originally provided for three generally available gTLDs: .com, .org and .net. .com was intended for use by companies and commercial enterprises, .org by non-commercial organisations and .net by network providers. In recent years, however, these restrictions have broken down so that all three have effectively become available for general use.

3–027

Registration of .com, .org and .net domain names was for a long time contracted out by the National Science Foundation under the auspices of the US Department of Commerce exclusively to a private company, Network Solutions Inc., (NSI, now Verisign, Inc.) for a period which was initially due to expire in March 1998. It was common at that time to refer to NSI as InterNIC, and to InterNIC as providing the registration of .com domain names, since that was the name under which NSI provided its registration services.[45] However, the US Department of Commerce reclaimed control of InterNIC as a neutral network information centre,

---

[42] See, for instance, the various IANA decisions on the delegation and re-delegation of ccTLDs listed at *www.iana.org/domain-names.htm*. However, the necessary changes to the authoritative root server root zone file to implement such a decision require the approval of the US Department of Commerce (see the explanation of the process for making changes to the root zone file, para. 3–021 above).

[43] The full root zone WHOIS database, listing all the ccTLD operators, is at *www.iana.org/ cctld/cctld- whois.htm*.

[44] See RFC 1591 and IANA ccTLD Delegation Practices Document (ICP–1) (May 21, 1999), both available at *www.iana.org/domain-names.htm*.

[45] See e.g. the 2nd edition of this book, at p.48.

stating that NSI was only one of several companies involved in the development of InterNIC as an integrated network information centre.[46]

Increasing the number of gTLDs

3–028   The lengthy process of debating the transfer of IANA's responsibilities and the migration away from NSI's exclusive registration rights was accompanied by vigorous debate over proposals to expand the number of gTLDs beyond the existing three available for general use (.com, .org and .net).[47]

Jon Postel had originally proposed in May 1996 a great expansion, allowing 150 new gTLDs to be established by up to 50 new competing registries, for a wide variety of business areas.[48] The Internet Society then promoted the formation of the Internet International Ad Hoc Committee[49] to consider this and other issues. The IAHC included representatives from the World Intellectual Property Organisation (WIPO), the International Telecommunications Union (ITU) and the International Trade Mark Association (INTA).

The IAHC process culminated in the signature of a gTLD Memorandum of Understanding (gTLD-MoU)[50] on May 1, 1997, upon the signature of which the IAHC dissolved. This recommended the establishment of seven new gTLDs: .firm, .store, .web, .arts, .rec, .nom and .info. It also recommended a worldwide system of competing registrars, to replace the exclusive right held by NSI, after the expiry of NSI's contract with the US Government National Science Foundation. The competing registrars were to be members of a Council of Registrars, which would be incorporated in Switzerland. There would also be a Policy Oversight Committee. WIPO would organise a dispute resolution procedure. The IAHC was succeeded on its dissolution by an interim Policy Oversight Committee.

3–029   The US Government at this point became more actively involved in debating the appropriate mechanism for moving internet governance (including decisions about new gTLDS and competing registrars)[51] to the private sector.

This intervention started with a White House report[52] "A Framework for

---

[46] See *www.internic.net/faqs/domain-names.html* and Amendment 19 dated November 10, 1999 to the Cooperative Agreement between NSI and the US Government (fn. 26 above).

[47] The convoluted history of the process is well documented. *www.wia.org* (now expired—some pages available through *www.archive.org*) included in its reference materials a number of detailed graphical timelines. The 1998 US Government Green Paper and White Paper referred to in the text both contain useful technical descriptions and detailed histories from a US Government perspective, as did the US General Accounting Office report in 2000 "Department of Commerce: Relationship with the Internet Corporation for Assigned Names and Numbers" (*www.gao.gov/archive/2000/og00033r.pdf*). Comprehensive collections of contemporaneous documents are available at the old IAHC site (*www.iahc.org*) and at *www.gltd-mou.org*.

[48] The original Postel proposal was revised, and in June 1996 the Internet Society's board of trustees endorsed a version in principle.

[49] The IAHC was dissolved on May 1, 1997. See *www.iahc.org*.

[50] *www.gtld-mou.org*.

[51] See, for instance, the August 12, 1999 news item on the *www.gtld-mou.org* website.

[52] *www.technology.gov/digeconomy/framewrk.htm*.

Global Electronic Commerce" dated July 1, 1997, accompanied by a Presidential directive[53] tasking the US Department of Commerce to "support efforts to make the governance of the domain name system private and competitive and to create a contractually based self-regulatory regime that deals with potential conflicts between domain name usage and trademark laws on a global basis". The Department of Commerce issued a Green Paper on January 30, 1998,[54] followed by a White Paper on June 5, 1998.[55]

By this time, especially since the US Government papers were proposing that a not-for-profit body based in the US should take on the major co-ordinating, policy and oversight role, the debate had evolved into a geo-political controversy conducted at the highest levels in the US Government and the European Commission over whether the domain system and internet should be run from the US. This was resolved in July 1998, when the European Commission issued a communication[56] accepting the US Government White Paper proposals as a basis for the way forward. The process resulted in the acceptance of an application by ICANN to be the not-for-profit body.

A renewed challenge to ICANN's position and the role of the US Government occurred in the run-up to the World Summit on the Information Society, organised under the auspices of the United Nations, the final meeting of which was held in Tunis in November 2005. In the event the WSIS gave birth only to a new vehicle for debate, the Internet Governance Forum.

ICANN's actions—new gTLDs

ICANN started its formal work in 1999. ICANN was to be tasked with (among other things) deciding on the appropriate expansion of the gTLD name space, and on devising uniform domain name disputes procedures.   3–030

The uniform disputes resolution policy (UDRP) introduced by ICANN in December 1999[57] is discussed below.

Competing registrars were introduced, starting with testbed registrars in April 1999. After further long drawn out debate and the solicitation of applications from putative operators of new gTLD registries, a final decision was taken in November 2000 to select seven new gTLDs and to open negotiations with their proposed operators.[58]

The seven selected new gTLDs were .biz, .info, .name, .pro, .aero, .coop and .museum. Of these, the first four were unsponsored (i.e. operated by a neutral registry operator), and three were sponsored (i.e. run by industry or sector representative bodies). The only unsponsored gTLD intended for

---

[53] *www.fas.org/irp/offdocs/pdd-nec-ec.htm.*
[54] Published in the Federal Register on February 20, 1998: *www.ntia.doc.gov/ntiahome/ domainname/ 022098fedreg.htm.*
[55] *www.ntia.doc.gov/ntiahome/domainname/6_5_98dns.htm.*
[56] COM(1998) 476 Final, July 29, 1998.
[57] For a detailed timetable of the introduction of the UDRP see *www.icann.org/udrp/udrp-schedule.htm.*
[58] *www.icann.org/tlds/.*

unrestricted use was .info. .biz was intended for businesses, .coop for cooperatives, .name for individuals and .pro for professions such as accountants, lawyers and physicians.

3-031   The first new gTLD to come into operation was .info[59], which became operational in October 2001 followed shortly by .biz[60] and by the remaining new gTLDs over the next three years.

Several of the gTLDs (.biz, .info and .pro) put in place complex pre-launch procedures designed to reduce the initial potential for cybersquatting.[61] Thereafter each registered domain names on a first-come first-served basis and operates the ICANN UDRP procedures. Some of the gTLDs operate additional dispute resolution procedures, such as the Charter Eligibility Dispute Resolution Policy operated by .aero, .coop and .museum, and the Restrictions Dispute-Resolution Policy operated by .biz. These additional policies are designed to address disputes over compliance with eligibility criteria. Only .info, as an unrestricted gTLD, applies the UDRP alone.

In 2004 ICANN received applications for 10 more sponsored TLDs: .asia, .cat, .jobs, .mail, .mobi, .post, .tel, .travel, and .xxx. So far .cat, .jobs, .mobi, and .travel have been accepted and have launched. ICANN rejected .xxx in May 2006 and again in March 2007. Negotiations continue over .post. .tel, and .asia have been accepted and have announced launches.

The ".eu" domain space

3-032   Mention should also be made of the .eu domain space, promoted by the European Commission for use by European companies. A European Parliament and Council Regulation[62] to govern the operation of a .eu domain space was made on April 22, 2002. The .eu domain went live for general registrations in April 2006 following a four month sunrise period. Being neither a ccTLD (based on the ISO 3166 list of country codes)[63] nor a gTLD, the .eu domain is anomalous in terms of the TLD structure. It appears on the IANA list of ccTLDs. It operates a modified version of the UDRP.

The ".uk" domain space

3-033   For a long time responsibility for the .uk name space was delegated by IANA to Dr Willie Black, a UK academic, working in conjunction with a collection of industry representatives called the United Kingdom Naming Committee.

---

[59] Operated by Afilias, LLC (*www.afilias.info*).
[60] Operated by Neulevel Inc (*www.neulevel.biz*).
[61] For a summary of all the disputes policies and pre-launch procedures adopted by the various gTLDs see *http://www.icann.org/udrp*.
[62] Regulation (EC) No 733/2002 of the European Parliament and Council of April 22, 2002 on the implementation of the .eu Top Level Domain.
[63] *http://www.din.de/gremien/nas/nabd/iso3166ma/index.html*.

In August 1996 responsibility was transferred to Nominet United Kingdom, a company limited by guarantee,[64] whose chairman until 2004 was Dr Black. The members of Nominet are drawn from those persons with an interest in the internet. Those providing domain name registration services can become Tag Holder members, who alone are entitled to use Nominet's automatic domain name registration system.

The .uk domain space is divided into a number of second level domains (SLDs): .co.uk, .org.uk, .ltd.uk, .plc.uk, .ac.uk, .gov.uk and some others. Most of these are operated by Nominet and are open for registration of third level domain names (3LDs), such as twobirds.co.uk. Some of the SLDs are restricted and some of those (such as .ac.uk and .gov.uk) are not operated by Nominet. One SLD (.parliament.uk) has been allocated to a single organisation for use as its domain name. In January 2002 Nominet introduced a new SLD, .me.uk for personal use by living individuals.

Quasi-ccTLDs

Mention should also be made of certain types of domain name which, although they may appear at first glance to be a branch of the official domain space structure described above, are in fact rather different. An example is .uk.com. It is possible to apply to the proprietor of this domain name for allocation of a sub-domain, such as "twobirds.uk.com". This looks very much like a ccTLD. However, it is not a ccTLD. **3–034**

uk.com is an ordinary domain name registered under the .com gTLD. The arrangements to allocate sub-domains within it have been made autonomously by the owner of the uk.com domain name. So, if the owner of the uk.com domain name were to lose the rights to that domain name (e.g. by failing to renew the subscription[65]), then all sub-domain registrants beneath it would lose their sub-domains.

This is different from registering directly under .com, since the continuing existence of the .com TLD depends directly on ICANN which is a consensus-based body. It is also different from registering directly under a ccTLD such as .co.uk, since although the continuing existence of the .uk TLD (and of the second level domains within it such as .co.uk) depends to some extent on Nominet, that is also a consensus-based body whose delegation of the .uk domain space could only be changed by a decision of

---

[64] Nominet's website is at *www.nominet.org.uk*.
[65] Forgetting to renew an important domain name is not necessarily a fantastic notion. In a famous incident in 1999, Microsoft forgot to pay the renewal fee for hotmail.com, with the result that the Hotmail service went down. A public-spirited computer consultant paid the $35 renewal fee by his credit card, and service was restored. J.P. Morgan & Co suffered a similar lapse in June 2000.

IANA.[66] IANA (now operated under the auspices of ICANN—see discussion above), has a recognised place within the structure of internet governance, has designated ".uk" as the appropriate name space for the UK in accordance with ISO 3166 and co-ordinates the operation of the root servers which recognise the relevant domain name spaces.

The contracts between ICANN and the new gTLDs prohibit the operators of the new gTLDs from permitting the registration of two letter second level domains such as ISO country codes.

3.4 HOW DOES SUBSTANTIVE LAW APPLY TO DOMAIN NAMES?

3.4.1 The functions of a domain name

3–035   We have already alluded to the potential for increased trade mark clashes on the internet. Most of the clashes that have occurred have been sparked by disputes over the use of domain names.

Address

3–036   As we have described, a domain name is an unique alphanumeric address which resolves to the unique numerical (IP) address of a server on the internet. For the web, a domain name is the basis of an address for any given website.[67] So, for example, Bird & Bird has the domain name "twobirds.com". This means that Bird & Bird's website has the unique address *http://www.twobirds.com*.

Identifier

3–037   In addition to its function as an address a domain name often also has a second role which is of great legal significance. Since it is generally an

---

[66] However, if the UK were to legislate for a different body to operate the .uk domain space, then under its promulgated delegation policy IANA would respect that and re-delegate to the new body. No such steps have been proposed in the UK. However, in its Electronic Commerce Act 2000 (s.31) the Irish Government took powers to authorise, prohibit or regulate the registration and use of the .ie domain name in Ireland. The Governmental Advisory Committee of ICANN has adopted as a principle that "ultimate public policy authority over the relevant ccTLD rests with the relevant government or public authority". According to the GAC this may be exercised in any appropriate way, ranging from contract to laws or regulations. (GAC Principles and Guidelines for the Delegation and Administration of Country Code Top Level Domains, April 5, 2005 (*http://gac.icann.org/web/index.shtml*). While the notion that a ccTLD operator should be subject to the general laws of the country in which it is established is unexceptional, the idea that the local government should be directly involved at a policy level in the operation of a ccTLD is controversial.

[67] Domain names are also, of course, used for internet purposes other than the web. They form the second part (after the @ symbol) of internet email addresses, and also serve as addresses for other internet sites, such as those for downloading files using the ftp protocol.

alphanumeric address, a URL incorporating the domain name can also act as a memorable way for people to access any given website. It can, therefore, be not only an address but also a specific identifier. One analogy is with the freephone 800 numbers used for voice telephony which spell a word using the letters associated with a telephone keypad (e.g. (1)–800-AIRWAYS).

The significance of the role as an identifier may vary from one domain name to the next. A domain name may correspond to a company's trading name or one of its brand names, represent the name of a non-profit organisation, represent a generic class of goods, services or interests, identify a topic of debate or controversy, represent an allegiance of the website owner[68] or be used in numerous other ways.[69]

3.4.2 Trade marks, passing off and instruments of fraud

Given its potential role as an identifier, the immediately obvious methods of restraining misuse of a domain name are by asserting infringement of a UK or Community registered trade mark, or by alleging that the use of the domain name amounts to passing off.[70]   3–038

In a blatant case it may also be possible to establish that the domain name amounts to an instrument of fraud, whose owner can be subjected to legal remedies even if trade mark infringement or passing off has not been established.

However, domain names and registered trade marks are not coterminous. They differ from each other in at least four significant ways. These are summarised in the following table:

---

[68] *E.g.* pop group or film star fan sites.

[69] In *One in a Million* (para.3–066 below), Aldous L.J. in the Court of Appeal made the bald statement, when considering registered trade mark infringement, that "The domain names indicate origin. That is the purpose for which they were registered." That could be taken as suggesting that all registered domain names (in whatever domain space) always and inevitably indicate origin. That, we suggest, overstates the position. It should always necessary to consider in each case whether the domain name in question in fact acts as an indicator of origin. See, for references to US cases emphasising the need for a factual inquiry in each case rather than a *per se* rule, the ICANN UPRD decision in *Bridgestone Firestone Inc, v Myers* (WIPO D2000–0190). And note the contrasting comments made by Aldous L.J. in the *One in a Million* case concerning the use of websites for criticism and the promotion of hobbies (see discussion at para.3–074 below).

[70] It is most unlikely that the use of a domain name would amount to copyright infringement, given the difficulties of proving that the name of a company constitutes an original literary work *Exxon Corp v Exxon Insurance Consultants International Ltd* [1982] Ch. 119 CA.

Trade mark	Domain name
Trade mark registrations are national or regional.	Domain names (whether gTLDs or ccTLDs) are visible in all countries, especially when pointed to live websites.[71]
Trade mark registrations protect use of the mark in the course of trade.	The purpose of the domain name registrant may be commercial or non-commercial.
A trade marks is registered for specified categories of goods or services.	The registration of a domain name (at least in open TLDs) is not linked to any specific class of goods or services.
The same trade mark can be registered for different goods and services by numerous different applicants.	Only one instance of a domain name can be registered.[72]

We draw attention to these differences not to criticise their existence, but to illuminate some of the underlying distinctions between registered trade marks and domain names (see also the discussion below at Section 3.8 on scrutiny of domain name registrations, in which we elaborate on the reasons why these distinctions exist).

The lack of congruence between registered trade marks and domain names means that a trade mark registration cannot be (or ought not to be capable of being) brought to bear on the registration of a domain name without some consideration of the use to which the domain name registration is likely to be, or is being, put.

3–039　　When considering the likely use of a domain name, it would be naïve to think of domain names only as technical addresses, with no potential for wider characteristics as identifiers. It is equally inappropriate to assume that

---

[71] Even when not pointed to a live website, the domain name has limited visibility through a WHOIS search. This was relied upon by the Court of Appeal in the *One in a Million* case (para.3–066 below).

[72] While each domain name is unique, so that only one instance of the domain can be registered, there are often possibilities for avoiding the blocking effect of an existing domain name registration by registering a minor variation, such as with a hyphen, or with an additional word incorporated in the domain name, or by registering under a different TLD. When the domain names in question correspond to a trade mark, especially a well-known trade mark, and are registered for nefarious purposes by someone with no legitimate interest in the mark, this would most likely be regarded as cybersquatting and be restrainable. Where the registration is done for legitimate purposes, by someone who either has a legitimate interest in the mark or who credibly does not intend to use the domain name in a way that would infringe the trade mark or amount to passing off or as an instrument of fraud, then the practice is (or at least ought to be) unexceptionable.

every domain name is registered for a commercial purpose and therefore potentially falls within the scope of someone's registered trade mark. The proper application of trade mark law should require evidence of actual or intended use, or grounds on which relevant use can properly be inferred.

Not every potential use of a domain name, even as an identifier, necessarily falls within the ambit of trade mark protection (e.g. identifying a topic of controversy, or exercising rights to criticise a company or its products[73]). So it should not be assumed that the mere registration of a domain name which includes someone's trade mark will automatically result in a finding of trade mark infringement or passing off.

However, especially in the case of domain names incorporating very well known trade marks, a court would almost certainly require convincing evidence to displace the natural suspicion that the domain name has been registered for nefarious purposes. Protestations of innocent purposes are likely to be disbelieved, even on an application for summary judgment, if they are inconsistent with surrounding evidence.[74] As we shall see from the caselaw discussed below, English courts have generally been ready to draw an inference of a nefarious purpose from appropriate evidence of surrounding conduct.[75]

3.5 THE TRADE MARKS ACT 1994[76]

3.5.1 Elements of registered trade mark infringement

Section 9(1) of the Trade Marks Act 1994 provides that the proprietor of a registered trade mark has exclusive rights in the trade mark which are

3–040

---

[73] The practice of establishing "grudge" or "lemon" sites for the purpose of airing grievances about a company or its products has become widespread (see, for instance, "Wide Open to the Web Warriors", *Marketing* February 4, 1999; "Surfers seek vengeance on corporate enemies", *Times* May 10, 1999). These are often established under a domain name incorporating the epithet "sucks" to indicate the nature of the site. For examples of caselaw and ICANN UDRP decisions on "sucks" cases see paras 3–057 and 3–075 below.

[74] See, for instance, *Britannia Building Society v Prangley* Ch.D, June 12, 2000 (unreported), *easyJet Airline Co. Ltd v Dainty* Ch.D, February 19, 2001 (unreported) and *Global Projects Management Ltd v Citigroup Inc* [2005] EWHC 2663 (Ch).

[75] See e.g. Aldous L.J. in *One in a Million* (para.3–066 below) "If it be the intention of the defendant to appropriate the goodwill of another, or to enable others to do so, I can see no reason why the court should not infer that that will happen, even if there is a possibility that such an appropriation would not take place."

[76] In the field of UK registered trade marks it is now the practice of the English courts to refer to the provisions of the underlying Trade Marks Directive and generally to ignore the text of the UK transposition as set out in the Trade Marks Act 1994. However, in a book such as this, concerned only with identifying issues specifically related to the internet, for the purposes of simplifying this general introduction to trade marks we have recited only the main provisions of the 1994 Act. Neither have we set out the provisions of the Community Trade Marks Regulation (Council Regulation (EC) No 40/941 of December 20, 1993 on the Community trade mark). We have also refrained from considering issues such as comparative advertising and the relationship between trade mark law and the Comparative Advertising Directive (as to which, see *O2 v Hutchison 3G Ltd* [2006] EWCA Civ 1656).

infringed by use of the trade mark in the UK without his consent; and that the acts amounting to infringement are specified in s.10. Section 10 (1) to (3) provides as follows:

> "(1) A person infringes a registered trade mark if he uses in the course of trade a sign which is identical with the trade mark in relation to goods or services which are identical with those for which it is registered.
>
> (2) A person infringes a registered trade mark if he uses in the course of trade a sign where because—
>
> (a) the sign is identical with the trade mark and is used in relation to goods or services similar to those for which the trade mark is registered, or
>
> (b) the sign is similar to the trade mark and is used in relation to goods or services identical with or similar to those for which the trade mark is registered,
>
> there exists a likelihood of confusion on the part of the public, which includes the likelihood of association with the trade mark.
>
> (3) A person infringes a registered trade mark if he uses in the course of trade, in relation to goods or services, a sign which—
>
> (a) is identical with or similar to the trade mark,[77]
>
> where a trade mark has a reputation in the United Kingdom and the use of the sign, being without due cause, takes unfair advantage of, or is detrimental to, the distinctive character or the repute of the trade mark...."

Certain definitions and qualifications to these provisions are set out in ss.10(4) to (6) and in ss.11 and 12. While these are of general importance, we do not address them in this short introduction to the rights granted under the Act.

Identical mark, identical goods or services

3–041 A claimant has to overcome a lower hurdle under s.10(1), where the defendant's sign is *identical* with the trade mark and is used in relation to goods or services which are *identical* to those for which the mark is registered, since there is no requirement to establish a likelihood of confusion.

---

[77] Section 10(3) was amended with effect from May 5, 2004 by the Trade Marks (Proof of Use) Regulations 2004, SI 2004/946, following the decisions of the European Court of Justice in *Adidas v Fitness World Trading* C–408/01 (October 23, 2003) and *Davidoff v Gofkid* C–292/00 (January 9, 2003).

Similar mark, similar goods or services

Where one or the other is not identical but similar, then under s.10(2) the claimant has to show a likelihood of confusion. For this purpose a mere association between the two marks as a result of their analogous semantic context is insufficient. While the greater the distinctiveness of the mark, the greater the likelihood of confusion, the assessment of confusion is a matter of global appreciation of a number of factors.[78]   **3–042**

Marks with a highly distinctive character, either *per se* or because of the reputation they possess on the market, enjoy broader protection in practice under s.10(2) than marks with a less distinctive character. A greater degree of similarity between the marks may offset a lesser degree of similarity between the goods and services, and vice versa.

The likelihood of confusion includes the risk that the public might believe that the goods or services in question come from the same undertaking (or economically linked undertakings).[79] Under s.10(2), therefore, there may be in some respects dissimilarity between the goods and services in question, yet confusion may still be proved. However, confusion must still be as to the origin of the goods or services.[80]

Identical or similar mark, dissimilar goods or services

Where the sign used is either identical or similar to the registered mark, but the goods or services are not similar, then infringement is possible only under s.10(3). For s.10(3) the trade mark must be shown to have a reputation in the UK, and while there is no requirement to prove likelihood of confusion[81] the use of the sign must be without due cause, take unfair advantage of, or be detrimental to, the distinctive character or the repute of the trade mark. The degree of similarity required between the mark with a reputation and the sign is that it has the effect that the relevant section of the public establishes a link between the sign and the mark.[82]   **3–043**

Use as a trade mark

An issue potentially of great significance to infringement by use of domain names is whether it is a requirement of s.10 of the Act that the allegedly infringing sign be used "as a trade mark" (i.e. in a way that indicates trade origin).   **3–044**

If there is no such requirement, then (subject to the defences set out above), trade mark registrations may be used to restrain a variety of types of use in the course of trade that would not have amounted to infringement under the pre-1994 UK trade mark law. For instance, under the old law it

---

[78] *Sabel v Puma* [1998] 1 C.M.L.R. 445; *L'Oreal v OHIM* (Case C–235/05 April 27, 2006); and see *O2 v Hutchison 3G Ltd* [2006] EWCA Civ 1656 at para.17.

[79] *Canon Kabushiki Kaisha v Metro Goldwyn Mayer Inc* [1999] 1 C.M.L.R. 77.

[80] *Pfizer Ltd v Eurofood Link (United Kingdom) Ltd* [2001] F.S.R. 17.

[81] *Premier Brands United Kingdom Ltd v Typhoon Europe Ltd*; [2000] F.S.R. 767; *Sabel v Puma* (above).

[82] *Adidas v Fitness World Trading* E.C.J. C–408/01 (October 23, 2003).

was held to be unarguable that the use of the words "Mother Care" in the title of a book about the problems facing working mothers was use in a trade mark sense.[83]

This issue was considered by the European Court of Justice in *Arsenal Football Club Plc v Reed*.[84] The Court held that it was not necessary for infringement to be found under s.10(1) of the Trade Marks Act 1994 that the mark be used so as to indicate the origin of the goods or services. The relevant consideration was whether the use complained about was likely to affect or jeopardise the guarantee of origin which constitutes the essential function of the trade mark.

Use in the course of trade

3–045 Even if use in a trade mark sense as traditionally understood is not required, it is still necessary to show "use" (or threatened use) of the sign "in the course of trade" and "in relation to" goods or services.

In the case of domain names these are real hurdles. It is not immediately obvious, for instance, how the mere registration of a domain name with no surrounding evidence as to its proposed use by the registrant might constitute use (or threatened use) in the course of trade. In the absence of evidence, the court has to fall back on inference. However, especially given the fact that it is no longer (if it ever was) realistic to infer intended commercial use from registration in .com or in .co.uk, in the absence of evidence such inference may be hard to draw.

Use in relation to goods or services

3–046 The requirement to show that the threatened use is "in relation to" goods or services may be difficult to satisfy in the case of mere registration if there is no evidence of the intended use of the domain name. For instance, the mere facts that the registration of the domain name will be visible via the internet (via a WHOIS search), and that if pointed to a website the website will be accessible over the internet, do not of themselves mean that the domain name will be used in relation to the provision of internet-related services. In the case of trade marks sufficiently well known to satisfy the requirements of s.10(3), while it does not matter whether the goods or services are similar or dissimilar, it is still necessary to show use or threatened use in relation to goods or services.

3.5.2 Inferring and evidencing the nature of the use

3–047 In practice, in domain name cases involving obvious cybersquatters, the requirements of, for instance, s.10(3) have tended to be easily satisfied.

---

[83] *Mothercare United Kingdom Ltd v Penguin Books Ltd* [1988] R.P.C. 113.

[84] ECJ November 12, 2002, explained in *Arsenal Football Club Plc v Reed* [2003] EWCA Civ 696.

Thus, in *British Telecommunications Plc v One in a Million Ltd*,[85] the Court of Appeal held that even assuming that there was a requirement for the purposes of s.10(3) that the use be trade mark use, that requirement was satisfied in that case:

> "Upon that basis I am of the view that threats to infringe have been established. The appellants seek to sell the domain names. . . . The domain names indicate origin. That is the purpose for which they were registered. Further, they will be used in relation to the services provided by the registrant who trades in domain names".

In most cases the claimant trade mark owner will have some evidence of the registrant's intended use of the domain name. Although not strictly relevant to the question of infringement, intention is relevant to ascertaining any threatened use and to consideration of appropriate remedies.

Further, the court may readily infer that intended passing off is likely to occur, even if there is a possibility that it would not occur.[86] Common scenarios are that the domain name may be pointed ("delegated") to a website, or the registrant may have communicated with the trade mark owner and, typically in the case of cybersquatters, have offered to sell the domain name to the trade mark owner or threatened to sell it to a third party. Or the claimant may be able to gather evidence of a pattern of conduct on the part of the registrant in relation to other domain names registered by him. Such evidence may enable the court to make findings or to draw inferences as to the intended conduct of the registrant.[87]

Does selling the domain name amount to use in the course of trade?

Often, the evidence will reveal an attempt or threat to sell the domain name. Since that may be the only evidence of commercial activity on the part of the registrant, it will be important to consider whether an attempt to trade in the domain name itself is sufficient to constitute use of the relevant sign "in the course of trade". If so, then in many cases of mere registration, the attempt or threat to sell the domain name will be sufficient to satisfy the requirement. In *One in a Million* the deputy judge at first instance found that trading in domain names was sufficient to constitute use in the course of trade for the purposes of s.10(3):

3–048

> "The use of a trade mark in the course of the business of a pro-
> fessional dealer for the purpose of making domain names more

---

[85] [1999] F.S.R. 1, CA.
[86] See e.g. the comments of Aldous L.J. in *One in a Million*, fn 75 above.
[87] Note for instance the remarks of Deputy Judge Jonathan Sumption Q.C. in *British Tele-communications Plc v One in a Million Ltd* [1998] F.S.R. 265 at first instance, commenting on the defendants' argument that a .org suffix differentiated the domain name from the trade mark: "The defendants make much of this point, but I am not impressed by it for the simple reason that although the words are probably capable of an innocent use, that is not the use that these defendants intend."

valuable and extracting money from the trade mark owner is a use in the course of trade."[88]

On appeal, the Court of Appeal did not specifically address the point. However, it explicitly affirmed the reasoning of the court below on the question of registered trade mark infringement.

3.6 PASSING OFF

3–049　To avoid the risk of failing to satisfy the statutory requirements of the Trade Marks Act, claimants in domain name cases typically also assert a case of passing off. Passing off, being a common law tort, is flexible and can be adapted to the needs of the moment.

3.6.1 Elements of passing off

3–050　The traditional requirements of passing off are threefold: that the claimant has established goodwill among the public in relation to its goods or services, such that its mark is distinctive of the goods or services; a misrepresentation by the defendant likely to lead persons wishing to buy the goods or services to be misled into buying the goods or services of the defendant; and that the claimant is likely to suffer damage.[89]

3.6.2 Passing off and instruments of fraud

3–051　As with registered trade mark infringement, in the case of a mere domain name registration with no surrounding evidence it is not immediately obvious how all the requirements of the tort of passing off can be satisfied.

　　However, it will be seen from the discussion below (paras 3–066 et seq) that in the One in a Million case the Court of Appeal overcame such difficulties in a number of ways. First, in that case there was surrounding evidence of the intentions of the defendants. Second, the court held (perhaps surprisingly, in the light of the second element of the tort), that the availability of the domain name registration details on a WHOIS search were sufficient to constitute passing off.[90]

---

[88] fn.87 above.

[89] *Reckitt and Colman Products Ltd v Borden, Inc* [1990] R.P.C. 341 HL.

[90] Contrast this finding with the comments of Jacob J. in *Avnet Incorporated v Isoact Ltd* [1998] F.S.R. 16. He stated that it is a general problem on the internet that it works on words (alone) and not on words in relation to goods and services, so that someone searching using a word may find web pages or data in a wholly different context from that which he was seeking. He said that users of the internet know that that is a feature of the internet and that their search may produce an altogether wrong web page or the like. He went on to say that that might be an important matter for the courts to take into account when considering trade mark and like problems. Clearly the Court of Appeal in *One in a Million* made no such allowance when considering WHOIS searches.

Third, the court applied an old doctrine of equipping oneself with an instrument of fraud, holding that the domain names in question were instruments of fraud in the hands of the defendants. For the purpose of the "instrument of fraud" doctrine it is unnecessary to show a threat to pass off by the possessor of the instrument. The court was even prepared to hold that some of the domain names in the case were "inherently deceptive", enabling remedies to be applied with no evidence of intended use.

It should be emphasised that the evidence in *One in a Million* was severely prejudicial to the defendants, establishing a blatant case of cybersquatting.

In *Global Projects Management Ltd v Citigroup Inc*[91] the dispute was over the domain name citigroup.co.uk, which the claimant had registered (the claim was for unjustified threats of trade mark infringement proceedings, which was met with a counterclaim for trade mark infringement and passing off, both against GPM and its sole owner and controller, a Mr Davies). 3–052

In this case there was no evidence of a pattern of conduct over time, no use in its business and no attempt to sell the domain name. It was to all intents and purposes a blocking registration. However, the court was able to draw appropriate inferences from the timing of the claimant's application for the domain name (a matter of hours after the announcement of the merger of Citibank and Travelers Group Inc) and Mr Davies' failed attempt the next day to register citigroup.com. The court was also unimpressed with the fact that Mr Davies had been receiving emails intended for Citigroup at the rate of about 13 a day and admitted having read some of them (although there was no evidence that he had misused any of the information).

Mr Davies denied being a cybersquatter. The judge concluded that he had no credible reason for holding on to the domain name and was biding his time.

3.7 APPLYING UK LAW TO OVERSEAS DOMAIN NAME REGISTRATIONS

The potential interaction between the Court of Appeal's approach in *One in a Million* and the treatment of cross-border trade mark issues in *Crate & Barrel*[92] (discussed fully in Chapter 6) has yet to be explored in England. In *Crate & Barrel*, Jacob J. suggested that for a trade mark to be held to be used within the jurisdiction, there had to be more than mere visibility. Some element of directing towards or targeting the UK was necessary. In that case, he regarded a .ie domain name as either indicating that the local Dublin shop advertised on the website was in Ireland, or as neutral. That 3–053

---

[91] [2005] EWHC 2663 (Ch), Park J.
[92] Above, fn.3.

approach was also adopted by the Court of Appeal in *1–800 FLOWERS* (see Ch.6, para.6–060).

So what is the approach if a cybersquatter registers a domain name in a non-UK ccTLD? If (apart from the suffix) it is identical to a well-known UK trade mark consisting of an unique word, does it follow from *One in a Million* that it is inherently deceptive and that passing off is occurring because of the availability of proprietorship details in a WHOIS search? Or does the court, following *Crate & Barrel*, have to consider whether there is evidence of directing or targeting to the UK? How would this be proved in the case of a mere registration?

If the registrant has approached the UK trade mark owner with an offer to sell, then that is likely to be persuasive if the usual implicit threat to misuse or dispose of the domain name elsewhere can be inferred so as to threaten damage to the trade mark owner's UK goodwill.

In the absence of evidence from which intent can be inferred, there must be a real doubt whether mere registration of a non-UK ccTLD domain name is sufficient to constitute use or threatened use within the UK. Usually, however, in a true cybersquatting case the perpetrator will have acted in some way that will enable the court to draw an appropriate inference.

3–054   It should also be borne in mind that some ccTLDs are marketed for the non-territorial connotations of their suffixes. For instance, .tv is the ccTLD for Tuvalu. It is of particular interest to the media sector. As such, it is in practice more like a gTLD than a ccTLD.

In the Scottish case of *Bonnier Media Ltd v Smith*[93] one of the defenders (who were outside the jurisdiction) had registered a number of domain names containing or comprising variations on the name of a Scottish newspaper published by the pursuers. The court was able, on the facts, to infer that the defenders, acting together, intended to set up a website designed to pass themselves off as the pursuers, or to make use of a name sufficiently close to the pursuers' trade mark as to be an infringement.

As to whether any of those threatened acts had delictual consequences within the Scottish jurisdiction, the court (after reviewing *1–800-FLOW-ERS* and *Crate & Barrel*) decided that the test was whether the website was unlikely to be of significant interest within the jurisdiction: "if the impact of a website in a particular country is properly to be regarded as insignificant, no delict has been committed there." (See also discussion in Ch.6, para.6–063, below.)

---

[93] [2002] S.C.L.R. 977.

3.8 SCRUTINY OF DOMAIN NAME APPLICATIONS

3.8.1 The practice of domain name registries

Each national or regional registry has its own rules for handling domain name applications and disputes. The rules for much of the .uk domain space were substantially loosened when Nominet assumed responsibility in August 1996. However, the underlying rule for allocating domain names, at least in open domain spaces available for general use, has always tended to be "first come, first served".

3–055

Domain name registries generally do not behave like a trade marks or patents registry. There is little or no detailed examination procedure such as would be appropriate for an application for a registered trade mark or other registered intellectual property right.[94] The primary concern of a domain name registry is to ensure that domain names registered are unique, as this is a fundamental technical requirement of the internet.

This is similar to the basic checks made by the UK Companies Registry when registering the names for companies, which are at present[95] largely restricted to eliminating identical or closely similar applications. The commercial imperatives with company names and domain names are identical: they need to be available for use immediately and at minimal cost, rather than after the months and with the significant cost typically required to register a trade mark.

Over time, various domain name registries have developed rules which they enforce by way of contract with anyone registering a domain name with them. These may provide, for example, that the applicant will not register a domain name where it is clearly not commercially entitled to use such a name, or that the applicant can only register a domain under that particular country designation if it has an established place of business in that country.

3–056

There has been considerable pressure from some trade mark owners, as the incidence of cybersquatting has increased, to introduce closer scrutiny of domain name applications. The main result of this has been the introduction of the post-registration ICANN Uniform Disputes Resolution Procedure. As discussed above (para.3–031) some new gTLD operators implemented pre-launch procedures designed to reduce the incidence of cybersquatting in the start-up phase of these new gTLDs. After launch,

---

[94] For domain spaces which are restricted in their use, or in who can apply for them, there may be some examination of the applications. For instance some gTLDs are restricted, and ccTLDs may operate restriction policies for part or all of their domain spaces.

[95] The Companies Act 2006 (yet to be brought fully into force) includes (ss.69 to 73) provisions enabling application to be made to a company names adjudicator objecting to a company name on the ground that it is the same as a name associated with the applicant in which he has goodwill, or that it is sufficiently similar to such a name that its use in the UK would be likely to mislead by suggesting a connection between the company and the applicant. A successful application would result in an order for the name to be changed.

however, there was to be no examination of applications. Domain names are still available for use within minutes of being applied for.

3.8.2 Should domain name registries scrutinise for trade mark infringement?

3–057 Some may think that a domain name simply should not be accepted for registration if it is the same as or similar to an existing registered trade mark, or at least a well-known mark. However, this is an over-simplistic view. This argument partly stems from an assumption that a name can be inherently deceptive, simply by reason of its similarity to a trade mark,[96] so that a domain name similar to a registered trade mark would be bound to infringe. But if that were correct, then (for instance) a journalist mentioning a product name (or domain name) in a newspaper article would infringe by mere mention of the name.[97] That would lead to monopolisation of the language, which is not the function of trade mark law.

It is the context within which, and the purposes for which, a name is used, as well as the degree of similarity to the mark, that determines whether (as appropriate) it is confusingly similar, deceptive, establishes a link between the mark and the sign, or takes unfair advantage of, or is detrimental to, the distinctive character or repute of the mark.[98]

That context does, of course, include the fact that domain names generally fulfil an identifying function, and other factors inherent in the domain name and internet system: the ubiquity of search engines, and the existence of WHOIS searches to ascertain the registrants of domain names. However, care needs to be taken to ensure that, in the enthusiasm to punish bad actors, the essential step of determining whether the accused domain name is in fact confusingly similar, deceptive and so on is not overlooked or reduced to a vestigial test.[99]

---

[96] Indeed, the Court of Appeal apparently fell into this trap in the *One in a Million* case. It is notable that in *Global Projects Management Ltd v Citigroup Inc* [2005] EWHC 2663 (Ch) Park J. decided that points argued by the domain name registrant that he might otherwise have found quite persuasive in relation to s.10(3) of the 1994 Act were not open to him since he was bound by *One in a Million*. In *Mastercard International Inc v Hitachi Credit (UK) Plc* [2004] EWHC 1623 (Ch) Peter Smith J. held that establishing unfair advantage or detriment still required real, not theoretical, evidence.

[97] See e.g. *Trebor Bassett Ltd v The Football Association* [1997] FSR 211.

[98] See *Musical Fidelity Ltd v David Vickers* [2002] EWCA Civ 1989 for an example of the court having regard to the context within which the domain name was used in order to determine the nature of the representation made and whether the use was deceptive.

[99] See, for instance, the Panelist's finding in UDRP decision WIPO D2000–0996 October 22, 2000 that the domain name "guinness-beer-really-sucks.com" was confusingly similar to the trade mark GUINNESS. See also the other UDRP panel decisions and US cases referred to in that decision, including WIPO case D2000–0636 July 4, 2000 which concerned exclusively English parties. Other "sucks" cases are mentioned in fn.17 below.

3.8.3 Are domain names intellectual property?

Domain names as the object, not the subject, of intellectual property protection

It may be thought that domain names are a species of intellectual property, and so (like some registered intellectual property rights) should be subjected to close scrutiny and examination before the domain name is issued. But as a matter of principle the analogy is false.

3–058

Domain names are not intellectual property rights. Domain names can be the object against which intellectual property rights are asserted, but they are not the subject of intellectual property rights.

So a trading name may be the subject of registered trade mark. The trade mark registration may be infringed by someone who (broadly) uses a mark, or a confusingly similar mark, in the course of trade in relation to the goods or services for which it is registered. The mode of use of the mark is the object against which the registered mark is brought to bear. The mode of use may be in manifold different ways: by advertising, shop front hoarding, business circular, packaging, letterhead, company name or, indeed, domain name. Whichever the vehicle, it is the use (actual, threatened or inferred) of the trade mark in a prohibited way that triggers the infringement, not the mere existence in some form in the hands of the defendant of the word or other sign corresponding to the trade mark.

The registered mark may be a means by which the defendant can be forced to deliver up infringing materials,[1] or to change the name of a company[2] or transfer a domain name, or (in extreme circumstances) have the domain name transferred on his behalf by a court official.[3] None of that, however, renders a domain name the subject of intellectual property rights.

It makes as little sense to speak of a domain name being intellectual property as it does a letterhead.[4] Possession of a letterhead *per se* confers no rights on its possessor other than possessory title to the physical letterhead. Registration of a domain name *per se* confers no rights, other than those limited quasi-possessory rights granted contractually by the registrar who issues the domain name.[5]

Registration of a domain name does result in a practical blocking effect against anyone else seeking to register the identical domain name, but that of itself confers no legal right. Its utility (or otherwise) depends on whether

3–059

---

[1] Trade Marks Act 1994, s.16.

[2] *Glaxo Plc v Glaxowellcome Ltd* [1996] F.S.R. 388 (fn.16 above).

[3] *Marks & Spencer Plc v Cottrell* (fn.17, above).

[4] It is sometimes loosely said that, for instance, computer software forms part of the intellectual property of a computer company. As an economic statement that is true. As a legal statement it is not. It would be legally correct to say that the exclusive right to copy (etc.) the computer software forms part of the intellectual property of the company.

[5] To the extent that a registrar might be regarded as exercising a public law function the registrant could also assert such public law rights against the registrar as might be available to him.

the registration and use of the domain name infringes the intellectual property rights of some third party.

Indeed, inferences drawn from the blocking effect and surrounding circumstances may constitute a ground for finding that the registration does infringe the intellectual property rights of others.[6] The use of letterhead and domain name alike may be protected or restrained by intellectual property rights, but they themselves are not the subject of intellectual property rights.

Comparison between domain names and company names

3–060 It is appropriate to scrutinise applications for registered intellectual property rights which, if granted, confer powerful and wide ranging exclusionary legal rights which can be used as the basis for litigation against third parties. But as we have seen, a domain name confers no such legal rights. The appropriate analogy is with the traditional approach to registration of company names, which in the UK have until now been granted with minimum scrutiny and maximum speed.[7] Like domain names, company names confer on the registrant no rights against third parties, but have a practical blocking effect against registration of identical company names. Like domain names, they confer no legal right to use the registered company name.

Like domain names company names are the object, not the subject of intellectual property rights. Whether they infringe third party rights depends on how they are used. Since (apart from any inference as to likely use that a court may be prepared to draw in the circumstances of a particular case) the proposed use cannot be ascertained from the mere fact of registration, company names are subject to minimal scrutiny before registration.[8]

The starting point in principle for domain names has to be that it is similarly inappropriate to subject applications to anything other than scrutiny for compliance with formal requirements and that, given the commercial undesirability of introducing cost and delay into the domain

---

[6] See Aldous L.J. in *One in a Million*: "The purpose of the so-called blocking registration was to extract money from the owners of the goodwill in the name chosen. Its ability to do so was in the main dependent upon the threat, express or implied, that the appellants would exploit the goodwill by either trading under the name or equipping another with the name so he could do so." Also see *Global Projects Management Ltd v Citigroup Inc* (para.3–052 above).

[7] The provisions of the Companies Act 2006 (see fn.95 above) will create a procedure for objecting to a registered company name, but would not affect the speed with which a company could be registered.

[8] The prohibition on registering a company name the same as one already registered (not, it should be noted, the same as a registered trade mark) is contained in s.26(1)(c) of the Companies Act 1985. The Act also provides a post-registration procedure whereby if a company name has been registered under a name which is the same as an existing one or, in the opinion of the Secretary of State, too like an existing name, then the Secretary of State can, within 12 months, direct the company to change the name (s.28). Companies House does not undertake any investigation of trade mark rights when registering company names. See fn.95 above for the forthcoming changes when ss.69 to 73 of the Companies Act 2006 are brought into force.

name application process, any proposed departure from that has to be strongly justified.

This is not to ignore the magnitude of the problem of cybersquatting. However, the remedies for that ill should not be founded on a misconception that domain names are a variety of registered intellectual property right and so should be scrutinised before grant.

3.9 TRADE MARKS AND DOMAIN NAMES—THE FUTURE

Quite apart from the difficult cross-border trade mark issues thrown up by the internet, domain names have acted as a lightning rod for a wider debate about the proper scope, function and limits of trade marks and related rights.

3–061

Should the proprietor of a well-known mark have rights to prevent use of the mark in areas beyond those for which he uses the mark himself (such as provided in s.10(3) of the 1994 Act)? If so, how far should that protection extend? Should such rights extend to use which, while not use as a trade mark, could arguably harm the reputation of the trade mark owner? Should well-known (or even less well-known) people, such as politicians, be granted protection for the use of their mere names, even if they do not exploit their names commercially?

For instance, the US has granted a specific right against registration of a living person's name as a domain name with intent to profit from the name by selling it—probably a broader right than any in the offline world. This was introduced in the US Anticybersquatting Consumer Protection Act. An inkling of some of the activities that may have been of particular concern to the US Congress can perhaps be discerned from the fact that ACPA mandated the Secretary of Commerce to prepare a report recommending guidelines and procedures in connection with the registration of personal names, including (specifically) domain names that included the personal names of government officials, official candidates and potential candidates for political office.[9]

The controversy that has surrounded the introduction of new gTLDs has been fuelled by concern over the potential for aggravating the problem of cybersquatting. There was concern that trade mark owners would be put to further expense in policing new gTLDs. Some parties favoured limited expansion of domains and closer scrutiny of domain name applications. On the other hand, the existing domain space was nearing capacity. The debate has also been fuelled by disagreement about the extent of bad faith, abusive registration (cybersquatting properly so-called), as opposed to registrations

3–062

---

[9] The report to Congress, dated January 18, 2001, is available at www.uspto.gov/web/offices/dcom/olia/tmcybpiracy/repcongress.pdf. It recommends no new guidelines and procedures and counselled "legislative restraint at this time". This is perhaps unsurprising, given that the public consultation prior to the report generated a total of 14 responses.

that have given rise to disputes for other reasons, such as between pre-existing good faith competing trade mark owners in different countries or different market sectors. There has been an unfortunate tendency to blame the domain name system for both types of dispute, when the latter type in reality derives from the need for trade mark registration systems generally to evolve to cope with low cost cross-border e-commerce.

Even with cybersquatting, care has to be taken if measures to combat it are not to put into the hands of trade mark owners rights of broader scope than they possess by virtue of their trade mark registrations, leading to problems such as "reverse domain name hijacking" (when domain name registrants are wrongly deprived of their domain names by a third party's invocation of, say, a disputes procedure).

The debate over this and other aspects of internet governance will continue, not least in the context of the Internet Governance Forum[10] established following the World Summit on the Information Society meeting in November 2005.

3.10 THE RISE OF THE DOMAIN NAME DISPUTE

3.10.1 Early history

3–063 The immediate availability of domain names, together with the slowness in the early days of the web of many companies to wake up to the significance of the internet as a commercial medium, provided an environment in which the first serious domain name disputes could arise.

The first incident to receive public attention occurred in 1994 when journalist Josh Quittner registered the domain "mcdonalds.com" and wrote about it in *Wired* magazine.[11] McDonalds, the hamburger chain, did not see the amusing side of this and instructed their lawyers to take action on the basis of their trade mark registration. This dispute was settled on payment by McDonalds of a sum of money to charity. Other companies regretted their tardiness in embracing the internet when they discovered that their rivals had already taken what, in their view, should have been their domain name.

The same October 1994 article in *Wired* revealed that 14 per cent of the US Fortune 500 companies had their names registered by others.[12] Since those early days the need to nurture and protect a company's brands on the internet has become well appreciated. From something that started as an obscure preserve of the company IT department, domain names have risen to a topic high on the agenda of corporate intellectual property strategists.

---

[10] *www.igfgreece2006.gr* is the website for the first meeting of the Forum.
[11] "Billions registered", *Wired* October 1994 (*www.wired.com/wired/archive/2.10/mcdonalds.html*).
[12] Of course, especially given the lack of uniqueness of some of the names, not all of these were necessarily instances of cybersquatting.

3.10.2 Domain name disputes—UK caselaw

There has been a lengthening series of UK court cases concerning domain 3–064
names. One has reached the Court of Appeal: the *One in a Million* case in
which the Court of Appeal stamped firmly on blatant domain name piracy.
The bulk of the reasoned judgment concerns passing off and instruments of
fraud, rather than registered trade mark infringement. Although findings of
registered trade mark infringement were made, they were not as fully reasoned as the remainder of the judgment.

The first cybersquatting case to come before the English courts was the
Harrods case. This was heard by the High Court in December 1996. In this
instance, the department store Harrods sued not only the domain name
owner (Mr Lawrie), but also NSI and the various computer/internet companies that allegedly "conspired" with the domain name owner in his
registration of the "harrods.com" domain name. NSI provided a statement
to the effect that it would abide by the decision of the English court.

Harrods claimed infringement of registered trade marks, passing off and 3–065
conspiracy. The conspiracy claim was based on the allegation that the
purpose of the defendants could only be to demand money from Harrods or
to prevent Harrods' own use of the name. Although the defendants served a
defence, most of them did not appear at the hearing of Harrods' application
for summary judgment. In this instance, the relief sought was an injunction
against the defendants using the Harrods mark and an order that the
defendants "take all steps as lie within their respective powers to release or
facilitate the release of the domain harrods.com". Lightman J. found no
difficulty with the suggestion that there was registered trade mark infringement and passing off and granted the order sought. In the absence of the
defendants no reasons were given.

The *One in a Million* case

In July 1998 the Court of Appeal handed down its decision in *British* 3–066
Telecommunications Plc v One in a Million Ltd.[13] The plaintiffs were
Marks & Spencer Plc, Ladbroke Group Plc, J Sainsbury Plc, Virgin
Enterprises Ltd and British Telecommunications Plc—all well-known
business enterprises. The defendants were dealers in internet domain names
who, over an extended period, specialised in registering the names and
marks of well known commercial or other enterprises without their
consent.

In this case domain names registered by one or other of the defendants
included "sainsburys.com", "j-sainsbury.com", "ladbrokes.com", "mark-
sandspencer.com", "marksandspencer.co.uk", "virgin.org", "bt.org" and
others. Except in one case (which was said to have arisen as a result of an
administrative mistake) none of the domain names was in use as the name

---

[13] [1999] F.S.R. 1, CA.

of an active internet site. They had simply been registered by the defendants and were available for such use.

The plaintiffs alleged passing off and infringement of their registered trade marks under the Trade Marks Act 1994. They sought summary judgment and succeeded at first instance. The defendants appealed to the Court of Appeal. Aldous L.J. delivered the judgment of the court. The defendants' appeal was dismissed.

3–067   The Court of Appeal found four different grounds on which to hold against the defendants: two varieties of passing off and two varieties of creating instruments of fraud. It also found that the defendants had infringed the plaintiffs' registered trade marks. However, the judgment contained comparatively little analysis of that finding.

In the case of both passing off and creating an instrument of fraud the Court distinguished between unique or inherently deceptive names and non-unique names. The significance of finding the defendants liable for creating instruments of fraud is that a defendant may be restrained from possessing or disposing of an instrument of fraud even if the defendant is itself not guilty of passing off or threatened passing off.

For instance, in the old case of *Singer Manufacturing Co. v Loog*,[14] the defendant was an importer of sewing machines who wrote a leaflet describing the machines as using the Singer mechanism, which he supplied to retailers with the machines. The importer was not himself passing off as there was no deception in relation to the retailers. The question was whether the importer had created an instrument of fraud (namely the leaflet) which would enable to retailer to pass off to ultimate customers. In that particular case it was held that the leaflet was not an instrument of fraud, the context in which the Singer name was used being such that the possibility of passing off by the retailer was too remote.

The four main grounds on which the Court of Appeal held the defendants liable can be categorised as follows.

3–068   **Passing Off—Unique name**   The Court of Appeal held that in the case of unique names, i.e. names which denoted only the plaintiff (such as "marks&spencer.com" and "burgerking.co.uk") the registration of the name constituted passing off. This created a false suggestion of association or connection with the name. Aldous L.J. illustrated this by means of the example of a WHOIS search, whereby a person looking up a domain name by means of a WHOIS search would be misled into believing that the indicated proprietor of the domain name was connected or associated with, for instance, Marks & Spencer Plc. This also constituted an erosion of the exclusive goodwill of Marks & Spencer Plc.

The Court also considered separately the evidence of intended or threatened use and held that there was an express or implied threat to trade using the domain name or to equip another to do so and that this amounted to a threat to pass off.

---

[14] [1882] 8 App. Cas. 15.

Passing Off—Name not unique In this category, for instance "virgin. 3–069 co.uk", the defendants argued that the domain name did not necessarily denote the plaintiffs. In this case the Court held that there was sufficient evidence of intended or threatened use of the domain name to constitute passing off.

Instrument of Fraud—Name inherently deceptive The Court of Appeal 3–070 held that in the case of unique names (such as "marks&spencer.com" or "burgerking.co.uk") the name was inherently deceptive so that any realistic use would result in passing off. That of itself constituted an instrument of fraud and could be restrained by the Court. The Court described an inherently deceptive name as one which "will, by reason of its similarity to the name of another, inherently lead to passing off".

Instrument of fraud—Name not inherently deceptive In the case of other 3–071 names, which would not inherently lead to passing off, the Court would assess whether the name was registered with a view to fraud. The Court should consider the similarity of the names, the intention of the defendant, the type of trade and all the surrounding circumstances.

This classification suggests that if a name is inherently deceptive the Court should ignore any evidence put forward by the defendant regarding the purpose for which the name was registered. However, it is difficult to understand the characterisation of an inherently deceptive name as being a name which "will by reason of its similarity to the name of another, inherently lead to passing off". It cannot be the case that similarity to the name of another is the only criterion to determine whether a domain name is inherently deceptive. For instance, it must be necessary to consider at least the uniqueness or fame of the trade mark. If similarity were the only criterion then, for instance, virgin.co.uk would be inherently deceptive.

The significance of context when considering inherent deceptiveness

It should, we suggest, also be necessary to consider the context of the 3–072 domain name registration. The case of *Singer v Loog* (see above) was the first case in which the distinction was drawn between documents which were inherently deceptive and those in which it was relevant to consider the surrounding circumstances. Lord Selborne in that case said:

> "...unless the documents were fabricated with a view to such a fraudulent use of them, or unless they were in themselves of such a nature to suggest, or readily and easily lend themselves to, such a fraud (which in my opinion they were not), the supposed consequence is too remote, speculative and improbable to be imputed to the defendant, or to be a ground for the interference of a court of justice with the course of the defendant's business. There is no evidence that, in point of fact, any such use was ever made of

them. The 'directions for use' spoke unmistakeably of 'Frister and Rossmann's shuttle sewing machine'; and no one, however, careless, could read in that document, the words 'on Singer's improved system' without seeing and understanding their context."

It is apparent from that quotation that the context within which the use of the Singer name was made was crucial to the Court's finding that neither were the documents fabricated with a view to a fraudulent use, nor were they inherently deceptive.

3–073   It is, therefore, a little surprising to find that the Court of Appeal in *One in a Million*, describing that passage, said:

"the Lord Chancellor contemplated that even where a party is not himself passing off an injunction would be granted in two circumstances; first, when fraudulent use was intended; secondly, when the name was inherently deceptive, and the name readily and easily lent itself to such a fraud".

It can be seen from the passage quoted above that the court in *Singer v Loog* was discussing not the name alone, but the document which provided the context for the use of the name. The court's finding was about whether the document was inherently deceptive, not whether the name was inherently deceptive.

We suggest, therefore, that it is wrong to look at a domain name purely as a "naked name"; and that just as the document in *Singer v Loog* provided context for the use of the name, so in some circumstances the nature of the particular domain name may provide context which can affect whether the name is to be regarded as inherently deceptive. Although that qualification is not apparent on the face the broad statement made by the Court of Appeal, we suggest that it should be applied to it.

The significance of this qualification can be illustrated as follows. Some of the domain names in question in the *One in a Million* case were .org domain names. The Court of Appeal stated that "there is an argument, which does not matter, about whether [.org] is confined to non-profit making organisations". Clearly, given the overwhelming evidence against the defendants in the *One in a Million* case about their intentions regarding the domain name, in this case that argument did not matter. And perhaps, in the case of .com registrations, the practice of companies registering their own names and brands as .com domain names is so well established that it is reasonable to conclude that a .com domain name can be inherently deceptive.

3–074   However, one can envisage situations in which the nature of the top level domain might be significant.[15] As Aldous L.J. pointed out early in his

---

[15] Note the commentary on potential differences between .com and .net in the ICANN UDRP decision in *Bridgestone Firestone, Inc. v Myers* (WIPO D2000–0190).

judgment, "websites are used for many activities such as advertising, selling, requesting information, criticism, and the promotion of hobbies". What if, for instance, ICANN decided to create a .discuss top level domain, with the intention that this be used for websites discussing, among other things, the products and activities of commercial organisations? Such discussion would almost certainly extend to criticism, as mentioned by Aldous L.J.

What would be the position if a person registered "well-knownname.discuss" as a domain name? This could be regarded as analogous to creating a Usenet newsgroup incorporating a well-known brand name. Such newsgroups do exist (see, for instance, the sub-groups of rec.autos) and appear not to have been the subject of trade mark litigation.

Is such a domain name to be regarded as inherently deceptive solely because of its similarity to a famous trade mark and therefore to be injuncted with no further consideration? Or does the nature of that particular top level domain provide context (as the surrounding document contents in *Singer v Loog* provided context) from which it could be concluded that the domain name is not inherently deceptive, allowing the defendant to adduce evidence of the purpose for which the domain name was registered?

We suggest that the holdings of the Court of Appeal in the *One in a Million* case ought not to provide the basis for automatic restraint of such a registration and that the context provided by the particular TLD in question should be taken into account in determining whether the domain name is or is not inherently deceptive.

A parallel can be drawn with "sucks" sites. These are websites set up by   3–075
disgruntled consumers, often using the domain name "wellknownname sucks.com".

In the US case of *Bally Total Fitness Holding Corp v Faber*[16] the defendant created a website called Bally Sucks, criticising the plaintiff. The court held that this did not constitute infringement of the BALLY trade mark and did not tarnish the mark under federal dilution law. Although the defendant did not own or use the "ballysucks.com" domain name, the court commented that if he had done so that would not necessarily be a trade mark violation.

ICANN UDRP decisions on "sucks" and similar domain names have shown little consistency, especially on the question whether a "sucks"

---

[16] C.D. Calif., No. CV 98–1278 DDP (MANx), 21.12.98.

domain name is confusingly similar to the trade mark concerned.[17]

One in a Million is a case in which the understandable enthusiasm of the Court of Appeal to provide a firm platform on which to find against domain name abuse and restrain mere registrations has resulted in some over-broad wording in the judgment. If taken literally, that wording could result in over-wide protection for trade mark owners. However, it is suggested that when one has regard to the main source of the distinction between inherently deceptive and other instruments of fraud, namely *Singer v Loog*, the importance of context as a basis on which to ameliorate those undesirable potential consequences becomes apparent.

One in a Million—registered trade mark infringement

3–076   As to registered trade mark infringement, the Court of Appeal decision in *One in a Million* contained relatively little reasoning in support of the finding of infringement under s.10(3) of the 1994 Trade Marks Act.

At first instance[18] Deputy Judge Mr Jonathan Sumption Q.C. stated that the plaintiffs' argument was that "Marks & Spencer" was registered for a variety of goods and services; that the word "marksandspencer" as part of a domain name was clearly similar; that the trade mark "Marks & Spencer" clearly had a reputation in the UK; and that it was clear that the defendants' use of the mark was detrimental to the trade mark, if only by damaging the plaintiff's exclusivity.

The defendants resisted summary judgment for trade mark infringement on two grounds: first that there was no use "in the course of trade" as required by the Act, and secondly that s.10(3) implicitly required confusion and there had been none. (The question of whether confusion is a requirement of s.10(3) has now been resolved against any such requirement—see para.3–043 above)

On the first issue, the judge held that trading in domain names is suffi-

---

[17] So-called "sucks" sites have, from the earliest days of the ICANN UDRP, given rise to some of the most controversial decisions to emanate from the UDRP process (see, for instance, the undefended case of *Diageo Plc v John Zuccarini* (WIPO Case D2000–0996) and the decisions referred to therein). Inconsistent decisions continue to flow from UDRP panelists. A useful summary of the contrasting positions on this issue adopted by various WIPO UDRP panelists can be found in the WIPO Overview of WIPO Panel Views on Selected URP Questions (*http://arbiter.wipo.int/domains/search/overview*). For examples of early contrasting decisions on "sucks" domain names involving the same company see *Wal-Mart Stores, Inc. v wallmartcanadasucks.com and Kenneth J. Harvey* (WIPO D2000–1104) and *Wal-Mart Stores, Inc. v Walsucks and Walmart Puerto Rico* (WIPO D2000–0477). Another decision in favour of a complainant is *Koninklijke Philips Electronics v Kurapa C. Kang* (WIPO D2001–0163). The panelist held that the domain name "antiphilips.com" was confusingly similar to the trade mark Philips, mainly on the grounds that although English speakers might not be confused, non-English speakers could be—a line of reasoning first used in *Direct Line Group Ltd v Purge I.T. Ltd* (WIPO D2000–0583). See also decisions concerning plain domain names, e.g. *Bridgestone Firestone Inc, v Myers* (WIPO D2000–0190) ("bridgestone-firestone.net" used for purposes of criticism, complaint denied); and *Shell International Petroleum Co Ltd v Donovan* (WIPO D2005–0538) ("royaldutch-shellgroup.com" and others used for purpose of criticism, complaint denied). See also fn.99 above.

[18] Above, para.3–087.

cient to constitute "use in the course of trade". He followed the then authority of *British Sugar Plc v James Robertson & Sons Ltd*[19] in finding that there was no requirement that the use be "as a trade mark". The judge did not decide whether likelihood of confusion was a requirement of s.10(3), but found in the Marks & Spencer case that if there was such a requirement it was satisfied by the inherent propensity of the domain name to confuse. In the other cases he found that the likelihood of confusion was made out beyond argument on the evidence of the history of the defendants' activities. As mentioned above, the Court of Appeal explicitly approved the judge's reasoning on this part of the case.

Cases after *One in a Million*

One in a Million has been applied in several further cases.   3–077

In *Britannia Building Society v Prangley*,[20] the claimant was a substantial and well-known building society. It applied for summary judgment for passing off against the defendant, who had registered britanniabuildingsociety.com. The defendant had not yet delegated the domain name to a website, but claimed that he intended to use the domain name to advertise a business that he was in the process of establishing to provide British builders to Iranians.

The court found the defendant's evidence to be "wholly incredible" and relied on certain statements in the defence to support the finding that the defendant regarded the domain name as a commercially usable instrument (there was a dispute on the evidence as to whether the defendant had or had not offered to sell the domain name to the claimant).

The judge also found the domain name in question to be inherently deceptive and an instrument of fraud. He indicate that there might be rather more doubt about the cause of action in trade mark infringement, but found it unnecessary to reach a conclusion on that. He granted injunctions ordering the transfer of the domain name to the claimant and restraining further misuse of the claimant's name.

In *easyJet Airline Co. Ltd v Dainty*,[21] the claimants were a well known   3–078
airline (easyJet) and various associated companies including easyEverything and easyRentacar. easyEverything promoted internet cafes, and easyRentacar rented vehicles. Both the airline and the car rental company took bookings largely over the internet. The defendant was an individual who registered the domain name "easyrealestate.co.uk",[22] which he wanted to

---

[19] [1996] R.P.C. 281. See discussion above as regards the current position on the question whether use as a trade mark is required for infringement.
[20] Ch.D Rattee J., June 12, 2000 (unreported).
[21] Ch.D Mr Bernard Livesey Q.C., February 19, 2001 (unreported).
[22] The judgment refers to the defendant having registered "easyRealestate.co.uk" as a domain name. However, the use of the capitalised "R" in a domain name is meaningless, since domain names are case insensitive. Nothing in the conclusions appears to turn on the use of the capitalised R, although the judge does refer to it as one of the distinctive features of the get-up used by the claimants.

use for a cut-price estate agency that he wished to establish. The claimants sued for passing off and applied for summary judgment.

It was noteworthy that the claimants did not have a business in the property field. The question therefore arose whether the claimants could establish the likelihood of damage, an essential element of passing off. The deputy judge held, relying on *Harrods Ltd v Harrodian School Ltd*[23] that although the claimants would not lose any prospective customers, it was legitimate to consider possible damage to the claimant's goodwill and to their own reputation in the conduct of their various business enterprises.

As to deception, the deputy judge (while agreeing that the claimants were not entitled to appropriate the word "easy" and prevent any businessman from using any name which includes the name "easy"), relied upon the close resemblance of the defendant's website to the claimants' get-up. He also relied on surrounding factual circumstances, including a previous approach to easyJet and certain misrepresentations made by the defendant to easyJet designed (so the judge held) to increase the price at which easyJet might be prepared to pay for the domain name. For both reasons he concluded that the likelihood of deception was made out.

As to remedies, the judge in addition to restraining injunctions ordered the transfer of the domain name to the claimants. While the domain name itself was not inherently deceptive, the get-up of the website in total was adapted to be used for passing off and, if used in any of a variety of manners indicated by the defendant probably would lead to passing off. The deputy judge was also concerned that the defendant might sell the domain name to a third party who might be a malefactor. Since the judge was satisfied on the evidence that the domain was a vehicle of fraud, he concluded that notwithstanding that the domain name was not inherently deceptive, an order for transfer should be made.

3–079   The third case was *Global Projects Management Ltd v Citigroup Inc*, discussed at para.3–052 above, in which the judge held that the claimant registrant held the domain name "citigroup.co.uk" as an instrument of fraud and that as regards passing off and registered trade mark infringement the case was on all fours with *One in a Million*. The registrant's explanations of his purpose in registering the domain name were dismissed as not credible.

Other cases in which *One in a Million* has been successfully invoked on an application for summary judgment or for an interim injunction include *Metalrax Group Plc v Vanci (t/a Disability UK)*,[24] *Easygroup IP Licensing Ltd v Sermbezis*[25] and *Tesco Stores Ltd v Elogicom*.[26]

One in a Million was also applied in a case that went to trial in *Phones 4u Ltd v Phone4u.co.uk Internet Ltd*.[27] In this case the judge at first instance found that at the operative date the claimant had no goodwill protectable

---

[23] [1996] R.P.C. 697.
[24] [2002] All ER (D) 299 (Jan).
[25] [2003] All ER (D) 25 (Nov).
[26] [2006] EWHC 403 (Ch).
[27] [2005] EWHC 334 (Ch); [2006] EWCA Civ 244.

by passing off. The Court of Appeal disagreed. They found that once that existence of goodwill was established it inevitably followed that albeit the domain name was registered innocently, there was no realistic use of it that would not cause deception. The defendant's later conduct in trying to sell the domain name once he knew of the claimant's shops and without having traded was not materially different from that of the *One in a Million* defendants.

By way of contrast with these cases, in *MBNA America Bank NA v Freeman*[28] the application was for an interlocutory injunction pending trial against the defendant who had registered "www.mbna.co.uk". The claimants, the world's largest independent credit card issuer, claimed infringement of a Community Trade Mark for a stylised representation of "mbna", and passing off. The interlocutory injunction claimed was to restrain the defendant firstly from operating or using any website with the domain name or any domain name including "mbna" and secondly from selling or offering for sale or otherwise dealing with the domain name "www.mbna.co.uk". 3–080

The defendant's evidence was that he chose the domain name for a future "banner exchange" business, and that mbna stood for Marketing Banners for Net Advertising. He also produced evidence of an existing website that he had operated for the previous 18 months.

The claimants suggested that the acronym was not properly descriptive of a banner exchange business, and that in the absence of a credible explanation for the use of the domain name it should be inferred that the defendant had deliberately chosen to use it in order to take advantage of the claimants' goodwill to increase the number of visitors to his website. They also claimed infringement in respect of a dissimilar business under s.10(3) of the Trade Marks Act 1994.

The judge found that the claimants had an arguable case, but that he was in no position to decide whether it was more likely to succeed or to fail at trial. As to remedies, having considered the balance of convenience he granted an interlocutory injunction pending trial restraining the sale or other dealings with the domain name, but declined to restrain the defendant from activating his website. In this he was at least partially influenced by the "impression of business competence" that the defendant, who represented himself, made at the hearing. This impression was reinforced by positive publicity in a national newspaper.

It can be seen from the above cases that credibility is crucial. For a defendant to stand any chance of succeeding in these cases, it is imperative that his evidence of why he chose the domain name and his intentions for it be credible and consistent with the surrounding circumstances. 3–081

In the case of a wholly recalcitrant defendant who wilfully disobeys court

---

[28] Ch.D Mr Nicholas Strauss Q.C., July 17, 2000 (unreported).

orders for transfer of a domain name, the court may invoke its power to order that a court official execute the transfer.[29]

Following the advent of the ICANN UDRP, discussed below, there are relatively few court cases involving bad faith gTLD registrations. Similarly, there is little reason to litigate over bad faith .uk registrations following the introduction in September 2001 of Nominet's Dispute Resolution Service.[30] However, *Global Projects Management*, discussed at para.3–052 above, in which the Nominet DRS procedure was halted after the domain name registrant issued threats proceedings under s.21 of the Trade Marks Act 1994 against the complainant, illustrates that litigation may still arise.

Other UK cases involving internet and domain name issues

3–082   For cases on the question whether the mere availability of a foreign website constitutes use of a trade mark within the UK, see the discussion in Chapter 6.

As we have discussed above (para.3–038), the lack of congruence between the scope of registered trade marks and the use of domain names mean that two persons who might quite legitimately wish to use the same domain name in areas of trade which do not clash cannot do so, since only the first one of these will actually obtain the domain name it wants. So a Scottish car repairer and a worldwide hamburger chain cannot both use "mcdonalds.com".

This situation arose in the UK and came to the attention of the UK courts in *Pitman Training Ltd v Nominet United Kingdom and Pearson Professional Ltd.*[31] In this case a dispute arose between two companies, both entitled to use the Pitman name in different fields of business.

One of the companies, Pearson Professional, had registered "pitman. co.uk" in February 1996 for the use of its Pitman Publishing division. It was the intention of Pitman Publishing in due course to set up a website, but it did not immediately intend to use the domain name. In March 1996 Pitman Training, through its ISP, checked whether "pitman.co.uk" was available and was informed that it was. "pitman.co.uk" became delegated to Pitman Training, who started to use it in July 1996 (no one was able to offer any clear explanation to the court as to how this was possible).

In December 1996 Pitman Publishing discovered that it no longer had the domain name. Its solicitors wrote to Nominet, relying on the fact that it had been first in time to register. Nominet in due course wrote to Pitman Training informing them that the domain name was being transferred back to Pitman Publishing.

Pitman Training sued, alleging against Pitman Publishing passing off, interference with contract and abuse of process. At the full hearing of Pitman Training's application for an interlocutory injunction, the judge

---

[29] As occurred in *Marks & Spencer Plc v Cottrell* Ch.D Lightman J., February 26, 2001 (unreported). The defendant was found to have committed 13 breaches of various court orders, including an order to assign various domain names to the claimant.

[30] See para.3–092, below, for a description of Nominet's disputes procedures.

[31] [1997] F.S.R. 797.

held that none of the causes of action were reasonably arguable and thereby gave practical effect to Nominet's "first come, first served" rule.

An interesting dispute over the domain name "prince.com" arose in **3–083** *Prince Plc v Prince Sports Group Inc*.[32] The English High Court considered whether the defendant Prince Sports Group Inc issued unjustified threats of trade mark infringement proceedings against Prince Plc, arising out of its use of the domain name "prince.com".

Prince Plc, which is in fact a computer company, had registered "prince.com" in 1995. On January 16, 1997 attorneys for Prince Sports Group, a sports equipment company, wrote to Prince Plc stating that the registration had come to their clients' attention, informing it of various US trade mark registrations owned by them and also stating that their client had registered the PRINCE mark in many other countries throughout the world including the UK. The letter demanded immediate agreement to assign "prince.com" to avoid litigation.

On January 29, 1997 Prince Sports' attorneys wrote to NSI, copied to Prince plc, setting out its US trade mark registrations and asking for the domain name to be put on hold. NSI wrote to Prince Plc on February 25, 1997 and on April 28, 1997 Prince Plc commenced proceedings against Prince Sports Group Inc alleging unjustified threats of trade mark proceedings and applied for summary judgment.

Prince Sports Group did not contend at the hearing that there was **3–084** infringement of any UK trade mark, and the arguments mainly concerned whether the letter in fact amounted to an unjustified threat and whether Prince Plc should be granted any relief. The judge held that the letter was an unjustified threat and granted a declaration to that effect and an injunction restraining the issuance of further threats.

The "prince.com" dispute, when it was first reported in the media, was widely thought to show that the then NSI disputes policy favoured US-based companies. This was because Prince Plc, having used the domain name for well over a year (and their trading name in the UK previous to that), were suddenly faced with the prospect of losing the use of it if NSI put it "on hold" as a result of the US company's citation of its US registered trade marks. The ICANN UDRP (which succeeded the NSI procedures) does take account of rights in unregistered marks.[33]

eFax.com Inc v Oglesby[34] was a straightforward application to internet **3–085** facts of established principles governing passing off and the grant of interim injunctions. Perhaps the main lesson to be drawn from this case is that, just as in the off-line world, the choice of a descriptive name for an internet or e-commerce service is likely to render the protection of that name difficult, at least until sufficient advertising, marketing and trading has taken place to render the name distinctive of the services offered. (For contrasting cases see

---

[32] [1998] F.S.R. 21.
[33] See for instance *Jeanette Winterson v Hogarth* (WIPO D2000–0235).
[34] [2000] 23(4) I.P.D. 29031.

Lawyers Online Ltd v Lawyeronline Ltd[35] and *French Connection Ltd v Sutton.*[36])

The *eFax.com* case involved an application by the claimant eFax.com Inc for an interim injunction restraining the defendant Mr Mark Oglesby pending trial of the action from passing off his services as and for those of the claimant by use of the name "efax". The defendant had registered and was using the domain name efax.co.uk.

The judge found that on the evidence presently available (and to put it at its lowest) the claimant might well have a difficult task at trial in establishing a distinctive goodwill in the word "efax" sufficient to support a case in passing off. However, that did not lead to the conclusion that the claim was bound to fail or that there was no serious issue to be tried. He, therefore, refused to strike out the claim.

In assessing the likelihood of confusion if no interlocutory injunction was granted, since the only confusion relevant is that which results from a misrepresentation by the defendant it was necessary for the judge to revisit the arguments and the evidence as to the allegedly descriptive and generic nature of the word efax. This was because since, to the extent that the word was descriptive of and generic in relation to the defendant's business, the use of it by the defendant in relation to his business could not amount to a misrepresentation or deception and any resulting confusion from mere description could not be relied upon in support of the claim in passing off.

3–086   The Judge concluded that any confusion which might hereafter result from the fact that both claimant and defendant were offering similar services in the UK under the name "efax" would in all likelihood be attributable to the descriptive nature at the name rather than to any "misrepresentation" by the defendant to the effect that he was carrying on the claimant's business. The judge also took into account other differences such as the fact that the defendant charged for his service while the claimant did not and that the two websites were different in appearance.

Taking into account the status quo as at November 12, 1999 when the action was commenced, and also the fact that the defendant acquired the "efax.co.uk" domain name a full year before the claimant first launched its service worldwide in February 1999, the judge declined to grant an interim injunction.

3.11 DOMAIN NAME REGISTRY DISPUTE POLICIES

3.11.1 History

3–087   As domain name disputes became more of a problem the domain name registries introduced registration fees, rules about how they would act when

---

[35] Ch.D. HH Judge Boggis Q.C., July 7, 2000 (unreported).
[36] [2000] E.T.M.R. 341.

disputes arise and, to a certain extent, rules on when they might refuse to register a domain name.

Typically, applicants seeking to register a domain name with the relevant domain name registry were required to enter into a contract incorporating the terms of these dispute policies so that the registry in question could enforce those policies by way of the law of contract. Applicants were often also required to give warranties to the registry, for instance that the use of the domain name would not contravene any third party's rights.

Before the creation of ICANN and the subsequent introduction of competing gTLD registrars there was only one registrar (NSI, now Verisign, Inc) issuing .com, .net and .org domain names. NSI had its own disputes policy which went through a number of iterations. That was discontinued when NSI adopted the ICANN Uniform Dispute Resolution Policy (UDRP), to which all ICANN-accredited registrars issuing gTLD domain names have to adhere.

Country code domain name registries generally continue to have their own disputes policies and rules relating to what can and cannot be registered, although some have voluntarily adopted the ICANN UDRP or policies modelled on it.

3.11.2 ICANN Uniform Dispute Resolution Policy

The Uniform Dispute Resolution Policy was adopted by ICANN in August 1999. It was implemented by registrars in the gTLDs (global top level domains) .com, .org and .net during December 1999 and January 2000. It provides third parties who would otherwise have to prove in court that registration of a domain name infringes their trade mark rights with an alternative to litigation in the case of abusive registration of domain names, i.e. those registered in bad faith. It is not intended for disputes between parties each of whom may have legitimate claims to the domain name. **3–088**

A domain name registrant is bound to the UDRP by his contract with the issuing registrar. The contract requires the registrant to submit to a mandatory administrative proceeding in the event that a third party asserts to the registrar that:

- (i) the registrant's domain name is identical or confusingly similar to a trademark or service mark in which the complainant has rights; and
- (ii) the registrant has no rights or legitimate interests in respect of the domain name; and
- (iii) the registrant's domain name has been registered and is being used in bad faith.

In the administrative proceeding, the complainant must prove that each of these three elements are present. The UDRP goes on the provide that the following circumstances, in particular but without limitation, if found by **3–089** the Panel to be present, shall be evidence of the registration and use of a domain name in bad faith:

   (i)   circumstances indicating that the registrant has registered or has acquired the domain name primarily for the purpose of selling, renting, or otherwise transferring the domain name registration to the complainant who is the owner of the trade mark or service mark or to a competitor of that complainant, for valuable consideration in excess of the registrant's documented out-of-pocket costs directly related to the domain name; or

   (ii) the registrant has registered the domain name in order to prevent the owner of the trade mark or service mark from reflecting the mark in a corresponding domain name, provided that the registrant has engaged in a pattern of such conduct; or

   (iii) the registrant has registered the domain name primarily for the purpose of disrupting the business of a competitor; or

   (iv) by using the domain name, the registrant has intentionally attempted to attract, for commercial gain, internet users to the registrant's website or other on-line location, by creating a likelihood of confusion with the complainant's mark as to the source, sponsorship, affiliation, or

   (v)   endorsement of the registrant's website or location or of a product or service on the registrant's website or location.

3–090   The UDRP then goes on to set out a number of circumstances, in particular but without limitation, any of which if found by the Panel to be proved based on its evaluation of all evidence presented, shall demonstrate the registrant's rights or legitimate interests to the domain name:

   (i)   before any notice to the registrant of the dispute, the registrant's use of, or demonstrable preparations to use, the domain name or a name corresponding to the domain name in connection with a bona fide offering of goods or services; or

   (ii) the registrant (as an individual, business, or other organisation) has been commonly known by the domain name, even if the registrant has acquired no trade mark or service mark rights; or

   (iii) the registrant is making a legitimate non-commercial or fair use of the domain name, without intent for commercial gain to misleadingly divert consumers or to tarnish the trade mark or service mark at issue.

Up to May 10, 2004, 9,377 proceedings had been commenced under the UDRP involving 15,710 domain names. Of those proceedings, 8,761 had been resolved (7,790 by decision, 971 otherwise).

3–091   A complainant may select the dispute-resolution service provider to which to submit his complaint from among those approved by ICANN. At the time of writing three providers have been approved and are active: WIPO, The National Arbitration Forum and the Asian Domain Name

Dispute Resolution Centre. Proceedings generally take place in writing (including on-line), with no in-person hearings unless exceptionally ordered by the panel. ICANN maintains a complete database, accessible on its website,[37] of all UDRP panel decisions.

The panel is given discretion under UDRP Rules of Procedure para. 15(a) to apply any rules and principles of law that it deems applicable.[38]

A UDRP panel decision to transfer or cancel a domain name will be implemented by the domain name registrar unless, within 10 business days, the domain name registrant files with the registrar official documentation evidencing the commencement of legal proceedings against the complainant in one of the jurisdictions to which the complainant has submitted under the UDRP Rules of Procedure.[39] The complainant is required to submit to the jurisdiction of at least one of a court jurisdiction at the location of either:

- the principal office of the domain name registrar with which the registrant registered a domain name the subject of the complaint (so long as the registrant submitted in its registration agreement to that jurisdiction for court adjudication of disputes concerning or arising from the domain name); or
- the registrant's address as shown in the domain name registrar's WHOIS database at the time the UDRP complaint is submitted to the UDRP dispute-resolution provider.

The decisions record of the various UDRP dispute-resolution service providers is attracting unprecedented academic and professional scrutiny, addressing issues such as the consistency and quality of decision-making, forum-shopping between providers and so on.[40]

---

[37] *www.icann.org.*

[38] The question of what law the panel should apply has excited surprisingly little controversy, given that the applicable law and the territoriality of the complainant's rights tend to go hand in hand. It is eapecially relevant where unregistered rights are relied upon (see e.g. *Antonio de Felipe v Registerfly.com* WIPO Case No. D2005–0969). It is also potentially important in cases where a complainant has secured a trade mark registration in only one or two countries and deploys those against a respondent in a country where the complainant has, and could obtain, no registration. See the concerns about this expressed by the dissenting panelist in *Ty Inc. v Parvin* (WIPO D2000–0688).

[39] UDRP, Rule 4(k).

[40] For a somewhat critical early appraisal of the UDRP record, see *Rough Justice—An Analysis of ICANN's Uniform Dispute Resolution Policy* by Dr Milton Mueller (*http://dcc.syr.edu/miscarticles/roughjustice.htm*). Dr Mueller issued a further paper in 2002, *Success by default: A new Profile of Domain name Trademark Disputes under ICANN's UDRP*. Also in 2002, the Max Planck Institute for Foreign and International Patent, Copyright and Competition Law published a comprehensive study of the operation of the UDRP system. The study concluded that as a matter of principle, the UDRP was functioning satisfactorily and that no major flaws had been identified in the course of the evaluation. Several issues were identified where the application of the Policy was unclear and needed further consideration. These were, in particular, the conditions under which a domain name should be found to be confusingly similar with a mark, measures to safeguard free speech, and rules about burden of proof and the standards to be applied in the assessment of the parties' contentions. See also Prof. Michael Geist, *Fair.com?: An Examination of the Allegations of Systematic Unfairness in the ICANN UDRP.* (*http://aix1.uottawa.ca/~geist/geistudrp.pdf*); and M. Scott Donahey, "The UDRP: Fundamentally Fair, But Far From Perfect" (2001) *Electronic Commerce and Law Report* Vol. 6 No. 34 p.937.

3.11.3 The Nominet DRS

3–092   In the UK, Nominet until September 2001 operated a policy whereby any disputes which arose were first addressed by an expert chosen from a panel put together by Nominet. If the opinion of that expert did not satisfy the parties then Nominet proposed some form of mediation.

    In September 2001 Nominet introduced a new disputes procedure.[41] Rather than adopt the ICANN UDRP, Nominet adopted an independent procedure, the Dispute Resolution Service (DRS). The DRS contains significant differences, both in substance and procedure, from the ICANN UDRP. The most obvious procedural differences are a mediation phase before referral to an independent expert, and the provision of a right of appeal to a three person panel of independent experts. The substantive differences include the lack of an explicit requirement on the Complainant to prove bad faith, in favour of a requirement to show that registration, acquisition or use of the domain name "took unfair advantage of, or was unfairly detrimental to, the Complainant's rights".

    The Nominet DRS was amended as from October 25, 2004,[42] the biggest change being the introduction of a category of abusive registration where a third party such as a web agency had retained a domain name having registered it as a result of a relationship with, for example, a customer who had paid for it.

3.12 CORPORATE TRADE MARK AND DOMAIN NAME PROTECTION POLICIES

3–093   Corporate policies concerning registrations of domain names differ quite substantially. Some companies may have registered only one or two domain names for their main trade mark or trading name, while others have created large domain name portfolios. For example, by late 1995 Proctor & Gamble had registered a whole series of domain names referring to certain common complaints such as badbreath.com, headache.com and diarrhoea.com. Meanwhile Kraft had also registered over 150 of its product names as domain names.[43]

    Clearly, it would be a mammoth task to register every trade mark which a company has in each top level domain, i.e. "twobirds.co.uk", "twobirds.fr", "twobirds.de" etc, even if this were permitted by each country's local registration rules. At present there are over 250 such top level domains. With the new gTLDs this growth in domains will continue. This leads to the conclusion that a company must largely rely on its registered trade mark rights for domain name protection.

---

[41] *www.nominet.org.uk/disputes/drs/oldpolicy.*
[42] *www.nominet.org.uk/disputes/drs/policy.*
[43] "Welcome to paranoia.com", *The Economist*, September 16, 1995.

However, one should also look at this in the light of the way in which domain names are used. If a user is seeking to find a particular website, he may go about it in a number of different ways. He may type in the correct URL to his browser, he may jump from a link on another website to the site in question, or he may carry out a search using one of the search engines such as Google. Quite often, if there is a particular company whose website a user wishes to find, he might first simply try typing in the company's name with either the .com extension or the commercial extension for the country in which that company normally resides.

This is possibly the major reason why domain names are so seriously fought over, since this ad hoc access is specifically facilitated by an appropriate domain name. At one time it was thought that the advent of enhanced keyword services such as RealNames would diminish the importance of domain names as identifiers. However RealNames ceased operations in 2002 and the focus of keyword systems has since shifted to search engines.

A good rule of thumb when trying to formulate a domain name regis-   3–094
tration policy is to identify the "crown jewel" trade marks of the company and then to register these at least in the commercial designation for the country where the company normally trades and, if the company is an international one, to register them as a .com domain name as well. This will not stop others registering similar marks with, for example, simply an addition of an "s" or a hyphen but it will guard against the most blatant domain name grabbing and blackmail activities.

Then one needs to review the company's trade mark registrations to ensure that they adequately back up the trading activity of the company on the internet. In view of the speed of change presently being seen on the internet, for the immediate future it would also be wise to repeat this review on at least an annual if not, six monthly basis.

Clearly, trade mark registrations in relevant territories for the main stem of the domain name will afford considerable protection. However, in some, but not all, countries it is also possible to register the full domain name (including the extension) as a trade mark provided that it will itself be used in a trade mark sense. An example would be using the full domain name in advertising the relevant website, so that the domain name is clearly used as branding for the website.

Certainly, in the UK Trade Marks Registry full domain names will be accepted for registration as a trade mark. Thus "twobirds.com" could be registered as a UK trade mark in relation to legal services. However, the Trade Mark Registry makes clear that the extension (in this case .com) cannot be regarded as a distinctive element of the mark.

Avnet Incorporated v Isoact Ltd[44] gives a useful indication of the   3–095
appropriate classes in which to register trade marks for internet-related services. The plaintiffs unsuccessfully applied for summary judgment for trade mark infringement under s.10(1) of the Trade Marks Act 1994. The

---

[44] [1998] F.S.R. 16.

requirement for infringement under s.10(1) is that the defendant's use be of a mark and services identical to those for which the plaintiff's mark is registered.

The plaintiff had the mark AVNET registered in Class 35 for "advertising and promotional services ... all included in Class 35". Its business was selling technical goods through a physical catalogue. The defendant's business as an internet service provider was quite different from that of the plaintiff and was not commercially in conflict with it. The defendant specialised in aviation, using the names Aviation Network and Avnet. The defendant had a website address "www.avnet.co.uk". They provided a service to their customers which included giving customers an email address and their own web page.

Jacob J. had to consider whether what the defendant was doing constituted providing advertising and promotional services. He decided that it did not do so. The defendant did no more than provide a place where their customers could put up whatever they liked. They did not assist their customers to write their copy. They did not require or expect their customers to put up advertisements.

3–096   The judge went on to consider whether, if he were wrong on this, the services were "included in Class 35". The informal view of a Trade Mark Registry officer provided over the telephone was that if an ISP were renting out advertising space on a website to customers, then it might possibly fall within Class 35. However, if it were providing only the usual services of an ISP by providing users with access to the internet then it would fall within Class 42. The judge commented that whilst this could not be the last word on the subject, he did not think that the defendant's activities fell within Class 35 as explained by the Registrar's officer—certainly not to the standard required for summary judgment.

The *Avnet* case therefore gives some guidance on the appropriate class for registration of trade marks for some internet-related services, particularly those provided by an internet service provider.

It also illustrates that the fact that a company is described as an "internet service provider" is not determinative of its potential liability for its activities. The court in this case looked at what the defendant actually did—in this case, whether or not it provided advisory services to its customers as well as providing email and hosting services—in determining whether it infringed the trade mark. If, for instance, the defendant had provided copywriting services and advice on how to advertise most effectively on the web, the result might well have been different.

3.13 METATAGS, WORDSTUFFING AND KEYWORD SALES

3.13.1 Metatags

What are metatags?

Two practices against which trade mark laws may be invoked are the misuse of metatags and the related practice of "wordstuffing". Both involve the use of text that is hidden from the casual user of the website, but is visible to search engines and to anyone who peruses the HTML or similar source code[45] of the site.

3-097

Metatags are contained in the "Meta" section of a web page. This section contains metadata, i.e. information about the web page. The web browser understands that this data is not to be presented to the user and keeps it hidden in normal browsing.

The "Meta" section is itself divided into a number of sub-sections, including "Description" and "Keywords". "Description" is used to provide a short abstract describing the site or page. That abstract will appear on the results page of a search engine that lists the site or page as a hit. "Keywords" is used by search engines to assess the relevance of the page or site to the search term that the user has entered into the search engine. Intelligent use of keywords can result in a higher relevance ranking on a search engine listing. The term "metatags" is generally used to indicate the "Keywords" sub-section of the "Meta" section.

Why do metatags give rise to disputes?

Keywords in particular are open to controversial uses. Some businesses have been tempted to attempt to divert business to their sites by including their competitors' names and brands in their own keywords. The result of this is that when a user types the competitor's name into a search engine, the resulting list of hits will include both companies.

3-098

The user will not know why the company has appeared in the list of hits, since the metatag keywords remain hidden (although of course the search term entered by the user will most likely appear at the top of the list as a reminder of the search term that he has entered). And it is likely to be clear to the user (unless the perpetrator has also adopted a confusingly similar

---

[45] The source code of a website page differs from that of an ordinary computer program in that it is easily accessible to the user. Website pages consist of text incorporating various codes which are interpreted, as the page is loaded, by the user's web browser. The web browser formats and presents the text in accordance with the codes and hides the codes from the user. It is trivial task in any browser or web page authoring program to view the codes. (In Internet Explorer the command is View|Source.) The source code of a computer program, on the other hand, is normally "compiled" into object code (i.e. a series of 1s and 0s that can be understood only by a computer). The object code version is released to purchasers, but the source code is normally retained by the software developer and treated as highly confidential.

company name) that the company is not the competitor, especially since as judicially noted by Jacob J. in *Avnet Incorporated v Isoact Ltd*)[46]:

> "someone searching using a word may find web pages or data in a wholly different context from that which he was seeking. Users of the internet know that that is a feature of the internet and that their search may produce an altogether wrong web page or the like. That might be an important matter for the courts to take into account when considering trade mark and like problems."

As with domain names, there is in principle a broad range of uses to which metatags may be put, and the question of trade mark infringement or passing off should be considered in the light of the particular use. The cases of a dealer who lists the brand names of goods that he supplies, or of a specialist magazine that lists the brands and manufacturers that it writes about, have to be considered differently from the company who lists its competitors' names.

In the US, for instance, use of a competitor's trade mark as a metatag has been held to violate the Lanham Act.[47] However, a former Playmate of the Year 1981 who included the words Playboy and Playmate in the metatags of her personal website was held entitled to do so.[48]

Can metatags infringe trade marks?

3–099   In *Reed Executive Plc v Reed Business Information Ltd*,[49] the Court of Appeal ruled that the defendants' use of metatags and search keywords incorporating a mark similar to that of the claimant did not amount to trade mark infringement underr s.10(2) of the Trade Marks Act 1994 or passing off. The court reached that conclusion on the basis of a finding of lack of confusion. It left open the question of whether invisible metatags and keywords can amount to use of a trade mark for the purposes of infringement of a registered mark.

The claimants were a recruitment agency. They owned the registered trade mark REED for employment agency services. The defendants were a large publishing group. Both groups of companies had co-existed for many years. The defendants, who had previously carried job advertisements in their journals and magazines, set up in 1999 a jobs website called totaljobs.com.

The claimants commenced proceedings for trade mark infringement and passing off, based on various alleged uses by the defendants of the words "Reed Business Services" and variations on that in connection with the totaljobs.com website.

---

[46] [1998] F.S.R. 16.

[47] *Brookfield Communications, Inc. v West Coast Entertainment Corporation*, 174 F.3d 1036 (9th Cir. 1999).

[48] *Playboy Enterprises, Inc. v Terri Welles* 78 F. Supp. 2d 1066 (S.D. Cal. 1999).

[49] [2004] EWCA Civ 159.

Among the complaints made by the claimants was one about a click-through "totaljobs" banner advertisement on the Yahoo! search portal. The banner was linked to search keywords entered by the user of the Yahoo! site. The defendant paid Yahoo! for a banner linked to the search terms "recruitment" and "job". They were also given a free extra keyword of their own name, for which Yahoo! chose "reed". If a user entered the word "reed" the totaljobs banner would appear on the results page and the user could click through to the totaljobs website. The word "Reed" did not appear on the banner advertisement itself.

The claimants also complained that the defendants used the words "Reed Business Information" as a metatag in the totaljobs website. Evidence was adduced about what happened when a search was entered for "Reed jobs". In all case where totaljobs was listed, it came below the claimant's site in the search results.

As well as considering many general issues of trade mark law, the court had to consider the particular issues raised by the use of search keywords and metatags.

Jacob L.J., with whom Auld and Rix L.L.J. agreed, held that this was a case of similar marks and similar services, which fell to be considered under Art.5.1(b) of the Trade Marks Directive. In order to demonstrate trade mark infringement under Art.5.1(b) the claimants had to establish that the similarity of the marks and services resulted in a likelihood of confusion on the part of the public.

The court had no hesitation in finding that both for keywords and metatags there was no likelihood of confusion. As for passing off, the court found that in both cases there was no misrepresentation. In the case of keywords, the court commented that if the banner click-through had led to a site bearing infringing material, that could be trade mark infringement and passing off.

If the case had been one concerning an identical mark and identical services, then to establish trade mark infringement the claimant would not have had to prove likelihood of confusion. It would have been sufficient to show that the defendant was using the mark in the course of trade. The court left open the question whether the use of keywords or metatags, which were readable only by computer and were not visible to human beings, would constitute infringement. Jacob L.J., while reserving his view, pointed out three difficult questions arising out of the invisibility of metatags: **3–100**

- Does metatag use count as use of a trade mark at all? Here he pointed out that use is important not only for infringement but also for saving a mark from non-use, and that it would be odd that a wholly invisible use could defeat a non-use attack
- If metatag use does count as use, is there infringement if the marks and goods or services are identical but no-one is misled?
- If metatag use can fall with the infringement provisions, can defences such as the own name defence apply? The judge at first

instance had thought not because the use was invisible. Why should that be relevant to the defence but not to infringement?

3–101 As illustrated by *Reed*, the requirement to show likelihood of confusion for the purposes of s.10(2) may cause problems. It was pointed out in both *Reed* and *Avnet* that internet users are accustomed to obtaining search results that "contain hits of varying degrees of irrelevance". On the basis of *Reed*, English courts ought to be unwilling to find confusion on the basis that the user is taken to the website as a result of the search engine hit, if it is clear when the user reaches the site that it is not connected with that of the trade mark owner ("initial interest confusion").

The problem with an initial interest confusion doctrine is in showing that the use of the metatag has caused any confusion when the user does not expect only to receive hits for sites connected with the company whose name he has entered into the search engine. Indeed, the typical user is likely to expect to receive hits for sites containing references to the company, and would be most disappointed to receive hits only for sites emanating from or commercially connected with the company.

The user cannot know whether the site is listed as a "hit" on the results page because of misuse of a metatag, some idiosyncrasy of the search algorithm, or because the word is included in the site for some innocent reason (such as quoting a newspaper article that mentions the word). Since the user is most unlikely to assume that every "hit" on the list emanates from the trade mark owner, why should the user make that assumption in the case of the particular "hit" that appears as a result of the misused metatag?

For passing off, it is not immediately easy to see exactly where or when the deception or misrepresentation arises in metatag and similar cases. In *Reed*, passing off was not found to have occurred.

In Italy a court has held that the use of a competitor's name in a metatag may constitute unfair competition.[50] In Germany the Dusseldorf Regional Appeals Court held in February 2004 that use of trade marks and a firm name in metatags did not violate trade mark or competition law.[51] An opposite conclusion was arrived at by the Munich regional court in June 2004.[52]

3.13.2 Wordstuffing

3–102 "Wordstuffing" is a simple way of hiding text in a web page. It involves formatting text so that it appears in the same colour as the page background—or rather does not appear, since the text merges invisibly into the

---

[50] *Genertel SpA v Crowe Italia Srl* Court of Rome, January 18, 2001 (World Internet Law Report August 2001, p.19).

[51] Case No. I 20 U 104/03, February 17, 2004 (E.C.L.R. Vol. 9 No. 12, p.289).

[52] *Impuls GmbH v C&W Media GbR*, LG Muenchen, 17HK 0 10389/04, June 24, 2004 (E.C.L.R. Vol. 9 No. 30, p.679).

background. The text is still present on the page, so that it will be indexed by search engines, but is invisible on the page itself. It is difficult to envisage circumstances in which deliberate hiding of text will do other than raise suspicion as to the purpose of the concealment.[53]

3.13.3 Search engine keyword sales

The selling of keywords by search engines has become an enormously 3–103 lucrative form of advertising. The practice consists of agreeing, for a fee, to tie banner advertisements or sponsored links to the keyword entered by the user, so that particular advertisements (or links to them) appear on the search results page for a particular keyword.

A problem arises if the search engine sells a keyword consisting of a trade mark to a competitor, so that the competitor's advertisement (or a link to it) appears on the results page when the keyword has been entered.

This issue has been considered by the Dutch courts in *VNU Business Publications BV v The Monster Board BV.*[54] The claimants were the proprietors of Benelux registered trade marks INTERMEDIAIR and INTERMEDIAIR ONLINE, for magazines and on-line services relating to the advertisement of employment vacancies. The claimants operated a website under the INTERMEDIAIR ONLINE trade mark.

The defendants, who operated a Dutch career site in competition with the claimants, concluded an agreement with a search engine, Vindex, whereby when (among others) the word "Intermediair" was entered into the search engine, a large click-through colour advertisement for the defendant's career site appeared on the upper part of the screen.

The claimants sued for trade mark infringement in summary proceedings. At first instance the court provisionally held that, contrary to s.13A, para.1(a) of the Benelux Trade Mark Act, the use of the trade mark constituted "economic trafficking" of the trade mark. The defendants' argument that any infringement was by the user of the search engine failed. The decision was reversed on appeal to the Court of Appeal in The Hague.

The Court of Appeal considered whether The Monster Board had only used the word "intermediair" within the general meaning of the word in the Dutch language of "party in between/mediator" in order to indicate the nature/quality of its services. Among the factors that the Court considered

---

[53] Wordstuffing featured for the first time in an English case in *Phones4u* (see above para.3–079). The evidence was that for a period the defendant Mr Heykali, in retaliatory response to various measures taken by the claimants, had used both metadata and hidden text (which the judge regarded as a form of metadata) on his own website including words such as "Phones 4 U" and "phones4u". At first instance the judge held that the claimants had not, due to lack of evidence, made out a case of deception in this and other respects. On appeal ([2006] EWCA Civ 244) his general approach to the evidence of deception was overturned. However, the wordstuffing aspects were not specifically referred to in the Court of Appeal judgment.

[54] [2000], E.T.M.R, 111, District Court of the Hague (Civil Law Division); on appeal, [2002] E.T.M.R.1, 1.

were that the reservation of the search term only had the consequence that The Monster Board's banner advertisement would appear above the list of results. The list of results itself was not changed. The banner was not dominant in the entire image. Further, in the banner advertisement the word "intermediair" did not occur.

In view of these and other circumstances considered by the Court of Appeal, the court did not deem it plausible that the way in which the word was used created the impression on the part of the internet user who entered the word "intermediair" and subsequently saw The Monster Board's advertisement appear on top of the page of results, that The Monster Board was using this word to distinguish goods or services. The court therefore concluded that there was no infringement.

3–104   In Germany the cosmetics manufacturer Estée Lauder sued the search engine Excite Inc over its sale of the keywords "Estee Lauder", "Clinique" and "Origins" to a discount outlet, Fragrance Counter, whose banner advertisements would appear in response to entry of the keywords. The banner advertisements in this case included Estée Lauder trade marks, in a form such as "Clinique@fragrancecounter".

The court found trade mark infringement by the use of the marks in the banner advertisements. As to the keywords, the court declined to hold that there was trade mark infringement, basing its decision instead on unfair competition. The court expressed doubts regarding trade mark infringement where the mark was not used visibly.[55]

Estée Lauder commenced similar proceedings against the same parties in the US. The dispute then settled, with iBeauty (as Fragrance Counter became called) voluntarily agreeing not to use Estée Lauder trade marks as internet keywords.

In a US case, *Playboy Enterprises, Inc. v Netscape Communications Corporation*[56] the US Court of Appeals for the 9th Circuit held that where the defendant had made trade marked search keywords available to persons other than the plaintiff trade mark owner, there was potential liability for direct or indirect contributory trade mark infringement. The court over-turned the lower court's finding of summary judgment in favour of the defendants and allowed the matter to proceed to trial. In doing so the court held that there was a genuine issue of material fact as to whether the defendant's activities would be likely to cause initial interest confusion, i.e. confusion that creates initial interest in competitor's product, but which is dispelled before a sale is made. The plaintiff's trade mark dilution claim was also allowed to proceed. The case is reported to have settled subsequently on undisclosed terms.

A rash of litigation has erupted around the Google search engine's AdWords service. This service also makes use of paid-for search keywords. But instead of tying them to banner advertisements AdWords uses them to

---

[55] "Sale of Keywords: Trademark violation, Unfair Competition or Proper E-Advertising?", R. Mann, [2000] E.I.P.R. 378.
[56] 354 F.3d 1020, 69 USPQ2d 1417, January 14, 2004.

create a ranked list of sponsored search results, shown separately from the main listing of non-keyed search results.

In France, the Tribunal de Grande Instance in Nanterre held in 2003[57] **3–105** that sale of keywords that resulted in links to competitors' websites appearing in the sponsored rankings when the plaintiff's trade mark "bourse des vols" or "bourse des voyages" was entered as a search term constituted trade mark infringement. This was so even where the keyword that triggered the appearance of the link to the competitive site was only the generic term "vols" or "voyages". The decision was upheld on appeal to the Paris Appeals Court in October 2005.[58]

Other litigation over Google's AdWords service has included suits brought by AXA and LVMH[59] in France; an interim injunction granted in Germany in November 2003, at the behest of Metaspinner GmbH; a suit brought by the Geico insurance company in Virginia (dismissed on summary motion as regards the word GEICO in keywords, but permitted to continue to trial in respect of the word appearing in the text of the sponsored advertisement itself[60]); a claim for a declaratory judgment brought by Google against American Blind & Wallpaper Factory, Inc in California; and a related counter-suit for trade mark infringement commenced in New York.

There is generally little consensus in the US cases over whether sale of trademarked keyword search terms constitutes a use in commerce for trade mark infringement purposes.[61]

In Germany the Dusseldorf Regional Court has held that a search site that displayed on its results page sponsored links provided by Google's AdSense programme infringed a trade mark where the trade mark owner's link was placed in a less prominent location (in the non-sponsored results section at the bottom of the page) than the sponsored link.[62]

3.13.4 Pop-up advertising

Another bout of US litigation was provoked by the emergence of pop-up **3–106** advertising. The typical model is that the user installs free software (often called adware) which, when the user visits a website, pops advertisements onto the user's screen which obscure the banner advertisements on the

---

[57] *Viaticum and Luteciel v Google France*, October 13, 2003. Three further French decisions against Google France and Overture in 2004 and 2005 are reported at E.C.L.R. Vol. 10, No. 5 p.93 and Vol. 10 No. 7 p.150.

[58] E.C.L.R. Vol. 10, No. 12 p.296.

[59] A finding of infringement against Google France in the LVMH case was upheld by the Paris Appeals Court on June 28, 2006 (E.C.L.R. Vol. 11, No. 27 p.755).

[60] *Government Employees Ins. Co. v Google, Inc.* E.D. Va., No. 1:04cv507, December 15, 2004 (E.C.L.R. Vol. 9, No. 48, p.1070).

[61] For a review of some US keyword advertising cases expressing divergent views see *Buying for the Home v Humble Abode LLC* (D.N.J. No 03–2783, October 20, 2006) (E.C.L.R. Vol. 11, No. 42 p.1061).

[62] *Zinke v Placht*, Landgericht Dusseldorf, No. 2a O 20/05, March 30, 2005 (E.C.L.R. Vol. 10, No. 18 p.464).

website. The pop-ups are keyed to elements such as the URL of the website that the user is visiting, the website's content, or search terms that the user has entered.

Many website proprietors assert the right to control the appearance of their site on the user's screen, and have invoked various causes of action including trade mark infringement in support. The pop-up software vendors assert the right of the user to control what appears on his screen, and deny that the website owners have any legal remedy that can be deployed to restrict that.

So far the pop-up vendors have mostly prevailed in the US, most recently with the decision of the US Court of Appeals for the Second Circuit in *1–800 Contacts, Inc v WhenU.com*.[63]

3.14 NON-UNITED KINGDOM DOMAIN NAMES— AUSTRALIA

3.14.1 The .au domain

Administrator

3–107   The administrator of the .au domain is auDA. auDA is a not for profit organisation formed in 1999 and endorsed by the Australian Federal Government as the body responsible for granting licences to registry operators. It accredits and licences registrars who can sell licences for domain names to eligible individuals, companies and organisations.

The Government holds reserve powers in relation to domain names under the Telecommunications Act 1997.

3.14.2 Registration Process

3–108   The registration process for the .au ccTLD differs from those generally applied by the various International Corporation for Assigned Names and Numbers (ICANN) endorsed registrars for the .com and other gTLD's.

The domain name registry holds the database of domain names and operates the "nameservers" that make the domain names visible on the internet. The registry for .com.au, .net.au, .org.au, .asn.au, .gov.au and .id.au is AusRegistry.

A registrar issues the domain name licenses to registrants. There are currently 22 auDA accredited registrars providing customer services to people who want to register a new domain name, and to people who want to either renew their existing domain name or make changes to their domain name record.

---

[63] June 27, 2005, (E.C.L.R. Vol. 10, No. 27 p.678).

Eligibility

Certain eligibility requirements apply depending on which second level domain (2LD) is chosen. For example, in order to register under the .com.au 2LD, the applicant must be an "eligible commercial entity". That is, a commercial entity registered in Australia, such as a company incorporated in Australia or a business registered with the relevant State government. In addition, the domain names under the .com.au 2LD "must" be identical to or an abbreviation of the name of the commercial entity, or be otherwise "closely associated" and "substantially connected" to the registrant's company, business, organisation or association name or trade mark.

3–109

As a measure to discourage "typosquatting", auDA will also refuse to register domain names regarded as misspellings or variations of a well-known company name or trade mark—for example, *www.yahhoo.com.au* or *wwwyahoo.com.au*. auDA publishes a list of prohibited variations that have been refused registration under this policy.

Accordingly, individuals are not able to register a domain name under the .com.au 2LD unless they have a business name registration or own a trade mark. However, individuals are able to register personal names under the .id.au 2LD.

Some of the other more common 2LDs are .net.au for network service providers, .edu.au for educational institutions, .gov.au for government bodies and .asn.au for unincorporated bodies, political parties, trade unions and clubs. The 2LD .org.au can be used by registered organisations that do not fall within the other 2LDs. Some of these 2LDs, such as .com.au, are "open" domains that are open to the general public, provided the other eligibility requirements are met. On the other hand, 2LDs such as .gov.au, are "closed", so that registrations of domain names will only be granted to those within a defined community with a common interest.

Originally, generic words such as "cars" or "winery" or "mining" that represented commercial categories or sectors could not be registered as a domain name in the .com.au 2LD. However, in 2002 auDA removed this restriction and generic names were released via an auction.

Similarly, auDA's restriction on Australian place names has also been removed. From June 1, 2005, Australian businesses were able to apply for the registration of geographic domain names for commercial purposes in .com.au and .net.au. Examples of these names include *stkilda.com.au* and *bondi.net.au*. Some such geographic domain names are available in both .com.au and .net.au, while some are only available in either .com.au or .net.au.

auDA has recently released "community" geographic names with the .domain structure "placename.state/territory.au". For example, bathurst.nsw.au or ballarat.vic.au. Use of these domain names is restricted to community website portals that reflect community interests, such as local business, tourism, historical information, special interest groups, and cultural events.

auDA has also removed the restriction of only allowing one domain name licence per entity. There is currently no restriction on the number of domain names that may be licensed by a registrant.

3.14.3 Dispute Resolution Process

3–110 The .au Dispute Resolution policy (auDRP) was adopted by auDA in August 2001. The purpose of the auDRP is to provide a speedier "alternative" to litigation for the resolution of disputes between the registrant of a .au domain name and a party with competing rights in the domain name, specifically:

(i) a domain name which is identical or confusingly similar to a name, trade mark or service mark in which the another party has rights;

(ii) a party to the complaint claims that the other party has no rights or legitimate interest in respect of the domain name; and

(iii) a domain name has been registered or subsequently used in bad faith.

The auDRP is closely modeled on the Uniform Dispute Resolution Policy (UDRP) administered by the Internet Corporation for Assigned Names and Numbers (ICANN). However, auDRP differs from the UDRP in a number of important respects, as follows.

(a) There is an expansion of the grounds on which a complaint can be made to include business names or other names, not just trade marks and service marks.

(b) The domain name holder does not need to have engaged in bad faith registration *and* use of the domain—bad faith registration or bad faith use of the domain name will suffice, and there is a relaxation of the requirements necessary to establish bad faith.

(c) There is a clarification of the defence of bona fide offering of goods and services by the specific exclusion of "offering of domain names".

(d) There is a limitation that the domain name can be transferred to a successful complainant only if the complainant is otherwise eligible to obtain a licence for the domain name, in keeping with the eligibility requirements applying to the .au namespace.

3.14.4 Other means of resolving "cybersquatting" disputes

The consumer protection provisions of the Trade Practices Act 1974 and the common law tort of passing off

3–111 There have not been any court decisions in Australia to date concerning domain name disputes. The common law tort of passing off and the consumer protection provisions of the Trade Practices Act 1974 and equivalent State Fair Trading Acts which prohibit misleading or deceptive conduct and the making of false or misleading statements can provide some protection against cybersquatting. It is likely that the English decision in *British Telecommunications Plc v One in a Million Ltd*[64] will be given some (albeit, not binding) weight by any Australian court which addresses this issue.

Trade Marks Act 1995

Proceedings would rarely be brought in Australia under the Trade Marks Act 1995 in a domain name dispute as misleading and deceptive conduct would commonly be more easily made out.

3–112

If proceedings were brought under the Trade Marks Act 1995, it may be quite difficult in Australia to successfully argue that the mere act of the registration of a domain name incorporating a trade mark constitutes trade mark infringement.

Mere registration of a domain name incorporating the trade mark without further actual use of it will not constitute trade mark infringement, as the threshold requirement of "use as a trade mark" under the Trade Marks Act 1995 will not have been made out. In other words, the name must have been used in relation to goods or services.

Where the domain name is being used in respect of a site that offers goods and/or services, it may be possible to argue that the domain name is used as a trade mark. In addition, to establish infringement, it needs to be shown that the trade mark has been used for goods or services in respect of which the trade mark has been registered.[65] The only exception may be for "well-known" marks which may be infringed by the use of the mark as a trade mark for unrelated goods or services, i.e. goods or services that are not of the same description or closely related to the registered goods or services. This is quite likely to be so in a cybersquatting case where the fame of the mark provides the incentive for the cybersquatter to register the domain name in the first place. However, a cybersquatter is probably less likely to actually be offering goods and services on any website associated with the domain name.

---

[64] (1998) 42 I.P.R. 289.

[65] The wider infringement test also covers goods of the same description as the registered goods, services that are closely related to the registered goods, services of the same description as the registered services and goods that are closely related to the registered services. However, in relation to this wider infringement test, there is a defence if the use will not deceive or cause confusion.

3.15 NON-UNITED KINGDOM DOMAIN NAMES— BELGIUM

3.15.1 Registration

3–113 From the end of the 1980s until the end of 1999, the top-level domain .be was managed by the computer department of the Catholic University of Louvain (KUL). However, following the exponential increase in the number of requests for registration of Belgian domain names during the 1990s,[66] the management of the domain .be was transferred to a non profit organisation, DNS Belgique (or DNS.be), established at the beginning of 1999.[67]

Major changes were effectuated as to the role of DNS Belgium and to the conditions of registration of the .be domain names. Those changes entered into force on December 11, 2000 and have led to a significant increase in registrations.[68]

Indeed, before that date, applications for .be domain names were reserved for legal commercial entities, corporations, public institutions, and public or private organisations. Consequently, applications for .be domain names by private individuals for non-commercial matters or by informal groups were not accepted. Besides, prior to any registration, the applicant had to evidence his right to the domain name.

Common nouns and generic names were not accepted unless they referred to a registered trademark. Moreover, applications were only accepted if the applicant was established in Belgium. In addition, applications for domain names based on a trademark were only accepted if the trademark was registered in Belgium.

3–114 From December 11, 2000, the system was liberalised. As to the role of DNS Belgium, it has been reduced to the sole management of the .be domain. DNS Belgium does not take registrations any more: the registration procedure was transferred to registrars. As to the conditions of registration, they have been removed. Only the "first come, first serve" principle applies. The registration of a domain name only gives right to an annual license to this domain name. There is therefore no possibility to "buy" a domain name. In order to deal with disputes arising from the liberalisation, DNS Belgium has developed a fast dispute settlement procedure, which follows the rules of the Belgian Arbitrage Centre, the CEPANI.

---

[66] In January 1994, only 129 domain names ".be" were registered against 25,000 six years later; *cf.* the site *http://www.dns.be*.

[67] The non profit association DNS Belgium started its activities at the beginning of the year 2000.

[68] Between November 2000 and July 2001, the total number of .be domain names went from 40,000 to almost 150,000, due to the changes of the conditions for registration.

3.15.2. Conflicts regarding domain names

Abusive registration of domain names

Unfair trade practices and alternative dispute settlement procedure   Due   3–115
to the liberalisation of the conditions to register .be domain names and the
growing economic value of domain names, an increasing number of domain
names were registered with the consequence of multiplying conflicts
regarding domain names.

In the absence of any specific legislation, Belgian Courts first had to rule
on abusive registration of domain names on the basis of existing laws.
Established jurisprudence sanctioned cybersquatting pursuant to Arts. 23
and/or 93 of the Act on fair trade practices[69] as an act contrary to fair trade
practices. For instance, the owner of a trade name protected by Art.8 of the
Treaty of Paris or the owner of a Benelux or Community trade mark could
sue a person who registered (and *a fortiori* who used) without authorisation
a domain name corresponding to this trade name or trade mark on the basis
that this registration could damage the professional interests of the plaintiff
and was therefore contrary to fair trade practices.

As an alternative to judicial recourses, DNS Belgium developed a fast   3–116
dispute settlement procedure directly inspired from the UDRP (Uniform
domain name Dispute Resolution Policy) procedure organised by ICANN
at the international level.

Article 10 of the Terms and Conditions of domain name registrations
under the .be domain operated by DNS, Version 3.1, of September 20,
2004[70] provides for the rules applying to dispute settlement.

Article 10(b)1 provides that the licensee must submit a dispute to alternative dispute resolution proceedings if a third party (a "Complainant")
asserts to an accredited Dispute Resolution Entity (listed at the website of
DNS Belgium) and proves that: (1) the licensee's domain name is identical
or confusingly similar to a trade mark, a trade name, a social name or
corporation name, a geographical designation, a name of origin, a designation of source, a personal name or name of a geographical entity in which
the Complainant has rights, (2) the licensee has no rights or legitimate
interests in the domain name, and (3) the licensee's domain name has been
registered or is being used in bad faith.

Article 10(b)2 provides for a non exhaustive list of circumstances that
can demonstrate the evidence of such in bad faith registration or use of a
domain name, while Art.10(b)3 lists the circumstances by which the
licensee can demonstrate his rights or legitimate interests to the domain
name. As soon as a request for alternative dispute resolution is filed and the
appropriate fee is paid, the Dispute Resolution Entity must inform DNS

---

[69] Act of July 14, 1991 on fair trade practices and information to, and protection of, consumers, *M.B.*, August 29, 1991.
[70] Available at: *http://www.dns.be/en/home.php?n=51.*

Belgium and the latter must immediately put the domain name involved "on hold" until the end of the proceedings (Art.10(j)).

The remedies available to a Complainant are limited to requiring the cancellation of the domain name registration or the transfer of the domain name to the Complainant (Art.10(e)). Article 10(g) provides that submitting the dispute to the alternative dispute resolution procedure does not prevent the parties from submitting the dispute to a court of competent jurisdiction for independent resolution before, during or after those proceedings.

3–117   **Act on Cybersquatting**   On June 26, 2003, Belgium adopted a new Act on Cybersquatting.[71] This Act aims at protecting intellectual property right holders and other right holders against the abusive registration of domain names by third parties who have no rights in the distinctive signs specified in the Act.

This Act on Cybersquatting does consequently not apply to conflicts between holders of competing rights, for instance conflicts between a trade mark owner and a trade name owner or the holder of a patronymic name. The resolution of this type of conflict will be briefly analysed in another section (see para.3–123).

3–118   The Act on Cybersquatting creates a cease and desist action and allows the President of the court to order the registration of the domain name or the transfer of this domain name to the person he designates.[72] The President of the court may also order the publication of the judgment, as long as this measure contributes to the cessation of the registration or of its effects.[73] The following cumulative conditions must be found for the Act on Cybersquatting to apply[74]:

(1) the registrant of the domain name must be domiciled or established in Belgium (regardless of the type of first level domain) *or* the domain name is registered under the first level domain corresponding to the country code .be;

(2) the plaintiff can assert a legitimate interest in the domain name at issue;

(3) the plaintiff can assert a right on a distinctive sign, such as a trade mark, a geographical indication or designation of origin, a trade name, an original creation, a company name or association name, a patronymic name or the name of a geographical entity[75];

(4) the registrant of the domain name has no right or legitimate interest in said domain name;

---

[71] Act of June 26, 2003 on abusive registration of domain names, *M.B.*, Sept. 9, 2003, p.45225.

[72] Art.6 of the Act on Cybersquatting.

[73] Art.7 of the Act on Cybersquatting.

[74] See Arts. 4 and 5 of the Act on Cybersquatting.

[75] The presence of the word "notably" in Art.4 of the Act indicates that this list of distinctive signs is not exhaustive.

(5) the registrant of the domain name has registered it in order to cause prejudice to a third party or take unfair advantage of it;

(6) the domain name at issue must be identical to, or be similar as to create a likelihood of confusion with, the distinctive signs specified above.

It has been ruled that the registrant of a domain name may have a legitimate interest regarding this domain name when it is used solely for a non-commercial website.[76]

The condition that the registration is made in order to cause prejudice to a third party or take unfair advantage of it does not request the existence of an actual damage. It is sufficient to prove the intention to damage and the fact that the abusively registered domain name is not actually used is not elusive of bad faith.[77]

In order to assess whether the similarity between the domain name and the distinctive sign can create a likelihood of confusion, the court must consider the denominations themselves, the activities exercised under these denominations, and the location where these activities are exercised.[78] The fact that the distinctive sign is written in two words while the domain name is written in one word is not relevant in assessing the identity or similarity of the denominations. The content of the website available under the litigious domain name should also be taken into account.[79] The likelihood of confusion may notably appear from a search of the distinctive sign via search engines such as Google.[80]   **3–119**

Since the provisions of the Act on Cybersquatting are largely based on the works of WIPO that served as guidance for the creation of the UDRP procedure, one can also usefully refer to the jurisprudence of the ICANN as well as of DNS Belgium in order to interpret said provisions.

A typical application of the Act on Cybersquatting is the following: the claimant is active in the travel sector and registered the domain name *www.connections.be*. The defendant registered the domain name *www.conections.be* and was also offering travel services. In the course of the proceedings, the content of the defendant's website changed and referred to an "adult dating site", while the litigious domain name was offered for sale. The Court ruled that the litigious domain name was clearly similar as to create a likelihood of confusion with the claimant's domain name and has been registered in bad faith since it was offered for sale on the

---

[76] Pres. Brussels, May 11, 2004, RABG, 2005, 10, p.948. See also for instance Pres. Comm. Liège, November 8, 2005, available at: *http://www.dns.be/pdf/re20051108.pdf*, where the President of the court rules that the defendant has a legitimate non commercial interest in the domain name *www.gemini.be* and is not acting in order to take unfair advantage of the company name Gemini S.A.

[77] Pres. Civ. Furnes, August 6, 2004, IRDI, 2005, p.506.

[78] Ghent, February 9, 2004, IRDI, 2004, p.235. In this case, both parties were exercising their activities on the internet.

[79] Pres. Civ. Brussels, May 11, 2004, RABG, 2005, p.948.

[80] Pres. Comm. Antwerp, March 30, 2004, IRDI, 2004, p.244.

defendant's website. The President of the court ordered the transfer of the domain name to the claimant.[81]

3–120   Article 11 of the Act recites that this Act does not apply to freedom of speech disputes. It has been argued, notably on the basis of the parliamentary works, that this provision created a defence that could be brought prior to any argument on the merits on the case.[82] If the registrant could prove that he chose the litigious domain name in order to convey an opinion and as a part of the exercise of his freedom of speech, the Act on Cybersquatting will not apply and the claim will be declared inadmissible on this ground.[83] It has, however, been ruled by the President of the Court of Commerce of Ghent that a cease and desist order to use a domain name does not create any limitation to the freedom of speech.[84]

3–121   The cease and desist action is organised as an urgency proceeding (*"comme en référé"*),[85] i.e. it follows the procedural rules of an urgency proceeding but the President of the court rules on the merits of the claim. This action must be brought before the President of the Court of First Instance except when the plaintiff bases its action on a trade mark, a geographical indication or designation of origin, a trade name or a company name. In these cases the action must be brought before the President of the Court of Commerce.[86]

3–122   The Act on Cybersquatting came into force on September 19, 2003. Considering the definition given in the Act of the word "registration", and pursuant to the principle of non-retroactivity of new laws, it has been argued that this Act could not apply to abusive registration made before its entry into force.[87] Some courts have, however, considered that this Act was applicable to disputes arising before September 19, 2003, on the basis that the *effects* of the abusive registration continued after its entry into force.[88]

The Act on Cybersquatting does not prevent the application of other existing legislations, such as, notably, the legal provisions protecting trade marks, trade names and the other distinctive signs mentioned in the Act, as well as legal provisions regarding unfair competition, fair trade practices and information and protection of consumers.[89] Since these laws already offered a protection against cybersquatting prior to the adoption of the Act on Cybersquatting, it has been questioned whether the new Act had any utility. In this regard, the new Act presents two advantages: the cease and desist action can be launched against any individual and not only against

---

[81] Pres. Civ. Brussels, January 18, 2006, available at: *http://www.dns.be/pdf/re20060118.pdf*.

[82] A. Cruquenaire, "La loi du 26 juin 2003 relative à l'enregistrement abusif des noms de domaine: et la montagne accoucha d'une souris …", *J.T.*, 2004, p.549.

[83] An example of this type of dispute is the famous "jeboycottedanone" case.

[84] Pres. Comm. Ghent, September 12, 2005, TGR, 2005, p.345.

[85] Art.8 of the Act on Cybersquatting.

[86] See Arts. 9 and 10 of the Act on Cybersquatting modifying the Belgian Code for civil procedure.

[87] A. Cruquenaire, *ibid*, p.547.

[88] Ghent, February 9, 2004, *ibid*; Pres. Comm. Antwerp, March 30, 2004, *ibid*.

[89] Art.3 of the Act on Cybersquatting.

sellers as is the case for the provisions concerning fair trade practices; and the plaintiff can claim the transfer of the domain name abusively registered.

Conflicts between holders of competing rights

The use of a domain name can be perceived by the public either as the use of **3–123** a trade name or as the use of a trade mark. It will be perceived as a trade name if the domain name is used to distinguish the company, for instance to give information on that company and its activities.[90] The domain name may instead be perceived as a trade mark when the website itself is a product or a service or when the domain name corresponds to the trade mark under which the products or services are put on the market.[91]

The conflicts between domain names and trade marks or trade names will consequently be dealt with differently according to the legal qualification that is given to the domain name in view of the circumstances. Considering this issue from the hypothesis that the domain name is perceived as a trade name, the following situations may occur.

(a) The trade mark is registered before the use of the domain name as a trade name.[92] The owner of a Benelux trade mark will be able to successfully bring a trade mark infringement action against the registrant of the domain name pursuant to Art.2.20(1)(d) of the new Benelux Convention on Intellectual Property[93] (former Art.13(A1d) of the Benelux Trade Mark Act), provided that the use by the registrant is made without due cause and takes unfair advantage of, or is detrimental to, the distinctive character or the repute of the mark.[94] The trade mark must consequently have a certain reputation in order for its owner to claim protection under this provision.

As a defense, the registrant of the domain name may invoke a due cause for the use of the sign alleged of infringement. In a decision of March 9, 2005, for instance, the owner of a prior trade mark "SWIFT" successfully opposed the use of the signs "SWIFT", "SWIFTPAY" and "Swiftpay.com" as trade names and domain names by defendant pursuant to former Art.13(A1d) of the Benelux Trade Mark Act. It has been ruled that taking into account the reputation of the "SWIFT" trade mark, it was certain that the defendant, who was active in the same commercial sector, was

---

[90] Pres. Comm. Malines, March 6, 2001, *Annuaires Pratiques du Commerce & Concurrence*, 2001, p.591; Pres. Comm. Malines, June 26, 2001, *Annuaires Pratiques du Commerce & Concurrence*, 2001, p.643.

[91] P. Maeyaert, "Conflits entre marques, dénominations sociales, noms commerciaux et noms de domaine", RIC, 2002, p.28.

[92] For the purpose of this presentation, it is assumed that the trade name has not been used otherwise than as incorporated to the domain name prior to the use of this domain name.

[93] Benelux Convention on Intellectual Property (trade marks and designs) of February 25, 2005, approved in Belgium by the Act of March 22, 2006.

[94] A corresponding provision is not provided for in Regulation 40/94 of December 20, 1993 on the Community trade mark.

taking unfair advantage of the distinctive character of the trade mark.[95]

(b) The use of the domain name as a trade name predates the registration of the trade mark. The registrant of the domain name perceived as a trade name can oppose the use of an identical or similar trade mark pursuant to the Act on Fair Trade Practices (Art.93). Besides, the owner of a Benelux trade mark cannot oppose to the use, in the course of trade, of an identical or similar domain name that predates the trade mark and that has only a local scope of protection, to the extent that the trade name (or the domain name used as a trade name) is protected in Belgium pursuant to Art.8 of the Paris Convention, and within the limits of the geographical scope of this protection.[96] The registrant of the domain name could also benefit from some protection against a subsequent Community trade mark.[97]

3.16 NON-UNITED KINGDOM DOMAIN NAMES— CANADA

3.16.1 Domain name registration

3–124　Since December 1, 2000, the Canadian .ca domain name registry has been operated by the Canadian Internet Registry Authority (CIRA). CIRA is a not-for-profit registry. CIRA's mandate is to provide professional registry services and to preserve the .ca domain as a Canadian resource that is operated for and managed by Canadians for Canadians. CIRA operates the .ca domain name registry, maintains the .ca database, handles complaints by Registrants about Registrars and is charged with implementing and administering a domain name dispute resolution service.

History

3–125　Before 2000, the .ca domain was administered by the CA Domain Committee, established at the University of British Columbia by John Demco, CA Registrar. The CA Domain Committee was comprised of 30 members representing various internet organisations, service providers, universities

---

[95] Pres. Comm. Nivelles, March 9, 2005, IRDI, 2005, p.322.

[96] Art.2.23–2 of the Benelux Convention on Intellectual Property, formerly Art.13A8 of the Benelux Trade Mark Act.

[97] Art.8.4 of Regulation 40/94 provides for instance that the owner of a sign used in the course of trade and of more than mere local significance can oppose to the registration of a community trade mark.

and defence establishments.[98] The .ca domain was registered with InterNIC by CDNnet in May, 1987.[99] It was based on a combination of the Domain Name System (DNS) framework and the CCITT X.500 directory service standard.

Previously, .ca domains were distributed pursuant to a policy which attempted to structure Canada's domain name space according to Canadian federal and provincial political jurisdictions. Canadian subdomain names frequently read as follows: "entity.city.province.ca."[1] Applications for subdomain names at the national level ("entity.ca") were required to include documentation showing that the entity was federally incorporated or maintained business offices in more than one province or territory (international offices were not considered). A business could also avoid being restricted to use of a provincial subdomain if it owned a federally registered trade mark.[2] This restrictive policy requiring the use of sub-domains is no longer mandatory.

Formerly, it was CA Domain's policy to limit individuals and organisations to a single domain name, regardless of the number of trade marks that the organisation owned or the number of business divisions the organisation may have had.

Entitlement

CIRA has implemented rules and procedures for new domain name registrations. Now, in order to be eligible to obtain a .ca domain name, the applicant must comply with CIRA's "Canadian Presence Requirements".   3–126

CIRA's Canadian Presence Requirements provide that the applicant must be any of:

(a) a Canadian citizen;

(b) a permanent resident of Canada;

(c) a legal representative of (a) or (b);

(d) a corporation under the laws of Canada or any province or territory of Canada;

(e) a trust established and subsisting under the laws of a province or territory of Canada, more than 66 and 2/3 percent of whose trustees meet one of the conditions set out in paragraphs (a) to (d) above;

(f) a partnership, more than 66 and 2/3 percent of whose partners meet one of the conditions set out in paragraphs (a) to (e) above, which is registered as a partnership under the laws of any province or territory of Canada;

---

[98] CA Domain Committee, *ftp.cdnnet.ca/ca-domain/committee-members*, April 4, 1997.

[99] The Ca Domain: An Introduction, *ftp.cdnnet.ca/ca-domain/introduction*, July 1, 1994. InterNIC, Network Solutions, Inc is a US corporation which functions as a central domain name registry under contract with the National Science Foundation (NSF).

[1] *Ibid.* CCITT is an international standards organisation similar to ISO.

[2] *Ibid.*

(g) an association (an unincorporated organisation, association or club):

  (i) at least 80 per cent of those members:

    (1) are ordinarily resident in Canada (if such members are individuals); or
    (2) meet one of the conditions set out in paragraphs (a) to (f) above (if such members are not individuals); and

  (ii) and at least 80 per cent of whose directors, officers, employees, managers, administrators or other representatives are ordinarily resident in Canada;

(h) a trade union which is recognised by a labour board under the laws of Canada or any province or territory of Canada and which has its head office in Canada;

(i) a political party registered under a relevant electoral law of Canada or any province or territory of Canada;

(j) an educational institution (a university or college which is located in Canada and which is authorised or recognised as a university or college under an Act of the legislature of a province or territory of Canada; or a college, post-secondary school, vocational school, secondary school, pre-school or other school or educational institution which is located in Canada and which is recognised by the educational authorities of a province or territory of Canada or licensed under or maintained by an Act of Parliament of Canada or of the legislature of a province or territory of Canada;

(k) a library, archive or museum that:

  (i) is located in Canada; and
  (ii) is not established or conducted for profit or does not form part of, or is not administered or directly or indirectly controlled by, a body that is established or conducted for profit, which is held and maintained a collection of documents and other materials that is open to the public or to researchers;

(l) a hospital which is located in Canada and which is licensed, authorised or approved to operate as a hospital under an Act of the legislature of a province or territory of Canada;

(m) Her Majesty Queen Elizabeth the Second and her successors;

(n) an Indian band and any group of Indian bands;

(o) Aboriginal Peoples (Any Inuit, First Nation, Metis or other people indigenous to Canada, any individual belonging to any Inuit, First Nation, Metis or other people indigenous to Canada and any collectivity of such Aboriginal peoples;

(p) Her Majesty the Queen in right of Canada, a province or a territory; an agent of Her Majesty the Queen in right of Canada, of a province or of a territory; a federal, provincial or territorial Crown corporation, government agency or government entity; or a regional, municipal or local area government;

(q) a person which does not meet any of the foregoing conditions, but which is the owner of a trade mark which is the subject of a registration under the Trade-marks Act (Canada) R.S.C. 1985, c.T–13 as amended from time to time, but in this case such permission is limited to an application to register a .ca domain name consisting of or including the exact word component of that registered trade mark; or

(r) a person which does not meet any of the foregoing conditions, but which is a Person intended to be protected by subs.9(1) of the Trade-Marks Act (Canada) [the owners of certain official marks] at whose request the Registrar of Trade-marks has published notice of adoption of any badge, crest, emblem, official mark or other mark pursuant to subs.9(1), but in this case such permission is limited to an application to register a .ca domain name consisting of or including the exact word component of such badge, crest, emblem, official mark or other mark in respect of which such Person requested publications.

Registration Procedure

Registration requests are dealt with on a first-come first-served basis. CIRA **3–127** offers registration services through approved Registrars. The Applicant must select a CIRA Certified Registrar who will act on its behalf in submitting a Registration Request for the registration of a domain name to CIRA. A domain name may be registered for a period of one to ten years.

Domain names are not case sensitive. The domain name must be between two and 50 characters long. CIRA maintains a registry of reserved domain names that are not available for registration (including country code TLDs, and gTLDs, to prevent registration of Asomething.com.ca@, etc.), names that might indicate an association with a municipality (such as .city.ca, .ville.ca), and major Canadian municipalities and landmarks.

A domain name will not be registered if the domain name is an exact match in all respects to a previously registered .ca domain name which is registered in the name of another person at any level, whether second, third or fourth, unless such other person consents in writing to the registration. For example, if abc.on.ca (third level) is registered, another person cannot obtain a Registration for abc.on.ca, abc.ca (second level) or abc.ottawa. on.ca (fourth level) without the written consent of the registrant of abc.on.ca. Third or fourth level domain names may be "upgraded" to second level names only with the consent of others who own domain names having the same prefix.

The obligation is on the Applicant to ensure that it has the right to use the domain name which is the subject of the Registration Request and that the registration or use of the domain name does not violate any third party intellectual property rights or other rights, does not defame any person and does not contravene any applicable laws including Canadian federal, provincial and territorial human rights legislation and the Criminal Code.

The Canadian Intellectual Property Office is now accepting registration of domain names as trade marks. To date, all applicants have been forced to disclaim the top level domain name suffix.

3.16.2 Domain name disputes

CIRA's Dispute Resolution Policy

3–128 The CIRA Domain Name Dispute Resolution Policy (CDRP) came into effect on November 29, 2001. The CDRP applies to all .ca domains including those first entered in the predecessor registry operated by the University of British Columbia. The purpose of the CDRP is to provide a forum in which cases of bad faith registration can be dealt with relatively inexpensively and quickly. The CDRP is not intended to apply to disputes between parties who have registered domain names in good faith and based on legitimate interests.

Specifically, under the CDRP a complainant satisfying Canadian Presence Requirements must show: (a) the registrant's .ca domain name is confusingly similar to a mark in which the complainant has rights prior to the date of registration of the domain name and continues to have such rights; (b) the registrant has no legitimate interest in the domain name; and (c) the registrant has registered the domain name in bad faith.

Each of the terms "confusingly similar", "mark", "rights", "legitimate interest" and "bad faith" are more particularly explained in the policy. A domain name is "confusingly similar" to a mark if the domain name so resembles the mark in appearance, sound or the ideas suggested as to be likely to be mistaken for the mark.

The registrant has a "legitimate interest" in the domain name if, prior to the complaint, the domain name was : (1) a mark used by the registrant; (2) clearly descriptive; (3) generic; (4) used non-commercially; (5) part of the registrant's name; or (6) the geographical location of the registrant's non-commercial activity.

The CDRP provides that there is "bad faith" if and only if the registrant obtained the domain name (1) primarily for the purpose of selling, renting, licensing or otherwise transferring the registration to the complainant or a competitor of the complainant for profit; (2) in order to prevent the complainant from registering its mark as a domain name provided that the registrant engages in a pattern of this type of conduct; or (3) primarily for the purpose of disrupting the business of the complainant provided that the registrant is a competitor.

3–129 The CDRP refers to bad faith registration, whereas the UDRP refers to bad faith registration or use. Some commentators have observed that this choice of language in the CDRP leaves open the question of whether it is permissible for an individual to register a domain name solely to prevent the holder of a mark from using it as a .ca domain.[3]

---

[3] Teresa Scassa and Michael Deturbide, *Electronic Commerce and Internet Law in Canada* (Toronto: CCH Canadian, 2004) at 200.

Once a complaint is filed, no changes can be made to the registration of the domain name. The remedies available are cancellation or transfer of the registration. The CDRP does not exclude other legal remedies—either party can at any time submit the dispute to a judicial or administrative proceeding, arbitration, mediation or any other procedure for independent resolution. Courts are not required to give CDRP panel decisions any weight at all.[4]

The accompanying CIRA Domain Name Dispute Resolution Rules (Rules) address the procedural issues involved in resolving a complaint under the CDRP. In a significant departure from the ICANN UDRP, the Rules require the complainant to pay for a three-member panel unless the registrant fails to respond in which case a less costly, one-member panel may be requested.

Since June 2002, two dispute resolution providers have been appointed to 3–130 administer CDRP proceedings. Over 40 cases have been decided by panellists on complaints initiated under the CDRP. Significant cases are set out below.

- *Red Robin Inc. v Greg Tieu* where the single panellist concluded that there was confusing similarity in that the complainant's trade name was identical to the domain name redrobin.ca.[5]
- *Browne & Co. Ltd. v Bluebird Industries* where the single panellist found the domain name browneco.ca had a great resemblance to the trade name such that there was confusing similarity.[6]
- *Government of Canada v David Bedford* which dealt with the domain names canadiancustoms.ca, ecgc.ca, governmentofcanada. ca, and so on. The three-member panel concluded that the government had rights in its official marks, and adopted a test of resemblance based upon first impression and imperfect recollection to support its finding of confusing similarity (with the exception of canadiancustoms.ca). The CDRP panel said that UDRP decisions were of little or no assistance in interpreting "confusingly similar" because the UDRP refers to marks that are "identical or confusingly similar." Further, the panel noted that the term echoes wording used in ss.9(1) and 6(5)(e) of the Trade-marks Act, but other aspects of s.6(5)(a)–(d) are absent, suggesting that the threshold for a finding of "confusingly similar" is much lower than the threshold for a finding of confusion for registered trade marks.[7]
- *Air Products Canada Ltd. v Index Quebec Inc.* in which the three-member panel decided that the term "air products" was insufficiently distinctive to find the registrant's domain name airproducts.ca "confusingly similar".[8]

---

[4] *Ibid.* at 209.
[5] 22 C.P.R. (4th) 204 (Canadian Internet Registration Authority, October 7, 2002).
[6] 22 C.P.R. (4th) 208 (Canadian Internet Registration Authority, October 22, 2002).
[7] 27 C.P.R. (4th) 522 (Canadian Internet Registration Authority, May 27, 2003).
[8] 30 C.P.R. (4th) 212 (Canadian Internet Registration Authority, April 15, 2003).

Traditional Legal Remedies

3–131   While a body of Canadian case law on domain name disputes is slowly developing, the law of trade marks and unfair competition remains generally applicable and of particular relevance in these matters. In Canada, a trade mark is used in association with services when the trade mark is used in advertising the service or displayed during the performance of the service. It is used in association with wares if it is marked on the wares or otherwise associated with the ware at the time of transfer in the property or possession of the ware, in the normal course of trade.[9] If the trade mark is not registered, then a common law action of passing off would apply and a determination would be made as to whether customers or consumers would be confused by a defendant's use of its trade mark.

The owner of a registered trade mark has the exclusive right to use the mark in relation to the goods and services for which the mark is registered.[10] Use of a confusingly similar trade mark constitutes an infringement of the trade mark owner's exclusive right.[11] The owner of a registered trade mark can also prevent use of the trade mark which results in the depreciation of the value of the goodwill associated with the registered mark.[12]

In order to establish infringement, or depreciation of the goodwill in a registered mark, a plaintiff must show that the offending mark was used in relation to the provision of goods or services in Canada. Services are often provided on the internet in conjunction with the display of trade marks and trade names. If the site provides services to, and is regularly accessed by, customers in Canada, in the normal course of trade, then the mark would be considered to be in use in Canada.[13] A mark would be used in respect of a transaction on the internet in respect of wares if the mark is displayed at the time of transfer of the property or possession of the goods (such as an electronic text). Software, documents, videos, music and other such products transferred over the internet in association with a trade mark would likely constitute use of the trade mark.[14]

3–132   In order for a trade mark to be registered in Canada, it must either be in actual use in Canada, or the registrant must intend to use the trade mark in Canada or it must be used and registered abroad, in the country of origin of the applicant.

If the trade mark is not registered, rights can be asserted under the common law tort of passing off. In order to sustain an action, the plaintiff has to demonstrate the existence of a requisite level of goodwill in the minds of the public, and that a misrepresentation was made by the defen-

---

[9] Canadian Trade Marks Act, RSC c.T.13, s.4.
[10] Trade-marks Act, s.19.
[11] Trade-marks Act, s.20.
[12] *Ibid.*, s.22.
[13] *Riches, McKenzie & Herbert v Source Telecomputing Corp.* (1992), 46 C.P.R. (3d) 563 (TMBd). Discussed by Andrea Rush in "Internet Domain Name Protection: A Canadian Perspective" (1996), 11 I.P.J. 1.
[14] *BMB Compuscience Canada Ltd v Bramalea Ltd* (1989), 22 C.P.R. (3d) 561 (FCTC). See discussion in *Internet Study*, pp.112, 113.

dant to the public resulting in actual or potential damage to the plaintiff.[15]

Canadian courts have resolved claims to domain names in both the gTLDs as well as the .ca domain. Significant Canadian cases on domain name disputes are set out below.

Interlocutory Relief

Typically, domain name claimants will seek an interlocutory injunction preventing the domain name registrant from using the domain name pending trial. Interlocutory relief has, generally, been difficult to obtain in Canadian domain name disputes.

3–133

No infringement established:

- In *PEINET Inc. v O'Brien*[16] the plaintiff, the owner of the peinet.pe.ca domain name, sued a former employee who had obtained the domain name pei.net and applied for an interlocutory injunction to prevent the use of the domain name. The application was dismissed, the plaintiff having failed to establish infringement or passing off. In passing, the court remarked that the plaintiff had not explained the internet very well.

No irreparable harm proven:

- In *ITV Technologies Inc. v WIC Television Ltd*[17] the Federal Court of Canada first granted an interim injunction and then dismissed an interlocutory injunction against ITV Technologies.[18] ITV Technologies was trying to expunge WIC's trade mark registrations for the mark "ITV" in order to undermine WIC's case before NSI against ITV Technologies over the domain name itv.net. WIC had used ITV as a trade mark since 1974 for television broadcasting and program production. WIC had also registered itv.ca as a domain name. ITV Technologies was "net-casting" from its website since late 1995. ITV Technologies posted a disclaimer on its website stating "ITV.net has no affiliation with CITV" and provided a link to the WIC site. In dismissing WIC's application for an interlocutory injunction, the court was not satisfied that irreparable harm would be caused.
- Irreparable harm was not made out in *Toronto.com v Sinclair (c.o.b. Friendship Enterprises)*[19] and toronto2.com was not prevented from using its domain name pending trial.

---

[15] *Ibid.*, at p.9.
[16] (1995), 61 C.P.R. (3d) 334 (P.E.I.S.C.).
[17] (1997), 77 C.P.R. (3d) 486 (F.C.T.D.).
[18] (1997), 77 C.P.R. (3d) 495 (F.C.T.D.).
[19] (2000), 6 C.P.R. (4th) 487 (F.C.T.D.).

Permanent Relief

3–134   In *Law Society of British Columbia v Canada Domain Name Exchange Corp.*,[20] the Law Society sought to prevent the registrant of lawsocietyofbc.ca and lsbc.ca from using or disposing of the domains. The court found that the domain names were being used to attract members of the public to visit the sites, which offered adult content, and to generate income at the expense of the Society's goodwill. The court ruled that the three elements of passing off had been established (goodwill, misrepresentation, and damage), and granted the Law Society a permanent injunction and damages.

The ease with which domain names can be transferred to parties beyond the jurisdiction of the Canadian courts has been a factor taken into consideration when injunctions have been granted:

- In *Innersense International Inc. v Manegre*[21] an Alberta Court granted an ex parte interim injunction restraining the defendants from directly or indirectly selling or transferring registration of the domain name innersense.com. Apparently, one of the defendants, a former employee, was responsible for registering the domain name with NSI. The domain name registration expired and the domain name was registered by the second defendant, the brother of the former employee. The defendants then offered the domain name for sale in the press. Applying the traditional test of (1) serious issue, (2) irreparable harm, and (3) balance of convenience, in determining whether or not to grant the injunction, the Court found that "problems with the possibly simple and quick transferability and marketability of this internet domain site and with respect to internet domain sites generally literally to any point in the world, lead me to believe that the balance of convenience or inconvenience is best served by granting the Application."
- In *Itravel2000.com Inc. (c.o.b. Itravel) v Fagan*[22] the Court granted an interlocutory injunction which prevented the defendant from transferring the domain name itravel.ca pending trial (an order analogous to a *Mareva* injunction where assets are ordered not to be removed from the jurisdiction pending the trial). Although the defendant was an admitted cybersquatter, of particular interest in this case was the fact that there were numerous potential legitimate claimants to the domain name. Presumably, the plaintiff could not recover the domain name from one of these third parties and so used the interlocutory injunction to make sure that it was first in line for the domain name.

However, in *Molson Breweries v Kuettner*[23] the Court would not

---

[20] [2004] B.C.J. No. 1692 (B.C.C.A.).
[21] (2000), 47 C.P.R. (4th) 149 (Alta Q.B.).
[22] [2001] O.J. No. 943 (Ont. S.C.J.).
[23] (1999), 3 C.P.R. (4th) 479 (F.C.T.D.).

accept deposit of the domain name into Court to ensure its "safe-keeping" pending trial.

If these *Mareva*-like orders become commonplace, then it will be imperative to file suit as early as possible to prevent other legitimate claimants to the domain name in question from gaining an advantage.

- In *Saskatoon Star Phoenix Group Inc. v Norton*[24] the plaintiff was the publisher of *"The Star Phoenix"*, a daily newspaper, in Saskatchewan. The plaintiff also operated a website at *thestarphoenix.com* which displayed news stories and banner ads. The defendant registered the domain name saskatoonstarphoenix.com and displayed the same material as found on the plaintiff's site except that the defendant replaced the plaintiff's banner ads with its own. The Court found that the defendant was in the business of registering domain names. One of the defendant's other websites had a "courtesy link" to *"The Star Phoenix"* which took a browser to the defendant's website.

  The plaintiff commenced an action in passing off. The plaintiff had evidence, in the form of emails, of browsers actually being confused by the defendant's site. The plaintiff was granted an interlocutory injunction. The defendant did not defend the passing off action, was noted in default, and the court ordered $5,000.00 in damages (despite no actual loss being shown), a permanent injunction, transfer of the domain name registrations and costs against the defendant. The Court considered, but refused to award punitive damages because domain name actions were relatively new. The Court did find that, in the future, punitive damages could be awarded on the facts of this case.

- In *Vulcan Northwest Inc. et al. v Vulcan Ventures Corp.*[25] the plaintiffs, two venture capital firms affiliated with Paul Allen, billionaire and former partner of Bill Gates, brought a passing off action against a penny stock mining exploration company that traded on the CDNX. The plaintiffs applied for an interlocutory injunction restraining the defendant from identifying itself as Vulcan Ventures. The plaintiff had applied for, but not yet registered the trade mark VULCAN VENTURES.

  In granting the interlocutory injunction, the Court found that: "[t]he potential for confusion is obvious and much of it may never come to the plaintiffs' attention thus making the damages unknown and irreparable." (at 100) The Court specifically found that the defendant "has an investor internet site, Stockhouse.com" that contained links to news about the plaintiffs. The affiliation between Stockhouse.com and the defendant was unclear. This case seems to have lowered the threshold for an interlocutory injunction.

---

[24] (2001), 12 C.P.R. (4th) 4 (Sask. Q.B.).
[25] (2001), 12 C.P.R. (4th) 95 (F.C.T.D.).

"Use" of a trade mark by internet access in Canada

3–135   The situation is relatively straightforward where the trade mark user's website is based in Canada.[26] An interlocutory injunction was granted in *Bell Actimedia Inc. v Puzo (Communications Globe Tête)* prohibiting the use of lespagesjaunes.com or any other domain name confusingly similar with it. The plaintiff, Bell Actimedia, is the company that produces and distributes trade and telephone directories in Canada. Bell Actimedia also provides business listings on the internet through the domain names yellowpages.ca, pagesjaunes.ca, canadayellowpages.com and pagesjaunes canada.com. Bell has owned registered trade marks for YELLOW PAGES and PAGES JAUNES for over 50 years.

The defendant, Communications Globe Tête registered the domain name lespagesjaunes.com and used its site to market a business directory of the French-speaking world. Communications Globe Tête claimed that Bell's trade marks only protected against use of a confusingly similar name in Canada and that Communications Globe Tête was entitled to use their domain name in any country other than Canada despite the fact that the impugned website was hosted in Montreal, Canada. Unfortunately, the court did not take the opportunity to address the territorial argument in granting the injunction.

British Columbia Automobile Association v Office and Professional Employees' International Union, Local 378[27] was an action for passing off, trade mark infringement and copyright infringement in relation to internet websites. The plaintiff, British Columbia Automobile Association (BCAA) claimed that the defendant, Office and Professional Employees' International Union, Local 378 (the "Union"), a union representing 170 office employees of BCAA, copied design elements and trade marks from BCAA's website and posted those copies on the Union's own website. BCAA also complained that the Union was guilty of passing off and had depreciated the goodwill of BCAA's trade marks by using them in domain names and metatags.

3–136   In March of 1999, the Union registered the domain names bcaaonstrike. com and picketline.com and later bcaabacktowork.com. All three of the Union's domain names took a browser to the Union's website. BCAA alleged that the Union copied fundamental design elements from the BCAA website. BCAA sent the Union a cease and desist letter. In response, the Union modified certain portions of their website and the metatags coded into their website. However, the Union continued to reproduce a substantial part of the BCAA website metatags.

Although BCAA alleged that the Union's unamended site infringed BCAA's copyright in its own website, BCAA did not advance that claim in respect of the amended site. The causes of action advanced against the amended site were passing off and depreciation of goodwill under s.22 of

---

[26] (1999), 2 C.P.R. (4th) 289 (F.C.T.D.).
[27] (2001), 10 C.P.R. (4th) 423 (B.C.S.C.).

the Trade-marks Act. BCAA alleged that use of the domain names bcaaonstrike.com and bcaabacktowork.com and the use of BCAA and other BCAA trade marks in metatags constituted passing off because the Union was intercepting people looking for the BCAA website. It is important to note that by October of 1999, and well in advance of trial, the Union had removed the metatags which included BCAA trade marks from its website and had also inserted commas between the words "British Columbia Automobile Association".

The Court considered the law of passing off as well as the developing body of British, American and Canadian law on passing off through the use of domain names and metatags.

The Court took notice of the fact that the Union was not making a commercial use of the website and was using BCAA's trade marks in connection with a labour relations dispute. The Court found that the Union's current website was not passing itself off for the BCAA website because there was no confusion or possibility of confusion in the mind of an internet user that the Union's website was associated with or belonged to BCAA.

The Court based this conclusion on the following facts: (1) the Union's **3–137** domain name was not identical to BCAA's trade marks; (2) the Union is not using metatags identical to BCAA's trade marks; (3) the Union's website is not competing commercially with BCAA; (4) the use of similar metatags or domain names is of less significance in a labour relations or consumer criticism situation, partly because there is less likelihood of confusion; and (5) even though the incorporation of the acronym BCAA into the Union's domain name was intentional, it is not a misrepresentation as long as the Union doesn't represent that its website belongs to, or is associated with, BCAA.

The Court found that in the context of a labour dispute, there was a reasonable balance to be struck between intellectual property rights and freedom of expression. The Court also found that an earlier version of the Union's website was inherently confusing and that Union was guilty of passing off based on the earlier version of the website. The Court refused to grant an injunction or to order the Union to deliver up the domain names which incorporated the BCAA trade mark.

The Court also found that the Union was not making a commercial use of BCAA's marks, they were only providing information and, therefore, the Union was not "using" BCAA's marks as required for the purposes of s.22 of the Trade Marks Act (which defines "use" as "use in the normal course of trade").

A similar finding was made of "non-commercial use" in *Bell ExpressVu Limited Partnership v Tedmonds & Co. Inc.*[28] where the Court refused to grant summary judgment enjoining the defendant from using the domain name expressvu.org on the basis that there was no evidence that the defendant was making a "commercial use" of the plaintiff's trade mark.

---

[28] [2001] O.J. No. 1558 (Ont. S.C.J.).

The defendant was allegedly selling US satellite decoding technology in Canada. The plaintiff held the registered trade mark EXPRESSVU and had registered the domain name expressvu.com. The defendant was using expressvu.org to post information relating to the legal action. Of significant interest for future disputes, the Court found authority for its reasons in an administrative decision issued under the UDRP implicitly recognising the value of these decisions as precedent.

Foreign websites "Using" trade marks in Canada

3–138 Where a foreign website "purposely targets" Canadian customers, Canadian courts may consider the Canadian website to be using trade marks in Canada. The *Tele-Direct (Publications) Inc. v Klimchuk*[29] case suggests that the Canadian Federal Court considers trade mark rights to be infringed in Canada (and therefore a trade mark to have been used in Canada) when an American website purposely targets Canada with the use of trade marks registered in Canada.

In *Tele-Direct*, the court found that the American defendants had knowingly used Tele-Direct's registered Canadian trade marks YELLOW PAGES and/or Walking Fingers design trade marks on their internet site located in the US and were purposely attempting to find customers in Canada. While use of the trade marks in the US was permissible (the marks had become generic there), the court found that the American companies were attempting to circumvent Canadian trade mark law by using the plaintiff's registered trade marks in Canada.

3–139 On the other hand, where a foreign website is passive, it appears the court will not assert jurisdiction over its operators. In *Canadian Kennel Club v Continental Kennel Club*[30] the Federal Court indicated that it would not assert jurisdiction over a US website that was not actively soliciting customers from Canada.

An apparent "trans-national border order" was granted by the Federal Court of Canada in *Canada Post v Sunview Management Group*[31] Sunview, an American corporation with registered offices in New York registered the domain name mailposte.com with NSI in the US. Canada Post is the owner of several Canadian registered trade marks and official marks, including MAIL POSTE & Design and POSTE MAIL & Design.

On October 19, 1998, Canada Post obtained an interim and interlocutory injunction against Sunview's use of the mark. This injunction was made permanent on January 11, 1999. The order prohibited Sunview from using the words MAIL POSTE or any other words likely to be confusing therewith in connection with its website or domain name.

Two aspects of the judgment are interesting. First, the court ordered that the original domain name declaration be deposited with the Canadian court. Second, the court directed that the domain name be transferred,

---

[29] (1997), 77 C.P.R. (3d) 23 (F.C.T.D.).
[30] (1997), 77 C.P.R. (3d) 470 (F.C.T.D.).
[31] (unreported) (Court No. T–1800–98) (F.C.T.D.) (per Dube J., January 11, 1999).

conveyed or assigned to Canada Post. It is somewhat surprising to see the Federal Court of Canada granting an order such as this, particularly where the Federal Court does not have the means to ensure compliance with NSI, the American based registry. Nevertheless, the order was enforced and Canada Post now owns the domain name.

3.17 NON-UNITED KINGDOM DOMAIN NAMES— CHINA

3.17.1 Registration

The registration of domain names in China is divided into three separate areas. The Ministry of Information Industry (MII) is responsible for the administration of Chinese domain names including the formulation of regulations and policies concerning the administration of domain names and supervision of the domain name registry and registrars in China. China's sole domain name registry, the China Internet Network Information Center (CNNIC) is responsible for maintaining the central database of .cn domain names, researching relevant technical and policy issues and providing domain name dispute resolution services. Actual registration services are provided by a number of accredited domestic domain name registrars that have been certified by the CNNIC. **3–140**

An applicant for a Chinese domain name must sign a registration agreement or file forms on-line or by email with the registrar of his choice, agreeing to submit accurate and complete registration information and comply with the various rules and regulations relating to the system of China internet domain names including the China Internet Domain Name Regulations and the CNNIC Domain Name Dispute Resolution Policy. The system for registering domain names in China is on a "first-come, first-served" basis.

It is possible to register domain names under the country code top level domain .cn or under two different categories of second level domains, namely domain names denoting the applicant's organisation or regional domain names. Domain names for organisations include .com.cn, .edu.cn, .gov.cn, .net.cn, .org.cn and .ac.cn (for scientific research institutions). There are 34 regional domain names which represent provinces and districts directly under the central government, such as .bj for Beijing and .sh for Shanghai. It is also possible for both national and overseas applicants to register internet domain names completely in Chinese characters. Organisations applying for .gov.cn or .edu.cn domain names, for example, must submit evidence of their status as a governmental or educational institution. Individuals cannot currently apply for .cn, .com.cn or .net.cn domain names.

There are a number of restrictions on the types of domain names that can be registered, including a prohibition against registering domain names that threaten national security, disturb public order, infringe other people's legal rights or interests, instigate crime or encourage pornography, obscenity, gambling or violence.

Term & Fees

3–141   Domain names can be registered for an initial period of one year and are renewable annually thereafter. The fee for registering a domain name varies according to the registrar used.

Transfer

3–142   A domain name can be transferred or cancelled by submitting to the registrar of the domain name an application form which either bears a company seal or has been duly notarised.

A domain name cannot be transferred in the following circumstances:

(1) it is less than 15 days since the domain name was registered;
(2) there are less than 15 days until the expiry date of the domain name;
(3) fees for the domain name are overdue;
(4) there is a dispute over the identity of the domain name holder;
(5) during adjudication, arbitration and dispute resolution proceedings.

3.17.2 Domain name disputes

Arbitration

3–143   The CNNIC has appointed two neutral domain name dispute resolution service providers—the China International Economic Trade Arbitration Center (CIETAC) and the Hong Kong International Arbitration Center (HKIAC). These two institutions have formally accepted .cn and Chinese language domain name disputes since September 30, 2002. Such disputes are governed by the CNNIC Domain Name Dispute Resolution Policy (CNDRP) issued by the CNNIC in September 2002.

As well as being appointed by the CNNIC to resolve .cn disputes, CIE-TAC represents the Beijing Office of the Asian Domain Name Dispute Resolution Center (ADNDRC), which is one of the four domain name dispute resolution providers approved by the Internet Corporation for the Assignment of Names and Numbers (ICANN). In this capacity CIETAC provides domain name dispute resolution services in respect of top level domain names such as .com, .org and .net. Such disputes are governed by the Uniform Domain Name Policy (UDRP) issued by ICANN on August 26, 1999.

Any person or company is entitled to commence a domain name dispute and the parties are required to submit to mandatory arbitration. The proceedings are based only on the documents provided by the parties with an *inter partes* hearing occurring only in exceptional cases.

The CNDRP requires a complainant to prove all three of the following elements:

(i)   the disputed domain name is identical with or confusingly similar to the Complainant's name or mark in which the Complainant has civil rights or interests;

(ii) the disputed domain name holder has no rights or legitimate interest in respect of the domain name or major part of the domain name;

(iii) the disputed domain name holder has registered or is using the domain name in bad faith.

It should be noted that the third element requires registration *or* use of the domain name in bad faith. Under the UDRP, the requirement is for the disputed domain name to be both registered in bad faith *and* used in bad faith. It is unclear whether CIETAC would apply the strict wording of the CNDRP as opposed to the UDRP with the result that there is a lower burden of proof upon the complainant in a Chinese domain name dispute. There do not appear to have been any cases specifically discussing this issue to date.

3–144

A .cn administrative proceeding should normally take less than 60 days from the date the complaint is filed until the parties and the relevant registrar are notified of the decision of the panel conducting the proceedings. The language of the proceedings will be Chinese, unless otherwise agreed by the parties or determined by the panel conducting the proceedings.

On March 17, 2006, the Measures of the China Internet Network Information Center for Resolving Disputes Regarding Domain Names (the "Measures") came into force, making a number of amendments to the CNDRP.

The Measures set out the requirements for proving that a domain name has been registered in bad faith, including the registration or acquisition of the domain name "for the purpose of selling, leasing or transferring the domain name to the complainant who is the owner of civil rights and interests relating to the domain name or to a competitor of the complainant to obtain unjustified benefits". The addition of the requirement that the sale etc. of the domain name must be *to the complainant or its competitor* has narrowed the scope of the existing bad faith requirement since evidence obtained through anonymous approaches (as opposed to direct offers to sell etc. to the complainant or its competitor) would no longer appear to be sufficient.

The Measures also provide that a domain name holder can establish that it has legitimate interests in the domain name through (i) honest use of the domain name to provide goods or services; or (ii) acquiring reputation in respect of the domain name through use (even if the domain name holder has not obtained a trade mark or service mark in respect of the domain name); or (iii) the domain name has been legitimately used with no intention of obtaining commercial gain or misleading the public.

The Measures have imposed a time bar of two years from registration of a .cn domain name for bringing an action by way of dispute resolution procedure in respect of the domain name. If more than two years has elapsed since registration of the domain name, the only course of action open to the rights owner is to bring a civil action in the Chinese People's Court.

Fees

3–145   The fees for .cn or a Chinese language domain name dispute with CIETAC or HKIAC are currently RMB4000 for a single panelist and RMB7000 for three panelists.

The fees for top level domain names disputes with ADNDRC are currently US$1000 for a single panelist and US$2500 for three panelists.

The fees increase if there are more than two domain names in dispute.

Case Law

3–146   The Chinese People's Court has built up a large body of case law in relation to domain name disputes. There are generally two causes of action in domain name disputes, namely trade mark infringement and unfair competition.

Often a registered trade mark owner will take action against the registrant of an unauthorised domain name on the basis of trade mark infringement. However, where an unauthorised domain name is used in relation to goods or services that are sufficiently different from those marketed under the registered trade mark, a trade mark infringement action is inappropriate and the trade mark owner would have to seek redress under the law of unfair competition.

For instance, in the landmark case of *Inter-Ikea Systems B.V. v Beijing CINET Information Co. Ltd*,[32] the plaintiff was the owner of famous household wares stores and had registered the mark "IKEA" in a number of classes in 90 countries across the world. The defendant, a Beijing internet service provider and notorious cybersquatter, registered the domain name *www.ikea.com.cn* for the purpose of launching voicemail services over the internet.

Since the goods and services offered by the defendant under the IKEA mark were different from the plaintiff's goods and services, the People's Court could not find trade mark infringement but ruled instead that the act of registering and using the domain name in bad faith was punishable under the Law Against Unfair Competition and the General Principles of Civil Law in China as a breach of the principles of honesty, fair competition and commercial morality.

---

[32] (1999), Beijng 2nd Intermediate Court.

There have been a number of cases where the Court has recognised a   **3–147**
trade mark as having well-known status which entitles the plaintiff to
pursue both causes of action. In *E.I Dupont de Nemours and Company v
Beijing Guowang Information Ltd*,[33] the defendant registered the domain
name *www.dupont.com.cn* while the plaintiff had previously registered the
trade mark "Dupont" in a number of different classes in China. The
plaintiff had established 11 enterprises in China which traded under the
Dupont mark and had extensively advertised the mark in the Chinese
media.

The Court held that the Dupont mark was well-known by the relevant
section of the public in China and, in accordance with the Paris Convention, a well-known mark should enjoy a higher level of protection than an
ordinary mark. Accordingly, the registration of the well-known mark as a
domain name, even though the domain name was not used in relation to
similar goods or services and, in fact, was never used at all by the defendant, could have caused confusion amongst the public and thus constituted
trade mark infringement.

The Court also found that since the defendant had no justified reason for
registering a domain name that was confusingly similar to the Dupont mark
and the non-use of the domain name indicated an intention to prevent the
plaintiff from identifying itself through the disputed domain name, the
defendant had breached the Law Against Unfair Competition.

It should be noted that in determining whether a trade mark owned by a   **3–148**
foreign organisation is a well-known mark, the Chinese People's Court
generally follows the TRIPS agreement and considers whether there is
sufficient evidence to prove reputation in the mark in the Chinese market,
whether or not the mark is actually registered in China.

In a case brought by the multinational pharmaceutical company Pfizer
Inc,[34] the Court held that the plaintiff's registered trade mark "Viagra" was
not a well-known mark in China because the plaintiff's product had only
been marketed in China under its Chinese name and the English name
"Viagra" did not have sufficient reputation amongst the Chinese public to
be considered a well-known mark.

Where a trade mark does not have well-known status, the Court will not
necessarily find trade mark infringement and unfair competition where the
trade mark is registered as part of a domain name. In a case before the
Beijing 1st Intermediate Court,[35] the plaintiff was the proprietor of the
"PDA" trade mark in relation to computer-related goods and the defendant
was the registrant of the domain name *www.pda.com.cn*.

The Court held that trade mark infringement and unfair competition had
not been established because using a registered trade mark as part of a
domain name is not the exclusive right of the trade mark owner. The Court

---

[33] (2000), Beijing 1st Intermediate Court, (2001), Beijing Higher People's Court.
[34] (2000), Beijing 2nd Intermediate Court.
[35] *Shijiazhuang Fulande Business Development Company v Beijing Mitianjiaye Technology and Trade Ltd* (1999), Beijing 1st Intermediate Court.

also found that "PDA" is a generic term used for laptop computers and the defendant was unable to prove that its mark was a well-known trade mark or that the public had been misled because of the defendant's act.

Chinese Language Domain Names

3–149   The first Chinese language domain name case[36] to be decided in China involved the well-known "Alibaba" website. The internet company Alibaba had registered the English language domain name *www.alibaba.com* and other domain names containing the word "alibaba" and used them to launch both an English and Chinese language version of its successful trading website.

The plaintiff, Beijing Zhengpu Technology Development Ltd, later filed trade mark applications for the Chinese characters and Chinese Pin-yin for "Alibaba". When Zhengpu then applied to register a domain name containing the Chinese language version of "alibaba", the CNNIC rejected the application on the grounds that the domain name was reserved for Alibaba as a well-known name in order to prevent acts of cybersquatting.

Zhengpu was unable to take action under the Trade Mark Law since its trade mark applications had not yet matured to registration, so it filed a lawsuit against the CNNIC and Alibaba claiming that the CNNIC, as registrar, did not have the authority to determine when marks were well-known and to reserve domain names (other than the names of governmental bodies and educational institutions) where the owner of the trade mark or enterprise name had not yet applied for the domain name.

The Court held that only the owner of a trade mark or enterprise name had the right to decide whether to register it as a domain name and the CNNIC had breached its authority by reserving the Chinese "alibaba" domain name. However, the Court recognised that the Alibaba website was very famous among Chinese internet users and the registration of the Chinese language "alibaba" domain name by Zhengpu would lead to confusion amongst the public and breach the Law Against Unfair Competition. Accordingly, the Court refused to transfer the disputed domain name to Zhengpu.

3.18 NON-UNITED KINGDOM DOMAIN NAMES— FINLAND

3.18.1 Registration

3–150   Finnish domain names under the .fi root may be applied for by a legal person, a private entrepreneur, a Finnish public body, an unincorporated

---

[36] *Beijing Zhengpu Technology Development Ltd v Computer Network Information Center of Chinese Academy of Science and Alibaba (China) Network Technology Ltd*, (2001) Beijing First Intermediate Court, (2002), Beijing Higher People's Court.

state enterprise, an independent public corporation, a public association and a diplomatic mission of a foreign state registered in Finland. Thus, foreign businesses may register a Finnish domain name only upon establishing a branch office duly registered in Finland. As of March 1, 2006, individuals 15 years of age and over, with a Finnish identity number and place of domicile in Finland, may also apply for Finnish domain names.

The Finnish Domain Name Act (228/2003) allows applicants to freely choose the domain name to be registered. The domain name does not need to correspond to the applicant's name. However, the domain name may not be based on the protected name or trade mark of another party. A name or a trade mark is protected, as to cause a rejection, when duly registered in the Finnish Trade Register, the Finnish Register of Associations, the Finnish Register of Foundations, the Finnish Trade Mark Register or the European Community Trade Mark Register. Names of Finnish public bodies and duly established company names and trade marks, as defined in the Finnish Company Name Act and the Finnish Trade Mark Act, are also protected. Domain names may not contain offensive expressions or incite to commit an offence.

A domain name may consist of 2–63 characters, letters from a to z, numbers from 1 to 9 and hyphens. As of September 1, 2005 it is possible to apply for Internationalised Domain Names (IDN) in Finland, i.e. domain names containing national special characters such as å, ä and ö. All browser and email programs do not, however, support such domain names.

The registration of Finnish domain names under the .fi root is admini- **3–151** strated by the Finnish Communications Regulatory Authority ("FICORA"). Domain names are applied for through the domain name service on FICORA's website. The applicant first needs to register online and fill in a contact information form. FICORA then provides the applicant with an identification code and passwords for the domain name service, after which the application for registration of a domain name can be made online at the website of FICORA. Information on name servers needs to be given in the application form. In case the applicant does not have name servers configured for the domain name, he can turn to an internet service provider who provides name server services and forwards applications on behalf of applicants.

The domain name registration is in force for three years, after which it can be renewed by paying a renewal fee prior to the expiry of the registration.

3.18.2 Disputes

Legal proceedings in relation to Finnish domain names can be instituted **3–152** based on the Domain Name Act or based on the Trade Mark Act and/or the Trade Name Act.

The Domain Name Act

3–153   FICORA may suspend or revoke a domain name under the .fi root which infringes the protected name or trade mark of another party. FICORA's rulings are based on the Domain Name Act, and the rulings may be appealed to the Administrative Court of Helsinki and further to the Supreme Administrative Court of Finland.

According to the Domain Name Act, a domain name under the .fi root may not without authorisation be based on someone else's protected name or trade mark. FICORA does not carry out a proper examination of name and trade mark registers in advance, even if the domain name service automatically examines the applications to a limited extent before the domain names are granted. Thus, the applicant is responsible for ensuring that the domain name does not infringe a registered name or trade mark.

At the request of a rights holder, FICORA may suspend or revoke a domain name that infringes a protected name or trade mark. The procedure is designed to be a fast and cost-effective way to intervene in clear infringement cases. A domain name may be revoked or suspended for a maximum of one year in two cases. Firstly, revocation or suspension may follow if there are weighty reasons to suspect that the domain name is a protected name or trade mark. Secondly, a domain name may be revoked or suspended if there are weighty reasons to suspect that the domain name is a derivative of a protected name or trade mark, and the domain name has been obtained with the obvious intent of gaining benefit from or harming the protected name or trade mark of another party.

When considering whether the conditions for revocation or suspension are met, FICORA requests a clarification from the domain name holder on the holder's right to the domain name in question. In practice, the right of the holder should be based on a registered trade name or trade mark in order to succeed against a request for revocation or suspension by the holder of a protected trade name or trade mark.

3–154   The written administrative process does not allow extensive evaluation of evidence submitted by the parties. Consequently, FICORA will take non-registered names or trade marks into account only when it is unquestionable that the relevant name or trade mark has been established. The establishment of a name or a trade mark has to be so evident that FICORA can, without evidence of establishment, find that there is probable cause or weighty reasons to suspect the domain name to be a protected name or a trade mark.

The position of a trade mark or name identical with the domain name is very strong. Trade marks or names slightly different from the domain name have proved to be in a weak position. In practice, it has been difficult to prove that the holder has acted "with an obvious intent of gaining benefit from or harming the protected name or mark of another party". Hence, if a domain name is not identical with the protected trade mark or name of another party, the domain name will in all likelihood not be suspended or revoked.

If a domain name has been granted prior to the entry into force of the Domain Name Act on September 1, 2003, the domain name cannot be revoked or suspended on the grounds of it being based on a protected name or trade mark. This is because FICORA examined the applications before granting a right to a domain name prior to the Domain Name Act.

The decision of FICORA can be appealed to the Administrative Court of Helsinki. Despite an appeal to the Administrative Court, FICORA may decide that the decision on suspension or revocation can be put into effect immediately. In its practice, the Administrative Court has not approved requests for suspension of such enforcement.

Trade Mark Act and Trade Name Act

Legal proceedings regarding a trade name or trade mark are to be initiated **3–155** at the District Court of Helsinki. The decision of the District Court can be appealed to the Court of Appeal of Helsinki and further to the Supreme Court of Finland, if the latter grants leave to appeal.

The Trade Mark Act and Trade Name Act give an exclusive right to the owner of a trade mark or name to use it in order to identify its products or services. If a protected trade mark or name, or a mark confusingly similar to these, is used commercially in order to identify the products or services of another party without proper consent, this may constitute trade mark or trade name infringement. As a rule, the use of a protected trade mark or name of another party as a domain name for a commercial entity constitutes trade mark or trade name infringement.

3.18.3 Comments

Disputes regarding domain names have been relatively rare in Finland **3–156** because of the strict registration practice previously applied. However, the entry into force of the Domain Name Act in September 2003 introduced a lighter registration procedure, which has lead to the development of case law. The majority of domain name disputes in Finland relate to unlawfully registered domain names under the .fi root and therefore fall into the scope of FICORA's authority.

A domain name that is identical with a registered word of someone else can most likely be suspended and/or revoked. As regards figurative marks, FICORA has in its practice compared texts included in such marks with word marks. It has been held that a text included in a figurative mark can base a right referred to in the Domain Name Act. However, a trade name which exactly matches a domain name will outrun a text of a figurative trade mark, which also matches the domain name. A domain name which exactly matches the text of a figurative mark will also in all likelihood be considered as only a derivative of the protected mark in question.

The consideration whether a domain name infringes a trade mark or name is based on the situation at the date of the domain name application.

If the parties possess equal rights to a sign, the principle of first come, first served is applied.

3.19 NON-UNITED KINGDOM DOMAIN NAMES— FRANCE

3–157   Over the last few years, domain names seem to have become an important aspect of international trade, which is fully understood by French companies. As communication via internet is perceived as an open door to the entire world of corporate activities and the domain name as the sole means of identifying such communication for the user, it is not surprising that domain names have become objects of trade and have acquired a real economic value to the benefit of their holders.

3.19.1 Registration

3–158   In September 1986, INRIA (Institut National de Recherches en Informatique et en Automatique) was responsible for the .fr domain names on behalf of the SRI-NIC and then the INTERNIC. In December 1997, INRIA and the French Government created AFNIC (French Network Information Center), a non-profit organisation which is now the only registry for the internet .fr (France) and .re (Reunion Island).

The requirements and procedure to register a .fr domain name are set forth in the Registration Rules ("Charte de Nommage") drafted by AFNIC and last modified on May 2005.

From a practical point of view, to register a .fr domain name, an applicant which complies with the requirements of the Registration Rules has to enter into an agreement with a registrar (*"prestataire technique"*) accredited by AFNIC. The list of accredited registrars is available on the AFNIC website *www.afnic.fr*.

Finally, it is worth noting that the Registration Rules prohibit the registration of various domain names, in particular those composed of terms which are insulting, racist or obscene terms, technical internet terms, or terms used for international organisations.

3–159   The allowed domain names are divided into three categories: the public, the sectorial and the conventional domain names.

The public domain corresponds in particular to .fr, .asso.fr, .tm.fr and .com.fr extensions.

Until May 11, 2004 all applicants in .fr domain names had to establish that they had a prior right over the domain name such as a company name or a trade mark.

As from May 11, 2004, the .fr domain names allocation was liberalised so that any entity which can be identified in public and national databases can apply for the registration of a .fr domain name without establishing a prior right over the domain name.

As a consequence, any French registered entity (company, association, institutions ... etc.) any French trade mark applicants, holders of an International registered trade mark covering the French territory, holders of a Community Registered trade mark, a French national and a foreign national domiciled in France may apply for the registration of a .fr domain name.

The .tm.fr domain name is available to trade mark holders who want to register as a domain name all or part of their trade mark. The applicant for such a domain name must provide the INPI registration application concerning a French trade mark or the definitive OHIM or WIPO trade mark certification concerning an International or Community trade mark.

The .asso.fr domain name is available to associations who want to register as a domain name all or part of the name of the association. The applicant must provide a copy of publication in the Official Journal, a copy of the declaration to the Prefecture, or a copy of the identifier in the INSEE directory.   **3–160**

There are no specific requirements with respect to the registration of .com.fr domain names. Such a registration is not permitted if the identical term has already been registered under one of the public domain extensions. However, the .com.fr registration does not prevent the same applicant from registering the same term under one of the public domain extensions.

Sectoral domain names concern regulated professional activities such as lawyers (.avocat.fr), doctors (.medecin.fr), pharmacists (.pharmacien.fr) ... etc.

Conventional domain names were created by AFNIC for specific authorities such as academies (.ac-nom.fr), embassies (.amb-nom.fr), etc. For both sectoral and conventional, the applicant must carry out certain registration formalities.

Although the registration of the public, sectoral and conventional domain names is regulated, the Registration Rules do not prevent conflicting situations.

3.19.2 Disputes

With respect to domain names disputes, action can be brought before French Courts based on trade mark and/or unfair competition law and/or before WIPO and CMAP (Centre de Médiation et d'Arbitrage de Paris).   **3–161**

Regarding registration of .fr domain names, AFNIC only verifies the availability of the domain name requested and not its validity. This means that the domain name is granted without assessing whether or not there is a conflict with prior rights such as trade mark, trade names, copyrights ... etc.

However, AFNIC has some control over .fr registered domain names. For instance, recently AFNIC noticed massive registrations of .fr domain names infringing third party's prior rights and decided to block all the registrations on the basis of Art.36 of the Registration Rules, so as to allow the legitimate owners to take any measures to protect their prior rights.[37]

Actions before the French Courts

3–162   As regards cases involving domain names and trade marks, it is first necessary to assess as to whether or not the trade mark was registered before or after the creation date of the domain name.

If the domain name is registered *after* the trade mark, trade mark law applies and the registrant of the trade mark may be in a position to bring a trade mark infringement action against the registrant of the domain name provided that there is a likelihood of confusion between the website run under the domain name and the products and/or services referred within the registered trade mark.[38]

In this regard, the sole fact that the trade mark is registered for telecommunication services (class 38) does not confer protection against the registration and/or use of a domain name since it is necessary to assess the likelihood of confusion between the website of the disputed domain name and the products/services referred to within the registration.

Furthermore, the sole registration of a domain name does not amount to trade mark infringement since it is considered as a neutral act.[39]

If the domain name is registered *before* the trade mark, the owner of such a domain name may be in a position to challenge the registration of the said trade mark[40] since French courts consider that it has an economic value and can be compared to a shop window.[41] Consequently, a domain name may constitute a valid prior right.

Finally, there are specific rules with respect to well-known trade marks, which benefit from a larger scope of protection and are protected under trade mark or tort law.[42]

3–163   For instance, in the *"Milka"* case, Mrs Milka, a dressmaker, had registered and was using the domain name "milka.fr", "Milka" being her surname, leading to her website presenting her activity on a mauve background. Judges ordered the transfer of the domain name since the use of the

---

[37] *Laurent N., EuroDNS/AFNIC* October 21, 2004; *KLTE Ltd/AFNIC* July 18, 2005 in *http://www.afnic.fr*.

[38] TGI Paris, March 23, 1999 *SNC Alice v Alice* in *http://www.legalis.net*; TGI Nanterre January, 21 2002 *Publications Bonnier v Saveurs creations* in *http://www.legalis.net*; CA Versailles, November 22, 2001, *SA Zebank v SA 123 Multimédia* in Com. Electr April 2002 ab. 56.

[39] TGI Nanterre, January 21, 2002 *Publications Bonnier v Saveurs creations* in *http://www.legalis.net*.

[40] TGI Le Mans, June 29, 1999 *Microcaz v/ Océanet et S.F.D.I.*

[41] TGI Paris, April 8, 2005.

[42] TGI Paris, March 27, 1998 *L'Oréal, Parfums Guy Laroche, The Polo Lauren Company, Cacharel et Ralph Lauren v PLD Enterprises*; TGI Nanterre, Référé, September 16, 1999 *La S.N.C Lancôme Parfums et beauté v La S.A Grandtotal Finances Ltd;* TGI Nanterre January 18, 1999 *SFR v Sté Systems Inc*, TGI Nanterre, March 14, 2005 *SA Kraft Foods Schweiz Holding AG c/ Milka B*, in *http://www.legalis.net*

Milka trademark was unjustified and weakened the distinctive nature of this well known trade mark

In the case of a conflict between a company name, trade name ... etc and a domain name, tort law shall apply. Indeed, when the domain name is identical or similar to such a prior right, the owner of such right may be in a position to bring an unfair competition action subject to the presence of a likelihood of confusion between the activity carried out by the company and the content of the website of the domain name.[43]

The same solution was reached concerning litigation involving two domain names (*www.hotel.fr v www.hotels.fr*).[44]

Alternative Dispute Resolution (ADR) and Mediation

Since May 11, 2004, .fr domain name disputes can also be brought before WIPO or before the CMAP (Centre de Médiation et d'Arbitrage de Paris) which is not *stricto sensu* an ADR.   3–164

Before WIPO, the .fr domain name ADR rules are specific since the complainant has to establish that "the registration or use of the domain name constitutes an infringement of rights protected in France" which include, in particular trade marks, and author's rights, in order to get a domain name transferred or cancelled.

The .fr domain name CMAP procedure is also specific since the decisions rendered by CMAP differ from the WIPO decisions. Indeed, they are only recommendations which bind the parties if they have both expressly consented.

3.20. NON-UNITED KINGDOM DOMAIN NAMES— GERMANY

3.20.1 Domain Name Registration

The approval and registration of domain names under the national top level domain .de is granted by DENIC (in full: DENIC Domain Verwaltungs-und Betriebsgesellschaft eG—*www.denic.de*). More than 200 internet service providers, both German and non-German, are members of this Frankfurt located registered co-operative. A list of all providers is available at the above-mentioned website.   3–165

A domain name registration can either be handled by the chosen provider or by using DENIC. However, DENIC itself advises registration through service providers as it is less complicated and bears lower costs.

In order to have a domain name registered the applicant does not need a domicile or residence in Germany. It is sufficient naming an administrative

---

[43] Com., July 7, 2004; Com. February 22, 2005 in *http://www.legifrance.fr*.
[44] TGI Paris January 29, 2003 in Petites affiches 05/23/2005 n°101 p.15.

contact ("admin-c") who is a natural person domiciled or resident in Germany. Having such an administrative contact acting as the authorised representative of the domain holder any foreign company can have its name registered under the German top level domain .de. Also the admin-c is the person to receive any kind of official or court documents. Regarding the registration process DENIC's website provides all necessary information—also in English.

This homepage also renders the "WHOIS search" service offering all relevant information on all registered .de domains, which by July 31, 2005 numbered more than 8.9 million.[45]

3.20.2 DENIC, German Courts and domain name disputes

3–166   Domains are registered in accordance with "first come, first served"—principally meaning that any domain is registered provided that is has not already been registered for someone else. No distinction is made between business and private names. When processing the registration of a domain name DENIC does not validate whether there are conflicting rights of third parties. Only in evident cases of infringement DENIC will deny the registration. In any other case the matter is to be settled by the domain holder and the third party.

There is no dispute resolution policy like the UDRP policy for .com domains in Germany. Disputes are handled by the civil courts. It is, therefore, advisable to check the trade mark and company name situation before using a domain name in the course of business for goods and services.

The only interference of DENIC regarding court proceedings is the possibility to ask DENIC for a so called "dispute" entry. A trade mark or company name owner who learns about a domain registration which infringes its IP rights can raise a "dispute". DENIC will enter that "dispute" provided that the claimant can demonstrate his possible rights and that measures (e.g. warning letter, preliminary injunction) are taken against the infringer to enforce these rights. Demonstrating its own rights is done by presenting *prima facie* evidence like extracts from trade mark databases, documents etc. The effect of such a dispute entry is that the registered owner can no longer transfer the domain and if the owner cancels the registration, the domain will automatically be registered for the party that submitted the dispute.

Many of the decisions granted by the German courts are preliminary injunctions which are granted "ex parte" and therefore without the possible infringer having a chance to present his view before the injunction is granted. In clear-cut cases regarding the infringing use of a domain name in the course of business, the courts are ready to grant a preliminary injunction within 1 or 2 days. If the claimant has been aware of the infringement

---

[45] *http://www.denic.de/en/domains/statistiken/domainentwicklung/index.html.*

for more than approximately one month (the length of this time frame depends on the court that the claimant chooses), the case is not considered to be "urgent" anymore and therefore no preliminary injunction proceeding is possible any longer.

In regular civil proceedings, one has to serve a writ of summons to the court and can expect a first instance decision within approximately six months depending on the court chosen. **3–167**

Since, in the case of an infringing use of a domain name in Germany, the connected website is accessible all over Germany, one can choose among various competent courts (so called forum shopping). Germany has installed specialised Trademark Infringement Chambers (Kennzeichen-streitkammern) at various civil courts which are competent. Besides those courts, in most cases involving companies the specialised Chambers for Commercial Matters (Kammern für Handelssachen) are also competent. Courts used very often for domain proceedings are the specialised Trademark Infringement Chambers in Munich, Hamburg, Cologne and Frankfurt.

In many cases a warning letter is sent to the possible infringer before going to the courts. Especially for those cases it is important to know, that stopping the use of the domain by disconnecting the relevant website does not stop the infringement. Because if the domain has once been used in the course of business or if there has been the proven danger of an initial use the so called danger of repetition (Wiederholungsgefahr) continues to exist. Such a danger of repetition can only be stopped by signing a cease and desist declaration including a contract penalty. If a legitimate warning letter is sent through a law firm the infringer has to pay the costs that arise due to sending this warning letter (approx. €2000–3000).

3.20.3 Relevant laws

There is no law or explicit regulation on domain names. The question of alleged trade mark or company name infringements is dealt with on the basis of ss.14 and 15 German Trademark Act (§§ 14, 15 Markengesetz, MarkenG). Also, any obligation of the domain holder to cease and desist the use of the domain or to pay damages results from that law. **3–168**

Section 12 German Civil Code (§ 12 Bürgerliches Gesetzbuch, BGB) grants protection to the names of individuals as well as companies or other legal entities. According to that rule a person or company entitled to bear a name has the right to exclude anybody else from using that name without authorisation. It becomes particularly relevant when a domain is not used in trade and business. Furthermore the general laws of unfair competition (UWG) apply.

3.20.4 Possible legal actions based on the German Trademark Act

3-169 The use of a domain name can result into a successful infringement claim if:

- The domain name is identical or similar to the protected trade mark
- The trade mark or company name is protected for identical or similar goods and services as offered under the relevant domain
- The domain is connected to a website; and
- The domain is used in the course of business (i.e. goods and services are offered on the website (proven intended use can be enough))

Therefore, the contents of a website and its actual use are important. If the usage does not involve any identical or similar goods and/or services that are protected by the trade mark the chances of success based on the German Trademark Act are low. The courts have to make an overall evaluation if, from their point of view, the concrete use of the domain causes a likelihood of confusion among the trade mark and the used domain.

If a well-known trade mark is concerned it is not necessary that the domain is used for goods and services that are similar or identical with the goods and/or services that are offered on the website. However, it is still necessary that the domain is connected to a website and that this is used in the course of business.

Yet, the issue remains as to whether only the registration of an identical or confusingly similar domain name, without any use of the website, infringes the rights of the affected trade mark owner. Courts disagree on that topic. Several courts held that the registration indicates the intended use, in cases of companies as domain holder intended use in trade and business. Other courts stated that the registration itself without any use does not represent an infringement. On this question it is at the moment hard to find any clear trend in German jurisdiction.

3.20.5 Claims based on unfair competition law and the law regarding names

3-170 Since the German Trademark Act does, not, for the most part, offer a solution for cases regarding domain names that have only been reserved but not put into use or only into private use, sometimes both, the unfair competition law (UWG) as well as the law protecting names (s.12 of the German Civil Code) can sometimes base a claim.

To some extent, the claims based on the laws of unfair competition are especially relevant in cases of "bad faith". If, for example, someone has registered a domain that resembles the trade mark of a competitor and cannot prove any real interest in having the domain registered, the courts would probably order the cancellation of the domain. The same could happen if one can prove that someone has registered a huge number of domains that resemble trade marks just to sell it to the trade mark owner.

In a landmark decision, the Federal Supreme Court decided that even the private use of a domain (shell.de) could result in an infringement of the right to a name of a company with the same name. The claimant was the German branch of Shell and the defendant was Andreas Shell, a private person. Although Andreas Shell did not use the domain for a business the court took the view that the interests of the parties in this dispute were of such different weight, that, exceptionally, this time the priority rule could not be followed. As far as Deutsche Shell's claim to a transfer of the internet address "shell.de" was concerned, the court rejected that claim. The claimant could only demand that the defendant cancels the address. Thereafter, Deutsche Shell was in a position to register it.

3.20.6 Recent relevant legal cases

The question of the registration of generic terms as domain names was dealt   3–171
with in several proceedings. As regards the registration of generic terms some lower courts held that a generic term must not be registered as a domain for a company due to the monopolisation this would mean.

The Federal Supreme Court, however, ruled that although it presents an advantage in competition, there is no reason to prohibit such registrations. These days all internet users are aware of the fact that, when logging into a domain consisting of a generic term, this is nothing more than the homepage of one single provider who managed to have that term registered.[46]

The registration of a generic term is not illegal either, even if a company might like to use that domain name for its website. In the case of the widely-known German newspaper "Die Welt" the court could not see any conflict in the registration of *www.weltonline.de* as long as there are no grounds for any suspicion of an intended infringing use in trade and business.

In terms of rights to a name, the Federal Supreme Court in 2004 held that even if the bearer of a name—in that case Kurt Biedenkopf, a well-known politician—has had a domain name cancelled on grounds of infringement he is not entitled to "block" that domain name for any further registration by a third party. The court stated that DENIC basically is not required to test whether the designation applied for infringes rights of the name bearer. However, this could be solved by keeping the domain registered.[47]

Also dealing with the question of a legitimate name use a court had to decide whether an advertising company bearing the name "mho", (for Medienhaus Osnabrück), is entitled to have the domain *www.mho.de* registered although a longer existing hospital is named MHO (for Marienhospital Osnabrück). The court decided that in the case of a company

---

[46] BGH IIC 2003, vol. 4, p.455–460—*mitwohnzentrale.de*.
[47] BGH IIC 2004, vol. 2, p.271–273—*kurt-biedenkopf.de*.

start-up using that name legally the registration of an identical domain in connection with the business start does not infringe any rights.[48]

3–172   The hotel company Maritim hotels went to a German court to have the use of the Danish domain *www.hotel-maritime.dk* stopped. On this website, run by a Copenhagen hotel named Maritime, information is also available in German and information brochures in the German language can also be ordered. The court held that although there is a risk of confusion with the registered trade marks of the plaintiff, the trade mark holder has no rights on grounds of infringement as long as the foreign offer does not have an economically relevant connection to Germany. In this case it was not considered to be a sufficient connection that it is possible to have a look at the homepage in a German version as well, and to order a brochure in the German language.

3.21 NON-UNITED KINGDOM DOMAIN NAMES— HONG KONG

3.21.1 Registration

3–173   Hong Kong's domain name registry is known as the Hong Kong Domain Name Registration Company Limited (HKDNR). The HKDNR is the operations arm of the Hong Kong Internet Registration Corporation (HKIRC) and its role is to oversee the registration and assignment of internet domain names ending with .com.hk, .org.hk, .gov.hk, .edu.hk, .net.hk and .idv.hk and any other categories to be introduced from time to time in Hong Kong. Since May 31, 2004, it has been possible to register domain names under the .hk country code top level domain for which there is a simplified application procedure since no documentation is required for new domain name registrations.

The Hong Kong system for domain name registration is essentially on a "first come, first served" basis. HKDNR does not check domain names applied for against registered trade marks, neither does it pre-vet applications for domain names. HKDNR is not obliged to enquire at the registration stage whether an applicant is entitled to register the domain name for which it has applied in Hong Kong. Furthermore, HKDNR's domain name registration agreement expressly states that the domain name applicant shall be responsible for use of the domain name once registered.

3–174   In order to apply for a third-level .hk domain name (other than .idv.hk which is designated for individuals) the applicant must prove that it is a commercial entity, a not for profit organisation, an entity managing network infrastructure machines and services, a bureau or department of the Government of HKSAR or a school or educational institution in HKSAR. For example, an applicant who wants to register a .com.hk domain name

---

[48] BGH GRUR 2005, vol. 5, p.430–431—*mho.de.*

must submit its Business Registration Certificate issued by the Inland Revenue Department or Certificate of Registration of Overseas Company issued by the Companies Registry as documentary proof. HKDNR's domain name registration rules allow an applicant to register multiple domain names. Since February 21, 2003, any Hong Kong Identity Card holder aged 11 or above may apply for an individual domain name (.idv.hk).

HKDNR accepts applications for top level .hk domain names from organisations and individuals from Hong Kong and from overseas, and generally no documentary proof is required. It is now possible to register Chinese language domain names containing at least one or more Chinese characters with the country code .hk. In September 2006, the HKDNR introduced a "Soft Launch" period for registration of Chinese domain names, to give priority registration to various categories of registrant such as trade mark/service mark owners and existing .hk Roman letter domain name holders. The "Soft Launch" period ended on February 9, 2007, and applications for Chinese domain names are now also on a "first-come, first-served" basis.

Under HKDNR's domain name registration agreement each applicant is required to warrant and represent that all statements in its application are true, that it has the right to use the domain name, that it intends to use the domain name (which use shall be bona fide for its own benefit), that the use or registration does not interfere with or infringe the rights of any third party in any jurisdiction and that it is not seeking to use the domain name for any unlawful purpose.

To register a domain name, customers must have two name servers, **3–175** which can be provided by ISPs and web hosting companies or managed by in-house system administrators (although HKDNR can provide temporary name servers during the registration period). HKDNR levies a nominal non-refundable fee (currently HK$200, or HK$150 for .idv.hk domain names) for registration of a new domain name or modification of an existing domain name. Domain names can be registered for a period of one, two, three or five years depending on the applicant's choice of contract and payment of fees.

An applicant may transfer the registration of its domain name to another party. However, both parties (i.e. the transferor and transferee) must mutually consent to the transfer and sign HKDNR's Transfer Form. Furthermore, the transferee must provide the same documentary proof which an applicant for a domain name would be required to produce when applying for a fresh domain name, for example, proof of incorporation and registration. It must also agree to be bound by the terms and conditions of the domain name registration agreement. A fee (currently HK$700 for applications from organisations and HK$650 for applications from individuals) will be charged for the transfer. This fee includes the initial registration fee for the new domain name.

3.21.2 Disputes

3–176   HKDNR has adopted a Domain Name Dispute Resolution Policy ("Dispute Resolution Policy"). The Dispute Resolution Policy sets forth the terms and conditions in connection with a dispute between the applicant and any party other than the HKDNR with regard to the registration and use of the applicant's .hk domain name. The Hong Kong International Arbitration Centre (HKIAC) has been appointed as the sole .hk domain name dispute resolution service provider. All domain name disputes will be resolved by mandatory arbitration proceedings.

In addition, under HKDNR's domain name registration agreement, the domain name applicant is required to defend, indemnify and hold harmless HKDNR, its directors, officers, committee members, employees and agents from all liabilities, losses, damages, costs, legal expenses, professional and other expenses of any nature resulting from any claim, action or demand arising out of, or related to, the registration or use of the domain name. Such claims shall include, without limitation, those based upon trade or service mark infringement, dilution, tortious interference with contract or prospective business advantage, passing off, defamation or injury to business reputation.

Arbitration

3–177   The HKIAC is the sole provider of dispute resolution services for .hk domain names. It is also one of four providers in the world of dispute resolution services for generic top level domain names such as .com, .net etc. and has been appointed by the China Internet Network Information Center (CNNIC) to resolve disputes for .cn domain names. It can also resolve disputes relating to .pw and .ph domain names.

Under HKDNR's dispute resolution policy, the owner of a .hk domain name will be subject to a mandatory arbitration proceeding if HKDNR receives a complaint from a third party asserting that:

(i)   the domain name is identical or confusingly similar to a trade mark or service mark in Hong Kong in which the complainant has rights; and

(ii)   the owner of the domain name has no rights or legitimate interests in respect of the domain name; and

(iii) the domain name has been registered and is being used in bad faith.

It is expressly stated under the policy that the acquisition of a domain name primarily for the purpose of selling the domain name to the complainant or a competitor of the complainant for consideration exceeding the actual out-of-pocket expenses directly related to registration of the domain name shall be considered as evidence of bad faith.

3–178   The complainant shall be responsible for paying the fees of the arbitration. The exception is where the complainant elects to have the dispute heard by a single arbitrator, but the respondent exercises its right to have the dispute heard by a panel of three arbitrators. In this case, the arbitration fees will be payable in equal shares by the complainant and the respondent. Under the current policy, the fees for resolving a dispute will be HK$8,000 by one arbitrator or HK$16,000 by three arbitrators. The arbitrators will be appointed by HKIAC.

The complainant must prove all of the three requirements as stated above in order to succeed in an arbitration. As the aim of the dispute resolution policy is to expedite the resolution of cybersquatting disputes and to allow the rightful owner to re-claim a domain name with minimal costs, the only remedies to which a complainant is entitled under such policy will be either an order to cancel the registration of the domain name or an order to transfer the domain name to the complainant. A complainant who wishes to seek remedies beyond this scope must go through the Court unless both parties agree to submit the whole of the dispute to arbitration.

Court Proceedings

Misuse of a domain name in Hong Kong could lead to legal liability in one of three ways: as infringement of a registered trade mark, as passing off or as a criminal offence under the Trade Descriptions Ordinance.   3–179

Infringement of a registered trade mark may arise on the basis that the use of the domain name by its holder is use of such name as a trade mark, or that it imports a reference to the proprietor of the registered mark, in circumstances where the use is made in relation to goods or services which are the same as, or of the same description as, those specified in the trade mark registration. Such use of the domain name will only be actionable if it results in a likelihood of confusion. Likelihood of confusion does not have to be shown, however, if the domain name is used for the goods or services actually specified in the trade mark registration and the domain name is identical to the registered mark.

Passing off may arise where the trade mark (whether or not it is registered) has a protectable goodwill in Hong Kong which will be damaged by confusion arising from use of the domain name.

It is also an offence under the Trade Descriptions Ordinance in Hong Kong to apply a trade mark to goods falsely. This includes using a trade mark in any manner which is likely to be taken as referring to those goods. Use of a domain name to advertise goods, for which the same name is registered as a trade mark by another party, would arguably fall within the scope of this offence. The criminal penalty is a fine of up to HK$500,000 and up to five years imprisonment on conviction on indictment, and a fine of up to HK$100,000 and up to two years imprisonment on summary conviction.

In addition to the above causes of action, any persons attempting to register potentially desirable domain names, with a view to selling them on at a profit, may also be susceptible to a *quia timet* action on the basis that

3–180   there is a serious and immediate risk of wrongdoing, even though there may yet have been no infringing act within Hong Kong. It is likely that the decision of the English Courts in the *One in a Million* case (see para.3–066 above) would also be followed in Hong Kong.

3–180   There have been several domain name disputes in Hong Kong where the parties in dispute have attempted to resolve the matter through legal proceedings since the *MTR* case, Hong Kong's first passing off action arising from the registration of a domain name.

In the *MTR* case, the Mass Transit Railway Company (commonly abbreviated to MTR or MTRC) sued a local company, Beezweb Productions Ltd, for registering the domain name "www.mtrc.com" with InterNIC.

In *Sun Microsystems Inc v Lai Sun Hotels International Ltd*,[49] Sun Microsystems, a renowned information technology company which conducts its internet business using the domain name www.sun.com, claimed against Lai Sun, a public listed company in Hong Kong, for passing off. One of the factors Sun Microsystems relied on was the fact that Lai Sun had registered and used the domain name "www.esun.com".

Sun Microsystems applied unsuccessfully for an interim injunction against Lai Sun. The judge held that the plaintiff had failed to establish a blanket reputation that would cause confusion amongst prospective customers of the defendant. It is believed that both of the above cases were settled out of court. Most cases involving domain name disputes in Hong Kong are settled through arbitration and do not reach the Hong Kong courts. Any decision made by the panel of arbitrators in accordance with the dispute resolution policy will be published on the HKIAC's website at *www.hkiac.org*.

3.22 NON-UNITED KINGDOM DOMAIN NAMES—ISRAEL

3.22.1 Registration

Israel domain name registry

3–181   The organisation responsible for administering internet domain names under the national top level domain name for Israel is the Israel Internet Association ("ISOC-IL"), which is a member of the international Internet Society.[50] It derives its authority to operate the Israel domain name registry from IANA. ISOC-IL is a registered non-profit organisation and there is no governmental regulation of the registry's operations.

---

[49] [2000] 2 H.K.L.R.D. 616.
[50] Further information regarding ISOC-IL is available on its website at *http://www.isoc.org.il*.

Domain name registration policy

ISOC-IL's current rules governing the registration of domain names (the **3–182**
"Rules") came into effect on January 1, 1999 and were most recently
amended in December 2006.[51] ISOC-IL, or in some cases a government
authority or accredited registrar acting under authority delegated by ISOC-
IL, allocates third level domain names under the top .il level. The domain
names are divided into eight second level domain name categories; .ac.il,
.k12.il, .net.il, .muni.il, .gov.il, .idf.il, .co.il and .org.il.[52] Commercial
entities are allocated domain names in .co.il. The registry accepts generic
domain names for registration, but not (i) names which contain obscene or
foul language, which would injure public order or sensibilities, or which do
not comply with the laws of Israel, (ii) the name "www", (iii) names
containing less than three characters, and (iv) names which are identical to
top level domain names.

Domain name registrations must be renewed every two years.[53] Registrations are transferable, and domain names are portable from one internet
service provider to another.

3.22.2 Resolving questions of rights to domain names at the registration stage

The Rules do not provide for examination of the availability of a domain **3–183**
name before its allocation.[54] However, the applicant must state in the
application form that to the best of his or her knowledge the domain name
sought is available and does not infringe the rights of any other party. Each
applicant must also consent to be bound by the Rules, which, *inter alia*,
grant authority to ISOC-IL to refuse or to cancel domain name allocations
on the grounds of misrepresentation, or the submission of inaccurate
information. ISOC-IL may exercise this authority against applicants who
knowingly request allocation of a domain name to which a third party has
better rights.

---

[51] The rules are posted on the ISOC-IL website. The previous ISOC-IL rules govern domain
names registered between April 1996 and December 1998.

[52] Restricted for use by recognised academic institutions, kindergartens and schools, licensed
internet service providers, municipal and local government authorities, government entities,
military entities, commercial entities and non-commercial organisations respectively.

[53] Registrations for domain names under .co.il and .org.il may be for either one or two year
periods and are renewable at the end of the period chosen.

[54] ISOC-IL allocates domain names on a "first come, first served" basis. This rule is purely
technical, and registration *per se* does not establish rights to a domain name. See Rule 6.2,
formerly Rule 3.3c, which was first applied in *Cellcom Israel Ltd v T.M. Aquanet Computer
Communications Ltd*, District Court Reports Vol. 33(3), p.424 (1999).

3.22.3 Domain name disputes

ISOC-IL Dispute Resolution Panel

3–184 An external Dispute Resolution Panel established under the Rules offers resolution of disputes over domain name allocations within three to four months from the date of submission of a petition. The parties to the dispute retain the right to institute court proceedings.

The Dispute Resolution Panel must decide domain name disputes in accordance with the Rules. ISOC-IL is bound to implement Panel decisions pending any court or final arbitration decision on the disputed domain name.

Grounds of Challenge

3–185 Since the Rules were last amended in December 2006, the dispute resolution process has been limited to third party challenges to domain name allocations.[55] The sole ground of challenge is that the domain name is the same as or confusingly similar to a trade mark or registered name of the complainant, and was applied for or used in bad faith. The new Rules provide a non-exhaustive list of circumstances that are deemed to constitute evidence of bad faith:

1. The holder continues to hold the domain name during or after termination of employment or a work for hire contract where the domain name allegedly should have been allocated to the employing/contracting party; or
2. the holder has requested allocation of the domain name primarily for the purpose of disrupting the business of a competitor; or
3. circumstances indicate that the holder has requested allocation of or holds the domain name primarily for the purpose of selling, renting, or otherwise transferring the domain name allocation to the complainant who is the owner of the trade mark or service mark or to a competitor of that complainant, for valuable consideration in excess of documented out-of-pocket costs directly related to the domain name; or
4. the holder has requested allocation of the domain name in order to prevent the owner of the trade mark or service mark from reflecting the mark in a corresponding domain name, provided that there is evidence of having engaged in a pattern of such conduct; or
5. by using the domain name, the holder has intentionally attempted to attract, for commercial gain, internet users to its website or other on-line location, by creating a likelihood of confusion with the complainant's name or as to the source, sponsorship, affilia-

---

[55] Prior to December 2006, standing was also given to applicants and domain name holders seeking to overturn allocation decisions made by ISOC-IL, and to ISOC-IL in cases where it wished to obtain an advisory opinion regarding an allocation.

tion, or endorsement of its website or location or of a product or service on its website or location.

One of the last cases decided before the latest amendment to the Rules was **3–186** *THK.co.il*. The opinion by one of the majority members of the Committee presents an analysis of appropriate legal bases for resolving domain name disputes.

The opinion served to justify the Committee's use of laws that are not related to trade marks in order to resolve the dispute over the THK.co.il domain name in THK's favour. It argued that by virtue of its Rules, ISOC-IL has a duty to protect both the external integrity of the domain name system (i.e. to ensure that domain names do not violate the social norms of the community) and the internal integrity of the system (i.e. to ensure that domain names function as they are intended to, for example, by leading users to the website they wish to access). In accordance with this principle, the Committee determined that ISOC-IL should resolve domain name disputes using any cause of action relevant to the integrity of the domain name system, in the light of the facts of the particular case.

All three members of the Advisory Committee held that the complainant THK did not possess any trade mark rights in Israel, but that the holder of the domain name had acted in bad faith. The majority of the Committee also determined that the holder had infringed the complainant's copyright by posting material from THK's website on its own site, and had unfairly interfered with customers' access to THK's business in contravention of s.3 of the Commercial Torts Law 1999. The domain name was transferred to THK.

A year after this decision, ISOC-IL amended its rules, and as stated previously, restricted the jurisdiction of its new dispute resolution body, the Dispute Resolution Panel. The Panel can only resolve domain name disputes based on a claim that the domain name is the same as or confusingly similar to a trade mark or registered name of the complainant, and was obtained or is used in bad faith.

Determinations made to date

Between 1999 and 2007, 14 determinations were made under the previous **3–187** version of the Rules by the Advisory Committee, which was the predecessor of the Dispute Resolution Panel.[56] The Advisory Committee generally had regard in its determinations to its previous rulings. The Dispute Resolution Panel has not made any determinations to date.

Thirteen out of the 14 determinations arose from a petition by trade mark owners, and in 12 cases, a domain name that was identical to a registered or unregistered trade mark was transferred from the domain name holder to the owner of the trade mark. In eight instances bad faith

---

[56] Advisory Committee decisions are published on the ISOC-IL website at *www.isoc.org.il/ domains/ildrp.html.*

was a factor in the decision to transfer the domain name[57] and in four cases the determination was published without reasons or was made with the respondent's consent. In the 13th case, lack of a finding of bad faith led to a decision not to transfer the domain name.[58] In the remaining case, *THK.co.il*, which is discussed in the previous section, the domain name was transferred to the complainant despite the finding that it did not possess any trade mark rights in "THK" in Israel.

Under the previous Rules, bad faith was not a necessary element for a challenge, or defined by the Rules. Nonetheless, bad faith was the predominant factor in the determinations. The Advisory Committee decided that since the allocation and use of domain names have global implications, it was appropriate to apply international standards that outlaw cybersquatting[59] when judging whether a domain name holder had complied with good faith obligations imposed by Israeli law.[60] In ordering the transfer of domain names, the Advisory Committee also relied on the existence of the law against trade mark infringement and the torts of passing off, unfair intervention with access to a business, unjust enrichment (these causes of action are described in the next section), and in one instance, on copyright law, as well as on Rule 13 (formerly Rule 9.2.1(b)), which requires an active domain name server to be established within one year of the date that the domain name is allocated.

Legislation and Case Law

3–188   A wide variety of laws is applicable to domain name disputes. The Trademarks Ordinance (New Version) 1972 regulates domain names that operate as trade marks. The Commercial Torts Law 1999 and the Unjust Enrichment Law 1979 proscribe use of a domain name that creates a likelihood of confusion, and certain kinds of unfair behaviour. In some circumstances, laws that focus on property rights (the Property Law 1969 and the Chattels Law 1971), or on the public interest (the Consumer Protection Law 1981 and the Contracts (General Parts) Law 1973), will apply.

Existing judicial standards indicate that the following doctrines may influence the resolution of domain name disputes.

---

[57] For instance, "*waltdisney.co.il*" (Decision dated January 28, 2000), "*habitat.co.il*" (Decision dated August 18, 2000), "*snapple.co.il*" (Decision dated February 25, 2001), and "*windows.co.il*", (Decision dated February 6, 2005).

[58] "*utopia.co.il*" (Decision dated November 7, 2002).

[59] The Advisory Committee generally applied a test of bad faith that it derived from ICANN rules UDRP (Uniform Domain Name Dispute Resolution Policy), WIPO policy, and provisions of the US Anti-CyberSquatting Consumer Protection Act 1999.

[60] In the cases where the Advisory Committee determined that the domain name holder was acting in bad faith it held that the holder was subject to ss.39 and 61(b) of the Contracts (General Part) Law, 1973. Section 39 provides that "In carrying out an obligation pursuant to a contract, one must act in an acceptable manner and in good faith; such is also the case in using a right derived from a contract". Section 61(b) extends the Law, where deemed appropriate and with relevant changes, to non-contractual acts and obligations. In making its orders, the Committee relies on Supreme Court authority that allows quasi-judicial bodies to revoke legal actions performed in bad faith.

Trade mark infringement

Use of a domain name which is the same as or similar to a trade mark   **3–189**
registered in Israel, in relation to goods and services for which the trade
mark is registered or which are of the same description, will constitute trade
mark infringement. The District Court case of *Israel Bar Association v Yair
Ben David et al* is often cited as the classic example of judicial support for
this rule.[61]

The rule is sufficiently broad to outlaw use of a domain name even where
it denotes products sold on the domain name owner's website. In the case of
Dead Sea Laboratories Ltd v Leshno Felix et al.[62], the owner of the trademark "Ahava" for cosmetic products produced from Dead Sea minerals,
and operator of the website *"www.ahava.co.il"*, was granted an interlocutory injunction against use of its trade mark by the respondent, who
operated the website *"www.ahavashop.com"*, through which he sold
genuine "Ahava" products. The court held that the sale of genuine products
over the internet does not constitute trade mark infringement in Israel, but
that the respondent's use of the name "Ahava" as part of his domain name
does.

As a general rule, trade mark suits in Israel relating to domain names
involve multiple causes of action. One early instance of this phenomenon is
the case of *Bouquet 4 U Ltd v Chen Boulevard Flowers Ltd*, where it was
held that use of a domain name that is similar to a trade mark may constitute trade mark infringement, passing off, and unjust enrichment. The
names involved were "Bouquet4U.co.il" and Bouquet4Me.co.il".[63]

Evidence of confusion of the public is not always required in order to   **3–190**
establish infringement.[64] Neither is proof of damage suffered by the registered owner.[65]

Despite this protective approach, according to the Supreme Court, likelihood of confusion with an existing trade mark will be required in order to
refuse the registration of another trade mark intended for internet use.[66]
The same court held that the connection between a consumer and internet
supplier is primarily visual, and therefore the appearance of the marks
should be compared in preference to comparing their respective sounds.
This raises the question of whether future litigants may show that a different test of similarity is more appropriate in their circumstances.

A new limitation was imposed on the theoretical rights of trade mark

---

[61] Trademarks Ordinance (New Version) 1972, s.1 and Tel Aviv District Court File 810/01, decision dated August 28, 2003.
[62] Tel Aviv District Court Civil Files 2176/04, 18216/04, 20936/04, decision dated January 4, 2005.
[63] Tel Aviv District Court Civil File 2308/02, decision dated December 8, 2002. The case was affirmed in Rishon L'Zion Civil File 1632/04, Decision dated June 20, 2004.
[64] *A Elionel Ltd v Ariel MacDonald*, Supreme Court Reports Vol. 58(4), p.314, 2003.
[65] *Gillette Co. v Adi Z.S. Import Marketing & Distribution Ltd*, District Court Reports, Vol. 96(6), p565, 1996.
[66] *E! Entertainment Television Inc. v Deutsche Telekom AG*, Supreme Court Civil Appeal 1677/05, decision dated June 29, 2006. The respective marks were T-ONLINE and E! ONLINE.

owners in July 2006, when the District Court sanctioned "abuse" of metatags. Companies may now be entitled to use competitors' names as keywords linking to their own advertisements.

In *Matim Li v Crazy Line*, the court considered the actions of the Crazy Line fashion chain, which used the keywords "Matim Li" (which means "Suits Me") and "ML" for an advertisement in Google AdWords. Crazy Line was sued by the Matim Li fashion chain, which owned registrations for the trademark "ml-" (the initials of the Hebrew translation of the phrase "suits me") and for the "Matim Li" ("Suits Me") logo.

3–191   The Tel Aviv District Court held that neither Crazy Line nor co-defendant Google Israel Ltd had infringed any right of Matim Li. The judge based his decision on his findings that the keywords were not identical to the registered trade marks, that the keywords were not visible in Crazy Line's advertisement, that the advertisements were clearly identifiable as such and as distinct from Google's search results, and that furthermore, users who had entered these keywords could elect not to view Crazy Line's advertisement. He held that no confusion was caused, and that the principles of free competition and freedom to conduct one's occupation outweigh any rights of the plaintiff that might arise from the existence of "initial interest confusion".[67]

Use of a domain name which is the same as or similar to a "famous mark", may also constitute trade mark infringement.[68] Where the famous mark is registered in Israel, use of the same or a similar domain name in relation to any goods and services will be prohibited, if such use is likely to indicate an association between the website and the proprietor of the famous mark and will probably result in injury to the proprietor of the famous mark. Where the famous mark is not registered in Israel, protection will be afforded against third party use of a domain name in relation to the same or similar goods or services, as those for which the mark is famous.

3–192   The application of "famous mark" rules to domain name disputes was approved in *Cellcom Israel Ltd v T.M. Aquanet Computer Communications Ltd*[69] and in *Israel Bar Association v Yair Ben David et al*,[70] although in the first case the judge did not consider the trade mark infringement claim, having decided that there were sufficient grounds to grant an interlocutory injunction on the basis of other causes of action, namely passing off and theft of goodwill, and in the second case, the domain name was transferred to the trade mark owner without a decision on the question of whether the mark was famous.

---

[67] *Matim Li Fashion Chain for Large Sizes Ltd et al v Crazy Line Ltd et al*, District Court Civil File 506/06, decision dated July 31, 2006.

[68] Trademarks Ordinance (New Version) 1972, s.46a.

[69] District Court Reports Vol. 33(3), p.424 (1999).

[70] fn.61 above.

Passing off

A dealer that causes its assets or services to be mistaken for those belonging   **3–193**
to, or connected to, another dealer, is liable for the tort of passing off.[71]

This law has been applied in cases where the applicant was held to possess a reputation in its mark for the goods or services that were being offered by the respondent under an identical or similar domain name.[72] According to the judgment in the *Cellcom* case, .co.il and .com are insufficiently distinct to prevent confusion between two domain names.

In the case of a "famous mark", anti-dilution protection is afforded even where the domain name is used in relation to goods or services dissimilar to those sold by the proprietor of the famous mark. This principle is well established in Israeli law for non-internet related use. In relation to domain names, only the Advisory Committee of ISOC-IL has applied the rule to dissimilar services, in the *Snapple* and *Windows* decisions.[73]

The Jerusalem District Court set out several prerequisites for protecting a famous mark in the case of *Katan v Yariv*.[74] The Court refused to grant the owner of the website "Jerusalem-Mall.co.il", on which Judaica products were sold online, an interlocutory injunction that would have prohibited use of the domain name "Jerusalem Mall" by the owner of a website called "Jerusalem-Mall.com". The respondent's website provided links to other websites. The court held that "Jerusalem-Mall" was not a famous mark entitled to protection, due to (i) a lack of advertising, reputation or even minimal public recognition of the name, (ii) the lack of likelihood of confusion between the respective websites, since they had different functions; and (iii) the descriptive nature of the mark.

Further authority for the proposition that a descriptive domain name is a weak target for the law of passing off, is found in the decision in *Parents & Children Publications Ltd v First Step Corp*. The judge held that when the mark in question is descriptive, the petitioner's claim will be considered only if it can show that the descriptive name has acquired a secondary meaning established by the length of time that the mark has been in use, and by the extent of its public recognition and association.[75]

Misappropriation of Goodwill

The Property Law 1969 and the Chattels Law 1971, when read together,   **3–194**

---

[71] Commercial Torts Law 1999, s.1.

[72] For instance, *Bouquet 4 U Ltd v Chen Boulevard Flowers Ltd*, fn.63 above, and *Pais Lottery v Gandur* Tel Aviv District Court Civil File 3885/02, decision dated March 3, 2003.

[73] fn.57 in the *Cellcom* case, the District Court held that the trademark "Cellcom" had a reputation for internet-related services even though the trademark owner was not engaged in an internet-related business. However, as the court noted, the applicant's telecommunication services and the respondent's email delivery services to cellular telephones were similar.

[74] *Katan v Yariv*, Jerusalem District Court Civil File 226/03, decision dated September 9, 2003.

[75] *Parents & Children Publications Ltd v First Step Corp*, Tel Aviv District Court File 317/01, decision dated November 19, 2003.

proscribe the act of trespass on an incorporeal property right such as goodwill.[76] The courts have frequently resorted to these property laws in order to prevent damage to trade mark owners, particularly in cases involving misappropriation of famous marks. The *Cellcom* case is the only instance where these laws have been used to grant a remedy in a domain name dispute. The judge held that the respondent's use of the domain name "cellcom.co.il" caused damage to Cellcom Israel Limited's proprietary rights.[77]

Unfair intervention

3–195 In 1999, the legislature created a new tort of unfair intervention. Pursuant to s.3 of the Commercial Torts Law 1999, a dealer may not unfairly impede the access of customers, employees or agents to the business, asset, or service, of another dealer.

In *Magnetics Ltd v Discopy (Israel) Ltd*,[78] the court created two now well established rules regarding the application of the tort to domain name disputes. First, "access" includes electronic access. Secondly, no company or individual engaged in business may register a domain name that is *identical* to a competitor's *trade mark* if this prevents the competitor from using its trade mark for the purposes of internet activity. The parties to this case were competitors, but the rules have also been applied to dealers who are not competitors.[79] The *Magnetics v Discopy* decision was distinguished in interlocutory proceedings involving generic domain names. The judge ruled that where the domain names are generic there is no unfair intervention if users can reach the plaintiff's website by entering the entire domain name, including the top level domain.[80]

It is feasible that in cases where s.3 of the Commercial Torts Law is the most relevant legislation, the courts will use it in order to prohibit cybersquatting. There is no judicial ruling on the question of whether a

---

[76] Property Law 1969, s.17 and Chattels Law 1971, s.8.

[77] fn.69 above.

[78] *Magnetics Ltd v Discopy (Israel) Ltd*, Tel Aviv District Court Civil File 1627/01, decision dated June 3, 2001 (unreported).

[79] *Pais Lottery v Gandur*, fn.72 above. In the case of *Paradise Mombasa Tours (1997) Ltd v New Soil Technologies Ltd* the Tel Aviv District Court held that the respondent was unfairly impeding customer access to the applicant's business, and granted an interlocutory injunction to halt the operation of a website. The respondent had operated an internet site on which it conducted marketing activities for the applicant. The applicant's name was used as the domain name for the site. Despite the termination of the relationship, the respondent continued to make the website, which contained outdated information, available to the public. The judge held that the respondent had contravened s.4 (entitled "Perpetrator and Injured Party") of the Commercial Torts Law 1999. However, s.4 simply adds conditions to the requirements of ss.1 to 3 of the Law, and the judge in fact used the language of s.3 when describing the tort committed by the respondent. *Paradise Mombasa Tours (1997) Ltd v New Soil Technologies Ltd*, Tel Aviv District Court Civil File 1509/01, decision dated May 8, 2001 (unreported). The court refused to grant a remedy under the law in *Katan v Yariv* (fn.74). It held that unfair intervention demands severe hindrance caused in an unfair manner, and that these elements were not present.

[80] *Interlogic Ltd v Empire Online Ltd et al*, Tel Aviv District Court Civil File 2285/05, decision dated November 20, 2005.

cybersquatter is a "dealer". However, the Advisory Committee of ISOC-IL has determined that acquiring and holding a domain name without making use of it may constitute unfair intervention.[81]

Unjust Enrichment

The Unjust Enrichment Law 1979 provides that a person from whom a **3–196** benefit is unlawfully obtained can claim restitution.[82] Prior to the enactment of the TRIPS related amendments to the Trademarks Ordinance in relation to famous marks, the courts frequently resorted to this law in order to prevent damage to trade mark owners, particularly in cases involving misappropriation of famous marks.

This Law has also been interpreted as granting a right of redress in domain name litigation. The owner of the website "Bouquet4U.co.il" was able to prevent a competitor from operating a website with the name "Bouquet4Me.co.il".[83] Outside the court system, the ISOC-IL Advisory Committee applied the unjust enrichment law in ordering the transfer of the domain name "snapple.co.il" to the registered trade mark owner. Nonetheless, in the Matim Li metatag case, a claim that the respondent's actions constituted unjust enrichment claim was rejected.[84]

Consumer protection legislation

The Commercial Torts Law and the Consumer Protection Law both outlaw **3–197** misleading advertising.[85] This may cover use of a domain name by anyone other than the company with which Israeli consumers associate the name. The Commercial Torts Law grants "dealers" who suffer damage as a result of the publication of a false description standing to sue another "dealer" who is responsible for the publication. The only related case is the *Matim Li* decision, in which it was held that triggering the appearance of an advertisement via keywords that consisted of elements from a competitor's registered trade marks, and which were identical to its unregistered trade mark, was not misleading for the purposes of the Consumer Protection Law.[86]

---

[81] *Amdocs* and *Habitat* ISOC-IL decisions.
[82] Unjust Enrichment Law 1979, s.1.
[83] fn.63 above.
[84] fn.67 above.
[85] Commercial Torts Law 1999, s.2, and Consumer Protection Law 1981, s.7.
[86] fn.67 above.

3.23 NON-UNITED KINGDOM DOMAIN NAMES—ITALY

3.23.1 Introduction

3-198   The Italian domain name system is operated by the Italian Registration Authority (RA), the institution that carries out the actual assignment of the Domain Names with the .it ccTLD. The RA is the body in charge of entering the contracts with website providers or maintainers, be they acting on behalf of third parties or for themselves respectively.[87]

An ancillary role is played by the Registry, which sets out the procedures and the rules to be strictly adhered to for successfully lodging a registration.

The Registry administers the domain names archive and performs its functions under the authority of the CNR, The National Institute of Research (CNR, that is, a public body aimed at supporting research in technological/scientific sectors and fostering knowledge for the social and economic advancement of the country).

This is also known as the "Registry of Assigned Names", hereafter the "RNA". Its task, *inter alia*, is to verify whether the domain name is available and assignable for an applicant in compliance with the "Regulation on the Assignment and Management of Domain Names with .it ccTLD 2004".

Domain Names are assigned by the Registry on a "first-come first-served" basis. The .it ccTLD can solely be distributed to EU citizens. The applicant is granted the use of the domain name only, for he does not acquire any property. Domains are not reserved in advance. They can be transferred by means of a deed between the concerned parties.[88]

In addition, there is a specific set of names, which by virtue of their nature, are not registrable such as those relating to i.e. geographic terms or governmental bodies.[89] Thus, these domain names are reserved and made available only to pre-determined categories entitled to their use[90] (such as, for example, *www.toscana.it*, *www.RepubblicaItaliana.it*, *www.governo.it* etc.).

---

[87] The legal provisions considered in this essay are: Internet Code, Regulation on the Assignment and Management of domain names with .it ccTLD, version 4.0 2004 (a new version 5.0 is being passed; the date of its coming into force is still unknown), Electronic Communications Code: Art.15, Legislative Decree No.259, August 2003, Technical Procedures for Registration, version 4.0, 2004, Italian Civil Code Art.6–Art.7–Art.8–Art.9–Art.2569 and consequent articles–Art.2598, Industrial Property Code: Art.22.

[88] Paolo Cerina and Maria Francesca Quattrone, "*Electronic Commerce in Italy*" 1999 ICCLR (Sweet and Maxwell), 42.

[89] Reserved domain names: see following website to read the full list *http://www.nic.it/RA/domini/regole/nomi-riservati.pdf*

[90] Regulation on the Assignment and Management of domain names with .it ccTLD, version 4.0, 2004: see for reference Art.1–Art.2–Art.3–Art.4–Art.6–Art.7–Art.9–Art.10–Art.13–Art.13.1.

The entire system is under the supervision of the Ministry of Communications in co-operation with the Communications Regulatory Authority, which enforces strict control over the assignment of domain names.[91]

3.23.2 The registration process

In the first place, the applicant—be it an undertaking or an individual— **3–199** must fill in an "Inducement letter" (*lettera di assunzione di responsabilità*) whereby they expressly state they are responsible for any criminal and civil liability which may arise therefrom.

This form requires the applicant to identify and provide the necessary information regarding itself and the provider in question. In the event that the application is submitted by a company or an individual, then the information provided differs in terms of content—usually more details shall be requested in the former case. Also an individual can only be in possession of one domain name, whilst a company is subject to no such limitation. The website provider also has a duty to fill in a Registration form for the domain names: its content is saved onto the RNA where it is made accessible to the public.

Once the Registry receives the two forms, the registration procedure begins. In spite of the first-come first-served policy the Registry is obliged to verify whether the domain name at issue complies with the formal and technical requirements.

The primary step is to check and compare the domain name for which registration is sought with pre-existing ones and those whose applications are pending. However, it must be stressed that the Registry does not carry out a substantial analysis as to the existence of trade marks or names which may give rise to conflicts with the domain name for which an application was submitted.

This rule was supported by a court decision establishing that the Registry need not set out pre-emptive rules as regards conflicts which may arise among domain names that are the subject of a registration process.[92]

The next step in the registration process is to ensure that the two forms have been completed properly. Only afterwards, the Registry has to ascertain that the configuration of the name-server is effective and correct; any mistake may delay the process and the registration.

Rejection of an application can occur in several instances: i.e. where the domain name that is being sought has already been assigned or applied for, if formal and technical formalities have not been complied with properly, if the relevant documents have not been provided or if the provider is in default with the CNR.[93]

---

[91] See Electronic Communications Code: Art.15, Legislative Decree No. 259, August 2003.
[92] *Poste.it v Malavasi*, Tribunal of Modena, September 27, 2004.
[93] Technical Procedures for Registration, version 4.0, 2004.: see for reference Art.1.3-Art.2.1-Art.2.2-Art.2.2.1-Art.2.2.2-Art.2.2.3-Art.2.2.4-Art.2.4.

Fees

3–200   A provider, whose task is to register domain names on behalf of third parties will be charged a yearly fee of €2500.00 excluding VAT. For a maintainer who has entered into a direct contract with the RA, registration and maintenance of the domain name amounts to €258.93 excluding VAT for the first year; as from the second year, the fee will solely be related to maintenance of the domain name equal to €103.29 excluding VAT.

3.23.3 Disputes Settlement

3–201   In Italy, anybody can submit a complaint against the Registry as regards the assignment or the use of a domain name. The dispute settlement is regulated by the above mentioned Regulation.

   A party who is suffering damage because of the assignment of a domain name to another party can commence proceedings by addressing a complaint to the Registry. The panel in charge of delivering a decision over a dispute consists of three arbiters, each selected by the two parties to the dispute respectively and the third—acting as president of the panel—is chosen by both arbiters. Failure to elect one will lead the registry to appoint the third arbiter.

   Once the panel has been formed, a decision is expected to be delivered within 90 days. The parties involved are given the right to supply all the necessary evidence to build up a prosecution or defence motion.

   In the event of serious matters the panel, on request by one of the parties, is entitled to take all disciplinary actions it deems reasonable in respect of the domain name in question. When a decision is finally reached—based upon both the Regulation and Italian legal provisions on the matter—there is no appeal against it on the merits.[94] Clearly, it is always possible to bring proceedings before an ordinary judge.

Legislation

3–202   Domain names are afforded several kinds of protection.[95] From a civil law perspective, we encounter the provisions on the use of names and marks and distinctive signs laid down in the civil code. In the former case, any individual enjoys the right to contend the prejudicial use by others of his/her name and demand such use to cease.[96] In the latter case, instead, it is forbidden to unduly use registered and unregistered trade marks of others

---

[94] Regulation on the Assignment and Management of domain names with .it ccTLD, version 4.0, 2004: see for reference Art.14-Art.15-Art.15.1-Art.15.2-Art.15.3-Art.15.4-Art.15.5-Art.15.6.

[95] For a complete collection of provisions on the internet, see "*The Internet Code*", G. Cassano, Giuffré Editore, 2006.

[96] Italian Civil Code, Art.6–Art.7-Art.8-Art.9.

as well as distinctive characters or names which could mislead the public and link the goods or services of one undertaking with those of another.[97]

A great novelty in the Italian legal system has been the introduction of Art. 22 of the Industrial Property Code. This establishes that it is forbidden for an undertaking to use the sign or domain name of the trade mark of another if the activities of the parties are either similar or dissimilar, and in the latter case the trade mark enjoys a great reputation within the State, so as to lead consumers to believe that there is a possible link between the two undertakings, thus causing detriment to the distinctive character of the legitimate trade mark.[98]

This Code has conferred on domain names the same protection granted to distinctive signs under Industrial Property Law, also known as the "principle of unity for distinctive signs".

It must be borne in mind that a right on distinctive signs and trade marks, allows the holder to enforce that right against whoever uses them in a misleading way, regardless of the latter having formally applied for registration.[99]

Furthermore, the Tribunal of Rome has declared that domain names are afforded protection by the provisions on competition law within the Italian Civil Code.[1] Specifically, provisions on unfair competition provide practical guidelines in this sense such as Art.2598 of the Civil Code which provides that, *inter alia*, anyone who uses the names or signs so as to give rise to a likelihood of confusion with the distinctive names or signs legitimately used by others—as well as causing financial detriment to the legitimate owners— is committing an infringing act.

Case Law

Courts have often delivered judgments regarding the use or abuse of   3–203
domain names as opposed to the rights of the trade mark owners. The assignment of domain names which correspond to trademarks can amount to an infringement of trade mark law or passing off and unfair competition.

Exploiting a famous trade mark, in fact, deceives the consumers who mistakenly attribute the goodwill of the complainant to the party in breach to the detriment of the former.[2] This concept was reiterated in the celebrity case *Giorgio Armani s.p.a c. Armani Luca*. The defendant had in fact registered *Armani.it* to promote his business, dissimilar from the plaintiff's,

---

[97] Italian Civil Code, Art.2569 and consequent articles.

[98] Industrial Property Code: see Art. 22, for more in-depth analysis see "Codice della Proprietà Industriale", G.Ghidini/F.De Benedetti, ed. Il Sole 24 Ore S.p.A., 2006; "Il Codice della proprietà industriale", M.Scuffi/M.Franzosi/A.Fittante, ed. CEDAM 2005.

[99] "I domain name ed i diritti sui segni distintivi: una coesistenza problematica", Mayr in AIDA 1996, 223 ss., Giuffré Editore; also see "Internet e i segni distintivi", Frassi, in Riv.dir.ind., 1997, II, 178.

[1] *Soc. Italia Invest Com v Soc. Worldnet Financial Informations*, Tribunal of Rome, July 18, 2000.

[2] Tribunal of Modena, sez. I, October 18, 2005, local jurisprudence.

yet for commercial purposes. Consequently, that was held to be detrimental to Giorgio Armani's famous mark and repute.

These decisions are perceived as a paradox having regard to the general rule that does not compel applicants to declare that they are owners of equivalent trademarks when attempting to register a domain name.[3] If there was an obligation in that sense, there would be an *a priori* control by the RA, with a view to avoiding a flood of cases being brought before courts where individuals who are not trade mark holders have accomplished registration of names not belonging to them.

In another case *Soc. Fila Sport c. Soc. Blu ed.*[4] it was concluded that "domain grabbing" (aposquatting), an illegal practice which consists of registering the mark of another as a domain name with a view to benefiting from the repute of the mark, amounts to counterfeiting, regardless of the effective use of that domain name, as this prevents the trade mark holder from using it on the internet.

On the same pattern, *Playboy Enterprises Inc. c. Giannattasio* focuses on the role played by the provider. This was a case where an individual had managed to register the domain name of the world famous magazine *Playboy*, a registered mark in Italy. The defendant had in fact created a porn website with a monthly subscription.

3–204   The internet provider that had activated the website was deemed liable together with the website holder for a counterfeiting action brought against them by Playboy, even if the provider had acted in good faith. The RA was also deemed liable for registering the domain name of this famous trade mark. Such liability originated outside the contract in respect of the trade mark holder whereas it originated from within the contract in respect of the provider who had acted in reliance of a guarantee by the RA.[5]

Most importantly, infringement of a trade mark brought forward through its use as a domain name is committed also when the RA has authorised registration of the domain names—on a request by the defendants—or when the trade mark holder has not registered the same domain name yet.[6]

3.24 NON-UNITED KINGDOM DOMAIN NAMES— JAPAN

3.24.1 Registration

3–205   Most of the computers connected to the internet which are located in Japan are administered under the .jp domain. The two letter code .jp represents

---

[3] *Poste.it v Malavasi*, Tribunal of Modena, September 27, 2004.
[4] *Soc. Fila Sport c. Soc. Blu ed.*, Tribunal of Parma, February 26, 2001.
[5] *Playboy Enterprises Inc. c. Giannattasio*, Tribunal of Naples, February 27, 2002.
[6] *Soc. Tiscali v Marcialis*, Tribunal of Cagliari, March 30, 2000.

Japan in accordance with ISO 3166. .jp is a hierarchical domain where .jp is on the topmost level.

In order to contribute to the development of computer networks, the organisation JPNIC allocated and maintained internationally unique .jp domain names to organisations that possess or administer computer networks till 2001. JPNIC is the country Network Information Centre (NIC) of Japan. All information concerning .jp domain names, IP network numbers, name servers, contact persons, and network providers in Japan were collected into the JPNIC database.

A general-use .jp domain (e.g. *http://www.comit.jp*) has been available since May 21, 2001. Allocation of General-Use .jp domains has been managed by Japan Registry Services Co. Ltd (JPRS). JPRS was incorporated on December 26, 2000, to administer .jp domain name registration and management, and to carry out operation of the domain name system. The management and administration of the .jp domain names was transferred to JPRS from JPNIC (*http://www.nic.ad.jp/en/*) in 2001. JPRS undertake the registration, maintenance and management services of the .jp domain name. JPNIC still also maintains a responsibility for the development of .jp Domain Name Dispute Resolution Policy and related services.

A domain name consists of several levels. For example the service provider's domain name "sphere.ne.jp" consists of three parts. .jp is the top level domain. .or is a generic term for an organisation. "Infosphere" is the third level domain.[7] .jp domain name is the domain name space for the organisations and individuals in Japan.

.jp domain names are divided into two categories.

(1) General-use .jp domain name: (Domain name type without restrictions on the number of registration per registrant.)

.jp Any individual, group, or organisation that has a permanent postal address in Japan may apply for a second level, i.e., general-use .jp domain name. (e.g. example .jp)

(2) Organisational/Geographic type .jp domain name: (Domain name types in which the number of registration is limited to one per registrant.[8])

co.jp	Companies (kaisha) having an official corporate registration in Japan. Non-Japanese companies that are registered as "Gaikoku Kaisha" may also apply. (e.g. example .co.jp)
or.jp	Judicial persons (other than kaisha) established under the laws of Japan. (e.g. example .or.jp)
ne.jp	Network service providers in Japan, offering network services to the general public on either profit or non-profit basis. (e.g. example .ne.jp)

3–206

---

[7] *http://jprs.co.jp/en/jpdomain.html.*
[8] Quoted from *http://jprs.co.jp/en/jpdomain.html.*

ac.jp	Schools established under the School Education Law or other laws, institutions used by several different universities, universities, technical schools (shokugyo kunren-ko), incorporated schools, incorporated technical schools. (e.g. example .ac.jp)
ad.jp	JPNIC members. (e.g. example .ad.jp)
ed.jp	Nurseries, kindergartens, primary schools, junior high schools, middle educational schools, high schools, schools for handicapped children, vocational schools (senshu gakko), and other types of schools which are mainly for people under the age of 18. (e.g. example .ed.jp)
go.jp	Japanese government authorities, research institutes under Japanese authority's jurisdiction, and government-affiliated corporations. (e.g. example .go.jp)
gr.jp	Groups which consist of two or more individuals residing in Japan, or groups of two or more corporations established under the laws of Japan. (e.g. example .gr.jp)
lg.jp	Japanese local authorities. (e.g. example .lg.jp)
geo	Geographic Type .jp Domain Name. Japanese local public bodies and their organs, special wards and their organs, hospitals, individuals residing in Japan, and organisations having registration eligibility for any of the organisational type domain names: .ac, .co, .ed, .go, .or, .ne, .gr.

As mentioned above, the domain used for commercial purposes is the .co.jp domain. Domain names are allocated in the order of arrival at JPRS.

3–207 A corporation wanting to be allocated a domain name should apply to JPRS. The contents of the application form involve information such as name and addresses of the organisation, technical administrator, persons in charge of technical matters and persons in charge of financial matters.

JPRS checks the application form and informs the applicant whether the domain name is allocable or not within ten days from the date of the application. According to the public documents of JPRS, JPRS allocates the requested domain name if the generic name of the domain name conforms to the JPRS structure and the requested domain name does not conflict with registered domain names.

The registration of the company must be submitted in the case of the .co domain. But it does not follow that applicants must have the same company name as the domain name.

3.24.2 Disputes Resolution Policy

Rules for the .jp Domain Name Dispute Resolution Policy[9] ("DRP") were made public on July 19, 2000, revised on October 10, 2000 and implemented on November 10, 2000.

3–208

Structure

An applicant in the .jp domain should agree on this DRP (Art.2 of DRP rule) and when an administrative panel makes a decision about the disputes (Art.3), the parties should obey the decision.

3–209

According to Art.3 of the DRP rule:

"The Center will transfer or cancel the domain name registration under the following circumstances:

(1) Subject to the provisions of Art.8, the receipt by the Center of written instructions from the Registrant or its authorised agent to take such action;

(2) The receipt by the Center of the original (a copy of the original may be acceptable if circumstances require) of an order from a court or arbitration tribunal, in each case of competent jurisdiction, requiring such action; and/or

(3) The receipt by the Center of a decision of an Administrative Panel requiring such action in .jp Domain Name Dispute Resolution Proceedings to which the Registrant was a party and which was conducted under this Policy or a later version of this Policy adopted by the Center (See Art.4(i) and (k) of the Policy below.)"

Cause of action

The complainant should prove the three following elements;

3–210

"(1) the domain name of the Registrant is identical or confusingly similar to any mark such as trade mark or service mark in which the Complainant has rights or legitimate interests; and

(2) the Registrant has no rights or legitimate interests in respect of the domain name registration; and

(3) the domain name of the Registrant has been registered or is being used in bad faith (unfair purpose)."

As to "bad faith", the rule says that

"To determine whether or not there are factual elements provided by this Article (a) (iii), the panel of the dispute-resolution service

---

[9] *www.nic.ad.jp/en/regist/dom/doc/jp-drp-rule-e.html.*

provider shall consider that the registration or use of a domain name is in bad faith (unfair purpose) if the Panel found especially the following circumstances, in particular but without limitation.

(1) circumstances indicating that the Registrant has registered or has acquired the domain name primarily for the purpose of selling, renting, or otherwise transferring the domain name to the Complainant or to a competitor of that Complainant, for valuable consideration in excess of the out-of-pocket costs (amount to be confirmed by documentation) directly related to the domain name; or

(2) the Registrant has registered the domain name in order to prevent the Complainant from reflecting any trade marks or other indication in a corresponding domain name, provided that the Registrant has engaged in plural numbers of such interference; or the Registrant has registered the domain name primarily for the purpose of disrupting the business of a competitor; or

(3) by using the domain name, the Registrant has intentionally attempted to attract, for commercial gain, internet users to the website or other on-line location of the Registrant, by intending to make confusion as to the source, sponsorship, affiliation, or endorsement of the website or location or of a product or service thereon."

Defence

3–211   The defence of the domain name holder is described in subsection (c) of Art.4:

"(1) before the Registrant receives any notice of the dispute related to the subject domain name by any third party or the dispute-resolution service provider, the Registrant uses, or apparently demonstrate preparations to use, the domain name or a name corresponding thereto, in order to offer goods or services without any bad faith (unfair purpose); or

(2) the Registrant has been commonly known by any name under the domain name, regardless of registration or others by the Registrant of any trade mark and other indications.

(3) The Registrant is using the domain name for a non-commercial purpose or is making fair use of the domain name, without intent for commercial gain to misleadingly divert consumers by utilizing the trade mark and other indications of the Complainant or to tarnish any trade mark and other indications of the Complainant."

3.24.3 Legal cases

Although many examples of domain name problems are reported in Japan, **3–212**
the number of reported legal case are very limited.[10] The leading case is
"*jaccs* case" in Toyama district court. The details of the case are as
follows.

Facts

The plaintiff (Japan Consumer Credit Service) is a company whose main **3–213**
business is consumer credit services and uses "jaccs" as a trade mark. The
Defendant (Nippon Kaisyo, Inc.) is a company which sells portable toilets
and is the holder of the domain name "jaccs.co.jp". The defendant has a
home page under the domain name which has link text which links to a web
page which shows their selling goods, mobile phone and company name.

The Plaintiff filed a suit that request injunction of use of "http://
www.jaccs.co.jp" as the domain name and prohibition of indication of the
"jaccs" on the home page based on the Unfair Competition Prevention law.

Judgment

The Toyama District Court granted the Plaintiff's request on December 6, **3–214**
2000. Three issues are disputed in this proceeding;

  (a) Is the domain name use "use of the indication of goods and so
      on"?

The Unfair Competition Prevention Law prohibits the use of the mark as
the "indication of the goods". The court said that whether the domain
name use is regarded as the "indication of the goods" or not is decided by
the total consideration of the meaning of the characters of the domain
names and the contents showed in the web pages reached by the domain
name. The court said that the domain name use is considered as the indication of goods in this case.

  (b) abuse of right defence

The defendant made an abuse of right defence saying that the domain name
is registered only on the "first-come first-served" theory. The court did not
admit this defence because JPNIC can cancel the registration of the domain
name and the defendant had bad faith.

  (c) Is it appropriate for the injunction of the use of "jaccs" on the
      home page?

---

[10] *J-Phone* case (Tokyo district court judgement, April 24, 2001 injunction admitted, Tokyo
high court October 25, 2002 held), *goo.co.jp* case (Tokyo district court April 26, 2002,
Tokyo high court October 17, 2002 held), etc.

The court prohibited the defendant to use the "jaccs" on his web page saying it is obvious the use of "jaccs" on his web page is use for "indication of goods".

Nagaya High Court Kanazawa branch upheld this judgment on September 10, 2001.

3.24.4 Legislation

3–215 Generally speaking, the Trade Mark Law and the Unfair Competition Law are relevant to a Japanese domain name dispute.

Trade Mark Law

3–216 As mentioned above, a "pirate" can register the famous trade mark of another as his own domain name in Japan. Whether such pirate would infringe the trade mark or not depends on the actual usage of the domain name. According to Art.30 of the Trade Mark Law of Japan, "A trade mark owner may establish an exclusive use right with respect to the trade mark concerned". Prohibited "use" includes: "Acts of displaying or distribution of advertisements, priced catalogues or transaction papers relating to goods, to which mark is applied."

When a domain name is used on a web page in such a way that, for instance, the domain name is used as the advertisement of goods of a similar kind to the goods of the registered mark, that will be an infringement of the registered trade mark. However, the Trade Mark Law does not apply when the domain name is shown only in the window of the browser. Nor does it apply when the domain name is used in a way which is not related to goods or services.

3–217 Trade Mark Law is of no assistance in some cases. One situation is the case in which the pirate uses the domain name in an advertisement of goods which are not of a similar kind. Another is the case in which the pirate uses the domain name just to catch the eye.

The Unfair Competition Protection Act (hereinafter "UCPA") provides some heads of protection.[11]

Before it was amended in 2001, the UCPA provided protection only for a "well-known badge of recognition" and a "distinguishing badge of recognition". The plaintiff had the burden of proof that its badge of recognition was "well-known" or "distinguishing" and, in case of "well-known badge", that the defendant's registration of the domain name actually caused confusion.

These burdens proved to be too heavy for plaintiffs. The UCPA was amended in June 2001 and enacted on December 25, 2001.

According to the amendment, activity consisting of obtaining the right to use, hold and/or use the same or similar domain name to the indication of

---

[11] *http://drwww.cas.go.jp/jp/seisaku/hourei/data/ucpa.pdf.*

the goods of another other person for the purpose of unfair profit or harm to the other should be prohibited as unfair competition.

That is, Art.2(1)(xii) of UCPA set out that "acts of acquiring or holding a right to use a domain name(s) that is identical or similar to another person's specific indication of goods or services (which means a name, trade name, trade mark, mark, or any other indication of a person's goods or services), or the acts of using any such domain name(s), for the purpose of acquiring an illicit gain or causing injury to another person;" shall be defined as "unfair competition". The plaintiff can seek injunction and damage against "unfair competition" (Arts. 3 and 4).

3.25 NON-UNITED KINGDOM DOMAIN NAMES—THE NETHERLANDS

3.25.1 Registration

In The Netherlands the authority that grants access to the internet by providing uniform resource locators is the Foundation Internet Domain Registration Netherlands (Stichting Internet Domein Registratie Nederland "SIDN"), established in 1996. This foundation has the exclusive right to register domain names for the top-level domain .nl. SIDN has its own website (*www.sidn.nl*) and was established in 1996 as a private non-profit organisation to ensure efficient and fair registration of domain names. Before 1996, domain names were registered by volunteer organisations within the University of Amsterdam (i.e. Centrum voor Wiskunde en Informatica). 　**3–218**

SIDN has established and published a Regulation for the registration of .nl domain names (Reglement voor registratie van .nl-domeinnamen), which sets out the rules with regard to the registration of domain names for the .nl top-level domain. In addition to this, the terms of the standard registration contract apply.

There has been some discussion in parliament whether internet access is an essential service that should be regulated by law and administered by a government institution. For the time being, the position is that the current self-regulation by a private non-profit entity sufficiently guarantees the availability of internet access.

The nature of domain names

There also is a debate on the nature of domain names in The Netherlands. The prevailing view is that domain names are issued on the basis of a contractual relationship between SIDN and the applicant, very much like a telephone number is issued. Thus SIDN undertakes the contractual obligation to grant and maintain access to the internet through a uniform resource locator. 　**3–219**

However, a minority view, which we believe to be wrong, holds that domain names are "absolute rights" and thus a new form of property rights. So far, this minority view has been shared by SIDN. The main consequence is in the way domain names can be seized to prevent their transfer pending the outcome of a law suit. In order for SIDN to block such transfers, the seizure should be effected in the same way as the seizure of property. The courts might find such a seizure invalid, but so far this has not been tested in court. If a court were to find such a seizure invalid, it could at the same time either grant an order to transfer the domain name to the plaintiff or for a seizure in the way the court would find appropriate.

Therefore, it is prudent to follow the format for seizures as described on the SIDN website. It may be legally incorrect, but it is the only way to effectively block transfer of domain names pending litigation. SIDN may review its position in the near future.

Applications

3–220   Applications for the registration of a domain name can only be submitted on-line by a service provider registered with, and participating in, SIDN. A .nl domain name can be registered by or on behalf of a company or private person anywhere in the world. For administration purposes, the applicant needs to choose an address in The Netherlands where SIDN can send official communications, an administrative contact and provide an email address.

The application will be made by the internet service provider chosen by the domain name applicant. The applicant needs to agree to SIDN's regulations and to its registration contract and terms. This is done through the ISP in a way that may vary per provider. SIDN advises to first check through its database at *www.sidn.nl* whether the desired domain name is still available. Only domain names that are not yet registered can be applied for.

Currently the registration of personal names (the applicant's last name) as second level domain names is suspended pending a strategic debate on the future of SIDN.

Before processing the application, SIDN will check whether the domain name has already been registered by a third party, but SIDN does not check whether the application infringes any third party rights. However, the applicant is required to declare by signing the registration contract that he does not infringe such rights and is also required to indemnify SIDN against any third party claims.

The registration and maintenance fees vary per internet service provider, but are approximately €25 to €50 per year. The registration process may take some two weeks.

3.25.2 Domain name disputes

Claiming a registered domain name

If the domain name is identical or similar to the applicant's trade mark or **3–221** trade name, but has already been registered by a third party, it may be claimed by the applicant. This can be done through a UDRP procedure, as agreeing to that is a condition for registration, so almost any current holder of a domain name has agreed to it, except for some early registrants that registered their domain names before the current regulation came into force. This UDRP procedure is almost identical to the WIPO UDRP procedure.

Dutch law applies to the procedure. Under Dutch law there is a specific intellectual property right that protects trade names, that is, the name that a company actually uses in the course of its trade. The claim can be based on infringement, which includes all types of trade mark or trade name infringements recognised under Dutch law, so it is not limited to just identical signs, but also includes similar signs. The plaintiff can claim that the domain name should be transferred to him (which can be executed without the co-operation of the defendant), that the domain name should be cancelled and/or that the defendant should be injuncted from registering similar domain names in future, subject to a monetary penalty.

Being introduced in 2003, by the end of 2006 some 35 UDRPs had been instigated, of which 16 were in 2006 itself. In 18 cases the claim was awarded, in two it was rejected and the remainder were terminated during the procedure. It is most likely in a relevant number of the cases that were terminated a settlement had been reached.

Instead of using the UDRP, an applicant can also bring an action in court. This is done quite often, especially if the plaintiff also wants an injunction on trade mark or trade name infringements other than through registering a domain name. Such an action can be brought by way of preliminary injunction proceedings, which takes 4–8 weeks. In intellectual property cases, urgency is not really a requirement, as ongoing infringements are deemed to create the required urgency. Courts regularly issue orders to transfer a domain name in preliminary injunction proceedings. Under Art.50 TRIPs and its Dutch implementation, full proceedings have to follow and the term for starting those is normally set at six months in the preliminary injunction judgment. However, many cases are settled once the preliminary injunction is granted.

A large number of domain name disputes have been decided by the courts. The website *www.domjur.nl*, a joint project of SIDN and Tilburg University, contains over 300 decisions (including the UDRP decisions).

3.26 NON-UNITED KINGDOM DOMAIN NAMES—NEW ZEALAND

3.26.1 Introduction

3–222 Domain name registration in New Zealand remains an area subject to industry self regulation rather than specific legislation. InternetNZ (formerly the Internet Society of New Zealand), a non-profit industry organisation, is the body responsible for the .nz country code Top Level Domain.

3.26.2 Registration of domain names

3–223 In 2002, the New Zealand internet registry changed from one dominated by a monopolist registrar to a Shared Registry System (SRS) with multiple registrars.

Immediately prior to the SRS, a subsidiary of InternetNZ (The New Zealand Internet Registry Ltd, trading as Domainz) was the sole body charged with running the domain name register.

Since the SRS went live in 2002, InternetNZ created two bodies splitting the management and the operational functions of the domain name registry. The management function is now performed by the Office of the Domain Name Commissioner (DNC), whereas the operational function is performed by the New Zealand Domain Name Registry Ltd, trading as .nz Registry Services (NZRS). The DNC is the body responsible for granting authorisation for entities to become registrars, permitting those entities to access the .nz register to register and maintain domain names on behalf of registrants.

The domain name system in New Zealand is similar in structure to systems adopted in other countries. The New Zealand domain name space has three elements:

- the country code Top Level Domain (ccTLD) .nz;
- a second level domain (denoting a "community of interest", such as .co), and
- a third level domain (selected by the domain holder and usually a word or words, such as "mgfwebb").

Each element is separated by a full stop. Each complete name (for example "mgfwebb.co.nz") may only consist of alpha-numeric characters, but may include a hyphen, and must be unique.

3–224 InternetNZ adopts the Internet Corporation for Assigned Names and Numbers (ICANN) policy and develops local policy for the .nz domain space.

The .nz namespace currently has 13 2nd Level Domains (2LDs). The creation of further 2LDs is subject to policy administered by the DNC and is based on a concept of "communities of interest". Registration of domain names under a moderated 2LD is limited by requiring certain criteria to be fulfilled before a successful application can be approved by a delegated moderator.

The current 2LDs are:

2LD	Community of interest
.ac	Tertiary educational institutions and related organisations
.co	Organisations pursuing commercial aims and purposes
.cri	*Crown Research Institutes*
.gen	Individuals and other organisations not covered elsewhere
.geek	For people who are concentrative, technically skilled and imaginative who are generally adept with computers
.govt	*National, regional and local government organisations operating with statutory powers*
.iwi	*A traditional Maōri tribe, Hāpū that belongs to a traditional Maōri Iwi or taura here Iwi group operating with the permission of the main Iwi*
.maori	Maōri people, groups, and organisations
.mil	*Military organisations of the NZ Government*
.net	Organisations and service providers directly related to the NZ Internet
.org	Not-for-profit organisations
.school	Primary, secondary and pre-schools and related organisations
.parliament	*Agencies and individuals who are a part of the parliamentary system but not a part of the executive government*

(Italicised 2LDs are moderated.)

Of these 13 2LDs, InternetNZ has granted permission to organisations to moderate membership of five specific 2LDS: .cri.nz, .govt.nz, .iwi.nz, .mil.nz and .parliament.nz.

Moderation means that applicants need to meet specific additional cri- **3–225** teria in order to be included in that community of interest.

When accepting an application for a third level name, registrars may not

269

register the domain name unless it is unique within the selected second level domain. In other words, the domain name to be registered must not be identical to the second and third levels of a domain name that is on the records of the register. Registrars are not obliged to accept any application for a domain name.

Registrars are not otherwise obliged to pre-vet applications for domain names; nor do they require applicants to declare they are the owners of the equivalent trade marks. Instead, InternetNZ requires applicants who lodge a request for a name to warrant that they are "entitled to register the name".

The registration of domain names is carried out on a "first come, first served" basis. That is, the registration of a name within any second level domain in the .nz domain space is simply a case of being first to apply.

InternetNZ provides that names are delegated to specific registrants and that delegation confers no rights on the registrant. Registration does not mean that the registrant has any rights to be associated with the name, nor even to publish the name for any purpose.

The DNC provides that a domain name may be cancelled at any stage where the registrant does not comply with published policies or fails to meet any fees in relation or other liabilities in connection with the registration or use of the domain name.

3.26.3 Domain name disputes

3–226 Prior to June 1, 2006, there was no separate legislative or industry process for the resolution of .nz domain name disputes in New Zealand. As a result, aggrieved individuals had recourse only through ordinary court processes, where they had to rely on conventional causes of action.

Since June 1, 2006, the DNC has administered an independent and impartial dispute resolution service as an alternative to the courts in situations where two parties are in dispute over who the registrant of a .nz domain name should be.

Broadly, under the Dispute Resolution Service Policy, complainants must demonstrate that:

- they have rights to a name which is identical or similar to the domain name in dispute; and
- the registration of the domain name by the current registrant is unfair.

The complainant is required to prove to an appointed independent expert that both elements are present on the balance of probabilities.

The DRS operates three tiers of resolution:

- informal mediation (applicable only if there is a response to a complaint);

- expert determination; and
- (for appeals) a panel of three experts to make a final decision.

If the parties resolve their dispute using mediation, this process is free to use. On the other hand, expert determinations and appeals require a fee from the person making the application.

However, the dispute resolution service provided by the DNC is merely an alternative to ordinary court processes, and therefore the common law cases relating to domain name disputes are still relevant.   **3–227**

There have been a number of disputes in New Zealand over the ownership of domain names, several of which have been heard in the High Court, mainly at interlocutory level. Litigants in such disputes have primarily relied on a combination of three causes of action: the tort of passing off, misleading or deceptive conduct in the course of trade under s.9 of the Fair Trading Act 1986, and breach of a registered trade mark under the Trade Marks Act 2002.

Most of these cases have been decided in favour of the trade mark owner (whether a registered trade mark or not) seeking to prevent use and ongoing registration of domain names by cybersquatters or parties the plaintiff believes have no right to hold or use the domain name.

The test of passing off in this context is wider than its traditional elements. The underlying principle in cases of alleged cybersquatting is the jurisdiction to grant injunctive relief where the defendant is equipped with, or was intended to equip another with, an instrument of fraud[12] or an instrument of deception[13]; that is, that the domain name is of such a nature that any use of it would inherently lead to passing off.

The two most notable New Zealand cases involving domain name disputes are *Oggi Advertising Ltd v McKenzie*[14] and *New Zealand Post Ltd v Leng*,[15] both of which were interlocutory decisions.

The *Oggi* case is often regarded as the starting point in New Zealand for a passing off action involving domain names. That case endorsed the application of the test of passing off as recorded by Lord Diplock in *Erven Warnick BV v J Townend & Sons (Hull) Ltd.*[16] Five elements must be present in order to create a valid cause of action for passing off: **3–228**

1. a misrepresentation;
2. made by a trader in the course of trade;
3. to prospective customers of his or ultimate consumers of goods or services supplied by him;
4. which is calculated to injure the business or goodwill of another

---

[12] *British Telecommunications Plc v One in a Million Ltd* [1998] 4 All E.R. 476 at 493 and 497.
[13] *New Zealand Post Ltd v Leng* [1998] 3 N.Z.L.R. 219 at 231.
[14] [1999] 1 N.Z.L.R. 631.
[15] [1998] 3 N.Z.L.R. 219.
[16] [1979] A.C. 731 at 742.

trader (in the sense that this is a reasonably foreseeable consequence); and

5. which causes actual damage to the business or goodwill of the
   trader by whom the action is brought or (in a quia timet action)
   will probably do so.

The learned judge also applied *Marks & Spencer Plc v One in a Million
Ltd*,[17] in which the Court—on the balance of convenience—could not
support the defendant's registration of a domain name, when the plaintiff
had the goodwill in that name and the defendant demanded a price for
handing over the name to the plaintiff. Although mere registration of a
domain name was not passing off, the judge in the *One in a Million* case
found that, for the purposes of an injunction, it was sufficient that the
defendant's conduct was calculated to infringe the plaintiff's rights in the
future.[18]

Subsequently, in the *Oggi* case, the judge made an order for assignment
of the domain name, rather than the more conventional order to withdraw
the registration. In doing so, his Honour was influenced by the possible
intervention of a third-party during the interval between deletion of the
domain name and any attempt by the plaintiff to register that domain
name.

3-229   *NZ Post v Leng* dealt with the issue of jurisdiction in domain name
disputes. Generally, in cases involving global top level domain names, the
Courts have applied the well-established principles of *forum conveniens*.[19]
No question of jurisdiction will arise for disputes involving .nz country
code domain names, as the registration of these domain names are made
subject to the laws of New Zealand.

The judge in the *NZ Post* case found that the Court had jurisdiction over
the use of the global domain name "nzpost.com" as the defendant was
resident in New Zealand, despite the domain name having been registered
in the US. Further, the judge had little difficulty in concluding that since the
domain name used the trade mark of New Zealand Post the defendant's use
of the domain name was an instrument of deception if not an instrument of
fraud. The case is interesting as it demonstrates the ability of the Court to
make an order of potentially global effect by requiring the relinquishment
of a global top level domain name, although the plaintiff only had goodwill
in New Zealand.

Other significant New Zealand cases involving disputes over domain

---

[17] [1998] F.S.R. 265 at 271. Confirmed on appeal: *British Telecommunications Plc v One in a
Million Ltd* [1998] 4 All E.R. 476.

[18] The New Zealand courts seem to endorse the "instrument of fraud" concept: see, for
example, *Qantas Airways Ltd v The Domain Name Company Ltd* (unreported, HC
Auckland, CP26-SD99, December 9, 1999, Anderson J.) and *DB Breweries Ltd v The
Domain Name Company Ltd* (unreported, HC Auckland, M724-SW00, August 2, 2000,
Salmon J.).

[19] ICANN Uniform Dispute Resolution Process remains an available method for determining
disputes involving global top level domain names.

names include: *DS Ltd v Clifton*,[20] *Telecom Corporation New Zealand Ltd v Yellow Web Ltd*,[21] *Qantas Airways Ltd v The Domain Name Company Ltd*,[22] *New Zealand City Ltd v Baseline E-Com Ltd*,[23] *DB Breweries Ltd v The Domain Name Company Ltd*,[24] *Hirepool Auckland Ltd v Uren*,[25] and *Containerlift Services Ltd v Maxwell Rotors Ltd*.[26]

The ICANN Uniform Domain-Name Dispute Resolution Policy (UDRP) is also available as an avenue for the resolution of domain name disputes involving global TLDs. Dispute proceedings arising from alleged abusive registrations of domain names (for example, cybersquatting) may be initiated by a holder of trade mark rights.

Under the UDRP, the complainant must establish that: 3–230

- the domain name registered by the other party is identical or confusingly similar to a trade mark in which the complainant has rights; and
- the other party has no legitimate rights in respect of the domain name; and
- the domain name has been registered and used in bad faith.

The majority of such disputes are heard by the World Intellectual Property Organisation's (WIPO) Arbitration and Mediation Centre in Geneva.

Examples of some recent New Zealand complaints heard in this forum include *Museum of New Zealand Te Papa Tongerewa v Greg Nicholas*,[27] which resulted in a transfer of the domain name "te-papa.com" to the Museum of New Zealand, commonly known as "Te Papa", and *Maori Television Service v Damien Sampat*,[28] for "maoritv.com".

3.27 NON-UNITED KINGDOM DOMAIN NAMES— SINGAPORE

3.27.1 Registration

At present, the Singapore domain name registry is administered by the   3–231
Singapore Network Information Centre Pte Ltd, or SgNIC. This is a private limited company which is wholly owned by the Infocomm Development Authority of Singapore (IDA). IDA is a statutory board created by the merger of the former National Computer Board (NCB) and Telecommunication Authority of Singapore (TAS) to build upon the synergies

---

[20] Unreported, HC, Auckland, CP452-SW99, October 28, 1999, Potter J.
[21] Unreported, HC, Auckland, M 316-SW99, April 14, 1999, Potter J.
[22] Unreported, HC, Auckland, CP26-SD99, December 9, 1999, Anderson J.
[23] Unreported, HC, Wellington, CP300/99, December 20, 1999, Heron J.
[24] Unreported, HC, Auckland, M724-SW00, August 2, 2000, Salmon J.
[25] Unreported, HC, Auckland, CP292/00, September 11, 2000, Cartwright J.
[26] (2003) 10 T.C.L.R. 807.
[27] Case No. D2004–0288, June 15, 2004, WIPO, Sir Ian Barker QC.
[28] Case No. D2005–0524, August 1, WIPO, Clive Elliot.

derived from the respective converging industries. One of its objectives is to promote the use of information technology in Singapore.

SgNIC took over Technet's domain name registry function when it decided to sell and thereafter transform Technet into Singapore's second commercial internet service provider. Currently, the three main local ISPs are StarHub, Pacific Internet and SingTel. SgNIC regularly consults members of the industry for feedback.

When SgNIC was first formed, it undertook the task of registering domain names itself. However, in recent years, SgNIC has followed the worldwide trend of "devolving" the registration and certain operations of domain names to a panel of accredited registrars. However, SgNIC remains in control of the registry and its decision whether or not to accept an application for a particular domain name is final.

At present, there are seven accredited commercial domain name registrars and it is understood that SgNIC wishes to encourage greater competition in the domain name registration market. Recently, SgNIC has made it easier for companies to register themselves as a domain name registrar. SgNIC would welcome more players in the market (and have indicated that they would not be setting a limit on the number of registrars it will accredit) even if they have set up stringent criteria which registrars must satisfy in order to remain accredited.

All accredited registrars will need to enter into a "Registrar Accreditation Agreement" with SgNIC. Additionally, SgNIC has a set of "Registration Policies, Procedures and Guidelines" which the registrar and anyone who wishes to register a domain name with SgNIC would need to abide.

3–232   Applications to register a domain name must be made electronically and through one of the accredited registrars. Exceptionally, SgNIC may itself register a domain name directly. At present, there are six types of second level domain names under the .sg top level. The following three second level names would be most relevant to commercial organisations:

- .com.sg—Applicants for this domain must be commercial entities registered with the Singapore Accounting and Corporate Regulatory Authority, IE Singapore or the appropriate professional body in Singpapore. A foreign company which is not so registered may only apply for such a domain name if it appoints a Singapore registered entity as its Administrative Contact.
- .net.sg—This domain is for network providers in Singapore. Essentially, all applicants under this category must have been licensed with the iDA.
- .org.sg—Non-profit organisations would apply under this category. However, such organisations would generally also be registered with the Singapore Registry of Societies.

3–233   In September 2004, SgNIC launched second-level domain names under the .sg top level domain which is opened to all interested parties. These domain names are shorter and easier to remember. As with the .com.sg domain name, foreign-based registrants need only designate a local contact in order to obtain a second-level domain name. During the soft launch phase due priority was given to registered trade mark proprietors, government bodies and existing registrants (in that order); second-level domain names may now be registered on a "first-come first-served" basis with any of the seven SgNIC accredited registrars.

However, for all registrations, applicants have to warrant that the use of the domain name requested will not give rise to a cause of action in passing off in Singapore, infringe the trade mark of others or the rights of third parties under any treaties or agreements.

3.27.2 Disputes

The Singapore Domain Name Dispute Resolution Policy (SDRP) was **3–234** introduced by the SgNIC on November 6, 2001, and took effect on January 1, 2002. Since its inception, the SDRP has successfully established an efficient framework for Alternative Dispute Resolution of .sg domain name disputes. The SDRP is closely modelled after the Uniform Dispute Resolution Policy (UDRP) of the Internet Corporation for Assigned Names and Numbers (ICANN) and is administered by a Secretariat under the auspices of the Singapore Mediation Centre and Singapore International Arbitration Centre.

The SDRP offers parties the benefit of a convenient, swift and affordable procedure to settle domain name disputes. Under para.4(a) of the SDRP, a Complainant can make an application to cancel or transfer a .sg domain name if the following requirements are satisfied:

(i) the Registrant's domain name is identical or confusingly similar to a name, trade mark or service mark in which the Complainant has rights;

(ii) the Registrant has no rights or legitimate interests in respect of the domain name; and

(iii) the Registrant's domain name has been registered or is being used in bad faith.

It is important to note that the remedy of cancellation or transfer of domain names is only available if Complainants are able to prove, on a balance of probabilities, the clear and unequivocal existence of all three of the above-mentioned elements.

Since graphic elements of marks are not reflected in domain names, domain name disputes are primarily concerned with the word elements of trade marks, and from the outset there appears to be a clear dichotomy between unique and distinctive (and famous) marks and generic or descriptive marks. Over the years, several decisions have been made based on the principles espoused in the SDRP, shedding light on the inherent inter-relationship between the SDRP and the laws of trade marks and passing off in Singapore. Case law also offers valuable guidance as to the nature and quality of evidence that a Complainant must adduce in order to succeed in its action under the SDRP, depending on the type of marks concerned.

3–235   We examine in turn, each of the three elements:

(i) The Registrant's domain name is identical or confusingly similar to a name, trade mark or service mark in which the Complainant has rights

The term "rights" in para.4(a)(i) of the SDRP encompasses all rights of the Complainant on or before the date of the commencement of the administrative proceeding, and includes rights arising from registration of trade marks as well as the common law tort of passing off.

If a Complainant were to have a registered trade mark consisting of both graphic and word elements that are generic or descriptive, registration of that trade mark would afford the Complainant exclusive rights to use and authorise the use of the trade mark as a whole in relation to the goods and services for which it is registered.[29]

However, those exclusive rights do not automatically translate into a corresponding exclusive right to use the word elements of the mark.[30] Furthermore, if the word elements of the mark or their common abbreviations have already been adapted into the mainstream language, the word(s) concerned would be deemed to have become "customary in the current language or in the *bona fide* and established practices of the trade".[31] This would diminish the strength of the Complainant's assertion that it has exclusive rights to the word(s).

3–236   In such a situation, a Complainant would also be hard-pressed to demonstrate the necessary misrepresentation and damage required to support an action for passing off, as it has been held that the mere fact that significant internet traffic flowed through the Registrant's website bearing the disputed domain name does not in itself establish misrepresentation or damage to the Complainant.[32] Where domain names comprising common or generic words are concerned, it is simply not possible to gauge whether the internet traffic actually intended to access the Complainant's website in the first place.

This is in stark contrast to a situation where the word elements of a mark are distinctive and fanciful, as such marks are far more likely to be registered as trade marks not only in Singapore, but in other countries as well.

The inclusion of descriptive words in the Registrant's domain name in addition to the unique mark also does not preclude a finding that the domain name is confusingly similar to the Complainant's trade mark. In fact, in determining the scope of the Complainant's rights in para.4(a) of

---

[29] Section 26(1) of the Trade Marks Act (Cap 332, 1998 Rev Ed) [hereinafter "TMA"].

[30] Phang Hsiao Chung, *Resolving Domain Name Disputes—A Singapore Perspective*, 14 Sa.C.L.J. 85 at 129.

[31] *Supra* fn.30, s.7(1)(d).

[32] *Viacom International Inc v Elitist Technologies Co Ltd* (SDRP–2002/0001(F)) at para.6.2.32.

the SDRP, it is irrelevant that the Complainant's goods, services or business are different from the Registrant's.[33]

Even if the Complainant's mark is not registered as a trade mark, the Administrative Panel is far more likely to find the three requisite elements to constitute passing off where a mark is distinctive and unusual:

    3–237

(a) goodwill—through business activities and use of the mark;

(b) misrepresentation—confusion when internet users are misled and diverted to the Registrant's website, notwithstanding any disclaimers they may encounter upon arrival; and

(c) damage—the erroneous belief of internet users, especially since the Complainant has no control over the content of the Registrant's website

and conclude that the Registrant has infringed the Complainant's rights in its mark by registering a confusingly similar domain name.

(ii) The Registrant has no rights or legitimate interests in respect of the domain name Paragraphs 4(a)(i) and (ii) of the SDRP appears to contemplate a situation where both the Complainant and Registrant have "rights" to a domain name.[34] In such a scenario, the rights of the Registrant, who was first in time to register the domain name, prevails, especially if the Registrant is able to offer cogent evidence proving the continued development of an established website as part of a genuine going concern, *prima facie* rebutting the Complainant's claim that the Registrant does not have any rights or legitimate interests in its domain name.

    3–238

Paragraph 4(c) of the SDRP provides some general guidelines on determining Registrants' rights to and legitimate interests in domain names in response to such complaints. The Administrative Panel has fine-tuned the provision in the cases, refusing to recognise the offering of products and services which are compatible with the Complainant's goods as a legitimate interest, especially where it is shown that the Registrant is exploiting the domain name for commercial gain and benefiting from attracting internet users to its website.[35]

This is even more so where the Registrant has not started to use the registered domain name in connection with any *bona fide* commercial activity, and is unable to demonstrate any concrete preparations to commence business at the time of the hearing.[36]

It is therefore evident that the Administrative Panel is clearly not fettered by a rigid and restrictive interpretation of the Registrant's "rights" and "interests", but instead employs commercial and pragmatic considerations to guide its ruling.

---

[33] *Google, Inc. v Googles Entertainment* (SDRP–2002/0003(F)) at para.6.6.

[34] *Supra* fn.30 at 131.

[35] *Samsung Electronics Co Ltd v Funexpress.com.sg Pte Ltd* (SDRP–2002/0004(F)) at paras 6.18 and 6.24.

[36] *Supra* fn.34 at para.6.16.

3–239 (iii) **The Registrant's domain name has been registered or is being used in bad faith** Evidence of good faith or lack thereof on the part of the Registrant is critical to determining whether the registration of the domain name was *bona fide* under the SDRP.

A list of circumstances evidencing bad faith is set out in para.4(b) of the SDRP, but this list is by no means exhaustive—Administrative Panels are tasked with scrutinising the circumstances of each case and conduct of Registrants to determine their true motives and intention in registering the disputed domain name.

So the fact that a Registrant offers to sell the disputed domain name to the Complainant for a price greater than that at which it was bought does not necessarily indicate bad faith or that the Registrant purchased the domain name primarily to profit from its re-sale, unless it transpires that the Registrant owns a bank of domain names which it registered with the intention of blocking subsequent applications so that it may then sell, rent or otherwise transfer the domain name registration for profits—speculation in the sale of domain names corresponding to the marks of others is not a legitimate interest.[37]

The Administrative Panel takes into consideration the role the domain name plays in the Registrant's business, as well as the amount of time and resources invested in developing and maintaining the website.[38] Other factors which tend to imply bad faith on the Registrant's part include the fact that: the Registrant has made no use of the registered domain name; the Registrant is unable to explain why it chose to register a unique name not naturally associated with its business; and the Complainant's business is well-known and the mark is so distinctive that it is most unlikely that the Registrant was unaware of it.[39]

Again, the implications of these factors are more significant where the domain name concerned is distinctive or famous. Where the domain name is generic or descriptive, it appears Administrative Panels are more likely to find that the Registrant either has a legitimate right or interest in respect of the domain name, or that it has acted in good faith in registering the domain name.[40] Any evidence of at least an intention on the Registrant's part to make proper use of the domain name could weigh in its favour, placing a heavy burden on the Complainant to prove its case.

Recognising the inherent close connection between the SDRP and the law of trade marks and passing off in Singapore, para.4(k) of the SDRP provides for the possibility of Panel decisions being reviewed by the courts for independent re-examination and resolution. At the time of writing there does not appear to be any reported judgments by the courts concerning the ownership of domain names in Singapore. It will be interesting to observe how the courts reconsider the decisions of the Administrative Panel

---

[37] *McDonald's Corporation v Naturerise, Inc* (SDRP–2005/0001(F)) at para.6.3.2.
[38] *Supra* fn.33 at para.6.4.4.
[39] *Supra* fn.34 at paras 6.21–6.25.
[40] *Supra* fn.33 at para.6.4.8.

according to the different principles under the law of trade marks and passing off.

3.28 NON-UNITED KINGDOM DOMAIN NAMES—SPAIN

3.28.1 Introduction

.es Governing Body

The governing body of the .es domain name is the entity Red.es. It is in charge of managing the registration of the .es domain name, as well as of setting up, maintenance and operation of the equipment, application and databases which may be necessary for the operation of the internet domain name system under the country code corresponding to Spain (.es).   **3–240**

This entity, which also participates in the bodies that co-ordinate the management of ICANN domain name registration, is attached to the Science and Technology Ministry through the Telecommunications State Secretariat, and acts as advising body before the Ministry, representing the same before ICANN and GAC (ICANN's Governmental Advisory Committee).

3.28.2 Registration

Who may apply for a .es domain name

The criteria for the assignment of .es domain names are established in Act 34/2002, of July 11, on *Information Society Services and Electronic Commerce* (Spanish acronym, "LSSI"). The first regulatory development of this Act was carried out through Order CTE/662/2003, of March 8 which approves the *National internet domain name plan under the country code corresponding to Spain, .es*, which was subsequently repealed by Order ITC/1542/2005, of May 19, 2005.   **3–241**

By means of those statues the registration process of the .es domain names has been simplified; more specifically, the criterion followed to determine the legitimacy which, contrary to what was previously the case, no longer depends on whether the domain name applicant has legal personality or not, or whether s/he owns earlier intellectual property rights or not.

Quite to the contrary, in order for the applicant of an .es domain name to be recognised as having legitimacy, it must have a "link to Spain".

Indeed, in accordance with the provisions of the LSSI and the Order of May 2005, all individuals and entities, with or without legal personality, who have interests or keep ties with Spain are able to request the assignment of an .es domain name, provided that they also meet the other mandatory requisites to obtain a domain name.

In this regard, and pursuant to Article Ten of the *"Instruction of the Director General of Red.es of 8 November 2006 which develops the applicable procedures for the assignment and other operations associated to the registration of .es domain names"* it can be inferred that the following personae have interests or maintain ties with Spain:

- Individuals or entities established in Spain;
- Individuals or entities who wish to direct all or part of their services to the Spanish market;
- Individuals or entities who wish to offer information, services and/ or products which are culturally, historically or socially linked to Spain.

3–242 Likewise, through the National Plan of May 2005 the prohibitions applicable to the assignment of second level domain names have been simplified; individuals are now allowed to apply for any type of domain name, as well as compound names comprised exclusively of their last name or of a combination of their first and last name provided that these are directly linked to applicant.

As for third level domain names, the National Plan of May 2005 distinguishes between "open registration" (.nom.es and .org.es) which are those domain names assigned without previously checking the applicable requisites, and "restricted" domain names (.gob.es and .edu.es), where compliance with the applicable requisites and prohibitions is verified beforehand.

In sum, regardless of the nationality of the applicant, but always provided that they have ties with Spain, in the above mentioned sense, it will be possible to apply for the following .es domain names:

- Individuals or entities and entities without personality, shall be allowed to apply for any .es or .com.es domain name
- Individuals shall also be allowed to apply for .nom.es domain names
- Non-profit entities, institutions or groups shall be allowed to apply for .org.es domain names
- The Spanish Public Administration and public entities depending from them shall be allowed to apply for .gob.es domain names
- Lastly, entities, institutions or groups with or without legal personality which have been officially recognised and carry our activities related to teaching or researching in Spain are allowed to register .edu.es domain names.

Criteria followed in the registration process

As mentioned earlier, by means of the LSSI and the Order of May 2005 the   **3–243**
.es domain name assignment system has been progressively simplified, and
is currently governed by the following criteria:

- First-come first-served basis—According to the provisions of Articles
  Five and Eight of the Plan of May 2005 and Article Six of the
  Instruction of the Director General of Red.es of November 2006,
  second and third level domain names shall be assigned taking on a
  first-come first-served basis. The time priority shall be determined by
  the reference number indicated in the application upon its receipt.
- Exclusivity—No applications can be filed for .es domain names
  which have been previously assigned.
- No previous check—The assignment of an .es domain name shall
  occur once it has been verified that the syntax rules established in
  Art.11 of the National Plan have been complied with, that none of
  the terms included in the list of prohibited terms of the National
  Plan has been included, and also that the specific limitations and the
  list of second level prohibited or reserved envisaged in Art.7 of the
  aforementioned Plan have been respected.

3.28.3 Alternative Dispute Resolution System

In accordance with the Single Additional Provision of the National Plan of   **3–244**
May 2005, the entity Red.es has created an alternative dispute resolution
system aimed at preventing the registration of abusive or speculative
domain names.

In this regard, the registration of a domain name is considered abusive or
speculative when the registered domain name is identical or similar—to the
point of creating confusion—with an other term protected by earlier intellectual property rights and the owner of the domain name lacks rights or
legitimate interests on said term, or has registered or is using it in bad faith.

There are currently four entities authorised to provide alternative dispute
resolution services:

- (AECEM), Asociación Española de Comercio Electrónico y Mar-
  keting relacional (Spanish Electronic Commerce and Relational
  Marketing Association).
- (Autocontrol), Asociación para la Autorregulación de la Comuni-
  cación Comercial (Association for the Self-Regulation of
  Commercial Communications).
- Consejo Superior de Cámaras de Comercio, Industria y Navegación
  de España (Spanish High Council of Commercial, Industry and
  Navigation Chambers).
- WIPO Arbitration and Mediation Center.

It is important to point out that the holdings of the above referenced bodies shall be binding on the parties, unless any of them decides to institute legal proceedings within 30 days from the date when the decision has been served on the parties.

3.28.4 Disputes concerning domain names—notable decisions

3–245   Although domain names are not properly a distinctive sign—there was a failed attempt to include them in the relative grounds for refusal envisaged in Art.9.1.d) of Act 17/2001, on Trademarks, the truth is that they have been often used to pirate known marks. The practices are very diverse:

- There are cases where the registration of the domain name consisting of a term previously registered as mark by a third party is sought, with the purpose of obtaining a consideration from said third party (*Viagra* Case, Court Order of the Community Trade Mark Court at Alicante, 19-X–2004 (AC 2005/95); *Dreamworks* case, Judgment of the High Court Madrid, 17-IX–2004) .
- In other cases, the term which forms the domain name consists of the name of a third party competitor company, with the purpose of preventing said third party competitor from using it in the marketplace ("*La Tienda del Espía*" Case, Judgment of the Madrid High Court 20-IV–2006).
- Likewise, there are cases where the domain name consists of a term which is not comprised of a third party business name or mark, but of a very similar term which only differs from them in certain letters. They are the so-called *oops! Domain names*.

3–246   Also frequent is the practice known as "*reverse domain name hijacking*" where a third party registers a domain name as mark with the purpose of preventing its owner from accessing the market.

In all these cases the owner of the sign affected by the registration of the domain name can invoke the infringement on its trade mark or business name rights, or the violation of unfair competition laws, as undoubtedly the abusive or fraudulent registration can constitute, for instance, an act of taking unfair advantage of the reputation of a third party, or an act of hindering access to the market.

An example of the aforementioned is the case "*Carrefour*", decided on appeal by the Provincial Court of Barcelona in its judgment of June 21, 2005 (JUR 2005\180742). In this case, the defendant had registered a series of domain names containing the terms "Carrefour" and "champion", seeking protection in the names of two companies incorporated in the Virgin Islands, which were merely instrumental companies to confer legitimacy to the registration of the domain names. In this case, both before the trial courts and on appeal, the court considered that the use by the defendant of names which were identical to plaintiffs named websites on the internet misled consumers and, therefore, amounted to an infringement on the plaintiffs' trademark rights.

However, Spanish case law follows on occasion somewhat lax criteria, which lead to dismiss complaints concerning the registration of a domain name on the basis of an infringement on earlier third party rights.

A clear example thereof is the "*CITI*" case, where the Provincial Court of Madrid held that the use and registration of the mark CITI and Design and of the domain name .citi.es by Compañía Internacional de Transportes e Inversiones, S.L., did not infringe on the intellectual property rights of Plaintiffs CITICORP, CITIBANK, N.A., CITIESPAÑA, S.A. and CITI-HOUSE, S.A. According to the Court's decision, although the opposed signs shared the same root "citi", other elements distinguished the marks and avoided the risk of confusion on the part of the consumers.

3.29 NON-UNITED KINGDOM DOMAIN NAMES— SWEDEN

3.29.1 Introduction

The registry and co-ordinating function of the Swedish national TLD .se   **3–247** (the .se domain) is performed by Stiftelsen för Internetinfrastruktur (the "IIS").

The IIS was formed in 1997 by the Swedish Chapter of the Internet Society, ISOC-SE. Previously, the .se domain had been the responsibility of a private individual, Mr Björn Eriksen, to whom the top level domain had been delegated by NIC (a precursor to the IANA function under ICANN) in 1986. Mr Eriksen was at this time employed in the IT industry, but maintained the registry independently, a practise he continued when he later moved to the Royal Institute of Technology. Mr Eriksen met the increased demands made by this task with the support and tacit approval of the university, but was in effect entirely unregulated by external powers.

Eventually, the demands on the registry became heavy enough to require the management of the domain to be transferred to a special purpose organisation. At the time of the inception of the IIS, the .se domain had circa 50,000 registered domain names. On January 1, 2007, the .se domain had close to 567,000 registered domain names.

The governing instruments of the IIS set out the objective of the foundation as promoting the stability of the internet infrastructure in Sweden, and to promote research, education and training in computer and telecom communications with particular emphasis on the internet. The continued development of the management of domain names in the .se and other national TLD is indicated as being of particular importance. The IIS, though a non-profit organisation, thus operates the .se domain to generate a reasonable surplus, which is used to promote the foundation objectives. This is mainly performed through granting financial support to research institutions, and supporting internet-related projects in Civil Society organisations.

3.29.2 Applicable legislation

3–248   As of July 1, 2006 the .se domain is regulated by the Act (2006:24) on National Top Level Domains for Sweden on the internet. The Act regulates all TLD "for Sweden", but is presently only applied to the .se domain. The Act requires the domain administrator (IIS) to notify the supervisory authority of its operations. The Swedish National Post and Telecom Agency (PTS), the telecom national regulatory authority, constitutes the supervisory authority.

The Act can be described as light-handed regulation. It requires the domain administrator to carry out domain operations in a safe and efficient manner in the public interest, to maintain and securely keep a registry database of allocated domain names and their registrants, and to deposit and keep updated a copy of this registry database with the PTS. The purpose of the deposit requirement is to safeguard the domain operations in the event the administrator ceases to function.

The Act does, however, not regulate the criteria under which the PTS may or must take action to maintain the .se domain operating, beyond authorising the PTS to supervise that the requirements of the Act are fulfilled. The Act also authorises the PTS to issue regulations supplementary to the Act, and to gain access to the domain administrator's premises for the purpose of carrying out inspections and other actions pertaining to its supervision.

3–249   On domain names, the Act requires that the administrator adopt and publish regulations on allocation, registering, de-registering and transferring of domain names. Such regulations are required to ensure a transparent, non-discriminatory procedure and to take into regard the protection of privacy, user interests and other public interests and finally internet developments.

The Act does not regulate how domain names are to be allocated, but requires the administrator to maintain a procedure for alternative dispute resolution (ADR). Furthermore, the Swedish Trade Mark Act (1960:644), the Swedish Trade Names Act (1974:156) and the Swedish Marketing Practices Act (1995:450), for example, all apply to the use of domain names.

As the IIS is a registered foundation, it is also subject to supervision under the Foundations Act (1994:1220). Supervision under the Foundations Act is focussed on the finances and assets management of foundations, and that foundations adhere to their internal governing instruments. Supervisory activities are the responsibility of the County Administrative Board where a foundation is registered as having its base; Stockholm in the case of IIS.

3.29.3 Domain Name Regulations for the .se domain

From the inception of the .se domain the regulations on who was permitted   **3–250**
to register which domain name were very restrictive. The administrator's
stated objective in this regard was to avoid conflicts and, as far as possible,
forestall legal liability. The administrator's regulatory framework was later
liberalised in steps. With the introduction of version 3.0 in April 2003, it
became possible for anyone to register virtually any .se address providing
that the domain name is available.

The domain name regulations

The II-Foundation's vision for the allocation of domain names under the .se
top level domain is that

> *"The national top domain .se shall be the natural home address
> for all users who have a connection to Sweden. This shall be
> effected without any risk to or deterioration of future technical
> developments or the emergence of new services. The domain shall
> be distinguished by stability and security, at the same time as the
> administration shall be quick, flexible, predictable and
> unbureaucratic."*

IIS domain name regulations, "General Conditions for Registration of .SE
Domain Names", are available in English from the IIS website *www.iis.se*.
The present version 3.0.6 came into force on February 12, 2007.

According to the regulations all applications for domain names must be   **3–251**
filed through one of IIS certified registrars. There are currently around 200
certified registrars. A complete list of official registrars is maintained on the
IIS website. Any natural or legal person who professionally conducts
operations of an economic nature, and whose operation is listed in an
official or trade register, may become a registrar. Registrars are subject to
entry and annual fees, and are required to submit a deposit. An English-
language version of the Registrar Agreement is available on the IIS website.

A domain name can only consist of the letters a–z, the numbers 0–9 and
the hyphen. It must begin and be ended by a letter or a digit, and may not
consist exclusively of hyphens. For technical reasons, it is not possible to
register a domain name that begins with two letters followed by two
hyphens. Purely numeric domain names are permitted since March 2006.
The domain name must contain at least two characters, and may have a
maximum of 63 characters. The .se domain supports the IDN standard,
whereupon many non-ASCII scripts can be registered as domain names
through the conversion to ASCII letters as set out by the standard.

Certain domain names are reserved by IIS, e.g. geographic words intended for use by municipalities or embassies, and therefore can not be
registered. A list of reserved domain names is available on the IIS website.

There is no limitation on the number of domain names possible to register per legal or private person.

IIS does not examine if an applicant's domain name infringes any third party rights or otherwise is inconsistent with legislation or regulation. The responsibility regarding the legal consistency rests solely on the applicant. IIS applies a "first come, first served" principle for the allocation of domain names, i.e. applications will be dealt with in the order they are received by IIS.

3–252   Trade marks can be registered directly under the .se domain but also under the .tm.se second level domain. In order for a trade mark to be registered under the .tm.se level it must be protected as (i) a national distinctive mark for goods or services, which is registered with the Swedish Patent and Registration Office (the "PRV") and has acquired legal force in Sweden, (ii) an international distinctive mark, which is protected in accordance with the so-called Madrid protocol and after designation has been registered *and* the registration has acquired legal force in Sweden, or (iii) a distinctive mark, which by means of registration, such as the European Community trade mark (the "EC mark") with the OHIM registration authority in Alicante, Spain, has legal force in Sweden.

There are also a number of other second level domains, such as .org.se for non-profit organisations, .parti.se for political parties, .press.se for periodical publications (magazines) and .pp.se for private individuals. There are, however, few names registered under most of the second level domains.

3.29.4 ADR under the .se Domain

3–253   IIS is entitled to cancel a registration after completed ADR proceedings, if the Holder does not satisfy the obligations laid down in the registration-conditions, or if the registered domain name should conflict with applicable laws or a final judgment or decision on infringement.

Following the liberalisation of the IIS domain name regulations, the .se domain became of interest for so called "cybersquatters". This has resulted in some 130 procedures before the ADR from 2003 through 2006. The ADR procedures only handle apparent cases of abuse and is also intended as a deterrent to prevent registrations made in bad faith. Disputes raised for ADR are settled by an adjudicator who is an independent lawyer approved by the IIS. Either party to the dispute has the right to demand that three adjudicators decide the ADR, where each party may designate one of them.

The ADR carries a SEK 10,000 cost, paid for by the party initiating the procedure. Should one of the parties demand the use of three adjudicators, the party is liable for a further SEK 10,000 charge. A 25 per cent surcharge is added for legal persons. Reduced rates are available when larger number of domain names are to be processed at the same time.

Many of the problems for the .se domain, following the liberalisation, are known from other liberal domain name systems in the world such as companies that on a large scale register misspellings of popular websites, company names and municipality names as their domain name.

A party that feels they are entitled to a registered domain name held by another party can use the ADR in order to have the name transferred from the holder to the claimant. The three factors taken into account in the ADR proceedings are (i) if the domain name is identical to or easily confused with a protected name or distinctive mark, (ii) if the holder does not have any right or legitimate interest in the domain name, (iii) if the domain name has been registered or used in bad faith.

There are also a few Swedish court decisions on domain names under the 3–254 "net" and "com" domains. In 2001 a Swedish district court found that a company that had registered "volvo-tuning.com" and informed the public that it was in the business of tuning Volvo cars was infringing the rights of the car manufacturer Volvo.

Both the Swedish Trade Mark Act and the Swedish Trade Names Act prohibits unauthorised use of a protected name in the course of business. The mere registration of a domain name, without adding any content to the relevant domain, would probably not constitute an infringement according to the abovementioned acts. In the "*volvo-tuning*" case mentioned above the registrant had added some content trying to market its services and it was found that the registrant was infringing another party's right. The registrant was ordered by the court either to de-register or change the domain name under a penalty.

Furthermore, the Swedish Marketing Practices Act could be used in some cases since it states that all marketing practices must be consistent with generally accepted marketing practices and otherwise fair in relation to consumers and undertakings. For example if someone uses a trademark belonging to someone else and such use causes confusion as to the origin of a product in its marketing, it can be seen as a violation of the requirement referred to above.

3.30 NON-UNITED KINGDOM DOMAIN NAMES— SWITZERLAND

3.30.1 Status of Switzerland's domain name registry

In Switzerland the registration of domain names is carried out by SWITCH, 3–255 a foundation constituted under private law. The main function of SWITCH is to operate high-performance telecommunications networks for Switzerland's universities. However, since 1987 SWITCH has also been responsible for the registration of second-level domain names in Switzerland (the .ch domain) and since 1993 has also had responsibility for the Principality of Liechtenstein (the .li domain). Domain name registration is managed by a department within SWITCH which is partly autonomous.

Until the completely revised Telecommunications Act (or FMG) came into effect in 1997, the assignment and administration of domain names in Switzerland was not regulated as a sovereign function. SWITCH carried out its activities solely on the basis of private law. Under the 1997 FMG (Art.28), however, domain names became subordinated as so-called addressing resources under government control through a Federal authority, the Federal Office of Communications (OFCOM).

However, taking special account of SWITCH's well-tried and tested system of domain name registration, Art.28, para.2 FMG included a provision enabling the administration of addressing resources to be delegated to third parties by OFCOM.

3–256 With reference to Art.28, para.2 FMG, OFCOM initially commissioned SWITCH to administer and assign .ch domain names in accordance with the principles previously established. It was only with effect from April 1, 2002 that the administration and assignment of .ch domain names became regulated through government regulations as a result of a supplement to the Ordinance concerning Addressing Resources in the Telecommunications Sector (OARTS).

On the basis of the OARTS, OFCOM delegated the administration and assignment of .ch domain names to SWITCH in an administrative law agreement which preserved OFCOM's supervision of the activities of SWITCH. This agreement, which was entered into initially up until March 31, 2007, was extended at the start of 2007 until March 31, 2015.

The basic principles for the administration and assignment of .ch domain names are now defined by the OARTS and by detailed technical and administrative implementation regulations issued by OFCOM, which are based on the OARTS. No distinction is made between Registry and Registrars, which is not the case with other TLDs. SWITCH is responsible for both the operation and maintenance of the database containing the registered domain names and for providing internet users with services related to the administration and assignment of .ch domain names. Pursuant to Art.14b of the OARTS, SWITCH is also obliged to make wholesale offers to companies wishing to provide third parties with services related to the administration and assignment of .ch domain names.

The relationship between SWITCH and the domain name owners is regulated by means of private law contracts and to this end, SWITCH has laid down General Terms and Conditions (GTC) within the parameters defined by the OARTS and the implementation regulations associated therewith, which have been approved by OFCOM. Not only the GTCs, but also the fees charged by SWITCH are subject to approval by OFCOM.

The GTCs and the charges payable are published on the SWITCH website.[41]

---

[41] http://www.switch.ch/id/terms/.

3.30.2 General description of Switzerland's domain name system

Domain names can be registered both by private individuals and by companies subject to the same conditions. Individuals and companies resident outside Switzerland may also register. **3-257**

An annual fee is payable in return for registration. In the event of late payment, SWITCH reserves the right to delete the domain name in question if the overdue payment is not received despite repeated reminders.

Unlike the .uk or .fr domains in the UK and France, the .ch domain is not subdivided into special sub-domains for companies, public bodies, universities or private individuals, for example. The domain name may be constituted as desired, provided that it, or rather its ACE string (ASCII Compatible Encoding String), consists of a minimum of three and a maximum of 63 characters and abides by the general rules which apply for technical reasons in relation to domain names (e.g. no special characters other than those listed in Annexes 1 and 2 of SWITCH's GTCs may be used).

There is no limitation on the number of domain names which may be registered for a particular owner. However, in its policy, SWITCH reserves the right to refuse applications for registration which are clearly improper.

SWITCH can register both active and inactive domain names. "Inactive" means that a domain name is registered for an individual or a company and thus cannot be registered by any third party even though the domain name concerned is not yet being effectively used.

3.30.3 Disputes

SWITCH registers domain names on a "first come, first served" basis. In so doing it does not carry out any check on the entitlement of the applicant to the domain name in question, e.g. to establish whether the applicant is the owner of an identical or similar trade mark or trade name. The applicant himself/itself is solely responsible for ensuring that the rights of third parties are not infringed. **3-258**

On the basis of the corresponding regulation in the technical and administrative implementation provisions and an associated list of names, SWITCH will only check in the case of names of villages and towns whether the relevant local authority has given its consent to registration.

On March 1, 2004 an out-of-court Dispute Resolution Service was set up for the .ch domain. The WIPO Arbitration and Mediation Center was charged with the duty to act as Dispute Resolution Provider and is responsible for appointing Conciliators and Experts, and also for the administrative handling of proceedings.

Proceedings take place in two stages.[42] A Conciliator first attempts to effect an amicable settlement between the parties in dispute by means of a conciliation process. This process normally consists of a telephone conference lasting one hour unless the parties agree on a longer duration or additional negotiations. If the conciliation process is not successful, in a second stage an Expert is appointed to settle the dispute by means of a decision. This second stage only comes about, however, if requested by the applicant at the beginning of the proceedings to cover the eventuality of the conciliation process being unsuccessful.

As soon an application has been submitted to the Dispute Resolution Provider, the latter must inform SWITCH immediately. SWITCH will in turn immediately block the appropriate domain name for the duration of the dispute resolution proceedings so that it can no longer be transferred to a third party by the current owner.

3–259 The time needed for the conciliation process is normally 63 days and for the decision process by an Expert, including the implementation of the Expert's decision, 39 days. Both stages together thus take 102 days.

The costs for the services of the Dispute Resolution Provider and of the Conciliator and Expert amount to CHF 600 for the conciliation process and for the decision process by an Expert CHF 2,000 (1–5 domain names) or CHF 2,500 (6–10 domain names). If more than 10 domain names are involved in the proceedings, the costs will be determined by the Dispute Resolution Provider on a case-by-case basis.

The Dispute Resolution Service is available to defend the infringement of any kind of distinctive sign protected under Swiss law by domain names registered in the .ch domain. These include in particular registered business names, personal names, trade marks, geographical indications and defensive rights devolving from unfair competition law. In the application for dispute resolution, the owner of a protected distinctive sign may request either deletion of the infringing domain name or the transfer thereof. In order for an application for deletion or transfer to be approved by the Expert, however, there must have been a clear infringement of a right in a distinctive sign belonging to the applicant.

Dispute resolution proceedings are not mandatory. The parties may bring an action in a public court at any time. This is even possible in the course of dispute resolution proceedings (and the Conciliator or Expert must then decide whether the dispute resolution proceedings should be suspended, ceased or possibly continued in parallel with the judicial proceedings).

If the decision by the Expert approves deletion of a domain name or its transfer to the applicant, SWITCH will implement the decision within 20 working days, unless the owner of the domain name in question brings a court action within this period of 20 working days with the object of

---

[42] The procedure is regulated in the Rules of Procedure for Dispute Resolution Proceedings for .ch and .li Domain Names, which are published on the SWITCH website (*http://www.switch.ch/id/disputes_rules_v1.html*).

obtaining a court ruling determining that, contrary to the decision by the Expert, registration of the domain name in question was legitimate.

An action of this kind must be brought at the competent court in Zurich, 3–260 the city where the SWITCH office is located. When submitting an application for dispute resolution, the applicant must specifically acknowledge the jurisdiction of this court. The bar placed on the domain name by SWITCH at the commencement of dispute resolution proceedings remains in place for the duration of the judicial proceedings.

A total of 38 cases were settled through decision by an Expert in the period between March 1, 2004 and the end of 2006. The applicant was successful in 25 cases and orders for either transfer (24 cases) or deletion (1 case) of the domain name, depending on the applicant's request, were issued. The application was rejected by the Expert in 12 cases, and in one case concerning several domain names, the application was partially approved and partially rejected.

The decision concerning the domain names "schweiz.ch", "suisse.ch" and "svizzera.ch" generated a great deal of interest. These domain names were allocated to the Swiss Confederation, which started dispute resolution proceedings against the owner of the websites operated under these names. The Expert justified his decision chiefly on the grounds that the names "Schweiz", "Suisse" and "Svizzera" are not just geographical designations but also recognised and legally protected names belonging to the Swiss Confederation. The names are, for instance, used in the signing of international treaties.

3.30.4 Legal cases in Switzerland

The Swiss courts have had the opportunity, in a series of judgments, to 3–261 clarify some fundamental principles relating to domain name disputes.

The basis behind these decisions has been the awareness that, although they are technically nothing more than transcriptions of computer IP addresses, domain names are perceived by internet users as distinctive signs representing websites, the individuals, companies, authorities and organisations operating them, or the goods and services distributed through them. Domain names thus fulfil a designation function comparable with that performed by legally protected distinctive signs, especially trade marks, registered business names and personal names.

Due to this function as distinctive signs, the domain names must be sufficiently distinct from older protected signs, in order to avoid the possibility of confusion. If this is not the case, the owner of a legally protected sign can prohibit the use of the domain name or demand that it be transferred.

When there is a conflict between different sign rights, in other words when the domain name corresponds to a legally protected sign belonging to the owner, for instance his surname, and conflicts with a legally protected sign belonging to someone else, for instance a trade mark, jurisprudence dictates that the interests of the two owners of the signs must be weighed up in order to establish which has a superior right to the domain name.

Again due to their function as distinctive signs, domain names must also abide by the principles of unfair competition law, which also prohibits the use of distinctive signs that might generate confusion and, in general terms, bars modes of conduct that offend against fair competition.

Taking these general principles as a basis, various types of cases can be identified.

3–262 In a series of cases,[43] the courts have defended actions brought by trade mark owners against website operators offering under a domain name that was identical with the trade mark, or so similar to it as to cause confusion, goods or services that were identical or similar to the goods and services for which the trade mark had been registered.

In this connection it should be stressed that for the purposes of assessing whether or not the website operator has, through its domain name, created a risk of confusion with the trade mark, comparison was made by the courts between the domain name and the trade mark only. The courts refused to take the content of the websites into account. It was thus of no help to the operator of the website that the latter contained a notice to internet users advising them that the goods and services on offer were not those of the trade mark owner.

In all these cases, the website operator was unable to assert any protectable interest that would allow it to operate the website under a domain name confusingly similar to the trade mark. In some of the cases it was even proved that the website operator deliberately intended to exploit the likelihood of confusion with the trade mark for its own benefit.

This was not so in the case of *rytz.ch*. In a decision on February 11, 1999 the Swiss Federal Court ruled that a company called Rytz Industriebau AG, which had been registered under this name in the Commercial Register since 1983, might continue to use the domain name rytz.ch, which it had registered in 1997, although another company, Rytz et Cie SA, had registered the trade mark "Rytz" in 1995. The Court came to this decision on the grounds of a balance of interests: It took the view that it would be unacceptable, if a company who had openly used the same family name for the last twenty years were unable to use this name as a domain name solely because of the existence of a more recent trade mark.

If the domain name is not used for the purposes of distributing goods and services that are similar to those for which the trade mark has been registered, an essential prerequisite of trade mark protection is lacking. In such cases it is harder for the trade mark holders to take action against the owner of a domain name identical or confusingly similar to the trade mark. The

---

[43] Decisions by the Swiss Federal Court concerning *tonline.ch* dated May 19, 2003 and *stockx.ch* dated October 5, 2001; decision (preliminary injunction) by the Lucern Higher Court concerning *elcotherm.ch* dated July 13, 2000; decision by Basel-Landschaft Higher Court concerning *hotmail.ch* dated May 2, 2000.

trade mark owners must therefore present additional facts justifying support for their action.

In a decision dated June 25, 2002 concerning *breco.ch*, the Commercial Court of the Canton of St Gallen did not refer to trade mark law to support the claim brought by the holder of the trade mark "breco" against the owner of the domain name breco.ch, since the domain name owner was not using, nor intending to use, the domain name in order to distribute similar goods. Instead, the court upheld the claim on the basis that the trade mark holder had succeeded in proving that the main purpose of the domain name owner was to hamper the use of the domain name by the trade mark holder. The court regarded this barring of the domain name, in the absence of any protectable interest on the part of the domain name owner in using the domain name, as an infringement by it of the Law against Unfair Competition.   **3–263**

In the decision (preliminary injunction) handed down by the Berne Higher Court on May 7, 1999, the action brought by the owner of the trade mark "Artprotect" was also defended through reference to the unfair competition law, since the domain name owner had hindered the trade mark holder in his use of the domain name *artprotect.ch* without any legitimate interest of his own.

In this case the domain name owner had also originally registered the trade mark at the behest of the trade mark holder and made it available to him for use to designate a database for lost and stolen works of art. After a disagreement between the parties, the owner of the domain name deactivated it with SWITCH, meaning that internet users could no longer access the database. By so doing, the domain name owner had also breached the contract he had entered into with the trade mark owner.

In what appears to be the only genuine instance of domain name grabbing decided by a Swiss court, the Higher Court of the Canton of Thurgau also referred to unfair competition law rather than trade mark law in a decision handed down on February 19, 2002. The defendant had registered dozens of domain names that corresponded to vehicle marques, or used them as a component part of the name, and was offering them for sale at CHF 1,000 each. The respective vehicle importers with the right to use those trade marks in Switzerland lodged a joint claim.

The court judged the conduct of the domain name holder to be unfair because he could not assert any legitimate interest of his own in the vehicle trade marks registered by him as domain names and his only purpose was clearly to sell the domain names. The court also considered that there was a risk of confusion, since internet users could be given the incorrect impression that the domain name owner had some kind of relationship with the vehicle importers or manufacturers. But the court judged this risk of confusion, too, on the basis of unfair competition law rather than trade mark law.

It becomes particularly difficult for trade mark holders if the domain name owner himself has a protected distinctive sign which he can use to legitimise registration of a domain name. Thus, in a decision dated   **3–264**

November 8, 2004, the Federal Court did not support the claim brought by the owner of the trade mark "Riesen", who had initiated an action against the owner of the domain name *riesen.ch*. The surname of the domain name owner was also Riesen, and the latter used it in connection with the operation of his company Riesen GmbH in the IT sector. In this case there was no use of a domain name for the purposes of distributing similar goods and services, nor was the use of the domain name unfair, since its owner had a legitimate interest in operating a website with the name riesen.ch.

In this case the Federal Court noted in particular that in judging the level of potential confusion between a domain name and a trade mark, only the comparison of the two signs is relevant, not of the contents of the websites. However, this did nothing to change the view of the court that trade mark law affords protection only against signs likely to cause confusion if such signs are used in connection with goods or services that are identical with those goods and services for which the trade mark was registered. In judging the existence of this precondition, therefore, the specific nature of the use of a domain name is decisive, and thus also the content of the website operated thereunder.

3–265 In a case decided shortly thereafter, on January 21, 2005, concerning *maggi.com*, the Federal Court ruled differently, however, and supported the trade mark holder, the Nestlé Group, in its action against the domain name holder bearing the surname Maggi, who was operating a family website with the domain name maggi.com.

The court found that the decisive difference lay, in the case of "Maggi", in the long-term use and the high degree of advertising for a famous brand, which it had explicitly rejected with regard to the trade mark "Riesen" in the case of riesen.ch. Famous trade marks are not subject to the restrictive precondition that protection is only available in respect of readily confusable distinctive signs used in conjunction with similar goods and services. This provided the court with grounds to uphold Nestlé's claim.

It was the court's view that internet users would expect to find that the domain name maggi.com would direct them to a website containing Maggi products. Moreover, it would be reasonable to expect the domain name owner to operate his family website under another domain name containing a distinguishing additional feature alongside the surname Maggi.

In some cases the action against the domain name owner was based not on trade mark law but on the right of protection for registered business names.

3–266 In its decision dated July 16, 2002, the Federal Court upheld the claim of Experteam AG against the younger XPERTEAM Management Consultants AG on the grounds of ease of confusion of the registered business names as regards the distinguishing components "Experteam" and "XPERTEAM" respectively. In the context of this action, the accused company was also forbidden to use the readily confusable domain name xperteam.com.

In the decision (preliminary injunction) handed down by the Lausanne District Court on July 23, 2001, the action brought by Cofideco SA against the owner of the domain name *cofideco.ch* was upheld. The domain name owner stated that it wanted to use this name to operate the website of a company with the object of promoting real estate. The court could see a potential risk of confusion with the plaintiff's registered business name. It also considered the action of blocking use of the domain name by Cofideco SA to be an infringement of unfair competition law.

Protection of registered business names requires that the domain name is used as a company's business name in the same way that, in the case of trade marks, similarity of the goods and services is a prerequisite for protection for readily confusable domain names. Thus, if a company is not using a domain name to operate a company website, protection of registered business names will not apply.

It was for this reason that on June 6, 2002, the Thurgau Higher Court handed down a decision in which it dismissed the action brought against the owner of the domain name *emarket.ch*. No company website was being operated under that name. The question as to whether the domain name owner acted in an unfair manner in blocking the plaintiff company from using its own registered name as a domain name was presumably not considered in this case because the domain name had been registered before the plaintiff had chosen the name eMarket as its registered business name.

Finally, in a number of cases decisions have been handed down where conflicts between domain names and the names of individuals or institutions were involved.

In a decision dated November 7, 2002, the Federal Court upheld a claim **3–267** by the pop star DJ Bobo against the owner of the domain name *djbobo.de*. Firstly, the court affirmed that there was a risk of confusion with DJ Bobo due to the owner's choice of domain name. Secondly, the court considered that there was also an infringement of the law of personal names by virtue of the fact that DJ Bobo was prevented from using his own name as a domain name on the important German market. Since both the domain name owner and DJ Bobo were resident in Switzerland, jurisdiction lay with the Swiss courts, and the Swiss law of personal names was applicable, despite the fact that the subject matter of the dispute was a domain name registered in Germany.

A similar conclusion had been reached in a previous decision dated July 23, 2002 handed down by the Federal Court in relation to the domain name *luzern.ch*. The court upheld the claim by the City of Lucerne against the owner of the domain name luzern.ch, who had been operating a website under that name providing information about the region of Lucerne.

In two further cases, both the domain name owner and the plaintiff **3–268** asserted rights ensuing from the law of personal names in respect of the domain names in question. In both cases the plaintiffs were municipalities.

In *montana.ch*, the municipality of Montana brought an action against the Institut Montana private school, which had registered the domain name montana.ch. In its decision dated July 23, 2002, the Federal Court valued the interest of the municipality in the domain name more highly than that of the private school, and upheld the claim. Of particular relevance in this instance was the level of fame of the municipality of Montana, which is an internationally well-known mountain resort. It was the court's view that internet users would expect to find at montana.ch a website about the municipality of the same name.

In its decision dated August 30, 2001, the Aargau Higher Court had for similar reasons previously upheld a claim by the municipality of Frick against a company that had registered the domain name *frick.ch* for its general manager, whose surname was Frick. In this case, too, the court valued the interests of the municipality more highly, again arguing that internet users would expect to find at frick.ch a website about the municipality.

3–269   In the case of *berneroberland.ch* the circumstances were rather special. There is no legal right to the name "Berner Oberland", since it is a geographical designation rather than a protected name of a municipality. The decision of the Federal Court in this matter, handed down on May 2, 2000, was therefore based on unfair competition law.

The domain name berneroberland.ch had been registered in 1996 by an IT company who had already registered other domain names with geographic designations from the well-known tourist region of Berner Oberland. "Berner Oberland Tourismus", the association representing tourist bodies in the Berner Oberland, successfully applied for a deletion of the registration.

The Federal Court concluded that the use of the domain name created a risk of confusion—as defined by the Law against Unfair Competition—with the applicant, Berner Oberland Tourismus. This was because users searching for tourist products would assume that behind the domain name berneroberland.ch was an official tourism provider representing the entire region of the Berner Oberland. Moreover, this was a reasonable assumption, because official tourist bodies in many other regions and locations operate websites both inside and outside Switzerland under domain names that are the same as their geographic designation.

Special circumstances also lay behind the decision of the Civil Court of the Canton of Basel-Stadt of March 10, 2005 in the case concerning "*www.tax-info.ch/www.info-tax.ch*". In this case, a publishing company in the tax law field was operating a database under the name www.tax-info.ch. Some time later, a competitor used the domain name www.info-tax.ch for a database of a similar type that it was operating. The publishing house brought an action.

The court refused protection of the domain name www.tax-info.ch since it was only a description of the database offered and did not constitute an individualising designation. However, it took the view that the competitor was acting unfairly since it had chosen a domain name easily confusable with www.info-tax.ch, and composed of the same elements, with the aim of redirecting customers to its site, since they could easily confuse www.tax-info.ch with www.info-tax.ch. The court therefore ordered the transfer of the domain name www.info-tax.ch to the publishing house that brought the action.

3–270   In conclusion, mention should be made of the decision involving *bundesgericht.ch*. In this case, the Federal Court upheld a criminal law conviction against the owner of this domain name imposed by the courts of the Canton of Lucerne. Registration of the domain name constituted a violation of the law protecting coats of arms, which, amongst other things, restricts the use of official designations incorporating the element "Bund" [= Federal] by private individuals and companies.

3.30.5 Relevant Laws

The laws which are relevant to domain name disputes are trade mark law, the law on registered business names, the law of personal names and the law relating to unfair competition.   **3–271**

The owner of a trade mark is protected against the use of a domain name which is identical or similar to its trade mark for designating a website which displays advertising or offers for goods or services which are identical or similar to the goods or services for which the trade mark is registered. However, trade mark law does not offer any protection if the domain name was registered and used before the trade mark was registered. Trade mark protection is not enforceable against brands, which have been used prior to trade mark registration to the extent of this prior use.

Trade mark law offers no protection against the simple registration of a similar domain name (without using it in the context of advertising or offering goods or services) and thus specifically not against domain name grabbing. This was explicitly stated by the Federal Court in the case *riesen.ch* mentioned above.

Protection for registered business names entered in the Commercial Register exists only in relation to identical or similar brands which are also used as the name of companies. The extent to which a domain name can be understood to be the name of a company due to the circumstances of its use, and thus the extent to which trade name law can be applied at all, has to be considered in each individual case.   **3–272**

The law of personal names protects private individuals (including artists' pseudonyms), companies and public bodies (e.g. villages and cities) against the use of their names or substantial parts of their names by third parties, which use the names or parts of names as domain names. The courts have affirmed that the simple registration of a name as a domain name, without its active use, constitutes an infringement of the law of names. The rightful bearer of a name has a claim to the use of its name, and as the law of names provides for a special complaint if the use of a name is contested, actions against domain name grabbing can be brought on the basis of the law of personal names.

In addition to the possibility of protection for trade marks, registered business names and personal names mentioned above, there is protection under the Law against Unfair Competition. Specifically, generating the risk of potential confusion through the use of brands which are identical or similar to those used by others, is deemed to be unfair.   **3–273**

This protection is very important for all brands which are not registered as trade marks and for trade marks which are only registered abroad but not in Switzerland, but are at least familiar here.

Under the terms of the Law against Unfair Competition, it is not only the generation of confusion which is unfair. Any conduct which results in the influencing of competition through unfair means is prohibited. Preventing individuals who are legitimate holders of trade marks or registered business names from using their distinctive signs as domain names, and thus in particular also domain name grabbing, is unfair, as the courts have ruled. This is because it makes it impossible for the rightful owner of a trade mark to register this as its domain name, a situation which may be detrimental to its market position.

3.31 NON-UNITED KINGDOM DOMAIN NAMES— UNITED STATES OF AMERICA

3–274   The conflict between the current system of domain name registration and the rights of trade mark holders is the subject of much discussion. This issue has given rise to a growing number of disputes between trade mark holders and registrants of domain names. In 1999, the domain name management system and the domain name dispute resolution process were significantly modified and a new US cybersquatting law was enacted. Disputes continue to arise.

3.31.1 Domain names

3–275   A domain name serves a dual purpose. It marks the location of a website within cyberspace, much like a postal address in the real world, but it may also indicate to users some information as to the content of the site, and, in instances of well-known trade names or trade marks, may provide information as to the source of the contents of the site.

Unlike the traditional trade mark environment, however, where identical trade marks can co-exist in different markets, in the current domain name system a unique trade mark can only be used by one entity within a particular top-level domain (e.g., .com). For example, there can only be one "www.apple.com" in cyberspace, but there could be trade marks used by Apple Computers, the Apple Grocery Store, Apple Clothing and Apple Records for their separate products without creating consumer confusion as to source.

Internet users often rely on domain names to search for particular home pages on the World Wide Web and other resources on the internet. Thus, the use of a well-known trade mark in a domain name can be an important source of visitors to a given website. The number of disputes over the registration of known trade marks as domain names has escalated in the past several years.

3.31.2 Registration

While most of the controversy in the US is focused on the generic top-level domains (gTLDs),[44] such as .com, the US, like most other countries, has its own country-code top-level domain (ccTLD), designated by .us.[45] As of July 2006, the US top-level domain is administered by NeuStar, Inc. VeriSign, Inc. is the registry for the .com and .net gTLDs, while the Public Interest Registry (PIR) manages all .org gTLDs. With few exceptions, the naming hierarchy under the .us TLD is based on geography: the second-level domain corresponds to a state, the third-level domain to a locality, such as a city or county, and the fourth-level domain to an organisation or individual. For example, under this system, the domain name of New York City's Metropolitan Transportation Authority is "mta.nyc.ny.us." Although any computer in the US may be registered under the .us TLD, it has been unpopular with businesses. Instead, state and local government entities, libraries and local public schools have been the predominate users.

3–276

On April 24, 2002, NeuStar launched the expanded second-level .us domain. This expanded .us domain enables companies, nonprofits, government entities and individuals to establish .us domain names and be able to register, for example, "company.us."[46]

3.31.3 ICANN domain name dispute resolution policy

On October 24, 1999, the Internet Corporation for Assigned Names and Numbers (ICANN) adopted the Uniform Domain Name Dispute Resolution Policy (UDRP), which incorporates by reference the Rules for Uniform Domain Name Dispute Resolution Policy.[47] The policy and rules provide mechanisms to contest the propriety of domain name registrations in the .com, .net and .org generic TLDs and certain country-code TLDs.[48]

3–277

The policy adopted by ICANN sets forth an arbitration-like procedure for resolving domain name disputes. To invoke the policy, a complainant must describe the grounds on which the complaint is made including in

---

[44] Please see section 3.3 for further information on registration of gTLDs.

[45] There are three other TLDs reserved for the exclusive use of certain US entities: .gov is reserved for US federal government agencies, .mil is reserved for the US military, and .edu is reserved for educational institutions in the US. For further information, see the gTLD page of the Internet Assigned Numbers Authority's website available at *http://www.iana.org/gtld/gtld.htm.*

[46] Information on the expanded .us domain is available at *http://www.nic.us/index.html.*

[47] The policy and rules are available at *http://www.icann.org/udrp/udrp.htm.*

[48] Country-code TLD dispute resolution policies vary. For more information, contact the manager of the ccTLD of interest. Contact information for each ccTLD is available at *http://www.iana.org/cctld/cctld-whois.htm.*

particular: "(1) the manner in which the domain name(s) is/are identical or confusingly similar to a trade mark or services mark in which the [c]omplainant has rights; and (2) why the respondent (domain name holder) should be considered as having no rights or legitimate interests in respect of the domain name(s) that is/are the subject of the complaint; and (3) why the domain name(s) should be considered as having been registered in bad faith."[49] In order to prevail, a complainant must prove each of these three elements. When a complainant asserts the presence of these three elements, the registrant is required to submit to the mandatory administrative proceeding. A trade mark holder is not required to have a trade mark registration in order to initiate the dispute resolution process, i.e. even common law trade mark right-holders may invoke ICANN's dispute resolution policy against alleged infringers who adopt confusingly similar variations of a common law mark.

3–278   The Policy sets forth a number of factors to be considered as evidence of registration and use in bad faith. Such factors include: (1) facts indicating that the registrant has registered the domain name "primarily for the purpose of selling, renting, or otherwise transferring the domain name registration to the complainant who is the owner of the trade mark or service mark or to a competitor of that complainant, for valuable consideration in excess of [the registrant's] documented out-of-pocket costs directly related to the domain name;" (2) facts indicating that the registrant has "registered the domain name in order to prevent the owner of the trade mark or service mark from reflecting the mark in a corresponding domain name" provided that v registrant has "engaged in a pattern of such conduct;" (3) facts indicating the registrant has registered the domain name "primarily for the purpose of disrupting the business of a competitor;" or (4) facts indicating that the registrant, by using the domain name, intentionally attempted to attract, for commercial gain, internet users to its website or other on-line location, "by creating a likelihood of confusion with the complainant's mark as to the source, sponsorship, affiliation, or endorsement" of the registrant's website or location, or of a product or service on its website or location.[50] Remedies under the ICANN policy are limited to the cancellation or transfer of an infringing domain name.

3.31.4 Relationship between UDRP proceedings and remedies under other US law

3–279   Domain name dispute remedies for trade mark owners in the US are not limited to UDRP proceedings. In fact, even during the pendency of a UDRP proceeding, a mark owner may be able to utilise judicial remedies. For example, in *BroadBridge Media LLC v Hypercd.com*,[51] the plaintiff had

---

[49] UDRP Rule 3(b)(ix)(1) to (3).
[50] UDRP 4(b).
[51] *BroadBridge Media, LLC v Hypercd.com*, 106 F. Supp. 2d 505 (S.D.N.Y. 2000).

registered the "hypercd.com" domain name and then mistakenly allowed it to lapse, whereupon an individual in Canada registered the name and refused during subsequent negotiations to relinquish it back to plaintiff. The plaintiff instituted a UDRP proceeding contesting the registration and simultaneously filed an *in rem* proceeding under the Anticybersquatting Consumer Protection Act (ACPA)[52] seeking immediate return of the domain name.

In addressing plaintiff's motion for preliminary relief, the court in *BroadBridge* cited UDRP 4(k) and UDRP Rule 18 in concluding that the plaintiff had not waived its right to proceed in federal court by filing the UDRP proceeding. In fact, the court noted that by the time of the judicial hearing, the arbitration panel had exercised its discretion to suspend the administrative proceeding pending the outcome of the litigation. Under the unique circumstances of the case, including the fact that the plaintiff had already expended substantial funds in reliance on its use of the domain name and that plaintiff's ability to provide customer support through its "hypercd.com" email address was impaired, the court ordered the immediate transfer of the domain name back to plaintiff.[53]

Weber-Stephen Products Co. v Armitage Hardware[54] was the first federal   **3–280** case to touch on the question of what weight should be given to the decisions of UDRP arbitrators. In that case, the defendant sought to stay plaintiff's UDRP proceeding, arguing that it would be irreparably harmed if the decision of the arbitrators foreclosed its ability to litigate its defenses in the federal court proceeding. The district court refused to stay the UDRP proceeding, concluding that the proceeding would not harm the interests of the defendant because the court was not bound by the decision of the UDRP arbitrators. The court left open the issue, however, of what weight, "if any," it would give to the arbitration decision once it was rendered.[55]

One US court that was presented squarely with the deference issue, *Referee Enterprises v Planet Ref Inc.*,[56] appears to have accorded no deference at all to the UDRP proceeding. The plaintiff, Referee Enterprises, owner of the mark "Referee" for a magazine, was the unsuccessful complainant in a UDRP proceeding against the assignee of the "eReferee.com," "eReferee.net" and "eReferee.org" domain name registrations. The UDRP arbitrator ruled that Planet Ref had a legitimate interest in the domain names and was not using them in bad faith.[57] Referee Enterprises then filed an action in federal court under the Lanham Act claiming trade mark infringement, dilution, unfair competition and false designation of origin in the defendant's use of the eReferee domain names. In January 2001, the

---

[52] For information regarding the ACPA, see *infra* section 3.19.5.
[53] *BroadBridge Media, LLC v Hypercd.com*, 106 F. Supp. 2d 505, 509–512.
[54] *Weber-Stephen Products Co. v Armitage Hardware*, 2000 U.S. Dist. LEXIS 6335, 54 U.S.P.Q.2d 1766 (N.D. Ill. May 3, 2000).
[55] *Ibid.* at *7.
[56] *Referee Enters., Inc. v Planet Ref Inc.*, 2001 U.S. Dist. LEXIS 9303 (E.D. Wisc. Jan. 24, 2001).
[57] *Referee Enters., Inc. v Planet Ref Inc.*, No. FA0004000094707 (N.A.F. June 26, 2000).

federal district court reversed the outcome of the UDRP proceeding and preliminarily enjoined Planet Ref from any use of the eReferee domain names, as well as any other domain name including the term "referee" in any form. The court's summary order contains no reference to the UDRP proceeding, suggesting both by the contrary result and the absence of discussion that it was given no deference whatsoever.

3–281   *Parisi v Netlearning Inc.*[58] confirmed the development that had been apparent in these earlier decisions: US courts will not consider themselves bound by the decisions of UDRP arbitrators. In *Parisi*, the plaintiff, holder of the "netlearning.com" domain name, sought a declaration of lawful use under the ACPA and a declaration of non-infringement under the Lanham Act. The defendant, Netlearning, Inc., argued that it was entitled to the disputed domain name pursuant to the prior decision of a UDRP panel[59] and that the plaintiff's complaint constituted an improper motion to vacate an arbitration award in violation of the Federal Arbitration Act (FAA).[60] The US District Court for the Eastern District of Virginia ruled that, among other things, ICANN's UDRP was intended to permit "comprehensive, *de novo*" court review of arbitration decisions, and that the FAA did not bar the relief sought by the plaintiff. The court therefore refused to dismiss the plaintiff's complaint.[61]

3.31.5 The Anticybersquatting Consumer Protection Act

3–282   In 1999, the US Congress passed the Anticybersquatting Consumer Protection Act (ACPA),[62] amending §43 of the Trademark Act of 1946 (also known as the Lanham Act). The ACPA establishes that a person who registers, traffics in or uses a domain name that is identical or confusingly

---

[58] *Parisi v Netlearning, Inc.*, 139 F. Supp. 2d 745 (E.D. Va. 2001).

[59] *Netlearning, Inc. v Parisi*, No. FA0008000095471 (N.A.F. Oct. 16, 2000).

[60] 9 U.S.C. § 1, et seq.

[61] More recent cases continue to rely on *Parisi* and find that UDRP decisions are not binding on subsequent judicial proceedings. See *Storey v Cello Holdings, LLC*, 347 F.3d 370, 381 (2d Cir. 2003); *Dluhos v Strasberg*, 321 F.3d 365, 373 (3d Cir. 2003); *Hawes v Network Solutions, Inc.*, 337 F.3d 377, 386 (4th Cir. 2003); *Sallen v Corinthians Licenciamentos LTDA*, 273 F.3d 14, 28 (1st Cir. 2001); *Stenzel v Pifer*, 2006 US Dist. LEXIS 32397, 8–9 (D. Wash. 2006); *Oneida Tribe of Indians of Wisconsin v Harms*, 2005 US Dist. LEXIS 27558 (E.D. Wis. Oct. 24, 2005). See also *Barcelona.com Inc. v Excelentisimo Ayuntamiento De Barcelone*, 330 F.3d 617 (4th Cir. 2003) (stating that "because the administrative process prescribed by the UDRP is 'adjudication lite' as a result of its streamlined nature and its loose rules regarding applicable law, the UDRP itself contemplates judicial intervention, which can occur before, during, or after the UDRP's dispute resolution process is invoked").

[62] Anticybersquatting Consumer Protection Act of 1999, Pub. L. 106–113, div. B, Sec. 1000(a)(9) (title III), November 29, 1999, 113 Stat. 1536, 1501A–545 (enacted by reference in the District of Columbia Appropriations Act, which incorporated by reference S. 1948, 106th Cong. §§ 3001–3010 (1999) (see Title III Trademark Cyberpiracy Prevention), codified at 15 U.S.C. §§ 114, 116, 117, 1125, 1127, 1129 (1999).

similar to a protected mark, or that is dilutive of a famous mark, will be subject to civil liability if he has a bad faith intent to profit from that mark.[63]

The Act outlines nine factors that may lead to a finding of bad faith. A court may consider, but is not limited to consideration of, any of the following factors[64]:

- any rights to the domain name the registrant may have;
- whether the domain name consists of the registrant's legal name or a name by which the registrant is known;
- any prior use of the domain name by the registrant in connection with the bona fide offering of goods or services;
- the registrant's bona fide non-commercial or fair use of the mark in a site accessible under the domain name;
- any intent on the part of the registrant to divert consumers from the mark owner's site to a location that will harm the goodwill of the mark owner;
- any offer made by the registrant to sell the domain name, without having used the domain name, as well as any pattern of this behaviour;
- the registrant's provision of false contact information when applying for the registration of the domain name, the registrant's intentional failure to maintain accurate contact information, or the registrant's prior conduct indicating a pattern of such conduct;
- whether the registrant has registered multiple domain names that are identical or confusingly similar to protected marks, or which dilute famous marks; and
- the extent to which the mark incorporated in the person's domain name registration is or is not distinctive and famous.

The Act provides that there shall be no finding of bad faith if the court determines that the registrant reasonably believed the use of the domain name was fair or was otherwise lawful.[65]

A finding of liability may lead to forfeiture or cancellation of the domain **3–283** name, or transfer of the domain name to the owner of the mark.[66] Moreover, plaintiffs are entitled to actual damages and profits, or if they so elect at any time prior to a final judgement, statutory damages in the amount of not less than US$1000 and not greater than US$100,000 per domain name.[67]

---

[63] 15 U.S.C. § 1125(d)(1)(A). The Act also specifically provides protection for trade marks, words, or names associated with the American Red Cross and the United States Olympic Committee. 15 U.S.C. § 1125(d)(1)(A)(ii)(III).
[64] 15 U.S.C. § 1125(d)(1)(B)(i).
[65] 15 U.S.C. § 1125(d)(1)(B)(ii).
[66] 15 U.S.C. § 1125(d)(1)(C).
[67] 15 U.S.C. § 1117(d).

The Act specifically affords protection to personal names.[68] A person who (1) registers a domain name consisting of, or similar to, the name of another living person, (2) without that person's consent, and (3) with the specific intent to profit from that person's name by selling the domain name to that person or to any third party, will be subject to civil liability.[69] However, an exception exists for a person who registers such a domain name in good faith if: (1) the name is used with, affiliated with, or related to a copyrighted work, (2) the person registering the name is the copyright owner or licensee of the work, (3) the person intends to sell the domain name in conjunction with the lawful exploitation of the work, and (4) such registration is not prohibited by contract between the registrant and the named person.[70] Successful plaintiffs are entitled to injunctive relief and, at the court's discretion, costs and attorney fees.[71]

3–284   An additional right created by the Act is the right of a mark owner to file an *in rem* action against the domain name itself (as opposed to the registrant of the domain).[72] An *in rem* action can be brought only if *in personam* (i.e., personal) jurisdiction cannot be obtained or if the appropriate defendant can not be found after notice is sent and published by means directed by the court.[73] Remedies in an *in rem* action are limited to forfeiture, cancellation or transfer of the domain name.[74]

Under the Act, a domain name registrar, domain name registry, or other domain name registration authority is not liable for damages, for the registration or maintenance of a domain name for another absent, a showing of bad faith intent to profit from such registration or maintenance of the domain name.[75]

3.31.6 Disputes under the ACPA

3–285   Prior to enactment of the ACPA, the central legal tools for resolving domain name disputes were federal trademark infringement and anti-dilution

---

[68] 15 U.S.C. § 1129.
[69] 15 U.S.C. § 1129(1)(A).
[70] 15 U.S.C. § 1129(1)(B).
[71] 15 U.S.C. § 1129(2).
[72] 15 U.S.C. § 1125(d)(2).
[73] 15 U.S.C. § 1125(d)(2)(A).
[74] 15 U.S.C. § 1125(d)(2)(D)(i).
[75] 15 U.S.C. § 1114(2)(D)(iii).

statutes.[76] However, this legal framework was often considered to be inadequate and to provide unsatisfying results.[77] The ACPA has removed what some had considered to be burdensome hurdles, such as proving that the alleged internet infringer made "commercial use" of the registered mark. The Act has been invoked regularly to deal with domain name disputes.[78]

In one of the first appellate court rulings under the ACPA, a panel of the

---

[76] In a claim for trade mark infringement under the Lanham Act, the trade mark owner must show that the defendant is using a mark confusingly similar to a valid, protectible mark. 15 U.S.C. § 1114, 1125(a). A trade mark owner can also file a claim for trade mark dilution under the Federal Trademark Dilution Act. Under that Act, a trade mark owner must establish that its mark is famous, that the defendant used the mark in commerce after the mark became famous, and that the defendant's use dilutes the distinctiveness of the mark. 15 U.S.C. § 1125(c). Unlike a claim for trade mark infringement, in a dilution case a plaintiff need not show competition between the parties or a likelihood of confusion resulting from the defendant's use of the mark. The Dilution Act has been applied to a number of domain name disputes. In several cases, courts have held that defendants who registered plaintiffs' trade marks as domain names had diluted the plaintiffs' trade marks. See, e.g., *Panavision Int'l, L.P. v Toeppen*, 945 F. Supp. 1296 (C.D. Cal. 1996), aff'd 141 F. 3d 1316 (9th Cir. 1998) (registration of "panavision.com" and "panaflex.com'" domain names diluted Panavision's trade marks); *Intermatic, Inc. v Toeppen*, 947 F. Supp. 1227 (N.D. Ill. 1996) (registration of "intermatic.com" diluted Intermatic's trade mark); *Hasbro, Inc. v Internet Entm'tt Group*, 1996 U.S. Dist. LEXIS 11626 (W.D. Wash. Feb. 9, 1996) (registration of "candyland.com" domain name probably diluted Hasbro's trade mark in the famous board game).

[77] In general, courts have held that the mere registration of a domain name that incorporates someone else's trade mark is not a "use in commerce." See, e.g., *Lockheed Martin Corp. v Network Solutions, Inc.*, 985 F. Supp. 949, 957 (C.D. Cal. 1997), aff'd, 194 F.3d 980 (9th Cir. 1999); *Jews for Jesus v Brodsky*, 993 F. Supp. 282, 307 (D.N.J. 1998), aff'd, 159 F.3d 1351 (3d Cir. 1998); See also *Bird v Parsons*, 289 F.3d 865, 880 (6th Cir. 2002) (stating that "simply posting a domain name on an internet auction site is insufficient to establish the commercial use of a trade mark sufficient to support a trade mark dilution claim. This reasoning also applies to an entity . . . that operates an online auction site"). However, when a domain name registrant has registered a domain name incorporating a trade mark with the intent to sell the name to the trade mark owner, courts have held that registration is a use in commerce for Lanham Act purposes. See *Panavision Int'l, L.P. v Toeppen*, 141 F. 3d 13161324 (9th Cir. 1998). Courts have also found trade mark infringement when a party registers a domain name containing the trade mark of a competitor. See *Washington Speakers Bureau, Inc. v Leading Authorities, Inc.*, 33 F. Supp. 2d 488 (E.D. Va. 1999), aff'd, 217 F.3d 843 (4th Cir. 2000).

[78] See, e.g., *Audi AG v D'Amato*, 2006 U.S. App. LEXIS 29127, 2006 FED App. 0439P (6th Cir. 2006) (affirming a district court decision awarding plaintiff injunctive relief and attorneys fees in an action alleging trade mark infringement, dilution, and cyberspiracy claims under ACPA where defendant used plaintiff's trade marks in its domain name and in the goods and services sold on the website); *E. & J. Gallo Winery v Spider Webs, Ltd.*, 286 F.3d 270 (5th Cir. 2002) (affirming a district court decision awarding a permanent injunction and statutory damages in an action alleging violation of trade mark laws and the ACPA where the defendant registered a domain name including plaintiff's trade mark in bad faith); *Porsche Cars N. Am., Inc. v Spencer*, 2000 U.S. Dist. LEXIS 7060, 55 U.S.P.Q.2d 1026 (May 18, 2000 E.D. Cal. 2000) (novel pre-ACPA *in rem* action was dismissed; on appeal, court held ACPA applies retroactively and remanded, effectively resurrecting Porsche's claims); *Electronics Boutique Holdings Corp. v Zuccarini*, 2000 U.S. Dist. LEXIS 15719, 56 U.S.P.Q.2d 1705 (E.D. Pa. Oct. 30, 2000) aff'd, 2002 U.S. App. LEXIS 9247 (3d. Cir. 2002) (imposing ACPA statutory damages in a cybersquatting case where defendant had registered five domain names that were slight misspellings of plaintiff's trade marks); *United Greeks, Inc. v Klein*, 2000 U.S. Dist. LEXIS 5670 (N.D.N.Y. May 2, 2000) (awarding ACPA statutory damages and attorneys' fees in a cybersquatting case where defendant had registered five domain names containing plaintiff's trade marks).

US Court of Appeals for the Second Circuit in *Sporty's Farm L.L.C. v Sportsman's Market Inc.*[79] ruled unanimously that a Christmas tree company's domain name, "sportys.com", was registered with a bad faith intent to profit from a distinctive mark. "Sporty's" was a trade mark registered by a mail order company, Sportsman's Farm, in conjunction with its aviation products. "Sportys.com" was registered by another aviation catalog company, then sold to a wholly-owned subsidiary called Sporty's Farm, which sold Christmas trees.

3–286   After a bench trial to resolve the ensuing domain name dispute, the district court ordered Sporty's Farm to relinquish the domain name, but limited the judgment on Sportsman's Market's trade mark dilution claims to such injunctive relief. On appeal by both parties, the Second Circuit panel applied the then-new anticybersquatting law, finding it "clear that the new law was adopted specifically to provide courts with a preferable alternative to stretching federal dilution law when dealing with cybersquatting cases." The panel affirmed the judgment below, holding that "sporty's" was a distinctive mark, and that the domain name was "confusingly similar" to the mark. On the issue of bad faith, the court found overwhelming evidence that "sportys.com" was registered in the first place to keep Sportsman's from using that domain name, and that the Christmas tree subsidiary was created so that the domain name could then be used in a commercial fashion to protect against infringement claims. The Second Circuit panel also found the injunction issued by the district court to be proper under the ACPA, but that damages under the Act were unavailable because "sportys.com" was registered and used by Sporty's Farm prior to the passage of the Act.

3–287   In another case, the court in *Virtual Works, Inc. v Volkswagen of America, Inc.*[80] found that plaintiff had violated the ACPA by registering a domain name with a bad-faith intent to profit from a previously registered trade mark. The court found the following to be direct evidence of bad faith: (1) Virtual Works' statement at deposition that, when registering "vw.net," two of its principals acknowledged that "vw.net" might be confused with Volkswagen and left open the possibility of someday selling the domain for "a lot of money"; and (2) the terms of Virtual Works' offer to sell the domain to Volkswagen, where it threatened to sell the domain at auction to the highest bidder unless Volkswagen made Virtual Works an offer within 24 hours. In addition, the court found the following facts to be circumstantial evidence of bad faith: (1) the famousness of the VW mark; (2) the similarity of "vw.net" to the VW mark; (3) the admission that Virtual Works never once did business as VW nor identified itself as such; and (4) the availability of "vwi.org" and "vwi.net" at the time Virtual Works registered "vw.net", either of which name would have satisfied Virtual Works' own stated criterion of registering a domain name that used

---

[79] *Sporty's Farm L.L.C. v Sportsman's Market, Inc.*, 202 F.3d 489 (2d Cir. 2000).
[80] *Virtual Works, Inc. v Volkswagen of Am., Inc.*, 238 F.3d 264 (4th Cir. 2001).

only two or three letters, but would have eliminated any risk of confusion with respect to the VW mark.

Another way in which cybersquatters have attempted to profit from famous marks is by "typosquatting", i.e. registering likely misspellings of those marks. In *Shields v Zuccarini*,[81] the US Court of Appeals for the Third Circuit upheld a lower court's grant of summary judgment, a permanent injunction, and award of statutory damages and attorneys' fees to the plaintiff under the ACPA. The defendant had registered five variations of the plaintiff's website "joecartoon.com": "joescartoon.com", "joecarton.com", "joescartons.com", "joescartoons.com" and "cartoonjoe.com". Once a user entered one of these sites, he was unable to exit without clicking through a series of advertisements, each of which paid between 10 and 25 cents to the defendant. The court found the defendant's behaviour to be a "classic example of a specific practice the ACPA was designed to prohibit."

3–288

3.31.7 Damage awards

Domain name disputes have occasionally resulted in substantial damage awards.[82] For example, in *Kremen v Cohen*,[83] the court awarded US$65 million for damages resulting from fraud and forgery in connection with the appropriation of the "sex.com" domain name. In that case, the defendant fraudulently obtained the registration of the domain name by sending a forged letter to Network Solutions, Inc., the domain name registrar. The court found that defendant had reaped profits exceeding US$40 million in the five years he operated the "sex.com" website. The damage award included US$25 million in punitive damages.

3–289

In *E-Cards v King*[84] E-Cards, a San Francisco-based electronic greeting card company, was awarded US$4 million by a jury in the Northern District of California, which found that a Canadian competitor, Ecards.com, had engaged in unfair competition. According to the companies' websites, E-Cards was founded in 1995, and Ecards.com was started in 1996. The jury apparently agreed with E-Cards' charge that the similarity of the names was causing confusion in the marketplace, although the verdict may be viewed as granting the plaintiff exclusive rights to a generic term.[85]

---

[81] *Shields v Zuccarini*, 254 F.3d 476 (3d Cir. 2001). See also *PetMed Express, Inc. v Med-Pets.Com, Inc.*, 336 F.Supp.2d 1213 (S.D. Fla. 2004) (stating that "liability for federal cyberpiracy occurs when a plaintiff proves that (1) its mark is a distinctive or famous mark entitled to protection, (2) the defendant's domain names are identical or confusingly similar to the plaintiff's marks, and (3) the defendant registered the domain names with the bad faith intent to profit from them," citing *Shields v Zuccarini*, 254 F.3d 476, 482 (3d Cir. 2001)).

[82] In addition to cases awarding compensatory damages, see *Shields v Zuccarini*, 254 F.3d 476 (3d Cir. 2001) (awarding US$50,000 in statutory damages plus US$40,000 in attorney fees in a cybersquatting case).

[83] *Kremen v Cohen*, No. C 98–20718 JW (N.D. Cal. April 3, 2001).

[84] *E-Cards v King*, No. 99-CV-3726 (N.D. Cal. May 10, 2000).

[85] The defendant Ecards.com filed an appeal to the Ninth Circuit, but the matter was settled in September 2000.

3.31.8 Domain names used for criticism or as parody

3-290   Companies have attempted to use the ACPA, traditional trade mark law and the UDRP to stop websites that are critical of their products or services, but with mixed results. The developing trend appears to be that courts will permit domain names to be used for sites that are used exclusively to criticize or parody the trade mark owner, but will afford less protection to sites that directly or indirectly engage in some type of commercial activity.

For example, in *Northland Insurance Cos. v Blaylock*,[86] a federal district court declined to grant preliminary relief to Northland Insurance Companies, the owner of the mark "Northland Insurance" in a suit brought against an individual who maintained a website critical of the company at "www.northlandinsurance.com." The plaintiff, which maintained its own website at "www.northlandins.com," sought relief under the ACPA, common law of trade mark infringement, and federal and state trade mark anti-dilution statutes. The domain name in question linked to a second website containing an account of the defendant's ongoing insurance claim disputes with the company. The defendant admitted that he had chosen the domain name deliberately to attract the attention of internet users who were searching for the plaintiff's website. The site offered no competitive products, nor did it solicit any commercial activity. The district court rejected plaintiff's argument that the use of the domain name created "initial interest" confusion based upon its close proximity to the domain name of the plaintiff's actual website because, the court found, the defendant did not appear situated to benefit financially or commercially from his website. The court also rejected the plaintiff's ACPA claim on the ground that there was insufficient evidence in the record that the defendant intended to profit from the sale of the domain name or to use it for any purpose other than commentary.[87]

---

[86] *Northland Insurance Cos. v Blaylock*, 115 F. Supp. 2d 1108 (D. Minn. 2000).

[87] See also *Lamparello v Falwell*, 420 F.3d 309, 315 (4th Cir. 2005) (stating that "a gripe site, or a website dedicated to criticism of the markholder, will seldom create a likelihood of confusion"); *Lucent Technologies, Inc. v Lucentsucks.com*, 95 F. Supp. 2d 528 (E.D. Va. 2000) (noting in *dicta* that domain names signaling parody or criticism of a company "seriously undermine" the necessary claims under the ACPA of bad faith and likelihood of confusion). In *Bally Total Fitness Holding Corp. v Faber*, 29 F. Supp. 2d 1161 (C.D. Cal. 1998), the defendant created a website called Bally Sucks (at *http:// www.compupix.com/ ballysucks/*) that criticised the health club company. Bally sued, alleging trade mark infringement and dilution and unfair competition. The court granted defendant Faber's motion for summary judgment on the trade mark infringement claim, explaining that there was no likelihood of confusion because "no reasonable consumer comparing Bally's official site to Faber's site would assume Faber's site [came] from the same source" or was affiliated with or sponsored by Bally. The judge also granted defendant's motion for summary judgment on the trade mark dilution claim because Bally failed to show Faber's use of the Bally mark was a commercial use. But see *Fairbanks Capital Corp. v Kenney*, 303 F. Supp. 2d 583 (D. Md. 2003) (finding a likelihood of confusion and granting a preliminary injunction because people landing on defendants' criticism website, which included plaintiff's name in the domain name, would likely be confused as to the source of information on defendants' website).

In contrast, the court in *People for the Ethical Treatment of Animals v Doughy*[88] ordered the owner of the domain name "peta.org" to relinquish the registration to the non-profit organisation People for the Ethical Treatment of Animals (PETA), even though he claimed his website was a parody. The defendant's website contained information captioned "People Eating Tasty Animals" and included a statement that the purpose of the website was to be a "resource for those who enjoy eating meat, wearing fur and leather, hunting, and the fruits of scientific research." The site also contained numerous links to commercial websites advertising leather goods and meats. The court found that the inclusion of even one link to another commercial site was sufficient to constitute a commercial use of the plaintiff's registered mark, even though the defendant himself did not actually place goods and services in the stream of commerce. The defendant was found to have both diluted and blurred the PETA mark, and to have caused actual economic harm to the PETA mark by lessening its selling power as an advertising agent for PETA's goods and services.

3–291

3.31.9 State anticybersquatting statutes

State anticybersquatting statutes need to be considered as well. For example, in August 2000, California enacted an anticybersquatting law that makes it unlawful for a person acting in bad faith to register, use or traffic in an internet domain name that is identical or confusingly similar to the personal name of another living person or "deceased personality".[89] The legislation is intended to apply to personal names that are not necessarily famous or registered as trade marks and thus may not fall under the federal ACPA. The statute includes a list of factors to be used in evaluating "bad faith" which is nearly identical to the list of factors in the federal ACPA. The remedies for violation of the law include injunctive relief, restitution and civil penalties of up to US$2,500 per violation.[90]

3–292

3.31.10 Metatags and other forms of internet trade mark infringement

Metatags are text embedded in the hypertext markup language (HTML) used to create websites. The tags, which are not visible to viewers of a web

3–293

---

[88] *People for the Ethical Treatment of Animals v Doughy*, 113 F. Supp. 2d 915 (E.D. Va. 2000).

[89] Cal. Bus. & Prof. Code §17525–17528 (Deering 2001).

[90] As of 2006, at least one case has been brought under Cal. Bus. & Prof. Code § 17525 et seq. (2002). See *Wright v Domain Source, Inc.*, 2002 U.S. Dist. LEXIS 16024 (D. Ill. 2002) (*Pro se* plaintiff sued defendant corporation alleging violation of the Anticybersquatting Consumer Protection Act, 15 U.S.C.S. § 1129, and Cal. Bus. & Prof. Code § 17525 et seq. (2002), and seeking damages, injunctive relief, costs, and an attorney's fee based on alleged piracy of his registered domain name on the internet).

page but can be seen by viewing the source of the HTML, contain data such as keywords that are used by search engines to locate websites.

Courts have ruled that a defendant who uses someone else's trade mark in metatags or in some other unauthorised way in conjunction with e-commerce may be infringing the trade mark.[91] For example, in *Brookfield Communications v West Coast Entertainment*,[92] the US Court of Appeals for the Ninth Circuit held that the defendant's use of the plaintiff's registered service mark "moviebuff" in its metatags caused "initial interest" confusion under the Lanham Act. The defendant owned the trade mark "The Movie Buff's Movie Store," registered the domain name "movie-buff.com," and used "moviebuff" in its website metatags. Brookfield owned the trade mark "Moviebuff" and sued for trade mark infringement and unfair competition. The court held that "by using 'moviebuff.com' or 'MovieBuff' to divert people looking for 'MovieBuff' to its website, West Coast improperly benefits from the goodwill that Brookfield developed in its mark." The court compared the use of another's trade marks in one's metatags to Company A posting a sign on the highway indicating that Company B's store is at Exit 7 (while Company B is really at Exit 8), hoping that consumers who get off at Exit 7 looking for Company B will see Company A's store and shop there.

3–294   In another case involving metatags, *Eli Lilly & Co. v Natural Answers Inc.*,[93] the US Court of Appeals for the Seventh Circuit upheld the district court's grant of a preliminary injunction sought by Eli Lilly & Co., manufacturer of Prozac, a prescription drug used to treat clinical depression. The district court enjoined the defendant Natural Answers' use of the name "Herbrozac" on a non-prescription, herbal "mood elevator" marketed on the defendant's website. The website contained source code that included the term "Prozac" as a metatag, and described Herbrozac as "a powerful, and effective all-natural and herbal formula alternative to the prescription drug Prozac." Citing the phonetic similarity of Herbrozac to Prozac, as well as the defendant's references to Prozac in the website metatags, the district court found a risk of initial interest confusion under the Lanham Act. On appeal, the circuit court found that the use of Prozac in the metatags, while not evidence of actual confusion, was nevertheless "significant evidence" of the defendant's intent to confuse and mislead: "The fact that one actively pursues an objective greatly increases the chances that the objective will be achieved".[94] In so ruling, the court cited the *Brookfield Communications* opinion for its comparison of defendant's use of metatags to "posting a sign with another's trade mark in front of one's store."

---

[91] Note, however, that at least one court has held that the ACPA does not apply to metatags. *Bihari v Gross*, 119 F. Supp. 2d 309 (S.D.N.Y. 2000).

[92] *Brookfield Commc'ns. v West Coast Entm't*, 174 F.3d 1036 (9th Cir. 1999).

[93] *Eli Lilly & Co. v Natural Answers, Inc.*, 233 F.3d 456 (7th Cir. 2000).

[94] *ibid.* at 465.

The use of another's trade mark in metatags does not always constitute infringement. In *Playboy Enterprises, Inc. v Terri Welles Inc.*,[95] the defendant was a model who had appeared in *Playboy* magazine several times, had been awarded the title of "Playmate of the Year 1981," and had identified herself as a "playmate" and a "playmate of the year" since 1980 with plaintiff's knowledge. The code for defendant's website at *http:// www.terriwelles.com* included the words "Playboy," "Playmate" and "Playboy Playmate of the Year 1981" in the metatags. Playboy, which owned federally registered trade marks for the terms "Playboy," "Playmate" and "Playmate of the Year" alleged, among other things, that defendant's use of Playboy's registered trade marks in its metatags infringed Playboy's trade marks by causing "initial interest confusion." The court disagreed, finding "fair use" in defendant's use of the words in a descriptive sense, with no intent to deceive. The court noted that if someone was attempting to find Welles's website, but didn't remember her name, they might enter key words such as "Playboy," "Playmate" or "Playboy Playmate of the Year 1981" because such terms "identify her source of recognition to the public." While crafting its analysis, the court cautioned that it must "be careful to give consumers the freedom to locate desired sites while protecting the integrity of trade marks and trade names".[96]

3–295

Playboy Enterprises, Inc. v Netscape Communications[97] involves a different use of plaintiff's trade marks on the internet. This case involves "keying" which "allows advertisers to target individuals with certain interests by linking advertisements to pre-identified terms".[98] Thus, if a person performs a search with a particular term, advertisements with that particular term will appear on the search results page. In this case, the district court granted defendants' motions for summary judgment on Playboy's trade mark infringement, trade mark dilution and unfair competition claims against Excite, Inc. and Netscape Communications. Playboy alleged that Excite and Netscape sold Playboy's trade marks to hard-core pornography advertisers and then targeted their banner ads to appear whenever a user searched for "Playboy" or "Playmate" on defendants' search engines. The court denied Playboy's claim of trade mark dilution, ruling that the defendants did not make a trade mark use of Playboy's marks. In addition, while the court admitted Playboy's survey evidence showing that consumers were confused by the banner ads, it nonetheless ruled that defendants' use of Playboy's trade marks created no likelihood that consumers would be confused as to the source of defendant's search services.

3–296

In 2004, the Ninth Circuit reversed and remanded the district court decision, finding genuine issues of material fact regarding the trade mark

---

[95] *Playboy Enters., Inc. v Terri Welles, Inc.*, 297 F.3d 796 (9th Cir. 2002) (affirming the district court's grant of summary judgment as to claims for trade mark infringement and trade mark dilution, with the sole exception of the use of the abbreviation "PMOY").
[96] *ibid.* at 1095.
[97] *Playboy Enters., Inc. v Netscape Commc'ns. Corp.*, 354 F.3d 1020 (9th Cir. 2004).
[98] *Ibid.* at 1022.

infringement and dilution claims. The court found that the Playboy established a genuine issue with respect to the trade mark infringement claim due to the likelihood of confusion that a consumer might experience resulting from the defendant's use of Playboy's marks.[99] The court examined a specific type of confusion, namely "initial interest confusion".[1] The court described "initial interest confusion" as "customer confusion that creates initial interest in a competitor's product".[2] The court looked to *Brookfield* for guidance and indicated that the defendants misappropriated the goodwill of Playboy's marks by leading internet users to competitors' websites just as in *Brookfield*.[3] The court noted that this activity was actionable trade mark infringement.[4]

Even though the court indicated that analogies to *Brookfield* alone would defeat a summary judgment,[5] the court applied an eight factor test for likelihood of confusion as stated in *AMF, Inc. v Sleekcraft Boats*.[6] The court held that the majority of the factors favored Playboy.[7]

3–297 Additionally, the court found that Playboy established a genuine issue with respect to the dilution claim as to the nature and extent of the use of similar marks by third parties for purposes of the famousness of the marks.[8]

This decision appears to expand trademark protection in cyberspace although the scope is not entirely clear. Under this case, linking an advertisement to a trademark may lead to liability.

---

[99] *Ibid.* at 1029.

[1] *Ibid.* at 1024–25.

[2] *Ibid.* at 1025.

[3] *Ibid.* at 1026.

[4] *Ibid.* at 1025.

[5] *Ibid.* at 1026.

[6] *AMF, Inc. v Sleekcraft Boats*, 599 F.2d 341, 348–349 (9th Cir. 1979) (stating that the factors that are relevant to determine confusion between related goods are: "1. strength of the mark; 2. proximity of the goods; 3. similarity of the marks; 4. evidence of actual confusion; 5. marketing channels used; 6. type of goods and the degree of care likely to be exercised by the purchaser; 7. defendant's intent in selecting the mark; and 8. likelihood of expansion of the product lines.").

[7] *Playboy Enters., Inc. v Netscape Commc'ns. Corp.*, 354 F.3d 1020, 1029 (9th Cir. 2004).

[8] *Ibid.* at 1034.

CHAPTER 4

Defamation

4.1 INTRODUCTION

Defamation liability was one of the first areas of law to come before the **4–001** courts in the field of on-line services. It continues to be a lively source of activity.

Two decisions in 1991 and 1995 (*Cubby v CompuServe* and *Stratton Oakmont v Prodigy*[1]) set the pace in the US. The first reported UK internet defamation litigation occurred in 1994. The plaintiff, Dr Laurence Godfrey, sued another academic, Dr Phillip Hallam-Baker, alleging that he had caused defamatory Usenet postings to be published. That litigation was subsequently settled.

Dr Godfrey was subsequently the plaintiff in the first reported judgment under the Defamation Act 1996.[2] In 1996 a judge in an English defamation case was reported to have allowed a plaintiff to serve notice of a writ and an *ex parte* injunction out of the jurisdiction on a defendant via internet email, when only the defendant's email address was known.[3] Significant damages have been paid out in defamation actions concerning internal company emails.[4]

The Defamation Act 1996 included specific provisions designed to address the question of who is liable, and to what standard, for defamatory

---

[1] *Cubby Inc v CompuServe Inc*, 776 F Supp 135 (SDNY 1991) and *Stratton Oakmont v Prodigy Inc.*, 1995 NY Misc LEXIS 229. See section 4.5 for an account of these cases.
[2] *Godfrey v Demon Internet Ltd* [1999] 4 All E.R. 342.
[3] On-Line in Print, June 1996.
[4] The first reported UK settlement of a defamation claim concerning company internal emails was the Asda case in 1995 (*The Lawyer*, April 25, 1995). This concerned a policeman who was refused service at an Asda store as a result of having being identified in an email circulated to stores. The case was settled with an apology and undisclosed damages. In 1997 a defamation claim brought by Western Provident Association against Norwich Union Insurance Company concerning an internal Norwich Union email was settled on payment of £450,000 damages by Norwich Union. In 1999 a defamation case brought by Exoteric Gas Solutions and its owner Mr Andrew Duffield against British Gas was settled when the plaintiffs accepted a payment into court of £101,000. The case concerned an internal email circulated by a British Gas area manager after Mr Duffield left British Gas to set up EGS (*Legal Week*, July 1, 1999). The question of liability for internal emails and the Norwich Union case are discussed further in Ch.5.

statements disseminated over computer and telecommunications networks such as the internet. These now co-exist with the defences for on-line intermediaries introduced in 2002 as a result of the implementation of the Electronic Commerce Directive.

4–002   The relative abundance of decisions and legislative activity in this area reflects a combination of factors: the endemic informality of email and similar communications, a tradition of robust and uninhibited discussions (originally in Usenet newsgroups and carried through into all types of discussion forum) and a wide selection of potential defendants (in addition to the author) for a prospective claimant to consider suing. Publication and dissemination of any information on the internet requires the involvement of many different entities including hosts, network providers and access providers. As these will often have deeper pockets than the author, the extent of their liability for defamatory content handled by them is of great significance.

The Defamation Act 1996 was one of the first attempts anywhere in the world to legislate for the liability of on-line intermediaries such as internet hosts and access providers. It remains on the statute book, but now co-exists with the set of defences for conduits, caches and hosts introduced by the Electronic Commerce (EC Directive) Regulations 2002,[5] the relevant provisions of which came into force on August 21, 2002.

The Electronic Commerce Regulations implement the Electronic Commerce Directive.[6] This lays down common European threshold liability standards for on-line intermediaries in respect of most types of civil and criminal activity, including defamation.

Since, generally, the Electronic Commerce Regulations provide greater protection than the 1996 Act, a defendant will normally wish to rely on those. However, for some defendants they will not be available, such as for a defendant who is not an information society service provider, or does not fall within the Regulations' definitions of conduit, cache or host. In such a case the 1996 Act defences will remain significant.

4–003   In June 2005 the Department of Trade and Industry issued a consultation paper on whether any of the protections for conduits, caches and hosts under the Electronic Commerce Directive should be extended to hyperlinks, location tools (such as search engines) and content aggregators.[7] In December 2006 it issued a Response[8] stating that there was currently insufficient evidence to justify any extension to the limitations.

The cross-border nature of the internet raises the liability stakes in two

---

[5] SI 2002/2013.

[6] European Parliament and Council Directive 2000/31 O.J. L178 on certain legal aspects of information society services, in particular electronic commerce, in the Internal Market (Directive on Electronic Commerce). See Ch.5 for full discussion of the provisions for liability of intermediaries. See also, as regards certain acts in relation to copyright, the discussion in Ch.2 para.2–014 of the provisions of Art.5(1) of the Copyright in the Information Society Directive.

[7] DTI Consultation Document on the Electronic Commerce Directive: The Liability of Hyperlinkers, Location Tool Services and Content Aggregators, June 2005.

[8] The DTI Response is available at *www.dti.gov.uk/files/file35905.pdf*.

ways: since publication is potentially to the whole world, that could increase the level of damages[9]; and the claimant could have a wide choice of jurisdictions in which to pursue a defendant.[10]

4.2 DEFAMATION—GENERAL[11]

A defamatory statement is one which would tend to lower the claimant in **4–004** the estimation of right-thinking members of society generally or cause him to be shunned or avoided. A defamatory statement may constitute either slander or libel. A slanderous statement is one which is issued verbally, or not committed to permanent form. If the statement is in permanent form it will amount to libel.

The importance of the distinction lies in the fact that a claimant alleging slander must prove special damage, in other words some actual financial loss. A claimant alleging libel need not do so.

Libel or slander?

In general, electronically disseminated communications are likely to **4–005** amount to libel rather than slander. A person who posts a Usenet article, sends an email or creates a web page, is committing content to a host computer. The electronic data resides on that computer until deleted. That is true whether the data is text, graphics, audio or video. This is more than a transient form and is likely to be libel, not slander.

The position may perhaps be more doubtful in the case of more transient and ephemeral forms of communication over the internet, such as Internet Relay Chat, instant messaging or video-conferencing.

Section 166 of the Broadcasting Act 1990 provides that the publication of words in the course of any programme included in a programme service shall be treated as publication in a permanent form. It is possible that

---

[9] See, for instance, the Australian case of *Cullen v White*, in which the judge awarding compensatory and exemplary damages commented that the on-line dissemination was plainly designed to maximise its detrimental effect (World eBusiness Law Report November 4, 2003).

[10] Jurisdiction questions are discussed in Ch.6. In Australia, damages of AUS $95,000 were awarded in 2003 to an academic as a result of a series of libels published on a number of websites. The award took into account the potential present-day audience of a website. Both liability and assessment of damages were adjudged in default of defence. In an undefended Canadian case in 2002 damages of CAN $400,000 were awarded over defamatory statements published on a series of websites. In England a teacher who brought defamation proceedings in the county court against an ex-pupil who had libelled him on a Friends Reunited bulletin board was awarded £1,250 in May 2002.

[11] For a detailed exposition of the law of defamation generally, see *Gatley on Libel and Slander* (10th edn, Sweet & Maxwell, 2003).

certain services containing sounds or visual images provided over the internet could constitute programme services (as defined in the Act[12]) and that items included within them could fall within this provision. (See Ch.8 for a discussion of what services may be covered by this.)

Single or multiple publication?

4–006   English law has long held that each individual publication of a libel gives rise to a separate cause of action. In *Loutchansky v The Times Newspapers Ltd*[13] the defendant newspaper sought to overturn this rule for publication of newspaper archives on the internet. The newspaper relied on a Limitation Act defence, arguing that the one year limitation period for libel should begin to run as soon as the allegedly defamatory article was first posted on the newspaper's website. Subsequent occasions upon which the website was accessed should not give rise to separate causes of action, each with its individual limitation period.

The newspaper argued that this area of the common law had developed to suit traditional hard copy publication and was inimical to modern conditions. The law should develop to reflect those conditions and to accommodate the requirements of the Human Rights Act 1998 and the European Convention on Human Rights.

The newspaper pointed out that every day during which a back number remained on the website potentially gave rise to a new publication of that issue of the newspaper, and therefore a new cause of action. The maintainer of the website was therefore liable to be indefinitely exposed to repeated claims in defamation. It was argued that if it were accepted that there is a social utility in the technological advances which enable newspapers to provide an internet archive of back numbers, then the law must evolve. If a newspaper defendant which maintained a website of back numbers was to be indefinitely vulnerable to claims and defamation for years and for even decades after the initial hard copy and internet publication, such a rule was bound to have an effect on the preparedness of the media to maintain such websites, and thus to limit freedom of expression. The court was urged to adopt the "single publication rule" used in the US.

4–007   The court rejected the newspaper's assertion that the multiple publication rule was in conflict with Art.10 of the European Convention on Human Rights because it had a chilling effect upon the freedom of expression that goes beyond what is necessary and proportionate in the democratic society for the protection of the reputation of others. Lord Phillips M.R., giving the judgment of the court, stated:

---

[12] The definition of "programme services" in s.201 of the Broadcasting Act 1990 includes not only "programme services" as defined in s.405 of the Communications Act 2003, but some other services of a broadly interactive nature consisting of the sending of sounds or visual images or both by means of an electronic communications network, as defined in s.201(c) of the Broadcasting Act 1990.

[13] [2001] EWCA Civ 1805.

"we accept that the maintenance of archives, whether in hard copy or on the internet, has a social utility, but consider that the maintenance of archives is a comparatively insignificant aspect of freedom of expression. Archive material is stale news and its publication cannot rank in importance with the dissemination of contemporary materials. Nor do we believe that the law of defamation need inhibit the responsible maintenance of archives. Where it is known that archive material is or may be defamatory, the attachment of an appropriate notice warning against treating it as the truth will normally remove any sting from the material."

The newspaper also relied upon a defence of qualified privilege under the principle in *Reynolds v Times Newspapers Ltd.*[14] The newspaper argued that it remained under a duty to publish the articles over the internet. The Court of Appeal affirmed the judgment at first instance that the republication of back numbers of *The Times* on the internet was made in materially different circumstances from those obtaining at the time of the publication of the original hard copy versions. The court commented that the failure to attach any qualifications to the articles published over the period of a year on *The Times*' website could not possibly be described as responsible journalism and that it could not be convincingly argued that the newspaper had a *Reynolds* duty to publish those articles in that way without qualification.

The decision in *Loutchansky v The Times* was considered by the Law Commission in its December 2002 Scoping Study entitled "Defamation and the Internet—A Preliminary Investigation". As to the interaction of the multiple publication rule with the limitation period applying to archived material, the Law Commission commented that it was potentially unfair to defendants to allow actions to be brought against newspapers decades after their original publication, simply because copies had been placed in an archive. The Study concluded that further consideration should be given to the issue, either through the adoption of a US style single publication rule, or through a more specific defence that would apply to both traditional and on-line archives.

When considering the law of defamation it should always be remembered that defamation cases have generally been tried before a judge and jury, and that the jury has been the arbiter of questions of fact.[15] In a jury trial the judge directs the jury on what the law is and should leave to the jury questions of fact, including facts that must be decided in order that the judge may determine a question of law (such as whether the facts amount to publication).

---

[14] [2001] 2 A.C. 127.

[15] Under the Defamation Act 1996 there is now greater scope for the trial of defamation actions by a judge alone.

4.3 WHO IS LIABLE FOR DEFAMATORY STATEMENTS OVER NETWORKS

4.3.1 Nature of the problem posed by dissemination over networks

Publication at common law

4–008   Before the Defamation Act 1996,[16] English law cast a wide net of liability for publication of a defamatory statement. Anyone who participated in or authorised the publication was liable. So in hard copy publishing the author, the editor, the publisher, the printer, the distributor and the vendor were all potentially liable, albeit (as explained below) subject to different standards of liability. But someone who merely facilitated, as opposed to participated in, publication did not publish the statement at all and would escape any liability. So the supplier of newsprint would not have been held to have published the statement, whereas the printer would have been.[17]

The first issue to consider in the context of networks such as the internet is where the line is to be drawn between authorising or participating in publication on the one hand, and mere facilitation on the other.

We discuss first the position at common law. The enactment of s.1(3) of the Defamation Act 1996 may, however, possibly have had the practical effect of bringing within the scope of potential liability some persons who at common law were only facilitators. This is discussed in para.4–022 below.

4–009   *Godfrey v Demon Internet Ltd*[18] provided the first specific judicial guidance as to who participates in or authorises publication on the internet. The case established that an internet service provider who hosts and makes newsgroups available publishes the contents of those newsgroups at common law. The judge found that the defendant, because it had chosen to store the newsgroup in question on its servers, and was able to obliterate postings to the newsgroup, was a publisher at common law.

After reviewing the authorities the judge concluded:

> "in my judgment the Defendants, whenever they transmit and whenever there is transmitted from the storage of their news

---

[16] The relevant provisions of the Defamation Act 1996 apply to causes of action which arose on or after September 4, 1996.

[17] *Gatley*, para.6.15. Even so, "participate" may have a broad meaning. In *Marchant v Ford* [1936] 2 All E.R. 1510 the Court of Appeal refused to strike out a pleading that the printer of the book jacket containing the "blurb" for a book had published the book. The Court of Appeal held that the matter should be left for evidence at the trial. See para.4–022 below *as to whether the provisions of s.1 of the Defamation Act 1996 may influence the common law meaning of "publish"*.

[18] See above, fn.2. The case has also been taken as supporting the proposition that the contents of the newsgroups are published where they are read or downloaded See the Australian case of *Gutnick v Dow Jones, Inc.* ([2002] HCA 56), *Harrods Ltd v Dow Jones & Co Inc* [2003] EWHC 1162, *King v Lewis* [2004] EWHC 168 (QB) and *Richardson v Schwarzenegger* [2004] EWHC 2422 (QB) and further, Ch.6. However, it is doubtful whether the judge was addressing place of publication, since that was not in issue in the case.

server a defamatory posting, publish that posting to any subscriber to their ISP who accesses the newsgroup containing that
posting. Thus every time one of the Defendant's customers
accesses 'soc.culture.thai' and sees that posting defamatory of the
Plaintiff there is a publication to that customer. ... I do not accept
Mr Barca's argument that the Defendants were merely owners of
an electronic device through which postings were transmitted. The
Defendants chose to store 'soc.culture.thai' postings within their
computers. Such postings could be accessed on that newsgroup.
The Defendants could obliterate and indeed did so about a fortnight after receipt."

The judgment does beg the question whether if a defendant (such as a **4–010**
telephone company who had done nothing other than passively transmit
data through its system) were able to establish that it was "merely [the
owner] of an electronic device through which postings were transmitted" it
could successfully argue that it did not publish the offending statement.[19]
However, commenting on the US *Lunney v Prodigy*[20] case, Morland J.
stated that (unlike in the *Lunney* case) in English law Prodigy would clearly
have been the publisher of an email message sent over its system.

If that is the case it is difficult to see why the same should not apply to a
telephone company transmitting voice traffic. The transmissions of the two
are both passive and to all intents and purposes indistinguishable. Indeed in
the era of digital networks voice and data may form part of the same digital
bitstream. Both are passive conduits. Yet it had been thought that at
common law a telephone company could argue that it merely facilitated,
and did not participate in, publication of voice traffic.[21]

The position of passive conduits has now been addressed in *Bunt v Tilley*.[22] In this case Eady J. held that the passive role of affording a connection
to the internet did not render the provider a publisher at common law of a
statement transmitted across the connection. This, unless they can be
regarded as referring to Prodigy's storage of emails on its system, implicitly
contradicts the observations made by Morland J. about the *Lunney* case.

Eady J. held that the crucial consideration was whether a person had "a
knowing involvement in the process of publication of the relevant words."
In order to impose legal responsibility upon anyone under the common law
for the publication of words, it was essential to demonstrate that they had a
degree of awareness that such words existed, or at least an assumption of
general responsibility.

The judge commented that in relation to pure conduits the practical
threshold is likely to be knowledge of the actual postings. When dealing

---

[19] As is the case in US law (*Anderson v New York Telephone Co.* 1974 35 N.Y. 2d 746). But
see section 4.5 below as to the dangers of comparisons with US caselaw.
[20] Main text, s.4.5.
[21] *Gatley*, para.6.8.
[22] [2006] EWHC 407 (QB).

with ISPs who host information, knowledge of "the process of publication" is more likely to be sufficient.

Hence the ISPs in *Bunt* (who were accused only of providing connections to the internet) could not be held accountable as they had no knowledge of the actual postings on which the claimant was basing his case. This is in contrast to the position of Demon Internet in *Godfrey*, for whom knowing involvement in the hosting of the discussion group was sufficient to found participation in the publication.[23]

Primary and subordinate disseminators at common law

4–011   We have mentioned that although a wide variety of actors were held to be publishers at common law, they were subject to different standards of liability. The common law distinguished between the "first or main" publisher and subordinate disseminators. The first or main publisher was strictly liable, whether or not it knew of the defamatory statement. Thus the proprietors of a newspaper would be liable for a libel contained in a classified advertisement, even if there were thousands of such advertisements in the publication. The fact that it might be very difficult to check each and every advertisement did not relieve the newspaper of strict liability.

Subordinate disseminators could take advantage of a defence of innocence. This common law "distributors' defence" was available to a defendant who could show that it did not know that the publication contained the libel; that it was not by reason of any negligence that it did not know that there was a libel in it; and that it did not know, nor ought to have known, that the publication was of a character likely to contain libellous matter.

The Defamation Act 1996 updated the common law distributors' defence by introducing a statutory scheme covering all types of media including electronic dissemination. However, the Act did not expressly abolish the common law subordinate disseminator's defence and it may have survived the introduction of the Act.[24]

---

[23] It should be noted that this finding renders it unnecessary to invoke the doctrine in *Byrne v Deane* ([1937] 2 All E.R. 204) in order to render a hosting ISP a participant in the publication. In that case it was held that a person who has the right to remove defamatory material that someone else has put up on their property, but permits it to remain displayed, then becomes a participant in the publication.

[24] The Consultation Paper "Reforming Defamation Law and Procedure" (Lord Chancellor's Department, July 1995) stated (s.2.6) that the new defence was to "replace and modernise innocent dissemination". In moving the Second Reading of the Bill in the House of Lords the Lord Chancellor stated that Clause 1 was a "new statutory defence which will supersede the common law defence of innocent dissemination" *Hansard*, H.L. March 8, 1996 col. 577. The Parliamentary Secretary, Lord Chancellor's Department made an identical statement when moving the Second Reading of the Bill in the House of Commons *Hansard*, H.C. May 21, 1996 col. 129. However, in Commons Committee the Parliamentary Secretary used slightly different words when moving amendments to Clause 1 of the Bill: "a new statutory defence to defamation proceedings that will *effectively* supersede the common law defence of innocent dissemination" (emphasis added) *Hansard* H.C. Standing Committee A June 6, 1996 col. 4.

Primary and subordinate dissemination over networks

Before the internet there were already difficulties in applying the common law distributors' defence to print media.[25] The distinction between primary publisher and subordinate disseminator then had to be revisited with the advent of electronic dissemination over networks. **4–012**

Applying the traditional distinction to electronic dissemination is not easy. In hard copy publishing the content tends to be selected, collated and conveniently wrapped inside discrete covers. The first or main publishers can be identified as those who participate in creating the wrapped product, and subordinate disseminators or distributors as those who receive the wrapped product and pass it down the chain to the ultimate purchaser.

Much (but by no means all) electronically disseminated content is created and distributed in unwrapped form, just as the author provides it. So in many cases it is no longer easy or even possible to distinguish between publication and distribution. A typical example of this is an on-line discussion forum or a Usenet newsgroup, where members of the public can place messages directly onto a database accessible by anyone else equipped with the appropriate software. The collation and wrapping function of the traditional publisher has disappeared, or at least has been reduced to the routine task of maintaining the organisation of the messages by topic, date order or author. The discussion forum proprietor may choose whether or not to exercise the remaining function of selecting content.[26]

The proprietors of on-line discussion forums emphasise the practical impossibility of vetting messages placed on their services[27]—which under the old common law begged the question: are they akin to distributors for whom this is a relevant matter,[28] or to primary publishers for whom it is

---

[25] The Faulks Committee in 1975 recommended that the ambit of the innocent dissemination defence be extended to printers.

[26] The potential significance of the disappearance of the wrapping function is illustrated by the *Lunney v Prodigy* case (below at para.4–057), in which the court's third reason for disagreeing with the earlier *Prodigy* decision relied upon treating each message transmitted across its system as being separate and distinct from the rest.

[27] See, for instance, the Response of CompuServe, Europe Online and Microsoft to the Lord Chancellors' Department on the July 1995 Consultation Paper: "Technology permits on-line services to edit or delete content when problems are pointed out to the service provider, but the sheer volume of works, services and communication prevents this being done in advance".

[28] See, for instance, on the question of negligence, *Weldon v "The Times" Book Co Ltd* (1912) 28 T.L.R.143 "It was quite impossible that distributing agents such as the respondents should be expected to read every book they had. There were some books as to which there might be a duty on the respondents or other distributing agents to examine them carefully because of their titles or the recognised propensity of their authors to scatter libels abroad. Beyond that the matter could not go." (Cozens-Hardy, M.R.). But volume and lack of time to inspect were not exonerating if no care was taken. See *Sun Life Assurance Company of Canada v W.H. Smith and Son Ltd* (1934) 150 L.T.R. 211, C.A. "... by the system they have adopted, Messrs. W.H. Smith & Son Ltd have made it next to impossible that they should exercise any care whatever in seeing whether posters they put up for reward for themselves contain defamatory statements against some other person ... It is not sufficient for the defendants to say that it is inconvenient for them and difficult for them, having regard to their large business, to make any other arrangements than the arrangements which they have in fact made." (Greer L.J.).

not? The practical impossibility of vetting messages did not of itself determine the legal status of an on-line provider. Only if it could claim subordinate disseminator status in the first place would that become a relevant factor in determining negligence.

Variety of relationships between internet actors and content

4–013   The illustration of the Usenet newsgroup, with its individual messages made instantly available by their authors, is only one aspect of publication on the internet. Many variations are possible, ranging from permanent to ephemeral, with differing relationships between the parties involved. Some publishing on the internet, when carefully crafted and vetted copy is placed on permanent websites or where electronic versions of well-known journals and magazines are created, is more like hard copy publishing and advertising.

Some examples of the variety of relationships between disseminator and content are:

- An internet service provider hosts and makes available Usenet newsgroups, receiving automatic updating feeds from other Usenet hosts and disseminating postings made by its own customers.
- The proprietor of a web journal includes a "letters to the editor" feature on the journal's website. Unlike the print version of the journal, in which letters to the editor are selected and edited for periodic publication, on-line readers are free to post "letters" directly to a forum on the website. Other readers can reply in like manner.
- An academic collates interesting postings from a Usenet newsgroup and periodically emails them to subscribers to an electronic mailing list.
- An internet service provider provides both internet access and free web hosting facilities to its customers.
- A telecommunications operator agrees to provide and manage a virtual network to enable a group of companies to operate an intranet. All the group's email traffic and requests for documents flow over the network.
- A web design company receives text from its customer, codes the text using HTML and Java, and passes the finished product by email to another company which will host the website.
- A search engine indexes websites and displays a customised list of links to relevant web pages in response to search terms entered by the user.

These examples raise issues both of whether the person has participated in the publication (as opposed to merely facilitating it) and also whether it has done so as a primary or secondary publisher.

4–014   In some of these examples the collation and wrapping functions of the

322

original publisher (content provider) remain, although the person disseminating the material may be more or less removed from the content provider. In other examples no collation takes place at all, for instance in the case of email traffic. In all cases distribution from the originating site or person to the end-user is an even more mechanical procedure than in the case of hard copy works, the electronic material simply becoming part of the general packet data traffic transmitted through the internet.

Interesting questions could also arise as to the status of mirror sites—sites which agree to act as a local duplicate host for a foreign site, to enable local users to obtain faster access—or sites which, say, hold duplicates of a number of different third party electronic magazines and newspapers. Such sites have features both of distributors and primary publishers in the traditional analysis. They are distributors in the sense that they receive a third party's publication. But in another sense they are doing nothing different from the original host who agrees to hold a publication.

4.3.2 Defamation Act 1996—the section 1 defence for secondary disseminators

The Defamation Act 1996 introduced a codified scheme of responsibility 4–015
for publication of defamatory statements. The Act not only addressed liability for electronic dissemination, but also reformed the law relating to liability for print publications, for instance by moving printers into the category of secondary publishers. Although the scheme of the Act is clearly inspired by the common law distinction between primary and subordinate disseminator, the Act created such a new and complex statutory structure that old cases on distributors' liability may be of little assistance, other than in broad terms, in determining the boundaries of liability. The Act was subject to various amendments to the responsibility for publication provisions during its passage through Parliament.

The Section 1 defence under the 1996 Act

Under s.1(1) of the Act a person has a defence in defamation proceedings if 4–016
he can show that:

(a) he was not the author, editor or publisher of the statement complained of,
(b) he took reasonable care in relation to its publication, and
(c) he did not know, and had no reason to believe, that what he did caused or contributed to the publication of a defamatory statement.

In determining whether a person took reasonable care, or had reason to believe that what he did caused or contributed to the publication of a defamatory statement, regard is to be had to:

(a) the extent of his responsibility for the content of the statement or the decision to publish it;

(b) the nature or circumstances of the publication; and

(c) the previous conduct or character or the author, editor or publisher.

Section 1(2) of the Act defines "author", "editor" and "publisher". It provides that:

> An "author" is the originator of the statement (but does not include someone who did not intend that his statement be published at all).
> An "editor" is a person having editorial or equivalent responsibility for the content of the statement or the decision to publish it.
> A "publisher" is a commercial publisher, that is, a person whose business is issuing material to the public, or a section of the public, who issues material containing the statement in the course of that business.

These definitions are "further explained" in s.1(3), which sets out five categories of persons who are not to be considered the author, editor or publisher of a statement. In a case not within these categories the court may have regard to them by way of analogy in deciding whether a person is to be considered the author, editor or publisher of a statement. These categories are the equivalent of the common law subordinate disseminators.

4–017   The five categories are persons who are "only" involved:

"(a) in printing, producing, distributing or selling printed material containing the statement;

(b) in processing, making copies of, distributing, exhibiting or selling a film or sound recording (as defined in Pt 1 of the Copyright, Designs and Patents Act 1988) containing the statement;

(c) in processing, making copies of, distributing or selling any electronic medium in or on which the statement is recorded, or in operating or providing any equipment, system or service by means of which the statement is retrieved, copied, distributed or made available in electronic form;

(d) as the broadcaster of a live programme containing the statement in circumstances in which he has no effective control over the maker of the statement;

(e) as the operator or provider of access to a communication system by means of which the statement is transmitted, or made available, by a person over whom he has no effective control."

For transmission across networks the most relevant categories of subordinate disseminators are likely to be (b), (c), (d) and (e), although (a) may possibly be relevant if resort is to be had to the analogy provision.

4.3.3 Judicial analysis of the Section 1 defence

The *Demon Internet* case

The courts have now considered the categories of subordinate disseminator on several occasions. In *Godfrey v Demon Internet Ltd* (see para.4–009 above), Morland J. had no hesitation in finding that Demon, when hosting Usenet newsgroups, was not a publisher within the meaning of ss.1(2) and (3) of the Act. He found that Demon was "clearly" not a publisher within the meaning of ss.1(2) and 1(3) and could "incontrovertibly" avail itself of s.1(1)(a).   **4–018**

However, the judge undertook no analysis of the explanatory categories. Presumably he considered that Demon's activities came within either or both of ss.1(3)(c) or (e). It is implicit in the decision that some degree of selection of content does not preclude a person from "only" being involved in those categories. This follows from the judge's reliance, in finding that Demon published the contents of the newsgroups within the common law meaning, on the fact that Demon's activities were more than passive in that they chose to host the particular newsgroup to which the offending article was posted.

Similarly, in *Bunt v Tilley* (para.4–010 above) BT successfully relied on ss.1(3)(c) and (e) in respect of newsgroup hosting.

The live broadcast exception—section 1(3)(d)

The scope of the live broadcast exception has been judicially considered. In *Market Opinion and Research International Ltd v BBC*[29] Gray J. ruled that the use of a time delay device whereby a broadcast could be delayed by 7–10 seconds would not mean that the broadcast ceased to be live, notwithstanding that the use of the delay device entailed recording the programme and broadcasting the recording.   **4–019**

The judge held that the contrary conclusion would run counter to the ordinary understanding of what is meant by a live broadcast. He went on to say that it would also run counter to the legislative purpose underlying the Act and in particular s.1, because whenever such a mechanism was used the broadcaster would lose the protection of s.1. The legislative purpose of s.1 of the Act was to narrow the scope of the liability of publishers in certain defined circumstances.

In considering the potential wider implications of the rulings, it should be noted that "broadcaster" and "programme" are not defined in the Act. These may, therefore, bear different, possibly wider, meanings from in the

---

[29] Transcript of reasons for ruling given during trial, June 17, 1999.

Broadcasting Act 1990, especially given the statutory encouragement to argue by analogy from the explanatory sub-sections.

"Effective control" in the live broadcast exception

4–020 The meaning of "effective control" in the live broadcast exception was also considered in the *MORI v BBC* case. The case concerned defamatory comments made by an interviewee during the course of a live television interview. The BBC relied upon s.1 for its defence.

The claimant argued that the BBC could rely on subs.(d) only in the absence of any ability to prevent the maker from making the statement and that if a degree of effective control were possible, then the BBC could not rely on the defence. The claimant argued that in a pre-arranged studio interview with a known participant it would be possible to lay down ground rules in advance, or intervene or moderate what was said by the interviewee.

The BBC argued that the subsection referred to effective control over the maker of the statement rather than over the statement made by him or its transmission. It argued that the issue was not whether the BBC could have taken steps to achieve effective control, but whether in fact such control existed at the time of the broadcast.

4–021 The judge held that s.1(3)(d) was addressing the relationship between the broadcaster and the individual who made the allegedly defamatory statement; and that the word "control" in this context connoted the "power of the broadcaster in relation to that individual as regards his conduct during the interview, in particular to direct or determine what is and what is not said by that individual". The judge went on to say that qualifying "control" by use of the word "effective" was intended to do no more than indicate that the power of control must be real and not theoretical or illusory.

The judge decided that the relevant question was the control in fact possessed by the BBC at the time of the interview, not what the BBC could have done to acquire control. So the possibility of laying down ground rules was not relevant to the issue of effective control.[30] The judge decided that there was sufficient evidence of effective control by ability to direct the interview so as to avoid provoking the interviewee and to intervene when he embarked on his attack on MORI and if necessary cut him off, for this question to be considered by the jury.

The judge also commented that one situation where effective control might be said to exist would be where the maker of the statement was the employee of the broadcaster, so that the broadcaster could stipulate what might or might not be said and impose sanctions which would have the effect of conferring control over the employee; and that there would be other situations where, by virtue of a contractual relationship or perhaps by means of volunteer consent on the part of the interviewee, it could be said

---

[30] Although it was relevant to the issue of reasonable care under s.1(1)(b).

that the broadcaster had or had available to him the means of obtaining effective control over the maker of the allegedly defamatory statement.

It is notable that the words "effective control" are also used in s.1(3)(e), in connection with the relationship between the operator of, or provider of, access to a communications system and a person by whom the statement is transmitted, or made available by means of the system. The extent to which the *MORI* analysis would be relevant to a case falling within s.1(3)(e) would depend upon the particular facts of the case.

4.3.4 Publication at common law and the 1996 Act

The meaning of "publisher" for the purposes of s.1 of the Act is confined to that section. It is very different from the normal meaning of publisher (i.e. one who publishes) in defamation, and does not affect the normal meaning of "publish" or "publication" either in the Act or for other defamation purposes (s.17(1)).   4–022

It therefore remains necessary to show that a defendant has published the offending statement in the common law sense before proceeding to consider the question of whether he is a primary or secondary publisher within the meaning of the Act.[31]

However, notwithstanding the explicit preservation of the common law meaning of "publish", it may yet be influenced in practice by the terms of the Act. For in making the innocent dissemination defence available to, for instance, a person involved only "in operating or providing any equipment, system or service by means of which the statement is retrieved, copied, distributed or made available in electronic form" (s.1(3)(c)) or "as the operator or provider of access to a communication system by means of which the statement is transmitted, or made available, by a person over whom he has no effective control" (s.1(3)(e)) the Act contemplates that all such activities would have constituted publication at common law.

That is debatable. Liability at common law did not extend to those who merely facilitated publication.[32] Although the boundary between participation and facilitation was by no means easy to draw, the categories of secondary disseminators under the Act would appear to include some (in particular those who merely transmit information) who were mere facilitators at common law.

As discussed in para.4–010 above, in *Bunt v Tilley*[33] Eady J. has held that the passive role of affording a connection to the internet does not render the provider a publisher at common law of a statement transmitted across the connection.

Although the decision in *Bunt v Tilley* is clear on this point and accords with established principles, it has to be recognised that the claimant con-

---

[31] *Godfrey v Demon Internet Ltd* (fn.2 above); *Bunt v Tilley* (fn.22 above).
[32] para.4–008 above.
[33] [2006] EWHC 407 (QB).

ducted his own case without the benefit of legal representation. The judgment contains no discussion of the underlying contradictions between s.1 and the scope of responsibility for publication at common law.

It could therefore still be open to a claimant to argue that the inclusion of mere conduits within s.1 implies that they should not be regarded as facilitators at common law.

4.3.5 Authors, editors and publishers under the 1996 Act

4–023   It can be seen that there are three ways in which someone can be held strictly liable for a defamatory statement—if he is the author, editor or publisher. This immediately highlights one respect in which the Act requires careful analysis—the distinction between editor and publisher. Under the Act the risk attached to exercising editorial control, or more accurately of assuming editorial responsibility, is of being found to be an editor, not a publisher. Conversely the definition of publisher appears to have nothing to do with whether editorial control is exercised, so that someone who falls within the definition of "publisher" may be held liable whether or not he assumes editorial responsibility.

Thus a commercial publisher who hosts a discussion forum may be in a different position from someone whose business is not commercial publishing. As noted above, in *Godfrey v Demon Internet Ltd*, the judge held that the defendant, an internet service provider which hosted newsgroups, was "clearly" not a publisher within the meaning of ss.1(2) and 1(3) and could "incontrovertibly" avail itself of s.1(1)(a).

Authors versus subordinate disseminators

4–024   The scope of the explanatory subsections which define the categories of subordinate disseminators is not easy to discern. In particular, it is unclear how the subsections "explain" each of the primary definitions. It does not seem possible that they operate on each primary definition in the same way. For example, it seems tolerably clear that an author can never fall within any of the subsections. Someone who originates the defamatory statement can surely never "only" be involved in any of the activities described in the subsections. The act of originating the statement must of itself disentitle the author from the protection of the subsections. Any other result would be absurd.

Publishers versus subordinate disseminators

4–025   However, the same does not appear to apply to a publisher. "Issuing" material is on its face a wide concept, apt to cover much of the activity contemplated in the explanatory subsections. So unless "issue" is intended to have a very restricted meaning, it would seem that a person whose business is in the wide sense issuing material to the public may yet be able to qualify as a subordinate disseminator if he "only", for instance, provides a service by means of which a defamatory statement is made available.

This is different from the case of the author, where the act of origination in the primary definition must be taken to preclude subordinate disseminator status. However, the questions of how narrow is the residual definition of commercial publisher, and what activities would disqualify a potential commercial publisher from being held to be "only" carrying on the activities in the subsections, and their relationship to the activities described in the primary definition, are obscure.

Editors versus subordinate disseminators

The case of the editor appears to work differently again. The definition of "editor" describes a status—someone who has assumed editorial or equivalent responsibility. It is not dependent on an act of editing. Yet the explanatory subsections describe acts, not a status. How do the subsections relate to the primary definition, and how can one discern whether someone has assumed editorial responsibility? The relationship may simply be that assumption of editorial responsibility is not to be inferred from only carrying on the activities described in the subsections. That leaves at large, to be answered without any real assistance from the Act, the question of what activities may result in actual or inferred assumption of editorial responsibility.   4–026

The consequence appears to be that, whatever may have been the position before the Act, activities from which assumption of editorial responsibility may be inferred are now to be avoided if subordinate disseminator status under the Act is to be preserved. Of course, if a person has assumed that responsibility (e.g. by undertaking a contractual obligation to edit), failing to discharge it will not permit him to claim subordinate disseminator status.

As to what activities could result in an inference of editor status, some assistance may now be gained from *Market Opinion and Research International Ltd v BBC*.[34] In this case Gray J. ruled that to use a time delay device in a live broadcast so as to enable the producer to cut out swear words or, if he thought quickly enough, a libellous comment would not render the broadcaster an "editor" within the meaning of s.1(1)(a). He said: 4–027

> "I consider that the function of an editor is to adapt, fashion and organise information so as to enable it to be communicated to the public in a journalistically acceptable or desirable fashion. An equivalent function is a function closely allied to an editorial function in the sense which I have described. The person who presses the button of the delay mechanism in order to cut out the profanity or libel is not, in my judgment, exercising an editorial function in the sense I have described. It is the function akin to

---

[34] fn.20 above.

that of a lawyer vetting material prior to publication. I do not consider that lawyers performing that task are exercising an editorial function."

That may be compared with the US case of *Stratton Oakmont v Prodigy*,[35] in which the screening of offensive words from messages posted to discussion forums was held to involve editorial control and render Prodigy a primary publisher.

However, the apparent contrast is illusory. In the *Prodigy* case there were journalistic reasons for screening offensive words, since Prodigy made a selling point of the fact that it was family-oriented and controlled the contents of its bulletin boards. In an article quoted in the judgment Prodigy stated:

"We make no apology for pursuing a value system that reflects the culture of the millions of American families we aspire to serve. Certainly no responsible newspaper does less when it chooses the type of advertising it publishes, the letters it prints, the degree of nudity and unsupported gossip its editors tolerate."

The judge commented that Prodigy had made a conscious choice to gain the benefits of editorial control and that "presumably Prodigy's decision to regulate the content of its bulletin boards was in part influenced by its desire to attract a market perceived to exist consisting of users seeking a 'family-oriented' computer service."[36]

Such removal of profanity for journalistic, as opposed to legal, reasons would fall within Gray J.'s definition of the function of an editor.

4.3.6 Which internet players can claim subordinate disseminator status?

4–028 We listed above some examples of the different varieties of relationship between disseminator and content. Which of these could claim "subordinate disseminator" status under the 1996 Act?

The Usenet host

4–029 The first example was the Usenet host. As discussed above, that was considered in *Godfrey v Demon Internet Ltd*. Demon was found to have subordinate disseminator status in relation to its hosting of newsgroups.

---

[35] fn.1 above.
[36] Prodigy abandoned editorial control in 1994—see *Lunney v Prodigy* (section 4.5 below). The policy implications of the earlier *Prodigy* decision also were criticised in *Lunney*. Similar policy concerns may lie behind Gray J.'s formulation of the editorial function in *MORI v BBC*.

The web journal discussion forum

The second example was the proprietor of a web journal who included a **4–030**
"letters to the editor" feature on the journal's website, in which on-line
readers were free to post "letters" directly to a forum on the website. Other
readers could reply in like manner.

The proprietor would have to overcome a number of serious obstacles to
take advantage of a defence. The first is that the proprietor of such a journal
is quite likely to be a "commercial publisher" within the ordinary meaning
of s.1(2), namely a person whose business is issuing material to the public,
or a section of the public, who issues material containing the statement in
the course of that business.

There is, however, some ambiguity in the phrase "issues material
containing the statement". This fails to recognise that (as discussed in
para.4–012 above) much material on the internet, especially the contents of
discussion forums, is "unwrapped". It makes little sense to speak of
material containing the statement, since it is extremely difficult to ascertain
where any item of material begins and ends in a seamless, dynamically
changing, linked environment.

The proprietor could seek to argue that the discussion forum on the
website was of a different nature from the material in the journal issued by
him and should be treated separately from it, so that the statement was not
contained in that material. The material within which the statement was
contained could be argued to be the remainder of the message posted by the
third party to the discussion forum. It could also be open to argument
whether the proprietor of the journal had "issued" the offending posting at
all.

The proprietor would also have to argue that he was not an "editor"
within the meaning of the Act. Clearly he (or his employed editor) would be
an editor in relation to the main content of the journal. Would that
necessarily extend to the content of the discussion forum included in the
journal? Or would he be able to argue that, in relation to the discussion
forum alone, he undertook no function of adapting, fashioning and organising the information to enable it to be communicated to the public in a
journalistically acceptable or desirable fashion?[37]

As to the explanatory categories of s.1(3), if necessary he would probably **4–031**
have to bring himself within s.1(3)(c), arguing that he was only providing a
service by means of which the statement was made available in electronic
form. In concept, if separation from the edited parts of the journal can be
established, the provision of the website discussion forum is little different
(volume of messages apart) from the hosting of newsgroups considered in
Godfrey v Demon Internet Ltd.

A proprietor of a website discussion forum seeking to rely on an innocent
dissemination defence could seek to draw comfort from the statements of

---

[37] See *MORI v BBC*, para.4–027 above.

Owen J. in *Totalise Plc v The Motley Fool*[38] regarding the responsibility, for the purpose of s.10 of the Contempt of Court Act 1981, of the defendants in that case for discussion fora on their websites (see Ch.6). However, while the judge's comments may be helpful in showing that no editorial responsibility was assumed, they do not address the question of being a publisher.

The academic mailing list

4–032   The third example was of an academic who collated interesting postings from a Usenet newsgroup and periodically emailed them to subscribers to an electronic mailing list. It is difficult to see how the academic could avoid being categorised as an editor. He performs the traditional editorial functions of selection and collation and has clear responsibility for the decision to publish the selected postings by emailing them on to his mailing list subscribers.

The internet access and web hosting ISP

4–033   This example was of an internet service provider who provided internet access and free web hosting facilities to its customers. In relation to internet access, the ISP would be able to argue that, as its activities were entirely passive, at common law it did not publish the material transmitted across its facilities in response to its customers' commands and requests (see the discussion above of *Bunt v Tilley*). If it did not succeed in that, it would almost certainly fall within the scope of s.1(3)(c). Its web hosting activities would also do so.

As the operator of a communications system its internet access activities would also potentially fall within s.1(3)(e), which carries the further condition that it had no effective control over the person who transmitted or made the statement available by means of the system. On the face of it, if s.1(3)(c) applies that should be the end of the matter. Could, however, it be argued that if s.1(3)(e) is applicable, the person should not be able to escape the "effective control" condition by relying on s.1(3)(c)? The interrelationship of these explanatory subsections is obscure.

Section 1(3)(e) does contain a potential trap, in that an ISP will have contracts in place with its internet access and web hosting customers. If the defamatory statement for which it is sought to make the ISP liable was generated by one of its customers, then there may be a question whether the contractual arrangements give the ISP "effective control" over the customer.[39]

In the case of web hosting, the questions of whether in the factual circumstances the ISP took reasonable care and did not know or have reason

---

[38] [2001] E.M.L.R. 29. The costs order against the second defendant was reversed by the Court of Appeal ([2001] EWCA Civ 1897). However, the Court of Appeal made no comment on the remarks of Owen J. regarding s.10 of the Contempt of Court Act 1981 referred to in the main text. A full discussion of the case is contained in Chs. 6 and 7.

[39] See *MORI v BBC*, para.4–020 above.

to believe that what it did caused or contributed to the publication of a defamatory statement are likely to be far more contentious than in the case of a statement merely transmitted across its network.

The managed virtual network

In this example, a telecommunications operator agreed to provide and manage a virtual network to enable a group of companies to operate an intranet. All the group's email traffic and requests for documents flow over the network. **4–034**

The telecommunications operator is in an excellent position to take advantage of s.1(3)(c) and (e). The "effective control" condition of s.1(3)(e) should be less of a concern, as it is difficult to conceive of a contractual arrangement that would give the telecommunications company "effective control" over all the staff of the group of companies using the network.

The web design company

In this example a web design company receives text from its customer, codes the text using HTML and Java, and passes the finished product by email to another company which will host the website. **4–035**

At common law the web design company is probably participating in the publication on the website. Because of its direct involvement with the text its activity is more akin to a printer than to, say, a designer who may not have been a publisher at common law.[40]

On the plain reading of "author, editor, or publisher" as defined by s.1(2) of the Act, the web designer appears to have a good argument that he is none of those (assuming that he resisted the temptation to improve the text while coding it). Unfortunately, none of the explanatory subsections read directly on to his activity, and if necessary he may have to argue by analogy from s.1(3)(a) "in printing, producing, distributing or selling printed material containing the statement".

The search engine

Last, let us consider the position of search engines.[41] Search engines set out to index the web. They do this by sending out automated "crawlers" which are pre-programmed to seek out websites and index their contents on a mammoth full-text database. The search engine's database is likely to contain a short term (probably about two to three weeks) cache of the whole text content of the web pages, a list of words contained in them and pointers to their location on the web. **4–036**

A user enters search words and the search engine will respond by displaying a page of links, page headings and short extracts. The search engine

---

[40] And see *Marchant v Ford*, fn.7 above.
[41] Note that Art.21 of the Electronic Commerce Directive (2000/31) requires a periodic re-examination of the Directive 2000/31 [2000] O.J. L178/1, encompassing the liability position of search engines.

is certainly publishing, at common law, the page headings and short extracts. It is more debatable whether, for each link, it is publishing the target page or site (see discussion of linking, section 4.4.2 below). Assuming that it is, can the search engine rely on the subordinate disseminator exceptions?

The first hurdle it has to overcome is to demonstrate that it is not a commercial publisher within the definition of s.1(2). The trouble is that there is no wholly analogous off-line equivalent to the search engine. However, given that the pure search engine will be providing access only to third party material with which it has no direct connection,[42] it should have reasonable arguments that it is not a commercial publisher.

Is it an editor? The search engine undoubtedly selects the material that it indexes, if only to the extent that the search algorithm instructs the crawler to seek out websites according to certain rules. It also has careful programming in place to determine the order in which "hits" are displayed to the user. However, all this is done automatically by software. Does this amount to editorial responsibility for the decision to publish, especially when the search criteria are keyed in by the user?

4–037   The Act appears to envisage that someone may be an editor even if they have only partial responsibility for the decision to publish. Otherwise the factors to be taken into account in assessing "reasonable care" would make little sense. On the other hand, can a purely automated process amount to editorial responsibility?[43]

Perhaps the most powerful argument in favour of the search engine is that it is doing no more than putting a sophisticated tool in the hand of the user to enable the user to locate sites; and that as such it is no different from a library transposed onto the internet, with a more sophisticated card index; and that it therefore either falls squarely within the provisions of s.1(3)(c), or should benefit from subordinate disseminator status by virtue of the analogy provisions.

4.3.7 Defamation Act 1996—standard of care

4–038   As mentioned above, even if a person is able to show that he is not an author, publisher or editor within the meaning of the Act, to escape liability for a defamatory statement he has to show that he took reasonable care in relation to its publication and that he did not know, and had no reason to believe, that what he did caused or contributed to the publication of a defamatory statement.[44]

---

[42] This may exclude "portals", which seek to combine search engines with direct content.

[43] Note that in the US case of *Lunney v Prodigy* (section 4.5 below) the court held that "intelligent editorial control involves the use of judgment, and no computer program has such a capacity".

[44] Defamation Act 1996 s.1(1)(b) and (c).

Notice and take-down

In *Godfrey v Demon Internet Ltd* the court, having found (as discussed **4–039** above) that Demon Internet had published the newsgroup posting in question and was not a publisher within the meaning of s.1(2) and (3) of the 1996 Act, considered whether it satisfied these conditions.

The factual background was that Demon carried the Usenet newsgroup "soc.culture.thai" and stored postings within the "soc" hierarchy for about a fortnight. On January 13, 1997 someone unknown made a posting in the US on the soc.culture.thai newsgroup. The posting was "squalid, obscene and defamatory of the Plaintiff". It purported to come from the plaintiff and invited replies to the plaintiff's email address. The posting was in fact a forgery. The posting was replicated from the originating American ISP through the newsgroup system to Demon's news server.

On January 17, 1997 Dr Godfrey sent a fax letter to the managing director of Demon, informing him that the posting was a forgery and requesting Demon to remove the posting from its Usenet news server. Demon admitted that the posting was not removed, but stayed on the server until it expired on about January 27, 1997. There was no dispute that Demon could have obliterated the posting from its news server after receiving Dr Godfrey's request. Dr Godfrey claimed libel damages for the period after January 17, 1997.

The judge held that because after January 17, 1997 Demon knew of the defamatory posting but chose not to remove it that posed an "insuperable difficulty" for their defence. The judge concluded that Demon's defence under s.1 of the Act was "hopeless" and struck it out.

In *Bunt v Tilley*,[45] on the facts the notifications given by the claimant were insufficient to fix the defendants with knowledge.

It should be noted that the test of knowledge is whether the defendant can establish that he did not know and had no reason to believe that what he did contributed to the publication of a *defamatory* statement—not an actionable statement. This means that if the defendant takes the view that the defamatory statement can be justified, that will not assist him in establishing an innocent dissemination defence. The practical consequence of this is that once a defendant has had the existence of a defamatory statement on his system drawn to his attention (for instance by the potential claimant, as in *Godfrey v Demon Internet*), he will no longer be able to rely on s.1 of the 1996 Act even if he makes inquiries of the author and has good grounds to believe that a defence of justification, fair comment or privilege would succeed.

Whether this "notice and take-down" regime draws the right balance **4–040** between the interests of potentially libelled claimants and freedom of speech may be open to question. The Lord Chancellor, during the debate on the Bill, took the view that the formulation in the Act reflected the common law. He said that to give an innocent dissemination defence to an inter-

---

[45] See above, para.4–010.

mediary because he formed the view that some other defence might be available would be to "create an entirely new defence".[46]

In *Goldsmith v Sperrings Ltd*[47] Bridge L.J. adopted a formulation of the common law defence similar to that of the Act. On the other hand Lord Denning M.R., in a dissenting judgment, referred to "a libel on the plaintiff which could not be justified or excused". If this formulation is correct, the possible survival of the common law defence of innocent dissemination may be significant. Lord Denning's judgment also contains a trenchant criticism of the consequences for freedom of speech of visiting too stringent a defamation liability regime on distributors.[48] It could be applied with little modification to the consequences of strict "notice and take-down" regimes on the internet.

Since the coming into force on October 2, 2000 of the Human Rights Act 1998 these issues have assumed greater significance than previously. As regards the statutory provisions of the Defamation Act 1996, the courts are bound under the Human Rights Act to read and give effect to them as far as possible in a manner compatible with the Convention rights[49] or, if that is not possible, the court may make a declaration of non-compatibility.[50]

If the common law defence survives, then the obligation on the courts to act themselves in a manner compatible with Convention rights[51] would require the courts to consider again the questions discussed by Lord Denning and, if necessary for Convention compliance, to reformulate the common law defence so as to make actionability the touchstone of the defence.

4–041   In December 2002 the Law Commission published a preliminary study on Defamation and the internet,[52] which included a review of the liability position of ISPs. It concluded that there was a strong case for reviewing the way that defamation law impacts on internet service providers, since the law places them under some pressure to remove material without considering whether it is in the public interest, or whether it is true. The problem is more pressing with ISPs than with traditional booksellers.

The impression from the evidence given to the Law Commission was that ISPs will almost invariably remove a site rather than risk litigation, at least when faced with a solicitor's letter sent on behalf of a well resourced company. The Law Commission noted a possible conflict between the pressure to remove material, even if true, and the emphasis placed upon freedom of expression under the European Convention on Human Rights.

It should also be noted that the "notice and take-down" provisions of the

---

[46] *Hansard* H.L. April 2, 1996 col. 214.
[47] [1977] 2 All E.R. 566.
[48] At p.573. For an account of libel actions against bookshops following the passage of s.1 of the 1996 Act see "A triumph that cost us dear" *Times*, August 20, 2002.
[49] Human Rights Act 1998, s.3(1).
[50] Human Rights Act 1998, s.4(2).
[51] Human Rights Act 1998, s.6(1) and (3).
[52] Defamation and the Internet—A Preliminary Investigation—Law Commission Scoping Study No 2, December 2002.

Electronic Commerce Directive concerning the liability of hosting inter-mediaries[53] refer to knowledge of "illegal" activity or information. The implementing Regulations (see para.4–002 above) use the word "unlawful".

The question arises whether this wording requires actionability rather than mere defamatory meaning. The Law Commission, in its Preliminary Investigation on Defamation and the Internet,[54] inclined to the view that awareness of a statement with defamatory meaning would be sufficient to remove the hosting immunity, since it is *prima facie* unlawful to publish a defamatory statement. However, in *Bunt v Tilley* (see para.4–010 above) Eady J. made comments suggesting that knowledge of actionability is the test: "In order to be able to characterise something as "unlawful" a person would need to know something of the strength or weakness of available defences."

Previous conduct or character

The requirement under s.1(1) of the 1996 Act to have regard to the previous **4–042** conduct or character or the author, editor or publisher raises the question of whether the defendant is required to take positive steps to make some investigation of the antecedents of, for instance, subscribers to an on-line or internet access service, or of those to whom web space is offered. This places service providers and web hosts in the difficult position of trying to avoid activities which would disqualify them from secondary disseminator status, but at the same time do enough to be held to satisfy the requirement to take reasonable care.

The emphasis on the previous conduct or character of the author may have particular implications for a Usenet host, who may be able to make a distinction between receiving individual messages from its direct sub-scribers and receiving a feed containing a stream of messages collated from the rest of the internet.

In the *Demon* case the offending posting was made in the US and sent to Demon via the updating Usenet feed. The *Netcom* copyright case (see Ch.2) also contains a good description of a typical arrangement. The defendant subscribed to a bulletin board service (BBS), which in turn connected to an internet access provider (Netcom). When the defendant posted an article to the alt.religion.scientology newsgroup the message was held initially on the BBS's version of the newsgroup (where other subscribers to the BBS could read it), then copied on to Netcom, who also stored it and forwarded it. The BBS kept messages for three days, Netcom for 11 days. So the BBS received and made available a message received direct from its subscriber, whereas Netcom received a general feed of all articles posted to that BBS.

The standard of care could effectively be more onerous in relation to the

---

[53] Art.14.
[54] Scoping Study "Defamation and the Internet—A Preliminary Investigation", December 2002.

Usenet host's direct subscribers than in relation to other contributors to newsgroups.

What is reasonable care?

4–043 Before the Defamation Act 1996 there were a number of cases dealing with the liability of traditional distributors of printed matter. There was at least one example of a distributor or other subordinate disseminator being held liable having failed to establish that it was not negligent. In *Vizetelly v Mudie's Select Library Ltd*[55] the proprietor of a circulating library was held liable for a book that he lent out containing a libel. Following litigation, the publishers had placed notices in the trade press asking for the book to be withdrawn. Although the proprietors took the trade papers, they were not checked for notices. The Court of Appeal found that the proprietors admitted that they ran their business on the basis that it was cheaper to run the risk of an occasional libel suit than to employ someone to read the books for libel. The proprietors' contentions that the number of books circulated was so great that it was impossible in the ordinary course of their business to read them did not avail them.

The question remains whether the positive obligation to take reasonable care in relation to publication of a defamatory statement can be discharged by an ISP who takes no positive steps to make any checks on content that it carries or hosts. In this regard, it is arguable that the wording of the Act places a more onerous burden on the defendant than did the common law defence, since the Act appears to place a positive burden on the defendant. Even in *Vizetelly* notices had been issued of which the defendant ought to have been aware.

The question could be asked, for instance, whether an ISP should make any random checks on content (to be required to check everything would be wholly unreasonable in view of the volumes of messages and websites carried by most ISPs).

In other contexts, traditional magazine distributors have been found to have satisfied a due diligence requirement where they had traded over a long period of time with a reputable publisher and made no checks themselves (see *e.g. London Borough of Harrow v W H Smith Trading Ltd*, discussed in Ch.5). However, while that is helpful in establishing that there is no rule of law that some steps must always be taken in order to satisfy a due diligence requirement, that leaves unanswered the question of whether any positive steps need to be taken where the ISP is receiving content direct from the public, as opposed to from a reputable publisher.

Reasonable care and Article 15 of the Electronic Commerce Directive

4–044 The reasonable care condition may now have to be read in the light of Art.15 of the Electronic Commerce Directive. This prohibits Member States from imposing a general obligation on information society service provi-

---

[55] [1900] 2 QB 170.

ders, when providing the conduit, caching or hosting services covered by Arts. 12, 13 and 14, to monitor the information which they transmit or store, or a general obligation actively to seek facts or circumstances indicating illegal activity. Recital (47) stresses that this applies only to obligations of a general nature and does not concern monitoring obligations in a specific case and, in particular, does not affect orders by national authorities in accordance with national legislation.

The question is whether, if an ISP is obliged to undertake a degree of general monitoring as a condition of being able to invoke a defence under the 1996, that breaches the prohibition under Art.15.

One answer is that since under the 1996 Act an ISP does not put itself in breach of any obligation by failing to monitor, no obligation is imposed on it on which Art.15 could bite. The only consequence of failing to monitor is the possible non-availability of the defence under the 1996 Act through failure to exercise reasonable care. Even if that could in theory be a breach of Art.15, it is of no significance since an ISSP providing conduit, caching or hosting services (within the meaning of the Directive) will always be able to have recourse to the separate defences under the Electronic Commerce Regulations. Those defences do not require any positive monitoring to be undertaken in order for an ISSP to be able to invoke them.

An alternative view is that if the UK chooses to provide an additional, home grown, defence which is capable of being invoked by persons who provide conduit, caching or hosting services covered by Arts. 12, 13 and 14 of the Directive, then it cannot with one hand provide the defence but with the other hand take it away by imposing a condition that conflicts with Article 15. The policy embodied in Art.15 is clear and the obligation to take reasonable care under s.1 of the 1996 Act ought, for consistency with Art.15, to be read so as to avoid placing on the defendant a positive obligation to monitor content that it carries or hosts.

Since there is, in any event, room for debate about whether the formulation of the reasonable care obligation in the 1996 Act was or was not intended to change the common law position by placing a positive burden on the secondary disseminator, it may well be that a court looking at the matter now would at least have regard to Art.15 when considering that question.

4.4 WHAT CONSTITUTES PUBLICATION?

The essence of publication is communication of the defamatory statement to someone other than the person defamed. This superficially simple statement has, however, to be considered in conjunction with issues such as burden of proof and intention to publish.   4–045

In the context of the internet, this raises several issues in addition to the question of publication by an ISP already discussed in para.4–008 above: first, whether an email is published to anyone other than the recipient of the email; second, whether on the World Wide Web there can be liability for linking to other sites containing defamatory material. The third question of in what circumstances the content of a foreign site will be taken to have been published within the English jurisdiction or, if not published here, may yet be actionable here, is dealt with in Ch.6.

4.4.1 Email

4–046 There is no liability for a defamatory statement sent only to the defamed person. So at first sight an email sent only to the defamed person ought not to found any liability. However, internet emails pass through intermediate routers on the way to their destination and are capable of being read by technicians at those intermediate sites. Could this constitute publication to a third party?

Two different situations need to be considered: first, where it is proved that a third party did in fact read the email; and secondly, where the court is being asked to infer publication without actual proof that someone read it.

If a third party does read the email, the court will have to consider whether the defendant intended, or ought to have foreseen, that the email would or could be read by someone other than the intended recipient. If, for instance, the defendant knows that the plaintiff is in the habit of letting his assistants open his emails, the defendant will be liable for publication to the assistant who opens it. On the other hand, if it is opened by someone at an intermediate router, much may depend on whether the defendant knew that this was possible, whether it was proper for the person at that intermediary to do so and other factual circumstances.

A claimant would most probably make great play of the much-publicised insecurity of internet email. If the email were encrypted before transmission and some third party managed to decrypt and read it, the defendant would have a strong case that he neither intended nor ought to have foreseen that publication.

The second situation is where there is no proof that anyone other than the recipient read the email, and the plaintiff instead asks the court to infer from the facts that some third person read it.

So, for instance, if a libel is written on the back of a postcard that will be evidence of publication, the words being visible to anyone through whose hands it passes. The same applies to a telegram, as the contents will have been communicated to the clerks who transmit it. But the presumption will not be made in the case of an unsealed envelope sent through the post, as there is no presumption that the post office staff will have opened it.[56]

It is submitted that an unencrypted email is more analogous to the unsealed note than to a postcard, so that the inference of publication ought not to be drawn; and that the inference will certainly not be drawn in the case of an encrypted email. However, if an unencrypted email is in fact read

---

[56] *Huth v Huth* [1915] 3 K.B. 32.

by a third party the sender may find himself liable for that publication as described above.

In *Al Amoudi v Brisard*[57] it was held that a claimant in an internet case is not entitled to rely on a presumption of law that there has been substantial publication. The claimant will be required to prove substantial publication within the jurisdiction, whether by direct evidence or by inference from the surrounding circumstances. Such an inference was drawn in *Pritchard Englefield v Steinberg* [2005] EWCA Civ 824.

4.4.2 Liability for linked content

A website can provide access to a collection of journals and periodicals   **4–047** without any of the content being physically on the site at all. A web page has a series of links, which when clicked will take the user to the linked material. These links may be "internal", leading to material held on the same site, or "external", leading to material held on someone else's site held elsewhere on the internet. So a site can be created consisting of nothing but external links to other sites. To the user it will look superficially identical to a site on which the same materials are held internally on that site.

What is the status and liability of such a site, with regard to defamatory material contained on one of the linked sites? Should the liability be any different from someone who holds the materials themselves? There is old authority[58] that drawing attention to an existing defamatory statement can amount to publishing it. In that case someone sat in a chair pointing out to passers-by a defamatory sign erected over the road. The author of the sign was unknown, but the person pointing it out was found thereby to have published it. That would seem to suggest that providing a link to another site can amount to publishing material contained on it.[59] Much may depend on the facts. For instance, was the link to the site as a whole, or to a particular article on it?[60]

Whether the person providing the link could rely on the innocent dissemination defence of the Defamation Act 1996 must be a matter of speculation. The activity does not obviously fall within any of the explanatory categories of s.1(3). It would be necessary to rely on the plain words of s.1(3) to argue that the person creating a link is neither an author, an editor, nor a commercial publisher, reinforced if necessary by reliance on the "analogy" provision of s.1(3).

If this hurdle is overcome, greater difficulty may be encountered in dis-

---

[57] [2006] EWHC 1062 (QB).

[58] *Hird v Wood* [1894] 38 S.J. 234.

[59] In Germany a website owner has been held liable in defamation for providing a link to third party sites containing defamatory statements about the plaintiff, notwithstanding a disclaimer stating that responsibility for linked third party statements would lie only with the respective authors. The defendant's claim that he was only providing a "market of opinions" failed. [1998] C.T.L.R. 7 N–113.

[60] See also the discussion in Ch.2 of common law principles of joint tortfeasorship (common design and procurement) applied to liability for linking to content that infringes copyright.

charging the standard of care requirements. In the case of a direct link to a defamatory article it is difficult to see how a person could establish reasonable care without proving that they read the offending page before linking to it. In that event (unless the fact that it was defamatory was not apparent from the text) how could they establish that they did not know and had no reason to believe that what they did contributed to the publication of a defamatory statement? The situation may be less clear in the case of a link to a website containing defamatory text elsewhere within it.

4–048   Although the Electronic Commerce Directive does not address the question of linking liability, Art.21 of the Directive requires the European Commission before July 17, 2003 and then at two yearly intervals to submit a report on the application of the Directive, which is required (among other things) to analyse the need for proposals concerning the liability of providers of hyperlinks.[61]

The First Report of the Commission was issued in November 2003.[62] While noting that some Member States[63] had addressed linking liability in their national laws, the Commission stated only that it would continue to examine any future need to adapt the existing framework.

The UK Department of Trade and Industry issued a consultation paper in June 2005 to explore whether the UK should extend the Directive's intermediary liability provisions to hyperlinkers, location tool services and content aggregators. It concluded in December 2006[64] that there was currently insufficient evidence to justify any extension to these limitations. The DTI observed that the second review of the Electronic Commerce Directive by the European Commission is due in 2007 and said that it would encourage the Commission to take on board the important issues raised during the consultation.

4.5 SOME US COMPARISONS

4–049   In the field of defamation analogies with US law are dangerous: "... I refer to [the American authorities] but only shortly because I found them only of marginal assistance because of the different approach to defamation across the Atlantic" (Morland J., in *Godfrey v Demon Internet Ltd*). However, the earliest on-line defamation judgments were delivered in the US and com-

---

[61] The report is also required to address the liability of the providers of location tool services, "notice and take-down" procedures and the attribution of liability following the taking down of content, as well as the need for additional conditions for the exemption of liability under Arts. 12 and 13 (mere conduits and caching) and the possibility of applying internal market principles to unsolicited email.

[62] *http://europa.eu.int/comm/internal_market/e-commerce/directive_en.htm#firstreport.*

[63] Spain and Portugal extended the hosting model of liability to search engines and hyperlinks, whereas Austria and Liechtenstein (an EEA state) had applied the conduit model to search engines and the hosting model to hyperlinks.

[64] "Government Response and Summary of Responses to Consultation Document on the Electronic Commerce Directive: the Liability of Hyperlinkers, Location Tool Services and Content Aggregators" (*www.dti.gov.uk/consultations/page13985.html*).

manded considerable attention worldwide. Those and some later decisions are of interest as examples of how another jurisdiction has approached the problem of determining on-line liability of intermediaries.

The two early US cases were *Cubby Inc v CompuServe Inc.*[65] and *Stratton Oakmont v Prodigy Inc.*[66] These cases concerned on-line discussion forums of the traditional pre-internet type, provided by CompuServe and Prodigy respectively. The main difference from an internet newsgroup is that rather than being replicated around publicly available hosts on the internet, a Prodigy or CompuServe forum of that era was held only on the provider's computer and was accessible only by subscribers to the service.

In *Cubby*, CompuServe agreed with a third party publisher to provide, as part of CompuServe's Journalism Forum, a magazine called *Rumorville USA*. The contract stated that the publisher would have responsibility for *Rumorville*'s contents. The magazine was produced regularly by the third party publisher, loaded direct into the Journalism Forum and made available to those CompuServe subscribers who had made arrangements with *Rumorville*'s publishers. CompuServe had another contract with a company whose job it was to manage the Journalism Forum in accordance with CompuServe's editorial and technical standards and conventions of style. The manager had the ability under the contract to edit, delete and control the contents of the Forum. On the evidence CompuServe had no opportunity to review the contents of *Rumorville* before the publishers placed it on the forum.

Cubby alleged that *Rumorville* contained a defamatory statement and sued CompuServe, claiming that it was a publisher. CompuServe maintained that it was a distributor and was innocent.

The court held that CompuServe was indeed a distributor in this case and subject to the same standard of liability as a traditional public library, bookstore or newsstand. The judge described it as an "electronic, for-profit library that carries a vast number of publications". He emphasised that although CompuServe could decide not to carry a publication, once it had decided to carry the publication it would have little or no editorial control over its contents. He also laid some emphasis on the management of the forum by a company unrelated to CompuServe.

The facts of the case were closely analogous to hard copy publication and 4–050 distribution, involving as they did the uploading of a pre-edited third party magazine to CompuServe's system. There was no consideration in the case of the position regarding posting of individual messages to a discussion forum.

The question of discussion forums came before the courts in the second US case, *Stratton Oakmont v Prodigy Inc*. This time the complaint was about a message posted to a discussion forum, hosted by Prodigy. The plaintiff sued Prodigy. On a preliminary point the court held that Prodigy was liable as a primary publisher, as it had exercised some editorial control

---

[65] fn.1 above.
[66] fn.1 above.

over the content of postings. It had, for instance, screened postings for offensive material and also held itself out as controlling the content of its bulletin boards. Prodigy, like CompuServe, contracted out management of the forum to a third party, but that was held not to prevent liability arising.

4–051   Since then, in *Lunney v Prodigy Services Company*[67] Prodigy have been held not liable in defamation for the contents of an email and two bulletin board messages sent using its system. The court found that Prodigy did not publish the messages.

The court put forward four reasons for disagreeing with the first Prodigy case: (1) insofar as the current case concerned email, the rationale of the original case would not apply to that since Prodigy clearly could not screen all the email sent by its subscribers; (2) on the evidence Prodigy abandoned in 1994 the efforts at editorial control which formed the factual basis of the earlier case; (3) the decision in *Anderson v New York Telephone Co.*[68] stated that a telephone company was to be considered a publisher only of those messages in whose transmission it actually participated. It would not matter if Prodigy exercised power to exclude vulgarities from certain messages, if there was no proof that it exercised such control in connection with transmission of the messages complained of by the plaintiff; (4) Even a telephone company which participated in the transmission of a libellous message could not be held liable unless it knew it was libellous.

Bracken J.P. held that Prodigy did not publish the statement and that even if it could be considered a publisher of the statement it attracted qualified privilege in the absence of proof that Prodigy knew such a statement would be false. Bracken J.P. also criticised the policy implications of the earlier *Prodigy* case:

> "... in *Stratton Oakmont* Prodigy was punished for allegedly performing in an inadequate way the very conduct (exercise of editorial control) which, initially, it had no legal duty to perform at all. The rule of law announced in *Stratton Oakmont* discourages the very conduct which the plaintiff in *Stratton Oakmont* argued should be encouraged."

4–052   In the *Demon Internet* case Morland J. observed that, unlike in the *Lunney* case, in English law Prodigy would clearly have been the publisher of the email message.

It should also be noted that s.230 of the Communications Decency Act now provides that no provider or user of an interactive computer service shall be held liable on account of "any action voluntarily taken in good faith to restrict access to or availability of material that the provider or user considers to be obscene ... or otherwise objectionable" or on account of "any action taken to enable or make available to information content providers or others the technical means to restrict access to [such mate-

---

[67] 250 A.D. 2d 230. Upheld on appeal to the Supreme Court of New York, 94 N.Y. 2d 242.
[68] fn.12 above.

rial]". It also provides that "No provider or user of an interactive computer service shall be treated as the publisher or speaker of any information provided by another information content provider". This was applied in *Zeran v America Online, Inc.*[69] so as to render the defendant immune from suit.

4.6 ON-LINE RIGHT OF REPLY

Moves have been afoot for some time to extend the right of reply that exists in most EU Member States to the whole EU, and to include on-line publications. On December 15, 2004 the Council of Europe adopted a Recommendation[70] specifically aimed at extending rights of reply to on-line media.   **4–053**

In the form adopted the Recommendation is more limited than in earlier drafts, but nevertheless starts from the audacious premise that:

> "the right of reply is a particularly appropriate remedy in the online environment due to the possibility of instant correction of contested information and the technical ease with which replies from concerned persons can be attached to it".

It is indeed true that the internet offers unrivalled opportunities for individuals to publish information to the world—which is why it is unnecessary, indeed damaging, to shoehorn the internet into a bureaucratic model of statement and counterstatement more appropriate to a set of litigation pleadings than to a vibrant discussion medium.[71]

The Recommendation applies to "any means of communication for the periodic dissemination to the public of edited information, whether on-line or off-line, such as newspapers, periodicals, radio, television and web-based news services". There is no requirement that the service be a commercial service. The monthly church newsletter would be caught.

So would a daily blog, if it is regarded as "edited". But what does "edited" mean? If it means edited by someone other than the author, then a blog would not count. If, on the other hand, the author can be regarded as performing the journalistic role of editing his own materials and presenting them to the reading public, then the blog would be caught. And to what end, when the obvious riposte is "go write your own blog" (conceivably at less cost than the burden to the original blogger of complying with the Recommendation's suggested procedures)? Could the Recommendation   **4–054**

---

[69] 1997 129 F3d 327; followed in *Blumenthal v Drudge*, 1998 992 F.Supp. 44 (D.C., D.C.).
[70] Recommendation Rec(2004)16 of the Committee of Ministers to Member States on the right of reply in the new media environment (*http://www.coe.int/T/E/Com/press/News/2004/rec(2004)16.asp*). The UK and the Slovak Republic reserved their rights to comply or not with the Recommendation, in so far as it referred to on-line services.
[71] See "Why Europe still doesn't get the Internet" CNet News.com June 16, 2003 for a trenchant criticism of an earlier draft of the Recommendation.

apply to moderated discussion forums (whether pre-vetted or post-vetted)? If so, to what possible purpose when the whole point of a discussion forum is to enable a continuing thread of comment and reply?

The recommended right of reply, which would be available to a natural or legal person, is restricted to "inaccurate facts about him or her and which affect his/her personal rights". A Recital records that dissemination of opinions and ideas must remain outside the scope of the Recommendation. Given the potential chilling effect on on-line speakers, there is no justification for placing on everyday on-line actors the burden of trying to understand the boundaries of this distinction, or of figuring out what personal rights a legal person can have, or of putting in place compliance mechanisms, when the whole internet is there for anyone who wants to have their say.

The concept of a mandated right of reply is a dinosaur that has survived from an age when the means of publication to the world were concentrated in the hands of the few. Even then, outside the anomalous field of television the need for a right of reply has never been accepted by the UK. Now that anyone can publish to the world at the touch of a mouse-click, any justification for a right of reply that might once have existed has evaporated.

Following the Recommendation the question of an on-line right of reply surfaced again in connection with the proposed revision of the Television without Frontiers Directive.[72] The European Commission originally suggested that a right of reply should be extended beyond traditional broadcast television to "non-linear" audio-visual services (which would include a broad swathe of internet content). However that proposal, which was opposed by the UK government, did not appear in the draft Directive issued on December 13, 2005.

---

[72] Television without Frontiers Directive (89/552/EC) of October 3, 1989, amended on June 30, 1997 by Directive 97/36/EC of the European Parliament and the Council; European Commission proposal for draft amending Directive adopted December 13, 2005 (*http://ec.europa.eu/comm/avpolicy/reg/index_en.htm*).

CHAPTER 5

Content Liability and Protection

5.1 INTRODUCTION

The content available on the web and other internet sources ranges from **5–001** pure entertainment to information that verges on professional advice. Tax sites, offering tips and tax calculation facilities, are one example of the latter. Medical and health sites have proliferated. It is easy to envisage sites providing legal advice, do-it-yourself hints and all manner of content on which the user may rely.[1] If the information were inaccurate and the user suffered harm, could the content provider (or the host) be liable? Can anything be done to minimise liability?

Negligence is the main legal basis on which liability for incorrect information on websites could accrue. The more remote possibility of strict liability under the Consumer Protection Act 1987 is also discussed.

We address the increasingly important topic of the liability of employers for use by their employees of email and the internet. This includes the development of staff policies to reduce and manage the risk of liability and the ability of employers and other network operators to access and make use of electronic communications on their networks, both for the purposes of their businesses and to police the use of their networks.

---

[1] The automation and electronic delivery of advice services formerly the preserve of professional advisers can also give rise to regulatory problems. In Texas the publishers of a software product, "Quicken Family Lawyer", were held to have contravened a Texas statute prohibiting the unauthorised practice of law (*Unauthorized Practice of Law Committee v Parsons Technology, Inc*, 1999 US Dist. LEXIS 813; on appeal, injunction vacated after amendment of the statute in question, 179 F.3d 956). In the UK, the sale of a software product generating buy, sell or hold signals in relation to specified traded stock options was held to constitute not mere software retailing, but the giving of investment advice. Authorisation under the Financial Services Act 1986 was therefore required (*Re Market Wizard Systems (UK) Ltd* [1998] 2 B.C.L.C. 282).

5.2 INCORRECT INFORMATION—NEGLIGENCE LIABILITY

5.2.1 General principles of negligence liability

5–002 The prerequisite for negligence liability is that the person accused owed a duty of care to the person harmed to take reasonable care to avoid the harm that occurred. The mere fact that a person has suffered harm as a result of another person's actions or omissions does not mean that a duty of care existed so as to found liability.

Dangerously defective products

5–003 There are two main strands of negligence liability, which to an extent coalesce when considering liability for on-line information. The first originates from liability for dangerously defective products. In 1932 in *Donoghue v Stevenson*[2] the House of Lords for the first time imposed direct liability to the end-user on the manufacturer of defective products causing physical injury.

The liability arises directly from acts or omissions such as one-off manufacturing defects in products, design defects, or incorrect labelling on hazardous materials.[3] The class of persons to whom the duty of care is owed is very wide; in effect to all those who could foreseeably be damaged by a defect in the product. The liability principles apply equally to personal injury and physical damage to property. However, the courts have not been willing to allow a claimant to recover pure economic loss, i.e. financial loss where the product defect did not cause any physical damage to property or persons. Nor can the claimant recover for the loss of the defective product itself.

Incorrect information and advice

5–004 The second strand of liability concerns information and advice. This differs from product liability in three respects: the nature of the damage recoverable, the size of the class to whom the duty of care is owed and the significance of reliance. Where a person has suffered damage as a result of relying upon incorrect information, the courts have (unlike in a product liability case) been prepared to allow recovery for pure economic loss where it would be fair, just and reasonable to do so.

But that is balanced by a drastic reduction in the size of the class of persons to whom the duty of care is owed. The courts have been unwilling to impose a duty of care to the world at large in respect of reliance on information. Liability has tended to be imposed only in respect of a small class of known persons with a sufficiently close relationship to the giver of

---

[2] [1932] A.C. 562.
[3] E.g. *Vacwell Engineering Co. Ltd v BDH Chemicals Ltd* [1971] 1 Q.B. 111.

the information that the duty of care should apply. This type of liability was established in 1964 in *Hedley Byrne & Co Ltd v Heller & Partners Ltd*.[4]

While the formulation of the test for determining whether a duty of care exists has tended to fluctuate, most recently it has been stated in terms harking back to the *Hedley Byrne* case, namely whether the provider of the information has assumed responsibility for it to the plaintiff.[5]

5.2.2 Liability for incorrect information

Duty of care

Other than cases of close proximity (such as in a professional relationship), there have been no English cases dealing directly with incorrect information causing physical injury or damage. Where there is sufficient proximity and it is fair, just and reasonable to impose a duty of care, a duty of care will be owed.[6] Recovery for economic loss is permitted if there is a sufficiently close relationship, so it would be surprising if recovery for physical damage or personal injury was not permitted. The difficult and uncertain question is whether in the case of physical damage the class of persons to whom the duty of care is owed is wider than for economic loss, and if so how much wider. Could, for instance, the duty of care extend to anyone who reads a web page and suffers physical injury as a result of acting on the information?   5–005

Interactivity

The question is not unique to on-line information. It applies to books and newspapers. But the potential for liability is exacerbated by two things. First, the scope for interactivity on an electronic site allows information to be provided that responds closely to a request made by the user. Such information could be provided by an expert system sitting behind the web page analysing requests. This begins to look more like personal advice than does the plain information available from a passive book. It could thus lead to liability.   5–006

For instance in *De La Bere v Pearson Ltd*,[7] a case decided early last century, a newspaper advertised that its City editor would answer inquiries from readers of the paper desiring financial advice. The paper published a reader's question asking for the name of a good stockbroker, together with a reply recommending someone who the editor ought to have known, if he

---

[4] [1964] A.C. 465.
[5] *Henderson v Merrett Syndicates Ltd* [1994] 3 All E.R. 506, H.L.; and see *First National Commercial Bank Plc v Loxleys (a Firm)* [1996] E.G.C.S. 174.
[6] For an example of a case in which it was held not fair, just and reasonable to impose a duty of care notwithstanding the reasonable foreseeability of physical damage, see *Marc Rich & Co. v Bishop Rock Marine* [1995] 3 All E.R. 307.
[7] [1908] 1 K.B. 280.

had made proper inquiries, was an undischarged bankrupt. The reader dealt with the stockbroker and lost his money.

The case was brought in contract, the consideration for the contract being said to be either the publication of the reader's question or the addressing of the inquiry. The newspaper was found liable. That was described by Lord Devlin in *Hedley Byrne* as a "just result". Nowadays, given the development in negligence liability since *Pearson*, it would probably be unnecessary to force the facts into the straightjacket of contract theory.

Mass advice

5–007 The second exacerbating factor is that the lower cost of providing information electronically permits wider and easier dissemination of the information. The result is that it becomes economic to provide, electronically, the sort of information and quasi-advice that has previously had to be custom-made and delivered personally by professional advisers. This may parallel the developments in the market for goods which preceded the imposition of manufacturers' liability for defective goods in *Donoghue v Stevenson* in 1932.

It is possible to glean some pointers to these liability issues from more recent decided cases, although these are all *obiter dicta* in cases not directed specifically to the question. Lord Oliver in *Caparo v Dickman*,[8] a case concerning reliance on audited company accounts, commented that:

> "...reliance upon a careless statement may give rise to direct physical injury which may be caused either to the person who acts on the faith of the statement or to a third person. One only has to consider, for instance, the chemist's assistant who mis-labels a dangerous medicine, a medical man who gives negligent telephone advice to a parent with regard to the treatment of a sick child, or an architect who negligently instructs a bricklayer to remove the keystone of an archway ... In such cases it is not easy to divorce foreseeability simpliciter and the proximity which flows from the virtual inevitability of damage if the advice is followed."

If the doctor is liable, why not the publisher of a website that provides information in response to a description of the symptoms? Is the greater degree of anonymity sufficient to take the case beyond the bounds of a duty of care? But if the reader in *De La Bere* could sue for his financial loss, why not the user of a website who suffered physical injury?

5–008 In *Candler v Crane, Christmas & Co*,[9] another case concerning liability for accounts, Lord Denning commented that:

---

[8] [1990] 2 A.C. 605.
[9] [1951] 2 K.B. 164.

"...a scientist or expert (including a marine hydrographer) is not liable to his readers for careless statements in his published works. He publishes his work simply for the purpose of giving information, and not with any particular transaction in mind at all. But when a scientist or an expert makes an investigation and report for the very purpose of a particular transaction, then, in my opinion, he is under a duty of care in respect of that transaction."

This suggests that there is no liability for mere information made available to the world at large. However, the question has never been decided in an English court and remains open.

Physical damage and economic loss

There has been a number of cases in other countries in which the question of liability for books and charts has been litigated. Courts in different countries have reached different conclusions. In the US the publishers of aeronautical charts have been held liable under US product liability laws, whereas the publishers of an encyclopaedia of mushrooms were held not liable. In France, on the other hand, a publisher of a book on edible plants is reported to have been held liable for injury caused by eating hemlock instead of wild carrot.[10]

Given the uncertainty over liability for physical damage caused by incorrect information, the possibility of liability for pure financial loss must be remote for information made generally available (as opposed to advice given in response to a request). There have been many cases concerning financial loss suffered as a result of reliance on audited accounts, profit forecasts and similar information. The courts have consistently restricted liability to a narrow class of persons.

The courts have resisted imposing liability for pure economic loss "in an indeterminate amount for an indeterminate time to an indeterminate class".[11] In the present state of English law it is most unlikely that liability would be incurred for pure economic loss caused by general information made available for free on a website.

One sure prediction, however, is that at least some of today's personal, custom-tailored, individually provided professional advice services will be tomorrow's branded, mass-provided interactive information services. That trend can only increase the pressure to widen the scope of liability for economic loss caused by incorrect information. The courts are currently set against this. But only a few years before *Donoghue v Stevenson* imposed product liability on manufacturers, judges were insistent that such liability should not be contemplated. In *Mullen v Barr*[12] Lord Anderson said:

5–009

5–010

---

[10] See section 7 (non-contractual liability) of the *Encyclopedia of Information Technology Law* (Sweet & Maxwell) for further details.
[11] *Caparo Industries Plc v Dickman* [1990] 2 A.C. 605, at p.621 *per* Lord Bridge.
[12] [1929] S.C. 461.

"In a case like the present, where the goods of the defenders are widely distributed throughout Scotland, it would seem little short of outrageous to make them responsible to members of the public for the condition of the contents of every bottle which issue from their works. It is obvious that, if such responsibility attached to the defenders, they might be called upon to meet claims of damages which they could not possibly investigate or answer."

The imposition of liability on manufacturers was preceded by the advent of mass-marketed, branded, advertised consumer products. These created an economic link between the consumer and the manufacturer, which was eventually recognised and reflected in the *Donoghue v Stevenson* decision. A move from personal advice to mass-marketed quasi-advice could presage a similar change in liability for the provision of information services.

To the extent that quasi-advice services are provided to known, individual, paying users, liability to those users is likely under present law and will also most likely be governed by express contracts.

However, information provision on the World Wide Web may not always follow that commercial model. Many sites are free to the user and paid for by advertising and sponsorship. Even those sites that do charge the user tend to have a substantial amount of free information available. In this situation it is less easy to hold the user to contractual terms; and the steps necessary to do so may be regarded from a marketing point of view as creating too great a deterrent to users.

Even if there is a paying user, the possibility of liability to others who may use the information but who are not in a contractual relationship with the content provider, friends and family members for instance, has to be considered.

5.3 INCORRECT INFORMATION—STRICT LIABILITY

5–011   Part I of the Consumer Protection Act 1987 implemented the EC Directive on Product Liability.[13] It established a regime, parallel with negligence liability, for liability for defective products irrespective of whether there was fault on the part of the manufacturer.

It is unlikely that any liability would accrue under the Act for "information defects" such as incorrect information contained on a website. On the other hand, it is more arguable that program files do fall within the Act as being products within the meaning of the Act. However, this is not at all clear and the question remains a matter of debate.[14] The Act applies only to defects causing death or personal injury; or physical damage to

---

[13] Directive 85/374 [1985] O.J. L210/29.
[14] See section 7 of the *Encyclopedia of Information Technology Law* for a detailed discussion.

non-business property exceeding £275 (which could include damage to data on the recipient's disk).[15]

Section 7 of the Act prohibits limitation or exclusion of liability under the Act to a person, or to a dependant or relative of such a person, who has suffered damage caused wholly or partly by a defect in a product.

5.4 VIRUSES

In addition to damage caused by human beings relying on incorrect information, electronic communication gives rise to the possibility of damage to data as the result of receiving maliciously written computer programs, or viruses. There are many varieties of virus, some verging on the playful, many capable of causing serious damage to the functioning of computer systems. Originally viruses existed only within executable program files. The prevailing wisdom was that data files, such as word processed documents, were safe.   **5–012**

Now, however, the sophistication of macro languages incorporated in word processor and other document production software is such that even ordinary documents are capable of containing viruses. These macro viruses can be especially lethal when distributed as attachments to email.[16]

The authors and originators of viruses may be subject to criminal liability. Virus authors have been successfully prosecuted under the Computer Misuse Act 1990.[17] Our concern here is with the possible civil liability of those who unintentionally disseminate viruses, now sometimes known as "downstream liability".

Potential liability may arise in three main ways: negligence, strict liability under the rule in *Rylands v Fletcher* and trespass.[18]

---

[15] This conclusion is based on the logic of the decision in *R v Whiteley* [1993] F.S.R. 168, a case concerning criminal liability of a computer hacker under the Criminal Damage Act 1971. Although such liability is now governed exclusively by the Computer Misuse Act 1990, the reasons employed to support the finding of liability remain relevant to questions of civil liability concerning damage to property.

[16] The first demonstration that macro viruses could be written was the Concept virus for Microsoft Word documents. Since then macro viruses such as the Melissa and Ethan email viruses have been distributed.

[17] "Prosecutions under the Computer Misuse Act 1990", R. Battock, *Computers and Law* Feb/March 1996.

[18] We should also note *Ashton Investments Ltd v OJSC Russian Aluminium* [2006] EWHC 2545 (Comm). The claimants alleged that overseas defendants had hacked into their server located in London in order to obtain confidential and privileged information. The claimants obtained permission to serve out of the jurisdiction based on pleas of unlawful interference with business and breach of confidence. The jurisdictional aspects of this case are discussed in Ch.6.

5.4.1 Negligence liability for virus dissemination

Duty of care and physical damage

5–013 As discussed above, for negligence it is generally easier to establish the existence of a duty of care owed to the world at large where the case involves the foreseeable risk of physical damage or personal injury. It is strongly arguable that a malicious virus causes foreseeable physical damage to any computer affected by it.

In *R v Whiteley*,[19] a prosecution of a hacker under the Criminal Damage Act 1971, the prosecution had to establish that the defendant had caused damage to tangible property. The Court of Appeal found that this requirement was satisfied. The defendant's argument that his activities had affected only the intangible information contained in the disk, and not the disk itself, failed. Lord Lane C.J. said:

> "It seems to us that the contention contains a basic fallacy. What the Act requires to be proved is that tangible property has been damaged, not necessarily that the damage itself should be tangible. There can be no doubt that the magnetic particles upon the metal disks were a part of the disks and if the appellant was proved to have intentionally and without lawful excuse altered the particles in such a way as to cause an impairment of the value or usefulness of the disks to the owner, there would be damage within the meaning of section 1. The fact that the alteration could only be perceived by operating the computer did not make the alterations any the less real, or the damage, if the alteration amounted to damage, any the less within the ambit of the Act."

The finding that a requirement of "damage to tangible property" was satisfied, suggests that in the context of negligence a requirement of physical damage would also be satisfied. This would provide a foundation on which to claim for consequential economic loss. Pure economic loss would remain irrecoverable.[20]

Foreseeability of physical damage

5–014 As to foreseeability, since the very purpose of a virus is to spread and to cause such physical damage, the element of foreseeability appears to be satisfied. The question of whether it is "fair, just and reasonable" to impose a duty of care on all classes of persons (including, for instance, private individuals), would require careful consideration by the courts.

---

[19] [1993] F.S.R. 168, CA. Although the application of the Criminal Damage Act 1971 to hacking has now been largely excluded by s.3(6) of the Computer Misuse Act 1990 the principle established in *R v Whiteley* may still be applied by analogy to civil liability.

[20] For a case in which recovery of pure economic loss was denied following the release of a real life virus into the wild, see *Weller v Foot & Mouth Disease Research Institute* [1966] 1 Q.B. 569.

Standard of care

A difficult question with negligence liability for distribution of a virus is that of the standard of care to be expected of the defendant. Is everyone who handles electronic files expected to take precautions by virus-checking files and emails before passing them on? Or must they do so only when, for instance, they knew or should have known that there was, or that there was a real risk of, a virus being present? Does the same standard apply to everyone? Or should software publishers, IT professionals, business people and private individuals (assuming a duty of care to have been imposed) be held to different standards of care? These questions remain to be answered.

5–015

5.4.2 *Rylands v Fletcher* and virus dissemination

General

The rule in *Rylands v Fletcher*,[21] now regarded as a variety of the law of nuisance applicable to an isolated escape,[22] imposes strict liability for foreseeable damage on someone who brings onto his land an inherently dangerous thing which subsequently escapes to some other place not under his control and which causes damage.

5–016

While there appears to be no reason in principle why recovery should not extend to economic loss consequent upon the physical damage, so long as the relevant type of damage is foreseeable, pure economic loss would be regarded as too remote.[23]

The fact that *Rylands v Fletcher* is properly regarded as a variety of the law of nuisance suggests that, like nuisance, it is a tort to land. It is thus restricted to claims for injury to interests in land, including the use and enjoyment of land. Not everything that is done on land is regarded as use of the land. If the action complained of could equally well cause the same injury to the claimant when the claimant is elsewhere than on the land in question, then it is unlikely to be regarded as an injury to the use and enjoyment of the land.[24] Given the prevalence of mobile computing, that ought to provide a powerful argument against the applicability of *Rylands v Fletcher* to computer virus cases.

A further argument against the applicability of the rule is that the like-

---

[21] (1866) L.R.I.Ex. 265.

[22] *Cambridge Water Co. v Eastern Counties Leather Plc* [1994] A.C. 264.

[23] *Cattle v Stockton Waterworks* (1875) 10 L.R. 453 QB.

[24] *Hunter v Canary Wharf Ltd* [1997] 2 All ER 426, H.L., *per* Lord Goff at p. 437: "If a plaintiff, such as the daughter of the householder in *Khorasandjian v Bush*, is harassed by abusive telephone calls, the *gravamen* of the complaint lies in the harassment which is just as much an abuse, or indeed an invasion of her privacy, whether she is pestered in this way in her mother's or her husband's house, or she is staying with a friend, or is at her place of work, or even in her car with a mobile phone. In truth, what the Court of Appeal appears to have been doing was to exploit the law of private nuisance in order to create by the back door a tort of harassment which was only partially effective in that it was artifically limited to harassment which takes place in her home. I myself do not consider that this is a satisfactory manner in which to develop the law...".

lihood of damage from a computer virus bears little relation to the proximity of the claimant to the defendant's land. The virus, once escaped, could as easily strike a computer next door or on the next continent (although it is true that the further apart the computers, the greater the number of "hops" across the internet the virus would probably have to negotiate in order to complete its journey.)

The following discussion should be read subject to these general caveats regarding the applicability of the rule to computer viruses.

Accumulation of dangerous material

5–017 The rule primarily imposes liability on someone who accumulates dangerous material on his land. The manufacturer of anti-virus software or the university computer science department maintaining a collection of computer viruses would constitute precise analogies with traditional categories of persons subject to the rule. However, most people do not set out to maintain collections of computer viruses. Their systems become infected by accident and they pass on the viruses by accident or neglect.

Third party acts

5–018 The rule recognises that where the dangerous thing has been brought onto the land, or the escape has occurred, through the unforeseeable act of a third party, then the defendant is not liable. However, he may become liable if he was himself negligent. So in the case of fire, a person is not liable to a neighbour whose house is destroyed by fire that escapes from his own property if the fire on his own property was started by a third party.[25] However, if the person negligently fails to prevent the spread of the fire, he then becomes liable.[26]

This reasoning suggests that even if a person's computer systems become infected with a virus due to the act of some third party, he may become liable for the onward transmission of the virus if, through the exercise of reasonable care, he could have prevented its further spread.

Natural or ordinary use of land

5–019 The rule in *Rylands v Fletcher* does not apply if the use of the land in question is a "natural use", which in *Rickards v Lothian*[27] the Privy Council interpreted as meaning that the rule only came into play if there were "some special use bringing with it increased danger to others, and must not merely be an ordinary use of the land or such a use as is proper for the general benefit of the community".

It might have been thought that since the House of Lords held in *Cambridge Water Co. v Eastern Counties Leather Plc*[28] that foreseeability of

---

[25] *Turberville v Stampe* (1697) 1 Ld.Raym. 264.
[26] *Job Edwards Ltd v Birmingham Navigations* [1924] 1 K.B. 341.
[27] [1913] A.C. 263, *per* Lord Moulton at p.280.
[28] Fn. 22 above.

harm of the relevant type is a necessary ingredient of liability in damages under *Rylands v Fletcher*, the natural use exception might be easier to control in the future[29] and so become less important.

However, in *Transco Plc v Stockport MBC*[30] Lord Bingham thought it clear that "ordinary user" is a preferable test to "natural user", making it clear that the rule is engaged only where the defendant's use is shown to be extraordinary and unusual. The question, as stated by Lord Bingham, is whether the defendant has done something which he recognises or ought to recognise, as being quite out of the ordinary in the place and at the time when he does it. Lord Hoffmann commented that the criterion of exceptional risk must be taken seriously and creates a high threshold for a claimant to surmount.

5.4.3 Liability in trespass for virus dissemination

The tort of trespass to goods may in some circumstances be prayed in aid by someone whose property has been damaged by a computer virus. Trespass to goods is an unlawful disturbance of the possession of goods by seizure or removal, or by a direct act causing damage to the goods.[31]　5–020

The logic of the decision in *R v Whiteley*, discussed above, suggests that virus damage to the data on a computer disk would constitute damage to goods for the purposes of trespass. The tort of trespass certainly includes intentional conduct (such as that of a person who deliberately releases a virus into the wild) and may include negligent conduct.[32] However, no liability will attach if the conduct of the defendant involved no fault.

5.5 RESTRICTING LIABILITY

5.5.1 Unilateral notices and contractual terms

Disclaiming or restricting liability for internet content usually takes the form of preventing a liability-inducing situation arising or disclaiming or restricting liability that may exist, and restricting the territories at which the content is aimed. These are done either by means of unilateral notices or as part of a broader attempt to bind the user to contractual terms. The latter is often achieved by requiring the user to signify acceptance of a set of terms and conditions by clicking on a button. These are known as "web-wrap" or "click-wrap" contracts, by analogy with software shrink-wrap licences, and are discussed in Ch.10. Here we discuss unilateral disclaimer notices.　5–021

The unilateral notice approach may be appropriate on a free site where

---

[29] *ibid., per* Lord Goff, at p.309.
[30] [2003] UKHL 61.
[31] *Halsbury's Laws of England*, Vol 45(2) 4th edn (Reissue) 1999 para.659.
[32] *ibid.*, para.660.

the only likely liability is tortious.[33] But a unilateral notice can do no more than restrict, or prevent arising, such liability as would otherwise exist. If the site owner wishes the user to assume specific obligations to the owner (such as by indemnifying the owner for liabilities that could occur through the user's use of the site), then the owner must create a contract with the user.

Even on free sites many owners seek to bind their users to lengthy contracts governing their use of the site. These have to be implemented with especial care. It is all too common to find a carefully (and no doubt expensively) drafted site use contract, complete with indemnity and exclusion clauses rendered in capital letters to draw them to the attention of the reader, hidden behind inconspicuous, anodyne or even misleading buttons and links.[34]

Such practices are likely to achieve little other than to provide the legal profession with the pleasure of conducting modern day re-enactments of the Victorian ticket cases.[35] While the site user may fairly expect that a purchase made from a site will be governed by some terms and conditions, many users would be surprised to find that the site owner was purporting to govern their use of the site itself under a detailed set of contractual terms and conditions including, for instance, indemnities on the part of the user.

5–022   By their very nature, contractual site use terms have to be incorporated at the entry point or home page of the site. Insofar as they purport to govern the provision of an "information society service" (e.g. the use of a commercial site) under the EU Electronic Commerce Directive, the question could arise of compliance with the contractual transparency requirements of Art.10 of the Directive[36] (as to which, see Ch.10). However, since those requirements are predicated on the placing of an "order" by the recipient of the service, their potential application to general site use contracts must be doubtful.

---

[33] The boundary between tort and contract may be different in other jurisdictions such as the US.

[34] It is not unknown to find such purported contracts lurking behind links marked "copyright" or "privacy notice".

[35] These are the Victorian cases concerning the legal effect of seeking to incorporate, typically, railway company general terms and conditions by reference on the back of a ticket. They are now rivalled by the volume of US cases dealing with incorporation of website terms and conditions, a well known example (in which the terms were held not to have been incorporated) being *Specht v Netscape Communications Corporation* No. 01–7860 (L) (2d Cir., October 1, 2002). See further, Ch.10.

[36] Implemented in the UK by the Electronic Commerce (EC Directive) Regulations 2002 (SI 2002/2013), which (with the exception of reg.16, which came into force on October 23, 2002) came into force on August 21, 2002.

Unilateral notices must also be properly drawn to the attention of the relevant person if they are to be effective.

Both unilateral notices and contracts are subject to consumer protection legislation, which affects the degree to which liability can be excluded and may prohibit some types of exclusion. This causes great difficulties. Each jurisdiction has its own consumer protection legislation, and exclusions that are lawful in one jurisdiction may be unlawful in another.[37] A website owner may well have no reliable indication of the country from which a particular user is accessing the site, or of the residence or domicile of the user.[38]

There are great difficulties in drafting disclaimers of worldwide validity. Software publishers have resorted to printing booklets of licences tailored for each jurisdiction. A similar approach on a website would require an elaborate screen with questions designed to ascertain the country from which the user was accessing the site (or the domicile or habitual residence of the user, as appropriate) and displaying the appropriate disclaimer. The practical problem with this approach, apart from the obvious expense, is that it may deter users. But anything less risks being ineffective.

One approach that may be an acceptable compromise is to divide the site into free and restricted access sections. The free access section includes the opening screen and any other sections with risk-free content. The restricted access sections are gated with a contract acceptance screen, the user answering whatever questions are required to ascertain the relevant juris-diction and to serve up an appropriate form of contract.

---

[37] Although attempts continue to be made to bring greater uniformity to consumer protection legislation across the European Community, the Community legislators continue to permit Member States individually to enact stricter consumer protection laws. For an example of this see the Unfair Commercial Practices Directive (Directive 2005/29/EC of the European Parliament and of the Council of May 11, 2005 concerning unfair business-to-consumer commercial practices in the internal market). Such national laws will often have the status of mandatory rules and thus in some circumstances be enforceable notwithstanding attempts to exclude their effect by choice of law and jurisdiction clauses. See Chs. 6 and (for choice of law in contract) 10.

[38] In the case brought against Yahoo! in France for permitting French users to participate in auctions of Nazi memorabilia on its US Yahoo.com auction site, a three-person technical panel appointed by the French court concluded that Yahoo! would be able to exclude reliably 90 per cent of French users by a combination of technical means based on identi-fying the location of users' IP addresses and obtaining declarations of residence from users in the case of ambiguous IP addresses. An English translation of the judgment of November 20, 2000 is available at *www.cdt.org/speech/international/20001120yahoofrance.pdf*. Whether the effectiveness of such geo-filtering has increased since then is a question that has yet to be authoritatively determined. It is interesting to note that the European Commis-sion's Proposal for a Regulation on the Law Applicable to Contractual Obligations (COM (2005) 650) suggests that the Art.5 rule applying the law of the consumer's habitual resi-dence to consumer contracts would not apply if the professional "did not know where the consumer had his habitual residence and this ignorance was not attributable to his negli-gence". The potential relevance, if any, of geo-filtering to this test is unclear, since ascertaining the location of a user is by no means the same thing as ascertaining his or her habitual residence.

5.5.2 Preventing liability arising

Disclaimers

5–023 It will be seen from the discussion above that on the currently ascendant theory of negligence liability, one question that may determine the existence of a duty of care is whether the information provider assumed responsibility to the person who relied upon the information. Many disclaimers are aimed at preventing the inference being drawn that the content provider has assumed responsibility.

Thus, a typical disclaimer may state that the contents of the site are for general information only, that nothing on the site constitutes professional advice, that the reader should take advice from a suitable qualified professional in relation to any specific problem and that the site owner takes no responsibility for any loss caused as a result of reading the content of the site.

The bank reference in *Hedley Byrne* itself was given with a disclaimer of responsibility. The House of Lords held that this prevented a duty of care arising. It was at pains to state that this was not a case of seeking to contract out of a pre-existing duty. The disclaimer was part of the material from which one deduces whether a duty of care was assumed.

However, a website disclaimer is unlikely to be read in isolation from the content of the site. If the overall assessment of the site content leads to the conclusion that the owner has, in fact, assumed responsibility to the user, then the disclaimer may not defeat that. Nowadays, the need to take into account the effect of any disclaimer when considering whether a duty of care exists also leads to consideration of the Unfair Contract Terms Act 1977 as an integral part of the exercise.[39] The effect of such consumer protection legislation is considered in more detail below.

Boundary markers

5–024 Another aspect of preventing liability arising is the use of "boundary markers". As noted in Ch.1, one effect of the World Wide Web is to blur the boundaries between documents. It is very easy for a user to slip from one site to another without realising that the identity of the site proprietor has changed.

The problem occurs acutely with on-line shopping malls. If a site owner provides space on his own advertised site to other companies, it is very easy for the user to become unclear whether he is dealing with the site owner or the tenant. The site owner may not even hold any of the tenant's materials on his site, if all he provides is a web link to the tenant's own site held on some other host. The site owner will wish to make clear that he is not responsible for the content of the tenants, and will wish to make clear to the

---

[39] *First National Commercial Bank Plc v Loxleys (a Firm)* (fn.5 above).

user when he is moving from the site owner's content to the tenant's content.

Similar problems can occur when a site owner acts as an introducer to third party suppliers. The transition from dealing with the site owner to dealing with the third party has to be made clear to avoid confusion over who the user is contracting with.

Similar considerations will apply if a website contains links to wholly unconnected third party sites.

It is common practice to warn users by means of a suitably placed notice or buffer page that linked third party sites are not the responsibility of the site owner. The potential effectiveness of such a disclaimer should always be reviewed by reference to the type of liability being considered. A disclaimer making clear that the proprietor assumes no responsibility for third party linked material may be effective in relation to negligence liability based on a theory of assumption of responsibility. However, it is unlikely to be directly effective in relation to, for instance, defamation liability where liability accrues through the act of publication.

On the other hand, if for any purpose the site owner's degree of responsibility for content depends on whether the site owner has (say) assumed editorial responsibility for the material, then a disclaimer could be useful evidence about that.

If drawing attention to the defamatory statement by linking to it amounts to publication of the target material by the creator of the link,[40] it is difficult to see how any disclaimer of responsibility could affect that. An appropriately drafted disclaimer could affect liability for linked content based on authorisation or inducement of copyright infringement, although if it is inconsistent with material on the remainder of the site it could be disregarded.[41]

5.5.3 Territory statements

A territory statement specifies that the site may be accessed from, or that   **5–025** the goods or services advertised are available only in, certain jurisdictions. Territory statements have to date been of most relevance if there is a risk that the content of the site or the services advertised are illegal in certain jurisdictions (examples of this range from pornography to financial services).

Territory statements are likely to assume greater importance with increasing acceptance of the principle that the mere availability of a website in a country is insufficient to trigger that country's jurisdiction, and that jurisdiction should be triggered only if the site is targeted or directed at that country.

This principle is emerging in a number of different areas. Examples

[40] See Ch.4, section 4.4.2.
[41] See Ch.2, paras 2–145, 2–156.

include US inter-state jurisdiction cases,[42] the increasingly unified international approach to financial services regulation,[43] recent English case law on cross-border use of trade marks,[44] a report from the World Intellectual Property Organisation Standing Committee on Trade Marks, Industrial Designs and Geographical Origins,[45] Art.15 of the "Brussels I" Regulation on Jurisdiction and Enforcement of Judgments,[46] and Art.5 of the European Commission's proposed Rome I Regulation on the Law Applicable to Contractual Obligations.[47] Cases asserting national laws on a "mere availability" basis may not reflect a point of view that will stand the test of time,[48] although it will be many years (if ever) before a wholly settled approach is achieved.

The efficacy of a territory statement is unlikely to be considered in isolation from other aspects of the site. Its efficacy may vary, depending on the nature of the risk that is sought to be guarded against. In some cases a mere statement, with no attempt to discover the country from which the user is attempting to access the site, may be of little use. However, for potential negligence liability a statement making clear (assuming it to be the case) that the information is relevant only to certain countries excluding England could well influence a determination as to whether any responsibility was assumed in respect of users in England.

5.5.4 Consumer protection legislation

5–026   Consumer protection legislation is highly relevant to website disclaimers. The owner of a freely accessible site faces a dilemma. In general, the kind of information most likely to give rise to liability (e.g. information which, if incorrect, could cause personal injury), is precisely that in respect of which legislation is most likely to prohibit, or render ineffective, disclaimers of liability. The kinds of information for which disclaimers of liability are possible are those for which as the law currently stands liability is very unlikely: typically information which, if incorrect, is likely to cause pure economic loss.

---

[42] See Ch.6.

[43] See the International Organisation of Securities Commissions (IOSCO) reports "Securities Activity on the Internet" (Sept. 1998) (*www.iosco.org/library/pubdocs/pdf/IOS-COPD83.pdf*) and "Report on Securities Activity on the Internet II" (June 2001) (*www.iosco.org/library/pubdocs/pdf/IOSCOPD120.pdf*) and previous guidance from the US Securities and Exchange Commission and the UK Securities and Investments Board (as it then was).

[44] *800 FLOWERS Trade Mark, Euromarket Designs Inc. v Peters*, discussed in Ch.6.

[45] Protection of Industrial Property Rights in Relation to the Use of Signs on the Internet (*www.wipo.org/sct/en/documents/session_5/pdf/sct5_2.pdf*).

[46] See Ch.6.

[47] COM (2005) 650, December 15, 2005.

[48] For contrary views, see "Yahoo! brought to earth", by Jack Goldsmith, *Financial Times*, November 27, 2000; "Damn the Constitution: Europe must take back the Web" by Bill Thompson, *The Register*, August 9, 2002; "Will Web ruling promote unfair competition?" by Ian de Freitas and Tamara Quinn, *Times*, November 20, 2001.

The distinction between contractual disclaimers and unilateral disclaimers by notice is important in the context of consumer protection. Both are covered by the Unfair Contract Terms Act 1977. The UK has also implemented the EC Unfair Contract Terms Directive 1993[49] by means of the Unfair Terms in Consumer Contracts Regulations 1999[50]. These Regulations, which supplement the 1977 Act, apply only to terms in consumer contracts. Unilateral notices restricting tortious liability are still covered only by the 1977 Act.

The effect of the 1977 Act and of the Regulations on website contracts is dealt with in Ch.10. Here the discussion will be restricted to unilateral notices. A notice under the 1977 Act includes an announcement, whether or not in writing, and any other communication or pretended communication (s.14).

Section 2(1) of the 1977 Act provides that a person cannot by reference to a notice exclude or restrict liability for death or personal injury arising from negligence. Notices which exclude or restrict liability for negligence other than death or personal injury are valid only if reasonable.

These provisions apply to business liability, in other words breach of obligations or duties arising from things done or to be done by a person in the course of a business (whether his own business or another's). The requirement of reasonableness in respect of a non-contractual notice is (under s.11(3) of the 1977 Act) that it should be fair and reasonable to allow reliance on it, having regard to all the circumstances obtaining when the liability arose or (but for the notice) would have arisen. The burden of showing that a notice is reasonable is upon the person seeking to rely upon it.

The 1977 Act applies to notices which exclude or restrict the relevant obligation or duty (s.13(1)). This is especially relevant to notices designed to prevent a duty of care arising. In *Smith v Eric S Bush*[51] the House of Lords held that such a disclaimer was caught by the 1977 Act where a surveyor retained by a lender attempted to disclaim liability to the borrower who relied upon the survey.

In *McCullagh v Lane Fox and Partners Ltd*[52] the Court of Appeal held that a disclaimer of responsibility in a set of estate agents' particulars was effective to prevent a duty of care to the purchaser arising as regards the description of the area of the garden of the property. The form of the disclaimer was "none of the statements contained in these particulars as to this property are to be relied upon as statements of representations of fact". The court also found that the exclusion of liability was reasonable under the 1977 Act.

---

[49] Directive 93/13 [1993] O.J. L95/29.
[50] SI 1994/3159, SI 1999/2083, SI 2001/1186.
[51] [1990] 1 A.C. 831.
[52] [1996] 18 E.G. 104, CA.

The medical advice website

5–027   NetMed is a fully interactive website, driven by a database of medical information. It is provided as a free attraction by a newspaper. Users can key in symptoms and after a few seconds a suggested diagnosis appears, with possible home treatments. The proprietors are acutely aware of the liability implications of this site. It is more than a general information system, as it provides tailored responses to specific queries. They wish to disclaim liability for actions taken in reliance upon the information provided. However, they are advised that excluding liability for death or personal injury is prohibited by the Unfair Contract Terms Act 1977 and (insofar as relevant) the Consumer Protection Act 1987. They speak to their insurers.

In *First National Bank Plc v Loxleys (a firm)*[53] the Court of Appeal held that the existence of a duty of care could not be decided as a discrete point separately from whether it was fair and reasonable under the 1977 Act to allow the defendants to rely upon a disclaimer, since it was at least possible that the existence of a duty of care would be held to depend at least partly on the effect of the disclaimer.

5.6 PROTECTING CONTENT

5–028   Content owners are often concerned about the ease with which content on the internet can be downloaded and copied. The least that a content owner can do to ease these concerns is to ensure that suitable copyright notices, warnings against copying and express licences are prominently displayed on the website. These apply expressly limited permissions to the use of the web page.

Matters to be addressed might include: is temporary or permanent storage on the user's local hard disk permissible? For instance, most web browsers "cache" (i.e. store) pages on the local hard disk to speed up access to a site. Is that to be permitted? It is hardly practicable not to permit that, when many users may not even realise that the web browser is caching pages on their disks or know how to prevent it occurring. Can users send email extracts to others? If so, under what conditions? Can corporate users copy any content on to their intranets?

If the site owner wishes to assert any control over linking to the site, especially "deep-linking" to sub-pages, then that should be included in the notice. It is, however, wise to exercise a degree of moderation when drafting anti-linking notices. A website exists devoted to "stupid linking policies".[54]

Many sites now include "anti-scraping" provisions in their licences, intended to deter the types of automated content-gathering activity

---

[53] Fn.5 above.
[54] *www.dontlink.com* (sadly, not updated since November 2002).

described in para.2–119 of Ch.2. A fuller discussion of copyright issues is contained in Ch.2.

5.7 LIABILITY OF ON-LINE INTERMEDIARIES

The liability of on-line intermediaries such as access providers, network 5–029 providers and hosts originally had to be considered individually for each tort or criminal offence. The substantive components of the relevant wrong had to be assessed, together with any other relevant principles such as vicarious liability, joint tortfeasorship and so on. The result of this was that the potential liability of on-line intermediaries was complex to assess, and might vary as between different wrongs in a rather arbitrary fashion, depending on how the substantive components of the wrong read onto the activities of the on-line intermediary.

5.7.1 Electronic Commerce Directive and the Electronic Commerce (EC Directive) Regulations 2002

For a wide range of torts and crimes this piecemeal approach changed with 5–030 the implementation in the UK of the EU Electronic Commerce Directive on August 21, 2002, by the Electronic Commerce (EC Directive) Regulations 2002 (hereafter "the 2002 Regulations").[55]

Articles 12 to 15 of the Directive (2002 Regulations 17 to 22) establish a single set of threshold requirements for the liability of certain on-line intermediaries in respect of a broad range of wrongs. The relevant inter-mediaries are "conduits" (which equate broadly to network and access providers), "hosts" (storage providers) and "caches" (those who create temporary caches of material to make for more efficient operation of the network). The Directive establishes protections from criminal and pecuni-ary liability. It does not, however, affect the possibility of the grant of injunctions.[56]

It is easy to fall into the error of assuming that if the conditions for invoking a protection set out in the Directive are not met, then an on-line intermediary is necessarily liable. However, that is not correct. The only consequence under the Directive is that the defence provided by the Directive is not available.[57] It is still usually[58] necessary for a claimant to

---

[55] SI 2002/2013.

[56] Articles 12(3), 13(3) and 14(3)of the Directive; reg.20 of the 2002 Regulations.

[57] But see the discussion below regarding the possibility that for some types of liability the acquisition of knowledge sufficient to disapply hosting protection may also trigger the underlying liability.

[58] An exception to this rule is s.97A of the Copyright Designs and Patents Act 1988, intro-duced by the Copyright and Related Rights Regulations 2003. This enables an injunction to be granted against a service provider where it has actual knowledge of another person using its service to infringe copyright. This applies irrespective of whether there is infringement by the service provider. See Ch.2, para.2–017.

establish a cause of action against the intermediary. For instance, in a defamation claim it is necessary to show that the defendant has published the offending words. On the authority of *Bunt v Tilley*[59] a claimant would be unable to establish publication by an internet service provider who has only passively transmitted a statement, rendering unnecessary any consideration of the "conduit" defence under the Directive.

Information society services

5–031   The scope of the Directive is set out in Art.1, which in Arts 1(1) and (2) sets out the general objective of contributing to the proper functioning of the internal market by ensuring the free movement of information society services between Member States including, to the extent necessary to achieve that objective, approximating certain national provisions on (*inter alia*) liability of intermediaries.

The 2002 Regulations adopt by reference the definition of an "Information society service" set out in Art.2(a) of the Directive. The Directive in turn defines it as a service within the meaning of the EU "Transparency Directive".[60] Recital 17 of the Electronic Commerce Directive summarises the definition: "any service normally provided for a remuneration, at a distance, by means of electronic equipment for the processing (including digital compression) and storage of data, and at the individual request of a recipient of the service". The Recital goes on to state that those services referred to in the indicative list of Annex V to the Transparency Directive that do not imply data processing and storage are not covered by the definition.

Recital 18 goes on to provide examples of economic activities that do and do not fall within the definition. Some of these are as follows.

Activities falling within the definition:

- Selling goods on-line,
- Insofar as they represent an economic activity:

   - Offering on-line information or commercial communications,
   - Providing tools allowing for search, access and retrieval of data,

- Transmission of information via a communication network,
- Providing access to a communication network,
- Hosting information provided by a recipient of the service,
- Video-on-demand,
- Provision of commercial communications by electronic mail.

Activities not falling within the definition:

---

[59] [2006] EWHC 407 (QB). See Ch.4, para.4–010.
[60] Directive 98/34 as amended by Directive 98/48 [1998] L37/35.

- Delivery of goods as such,
- Provision of services off-line,
- Television and radio broadcasting (because they are not provided at individual request),
- Use of electronic mail or equivalent individual communications by natural persons acting outside their trade, profession or business including their use for conclusion of contracts between such persons,
- The contractual relationship between an employee and his employer,
- Statutory auditing of company accounts,
- Medical advice requiring the physical examination of a patient.

So, for instance, a solicitor giving advice at the request of a client through a website or email would be likely to fall within the provisions of the Directive. However, if the solicitor were to confirm the advice by letter, that confirmatory advice would fall outside the Directive.

Article 1(4) states that the Directive does not establish additional rules on private international law nor does it deal with the jurisdiction of courts. This Article is not transposed into the 2002 Regulations.

Exclusions from the scope of the Directive

Certain areas are by Art.1(5) excluded entirely from the scope of the Directive, so that the liability of intermediaries provisions will not apply to these areas. The exclusions are:

5–032

(a) the field of taxation;
(b) questions relating to information society services covered by Directives 95/46 and 97/66 (Data Protection Directive and the Telecommunications Data Protection Directive);
(c) questions relating to agreements or practices governed by cartel law;
(d) the following activities of information society services:

- – the activities of notaries or equivalent professions to the extent that they involve a direct and specific connection with the exercise of public authority,
- – the representation of a client and defence of his interests before the courts,
- – gambling activities which involve wagering a stake with monetary value in games of chance, including lotteries and betting transactions.

The exclusions from the scope of the 2002 Regulations are largely, but not precisely, copied out from Art.1(5) of the Directive. The differences are:

Data protection. The Directive on Privacy and Electronic Communications (Directive 2002/58/EC of the European Parliament and the Council of July 12, 2002) is added to the excluded areas.

Gambling. The wording of the exclusion has been amended, apparently to fit UK domestic legislation, to read: "betting, gaming or lotteries which involve wagering a stake with monetary value".

Article 1(6) provides that the Directive does not "affect measures taken at Community or national level, in the respect of Community law, in order to promote cultural and linguistic diversity and to ensure the defence of pluralism". The effect of this provision is obscure. Presumably the use of the word "affect" rather than "apply to" means that this provision is not intended to amount to a complete exclusion of the Directive. Article 1(6) is not transposed into the 2002 Regulations.

Territorial scope of the Directive and the 2002 Regulations

5–033   Recital (58) states that the Directive should not apply to services supplied by service providers established in a third country. This provision is not transposed into the 2002 Regulations. It does, however, give rise to real difficulty in interpreting the territorial scope of the Regulations.

The liability of intermediaries provisions of the 2002 Regulations (regs. 17 to 22) are stated to apply to "service providers", defined as any person providing an information society service. The protection provided by the 2002 Regulations is, therefore, on the face of it, not restricted to service providers established within the EEA.

This follows the substantive text of Arts. 12 to 15 of the Directive and, on the face of it, accords with the corresponding definition of "service provider" in the Directive. However, in the light of Recital (58) it is far from clear that Arts. 12 to 15 of the Directive should be construed so as to apply to non-EEA established service providers.

The main basis of the Directive is Art.95 of the EC Treaty, concerning the establishment and functioning of the internal market. Recital (40) states the justification of the liability provisions as being that existing and emerging disparities in Member States' legislation and case law concerning liability of on-line intermediaries "prevent the smooth functioning of the internal market, in particular by impairing the development of cross-border services and producing distortions of competition". However, the Directive is not intended to "harmonise the criminal law as such" (Recital (8)).

Since it is difficult to see how the provision of cross-border on-line services between EEA states could be affected by a disparity in the liability law applicable to a service provider established outside the EEA, it appears that the Directive should only require the liability of intermediaries provisions to be applied to EEA-established service providers. It is consistent with that underlying basis of the Directive for Recital (58) to state that services provided from outside the EEA are outside the scope of the Directive, leaving liability for such services to national law.

The Directive does not define either "service provider" or "established service provider" in territorial terms. An "established service provider" is simply one pursuing an economic activity using a fixed establishment for an indefinite period. If Recital (58) should be understood to limit generally the territorial scope of the Directive, then it would follow that both these defined terms, and the reference to "service providers" in Arts. 12 to 15 of the Directive, should be construed so as to exclude non-EEA service providers.

If that is right, should the use of the term "service providers" in the 2002 Regulations also be interpreted in the same way as the Directive? Consideration of this question is complicated by the fact that the framers of the 2002 Regulations have adopted slightly different definitions from the Directive.   5–034

The 2002 Regulations draw a territorial distinction between the defined terms "service provider" and "established service provider" which is not present in the Directive's definitions. The 2002 Regulations state explicitly that an "established service provider" is one established in a Member State, but as we have seen make no corresponding territorial limitation on the definition of "service provider".

Curiously the 2002 Regulations, like the Directive, having defined the term "established service provider" then make no use of it. However, it is likely that the framers of the 2002 Regulations, by defining and using the territorially unlimited term "service provider" (as defined in the 2002 Regulations) instead of the territorially limited "established service provider" (as defined in the 2002 Regulations), must have intended by so doing to include non-EEA service providers.

For what it is worth, there is nothing in the DTI consultation on the draft 2002 Regulations to suggest that non-EEA service providers were to be excluded from protection.

The question could arise whether, since the 2002 Regulations are made under s.2(2) of the European Communities Act 1972, by extending protection beyond the territorial scope of the Directive they are *ultra vires* and invalid. However, in the light of the very broad interpretation of s.2(2) of the 1972 Act adopted by the Court of Appeal in *Oakley, Inc v Animal Ltd*,[61] it is unlikely that an argument of *ultra vires* would succeed.

Non-prospective effect of the 2002 Regulations

The 2002 Regulations are stated (reg.3(2)) not to apply in relation to any Act passed on or after the date the Regulations were made or in relation to the[62] exercise of a power to legislate after that date. Extending regulations are, therefore, required both to reapply the 2002 Regulations when existing legislation is amended, and to apply the 2002 Regulations to any new legislation which may conflict with the provisions of the 2002 Regulations, for instance by failing to include appropriate liability defences for on-line intermediaries.   5–035

The Department of Trade and Industry Internet Regulation Policy Advisor has issued guidance to government departments on how to ensure

---

[61] [2005] EWCA Civ 1191.
[62] The words "relation to the" were added by reg.3 of the Electronic Commerce (EC Directive) (Extension) Regulations 2004, which came into force on May 14, 2004. The Explanatory Note states that the words were omitted in error.

that future legislation is compliant with the Electronic Commerce Directive: "Administrative Guidance on Consistency of Future Legislation".[63]

Notwithstanding that guidance, it is an unlikely assumption that all new legislation complies with the Directive. That can be seen, for example, from the Tobacco Advertising and Promotion Act 2002, which received Royal Assent on November 7, 2002. Although the Electronic Commerce Directive is stated, in Recital (11), to be without prejudice to Directive 98/43/EC on advertising and sponsorship of tobacco products, that Directive was held by the European Court of Justice to be invalid. The Act when originally passed was, therefore, purely domestic legislation which ought to have complied with the Electronic Commerce Directive.

However, the Act contained provisions addressing liability for electronic publication and distribution which did not conform to the Directive (see below para.5–056). Compliance with the Directive was subsequently achieved by means of a statutory instrument extending the 2002 Regulations to the Act.[64] The effect of this, according to the Explanatory Note to the extending Regulation, was that the legislation "must be read in a way that is compatible with the requirements of the E-Commerce Regulations. Where a provision in [the enactment] is in conflict with any of the requirements of the E-Commerce Regulations, the latter will prevail." A similar approach has been taken with some other legislation,[65] while home-grown attempts to replicate the safe harbours of the Directive continue occasionally to be included in primary legislation.[66]

5–036   This is hardly an ideal method of law-making. However, the alternative

---

[63] Available at *www.hgc.gov.uk/Client/Content_wide.asp?ContentId=506.*

[64] This has itself now been superseded by amendments to the 2002 Act introduced by the Tobacco Advertising and Promotion Act 2002 etc. (Amendment) Regulations 2006 (SI 2006/2369) which came into force on September 28, 2006.

[65] So far, statutory instruments applying the 2002 Regulations to subsequent legislation include: the Electronic Commerce (EC Directive) (Extension) Regulations 2003 (SI 2003/115) and the Electronic Commerce (EC Directive) (Extension) (No. 2) Regulations 2003 (SI 2003/2500); the former, which came into force on February 14, 2003, extended the original Regulations to the Copyright (Visually Impaired Persons) Act 2002 and to the Tobacco Advertising and Promotion Act 2002; the latter, which came into force on October 31, 2003, extended the original Regulations to a series of existing copyright statutes and instruments, as amended by the Copyright and Related Rights Regulations 2003, and to two new copyright instruments; the Price Marking Order 2004, which by reg.3(2) applied the 2002 Regulations to itself; the Uranium Enrichment Technology (Prohibition on Disclosure) Regulations 2004, which by reg.8 applied the 2002 Regulations to themselves; the Electronic Commerce Directive (Financial Services and Markets) (Amendment) Regulations 2004, amending the Electronic Commerce Directive (Financial Services and Markets) Regulations 2002 so that certain rules made by the Financial Services Authority do not apply to incoming information society services from another EEA State; and the Electronic Commerce (EC Directive) (Extension) Regulations 2004, which applied the 2002 Regulations to the Sexual Offences Act 2003; note also the Electronic Commerce Directive (Adoption and Children Act 2002) Regulations 2005, which created a self-standing set of Regulations applying the Directive to the Adoption and Children Act 2002, rather than extending the application of the 2002 Regulations.

[66] See for example s.166A of the Criminal Justice and Public Order Act 1994 as prospectively inserted by s.53 of the Violent Crime Reduction Act 2006. The section provides two (instead of three) safe harbours: a hosting defence and a defence combining features of the conduit and caching defences.

route of legislating for prospective effect would raise difficult questions as to the efficacy of such a provision if plainly contradictory legislation were to be enacted subsequently. On established principles later legislation impliedly repeals earlier inconsistent legislation, and a present Act cannot curtail the ambit of any future Act.[67]

However, these principles are rooted in considerations of Parliamentary sovereignty, in particular the inability of Parliament to constrain its future powers. Such considerations may now carry less weight where the legislative provision in question is intended to ensure future compliance with EU obligations, since membership of the European Community has of itself entailed a diminution in Parliamentary sovereignty, reflected in the ability of the courts to override a provision of national legislation in conflict with Community law.[68]

Interestingly, the Regulatory Reform (Unsolicited Goods and Services Act 1971) (Directory Entries and Demands for Payment) Order 2005 not only applies the 2002 Regulations to itself, but also purports to apply them to any subordinate provisions order (within the meaning of s.4(4) of the Regulatory Reform Act 2001) made in respect of the Schedule to the 2005 Order. The Order thus purports to give a measure of prospective effect to the 2002 Regulations, notwithstanding that the 2002 Regulations themselves are stated not to have prospective effect.

Mere conduits

Article 12 of the Directive addresses the liability of "mere conduits", which should be contrasted particularly with hosting liability addressed in Art.14. Article 12(1) provides that:

5–037

> "1. Where an information society service is provided that consists of the transmission in a communication network of information provided by a recipient of the service, or the provision of access to a communication network, Member States shall ensure that the service provider is not liable for the information transmitted, on condition that the provider:
>
> (a) does not initiate the transmission;
> (b) does not select the receiver of the transmission; and
> (c) does not select or modify the information contained in the transmission."

The typical telecommunications network provider will fall within this provision as regards its transmission services. If the same company also provides hosting services, those will fall under Art.14 notwithstanding that the company providing them is at first blush a traditional telecommunications company.

---

[67] *Ellen Street Estates Ltd v Minister of Health* [1934] 1 K.B. 590.
[68] *Kirklees BC v Wickes Building Supplies Ltd* [1991] 4 All E.R. 240, Dillon L.J. at p.246.

Article 12(2) goes on to state:

"2. The acts of transmission and of provision of access referred to in paragraph 1 include the automatic, intermediate and transient storage of the information transmitted in so far as this takes place for the sole purpose of carrying out the transmission in the communication network, and provided that the information is not stored for any period longer than is reasonably necessary for the transmission."

The purpose of this provision is to make clear that a mere conduit can still take advantage of Art.12 even though the transmission involves automatic, intermediate and transient storage of the information. The use of the word "transient" may be contrasted with the use of the word "temporary" in Art.13 concerning caching. "Transient" storage would presumably cover the storage of data in RAM as it travelled through a switch, or buffering of data to relieve transmission bottlenecks. However, the point at which storage ceases to be transient is not clear, save that it is governed by the requirement that the storage be no longer than reasonably necessary for the transmission.

For copyright, reference should also be made to the separate provisions of s.28A[69] of the Copyright Designs and Patents Act 1988, exempting from infringement certain temporary acts of reproduction enabling transmission in a network (see Ch.2, para.2–017).

5–038   Article 11(3) provides:

"3. This Article shall not affect the possibility for a court or administrative authority, in accordance with Member States' legal systems, of requiring the service provider to terminate or prevent an infringement."

Exposure to an injunction would, therefore, under Art.11(3), be assessed by reference to the underlying national law regarding an intermediary's possible liability for the tort or crime in question. Similarly for pecuniary or criminal liability, if, for some reason, an intermediary were to fall outside the protection of the Directive it would (if the national implementation is structured in this way) still be necessary to examine the underlying national law to ascertain whether the intermediary had done an act that attracted the relevant civil or criminal liability. For copyright, however, it is in some limited circumstances possible for an injunction to be granted against a service provider even where there is no underlying cause of action against it (see para.5–030 above).

The conduit defence of Art.12 is implemented in the UK by reg.17 of the 2002 Regulations:

---

[69] Section 28A was introduced into the 1988 Act on October 31, 2003 by the Copyright and Related Rights Regulations 2003.

"17(1) Where an information society service is provided which consists of the transmission in a communication network of information provided by a recipient of the service or the provision of access to a communication network, the service provider (if he otherwise would) shall not be liable for damages or for any other pecuniary remedy or for any criminal sanction as a result of that transmission where the service provider–

(a) did not initiate the transmission;
(b) did not select the receiver of the transmission; and
(c) did not select or modify the information contained in the transmission.

(2) The acts of transmission and of provision of access referred to in paragraph (1) include the automatic, intermediate and transient storage of the information transmitted where:

(a) this takes place for the sole purpose of carrying out the transmission in the communication network, and
(b) the information is not stored for any period longer than is reasonably necessary for the transmission."

Regulation 21 provides for the burden and standard of proof in criminal proceedings, applicable to all three defences (conduit, caching and hosting). It provides that where evidence is adduced which is sufficient to raise an issue with respect to the defence in question, the court or jury shall assume that the defence is satisfied unless the prosecution proves beyond reasonable doubt that it is not.   5–039

In *Bunt v Tilley*,[70] a defamation case, an English court for the first time considered the intermediary liability provisions of the 2002 Regulations. The usefulness of the decision in providing guidance for the future is limited by the fact that the claimant acted in person, without the benefit either of legal representation or of independent expert evidence, with the result that the factual basis on which the court made its findings is confusing and difficult to discern. However, some useful conclusions can be drawn from the case.

As regards the conduit provisions, the court came to the inevitable conclusion that activity of an internet service provider that consists only of internet access constitutes an information society service and falls within the conduit exception.

The judge went on to discuss, *obiter*, the potential applicability of the conduit exception to email, making a possible distinction between ordinary and web-based email on the basis that the latter may be stored more per-

---

[70] [2006] EWHC 407 (QB). See fn.59 above and Ch.4, para.4–010.

manently than the former,[71] and so engage the hosting rather than the conduit provisions. Several comments need to be made about this.

The difference between ordinary and web-based email is that ordinary email is intended to be downloaded from the ISP's email server and stored locally by the user, whereas an ISP's web-based email server is intended itself to be the long-term repository of the user's emails. However, while that certainly suggests that storage of web-based email is outside the conduit exception, it does not necessarily follow that the storage of ordinary email falls within it.

It is important to focus on the qualifications to the conduit exception, in particular that the storage must be "for the sole purpose of carrying out the transmission in the network".

All emails are, immediately upon receipt, stored in a database from which the individual recipient then downloads them (in the case of web-based email, only to the user's web browser while reading the email).

5-040   A typical ISP dial-up or broadband email account operated via an email client (such as Microsoft Outlook) allows the recipient to opt whether or not the email, when it is collected, is retained on the ISP's email database.[72] The ISP may provide a facility whereby an ordinary email account can also accessed through a web interface. In all these cases the user, when he collects the email, will pull it over a public internet connection from the email database of the ISP where he holds his account.

In a corporate environment an email sent to an employee is more likely to be stored on the company's own email server, and the download to take place over the company's internal network. However, an employee may also be able to download remotely, and in many cases the operation of the email server itself may be outsourced to a third party, and the server situated remotely from the office network.

Can it really be said that in these cases (or any of them) the storage of received email in the email database is taking place for the sole purpose of carrying out the transmission in the network? It seems far more realistic to say that the purpose of the storage is to enable the ultimate recipient of the email to download it at his convenience, and that the storage has nothing to do with a technical act of transmission.

It is also doubtful whether there is any real distinction to be drawn between ordinary and web-based email, particularly when it is understood that there is nothing in the nature of ordinary email that requires it to be deleted when the user downloads it. Even if email were to be deleted at that point, it is surely stretching language to characterise such storage as

---

[71] The distinction drawn by the judge is derived from a discussion at paras 17.07 and 17.08 of "The Law of Defamation and the Internet" by Dr Matthew Collins (Oxford University Press, 2nd edn 2005).

[72] Microsoft's Outlook Express, for instance, defaults to deleting messages on a POP3 email server when they are collected. However, it provides a user option to retain messages on the server. IMAP email servers store messages permanently by default. (See "Setting Up Mail Servers in Outlook Express" *www.microsoft.com/windows/ie/community/columns/mailserver.mspx*.)

"transient", when the period for which the email is stored is not fixed, is outside the control of the intermediary and depends entirely upon when the subscriber chooses to access the mailbox. The fact that deletion would depend upon the human intervention of the subscriber might also militate against the storage being regarded as "automatic".

We would also observe that if the correct analysis is that storing web-based (or any other type of) email for a subscriber amounts to hosting, that does not deprive the ISP of conduit protection for any transmission activities involved in receiving the email prior to storing it for collection by its subscriber. If it were the case that storing the email at one end of a chain of transmission caused the whole transmission by that ISP to be characterised as hosting, then the only ISPs who could benefit from the conduit exception would be those in the middle of a chain of networks, not at the end of it.

That would contradict the part of *Bunt v Tilley* in which the judge rejected the claimant's argument that only an ISP who passed data from one network to another could qualify as a conduit. It would go against the scheme of the Directive, which is to grant protection according to the particular activity under consideration, rather than to label the entity concerned as either "a host" or "a conduit".[73] There is no reason why one ISP should not be regarded as, in relation to the same data at different stages, a conduit for its acts of transmission and a host for its acts of hosting.

Hosting

Article 14 of the Directive addresses hosting liability. It provides:

5–041

> "1. Where an information society service is provided that consists of the storage of information provided by a recipient of the service, Member States shall ensure that the service provider is not liable for the information stored at the request of a recipient of the service, on condition that:
>
> (a) the provider does not have actual knowledge of illegal activity or information and, as regards claims for damages, is not aware of facts or circumstances from which the illegal activity or information is apparent; or
>
> (b) the provider, upon obtaining such knowledge or awareness, acts expeditiously to remove or to disable access to the information.

---

[73] Note the Commission proposal for the Directive (COM (1998) 586 final, 98/0325 (COD)), which stated in its commentary on the liability of intermediaries provisions: "The distinction as regards liability is not based on different categories of operators but on the specific types of activities undertaken by operators. The fact that a provider qualifies for an exemption from liability as regards a particular act does not provide him with an exemption for all of his other activities."

2. Paragraph 1 shall not apply when the recipient of the service is acting under the authority or the control of the provider.

3. This Article shall not affect the possibility for a court or administrative authority, in accordance with Member States' legal systems, of requiring the service provider to terminate or prevent an infringement, nor does it affect the possibility for Member States of establishing procedures governing the removal or disabling of access to information."

5-042 This Article, by contrast with the mere conduit provisions, provides a "notice and takedown" regime for immunity from liability for damages (the service provider remains vulnerable to an injunction). The reference to "illegal" information is unfortunate, since it could be taken to connote only criminal liability. However, the references to damages would be inappropriate if that were intended. The intent of the Directive is to provide immunity from both civil and criminal liability.

As we have mentioned, the effect of acquiring relevant knowledge is, under the Directive itself, only that the protection of the hosting provisions is lost. The host does not automatically become liable. However, it should be borne in mind that the acquisition of knowledge may in some circumstances also affect the underlying potential liability. For instance, in relation to copyright it has been suggested in the Canadian Supreme Court "*Tariff 22*" case[74] that an internet service provider, which would not ordinarily be regarded as authorising copyright infringement, might be regarded as doing so if it received notice of infringing material and failed to take remedial action.

This suggestion has similarities to the decision in the English defamation case of *Byrne v Deane*,[75] holding that a person who has the right to remove defamatory material that someone else has put up on their property, but permits it to remain displayed, then becomes a participant in the publication.[76]

In the sphere of criminal liability, if the underlying offence has a *mens rea* element then the acquisition of knowledge may both complete the underlying offence and also disapply the Directive's hosting protection if the material is not taken down expeditiously upon acquisition of relevant knowledge. However, mere awareness of the nature of the content, while that may suffice for the purposes of the underlying offence, is likely in many cases to be insufficient to negate the hosting protection of the Directive, which requires actual knowledge of the illegality.

Unlike for conduit or caching intermediaries the hosting provisions, in

---

[74] *SOCAN v Canadian Association of Internet Providers* [2004] 2 S.C.R. 427, 2004 S.C.C. 45. See Ch.2 above.

[75] [1937] 2 All E.R. 204.

[76] Note that for defamation liability it is unnecessary to apply this doctrine to hosting ISPs, since for defamation purposes they are at common law already regarded as publishing material that they host, regardless of their knowledge of the content of the material (*Godfrey v Demon Internet Ltd* [1999] 4 All E.R. 342). A hosting ISP's knowledge of the process of publication is sufficient to render it a participant in the publication (*Bunt v Tilley*, above).

addition to reserving rights to terminate infringement, permit Member States to establish procedures governing the removal or disabling of access to information.

The hosting defence is implemented by reg.19 of the 2002 Regulations:

> "Where an information society service is provided which consists of the storage of information provided by a recipient of the service, the service provider (if he otherwise would) shall not be liable for damages or for any other pecuniary remedy or for any criminal sanction as a result of that storage where–
>
> (a) the service provider–
>
>> (i) does not have actual knowledge of unlawful activity or information and, where a claim for damages is made, is not aware of facts or circumstances from which it would have been apparent to the service provider that the activity or information was unlawful; or
>>
>> (ii) upon obtaining such knowledge or awareness, acts expeditiously to remove or to disable access to the information, and
>
> (b) the recipient of the service was not acting under the authority or the control of the service provider."

It will be noted that the regulation specifically covers both pecuniary remedies and criminal liability. It, correctly in our view, transposes "illegal" as "unlawful".

Regulation 22 provides as follows:

5–043

> "In determining whether a service provider has actual knowledge for the purposes of regulations 18(b)(v) and 19(a)(i), a court shall take into account all matters which appear to it in the particular circumstances to be relevant and, among other things, shall have regard to–
>
> (a) whether a service provider has received a notice through a means of contact made available in accordance with regulation 6(1)(c), and
>
> (b) the extent to which any notice includes–
>
>> (i) the full name and address of the sender of the notice;
>>
>> (ii) details of the location of the information in question; and
>>
>> (iii) details of the unlawful nature of the activity or information in question."

Regulation 22 is a home-grown provision which has no equivalent in the Directive. Inserted after the consultation on the draft regulations as a result of lobbying by internet service providers, it seeks to provide assistance to the courts in determining whether a service provider is fixed with relevant knowledge.

The Directive itself does not expand on the meaning of knowledge. Any attempt in national legislation to introduce clarification risks being found to be contrary to whatever the European Court of Justice might finally decide is the meaning of actual knowledge. Where, as in this case, the implementation is by secondary legislation under the European Communities Act, the question of validity of the legislation also arises.

Regulation 22 apparently obliges the court to have regard, in all cases, to whether the service provider has received a notice, by what means and containing what information. Applying such a requirement to all cases presupposes that a service provider can only ever acquire the relevant knowledge by receiving a notice. However, there is nothing in the Directive to support such a narrow view of actual knowledge, and patently a service provider could acquire actual knowledge through means other than being sent a notice.

Either reg.22 is inconsistent with the Directive or, more likely, notwithstanding its mandatory terms it should be regarded as doing no more than giving an indication of factors that the court may wish to take into account when determining knowledge.[77]

Regulation 22 will nonetheless have some practical effect. A person giving notice to a service provider is unlikely to wish to become embroiled in a debate over whether or not reg.22 is valid, and so will wish as a matter of practice to serve a notice satisfying the requirements of reg.22.

5–044   Regulation 22 was considered in *Bunt v Tilley*. The notices in that case were obviously inadequate (they did not identify the postings complained of) and little emerges from that finding. Of more interest are the judge's observations on reg.22(b)(iii), which requires details to be given of the unlawful nature of the activity or information in question. Since this was a defamation case, that raised the question (discussed in Ch.4, para.4–039) of whether in order to disapply the hosting exception it is sufficient to have knowledge of the defamatory nature of the material, or whether the ISP has to have knowledge that it is actionable.

Eady J. preferred the latter view. He stated:

> "In order to be able to characterise something as 'unlawful' a person would need to know something of the strength or weakness of available defences".

If this is correct, reg.19 provides significantly more protection for ISPs than is available under the separate defences provided by s.1 of the Defamation Act 1996. Those defences are disapplied if there is knowledge of the mere

---

[77] Article 14 of the Directive does permit Member States to establish procedures governing the removal or disabling of access to information. However, nothing in that provision permits a Member State to tinker with the concept of actual knowledge.

defamatory nature of the content. If Eady J.'s view of reg.22 is followed, an ISP should not be deemed to have "actual knowledge" of an unlawful activity under the 2002 Regulations unless the person giving the notice has explained why any potential defences would not apply.

What is a host?

There are difficulties in determining the scope and the degree of protection given by Art.14. As to scope, it is debatable whether Art.14 applies only to the purely technical act of hosting, or includes a broader range of those who store, or have caused to be stored, information on behalf of third parties.

5–045

The difficulty is illustrated by considering a website that includes a discussion forum. Assume that the website proprietor self-hosts, in other words stores the contents of the website on its own servers. As far as its own content is concerned, it does not come within Art.14. But as regards the discussion forum, to which third parties make postings, it appears to come within Art.14. The third parties are recipients of an information society service. The website proprietor stores their postings at their request.

What, though, if the website proprietor outsources the hosting of the site to a specialist hosting company? The hosting company would, as regards all the content on the site, claim the protection of Art.14. But since the website proprietor no longer carries out the technical function of storing any content itself, can it still claim the protection of Art.14 in respect of postings to its discussion forum?[78]

The recitals to the Directive add to the confusion. Recital (42), taken at face value, would suggest that a narrow technical view of the liability exemptions should be adopted:

> "The exemptions from liability established in this Directive cover only cases where the activity of the information society service provider is limited to the technical process of operating and giving access to a communication network over which information made available by third parties is transmitted or temporarily stored, for the sole purpose of making the transmission more efficient; this activity is of a mere technical, automatic and passive nature, which implies that the information society service provider has neither knowledge of, nor control over, the information which is transmitted or stored."

However, although this recital commences with a general reference to the liability exemptions, upon closer analysis it is extremely difficult to regard it

5–046

---

[78] This appears to have been the position with the *Mumsnet* incident in 2006, which is an example of the real problems that can be encountered by the proprietors of website discussion forums. Lawyers for the complainant in that case (the babycare expert Gina Ford) wrote both to Mumsnet itself about postings to Mumsnet's discussion forums and also to Mumsnet's hosting ISP. Mumsnet felt it then had no alternative but to request its members not to discuss Gina Ford at all (see statement by Mumsnet at *www.mumsnet.com/lw/state.html*).

as applying to the hosting exception. The Recital is concerned only with (a) operating and giving access to a communication network, (b) transmission or temporary storage and (c) making the transmission more efficient. None of these conditions has any relevance to hosting, which within the terms of Art.14: (a) does not consist of connection to a network, (b) includes permanent storage and (c) has nothing to do with making transmissions more efficient.

The better view, we suggest, is that in spite of its general opening words the recital does not restrict the hosting exception to narrow technical activity of the kind described in the recital; and the exception should apply more broadly to those who, in a general sense, store third party information. This would potentially include the proprietor of the web discussion forum that we have discussed above, regardless of whether he has outsourced the technical hosting function.

This interpretation fits comfortably within the wording of Art.14 itself, if the matter is considered from the point of view of the recipient of the information society service. From that perspective, in the web discussion forum scenario two different information society services are being provided. First, as between the discussion forum proprietor and the outsourcing provider, the outsourcer is providing a storage service to the discussion forum proprietor. Second, from the point of view of the user of the discussion forum, the discussion forum proprietor is providing a storage service to the user. The discussion forum proprietor's internal arrangements are of no concern to the user. What matters to the user is that the service offered to the user is a storage service, regardless of whether the discussion forum proprietor contracts out its back end activities.

Even if this broad interpretation of Art.14 is adopted, uncertainties remain about the scope of the activities protected. German courts, for instance, have held that the structure and organisation of a site may be such that third party content is to be regarded as having been adopted as the proprietor's own, thereby falling outside the hosting provisions (see discussion at para.6–177, below).

5–047   A further problem arises with the reference in Art.14 (and, more so, with reg.19) to "storage". Article 14 provides that service providers are "not liable for the information stored . . .". Liability for information is not an easy concept to understand, since liability typically arises not from the mere existence of information, but from some act that a person does with it (transmission, publication, copying, making available to the public and so on).

It might be thought that protection under Art.14 is limited to liability arising from the act of storage. However, if that were intended one might have expected to see wording similar to that in Art.13, i.e. "not liable for the . . . storage of that information"—a formulation which much more clearly focuses on the act of storage.

What is more, if Art.14 does grant protection limited to the act of storage, the results would be arbitrary and would remove much of the utility of the provision. For instance, in the case of copyright the Article would provide protection from liability for an act of infringement consisting of copying (since that is what occurs when a work is stored), but not for making available to the public, since that occurs only when the material is made available to be served up to a user and not upon mere storage.

Similarly, defamation liability arises from publication, which occurs when material is read and comprehended by the recipient. Publication requires more than an act of storage. It requires a copy of the material to be sent out of storage to a recipient.

On a restrictive interpretation of Art.14 any liability, civil or criminal, that arose from an act beyond mere storage, such as transmission from storage or publication, would not be covered. Protection for the transmission aspects might be provided by Art.12, so long as a host could satisfy the requirements under Art.12 of not initiating the transmission, of not selecting the recipient, and of not selecting the information contained in the transmission. But even that would not protect against a resulting act, upon receipt, of publication or making available to the public.

It is unlikely that Art.14 was intended to have such a narrow meaning. The subject-matter of the Directive is the commercial business of making information publicly available through electronic networks and devices. The heading of Art.14 is "Hosting", which is universally understood to mean storing information so as to enable it to be accessed by others. Article 14 is in its own terms concerned with access to stored information as well as with the act of storage. That can be seen from Art.14(1)(b) under which it is sufficient, in order that a provider remains protected from liability after it becomes aware of illegality, for it to disable access to the information.

Article 14 ought properly to be understood as providing a host with protection from liability incurred as a result both of storing information and of providing access to the stored information.

Regrettably, the UK implementation under the Regulations does not use language that would make this interpretation clear. Instead, reg.19 uses a narrower language than Art.14. It adopts an approximation of the language of Art.14 which focuses on protection from liability arising specifically from the act of storage: "shall not be liable for damages or for any other pecuniary remedy or for any criminal sanction as a result of that storage ...". It is to be hoped that the courts will have regard to the Directive and construe these provisions in the broader sense that we have suggested.[79]

5–048

These are difficult questions, if only because the drafting of the Directive is so vague. However, overly narrow technical interpretations could leave many internet service providers and others unprotected for activities that, from a broad policy perspective, the Directive was surely intended to cover.

In its original Proposal[80] for the Directive the European Commission stated the problem that needed to be addressed as follows:

---

[79] See also s.166A(3)(b) of the Criminal Justice and Public Order 1994 (as inserted by s.53 of the Violent Crime Reduction Act 2006, but not yet in force at the time of writing). This is presumably an attempt to provide a hosting exception in similar terms to Art.14 of the Directive, but is drafted in terms that appear to tie the protection even more closely to the act of storage alone.

[80] COM (1998) 586 final. 98/0325 (COD).

"In view of the limited degree of knowledge providers have about the information that they transmit or store via interactive communication networks, the main problem that arises is the allocation of liabilities between on-line service providers transmitting and storing illegal information and the persons who originally put such information on line. Questions also arise as regards the ability of providers to control the information they transmit or store."

In its commentary on Art.14 the Commission stated:

"Article 14 establishes a limit on liability as regards the activity of storage of information provided by recipients of the service and at their request (e.g. the provision of server space for a company's or an individual's website, for a BBS, a newsgroup, etc)."

While the latter comment tends to focus on the technical activity of providing server space, the fact remains that providing protection for storage while not protecting the serving up of information from storage is, in the context of providing information society services, no protection at all. The former comment suggests that the Commission were looking at the problem in broad binary terms (on-line service providers versus content providers) and did not descend to the level of detail that we now have to consider. The 2003 European Commission Report on the Directive[81] commented:

"the limitation on liability for hosting in Article 14 covers different scenarios in which third party content is stored, apart from the hosting of websites, for example, also bulletin boards or 'chatrooms'."

The Commission might also have mentioned other types of operator such as on-line auction sites. They undoubtedly see themselves as providing no more than a platform on which users can auction goods, and so being no different from other intermediaries who can avail themselves of the hosting liability exception. There has been no UK case law on the position of auction sites under the Directive. However, in March 2006 the General Optical Council offered no evidence in a prosecution of eBay over unlawful offers for sale of contact lenses on its site. The GOC stated that they had been advised that under European law eBay could not be required to actively monitor its listings since it qualified as a hosting company under the E-Commerce Directive.[82]

---

[81] First Report on the application of Directive 2000/31/EC of the European Parliament and of the Council of 8 June 2000 on certain legal aspects of information society services, in particular electronic commerce, in the Internal Market (Directive on electronic commerce) COM (2003) 0702, November 21, 2003.

[82] General Optical Council press release March 6, 2006 (*www.optical.org/index_files/ news_room/documents/2006–03–06GOCprosecutionofeBay.pdf*).

Caching

Article 13 addresses liability for caching. It provides: 5–049

> "1. Where an information society service is provided that consists of the transmission in a communication network of information provided by a recipient of the service, Member States shall ensure that the service provider is not liable for the automatic, intermediate and temporary storage of that information, performed for the sole purpose of making more efficient the information's onward transmission to other recipients of the service upon their request, on condition that:
>
> (a) the provider does not modify the information;
> (b) the provider complies with conditions on access to the information;
> (c) the provider complies with rules regarding the updating of the information, specified in a manner widely recognised and used by industry;
> (d) the provider does not interfere with the lawful use of technology, widely recognised and used by industry, to obtain data on the use of the information; and
> (e) the provider acts expeditiously to remove or to disable access to the information it has stored upon obtaining actual knowledge of the fact that the information at the initial source of the transmission has been removed from the network, or access to it has been disabled, or that a court or an administrative authority has ordered such removal or disablement.
>
> 2. This Article shall not affect the possibility for a court or administrative authority, in accordance with Member States' legal systems, of requiring the service provider to terminate or prevent an infringement."

It may be noted that the wording of this provision differs from that of the 5–050
conduit and hosting provisions, in that the exemption is from liability for the defined act of "automatic, intermediate and temporary storage" of the information, rather than (in the case of the other two provisions) liability for the information generally. That could mean that the exemption in this case is only from liability that could attach to that act (such as copyright infringement), rather than liability attaching to the onward transmission of the information or its receipt by the ultimate recipient.

The reference to rules regarding updating information refers to the fact that caching of information may result in the recipient, without his knowledge, receiving out of date information. In time-critical cases such as stock prices this could be seriously misleading. The reference to technology used to obtain data on the use of the information recognises that websites rely on usage data to justify advertising rates. If a user "hits" a cache instead of the source site, then the site may not capture the hit and will underestimate the usage.

The reservation of infringement termination rights against a caching intermediary is in identical terms to that in respect of conduits.

Regulation 18 of the 2002 Regulations is as follows:

"18. Where an information society service is provided which consists of the transmission in a communication network of information provided by a recipient of the service, the service provider (if he otherwise would) shall not be liable for damages or for any other pecuniary remedy or for any criminal sanction as a result of that transmission where–

(a) the information is the subject of automatic, intermediate and temporary storage where that storage is for the sole purpose of making more efficient onward transmission of the information to other recipients of the service upon their request, and

(b) the service provider–

(i) does not modify the information;

(ii) complies with conditions on access to the information;

(iii) complies with any rules regarding the updating of the information, specified in a manner widely recognised and used by industry;

(iv) does not interfere with the lawful use of technology, widely recognised and used by industry, to obtain data on the use of the information; and

(v) acts expeditiously to remove or to disable access to the information he has stored upon obtaining actual knowledge of the fact that the information at the initial source of the transmission has been removed from the network, or access to it has been disabled, or that a court or an administrative authority has ordered such removal or disablement."

5–051   The distinction noted above between the wording of Art.13 of the Directive and that of Arts. 12 and 14 is not maintained in the same way in the Regulations. The text of reg.18 differs materially from that of Art.13 of the Directive.

The Directive provides protection from liability for the automatic, intermediate and temporary storage of information, performed for the sole purpose of making transmission more efficient.

The Regulations, on the other hand, provide protection from liability arising as a result of the transmission, where the information is the subject of automatic, intermediate and temporary storage and where that storage is for the sole purpose of making transmission more efficient.

The reason for this departure from the terms of the Directive is unclear. The intention may be to provide protection for both the storage and the onward transmission of the cached information. If so, the drafting of the Regulations does not unambiguously achieve that.

No obligation to monitor

Article 15 of the Directive prohibits Member States from imposing a general obligation on intermediaries to monitor the information which they transmit or store, or a general obligation actively to seek facts or circumstances indicating illegal activity.

5–052

Recital (47) states:

> "Member States are prevented from imposing a monitoring obligation on service providers only with respect to obligations of a general nature; this does not concern monitoring obligations in a specific case and, in particular, does not affect orders by national authorities in accordance with national legislation."

Recital (48) states:

> "This Directive does not affect the possibility for Member States of requiring service providers, who host information provided by recipients of their service, to apply duties of care, which can reasonably be expected from them and which are specified by national law, in order to detect and prevent certain types of illegal activities."

This leaves open the possibility, consistently with the savings for injunctions in Arts. 12 to 14 and Recital (45), of injunctions being granted that would require an intermediary to undertake a degree of monitoring in order to comply with it (see the discussion of the Belgian case *SABAM v Tiscali*[83] in Ch.2, para.2–014).

However, the more broadly framed the injunction the more likely that it would fall foul of the Art.15 prohibition. What is more, it could be argued that such an injunction could prejudice the ability of the ISP to rely on the mere conduit exception, since the ISP might no longer satisfy the requirement that it does not select the information contained in the transmission.

Article 15 has not been transposed into the 2002 Regulations, but a court would have to have regard to Art.15 when considering the grant of an injunction against an intermediary. The grant of injunctions against ISPs is the subject of the next section.

---

[83] *SABAM v Tiscali*, Court of First Instance, Brussels, June 24, 2004.

Other on-line intermediaries

5–053 The Electronic Commerce Directive does not provide defences for other actors that could be regarded as types of on-line intermediary, such as search engines or the providers of hyperlinks. Nor (unlike some European countries) does the UK national implementation of the Directive do so.

The Department of Trade and Industry issued a Consultation Paper in June 2005 to explore whether the UK should extend the Directive's intermediary liability provisions to hyperlinkers, location tool services and content aggregators. It concluded in December 2006[84] that there was currently insufficient evidence to justify any extension to these limitations.

Under Art.21 of the E-Commerce Directive the European Commission is required to review the Directive every two years, including considering the need for proposals concerning linking and location tool liability. The Commission's First Report, in 2003, did not make recommendations to extend the Directive. The Commission's Second Report is overdue. In its Response to Consultation the DTI said that it would encourage the Commission to take on board the important issues raised during its consultation.

5.7.2 Beyond the Electronic Commerce Directive

5–054 The question of on-line intermediary liability regularly comes to public attention when particular issues of topical interest arise. Examples have included internet advertising by overseas adoption agencies, liability for tobacco advertising, fake goods on auction sites, safety of minors in chatrooms and on social networking sites[85] and the application to internet service providers of injunctions granted against the whole world (such as the *Bulger* and *Maxine Carr* injunctions).

If they fall within the scope of the Electronic Commerce Directive, then a degree of uniformity will be brought to these issues. However, the Directive does not provide a complete protective mantle. In particular, as we have seen, the Directive does not affect the grant of injunctions. Nor does it specify the terms in which injunctions may be granted. Indeed, it specifically permits national courts to require an intermediary to "terminate or prevent" an infringement.

Taken at face value, this could allow an injunction to be cast in wide terms, so that an intermediary could be put at risk of breaching an injunction in circumstances in which it would otherwise gain the protection of the Directive. However, as we shall see when we examine the *Bulger* case

---

[84] "Government Response and Summary of Responses to Consultation Document on the Electronic Commerce Directive: the Liability of Hyperlinkers, Location Tool Services and Content Aggregators" (*www.dti.gov.uk/consultations/page13985.html*).

[85] The social networking site MySpace.com has been sued in the US by the mother of a teenager who alleges she was sexually assaulted by another MySpace user ("Internet sites seek to head off paedophilia concerns" *Financial Times* July 17, 2006).

the English courts have gone some way, when fashioning injunctions, towards recognising the special position of internet service providers.

Internet adoption advertising

The question of liability of internet service providers under the Adoption Act 1976 arose in the context of the publicity surrounding the "*Internet twins*" case. The only role of the internet in the case was enabling the putative UK adopters to identify a US adoption broker. Subsequently, the Department of Health wrote to UK ISPs suggesting that they faced criminal prosecution if they knew that they had material on their servers that contravened s.58(1) of the 1976 Act, but failed to remove it.[86] Although this letter caused concern in the ISP community, the stance of the Department (albeit based on the provisions of the 1976 Act) appears to have been in line with the hosting liability provisions of the Electronic Commerce Directive.

5–055

Subsequently, Parliament enacted the Adoption and Children Act 2002, which came into force at the end of 2005 and replaced the 1976 Act. Sections 123 and 124 created offences concerning adoption advertisements, which provisions did not comply with the Electronic Commerce Directive. Simultaneously, the Electronic Commerce Directive (Adoption and Children Act 2002) Regulations 2005 came into force. These provided the conduit and hosting defences missing from the Act and also added provisions to comply with the internal market aspects of the Directive.

Tobacco advertising

Consternation arose among ISPs at the beginning of 2001 as a result of the Tobacco Advertising and Promotion Bill, intended to prohibit tobacco advertising. Withdrawn before the General Election, it was reintroduced in July 2001 in the same form and received Royal Assent on November 7, 2002. The Bill contained broad definitions of publication and distribution, extending to publishing by any electronic means including the internet, and (in the case of distribution) transmitting in electronic form, participating in doing so and providing the means of transmission.

5–056

The Bill would have provided an internet service provider with a defence to an electronic publication offence that he was unaware that what he published was, or contained, a tobacco advertisement. This defence was removed before Royal Assent after lobbying by the ISP industry, which was concerned that the reference in the Bill to internet service providers publishing advertisements could lead to ISPs being regarded as publishers. (For the purposes of defamation liability, the courts have held that ISPs publish material that they host, but not material that they merely transmit.[87])

This left hosting ISPs with no defence equivalent to that required under the Electronic Commerce Directive. As to distribution, the Act provides an

---

[86] *Financial Times*, January 23, 2001.
[87] *Godfrey v Demon Internet* [1999] 4 All E.R. 342 (para.4–009 above), *Bunt v Tilley* [2006] EWHC 407 (QB).

electronic distributor with a a defence if he was unaware that what he distributed or caused to be distributed was, or contained, a tobacco advertisement; or that having become aware of it, he was not able to prevent its further distribution. Since the definition of distributor would clearly encompass a conduit within the meaning of the Directive, this defence would not provide a conduit with the protection required under the Directive.

The missing defences required by the Directive were provided by the Electronic Commerce (EC Directive) Extension Regulations 2003 which came into force on February 14, 2003, some three months after the primary legislation.

Parliament had a third stab at enacting the defences in September 2006. By the Tobacco Advertising and Promotion Act 2002 etc. (Amendment) Regulations, which came into force on September 28, 2006, the Act was amended to introduce the required safe harbours into the legislation itself. The 2003 Regulations were simultaneously disapplied.

The reason for this third round of legislation was that compliance with Directive 2003/33/EC on Advertising and Sponsorship of Tobacco Products required amendments to be made to the 2002 Act and also gave rise to uncertainties about the interaction of the 2003 Directive with the Electronic Commerce Directive.[88]

The *Bulger* injunction

5–057   In *Venables v News Group Newspapers Ltd*[89] Butler-Sloss P. granted an injunction restraining the publication of information that would reveal the identity or whereabouts of the claimants. In 1993 the claimants had been convicted (when both were aged 11) of the murder in February that year of a two year old boy, James Bulger. The claimants had spent their minority in detention and, having reached age 18, were likely to be considered for release during 2001.

The injunction granted by the judge was extremely unusual in being an injunction against the world at large, not merely against the newspapers who were defendants to the proceedings. As originally granted on January 8, 2001, the injunction (so far as relevant for these purposes) restrained:

> "1. ... the Defendants and any person with notice of this order (whether themselves or by their servants or agents or otherwise howsoever or in the case of a company whether by its directors or officers servants or agents or otherwise howsoever) from:
>
> (1) publishing or causing to be published in any newspaper or broadcasting in any sound or television broadcast or by

---

[88] Explanatory Memorandum to the Tobacco Advertising and Promotion Act 2002 etc. (Amendment) Regulations (*www.opsi.gov.uk/si/em2006/uksiem_20062369_en.pdf*).

[89] [2001] 1 All E.R. 908.

means of any cable or satellite programme service or public computer network: [the prohibited material]..."

The Order also provided for service on:

"(a) such newspapers and sound or television broadcasting or cable or satellite programme services and public computer networks as [the First and Second Claimants' Solicitors] may think fit, in each case by facsimile transmission or pre-paid first class post addressed to the Editor in the case of a newspaper, or Senior News Editor in the case of a broadcasting or cable or satellite programme service, or person responsible for any public computer network in the case of that network;..."

There was a clear possibility that an internet service provider could be in breach of this order if a third party posted material to its servers, even though the ISP did not know it was there. While contempt of court requires both *actus reus* and *mens rea*,[90] so that it may be doubted whether an ISP could in fact have been in contempt for an act that it did not know it had done, clearly the wording of the injunction would create considerable unease in an ISP served with a copy of it.

Thus Plc, the proprietors of the ISP Demon Internet, applied to court in July 2001 for a variation of the injunction to allay these concerns. The injunction was varied by consent, by insertion of the following proviso to para.1(1):   5–058

"in relation to any internet service provider ('ISP'), its employees and agents:

(a) an ISP shall not be in breach of this injunction unless it, or any of its employees or agents:

  i. knew that the material had been placed on its servers or could be accessed via its service; or

  ii. knew that the material was likely to be placed on its servers, or was likely to be accessed via its service; and in either case

  iii. failed to take all reasonable steps to prevent the publication;

(b) an employee or agent of an ISP shall not be in breach of this injunction unless he or it:

  i. knew that the material had been placed on its servers or could be accessed via its service; or

---

[90] *A-G v Punch Ltd* [2002] UKHL 50.

ii. knew that the material was likely to be placed on its servers or was likely to be accessed via its service; and in either case

iii. failed to take all reasonable steps to prevent the publication and to induce the ISP to prevent the publication;

(c) an ISP, employee or agent shall be considered to know anything which he or it would have known if he or it had taken reasonable steps to find out;

(d) 'taking all reasonable steps to prevent the publication' includes the taking of all reasonable steps to remove the material from the ISP's servers or to block access to the material."

The service provisions were also amended to permit service on a public computer network by email.

5–059 The amended order bears some similarities to the hosting liability provisions of Art.14 of the Directive, especially the combination of knowledge and failure to take reasonable steps to prevent publication. However, the knowledge standard as defined in the amended order—"anything which he or it would have known if he or it had taken reasonable steps to find out"— is certainly different from, and probably more onerous than, that in the Directive.

The Directive requires lack of actual knowledge and, for damages, lack of awareness of "facts or circumstances from which the illegal activity or information is apparent". The Directive does not imply, as the amended order appears to do, that there is a duty to take reasonable steps to find out. In fact such an implication would arguably be contrary to the Art.15 prohibition on imposing a duty to monitor. The formulation in the amended order also begs the question of what may constitute "reasonable steps to find out" within the user-generated content context of hosting.

Other comparisons could be made with the deemed knowledge standard for secondary infringement of copyright "knows or has reason to believe",[91] or with the defence under s.2(5) of the Obscene Publications Act 1959 "no reasonable cause to suspect".

As a matter of general English law, knowledge includes the state of mind of someone who deliberately shuts his eyes to the obvious or refrains from inquiry because he suspects the truth but does not want to have the suspicion confirmed.[92] That, however, is not satisfied by mere neglect to carry out reasonable inquiries. To reduce the threshold to a negligence standard invites the question whether positive steps must always be taken in order to discharge the duty, or whether in particular factual circumstances it can be reasonable to take no positive steps.

---

[91] Copyright, Designs and Patents Act 1988, s.23.
[92] *Westminster City Council v Croyalgrange Ltd* [1986] 2 All E.R. 353, at p.359 HL.

So, for instance, in *London Borough of Harrow v W H Smith Trading*   5–060
Ltd,[93] a case under the Video Recordings Act 1984, the Divisional Court
held that the Crown Court was entitled to acquit the respondent newsagents of a charge of supplying an unclassified video recording in the form of
a computer game covermounted on a computer magazine.

The Act provided a defence that the commission of the offence was due
to the act or default of a person other than the accused; and that the accused
"took all reasonable precautions and exercised due diligence to avoid the
commission of the offence by any person under his control". The magazine
was supplied by a reputable publisher with whom the respondents had dealt
for 20 years, which carried out its own checks.

The Divisional Court found that the only question was whether the
respondents should have made some checks. As to that, the court found:
"Checking on a random basis would not in itself provide any significant
protection for the respondent. And checking every item would be unrealistic. ... Random checking was a step which the court could properly
conclude was not required in relation to this publisher."

This, as with most cases assessing the reasonableness of conduct, was a
decision on its particular facts. It still leaves unanswered the question
whether, if a negligence or due diligence standard is applied to an ISP which
receives content direct from members of the public (as opposed to a distributor receiving magazines from a reputable publisher), that standard may
require the ISP to take any (and if so what) positive steps in relation to any
of that content. This is similar to the conundrum faced by ISPs in relation to
establishing the innocent dissemination defence under the Defamation Act
1996 (see Ch.4).

On May 13, 2004 the High Court granted an injunction, effective against
anyone with notice of it, prohibiting publication of specified information
about Maxine Carr upon her release from custody on May 14, 2004,
including her proposed new name, her whereabouts and various other
details. The injunction contained an ISP proviso in the same terms as that in
the *Bulger* injunction.

The *Bulger* form of proviso is constructed specifically around the hosting
and access provision roles of a traditional ISP. For instance it addresses
both the removal of material from the ISP's own servers and the blocking of
access to material from other sources (including, presumably, where the
material could be accessed in this country from an overseas website).

Third party injunctions

An on-line intermediary proviso is also likely to come under consideration   5–061
where an interim injunction, although addressed to individual defendants
rather than being an injunction *contra mundo*, is served on third parties so
as to bind them under the *Spycatcher* principle.

Strictly speaking the third party is not bound by the order itself, which is

---

[93] [2001] E.W.H.C. Admin 469, June 19, 2001.

directed only to the defendant. However, as enunciated in *A-G v Punch Ltd*,[94] once served with an interim injunction a non-party is in contempt of court if it either aids and abets a defendant to breach the order or, acting independently:

> "with the intention of impeding or prejudicing the administration of justice in an action between two other parties, himself [does] the acts which the injunction restrains the defendant in that action from committing if the acts done have some significant and adverse affect on the administration of justice in that action" (see further Ch.12, para.12–094).

Service of an interim injunction on an on-line intermediary is especially likely to occur in defamation and privacy actions. Claimants in such actions may seek to serve interim injunctions not just on traditional hosts and access providers, but on a wide variety of on-line intermediaries including, for instance, search engines and sites rich in user-generated content.

Quite apart from the reservations expressed above about the substance of the ISP proviso in *Bulger*, it should be appreciated that that proviso was not drawn with the broader categories of on-line intermediaries in mind. The proviso would require extensive reformulation to accommodate them.

5–062   As the practice of notifying interim injunctions to on-line intermediaries gains in popularity, at some point the question of the cost of complying with such orders is likely to arise. The lengths to which the on-line intermediary is expected to go in policing the injunction will depend on the substantive form of the order, including any on-line intermediary proviso. Whatever those lengths may be, under current practice the on-line intermediary is effectively an innocent third party who, when served with an interim injunction, is required to act as an unpaid policeman of the claimant's asserted rights.

In substance the position of an on-line intermediary notified of such an injunction is very similar to that of a non-party bank served with an asset freezing order. Both are third parties with no direct involvement in the wrongdoing. Both are being asked to contribute to the proper administration of justice by assisting in the preservation of some aspect of the status quo pending trial. Both will incur substantial administrative time and effort in complying with the injunction. Both will be rightfully concerned, if the extent of their obligation is not clear, about the possibility of being held in contempt.

Despite the similarities in the positions of banks and on-line intermediaries, there are significant differences in current practice between freezing orders and *Spycatcher* injunctions. A bank, unlike the recipient of a *Spycatcher* injunction, is entitled to be reimbursed its costs of complying with the freezing order. While freezing orders contain specific provisions addressing the position of the banks to be notified it does not appear to be

---

[94] [2002] UKHL 50, *per* Lord Nicholls at para.4.

established practice to include on-line intermediary provisos (whether along the lines of *Bulger* or in any other form) in *Spycatcher* injunctions. This can create great uncertainty for the on-line intermediary in knowing what it has to do to avoid being in contempt.

The historical explanation for the differences in current practice between   5–063
freezing orders and *Spycatcher* injunctions is that they have their roots in very different factual circumstances.

With freezing orders it was always understood that banks were innocent parties operating huge volumes of bank accounts who were being put to time and expense in identifying, or even searching for, relevant bank accounts.

The *Spycatcher* principle, however, arose in the context of newspapers who had full editorial control over the contents of their publications, and who were being asked to ensure that they did not publish certain specified material—material which if it were to be published would in the normal course of events go through their editorial decision-making process anyway.

While the *Spycatcher* principle raised many controversial issues, it did not have the logistical impact on newspapers that notifying a freezing order had on the banks. Hence no question arose of indemnifying the newspapers for their compliance costs. The logistical impact on on-line intermediaries, however, is far greater; and may sometimes raise questions about whether compliance is even possible at all.

When *Mareva* injunctions (as freezing orders were then known) were first introduced, the banks were uncertain about various aspects of their position when served with an order, including the standard of knowledge and diligence to which they would be held. In 1981 the clearing banks asked the Court of Appeal, in *Z Ltd v A*,[95] to consider these issues. This resulted in the Court of Appeal laying down a set of guidelines, which we discuss below.

Applying the *Spycatcher* principle to on-line intermediaries raises the   5–064
same issues that prompted the clearing banks to seek guidance from the courts. On-line intermediaries generally do not (and given the volumes of material mostly could not) exercise editorial control. They process vast quantities of information. Compliance with the order is not merely a matter of instructing the editor of a newspaper. It imposes a similar (or even greater) burden of search and vigilance as does the freezing order on a bank. That burden was described by Kerr L.J. in *Z Ltd v A*:

> "The special position of banks, in particular of the clearing banks before us, is that they cannot in practice ensure compliance with such an order without instituting what may be a very costly and elaborate search throughout all their branches in order to see whether they hold any assets of the particular defendant. If such an order is served on a bank, it is obliged, as a matter of self-defence for the purpose of complying with the order, to carry out

---

[95] [1982] 1 All E.R. 556.

such a search; and by virtue of his undertaking the plaintiff will then be liable to pay their reasonable costs. In this connection we were told that a full 'trawl' through all the branches of a clearing bank could cost as much as £2,000. However, a plaintiff may well be unaware, when applying for a *Mareva* injunction covering all the assets of a defendant which is then served on a bank, that this is the level of the liability which he may be incurring. This is the first problem. The second problem, which is faced by banks to a greater extent than other third parties, is that they may have no ready means of establishing through any central register or other records what assets of a particular defendant they in fact hold."

Although freezing orders and *Spycatcher* orders arose from very different factual circumstances, their juristic basis is remarkably similar. In *Z Ltd v A*, the Court of Appeal addressed the basis on which a bank might be in contempt if it honoured a cheque drawn on an account that was required to be frozen. If the defendant had been served with the injunction, the bank might be guilty of aiding and abetting the defendant's contempt. But often the banks would be served with the injunction before the defendant. At that stage there could be no breach by the defendant capable of being aided and abetted by the bank.

The Court of Appeal found that the bank could nevertheless be in contempt, on a different principle. Lord Denning held that the *Mareva* injunction operated *in rem* against the defendant's assets and therefore took effect immediately against those assets. He said:

"Every person who has knowledge of [the injunction] must do what he reasonably can to preserve the asset. He must not assist in any way in the disposal of it. Otherwise he is guilty of a contempt of court."

He went on to enunciate the juristic principle:

"As soon as the bank is given notice of the *Mareva* injunction, it must freeze the defendant's bank account. It must not allow any drawings to be made on it, neither by cheques drawn before the injunction nor by those drawn after it. The reason is because, if it allowed any such drawings, it would be obstructing the course of justice, as prescribed by the court which granted the injunction, and it would be guilty of a contempt of court."

In its focus on obstruction of the course of justice, Lord Denning's juristic principle is similar to that underlying the *Spycatcher* injunction, as enunciated in *A-G v Punch* quoted above. Eveleigh L.J. put it in terms that are even closer to the *Spycatcher* principle:

"the conduct will always amount to contempt of court by himself.

It will be conduct which knowingly interferes with the administration of justice by causing the order of the court to be thwarted"

Lord Denning set out a number of things that he said necessarily followed   5–065
from the juristic principle, in justice to the bank or other innocent third
party who is given notice of the *Mareva* injunction or knows of it. They
included:

1. "*Indemnity* In so far as the bank, or other innocent third party,
is asked to take any action, or the circumstances require them to
take any action, and they are put to expense on that account, they
are entitled to be recouped by the plaintiff; and in so far as they
are exposed to any liability, they are entitled to be indemnified by
the plaintiff. . . .
In addition . . . the judge, when he grants the injunction, may
require the plaintiff to give an undertaking in such terms as to
secure that the bank or other innocent third party does not suffer
in any way by having to assist and support the course of justice
prescribed by the injunction."
2. "*Precise notice* The bank, or other innocent third party,
should be told, with as much certainty as possible, what they are
to do or not to do. The plaintiff will, no doubt, obtain his *Mareva*
injunction against the defendant in wide terms so as to prevent the
defendant disposing, not only of any named asset, but also of any
other asset he has within the jurisdiction. . . . But, when the
plaintiff gives notice to the bank or other innocent third party,
then he should identify the bank account by specifying the branch
and heading of the account and any other asset of the defendant
with as much precision as is reasonably practicable."
3. "*Search* If the plaintiff cannot identify the bank account or
other asset with precision, he may request the bank or other
innocent third party to conduct a search so as to see whether he
holds any asset of the defendant, provided that he undertakes to
pay the costs of the search. . . . We are told that in one case the
Inland Revenue requested the bank to make a 'trawl' of all its
branches to see if the defendant had an account at any of them.
The bank could not be expected to do this, except on the footing
that all the expense was to be paid by the plaintiff."
4. "*Tell the judge* In view of the impact of the *Mareva* injunction on banks and other innocent third parties, it is desirable that
the judge should be told on the application the names of the banks
and third parties to whom it is proposed to give notice: but it
should not preclude the plaintiff from giving notice to others on
further information being obtained."
5. "*Undertakings* The plaintiff who seeks a *Mareva* injunction
should normally give an undertaking in damages to the defendant,
and also an undertaking to a bank or other innocent third party to

pay any expenses reasonably incurred by them. The judge may, or may not, require a bond or other security to support this undertaking...."

5–066   Kerr L.J. also provided a checklist of matters that the plaintiff and their legal advisers should consider.

The practice for freezing orders is now enshrined in the draft form of order attached to the Practice Direction for CPR Pt 25.

Rhetorically one can ask, if the list of matters enunciated by Lord Denning necessarily follow from the juristic principle underlying the enforceability of the *Mareva* injunction against innocent third parties, why do the same requirements not follow from the virtually identical juristic basis of the *Spycatcher* principle? For on-line intermediaries it is difficult to understand why the same consequences should not follow.

At some point a court is likely to be asked, on the application of an on-line intermediary third party, to address the issue. If the same principles were applied to on-line intermediaries, these are some of the practical consequences that could follow:

1. *Indemnity* and *undertaking*. There would seem to be no reason why a similar form of indemnity and undertaking should not be given to an on-line intermediary.

2. *Precise notice*. On-line intermediaries can be assisted by precision in identifying the offending material. For instance details of known file names, sizes and hash sums may assist some intermediaries in identifying material. An undertaking to provide such information on an ongoing basis as it becomes known to the claimant would also be useful. If the on-line intermediary is expected to go no further than to identify material by such technical criteria, that should be made clear.

3. *Search*. If the intermediary is expected to go further and actively search for material, that should be made clear. It may assist some intermediaries to be provided with a set of keywords by which the extent of the search that they are expected to carry out can be defined and limited.

4. *Tell the judge*. This requirement applies with equal force as regards on-line intermediaries, so that the judge can understand and properly consider what is being proposed. It should also be made clear what types of on-line intermediaries are intended to be served, and in respect of which functions that they perform.

   For instance, one on-line intermediary may host websites and another provide discussion forums to which users can post comments and files. What it is reasonable to expect of each may differ. Is the provider of the discussion forum expected only to delete files that it hosts, or to search out and remove user-submitted links to the same material on third party sites? None of these issues will be apparent to the judge, or reflected in the order, unless the claimant informs the judge of his intentions.

5.8 EMPLOYER LIABILITY, EMAIL AND INTERNET ACCESS POLICIES

5.8.1 Electronic communication risks

The civil and criminal liability of employers for the acts of their employees on electronic networks raises increasingly complex issues. The starting point is to consider in what circumstances an employer can be liable for illegal or unlawful acts of its employees when sending or circulating emails and attachments, or when downloading material from the internet and storing it on the employer's network, or indeed when using voicemail.[96]   5-067

The element common to all these technologies, and which distinguishes them from corridor chat or the ordinary telephone, is that they are self-recording. The act of communicating automatically creates and leaves behind electronic footprints as the message is stored and forwarded around the system. This has particular implications for informal behaviour in the workplace, which is precisely the area in which the risk of employer liability is greatest. Inappropriate behaviour formerly went unrecorded. Now it is routinely documented in an electronic trail that will have to be produced in any subsequent litigation.[97]

Reputations can also suffer. Embarrassing emails occasionally go viral, spreading to thousands and ultimately millions of email users in a matter of hours.[98]

Consequential issues arise from the steps that employers may wish to take to minimise their risk of liability or to ensure that they can discipline offending employees. We have to consider the extent to which employers are free to monitor and read their employees' communications made using the employer's network. The provisions of the Regulation of Investigatory Powers Act 2000 rendering operators of private networks (including employers) potentially liable to civil action for intercepting communications on their own networks are significant, as is the increasing emphasis on

---

[96] For an example of a voicemail incident, see M. Hart, Corporate Liability for Employee Use of the Internet and E-mail, C.L.S.R. Vol.14 No.4, 1998, p.223.

[97] A mini-industry in its own right is developing around the topic of electronic document disclosure. This has three main elements: the rules governing what has to be disclosed, the practicalities and cost of preserving and sifting through massive quantities of electronic documents and communications, and the forensic recovery of deleted electronic evidence. See CPR Rule 31 (in particular the draft form of disclosure statement) and the accompanying PD31 para.2A. Reference may also usefully be made to the Report of a Commercial Court Working Party on Electronic Disclosure of October 6, 2004 (*www.hmcourts-service. gov.uk/docs/electronic_disclosure1004.doc*).

[98] London law firms seem to be especially prone to such embarrassments. The notorious "Yum" email of December 2000 and the "Ketchup trousers" email of 2005 both originated in London solicitors' offices.

human rights, including a developing right of privacy, as a result of the Human Rights Act 1998. That is evident in the approach of the Information Commissioner to the data protection implications of monitoring electronic communications in the workplace.

An important aspect of content liability is that attaching to email messages, both those sent via the internet and internal emails. Postings to Usenet newsgroups, which are in effect emails published to the world at large, are also potentially high-risk. The *Netcom* copyright infringement decision,[99] the *Godfrey v Demon Internet* defamation case[1] and some aspects of the *Bunt v Tilley* defamation case[2] all concerned newsgroup postings.

The informal and uninhibited nature of email and newsgroups encourages unguarded comment which can and does attract lawsuits. Incoming material is also high risk. Some newsgroups are very likely to contain illegal or infringing material which an employer will not wish to find stored on its systems. However, it should not be forgotten that the largest UK email defamation damages paid to date (£450,000) arose from the circulation of emails internally within an organisation.[3] A more recent area of potential concern is employee blogs.

5–068   It is also possible for employees to bind the employer to contracts by means of email.[4] This may be what the employer wants. But if not, it represents a potentially significant area of risk.

In this section we look generally at employer liability: how an employer may be liable for the legal incidents of email sent by its employees using the company email system or of other employee internet activities, and what the employer can do to minimise the risk of liability.

The criteria for the existence of direct tort and criminal liability differ in respect of each type of liability (copyright, defamation, confidentiality, liability for virus damage etc). Reference should be made to the relevant discussions elsewhere in this book. A summary of some typical activities and corresponding statutory provisions and rules of law that may read onto such activities is contained in Table 5.1.

---

[99] See Ch.2.

[1] Above, para.4–009.

[2] Above, para.4–010.

[3] The *Norwich Union* case (see Ch.4).

[4] See Ch.10 for a detailed discussion of formation of contracts and requirements of form in the electronic environment. Where there are no statutory formalities the normal rules of offer and acceptance apply as much in the electronic environment as in any other. When considering the relatively uncommon cases in which statute imposes formalities, it should be borne in mind that "writing" is generally accepted to include documents in electronic form and that a statutory requirement for a signature can be satisfied by something as informal as a name typed at the end of an email.

Table 5.1

Activity	Consequence	Typical classes of liability-inducing act	Examples of applicable legislation
Downloading from websites, newsgroups, ftp sites etc; incoming email	Data stored on company's servers. Programs may execute on company's system	Possession (indecent photograph) Copying, storage	Criminal Justice Act 1988 Copyright Designs & Patents Act 1988
Internal emails	Information (both body text and attachments) circulated within company	Copying, storage Publication, receipt Transmission Possession (indecent photograph)	Copyright Designs & Patents Act 1988 Defamation, harassment/discrimination Obscene Publications Act 1959 (as amended) Criminal Justice Act 1988
Outgoing email	The email may conclude a contract, may be relied upon by the recipient, may damage data on the recipient's system if it contains a virus, or may trigger any liability founded upon communication of information to the recipient	Offer/acceptance Assuming responsibility for advice Publication Transmission Causing damage Unauthorised modification of contents of a computer	Contract Negligent misstatement Defamation (*cf.* passing off, trade mark infringement) Obscene Publications Act 1959 (as amended) Negligence, trespass Computer Misuse Act 1990

Uploading to website discussion forums, newsgroups, mailing lists	Information made available to worldwide audience.	Publication	Defamation
		Transmission	Obscene Publications Act 1959 (as amended)
		Issuing copies to the public, distribution, copying	Copyright Designs & Patents Act 1988

5-069   The potential risks have led many companies to enforce electronic communication policies. Following the introduction of the Tele-communications (Lawful Business Practice) (Interception of Communications) Regulations 2000, made under s.4(2) of the Regulation of Investigatory Powers Act 2000 (hereafter the "RIPA Lawful Business Practice Regulations" and "RIPA"), the desirability of having such a policy is even greater since it may enhance the company's ability lawfully to access communications on its network. This has two benefits: first, the avoidance of civil or criminal liability in connection with unlawful access; second, the ability to resist an argument in a court or tribunal that the evidence was unlawfully obtained and should excluded from consideration.

Although there is no general rule of law that unlawfully obtained evidence should be excluded, with the advent of the Human Rights Act 1998 the court should consider whether admitting such evidence will affect the fairness of the trial.[5]

However, if the evidence has been obtained by an interception of communications on a private network unlawful under RIPA, then under s.17 of RIPA the evidence cannot be adduced in legal proceedings, including civil proceedings. If the evidence was obtained by interception of communications on a public network, then whether obtained lawfully or unlawfully it cannot be adduced as evidence in legal proceedings. The prohibition on adducing interception evidence is subject to certain exceptions set out in s.18.

For an explanation of the purpose of these prohibitions, and a determination of what matters the court is permitted to investigate without offending against s.17, see *Attorney General's Reference (No 5 of 2002) sub nom, R v W*[6] in which Lord Bingham summarised the position as follows:

"I am satisfied that a court may properly enquire whether the interception was of a public or private system and, if the latter,

---

[5] See, for instance, *R v Khan* [1997] A.C. 558 and *Khan v UK* ECtH.R. 12.05.2000 No 35394/97; also *R v P* [2001] 2 W.L.R. 463 and *R v Wright* June 14, 2001 CA. Examples in the employment context include *Jones v University of Warwick* [2003] EWCA Civ 151, *McGowan v Scottish Water* (EAT) (2005) I.R.L.R. 167 and *XXX v YYY* (EAT) (2004) I.R.L.R. 137.

[6] [2004] UKHL 40.

whether the interception was lawful. If the court concludes that it was public, that is the end of the enquiry. If the court concludes that it was private but unlawful, that will also be the end of the enquiry. If it was private but lawful, the court may (subject to any other argument there may be) admit the evidence."

The wise company will also educate its staff to understand that sending an email is not (as they may think) akin to using the telephone, but is tantamount to sending written company correspondence. Like a letter or memo, email can be produced in court as evidence and may have to be disclosed to opponents in litigation during disclosure of documents. An email is also extremely difficult to delete from a system.[7]

5.8.2 Liability for acts of employees

Vicarious liability

The principle on which an employer may be held liable for a civil wrong   5–070
committed by one of its employees is simply stated, but not easily applied. The employer is vicariously liable for a wrongful act committed by an employee in the course of his employment.

Historically the test was whether the act was of a type which the employee was employed to carry out. If so, the employer was liable even if the act was done in an unauthorised way. But if the act was not one of a type which the employee was employed to carry out, then the employer was not liable.

The House of Lords re-stated this test in *Lister v Hesley Hall Ltd*.[8] Their Lordships held that the test is whether the tort is so closely connected with the employment that it would be fair and just to hold the employer vicariously liable. This test is more flexible, and probably broader, than the old one. It enables an employer to be held liable for acts done, as in the *Lister* case itself, "in the time and on the premises of the defendants" while the employee had also been busy carrying out his duties. The tort (in this case sexual abuse of pupils by the warden of a school boarding house) had been "inextricably interwoven" with the carrying out by the warden of his duties.

This approach perhaps increases the chance of an employer being held vicariously liable for infringing or defamatory employee personal emails sent on the employer's network and in its time. Even under the old test, merely prohibiting the sending of infringing or defamatory emails would

---

[7] For some vivid examples of emails disclosed on discovery, see "Big Brother is Watching" Computer Litigation Journal, Peter C. Spiel, July 1999. The effective use of disclosed emails in the *Microsoft* anti-trust litigation gave rise to the idiom "self-toasting". See also M. Hart, *op.cit.* on the surprise of Oliver North, testified to in the Iran-Contra hearings, that hitting the delete button did not erase the message from the system.
[8] [2001] 2 All E.R. 769.

not have relieved an employer of liability if the email was otherwise sent in the course of its business.

Following *Lister*, in *Majrowski v Guy's & St Thomas's NHS Trust*[9] the House of Lords held that the principles of vicarious liability could apply to statutory wrongs as well as to common law torts. In that case the proper interpretation of the Protection from Harassment Act 1997 was that an employer could be liable for an employee's wrongful conduct under the Act.

Criminal liability

5–071 A corporate employer's potential liability for its employees' criminal acts is more limited than that for civil wrongs. There may be liability if the employer authorised the act or turned a blind eye to it. Or a company may be vicariously liable on the clear words or construction of a statute.[10] Or if any necessary acts and mental state were those of individuals who represent the controlling mind and will of the company and therefore can be identified with it, the company can be liable for criminal acts of the individuals.[11]

Personal email

5–072 Difficult questions may arise with personal email. Many companies routinely tolerate a certain level of personal telephone calls, but would be very surprised if an employee were to use company headed paper for personal letters. Should a company tolerate or prohibit personal email? If a company explicitly permits its system to be used for personal email (even with appropriate disclaimers attached to the messages), then a claimant might try to argue (especially under the new, more flexible *Lister* test) that that brings it within the realm of vicarious liability. A prohibition honoured only in the breach could afford the claimant a similar opportunity.

Direct liability

5–073 A claimant seeking to make the employer liable for personal email could also rely upon other forms of liability specific to certain rights, such as participating in the publication of a defamatory statement or authorising copyright infringement. For defamation, in particular, there are several bases on which a claimant could seek to hold the employer liable:

1. Vicarious liability for the act of the employee in publishing the email by sending it to a recipient.
2. As a publisher in its own right through participating in the employee's act of publication by providing the computer system by means of which the publication took place.

---

[9] [2006] UKHL 34.
[10] See *e.g. Alphacell Ltd v Woodward* [1972] 2 All E.R. 475, *National Rivers Authority v Alfred McAlpine Homes East Ltd* [1994] 4 All E.R. 286.
[11] The "identification principle" was enunciated by Lord Reid in *Tesco Supermarkets Ltd v Nattrass* [1972] A.C. 153 at p.170.

3. As a publisher in its own right through participating, by providing the computer system, in any further acts of publication in which the email is further disseminated, or by means of which other users see the email.

As to the basis of holding an employer directly liable for defamation in its own right as a publisher, and the possible availability of the "innocent dissemination" defence, in defamation law anyone who participates in the first or main publication of a defamatory statement is liable for the defamation. In the traditional commercial publishing context this applies not only to the author, the editor and the publisher, but also to the printer and the distributor. Although subordinate disseminators such as printers, distributors and internet service providers have an "innocence" defence available to them under s.1 of the Defamation Act 1996, they have *prima facie* participated in the publication and so will be liable if they cannot make out the innocence defence.

The publication of an employee's email, using the employer's email system, undoubtedly takes place on and by means of the employer's network. The question then is whether the employer is thereby to be regarded as having participated in the publication, or having merely facilitated it. If the former, then the employer would be regarded as having published the email and be *prima facie* liable. If the latter, the employer would not be liable. This would apply to employees' personal emails as much as business emails, since it is irrelevant to the question of publication whether an email was sent in the course of employment.

5–074

The argument for employer liability on the basis of participating in the publication is untested, although in one Canadian case[12] a printing company was held liable for a defamatory newssheet printed on its presses by some of its employees. The court found that the company's manager knew about and made no effort to stop the printing of the newssheet.

We also discuss in Ch.4 whether the pre-Defamation Act 1996 distinction between participation and facilitation has been modified as a result of the innocent dissemination provisions of the 1996 Act.[13]

If the employer were found to have published the email, then it would be strictly liable for the defamation unless it can establish both that it is within the categories of those entitled to rely on the innocent dissemination defence and that it conformed to the necessary standard of care and other conditions laid down in the Act (see Ch.4).

An employer may also find that, even if it escapes vicarious liability for an act of harassment carried out by an employee, it may still, as a consequence of failing to control the type of material in circulation or viewed in its office, including electronic material, become vulnerable to direct liability

---

[12] *Lobay v Workers and Farmers Publishing Co.* [1939] 2 D.L.R. 272.

[13] The decision in *Bunt v Tilley* [2006] EWHC 407 (QB) suggests that the distinction survives unmodified. However, the claimant was not legally represented and the point that s.1(3)(e) of the Defamation Act 1996 is superfluous if mere transmission does not amount to publication does not appear to have been considered by the court.

for sexual or racial harassment.[14] The Employment Appeal Tribunal has held, in *Moonsar v Fiveways Express Transport Ltd*,[15] that where a group of male employees downloaded pornographic images onto a computer screen in close proximity to a female employee working in the same room, who was aware of what was happening, that was capable of amounting to discrimination under the Sex Discrimination Act 1975.[16]

5–075   In some circumstances negligence liability may have to be considered. In the US the New Jersey Superior Court, Appellate Division, has held that "an employer who is on notice that one of its employees is using a workplace computer to access pornography, possibly child pornography, has a duty to investigate the employee's activities and to take prompt and effective action to stop the unauthorized activity, lest it result in harm to innocent third parties. No privacy interest of the employee stands in the way of this duty on the part of the employer."[17]

The case concerned a negligence claim by a 10-year old girl (brought through her mother) against the former employer of her step-father. The step-father had photographed the girl in nude and semi-nude positions, stored them on his workplace computer and had transmitted from that computer three of the photographs to a child pornography website. There was no evidence that the employer had actual knowledge that the employee was accessing or transmitting child pornography, as opposed to adult pornography, but in the factual circumstances (credible reports of improper use had been made, but further investigations were not carried out) the court was prepared to find that the employer was on notice.

The employer was, therefore, under a duty, owed to the girl, to investigate further and to act, either by taking effective internal action to prevent the activities, whether by dismissal or otherwise, or by reporting his activities to law enforcement authorities, or both. The appeal court reversed the lower court's grant of summary judgment in favour of the defendant and remitted the case to the lower court to consider whether there the plaintiff had a case that the girl had suffered any harm from the alleged breach of duty.

As regards contracts, the increasing availability of access to the internet from employees' computers raises issues relating to the ability of those employees to bind their employer to contracts. Whereas contracts entered into in writing are likely to be subject to management procedures such as a review process and to formal signing off, such procedures may be circumvented in respect of contracts formed by email or in response to a web page.

---

[14] See, for instance, as regards racial harassment, *Tower Boot Co. Ltd v Jones* [1997] 2 All E.R. 406. See also ss.4(2A) and 32(3) of the Race Relations Act 1976, introduced by the Race Relations Act 1976 (Amendment) Regulations 2003.

[15] EAT September 27, 2004.

[16] The respondent employer did not appear in that case, so the question of whether it could rely on any defence such as having taken such steps as were reasonably practicable to prevent the employee doing the act or acts of that description (1975 Act, s.41) was not considered.

[17] *Doe v XYC Corporation* 887 A.2d 1156 (N.J. Super. 2005).

An employee may bind his employer in accordance with the general principles of agency. Of course, if the employee has actual authority to act in such a way, the internet raises no particular issues as regards agency. The real concern must be as to whether the granting of the right to an employee to send and receive internet emails and respond to web pages confers ostensible authority to contract. The test is whether the employee is being held out by the employer as having that authority.

Common sense would suggest that the mere granting of access to the internet does not confer ostensible authority to bind an employer. However, this must depend on the circumstances of each case. It would seem prudent for employers to review internal procedures and guidelines as to who is permitted access and for what purposes, to avoid the problem arising, and to ensure that the risks of creating a contract in this way are understood by all employees having access to the internet.

5.8.3 Employment Tribunal decisions

Some examples of industrial tribunal claims that have involved the use and misuse of electronic communications and reliance on email and internet access policies are as follows.[18]   5–076

In deciding whether unauthorised access to any computer system constitutes grounds for dismissal a Tribunal will look closely at the circumstances of the particular case.

Unauthorised access

In *Denco Ltd v Joinson*,[19] Mr Joinson's password only gave him access to a   5–077 particular part of the data held on his employer's computer system. He gained access to other more sensitive data by learning another password from his daughter who also worked for the same company. He was summarily dismissed. He had no improper motive. He had simply been "playing around with the system". Although at first instance his summary dismissal was considered unfair, on appeal the EAT overturned that decision ruling that if an employee deliberately uses an unauthorised password to enter a computer known to contain information to which he is not entitled, this in itself constitutes gross misconduct.[20] By contrast, in the case of *BT v Rodrigues*,[21] Mr Rodrigues was sum-

---

[18] Many of the pre-2000 cases mentioned are reported in *IDS Brief* 637, May 1999 (Incomes Data Services) (also available at *http://web.archive.org/web/20020601212424/http://www.incomesdata.co.uk/brief/ecases.htm*).

[19] [1991] I.C.R. 172.

[20] On the authority of *R v Bow Street Stipendiary Magistrates Exp. Government of the United States of America* [2000] 2 A.C. 216 such conduct also constitutes a criminal offence under the Computer Misuse Act 1990, since an offence is committed if an employee who is authorised to work on some accounts accesses other accounts to which she has access, but to which that authority did not extend.

[21] [1998] Masons C.L.R. Rep. 93.

marily dismissed for having obtained unauthorised access to computer data but his dismissal was found to have been unfair. He wanted access for legitimate work related purposes and although he had not been authorised to use the computer to access the information he had acquired, he would have been entitled to that information if he had asked for it over the telephone.

In both cases the Tribunal stressed that employers should make it abundantly clear to employees in disciplinary codes or other company literature that computer misuse would automatically result in summary dismissal so that employees should be aware of the seriousness of their actions.

5–078   In *Pickersgill v Employment Service*[22] the EAT found that the employee was fairly dismissed after having used her personal identification number to gain unauthorised access to her employer's computer system on some 70 occasions. The Tribunal found that the person dismissing the applicant genuinely believed that she was guilty of such unauthorised access, that he had reasonable grounds for that belief and had carried out a reasonable investigation, the procedure he had adopted had been fair and the decision to dismiss fell within the range of reasonable responses of a reasonable employer.

In *Taylor v OCS Group Ltd*[23] the claimant was an an employee in the company's IT department. He had been asked to assist a fellow employee with a database problem and was working on the problem via remote access. While doing so he emailed several emails from the fellow employee's terminal to his own. These were found not to be relevant to the work that he was doing. The EAT commented that "it is a very serious matter for an employee, particularly one based in the IT department with access to other staff members' computers, to forward emails from colleagues' terminals to their own, without permission, that are not related to the job in hand".

Pornography

5–079   Using internet facilities at work to access pornographic material may not necessarily justify dismissal on grounds of gross misconduct. Much will depend on the circumstances. In the case of *Parr v Derwentside DC* decided in 1998, the local authority employer did not accept the employee's claim that he had accessed a pornographic website by mistake when it could be established that he had accessed the site for a considerable period and had then re-visited it. In view of the fact that the employer was a local authority with standards to uphold, the Tribunal was satisfied that the dismissal was fair.

Dunn v IBM UK Ltd, also decided in 1998, the employee was summarily dismissed for gross misconduct. He admitted that he had accessed pornography via the internet and made print-outs of downloaded pictures.

---

[22] [2002] EWCA Civ 23.
[23] Employment Appeal Tribunal, May 23, 2005.

However, the Tribunal found that his dismissal was not fair because he had admitted the offences without appreciating that the consequence would be his dismissal and the Tribunal did not feel that any disciplinary procedure had been properly applied. In these circumstances summary dismissal was inappropriate but the Applicant's compensation was reduced by 50 per cent to take account of the fact that he had contributed by his behaviour to his own dismissal.

In *Thomas v Hillingdon London Borough*[24] the claimant employee was a lead personnel officer who had accessed pornography on the internet several times. The employer genuinely believed this on reasonable grounds and conducted a reasonable investigation. The employer regarded the employee's behaviour as gross misconduct and dismissed him. The Employment Appeal Tribunal held that the categorisation as gross misconduct was within the range of reasonable employer responses and that the dismissal was fair.

Harassment

Employees who access or transmit pornography while at work may use it to unlawfully harass their colleagues in the workplace. Their employers may be liable for their unlawful actions.

In the case of *Morse v Future Reality Ltd*, decided in 1996, the female Applicant was required to share an office with several men who spent a considerable amount of their time poring over sexually explicit or obscene images downloaded from the internet facilities available to them at work. She accepted that these activities were not directed at her personally, but they did cause her to feel uncomfortable. Eventually she resigned and made a claim against her employers of sex discrimination on the grounds of harassment citing the pictures, bad language and general atmosphere of obscenity in the office as the basis of her complaint. The Tribunal held that her claim was well founded. No one had taken any action to prevent the behaviour complained of. She was awarded three months' lost earnings and £750 for injury to feelings. A further example is *Moonsar v Fiveways Express Transport Ltd*, discussed above (para.5–074).

5–080

5.8.4 Electronic communication policies

An email and internet policy should extend to incoming messages and other forms of internet access using the employer's facilities. One issue here is protection of the employer's business systems from viruses or other similar damaging incomers, and seeking to prevent liability for illegal, infringing or other damaging material downloaded and stored on the company's system.

5–081

---

[24] Employment Appeal Tribunal, September 26, 2002.

Another issue is the reputational and possible legal liability risk to the employer arising out of external communications by employees. If employees (or some of them) have full internet access, the policy will need to go wider than just email, and extend to all forms of internet access including reading web pages and downloading files on to the employer's system. It may also need to extend to other forms of electronic communication, such as instant messaging, blogs, mobile text and video messaging and so on.

In theory it can be useful to draw a distinction between executable and non-executable files. A non-executable (text) file ought to be harmless, whereas an executable (or program) file can potentially harbour a virus. Unfortunately, the distinction is now not so clear. Word processed documents often contain macros capable of operating as viruses. Program files can be converted to text for transmission as email attachments and converted back to executable form on receipt. Java and ActiveX, programming languages commonly used to animate and drive web pages, require the recipient to download mini-programs to his computer, in addition to the page text.

So an electronic communications policy will need to address a variety of issues. Which employees can send email on behalf of the company? What materials (if any) may be downloaded from outside the company network? What procedures should be adopted to quarantine and check such materials before allowing them onto the company network? Is personal email permitted, and if so what signature file should be appended to indicate that? What signature tags should be appended to indicate the sending company and the position of the individual sender? Are postings to Usenet newsgroups permitted? What policy is adopted towards employee blogs?

A formal electronic communications policy should be promulgated to staff and other system users and made part of the employee handbook and preferably incorporated in the contracts of employment.[25] The seriousness of non-compliance should be emphasised and the potential sanctions made explicit. The reasons for the policy and the risks to the company of non-compliance should be communicated clearly to employees.

If the employer wishes be able to do anything that would otherwise constitute an unlawful interception of a communication on its network, then in order to take advantage of the RIPA Lawful Business Practice Regulations it must (among other things) make all reasonable efforts to inform all persons who may use the telecommunications system in question that communications transmitted by means of the system may be intercepted (see below, para.5–105 as to what this means). The policy should also take into account the requirements of data protection law.

The Information Commissioner's Employment Practices Code (discussed below, para.5–112) contains at s.3.2 a list of data protection features that

---

[25] If the contents of the policy are not properly communicated, then the employer may not be able to justify taking disciplinary action on the basis of it, for instance in employment tribunal unfair dismissal proceedings.

employers should consider integrating into their electronic communications policies.

5.9 EMPLOYER ACCESS TO WORKPLACE COMMUNICATIONS

The ability of an employer to gain access to and utilise the contents of employee electronic communications is now affected by up to three separate pieces of legislation. These are the Regulation of Investigatory Powers Act 2000, the Data Protection Act 1998 and the Human Rights Act 1998. Each of these came into force during the course of 2000.[26]   5–082

5.9.1 Regulation of Investigatory Powers Act 2000

The Regulation of Investigatory Powers Act introduced a new statutory regime, replacing the Interception of Communications Act 1985, governing the interception of telephone and electronic communications.   5–083

Sections 1(1) and 1(2) of the Act create criminal offences of intercepting communications on public and private telecommunications systems respectively. By s.1(6) of the Act interception on a private telecommunication system is excluded from criminal liability if it is carried out by a person with a right to control the operation or the use of the system, or by someone with the express or implied consent of such a person to make the interception.

However, such a person making such an interception may still be subject to civil liability under s.1(3). Under s.1(3) any interception of a communication in the UK by, or with the express or implied consent, of a person having the right to control the operation or use of a private telecommunication system is actionable if it is without lawful authority. The tort is actionable at the suit of the sender, recipient or intended recipient of the communication.

The Court of Appeal in *R v Stanford*[27] held that the person with the "right to control the operation or the use of the system" is a person who can authorise or forbid the use of the system by others. The mere right to use or operate the system, such as a system administrator equipped with broad privileges and the necessary passwords will have, is not sufficient to fall within s.1(6).

Further, there was no challenge to the ruling of the first instance judge

---

[26] The relevant part of the Regulation of Investigatory Powers Act 2000 came into force on October 24, 2000, the Human Rights Act 1998 (for England and Wales) on October 2, 2000 and the Data Protection Act 1998 on March 1, 2000. For a comprehensive and balanced discussion of employee privacy issues generally, see *Employee Privacy in the Workplace* (Incomes Data Services Employment Law Supplement) May 2001.

[27] C.A. (Crim Div) February 1, 2006.

that if the express or implied consent of a person with the right to control the system is to be relied upon, it must be consent to the specific interception, not a mere general authorisation to operate and run the system. The Court of Appeal rejected the argument that the civil remedies provided by the Act would suffice to protect privacy rights in the case of unauthorised interceptions by persons who had been granted administrator access: "The scheme of the legislation is that criminal sanctions should provide the primary protection against the interception of private communications."

5–084 "Private telecommunication system" is defined in s.2(1) as meaning:

> "any telecommunication system which, without itself being a public telecommunication system, is a system in relation to which the following conditions are satisfied—
>
> (a) it is attached, directly or indirectly and whether or not for the purposes of the communication in question, to a public telecommunication system; and
> (b) there is apparatus comprised in the system which is both located in the United Kingdom and used (with or without other apparatus) for making the attachment to the public telecommunication system."

"Public telecommunication system" means:

> "Any such parts of a telecommunication system by means of which any public telecommunications service is provided as are located in the United Kingdom."

"Public telecommunications service" means:

> "Any telecommunications service which is offered or provided to, or to a substantial section of, the public in any one or more parts of the United Kingdom."

"Telecommunications service" means:

> "Any service that consists in the provision of access to, and of facilities for making use of, any telecommunication system (whether or not one provided by the person providing the service)."

"Telecommunications system" means:

> "Any system (including the apparatus comprised within it) which exists (whether wholly or partly in the United Kingdom or elsewhere) for the purpose of facilitating the transmission of

communications by any means involving the use of electrical or electro-magnetic energy."

Since "private telecommunication system" includes only systems attached directly or indirectly to a public telecommunication system, any private network not so attached is excluded from the scope of the Act, since it is neither a private nor a public telecommunication system as defined. However, this is unlikely to exclude more than a small minority of physically isolated networks.

"Private telecommunication system" is likely to catch any private net-   5–085
work on which, for instance, it is possible to send or receive internet email, even by means of a dial-up connection. This will include most office networks. Since an employer will be a person with the right to control the operation or use of its own network, these provisions have clear potential to affect the ability of employers to read emails and other communications in their own systems.

The Explanatory Notes to the Act (para.27) state that "an office network, linked to a public telecommunication system by a private exchange, is to be treated as a private system. ... An entirely self-standing system, on the other hand, such as a secure office intranet, does not fall within the definition". The reference to a secure office intranet is puzzling. Most intranets, while located behind secure firewalls to prevent unauthorised access from the outside world, are nevertheless connected to the outside world and permit traffic to flow between the intranet and the public network beyond the firewall. According to the definition in the Act it would seem that a secure intranet would only fall outside the definition of "private telecommunication system" if it were completely physically isolated from the public network.

The distinction between "private" and "public" telecommunication systems was also commented on by the Home Office Minister during the House of Commons Committee debate. He stated:

> ". . . on the matter of public-private systems and domestic systems, I am advised, and we believe, that domestic systems are unequivocally private systems. The end of the public system is the network termination point, which is usually the white BT box just inside the front door of a house. Any extensions after that, whether to the PC or anything else, are part of the householder's private system."[28]

Unfortunately, while this explanation is certainly in accordance with   5–086
established telecommunications regulatory distinctions between public and private networks, it does not fully reflect the definition in the Act.

One of the determining factors under the Act is whether any public

---

[28] *Hansard* March 16, 2000, standing Committee F, House of Commons, Charles Clarke MP (Minister of State for the Home Office).

telecommunications service is provided by means of any part of the system. A telecommunications service includes provision of "access to" a telecommunications system. If offered or provided to a substantial section of the public it becomes a public telecommunications service.

So if someone in a household were to host a website or a collection of MP3 files on a domestic PC, or store webcam pictures, and make them available to the public through the domestic telephone line[29] that would appear on the face of it to constitute offering the public access to the system consisting of the domestic PC. If apparatus used for the provision of hosting services (as opposed to mere transmission) is to be regarded as apparatus for the purpose of "facilitating" the transmission of communications within the definition of "telecommunications system", that would render the parts of the domestic system used for that purpose a public telecommunications system for the purposes of the Act.

Interception in the course of transmission

5–087 To fall within the civil liability provisions of s.1(3) the interception must either be in the course of transmission by the private telecommunications system or by a public telecommunication system to or from the private system. These definitions have their genesis in the subject-matter of the old Interception of Communications Act 1985, which mainly concerned real-time tapping of communications such as telephone conversations.

The Court of Appeal in R v E[30] considered the meaning of "in the course of transmission". Police officers had secreted a recording device in the suspect's car, where the device picked up all conversation in the car including what the suspect said during mobile phone conversations. The device operated by picking up sound waves in the car. It was not attached to the mobile phone. It was argued that recording what was said into the mobile phone was an interception under RIPA. The Court of Appeal rejected this. Hughes J, giving the judgment of the court, said:

> "In our view, the natural meaning of the expression 'interception' denotes some interference or abstraction of the signal, whether it is passing along wires or by wireless telegraphy, during the process of transmission. The recording of a person's voice, independently of the fact that at the time he is using a telephone, does not become interception simply because what he says goes not only to the recorder, but, by separate process, is transmitted by a telecommunications system. ... The system begins at point A with the conversion of sound waves from the maker of the call into electrical or electromagnetic energy."

---

[29] This is an increasingly likely possibility with the advent of "always-on" telecommunication services to the home such as ADSL. Unlike traditional "dial-up" telephone services these provide a permanent connection from the home apparatus to the public telecommunication network.

[30] [2004] EWCA Crim 1243; followed in R v Allsopp [2005] EWCA Crim 703.

The Regulation of Investigatory Powers Act, somewhat ill-advisedly in the light of the anomalies thereby created, ventures beyond real-time interception into some aspects of storage.

The general definition of interception under s.2(2) is that:　　　　5–088

> "a person intercepts a communication in the course of its transmission by means of a telecommunication system if, and only if, he:
>
> (a) so modifies or interferes with the system, or its operation,
> (b) so monitors transmissions made by means of the system, or
> (c) so monitors transmissions made by wireless telegraphy to or from apparatus comprised in the system,
>
> so as to make some or all of the contents of the communication available, while being transmitted, to a person other than the sender or intended recipient of the communication."

Under s.2(6) references to the modification of a telecommunication system include references to the attachment of any apparatus to, or any other modification or interference with (a) any part of the system; or (b) any wireless telegraphy apparatus used for the making of transmissions to or from apparatus comprised in the system.

As regards storage, the times when a communication is being transmitted are extended by s.2(7) to include any time when the system is used for storing the communication in a manner that enables the intended recipient to collect it or otherwise have access to it.

So an incoming pending email stored in a mailbox would be covered. Curiously, to access a copy of an outgoing email stored in a mailbox appears unlikely to constitute interception, since as a separate archive copy it probably does not form part of the actual communication in the course of transmission. Nor is it covered by the s.1(7) extended meaning of "while being transmitted", which deals only with storage for access by intended recipients of communications.

A further issue that may require resolution by the courts is at what point in time (if at all) an incoming email ceases to be covered by the extended definition of s.2(7). For instance, once the intended recipient has accessed the email is it no longer within s.2(7)? Or does s.2(7) continue to bite until, for instance, the communication has been deleted from the mailbox?[31]

When is the purpose of an interception to be determined?

Under s.2(8) the cases in which any contents of a communication are to be　　5–089
taken to be made available to a person while being transmitted shall include

---

[31] Similar issues have arisen under US statutes. See G.Y. Porter, "Electronic Communication Tests Boundaries of Privacy Statutes", E.C.L.R. Vol.6 No.23, p.602; and "Voice Mail Message May Be 'Intercepted' Even If Already Heard by Intended Recipient", E.C.L.R. Vol.6 No.22, p.575.

any case in which any of the contents of the communication, while being transmitted, are diverted or recorded so as to be available to a person subsequently.

The Department of Trade and Industry, in its Response to Consultation[32] on the RIPA Lawful Business Practice Regulations, appears to suggest that the determining factor is the purpose for which the recording is made at the time it is made. So, the DTI suggests, if a consumer were to record a telephone call with a business for his own use, that would not amount to interception under the Act (presumably because the recording would not be "so as to be available to a person [other than the sender or intended recipient][33] subsequently").[34] But, says the DTI, nothing in the Act[35] would prevent the consumer from choosing subsequently to make use of the recording in, for instance, court proceedings.

Can the recipient be guilty of interception?

5-090 The DTI interpretation presupposes that the intended recipient of a communication can be liable for intercepting that communication, for instance by recording it so as to make it available to some other person.

This appears to be consistent with the wording of s.2(2), which places no obvious limitation on the class of person who may be found to have intercepted a communication. It differs, however, from Art.5 of the Telecommunications Data Protection Directive, which these provisions of the Act purport to implement.

Article 5 requires Member States to prohibit interception or surveillance of communications "by others than users", without the consent of the users concerned. The Directive, therefore, places no obligation on Member States to prohibit interception by a user in any circumstances. Unlike the Act, it draws no distinction based on the purpose for which the user intercepts the communication. The Directive is discussed further below.

Following the Court of Appeal decisions in *R v Hardy and Hardy*[36] and *R v E*,[37] it appears very doubtful that a recipient can be guilty of interception. However, the precise basis of the Court of Appeal's reasoning is unclear, and the point may require further consideration.

In *Hardy* undercover police officers tape recorded telephone calls that they had with one of the defendants. The Court of Appeal said:

---

[32] The Response was originally at *www.dti.gov.uk/cii/regulatory/telecomms/telecomms regulations/lawful_business_practice_response.shtm*. This document is no longer available on the DTI website. A DTI summary of the consultation procedure at *www.dti.gov.uk/files/ file31194.doc* contains the same statement.

[33] The words in square brackets derive from the main definition of interception in s.2(2).

[34] This interpretation presupposes that the tape recorder is attached in some way to the telephone. If the tape recorder is only recording sound waves (e.g. by being held close to the telephone earpiece) then there is no interception (*R v E*, considered in para.5-087 above).

[35] If personal data were involved, then subsequent use for a different purpose might be constrained under the Data Protection Act 1998.

[36] [2002] EWCA Crim 3012.

[37] Para.5-087 above.

"For present purposes the important words are 'while being transmitted'. What happened here was that one party to the telephone calls (the undercover officer) taped the calls. The contents of the calls were not made available whilst being transmitted to any third party. This is not a case of telephone tapping. It is exactly the same as the undercover officer secreting a tape recorder in his pocket or briefcase whilst meeting the suspect face-to-face, something which he also did in this case. It is surveillance and it requires regulation. The Act provides for it but it is not interception. . . . We regard that conclusion as the clearest possible result of the words of the statute."

Unfortunately that conclusion took no account of s.2(8), which extends the meaning of "while being transmitted" to include "any case in which any of the contents of the transmission, while being transmitted, are diverted or recorded so as to be available to a person subsequently". If the calls were recorded while being transmitted, that satisfies the section.

Even more unfortunately, the exact nature of the taping was not spelt out in the judgment. It is unclear whether the tape recorder was picking up sound waves or was connected to the telephone. If the former, then on the later authority of *R v E*[38] there was no interception and *Hardy* can be explained on that basis. If the latter, then the Court of Appeal seem to have been suggesting a broader proposition that a recipient can never be regarded as carrying out an interception by recording his own call.

The Court of Appeal in *R v E* approved the decision in *Hardy*, making   5–091
clear that in *Hardy* their main conclusion was that there was no interception; but that if there had been an interception it would have been lawful under s.3(2) (consent of one party plus official authorisation under Pt II of the Act). The comments in *R v E*, referring as they do to participant monitoring generally, suggest that the *Hardy* is authority for the broader proposition set out above.

The Court of Appeal in *Hardy* went on to say:

"If the submission made on behalf of the Defendants were correct, it would be an offence for any householder to put a tape recorder on his own private telephone. We are quite satisfied that Parliament intended to make no such provision and has made no such provision."

Whatever Parliament's intentions may have been, this passage is plainly wrong in its suggestion that the householder could be exposed to criminal liability. A householder could not be guilty of an offence in these circumstances. He or she would at most be liable to civil proceedings, since the householder's telephone is not part of the public network. If the householder's telephone were regarded as part of a private network, then the

---

[38] [2004] EWCA Crim 1243.

interception would have been undertaken by the person with the right to control the operation or use of the system and therefore be excluded from criminal liability by virtue of s.1(6). The comments of the court are also at odds with the interpretation apparently adopted by the Department of Trade and Industry (see para.5–089 above).

While it may be possible to criticise the route by which the Court of Appeal arrived at its conclusion in *Hardy*, it should be remembered that the House of Lords in *Attorney General's Reference (No 5 of 2002) sub nom, R v W*[39] described RIPA as "longer and even more perplexing" than its predecessor the Interception of Communications Act 1985, which the House of Lords had previously described as "short but difficult".

In any event the Court of Appeal's conclusion in *Hardy* does have the merit of according with commonsense in its application to private email systems. If the intended recipient of a communication is indeed among those who may be regarded as intercepting the communication, the consequences for users of voicemail and email verge on the bizarre and are certainly arbitrary.

5–092   Even if the recipient can be guilty of intercepting, it would presumably not constitute an interception for the recipient of an email to forward it to a colleague after reading it, either because the user having collected the email it is no longer caught by s.2(7),[40] or because no modification or interference with the system, or monitoring of transmissions, is involved.

Section 2(8) extends the cases in which a communication is taken to be made available to a person while being transmitted to include any case in which any of the contents of the communication, while being transmitted, are diverted or recorded so as to be available to a person subsequently. This could read well onto forwarding copies of emails to a colleague. However, it does not override the time requirement of s.2(7), nor on the face of it detract from the requirement that there be a modification or interference with the system, or monitoring of transmissions made by the system, "so as" to have the consequences described. "Monitor" is not defined in the Act. While its meaning is well understood for real-time communications such as telephone calls, it is inapt to describe activities such as forwarding an email, or even gaining access to an email box of stored communications.

However, what is the position if the user programs his email system automatically to forward incoming emails from a particular sender to the same colleague? The extended s.2(7) time limit does not fall away until, at the earliest (if at all) the intended recipient has collected his emails. The programming of the email facility could, more plausibly than the manual forwarding in the first example, be regarded as a modification or interference with the system or its operation. Alternatively, the colleague to

---

[39] [2004] UKHL 40.
[40] However, it is not at all clear whether s.2(7) does cease to have effect when the user has collected the email. It could readily be construed to have effect until such time as the user has deleted the message from the system.

whom the emails are forwarded could more plausibly be regarded as "monitoring" transmissions made by means of the system, even if he took no part in the decision or the steps necessary to forward the emails to himself.

Lastly, what if the user, instead of setting up an auto-forward system, configures his email software so as to grant access privileges to his colleague, or provides his colleague with a password to gain access? Again, could this be regarded as a modification or interference with the system or its operation? And would the colleague granted access privileges be regarded as monitoring?

If these examples, or any of them, do constitute interception under the Act and do apply to recipient users, then the Act has consequences that were certainly not alluded to by its government promoters. The Act would, for no discernible policy reason, restrict the ordinary, everyday use of email by users themselves.   5–093

If, on the other hand, at least the second and third examples (auto-forward and granting access privileges) do not constitute interception under the Act (whether done by users or third parties), then the Act would be unlikely to achieve its presumed intent. Since the system operator has complete control over system privileges and configuration, it would be a simple matter to set up auto-forwards, or to grant widespread email access privileges.

Even if some distinction could validly be made between acts of the intended recipient and of the network operator,[41] so that only when carried out by the user do the acts not amount to interception, it would still be a relatively simple matter[42] for the network operator to require any user of the system to permit other system users to have access privileges to their email box, if necessary constituting the employer the agent of the user for the purpose of configuring the system on behalf of the user to achieve that.

If such steps are effective, the practical impact of the Act on email and other self-storing, non-real-time, communications would become minimal and the RIPA Lawful Business Practice Regulations would be largely superfluous.

Ephemeral versus self-recording communications

Generally, the very concept of "interception" has implications that differ significantly as between ephemeral real-time communications such as telephone calls on the one hand, and self-recording communications such as email or voicemail on the other.   5–094

In the case of telephone calls, the act of interception creates a record where none would have existed but for the interception. To the extent that any party to the telephone call has a legitimate expectation of privacy in relation to it, the covert creation of a record of the call would raise

---

[41] For instance, by reading the words "other than the sender or intended recipient of the communication" into s.2(2) after the word "person" in the second line.

[42] At least it is simple with new users. The position with existing users may be more difficult.

understandable concerns as to whether that expectation had been respected.[43] The potential for privacy rights to be engaged by the creation of a permanent record of personal data where there is no expectation of that occurring has been recognised by the European Court of Human Rights, which has distinguished on that basis between non-recording CCTV monitoring and the making of a covert video recording.[44]

In the case of email and voicemail, however, the very sending of the communication creates a record of it. The position is far more akin to a person who sends a letter, and thereby places a record of the communication in the hands of the recipient organisation. The act of "interception" in this case bites not on the creation of a record where none would otherwise have existed, but on gaining access to or creating further copies of a record that has already been placed in the hands of the recipient organisation by the sender. Any legitimate expectation of privacy in this case is likely to be far weaker than in the case of recording a telephone call. This distinction has been recognised in some US cases on the interception of email.[45]

Much of the difficulty encountered in this area, not least the public controversy during the Department of Trade and Industry consultation on the RIPA Lawful Business Practice Regulations, can be traced back to the legislature treating these two different things (ephemeral and self-recording communications) as one and the same and attempting to create a single set of rules to fit both.

Who is a recipient?

5–095   Another example of this kind of difficulty stems from the fact that the Act does not define "sender", "recipient" or "intended recipient". In the case of a telephone call, it makes reasonable sense to assume that under the Act the recipient or intended recipient of the communication is the individual person who participates in the call, and not any organisation by whom that person is employed, or to whom the telephone apparatus belongs.

But if "recipient" or "intended recipient" under the Act always refers to an individual recipient, that creates severe difficulties in the case of email since there are common cases in which no intended individual recipient is

---

[43] In the case of telephone calls privacy concerns were long recognised by the restrictions on recording telephone calls contained in the Privacy of Messages condition in the Telecommunications Services Class Licence and the Self-Provision Class Licence issued under the Telecommunications Act 1984. The specific restrictions were removed from both Licences on April 9, 2001 following the implementation of the Regulation of Investigatory Powers Act 2000 and the Lawful Business Practice Regulations made under it. Each Licence contained a general obligation on the Licensee to take all reasonable steps to safeguard the privacy and confidentiality of any Message conveyed for a consideration by means of Applicable Systems and of any information acquired by the Licensee in relation to such conveyance.

[44] *Perry v UK*, ECtHR July 17, 2003, para.38.

[45] *Washington v Townsend*, Washington Court of Appeals, April 5, 2001 (World Internet Law Report, May 2001, p.22; E.C.L.R. Vol.6 No.16 p.416); *State of New Hampshire v Lott*, N.H., No. 2004–380, July 15, 2005 (E.C.L.R. Vol.10, No.31 p.794).

identifiable. By analogy with the post the sender (whose intent can be the only relevant intent for the purpose of ascertaining the "intended recipient") often intends to place the communication in the hands of the recipient organisation, even if it be marked for the attention of an individual within the organisation.

And what of the common case where someone sends an email to "info@companyname.com", or "support@companyname.com"? That will be routed to some email box or email management system within the organisation, to which one or more individuals within the organisation will have access. But no individual intended recipient of the email is identifiable.[46]

If the Act does not admit the concept of an organisational intended recipient, what is the status of such an email? Since an integral part of the definition of "interception" under s.2(2) is that there be an intended recipient, if no individual intended recipient can be identified does the email fall outside the scope of these provisions altogether? Or could the intended recipient(s) be regarded not as the organisation, but as all individuals within the organisation?

If the sender of the email receives a reply from an individual within the organisation, and sends a further email to that individual (either to "namedindividual@companyname.com", or still to "info@company name.com" but addressed to the individual within the body of the email), does the further email fall within the Act because there is now an identifiable intended recipient?

If, on the other hand, the Act does admit the concept of a recipient   5–096 organisation, then much of the protection against interception afforded by s.1(3) of the Act may fall away. That is because, as discussed above, it is easy to argue that the true intended recipient of most electronic communications sent to a business organisation (even those addressed to an individual mailbox) is in fact, as with business post, the organisation and not an individual within it. If that is so, then an organisation would fall foul of the interception provisions only if the interception were such as to make the communication available to someone outside the organisation.

The Information Commissioner has taken the view that some communications are addressed to the business and that to monitor them will not involve an interception:

> "Bear in mind that in many cases, for example customer enquiries, the intended recipient of a communication will be the business itself rather than a specific individual. Monitoring of such incoming communications by the business will not involve an

---

[46] It could be argued that the recipients are those individuals who have access to the relevant email box. However, s.2(2), defining "interception", requires that the content be made available to "a person other than the sender or intended recipient". The only relevant intent can be that of the sender. In the scenario under discussion the sender has no intent to send the email to any specific individual, so even if it were possible to identify individual recipients it is difficult to see how any of them could be "intended" recipients.

interception. There are, though, likely to be incoming communications, including but not limited to private ones, where the intended recipient is a specific individual. Monitoring that extends to the content of these before they have been opened by the intended recipient is likely to involve an interception."[47]

Article 5 of the Telecommunications Data Protection Directive

5–097   Since these provisions of RIPA purported to implement Art.5 of the then EU Telecommunications Data Protection Directive,[48] some clue as to the intent of the legislature may, perhaps, be gleaned from the Directive. However, Art.5 of the Directive arguably did not actually require any legislation to be implemented for communications on private networks.[49] Even if that is wrong, the Act clearly applies to a broader category of communications than those that fell within the scope of Art.5 of the Directive.

Article 5(1) of the Telecommunications Data Protection Directive, which had to be implemented by Member States by October 24, 2000, required Member States to:

> "1. ... ensure via national regulations the confidentiality of communications by means of a public telecommunications network and publicly available telecommunications services. In particular they shall prohibit listening, tapping, storage or other kinds of interception or surveillance of communications, by others than users, without the consent of the users concerned, except when legally authorised, in accordance with Article 14(1)."

Article 5(2) provided:

> "2. Paragraph 1 shall not affect any legally authorised recording of communications in the course of lawful business practice for the purpose of providing evidence of a commercial transaction or of any other business communication."

5–098   "User" was defined in Art.2 as:

---

[47] Section 3.2.2 of the Supplementary Guidance issued with the Employment Practices Code (*www.ico.gov.uk/upload/documents/library/data_protection/detailed_specialist_guides/ employment_practice_code_-_supplementary_guidance.pdf*).

[48] Directive 97/66 [1997] O.J. L24/1 concerning the processing of personal data and the protection of privacy in the telecommunications sector.

[49] The Dutch implementation of the Directive adopted the interpretation that it does not apply to communications on private networks. The Directive has since been replaced by the Directive on Privacy and Electronic Communications (2002/58/EC), which retains the emphasis on public telecommunications services and networks. It applies to "the processing of personal data in connection with the provision of publicly available electronic communications services in public communications networks in the Community" (Art.3).

"Any natural person using a publicly available telecommunications service, for private or business purposes, without necessarily having subscribed to this service."[50]

The first sentence of Art.5(1) of the Directive is a general obligation, making no reference to users. The second sentence, however, is clearly concerned with natural, not legal, persons. To the extent that the Act is to be regarded as implementing the Directive, this may suggest that "sender", "recipient" and "intended recipient" are intended to refer to natural persons.

The Department of Trade and Industry took the view that Art.5 of the Directive applied to any communications on a private telecommunication system that travel on a public telecommunication system before or after travelling on the private system.[51] The government also justified these provisions of the Act by reference to the Directive during the passage of the Bill through Parliament.[52]

This interpretation is not obvious from the terms of Art.5(1), which refer explicitly to public telecommunications networks and publicly available telecommunications services. It may be argued that the DTI interpretation is implicit in Art.5(2), since there could be no circumstances in which the activities described in Art.5(2) could be legitimately be exercised in relation to communications while on a public telecommunications network or while being conveyed by means of a publicly available telecommunications service.

However, this does not stand up to scrutiny. For instance, a financial **5–099** services company might wish to record telephone calls for compliance purposes. If it were to do that on its own network, on the private side of the public network termination point, then Art.5(1) would not apply. If it decided, instead, to employ the public network operator to record its calls at the public exchange, as part of a managed service provided by the public network operator, then without Art.5(2) that would be a breach of the prohibition in Art.5(1).

Thus Art.5(2) has a perfectly sensible purpose without the need to extend the ambit of Art.5(1) beyond its apparent scope so as to include communications on private networks. It is, therefore, open to serious question whether there was ever any obligation to enact s.1(3) at all in order to give effect to the Directive.

It may also be noted that, in its implementation, s.1(3) is not restricted to communications on a private telecommunications system that have also

---

[50] These definitions are repeated, extended to include traffic data and otherwise with minor amendments, in the Directive on Privacy and Electronic Communications.

[51] See e.g. para.6 of the DTI Public Consultation Exercise (August 1–25, 2000) on the draft Lawful Business Practice Regulations: "The requirement also extends to communications on private networks (e.g. office telephone networks or email systems) which will also travel or have also travelled on a public network."

[52] See e.g. *Hansard* March 16, 2000, Standing Committee F, House of Commons, Charles Clarke MP (Minister of State for the Home Office).

travelled or will travel on a public telecommunications system. It applies to all communications on a private telecommunications system. So even on the DTI's own interpretation of the Directive s.1(3) applies to a broader class of communications than would have been required by the Directive.

5–100 A further difference between the Directive and the Act is that Art.5 did not, on its face, require Member States to secure the confidentiality of stored communications. If on its true interpretation the obligation did extend to stored communications,[53] Art.5 made no distinction (unlike the Act) between stored copies of outgoing communications and stored incoming communications.

The significance of this comparison with the Directive is twofold. First, the degree to which the Act actually implemented the Directive may be relevant to any attempt to construe provisions of the Act by reference to the Directive.[54] Second, when we come to discuss the Lawful Business Practice Regulations we will see that the Regulations include a saving on the authority conferred by the Regulations by reference originally to the Directive and now to its successor, the Directive on Privacy and Electronic Communications. But since the original Directive and its successor may in truth be partially or wholly irrelevant to s.1(3), the references to these Directives in the Regulations may be of little or no significance.

5–101 Finally, it should be noted that there was no need to seek to extend the scope of Art.5 to communications on private networks, since such communications are covered by the Data Protection Directive. This was reflected in Recital (11) of the Telecommunications Data Protection Directive, which stated:

> "for all matters concerning protection of fundamental rights and freedoms, which are not specifically covered by this Directive, including the obligations on the controller and the rights of individuals, Directive 95/46/EC [the Data Protection Directive] applies; whereas Directive 95/46/EC applies to non-publicly available telecommunications services;"

Recital (10) of the Directive on Privacy and Electronic Communications is in similar terms:

> "In the electronic communications sector, Directive 95/46/EC applies in particular to all matters concerning protection of fundamental rights and freedoms, which are not specifically covered by the provisions of this Directive, including the obligations on the controller and the rights of individuals. Directive 95/46/EC applies to non-public communications services."

---

[53] There were general statements in, for instance, Arts. 1 and 3 of the Directive stating that the Directive was concerned with the "processing of personal data", an expression that is apt to cover storage. However, Art.5 did not include this wording and indeed, notwithstanding the general words referred to, was not limited to personal data.

[54] Consistency with the Directive was an issue in *R v E* (above, para.5–091).

Lawful authority

Interception is not actionable under s.1(3) of the Act if it has lawful   5–102
authority. Interception has lawful authority (so far as likely to be relevant
for the purposes of this discussion) in three situations.[55] First, under s.3(1)
of the Act it is authorised if the interception has, or the person intercepting
has reasonable grounds for believing it has, the consent of both the sender
and the intended recipient of the communication.

The usefulness of this exception differs significantly depending on the
nature of the communication. For a real-time communication that requires
the active participation of all concerned to initiate the connection (e.g. a
telephone call), it is at least feasible to obtain the prior consent of all
concerned to record the call. However, that is not the case for communications (such as email and, to a lesser extent, voicemail) which are sent
unilaterally to publicly available addresses and stored until such time as the
recipient decides to access his mailbox. In the case of internet email, at least,
it is (questions of implied consent apart) literally impossible to comply with
a requirement of prior consent.

Second, interception has lawful authority under s.3(3) of the Act if it is
conduct by or on behalf of a person who provides a telecommunications
service and it takes place for purposes connected with the provision or
operation of that service or with the enforcement, in relation to that service,
of any enactment relating to the use of telecommunications services. Since
this section applies to all telecommunications services, not just public telecommunication services, operators of private telecommunications systems
ought to be able to take advantage of it.

Third, interception has lawful authority if it is authorised by regulations
made by the Secretary of State under s.4(2). The Secretary of State may
make regulations authorising conduct that appears to him to be a legitimate
practice reasonably required for the purpose, in connection with the carrying on of any business, of monitoring or keeping a record of (a)
communications by means of which transactions are entered into in the
course of that business; or (b) other communications relating to that
business or taking place in the course of its being carried on.

5.9.2 The RIPA Lawful Business Practice Regulations

The Telecommunications (Lawful Business Practice) (Interception of   5–103
Communications) Regulations made under ss.4(2) and 78(5) of the Act
came into force at the same time as s.1(3) of the Act, on October 24, 2000.
Some assistance in understanding the intent of the Regulations may be
gained from the Notes for Business published by the Department of Trade
and Industry as Annex C to the Response to Consultation, which also

---

[55] For an example of other circumstances in which lawful authority may arise, see *R v Ipswich
Crown Court* Ex p, *NTL Group Ltd* [2002] EWHC 1585 (Admin).

included the final version of the Regulations. The final version of the Regulations differed significantly from the draft Regulations on which the DTI consulted in August 2000. The Response to Consultation made clear that there was a distinct policy change between the draft and final Regulations.

Paragraph 3(1) of the Regulations sets out various categories of conduct that are authorised for the purposes of s.1(5)(a) of the Act. That section provides that conduct is authorised for the purposes of s.1 if (*inter alia*) it is authorised under s.4 of the Act. It also provides that authorised conduct shall be taken to be lawful for all other purposes.

General preconditions to lawful interception

5–104 Paragraph 3(2) of the Regulations sets out certain general preconditions that must be satisfied before any of the categories of conduct under para.3(1) are authorised. The first of these is under para.3(2)(a), that "the interception in question is effected solely for the purpose of monitoring or (where appropriate) keeping a record of communications relevant to the system controller's business".

"Business", "system controller" and "relevant to the system controller's business" are defined in para.2 of the Regulations.

References to a business "include references to activities of a government department, of any public authority or of any person or office holder on whom functions are conferred by or under any enactment".

"System controller" "means, in relation to a particular telecommunication system, a person with the right to control its operation or use".

A reference to a communication as "relevant to a business" is a reference to:

> "(i) a communication—
>
>> (aa) by means of which a transaction is entered into in the course of that business, or
>> (bb) which otherwise relates to that business, or
>
> (ii) a communication which otherwise takes place in the course of the carrying on of that business."

The restriction of the authorisation to monitoring or (where appropriate) keeping a record of communications relevant to the system controller's business derives from the restrictions on the power to make Regulations contained in s.4(2) of the Act itself.

5–105 The second general precondition, under para.3(2)(b) of the Regulations, is that the telecommunication system in question is provided wholly or partly in connection with the system controller's business. This reflects a restriction on the power to make Regulations contained in s.4(3) of the Act.

The third general precondition is that "the system controller has made all reasonable efforts to inform every person who may use the telecommunication system in question that communications transmitted by means thereof may be intercepted".

This is a potentially far-reaching provision. It suggests that if it can be demonstrated that the system controller has failed to make all reasonable efforts to inform one user of the system, or one small category of users of the system, then the system controller's conduct is unauthorised in respect of all users, even those whom the system controller did inform. So it will be important for the system controller to be able to demonstrate, if called upon to do so, its procedures for discharging this obligation, and that such procedures cover all classes of users.

Users of the system extend wider than merely employees. They will include contract staff, secondees, temporary staff, extranet users (which could include customers and suppliers) and so on.

The Regulations do not define "use" of the system. On a broad inter-   5–106 pretation it might be thought that third parties who telephone or email in to the system, or leave a voicemail, are using the system.

The DTI Notes for Business take a narrower view:

> "The persons who use a system are the people who make direct use of it. Someone who calls from outside, or who receives a call outside, using another system is not a user of the system on which the interception is made."

It is to be hoped that the courts adopt this sensible interpretation, which reflects the policy change between the draft and final Regulations noted at para.30 of the Response to Consultation.

If they do not, then what is required to satisfy the "reasonable efforts" test in relation to external users will be judged in the light of what is practicable. This could require warnings to be incorporated in outgoing emails and proximate to website feedback facilities. If (as will often be the case) it is not possible to issue a warning to the external sender of an incoming email before the email is received, then it is difficult to see what "reasonable efforts" could be required of the system controller, at least in the case of interception that takes place upon receipt.

As to the time period over which the system controller needs to inform users of the system that interception may take place, clearly the precondition needs to have been satisfied prior to the particular interception whose legality is under scrutiny. Even though the Regulations contain no provision suggesting that a warning, once given, can expire, it would nonetheless be prudent to repeat it. Also, it could be argued that if a new network or email system is installed, or sufficiently major changes made to an existing one, then previous warnings are ineffective since they no longer relate to "the telecommunication system in question".

The Regulations do not state that the information to users should specify any particular kinds of interception that may take place. However, as we have seen "interception" within the meaning of the Act is a concept much broader than the ordinary understanding of the word. So if the information is to be capable of being understood by users, it may need to identify the telecommunication systems in question, illustrate the types of communications involved and explain what is meant by "interception". Also, the information will need to be prepared with the provisions of the Data Protection Act 1998 and any relevant Codes of Practice made under it[56] in mind. These may necessitate more detailed descriptions of the circumstances in which interception may take place.

Authorised categories of conduct

5–107   Subject to satisfying the three general preconditions (and any specific preconditions noted below), the categories of conduct authorised under para.3(1) of the Regulations are[57]:

> (1) interception effected by or with the express or implied consent of the system controller for the purpose of monitoring or keeping a record of communications in order to establish the existence of facts (para.3(1)(a)(i)(aa))
>
> (2) interception effected by or with the express or implied consent of the system controller for the purpose of monitoring or keeping a record of communications in order to ascertain compliance with regulatory or self-regulatory practices or procedures which are applicable to the system controller in the carrying on of his business or applicable to another person in the carrying on of his business where that business is supervised by the system controller in respect of those practices or procedures (para.3(1)(a)(i)(bb))
>
> "Regulatory or self-regulatory practices or procedures" means "practices or procedures:
>
>> (i) compliance with which is required or recommended by, under or by virtue of—
>>
>>> (aa) any provision of the law of a member state or other state within the European Economic Area, or
>>>
>>> (bb) any standard or code of practice published by or on behalf of a body established in a Member State or other state within the European Economic Area which includes among its objectives the publication of standards or codes of practices for the conduct of business, or
>>
>> (ii) which are otherwise applied for the purpose of ensuring

---

[56] The Information Commissioner's Employment Practices Code and related Supplementary Guidance contains a section on monitoring of staff, including electronic communications. The Code is discussed below (para.5–112).

[57] At the cost of some repetition, we have set out each category of authorised conduct *in extenso*. Some of the categories require consideration of double or treble purposes, which can more easily be understood by setting out the full text of each category of authorised conduct.

compliance with anything so required or recommended" (para.2(c))

(3) interception effected by or with the express or implied consent of the system controller for the purpose of monitoring or keeping a record of communications in order to ascertain or demonstrate the standards which are achieved or ought to be achieved by persons using the system in the course of their duties (para.3(1)(a)(i)(cc))

Conduct falling within items (1) to (3) above is authorised only to the extent that Art.5 of the Privacy and Electronic Communications Directive so permits (para.3(3)).[58]

We have discussed above the extent, if any, to which Art.5 of the   5–108
Directive and its predecessor the Telecommunications Data Protection Directive applies to communications on private networks.

(4) interception effected by or with the express or implied consent of the system controller for the purpose of monitoring or keeping a record of communications in the interests of national security, so long as the person by or on whose behalf whom the interception is effected is a person specified in s.6(2)(a) to (i) of the Act (para 3(1)(a)(ii) and 3(2)(d)(i))

The persons so specified include the Director-General of the Security Service, the Chief of the Secret Intelligence Service, the Director of GCHQ, the Director General of the National Criminal Intelligence Service, the Commissioner of Police of the Metropolis, the Commissioners of Customs and Excise and the Chief of Defence Intelligence.

(5) interception effected by or with the express or implied consent of the system controller for the purpose of monitoring or keeping a record of communications for the purpose of preventing or detecting crime (para.3(1)(a)(iii))

(6) interception effected by or with the express or implied consent of the system controller for the purpose of monitoring or keeping a record of communications for the purpose of investigating or detecting the unauthorised use of the system controller's or any other telecommunication system (para.3(1)(a)(iv))

(7) interception effected by or with the express or implied consent of the system controller for the purpose of monitoring or keeping a record of communications where that is undertaken in order to secure or as an inherent part of the effective operation of the system (including any monitoring or keeping of a record which

---

[58] The Regulations were amended on December 11, 2003 to substitute the original reference to the Telecommunications Data Protection Directive with a reference to its successor, the Privacy and Electronic Communications Directive (2002/58/EC).

would be authorised by s.3(3) of the Act if the conditions in para (a) and (b) thereof were satisfied) (para.3(1)(a)(v))

(8) interception effected by or with the express or implied consent of the system controller for the purpose of monitoring communications for the purpose of determining whether they are communications relevant to the system controller's business which fall within reg.2(b)(i)

5–109 A relevant communication within reg.2(b)(i) would be one by means of which a transaction is entered into in the course of that business, or which otherwise relates to that business, but not (due to the exclusion of reg.2(b)(ii)) a communication which otherwise takes place in the course of the carrying on of that business.

For conduct to be authorised under this provision the communication must be one which is intended to be received (whether or not it has been actually received) by a person using the telecommunication system in question (para.3(2)(d)(ii)).

The provision is thought to be aimed at the difficulties that could otherwise be encountered by an employer who wished to access an employee's email box, perhaps during the employee's absence from the office, to check for business correspondence. This is the example give by the DTI in their Notes for Business. The use of the word "monitoring" to describe such activity is inapt. However, that derives from the equally inapt use of the same wording in the enabling provision of the Act. "Monitoring" is undefined in both the Act and the Regulations.

The provision is limited to interception for the purpose of monitoring, and not for the purpose of keeping a record. Does it prevent an employer who accesses an employee's email box and reads a business communication for the permitted purpose, from creating a new record by printing it out or forwarding it to another email box?

This arguably involves two acts of interception in the course of transmission: the accessing of the email box (an interception under the ordinary definition of interception in the course of transmission in s.2(2) of the Act as extended to stored communications by s.2(7)); and the forwarding or printing (which arguably constitutes interception under the extended definition of s.2(8), which includes any case in which any of the contents of the communication are diverted or recorded so as to be available to a person subsequently).

It could perhaps be argued that printing out the email did not constitute recording it under s.2(8). It is difficult to see how forwarding it would not constitute "diverting" it, unless in order to constitute diversion the diverted communication must be prevented by the diversion from reaching the intended recipient.

As to whether forwarding constitutes "recording", that could depend on whether the technology used caused a new copy of the email to be made, or simply resulted in another person gaining access to an existing copy in a central email database. The Act contains no definition of "diverted" or "recorded". Nor do the Explanatory Notes to the Act make any comment on s.2(8).

So long as the purpose for which the interception is carried out is permitted by the Regulations, then conduct consisting of the interception is authorised and there is no actionable interception under the Act (since it is not without lawful authority). So it could be argued that so long as the purpose remains a permitted purpose throughout the two acts of interception involved in accessing an email box and printing out or forwarding the email, all the conduct is authorised.

5–110

On the other hand, it could powerfully be argued that once the employer has accessed the email box and read the business email, then at that point he will have ascertained whether the email relates to the business or not. Having done so, any further act of interception involved in forwarding or printing the email cannot be for that purpose and can only be for the purpose of keeping a record, which is specifically excluded from the permitted purposes for which conduct is authorised under this paragraph.

A result that would prevent the employer from printing or forwarding an email which, by definition, relates to his business would be absurd. It may be that having justified the initial access under this paragraph, the making of a record could then be justified under one of the other provisions of the Regulations.

(9) interception effected by or with the express or implied consent of the system controller for the purpose of monitoring communications made to a confidential voice-telephony counselling or support service which is free of charge (other than the cost, if any, of making a telephone call) and operated in such a way that users may remain anonymous if they so choose (para.3(1)(c)).

5.9.3 The Data Protection Act 1998

For a full discussion of the Data Protection Act the reader is referred to Ch.7. Here, it is sufficient to note that even if the interception is lawful under RIPA, the use that can be made of personal data to which the system controller gains access is constrained by the Data Protection Act. In particular, the First Data Protection Principle requires that personal data shall be processed fairly and lawfully. Although compliance with the RIPA Lawful Business Practice Regulations can ensure that personal data is accessed lawfully, it does not guarantee that the data has been processed fairly.

5–111

On May 29, 2002 the Data Protection Working Party established under Art.29 of the Data Protection Directive adopted a working document on the surveillance of electronic communications in the workplace.[59] This document places heavy emphasis on employee rights of privacy, yet fails to

---

[59] 5401/01/EN/Final WP 55.

explain adequately when and how such rights may arise. Nor does it deal more than cursorily with arguments that expectations of privacy may be displaced by the employer (see below, para.5–119).

The Information Commissioner's Employment Practices Code—Part 3 (Monitoring at Work)

5–112   In October 2000 the Data Protection Commissioner (now the Information Commissioner) issued for consultation a draft Code of Practice under s.51(3)(b) of the Data Protection Act 1998 on the Use of Personal Data in Employer/Employee Relationships. After intense debate and several revisions Pt 3 "Monitoring at Work" of the Employment Practices Data Code was issued in June 2003. The Code was then rewritten as the Employment Practices Code with related Supplementary Guidance and re-issued on June 14, 2005.

The theme of Pt 3 of the Code is that while monitoring is a recognised component of the employment relationship, where monitoring goes beyond one individual simply watching another and involves the manual recording or any automated processing of personal information, it must be done in a way that is both lawful and fair to workers.

The Code emphasises that monitoring may have an adverse impact on workers. It may intrude into their private lives, undermine respect for their correspondence or interfere with the relationship of mutual trust and confidence that should exist between them and their employer. Broadly, the Act requires that any adverse impact on workers is justified by the benefits to the employer and others. The Code is designed to help employers determine when this might be the case.[60] It generally recommends the use of formal or informal[61] impact assessments to achieve this.[62]

Impact assessments involve a five step process of identifying the purpose and benefits of the monitoring arrangements, identifying any likely adverse impact, considering alternatives, taking into account any obligations that arise from monitoring and judging whether monitoring is justified.[63] Employers who can justify monitoring on the basis of an impact assessment will not generally need the consent of individual workers.[64]

5–113   The Code applies to both systematic monitoring done as a matter of routine and occasional monitoring put in place to address a particular problem or need.[65] The Code states that is not concerned with business records that are not collected primarily to keep a watch on their performance or conduct. Examples given include records of customer transactions, including paper records, computer records or recordings of

---

[60] Employment Practices Code, p.54.
[61] The Code suggests that it will often be enough for this to be done mentally, but in some cases it would be advisable to document the impact assessment (Employment Practices Code, p.59).
[62] Employment Practices Code, p.56.
[63] Employment Practices Code, p.57.
[64] Employment Practices Code, p.59.
[65] Employment Practices Code, p.55.

telephone calls. The Code emphasises that it is not concerned with occasional access to records of this type in the course of an investigation into a specific problem, such as a complaint from a customer; or checking a collection of emails sent by a particular worker which is stored as a record of transactions, in order to ensure the security of the system or to investigate an allegation of malpractice.[66]

It might be thought that this would exclude matters such as accessing employees' email boxes in their absence, since such emails are part of the ordinary business records of the company, not collected primarily to keep watch on performance or conduct. But no. The Code includes detailed recommendations on checking email accounts of employees in their absence (presumably because email boxes typically contain a mixture of email subject matter).[67] So the professed exclusion from the Code should not be read too literally. In any event, the fact that something is outside the Code does not mean that it is outwith the scope of the Act.

The Code gives examples of monitoring to which the Code applies. Some of those relevant to electronic communications include:

- Randomly opening up individual workers' emails or listening to their voicemails to look for evidence of malpractice
- Using automated checking software to collect information about workers, for example to find out whether particular workers are sending or receiving inappropriate emails
- Examining logs of websites visited to check that individual workers are not downloading pornography.[68]

The Code sets out a set of Core Principles that underlie its Good Practice Recommendations in respect of monitoring generally. These are:

- It will usually be intrusive to monitor workers.
- Workers have legitimate expectations that they can keep their personal lives private and that they are also entitled to a degree of privacy in the work environment.
- If employers wish to monitor their workers, they should be clear about the purpose and satisfied that the particular monitoring arrangement is justified by real benefits that will be delivered.
- Workers should be aware of the nature, extent and reasons for any monitoring, unless (exceptionally) covert monitoring is justified.
- In any event, workers' awareness will influence their expectations.

The second and fifth principles in this list touch on the extremely contentious area of the extent to which employees by default have a reasonable expectation of privacy in the workplace, and the extent to which an **5–114**

---

[66] Employment Practices Code, p.56.
[67] Employment Practices Code, p.67.
[68] Employment Practices Code, p.55.

employer can displace any expectation of privacy by publishing a set of "no privacy" groundrules. Unlike the early consultation drafts of the Code, this version recognises that expectations may at least be influenced in this way, if not completely displaced.[69] It also recognises that the degree of privacy to be expected in the workplace is not the same as that in the home.[70] This issue is closely related to the impact on the workplace of the Human Rights Act 1998 and the extent to which it applies to private as well as public employers. These issues are discussed below.

The Good Practice Recommendations specific to monitoring electronic communications are, in summary:

- If you wish to monitor electronic communications, establish a policy on their use and communicate it to workers.
- Ensure that where monitoring involves the interception of a communication it is not outlawed by the Regulation of Investigatory Powers Act 2000.[71]
- Consider—preferably using an impact assessment—whether any monitoring of electronic communications can be limited to that necessary to ensure the security of the system and whether it can be automated.[72]
- If telephone calls or voicemails are, or are likely to be, monitored, consider—preferably using an impact assessment—whether the benefits justify the adverse impact. If so, inform workers about the nature and extent of such monitoring.
- Ensure that those making calls to, or receiving calls from, workers are aware of any monitoring and the purpose behind it, unless this is obvious.
- Ensure that workers are aware of the extent to which you receive information about the use of telephone lines in their homes, or mobile phones provided for their personal use, for which your business pays partly or fully. Do not make use of information about private calls for monitoring, unless they reveal activity that no employer could reasonably be expected to ignore.
- If emails and/or internet access are, or are likely to be, monitored, consider—preferably using an impact assessment—whether the benefits justify the adverse impact. If so, inform workers about the nature and extent of all email and internet access monitoring.
- Wherever possible avoid opening emails, especially ones that clearly show they are private or personal.
- Where practicable, and unless this is obvious, ensure that those

---

[69] The Supplementary Guidance at p.51 explicitly recognises this in the case of emails.
[70] Employment Practices Code, p.66.
[71] As to compliance with the Regulation of Investigatory Powers Act 200, see discussion above.
[72] The Code suggests that automated systems, since they only involve communications being "read" by a machine, may be less intrusive than monitoring by human beings.

sending emails to workers, as well as workers themselves, are aware of any monitoring and the purpose behind it.

– If it is necessary to check the email accounts of workers in their absence, make sure that they are aware that this will happen.

– Inform workers of the extent to which information about their internet access and emails is retained in the system and for how long.

The Supplementary Guidance published with the Code contains further discussion of these issues, focusing in particular on the circumstances in which employers may open personal emails, how such emails are to be distinguished from business emails and the effect of a ban on personal emails.

5.9.4 The Human Rights Act 1998

Public v private employers

The ability of employers to access and make use of employee commu- 5–115
nications on their networks may be affected by the Human Rights Act 1998, which incorporated the European Convention on Human Rights into UK domestic law. The Act came into force in England and Wales on October 2, 2000.

The Act directly affects the activities of public bodies (including "any person certain of whose functions are of a public nature"),[73] for whom the Act renders it unlawful to act in a way incompatible with Convention rights.[74] It also requires that, so far as it is possible to do so, primary legislation and subordinate legislation must be read and given effect in a way which is compatible with Convention rights.

Whether the Act affects the activities of private bodies depends on the extent to which the Act creates a positive obligation on the State to secure the relevant Convention rights as between private individuals, as opposed to creating rights only as against the State. This is a difficult and controversial topic.[75] The Lord Chancellor in the Third Reading of the Bill in the House of Lords stated:

"We have not provided for the Convention rights to be directly justiciable in actions between private individuals. We have sought

---

[73] Human Rights Act 1998, s.6(3)(b). Note, however, that under s.6(5) "in relation to a particular act, a person is not a public authority by virtue only of subs.(3)(b) if the nature of the act is private". This still leaves open the possibility that in the case of a clearly public body whose public body status is not dependent on the operation of subs.(3)(b), private acts of the body are subject to the Convention.

[74] *ibid.* s.6(1).

[75] M. Hunt, "The 'Horizontal Effect' of the Human Rights Act" [1998] Aut. P.L. 423; Buxton L.J. (writing extra-judicially) "The Human Rights Act and Private Law" [2000] 116 L.Q.R. 48; H.W.R. Wade. "Horizons of Horizontality, [2000] 116 L.Q.R. 217.

to protect the human rights of individuals against the abuse of power by the state, broadly defined, rather than to protect them against each other."[76]

However, this does still leave open the possibility that rights as between private individuals may indirectly have been created, in circumstances where the State is held to have abused its power by failing to protect one individual against another. Whether such a positive obligation is placed on the State depends very much on the particular circumstances, the particular Convention right under consideration and the effect of the mode of incorporation of the Convention into domestic law adopted in the 1998 Act.

The most relevant question for our purposes is the extent to which Art.8 of the Convention, which secures (subject to various possible derogations by a public authority) the right to respect for private and family life, home and correspondence, has horizontal effect.

5–116   In particular cases the European Court of Human Rights has sometimes found for a positive obligation to secure rights under Art.8,[77] and sometimes against.[78] *Von Hannover v Germany* is significant in that it applied such a positive obligation to the privacy aspect of Art.8, finding that the German courts had failed to provide adequate protection to Princess Caroline of Monaco in respect of the publication of paparazzi photographs taken in various public places when she was not on official business. The Court in that case stated, as regards the applicability of Art.8:

> "50. The Court reiterates that the concept of private life extends to aspects relating to personal identity, such as a person's name...
>
> Furthermore, private life, in the Court's view, includes a person's physical and psychological integrity; the guarantee afforded by Art.8 of the Convention is primarily intended to ensure the development, without outside interference, of the personality of each individual in his relations with other human beings ... . There is therefore a zone of interaction of a person with others, even in a public context, which may fall within the scope of "private life"....
>
> 51. The Court has also indicated that, in certain circumstances, a person has a "legitimate expectation" of protection and respect for his or her private life. Accordingly, it has held in a case concerning the interception of telephone calls on business premises that the applicant "would have had a reasonable expectation of privacy for such calls"....
>
> 52. As regards photos, with a view to defining the scope of the

[76] *Hansard*, House of Lords, February 5 1998 col.840.

[77] See e.g. *Marckx v Belgium* (1979–80) 2 E.H.R.R. 330, *Airey v Ireland* (1979–80) 2 E.H.R.R. 305, *X and Y v Netherlands* (1986) 8 E.H.R.R. 235 and *Von Hannover v Germany* [2004] E.M.L.R. 379.

[78] See e.g. *Johnston v Ireland* (1987) 9 E.H.R.R. 203.

protection afforded by Art.8 against arbitrary interference by public authorities, the European Commission of Human Rights had regard to whether the photographs related to private or public matters and whether the material thus obtained was envisaged for a limited use or was likely to be made available to the general public. . . .

53. In the present case there is no doubt that the publication by various German magazines of photos of the applicant in her daily life either on her own or with other people falls within the scope of her private life.

. . .

57. The Court reiterates that, although the object of Article 8 is essentially that of protecting the individual against arbitrary interference by the public authorities, it does not merely compel the State to abstain from such interference: in addition to this primarily negative undertaking, there may be positive obligations inherent in an effective respect for private or family life. These obligations may involve the adoption of measures designed to secure respect for private life even in the sphere of the relations of individuals between themselves . . . That also applies to the protection of a person's picture against abuse by others. . . .

The boundary between the State's positive and negative obligations under this provision does not lend itself to precise definition. The applicable principles are, nonetheless, similar. In both contexts regard must be had to the fair balance that has to be struck between the competing interests of the individual and of the community as a whole; and in both contexts the State enjoys a certain margin of appreciation. . . ."

The court also alluded to the significance of new technology:

"70. Furthermore, increased vigilance in protecting private life is necessary to contend with new communication technologies which make it possible to store and reproduce personal data . . . . This also applies to the systematic taking of specific photos and their dissemination to a broad section of the public."

As regards English cases, following *von Hannover* the Court of Appeal in **5–117** *Douglas v Hello (No 3)* and *McKennitt v Ash* has now recognised that Art.8 can create a positive obligation on the State to secure a right of privacy as between private individuals, enforceable in an action between individuals.[79]

---

[79] *Douglas v Hello! Ltd (No 3)* [2005] EWCA Civ 595, at para.49; *McKennitt v Ash* [2006] EWCA Civ 1714, *per* Buxton L.J. at para.10; see also *A v B (a company)* [2002] EWCA Civ 337 in which Lord Woolf's analysis of the applicability of Art.8 to the action for breach of confidence was implicitly founded on the same basis.

The effect of combining *Halford* (discussed below) with *von Hannover* is that there is now room to develop the application of Art.8 rights in the private sector workplace. The question then arises, how are they to be applied? In the context of the media the courts have applied Art.8 rights by developing the action for breach of confidence. In the workplace, Art.8 rights may be recognised in other ways. Some of these are:

1. Taking Art.8 into account in considering the nature of the increasingly recognised implied duty of trust and confidence between employer and employee.
2. Considering the protection afforded by the Regulation of Investigatory Powers Act and the RIPA Lawful Business Practice Regulations (discussed above).
3. Taking Art.8 into account in the application of data protection principles (as is done in the Information Commissioner's Employment Practices Code, discussed above).
4. Taking Art.8 into account in unfair dismissal claims.

In whichever way effect is given to Art.8, it should not be forgotten that Art.8 does not confer an absolute right of privacy (even before the exercise of balancing Art.8 rights with other Convention rights is undertaken). In particular, the circumstances must be such as to give rise to a reasonable expectation of privacy before Art.8 can be engaged.

Reasonable expectation of privacy

5–118   The decision of the European Court of Human Rights in *Halford v UK*[80] establishes that communications (in that case telephone calls) made by an employee from business premises (in that case the Merseyside Police Authority, obviously a public authority) may be covered by the right of respect for private life under Art.8 of the Convention. Article 8(1) provides that "everyone has the right to respect for his private and family life, his home and his correspondence". Article 8(2) provides that there shall be no interference by a public authority with the exercise of this right except in accordance with the law in certain specified circumstances.

One of the factors that the court took into account when deciding that Ms Halford, who was bringing a sex discrimination case against her employers, had a reasonable expectation of privacy for her telephone calls was that she had not been warned that her telephone calls made using the internal telephone system were liable to be intercepted. Indeed, this was reinforced by the facts that a particular telephone in her office was designated for personal calls and she had received a positive assurance that she could use her office telephones for the purposes of her industrial tribunal case. The court found that no domestic law provided protection against interference by a public authority on a private network, so that any inter-

---

[80] [1997] I.R.L.R. 471.

ference by a public authority could not be "in accordance with the law".[81]

Displacing an expectation of privacy

The questions that *Halford* leaves unanswered are first, whether the default **5–119** position (if nothing is said) is that the employee has a reasonable expectation of privacy for any, and if so which, communications using the employer's equipment. If not, what conditions have to exist for such an expectation to arise? Secondly, if the conditions are such that a reasonable expectation of privacy would otherwise arise, can an employer displace any such reasonable expectation of privacy that might arise simply by so informing the employee, or are there situations in which the privacy right is so fundamental that it cannot be displaced?

This is a controversial topic. *Halford* appears to require a two stage process so that in the workplace context (at least as regards employee communications), one has first to ask whether the privacy right is in play at all, since it only arises if there is a reasonable expectation of privacy; and only then go on to consider whether interference is justified under Art.8(2).

That may suggest that if the employer takes sufficient steps to displace any expectation of privacy in respect of communications, Art.8 simply does not come into play. However, the court in *Halford* was silent on what steps would be required to displace the privacy expectation.

It is possible in the wider employment situation to envisage circumstances in which the employer would be unable to displace a reasonable expectation of privacy (e.g. CCTV monitoring of lavatories) by giving warnings. If that could apply in some circumstances to communications, then the employer might not have total freedom to set a "no privacy" rule. However, it is not at all obvious in what, if any, circumstances use of the employer's system for communications could give rise to any such non-displaceable expectation of privacy.

The issue is most likely to arise where an employer permits use of its computer system for personal emails, but explicitly states that they will not be regarded as private. If employees know the rules (and especially if they have the use of alternative means of communication for personal matters, such as an office telephone), then it would seem quite arguable that an employer should be able to displace any reasonable expectation of privacy.[82]

Because of concerns about the ability of an employer to displace a rea- **5–120** sonable expectation of privacy, some have argued for recognition of a broader concept of autonomy, which cannot be displaced by the

---

[81] At the time of the case the only legislation governing interception was the Interception of Communications Act 1985, which did not extend to communications on private telecommunications networks. The introduction of the Regulation of Investigatory Powers Act 2000 was at least partly motivated by the need, especially with the introduction of the Human Rights Act 1998, to put all interception on a legal footing.

[82] For a contrary view, see JUSTICE's Response to the Government Consultation Paper "Interception of Communications in the United Kingdom".

employer.[83] While from a broad human rights perspective it may be appropriate to view privacy as derived from notions of personal autonomy,[84] that does not of itself justify a separate legal concept of non-displaceable employee autonomy, especially if that concept were to amount to a purported right not to be supervised by the employer.

Compatibility of RIPA Lawful Business Practice Regulations with the 1998 Act

5–121   It has been suggested[85] that the RIPA Lawful Business Practice Regulations may not be compatible with the Human Rights Act, due to a failure to secure sufficient respect for the employee's right of privacy.

Another, less publicised, human rights aspect of the Regulations is that they have the potential directly to interfere with the employer's ability to access its own business correspondence. Since Art.8 of the Convention secures the right to respect for correspondence,[86] regulations that went too far in restricting a business's access to its own correspondence could infringe that right.[87]

Unlike in the case of the employee's right of privacy, there would be no need to show that the Convention imposes a positive obligation on the State to secure the Convention right. The argument would be the far simpler one that the regulations constituted a direct infringement by the State of the business's Convention right. Similarly, there would be potential for direct interference with the employer's Art.10 rights (freedom to impart and receive information) and possibly the First Protocol Art.1 right (protection of property).

---

[83] Michael Ford *Surveillance and Privacy at Work*, (Institute of Employment Rights), 1998 p.16–17. The concept of employee autonomy as something separate and different from privacy was endorsed in first draft of the Information Commissioner's Code of Practice on the use of Personal Data in the Employer/Employee Relationship (para.5–112 above). This was extremely controversial since it seemed to conflict with the employer's right to supervise its employees. The final version of the Code contains no mention of employee autonomy.

[84] *Douglas v Hello!* (fn. 79 above) *per* Sedley L.J. at para.126; and see the extracts from *Von Hannover* quoted (para.5–116 above).

[85] *Financial Times*, October 4, 2000.

[86] The case of *Niemitz v Germany* (1992) 16 E.H.R.R. 97 in the ECtHR establishes that this extends to business correspondence.

[87] Whatever the merits of the debate over whether companies can enjoy a right of privacy under Art.8 (see *R v Broadcasting Standards Commission Ex p., British Broadcasting Corporation* C.A, [2000] 3 All E.R. 989), it should not be forgotten that many employers are individuals and partnerships.

CHAPTER 6

Enforcement and Cross-border Liability

In this chapter we discuss two topics: what remedies are available to help   6–001
identify wrongdoers on the internet; what factors will influence where they
can be pursued and under which country's law?

Simply to characterise someone as a wrongdoer, however, glosses over
probably the single most difficult legal and policy issue raised by the
internet. If someone's on-line activities are lawful in his home country, but
unlawful in other countries in which his website is accessible, by which
country's rules is he to be judged?

In this chapter we address the existing law and analyse the outcomes that
the current rules produce. We also note the changes to applicable law rules
proposed by the European Commission in its Rome I and Rome II projects.
In Ch.12 we address the broad policies behind the rules, asking the question
"by which country's rules *ought* an on-line actor to be judged?", and discuss how cross-border liability rules should be framed in order to produce
the most desirable outcomes.

In previous editions we enumerated the increasing varieties of internet
litigation. That is no longer a useful exercise. The intrepid litigants whom
we previously described as creating the building blocks of the future law of
the internet have done their work and litigation has flourished. That is not
to say that the results have been uniformly good. Cross-border liability is
one area in which much remains to be done both to achieve greater legal
certainty and to evolve rules that produce good outcomes for the internet.

The internet does still present challenges. Technology continues to create
novel factual situations, and enforceability remains a concern. Historically,
English courts have shown themselves remarkably adept at devising new
remedies to maintain the potency of the law. The *Anton Piller* order, the
Mareva injunction, the worldwide *Mareva* injunction, the *Norwich Pharmacal* order, the "*ne exeat regno*" injunction, and the class injunction were
all fashioned by English courts who were not prepared to see the law
rendered powerless to assist rights owners against rogues. Neither have the
courts shirked the challenge of dealing with malefactors who lurk in the
dark corners of the internet.

6.1 ENFORCEMENT IN ENGLAND

6.1.1 Enforcement—identifying the defendant

6–002   The first challenge is to identify the wrongdoer. This may not be easy. Someone emailing infringing material or posting to a Usenet newsgroup or a web discussion forum may do so from behind an anonymous remailer, which offers the service of stripping identifying material from emails before sending them on. Even if that does not happen, the person with the account may be using a false email identity, and even masquerading behind a false IP address (a technique known as spoofing). Although a genuine IP address would in many cases enable the sending computer to be identified, it might only show that the sender was a subscriber to a particular commercial internet access provider.

In the case of infringing material held on a more permanent internet resource, such as a website or ftp site, it may be difficult to identify the person responsible for putting material onto the resource.[1]

The potential claimant will usually be able to identify the apparent source of the posting to a Usenet newsgroup; and should, with a little technical knowledge, be able to identify the apparent owner of the host on which a website is held. But that may be a university or commercial host. The identity and whereabouts of the individual or company responsible for the content may not be apparent.

English law is well able to help with this problem. In the case of material infringing copyright held on a third party host, it is possible that the host is itself committing infringing acts by storing the material on its computer and by making copies when users access it. As explained in Ch.2, even transient copies are generally considered to be copies for the purposes of UK copyright law.[2] Unless the host is regarded as having involuntarily copied,[3] it would therefore be a potential defendant to copyright infringement proceedings. For defamation, an internet service provider has published materials that it hosts[4] and so is perhaps a potential defendant.

It has long been established that English courts are, by way of "advance disclosure", able to order infringers to disclose information to enable the

---

[1] See, e.g. *Grant v Google* [2006] All E.R. (D) 243 (May), in which a *Norwich Pharmacal* order (see discussion in section 6.1.2) was granted against the defendant search engine when the alleged wrongdoer, who had advertised on Google, had registered its website with a company that specialised in cloaking the identity of domain owners. Commercial websites are now required, under reg.6 of the Electronic Commerce (EC Directive) Regulations 2002, to make certain information about themselves available including their name, geographic and email address.

[2] Since October 31, 2003, there has been an exception for certain transient copies created for the purpose of enabling either transmission in a network or a lawful use of the work (Copyright, Designs and Patents Act 1988, s.28A).

[3] See Ch.2, para.2–169.

[4] But it does not publish materials that it merely transmits (*Bunt v Tilley* [2006] EWHC 407 (QB)).

rights owner to track back up the chain to the source of the infringing material. At first sight there would, therefore, seem to be no reason why the university or commercial host should not be required to disclose the identity of the person who put the infringing or defamatory material on their host computer. However, in most situations it would have a hosting or (for defamation) innocent dissemination defence available to it.[5] The normal course is therefore to apply for a *Norwich Pharmacal* order, to which we now turn.

6.1.2 Identifying the wrongdoer—*Norwich Pharmacal* orders

Even if the host is not committing an infringing act itself, if it is sufficiently   6–003
mixed up in the commission of the tort and is within the jurisdiction of the court, the court has discretion to grant a disclosure order against it. In the case of *Norwich Pharmacal Co v Customs and Excise Commissioners*[6] the House of Lords held that such an order could be made against a third party who was mixed up in the commission of a tort, but otherwise innocent. The difference from being a normal defendant is that the claim is for disclosure only (not damages or a substantive injunction) and the claimant would normally have to pay the host's legal costs and its costs of complying with the order. A *Norwich Pharmacal* order should be available not only to ascertain the identity of the person who placed infringing material on a host, but also to disclose the identity of the holder of an email account used to disseminate infringing matter.

While the *Norwich Pharmacal* order originated in intellectual property cases it is also available in connection with other torts such as defamation, or indeed breach of contract and other civil or criminal wrongs.[7] However, an order cannot be made against someone who has no connection with the wrongdoing, or where an advance disclosure order is available against the intended defendant, or where the court is not satisfied that the making of the order is a necessary and proportionate response in all the circumstances.[8]

In *P v T Ltd*[9] Scott V.-C. held that the court could order discovery against a party so as to assist the plaintiff in bringing proceedings for malicious falsehood or libel against a third party, even where without that information the plaintiff could not determine whether it in fact had a cause of action against the third party. In this case a senior employee of a company

---

[5] Under Art.14 of the Electronic Commerce Directive and s.1 of the Defamation Act 1996 respectively—see Ch.4, section 4.3.2 and Ch.5, section 5.7.1.

[6] [1974] 1 A.C. 133.

[7] *Ashworth Hospital Authority v MGN Ltd* [2002] UKHL 29: [2002] 1 W.L.R. 2033; *Campaign against Arms Trade v BAE Systems Plc* [2007] EWHC 330 (Q.B.).

[8] *Ricci v Chow* [1987] 1 W.L.R. 1658; *Ashworth Hospital Authority v MGN Ltd (ibid.)*; *Mitsui & Co Ltd v Nexen Petroleum UK Ltd* [2005] EWHC 625 (Ch); *Nikitin v Richards Butler* [2007] EWHC 173 (Q.B.).

[9] [1997] 4 All E.R. 200.

had been dismissed after a third party had made allegations against him, the nature of which the company refused to disclose. The company also refused to disclose the identity of the informant. It was known in the industry that the plaintiff had been dismissed for impropriety, which he was unable to explain. He applied successfully for an order that the company disclose the identity of the informant and the nature of the allegations and that he be at liberty to use the information in proceedings against the informant for libel or malicious falsehood.

In a defamation case that went to a full trial, *Takenaka (UK) Ltd v Frankl*,[10] the defendant steadfastly denied that he was the author of the defamatory emails in question. The claimant obtained disclosure orders against various internet service providers in the course of identifying the defendant so as to enable it to commence proceedings.

In *Campaign against Arms Trade v BAE Systems Plc*[11] the respondents had received by email a copy of an internal email of the applicant containing privileged and confidential information. The respondents, through their solicitors, returned a hard copy of the email to the applicants with routing information redacted out. The respondent's solicitors stated that they and their client had undertaken all reasonable efforts to destroy any paper or electronic copies of the email that they or their client held. The applicant sought an order for disclosure of, *inter alia*, routing and addressing information for the email, so as to enable them to identify the source of the leak.

The judge held that it was a proper case for the making of a *Norwich Pharmacal* order. He also accepted the claimant's assertion that it is almost impossible to delete electronic data:

> "A 'deleted' email can normally be recovered by a competent professional. Computer imaging and data recovery orders are routinely granted to enable 'deleted' information to be recovered."

He accepted that the order should include a provision that where a document that would otherwise fall to be preserved under the terms of the order had been deleted, the respondent should take all reasonable steps to reconstruct such documents using a qualified independent computer professional, instructed by and under the supervision of the respondent's solicitors.

6–004   In *Totalise Plc v The Motley Fool*[12] the defendants were the proprietors of websites containing discussion forums. An anonymous contributor who went under the pseudonym Z Dust had made numerous postings about the claimant, which the claimant asserted were defamatory. The claimant applied for disclosure of the identity of Z Dust or of any material in the

---

[10] Unreported, Q.B., Alliott J. October 11, 2000. Upheld on appeal [2001] EWCA Civ 348.
[11] Above, fn.7.
[12] [2001] 4 E.M.L.R. 750.

defendants' possession which could lead to the identification of Z Dust. The first defendant had refused disclosure in correspondence, relying on the Data Protection Act 1998, but neither consented to nor opposed the disclosure application, stating that it was under an obligation to protect the privacy of the information of which disclosure was sought. The second defendant, Interactive Investor Ltd, also resisted disclosure, based on the Data Protection Act and its privacy policy incorporated in its customer terms and conditions.

The application proceeded on the basis that the court was exercising its *Norwich Pharmacal* jurisdiction. However, it is far from clear that this was in fact a true *Norwich Pharmacal* case. These defendants had clearly published the postings concerned[13] and, subject to an innocent dissemination defence, would have been liable for any defamation in their own right. Further, in the case of operators of a discussion forum on a website it is far less clear than in the case of an internet service provider that they would have been able to rely on the innocent dissemination defence at all (see discussion of this point in Ch.4, at para.4–030).

Lastly, on the facts the first defendant had allowed Z Dust back onto the forum after initially revoking his access following the claimant's complaint—a situation that could have prevented the first defendant from successfully relying on the innocent dissemination defence in respect of subsequent postings before revoking Z Dust's access for a second time. For all these reasons it appears from the facts set out in the judgment that the defendants could have been made defendants to substantive proceedings.[14]

For the issues under the Data Protection Act, see the discussion of this case in Ch.7, at para.7–049.

The first defendant sought to argue that s.10 of the Contempt of Court   **6–005** Act 1981 was relevant to the exercise of discretion. That, subject to exceptions for the interests of justice, national security or the prevention of disorder or crime, prohibits a court from requiring a person to disclose "the source of information contained in a publication for which he is responsible". The court found that this section had no application in this case:

> "It is concerned with the protection of a journalist's sources and is directed at resolving the tension that may arise between the public interest in a free press and in enabling justice to be attained by a party seeking to enforce or protect its legal rights. The journalist is responsible at law for the material which he publishes. The defendants take no such responsibility. They exercise no editorial control. They take no responsibility for what is posted on their discussion boards. ... [quotes second defendant's disclaimer] ... The defendants simply provide a facility by means of which the

---

[13] *Godfrey v Demon Internet Ltd* [2001] Q.B. 201.
[14] For an example of a case in which a claim for a *Norwich Pharmacal* order was made in the alternative to a claim for advance disclosure, see *Hughes v Carratu International Plc* [2006] EWHC 1791 (QB).

public at large is able publicly to communicate its views. In my judgment, they are not responsible for the publication of such material within the meaning of the section. But if I am wrong as to that, then, for the reasons which I will subsequently set out, I am satisfied that disclosure is necessary in the interests of justice."

In exercising his discretion, the judge stated:

"I am mindful of the fact that both defendants have a policy of confidentiality with regard to personal information relating to those using its websites and do not wish to deviate from that policy. But the claimant argues that it simply wants the author of the Z Dust postings to take responsibility for his actions, and that, when balancing the interests of the parties, the respect for and protection of the privacy of those who chose to air their views in the most public of fora must take second place to the obligation imposed upon those who become involved in the tortious acts of others to assist the party injured by those acts.

I have no hesitation in finding that the balance weighs heavily in favour of granting the relief sought. To find otherwise would be to give the clearest indication to those who wish to defame that they can do so with impunity behind the screen of anonymity made possible by the use of websites on the internet."

6–006   If the judge's conclusions regarding the responsibility of the defendants for their discussion fora for the purposes of s.10 of the Contempt of Court Act 1981 were to be translated into defamation liability, that would still not necessarily mean that the defendants could take advantage of the innocent dissemination defence. Certainly they would not be regarded as having assumed editorial responsibility, but that still leaves the difficult question of whether or not they would be a publisher within the special meaning of s.1 of the Defamation Act 1996.

When it came to costs, the judge departed from the usual *Norwich Pharmacal* order that the party seeking disclosure should bear the costs of a blameless defendant. He found that the situation was very different from the classic *Norwich Pharmacal* situation and that there was:

"considerable force in [the claimant's] argument that those who operate websites containing discussion boards do so at their own risk. If it transpires that those boards are used for defamatory purposes by individuals hiding behind the cloak of anonymity then in justice a claimant seeking to establish the identity of the individuals making such defamatory contents ought to be entitled to their costs."

The judge held that both defendants ought to have acceded to the claimant's requests and he ordered the defendants to pay the claimant's costs.

The order as to costs was reversed by the Court of Appeal.[15] The appeal proceeded on the basis that this was a true *Norwich Pharmacal* case, in which the web provider had become mixed up in tortious acts and was only concerned that duties and rights, such as duties of confidence and legitimate interests of privacy, were considered by the court. The Court of Appeal laid down a set of principles governing applications against on-line intermediaries.

The *Totalise v Motley Fool* principles

Although the appeal concerned only the costs of the second defendant,   6–007
Interactive Investor Ltd, Aldous L.J. giving the judgment of the court considered the general approach to disclosure applications. He concluded:

1. By virtue of s.35 and Sch.2, paras. 5 and 6 of the Data Protection Act 1998, no order is to be made for the disclosure of a data subject's identity, whether under the *Norwich Pharmacal* doctrine or otherwise, unless the court has first considered whether the disclosure is warranted having regard to the rights and freedoms or the legitimate interests of the data subject (para.24).
2. If s.10 of the Contempt of Court Act 1981 is applicable, a court must also be satisfied that disclosure is necessary in the interests of justice (para.24).
3. The court must be careful not to make an order which unjustifiably invades the right of an individual to respect for his private life, especially when that individual is in the nature of things not before the court. That protection is available to the anonymous as well as to the named and there are many situations in which the protection of the person's identity from disclosure may be legitimate (para.25).
4. Although it is difficult for the court to carry out this task in a contest between two parties, neither of whom is the data subject who is the person most concerned, the website operator can, where appropriate, tell the user what is going on and offer to pass on in writing to the claimant and the court any worthwhile reason the user wants to put forward for not having his or her identity disclosed. Further, the court could require that be done before making an order (para.26).
5. It is legitimate for a website operator not implicated or involved in the wrongful act, who has reasonably agreed to keep information confidential and private, to refuse to voluntarily hand over such information (para.28). It is for the applicant to satisfy the court that the order should be made, not for the defendant to take a view which could be wrong (para.22).

As to costs, the Court of Appeal considered that in general the costs of a   6–008
successful *Norwich Pharmacal* application should be paid by the applicant.

---

[15] [2001] EWCA Civ 1897.

There might be cases where the circumstances required a different order, but they would not include cases where:

    a.   the party required to make the disclosure had a genuine doubt that the person seeking the disclosure was entitled to it;

    b.   the party was under an appropriate legal obligation not to reveal the information, or where the legal position was not clear, or the party had a reasonable doubt as to the obligations; or

    c.   the party could be subject to proceedings if disclosure was voluntary; or

    d.   the party would or might suffer damage by voluntarily giving the disclosure; or

    e.   the disclosure would or might infringe a legitimate interest of another (para.30).

The court concluded that Interactive Investor Ltd should have recovered its costs and so allowed the appeal.

Aldous L.J. also commented that although the court was not convinced that a party was free to hand over material without coming to a view on the merits, and that was not the party's task, the position could have been different if it was in some way implicated or involved in the wrongful act. A party who supported or was implicated in a crime or tort, or who sought to obstruct justice being done, would be likely to have to bear its costs and, if appropriate, pay the applicant's costs.

Practice of ISPs in response to disclosure requests

6–009 Following the *Totalise* case the usual practice of ISPs and other intermediaries faced with a request to identify their customer is not to disclose voluntarily, but to take a neutral position if a properly supported application is made for a *Norwich Pharmacal* order.[16]

It is, we suggest, good practice for the respondent to such an application to scrutinise the application carefully in order:

    (a) To ensure that the evidence appears to justify the order sought and that there are no inconsistencies with the respondent's own records that might suggest flaws in the applicant's evidence.

    (b) To verify that the respondent is capable of complying with the precise terms of the order as drafted.

    (c) If the information sought goes beyond the name and address of the customer, to consider whether provision of the further information is justified by the evidence in support of the application.

---

[16] For an example of an order made against a search engine in respect of an advertiser see *Grant v Google* [2006] All E.R. (D) 243 (May), in which the court satisfied itself that an order should be made on the usual terms as to payment of the defendant's costs of providing the information. Google was not represented at the hearing.

(d) To satisfy itself that the evidence presented in support of the application presents a fair picture to the court.

The respondent may also wish to offer to notify its customer of the proposed application and to pass on (anonymously) any representations that the customer may wish to make so that they can be put before the court.

The evidence adduced by the applicant will normally include some explanation of the technical workings of the internet, for instance describing the function of an IP address where that is the basis on which the respondent has been identified. It is incumbent upon the applicant to ensure that technical explanations are accurate and comprehensible. However, since this is not always the case, the respondent should, as mentioned in point (d), review the evidence with care.

One typical omission is where the applicant's evidence does not make clear that an IP address identifies a device, not a person, and that the identifying details that the respondent can provide are not necessarily those of the alleged wrongdoer. An ISP can only provide information about its customer. The alleged wrongdoer might be the ISP's customer, but could easily be a member of the customer's household or a visitor. It could even be someone with no relationship at all with the customer, such as someone wrongfully accessing the customer's unsecured home wireless network in order to make use of the internet connection.

Given the essentially intrusive nature of a *Norwich Pharmacal* order, the court ought to be apprised of any such possibilities when considering whether it should make the requested order.

6.1.3 Transient nature of internet evidence

Infringing material often stays in one place on the internet only for very   6–010
short periods. Usenet hosts may retain postings only for a matter of days before deleting them. Sites may spring up, close down and pop up again elsewhere extremely rapidly. Even the content of websites is increasingly dynamic and may change rapidly. This undoubtedly poses challenges for rights holders and their lawyers, who must move fast if the evidence is not to disappear.

However, it should not be forgotten that once the person who is perpetrating a wrong within the jurisdiction has been identified, it should be possible in due course to obtain an injunction against that person. Because the injunction restrains the defendant personally from doing infringing acts, the effect of the injunction would not merely extend to the site that formed the basis of the complaint, but (subject to any questions of territorial jurisdiction) would also affect other sites on which the defendant thereafter placed the infringing material.

In July 1997 the Norwich Union insurance company made an agreed payment of £450,000 to the Western Provident Association (WPA) in settlement of defamation proceedings brought by WPA against Norwich

Union. The proceedings were based on a statement made in an internal Norwich Union email. WPA obtained an ex parte injunction requiring Norwich Union to preserve and deliver up a copy of the email. WPA also obtained an order that the company secretary of Norwich Union interrogate its salesforce as to whether they had repeated the defamatory statement to potential customers. The company secretary was then required to produce an affidavit setting out the results of his inquiries.

In the *Takenaka* case referred to above (para.6–003), a court-appointed expert conducted a detailed forensic examination of the computer, ultimately delivering an opinion that the emails had been sent by the defendant. The court accepted this opinion and liability was established.

It should also be borne in mind that internet service providers typically retain traffic data for relatively short periods.[17] So, if it is desired to require an ISP to disclose (say) the identity of the customer who was allocated a particular IP address at a particular time, swift action will have to be taken if the data is not to be lost.

6.1.4 Transportability of sites

6–011   The ability of sites to reappear, perhaps out of the jurisdiction, but equally available as if they were located in the jurisdiction, poses real problems for rights owners. If a rights owner has an injunction against an infringer, can he do anything to deny people access to the infringing site if it reappears out of the jurisdiction?

One possible approach would be to seek to have the infringing site's domain name and IP address removed from domain name servers and IP routing tables respectively. If notice of the injunction were to be given to the operator of a domain name server, the operator would be bound under the *Spycatcher* principle neither to aid nor abet the defendant to breach the injunction, nor wilfully to do acts that the injunction restrains, with the intention of impeding or prejudicing the administration of justice.[18] In the case at least of a wholly pirate site, it may be that the operator could be required to prevent access being granted to the site by removing the name from the domain name server. The same could be required of owners of routing tables as regards the IP address of the site.

The possibility of doing this is speculative. Operators of domain name servers and routers would have serious points to make about their ability to

---

[17] The formal position will change when the Data Retention Directive (2006/24/EC) is implemented. This Directive requires Member States to ensure that public communications networks and publicly available electronic communications services retain certain data for between six months and two years. It is due to be implemented in the UK by March 15, 2009.

[18] *A-G v Punch Ltd* [2002] UKHL 50, *per* Lord Nicholls at [4].

filter the defendant's site.[19] The defendant might retaliate by frequently changing the IP address of his site, or by asking others to mirror his content on other sites.

Nonetheless, the courts are concerned to ensure that their orders are effective and might be willing to contemplate requiring operators to take such steps. The effectiveness of the *Mareva* (asset freezing) injunction has been greatly assisted by the ability to give notice of the injunction to banks thought to hold relevant accounts of the defendant. The interests of the bank are preserved by various practice requirements, including that the claimant pay the reasonable costs of the bank in complying with the order. A similar approach may be possible with ISPs to ensure that injunctions against infringing internet site operators are effective while the interests of access providers are preserved.[20]

However it appears that third parties acting independently cannot be bound by the terms of a final injunction, as opposed to an interim injunction,[21] unless it be an injunction issued *contra mundo* (as has been done in cases where the protective jurisdiction of the court is being exercised, such as in the *Bulger* case[22]). That would not, however, affect their liability if they could be shown to be aiding and abetting a breach of the injunction.

In the *Bulger* case, broad injunctions preserving confidentiality were granted against public computer networks, as well as against newspapers, broadcasters, cable and satellite companies. However, the injunction was amended subsequently to recognise that ISPs should not be held in contempt of court for material placed on their servers or accessible via their services without their knowledge (see Ch.5, para.5–057, for the detailed terms of the injunction).

The *Bulger* injunction concerned broad categories of content, not an identified website. That is different from the position where the identity and location of a particular website is known. In that case there may well be scope for holding an ISP to a tighter standard of liability once notice of the injunction is given.

In *Marks & Spencer Plc v Cottrell*,[23] an application to commit the perpetrator of fake websites for contempt of court, Lightman J. commented (*obiter*):

6–012

---

[19] See for instance *SABAM v Tiscali* (Computer Law Review International, March 2005, p.87) in which the question of whether it is feasible for an ISP to filter illegal peer to peer activity is under investigation. In Germany an administrative order requiring ISPs in Westphalia to block access to certain foreign neo-Nazi sites has been upheld by several courts (*http://www.edri.org/edrigram/number3.12/blockingorder*). A French court has issued an order requiring 10 French ISPs to block access to foreign revisionist or anti-Semitic websites (*http://www.edri.org/edrigram/number3.12/blocking*). In Italy a decree was issued on February 21, 2006, creating a blacklist of over 600 foreign gaming sites which ISPs were required to block. See also Ch.2, para.2–019.

[20] See Ch.5, para.5–061, for a full discussion comparing the practice on freezing orders with that for *Spycatcher* injunctions.

[21] See discussion of third party injunctions in Ch.12.

[22] *Venables v News Group Newspapers Ltd* [2001] 1 All E.R. 908.

[23] Ch.D., Lightman J., February 26, 2001 (unreported).

"I am told that one of the problems that exist today for companies like Marks & Spencer faced with persons of the like of Mr Cottrell is that orders such as those that have been made in this case prohibiting an individual from using a particular domain name can be evaded by adopting a minuscule variation upon it. The domain name providers will comply with a court order prohibiting the use of a particular name but because all questions of registration and domain name and monitoring are computer driven, no scope at the moment is available to prevent colourable imitations of the names though they are prohibited from being used. I do not think it can or should safely be assumed by domain name providers, that they have no responsibility to monitor whether court orders prohibiting use, not merely of particular names, but of colourable imitations are being broken by registrations made with names that fall foul of the prohibition. That is not a matter that I need go into now but it does seem to me far from clear that they can abdicate responsibility in respect of the names which they permit it is registered on their sites. But that is a matter which requires very careful consideration on another occasion."

6.1.5 Mirror sites

6–013 A common tactic among defendants threatened with proceedings, especially where freedom of speech issues arise, is to issue a call for help to the internet community by requesting others to mirror (i.e. copy) the site.

This tactic is designed to nullify the effect of local legal proceedings by multiplying the site across numerous jurisdictions. This undoubtedly creates practical problems for claimants, who are then faced with the task of trying to put the genie back in the bottle by pursuing defendants, many of whom may regard themselves as performing a public service by mirroring the original threatened site, around the world.

The prospective claimant may, if the circumstances warrant, wish to consider moving for an injunction without notice, sufficiently broadly worded to put the defendant in contempt of court if it requests others to mirror the site or if it creates hypertext links to mirror sites.

The difficulties that can be encountered in pursuing website infringement cases with a freedom of speech element are well illustrated by the Nottinghamshire County Council "JET Report" case in 1997.

The JET Report was a report by a Joint Enquiry Team into the Broxtowe case, one of the first instances of a UK social services department forming a view that "satanic abuse" may have occurred. Three journalists published the report on a website.

Nottinghamshire County Council asserted copyright in the report and obtained an ex parte injunction restraining the reproduction of and other specified dealings with the JET Report.[24] The report appeared on various mirror sites around the world. The council wrote letters before action to a number of them objecting to both copying of the report and the inclusion of any hypertext links to it. This drew caustic responses from some of the overseas mirror sites. Ultimately the council accepted that it could not effectively prevent the availability of the report and dropped the action.

With the advent of the Human Rights Act 1998, in rare cases the Art.10 right of freedom of expression may come into conflict with the protection afforded by the Copyright, Designs and Patents Act 1988. In such cases a court may decline in its discretion to grant an injunction (either interim or final), leaving the claimant to its remedies of damages or an account of profits. In other rare cases the defendant may be able to rely on a substantive public interest defence wider than the specific defences provided in the Copyright, Designs and Patents Act 1988, so that the copyright work may be published by the defendant without sanction. In any event, the implications of the human rights will always be considered where the discretionary relief of an injunction is sought.[25]

6.2 JURISDICTION AND APPLICABLE LAW

6.2.1 Background

It was inevitable, with the advent of cheap cross-border communication for all, that questions of jurisdiction and applicable law would sooner or later bubble to the surface of the cauldron of legal and policy issues raised by the internet. They have done so now. Jurisdiction and applicable law have been at the heart of many internet-related policy debates. The broad concepts of country of origin, country of destination and other regimes are discussed in Ch.12. These are some of the specific areas in which they have been debated. **6–014**

Domain names

The protracted discussions about the ICANN dispute resolution procedures for global top level domain names encompassed some heavily debated jurisdictional and choice of law issues. The solution arrived at for jurisdiction was that a complainant using the ICANN Uniform Disputes Resolution Procedure (UDRP) is required to agree to submit, for the purpose of a challenge to a Panel decision, to at least one of the jurisdictions of the principal office of the Registrar who registered the domain name, or the domain holder's address as shown in the Registrar's WHOIS database at **6–015**

---

[24] The terms of the injunction are available at *www.linksandlaw.com/decisions–86.htm*. General information about the case can be found at *www.cyber-rights.org/jetrep.htm*.
[25] *Ashdown v Telegraph Group Ltd* [2001] EWCA Civ 1142.

the time of the filing of the complaint.[26] For applicable law the Panel decides a complaint on the basis of "... any rules and principles of law that it deems applicable".[27]

Consumer contracts

6–016 Various provisions of the 1968 Brussels Convention on Jurisdiction and Enforcement of Judgments in Civil and Commercial Matters[28] (now superseded in the UK by the Brussels Jurisdiction and Judgments Regulation[29]) and of the 1980 Rome Convention on the Law Applicable to Contractual Obligations[30] created a regime under which a consumer might in some circumstances invoke the protection of the courts of his domicile and the mandatory rules of his country of habitual residence, by way of exception to the otherwise applicable rules governing jurisdiction and choice of law. So in the Brussels and Rome Conventions there was an existing framework that favoured, for consumers, the country of destination over the supplier's chosen law or that of his country of origin.

The appropriateness of these existing rules was put in question by the advent of cheap cross-border on-line trade, where by default a website is available throughout the world. The website proprietor who wishes to trade only with certain jurisdictions must take positive steps to prevent transactions occurring with customers in other jurisdictions. This is the reverse of the position that obtained when the Brussels and Rome Conventions were written, when trade was domestic by default and a supplier would generally have to take positive steps to market overseas.

The Brussels Convention was superseded[31] in March 2002 by a Council Regulation on Jurisdiction and the Recognition and Enforcement of Judgments in Civil and Commercial Matters,[32] commonly known as the Judgments Regulation. The original Commission proposal,[33] which would have reinforced the existing consumer protection exceptions in the on-line context, sparked vigorous lobbying.

Trade bodies argued that any revisions should reflect the new country of origin philosophy which underlies, to an extent, the EC Treaty and the Electronic Commerce Directive; and that consumers would be harmed through suffering restricted choice if e-commerce providers were inhibited from providing their services across borders. Consumer organisations

---

[26] ICANN UDRP Rules, paras 1 and 3(xiii).

[27] ICANN UDRP Rules, para.15(a).

[28] Implemented by the Civil Jurisdiction and Judgments Act 1982.

[29] Council Regulation on Jurisdiction and the Recognition and Enforcement of Judgments in Civil and Commercial Matters (Council Regulation 44/2001 of December 22, 2000).

[30] Implemented by the Contracts (Applicable Law) Act 1990.

[31] The Regulation applies to all Member States except Denmark, which decided not to participate in the adoption of the Regulation. The Brussels Convention therefore continued to apply as between Member States and Denmark until July 1, 2007, when a bilateral agreement between the Community and Denmark extending the Regulation to Denmark came into effect.

[32] Council Regulation 44/2001 of December 22, 2000.

[33] COM (1999) 0348 dated July 14, 1999.

argued that consumers should not forfeit their existing legal protections when contracting electronically.

The final form of the Regulation represented something of a compromise on this issue, substantially retaining the principle of the consumer exceptions but basing their applicability on a new concept of directing activities towards one or more Member States. This is discussed in more detail below.

The Judgments Regulation was viewed by some as likely to become a precedent for future revisions to the 1980 Rome Convention on the Law Applicable to Contractual Obligations, and so it proved. On January 14, 2003, the European Commission issued a Green Paper on the conversion of the 1980 Rome Convention into a Community instrument, a project known as "Rome I".

The Green Paper addressed conflict of laws rules governing contracts. It set out eight different discussion options for consumer protection. At one extreme there was maintenance of the current position under the 1980 Rome Convention, under which a consumer could not be deprived by a choice of law clause of the benefit of consumer protection rules in his country of habitual residence, if he concluded the contract there and that was preceded by advertising or to a specific invitation addressed to him.

6–017

At the other extreme was a suggestion that the supplier could designate the law of its country of establishment (but no other law), if it could show that the consumer made an informed choice and that advance information was given to the consumer on the relevant provisions of the supplier's law. As with the existing 1980 Rome Convention, the proposed Regulation would apply universally, thus including US choice of law clauses litigated in European courts.

The Green Paper was followed by a Proposal[34] for a Regulation. The consumer protection aspects of the Proposal differ in a number of ways from the 1980 Convention, the main ones being:

– The existing trigger of advertising or specific invitation would be replaced by a directed activities test based on that of the Judgments Regulation, and like the Judgments Regulation lacking any proper definition of what would constitute "by any means" directing activities towards one or more Member States. Recital (10) would emphasise that the concept of targeting should be interpreted harmoniously with that in the Judgments Regulation, bearing in mind the joint declaration of the Council and the Commission regarding Art.15 of that Regulation (below, para.6–072).

– Rather than being confined to mandatory rules, the whole law of the consumer's habitual residence would apply to the the contract.

– The 1980 Convention trigger requiring the contract to be concluded in the place of the consumer's habitual residence would be replaced by a test based on the trader's actual or deemed knowledge of the consumer's habitual residence.

---

[34] Proposal for a Regulation of the European Parliament and Council on the law applicable to contractual obligations (Rome I) COM (2005) 650, December 15, 2005.

-   The reference in Recital (10) to the joint declaration of the Council and the Commission regarding Art.15 of the Brussels Jurisdiction Regulation suggests that it would be appropriate, when considering whether or not activities have been directed at a Member State, to take into account the fact that a contract has been concluded. This would be a departure from the 1980 Convention approach in which the consumer protection provisions are triggered only by activities that precede the making of the contract.[35]

While a properly limited concept of directing or targeting activities is likely to be a fruitful approach,[36] the version proposed by the Commission would expose on-line traders to greater risk than do the provisions of the existing 1980 Convention.

Regulated industries

6–018   Suppliers in licensed and highly regulated industries such as financial services and pharmaceuticals must typically comply with a detailed domestic compliance regime. Once such suppliers go online, the question arises whether the mere global availability, by default, of the website, is sufficient to trigger the compliance regimes of other jurisdictions. National regulators have tended towards evolving solutions which recognise that mere availability should not be sufficient to trigger a country's compliance regime, thus permitting peaceful co-existence of websites established under a variety of domestic regimes.

Hague Convention

6–019   The advent of e-commerce had an impact on the proposed Hague Convention on International Jurisdiction and Foreign Judgments in Civil and Commercial Matters. The negotiations came to a halt in 2001, at least partly as a result of disagreements over the rules that should apply to internet and e-commerce. The end result was a very limited Convention on Choice of Court Agreements, concluded on June 30, 2005.

Freedom of speech

6–020   The impact of applicable law rules on cross-border freedom of speech came to the fore during negotiations on the European Commission's proposed Regulation on the Law Applicable to Non-Contractual Obligations ("Rome II").[37] The current position is that agreement on a common position was reached between Member States on September 25, 2006.[38] However, due to the inability of Member States to reach agreement on an

---

[35] *Rayner v Davies* [2002] EWCA Civ 1880 (CA) *per* Waller L.J. at [24].

[36] For a more detailed discussion of this approach, see "Directing and Targeting – the Answer to the Internet's Jurisdiction Problems?" by G J H Smith, *Computer Law Review International*, 5/2004.

[37] Proposal for a Regulation of the European Parliament and the Council on the law applicable to non-contractual obligations ("Rome II") COM/2003/0427 final, July 22, 2003.

[38] *http://register.consilium.europa.eu/pdf/en/06/st09/st09751.en06.pdf.*

appropriate rule for privacy and rights relating to the personality, including defamation, that whole area has been excluded from the scope of the proposed Regulation.

Although the UK Government apparently regarded this as a good outcome,[39] it is perhaps more to the point that international lawmaking bodies are not yet ready to adapt to the changes that the internet has wrought in this field. The proposed Regulation returned to the European Parliament, which on January 18, 2007, voted to reinstate coverage of defamation and personality rights.[40] The subsequent Compromise Text restored the exclusions.

Mere availability

At the heart of many conflict of laws debates concerning the internet is the question whether the jurisdiction of the courts of a country, or its local laws, can be invoked by the "mere availability" of a website in that country, or whether more (such as targeting of the site to that country) is required. This regularly gives rise to controversy, such as over the case brought in France against Yahoo! Inc over the availability of Nazi memorabilia on yahoo.com auction sites (discussed in Ch.12). In our view the question of "mere availability" is a touchstone by which any conflict of laws rule should be judged in its applicability to the internet.   6–021

In this summary of English jurisdictional and applicable law rules special attention is paid to those rules that could be used to found jurisdiction over or apply English law to a "merely available" website and to examples of targeting tests.

6.3 JURISDICTION—DEFENDANT DOMICILED WITHIN A MEMBER STATE

The Brussels Jurisdiction and Judgments Regulation (the "Judgments Regulation") came into force on March 1, 2002. It applies generally to civil and commercial matters.[41] However, it does not extend to revenue, customs or administrative matters, nor to a variety of specifically excluded subject matter. The Brussels Convention has continued to apply to Denmark.[42] The Brussels Convention also continues to apply to certain territories of EU Member States excluded from the operation of the Judgments Regulation by Art.299 of the EC Treaty. The Lugano Convention continues to apply to Iceland, Norway, and Switzerland.   6–022

---

[39] See House of Commons Select Committee on European Scrutiny – Thirtieth Report (*www.publications.parliament.uk/pa/cm200506/cmselect/cmeuleg/34-xxx/3409.htm*).

[40] *http://www.europarl.europa.eu/sides/getDoc.do?pubRef=-//EP//TEXT+TA+P6-TA–2007–0006+0+DOC+XML+V0//EN&language=EN.*

[41] Art.1.

[42] See, however, the Agreement between the European Community and the Kingdom of Denmark on jurisdiction and the recognition and enforcement of judgments in civil and commercial matters O.J. 2005 L299 62–70 which came into effect on July 1, 2007.

6.3.1 The general rule

6–023　The general rule under Art.2 of the Brussels Regulation is that a defendant domiciled in a Member State shall be sued in the courts of that State.

This general rule is subject to a number of exceptions provided for by the Regulation, the most relevant of which for internet and e-commerce are described below. The general rule requires an English court to assume jurisdiction even where an English domiciled defendant is sued in England by a claimant domiciled outside a Member State. The court retains no discretion on grounds of *forum non conveniens* to grant a stay of such proceedings in favour of either a Member State or a non-Member State forum.[43]

The most relevant cases in which a defendant domiciled within a Member State may, exceptionally, be sued in the court of another Member State are as follows.

6.3.2 Jurisdiction agreements

6–024　Article 23 provides that if the parties, one or more of whom is domiciled in a Member State, have agreed that a court or the courts of a Member State are to have jurisdiction to settle any disputes which have arisen or may arise in connection with a particular legal relationship, that court or those courts shall have jurisdiction. Such jurisdiction shall be exclusive unless the parties have agreed otherwise.

Such an agreement is required to be either:

   (a) in writing or evidenced in writing, or
   (b) in a form which accords with practices which the parties have established between themselves, or
   (c) in international trade or commerce, in a form which accords with a usage of which the parties are or ought to have been aware and which in such trade or commerce is widely known to, and regularly observed by, parties to contracts of the type involved in the particular trade or commerce concerned.

The Regulation goes on to state that "Any communication by electronic means which provides a durable record of the agreement shall be equivalent to writing".[44]

The substantive provision of Art.23 does not apply to consumer contract proceedings,[45] for which jurisdiction is determined by Arts. 15–17. How-

---

[43] *Owusu v Jackson (trading as Villa Holidays Bal-Inn Villas)* (ECJ) [2005] 2 All E.R. (Comm.) 577. The decision of the Court of Appeal in *Re Harrods (Buenos Aires) Ltd* [1992] Ch.72 is no longer good law. See also *Antec International Ltd v Biosafety USA Inc* [2006] All E.R. (D) 208 (Jan).

[44] Art.23(2).

[45] Art.23, para.5.

ever, the requirements of form laid down by Art.23 are thought to apply to the limited jurisdiction agreements that Art.17 does permit for consumer disputes, even though not expressly stated to do so.[46]

6.3.3 Registered rights

Article 22 of the Regulation provides in certain cases for exclusive jurisdiction to be vested in designated Member State courts, regardless of domicile. For proceedings concerned with the validity of patents, trade marks, designs or other similar rights required to be deposited or registered, the courts of the Member State in which the deposit or registration has been applied for, or has taken place, or is under an international convention deemed to have taken place, shall have exclusive jurisdiction.

6–025

The English courts, now supported by the European Court of Justice, have taken the view that in patent proceedings where questions of validity and infringement both arise, since the infringement claim cannot not be determined without also determining validity, a claim for infringement of a UK patent comes within the exclusive jurisdiction of the English court.[47]

However, the general domicile rule under Art.2 of the Regulation can apply to non-registrable intellectual property rights. In *Pearce v Ove Arup Partnership*[48] it was accepted that under the terms of Art.2 of the Brussels Convention the court was required to accept jurisdiction in a case where an English company domiciled in England was sued for infringement of a Dutch copyright.[49]

An agreement conferring jurisdiction has no legal force if the courts whose jurisdiction it purports to exclude have exclusive jurisdiction by virtue of Art.22.[50]

---

[46] Schlosser Report O.J. C 59, March 5, 1979, at page 120, commenting on the identical provisions of the Brussels Convention.

[47] *Fort Dodge Animal Health Ltd v Akzo Nobel NV* [1998] F.S.R. 222, CA. See also *Coin Controls Ltd v Suzo International (UK) Ltd* [1997] 3 All E.R. 45. The European Court of Justice has now held in *GAT v LUK* (Case C–4/03 July 13, 2006) that the scope of the exclusive jurisdiction applies whether validity issues are raised directly by way of an action, or indirectly by way of a plea in objection (i.e. a defence). See also *Roche Nederland BV v Primus and Goldenberg* (ECJ Case C–539/03 July 13, 2006).

[48] [1999] 1 All E.R. 769, CA.

[49] However, the court went on to consider the question of justiciability as a separate matter from jurisdiction. It held that the *Mocambique* rule did not require the court to refuse to entertain the case and that the double actionability rule did not render the case bound to fail. The court declined to refer these questions to the European Court of Justice, holding that these were not questions of interpretation of the Brussels Convention but of the policy underlying the relevant rules of English private international law.

[50] Art.23(5), para.4.

6.3.4 Contract

6–026   Article 5(1) provides that in matters relating to contract, a person domiciled in a Member State may be sued in another Member State in the courts for the place of performance of the obligation in question. Ascertaining the place of performance of the obligation requires consideration of issues outside the scope of this text. It may sometimes be necessary to ascertain the law applicable to the contract before the place of performance of the obligation can be ascertained.[51] The Regulation lays down some general rules for ascertaining the place of performance.[52]

6.3.5 Tort—general considerations

The place of the harmful event under Art.5(3)

6–027   Article 5(3) provides that in matters relating to tort, delict or quasi-delict,[53] a person domiciled in a Member State may be sued in another Member State in the courts for the place where the harmful event occurred or may occur. The scope of Art.5(3) is especially relevant to the possibility of being sued in a Member State in which a website is "merely available".

The question where the harmful event occurs for the purpose of Art.5(3) has been elaborated in several decisions of the European Court of Justice. The phrase "harmful event" can include both the event giving rise to the damage and the damage itself.[54] So where a French company discharged pollutants into the Rhine in France, which flowed downstream and damaged the claimant's crops in the Netherlands, the damage occurred in the Netherlands and the claimant could sue there.[55]

However, the ECJ in the *Dumez* case held that the place where the "damage" occurs covers only "the place where the event giving rise to the damage, and entailing tortious, delictual or quasi-delictual liability, directly produced its harmful effects upon the person who is the immediate victim of the event".[56] So a different place where indirect victims suffer consequential loss as a result of the harm initially suffered by direct victims is not a place where damage has occurred within Art.5(3).[57]

Dumez also emphasised that the place where the initial damage manifests

---

[51] See, for instance, *Definitely Maybe (Touring) Ltd v Marek Lieberberg Konzertagentur GmbH* [2001] I.L.Pr. 29 QB.

[52] Art.5(1)(b).

[53] This expression has an autonomous meaning and should not be interpreted simply as referring to the national law of one or other Convention State (*Kalfelis v Schroder* [1988] E.C.R. 5565).

[54] *Handelskwekerij G J Bier BV v Mines de Potasse d'Alsace SA* [1976] E.C.R. 1735, ECJ.

[55] *ibid.*

[56] *Dumez France v Hessische Landesbank* [1990] E.C.R. 49, ECJ. See also *Domicrest Ltd v Swiss Bank Corp* [1998] 3 All E.R. 577, *ABCI v Banque Franco-Tunisienne* [2003] EWCA Civ 205 and *Newsat Holdings Ltd v Zani* [2006] EWHC 342 (Comm).

[57] See also *Marinari v Lloyds Bank Plc* (Case C–364/93) [1996] Q.B. 217.

itself is usually closely related to the other components of the liability and that in most cases the domicile of the indirect victim is not so related.[58]

In *Shevill v Presse Alliance SA*,[59] the ECJ held that the criteria for assessing whether the event in question is harmful and the evidence required of the existence and extent of the harm alleged are governed by the substantive law determined by the national conflict of laws rules of the court seised, provided that the effectiveness of the Convention was not thereby impaired.

There has always been a trickle of cross-border tort cases: waste released into the Rhine in France damaging crops in the Netherlands[60]; a defamatory newspaper article published in France finding its way into England[61]; assurances given by telephone from Switzerland to London,[62] are just some dating from the pre-internet era. But the true cross-border tort, in which the activities comprising the chain of constituent events cross national boundaries, has tended to be the exceptional case.

Receipt-oriented torts

However, the internet, by virtue of its inherently cross-border nature, has propelled the cross-border tort, founded on simultaneous multi-jurisdiction activity, into the mainstream. Art.5(3), being an effects-based rule, could open up forum-shopping based on internet activity as never before, particularly in the case of those torts which, in the context of transmitted information, may be characterised as "receipt-oriented".

6–028

By receipt-oriented torts we mean those in which the nature of the wrongful act is such that a court can easily hold that at least the damage, and perhaps all the components of the tort, have occurred in the destination country: the country in which information transmitted from outside the jurisdiction is received. Such torts could potentially include trade mark infringement, passing off, defamation, misrepresentation, negligent misstatement and some aspects of copyright.[63] We consider below the extent to which each of these is in fact receipt-oriented.

---

[58] Applied by Jacob J. in *Mecklermedia* (below, para.6–057), holding that in a case of passing off the harmful event occurred in England since the harm was to the plaintiff's goodwill in England and was the effect on the reputation in England. Referring to *Dumez*, he said that he was reinforced in that view by the quoted paragraph: "All the components of the tort take place in England. A trial would require proof of goodwill, misrepresentation and damage in England. It would not matter whether or not what DC were doing in Germany was, so far as German law and facts was concerned, lawful or not".

[59] [1995] 2 A.C. 18.

[60] *Handelswekerij GJ Bier BV v Mines de Potasse D'Alsace SA* [1976] E.C.R. 1735 ECJ.

[61] *Shevill v Presse Alliance SA* [1995] 2 A.C. 18 ECJ.

[62] *Domicrest Ltd v Swiss Bank Corp* [1998] 3 All E.R. 577.

[63] Those aspects of copyright that involve concepts such as "making available to the public" have the potential to be receipt-oriented. The aspects that dwell on the making of the copy are by nature not receipt-oriented, although the tendency of the internet to create a trail of copies along the information transmission path may result in discrete infringing acts in multiple jurisdictions.

Location of the tort compared with place of the harmful event

6–029   We have referred to the location of the components of the tort. Until 1987 the location of the tort was, in cases outside the then Brussels/Lugano Conventions, highly relevant since one of the grounds on which permission could be sought to serve English proceedings out of the jurisdiction was that a tort had been committed within the jurisdiction. However, in 1987 that ground was replaced by a provision[64] closely modeled on the Brussels/Lugano Convention requirement of a harmful event within the jurisdiction.

It is indeed the location of the tort and place of the harmful event are indeed two different concepts.[65] Identifying the place of the harmful event requires consideration of the place of the damage, or of the event which gave rise to the damage. Identifying the place of commission of the tort requires consideration of what comprises the substantive components of the tort and where they occurred.

It might reasonably be assumed that at least in an Art.5(3) case, apparently concerned only with the location of the event giving rise to the damage or the location of the damage itself, the location of the tort is now of no relevance. However, that is not always so. For at least these three purposes the location of the tort remains significant:

1. For territorial rights (such as registered trade marks) it is likely to be relevant, when considering whether there is a good arguable case on which to found jurisdiction, to consider the place of commission of the allegedly infringing act. So if the infringement is alleged to be of a UK registered trade mark, then it will be infringed only by use of the mark within the UK (see para.6–058 below).
2. When considering the applicable law in cases outside the Private International Law (Miscellaneous Provisions) Act 1995 the common law choice of law rules come into play only if the tort has foreign elements. This requires examination of the location of the tort. If the wrong can be regarded as entirely local, then English law will apply without having to consider choice of law rules. The main example of this is defamation, in which the substantive rule that publication takes place where the statement is read and comprehended results in defamation by material on a foreign website being regarded as a local English tort (see para.6–036 below).
3. The European Court of Justice ruling in *Shevill* requires that at

---

[64] Now CPR 6.20(8).
[65] So in *Newsat Holdings Ltd v Zani* [2006] EWHC 342 (Comm) David Steel J. held that the autonomous meaning of the place where the harmful event occurred did not turn upon whether, as a matter of English law, the event which gave rise to the damage incorporated all the necessary ingredients of the cause of action.

least a defamation claim[66] brought under Art.5(3) of the Judgments Regulation be restricted to damages for publication[66a] within the jurisdiction in which the proceedings are brought.

In non-Judgments Regulation cases the following further examples may be added:　　6–030

4.　Under CPR 6.20(2) a ground for granting permission to serve out of the jurisdiction is if a claim is made for an injunction ordering the defendant to do or refrain from doing an act within the jurisdiction. (The act sought to be prohibited may not fully coincide with the place of the commission of the tort,[67] but is likely to be closely related to it.)
5.　Identifying the place of the commission of the tort is the starting point for determining the most natural or appropriate forum in a *forum conveniens* dispute.[68]
6.　A defamation claim in a case in which permission to serve out of the English jurisdiction is required (i.e. a non-Judgments Regulation case) must apparently be limited to publication within the jurisdiction.[69]

Is a broad receipt-oriented approach to Art.5(3) consistent with the purpose of the Judgments Regulation?

If the receipt of information through the mere availability of the website were enough to satisfy Art.5(3), then in a Judgments Regulation case the potential claimant would have a choice, for receipt-oriented torts, of litigating in any Member State. He would be constrained only by the *Shevill*　　6–031

---

[66] The extent to which the *Shevill* principles may apply to types of liability other than defamation is yet to be fully determined. See, e.g. *Bank of Tokyo-Mitsubishi Ltd v Baskan Gida Sanaya* [2002] Lloyd's Rep. 395 in which Lawrence Collins J. left open the question whether *Shevill* might apply to claims for fraudulent and negligent misrepresentation. In *IBS Technologies (PVT) Ltd v APM Technologies SA* (Ch.D. April 7, 2003, unreported) the court held that *Shevill* did apply to a claim for copyright infringement.

[66a] Although *Shevill* itself restricts recovery to harm that occured within the jurisdiction, in an on-line defamation context this logically equates to publication within the jurisdiction. And see *Jahmed v Dow Jones* [2005] EWCA Civ. 75, at para.49.

[67] See, e.g. *King v Lewis* [2004] EWCA Civ 1329, in which although it was common ground that publication on a US controlled website took place where the text was downloaded, the court nevertheless commented that it must be at least problematic whether the application for an injunction could be said to require or prohibit anything being done within the jurisdiction.

[68] *King v Lewis, ibid.*, [24]. See discussion below under Non-Judgments Regulation cases.

[69] *King v Lewis, ibid.* For this proposition the judge referred to *Diamond v Sutton* (1866) L.R. 1 Ex. 130 and *Berezovsky v Michaels* (below, para.6–040). Although the rule in *Diamond v Sutton* was explicitly endorsed by Lord Steyn in *Berezovsky v Michaels*, the rule was formulated at a time when obtaining leave to serve out of the jurisdiction required proof of a tort committed within the jurisdiction. As explained in the main text, that is no longer the test. What is required now is proof of damage sustained within the jurisdiction or that the damage sustained resulted from an act committed within the jurisdiction (CPR Rule 6.20(8)). As discussed in the main text, this is a very different test closely modeled on Art.5(3) of the Brussels Regulation. This change was not considered by Lord Steyn in *Berezovsky*.

restriction, established in defamation cases and potentially applicable in others, that in an Art.5(3) case damages can be recovered only for a wrong committed within the chosen forum.

That would create greater exposure to foreign jurisdictions for on-line activity than for comparable off-line activity.

Such a result would be contrary to the scheme of the Regulation, in which Art.5(3) is intended to be a limited exception from the basic rule that a defendant is to be sued in the courts of his domicile.[70]

However, as can be seen from the *MARITIM* case discussed below, local courts are capable of interpreting Art.5(3) in such a way as to afford it a long reach in the on-line arena. In that case a German court explicitly took jurisdiction on a mere availability basis.

In order to preserve the objective that Art.5(3) is a limited exception from the domicile rule a means has to be found, for on-line activity, of restricting the reach of Art.5(3). As we discuss below, English courts are sometimes able to do this by applying a threshold requirement of a good arguable case, which can import an element of substantive law into determination of jurisdiction. In non-Judgments Regulation cases English courts can also invoke *forum non conveniens* considerations. However, in Judgments Regulation cases this is not possible, even where the convenient forum would be a non-EU country.[71] The *Shevill* restriction referred to above reintroduces the location of the tort as a relevant consideration, notwithstanding the focus of Art.5(3) on the "harmful event". That will have greater significance if *Shevill* has wider application than to defamation cases alone.[72]

The US "purposeful availment" approach

6–032 US courts in inter-state internet cases have used "purposeful availment of the jurisdiction" principles, derived from the US Constitution requirement of "minimum contacts", to hold that the mere availability of a website, with nothing more, does not found jurisdiction. Similar criteria apply to extraterritorial jurisdiction.[73]

At first sight, where the Judgments Regulation applies, an English court is not permitted to have regard to such considerations. Where the claimant claims jurisdiction under Art.5(3), then if a harmful event has occurred within the jurisdiction and the matter relates to a tort, delict or quasi-delict, the court *must* assume jurisdiction.[74] And in the case of receipt-oriented torts it may be relatively easy to show that a harmful event has occurred within the jurisdiction.

---

[70] *Kalfelis v Bankhaus Schroder, Münchmeyer, Hengst & Co* [1988] E.C.R. 5565.

[71] *Owusu v Jackson* ECJ Case C–281/02, [2005] Q.B. 801.

[72] See para.6–029 above.

[73] See, for example *Pebble Beach Company v Caddy*, CA 9th Cir. July 12, 2006 (Computer Law Review International, Issue 5 2006, p.145), a case involving an English defendant.

[74] Assuming that the claimant satisfies the requirements to show a good arguable case that the case comes within Art.5(3) and a serious issue to be tried on the merits, and that factors such as *lis pendens* (Art.21) are absent.

Article 5(3)—the impact of the English good arguable case requirement

That will be tempered in England by the fact that the claimant must demonstrate a good arguable case that the terms of Art.5 are satisfied.[75] He must also establish that there is a serious issue to be tried on the merits.[76]

6–033

These two requirements are succinctly set out in the judgment of Lightman J. in *Albon v Naza Motor Trading SDN BHD*.[77] Although this was not a case under the Judgments Regulation (hence the references to the differing Gateways under CPR Rule 6.20), as regards good arguable case and serious issue to be tried, the principles are essentially the same:

> "... (1) a good arguable case that each claim made fell within the one or more of the Gateways under CPR Rule 6.20.... What a good arguable case means depends on the Gateway concerned and whether the issue can or will be revisited at trial. Generally speaking the applicant for permission must show a strong probability that the claim falls within the letter and spirit of the Gateway, and this requirement is strict if once permission is given that issue will never thereafter be investigated; (2) on the merits that there was a serious issue to be tried, that is to say there is a real question to be tried. This is a lesser hurdle than good arguable case; ..."

As we have mentioned, this can raise the question whether the availability of the foreign website in England and Wales constitutes a substantive tort in this jurisdiction.[78] This, for some torts at least, allows the court to consider whether a website is directed to or targeted at this jurisdiction, even though Art.5(3) of the Regulation does not refer to this as a relevant factor. However, since this is a question of the substantive components of the tort in question, not a broad rule of jurisdiction, and different torts comprise different component elements, the relevance of targeting has to be considered individually for each tort.

The clearest example of the relevance to jurisdiction of the substantive elements of the tort is trade mark infringement, for which the courts have determined that a mark visible on a foreign website is not used in the UK unless the site is targeted at this country. Since use is an essential component of a trade mark infringement claim, failure to show a good arguable case of use within the UK will enable the court to decline jurisdiction.

---

[75] The same standard of proof should apply as under the non-Brussels Convention Rules: *Tesam Distribution Ltd v Schuh Mode Team GmbH* [1990] I.L.Pr. 149, CA and *Mülnycke AB v Procter & Gamble Ltd* [1992] 1 W.L.R. 1112, CA.

[76] *ABKCO Music & Records Inc v Music Collection International Ltd* [1995] R.P.C. 657, CA. This test also parallels the requirement in non-Brussels Convention cases.

[77] [2007] EWHC 9 (Ch), at [15].

[78] This assumes that the claimant is unable to demonstrate that the activity amounts to a tort in the defendant's home jurisdiction. This will usually be the case in a typical cross border internet dispute between companies whose websites are based on businesses conducted domestically in their home jurisdictions. The activity gives rise to complaint only when the business goes on-line and so becomes visible in other countries.

6–034   By way of contrast with trade mark infringement, for defamation the wrongful act is publication, not use. The English courts have so far held that publication takes place where the statement is downloaded, regardless of any question of targeting. On that analysis defamation is inherently a more receipt-oriented tort than trade mark infringement, enabling the court to take jurisdiction in circumstances where it could not do so for trade mark infringement.

Courts elsewhere in Europe that maintain a more rigorous separation between jurisdiction and substantive law may not, *Shevill* considerations apart, be able to introduce substantive law aspects at the jurisdiction stage.

This is illustrated by a German case in the Hamburg District Court, *Re the MARITIM Trade Mark*.[79] The proprietor of German and EU trade marks for MARITIM, which it used for a chain of hotels in Germany, sued in Germany a Danish defendant who ran a bed and breakfast establishment in Copenhagen. The defendant had registered HOTEL MARITIME as a trade mark in Denmark and ran a website using the domain name hotel-maritime.dk. The website included information in German about the hotel. It also had a brochure in several languages, including German, which was sent to prospective clients (but only on request).

The claimant asked for orders restraining (1) the defendant's use in business in Germany of the name Hotel Maritime to identify the hotel run by it, and (2) its use of the domain name *www.hotel-maritime.dk* insofar as its advertising was conducted under that domain name in the German language. The court held that it had jurisdiction to hear the claim, but dismissed the claim on its merits.

On jurisdiction, the court took an extremely broad view of Art.5(3):

> "In the case of trade mark infringements via the internet, the place of the tort is any place at which the internet domain can be called up. Websites used on the internet and their content are technically not restricted to specific countries, so that they can also generally be called up in Germany. This suffices for the court to be awarded jurisdiction. Any undertaking that is actively involved in the internet will be aware that its on-line content can be called up throughout the world and must therefore expect to be sued in foreign courts in accordance with Art.5(3) of the Convention."

The court made clear that as a matter of German law it was immaterial, when considering jurisdiction, whether infringement actually took place in Germany, or to consider the extent to which national trade marks should be given extraterritorial effect. These related to the substance of the claim and not to the jurisdiction of the court. That contrasts with the English requirement, before the court will assume jurisdiction, that the claimant should demonstrate a good arguable case.

---

[79] [2003] I.L. Pr. 17. The aspect of the decision dealing with the merits is discussed at para.6–062 below. See also the Belgian *Liberty tv.com* case discussed at para.6–123, below.

Determination of applicable law in tort claims

Where the substantive law is relevant to determining whether there is a **6–035** good arguable case, an English court should first determine the applicable law if this is in question. For non-contractual claims other than defamation and like claims[80] the court will apply the provisions of the Private International Law (Miscellaneous Provisions) Act 1995.[81] Unlike the Contracts (Applicable Law) Act 1990, which implements the 1980 Rome Convention on the law applicable to contractual obligations, the 1995 Act implements a home-grown UK set of conflicts rules.

Section 11(1) of the 1995 Act lays down the general rule that the applicable law is the law of the country in which the events constituting the tort in question occur. For many receipt-oriented torts, where the court can conclude that all the components of the tort were located in England, this will in practice be sufficient to enable the court to conclude that it is dealing with a domestic English tort.[82]

If the events constituting the tort occurred in different countries, then under s.11(2)(c) of the 1995 Act the general rule is that the applicable law is the law of the country in which the most significant element or elements of those events occurred. This has similarities to the former "substance" test (discussed below under defamation, to which the old test still applies).

However, under s.12 in both cases the general rule can be displaced by factors connecting the tort with another country, including factors such as those relating to the parties, to any events which constitute the tort in question or to any of the circumstances or consequences of those events. If it is substantially more appropriate for the applicable law to be the law of the other country, the general rule is displaced.

The Rome II Proposal for a harmonised pan-European set of applicable law rules for non-contractual liability has reached the stage of an agreed Compromise Text. We will discuss below under each specific type of liability the current and proposed rules. In general Rome II tends to favour effects-based conflicts rules, which as we have discussed tend to create greater exposure to foreign law for on-line activity than for offline.

The impression that insufficient attention has been paid in Rome II to the differential impact on on-line activity is reinforced by the fact that the

---

[80] Section 13 of the 1995 Act excludes any claim under the law of any part of the UK for libel or slander or for slander of title, slander of goods or other malicious falsehood and any claim under the law of Scotland for verbal injury; and any claim under the law of any other country corresponding to or otherwise in the nature of such claims.

[81] The relevant provisions of the Act came into force on May 1, 1996.

[82] Section 9(6) of the Private International Law (Miscellaneous Provisions) Act 1995 requires the conflicts rules of the Act to be applied even where the events occur within the forum. However in many cases there will be no real dispute about the application of English law. Thus in *Mecklermedia* (see below, para.6–057) the claimant's claim was for the English tort of passing off. There was no discussion of applicable law as such, but Jacob J.'s analysis in relation to "harmful event" under Art.5(3) of the Brussels Convention was that all the components of the tort had taken place in England. See also the discussion at para.6–037 regarding defamation, which is outside the 1995 Act and to which the common law rule still applies that if all the events occur within the forum no question of conflict of laws arises.

European Commission's original Proposal adopted on July 22, 2003 contained not a single mention of the internet or e-commerce. For a document prepared at a time when the most significant challenges for conflict of laws are presented by the internet, this was an extraordinary omission.

Since some torts are more receipt-oriented than others, and since in the English courts the substantive aspects of the tort are capable of having an impact on jurisdiction, we will consider both the substantive components of the tort (including determination of applicable law) and the existence of a harmful event on a tort by tort basis.

The appropriateness of this tort by tort approach is reinforced by the *obiter* comments of Buxton L.J. in the Court of Appeal decision in *800-FLOWERS Trade Mark*.[83] He thought it unlikely that there would be one uniform rule, specific to the internet, that could be applied to all cases of internet use.

It should be borne in mind that although the substantive components of the tort may be relevant to whether a good arguable case has been made out, and to the location of the tort where that is a relevant consideration, the "place where the harmful event occurred" has an autonomous Regulation meaning, so that the fact that under English law the place of commission of the tort would be England does not prevent the place of the event giving rise to the damage being another country.[84]

6.3.6 Defamation

Defamation—applicable law

6-036   For defamation, the applicable law is determined according to English common law principles, unaffected by the Private International Law (Miscellaneous Provisions) Act 1995 (which excludes defamation from its scope).

If the tort is found to have been committed in this country then it is a domestic tort and only English law is relevant. In traditional defamation cases this is very likely since they will usually be founded on evidence of actual publication by circulation of physical copies in this jurisdiction.[85]

In internet cases English courts have repeatedly confirmed the traditional rule that publication takes place where the statement is read and comprehended, which for the internet translates into the place where it is downloaded (see discussion below, para.6–041 *et seq.*). Since publication is

---

[83] [2001] EWCA Civ 721.

[84] This is most clearly illustrated in misrepresentation and negligent misstatement cases. See discussion in *Newsat Holdings Ltd v Zani* [2006] EWHC 342 (Comm).

[85] See, for instance, the *Berezovsky* case (below, para.6–040); and see also *Chadha v Dow Jones & Co Inc* [1999] E.M.L.R. 724.

the relevant act for establishing defamation, this leads to the same result as for hard copy publication, namely a domestic English law tort.[86]

If there were a foreign element, the court would apply the test of where in substance the cause of action arose. If the tort has in substance been committed abroad, then the rules of double actionability will be applied to determine whether an actionable tort has been committed.[87]

Defamation—place of the harmful event under Art.5(3)

As to jurisdiction and the place of the harmful event under Art.5(3) of the Judgments Regulation, in *Shevill v Presse Alliance SA*,[88] a defamation case under the Brussels Convention, the court stated that damage is caused in the places where the publication is distributed, when the victim is known in those places. The court also stated that the place where the event giving rise to the damage occurred is the place where the publisher is established, since that is the place where the harmful event originated and from which the libel was issued and put into circulation.

6–037

The court held that a claimant could therefore sue either in each or any country of distribution, pursuant to Art.5(3), or in the country in which the defendant publisher was established. If the claimant sued in the country of the publisher's establishment it could recover for harm occurring in all Convention countries. However, if the claimant chose to sue in the country of distribution under Art.5(3) it could recover damages only in respect of the harm occurring in that country. In the on-line context this equates to damages for publication in that country (see para.6–029 above).

The court also held that the criteria for assessing whether the event in question is harmful and the evidence required of the existence and extent of the harm alleged are governed by the substantive law determined by the national conflict of laws rules of the court seised, provided that the effectiveness of the Convention was not thereby impaired. When the case returned to the House of Lords it was held that the English law presumption of harm to the plaintiff from publication of a defamatory statement was sufficient to constitute a harmful event for the purpose of Art.5(3), without specific proof of damage.[89]

The presumption of harm means that in libel the requirement under

---

[86] See for instance *King v Lewis* [2004] EWCA Civ 1329, where there was no dispute that a defamation claim in respect of a US website, limited to publication in England, was governed by English law. See also Dicey, Morris and Collins *The Conflict of Laws*, 14th ed. (2006) at paras. 35–130–35–131.

[87] *Metall & Rohstoff v Donaldson Inc* [1990] 1 Q.B. 391, CA. One effect of the double actionability test is that it prevents an English court having to give effect to stricter foreign defamation laws. For claims within the co-ordinated field of the Electronic Commerce Directive the double actionability rule may have been removed (Law Commission Scoping Study on Defamation and the Internet – A Preliminary Investigation, December 2002 at para.4.41).

[88] [1995] 2 A.C. 18.

[89] *Shevill v Presse Alliance* [1996] 3 All E.R. 929.

Art.5(3) of the Regulation to prove that damage has been sustained in the jurisdiction will normally be easy to satisfy.[90]

Defamation—jurisdiction and applicable law in the English courts

6–038 The English courts have so far taken a robustly destination-oriented approach to applying English law in internet defamation cases and taking jurisdiction over defamatory content on merely available foreign internet sites. However, the House of Lords has yet to consider the matter and has acknowledged that defamation on the internet raises difficult questions.[91]

How did the courts arrive at their current position? This includes consideration of Australian and several English internet defamation cases. These are all non-Judgments Regulation cases. However, given the similarity between the conditions for granting permission to serve out of the English jurisdiction under CPR 6.20(8) and the requirements of Art.5(3) of the Regulation, it is convenient to introduce them at this point in the discussion.

Defamation—place of publication in pre-internet cases

6–039 The pre-internet principles were established with foreign newspapers and broadcasts. Even if only a few copies of a foreign newspaper are distributed in England, each will constitute a publication in England and the publisher of the newspaper will normally be taken to have authorised it,[92] thereby incurring liability for publication within the jurisdiction. A letter from abroad opened and read in England is published within the jurisdiction.[93]

A radio broadcast is published where it is received.[94] In the Canadian case of *Jenner v Sun Oil* McRuer C.J.H.C. said:

> "Radio broadcasts are made for the purpose of being heard. The programme here in question was put on the air for advertising purposes. It is to be presumed that those who broadcast over a radio network in the English language intend that the messages they broadcast will be heard by large numbers of those who receive radio messages in the English language ... The 'ears' of the recipients of a foreign broadcast are the receiving sets within the jurisdiction and such a set is not dissimilar in law to a hearing device such as may be used by one whose hearing is impaired or the glasses that one with defective vision puts on so that he may read.

---

[90] The presumption of damage is theoretically not irrebuttable, albeit before the coming into force of the Human Rights Act 1998 on October 1, 2000 it was so in practice (*Dow Jones & Co Inc v Jameel* [2005] EWCA Civ 75).

[91] See the comments of Lord Steyn in *Berezovsky*, below, para.6–040.

[92] We discuss below (para.6–045) the question of responsibility for publication and the impact that it has on applicable law and jurisdiction in internet cases.

[93] *Bata v Bata* [1948] W.N. 366.

[94] *Jenner v Sun Oil Co* [1952] 2 D.L.R. 526, an Ontario case.

I cannot see what difference it makes whether the person is made to understand by means of the written word, sound-waves or ether-waves insofar as the matter of proof of publication is concerned. The tort consists in making a third person understand actionable defamatory matter."

Although in defamation publication is sufficient to found liability, the question of whether jurisdiction can be taken based on mere availability on the internet has not yet been examined at the highest level in the English courts.   6–040

The closest that we have come is *Berezovsky v Michaels*.[95] This was a non-Brussels Convention libel case in which the House of Lords decided by a 3–2 majority not to stay libel proceedings brought by Russian businessmen against a US magazine with a small circulation in England. The magazine was stated also to be available on the internet within the English jurisdiction. However, their Lordships were able to come to a conclusion without reference to this aspect. Lord Steyn commented:

"In their statements of claim the plaintiffs relied on the fact that the Forbes article is also available to be read on-line on the Internet within the jurisdiction. The Court of Appeal referred to this aspect only in passing. During the course of interesting arguments it became clear that there is not the necessary evidence before the House to consider this important issue satisfactorily. Having come to a clear conclusion without reference to the availability of the article on the internet it is unnecessary to discuss it in this case." (p.996h–j)

In his dissenting speech Lord Hoffmann stated:

"... But that does not mean that we should always put ourselves forward as the most appropriate forum in which any foreign publisher who has distributed copies in this country, or whose publications have been downloaded here from the internet, can be required to answer the complaint of any public figure with an international reputation, however little the dispute has to do with England."

Defamation—place of publication in internet cases

Questions of jurisdiction over a foreign internet publication were addressed in detail for the first time in the Australian case of *Gutnick v Dow Jones & Co Inc*.[96] This was decided at first instance in August 2001 and subsequently by the High Court of Australia in 2002. The case concerned an   6–041

---

[95] [2000] 2 All E.R. 986, HL.
[96] [2001] V.S.C. 305; on appeal, [2002] H.C.A. 56.

article in the on-line version of *Barrons* magazine, alleged to be defamatory of a resident of the State of Victoria. The magazine was provided by means of a password access, subscription website. The website was operated from the USA, where the servers were located and maintained. It was admitted that the article had been downloaded by subscribers in the State of Victoria.

At first instance Hedigan J. considered the questions of what constituted publication and where publication took place; and who was responsible for the publication, the subscriber or the website proprietor? The court also considered the broader policy implications of country of origin versus country of receipt rules, for which see Ch.12.

As to what constituted publication, the defendant argued that publication took place not on reception by the user but on delivery, which in this case equated to the "uplift" (i.e. transmission) of the article upon receipt of a request from the user's browser. It therefore followed, argued the defendant, that publication took place in the US, where the servers were located, and that there was no publication in Australia.

The court held, following *Jenner v Sun Oil* and other authorities including *Godfrey v Demon Internet Ltd*,[97] that publication took place at the time and in the place where it was made manifest in a form capable of being comprehended by a third party. It rejected the argument that publication took place on delivery as being contrary to centuries of authority.

The defendant sought to distinguish *Godfrey v Demon Internet Ltd*, in which Morland J. had held that transmission of a defamatory posting from the storage of a Usenet news server constituted a publication of that posting to any subscriber who accessed the news group, whenever one of its subscribers accessed the newsgroup and saw that posting. The defendant contended that this case was of no assistance because it involved Usenet, not the internet. The judge rejected that, noting Morland J.'s reference to seeing the posting defamatory of the plaintiff and holding that that was equivalent to downloading in this case.

The judge said that even if he was wrong as to publication occurring on downloading, he rejected the defendant's contention that it was possible to separate uplift from download. In the court's view these were indivisible, the reception by the user taking place to all intents and purposes simultaneously with the transmission by the web server. Therefore, if delivery was the correct test, publication took place in both the US and Victoria at the same time. However, the judge decided the case on the basis that publication took place on downloading.

We discuss below (para.6–045) the judge's findings on responsibility for publication. He also rejected an application by the defendant to stay the proceedings on grounds of *forum non conveniens*.

6–042   Although the first instance judge's determination of place of publication would apply equally to a free website as to the subscription site considered in this case, the determination that the defendant caused the publication in Victoria was heavily reliant on the fact that this was a subscription website.

[97] [1999] 4 All E.R. 343.

It left open the question whether, and if so in what circumstances, the proprietor of a free website would be taken to have intended publication in all countries in which it is capable of being received.

However, that did not survive the subsequent appeal to the High Court of Australia, which made extraordinarily broad statements of the grounds on which a court could assume jurisdiction over any foreign website, whether subscription or free. Those statements have, as we shall see, been adopted by the English courts.

The appeal of Dow Jones in *Gutnick* was heard by a seven judge panel of the High Court of Australia.[98] The judges dismissed the appeal. Although the decision was unanimous in the result, one judge (Kirby J.) was markedly more sympathetic to the defendant than the majority, finding merit in the defendant's arguments that the internet was a sufficiently different medium to require a different approach. However he held that this had to be addressed by international discussion, not by the courts. The majority regarded the internet as no different in kind from previous media:

"...the problem of widely disseminated communications is much older than the internet and the World Wide Web. The law has had to grapple with such cases ever since newspapers and magazines came to be distributed to large numbers of people over wide geographic areas. Radio and television presented the same kind of problem as was presented by widespread dissemination of printed material, although international transmission of material was made easier by the advent of electronic means of communication. [38]

It was suggested that the World Wide Web was different from radio and television because the radio or television broadcaster could decide how far the signal was to be broadcast. It must be recognised, however, that satellite broadcasting now permits very wide dissemination of radio and television and it may, therefore, be doubted that it is right to say that the World Wide Web has a uniquely broad reach. It is no more or less ubiquitous than some television services. In the end, pointing to the breadth or depth of reach of particular forms of communication may tend to obscure one basic fact. However broad may be the reach of any particular means of communication, those who make information accessible by a particular method do so knowing of the reach that their information may have. In particular, those who post information on the World Wide Web do so knowing that the information they make available is available to all and sundry without any geographic restriction [39]."

According to the majority, any potential injustice in exposing a defendant to a theoretical risk of being sued around the world is ameliorated by a   6–043

---

[98] *Gutnick v Dow Jones Inc* [2002] H.C.A. 56.

number of factors: first, that a claimant will in practice be restricted to jurisdictions in which he has a reputation; secondly, that claimants are unlikely to sue unless a judgment obtained would be of real value, taking into account where it could be enforced; and thirdly, that identifying the person about whom material is to be published will, except in the most unusual cases, readily identify the defamation law to which that person may resort.

We may interject that the first and third observations fail to take account of claimants with international reputations (who are often precisely those with the resources and inclination to resort to defamation litigation). The point about enforcement is of little weight within Europe, where judgments are easily enforceable under the Judgments Regulation.

The *Gutnick* majority also commented that existing rules about vexatious litigation and *forum conveniens* could be used to prevent multiplicity of suits. Whether such optimism is justified may perhaps be doubted when, as in *Berezovsky v Michaels* (above, para.6–040), one sees a Russian claimant suing a US magazine in England on the basis of a few copies circulated here, and the House of Lords (by a 3–2 majority) refusing to stay the suit on the basis of *forum non conveniens*.

Further, *forum non conveniens* is not available to defendants in cases under the Judgments Regulation. As against that, English courts are now prepared to strike out or stay defamation cases where there is no real or substantial tort within the jurisdiction.[99]

The only deference that the majority of the seven judges in *Gutnick* showed to Dow Jones' arguments was a suggestion that it might be necessary to develop common law defences to defamation so as to take into account the reasonableness of the publisher's conduct, including where the conduct took place and what rule or rules about defamation applied in that place or in those places.

In *Harrods Ltd v Dow Jones & Co Inc*,[1] an English case, the claimants commenced defamation proceedings against the US defendant, Dow Jones & Co Inc, limited to damages for publication within the English jurisdiction. Dow Jones had published an article about the claimants in the US edition of The Wall Street Journal, following an April Fool joke perpetrated by Harrods designed to promote a new website.

The article did not appear in the European edition of the WSJ. The evidence before the court was that 10 copies of the US edition were sent to subscribers in the UK, and that there was a very small number of hits on the on-line edition at *www.wsj.com* and in an Interactive Publications Library.

Dow Jones had sought a ruling from a New York court that it could continue to publish the article. However the New York judge determined that a more appropriate alternative remedy existed for the parties in proceeding with the English action and declined to encroach upon the English court.

---

[99] *Dow Jones & Co Inc v Jameel* (above, fn.90).
[1] [2003] EWHC 1162 (QB).

Having found that the English proceedings had not been effectively   6–044
served in England, the court went on to consider a precautionary application by the claimant for permission to serve the proceedings outside the
English jurisdiction. The issues on this application overlapped considerably
with those on the defendant's application to stay the proceedings on
grounds of *forum non conveniens.*

Eady J. emphasised that this was a claim brought by an English company
to protect its trading reputation in respect of publications which, according
to English law, had taken place within the English jurisdiction. That
applied "both to the small number of copies of The Wall Street Journal
received by subscribers here and also to the apparently limited number of
hits emanating from this jurisdiction on the relevant page of the website".[2]

The judge also stressed that English law does not recognise the "single
publication" doctrine,[3] so that even though a newspaper's primary circulation may be in one or more foreign jurisdictions, under English law there
may also be separate publications in other jurisdictions, each sufficient to
found a separate cause of action. "Thus, however limited and technical it
may appear, there have been publications within this jurisdiction which are
arguably tortious and which give rise to a cause of action here."

The judge refused to stay the proceedings on grounds of *forum non
conveniens* (see para.6–076 below)

Don King v Lennox Lewis, Lion Promotions LLC and Judd Burstein[4]
was the first defamation case in which the English courts ruled on jurisdiction where the internet was the sole means of publication. It was
decided at first instance by Eady J. and then by the Court of Appeal. We
discuss it below under non-Judgments Regulation cases.

In *King v Lewis* there was no dispute, in the light of the authorities, that
the place of publication was the place of download. The same judge stated
in *Richardson v Schwarzenegger*[5] that it was now "well settled" that "an
internet publication takes place in any jurisdiction where the relevant words
are read or downloaded".

Defamation—responsibility for publication

Another aspect of the substantive law of defamation that has a major   6–045
impact on jurisdiction and applicable law is the question of responsibility
for publication.

The corollary of the position that publication takes place where the
statement is downloaded is that, for most types of internet publication, no
publication takes place until the reader accesses and downloads the article.

---

[2] The judge cited *Godfrey v Demon Internet* (see above, para.6–041), *Loutchansky v Times
Newspapers Ltd* [2002] 2 W.L.R. at [58] and *Gutnick* (see above, para.6–041) in support
of this proposition.
[3] In England each publication of a statement gives rise to a separate cause of action (*Duke of
Brunswick v Harmer* (1849) 14 Q.B. 185). In the USA there is one global act of publication.
An attempt in *Gutnick* to argue for the single publication doctrine was unsuccessful.
[4] [2004] EWHC 168 (QB).
[5] [2004] EWHC 2422 (QB).

The cause of action in libel arises when the words come to the attention of the reader. In order to attribute responsibility for that publication to the person who owns the website, it is necessary to hold that by putting the material on the website he caused the publication that takes place when the reader later downloads the material.

Material placed on the internet, such as on a public website, is prima facie available for viewing anywhere in the world. In the absence of any contrary factual circumstances someone who puts up a website would, on existing pre-internet principles, be taken to know that it can and will be read in England and to authorise that publication.[6]

We will see that the English and Australian courts have, so far, rigorously applied these pre-internet principles to publication on the internet. In particular, unlike in trade mark infringement, they have so far resisted any suggestion that directing or targeting of activities has any relevance to cross-border defamation liability.

In the *Gutnick* case at first instance (see para.6–041, above), the judge addressed in detail the question of who was responsible for, or caused, the publication. The defendant argued that the web was a "pull" rather than a "push" technology, so that the article was only sent into Australia in response to a request by the user, the defendant's web servers being effectively passive. The user was in effect "self-publishing" and the defendant did not cause the publication.

The judge rejected this argument. The defendant sought to contrast information obtained by the user's own deliberate actions, by clicking to request the defendant's web server to provide access to the relevant document, with persons listening to a radio or seeing and hearing a television broadcast. However, the judge stated that appreciation of the contrast between push and pull technologies could not dominate the question of publication for the law of defamation:

> "It would be otherwise just as relevant to say that a radio station has not done anything to facilitate the broadcast in the publishing sense because the listener turns the selection control to that station."

6–046   The judge also rejected, on the basis that this was a subscription site, the defendant's contention that the process of extracting the particular article from the Dow Jones web server involved requests for actions by persons "over whom Dow Jones has no control". The judge commented:

> "This is by no means wholly accurate as Dow Jones has programmed its computers ... to decline requests e.g. for Barrons in

---

[6] "Authorisation" is one aspect of the "unrespectable complexity" of causation rules in defamation law (*per* Laws L.J. in *McManus v Beckham* [2002] EWCA Civ 939). Competing causation formulations discussed in *McManus* include "natural and probable result" and "reasonably foreseeable".

the absence of a provided password and also to decline even with a password if the requestor is delinquent in the payment of his or her outstanding account at that time.".

The plaintiff argued that publication to persons in Victoria who read it was the intended natural and probable consequence of what the defendants had done and that the defendant was therefore liable for the publications that occurred in Victoria; and that:

"it was entirely foreseeable and to be expected that the article about the plaintiff, a prominent Victorian resident, would be published in Victoria and that in publishing the article the defendant was author, editor, printer, publisher and librarian".

The judge agreed: 6–047

"It is also absolutely clear that Dow Jones intended that only those subscribers in various States of Australia who met their requirements would be able to access them, and they intended that they should".

On appeal, the High Court made the broad comments that we have already noted to the effect that simply knowing the global reach of the medium is sufficient to render someone who publishes on the internet responsible for publication wherever it may take place.

The question of authorisation in the context of internet publication has been specifically addressed in one English case, *King v Lewis*.[7] The facts of this case are set out at para.6–076 below. The defendants were a promotions company and two individuals, one of whom (Mr Burstein) was said to have made the statements complained of in two articles that appeared on US-based websites. The defendants applied to set aside service out of the jurisdiction. They argued, among other things, that they had not authorised downloading in England. Eady J. (who was upheld on appeal) said:

"42. A closely allied point put forward by Mr Price [(the defendants' counsel)] was that the downloading in England was not something that was authorised by Mr Lennox Lewis or, for that matter, by Mr Burstein. He submits that authorisation has to be seen in terms of agency, and it would be absurd to suggest that any of his clients were in such a relationship with any of the relevant persons in this jurisdiction who downloaded or read the offending words. It is not enough, says Mr Price, merely to 'facilitate' the ultimate act of downloading. I am by no means persuaded that authorisation, in the context of publication, has to be seen in terms of agency. It may be true that someone who gives an

---

[7] [2004] EWHC 168 (QB); on appeal [2004] EWCA Civ 1329.

interview to a newspaper is not thereby creating the editor his agent or in any way binding the editor to publish the interview. He is nonetheless authorising the use of the information he provides and, to that extent, the law would regard him as responsible if a defamation is published as a result. Mr Price may no doubt wish to develop these arguments at trial, with particular reference to the way in which the law approaches internet publication, but the Claimant's case is that Mr Burstein caused the ultimate publications in England by virtue of having said what he did to fightnews.com and boxingtalk.com. That is plainly an arguable case in the context of the present application."

6–048   Eady J. also touched on causation in *Richardson v Schwarzenegger*,[8] in which he said:

"There is no warrant for drawing a distinction (as was tentatively canvassed in argument) between those who deliberately publish or put matters on the World Wide Web as part of their business and those who do so incidentally, and without intending to target any particular jurisdiction for the receipt of their communications: *Lewis v King* at [33] to [34]. It seems to be a question of applying or adapting settled principles as to legal responsibility for publication, including that relating to foreseeability: see e.g. *McManus v Beckham* [2002] EWCA Civ 939."

In the first sentence Eady J. confirms that targeting has no relevance to *forum* considerations (which were the topic of the paragraphs from *Lewis v King* to which he referred—see below, para.6–076). In the second sentence he confirms the relevance of general causation principles (the nature of which was in issue in *McManus*). It is unclear whether Eady J. is suggesting here that targeting cannot ever affect the question of causation.

The current approach of the courts amounts to holding that worldwide publication is the natural and probable (or reasonably foreseeable)[9] consequence of putting up a website and that the website proprietor has thereby authorised, or at least is to be held responsible for, every publication that takes place when a third party downloads an article from the website.

It is by no means obvious that every defendant should be automatically responsible for every publication that takes place when someone goes to its website and downloads an article. That approach may be superficially attractive when the defendant is an international American media company. But what of the church newsletter, the garden club magazine, the schoolgirl blogger? Are they to be characterised as a "global publisher"[10]

---

[8] [2004] EWHC 2422 (QB).
[9] For a full discussion of the appropriate formulation see *McManus v Beckham* [2002] EWCA Civ 939.
[10] *King v Lewis* [2004] EWCA Civ 1329, at [31]: "... a global publisher should not be too fastidious as to the part of the globe where he is made a libel defendant."

and exposed to worldwide liability because they are taken to know the reach of the medium on which they have chosen to publish?[11] The current doctrine can be seen to do less than justice when viewed in that context.

Should the English courts at some point wish to develop a directing and targeting approach for defamation, causation provides a suitable framework within which to do so. The judgments in *McManus v Beckham* emphasise that the question of causation is not merely a question of factual enquiry, but of achieving a just and reasonable result.[12] It is a "control mechanism"[13] in respect of defamation liability. That is precisely what is required to counterbalance the destination-oriented approach so far taken by the English and Australian courts.

6–049

It would be possible (and, we suggest, desirable) for the courts to develop a rule that when a third party downloads an article in a jurisdiction that the defendant has not targeted, that act is too remote for the defendant to be regarded as having authorised the publication. Such a rule would have the advantage that it would be applicable in all cases, regardless of whether *forum non conveniens* is available. Whether the defendant had targeted the jurisdiction would depend on consideration of the objectively ascertainable factual circumstances.[14]

Different types of internet publication may vary in the extent to which worldwide distribution is the inevitable result of the publication. In the case of Usenet newsgroups, for instance, the very nature and purpose of the Usenet system is to cause postings to be disseminated by replication to Usenet servers around the world where they are available for public consumption by downloading the postings.

In those circumstances it might be quite difficult, absent any circumstances suggesting that the likely audience was predominantly local, for the author to suggest that he did not authorise publication to the world at large, including England. A court might well be prepared, at least at the stage of determining whether it has jurisdiction, to infer publication in England without proof that anyone within the jurisdiction actually read the posting.[15]

If someone at the instigation of the claimant were to read the posting in order to provide evidence of actual publication for the purpose of legal proceedings, that is in principle sufficient to support the assertion that a tort has been committed within the jurisdiction. However, if that were the only publication then the action would be liable to be stayed or struck out for lack of a real or substantial tort within the jurisdiction.[16]

6–050

---

[11] "...the *dicta* in *Gutnick* ... emphasise the internet publisher's very choice of a ubiquitous medium." (*King v Lewis, ibid.*, [31]).

[12] Waller L.J., [34] Laws L.J., [39], [42].

[13] Waller L.J., [33].

[14] We discuss in para.6–054 the misconception that a targeting test necessarily involves ascertaining the subjective intention of the publisher.

[15] At trial, however, the claimant will be required to prove substantial publication within the jurisdiction, whether by direct evidence or by inference from the surrounding circumstances (*Al Amoudi v Brisard* [2006] EWHC 1062 (QB)). For an example of such inference, see *Pritchard Englefield v Steinberg* [2005] EWCA Civ 288 at [21].

[16] See discussion in *Dow Jones v Jameel* [56].

It might be thought that where a website is made available it is less inevitable than with Usenet newsgroups that worldwide publication will result, and therefore more arguable that the website publisher did not authorise publication in every country. However, it will have been seen from the cases discussed that this argument, indeed any arguments based on the degree of "push" and "pull", have not found favour with the courts.[17]

Questions of causation will inevitably have a part to play in some types of electronic publication. Assume, for instance, that an American sends an email from America to a recipient with a New Zealand email address. The email is defamatory of an English third party. The New Zealand recipient has a Blackberry device, to which the email is pushed automatically on receipt.[18] The New Zealand recipient happens to be travelling in England when he uses his Blackberry to open and read the email. According to existing principles, that is a publication in England upon which the English courts could take jurisdiction.

6–051 Is the American sender to be taken to have authorised or caused the publication in England? It is now common knowledge that emails can be accessed on the move, anywhere in the world. According to the *Gutnick* approach, the very choice of a ubiquitous medium carries with it the risk of worldwide liability.[19] That suggests that the American sender would be liable for the English publication.

But this communication was sent to a New Zealand email address. We suggest that in those circumstances, the communication having been targeted at New Zealand, the just result is that the American sender should not be taken to have authorised publication outside New Zealand. It cannot be right that the choice of a ubiquitous medium is itself sufficient to hold the

---

[17] See para.6–045. This is also true in other areas, such as obscenity. See, e.g. *R v Fellows, R v Arnold* (1996) October, 3 *Times*, CA. In this case one of the defendants to charges under the Obscene Publications Act 1959 and the Protection of Children Act 1978 argued that giving certain others password access to his archive of indecent pictures on his employer's computer did not amount to "showing" the pictures as contended by the prosecution. The defendant argued that "showing" is active rather than passive, and that he did nothing more than permit others to have access to his archive. The Court of Appeal accepted, for present purposes, that active conduct on the defendant's part was required. Evans L.J. said: "... it seems to us that there is ample evidence of such conduct on his part. He took whatever steps were necessary not merely to store the data on his computer but also to make it available worldwide to other computers via the internet. He corresponded by email with those who sought to have access to it and he imposed certain conditions before they were permitted to do so. He gave permission by giving them the password. He did all this with the sole object of allowing others, as well as himself, to view exact reproductions of the photographs stored in his archive."

[18] The technical mechanism involved is that a dedicated server at the (normally) corporate receiving end processes the incoming emails and forwards them immediately to the individual recipient's Blackberry device, where they are stored. This contrasts with the traditional email or webmail process, where the emails remain stored on the corporate or ISP server until the individual recipient accesses the email account and downloads the new emails to their local machine. The traditional email process can vary in details. For instance on a corporate network the list of emails visible in the inbox is likely to be updated in real time, whereas for remote access to the corporate email server, or for an account with an ISP, both the list and the emails themselves have to be downloaded by the user.

[19] See fn.11 above.

publisher responsible for every publication that results, in any part of the world.

On this basis, the proposition that targeting can never affect causation has to be rejected. Once it is accepted that targeting can be relevant to causation, then the door is opened to deploy objective directing and targeting criteria in internet defamation cases generally, so as to rein in the more extreme consequences of the existing Anglo-Australian approach.

We also note that in the context of publication for the purposes of the Obscene Publications Act 1959, the Court of Appeal in *R v Waddon*[20] hinted at the potential relevance of causation in determining questions of publication in cross-border internet cases:

> "[Counsel for the defendant] invited the Court, which invitation, in the course of argument, we did not accept, to rule upon what the position might be in relation to jurisdiction if a person storing material on a website outside England intended that no transmission of that material should take place back to this country. For the purpose of this appeal, it is unnecessary to embark on a consideration of the issues which may arise in relation to that matter, which will, no doubt, as [counsel for the defendant] accepted, depend upon questions of intention and causation in relation to where publication should take place."

Defamation—abuse of process

The English courts have, with *Jameel v Dow Jones & Co Inc*,[21] started to   **6–052**
display a willingness to strike out or stay defamation cases as an abuse of process where no real and substantial tort appears to have been committed within the jurisdiction. Although *forum conveniens* arguments cannot be deployed in cases within the Judgments Regulation, the Regulation presents no obvious bar to striking out or staying proceedings on the ground of no real or substantial tort.

In *Jameel* the publication complained of was wholly online. It concerned an article posted on the *Wall Street Journal On-line* subscription website hosted in New Jersey, which contained a hyperlink to a document in which the claimant was named in a list of people. The article remained on the website for about four days, when it was moved into an archive where it remained for another four months, after which it was removed altogether.

---

[20] [2000] All E.R. (D) 502, see para.12–063 below. But see also *R v Fellows, R v Arnold* (fn.17 above).

[21] [2005] EWCA Civ 75. In an earlier case, *Level 8 v Abbas* (unreported, July 6, 1999) the claimant in an English action alleged malicious falsehood based on a footnote in quarterly returns filed by the defendant with the US Securities and Exchange Commission and published on the SEC website. Jacob J. struck out the malicious falsehood claim, having found that there was no evidence that (1) anyone in the UK had accessed the website, (2) that even if they had, they would necessarily have made the connection with the claimant and (3) that if they did he would not suffer any significant or appreciable damage as a result of the publication.

The claimant obtained permission to serve proceedings on Dow Jones in the US. Dow Jones did not challenge the English court's jurisdiction. Dow Jones asserted, and the hearing proceeded on this assumption, that only five subscribers had followed the hyperlink. Of those, three were associated with the claimant. The remaining two did not know of the claimant and had no recollection of reading the claimant's name.

Dow Jones argued that the publication had been minimal and had done no significant damage to the claimant's reputation. In these circumstances pursuing the action was disproportionate and an abuse of process. The claimant argued that he was entitled to seek vindication of his reputation and an injunction restraining Dow Jones from repeating the libel. He argued that having raised no challenge to jurisdiction, Dow Jones could not now raise an objection of no real or substantial tort within the jurisdiction.

As to obtaining an injunction, the court on the particular facts did not regard this as as a sufficient reason to continue the litigation in this case.

As to vindication, the court emphasised that although the publication on the website was worldwide, the proceedings related only to the publication in England. It was not legitimate for the claimant to seek to justify continuing the proceedings by praying in aid the effect that they might have in vindicating him in relation to the wider publication. Any vindication that the claimant might achieve in relation to the publication in England would be minimal.

The court concluded that it would be an abuse of process to allow the claim to continue. If the court had been considering an application to set aside permission to serve proceedings out of the jurisdiction, it would have done so on the basis that the five publications within the jurisdiction did not amount to a real or substantial tort.

Defamation—is there room for a directing and targeting threshold?

6–053   It will be apparent that so far the English courts in defamation cases have adhered strongly to the view, most clearly expressed in *Gutnick*, that someone who puts up material on the web is taken to know the global reach of the medium and must take the consequences.

A New Zealand court has also taken a similar view, applying *Gutnick*:

> "To my mind, if a defendant chooses to upload information on the internet, being aware of its reach, then they assume the associated risks, including the risk of being sued for defamation. If it were otherwise, namely that publication occurred at the place of uploading, defendants could potentially defame with impunity by uploading all information in countries with lax, or no, defamation laws."[22]

---

[22] *University of Newlands v Nationwide News Pty* (2002) 210 C.L.R. 575; [2005] C.T.L.R. 2 N–17.

Taken together with the doctrine that publication takes place where the material is read and comprehended, this amounts to a full-blown country of destination rule, ameliorated only by *forum conveniens* considerations (where available) and the power to strike out for abuse of process in an extreme case such as *Jameel*. This makes for a striking contrast with, for instance, trade mark infringement, in which the courts have adopted a "directing and targeting" test (see below, para.6–058 *et seq.*).

In *King v Lewis* (para.6–047 above) the Court of Appeal roundly rejected an attempt by the defendant to argue that the courts should be more ready to stay defamation proceedings on *forum non conveniens* grounds where defendants did not target their publications towards the jurisdiction in which they have been sued.

In rejecting the notion of targeting, the Court of Appeal appear to have been under the misapprehension that a targeting test necessarily involves ascertaining the intention of the defendant. At [33] of their judgment they record the defendant's submission as being that the intention of the defendant should be taken into account.

The Court of Appeal went on to say: 6–054

"... it makes little sense to distinguish between one jurisdiction and another in order to decide which the defendant has 'targeted', when in truth he has 'targeted' every jurisdiction in which his text may be downloaded. Further, if the exercise required the ascertainment of what it was the defendant subjectively intended to 'target', it would in our judgment be liable to manipulation and uncertainty, and much more likely to diminish than enhance the interests of justice."

However it is quite possible to approach a targeting question on the basis of the objectively ascertainable conduct of the defendant. In *Euromarket Designs Ltd v Peters Ltd*[23] Jacob J. (as he then was), responding to counsel's criticism of his reference in a previous case[24] to the intention of the website owner, formulated an objective test for trade mark use:

"Would a reasonable trader regard the use concerned as 'in the course of trade in relation to goods' within the Member State concerned?"

In *Dearlove v Combs*[25] Kitchin J. approached the matter from the point of view of the consumer:

"The fundamental question is whether or not the average consumer of the goods or services in issue within the UK would regard

---

[23] [2001] F.S.R. 288.
[24] *800-FLOWERS Trade Mark* [2000] F.S.R. 697.
[25] [2007] EWHC 375 (Ch), at [25].

the advertisement and site as being aimed and directed at him. All material circumstances must be considered and these will include the nature of the goods or services, the appearance of the website, whether it is possible to buy goods or services from the website, whether or not the advertiser has in fact sold goods or services in the UK through the website or otherwise, and any other evidence of the advertiser's intention."

Although Kitchin J. did not elaborate on whether the advertiser's intention was to be regarded subjectively or objectively, the fact that he proceeded to grant summary judgment suggests that he had in mind an approach based on objectively ascertainable conduct. This is reinforced by his further comments[26]:

"I invited counsel to consider whether disclosure, further evidence or even cross-examination might assist a trial judge to decide whether or not the MySpace and YouTube web-pages and the *www.badboyonline.com* website constituted an advertisement of goods or services within the UK. Their submissions confirm my own view that it is most unlikely that anything useful will emerge before or at a full trial. This is a matter which I am as well placed as a trial judge to decide."

6–055   There is no reason why in a defamation case an objective approach could not be adopted, if a suitable legal basis for a targeting test can be found. As to that, we have discussed at para.6–049 above the possibility that causation can provide a suitable framework within which to develop a targeting approach.

The suggestion by the Court of Appeal in *King v Lewis* that a defendant has targeted every jurisdiction in which his text may be downloaded amounts to nothing more than a bare refusal to admit for consideration any factor other than the inherent worldwide availability of a website.

A different approach is certainly possible for defamation. US courts, when considering whether the defendant has "purposefully availed" himself of the jurisdiction, have regard to a variety of objective factors in defamation cases. These include not only factors such as the readership within the jurisdiction, but the focus of the story itself.[27]

The Law Commission in December 2002 published a Scoping Study entitled "Defamation and the Internet – A Preliminary Investigation". Among the areas addressed was jurisdiction and applicable law. The Study concluded that the problems posed by defamation across national bound-

---

[26] At [36].
[27] *Calder v Jones* 465 US 783 (1984); *Young v New Haven Advocate* F.3d, No. 01–2340, 2002 WL 31780988 (4th Cir., Dec 13, 2002); *Revell v Lidov* (5th Cir., No. 01–10521, December 31, 2002). For a discussion of targeting tests generally, see "Directing and Targeting – the Answer to the Internet's Jurisdiction Problems?", GJH Smith, *Computer Law Review International* 5/2004 p.145.

aries continued to present intractable problems.[28] The authors expressed some sympathy with the concern expressed about the levels of global risk, but observed that any solution would require an international treaty accompanied by greater harmonisation of the substantive law of defamation. The authors did not think that the problem could be solved within the short to medium term.[29]

Lastly, it should be noted that the defendants in the cases to date have mostly been the proprietors of the websites in question. If the defendant were, say, an internet service provider who hosted a third party's website, then additional questions concerning the liability of intermediaries would have to be taken into account when considering whether the defendant could be haled into the overseas jurisdiction, including the jurisdiction's own domestic laws on the liability of intermediaries.

Defamation—Rome II

Rome II (see above, para.6–035) would, as agreed upon in the Compromise Text, have no effect on defamation claims since they would be excluded from the scope of the Regulation. This followed the inability of Member States to agree a formulation that would give the media sufficient protection from restrictive foreign laws, particularly in the on-line field. **6–056**

6.3.7 Trade marks and passing off

In *Mecklermedia*,[30] a passing off case, the plaintiffs (successfully defending an application by the defendants to strike out the proceedings, or to set aside or stay the proceedings on jurisdiction grounds) established that there was a serious question to be tried that they owned goodwill in England in the mark "Internet World" at least for trade shows. The defendants, based in Germany, had organised their own "Internet World" trade shows in Germany and Austria. They had created English language promotional material and sent it out to people including some who appeared in the plaintiff's Internet World trade show catalogue in London. They also established a German website under the domain name "*www.internet-world.de*". **6–057**

Jacob J. found a serious issue to be tried as to whether what the defendants were doing would mislead the interested public in England and held that the court was entitled to infer damage to the plaintiff's goodwill. The judge commented:

---

[28] Para.4.30.
[29] Para.4.54.
[30] *Mecklermedia Corp v DC Congress GmbH* [1998] Ch. 40.

"To do acts here which lead to damage of goodwill by misleading the public here is plainly passing off. To do those same acts from abroad will not avoid liability."

The judge went on to find that for the purposes of Art.5(3) the harm was to the plaintiff's goodwill in England, so that a harmful event had occurred in England. He concluded, deciding that the proceedings should continue in England:

"...when an enterprise wants to use a mark or word throughout the world (and that may include an internet address or domain name) it must take into account that in some places, if not others, there may be confusion. Here it is clear DC knew that Mecklermedia used the name 'Internet World' and I do not think it is surprising that it is met with actions in places where confusion is considered likely."[31]

Trade marks—the interaction of trade mark use and jurisdiction

6–058　By contrast with defamation, which requires only publication, trade mark infringement requires the claimant to show that there has been use of the registered mark. The significance of this point in cross-border internet cases was considered by Jacob J. (as he then was) in *Euromarket Designs Ltd v Peters Ltd.*[32]

6–059　　Commenting on the Irish defendants' Irish website, he said:

"22. Now a person who visited that site would see 'ie'. That would be so, either in the original address of the website, 'crateandbarrel-ie.com', or the current form, 'crateandbarrel.ie'. The reference to four floors is plainly a reference to a shop. So what would the visitor understand? Fairly obviously that this is advertising a shop and its wares. If he knew 'ie' meant Ireland, he would know the shop was in Ireland. Otherwise he would not. There is no reason why anyone in this country should regard the site as directed at him. So far as one can tell, no one has.

23. Now almost any search on the net almost always throws up a host of irrelevant 'hits.' You expect a lot of irrelevant sites. Moreover you expect a lot of those sites to be foreign. Of course you can go direct to a desired site. To do that, however, you must type in the exact address. Obviously that must be known in advance. Thus in this case you could get to the defendants' site either by deliberately going there using the address, or by a search. You could use 'Crate' and 'Barrel' linked Booleanly. One could

---

[31] Contrast this with the same judge's comments in *800-FLOWERS Trade Mark* and *Euromarket* quoted in the next paragraph.
[32] Above, fn.23.

even use just one of these words, though the result then would throw up many more irrelevant results.

24. Whether one gets there by a search or by direct use of the address, is it rational to say that the defendants are using the words 'Crate & Barrel' in the UK in the course of trade in goods? If it is, it must follow that the defendants' are using the words in every other country of the world. Miss Vitoria says that the internet is accessible to the whole world. So it follows that any user will regard any website as being 'for him' absent a reason to doubt the same. ... In *800-Flowers* I rejected the suggestion that the website owner should be regarded as putting a tentacle onto the user's screen. Mr Miller here used another analogy. He said using the internet was more like the user focusing a super-telescope into the site concerned; he asked me to imagine such a telescope set up on the Welsh hills overlooking the Irish Sea. I think Mr Miller's analogy is apt in this case. Via the web you can look into the defendants' shop in Dublin. Indeed the very language of the internet conveys the idea of the user *going to* the site—'visit' is the word."

Thus it can be seen that the hurdle that a claimant has to surmount to prove use of a trade mark in a cross-border context is significantly higher than that for defamation (see previous section). Since to found jurisdiction the claimant must establish a good arguable case that a tort has been committed, the vulnerability to English jurisdiction of a "merely available" foreign website is likely to be much less for trade mark infringement than for defamation.

This conclusion is reinforced by the *obiter* comments of Buxton L.J. in   6–060
the Court of Appeal decision in *800 FLOWERS Trade Mark*,[33] in which he discussed trade mark use for both registrability and infringement purposes:

"136. The implications of internet use for issues of jurisdiction are clearly wide-ranging, and will need to be worked out with care in both domestic and private international law. ... I do venture to suggest that the essence of the problem is to fit the factual circumstances of internet use into the substantive rules of law applying to the many and very different legal issues that the internet affects. It is therefore unlikely, and it is nowhere suggested, that there will be one uniform rule, specific to the internet, that can be applied in all cases of internet use. That consideration is of importance in our present case, because it was a significant part of the applicant's submissions that, for instance, 'publication' of statements in a particular jurisdiction by downloading from the internet according to the rules of law of defamation or of misrepresentation was of at least strong analogical relevance to

---

[33] [2001] EWCA Civ 721.

whether a trade mark downloaded from the internet had been 'used' in the jurisdiction to which it was downloaded; and, even more directly, that when A placed a mark on the internet that was downloaded by B, the same criteria should apply in determining whether A thereby used the mark as determine whether A thereby infringed the same mark in the jurisdiction where B was located.

137. I would wish to approach these arguments, and particularly the last of them, with caution. There is something inherently unrealistic in saying that that A 'uses' his mark in the UK when all that he does is to place the mark on the internet, from a location outside the UK, and simply wait in the hope that someone from the UK will download it and thereby create use on the part of A. By contrast, I can see that it might be more easily arguable that if A places on the internet a mark that is confusingly similar to a mark protected in another jurisdiction, he may do so at his peril that someone from that other jurisdiction may download it; though that approach conjured up in argument before us the potentially disturbing prospect that a shop in Arizona or Brazil that happens to bear the same name as a trade marked store in England or Australia will have to act with caution in answering telephone calls from those latter jurisdictions.

138. However that may be, the very idea of 'use' within a certain area would seem to require some active step in that area on the part of the user that goes beyond providing facilities that enable others to bring the mark into the area. Of course, if persons in the UK seek the mark on the internet in response to direct encouragement or advertisement by the owner of the mark, the position may be different; but in such a case the advertisement or encouragement in itself is likely to suffice to establish the necessary use. Those considerations are in my view borne out by the observations of this court in *Reuter v Mulhens* [1954] Ch 50. The envelopes on the outside of which the allegedly infringing mark was placed as advertising matter were sent by post into the UK by the defendants. It is trite law that the Post Office is the agent of the sender of the letter to carry it, and thus it was the defendants who were to be taken to have delivered the letter to the recipients and to have displayed the mark to them within this jurisdiction. No such simple analysis is available to establish use by the applicant within this jurisdiction if he confines himself to the internet."

6–061   *Euromarket Designs v Peters* and *1–800 FLOWERS* were applied by Kitchin J. in *Dearlove v Combs*,[34] an application for summary judgment for breach of a settlement agreement compromising English passing off litigation. In the agreement the defendant had undertaken not to advertise, offer or provide certain goods and services within the UK under or with reference

---

[34] [2007] EWHC 375 (Ch), at [30] to [35].

to the word "Diddy". Kitchin J. had to decide whether a website (*www.badboyonline.com*) and certain web pages on YouTube and MySpace were directed at UK users. He said:

"34. In my judgment it is plain that the MySpace and YouTube web pages and *www.badboyonline.com* website do advertise and promote goods, namely recordings and, in particular, the 'Press Play' album, under and by reference to the name 'Diddy'. They also promote Mr Combs's activities as a recording artist and performer under and by reference to the same name. In the case of MySpace, the web pages also advertise his promotional tour, again under the name 'Diddy'.

35. I have also reached the conclusion that these web pages and website are directed at UK users. The following circumstances are material.

First, Mr Combs is an international celebrity and his new album 'Press Play' is sold here.

Secondly, Mr Combs is shortly to visit the UK in the course of his current tour and will performs at a series of shows in London, Cardiff, Manchester, Glasgow and Nottingham. These shows will no doubt promote and support the sales of his new album. Accordingly, it is quite clear that Mr Combs does have a substantial continuing business in the UK.

Thirdly and importantly, Mr Calvert says in paragraph 85 of his first witness statement that 'maintaining a page on MySpace and YouTube websites is a valuable promotional and marketing tool of many current artists' and that Mr Ferguson, the Chief Financial Officer of the Company, and Mr Asare, the New Media and Marketing Manager of Atlantic Records, have confirmed that the web pages concerning Mr Combs on MySpace and YouTube and his *www.diddy.com* website were the 'primary means' by which Mr Combs's 'Press Play' album was 'advertised and promoted'. Indeed, Mr Calvert also explains in paragraph 86 of that statement that the maintenance of Mr Combs's web-pages on MySpace and YouTube is a 'key piece' of his global marketing campaign and, in paragraph 87, that the websites are marketing tools used 'internationally' to 'promote the Defendant and his professional services and goods'. It is therefore clearly intended they should be accessed by users outside the US.

Fourthly, Mr Calvert's evidence is confirmed and supported by the fact that all three sites refer to UK visitors and the MySpace web pages specifically promote the forthcoming UK shows. It is right to acknowledge that the MySpace and YouTube web pages invite the UK users to click on an icon. But in the case of YouTube the icon is ineffective and in the case of MySpace it will only be seen by users on reviewing the whole page and there is much on the rest of the page that is apparently directed to them – most notably the UK shows.

Similarly, the *www.badboyonline.com* website contains separate icons which US and UK residents are asked to press but the presentation of the site suggests that the general site is intended for both and that for further information the user should press the appropriate icon depending upon his country of residence."

6–062 There appears to be a difference of approach as to whether the conduct that is under consideration should be regarded from the point of view of the reasonable trader or of the average consumer (see para.6–054 above). Whether there exist factual circumstances in which this would make any practical difference to the outcome remains to be seen.

In *V&S Vin & Sprit Aktiebolag AB v Absolut Beach Pty Ltd*[35] the claimant relied on the availability of an Australian website in the UK bearing the mark complained of; willingness to accept orders placed via the website; and (the judge commented probably most importantly) the circulation in the UK by the defendant of its brochure in response to orders from the website. Pumfrey J. found that there was, just, a good arguable case of trade mark infringement sufficient to found jurisdiction.

The approach of the Hamburg District Court in *Re the MARITIM Trade Mark*[36] to the substantive elements of trade mark infringement in a cross-border internet case is instructive. The facts of this case and the court's finding that it should take jurisdicrion are set out at para.6–034 above.

On the merits of the claim, the court found that there was no infringement. Where a potential infringement had been instigated abroad, there had to be a domestic connecting factor for there to be infringement. In this case there was no domestic connecting factor because the defendant's services could only be rendered abroad.

6–063 Further, the mere possibility of receiving foreign advertising content was not sufficient. A greater specific domestic link had to be established, otherwise any use of trade marks on the internet would constitute infringement in Germany.

Nor did the use of the German language on the website establish sufficient domestic connection. Multilingual hotel information and advertising material was normal in this sector and justified in view of the international clientele. Language per se was therefore not relevant. It would only be relevant if its stated aim was to reach consumers in Germany.

The website was directed to the Danish market and there were no elements, such as a German contact address, aimed at the German market.

The use of the .dk domain was also relevant, since a consumer would assume (unlike with a .com domain) that the information was tailored to that country. The external format of the website also made sufficiently clear that it was not targeting the German market.

---

[35] [2002] I.P. & T. 203, Ch D.
[36] [2003] I.L.Pr. 17.

As to the brochure material sent to Germany, again there was no service capable of being provided in Germany, and the brochures were only sent out on request. This was insufficient to establish a domestic connecting factor. Nor did the brochures constitute advertising for the website. (Contrast these findings with the conclusion of Pumfrey J. in *Absolut Beach*, discussed above.)

The Scottish Court of Session has considered the application of Art.5(3) to an internet trade mark case, in *Bonnier Media Ltd v Smith*.[37] In this case the claimants were the owners, printers and publishers of a Scottish newspaper known as "business a.m.", for which they had registered a UK trade mark. The claimants also operated a website under "*www.businessam.co.uk*".

The first defendant, who was resident and domiciled in Greece, was the managing director of the second defendant, a company incorporated in Mauritius. It was also averred that the second defendants had places of business in London and Athens; and that prior to residing in Greece the first defendant had had substantial business interests in Scotland. The first defendant had previously sued the claimant in England for defamation arising out of articles concerning the first defendant published in business a.m., which proceedings were defended.

The claimants alleged that the first defendant had intended (but failed) to 6–064 acquire businessam.com, and had registered 22 other domain names which included the words businessam, business-am or businesspm.

The claimants alleged that there was only one possible reason for registering such names, namely to pass themselves off as the pursuers, and that if any websites were set up members of the Scottish public seeking to find the claimants' website would be confused. The claimants had obtained an ex parte interim injunction and the defendants applied to discharge or restrict it.

The court would have jurisdiction to make an order to restrain a threatened wrong that was likely to produce a harmful event within Scotland. As to whether a wrong was threatened within Scotland, the defendants argued that merely putting up a website on a server outside Scotland was not a wrong that would occur in Scotland. The defendants relied upon *800-FLOWERS* and *Euromarket v Peters* (see above for these cases). The court held that:

> "the person who sets up the website can be regarded as potentially committing a delict in any country where the website can be seen, in other words in any country in the world. It does not follow that he actually commits a delict in every country in the world, however. It is obvious that the overwhelming majority of websites will be of no interest whatsoever in more than a single country or a small group of countries. In my opinion a website should not be regarded as having delictual consequences in any country where it

---

[37] [2002] S.C.L.R. 977.

is unlikely to be of significant interest. That result can readily be achieved by a vigorous application of the maxim *de minimis non curat praetor*; if the impact of a website in a particular country is properly regarded as insignificant, no delict has been committed there."

The court then went on to characterise the *Euromarket* case as one in which the defendant's trade with the UK was insignificant.

After reviewing the facts in the instant case, the court concluded:

"In my opinion an inference may readily be drawn from the foregoing facts that the defenders, acting together, intend to set up a website which is designed to pass themselves off as the pursuers, and to make use of a name sufficiently close to the pursuers' trade mark to amount to an infringement of that trade mark. Those acts are clearly aimed at the pursuers' business. That business is centred in Scotland, and it is in my opinion obvious that the defenders' actings are intended to have their main effect in Scotland. In these circumstances I am of opinion that the requirement that the effect in Scotland of the website should be significant is plainly satisfied, and that accordingly the defenders can be regarded as threatening a delict in Scotland. I accordingly conclude that the Scottish courts have jurisdiction over the defenders."

While the result of the case is unsurprising, it is doubtful whether a test based on "insignificance" is consistent with the English cases, or sets an appropriately high threshold.

Under the Rome II proposal the applicable law for infringement of intellectual property rights would be that of the country for which protection is claimed. For unitary rights such as the Community Trade Mark the applicable law would be that set out in the relevant Community legislation or, failing that, the law of the Member State in which the infringing act has been committed.

6.3.8 Misrepresentation and negligent misstatement

Applicable law

6–065   The law applicable to a negligent misstatement or misrepresentation is determined in accordance with the 1995 Act (see above, para.6–035). In *Morin v Bonham & Brooks Ltd*[38] the Court of Appeal observed that although the applicable law scheme of the 1995 Act might amount to much the same as the old "substance" test, particularly if it involved taking the

---

[38] [2003] EWCA 1802.

broad approach mentioned in *Metall und Rohstoff* at p.449C, it was inappropriate to complicate disputes by referring to cases on the old law.

The case concerned alleged negligent misstatement. The defendant, a Monaco company, had published a catalogue for an auction in Monaco. The defendant's London parent company, at the request of the claimant, sent the catalogue to the claimant in London, where he read it. He then travelled to Monaco, where he bid successfully in the auction. He claimed that the catalogue contained actionable misstatements. The court held that the applicable law was that of Monaco. The court commented that if the claimant had stayed in London and bid by telephone, that would have presented a "teasing question".

Under Rome II, misrepresentation and negligent misstatement would fall under the proposed general rule. Under this rule the applicable law would be the law of the country in which the damage occurs, irrespective of the country in which the event giving rise to the damage occurred and irrespective of the country or countries in which the indirect consequences of that event arise.

Where the claimant and defendant were both habitually resident in the same country when the damage occurred, the law of that country would apply.

However, where it is clear from all the circumstances of the case that the tort or delict is manifestly more closely connected with another country, the law of that other country would apply. A manifestly closer connection with another country might be based in particular on a pre-existing relationship between the parties, such as a contract that is closely connected with the tort or delict in question.

Place of the harmful event

As to jurisdiction and the place of the harmful event for the purposes of Art.5(3) of the Judgments Regulation, there has been no ECJ case directly on the point of the application of Art.5(3) to cases of negligent misstatement.   **6–066**

Several English cases have, however, considered this in the light of the general ECJ decisions. In *Domicrest Ltd v Swiss Bank Corp*,[39] the statement originated in Switzerland and was relied upon in England. Rix J. held that in the case of negligent misstatement the place where the harmful event giving rise to the damage occurred was where the misstatement originated, not the place where it was relied upon. On the particular facts of the case he held that although the statement was relied on in England, the damage was suffered in Italy and Switzerland, so that on no basis did the harmful event occur in England and the court had no jurisdiction under Art.5(3).

Domicrest has been approved by the Court of Appeal in *ABCI v Banque*

---

[39] [1998] 3 All E.R. 577.

Franco-Tunisienne[40] and followed in *Newsat Holdings Ltd v Zani*[41] and *London Helicopters Ltd v Heliportugal LDA-INAC*.[42]

6.3.9 Copyright

6–067　So far as copyright is concerned, a variety of acts can constitute infringement and these are set out in detail in Ch.2.

Particular attention should be paid to the "making available" right introduced by the Copyright and Related Rights Regulations 2003. The place of commission of an act infringing this right is not spelt out either in the Regulations or in the Copyright in the Information Society Directive that they implement. It is possible that the act is committed in both the place of upload and the place of download.[43]

The place of commission is significant in establishing a good arguable case of infringement of UK copyright, since UK copyright is a territorial right.

In some circumstances it is possible to bring a claim in an English court for infringement of a non-UK copyright.[44] However, if *Shevill* applies to copyright as well as to defamation, then the claimant would be restricted to claiming for harm that occurred within the jurisdiction, which given the territorial nature of copyright would limit the claim to infringements of UK copyright. Where a good arguable case of infringement of UK copyright is established, it follows inevitably that the court would accept that a harmful event within the jurisdiction has also been established.

These points are well illustrated by *IBS Technologies (PVT) Ltd v APM Technologies SA*.[45] In this case, under the Lugano Convention, the claimant alleged infringement of Swiss copyright by acts of copying during the development of computer software in Switzerland, and infringement of English copyright by testing and threatened sale of the software within the UK. The defendant was a Swiss company. The claimant relied upon Art.5(3) to support jurisdiction in England.

6–068　The deputy judge held that *Shevill* applied to the claim. Although the

---

[40] [2003] 2 Lloyd's Rep. 146.

[41] [2006] EWHC 342 (Comm).

[42] [2006] EWHC 108 (QB). In this case Simon J. held that because jurisdictional questions are decided on an autonomous basis under the Regulation he did not have to decide what law was applicable at the stage of determining a jurisdictional question. However, this is too broad a statement. While it is clear that the *place* of the harmful event is to be determined autonomously without recourse to domestic law, in *Shevill* the ECJ held that the criteria for assessing whether the event in question is harmful and the evidence required of the existence and extent of the harm alleged are governed by the substantive law determined by the national conflict of laws rules of the court seised, provided that the effectiveness of the Convention was not thereby impaired (see para.6–027 above).

[43] This was the conclusion of the Canadian Supreme Court in relation to the right of communication to the public in the Canadian copyright legislation in *SOCAN v Canadian Association of Internet Providers* [2004] 2 S.C.R. 427, 2004 S.C.C.45.

[44] *Pearce v Ove Arup Partnership Ltd* (1999) 1 All E.R. 769.

[45] unreported, April 7, 2003, ChD.

defendant's application for a declaration that there was no jurisdiction failed, the court declared that its jurisdiction was limited to adjudication upon actual or threatened damage to the claimant within the UK.

In *Vasarhelyi v Guinness World Records Ltd*,[46] a French case decided in the Tribunale de Grande Instance de Paris, the claimant sued a variety of defendants claiming that the French edition of the Guinness Book of Records infringed copyright in two works by Vasarhelyi. Among the defendants were Amazon.fr, Amazon.com International Sales and Amazon.com.

Amazon challenged the competence of the court, arguing that the accessibility of at least the Amazon.com site in France was insufficient to pinpoint the place of the damaging action, particularly as the site and the work were directed at an English-speaking public. The court held that the Amazon.com and Amazon.fr sites were accessible in France and they offered the book for sale, the offer for sale was thus made in France and the court was competent under the French Code of Civil Procedure to hear the claim.

In the Belgian case of *Copiepresse v Google Inc*[47] Google argued that the order against it should be restricted to the Belgian sites Google.be and Google.news.be. Copiepresse (representing a group of Belgian newspaper publishers) argued that the order should not be so limited, as the headlines, extracts and links to cached copies of the newspaper articles in dispute were accessible on Google's French site (google.fr) and on google.com. The judge found that since Google had stated that it was only possible to comply with the order by completely de-indexing the newspaper publishers' sites, and that would result in their being removed from all Google News sites worldwide, there was no point in limiting the order to Google's Belgian sites.

Under the Rome II proposal the applicable law for copyright would be that of the country for which protection is sought.[48]

6.3.10 Patents

In the case of a patent it is an infringement to make, dispose of, offer to dispose of, use, keep, or import a patented product in a country where the relevant patent subsists. In the case of the internet the issue is most likely to concern a technique of some sort and it will depend on the particular nature of the patented item as to where infringement might occur.

6–069

There will certainly be a number of situations where someone accessing some part of the internet where such a technique is used will technically be

---

[46] [2003] E.C.D.R. 14.

[47] Brussels Court of First Instance, February 13, 2007. See Ch.2 for a detailed account of this decision.

[48] This is similar to Art.5(2) of the Berne Convention. The French Cour de Cassation has interpreted that provision as referring to the law of the State or States on whose territory the infringing acts took place (*SISRO SV v Ampersand Software BV* [2004] E.C.D.R. 22).

infringing the patent for the technique providing such a patent is registered in the country from which that person is accessing the relevant part of the internet. There will also be cases in which different parts of the technique are operated in different countries.

In *Menashe Business Mercantile Ltd v William Hill Organisation Ltd*[49] the claimant alleged infringement of a European Patent (UK). The patented invention related to a computerised gaming system, the claimed elements including a host computer and a terminal computer, characterised in that the terminal computer is situated at a location remote to the host computer.

The claimants alleged infringement under s.60(2) of the Patents Act 1977, i.e. that the defendants had infringed by "supplying and/or offering to supply in the United Kingdom ... means relating to an essential element of the invention for putting the invention into effect when the defendant knew at all material times and/or it was obvious to a reasonable person in the circumstances that the said means were suitable for putting and were intended to put the invention into effect in the United Kingdom."

The defendants alleged (*inter alia*) that they did not infringe as the host computer was situated outside the UK in Antigua or Curacao. They asked the court to determine the point as a preliminary issue.

The agreed facts on which the preliminary issue was tried were that William Hill operated a gaming system available to punters in the UK who had a computer. The punters were supplied with a program usually by a CD which turned the punter's computer into a terminal computer which communicated via the net with a host computer located outside the UK.

The Court of Appeal held that on the agreed facts there would be infringement, since although part of the invention (the host computer) was situated outside the UK, the supply of the CD served to put the whole invention into effectiveness in the UK. Since it was irrelevant to the punter where the host computer was situated, it was not a misuse of language to say that the punter used the host computer in the UK.

6.3.11 Breach of confidence

6–070   Claims for breach of confidence, while certainly non-contractual, are an exercise of the court's equitable jurisdiction and do not arise in tort.[50] The question whether they are within Art.5(3) is unresolved.[51]

In *Kitechnology BV v Unicor GmbH Plastmaschinen*,[52] an English breach of confidence case, it was held at first instance that the damage to

---

[49] [2003] 1 W.L.R. 1462.

[50] *Kitechnology BV v Unicor GmbH Plastmaschinen* [1995] F.S.R. 765 at 777–778 CA.

[51] The point was left undecided in *Kitechnology*. After the subsequent House of Lords decision in *Kleinwort Benson Ltd v Glasgow CC* [1999] 1 A.C. 153, commenting on the ECJ decision of *Kalfelis v Schroder* [1988] E.C.R. 5565 and holding that unjust enrichment claims do not fall within Art.5(3), the point remains debatable. *cf. Douglas v Hello! Ltd (No.3)* [2005] EWCA Civ 595 [96].

[52] [1994] I.L.Pr. 559 Ch D; reversed on appeal [1995] F.S.R. 765 CA.

the owner of the right was a damage in his ability to exploit it wherever he wished and in particular in the country where he was based and therefore where he might well most wish to exploit it. The plaintiff was therefore able to maintain proceedings in England under Art.5(3), even though the breach of confidence was alleged to have occurred in Germany.

That conclusion was overturned on appeal. In the absence of any evidence that the defendants had publicised the information in England or elsewhere, or that they had exploited it otherwise than in Germany, there was no damage directly caused to the plaintiff in England and therefore no harmful event in England. If the plaintiff's argument was correct, the plaintiff would be able to establish jurisdiction in any country in which it was entitled to protect the confidentiality of the information, regardless of whether the defendants' alleged activities had any effect on their commercial interests there. That would be a major derogation from the general rule stated in Art.2.

The position of breach of confidence claims under the Rome II proposal is obscure. Privacy claims (which in England come under the umbrella of breach of confidence) are among those excluded from scope in the Compromise Text. Other breach of confidence claims might possibly be characterised as intellectual property claims or for unjust enrichment or, if not, they would fall under the general rule.

6.3.12 Consumer contracts

Jurisdiction

Articles 13–15 of the Brussels Convention determined jurisdiction in proceedings concerning a contract concluded by a person for a purpose which could be regarded as being outside his trade or profession ("the consumer"), in the following cases[53]: **6–071**

(1) A contract for the sale of goods on instalment credit terms.
(2) A contract for a loan repayable by instalments, or for any other form of credit, made to finance the sale of goods.
(3) Any other contract for the supply of goods or a contract for the supply of services, and:

    (a) in the State of the consumer's domicile the conclusion of the contract was preceded by a specific invitation addressed to him or by advertising; and

    (b) the consumer took in that State the steps necessary for the conclusion of the contract.

---

[53] Art.13 also contained provisions about branches and agencies within a Contracting State of parties not domiciled in a Contracting State; and also disapplied Arts. 13–15 to contracts of transport.

Article 14 provided that a consumer might bring proceedings against the other party to a contract either in the courts of the Contracting State in which that party was domiciled or in the courts of the Contracting State in which the consumer was domiciled.

Article 15 restricted the cases in which the terms of Arts. 13–15 might be departed from by agreement. In particular, Art.15 had the effect that the consumer could not, by means of a provision in the contract under dispute, be deprived of the right under Art.14 to sue in his home court.

The Judgments Regulation replaced these provisions. Article 15 provides that the general test for determining whether a consumer can bring proceedings in the courts of the place where the consumer is domiciled is whether:

> "the contract has been concluded with a person who pursues commercial or professional activities in the Member State of the consumer's domicile or, by any means, directs such activities to that Member State or to several countries including that Member State, and the contract falls within the scope of such activities."

The Regulation in its original proposed form contained a Recital (13) stating that: "... electronic commerce in goods or services by a means accessible in another Member State constitutes an activity directed to that State."

The UK Government opposed the inclusion of that recital. In the debate on the Second Reading of the Electronic Communications Bill on November 29, 1999, the Minister introducing the Bill stated[54]:

> "The Brussels convention has existed for 31 years and, in that time, almost no consumer has used it to sue for breach of contract. None the less, the Commission sought to extend its provisions to electronic commerce by providing in a draft recital that any web site that could be accessed from another Member State would thereby qualify as advertising directed at consumers in that Member State and could activate the convention's provisions. That, of course, misses the point that, on the internet, any web site is, by definition, accessible from anywhere else. I am pleased to be able to tell the House that there is growing agreement among Member States with our view that the new recital should be dropped."

6–072   Recital (13) was indeed dropped. However, that left the term "directs" in Art.15 wholly undefined. An attempt was made to remedy this by the minuting of a joint Council and Commission statement in relation to the Regulation.[55] The relevant part of the statement reads:

---

[54] *Hansard*, November 29, 1999, Col.48 (House of Commons).
[55] *http://register.consilium.eu.int/pdf/en/00/st14/14139en0.pdf.*

"... for Article 15(1)(c) to be applicable it is not sufficient for an undertaking to target its activities at the Member State of the consumer's residence, or at a number of Member States including that Member State; a contract must also be concluded within the framework of its activities. This provision relates to a number of marketing methods, including contracts concluded at a distance through the internet.

In this context, the Council and Commission stress that the mere fact that an internet site is accessible is not sufficient for Article 15 to be applicable, although a factor will be that this internet site solicits the conclusion of distance contracts and that a contract has actually been concluded at a distance, by whatever means. In this respect, the language or currency which a website uses does not constitute a relevant factor."

The OECD Consumer Protection Guidelines for e-commerce adopted on December 8, 1999[56] recognised that existing approaches to jurisdiction might have to be reconsidered. They state:

"Business-to-consumer cross-border transactions, whether carried out electronically or otherwise, are subject to the existing framework on applicable law and jurisdiction. Electronic commerce poses challenges to this existing framework. Therefore, consideration should be given to whether the existing framework for applicable law and jurisdiction should be modified, or applied differently, to ensure effective and transparent consumer protection in the context of the continued growth of electronic commerce. In considering whether to modify the existing framework, governments should seek to ensure that the framework provides fairness to consumers and business, facilitates electronic commerce, results in consumers having a level of protection not less than that afforded in other forms of commerce, and provides consumers with meaningful access to fair and timely dispute resolution and redress without undue cost or burden."

Applicable law

The law applicable to consumer contracts is governed by Art.5 of the 1980 **6–073** Rome Convention, implemented in the UK by the Contracts (Applicable Law) Act 1990. Article 5 contains provisions closely mirroring those of the 1968 Brussels Jurisdiction Convention (see above). The most relevant provision is that a choice of law made by the parties shall not have the result of depriving the consumer of the protection afforded to him by the mandatory rules of the law of the country in which he has his habitual residence if in that country the conclusion of the contract was preceded by a

---

[56] Available on the OECD website at *www.oecd.org*.

specific invitation addressed to him or by advertising, and he had taken in that country all the steps necessary on his part for the conclusion of the contract.

This provision, predating the internet, is a type of targeting test. The Guiliano/Lagarde Report, elaborating on what would count as specific invitation or advertising, made clear that in both cases the trader must have done acts aimed specifically at the country in question. In *Rayner v Davies*[57] Waller L.J., commenting on the Guiliano/Lagarde Report in the context of the identical provisions of the 1968 Brussels Jurisdiction Convention, said:

> " 'specific invitation' is coupled with 'advertising' preceding the conclusion of the contract. That seems to contemplate some positive conduct on the part of the seller of goods or services preceding the contract, and (I would suggest normally) preceding the involvement of the consumer."

The European Commission's Rome I proposal seeks to modernise Art.5 of the 1980 Convention. In doing so it has made significant changes. The proposal, in summary, is that consumer contracts shall be governed by the law of the Member State in which the consumer has his habitual residence, on condition that the contract has been concluded with a person who pursues a trade or profession in the Member State in which the consumer has his habitual residence or, by any means, directs such activities to that Member State or to several States including that Member State, and the contract falls within the scope of such activities, unless the professional did not know where the consumer had his habitual residence and this ignorance was not attributable to his negligence.

Recital (10) attempts to link the interpretation of directing activities back to the Judgments Regulation and its accompanying Council and Commission Declaration:

> "Harmony with Regulation (EC) No 44/2001 requires both that there be a reference to the concept of 'targeted activity' as a condition for applying the consumer-protection rule and that the concept be interpreted harmoniously in the two instruments, bearing in mind that a joint declaration by the Council and the Commission on Article 15 of Regulation No 44/2001 states that *'for Article 15(1)(c) to be applicable it is not sufficient for an undertaking to target its activities at the Member State of the consumer's residence, or at a number of Member States including that Member State; a contract must also be concluded within the framework of its activities'*. The declaration also states that *'the mere fact that an internet site is accessible is not sufficient for Article 15 to be applicable, although a factor will be that this internet site solicits the conclusion of distance contracts and that a*

---

[57] [2002] EWCA Civ 1880 (CA), at [24].

> *contract has actually been concluded at a distance, by whatever means. In this respect, the language or currency which a website uses does not constitute a relevant factor'."*

The result is not satisfactory. The Recital does suggest that mere accessibility is not sufficient to count as a directed activity. But it also permits the fact that a contract has been concluded to be taken into account as a factor. That would not be permissible under the 1980 Rome Convention, in which only activities preceding the contract can be taken into account. The fact that a contract has been concluded is, under the 1980 Convention and ought to be under the proposed Regulation, neutral.

The proposed text makes insufficiently clear that only positive conduct (see *Rayner v Davies*, above) can be regarded as targeting. The proposal is also controversial in substituting the whole law of the consumer's place of habitual residence for the previous mandatory rules, and in the proviso concerning the supplier's knowledge or deemed knowledge of the consumer's habitual residence.

At the time of writing the UK Government has declined to opt in to Rome I (mainly because of concerns over the separate issue of mandatory rules of third countries under Art.8.3). The Rome I proposal is in its early stages and the provisions of Art.5 are the subject of active lobbying.

6.4 JURISDICTION—DEFENDANT NOT DOMICILED WITHIN A MEMBER STATE

6.4.1 Jurisdiction over non-domiciliaries by virtue of the Judgments Regulation

The main provisions of Art.23 concerning jurisdiction agreements apply where one or more of the parties to the jurisdiction agreement are domiciled in a Member State.[58] A jurisdiction agreement is therefore capable,[59] by virtue of the Regulation, of conferring jurisdiction on the court of a Member State where the defendant is domiciled in a non-Member State.[60] Otherwise under Art.4 of the Regulation, if the defendant is not domiciled

6–074

---

[58] Art.23, para.2 also provides for the situation where an agreement under Art.23 conferring jurisdiction on the court or courts of a Member State is entered into by parties, none of whom is domiciled in a Member State. In that case the courts of other Member States shall have no jurisdiction unless the courts chosen under the agreement have declined jurisdiction.

[59] A jurisdiction agreement contained in a contract under dispute that did not comply with the formal requirements of Art.23 could still be relied upon for the purpose of seeking permission to serve proceedings out of the jurisdiction in a case not otherwise governed by the Regulation (CPR Rule 6.20(5)(d).

[60] The significance of jurisdiction being conferred by virtue of the Regulation is that in such a case it is unnecessary, since it is a Regulation case, to seek the permission of the English court to serve the proceedings outside the jurisdiction, even though service may be in a non-Member State. See Civil Jurisdiction and Judgments Act 1982 and CPR Rule 6.19(1)(b)(iii).

within a Member State the jurisdiction of the courts of each Member State shall be determined by the national law of that State. This is subject only to Art.22 of the Regulation, which provides in certain cases (such as proceedings concerned with the validity of patents, trade marks, designs or other similar rights required to be deposited or registered) for exclusive jurisdiction to be vested in designated Contracting State courts, regardless of domicile.

6.4.2 Cases outside the Judgments Regulation

6-075   In a case not within the scope of Art.1 of the Judgments Regulation, or in which Art.4 delegates the question of jurisdiction to national law, the substantive rules of English common law and the procedure of the Civil Procedure Rules will apply.

In such cases the English court will prima facie be competent if:

(1) the defendant is served within the jurisdiction[61]; or
(2) the defendant has submitted to the jurisdiction of the English court; or
(3) the defendant has been served with English proceedings out of the English jurisdiction pursuant to permission granted under r.6.21 of the Civil Procedure Rules.

Each of these cases is subject to the possibility of the defendant applying to stay the proceedings on grounds of *forum non conveniens*[62] and in the case of service out of the English jurisdiction also to apply to dispute jurisdiction and to set aside the permission to serve out of the jurisdiction.[63]

An application for permission to serve the proceedings outside the jurisdiction is made without notice to the intended defendant.[64] The claimant must show that it has a good arguable case that the court has jurisdiction under one of the categories set out in the CPR Rule 6.20[65]; and that there is a serious issue to be tried on the merits of the claim.[66] It must also

---

[61] As to which, note that a foreign company may be served in England if it has a branch here either by virtue of the Companies Act or under the CPR. See *Saab v Saudi American Bank* [1999] 4 All E.R. 321.

[62] A defendant may, by submitting to the jurisdiction, also forfeit its right to apply for a stay of exercise of the court's jurisdiction (see, e.g. *Ngcobo v Thor Chemicals* (*Times*, November 10, 1995)).

[63] CPR Rule 11 sets out the procedure for applying to dispute the court's jurisdiction to try the claim, or to argue that the court should not exercise any jurisdiction which it may have.

[64] The application is made under the provisions of CPR Rules 6.20–6.21.

[65] CPR Rule 6.21(1)(a) requires the claimant to state in written evidence the grounds on which the application is made and the paragraph(s) of Rule 6.20 relied on.

[66] *Seaconsar Far East Ltd v Bank Markazi* [1993] 4 All E.R. 456, HL. CPR Rule 6.21(1)(b) requires the claimant to state in written evidence that he believes that his claim has a "reasonable prospect of success".

demonstrate that England is clearly the appropriate forum in which to try the case for the interests of all the parties and for the ends of justice.[67]

Discretion of the court

The *Spiliada* principles will apply to the determination whether England is the most appropriate forum. However, it is not inconsistent with those principles to apply a *prima facie* assumption that the jurisdiction where in substance the tort is committed is the appropriate forum, or at least to treat that as a weighty factor.[68]

6–076

The court therefore retains a discretion whether or not to grant permission. So in a libel case, for instance, even if there is a publication within the jurisdiction, the court may yet in its discretion refuse leave to serve a defendant out of the jurisdiction. In *Kroch v Rossell*,[69] leave was refused on the ground that there was no question of substance in England. Only a small quantity of foreign newspapers had circulated here, the plaintiff was a foreigner and there was no evidence that he had a reputation or associations here.[70]

The Court of Appeal in *Dow Jones v Jameel*[71] observed that if it had been considering an application to set aside permission to serve out of the jurisdiction, it would have granted the application on the basis that the five publications that had taken place in the jurisdiction did not, individually or collectively, amount to a real or substantial tort.

In *Harrods Ltd v Dow Jones & Co Inc*[72] (discussed above, para.6–043), in considering the exercise of his discretion to give permission to serve proceedings out of the jurisdiction, or to stay the proceedings on grounds of *forum non conveniens*, the judge took into account the technical nature of the publications within the jurisdiction, for which the claimant appeared to have little to gain. He also took into account the considerable difficulty that might be encountered in enforcing an English defamation judgment in the USA. Against that was the legitimate public policy interest in a claimant being entitled to vindicate its reputation.

The judge concluded that however limited and technical these English publications, relating to an English company, were most conveniently dealt with in an English court. He therefore granted permission to serve the

---

[67] *Spiliada Maritime Corp v Cansulex Ltd* [1986] 3 All E.R. 843, HL. CPR Rule 6.21(2A) states that the court will not give permission for service out of the jurisdiction unless "satisfied that England and Wales is the proper place in which to bring the claim".

[68] *Berezovsky v Michaels*, para.6–040 above; see also *Schapira v Ahronson* [1999] E.M.L.R. 735, in which restriction of the claim to publication within the jurisdiction was a significant factor in considering the appropriate forum. The restriction appears to have been voluntary since although all three defendants were foreign, service of proceedings was accepted by English solicitors.

[69] [1937] 1 All E.R. 725, CA.

[70] Contrast with *Berezovsky v Michaels*, above, in which the House of Lords by a 3–2 majority allowed the proceedings to continue in England.

[71] See para.6–052 above.

[72] [2003] EWHC 1162 (QB).

proceedings out of the jurisdiction and refused a stay on grounds of *forum non conveniens*.

Don King v Lennox Lewis, Lion Promotions LLC and Judd Burstein[73] was the first defamation case in which the English courts ruled on jurisdiction where the internet was the sole means of publication. It was decided at first instance by Eady J. and then by the Court of Appeal.

The case concerned statements alleged to have been made by Mr Burstein, an attorney representing the boxer Lennox Lewis and his company Lion Promotions LLC in US litigation with the boxing promoter Don King. The statements were contained in an article and an interview published on *www.fightnews.com* and *www.boxingtalk.com* respectively. The defendants described these as "United States-based" publications. There was evidence that the two websites were popular and frequently accessed by people in the English jurisdiction; and that once news was placed on either website, it quickly went round the boxing community by phone calls, word of mouth or by forwarding via computers.

6–077   The proprietors of the websites were not parties to the proceedings.

The defendants applied to set aside service of the proceedings in the US. In order to resist this application the claimant had to establish that it was an appropriate case for service out of the jurisdiction (in this case, that damage was sustained within the jurisdiction, or resulted from an act committed within the jurisdiction under CPR 6.20(8)) and that England and Wales was the appropriate forum in which to hear the case.

The claimant deployed the following principles, which the judge described as "well-known":

- That the common law currently regards the publication of an internet posting as taking place when it is downloaded. (see para.6–041 above)
- That English law does not recognise a "single publication" rule. (see para.6–044 above)
- In defamation, damage is presumed to have occurred. (see para.6–037 above)
- That the claimant was not permitted to complain in these proceedings and did not seek to do so of any publication outside England and Wales.[74]

As regards the appropriate forum, the claimant argued that there was a general presumption that the natural forum was that of the jurisdiction where the tort was committed; that it gave a significant dimension to the case that he had a reputation to protect specifically in England; and that the English courts were the natural forum in which to vindicate an English reputation.

The defendants submitted, *inter alia*, that there had never been another

---

[73] [2004] EWHC 168 (QB).
[74] See para.6–030 above.

case in which a US resident obtained permission to serve English proceedings out of the jurisdiction against another US resident in respect of a US-based publication. However, the judge, Eady J., commented that that missed the point about the nature of the internet publications and the fact that English law regarded the website publications in question as having occurred in England.

The judge concluded that the claim should be allowed to proceed.

On appeal, the Court of Appeal upheld the judge's decision in respect of Mr Burstein (the other two defendants having settled with the claimant after the hearing of the appeal but before judgment). The appeal concerned mainly the question of *forum conveniens*.

The Court of Appeal stressed that although the place of the commission of the tort was the starting point for consideration of the natural *forum*, that fact that publication has taken place elsewhere will always be a relevant factor. The more tenuous the claimant's connection with the jurisdiction and the more substantial any publication abroad, the weaker this consideration becomes. Further, it was necessary in the case of transnational libels, such as on the internet, to consider the global picture. Because a defendant who publishes on the web may at least in theory find himself vulnerable to multiple actions in different jurisdictions, the place where the tort was committed ceases to be a potent limiting factor.

The Court of Appeal went on to cite the High Court of Australia's 6–078 decision in *Gutnick* as suggesting that:

> "... a global publisher should not be too fastidious as to the part of the globe where he is made a libel defendant. We by no means propose a free-for-all for claimants libeled on the internet. The court must still ascertain the most appropriate *forum*; ... in an internet case the court's discretion will tend to be more open-textured than otherwise; for that is the means by which the court may give effect to the publisher's choice of a global medium. But, as always, the case will depend upon its own circumstances."

As we have observed above (para.6–053) the Court of Appeal rejected the suggestion that the court should be more ready to stay proceedings where the defendant had not targeted its publications towards the jurisdiction.

Grounds for service out of the jurisdiction

The categories in CPR Rule 6.20 within which a claimant has to bring his 6–079 claim that are most relevant to the internet and e-commerce are:

- A claim is made for a remedy against a person domiciled within the jurisdiction (r.6.20(1)).
- A claim is made for an injunction ordering the defendant to do or refrain from doing an act within the jurisdiction (r.6.20(2)). For the court to grant leave on this basis the injunction must be a

genuine part of the substantive relief sought[75] and there must be a reasonable prospect of the injunction being granted at trial.[76]

- A claim is made in respect of a contract where the contract: (a) was made within the jurisdiction; (b) was made by or through an agent trading or residing within the jurisdiction; (c) is governed by English law; or (d) contains a term to the effect that the court shall have jurisdiction to determine any claim in respect of the contract (r.6.20(5)).

The question whether a contract was made in the jurisdiction will be determined by consideration of the point at which the contract was concluded, in particular whether it was concluded upon the sending (the "postal rule") or the receipt or deemed receipt (the "telex rule")[77] of the acceptance. Although it is tempting to assume that all internet transactions are instantaneous and so analogous to telex, the reality is that there is a variety of different types of internet communications, and that some (e.g. internet email, especially using dial-up accounts) is by no means instantaneous. While these differences may in some cases go more to the time of receipt, rather than to the question whether acceptance is effective at the place of sending or receipt, the application of these rules is still by no means fully worked out.

- A claim is made in respect of a breach of a contract committed within the jurisdiction (r.6.20(6)); or a claim is made for a declaration that no contract exists where, if the contract were found to exist, it would comply with the conditions set out in r.6.20(5) (r.6.20(7)).
- The claim is made against a person on whom the claim form has been or will be served and (a) there is between the claimant and that person a real issue which it is reasonable for the court to try, and (b) the claimant wishes to serve the claim form on another person who is a necessary or proper party to that claim (r.6.20(3)) In this case the claimant must state in written evidence the grounds on which the witness believes that there is a real issue which it is reasonable for the court to try (r.6.21(1)(c)).
- The claim is made in tort where (a) the damage was sustained within the jurisdiction; or (b) the damage sustained resulted from an act committed within the jurisdiction (r.6.20(8)). This head is similar to Art.5(3) of the Brussels Convention discussed above. However, the scope is restricted to tort alone, according to its English law meaning.

6–080 As with cases under Art.5(3) of the Judgments Regulation, the claimant will

---

[75] *Rosler v Hilbery* [1925] 1 Ch. 250, CA.
[76] *Watson v Daily Record* [1907] 1 K.B. 853, CA.
[77] *Entores v Miles Far East Corp* [1955] 2 Q.B. 327; *Brinkibon Ltd v Stahag Stahl* [1982] 1 All E.R. 293; and see *Schelde Delta Shipping BV v Astarte Shipping Ltd (The Pamela)* [1995] 2 Lloyds Rep. 249. See further, Ch.10.

have to show that he has a good arguable case that an actionable tort has been committed. The question of actionability has to be determined according to the relevant English law principles[78] and requires the court to consider substantively the tort alleged to have been committed.

- The whole subject matter of a claim relates to property located within the jurisdiction (r.6.20(10). This head is wider than the corresponding provision of the previous Rules of the Supreme Court, which related only to land. It could have application in, for instance, a dispute about rights to a *.uk* domain name registered at Nominet.[79] It has been held to apply to confidential information located within the jurisdiction.[80]

In *Ashton Investments Ltd v OJSC Russian Aluminium*[81] the claimant alleged that two Russian defendants (the Rusal defendants) had hacked into Ashton's London computer system from Russia and inserted a surreptitious keylogger program with the intention of obtaining privileged and confidential information about existing English litigation that was in progress between the parties. The Rusal defendants denied this and asserted that Rusal's own Wi-fi network must have been accessed and used by students at a nearby technical university to carry out the hacking.

Ashton started proceedings for breach of confidence, unlawful interference with business and conspiracy and sought an injunction.

It sought permission to serve the proceedings against the Rusal defendants in Russia. It relied upon (*inter alia*)   6–081

- CPR Rule 6.20(8) for the tortious claims of unlawful interference with business and conspiracy;
- CPR Rule 6.20(10) for the breach of confidence claim;
- CPR Rule 6.20(2) in relation to the injunction as being a claim for an order to refrain from doing an act within the jurisdiction.

As regards r.6.20(8), the deputy judge held that both limbs of the rule were satisfied:

"Ashton's computer server was in London. That is where the confidential and privileged information was stored. The attack

---

[78] In most cases the Private International Law (Miscellaneous Provisions) Act 1995 will apply, since s.9(4) of the Act states that the applicable law (as defined by the Act) shall be used for determining issues including the question whether an actionable tort has occurred. In those cases (e.g. defamation) excluded from its application the English common law rules continue to apply.

[79] The controversial question of whether a domain name constitutes property was considered in the US case of *Kremen v Cohen* (337 F.3d 1024). The 9th Circuit Court of Appeals held the "sex.com" domain name in issue in that case was a species of property susceptible to conversion.

[80] *Ashton Investments v OJSC Russian Aluminium* [2006] EWHC 2545.

[81] [2006] EWHC 2545, October 18, 2006.

emanated from Russia but it was directed at the server in London and that is where the hacking occurred. In my view, significant damage occurred in England where the server was improperly accessed and the confidential and privileged information was viewed and downloaded. The fact that it was transmitted almost instantly to Russia does not mean that the damage occurred only in Russia. If a thief steals a confidential letter in London but does not read it until he is abroad, damage surely occurs in London. It should not make a difference that, in a digital age of almost instantaneous communication, the documents are stored in digital form rather than hard copy and information is transmitted electronically abroad where it is read. The removal took place in London....

I also consider that substantial and efficacious acts occurred in London, as well as Russia. That is where the hacking occurred and access to the server was achieved. This may have been as a result of actions taken in Russia but they were designed to make things happen in London, and they did so. Effectively the safe was opened from afar so that its contents could be removed. It would be artificial to say that the acts occurred only in Russia. On the contrary, substantial and effective acts occurred in London."

As regards r.6.20(10), Ashton submitted that the claim related to the Ashton computer system and the confidential information contained on it, which were located in London. The judge held:

"In my judgment, Part 6.20(10) extends to claims in respect of confidential information if it can be established that the information was really located in the jurisdiction. Information contained in digital form on a server in London satisfies this test."

As regards r.6.20(2), the judge held:

"The information is now presumably in Russia and any documents are likely to be there. I am not satisfied that the injunction would in substance be ordering the Defendant to do or refrain from doing an act in the jurisdiction.

By contrast, if a claim were added for an injunction restraining the Defendants from interfering with the server (as I anticipate it will be), that would be restraining the Defendants from doing an act in the jurisdiction."

Ashton had also established that England was clearly the convenient forum for the dispute. Among other factors the judge noted that it was likely that the claim would be governed by English law, since the most significant element of the events—the unauthorised access to the server—occurred in

London. Events which occurred abroad were all directed at the server in London.

The judge therefore granted permission to serve the proceedings against the Rusal defendants in Russia. He refused permission to serve proceedings against the individual defendants against whom Ashton also proceeded, since Ashton had not established a good arguable case in conspiracy or that the individual defendants were necessary or proper parties to the litigation.

6.5 "COUNTRY OF ORIGIN" RULES

6.5.1 Background

We discuss in Ch.12 a variety of possible policy approaches to the problem of whether a website proprietor, due to the fact that his website is by its very nature available in any country with internet facilities, is potentially subject to the laws of all those countries.   6–082

We have also discussed above the development in the UK, in some areas of law on a piecemeal basis, of rules suggesting that only if a website is in some sense directed at the UK should it be subject to UK laws or jurisdiction.

Within the European Community an attempt has been made, in the internal market provisions of the Electronic Commerce Directive,[82] to provide for a broader "country of origin" rule. A pure country of origin rule would provide that a website proprietor would only be required to comply with the laws of the state in which it is established, thus protecting website proprietors established in a country within the European Union from the laws of other European Union countries even if they direct their activities to those countries.

The Directive was implemented generally in the UK by the Electronic Commerce (EC Directive) Regulations 2002[83] (hereafter "the Electronic Commerce Regulations"). With the exception of reg.16, which came into force on October 23, 2002, these came into force on August 21, 2002. The internal market provisions of the Directive are implemented by regs. 4 and 5.

We discuss in Ch.12 the political reasons why a pure country of origin regime is unlikely ever to be adopted. The Electronic Commerce Directive, containing a number of exceptions and derogations, does not embody a pure country of origin rule. We discuss here the scope of the country of origin provisions of the Directive and the exceptions and derogations from it.   6–083

The Directive does not purport to alter international jurisdiction or

---

[82] Directive 2000/31/EC of the European Parliament and of the Council of June 8, 2000, on certain legal aspects of information society services, in particular e-commerce, in the Internal Market (Directive on electronic commerce).
[83] SI 2002/2013.

applicable law rules. However, it can affect the ability of a Member State to enforce the domestic laws that would apply as a consequence of those rules, if to enforce those domestic laws would amount to a prohibited restriction on the freedom to receive "information society services" from another Member State. The precise relationship of the Directive with rules of private international law is obscure in the extreme.

6.5.2 The Electronic Commerce Directive

6–084   The Directive was promoted primarily by the old Commission Directorate DGXV and now the Internal Market Directorate, which have been responsible for Single Market initiatives. The focus of the Directive is on removing obstacles to cross-border e-commerce within the Community and on implementing, as far as possible, a regime of control of cross-border services by country of origin and concomitant mutual recognition of Member State national laws.

Information Society Services

6–085   The Directive applies to "Information Society Services". These are defined as services within the meaning of Art.1(2) of the "Transparency Directive"[84] (Art.2(a)). The full definition in the Transparency Directive is set out below. However, there appear to be some qualifications to this definition as a result of the recitals to the Electronic Commerce Directive. The Transparency Directive definition is:

> " 'service', any Information Society service, that is to say, any service normally provided for remuneration, at a distance, by electronic means and at the individual request of a recipient of services.
>
> For the purposes of this definition:
>
> 'at a distance' means that the service is provided without the parties being simultaneously present,
>
> 'by electronic means' means that the service is sent initially and received at its destination by means of electronic equipment for the processing (including digital compression) and storage of data, and entirely transmitted, conveyed and received by wire, by radio, by optical means or by other electromagnetic means,
>
> 'at the individual request of a recipient of services' means that the service is provided through the transmission of data on individual request.
>
> An indicative list of services not covered by this definition is set out in Annex V.

---

[84] European Parliament and Council Directive 98/34 [1998] O.J. L204/37 as amended by Directive 98/48 [1998] O.J. L37/35.

This Directive shall not apply to:
radio broadcasting services,
television broadcasting services covered by point (a) of Article 1
of Directive 89/552/EEC."

Annex V of the Transparency Directive provides: 6–086

"ANNEX V
Indicative list of services not covered by the second subparagraph
of point 2 of Article 1
1. Services not provided 'at a distance'
–Services provided in the physical presence of the provider and
the recipient, even if they involve the use of electronic devices

(a) medical examinations or treatment at a doctor's surgery
    using electronic equipment where the patient is physically
    present;
(b) consultation of an electronic catalogue in a shop with the
    customer on site;
(c) plane ticket reservation at a travel agency in the physical
    presence of the customer by means of a network of
    computers;
(d) electronic games made available in a video-arcade where
    the customer is physically present.

2. Services not provided 'by electronic means'
–Services having material content even though provided via
electronic devices:

(a) automatic cash or ticket dispensing machines (banknotes,
    rail tickets);
(b) access to road networks, car parks, etc., charging for use,
    even if there are electronic devices at the entrance/exit
    controlling access and/or ensuring correct payment is made,

–Off-line services: distribution of CD roms or software on
diskettes,
–Services which are not provided via electronic processing/
inventory systems:

(a) voice telephony services;
(b) telefax/telex services;
(c) services provided via voice telephony or fax;
(d) telephone/telefax consultation of a doctor;
(e) telephone/telefax consultation of a lawyer;
(f) telephone/telefax direct marketing.

3. Services not supplied 'at the individual request of a recipient
of services'
–Services provided by transmitting data without individual

demand for simultaneous reception by an unlimited number of individual receivers (point to multipoint transmission):

(a) television broadcasting services (including near-video on-demand services), covered by point (a) of Article 1 of Directive 89/552/EEC[85];

(b) radio broadcasting services;

(c) (televised) teletext."

6–087 The effect of the indicative list of excluded services in Annex V may be modified by Recital (17) of the Electronic Commerce Directive, which states:

"The definition of information society services already exists in Community law in Directive 98/34/EC[86] of the European Parliament and of the Council of 22 June 1998 laying down a procedure for the provision of information in the field of technical standards and regulations and of rules on information society services and in Directive 98/84/EC[87] of the European Parliament and of the Council of 20 November 1998 on the legal protection of services based on, or consisting of, conditional access; this definition covers any service normally provided for remuneration, at a distance, by means of electronic equipment for the processing (including digital compression) and storage of data, and at the individual request of a recipient of a service; those services referred to in the indicative list in Annex V to Directive 98/34/EC which do not imply data processing and storage are not covered by this definition."

This appears to restrict the Annex V exclusions to those in the Annex V indicative list which do not imply data processing (including digital compression) and storage. So although fax is on the Annex V list, it does utilise digital compression techniques and so according to the recital ought to be included in the definition. This approach does create considerable uncertainties.

A further indication of the scope of the definition is provided by Recital (18) of the Electronic Commerce Directive. This provides a list of services that do and do not constitute information society services. Those that do include selling goods online; insofar as they represent an economic activity, services which are not remunerated by those who receive them, such as those offering on-line information or commercial communications, search tools; transmission of information via a communication network, providing access to a communication network, hosting information provided by a

---

[85] Directive 89/552 [1989] O.J. L333/5.
[86] Directive 98/34 [1998] O.J. L204/37.
[87] Directive 98/84 [1998] O.J. L320/54.

recipient of the service; video-on-demand or the provision of commercial communications by electronic mail.

Those that do not constitute information society services are stated to include the delivery of goods as such or the provision of services off-line; television broadcasting within the meaning of Directive 89/552[88] and radio broadcasting, because they are not provided at individual request; the use of electronic mail or equivalent individual communications for instance by natural persons acting outside their trade, business or profession including their use for the conclusion of contracts between such persons; the contractual relationship between an employee and his employer; activities which by their very nature cannot be carried out at a distance and by electronic means, such as the statutory auditing of company accounts or medical advice requiring the physical examination of a patient.

The reference to the inclusion of email is obscure. It is unclear how, notwithstanding the terms of the recital, the sending of email can be characterised as a service normally provided at individual request as required by the main definition.

Place of establishment

The Directive defines the place of establishment of an information society service provider ("ISSP"). This is important for the principle of country of origin control, since a Member State is required to ensure that the information society services provided by a service provider established on its territory comply with the national provisions applicable in the Member State in question which fall within the co-ordinated field.

6–088

Article 2 provides that an "established service provider" is:

"a service provider who effectively pursues an economic activity using a fixed establishment for an indefinite period. The presence and use of the technical means and technologies required to provide the service do not, in themselves, constitute an establishment of the provider;"

This is further elucidated in Recital (19), which states:

"The place at which a service provider is established should be determined in conformity with the case-law of the Court of Justice according to which the concept of establishment involves the actual pursuit of an economic activity through a fixed establishment for an indefinite period; this requirement is also fulfilled where a company is constituted for a given period; the place of establishment of a company providing services via an internet website is not the place at which the technology supporting its website is located or the place at which its website is accessible but

---

[88] See fn.85 above.

the place where it pursues its economic activity; in cases where a provider has several places of establishment it is important to determine from which place of establishment the service concerned is provided; in cases where it is difficult to determine from which of several places of establishment a given service is provided, this is the place where the provider has the centre of his activities relating to this particular service."

The "country of origin" principle comes to the fore in the statement that the place of establishment is not where the website is accessible. Although the recital also states that a service provider is not established where the technology supporting its website is located, in cases of difficulty where the centre of activities relating to the particular service has to be ascertained it is difficult to resist the conclusion that the location of the technology supporting the website will often be at least one factor to be considered.

The definition of an established service provider in the Electronic Commerce Regulations is an amalgam of Art.2 and Recital (19):

"a service provider who is a national of a Member State or a company or firm as mentioned in Article 48 of the Treaty and who effectively pursues an economic activity by virtue of which he is a service provider using a fixed establishment in a Member State for an indefinite period, but the presence and use of the technical means and technologies required to provide the information society service do not, in themselves, constitute an establishment of the provider; in cases where it cannot be determined from which of a number of places of establishment a given service is provided, that service is to be regarded as provided from the place of establishment where the provider has the centre of his activities relating to that service; references to a service provider being established or to the establishment of a service provider shall be construed accordingly;"

Mutual recognition

6–089 The Directive lays down a regime of mutual recognition of Member State national laws and control by Member State of origin and for exclusions and derogations from the Directive and from the country of origin principle. Mutual recognition of the legal regimes of other Member States is achieved in Art.3.2, which states the general principle that Member States may not, for reasons falling within the co-ordinated field, restrict the freedom to provide information society services from another Member State.

The country of origin provisions reflect the general principles of free movement of goods, freedom of establishment and freedom to provide and receive services under the Treaty of Rome and the specific responsibility of DGXV and now the Internal Market Directorate of the Commission to promote the Single Market.

The mutual recognition principle expressed in Art.3.2 of the Directive is implemented by reg.4(3) of the Electronic Commerce Regulations. This states that subject to paras (4), (5) and (6) of reg.4:

> "any requirement shall not be applied to the provision of an information society service by a service provider established in a Member State other than the United Kingdom for reasons which fall within the coordinated field where its application would restrict the freedom to provide information society services to a person in the United Kingdom from that Member State."

Regulation 4(4) excludes the application of this principle to the fields set out in the Annex to the Directive (see below, para.6–096).

Regulation 4(5) excludes any requirement maintaining the level of protection for public health and consumer interests established by Community acts.

Regulation 4(6) limits the penalty for any new criminal offence created by the Regulations to two years' imprisonment or, on summary conviction, three months, or a fine of more than level 5 on the standard basis or a daily fine of £100. These are the maximum penalties allowed under para.1(1)(d) of Sch.2 of the European Communities Act 1972, the Act under which the Regulations are made.

EC Treaty

The EC Treaty contains provisions designed to ensure the free flow of goods and, most relevantly for the purpose of this Directive, services between Member States. **6–090**

Articles 28–30 (old 30–36[89]) of the EC Treaty prohibit quantitative restrictions on the free movement of goods between Member States. Article 28 (old 30) states:

> "Quantitative restrictions on imports and all measures having equivalent effect shall be prohibited between Member States."

Article 30 (old 36) states:

> "the provisions of Articles 28 and 29 shall not include prohibitions or restrictions on imports, exports or goods in transit justified on grounds of public morality, public policy or public security; the protection of health and life of humans, animals or plants; the protection of national treasures possessing artistic, historic or archaeological value; or the protection of industrial and commercial property. Such prohibitions or restrictions shall

---

[89] By virtue of the Treaty of Amsterdam, which came into force on May 1, 1999, the articles of the Treaty of Rome were renumbered. This article will use the new numbering with the old numbering in brackets.

not, however, constitute a means of arbitrary discrimination or a disguised restriction on trade between Member States."

As to freedom of services, Art.49 (old 59) states:

"Within the framework of the provisions set out below, restrictions on freedom to provide services within the Community shall be prohibited in respect of nationals of Member States who are established in a State of the Community other than that of the person for whom the services are intended ..."

Under Art.50 (old 60) services are within the meaning of the Treaty where they are:

"normally provided for remuneration, insofar as they are not governed by the provisions relating to freedom of movement for goods, capital and persons."

"Services" is defined in particular to include:

"a) activities of an industrial character; b) activities of a commercial character; c) activities of craftsmen; d) activities of the professions."

Under Art.55 (old 66) the provisions of Arts. 45–48 (old 55–58) apply. In particular, Art.46 (old 56) provides:

"1. The provisions of this Chapter and measures taken in pursuance thereof shall not prejudice the applicability of provisions laid down by law, regulation or administrative action providing for special treatment for foreign nationals on ground of public policy, public security or public health."

Thus it can been seen that under the Treaty itself the country of origin/mutual recognition regime applied by Arts. 28 (old 30) and 49 (old 59) is qualified by a number of exceptions which permit the destination Member State to restrict goods and services received from the Member State of origin.

Further, Art.153 (old 129A) places a specific obligation on the Community in relation to consumer protection:

"In order to promote the interests of consumers and to ensure a high level of consumer protection, the Community shall contribute to protecting the health, safety and economic interests of consumers, as well as to promoting their right to information, education and to organise themselves in order to safeguard their interests."

The Article specifies that consumer protection requirements shall be taken into account in defining and implementing other community policies and activities; and that measures adopted by the Council under Art.153(4) (old 129a(4)) shall not prevent any Member State from maintaining or introducing more stringent protective measures, albeit that such measures must be compatible with the Treaty.

The Electronic Commerce Directive as advertised

In promoting the proposed Electronic Commerce Directive, the European Commission placed most emphasis on the principle of country of origin control, for instance: 6–091

> "The proposal builds upon the tried and tested Single Market principles of free movement and freedom of establishment, and would ensure that providers of information society services based within the EU can provide their services throughout the EU if they comply with the law in their country of origin"[90]
>
> "[in the proposed electronic commerce directive] commercial communications emanating from a service provider established in the European Community would be subject to country of origin control. This means that the service provider will have to comply with the rules of the country in which he is established and will benefit from the free provision of services throughout the Community." ... "The expectation that consumers are adequately protected by the legislation of the country of origin of the service provider reflects the high level of integration among Member States of the European Community."[91]

The Directive in reality

However, if an ISSP were to believe that now the Directive is implemented he only has to worry about the laws of his home Member State, he would be mistaken. Although in principle a country of origin regime properly so called could achieve that ideal, the reality is that the Electronic Commerce Directive does not achieve that. This is hardly surprising when, as we have seen, exceptions from country of origin control are built into the very fabric of the EC Treaty. Politically, proposals for a true country of origin regime are always bound to encounter formidable obstacles.[92] After the Directive was adopted, statements began to emerge from the Commission that 6–092

---

[90] Commissioner Mario Monti, *Global Electronic Commerce—the Next Phase.*
[91] *US Perspectives on Consumer Protection in the Global Electronic Marketplace—Comments by the European Commission*, April 21, 1999.
[92] See Ch.12.

recognised the significance of the Directive's derogations from the country of origin principle.[93]

The broad principle of country of origin control is set out in Art.3 of the Directive. Article 3.1 states:

> "Each Member State shall ensure that the information society services provided by a service provider established on its territory comply with the national provisions applicable in the Member State in question which fall within the co-ordinated field."

Thus, a Member State must ensure that its laws apply to an ISSP established within its territory, even if the ISSP has so arranged matters that the services are delivered from a location outside the Member State's territory. The location of the web server, or the ability to access a site from within a Member State, do not determine the place of establishment.

This aspect of the Directive is implemented generally in the UK by regs 4(1) and 4(2) of the Electronic Commerce Regulations.

Regulation 4(1) provides that subject to reg.4(4) (see para.6–089 above) any requirement which falls within the co-ordinated field shall apply to the provision of an information society service by a service provider established in the UK irrespective of whether that information society service is provided in the UK or another Member State.

Regulation 4(2) provides that subject to reg.4(4) an enforcement authority with responsibility in relation to any requirement in reg.4(1) shall ensure that the provision of an information society service by a service provider established in the UK complies with that requirement irrespective of whether that service is provided in the UK or another Member State and any power, remedy or procedure for taking enforcement action shall be available to secure compliance.

This provision probably does not override existing statutory rules conferring discretion on enforcement authorities, but operates so that any such discretion cannot be exercised in a discriminatory way by reference to the place to which the information society service is provided.

An "enforcement authority" does not include courts, but subject to that means any person who is authorised, whether by or under an enactment or otherwise, to take enforcement action. "Enforcement action" includes in relation to any legal requirement imposed by or under any enactment, any action taken with a view to or in connection with imposing any sanction, whether criminal or otherwise, for failure to observe or comply with it; and in relation to a permission or authorisation, anything done with a view to removing or restricting that permission or authorisation.

6–093 The co-ordinated field of the Directive concerns:

---

[93] See, for instance, Commission Communication of February 9, 2001, on E-Commerce and Financial Services: "There are significant derogations in the e-commerce Directive from the internal market approach described above."

"requirements with which the service provider has to comply in respect of:

- the taking up of the activity of an information society service, such as requirements concerning qualifications, authorisation or notification,
- the pursuit of the activity of an information society service, such as requirements concerning the behaviour of the service provider, requirements regarding the quality or content of the service including those applicable to advertising and contracts, or requirements concerning the liability of the service provider;"

The co-ordinated field is stated not to cover requirements such as:

- requirements applicable to goods as such,
- requirements applicable to the delivery of goods,
- requirements applicable to services not provided by electronic means.

So although the co-ordinated field includes what may be thought of as regulatory requirements with which a service provider has to comply, it goes much wider than that, for instance extending to general content laws (insofar as they apply to services delivered by electronic means).

Regulation 2(1) of the Electronic Commerce Regulations copies out the Directive's definition of the co-ordinated field.

Article 3.2 of the Directive states:

6–094

"Member States may not, for reasons falling within the co-ordinated field, restrict the freedom to provide information society services from another Member State."

This reflects the primary mutual recognition provisions of the EC Treaty as regards freedom of services (Art.49 (old 59)).

The elevation of consumer protection to a primary objective of the Community under the EC Treaty may increase the potential for conflict between country of origin control and the traditional approaches to consumer protection involving preserving the mandatory rules of the consumer's country of habitual residence and exemplified in the Judgments Regulation and the 1980 Rome Convention (see above).

The prohibition on restricting incoming services is implemented in reg.4(3) (see para.6–089 above).

Some have taken the view that the internal market provisions of the Directive are unclear as to whether they extend to private law matters and that the Directive for that reason leaves open to Member States whether to apply them to private law disputes; that the internal market provisions of the Electronic Commerce Regulations are restricted to requirements of a regulatory nature and that reg.4(3) cannot be invoked in private law disputes.[94]

This is unconvincing. The Directive is on the face of it not generally restricted to public law matters, indeed the co-ordinated field definition specifically includes private law matters such as liability. Nothing in the internal market provisions of the Directive restricts them to public law matters. Various provisions of the Directive (notably Recital (25)) would be otiose if they were so restricted.[95] As for the Electronic Commerce Regulations it is significant that reg.4(3), unlike regs. 4(1) and 4(2)), is not limited to activities of public enforcement authorities and thus includes the courts.

It is true that applying the internal market provisions of the Directive to private law disputes raises difficult questions about the relationship of the Directive to private international law. We discuss these below. However, that is no reason to impose an artificially narrow interpretation upon the Regulations.

Exclusions and derogations

6–095 The Directive contains both exclusions from the complete scope of the Directive and derogations from the country of origin principle. The Commission, in its Explanatory Memorandum, justified the exclusions from the complete scope of application of the Directive on various grounds including undesirable clashes with areas covered by other Directives (e.g. data protection), or that work is in progress under other initiatives (e.g. taxation), or that "it is not possible to guarantee the freedom to provide services between Member States given the lack of mutual recognition or sufficient harmonisation to guarantee an equivalent level of protection of general interest objectives".[96]

As to derogation from the country of origin principle, the Commission put forward three reasons for derogating in specific areas from the country of origin principle:

> "(1) It is *impossible to apply the principle of mutual recognition* as set out in the case law of the Court of Justice concerning the principles of freedom of movement enshrined in the Treaty, or
>
> (2) It is an area where mutual recognition cannot be achieved and there is *insufficient harmonisation* to guarantee an equivalent level of protection between Member States,
>
> (3) There are *provisions laid down by existing Directives which*

---

[94] See, e.g. "The UK Perspective on the Country of Origin Rule in the E-Commerce Directive – A Rule of Administrative Law Applicable to Private Law Disputes?" J Hörnle, *International Journal of Law and Information Technology* (2004) 12: 333–363.

[95] See M Hellner "The Country of Origin Principle in the E-Commerce Directive – A Conflict with Conflict of Laws?" *European Review of Private Law* 2–2004 p.193.

[96] Explanatory Memorandum, p.32. See also Recitals (11) to (16) of the Directive.

are clearly incompatible with Article 3 because they explicitly require supervision in the country of destination."[97]

In addition to the exceptions and derogations specifically provided for, Art.3 of the Directive preserves the right, subject to a series of conditions relating to the characteristics of measures and the conduct of the Member State taking them, for Member States to take country of destination measures against given information society services emanating from other Member States. It also provides for an emergency procedure and for a supervision and veto procedure by the Commission. The Commission stated[98]:

"It goes without saying that the Commission's approach in this context will be flexible, and, in particular, will seek to avoid cases of disguised or disproportionate restrictions to the free movement of the relevant services. Having said this, the Commission will fully account for the Member States' need to enforce laws seeking to protection fundamental societal interests. It would, for example, be out of the question for the Commission to prevent a Member State from applying a law which would forbid the arrival of racist messages."

The Directive provides the following derogations from the country of origin principle[99]:   6–096

- Copyright, neighbouring rights, rights referred to in Directive 87/54/EEC[1] (legal protection of topographies of semi-conductor products) and Directive 96/9/EC[2] (legal protection of databases) as well as industrial property rights.
- The emission of electronic money by institutions in respect of which Member States have applied one of the derogations provided for in Art.8(1) of Directive 2000/46/EC[3] (Directive on the taking up, pursuit of and prudential supervision of the business of electronic money institutions).
- Article 44(2) of Directive 85/611/EC[4] (co-ordination of laws, regulations and administrative provisions relating to undertaking for collective investment in transferable securities).
- Article 30 and Title IV of Directive 92/49/EEC (direct insurance other than life insurance), Title IV of Directive 92/96/EEC (direct life insurance), Arts. 7 and 8 of Directive 88/357/EEC (direct

---

[97] Explanatory Memorandum, p.32.
[98] Explanatory memorandum, p.33.
[99] The Annex to the Directive.
[1] Directive 87/54 [1987] O.J. L45/43.
[2] Directive 96/6 [1996] O.J. L2/14.
[3] Directive 2000/46 [2000] O.J. L275/39.
[4] Directive 85/611 [1985] O.J. L375/3.

insurance other than life assurance) and Art.4 of Directive 90/619/EEC (direct life insurance).

- The freedom of the parties to choose the law applicable to their contract
- Contractual obligations concerning consumer contracts.
- Formal validity of contracts creating or transferring rights in real estate where such contracts are subject to mandatory formal requirements of the law of the Member State where the real estate is located
- The permissibility of unsolicited commercial communications by electronic mail.

Apart from these specific derogations from the country of origin principle, Art.3.4 of the Directive also lays down that Member States may take measures to derogate from Art.3.2 in respect of a given information society service if the following conditions are fulfilled:

(a) The measures shall be:

  (i) Necessary for one of the following reasons:

    - public policy, in particular the prevention, investigation, detection and prosecution of criminal offences, including the protection of minors and the fight against any incitement to hatred on grounds of race, sex, religion or nationality, and violations of human dignity concerning individual persons,
    - the protection of public health,
    - public security, including the safeguarding of national security and defence,
    - the protection of consumers, including investors;

  (ii) Taken against a given information society service which prejudices the objectives referred to in point (i) or which presents a serious and grave risk of prejudice to those objectives,

  (iii) Proportionate to those objectives.

6–097 These bases of derogation mirror and (in the case of public policy) amplify the derogations from country of origin for freedom of services set out in Art.46 (old 56) of the EC Treaty, with the addition of consumer protection.

The derogations are implemented in the Electronic Commerce Regulations by reg.5. The conditions under which such measures may be taken by an enforcement authority are set out in reg.5(1) and (3) to (7). These mirror the provisions of Art.3.4 of the Directive.

Regulation 5(2) sets out the circumstances in which a court (which is not an enforcement authority under the Regulations, and includes any court or tribunal) may take such measures.

Regulation 5(2) provides that in any case where an enforcement authority with responsibility in relation to the requirement in question is not party to the proceedings, a court may, on the application of any person or of its own motion, apply any requirement which would otherwise not apply by virtue of reg.4(3) in respect of a given information society service, if the application of that enactment or requirement is necessary for and proportionate to any of the objectives set out in reg.5(1). As with an enforcement authority, under reg.5(3) a court may take such measures only where the information society service prejudices or presents a serious and grave risk of prejudice to an objective set out in reg.5(1).

Article 3.4(b) of the Directive provides that prior to taking the measures **6–098** in question, and without prejudice to court proceedings, including preliminary proceedings and acts carried out in the framework of a criminal investigation, the Member State must have asked the Member State with country of origin control to take measures and the latter either did not take measures or they were inadequate; and also notified the Commission and the Member State in which the service provider is established of the intention to take such measures. The Member State may in the case of urgency, take measures without complying with those conditions so long as it notifies them in the shortest possible time afterwards to the Commission and the Member State in which the service provider is established, indicating the reasons for which the Member State considers that there is urgency.

The Commission under Art.3.6 shall, without prejudice to the Member State's possibility of proceedings with the measures in question, examine the compatibility of the notified measures with Community law in the shortest possible time. Where the Commission comes to the conclusion that the measure is incompatible with Community law, the Commission shall ask the Member State in question to refrain from taking any proposed measures or urgently to put an end to the measures in question. This formulation of the Commission's powers is significantly weaker than the Commission's original proposal, which required Member States to cease or refrain from measures in the event of a Commission negative decision.

Under the Electronic Commerce Regulations, court proceedings, including preliminary proceedings and acts carried out in the course of a criminal investigation, are under reg.5(5) exempt from the requirement of Reg.5(4) first to request the home Member State to take measures and to give advance notice to that Member State and the European Commission.

The derogation provisions potentially provide scope for Member States to seek to justify existing restrictions against a "given" service on one of the grounds set out in Art.3.4,[5] or to put in place new restrictions under the urgency procedure and then to fight a lengthy political campaign seeking to justify the measures taken. It is unclear whether a "given" service can

---

[5] The effect of the Directive on existing legislation is not spelt out. It is not clear whether Member States can seek to justify existing legislation under the Art.3.4 derogations, or whether any attempt to enforce existing legislation is a "measure" subject to the notification procedures of Art.3.4.

extend to a designated type of service, or means a particular service emanating from a particular provider. They may also provide scope for complex debates in the domestic courts over the justifiability of domestic laws when applied to services emanating from providers established in other Member States.

Given that the EC Treaty itself does not provide for pure country of origin control it is, perhaps, hardly surprising that the Directive is laden with exceptions and derogations.

Practical effect of the Directive

6–099   The practical effect of the derogations may usefully be considered in the light of the Commission's own survey of the key areas giving rise to legal costs associated with electronic commerce.[6] The Commission's survey showed that 64 per cent of those who had undertaken a legal analysis of the regulatory situation had evaluated legal aspects other than those in their own country. 57 per cent believed it was essential to evaluate how the activity would be treated in other Member States.

The key areas giving rise to legal costs were, in descending order of significance: copyright, general requirements on advertising, contracts, promotional offers, unfair competition, consumer protection, and liability regimes.

It is instructive to assess the effect of the country of origin provisions of the Directive on each of the main topics identified by the Commission's survey:

As to copyright, the country of origin provisions have no effect thanks to the derogation from the country of origin principle under Art.3.3 and the Annex. Other aspects of the Directive, especially the liability of intermediaries provisions, apply to copyright.

As to advertising, in principle the Directive could have considerable effect. However, the Art.3.4(a) derogations, particularly public policy and consumer protection, may give Member States scope to seek to defend advertising restrictions. Further, any advertising-related trade mark issues would appear to be derogated from the country of origin principle by virtue of the derogation for industrial property rights. Similar remarks could be made about unfair competition laws.

As to contracts, the effect of the country of origin provisions on the need to obtain legal advice on contracts will not be great. On the positive side, Art.9 of the Directive in many cases requires Member States to remove obstacles of form to on-line contract formation. The Directive also creates uniform requirements as to placing of orders and receipt of acknowledgments and information to be provided to the recipient service.[7] These apply to all contracts within the scope of the Directive, including consumer contracts.

---

[6] Explanatory Memorandum, p.9.
[7] Arts. 9–11.

Notwithstanding these harmonised rules, the derogations for Member States to exercise country of destination control, particularly for the purposes of consumer protection, and the derogation for contractual obligations concerning consumer contracts, mean that an ISSP cannot assume that his contract terms will comply with the law in all destination Member States.[8]

In principle, promotional offers should be protected by the country of origin provisions of the Directive, particularly as Art.6 of the Directive lays down harmonised minimum requirements for commercial communications, including promotional offers, competitions and games. Again, Member States may seek to rely on the consumer protection derogation to justify measures against a given service. On the other hand, one of the main effects of the Directive has been to force Germany to liberalise its notoriously restrictive rules against "two for one" offers and the like.[9] If these could not be enforced against incoming services, domestic traders were at a disadvantage. Rather than seek to defend the restrictions, the German Government changed the law.

As to differing liability regimes,[10] these could only be the subject of the country of origin principles of the Directive if a Member State's liability provisions could be characterised as a restriction on the freedom to provide Information Society services in that State. Since "requirements concerning the liability of the service provider" are stated to be within the co-ordinated field of the Directive, that could be found to be so. Of course, laws regarding the liability of information society intermediaries are harmonised by the Directive, but that does not affect the position of non-intermediary ISSPs. **6–100**

There are numerous other areas about which ISSPs might consider taking advice in destination Member States: e.g. defamation, privacy laws, obscenity, language laws and many others. Some of these, such as language laws, ought in principle to be among the strongest candidates for country of origin control (although see Recital (63) discussed below).

The Law Commission in its Scoping Study on Defamation and the Internet[11] suggested that defamation liability appeared to be within the co-ordinated field as a "requirement of a general nature covering publishers' liabilities". The authors thought that it would appear that imposing English defamation liability on a foreign ISP would constitute a restriction on an incoming service if the liability would not have been imposed in France, but noted that neither the Directive nor the Regulations were clear on the point. The extent to which defamation is affected by the Directive raises further

---

[8] There is of course a degree of harmonisation of consumer protection in contract by virtue of, among others, the Distance Selling Directive 97/7 [1997] O.J. L144/19 and the Unfair Contract Terms Directive 93/13 [1993] O.J. L95/29.

[9] The German Discount Act and the Free Gift Ordinance were repealed in 2001.

[10] It is assumed that this refers to issues such as liability for inaccurate content, possibly defamation and so on.

[11] Above, para.6–055.

questions about the relationship between the Directive and private international law, which we discuss below.

An early UK example of enforcement action against an incoming service claimed to be justified under the derogations from the country of origin principle was provided in October 2002 by ICSTIS, the UK Independent Committee for the Supervision of Standards of Telephone Information Services. ICSTIS took action to suspend web-related premium rate telephone services provided to the UK by two companies established in Spain and Germany. It barred access to the services for two years, fined the companies £75,000 and £50,000, issued a formal reprimand and instructed them to offer redress to all complainants.

In this case ICSTIS relied on the full urgency exception provided in Reg.5(6). On the basis of ICSTIS' account of the facts, the activities of the companies in question presented a serious danger to UK consumers. According to ICSTIS, the companies' websites downloaded dialler software to users' computers without their knowledge. The dialler program would then dial up a premium rate number charged at £1.50 per minute. The promotional material for one website is said to have contained references to paedophilia and sexual acts involving children.

It is open to question, on these facts, whether ICSTIS' action was constrained by the Directive at all. To constitute an information society service within the Directive, a service must be provided "at the individual request of a recipient of the service". The nub of the complaint here was that the dial-up occurred without the user's knowledge, which by definition can hardly have occurred at the user's individual request. However, ICSTIS proceeded on the basis that they had to justify their actions within the terms of the Directive.

There can be little doubt on the available facts that, assuming that the urgency requirement was satisfied, ICSTIS was justified in suspending the services, at least for a sufficient period to enable authorities in Germany and Spain to take appropriate action. That would have protected consumers and minors. As to the fines, would they be regarded as a "restriction" on the provision of services? If not, they would be outside the limitations of the Directive. But if they did constitute restrictions it could be questioned whether, once the services had been suspended, the additional imposition of fines of £75,000 and £50,000 could be said to be either necessary or proportionate to those objectives. That could be seen as going beyond what was necessary for the protection of consumers and minors, and instead to usurp the jurisdiction of the authorities in the home countries of the service providers: the very thing that the Directive set out to prevent.

In its First Report[12] on the operation of the Electronic Commerce Directive the European Commission stated that it had received only five formal notifications under the derogation provisions of the Directive. All five emanated from the same Member State (which we can confidently infer was the UK) and all concerned the fraudulent use of premium rate numbers.

---

[12] 21.11.2003, COM(2003) 702 final.

The Directive and private international law

Uncertain boundaries between the Directive and private international law   **6–101**
may cause problems. Article 1.4 of the Directive states: "This Directive
does not establish additional rules on private international law nor does it
deal with the jurisdiction of Courts." Similarly Recital (23) states: "This
Directive neither aims to establish additional rules on private international
law relating to conflicts of law nor does it deal with the jurisdiction of
Courts; provisions of the applicable law designated by rules of private
international law must not restrict the freedom to provide information
society services as established in this Directive."

The interaction between the Directive and private international law is not
easy to predict. If, for instance, French law provides that a consumer
contract is invalid if it is not in French, the 1980 Rome Convention on the
Law Applicable to Contractual Obligations would entitle a consumer
habitually resident in France to take advantage of a French "mandatory
rule" to that effect, if the conclusion of the contract was preceded by a
specific invitation to the consumer or by advertising. But if the Electronic
Commerce Directive means anything, such a law should be regarded as a
restriction on the freedom to provide services from another Member State
and thus, unless it can be justified under one of the derogations from Art.3,
contrary to the Directive. If the Rome Convention takes precedence, or if a
language law can be justified under one of the derogations (such as for
contractual obligations in consumer contracts), it becomes difficult to see
what is left of the "country of origin" principle that is supposed to underlie
the Directive. Interestingly, in its Communication on E-Commerce and
Financial Services issued in February 2001, the Commission makes the
following comment on the interaction between the Rome Convention and
the Directive:

> "The effect of the derogation in the field of contract law is to
> allow Member States other than the State in which a service
> provider is established to apply rules which restrict the freedom to
> provide information society services, subject to compatibility of
> such measures with Article 49 of the EC Treaty."

Further, if national sensitivities are to be given weight under the public
policy derogations, then it has to be questioned to what extent the Directive
would provide protection against incidents such as the action taken by the
German authorities against a left wing magazine hosted on a website in
Holland, which the German authorities regarded as contravening German
laws against encouraging terrorism.[13] The recitals to the Directive contain
language which might provide some comfort to a Member State seeking to
place a wide interpretation on, for instance, the public policy derogation.
Recital (63) states:

---

[13] The *Radikal* incident (see Ch. 12).

"The adoption of this Directive will not prevent the Member States from taking into account the various social, societal and cultural implications which are inherent in the advent of the information society; *in particular it should not hinder measures which Member States might adopt in conformity with Community law to achieve social, cultural and democratic goals taking into account their linguistic diversity, national and regional specificities as well as their cultural heritage*, and to ensure and maintain public access to the widest possible range of information society services; in any case, the development of the information society is to ensure that Community citizens can have access to the cultural European heritage provided in the digital environment." (emphasis added).

6–102 Whilst the Directive may have reduced the areas in which those risks exist and in which cross-border advice needs to be taken, it is unlikely to have eliminated either the risk or the need. At worst it has simply replaced one uncertainty (the nature of the laws of the destination Member State) with another (the justifiability of the destination Member State laws under the derogations from the Directive). At best, if the political will to embrace the Single Market in cyberspace is present among the Member States, it has established a bridgehead for a true European single market in the on-line world, taking advantage of the de facto destruction of national frontiers pioneered by the internet to transcend the traditional national boundaries of the off-line world.

The relationship of the Directive to private international law was hotly debated during the consultation on the UK implementation. Some argued that the internal market provisions of the Directive pre-empted private international law, relying in part on Recital (22) "moreover, in order to effectively guarantee freedom to provide services and legal certainty for suppliers and recipients of services, such information society services should in principle be subject to the law of the Member State in which the service provider is established." However, this can be understood as laying down a minimum requirement, not that the home State's domestic law should in all circumstances apply to the exclusion of another Member State's domestic laws. Recital (22) does not say that "only" the law of the Member State of establishment should apply.

If Recital (22) did mean that the Directive lays down the applicable law, Recital (23) would make no sense and Art.1.4 of the Directive would be contravened. Further, if private international law were not preserved, it is difficult to see how Art.3.2 could ever be relevant in a case with foreign elements[14] since it is only by application of local law to an incoming service

---

[14] However, not all cases that might appear to have foreign elements in fact do so. See for instance the discussion of defamation liability at para.6–036 above, where the English courts have held that if a defamatory foreign website is read in England, publication takes place in England and results in a domestic English tort.

that a restriction on an incoming service could be created. One interpretation of the Directive is that private international law is preserved but
that the domestic law found to be applicable (if it is other than the law of
the Member State of origin) should be disapplied if the result would be to
restrict incoming services. Determining whether it is restrictive may require
a cumbersome comparison between the law of the Member State of origin
and that found to be applicable.

Another possibility is that the Directive does indeed create an autonomous framework for deciding which Member State's law applies, which
overrides private international law. Since private international law
accommodates the concept of overriding mandatory rules,[15] if the Directive
has the status of a Community mandatory rule it would pre-empt, but not
create an additional rule of, private international law.[16] This interpretation
would therefore not offend against Art.1.4 of the Directive. The main
difficulty with this approach is that the internal market provisions of the
Directive do not lay down substantive rules,[17] but (assuming that they
mandate the law of the Member State of origin) rules about which country's
laws should apply. If that is not a choice of law rule, then it effectively
requires an English court to regard the domestic law of another Member
State as being mandatory. That is something that the UK has always
resisted, as evidenced by its derogation from Art.7(1) of the 1980 Rome
Convention.

Further, if the content of the Community mandatory rule is that the law
of the Member State of origin always applies within the co-ordinated field,
on what basis can the forum state ever invoke its own law and bring Art.3.2
into play? One answer could be that such a mandatory rule is subject to an
exception for the forum state's own mandatory[18] rules (but no others). That
would make some sense, since the conditions for derogating from the
internal market provisions are sufficiently stringent that only a local law of
mandatory status is likely to be regarded as sufficiently important to satisfy
the derogation conditions. The result of that would be that a local law of
non-mandatory status could never fall to be tested as to whether it constituted a restriction on incoming services under Art.3.2. That would
prevent, for instance, English defamation law ever being applied to an
incoming service from another Member State regardless of whether it might
or might not constitute a restriction on an incoming service.

6–103

The UK Electronic Commerce Regulations are silent as to what interpretation of the internal market provisions is favoured. Notably, they do
not require the English courts to apply the law of the Member State of

---

[15] See, for instance, Art. 7(2) of the Rome Convention.

[16] See M Hellner "The Country of Origin Principle in the E-Commerce Directive—A Conflict
with Conflict of Laws?" *European Review of Private Law* 2–2004 p.193.

[17] In this respect the Directive differs from the *Ingmar* case (Case C–381/98 *Ingmar GB Ltd v
Eaton Leonard Technologies Ltd* [2000] E.C.R. I–9305 in which the ECJ held that the
provisions of Arts 17–19 of the Agency Directive were of an internationally mandatory
character.

[18] In the sense of applying irrespective of the law otherwise applicable.

establishment of a non-UK ISSP. That perhaps suggests that they favour, or at least allow for, the preservation of private international law.

The last word on this topic should go the Law Commission, which in its Scoping Study on Defamation and the Internet in December 2002 tried valiantly to assess the impact of the internal market provisions on defamation claims:

> "... doubts remain about how far the Directive, as implemented, affects private international law rules about which law is applicable to defamation actions brought against ISP...
>
> The Regulations, as drafted, have not succeeded in their avowed aim of reducing the legal uncertainty over which national rules apply to ISPs. Confusion remains about how far they prevent an ISP based in another Member State from being held liable under English law for a defamation that takes place in England. It would appear that foreign ISPs are not subject to any additional restrictions imposed by English law unless the defamation is sufficiently severe so as to violate an individual's human dignity."

6.6 CROSS-BORDER LIABILITY—AUSTRALIA

6.6.1 Misuse of Registered and Unregistered Trade Marks

Available causes of action

6–104   A range of alternatives are open to an owner of a registered or unregistered trade mark which is used by an unauthorised user on a website. They are:

- Trade mark infringement;
- The consumer protection provisions of the Trade Practices Act 1974 and equivalent State and Territory fair trading legislation; and
- The common law tort of passing off.

The availability of trade mark infringement will generally be limited to a situation where the trade mark is used on the website to sell or advertise goods or services. The Trade Practices Act 1974 has a broader application applying even where there are no goods or services being promoted or sold.

Trade mark infringement

6–105   The Trade Marks Act 1995 offers protection to the owner of a registered trade mark against use of the trade mark as a trade mark in relation to goods and/or services in respect of which the mark has been registered or closely related goods and/or services. For marks which are "well-known" in Australia, use even in relation to unrelated goods or services may be infringing use.

The application of the Trade Marks Act 1995 is geographically limited to Australia and certain Australian territories. Accordingly, it will need to be shown that the infringing use of the trade mark took place within Australia. The offer for sale of goods or services on a website can be perceived as falling within one of three levels of accessibility to Australian consumers.

- At its highest, the goods or services can be offered specifically to Australian consumers and/or on a site which is hosted in Australia. Provided the other requirements were met, this would be a clear case of trade mark infringement.
- Where the goods or services are generally offered to the world at large without any specific targeting of Australian consumers, trade mark infringement is arguable.
- In a situation where the goods are not able to be purchased by Australian consumers (such as where the site contains a disclaimer), the situation is unclear. At present, a laissez faire attitude has been taken by trade mark owners towards use in this manner, with trade mark infringement not being pursued vigourously. However, this does not necessarily mean that there has been no trade mark infringement.

In order to have standing to sue for trade mark infringement, the person must be either a "registered owner" or an "authorised user" of the trade mark. An "authorised user" is defined under the Trade Marks Act 1995 as a person who "uses the trade mark in relation to goods or services under the control of the owner of the trade mark". Control may include quality control or financial control. However, the rights of an "authorised user" to sue for infringement (as set out in s.26) arise only if the registered owner refuses or neglects to bring infringement proceedings and are, in any event, subject to any agreement between the registered owner and the authorised user.

Consumer protection provisions of the Trade Practices Act 1974

Unauthorised use of a trade mark may also constitute a breach of the consumer protection provisions of the Trade Practice Act 1974. The application of the federal legislation is generally limited to corporations engaging in "trade or commerce" although a person who aids or abets a corporation's misleading conduct or is knowingly involved in such conduct may be liable. There are State and Territory based Fair Trading Acts which apply equivalent provisions to the conduct of individuals. 6–106

Section 52 of the Trade Practices Act 1974 prohibits misleading or deceptive conduct in trade or commerce or conduct in trade or commerce which is likely to mislead or deceive by a corporation.

Section 53 prohibits the making of false or misleading representations by a corporation in trade or commerce in connection with the supply or possible supply of goods or services or in connection with the promotion by any means of the supply or use of goods or services. Among the types of representations prohibited are those which represent that the corporation has a sponsorship, approval or affiliation it does not have. A misuse of a trade mark on a website or as a domain name can constitute this type of misrepresentation.

Passing off

6–107　Passing off involves the misrepresentation by one person that their goods, services or business are those of another or have some association or connection with them.

To successfully establish passing off, three elements must be satisfied. First, it will be necessary for a plaintiff to show that it has a *reputation* in Australia (although it is not necessary to actually have a business in Australia). So where a defendant has made a misrepresentation on a website which is accessible in Australia, but the plaintiff has no reputation here, the cause of action will be of no avail.

Secondly, the defendant must have made a *misrepresentation* to the public which leads the public or is likely to lead the public to believe that the goods or services offered by it are those of the plaintiff or that the defendant or its business is the plaintiff or has a licence or association or other connection with the plaintiff. This may occur through the use of the plaintiff's trade marks (whether registered or unregistered) or name on the site or as a domain name or even the appropriation of the "look and feel" of the plaintiff's website. Thirdly, the plaintiff must have suffered *damage* as a result.

There is almost total overlap between passing off and ss.52 and 53 of the Trade Practices Act 1974 (and equivalent the provisions of the State and Territory Fair Trading Acts). Every case of passing off will constitute misleading and deceptive conduct or a false and misleading representation, with an exception perhaps where the misrepresentation is not in trade or commerce. However, a key difference is that damage is required to be established in a passing off action, but not in an action under the Trade Practices Act 1974. Accordingly, passing off is used infrequently.

Both the Trade Practices Act 1974 and passing off also have the benefit of protecting unregistered trade marks.

Disclaimers

6–108　A sufficiently prominent disclaimer on a website may be effective to negate a breach of s.52 of the Trade Practices Act 1974 or passing off, where the disclaimer negates any misleading effect that the use of a trade mark may otherwise have had.

However, under the Trade Marks Act 1995, where the infringement alleged is in relation to the use of the mark in relation to the goods or services in respect of which the mark is registered, such a disclaimer will be ineffective. On the other hand, where the infringement alleged is in relation to goods of the same description as the registered goods, services closely related to the registered goods, services of the same description as the registered services or goods closely related to the registered services, a prominent disclaimer may be effective if the defendant can show that using the trade mark as it did is not likely to deceive or cause confusion.

6.6.2 Copyright

The Copyright Act 1968 protects original literary, artistic, dramatic or musical works. It also protects original sound recordings, films, television and sound broadcasts or published editions of a work. Owners of copyright have a number of exclusive rights in relation to the copyright material, including the right to reproduce, publish, perform, communicate to the public, adapt and in some cases enter into a commercial rental agreement. To have standing to sue for copyright infringement, the plaintiff must be either the owner of the copyright or an exclusive licensee of at least some of the rights comprised in the copyright.

    6–109

A single website may comprise many different copyright works: text, photographs, diagrams, computer programs, audio and video content may all be subject to copyright protection. Printing or downloading content from a website may constitute copyright infringement if there is no express or implied licence to do so, as all involve making a copy of part of the website. Many websites feature terms of use which contain an express licence to do these things. It is arguable that the act of making a website available on the internet constitutes an implied licence for internet users to print or download the website.

In 2001, a new exclusive right to "communicate to the public" was introduced into the Copyright Act 1968. The right replaced the traditional right to transmit and broadcast copyright works, and was intended to make the Act more technology neutral in light of the rise of the internet.

"Communicate" is defined as "to make available on-line or electronically transmit (whether over a path, or a combination of paths, provided by a material substance or otherwise) a work or subject matter". The Act defines "to the public" as the public within or outside Australia. The right is therefore an exclusive right to communicate a work to the public via the internet or by terrestrial, satellite or cable television or radio.

Temporary copies

An issue which has caused concern in the past is the issue of temporary copies made in the process of ordinary usage of the internet and whether that constitutes copyright infringement. The Copyright Act 1968 now contains explicit exceptions to what would otherwise be an infringement of copyright in a work for making a temporary reproduction of copyright material as part of the technical process of making or receiving a communication and for making a temporary reproduction of the copyright material as part of the technical process of using the material. Accordingly,

    6–110

the downloading of a web page onto an internet user's machine which occurs when the web page is viewed, does not constitute infringement of the copyright subsisting in the web page.

ISP safe harbour provisions

6-111   New amendments to the Copyright Act 1968 made in 2005 as a result of the Free Trade Agreement between Australia and the US feature "safe harbour" provisions for internet service providers (ISPs). These provisions provide protection from legal proceedings to ISPs who engage in on-line activities which involve the infringement of copyright, provided that the ISPs comply with certain requirements.

The provisions set out four categories of infringing activity:

- Category A activity—when an ISP acts as a conduit for copyright material, including by intermediate and transient storage of such material;
- Category B activity—when an ISP automatically caches copyright material;
- Category C activity—when an ISP stores copyright material on their systems or networks at the direction of a user; or
- Category D activity—when an ISP links users to on-line locations using information tools or technology.

The ISP must meet each of the relevant conditions in order to receive protection in relation to each category. These conditions are progressively more stringent from Category A through to Category D, to reflect the ISP's differing levels of control in relation to each type of activity. For instance in relation to Category C and D activities, before protection will be granted, there is, amongst other things, a specific requirement that the ISP must act "expeditiously" to remove or disable access to copyright materials if they either became aware of the fact the material is infringing, or alternatively were aware of circumstances which made this appear likely.

Electronic rights management information and technological protection measures

6-112   The Copyright Act 1968 contains a series of provisions offering protection against intentional removal or tampering with "electronic rights management information" in copyright works. "Electronic rights management information" is defined in the Act as "information attached to, or embodied in, a copy of a work or other subject-matter that identifies the work or subject-matter, and its author or copyright owner; or identifies or indicates some or all of the terms and conditions on which the work or subject-matter may be used, or indicates the use of the work or subject-matter is subject to terms or conditions; or any numbers or codes that represent such information in electronic form".

Common examples of "electronic rights management information" are the digital watermarks which are often embedded in digital video and audio recordings. Any attempt to remove a "digital watermark" from copyright material would constitute a breach of these provisions. New amendments to the Act made in 2005 which enacted the Free Trade Agreement between Australia and the US broaden the protection provided to electronic rights management information, and feature a new criminal offence in relation to distributing or importing electronic rights management information that has been removed or altered for a commercial advantage.

The Act also prohibits the manufacture, sale or distribution of devices or the provision of services which are capable of circumventing a technological protection measure. The Act defines a "technological protection measure" as a device, product, technology or component (including a computer program) that in the normal course of its operation:

- prevents, inhibits or restricts the doing of an act comprised in the copyright in a protected work; or
- controls access to a protected work in connection with the exercise of the copyright in that work (this second category is called an "access control technological protection measure" and is a recent addition to the definition).

However, a device, product, technology or component is not considered a technological protection measure to the extent that it controls geographic market segmentation or restricts the use of particular goods or services in connection with the device in which the technological protection measure is installed.

The High Court of Australia considered an earlier definition of "technological protection measure" in *Stevens v Kabushiki Kaisha Sony Computer Entertainment*.[19] The court held that a mechanism integrated into Sony Playstation video-game consoles which was designed to ensure that copied discs could not be played in the console was not a technological protection measure, and that therefore the sale of "mod chips" which disabled that mechanism was not in breach of the Act.

The court held that the operation of a technological protection measure must *directly* prevent or inhibit the infringement of copyright in the protected work—in other words, a technological protection measure must prevent the infringing act of copying a game disc, not the playing of copied discs (the court rejected Sony's argument that playing a copied disc was itself an infringing act).

However, subsequent amendments to the Act make it unclear whether *Stevens v Sony* would be decided the same way today. Amendments to the Act in 2005 provided that a reproduction of a work in RAM constitutes a reproduction "in a material form". This may mean that playing a copied disc is now an infringing act, although it would still need to be established that the reproduction in RAM was of a substantial part of the work.

---

[19] (2005) 221 A.L.R. 448.

In 2006, the definition of "technological protection measure" in the Act was extended to include access control technological protection measures. As an access control technological protection measure is a measure which controls access rather than infringement, it is arguable that a mechanism which prevents copied discs from being played is an access control technological protection measure, even if the playing of copied discs is not an infringing act.

6.6.3 Defamation

Defamation law in Australia

6–113 Defamation law in Australia is based on the common law and the uniform defamation legislation in each state and territory.

To succeed in an action for defamation, in general the plaintiff must be able to show that:

- The plaintiff was identified in the material complained of;
- The published material was "defamatory" of the plaintiff;
- The material complained of was "published" in the jurisdiction, that is communicated to a person other than the plaintiff; and
- The publication was not protected by any defence.

For material to be "defamatory" of a person, it must either directly, or by implication, tend, in the eyes of ordinary reasonable people, to injure the reputation of that person according to one of the following tests:

- Subjecting the person to "hatred, ridicule or contempt";
- Causing others to "shun or avoid" the person; or
- "Lower the plaintiff in the estimation of right-thinking members of society".

Some of the defences that may apply include:

- Justification (truth);
- The opinion defence;
- Qualified privilege (where a person has a legal, social or moral duty to report or publish something to others who have an interest in seeing it);
- The political free speech defence; and
- Qualified privilege (reports of parliament or courts).

Jurisdictions

6–114 An important element of defamation is that the defamatory imputation be "published" within the jurisdiction. In respect of publication on the internet, this issue was considered in the case of *Gutnick v Dow Jones*.[20] In a

---

[20] [2001] V.S.C. 305.

ruling which was subsequently approved by the High Court of Australia,[21] Hedigan J. of the Supreme Court of Victoria held that "publication" should be considered to occur where the allegedly defamatory material was accessed or downloaded, rather then where it was uploaded. Because of the differences in defamation law in different jurisdictions this decision was a key factor in the subsequent settlement of this dispute. However, the court rejected the concerns raised by Dow Jones that such a rule would facilitate "forum shopping" amongst plaintiffs.

Enforcement

One potential difficulty for plaintiffs in internet defamation cases is the prospect of obtaining an injunction to have the material removed from the website. In *Macquarie Bank v Berg*[22] a single judge in the New South Wales Supreme Court refused to grant an injunction on the basis that, as it is not technologically possible to prevent access to information on a website in a particular geographical location, the effect of granting an injunction would be to impose the law of New South Wales on other places around the world, which would be an unjustified imposition on the right to freedom of speech. This decision has been criticised by some commentators and was distinguished by Hedigan J in *Gutnick v Dow Jones*.[23] Accordingly, the availability or enforceability of injunctions under Australian law in internet defamation cases remains unclear.

6–115

6.6.4 Misleading information/False representations—Trade Practices Act 1974/State Fair Trading Acts

The consumer protection provisions of the Trade Practices Act 1974 and the State Fair Trading Acts, referred to in relation to trade marks above, cover not only a scenario involving the misuse of trade marks, but all misleading and deceptive conduct.

6–116

Elements of the Action

In order to establish a breach of s.52, the key elements which need to be shown are that:

6–117

- There was conduct engaged in by a corporation in trade or commerce; and
- That conduct misled or deceived the public or was likely to do so.

Section 53 is a specific provision, the breach of which would also contravene s.52. However, whilst a breach of s.52 attracts civil liability only,

---

[21] [2002] H.C.A. 56.
[22] [1999] N.S.W.S.C. 526.
[23] [2001] V.S.C. 305.

criminal liability may attach to a breach of s.53. A breach of s.53 is also punishable by a fine if prosecuted by the Australian Competition and Consumer Commission.

Section 53 prohibits, among other things, a corporation from "falsely representing that goods are of a particular standard, quality, value, grade, composition, style or model or have had a particular history ... " in trade or commerce in connection with the supply or goods or services.

Anyone can bring an action under the Trade Practices Act 1974 consumer protection provisions as there are no standing requirements. This is because the provisions are directed at maintaining a standard of conduct rather than enforcing a particular right the plaintiff has acquired. Accordingly, a person may bring an action even if they were not the particular consumer misled or deceived.

Each State Fair Trading Act has equivalents to ss.52 and 53 and each has the same absence of standing requirements.

Jurisdiction

6–118   Where the website is located or operated by a corporation somewhere other than in Australia, if it can be shown that members of the Australian public were deceived or misled, action could be taken against the website operator as the Trade Practices Act 1974 is defined broadly enough to encompass trade between Australia and places outside Australia and trade by foreign corporations in Australia. Section 6 of the Act extends the meaning of "trade or commerce" to include trade or commerce between Australia and places outside Australia. Despite this extraterritorial effect, there may, of course, be serious practical difficulties in enforcing judgments in such circumstances.

It is possible that a foreigner who was deceived or misled could take action against an Australian-based website as there is no limitation on the parties who are entitled to take action under the consumer protection legislation.

If the website is operated by an individual or an unincorporated association or other body that does not fall under the Commonwealth Trade Practices Act 1974, the equivalent State Fair Trading Acts will apply. These Acts also make some provision for extraterritoriality. For example, the Victorian Fair Trading Act 1999 will apply where the conduct occurred outside Victoria if the supplier is a body corporate whose principal place of business is in Victoria, or a person who is ordinarily resident in Victoria. It also applies where either the supplier or the consumer enters into the agreement in Victoria, or the goods or services are proposed to be supplied in Victoria. However, for the relevant State Act to apply, some nexus with the relevant State must be shown.

6.6.5 Liability of internet service providers for infringing content

The Broadcasting Services Act 1992 contains a system for classifying and **6–119** regulating internet content. The system does not have an automatic blanket application to *all* internet content, rather it is a mechanism for regulating content that has already been classified or for classifying and regulating content when a complaint is made about it. The Australian Communications and Media Authority (ACMA) has responsibility for overseeing the system.

A person may lodge a complaint with the ACMA about "prohibited content" or "potential prohibited content".

"Prohibited content" in Australia is either material that has been classified RC (Refused Classification) or X by the Classification Board, or material that is rated R and access to it has not been restricted by a restricted access system. "Prohibited content" outside Australia is material which has been classified RC or X by the Classification Board. The Classification Board is the entity responsible for classifying publications, films and computer games in Australia.

"Potential prohibited content" is content which has not yet been classified by the Board but there is a substantial likelihood that it would be prohibited content if it were to be classified.

If the content is hosted in Australia and is "prohibited content", the Authority can issue a "take down notice" to an internet content host (ICH) which must be complied with by 6 pm the next day.

If the content is hosted in Australia and is "potential prohibited content" the Board will be directed to classify the content and an interim "take down notice" will be issued.

If the content is hosted outside Australia, the Authority can require that access to that material be restricted by internet service providers (ISPs) in Australia by means of appropriate filtering technologies.

An ICH or ISP which acts in compliance with a notice or direction from the ACMA receives immunity from civil proceedings in respect of that action—this ensures, for example, that the ICH or ISP cannot be sued by a person whose website has been taken down.

6.6.6 Cybercrimes

Since the enactment of the Federal Cybercrime Act 2001, the Criminal **6–120** Code Act 1995 contains a number of "serious computer offences" including:

- Unauthorised access, modification or impairment with intent to commit a serious offence;
- Unauthorised modification of data to cause impairment; and

- Unauthorised impairment of electronic communication.

The Act also includes "other computer offences" including:

- Unauthorised access to, or modification of, restricted data;
- Unauthorised impairment of data held on a computer disk, etc.;
- Possession or control of data with intent to commit a computer offence; and
- Producing supplying or obtaining data with intent to commit a computer offence.

An example of conduct which would constitute unauthorised access, modification or impairment with intent to commit a serious offence is hacking into password protected data in a bank in order to facilitate the theft of large sums of money. Bombarding a website with large volumes of data so that it is prevented from functioning (a "denial of service" attack) could constitute breach of the prohibition of unauthorised impairment of electronic communication. The spreading of a virus by email that deletes or otherwise modifies data impairing the operation of a business would breach the prohibition on the unauthorised modification of data to cause impairment.

The Criminal Code Act 1995 (Cth) also contains a number of offences relating to accessing, possessing or making available child pornography. New amendments have recently been passed to the Act which require internet service providers and internet content hosts to promptly report to the Australian Federal Police any child pornography which they become aware can be accessed through the service provided by them. Although the provisions do not require internet service providers and internet content hosts to actively monitor internet content, they must promptly report any child pornography which is brought to or otherwise comes to their attention. A failure to refer such a matter to the Australian Federal Police can result in a large fine.

6.7 CROSS-BORDER LIABILITY—BELGIUM

6.7.1 Jurisdiction

Jurisdiction and applicable laws in criminal matters

6–121 In criminal matters, "Belgian law applies to offences committed in the territory of Belgium, by Belgians or foreigners" (Art.3, Criminal Code). Consequently it is important to determine whether the offence was committed within the territory of Belgium. In Belgium, as well as in France, judges interpret the principle of territoriality rather loosely and sanction the theory of extra-territorial jurisdiction ("ubiquity"). According to this theory, "the Belgian judge has jurisdiction if one of the constitutive elements of the offence occurs in Belgium".[24] Given the international nature of the internet, any person exhibiting content on the internet that would be deemed illegal under Belgian criminal law may be prosecuted and judged in Belgium in accordance with Belgian laws.[25]

In a recent case, a complaint was lodged against the (unknown) authors, interpreters and editors of a racist rap song available on the internet and against the service providers through which the distribution of this song on the internet was made possible. The claimants (three politicians) argued that they had standing to sue since they were as citizens suffering damage related to the threat the content of the song constituted to any democratic society. The Brussels Court of Appeal decided that the claim was admissible.

As for defamation and slander, it has been ruled that "texts appearing in chat rooms on the internet meet the conditions of publicity required by the law" to consider these texts as defamatory.[26] Indeed, even if these chat rooms are non-public places, "it is sufficient that [the writings] can be read in order to meet the condition of publicity".[27] The sending of slanderous or defamatory contents by electronic mail may also be prosecuted, based on Art.444 of the Criminal code, which includes "non public writings that are addressed or communicated to several persons".

Jurisdiction in civil and commercial matters

In civil and commercial matters, the most important enactments to take into account from a Belgian perspective are the Council Regulation 44/2001 (also called Regulation Brussels I)[28] and the Belgian Act on the Code on International Private Law.[29]   **6–122**

Regulation 44/2001 (hereunder "the Regulation"), which entered into force on March 1, 2002, establishes rules to determine which national court has jurisdiction as regards EU Member States. It applies as soon as the defendant is domiciled in a Member State. If the defendant is not domiciled in a Member State, the new Belgian Code on International Private Law will apply, pursuant to Art.4 of the Regulation.

Defendant domiciled in a Member State

If the defendant is domiciled in a Member State, the Regulation will apply, without prejudice to the application of provisions governing jurisdiction in   **6–123**

---

[24] P. Gerard and V. Willems, "Prévention et répression de la criminalité sur Internet", in *Internet face au droit*, Cahier du CRID, N812, 1997, E. Montero (ed.), p.157 (free translation).

[25] *Ibid.*

[26] Criminal Court of First Instance of Brussels, December 22, 1999, unpublished.

[27] O. Vandemeulebroeke in *Internet sous le regard du droit*, (ed., JB Bruxelles, 1997), p.221, quoted by the Magistrate's Court Brussels, December 22, 1999, unpublished.

[28] Council Regulation No.44/2001 of December 22, 2000, on jurisdiction and the recognition and enforcement of judgments in civil and commercial matters, O.J. L 12/1, 16.01.2001.

[29] Act on the Code on International Private Law of July 16, 2004, *MB*, July 27, 2004.

specific matters. As a general provision, the defendant, whatever its nationality, must be sued in the courts of the Member State where he is domiciled.[30] Sections 2 to 7 of the Regulation however provide for special jurisdiction according to which the defendant domiciled in a Member State may be sued in the courts of another Member State.

In matters relating to a contract, and in the absence of a specific provision to the contrary between parties,[31] the defendant may, in another Member State, be sued in the courts for the place of performance of the obligation in question (Art.5.1). Special rules are however applicable to consumer contracts.[32]

In matters relating to tort, delict or quasi-delict, the courts of the place where the harmful event occurred or may occur will have jurisdiction (Art.5.3 of the Regulation). In a cyberspace context, this provision is particularly relevant for issues of defamation, copyright infringement and unfair competition. The place where the damage occurred should be the place where the website is displayed (and downloaded) by the claimant.

In a case brought before the Court of Appeal of Brussels,[33] the holders of the domain name *"Liberty tv.com"* and of various trade marks including the word "Liberty", active in the travel sector, claimed that the use of the domain name *"Liberty-Voyages.com"* by a Swiss travel agency to promote its activities was infringing their trade mark rights.

The court considered that it had jurisdiction pursuant to Art.5.3 of the Convention of Lugano[34] since the fact that Benelux consumers could access the website in question caused or may cause prejudice in this territory and since the protection was claimed in that territory. On the merits, the court ruled that there was no likelihood of confusion because the Swiss travel agency, although using a website accessible to Belgian and Benelux surfers, was not present on the Belgian or Benelux market and was not targeting Benelux consumers. Indeed, the information on the website was only given in French, prices were in Swiss currency, the contact information was indicated to be in Geneva and the links were leading to Swiss websites. Additionally, travel departures were only possible from Swiss airports.

In another case, the President of the Court of Commerce of Brussels ruled that it was not sufficient that an internet website be technically accessible in Belgium to consider that its content is relevant for the Belgian territory and the relevant public.[35]

---

[30] Art.2.1 of the Regulation 44/2001. This provision will be applicable in the absence of express agreement between parties regarding jurisdiction.

[31] See Art.23 of the Regulation which provides for the freedom of choice regarding jurisdiction for the parties to a legal relationship.

[32] See Arts. 16 and 17. Article 15 defines the consumer contracts to which these special rules apply. The fact that the definition includes contract concluded with a person who *"by any means"* directs commercial or professional activities to the Member State of the consumer's domicile is of specific relevance for contracts concluded online.

[33] Brussels, December 2, 2004, *Ing.-Cons.*, 2004, p.537.

[34] Convention of Lugano of September 16, 1988 (88/592/CEE), O.J. L319, 25.11.88, p.9, extending to EFTA countries the Brussels Convention of September 27, 1968.

[35] Pres. Brussels, December 12, 2005, *Ing.-Cons.*, 2005, p.265.

These two cases illustrate the problems of the active/passive websites and of the so-called effects-based approach which analyses whether facts committed on-line have consequences in a country as to justify the jurisdiction of the courts of this country. However, this approach often means that the courts must consider the merits of the claims. In these two cases, the court ruled it had jurisdiction but dismissed the claims on the merits.

Defendant not domiciled in a Member State

If the defendant is not domiciled in a Member State, the new Belgian Code on International Private Law (hereafter the Code), which entered into force on October 1 2004,[36] will apply without prejudice to the application of international treaties, Community law or laws regarding particular matters. A series of rules in this Code use the criteria contained in Regulation 44/2001, sometimes incorporating the interpretation given by the European Court of Justice. The scope of these rules should thus, to a certain extent, be the same as the Community rules. The Code sets out as a general rule that Belgian courts have jurisdiction when the defendant is domiciled or has its usual residence in Belgium at the moment the action is brought to court (Art.5 of the Code).[37] [38]

6–124

An interesting provision is Art.10 which provides that in urgent matters, Belgian courts have jurisdiction for provisional or conservatory measures regarding persons or goods situated in Belgium at the moment the action is brought to court, even if these courts do not have jurisdiction on the merits.

The exceptional jurisidiction provided by former Art.638 of the Belgian Judicial Code (giving jurisdiction to the court where the plaintiff has his/her domicile or residence if no other rule can apply) has been withdrawn. Article 11 only provides that, notwithstanding the other provisions of the Code, Belgian courts will exceptionally have jurisdiction when the case presents close links with Belgium and when proceedings abroad appear impossible or when it cannot be required that the claim be brought abroad.

In matters relating to a contract, and in the absence of an agreement between parties on this aspect, Belgian courts will have jurisdiction if the claim concerns a contractual obligation that originated in Belgium or that is or must be executed in Belgium (Art.96.1 of the Code). As for consumer contracts,[39] Belgian courts will also have jurisdiction if: (1) the consumer accomplished in Belgium the acts necessary for the conclusion of the con-

---

[36] Except for some specific provisions regarding adoption which entered into force on September 1, 2005.

[37] This general rule can also be applied for specific matters for which special rules were provided (see below).

[38] Article 4 defines domicile as being, for an individual, the place where he/she is registered, and for a legal person, the place of its registered office. The usual residence is defined as being the place where an individual is principally established (notably according to personal or professional circumstances revealing long-lasting connection with this place), even without registration and notwithstanding any authorisation, or, for legal persons, the place where they have their principal establishment (according to the center of decision and activities).

[39] The consumer being an individual who acts for another purpose than his/her professional activity.

tract and had at that time his/her usual residence in Belgium, or if (2) the good or service was or had to be provided to a consumer who had his/her usual residence in Belgium at the time of the order, if this order was preceded by an offer or advertising in Belgium (Art.97 of the Code).[40]

6–125   In matters relating to tort, Belgian courts will have jurisdiction when the claim concerns an obligation deriving from a harmful event, (1) if the fact causing the obligation occurred or is about to occur, as a whole or in part, in Belgium, or (2) if *and to the extent that* the prejudice occurred or is about to occur in Belgium (Art.96.2 of the Code). The second option reflects the jurisprudence of the European Court of Justice in the *Shevill* case which concerned a compensation claim for defamation through the press.[41]

As to the question of the location where the prejudice occurred, the Court of First Instance of Brussels ruled in a defamation case that the litigious remarks "were largely disseminated through the internet" and that defamatory or slanderous messages made through the internet "must be considered as having being made wherever the dissemination of these remarks could be received and read".[42]

Specific provisions exist concerning intellectual property issues. Article 86 provides that Belgian courts will have jurisdiction regarding any claim concerning the protection of intellectual property rights, besides the general rules of the Code, when the protection claimed is limited to the Belgian territory.[43] This provision is however subsidiary since special rules (notably the Benelux Convention on Intellectual Property and Regulation 40/94 on the Community Trade Mark) contain specific provisions regarding jurisdiction for trade marks and designs.

The jurisdiction of a Belgian court in Benelux trade mark infringement cases is provided for under Art.4.6 of the Benelux Convention on Intellectual Property (BCIP).[44] Unless otherwise expressly stipulated in a contract, jurisdiction in respect of trade mark cases shall be determined by the domicile of the defendant or by the place where the undertaking giving rise to the litigation originated or was or is to be performed. The place where a mark was filed or registered can on no account serve in itself as a basis for the determination of jurisdiction. If these criteria are insufficient for the determination of jurisdiction, then the plaintiff may file the action before the court of his domicile or residence, or, if he has no domicile or residence within the Benelux territory, before the courts of Brussels, The Hague or Luxembourg, at his choice.

---

[40] The consumer can only depart from these rules in an agreement concluded after the dispute has arisen.

[41] Case 68/93, March 7, 1995, *CJCE*, I, p.415.

[42] Brussels, February 19, 2004, available at *http://www.droit-technologie.org/jurisprudences/ TPI_bruxelles_190204.pdf* and in R.T.D.I., 2005, n°21, p.75.

[43] Article 86 does consequently not grant jurisdiction for an extraterritorial protection. If such a protection is needed, the jurisdiction will have to be based on the general rules of the Code.

[44] Benelux Convention on Intellectual Property (trade marks and designs) signed in The Hague on February 25, 2005, and approved in Belgium by the Act of March 22, 2006, *M.B.*, April 26, 2006, p.21866.

A recent copyright case on the internet opposed Belgian daily press publishers (represented by Copiepresse S.C.R.L. that manages the publishers' rights) against the company under US law Google Inc. Copiepresse launched a cease and desist action before the President of the Court of First Instance of Brussels alleging that the activities of *Google News* and the provision of links to cached content by Google infringed the publishers' copyright[45] and database rights. Copiepresse was arguing that Google News was extracting daily press articles in order to copy them or make automatic summaries and to provide the surfers with a press review based on automatic selection of information. Copiepresse notably claimed that all the publishers' articles, photographs and graphic representations be removed from all Google websites (*Google News* and Google 'Cached' links). Although the court did not expressly mention it, it considered it had jurisdiction on this matter and applied Belgian law.[46]

6.7.2 Applicable laws

As a general rule, the laws applicable to contractual obligations, including electronic contracts, are determined by the 1980 Rome Convention.[47] Special legislation may however apply in priority to this Convention.[48] In particular, Belgium implemented the Directive on electronic commerce[49] in its Act of March 11, 2003, on certain legal aspects of information society services. Article 5 of this Act provides for the application of the country of origin rule regarding the provision of information society services. Article 3 however provides that this Act does not apply to a series of matters (such as tax, privacy and gambling) and Art.6 notably provides that Art.5 does not apply to the freedom of the parties to decide the law applicable to their contract, to consumer contracts and to matters of copyright, neighbouring rights and industrial property rights.

6–126

In matters relating to tort, the new Code establishes a "cascade" system.[49a] Belgian courts will apply the laws of the State in which both the person

---

[45] The Belgian Copyright Act of June 30, 1994, was amended by the Act of May 22, 2005, implementing in Belgian law the Directive 2001/29/EC of the European Parliament and of the Council of May 22, 2001, on the harmonization of certain aspects of copyright and related rights in the information society, *M.B.*, May 27, 2005.

[46] Pres. Brussels, September 5, 2006. This decision was however rendered by default and Google filed an opposition to this decision on September 19, 2006. Two decisions were rendered in opposition, on September 22, 2006 and the other on February 13, 2007, confirming the Jurisdiction of the court. These decisions are available at *www.droit-technologie.org/search/default.asp?checkALL=1&searchfield=Google&x=41&y=0*.

[47] This rule is repeated under Art. 98 of the Belgian Code on International Private Law.

[48] This is for instance the case for the Convention of Vienna of April 11, 1980, or Community legislation containing rules on the applicable law.

[49] Directive 2000/31 of the European Parliament and of the Council on certain legal aspects of information society services, in particular electronic commerce, in the internal market, O.J., L178, 17/07/2000, p. 1.

[49a] This contribution does not comment on the new Regulation 864/2007 of the European Parliament and of the Council of July 11, 2007 on the law applicable to non-contractual obligations (Rome II), O.J. L199, 31/07/2007, p.40.

responsible for, and the person injured by, the damage have their usual residence at the moment of the occurrence of the harmful event. If these persons do not have their usual residence in the same State, the court will have to apply the laws of the State where both the fact causing the obligation and the damage occurred or are about to occur in their entirety. In all other cases, the third level of this "cascade" system provides that the laws of the State with which the obligation has the closest links will have to be applied (Art.99 §1 of the Code).

The second paragraph of Art.99 however provides for important derogations from the above system. In cases of defamation, or of prejudice brought to privacy or to personality rights, the plaintiff will have the choice between the laws of the State where the fact causing the obligation, or the laws of the State where the damage occurred or is about to occur.[50] The plaintiff will not have this choice if the person responsible can establish that he/she could not have foreseen that the damage would occur in that State.

This provision specifically addresses the issue of tort caused through the internet and implements to a certain extent the "target-market" law theory that was already supported by part of the Belgian doctrine. According to this theory, if an internet site targets a particular country, then the law of that country should apply to the content of that site.[51] As regards internet sites, the target market is determined according to elements composing the site: presentation, language, content, payment system, etc.

As for unfair competition and unfair trade practices cases, the laws of the State where the (direct) damage occurred or is about to occur will be applicable (Art.99 §2, 2°). This provision confirms the ruling of the Brussels Court of Appeal in the Tractebel case.[52]

6–127 As for the laws applicable to intellectual property right issues that can arise through the internet, Art.93 of the Code provides that these rights are governed by the laws of the State in which the protection is claimed.

In an interesting case brought before the Court of Commerce of Liège, a company existing under the laws of Antigua and organising on-line gambling in 21 languages or more, was accused of using, for its on-line gambling activities, the names, image and/or trade marks of well-known football players and/or football clubs. The company had bought its activ-

---

[50] This provision expressly departs from the jurisprudence of the Belgian Supreme Court, which interpreted the *lex loci delicti* as being the law of the place where the fact causing the damage occurred. See Cass. May 17, 1957, *Pas.* I, p.1111; Cass. October 30, 1981, *Pas.* 1982, I, p. 306; Cass. April 29, 1996, J.T., 1996, p.842. For an application of this principle on a case of defamation and unfair trade practices on the internet, see Comm. Mons, June 15, 2001, available at *http://www.droit-technologie.org/jurisprudences/commerce_mons_150601.pdf*.

[51] P. Péters, "L'internet et la protection des consommateurs", *Internet sous le regard du droit*, Jeune Barreau de Bruxelles (ed.) 1997, p.138.

[52] Brussels, April 1, 1998, *J.L.M.B.*, 1998, p.1588. In this case, the court ruled that "the Trade Practices Act as a compulsory legal rule is applicable to all facts falling under its territorial field of application, that is, all unfair commercial practices occurring on Belgian territory. If a commercial practice is composed of a chain of facts of which part is situated abroad but which ends in Belgium, where moreover the damage is caused, the Belgian judge is competent and the Belgian law will be applied".

ities from another company existing under the laws of Malta and argued that the Belgian court (the jurisdiction of which was not disputed) had to apply the laws of Malta pursuant to the "internal market" clause and the country of origin rule introduced by the Directive on electronic commerce and implemented in Art.5 of the Belgian Act of March 11, 2003.

The court stated that this Act (as well as the Directive) does not apply to gambling games and applied Belgian law on the basis of Arts. 93 and 99 of the Code on international private law (intellectual property and unfair competition).[53]

6.8 CROSS-BORDER LIABILITY—CANADA

6.8.1 Jurisdiction

Introduction

Usually, for a matter to be actionable in Canada, the cause of action must **6–128** arise in Canada. Where the cause of action depends upon the breach of a statute, the statutory breach must have occurred in Canada. Where a cause of action is founded in tort, a sufficient nexus to Canada will have to be established before a Canadian court will assume jurisdiction. Additionally, an order or injunction is normally granted only where the court is satisfied that it could be enforced.

If the Canadian court can assume jurisdiction over a case, then it must do so, unless there is a more convenient forum for the action.

Rules exist within each of the superior courts of the provinces of Canada as well as the Federal Court of Canada providing certain procedural steps for the plaintiff to follow to serve foreign defendants (service *ex juris*).

Accessing a website from within Canada necessarily involves the display of the contents of the site in Canada. Depending upon the tort, this fact could place the infringing action in Canada and bring it within the jurisdiction of a Canadian court.

A Canadian or provincial action would only be stayed if a proceeding in another court or jurisdiction was more comprehensive (i.e. it included the cause of action in the jurisdiction in question as well as additional causes of action). If another action was pending in a jurisdiction outside of Canada relating to the same facts or circumstances, because the foreign court could not have jurisdiction over breach of a Canadian statue or the occurrence of a tort in Canada, a related Canadian action would likely not be stayed by the existence of such foreign proceedings.

Cases such as *Tele-Direct (Publications) Inc v Klimchuk, Canadian Kennel Club* and *Canada Post v Sunview Management Group* (discussed above, Ch.3, section 3.16) all suggest that Canadian courts will not hesitate

---

[53] Comm. Liège, November 24, 2006, available at : *http://www.droit-technologie.org/ 4_1.asp?jurisprudence_id=219.*

to assume jurisdiction over internet actors when there is a real and substantial connection between the activity and Canada.

The *Muscutt*[54] and *Leufkens*[55] cases, referring to *Morguard*,[56] considered eight factors (none determinative) that should be considered when deciding if there is a real and substantial connection to a Canadian jurisdiction:

(1) the connection between the forum and the plaintiff's claim;
(2) the connection between the forum and the defendant;
(3) unfairness to the defendant in assuming jurisdiction;
(4) unfairness to the plaintiff in not assuming jurisdiction;
(5) the involvement of other parties to the suit;
(6) the court's willingness to recognise and enforce an extra-provincial judgment rendered on the same jurisdictional basis;
(7) whether the case is interprovincial or international in nature; and
(8) comity and the standards of jurisdiction, recognition and enforcement prevailing elsewhere.

6.8.2 Defamation

6–129 Defamation is a tort at common law. In order to support a defamation action, a plaintiff must show that the offending statement was published, that it referred to the plaintiff and that the statement was false and had the effect of discrediting the plaintiff.

Publication merely requires that the offending statement be made known to people other than the author of the statement. This component would seem to be satisfied when the defamatory statement is made available on a website and the site is accessed by others who then read the statement.

Once publication is established, the contents of the statement are presumed by the court to be false, published maliciously, and it is further presumed that the plaintiff suffered damages.

The defendant may counter each presumption by contending that the statement consists of true facts, and by showing that, in speaking the truth, the defendant was not motivated by malice. Further, the defendant may be in a position to invoke parliamentary or some other privilege. However, it is far more likely in the context of the internet that an embattled defendant would invoke the defence of innocent dissemination.

The defence of innocent dissemination will be made out if the following three components are shown:

(1) the defendant was innocent of any knowledge of the defamatory nature of the work disseminated by him;

---

[54] *Muscutt v Courcelles* (2002), 60 O.R. (3d) 20 (CA).
[55] *Leufkens v Alba Tours International Inc* (2002), 60 O.R. (3d) 84 (CA).
[56] *Morguard Investments Ltd v De Savoye* [1990] 3 S.C.R. 1077.

(2) nothing in the work or the circumstances under which it came into his possession should have suggested its defamatory content; and

(3) the defendant was not negligent in failing to note the defamatory nature of the contents of the work.

In *Southam Inc v Chelekis*[57] the court applied the same rules to defamatory material distributed by electronic means as have been applied to other types of publications. Canadian law on defamation will apply equally to publications on the internet. An appeal from this decision to the British Columbia Court of Appeal[58] was dismissed and the Supreme Court of Canada refused leave to appeal without reasons.[59] **6–130**

Even if a foreign court can be persuaded to take jurisdiction over an online dispute, its decision will not necessarily be enforced. In *Braintech, Inc v Kostiuk*,[60] the British Columbia Court of Appeal refused to recognise the default judgment of a Texas court. Kostiuk was alleged to have made defamatory statements by posting them to a bulletin board. Braintech sued in Texas and relied on the service provisions of Texas law that provide that service can be effected on a non-resident by serving the Secretary of State (who is then statutorily obligated to effect service on the named party).

The court found that the principle of comity did not extend to the recognition of the order in the circumstances. The Canadian court found that the Texas court did not have personal jurisdiction over Kostiuk because the three-pronged test for determining whether assuming jurisdiction over the defendant was not satisfied. Adopting the reasoning in *Zippo*, the British Columbia Court of Appeal found that:

> "In these circumstances the complainant must offer better proof that the defendant has entered Texas than the mere possibility that someone in that jurisdiction might have reached out to cyberspace to bring the defamatory material to a screen in Texas. There is no allegation or evidence Kostiuk had a commercial purpose that utilized the highway provided by internet to enter any particular jurisdiction. A person who posts fair comment on a bulletin board could be haled before the courts of each of those countries where access to this bulletin could be obtained.
>
> It would create a crippling effect on freedom of expression if, in every jurisdiction the world over in which access to internet could be achieved."

Application for leave to appeal from this decision to the Supreme Court of Canada was dismissed without reasons.[61]

---

[57] [1998] B.C.J. No.848 (SC).
[58] (2000) 73 B.C.L.R. (3d) 161 (CA).
[59] [2000] S.C.C.A. No.177.
[60] (1999) 63 B.C.L.R. (3d) 156 (CA).
[61] [1999] S.C.C.A. No.236.

Conversely, in *Kitakufe v Oloya*,[62] ("Kitakufe"), the Ontario motions judge decided that an Ontario plaintiff could sue for defamation in Ontario based on material published in a Ugandan newspaper and republished on the internet. Although it is likely that the court was persuaded that Ontario was the proper forum to hear the action on the basis that the plaintiff and the defendant were both Ontario residents, the case is nevertheless important because of the way it has subsequently been interpreted.

6–131   In *Gutnick v Dow Jones & Co Inc*,[63] ("*Gutnick*") the Supreme Court of Victoria cited the *Kitakufe* decision as a "case [in] which a superior court assumed jurisdiction over a defamation suit on the basis of access to the website and its reception (that is, downloading) in Ontario, Canada." (*Gutnick* at a.47) It would seem that the Australian court has given the *Kitakufe* decision a very broad interpretation.

The Canadian courts have recently rendered decisions dealing with American newspapers and their on-line articles. A British Columbia court recently ruled against the New York Post who allegedly made defamatory remarks in published articles about Brian Burke, the general manager of a National Hockey League team.[64] The articles were posted on the New York Post website, which was accessible in British Columbia. The court stated that it was foreseeable that the article would be read on-line in British Columbia and that it would be unfair to force Burke to clear his name in New York.

In the case of *Bangoura v Washington Post*,[65] a court found that Ontario was not the appropriate jurisdiction for the proceedings. The articles that Bangoura alleged were defamatory were published in 1997 but were subsequently available online. The Ontario Court of Appeal stated that because Bangoura had no connection to Ontario until three years after the publication of the articles, no damages were suffered in Ontario and there was no significant connection between the Washington Post and Ontario, the Ontario courts were not the appropriate venue. The court stated that "[t]o hold [that there was a connection between the Washington Post and Ontario] would mean that a defendant could be sued almost anywhere in the world based upon where a plaintiff may decide to establish his or her residence long after the publication of the defamation."[66] An application for leave to the Supreme Court of Canada has been filed.[67]

6.8.3 Inaccurate information

6–132   In Canada, compensation for detrimental reliance on inaccurate information will result in situations where: (i) a duty of care based on a "special

---

[62] [1998] O.J. No. 2537 (SCJ).
[63] [2001] VSC 305 (August 28, 2001).
[64] *Burke v NYP Holdings Inc (c.o.b. New York Post)* [2005] B.C.J. No.1993 (SC).
[65] [2005] O.J. No. 3849 (CA).
[66] *ibid.*, at para.25.
[67] [2005] S.C.C.A. No.497.

relationship" between the representor and the representee is established; (ii) the representation in question is shown to be untrue, inaccurate or misleading; (iii) the representor has acted negligently in making the said representation; (iv) the representee has relied, in a reasonable manner, on the negligent representation; and, (v) the reliance has been detrimental in the sense that damages were incurred by the representee.[68]

There is a duty to exercise such reasonable care as circumstances require to ensure that representations made are accurate and not misleading.[69] In all cases, reliance must be *reasonable*. Liability will not arise in situations where the defendant has warned the plaintiff that it is not assuming any obligation with respect to the information given.[70]

6.8.4 Copyright

The reproduction of a copyrighted work "in any material form"[71] constitutes the making of a copy, which, if not authorised, would be copyright infringement. The copying of a copyrighted work into the central processing unit (CPU) of a computer constitutes copying.[72]   **6–133**

Because browsing a web page requires the downloading of a copy of that page onto the browser's CPU and screen, a copy is necessarily brought into Canada. There is probably an implied licence to download and store in random access memory (RAM), a copy of a work from a web page (assuming the owner of the web page has the right to permit such use). However, subsequent commercial distribution of the material by the recipient would be an infringement by offering to sell, selling, distributing, exhibiting and/or importing the work.[73] Knowledge of infringement is a prerequisite to collecting damages; registration of the copyright deems such knowledge to be present.[74]

Where material was not permitted to be posted on a web page, and the web page owner allowed Canadians to download copies of it into Canada, the web page owner may be liable for authorising infringement,[75] communicating the work to the public by telecommunications[76] or performing the work in public or authorising someone else to do so.[77]

It is an infringement under Canadian copyright law to "authorise" another to make a copy of a copyrighted work. Including a notice on a

---

[68] *Queen v Cognos Inc* [1993] 1 S.C.R. 87 at 117.
[69] *ibid.*, at 121.
[70] *Hedley Byne & Co Ltd v Heller & Partners Ltd* [1963] 2 All E.R. 575; [1964] A.C. 465 (HL).
[71] Copyright Act, s.3(1).
[72] *Apple Computer Inc v Mackintosh Computers Ltd* [1990] 2 S.C.R. 209; 30 C.P.R. (3d) 257 at 261.
[73] Copyright Act, s.27(4).
[74] Copyright Act, s.39.
[75] Copyright Act, ss.3(1) and 27(1).
[76] Copyright Act, s.3(1).
[77] Copyright Act, s.3(1).

website that prohibits browsing from other countries may protect the website owner from "authorising" the unauthorised copying of the web page into Canada. The person or persons who downloaded the web page would still be liable for infringement in Canada.

The Supreme Court of Canada has considered the role of internet service providers (ISPs) in the dissemination of copyrighted works over the internet. In the *SOCAN* case, it was decided that a real and substantial connection to Canada is sufficient to support the application of the Canadian Copyright Act to international internet transmissions (i.e. if the communication originated or is received in Canada).[78] Section 2.4(1)(b) of the Copyright Act provides that persons who only supply "the means of telecommunication necessary for another person to so communicate" are not themselves to be considered parties to an infringing communication. So long as an internet intermediary does not itself engage in acts that relate to the content of the communication, but confines itself to providing "a conduit" for information communicated by others, its actions will fall within s.2.4(1)(b).

The creation of a "cache" copy was deemed a necessary consequence of improvements in internet technology, content neutral, and not to have any legal bearing on the communication between the content provider and the end user. An ISP's knowledge that someone might be using content-neutral technology to violate copyright would not necessarily be sufficient to constitute authorisation, but the court stated that authorisation could be inferred in certain cases.

6.8.5 Trade marks

6–134 In order for there to be trade mark infringement in Canada, there would have to be "use" of the trade mark in Canada. As discussed above, the *Tele-Direct (Publications) Inc v Klimchuk* decision suggests that a website will be deemed to be using a trade mark in Canada if that site purposely targets Canadian customers.

One possible interpretation is for the court to consider the "imported" web page to be a "ware" (such as a publication, e-zine or electronic book) and the trade mark was marked on the web page and the web page was provided to the Canadian browser "in the normal course of trade", then there would be actionable use of the trade mark in Canada. The term "in the normal course of trade" normally relates to commercial transactions and not to giving away the ware.[79] Merely advertising wares on a website in the USA does not constitute "use" of a trade mark in Canada.[80] However, it

---

[78] *Society of Composers, Authors and Music Publishers of Canada v Canadian Assn of Internet Providers* [2004] 2 S.C.R. 427 [*SOCAN*].

[79] *Ports International Ltd v Canada (Registrar of Trade Marks)* (1983) 79 C.P.R. (2d) 191 (F.C.T.D.).

[80] *Pro-C Ltd v Computer City Inc* (2001) 55 O.R. (3d) 577 (CA); leave for appeal refused, [2002] S.C.C.A. No.5.

is infringement of a registered Canadian trade mark for a website based in Canada to use a trade mark even if the website is directed to those outside of Canada (e.g. the French speaking world).[81]

Merely advertising a service which is provided outside of Canada does not constitute trade mark use in Canada.[82] If a service is provided to Canadians from the foreign country through the web page utilising the trade mark, then the trade mark is being used in Canada for that service. For example, Saks Fifth Avenue maintained a Canadian trade mark registration for "retail department store services" by providing catalogue shopping services to Canadians from its US stores without ever operating a store in Canada.[83]

Jurisdictional issues with regard to domain names have been considered by Canadian courts as well. An Ontario court refused to exercise its jurisdiction over a registrant of a domain name even though the registrant was in Toronto, Ontario.[84] Domain names lack a physical presence and merely because the corporation was domiciled in Toronto, the domain name did not physically exist in Ontario.

The British Columbia Court of Appeal was faced with a case where the matter at issue was the right to use an internet domain name associated with on-line gambling, which is illegal in Canada.[85] The court affirmed the lower court's ruling that even though there was no tort committed in British Columbia, the claims were clearly related to the contract arbitration proceedings regarding the domain name between the parties in British Columbia; this was the basis for having the case heard in British Columbia.

6.9 CROSS-BORDER LIABILITY—CHINA

6.9.1 Introduction

The rules relating to jurisdiction over the internet in China are closely   6–135
connected with the traditional rules on the jurisdiction of the national courts. These traditional rules are supplemented by a range of complex laws and regulations conferring authority on different organisations and administrative bodies within China regarding access to and publication of material online.

---

[81] *Bell Actimedia Inc v Puzo (Communications Globe Tête)* [1999] F.C.J. No. 683 (F.C.T.D.).
[82] *Marineland Inc v Marine Wonderland and Animal Park Ltd* [1974] 2 F.C. 558 (F.C.T.D.).
[83] *Saks & Co v Canada (Registrar of Trade Marks)* (1989) 24 C.P.R. (3d) 49 (F.C.T.D.).
[84] *Easthaven Ltd v Nutrisystem.com Inc* (2001) 55 O.R. (3d) 334. (SC).
[85] *UniNet Technologies Inc v Communications Services Inc* (2005) 39 C.P.R. (4th) 1. (B.C.C.A.).

6.9.2 General Jurisdiction

Civil Jurisdiction

6–136 The main piece of legislation governing civil litigation and jurisdictional issues is Part Four of the Civil Procedure Law of the People's Republic of China (CPL), entitled "Special Provisions of Civil Procedure for Cases Involving Foreign Elements". The CPL contains measures providing for the commencement of litigation in courts at different levels (district court, intermediate court or higher court), the transfer of cases from non-competent to competent courts, and the designation of jurisdiction upon a lower by a higher court.

However, the most important parts of the CPL, when considering the jurisdiction of the Chinese courts over cases involving the internet, are the provisions that deal with territorial jurisdiction. Territorial jurisdiction under the CPL can be divided into the following categories:-

6–137 **(i) Exclusive Jurisdiction** The CPL expressly provides that the Chinese People's Court shall have exclusive jurisdiction over certain civil matters to the exclusion of foreign courts. For example, Art.246 of the CPL states that civil actions arising from disputes over the implementation of contracts of Chinese-foreign joint ventures, Chinese-foreign co-operative enterprises and Chinese-foreign joint exploration and exploitation of natural resources shall be under the exclusive jurisdiction of the People's Court in China. The CPL also confers exclusive jurisdiction on the People's Court over cases involving immovable property, harbour operations and inheritance disputes.

6–138 **(ii) Consensual Jurisdiction** Article 25 allows parties to a dispute involving foreign contracts or foreign property rights to select a court through agreement in writing, provided that the court chosen is in a place with actual connections with the dispute.

In addition, a non-resident defendant in a civil action involving foreign interests may be deemed to accept the jurisdiction of the People's Court if it files a defence to the complaint.

6–139 **(iii) General Jurisdiction** General territorial jurisdiction is determined by the defendant's domicile (or habitual residence where a defendant has both a domicile and a habitual residence). Unlike in some other civil law jurisdictions, the nationality of the defendant is not used as a basis for determining jurisdiction. The People's Court may also exercise jurisdiction over a defendant who conducts business within the territorial reach of the court. If the defendant is an institution or organisation, a civil action falls under the jurisdiction of the People's Court at the place where the defendant is registered.

Article 23 of the CPL provides that the plaintiff's domicile or habitual residence will be used to determine jurisdiction in actions concerning the identity of persons who do not reside within the domain of the People's Republic of China.

(iv) Specific Jurisdiction The CPL allows the People's Court to exercise 6–140
jurisdiction over foreign defendants who are not domiciled or resident within China where there is a sufficient connection with China (which must be more than "mere presence" in China). Such cases are usually determined by the location of the foreign defendant's conduct or property. These rules will be applicable in many cases involving civil offences committed over the internet where the offender is not actually a Chinese citizen.

Contract Article 243 of the CPL specifically relates to contractual disputes and disputes over property rights against non-resident defendants and provides that the plaintiff can select the place where the contract was signed or performed in China, the place where the subject-matter of the litigation is located, the place where the defendant has distrainable property, the place where the infringing conduct took place or the place where the defendant's representative office is located to be the forum, if these places are within the territory of the People's Republic of China.

Tort In a tort action, the plaintiff may choose the place of the defendant's domicile, the place where the tort was committed, or the place where the harm occurred as the forum.

Criminal Jurisdiction

The main legislation governing jurisdiction over Chinese citizens and for- 6–141
eigners in criminal law issues is Art.10 of the Criminal Law and Part I of the Criminal Procedure Law.

In summary, Chinese authorities have the right to exercise jurisdiction in the following circumstances:

(i) Personal jurisdiction Anyone who violates Chinese criminal law within the territory of the People's Republic of China or abroad is subject to the jurisdiction of the Chinese authorities.

(ii) Territorial jurisdiction The authorities have jurisdiction over crimes occurring within the territory of the People's Republic of China, including crimes started abroad but completed within Chinese territory or crimes causing serious harm to the social or economic order within Chinese territory.

6.9.3 Enforcement of Judgments

The CPL provides a number of measures for enforcing a judgment of the 6–142
People's Court. These include sequestration, freezing or transfer of assets,

search and seizure of belongings, distress and sale of property by auction, eviction, attachment of earnings, specific performance of the obligations set out in a judgment, issuance of certificates for the transfer of property rights and the imposition of fines for delayed payment of debts.

Where a judgment debtor or his/her assets are located outside China, the judgment creditor may apply directly to a competent foreign court for enforcement of a People's Court judgment. Recognition of the judgment by a foreign court will depend on the provisions of bilateral or international treaties between China and the relevant foreign country or the principle of mutual reciprocity.

A judgment creditor of a legally effective judgment made in a foreign court may directly request a competent intermediate People's Court to acknowledge its validity and execute it or the foreign court may request the People's Court to do so in accordance with the provisions of bilateral or international treaties to which China is a party or in accordance with the principle of mutual reciprocity. It is a requirement of Chinese law that a foreign judgment be translated into Chinese before it can be enforced.

On July 14, 2006, China and Hong Kong signed an "Arrangement on Reciprocal Recognition and Enforcement of Judgments in Civil and Commercial Matters by the Courts of the Mainland and of the Hong Kong Special Administrative Region Pursuant to Choice of Court Agreements between Parties Concerned" (the "Arrangement").

The objective of the Arrangement is to establish a convenient mechanism for the reciprocal enforcement of judgments made by the courts of mainland China and Hong Kong. However, the Arrangement will only apply to judgments for liquidated sums of money where the underlying dispute has arisen from a commercial contract and the parties must have agreed in writing that a court of mainland China or Hong Kong should have sole jurisdiction for resolving any disputes.

The Arrangement is expected to come into force in 2007/2008. Due to the restricted scope of the Arrangement, the only area in which it is likely to be of relevance in relation to jurisdiction and the internet is in the field of licensing.

6.9.4 Copyright

6-143 The Copyright Law of the People's Republic of China provides that "copyright" includes the right of communication of information on networks, that is, the right to communicate to the public a work, by wire or wireless means in such a way that members of the public may access these works from a place and a time individually chosen by them. This right was added to the Copyright Law in 2001 to make it clear that a work on the internet can qualify for copyright protection in China.

On November 22, 2000, the Supreme Court issued its "Interpretation on the Application of Law in Cases Involving Internet Copyright Disputes" (the "Interpretation") in order to clarify how the relevant provisions of the

Copyright Law should be applied in internet copyright cases. The Interpretation, which was amended in 2003 and 2006, contains rules on the jurisdiction of network copyright disputes.

Article 1 provides:

> "Cases involving copyright infringement disputes on the internet are subject to the jurisdiction of the court in the place where the infringing act occurs or where the defendant is domiciled. The place where the infringing act occurs includes the location of the equipment used for the alleged infringing act, such as the internet server or computer terminals etc. In cases where the place where the infringing act occurs or where the defendant is domiciled cannot be determined, the location of the equipment such as computer terminals etc through which the plaintiff discovers the infringing content may be considered as the place where the infringing act occurs."

The Interpretation therefore seeks to apply the normal rules concerning jurisdiction under Art.29 of the CPL to the on-line environment so that a copyright infringement action will come under the jurisdiction of the People's Court in the place where the infringing act occurred or where the defendant is domiciled.

Since it may be difficult to determine the domicile of an infringer in cyberspace, the Interpretation assists the plaintiff by defining the "place where the infringing act occurs" as including the location of the server or computer used for the infringing act. However, where neither the domicile of the infringer nor the location of the equipment used for the infringing act can be determined, a third alternative is available to the plaintiff in that the People's Court can assume jurisdiction in a place where the infringing material can be accessed. This third alternative is only to be adopted where the other two criteria cannot be established. It means that in theory, the People's Court can assert jurisdiction over a foreign infringer if the infringing material is accessible from computers in China within the court's territorial reach.

Liability of internet service providers

China's Copyright Law does not specifically deal with the liability of   **6–144**
internet service providers (ISPs), but the Interpretation contains a number of provisions clarifying the level of responsibility of service providers for copyright infringement on the internet.

The Interpretation only applies to ISPs that are involved in some way with the infringing activity, either by aiding and abetting the infringing act or by providing content services that infringe upon a person's copyright. Under Art.106 of the General Principles of Civil Law of the People's Republic of China, legal persons shall not bear civil liability where they are not at fault for the infringing acts (unless the law otherwise stipulates). In the case of internet service access providers that merely provide physical infrastructure services such as wiring and connection with no control over content, there is no subjective fault and therefore no liability for the infringing acts of their customers.

Where an ISP assists another person in committing an act of copyright infringement or where an ISP has editing control over content on the internet, the Interpretation provides that the ISP will be jointly and severally liable with the infringer in accordance with Art.130 of the General Principles of Civil Law. An ISP that provides content services is under an obligation to take measures to delete infringing content and prevent its dissemination after it has become aware of the infringing nature of the content or has received a warning from the copyright owner supported by evidence.

The Measures for the Administrative Protection of Copyright on the Internet (the "Measures"), issued by the National Copyright Administration and the Ministry for Information Industry in April 2005, set out an administrative procedure for a copyright owner to take action against an ISP. The Measures provide that a copyright owner can send a Copyright Owner's Notice to the ISP including certain information such as proof of ownership of the copyright work and evidence about the infringing material on the internet. An ISP that receives a Copyright Owner's Notice is required to immediately remove the infringing content from the web and retain the Copyright Owner's Notice for six months.

Where there is no evidence to indicate that an ISP is fully aware of an infringing act or where the ISP takes measures to remove infringing content after receipt of a Copyright Owner's Notice, the ISP will not bear any administrative liability. However, if the ISP wilfully disregards an infringing act or fails to take measures to remove relevant content after being notified by a copyright owner, the appropriate copyright administration department may order the ISP to cease the infringing act, confiscate any illegal gain and/ or impose a fine upon the ISP. On receiving a counter-notice from the content provider giving evidence of the legal nature of the removed content, the ISP has the discretion to restore the removed content without facing administrative liability.

Under the Interpretation, an ISP is obliged to provide the registration information and details of users alleged to have infringed copyright on the receipt from the copyright owner of evidence as to the copyright owner's identity, proof of ownership of the copyright and evidence of the alleged infringing activities of the ISP. If it refuses to do so, without justified reason, it can be held liable for infringement of the copyright owner's interest. The copyright owner may also apply to the court for an order requiring the ISP to provide the relevant information.

Where loss is wrongly caused to a content provider by removal of the content by an ISP, the ISP shall not be liable and cannot be sued by the content provider for breach of contract and the copyright owner shall bear responsibility. In these circumstances, the ISP is requested to restore the content that has been wrongly removed.

The Regulations on the Protection of the Right of Communication Through Information Networks, which came into force in July 2006, provide further clarification on the obligations and liabilities of ISPs and include a number of safe harbours for ISP activities.

Technological Evasion Measures

The 2003 amendment to the Interpretation added a new Art.7 (now Art.6) **6–145** which states that where an ISP knowingly uploads, transmits or provides the means to circumvent technological protection measures for copyright materials, the court may, depending on the allegations of the parties and the facts, impose civil liability upon the ISP for copyright infringement.

Hyperlinking

The Supreme People's Court has clarified that the provisions of the Inter- **6–146** pretation shall apply to the act of hyperlinking to infringing material by ISPs (both access and content providers).

Accordingly, where an ISP is aware of infringing content to which it provides access through hyperlinks or wilfully disregards a warning of infringement from a copyright owner, the ISP may be held jointly and severally liable with other direct infringers.

In November 2006, the Beijing First Intermediate Court dismissed an application by some of the world's largest record companies—including EMI, Warner, Universal and Sony—claiming infringement of copyright by Baidu.com, one of China's most popular music search engines[86]. Baidu.com posted links to sites offering unlicensed mp3 music downloads, a process known as deep linking. The court held that Baidu's activities did not constitute infringement since the unlicensed files were downloaded from servers belonging to third parties and the record companies failed to prove that Baidu knew or ought to have known that the files in question were infringing. The record labels are now appealing to the Beijing High Court.

The *Baidu* decision would appear to be at odds with the previous case law in China relating to infringement of copyright by ISPs. In 2004, Universal Records won a case[87] in the Beijing Higher People's Court against a Chinese search engine called *ChinaMP3.com*. The court held that the service provided by ChinaMP3 was a "channelling service" which facilitated third party websites to distribute infringing music files to the general public; ChinaMP3 did not make any attempt to find out whether the third party websites were authorised to distribute the music files and it should have known that the website embedded in the deep links were offering infringing files; the fact that ChinaMP3 further selected, processed and ranked the illegal deep links facilitated the infringement of copyright by the third party websites and ChinaMP3 was making a profit by providing such links.

---

[86] Beijing First Intermediate Court, Case No. [2005] Yi Zhong Min Chu No.7965.
[87] *Universal Records v ChinaMP3.com*, Beijing Higher People's Court, Case No. [2004] Gao Min Zhong No.713.

Accordingly, the court ordered ChinaMP3 to stop providing the deep links and to pay compensation to the plaintiff.

A similar decision was reached in *Shanghai Push Sound Music & Entertainment v Baidu.com, Inc.*,[88] a decision also involving the Baidu.com search engine which is currently being appealed to the Beijing Intermediate People's Court.

More recently, in April 2007, in a case brought by eleven members of the International Federation of the Phonographic Industry (IFPI), the Beijing Intermediate People's Court ruled that Yahoo China had infringed copyright by failing to take steps to remove links to infringing tracks from its search engines. The Court ordered Yahoo China to pay damages to the plaintiffs and delete the offending links.

6.9.5 Trade Marks

6–147 A registered trade mark in China gives the owner an exclusive right to use that mark in connection with goods or services in respect of which the trade mark is registered.

In China disputes between owners of trade marks and owners of trade names are common due to the fact that the Administration for Industry and Commerce (AIC) has jurisdiction over the registration of trade names at the local, regional, provincial and national levels while the Trade Mark Office has jurisdiction over the registration of trade marks.

In a case heard by the Beijing Second Intermediate Court,[89] a kitchenware company sued another company dealing in kitchen products, over the registration of the domain name "www.franke.com.cn" to market its goods online. The plaintiff had registered the Chinese language transliteration of "Franke" with the AIC.

The court held that "Franke" and its Chinese equivalent were the plaintiffs' official trade names through which it distinguished itself from other entities. Since registration of the domain name by the defendant was likely to cause confusion amongst the public, this act constituted unfair competition and the court ordered the defendant to revoke its domain name. This case shows that trade and enterprise names can be protected on the internet by the Law Against Unfair Competition even where the owner of the name has no registered trade mark.

Trade Mark Jurisdiction

6–148 Any party who is not satisfied with the decision of the Trade Mark Review Committee (the administrative body responsible for reviewing decisions of the Trade Mark Office concerning refusal of registration, opposition,

---

[88] *Shanghai Push Sound Music & Entertainment v Baidu.com Inc*, Beijing Haidian District People's Court Case No. [2005] Hai Min Chu No.14665.
[89] *Franke (Heshan) Kitchen Equipment Co Ltd v Fuoshan Modern Decoration Materials Company*, (2001), Beijing 2nd Intermediate Court.

revocation and cancellation, etc.), may initiate legal proceedings before the People's Court. Such cases are under the exclusive jurisdiction of intermediate courts in Beijing designated by the Beijing Higher People's Court. The People's Court at or above the intermediate level has jurisdiction over other trade mark related cases at first instance.

Liability of Internet Service Providers

In May 2005, a Danish clothing company, Aktieselskabet Af sued eBay EachNet, one of China's largest on-line auction websites, and its associates for trade mark infringement.[90] The plaintiff owned the trade marks ONLY and VERO MODA and discovered more than 3,000 products bearing these trade marks for sale on the defendants' websites without authorisation. The Danish company claimed that the defendants were joint tortfeasors since they had knowingly allowed the infringing acts to continue and had assisted the infringers by providing an on-line platform over which the unlicensed goods could be auctioned.   **6–149**

In September 2006, the Shanghai First Intermediate People's Court held that the defendants were not liable for trade mark infringement since they did not have the requisite degree of knowledge. As they were merely website operators, they could not control the information exchanged online by third parties. A similar decision was reached in *Beijing Yuzhouxing Trading Company v Chen*.[91]

6.9.6 Domain Names

Since July 2001, cases involving the infringement of an entity's registered trade mark or trade name through registration or use of a domain name have been within the scope of the People's Court's jurisdiction as civil lawsuits. The People's Court can assume jurisdiction in the place where the defendant is domiciled or the place of infringement. Where it is difficult to determine either of these criteria, the location of the equipment such as computer terminals and servers, etc. through which the plaintiff discovered the infringing domain name can be regarded as the place where the infringing act occurs.   **6–150**

This means that Beijing People's Court will almost always have jurisdiction over Chinese domain names, because Beijing is where the China Internet Network Information Centre (CNNIC), the organisation that manages Chinese domain names, is located, and is thus the place where infringing acts commonly occur. In *Re www.franke.com.cn* both parties to the dispute resided in Guangdong province, but the plaintiff chose to file the lawsuit in Beijing, where the CNNIC is located.

The People's Court at the intermediate level can still claim jurisdiction

---

[90] [2005] Hu Yi Zhong Min Wu Chu No.371.
[91] [2005] Qing Min San Chu No.404.

where either of the parties to a domain name dispute is a foreign national, a foreign enterprise or organisation, an international organisation or a stateless person.

Chinese courts have also accepted cases where domain names have been registered through overseas registrars. For example, in *Shenzhen Zhongxiangwong Satellite Network Ltd v Merion International Business Network (Beijing) Ltd*,[92] the disputed Chinese language domain names were registered through the US registration organisation Verisign Inc, but the parties to the dispute were both Chinese. In such cases, the People's Court's decision will be delivered to the foreign registration organisation for enforcement.

6.9.7 Defamation

6–151　Defamation is both a civil and criminal offence in China. A decision of the National People's Congress on Maintaining Internet Security issued in 2000 specifically brings offences of defamation over the internet within the scope of the criminal law. It is also an offence under the Telecommunications Regulations to produce, copy, publish or distribute defamatory information using telecommunication networks, and there are a host of other regulations prohibiting acts such as the viewing of defamatory information, the publication of defamatory information on electronic forums and chat rooms and the publication of defamatory information in news on internet websites.

Defamation cases fall under the jurisdiction of the People's Court in the place where the infringing act occurs or where the defendant is domiciled. The location of the infringing act includes both the place where the infringing act is committed and the place where the results of the infringement occur.

The first internet defamation case in China was *Max Computer Station Inc v Wang Hong Life Times & PC World*.[93] The case concerned the publication by a consumer of defamatory information on the internet about a computer manufacturer. The consumer also set up a website with hyperlinks to a forum for internet users to discuss their own discontent with the manufacturer's products. On appeal to Beijing No.1 Intermediate People's Court, it was held that the consumer was liable for the defamatory statements he made himself, but was not liable for the defamatory remarks posted on the website that was linked to his homepage.

Liability of internet service providers

6–152　According to the Measures on Internet Information Services issued in 2000, an ISP will be responsible for defamatory content on its website if the ISP

---

[92] (2001), Beijing 2nd Intermediate Court.
[93] (2000), Beijing 1st Intermediate Court.

knows or ought to know of its existence. These measures provide that if the ISP is a profit-making organisation, it can be ordered to suspend its services for internal rectification by the authority that issued its business licence, or its business licence can be revoked. Non-profit making ISPs can be ordered to temporarily or permanently shut down the website in question.

The Public Security Bureau (the police) is responsible for overseeing ISPs that provide internet access services. ISPs are required to assist the Public Security Bureau in investigations into cybercrimes and must provide monthly reports showing numbers of website users, numbers of viewings of website pages and user profiles. Any offences by website users may result in revocation of an ISP's business licence and network registration, fines and possible criminal prosecution of the ISP's staff.

6.10 CROSS-BORDER LIABILITY—FINLAND

6.10.1 Defamation

Defamatory statements are criminalised in the Finnish Penal Code. An **6–153** internet user may conduct such a crime through distribution of an offending statement publicly. There is no liability for a defamatory statement transmitted only to the defamed person. However, due to the nature of the internet the threshold for regarding a message publicly must be considered rather low.

The liability for defamatory statements lies primarily with the author of the statement. Internet service providers and bulletin board service providers are not liable through mandatory provision as is the case with publishers and broadcasters. It is, however, possible that certain services provided over the internet could be regarded as very similar to publishing and that service providers could thus be exposed to a strict liability together with the author.

Only individuals are subject to criminal sanctions under the Penal Code. Consequently, corporations and organisations are not liable for defamatory statements. However, the members of the board or the managing director may be subject to criminal sanctions on behalf of the corporation they represent. Accordingly, a corporation may not be subject to defamation as defined by the Penal Code, only individuals.

As the internet to an increasing degree is a format for commercial dealings and advertising, statements that are of a defamatory nature and may harm the business activities of a corporation can be dealt with under the provisions of the Act on Unfair Business Practices. Injunctions against activities contrary to the Act on Unfair Business Practices can be granted by the Market Court and significant wilful conduct contrary to the Act on Unfair Business Practices is also criminalised.

The penalty for defamation is a fine or maximum two years of imprisonment. Compensation to the defamed party may also be awarded by the court.

The Finnish Penal Code is applicable when an unlawful act has been conducted in Finland. With regard to the internet this would mean that if a defamatory message is received in Finland, the defamatory act has also been conducted in Finland. There does not exist court practice in this respect. If an overseas website can be accessed from Finland a Finnish court will most likely consider itself competent.

The problematic issues will in many cases be to find the defendant and to serve a summons upon such defendant. Unless multilateral or bilateral agreements on assistance between relevant authorities between Finland and the state of the defendant exist, the criminal act may in practice remain unsanctioned. Consequently, the responsibility of an internet service provider in Finland will be a critical issue which has not yet been tested in defamation lawsuits.

The Act on the Exercise of Freedom of Expression in Mass Media (460/2003) contains more detailed provisions on the exercise, in the media, of the freedom of expression enshrined in the Constitution. It applies also to the internet communication, provided that it falls within the scope of publishing or broadcasting. The Act which contains provisions on, e.g. liability, compensation and coercive measures applicable to disputes related to the exercise of freedom of expression does not apply to the communication of private citizens. Criminal liability for an offence arising from the contents of a message provided to the public lies in the Penal Code.

With regard to corporate liability for statements that may be harmful to a business entity, parallels could be drawn between satellite broadcasting and internet transmissions. The Market Court has held that the Finnish subsidiary of a foreign company was liable for satellite TV advertising made by the parent company as the Market Court considered that the Finnish subsidiary profited from such marketing when the satellite broadcasting transmission was received in Finland. In the same manner the Market Court could consider itself competent to handle a lawsuit based upon presentation of harmful statements through the internet made by a foreign commercial entity if such entity has a subsidiary or distributor in Finland profiting from the statement.

It is more problematic if individuals distribute harmful information concerning a commercial entity in Finland. The current Finnish laws have not properly taken into account such situations.

As a whole, defamatory statements on the internet and liability for the different internet service providers has not been properly addressed in current Finnish laws, which leaves room for interpretations and uncertainty. The lack of precedent cases also leaves room for interpretations.

6.10.2 Content liability

6–154   The content made available on a website may be of various types, including advertising, facts about the website owner and professional advice. The general principle of Finnish law is that the website owner is responsible for the information on the website administered by such company. Also, in such situations where the internet users have been entitled to store information on a company's website, the company remains responsible therefore and has an obligation to supervise the website on a constant basis.

The main principle under Finnish law is, consequently, that the company administering its website is held liable, for example, for copyright infringement or trade mark infringement if such infringement occurs on the website. If the negligence of the website owner is considered minor, the compensation awarded to the infringed party can be adjusted and in cases of no negligence, the compensation can be adjusted to nil.

If someone has relied upon incorrect information on the website, the owner of the website is primarily liable to compensate the harm suffered from relying upon such information. Especially with regard to consumer products and services, special attention must be paid as the Consumer Protection Act and the Product Safety Act provide for strict liability with regard to marketing and product information that may be harmful to the consumer. Here again the problematic issue might be to identify the providers of the incorrect information and establish court jurisdiction in Finland.

6.10.3 Copyright infringement

According to the Finnish Copyright Act, copyright protection subsists in a   6–155
wide variety of works, whether they are literary or artistic, fictional or descriptive representations in writing or in speech, or whether they be musical, dramatic or cinematographic works, works of fine art, architecture, artistic handicraft, industrial art or works expressed in some other manner. Maps and other descriptive drawings or graphically or three-dimensionally executed works, as well as computer programs, are considered literary works. Rules governing rights such as the rights of performing artists, producers of records, as well as radio and television organisations, are also encompassed in the Copyright Act.

Copyright protection originates automatically through the performance of the author. If the product of creativity fulfils a certain level of originality, the work is protected automatically without any registration or other formalities.

It is nevertheless usual and also recommended especially in the internet to emphasise the subsistence of copyright in a work by placing an appropriate copyright notice and the year of publishing on it. The author of a work may be one or several individuals. According to the Finnish copyright system, a legal entity, a computer or an animal cannot be considered as an author. Thus, a legal entity's copyright is always derived from an individual. If a work is created by two or more authors whose contributions do not constitute independent works, the copyright shall belong to the authors jointly. However, each of them separately may initiate an infringement action.

With regard to computer programs and associated works that have been created within the scope of ordinary duties in an employment situation, it is expressly stipulated in the Copyright Act that the copyright of such programs and works pass automatically to the employer, unless otherwise agreed.

Copyright protection in most cases now subsists until the end of the 70th year after the year in which the author died or, in the case of several authors, after the year after the last surviving author died. However, different treatment with regard to different types of works create some problems with regard, for example, to websites that may constitute a combination of text, film, photographs and sound. Under the Copyright Act, the rights of an author have been divided into moral and economic rights. Economic rights may freely be assigned or licensed to a third party.

6–156   For copyright to be infringed, a work or a substantial part of it, must have been made available to the public, imported for distribution or copied without authorisation. Wilful production of a copy of a work or making a work available to the public in violation of someone else's copyright is a criminal offence, as is the importation of an unauthorised copy of a work for distribution to the public, provided that the infringer has committed the infringement for gain. The penalty for such an offence is a fine or a maximum of two years' imprisonment. The author will receive fair compensation for any unauthorised use and, if such use is wilful or results from negligence, the infringer shall, in addition, pay damages for any other loss.

According to case law, "piracy" is generally considered to be a criminal offence. As the maximum penalty is two years' imprisonment, there are fair possibilities for a copyright owner to enforce confiscation, seizure or other interim measures as well as customs support. In criminal proceedings, confiscation and seizure can be obtained at an early stage of the proceedings, whereas interim measures are usually more difficult to obtain in civil proceedings.

The shortly incoming Copyright Act amendment may set forth stricter rules concerning piracy. According to the proposed amendment, the criminal liability for importation of an unauthorised copy of a work would no longer require distribution to the public. Therefore, the scope of the provision would be extended to also cover the importation of pirate products for private use. In addition, the amendment would outlaw the passage of pirate products via Finland to third countries.

If a website without proper authorisation contains a copy of someone else's original work, this would generally be considered a copyright infringement. However, copying of a published work (other than a computer program) which is protected by copyright is permitted for personal use. If the copy is made for a company, it would generally be regarded as non-personal use and subject to sanctions under the Copyright Act.

Making copyright protected work available to the public also constitutes copyright infringement and consequently, if an individual would use copyright protected material on his website without authorisation, this would be regarded as making the work available to the public and would thus constitute copyright infringement.

Based on the above, as Finnish law allows the making of copies of 6–157 published copyrighted works for private use, private persons may generally browse the internet without a fear of infringing someone's copyright. Companies should, however, be more careful as it is likely that their use is not deemed as personal and the making of copies without copyright owner's authorisation is therefore not allowed.

According to the proposed amendments to the Copyright Act implementing the Directive 2001/29/EC, temporary acts of reproduction which are transient or incidental and an integral and essential part of a technological process and whose sole purpose is to enable (i) a transmission of a work in a network between third parties by an intermediary, or (ii) a lawful use of a work or other subject-matter to be made, and which have no independent economic significance, shall be exempted from the reproduction right. This will verify the interpretation that copyright is not infringed when a temporary copy of a work is made by an intermediary as an integral part of a transmission process.

It is, however, important to point out that with respect to uses of works, the making of a temporary copy as an integral part of a process for instance to a personal computer's random access memory (RAM) would be allowed only in connection with lawful uses of works. If the use is not authorised by copyright owner or allowed by law, copyright would be infringed each time a temporary copy is made, for instance to a computer's RAM.

6.10.4 Trade mark infringement

Trade mark rights in Finland can be obtained through registration and/or 6–158 establishment. Registration that covers Finland is possible to obtain through a national registration, through registration of an EU trade mark or through the Madrid Protocol and the Madrid Agreement. It may be noted that unregistered international trade marks more rapidly than previously may become established in Finland through advertising in, for example, satellite broadcasts and on the internet.

There is no established court practice with regard to trade mark infringement through the internet, but the general perception is that if commercial use of a trade mark is accessible through the internet in Finland this will constitute trade mark infringement in Finland. In practice this means that the infringer may be subject to injunction and payment of compensation for trade mark infringement even if the use would be legal in other countries. Here again, one of the difficulties might be that the defendant is difficult to identify and serve a summons upon.

6.11 CROSS-BORDER LIABILITY—FRANCE

6.11.1 Introduction

6–159   As in most countries, the main issue in France is not so much the lack of laws likely to apply to the internet rather than their enforcement.

6.11.2 Governing law and jurisdiction for foreign websites

6–160   With respect to internet-related disputes, it is first necessary to determine (a) whether the French courts have jurisdiction to hear the case before, (b) deciding if French law can be enforced.

The jurisdiction of the French courts

6–161   In order to determine the jurisdiction of the French courts in an international dispute, both national laws and international conventions apply.

In the first place, French case law has decided that domestic laws which determine the jurisdiction of the French courts also apply to international disputes.[94] As a result, Arts 42 and 46 of the French Code of Civil Procedure will be applicable to international disputes.

Article 42 states that:

> "the territorially competent court is, unless otherwise provided, that of the place where the defendant lives".

Article 46 provides that:

> "the plaintiff may bring his case, at his choosing, besides the court of the place where the defendant lives, before:
>
> – in contractual matters, the court of the place of the actual delivery of the chattel or the place of performance of the agreed service;
> – in tort matters, the court of the place of the event causing liability or the one in whose district the damage was suffered;"

Alongside domestic rules, the European Regulation CE 44/2001 of December 22, 2000, which replaced the Brussels Convention of September 27, 1968, on international jurisdiction in civil and business matters, provides for the enforcement of the rule "*actor sequitur forum rei*" pursuant to which the court that has jurisdiction is the one from the country in which the defendant lives.[95]

---

[94] Civ. October 19, 1959 (arrêt Pelassa).
[95] Art. 2 of the European Regulation CE 44/2001.

With respect to internet-related cases, French courts generally consider that they have jurisdiction whenever the service available on the internet can be received on the French territory and the damage occured in France (*Faurrisson*,[96] *Payline*,[97] *St. Tropez*,[98] *Nart*,[99] *Yahoo!*,[1] *Louis Vuitton*[2] cases).

The *Yahoo!* case illustrated the possibility to pass judgment against a foreign provider in France. The case involved the availability of Nazi memorabilia on the US Yahoo! auction site. In a preliminary order, dated May 22, 2000, the court asserted its jurisdiction, considering that Yahoo's services could be accessed in France.[3] The court consequently ordered Yahoo! to prevent French people from accessing its unlawful service.

In another case involving Yahoo!, the court also acknowledged its jurisdiction on the grounds that since the website offering Nazi objects could be viewed in France, this represented a form of publicity necessary to constitute an act of apology of crimes against humanity considered a criminal offense under French law.

In another recent case concerning Yahoo for the same facts, the court decided to reject definitively the defendant's motion for declining the jurisdiction of French courts, thereby asserting the jurisdiction of French over the case.[4]

The French Supreme Court (*Cour de Cassation*) has also ruled that the French courts had jurisdiction to award damages to the plaintiff with respect to a damage suffered on French territory, due to the operation of an internet website in Spain, since this website could be accessed in France.[5]

The enforcement of French law

Civil grounds In determining the applicable governing law and jurisdiction under French civil law, a distinction must be made between (i) tort matters, and (ii) contractual matters.   **6–162**

---

[96] Proc. Rep, *UNADIF, FNDIR et autres c/ Robert F.*, TGI Paris, ch. Correctionnelle, November 13, 1998.

[97] Sté SG2 c/ *Brokat Informations Systeme GmbH (Allemagne)*, *Tribunal de Grande Instance de Nanterre*, Ordonnance de référé du October 13, 1997.

[98] 21/08/1997, TGI Draguignan, aff. Saint-Tropez c/ Eurovirtuel.

[99] *Chambre nationale des Commissaires-priseurs, Chambre de Discipline des Commissaires-priseurs de la Compagnie de Paris / NART SAS (société de droit français), NART Inc. (société de droit américain) et le ministère public*, Tribunal de Grande Instance deParis,1ère chbre,1ère sec. Jugement du May 3, 2000.

[1] *UEJF et Licra c/ Yahoo! Inc. et Yahoo France*, TGI Paris, Référé, May 5, 2000; *Amicale des déportés d'Auschwitz et MRAP c/ Yahoo! Inc.*, TGI de Paris, 17è ch. de la Presse, February 26, 2002; *Amicale des déportés d'Auschwitz et MRAP c/ Yahoo! Inc*, Cour d'Appel de Paris, 11è ch., sect. A, March 17, 2004.

[2] *SA Louis Vuitton Malletier c/ Société Google Inc.*, TGI de Paris, February 4, 2005.

[3] *UEJF et Licra c/ Yahoo! Inc. et Yahoo France*, TGI Paris, Référé, May 22, 2000.

[4] *Amicale des déportés d'Auschwitz et MRAP c/ Yahoo! Inc.*, TGI de Paris, 17è ch. de la Presse, February 26, 2002; *Amicale des déportés d'Auschwitz et MRAP c/ Yahoo! Inc*, Cour d'Appel de Paris, 11è ch., sect. A, March 17, 2004, *Amicale des déportés d'Auschwitz c/ Yahoo et Timothy KOOGLE*, TGI Paris February 26, 2002, *Amicale des déportés d'Auschwitz c/ Yahoo et Timothy KOOGLE* Cour d'appel de Paris 11ᵉ ch., sect. A, October 13, 2004

[5] Civ. 1ʳᵉ, December 9, 2003, *Société Castellblanch c/ Société Champagne Louis Roederer*.

6–163 **Tort matters** Under French international private law, the governing law with respect to tort matters is the law of the place where the event causing liability occurred (*lex loci delicti*). However, in cases where the wrongful act and the damage suffered occurred in two different countries, French legal authors and case law both hesitate between applying the law of either of such countries.

With respect to internet-related disputes, it is often difficult to determine the territory on which the event causing liability occurred, which may be any of the following:

- – the law of the country of origin (i.e. foreign law);
- – the law of the country of reception (i.e. French law);
- – the law of the country to which the website is directed or targeted ("country of destination") (i.e. either foreign or French law).

EU authorities adopted the principle of the country of origin in the European Directive on Satellites of September 27, 1993. Critics suggest that systematic application of this principle to the internet would be dangerous, as it could result in significant abuses and in the establishment of "informational havens" where the most harmful information could be carried out in complete impunity, and where copyright or other claims would be completely ignored.

On the other hand, the drawback to systematically enforcing the law of the country of reception is that any website would be subject to the laws of all countries worldwide.

French courts generally decide that as long as a website can be viewed by internet users in France, French law must therefore be enforced (see above the *Yahoo!* cases).

In conclusion, it appears that in France, when a court holds that French law is the governing law, generally, by way of consequence, it also acknowledges that French courts have jurisdiction.

6–164 **Contractual matters** In a contractual context, the question of the applicable governing law is easier to resolve, as the parties (in this case, the overseas site and the French user) may have already determined the governing law in a contract between them. If the contract does not designate any law, international conventions may apply, such as the Rome, Brussels or the Hague Conventions. In this case, the Rome Convention sets forth that when the parties have not expressly chosen a law, then the applicable law is the one of the country with which the contract is the most closely connected.[6]

The Trust in Digital Economy Act of June 21, 2004 contains specific provisions in relation to e-commerce.[7] Two situations must be distinguished

---

[6] Article 4 § 1 of the Rome Convention of June 19, 1980, on the law that applies to contractual obligations, signed between Member States of the European Community.

[7] E-commerce is defined in Art.14 of the Law on Digital Economy dated June 21, 2004, as any economic activity by which a person offers or ensures from a distance and through electronic means the supply of goods or services.

depending on whether the contract has been signed by two professionals or by a professional and a consumer.

In the first case, when a contract has been signed by two professionals, Art. 7 of the Act provides for a rule identical to that of the Rome Convention. The law states that any e-commerce activity is subject to the law of the Member State on the territory of which the person exercising this activity is settled, unless the parties have decided otherwise. Therefore, the law that applies is either the law chosen by the parties or, if no law has been chosen by the parties, the law of the State in which the goods or services are supplied (in other words, the law of the supplier).

The Trust in Digital Economy Act however provides for an exception where one of the parties is a consumer. In this case, the applicable law remains in principle the law chosen by the parties, or the law of the supplier. Nonetheless, the law chosen by the parties cannot result in depriving the consumer of the protection afforded by the law of the country where the consumer lives. The most protective measures of the law of the consumer of party will then apply as mandatory rules.

Criminal grounds

Article 113–2 of the New Criminal Code provides that: 6–165

> "French criminal law is applicable to all offences committed on the territory of the French Republic.
> An offence is deemed to have been committed on the territory of the French Republic where one of its constituent elements was committed on that territory".

Article 113–7 of the same Code provides that:

> "French criminal law is applicable to any felony, as well as to any misdemeanour punished by imprisonment, committed by a French or foreign national outside the territory of the French Republic, where the victim is a French national at the time the offence took place."

Therefore, French Criminal law applies when one of the constituent elements of the crime or felony has a connection with France. The general position is that French law is applicable and French courts are competent whenever a website on which potentially illegal or damaging content is displayed can be accessed from a computer situated in France. This applies to both tort and criminal matters.

However, some difficulties remain on both the question of evidence of the physical and intentional aspects of the offence and the enforcement of a French court decision against a foreign website (see *Yahoo!* cases).

6.11.3 Defamation

6–166 The law on freedom of press, of July 29, 1881, details the offences that can be committed by way of a publication. Any information that is defamatory or denigrating or infringes on a person's image or private life or is promoting crimes, offences or suicide, is punishable both on civil and criminal grounds.

With the development of the internet, it made no doubt that the sole accessibility in France of such information through the internet constitutes a publication under French law, even though it is not displayed by French sites.

The *BNP Banexi v Mr Yves Rocher*[8] decision is one of the first court decisions concerning defamation on the internet. In this matter, Mr Rocher was ordered to remove defamatory information from its website. Since this decision, other cases have been rendered, but to our knowledge, there is no case law in France concerning a foreign defamation.

In case of defamation, the law of July 29, 1881, limits to three months starting from the first day of publication the period during which an action can be brought.[9] Due to the nature of the internet, the question of the application of this period to publications made over the internet led to a debate.

At first, a judgment decided that a publication made on-line was a continuous or ongoing act and that as long as the defamatory content could be accessed on a website, this meant that a new publication was made each day, thus bringing the three month period to a new start each day.[10]

However, this position was not followed by the *Cour de Cassation* which decided in three decisions that the starting point of an action against defamation made on a website must be understood as the moment at which the message was made available for the first time to internet users.[11] Therefore, case law has decided that a publication made on the internet is instantaneous and that the law of July 29, 1881, which decides that the starting point of an action against defamation is fixed at the day of the first publication, applies indifferently to publications made on paper or online.

Since then, the law of June 21, 2004, on Digital Economy, has definitely put an end to this debate in considering that any legal action in case of defamation must be brought before the court within three months of the first day of publication on the internet. In recent cases, the Court of Cassation confirms the implementation of that rule, that is to say the three months prescription for defamation begins on the first day of publication on the internet.[12]

Furthermore, the law on Freedom of Press also provides for in its Art.13

---

[8] *BNP Banexi v Mr Yves Rocher*, TGI Paris, April 16, 1996.
[9] Article 65 of the law of July 29, 1881.
[10] Cour d'appel de Paris, 11e ch. Corr., December 15, 1999.
[11] Cass. Crim, January 30, October 16, November 27, 2001.
[12] Cour d'appel de Paris, 11è ch., sect. A, February 27, 2002 *Ministère public c/ MEYSSAN Raphaël*, Cass. crim. September 19, 2006 n° 05–87–230.

a right to answer which can be brought by the victim of defamation. At first, the judges considered that the right to answer was not applicable to on-line publications because this article only applied to daily press.[13]

However, since the law of June 21, 2004, on Digital Economy any person named or designated in an on-line service has a right of answer. The request to exercise this right of answer must be made to the editor in chief within a period of three months starting from the publication of the message justifying such a request. A decree, which has yet to be enacted, should bring more precise provisions on this question. While waiting for this decree, we can recall the decree of April 6, 1987,[14] which granted to natural persons a right of answer that can be sued upon, in case of death, by the direct heirs, the universal legatees, or by the spouse. Concerning legal entities, they can sue upon their right to answer by their legal representatives.

6.11.4 Copyright

The French Intellectual Property Code defines infringements as any repro- **6–167** duction, representation or broadcast, by any means whatsoever, of a creative work in breach of copyright as defined and regulated by the law.

In the well-known case of *Brel-Sardou*[15] the court held that the defaulting party had infringed several pieces of work protected by copyright (in this case, the words and extracts of songs by Jacques Brel and Michel Sardou) because this work had been, digitised and made available to the public on a web page on the website of a school in Paris without the authorisation of the artists.

This decision is important in that it officially recognises (for the first time) that making information available to the public on a web page is deemed a publication of such information. Since then, the Trust in Digital Economy Act has given a definition of a communication to the public through electronic means. The law defines it as any sign, signal, text, image, sound or message of all sorts that does not have the nature of a private correspondence, and that is made available to the public, or part of the public, through an electronic communication device.

In addition, Art.7 of the same law refers specifically to illegal downloading. It mentions that when internet service providers indicate in their advertising or commercial offers the possibility of downloading files which were not provided by them, they must therefore clearly remind, in this advertising, that illegal downloading is harmful to artistic innovation.

In case law, several court decisions in which internet users were sentenced for illegal downloading on peer-to-peer networks were recently

---

[13] *P de Hohenzollern c/ Stéphane Bern*, TGI de Paris, June 5, 2002.
[14] Decree of April 6, 1987 n° 87–240.
[15] *Brel-Sardou*, Tribunal de Grande Instance de Paris, August 14, 1996.

passed.[16] In all of these cases, the judge considered that the act of making available to the public protected work on the peer-to-peer networks constituted a copyright infringement. Nevertheless, it was not clear whether the act of downloading work made available on the internet for the sole purpose of private use (authorised by article L.122–3 of the Code on Intellectual Property) without making it available to others also qualified as a copyright infringement.[17]

The new Copyright Act[18] of August 1, 2006, which implements the directive of May 22, 2001,[19] addresses the exchange of files through peer-to-peer networks.

The law institutes criminal liability for persons who publish or make available to the public software which is specifically intended to be used for unauthorised downloading. Such persons may be punished by three years of imprisonment and €300,000 fine (Art. L.335–2–1 of the Intellectual Property Code).

6.11.8 Trade marks

6–168   In France, the holder of a registered trade mark has a right of ownership on such trade mark for certain designated products and services.

Accordingly, the reproduction, use, imitation or appropriation of a trade mark as well as its use for products that are identical or similar to the products or services designated in the registration, constitutes an infringement of both civil and criminal law. The appropriation of a domain name in violation of an existing trade mark right or the unauthorised use of a third party's trade mark reproduced on a website may constitute a trade mark infringement.[20]

In France, courts have acknowledged their own jurisdiction even if the reproduction of the trade mark was carried out by a non-French citizen or resident, provided that it was made on a website.[21] Even if the foreign party is not the holder of a trade mark, French courts have jurisdiction to assess the conflict and order a preliminary injunction.[22] However, in a recent case, the *Cour de Cassation* decided that the use of a famous brand on a foreign website could not be deemed a trade mark infringement to the extent that

---

[16]   Trib. Corr. de Pointoise, February 2, 2005; Cour d'appel de Montpellier, March 10, 2005; Trib. Corr. de Meaux, April 21, 2005; Trib. Corr. de Créteil, May 10, 2005; Trib. Corr. de Toulouse, May 19, 2005.

[17]   Cour d'appel de Montpellier, March 10, 2005.

[18]   Loi n° 2006–961 du 1ᵉʳ août 2006 relative au droit d'auteur et aux droits voisins dans la société de l'information.

[19]   Directive 2001/29, May 22, 2001 sur l'harmonisation de certains aspects du droit d'auteur et des droits voisins dans la société de l'information.

[20]   See Ch.3 above.

[21]   October 13, 1997, Référé, TGI Nanterre, aff. *Sté SG2 c. Brokat.Informations Systeme GmbH*.

[22]   January 1, 2000 Tribunal de commerce de Paris, aff. *ALTAVISTA Internet Solutions Ltd c/ Monsieur R P, Sarl Adar Web*.

the products offered on the website were not available in France and therefore the website was not destined to the French public.[23]

In order to determine the jurisdiction of French courts, the Paris Court of Appeal decided recently that "for each case (involving a trade mark infringement on the internet), a sufficient, substantial or significant link between the facts or acts and the damage alleged, should be evidenced".[24]

6.11.6 Content liability

In determining a person's liability with respect to content made available on a website, a distinction must be made between (a) civil liability, and (b) criminal liability.

6–169

Civil liability

The content of a website may cause damage when it adversely affects the rights and interests of others. Under French civil law, a person can be held liable on the grounds of either tort or contract law. In general, when two people are bound by an agreement, the plaintiff does not have the choice and must prove the breach of a contractual obligation. On the other hand, under French tort law, three elements must be proven for a person to be held liable: a wrongful act, a harm suffered, and a causal link between these two elements.

6–170

Therefore, the question to be addressed is that of the relationship between the parties (i.e. users, access providers, operators, content providers or hosting providers). While website operators generally insist that the users should review and comply with on-line terms of use, it is questionable whether such terms of use can be enforced against such users unless it can be evidenced without doubt that they have read the terms and agreed to them.[25] Contracts between users and access or hosting providers, which are more common, relate to the access to the internet or the content hosting, and not the content of the information released. Consequently, under civil law, individuals are more often held liable for the website content on tort rather than on contractual grounds.

The question of the liability of technical service providers gave rise to a very strong discussion involving market players, politicians and lawyers.

Originally, French case law acknowledged the possibility of holding host providers liable on the grounds of Arts. 1382 or 1383 of the French Civil Code if they did not remove the illegal content after having been informed of it (*Lacoste* and *Multimania* cases[26]).

Since then, the question of the liability of technical service providers has

---

[23] Com. January 11, 2005, *Hugo Boss c/ Reemstma Cigarettenfabriken Gmbh*.

[24] CA Paris, 4ᵉ ch., April 26, 2006, *Scherrer et SA Normalu c/ SARL Acet*.

[25] There is no case law available regarding this issue.

[26] *Madame L. / les sociétés Multimania Production, France Cybermedia, SPPI, Esterel*, Tribunal de Grande Instance de Nanterre Jugement December 8, 1999.

been clarified by the Trust in Digital Economy Act. The statute provides that internet service providers along with hosting providers do not have a general obligation to monitor the information that they convey or store, nor do they have a general obligation to search for facts or circumstances revealing illegal activities.

With respect to host providers, Art.6-I of the Trust in Digital Economy Act states that they are not liable on civil grounds provided that they were not actually aware of the illegal nature of the information stored, or of facts and circumstances revealing this nature, nor if they acted promptly to remove this data or make it impossible to access it as soon as they became aware of the illegal nature of the information.

In a recent case, France Télécom Services Company has been sued by the Comity of defence of Armenian genocide (CDSA) following the posting of documents denying the Armenian genocide. The Paris Court of Appeal confirmed that the hosting provider, France Télécom Services Company, could not be held liable to the extent it was not aware of the illegal nature of the information and since it reacted rapidly to remove the incriminating information.[27]

Criminal liability

6–171   Several provisions of French criminal law aim directly at content providers and the offences committed through making illegal content available on a website.

First of all, the law on Freedom of the Press dated July 29, 1881, provides for a list of criminal offences committed by way of communication to the public through electronic means. For instance, the apology of crimes of war or crimes against humanity, or the provocation of discrimination, hatred or violence against a person or group of people because of their origins, nationality, religion, ethnical background or sexual orientation are considered criminal offenses for purposes of Art.24 of said law.

Furthermore, according to Art.227–23 of the Criminal Code, the mere fact of holding, transporting, releasing or making available, a pornographic content representing a person underage is a criminal offence. In addition, the fact of manufacturing, transporting, and making available to people underage a message containing violent or pornographic content is also a criminal offence (Art.227–24, Criminal Code).

Concerning unlawful content originating from a foreign source, French courts generally acknowledge their own jurisdiction and apply French law. For example, French courts have jurisdiction to pass sentence on a website with racist or illegal content (see *Faurisson* and *Yahoo!* cases above).

With regards to hosting providers, the Trust in Digital Economy Act considers that they are not liable on criminal grounds if they were not actually aware of the illegal activity or information, nor if they acted

---

[27] CA Paris, 11ᵉ ch., November 8, 2006, *Comité de la défense de la cause arménienne (CDSA) c/ S. Aydin et autre.*

promptly to remove this data or make it impossible to access it as soon as they became aware of it (see the *CDSA c/S.Aydin* case above).

It is assumed that the host providers have knowledge of the contentious facts when relevant information has been notified to them (such as a description of the contentious facts or the reasons why the content must be removed).

In the case of child pornography, apology of crimes against humanity, and incitement to racial hatred, internet service providers and host providers have reinforced obligations. In particular, they must promptly inform the public authorities if they are aware that any of these activities are exercised by one of their clients.

Finally, Art.6-I-8 of the same law enables a judge to order all measures necessary to prevent or put an end to a damage caused by content posted online. This article was applied for the first time recently by the tribunal of Paris[28] regarding on-line betting prohibition and was confirmed by the Court of Appeal of Paris.[29]

6.12 CROSS-BORDER LIABILITY—GERMANY

6.12.1 Jurisdiction

Under German procedural law, for tortious acts jurisdiction lies with the locally competent court in whose circuit the respective act was committed, i.e. either where the cause of the act of tort occurred, or where its effects have materialised and resulted in a breach of provisions of material German law.   **6–172**

Given the ubiquitous nature of the internet, in a number of cases German courts have declared themselves competent to rule over alleged breaches of (German) law stemming from content providers using the internet, even though these may not necessarily have resided in Germany or otherwise have had a natural linkage to Germany or the German market.[30]

German courts have set considerably lower thresholds in order to declare themselves competent whenever this is necessary, from their point of view, to defend higher protective interests of public order. In the *Australian holocaust denial* case, an Australian citizen had denied the holocaust—which is a criminal offence under German law—on an English language website that was hosted in Australia, without any indications of specifically "targeting" German users. While travelling through Germany later, the man was arrested and prosecuted. The German Federal Court of Justice   **6–173**

---

[28] TGI Paris (réf.), March 25, 2005.

[29] Cour d'appel de Paris 14ème ch. Sect.A June 14, 2006 "*Bell Med Ltd, société Computer Aided Technologies Ltd c/ GIE Pari Mutuel Urbain*" n °05/22459.

[30] OLG Hamburg, May 2, 2002, court file no. 3 U 312/01, *Maritime*; OLG München, November 15, 2002, court file no. 29 U 3769/01, *Literaturhaus*; OLG Karlsruhe, July 10, 2002, court file no. 6 U 9/02, *Intel*.

("*Bundesgerichtshof*") confirmed the criminal charge, ruling that the criminal offence had materialised within its jurisdiction, solely because the website was accessible in Germany.[31] Given the general public and political sensitivity of this very specific criminal offence, criticism has been cautious. But looking at it in a wider context, with this decision the court has taken a considerable step regarding the (extraterritorial) reach of German criminal law, given that there was no specific connection to a specific German user community.

More recently, however, German courts—in particular confirmed by the German Federal Court of Justice in the *Doc Morris* case (the Dutch online-pharmacy had been selling pharmaceutical products from the Netherlands into the German market)—have started taking a rather focused view, introducing a test on the "designated effect" ("*Prüfung auf bestimmungsgemäßes Auswirken*"). In substance, this represents a form of "targeting test", looking at the content and scope of the respective (foreign) website in order to assess whether it is (objectively) intended to be perceived by German market participants.[32]

6–174 So far, some uncertainty remains as to the criteria for "targeting" of the German market. In general, "targeting" will require that—from an "objective user's perspective"—the respective on-line activity is perceived as directed towards the German market. This is obvious where services or goods are explicitly promoted to German customers.[33] Operating a website under the ".de" top level domain and use of the German language will typically count as (strong) indications to this end—but not necessarily under all circumstances.[34]

Likewise, it is obviously possible to target the German market from non-German top level domains,[35] both in German as well as in a foreign (i.e. English) language, given that in particular younger Germans are considered "web-educated" and sufficiently conversant in English in order to be targeted through such foreign websites.[36]

In its *Doc Morris* decision the Federal Court of Justice has opened a back door for foreign providers of (commercial) websites in order to avoid the impact of German jurisdiction: The court has hinted at the possibility for a foreign website operator to use a disclaimer stating that it is not targeting the German market, provided that such a disclaimer is not abusive, but sincere and correct.[37]

---

[31] BGH, December 12, 2000, court file no. 1 StR 184/00, *Auschwitz-Lüge*.
[32] OLG Bremen, February 17, 2000, court file no. 2 U 139/99, *Subventionsberatung Mecklenburg-Vorpommern*; OLG Frankfurt am Main, May 31, 2001, court file no. 6 U 240/00, *Doc Morris*; BGH, March 30, 2006, court file no. I ZR 24/03, *Doc Morris*.
[33] BGH, October 13, 2004, court file no. I ZR 163/02, *Maritime*.
[34] BGH, October 13, 2004, court file no. I ZR 163/02, *Maritime*.
[35] BGH, April 11, 2002, court file no. I ZR 317/99, *Vossius*.
[36] OLG Frankfurt am Main, December 3, 1998, court file no. 6 W 122/98, *Füllfederhalter*.
[37] BGH, March 30, 2006, court file no. I ZR 24/03, *Doc Morris*.

6.12.2 Country of origin rule

In 2001, Germany implemented the E-commerce Directive into the German **6–175** Teleservices Act (*"Teledienstegesetz"*, the TDG), including the country of origin rule as well as its related exemptions. In 2007, the TDG was replaced by the Telemedia Act) (*"Telemediengesetz"*, the TMG), now replacing the—materially unchanged—country of origin rule in a new s.3 of the TMG.

The German lawmaker did not clarify whether the country of origin rule affects the conflicts of law/applicable law rules, or changes the material law (e.g. by "overriding" it with foreign law), or does neither, but is to be seen as some kind of *sui generis* law instead.

In consequence, there has been much debate among legal writers about this question, however, with no definitive conclusion so far. Even the Federal Court of Justice, which would have had the opportunity in the *Doc Morris* case to comment on this by way of an *obiter dictum* has remained silent. Accordingly, the Court of Appeals of Hamburg explicitly noted in 2006 that the nature of the relationship between the provisions on conflict of laws/applicable law and the country of origin rule is not clarified yet.[38]

The country of origin rule does not apply to providers operating from outside the EU.[39] Furthermore, it only applies to matters regulated by the Telemedia Act. For example, whenever goods are delivered "off-line" after an order has been placed on-line, the country of origin rule will only apply to the order, but not to the actual delivery.[40]

Section 3, subss. 3 to 5, TMG contain ample exceptions from the country of origin rule, in accordance with the exceptions permitted under the E-commerce Directive. As much as the relationship between the country of origin rule and the provisions on conflict of laws/applicable law remains unclear, so does the relationship between the exceptions from the rule and the respective provisions. Legal writers emphasise the need to interpret those exceptions in strict accordance with the E-commerce Directive in order to avoid undercutting the goals of the Directive.

In practice so far, as a result of several lawsuits, most attention has been called to the exceptions concerning gaming law and intellectual property rights.[41] Additional aspects are still part of further (academic) debate, for example, whether the country of origin rule only applies to the (foreign) service provider, or also to its employees, which may in turn become a particular concern in regard to criminal offences.

---

[38] OLG Hamburg, December 6, 2006, court file no. 5 U 9/06, *Lotteriestaatsvertrag.*
[39] OLG München, September 21, 2006, court file no. 29 U 2119/06, *Lateinbuch.*
[40] BGH, March 30, 2006, court file no. I ZR 24/03, *Doc Morris.*
[41] OLG Hamburg, June 5, 2002, court file no. 5 U 74/01, *Die Hunde sind los*; OLG München, October 9, 2003, court file no. 26 U 2690/03, *geografische Herkunftsangaben.*

6.12.3 Liability for content

6–176 Sections 7 to 10 of the TMG have fully implemented the privileges on liability for mere conduit, caching and hosting as set forth in the E-commerce Directive. German courts and legal writers see these provisions to function as an "up-front filter system", which filters out liability claims before getting into a more detailed assessment of whether a specific content is in breach of (other) provisions of German law.

Proprietary and third party content

6–177 While in most cases it is clear what should be regarded as proprietary content, a number of court decisions have expanded on whether an ISP had "adopted as his own" ("*sich zu eigen machen*") certain third party content by reference and incorporation to its website.

The Court of Appeals of Cologne, for example, held Microsoft liable for defamatory content/images provided by users that had uploaded it onto a discussion board run by Microsoft, ruling that by providing the overall organisational structure of the board and embedding it into related contents, Microsoft had adopted its users' contents as its own.[42]

Since neither the E-commerce Directive itself, nor its recitals refer to the concept of "adopting third party content as own content", legal writers have strongly criticised this concept, arguing that the liability privileges regulated by the E-commerce Directive are essentially driven by technical modalities of providing information society services and not by the distinction between "adopted proprietary" and "true" third party content. However, given that the German legislator expressly mentioned this concept when implementing the E-commerce Directive into the Teleservices Act, German courts have continued applying it.[43]

No duty for internet service providers to monitor third party content?

6–178 Section 7 of the TMG provides that an internet service provider (ISP)—if he is acting as a mere conduit, or is caching or hosting third party content—is under no specific obligation to search proactively for unlawful third party content. However, upon becoming aware or being notified of such content, the ISP can come under an obligation to delete or bar access to such content. It is clear that mere circumstantial knowledge does not suffice to require action from the ISP. In other words, any third party claiming an infringement of his rights must notify the ISP specifically of the circumstances of the infringement and of his rights concerned.

Notwithstanding the liability privileges provided under ss.8 to 10 of the TMG, a problem remains unsolved for ISPs. In the *Rolex I* case—watch manufacturer Rolex had sued on-line auctioneer Ricardo because of users'

---

[42] OLG Köln, May 28, 2002, court file no. 15 U 221/01, *Steffi Graf.*
[43] OLG Brandenburg, December 16, 2003, court file no. 6 U 161/02, *Haftung eines Online-Auktionshauses.*

listings of counterfeit watches on its platform—the Federal Court of Justice ruled that the TDG's liability privileges, i.e. now the TMG's, could not apply to injunctive claims.[44] Ricardo was not held liable for infringing Rolex's trade marks or participating in such infringement by hosting and displaying the respective auctions on its website. But the court warned Ricardo that it could be held liable as a so-called "disquietor" ("*Störer*") if it did not refrain from allowing trade with such counterfeit watches in the future. The concept of liability as a *Störer* goes back to general principles of civil law where the *Störer* intentionally contributes by his omission to an infringement in an "adequate-causal" manner, as a consequence of which he comes under a subsequent "surveillance duty" ("*Kontrollpflicht*") in regard to his sphere of influence in order to avoid that further infringement can occur.

As a consequence, an ISP can come under an ongoing duty to control (for) a specific type of third party content following an initial respective notification that such content may infringe (other) third party rights—which stands in contrast to the intention set forth in Arts. 15 and 14 of the E-commerce Directive (no general obligation to monitor content; liability privilege for hosting), respectively its implementation into s.7, subs.2 and s.10 of the TMG.

Such "surveillance duty"—and related liability—is limited by a rule of reason to apply in each individual case concerned, taking particular account of the "technical feasibility" of appropriate measures. The Court of Appeals of Dusseldorf, for example, held that it is not reasonable for the provider of a privately run discussion board to monitor the board for defamatory content, even if such content had been posted several times before.[45]

The Court of Appeals of Munich, on the other hand, has held eBay liable on the grounds of the "*Störer*"-principle for repeated sales of non-authorised copies of a Latin schoolbook.[46] The Court of Appeals of Brandenburg required eBay to take appropriate measures against the repeated abuse of an individual's (the plaintiff's) personal data by unknown third persons who had opened accounts with eBay under the plaintiff's name.[47]

It is expected that German courts will have more opportunity to expand on the requirements on taking appropriate technical measures for an ISP to comply with his "surveillance duty".

Liability for hyperlinks, liability of search engines

Liability for unlawful content made available through hyperlinks is an **6–179** ongoing issue under German law. In various cases German courts have discussed the border line between the constitutional right of freedom of speech (as argued by those ISPs that predominantly provide journalistic or

---

[44] BGH, March 11, 2004, court file no. I ZR 304/01, *Rolex I.*
[45] OLG Düsseldorf, June 7, 2006, court file no. 15 U 21/06, *Foren-Haftung.*
[46] OLG München, September 21, 2006, court file no. 29 U 2119/06, *Lateinbuch.*
[47] OLG Brandenburg, November 16, 2005, court file no. 4 U 5/05, *Identitätsklau.*

similar content through websites) versus the liability for hyperlinks leading to third party websites containing unlawful content.

As a general rule and in lack of specific legislation addressing hyperlinks, it is the common understanding that the liability exemptions from the E-commerce Directive, respectively ss.8–10, TMG will not apply.[48] In fact, when replacing the TDG with the TMG in 2007, the German legislator emphasised that it did not want to pick up this issue but would rather wait for harmonisation at the European level. German courts have already developed extensive case law in assessing liability for hyperlinks, often arguing that setting hyperlinks is a form of "adopting content as one's own" (*"sich zu eigen machen"*).

In the prominent *heise*-case, the Court of Appeals of Munich confirmed the injunctive relief against an on-line computer journal which had reported on certain software tools as being capable of circumventing technical copyright protection devices; the software tools were available on a foreign website (operated from an offshore location) and not specifically targeted at the German market.[49]

Although the court denied that the article itself should be regarded as a kind of "manual" on how to circumvent technical copyright protection devices (which would have triggered direct criminal liability for the authors), the court declared illegal setting a hyperlink to the websites from where such tools could be downloaded. The court's ruling is a confirmation that any ISP located in Germany can be held liable for content that is unlawful under German law, if it is made available through a hyperlink—irrespective of whether that content may be lawful under a foreign jurisdiction.

As little as the German Telemedia Act is applicable to hyperlinks, it is applicable to search engines like Google or Yahoo! (another issue the German legislator leaves to further harmonisation efforts at the European level). Consequentially, the operators of internet search engines cannot rely on the liability privileges provided by the Telemedia Act either.[49a]

6.13 CROSS-BORDER LIABILITY—HONG KONG

6.13.1 Jurisdiction

Introduction

6–180   As Hong Kong is a common law territory, traditional *criminal* jurisdiction is generally (but not always) dependent upon the criminal act having been carried out at least in part within the geographical boundaries of the territory, and enforcement requires the presence of the individual in the

---

[48] BGH, April 1, 2004, court file no. I ZR 317/01, *Schöner Wetten*.
[49] OLG München, July 28, 2005, court file no. 29 U 2887/05, *heise*.
[49a] KG Berlin, March 20, 2006, court file no. 10W 27/05, Admin C.

territory or the individual being susceptible to extradition.[50] A person generally becomes subject to the *civil* jurisdiction of the territory's courts if the person is present in the territory (even fleetingly) and can be served with or notified of "originating process" such as a writ regardless of whether the transaction in question has anything to do with the territory. However, in both criminal and civil matters, the courts' traditional jurisdictional reach has been extended by statute.

Criminal Jurisdiction

Any person using the internet in Hong Kong to commit a criminal act will be liable to criminal prosecution. For example, sending an intimidating or blackmailing message by email from a PC in Hong Kong renders the sender liable to prosecution for criminal intimidation[51] or blackmail.[52] In a 1998 case[53] an individual (who happened to be a foreigner) in Hong Kong loaded paedophile pornographic images onto a web server in Hong Kong and was duly prosecuted for an offence contrary to Control of Obscene and Indecent Articles Ordinance.[54]

6–181

In another 1998 case[55] the court looked in some detail at how loading pictures onto a web server constituted "publishing" under the Ordinance in view of the fact that the Ordinance was enacted in 1987 before the internet (as it now operates) was contemplated. It was expressly held that the "publication" was complete when the appellant uploaded the files to the web server and his actions thereby constituted "publishing". It was further held that as the images could be seen on screen during downloading they were also "shown and projected" within the meaning of another section of the Ordinance. The finding on uploading may have jurisdictional consequences. The court also held that once the files were uploaded they were available on the internet to users: there was no requirement that "publication" be "in public". A similar case occurred in 2000.[56]

The Hong Kong Internet Service Providers Association, a body which represents the internet industry in its relations with the public and the government, has issued a Code of Practice in relation to obscene and indecent material transmitted over the internet. The Code requires internet service providers to take reasonable steps to prevent users of their services committing offences under the Ordinance by means of the internet.

In another 2000 case[57] the defendants had used Back Orifice software to access the computers in question through the internet. The first two defendants were convicted of misuse of computer offences under the Crimes

---

[50] *Air India v Wiggers* [1980] 1 W.L.R. 815.
[51] S.24, Crimes Ordinance, Ch.200, Laws of Hong Kong.
[52] S.23, Theft Ordinance, Ch.210, Laws of Hong Kong.
[53] *HKSAR v H Takeda* [1998] 1 H.K.L.R.D. 931.
[54] Ch.390, Laws of Hong Kong.
[55] *HKSAR v Cheung Kam Keung* [1998] 2 H.K.C. 156.
[56] *HKSAR v Wong Tat Man* [2000] H.K.E.C. 915.
[57] *HKSAR v Tam Hei Lun* [2000] H.K.E.C. 1178.

Ordinance[58] (similar to the UK offences) and the Organised and Serious Crimes Ordinance[59] as well as criminal damage contrary to the Crimes Ordinance.[60] A third defendant was found guilty of the criminal offence of making infringing copies of copyright works for sale or hire contrary to the Copyright Ordinance.[61]

(The judgments in the foregoing reported cases other than *HKSAR v Cheung Kam Keung* are appeals against sentence.)

6–182   The Hong Kong Government enacted the Criminal Jurisdiction Ordinance[62] in December 1994 to address jurisdictional problems associated with international fraud. The Ordinance extends the court's jurisdiction over certain dishonesty and fraud offences as follows:

- Where any part of the offence or of the results required to be proved take place in Hong Kong, the offence is triable in Hong Kong;
- An attempt to commit a Hong Kong offence will be triable whether or not the attempt was made in Hong Kong;
- An attempt or incitement in Hong Kong to commit an offence elsewhere is an offence in Hong Kong;
- A conspiracy wherever made to commit an offence in Hong Kong is a Hong Kong offence, whether or not anything in furtherance of the conspiracy is done in Hong Kong; and
- A conspiracy in Hong Kong to do elsewhere something that if done in Hong Kong would be an offence in Hong Kong, is an offence in Hong Kong.

The Ordinance only applies to certain offences but the Chief Executive may extend the list by Order. Of the various offences created by the Computer Crimes Ordinance, the Criminal Jurisdiction Ordinance so far only covers "false accounting done through a computer".

In November 2002, the Hong Kong Government introduced the Criminal Jurisdiction Ordinance (Amendment of s.2(2)) Order 2002 into the Legislative Council. The Order brings the offences of unauthorised access to a computer, destroying or damaging property (limited to the misuse of computers) and access to a computer with criminal or dishonest intent within the scope of the Criminal Jurisdiction Ordinance.

The Order also proposes amendments to address the traditional jurisdictional problems associated with cross-border computer related crimes. The amendments have not yet been approved, but if they are, they will allow Hong Kong courts to assume jurisdiction over computer-related crimes committed or planned outside Hong Kong but which are connected to, or intended to cause damage, in Hong Kong.

---

[58] S.161, Ch.200, Laws of Hong Kong.
[59] S.25, Ch.455, Laws of Hong Kong.
[60] S.60, Ch.200, Laws of Hong Kong.
[61] S.118, Ch.528, Laws of Hong Kong.
[62] Ch.461, Laws of Hong Kong.

Civil Jurisdiction

Generally a person who commits a civil wrong in Hong Kong using the **6–183** internet will be liable to be sued here on being served with local process in Hong Kong, either personally or under the rules permitting postal service within the territory. Certain substantive wrongs are considered below.

As regards procedure, as in many common law territories, in Hong Kong the general rules on civil jurisdiction by way of personal or postal service have been extended by so-called "long arm" legislation. Under the extended procedural rules, Hong Kong process may in certain cases be served on a defendant outside the territory if the transaction in question had certain points of connection with Hong Kong. Once a defendant to an action resident abroad has been served outside the territory with process from the court, the defendant must decide whether to participate in the proceedings, or ignore them and face the risk of a default judgment.

The Hong Kong Order 11 of the Rules of the High Court[63] enables persons resident or incorporated outside Hong Kong to be sued in Hong Kong and served with Hong Kong process at their foreign place of residence or business where, amongst other things, they have made contracts in Hong Kong, have committed breaches of contract in Hong Kong or have committed torts in Hong Kong or torts the resulting damage from which is suffered within Hong Kong or the case concerns Hong Kong real property.

In most cases involving Order 11 the key question for the court in deciding whether to grant leave to "serve out" will be whether the case in question falls factually within any of the limbs of Order 11(1), and there is an important subsidiary question in each case of service out as to whether it is a "proper" case for service out. This depends on the convenience of the parties and other *forum non conveniens* considerations.

There is at present in Hong Kong and the Commonwealth a dearth of case law relating to e-commerce and jurisdictional issues.

The Hong Kong Electronic Transactions Ordinance[64] (ETO) provides answers to some of the questions that will inevitably arise in service out cases involving e-commerce. Section 17 confirms, in case anyone doubted it, that electronic records (which term includes emails or messages sent between web servers and PCs) may be used to conclude contracts. Section 18 provides guidance as to the *attribution* of electronic records and s.19 deals with the *timing* and *place* of dispatch and receipt of electronic records.

Tort The basic rule is that a tort (which includes infringement of intel- **6–184** lectual property rights) is considered to have been effected in the place where the relevant acts took place. In the case of misrepresentation, deceit or negligent misstatement that will probably be the place where the statement comes to the attention of the addressee. So where a Hong Kong party

---

[63] Under the High Court Ordinance, Ch.4, Laws of Hong Kong.
[64] Ch.553, Laws of Hong Kong.

is in negotiations with, or is being advised by, a non-Hong Kong resident, and a misstatement is made to the Hong Kong party, the location of the tort constituted by the misstatement will probably be Hong Kong. In the case of defamation, the tort occurs in the place of publication.

6–185 **Contract** The basic rule at common law is that a contract is made when and where the acceptance of an offer is received by the offeror. This rule can be applied easily enough to contracts concluded by instantaneous means of communication. For non instantaneous means of communication the rule has historically been subject to the common law exception known as the "postal acceptance rule" under which when an offer is accepted by post, the contract thereby concluded is deemed to have been made when, and therefore where, the acceptance is put in the post which is logically before the offeror will in fact receive it.

There are as yet no reported Hong Kong cases on whether or how the postal acceptance exception applies to email or interaction through a website. Some recent UK texts treat email as an instantaneous form of communication,[65] although the difficulties with email are acknowledged.

Section 19 of the ETO provides that an electronic message is regarded as having been sent at the place of business of the originator and to have been received at that place of business of the addressee with which the underlying transaction is related, or if the addressee has no place of business then where the addressee ordinarily resides.

Apart from that, the ETO is silent on when and where contracts concluded over the internet or otherwise using electronic messages will be regarded as having been made. The general contract rules on these questions will therefore apply.

It seems that by focusing on individual messages themselves, rather than *exchanges* of messages, the drafters of the ETO deliberately avoided providing new substantive contract law rules or clarifying how existing ones apply, and intentionally left open the question of whether the postal acceptance exception will apply to exchanges of internet communications.

The only provision that touches on contract law is s.17(3) that states expressly that s.17 does not affect any rule of law to the effect that an offeror may prescribe the method of accepting an offer.

This approach contrasts with other legislative measures dealing with contracts formed electronically. For example, the US Uniform Computer Information Transactions Act of 1999 provides in s.203(4) that a contract formed by exchange of email is formed when the acceptance is received. That clearly excludes the postal acceptance exception.

It was said in *Brinkibon v Stalag Stahl*,[66] a well-known UK case dealing with telexes, followed in *Eastern Power Ltd v Azienda Communate Energia*

---

[65] See for example Dicey & Morris, *The Conflict of Laws* (14th ed., 2006), p.377 and *Chitty on Contracts*, (29th ed., 2004), para.2–051.
[66] [1983] 2 A.C. 34.

and Ambiente[67] as regards faxes, that there can be no general rule applicable to all instantaneous or "virtually" instantaneous communications, and the questions of whether and when a contract is concluded by such means will depend on all the circumstances, including the interacting parties' intentions.

It may be that as between two parties dealing on a "B2B" basis and using **6–186** "always on" email systems the postal acceptance exception will not apply, but the exception may apply in the "B2C" situation where it is likely that the consumer is using dial-up or other non instantaneous email access. It seems unlikely that the postal acceptance exception would apply to a contract concluded via interaction on a website where an order is acknowledged immediately as the communication is sufficiently instantaneous. On the other hand, if a transaction on a website requires a delayed confirmation email sent by the operator to the customer before the contract is concluded, the exception may apply.

If matters are left uncertain by poorly drafted terms of business on an e-commerce website, then where an email or website contract is entered into by a Hong Kong resident with a non-resident website operator, the contract is probably made in Hong Kong when the Hong Kong resident receives the website operator's acceptance of the resident's order.

The Hong Kong resident may therefore be able to sue the other party for subsequent breaches in Hong Kong by relying on the combined effects of s.19(4) and 19(5)(b) of the ETO and Order 11, Rule 1(d)(i) of the RHC.

In the perhaps unlikely event of the postal acceptance exception applying, the contract would be made abroad when and where the operator dispatched its acceptance of an order.

Conversely, a Hong Kong website operator may find that it enters into contracts abroad, and is therefore liable to be sued abroad, when sending acceptances to customers abroad.

A Proper Case for Service Out or Prosecution?

As stated above, where a Hong Kong plaintiff sues a foreign party in Hong **6–187** Kong alleging that certain website content or functionality has constituted a civil wrong against that plaintiff or an infringement of that plaintiff's rights in Hong Kong, the plaintiff will, as well as having to show that the case falls within one of the categories of cases for service out, need to satisfy the court that the case is a "proper" one for service out.

Where the alleged wrong is, for example, a breach of local Hong Kong trade or advertising laws, infringement of a trade mark or passing off by use of the plaintiff's trade get up, the foreign defendant may well say in its defence that even if what the plaintiff says is correct, the alleged wrong is only incidental to its activities and the defendant has not intentionally "directed" any of its activities towards Hong Kong such that the defendant should attract the jurisdiction of the Hong Kong courts.

In the US many states have long-arm statutes that permit service out of

---

[67] [1999] O.J. 3275, Ontario CA.

local process in all cases where that is constitutionally permissible. US federal constitutional case law holds that it is constitutional for a state to exercise long-arm jurisdiction over out-of-state defendants who have engaged in "minimum contacts" with the state. There is now a substantial body of US constitutional case law on what types of activities meet this test.

It is clear that merely establishing a website that is only viewable in a state because websites are viewable anywhere will not constitute deliberate engaging in minimum contacts with the state or its residents so as to justify the exercise of long-arm jurisdiction by that state.

It is likely that in the emerging case law of the various Commonwealth jurisdictions and Hong Kong a similar test will evolve focusing on whether the defendant has "directed" any of its activities, including those on the internet, to the jurisdiction in question.

In the case of defamation, where web content has defamed a Hong Kong plaintiff, the defendant is likely to have little success in arguing that while the content was viewable in Hong Kong the defendant had not deliberately directed the content at Hong Kong.

In the case of trade mark infringement, the plaintiff will have to demonstrate that the foreign defendant had used the plaintiff's Hong Kong trade mark or something similar in "the course of trade" in Hong Kong. To do this the plaintiff will have to show a "sufficient link"[68] with Hong Kong. Merely establishing a website abroad aimed primarily at other markets without any intent to use a trade mark similar to an established Hong Kong trade mark amongst Hong Kong clientele would probably not amount to a sufficient link for the plaintiff to overcome the service out discretionary hurdle.

Similarly in the criminal sphere, putting aside the issue of whether as a practical matter the intended defendant is amenable to the Hong Kong criminal process by visiting here or by being liable to extradition, where web content amounts to a Hong Kong criminal offence, the Hong Kong authorities are unlikely to mount a prosecution unless there is some intentional act on the part of the defendant to "direct" the website in some way to the Hong Kong community.

A New Convention?

6–188   A Special Commission of the Hague Conference on Private International Law has been convened with the task of producing a Convention on International Jurisdiction and Enforcement and Recognition of Judgments in Civil and Commercial Matters. A representative of the Hong Kong SAR Government has taken part as a member of the Chinese delegation. A "Preliminary Draft" of the Convention was completed in 1999. If a Convention is produced it is likely that the Hong Kong SAR Government would give serious consideration to implementing it by way of local enacting legislation.

---

[68] *Euromarket Designs Inc v Peters* [2001] F.S.R. 20.

Any convention produced is likely to be influenced by the existing Brussels and Lugano Conventions in force in certain European countries.

Constitutional Considerations

In the US and increasingly in the UK, the exercise of the so-called long-arm jurisdictional powers is subject to constitutional challenge on the ground that such exercise (or the power itself) is a breach of the defendant's human rights or is a failure of "due process" guaranteed by some embedded law.   **6–189**

Foreign case law on these issues is unlikely to be relevant in Hong Kong. It has not yet been suggested by a non resident sued in Hong Kong, at least in any reported case, that the Criminal Jurisdiction Ordinance or Order 11 is unconstitutional under the Basic Law[69] or contrary to the Hong Kong Bill of Rights.[70]

6.13.2 Defamation

The essence of defamation is the publication of a statement that tends to lower the plaintiff in the estimation of right thinking members of society generally or cause the plaintiff to be shunned or avoided. Under the law relating to defamation in Hong Kong (English common law and the Defamation Ordinance[71]), any person who participates in the publication of a defamatory statement is liable for the defamation.   **6–190**

However, there is a possible defence for a website operator under s.8 of the Defamation Ordinance. This provides that where a presumptive case of publication by the act of any other person by his authority is established against a defendant, the defendant may prove that the publication was made without his authority, consent or knowledge *and* that the publication did not arise from want of due care or caution on his part. Section 25 of the Ordinance also provides a defence of innocent defamation provided the defendant makes an offer of amends to the defamed person as soon as practicable after receiving notice that the publication in question is or might be defamatory.

The case law of defamation provides one of the few examples, if not the only example, of consideration of internet jurisdiction as such by a Hong Kong court. In *Investasia Ltd v Kodansha Co Ltd*[72] the plaintiff commenced proceedings against the defendants for two libellous articles in Japanese written by the first defendant and published by the second defendant. The plaintiffs alleged that one article that was posted on the internet and another that was published in a magazine distributed in several

---

[69] The Basic Law Of The Hong Kong Special Administrative Region Of The People's Republic Of China (Adopted at the third Session of the Seventh National People's Congress on April 4, 1990), reprinted at Ch.2101, Laws of Hong Kong.
[70] Hong Kong Bill of Rights Ordinance, Ch.383, Laws of Hong Kong.
[71] Ch.21, Laws of Hong Kong.
[72] [1999] 3 H.K.C. 515.

jurisdictions, including 157 copies in Hong Kong, were defamatory of them.

The court granted leave to serve a Hong Kong writ on the defendants in Japan under Order 11 on the basis that the claim was founded on libel and damage was sustained within Hong Kong. The defendants applied to set aside the writ. The plaintiffs filed evidence showing they had substantial connections with Hong Kong and that they had suffered damage to their reputations in Hong Kong by reason of the publications.

6–191 The evidence was that Mr Wada, the second plaintiff, who had a "controlling hand" in the first plaintiff, had kept a residence in Hong Kong since 1994, was a Japanese national, had had investments in Hong Kong since 1994, was a facilitator whose business depended on the trust his clients could place in him, had built a good reputation in Hong Kong, had the right relationships with financial institutions in Hong Kong, spent four to six months a year in Hong Kong and had no residence elsewhere and that the first plaintiff had bank accounts in Hong Kong and a liaison office in Hong Kong.

The judge refused to set aside the writ. He held that if a plaintiff has a reputation in Hong Kong, as the plaintiffs in this case had, it was not right to tell him or her to go elsewhere to vindicate that reputation because the place to vindicate a damaged Hong Kong reputation is in Hong Kong. Where the circulation of a foreign publication gives rise to a tort in Hong Kong it would be necessary to consider the scale of publication in Hong Kong and elsewhere in deciding whether or not Hong Kong was the natural forum for the resolution of the dispute. The court considered that 157 magazines containing sensational material was sufficient to sustain a complaint within Hong Kong.

On converse facts, the case *Emperor (China Concept) Investments Ltd v SBI E–2 Capitol Securities Ltd*[73] involved proceedings brought in Hong Kong that were stayed to Singapore. The only evidence of publication of a defamatory statement was receipt of an email in Singapore that had been sent from Hong Kong.

The *Investasia* decision followed *Berezovsky v Forbes Inc* in the English Court of Appeal.[74] That case subsequently proceeded to the House of Lords in England[75] and also involved a publication in a magazine and on the internet and evidence of low circulation in the jurisdiction where the plaintiff wished to proceed and little or no evidence of how many times if at all the internet version of the publication had been accessed. The Hong Kong and English courts reached the same conclusion.

Similar decisions were reached in the Australian case of *Gutnick v Dow Jones & Co Inc*[76] and the English cases of *Lewis v King*[77] and *Anna*

---

[73] [2005] H.K.L.R.D. L13.
[74] [1999] E.M.L.R. 287.
[75] [2000] 2 All E.R. 986 (see above, section 6.2.2).
[76] [2001] V.S.C. 305 (August 28, 2001), Supreme Court of Victoria. This case is discussed further in Ch.12.
[77] [2004] EWCA Civ 1329.

Richardson v Arnold Schwarzenegger[78]. All three cases held that internet publication takes place in the jurisdiction where the defamatory words are read or downloaded.

6.13.3 Liability for Erroneous or Misleading Content

There have been no reported cases to date in Hong Kong relating to reliance   **6–192** on incorrect information placed on a website causing loss or damage. It is unlikely that the Hong Kong courts would have difficulty in treating such information as published in Hong Kong; however, they would retain a discretion whether or not to accept jurisdiction on the grounds discussed above.

Of particular relevance would be whether there was a good arguable case on the merits. In this regard, the court would consider the proximity of the relationship between the plaintiff and the party which placed the information on the website and whether, following the line of cases beginning with *Hedley Byrne v Heller*, the plaintiff came within the limited class of persons entitled to rely on the information.

Website operators and content providers would presumably be liable under the Misrepresentation Ordinance[79] for untrue statements contained in websites or emails. Where information is mistakenly presented on a website, an on-line seller or customer may be able to rely on mistake at common law to render a contract void *ab initio* and release both parties from their respective obligations under the contract.

6.13.4 Copyright

As mentioned above, Hong Kong's copyright law (contained in the Copy-   **6–193** right Ordinance)[80] is founded principally on the UK Copyright, Designs and Patents Act 1988. It is, among other things, an infringement of a copyright work to copy it, which includes storing the work by electronic means in any medium.

However, making transient copies of the work (such as would be made temporarily in a computer's RAM) for the purpose of viewing and listening to a copyright work is not an infringement.

Section 26 of the Copyright Ordinance makes it an infringing act to make available copies of works to the public by wire or wireless means such as the internet where no permission of the copyright owner has been obtained.

In Hong Kong, copyright infringement can be a criminal offence, as well as lead to civil liability.

There has been an internet-related case in Hong Kong concerning alle-

---

[78] [2004] EWHC 2442.
[79] Ch.284, Laws of Hong Kong.
[80] Ch.528, Laws of Hong Kong.

gations of copyright infringement. *Action Asia*, a Hong Kong published magazine, claimed that its copyright in a number of articles had been infringed by a California-based diver who posted extracts from *Action Asia's* articles on his home page.

The alleged infringement was only discovered by *Action Asia's* editorial staff because, while "surfing" the internet for interesting websites, they discovered their own material on Mr Taylor's site. *Action Asia* offered Mr Taylor a solution whereby he could, on terms, continue to use the offending material, but he declined the offer. *Action Asia* issued proceedings against Mr Taylor and named Mr Taylor's internet service provider, Best Internet Communications, as a co-defendant. The case against Best Internet was settled three months after proceedings were issued. Thereafter, *Action Asia* did not pursue Mr Taylor personally, since he removed the offending content from his home page.

6–194   More recently in 2005, the Hong Kong Magistrates' Court handed down its first criminal conviction and custodial sentence for the crime of attempting to distribute an infringing copy of a copyright work (otherwise than for the purpose of, or in the course of, any trade or business) to such an extent as to affect prejudicially the owner of the copyright. In *HKSAR v Chan Nai Ming*[81], the defendant Mr Chan had used BitTorrent software to upload copyrighted films onto a computer linked to the internet, allowing third parties to link their own computers to his and download the copyright files.

The court held that Mr Chan had committed an offence by illegally distributing copies of the films under ss.18(1)(f) and 119(1) of the Copyright Ordinance and s.159G of the Crimes Ordinance.[82] Mr Chan unsuccessfully appealed his conviction in 2006.[83] The judgments in this case are interesting since they suggest that a person who uploads copyright works onto a file-sharing system in Hong Kong will be liable for copyright infringement regardless of where in the world and by whom the material is actually downloaded. The same principles would appear to apply to material posted on a website operated in Hong Kong, even if the website is only available overseas and whether or not the website is actually accessed by anyone overseas. Conversely, in the US case of *Playboy Enterprises Inc v Chuckleberry Publishing Inc*,[84] the uploading of infringing copies of works onto an Internet server located in Italy amounted to distribution of the copyright works within the US since the defendant "caused and contributed to their distribution".

Following a public consultation exercise in early 2005, the HKSAR Government proposed a package of legislative amendments to the local copyright regime and the Copyright (Amendment) Bill 2006 (the "Bill") was introduced into the Legislative Council in March 2006. The Copyright

---

[81] TMCC 1268/2005.
[82] Ch.200, Laws of Hong Kong.
[83] *HKSAR v Chan Nai Ming* [2006] H.K.E.C. 2269.
[84] 1996 WL 337276 (SDNY); 1996 WL 396128 (SDNY).

(Amendment) Ordinance came into force on July 6, 2007, making a number of changes to the law relating to copyright protection, exemptions and parallel importation.

A further round of consultation began in December 2006 when the government issued a consultation document seeking the views of the public on the question of whether the existing legislative framework needs to be improved for more effective copyright protection in the digital environment. The document covers various issues related to copyright in the digital era, including the liability of internet service providers and the question of whether an all-embracing right of communicating copyright works to the public should be given to copyright owners.

It is expected that further amendments will come into force in 2007/2008. Since the most recent consultation is specifically aimed at bringing Hong Kong's copyright law up to date with new digital technology and since the use of the internet is becoming ever more widespread, allowing the transmission of copyright material almost instantaneously over an environment virtually without borders, it is likely that the amendments will have some kind of substantive effect on the law of Hong Kong relating to jurisdiction and the internet.

6.13.5 Trade marks

A website operated from outside Hong Kong that displays a mark identical **6–195** or substantially similar to a trade mark or service mark registered in Hong Kong could be susceptible to a claim for infringement if such website offers goods or services in a class for which the mark has been registered and it can be said that the Hong Kong trade mark has been used in Hong Kong without permission.

The English case of *Euromarket Designs Inc v Peters*[85] is likely to be followed in Hong Kong as the relevant provisions of the Hong Kong Trade Marks Ordinance[86] are similar to the provisions considered by the English court in that case. In the *Yakult* case,[87] the court did not decide whether use of a trade mark on a foreign website would be use in Hong Kong and therefore constitute trade mark infringement in Hong Kong. The judge chose instead to regard the defendants' website and email address as instruments of fraud in the passing off sense and held that the court has jurisdiction to grant injunctive relief where a defendant is equipped with an instrument of fraud.[88] The court granted injunctive relief on a *quia timet* basis to restrain the defendants' threatened acts of passing off.

---

[85] [2001] F.S.R. 20 (see above, section 6.2.2).
[86] Ch.559, Laws of Hong Kong.
[87] *Kabushiki Kaisha Yakult Honsha v Yakudo Group Holdings Ltd* [2003] 1 H.K.L.R. 391.
[88] *British Telecommunications Plc v One in a Million Ltd* [1999] F.S.R. 1 at p.18.

6.13.6 Online gambling

6–196 The current law on all forms of gambling, gaming and bookmaking is contained in the Gambling Ordinance.[89] The Gambling (Amendment) Ordinance 2002[90] extended the scope of the Gambling Ordinance to gambling offences over the internet, making it an offence for persons in Hong Kong to bet with bookmakers located overseas and for overseas bookmakers to accept bets from persons in Hong Kong by any means, including over the internet.

There are a number of separate offences under the Ordinance. These include:

- *bookmaking* any person who ... holds out in any manner that he solicits, receives, negotiates or settles bets by way of trade or business whether personally or by letter, telephone, telegram, or on-line medium (including the service commonly known as the internet) or by any other means; or ... in any capacity assists, either directly or indirectly, another person in bookmaking;
- *betting with a bookmaker* any person who bets with a bookmaker ...;
- *promoting lotteries* any person who ... promotes, organises, conducts or manages, or otherwise has control of, an unlawful lottery ... in any capacity assists, either directly or indirectly, in the promotion, organisation, conduct, management or other control of an unlawful lottery ...;
- *publicising lotteries* any person who in any manner ... provides or publishes, or causes to be provided or published, expressly or otherwise ... any tip, hint or forecast relating to the result of an unlawful lottery; or ... any announcement of the result of an unlawful lottery ...; and
- *gambling* in a place other than a licensed gambling establishment.

6–197 One of the key new offences introduced by the Gambling (Amendment) Ordinance is "promoting or facilitating" bookmaking. This offence is not committed if the bookmaking takes place wholly outside Hong Kong and both/all of the parties to the transaction are outside Hong Kong. However, it is quite clear that it will be an offence to do acts in Hong Kong to promote bookmaking on websites based offshore that accept bets from punters located in Hong Kong.

The government has stated that it is aware of the following promotional activities being conducted by offshore gambling websites:

(a) advertising in the mass media in Hong Kong, including in popular newspapers and sports magazines and on buses, handing out

---

[89] Ch. 148, Laws of Hong Kong.
[90] Ord. No.12 of 2002.

     leaflets to the public and sending information to the media to promote their business and attract bets;

(b) setting up on local websites hypertext links to gambling websites;

(c) broadcasting on local television or radio stations offshore events (and related betting information) on which they take bets; and

(d) providing betting information (for example, odds on overseas soccer matches) in the local media to stimulate betting interest.

The purpose of the new "promoting" offence is to criminalise activities that promote a bookmaker but which fall short of assisting a bookmaker in bookmaking. Accordingly, where an associate or employee may not be regarded as assisting bookmaking or assisting unlawful gambling, he or she might very well be regarded as promoting such activities.

The term "facilitating" potentially has very broad implications. The Home Affairs Bureau indicated that one of the aims of the provision is to prevent punters from using their credit cards to place bets. The argument is that the issuer of the credit card would be facilitating the transaction and would thereby commit an offence if it authorised the transaction. The Home Affairs Bureau also anticipated being able to use Hong Kong's anti-money laundering legislation to prevent local banks from providing banking services to known operators of offshore gambling sites.

An ISP based in Hong Kong maintaining internet access for its customers would arguably commit an offence of facilitating bookmaking in the event that any of the ISP's customers places a bet on an offshore website. The risk to ISPs may be such that they decide to block access to such websites.

There are currently no reported Hong Kong cases dealing with internet gambling.

6.13.7 Reunification

The handover of Hong Kong's sovereignty to the People's Republic of **6–198** China (PRC) at midnight on June 30, 1997, and the conversion of the former British Dependant Territory into the Hong Kong Special Administrative Region of the People's Republic of China has been well-documented. Since the handover, the PRC has remained committed to the "one country, two systems" legal doctrine. Under this doctrine, Hong Kong, except insofar as national security, nationality, defence and certain other matters may be affected, is allowed to continue its former laws and make new laws separately from the rest of the PRC, subject where necessary to the adaptation of pre-handover laws to Hong Kong's new status.

These principles are embodied in Hong Kong's mini constitution, the Basic Law, and have been implemented by way of the Hong Kong Reunification Ordinance[91] and an ongoing series of "Adaption of Laws" Ordinances. None of these have affected substantive commercial or crim-

---

[91] Ch.2601, Laws of Hong Kong.

inal law in any significant way and the great majority of pre-handover legislation modelled closely on UK legislation remains in force. The handover did not affect the laws of Hong Kong insofar as they are relevant to the internet.

Since the handover, the procedural law of England and Wales, on which Hong Kong procedure is very closely based, has undergone a radical change commonly referred to as the "Woolf Reforms". The Hong Kong judiciary and the Law Society of Hong Kong have since set up working parties to review civil procedure in Hong Kong and, amongst other things, consider whether any or all of the Woolf Reforms, or similar initiatives in Singapore, Australia and other commonwealth jurisdictions, should be adopted in Hong Kong. It is unlikely that it will be considered appropriate or politically acceptable for the English reforms to be adopted *en masse* in Hong Kong.

6.13.8 Conclusions

6–199   The Hong Kong courts and those in other Asian commonwealth jurisdictions with similar procedural laws may have considerable jurisdiction over internet activities in which non residents are involved. Where a Hong Kong resident deals with a non-resident provider of goods or services or publisher, and unlawful acts take place or a dispute arises in relation to the contract formation process or performance, the Hong Kong courts may be willing to exercise jurisdiction if the non resident comes here or is liable to be served under Order 11. Whether any particular case will be a "proper" one to be determined in Hong Kong will depend on all the facts of the case.

6.14 ISRAEL

6.14.1 Jurisdictional issues relating to foreign website proprietors and other entities

6–200   Civil jurisdiction in Israel is founded upon service on the defendant of a summons.[92] Under the civil procedure rules,[93] service may be effected upon a defendant outside of Israel, or upon his solicitor in Israel,[94] if the court has granted leave under its discretionary power for service outside the jurisdiction in one or more of the circumstances provided for in r.500. If the defendant is a foreign website proprietor, or it is alleged that a foreign person or entity has committed unlawful acts related to a website, any of the following are likely to apply:

---

[92] Civil Law Procedure Regulations 1984, r.477.
[93] Civil Law Procedure Regulations 1984, r.500.
[94] Civil Law Procedure Regulations 1984, r.477.

(1) *Injunctive relief*: An injunction is sought, in respect of an act performed or about to be performed within Israel.[95]

The court may assume jurisdiction for the purpose of granting a temporary injunction in order to prevent damage from occurring pending final resolution of the dispute in the forum where the action will ultimately be tried.[96] The court must be satisfied that the application, whether for an interim or final injunction, has not been made solely so that the court will acquire jurisdiction.

The injunction may be sought against either the local ISP, or against the foreigners who are responsible for the material reaching Israel, foremost among whom will be the foreign website proprietor. An action for an injunction against the ISP may well be sufficient for the court to assume jurisdiction over a foreign entity, against which damages are claimed, as a joint defendant.

(2) *Tort*: The action is based on an act or omission within Israel.[97] The rule is that the court may assume jurisdiction over a foreign defendant when the act or omission takes place within Israel.[98] The occurrence of the damage within Israel is not sufficient.[99] Therefore, a foreign website proprietor will only be subject to the court's jurisdiction when the commission of the alleged tort has a connection to Israel. For instance, an e-commerce sale of books to an Israeli customer is likely to constitute an act within Israel.[1] A negligent misstatement may constitute an omission within Israel. The sale or promotion of goods marked with an Israeli trade mark to customers in Israel, via the internet, is highly likely to constitute an act within Israel.[2]

(3) *Contract*: The plaintiff is seeking a remedy for breach of contract, and the contract was made in Israel by, or on behalf of, the foreign defendant, or the breach of contract occurred in Israel.[3] As yet, there are no cases related to internet purchases from foreign websites. The rule for local jurisdiction cases is that a contract for

---

[95] Civil Law Procedure Regulations 1984, r.500(6).

[96] *Unger v Paris Israel Movies Ltd*, Supreme Court Reports, Vol.20(3), p.6 (1966).

[97] Civil Law Procedure Regulations 1984, r.500(7).

[98] *Mizrachi v Nobel's Explosives Co Ltd*, Supreme Court Reports, Vol.32(2) p.115 (1977). In *Lang v Marks*, the court stated that the place of the alleged tort was of only secondary importance in light of all of the circumstances of the case, but this statement was *obiter*, because the court assumed jurisdiction over the foreign entities as necessary or right parties to the action under r. 500(10). Supreme Court Reports, Vol.56(1), p.118 (2001).

[99] *Mizrachi v Nobel's Explosives Co Ltd, supra.* Followed in *Hoida v Hindi*, Supreme Court Reports, Vol.44(4), p.545 (1990).

[1] *Eisenman v Qimron*, known as the "The Dead Sea Scrolls Case", Supreme Court Reports, Vol.54(3), p.817 (2000). The court held that mail order sales of three copies of a book from the US to customers in Israel sufficed as evidence of publication of the book in Israel. This decision may establish a low threshold for an act to be considered as having occurred within the jurisdiction.

[2] *Ahava USA Inc v J Dablin Jay Ltd*, Jerusalem District Court Civil File 3137/04, decision dated October 10, 2004. For details of the case, see the trade marks section of this chapter below.

[3] Civil Law Procedure Regulations 1984, r.500(4) and r.500(5).

goods sold via the internet is made at the place of the purchaser. If the courts adopt the logic of this rule for cross-border cases, then the contract underlying e-commerce sales of goods to Israeli customers may expose a foreign internet vendor to Israeli jurisdiction.

(4) *Necessary/right party*: The person abroad is a necessary party or the right party in an action duly submitted against another person, on whom a summons was duly served within Israel.[4]

The plaintiff can apply for leave to serve the foreign website proprietor or other foreign entity as a necessary party or the right defendant to the proceedings if it can identify and serve a potential defendant in Israel, such as an ISP. The court will not grant leave if it determines that there is no real issue to be tried against the Israeli defendant, or that the proceedings have been brought against the Israeli defendant solely to gain jurisdiction against the foreign website proprietor. The rule will be most useful in cases where the plaintiff cannot otherwise obtain leave for service under r.500 (such as in an action regarding defective software downloaded from a foreign website), or to found a third party action by the local ISP against a foreign website proprietor.

Procedure

6–201   The application for leave must be supported by affidavit evidence demonstrating that the plaintiff has good grounds for its action, together with evidence supporting the grounds of the application. Given the ex parte nature of the application, the plaintiff is obliged to disclose all relevant facts in his possession to the court.

Connection to the website owner

6–202   The likelihood that a court will assume jurisdiction over a foreign website owner or other entity involved in an internet dispute will depend on the circumstances of the application. The court will refuse leave where the case is outside the spirit of r.500.[5]

A recent line of Supreme Court cases demonstrates an increasing willingness by Israeli courts to assume jurisdiction over foreign businesses trading with Israeli customers.[6]

The Jerusalem District Court has held that enforcement of intellectual property law in Israel is in the public interest, notwithstanding that choice of law rules may lead to the application of the law of another jurisdiction.[7]

---

[4] Civil Law Procedure Regulations 1984, r.500(10). See for example, *Lang v Marks*, fn.98.

[5] *Rad v Chai*, Supreme Court Reports, Vol.40(2), p.141 (1986).

[6] See for example, *Hageves A Sinai (1989) Ltd v The Lockformer Co*, Supreme Court Reports, Vol.52(1), p.109 at 119 (1998), followed in later cases, for example, *Lang v Marks*, fn.98.

[7] fn.2 above.

On the basis of current case law, mere accessibility of the website in Israel is not likely to be sufficient to found jurisdiction[8] in the absence of a tangible connection between the website and Israeli users.[9] The location of the server from where data is uploaded to the internet is unlikely to be a critical factor.[10]

In relation to domain name disputes, a District Court ordered the transfer by the US based registry of a domain name registered under the .com gTLD, without any discussion of the jurisdictional question.[11]

6.14.2 Forum non conveniens

Discretion to determine whether forum is appropriate

The court, in exercising its discretion whether or not to grant leave to serve proceedings on a defendant outside the jurisdiction under r.500, will consider whether, in the circumstances of the case, Israel is the appropriate forum for the case to be heard.[12] As the application for leave under r.500 is made ex parte, the foreign defendant upon whom service has been effected is granted two opportunities (motion to cancel, and in the pleadings) to move for a stay of proceedings, by persuading the court that Israel is not the *forum conveniens* for the trial of the matter. The chances of so persuading the court have decreased over the past decade, as the judges take into account the modern methods of communication that continue to reduce the difficulty and cost of defending an action in a foreign jurisdiction.[13] **6–203**

The defendant is bound to raise the issue of *forum non conveniens* at its earliest opportunity. Lack of a case at trial will not lead to the jurisdiction issue being reopened; being wrongfully joined to the proceedings will not assist either.[14]

The circumstances of each case will determine the weight given to different factors. The general principles are set out below.

The Israeli law is very close to the English law,[15] although the courts have

---

[8] *Rambam v Levy*, Jerusalem Magistrates' Court Criminal Complaint 117/00 (Rehearing), Decision dated February 10, 2004.

[9] For authority that in certain forms of e-commerce, transactions may occur at the user's location, rather than at the location of the foreign website's server, see *Ahava USA Inc v J Dablin Jay Ltd*, fn.2. The case also supports the proposition that the logic of the regular civil procedure rules should be applied to jurisdictional issues arising from use of the internet.

[10] *Reut Electronics and Components Ltd v Mirrors Image Ltd*, Jerusalem District Court Civil Files 2841/03 and 5242/03, Decision dated December 14, 2003. The case involved an internet site located *within* Israel.

[11] *Israel Bar Association v Yair Ben David*, Tel Aviv District Court File 810/01, decision dated August 28, 2003.

[12] *Abu Jihalah v East Jerusalem Electric Co Ltd*, Supreme Court Reports, Vol.44(1), p.554 (1993).

[13] *Hageves A Sinai (1998) Ltd v The Lockformer Co*, Supreme Court Reports, Vol.52(1), p.109 (1988) at 119, and later cases.

[14] *Rad v Chai*, Supreme Court Reports Vol.40(2) p.141 (1986) at 147.

[15] As enunciated in *Spiliada Maritime Corp v Consulex Ltd* [1987] A.C. 460.

at times adopted the public interest aspects of the approach taken by the US courts.[16] The test applied is whether the natural forum for resolution of the dispute is Israel or another jurisdiction.[17] The reasonable expectations of the parties, and the public interest in achieving justice, are the major issues to be considered in determining the natural forum.

The court considers all of the circumstances, and the strength of the connections of each forum to the issues raised by the dispute. The court will also give due weight to the reasonable expectations of the parties.[18] All the relevant facts and causes important to the question must be balanced. These include, *inter alia*, nature of the dispute, relevant law in the *fora*, *lis alibi pendens*, nexus between each forum and the evidence, location of the parties and witnesses, place where the actionable event occurred, costs, availability of similar defences in each forum, ability to enforce a judgment, and the public interest, which includes matters such as the court's familiarity with the applicable law and the absence of an impartial judicial system in the other forum.[19]

If the defendant has convinced the court that there is another forum that may be more appropriate than Israel, the burden of proof rests on the plaintiff to show that there are special reasons why the Israel court should hear the matter.[20]

6.14.3 Defamation

6–204   Liability for defamation is based on publication of a defamatory statement. "Publication" is defined as any statement directed to a person other than the injured and which has reached that person, and in the case of written material, which is likely to reach any person other than the injured party.[21] A statement published on a popular website is presumed likely to have reached this other person.[22]

For defamation to be actionable, its commencement must occur within Israel.[23] The court acknowledged the reach of the defamation law outside the country, when a defamatory letter sent from Israel to the US was held to fall within the scope of the law. Similarly, the Israeli Supreme Court has ruled that a statement made by an Israeli to the Jordanian Government, and

---

[16] See for instance, *Shechem Arabic Insurance Co v Abed Zerikat*, Supreme Court Reports, Vol.48(3), p.265 (1994).

[17] *Abu Attiah v Arbitisi*, Supreme Court Reports, Vol.39(1), p.365 (1985).

[18] The two conditions of the old English test are subsumed into the "expectations of the parties". See *Abu Jihalah v East Jerusalem Electric Co Ltd*, fn.12.

[19] *ibid.*

[20] *ibid*, at p.568.

[21] Defamation Law 1965, s.2(b).

[22] *Yoav v Halevy*, Tel Aviv District Court Civil File 33613/03, decision dated October 28, 2004.

[23] Defamation exists only if the material is published to at least one person other than the injured (Defamation Law 1965, s.7). As the tort of defamation is subject to s.3 of the Civil Wrongs Ordinance (New Version) 1968, the tort must occur within Israel in order for the defamation to be actionable.

its publication in a Jordanian newspaper that was also distributed in Israel, are subject to the statute.[24] These precedents provide grounds to argue that defamatory statements posted on bulletin boards, newsgroups, chat rooms or publicly available websites may well be viewed as intended for publication in Israel (as in the case of the Jordanian newspaper), when such services are provided worldwide.

There is however authority for a contrary position in criminal defamation trials. In *Rambam v Levy*,[25] the Jerusalem Magistrates' Court held a rehearing relating precisely to this question of the circumstances in which an Israeli court has jurisdiction over foreign website owners. The suit was a private criminal prosecution for defamation based on material published on a US operated website. The court held that "publication" of a passive website occurs solely at the location of the server. Publication in Israel requires the existence of a subscriber/information provider relationship, or similarly tangible connection between the foreign website operator and Israeli users.[26]

The decisions in local civil defamation cases are not uniform in their approach to the internet, or in their interpretation of the law on local jurisdiction. Moreover, these cases are mostly irrelevant to international disputes, because Israel is a small country, because the substantive law is the same in every jurisdiction, and because the regulations that govern local jurisdiction are different from r.500 of the Civil Procedure Rules 1984, which applies to defendants outside of Israel. However, it is worth noting a local court ruling, that a defamatory statement placed on the website of a national newspaper at its headquarters in one area of Israel was "published" in all areas of the country, and is actionable in every region.[27]

Besides the primary liability of the person who places a defamatory statement on a website, it is a matter of debate whether, and to what extent, an ISP, website proprietor, or newsgroup owner will be liable for defamation. The author, editor, and publisher of such services may be subject to primary liability if they are deemed to be media persons for the purposes of the Defamation Law[28] or fall within the definition of a "newspaper" in the

---

[24] *Shaha v Serderian*, Supreme Court Reports, Vol.29(4), p.734 (1985).

[25] fn.8. Although *Rambam v Levy* is a criminal decision, in the civil trade mark infringement case of *Ahava USA Inc v Dablin Jay Ltd* (see fn.2), the Jerusalem District Court referred to *Rambam v Levy* as authority for the proposition that publication of defamatory statements solely by means of its distribution via a foreign website, without any further connection to Israeli users, does not constitute defamation within Israel.

[26] *ibid.* The judge found that a Jerusalem newspaper advertisement that invited the Israeli public to read the offending internet article was insufficient connection between the US website owner and Israeli users in order to found jurisdiction in Israel.

[27] *Landau v Hasson*, Kiryat Gat Magistrates Court Civil File 884/02, decision dated May 1, 2002.

[28] Two bills proposing the addition of "internet sites" to the definition of "mass media" in s. 11 of the Defamation Law were tabled during the terms of previous parliaments.

Press Ordinance, or, alternatively, if a court applies general tort principles to fill any lacunae in the current definitions. There are conflicting rulings on the issue in local cases.[29]

Distribution of a defamatory statement may be caused by the actions of the foreign website owner, the owner of the host server, the service providers who own the routers, or the access provider in Israel. Providers of such services may also be subject to secondary liability if they are found by the court to be "printers", "distributors", or "vendors" of the publication. If so, they may be subject to liability only if they knew or should have known that the publication contained defamatory matter.[30]

An ISP may be ordered to provide details of its customers for the purpose of identifying potential defendants in a defamation suit. In *A v Bezeq International Ltd*, the judge stressed the importance of protecting the privacy of internet users as a means of promoting the principle of free expression. Accordingly, she held that such details would only be provided to a plaintiff in a *civil* defamation suit who can establish a likelihood that the person or persons responsible for placing the material on the internet would lose a *criminal* defamation action.[31]

6.14.4 Content liability

6–205 Incorrect information that causes damage may be actionable under the Civil Wrongs Ordinance (New Version) 1968, either as negligence or fraud. Section 3 of the statute provides that remedies are available to any person injured by a civil wrong (act or omission), which has been committed in Israel.[32]

---

[29] Defamation Law 1965, s.11. Press Ordinance, Laws of Palestine, Ch. 116, Vol.B, p.1191. In *Weisman v Golan*, Magistrates Court Reports 2001(3) p.112, which related to an editor's liability for statements published on *Globes Online*, the internet website of the national daily financial newspaper, *Globes*, the court held that websites clearly fall within the scope of the Defamation Law. The cases that do not relate to publication in an internet newspaper, tend to the other direction. In *Borochov v Foren*, Kfar Saba Magistrates' Court Civil File 7830/00, decision dated July 14, 2002, the judge was not persuaded that *Weisman v Golan* was a correct decision. *Borochov v Foren* was a harder case, concerning the liability of the administrator of an on-line forum. The administrator was held not to be an editor for the purposes of the law. Editors are liable only for publication in the "mass media", the definition of which was restricted by the judge in accordance with the precise wording of the statute, to newspapers, radio, and television. *Borochov v Foren* has been accepted as the authority that releases website proprietors from liability in cases where a user uploads the defamatory material onto the website.

[30] Defamation Law, s.12. In *Borochov v Foren, supra*, the judge enunciated a stricter three part test, whereby an ISP will be liable for publication of defamatory statements if: (i) the complainant informs it of the offending statement(s) and requests that it be removed; (ii) the statement(s) is patently defamatory; and (iii) by exerting reasonable effort it could remove the statement(s), and fails to do so. It is likely that a forum administrator may be more easily held liable than a primary ISP on this third leg of the test. In an interlocutory decision in *A v Bezeq International Ltd*, below fn.31, the judge stated as obiter that she did not consider website proprietors to be distributors for the purposes of the Defamation Law.

[31] Jerusalem Magistrates' Court Civil File 4995/05, decision dated February 28, 2006.

[32] The wording here is "civil wrong" rather than the "act or omission" of r.500(7). See fn.97.

Liability for misleading advertisements under the Consumer Protection Law 1981[33] applies to any advertisement that might mislead a consumer in Israel, regardless of whether it was made in Israel. Any person who originated the advertisement or arranged for its publication may be liable. Distributors may be liable for distributing a misleading advertisement if it is misleading at first glance, or if they knew it to be misleading. Note that misleading advertisements include advertisements that do not appear to be advertising materials at first glance.[34]

It is also a tort under the Commercial Torts Law 1999 for a dealer to publish false information about a business, profession, asset or service, including his own, where he knows or should know that the information is incorrect.[35] Distributors of such information may be liable if they knew the information to be false, or if it is obviously false.[36]

In cases where a computer virus downloaded from a website unlawfully affects use of a computer or of computer material, compensation for damage suffered as a result may be recoverable under the Computer Law from the person responsible for causing the damage.[37]

To date, the only judgment that has dealt with incorrect information published on the internet is *Paradise Mombasa Tours (1997) Ltd v New Soil Technologies Ltd*.[38] Following the termination of a business relationship between the parties, the defendant retained outdated descriptions of the plaintiff's business activities on the defendant's website. The court held that the defendant was unduly intervening with customers' access to the plaintiff's business, and granted an interlocutory injunction under s.4 of the Commercial Torts Law 1999. *Paradise Mombasa* concerned a local website, and did not involve reliance on the incorrect information. Where there is reliance in an extra- jurisdictional situation, the courts may apply s.2 of the Commercial Torts Law, or the provisions of the Consumer Protection Law and Civil Wrongs Ordinance (New Version) discussed above.

6.14.5 Copyright

Copyright works are protected in Israel under the Copyright Act 1911[39] **6–206** and the Copyright Ordinance 1924.[40] A new Copyright Bill was laid before parliament on July 20, 2005, and is now at the committee stage. The bill is

---

[33] Consumer Protection Law 1981, s.7.
[34] *ibid.*, s.7(c).
[35] Commercial Torts Law 1999, s.2(a).
[36] *ibid.*, s.2(b).
[37] Computer Law 1995, s.7.
[38] Tel Aviv District Court Civil File 1509/01, decision dated May 8, 2001. For a more detailed discussion of the case, refer to Ch.3, fn.79.
[39] Copyright Act 1911, which dates from the British mandatory period.
[40] Copyright Ordinance 1924, also dating from the British mandatory period, as amended on several occasions by the Israeli Parliament.

intended to deal with the issues raised by the internet era,[41] however, until it is enacted, there is no legislation that regulates the use of works with modern technology. Consequently, the present law in this area, which is set out below, is primarily case law, and still relies in fair measure on foreign precedents.

Posting an infringing copy of a copyright work on a website may constitute copyright infringement under Israeli law on several grounds. These are discussed below. The term "infringing copy" under the Act is broad enough to include copies created outside Israel.[42]

Downloading a copy of a work onto a device such as a DVD or iPod will infringe reproduction rights. Devices intended for use in a computer are specifically excluded from the exemption granted to recording or copying works for private and domestic use on other recordable media.[43]

Placing a copy of a work in the RAM of a user's computer may infringe the reproduction rights of the copyright owner.[44] In the absence of direct authority under Israeli case law, it is unclear whether reproduction rights apply to unlicensed transient copies made on the servers of search engines, the user's ISP, and the like during the transmission, or when such copies arrive at their destination.[45]

The right to publicly perform the work[46] may also be infringed where the work is delivered by means of a mechanical instrument.[47] Israeli courts interpret this section broadly, as applying to any broadcast or transmission,

---

[41] The Supreme Court has called for legislation that addresses specific issues created by technological advances. The Copyright Bill 2005 introduces a new right of "making available to the public", derived from the 1996 WIPO Treaties relating to copyright (WCT), and to phonograms and performances (WPPT). The explanatory memoranda to ss.11 and 15 of the Bill state that the new right has been drafted to encompass acts making copyright works available via the internet. However, it could be argued that the existing reproduction and performance rights cover the uploading of works, and that light of the exemption proposed in s.26 of the Bill (see fn.42) the new right does not materially extend the scope of protection currently granted by the law.

[42] Copyright Act 1911, s.35(1). "Infringing copy" means "any copy, including any colourable imitation, made, or imported in contravention of the provisions of this Act".

[43] ibid., s.1(2), Copyright Ordinance 1924, s.3b (1996 amendment).

[44] Copyright Act 1911, s.1(2). The Copyright Bill 2005 expressly states that reproduction includes electronic or other technological means of storing a work.

[45] The Copyright Bill 2005 distinguishes between the end user and intermediaries. If enacted, s.26 will sanction the creation of temporary transmission copies, based on the approach of Art.5 of the European Union 2001 Copyright Directive. The latest published version of the bill states: "s.26 Incidental Reproduction—Incidental or transient reproduction of a work is permitted, if the reproduction is an integral part of a technological process whose sole purpose is to enable one of the following, and on condition that such reproduction has no significant economic value of itself: (1) transmission of the work between third parties in a communications network by an intermediary; (2) other lawful use of the work."

[46] Copyright Act 1911, s.1(2).

[47] ibid., s.35(1).

or distribution of the work by any other means.[48] Re-transmission of satellite television broadcasts by cable companies also constitutes public performance. The courts have distinguished between a "viewer", namely a passive transmitter of a broadcast, and a "broadcaster", who plays an active role in distributing the broadcast.[49] ISPs and other service providers may thus be liable for public performance. An individual user, who merely views a copy of an infringing work, is unlikely to be liable for public performance. Given the broad interpretation of the right, and depending on such networks' physical modes of operation, it may also be relevant to the issue of P2P file sharing networks in Israel.

Another way to establish liability is to show that a service provider allowed the use of a "place of entertainment" for the infringing performance of a work in public, unless there is no reasonable ground for suspecting that the performance would be an infringement of copyright.[50] It is not clear whether the courts will apply this section to virtual spaces such as websites.

Posting an infringing copyright work on a website may expose the website proprietor, the person responsible for uploading the work, or the ISP, to indirect liability for the sale, hiring, or distribution for the purpose of trade, exhibition or importation of a work "which to his knowledge infringes copyright". P2P network operators and file sharers may be held liable for distributing infringing works "to such an extent as to affect prejudicially the owner of the copyright".[51]

In 2005, one of the battles in the long war between music and film 6–207

---

[48] See, for instance, *Ernest Bloomers v The Israeli Chapter of the International Federation of Record Industry*, District Court Reports, Vol.1982(2), p.156. The district court of Tel Aviv held that the delivery of radio broadcast to hotel guests' rooms constituted a public performance. The court found that any distribution of a work, by whatever means, constitutes a performance, and that a broadcaster is a performer even if it only transmits and broadcasts the work. In internet related cases, this case has been regarded as authority for the wider proposition that the act of "facilitating" copyright infringement on the internet is illegal. See, for instance, *Mirror Images Ltd v Care Medical Services Group Ltd*, Tel Aviv District Court Civil File 6420/04, decision dated February 3, 2005.

[49] *Golden Lines v Tele-Event Ltd & Co*, Supreme Court Civil Appeal 6407/01, decision dated June 16, 2004. The court considered that use of a sophisticated technical procedure and of expensive equipment that is not regularly used by individual users, and the commercial purpose of the broadcast, each indicated the function of a "broadcaster" rather than a "viewer".

[50] Copyright Act 1911, s.2(3):
   "Copyright in a work shall also be deemed to be infringed by any person who for his private profit permits a theatre or other place of entertainment to be used for the performance in public of the work without the consent of the owner of the copyright, unless he was not aware, and had no reasonable ground for suspecting, that the performance would be an infringement of copyright."

[51] Copyright Act 1911, s.2(2):
   "Copyright in a work shall also be deemed to be infringed by any person who:
   (a) sells, or let for hire, or by way of trade exposes or offers for sale or hire, or
   (b) distributes either for the purposes of trade or to such an extent as to affect prejudicially the owner of the copyright, or
   (c) by way of trade exhibits in public, or
   (d) imports for sale or hire
   any work, which to his knowledge, infringes copyright".

copyright owners and the Israeli collecting societies on the one hand, and owners of sites offering free downloads on the other, reached the court. Israeli music publishers joined the anti-piracy organisation ALIS, which represents several large US studios and Israeli film and video companies, in suing local P2P file sharing network operators, two ISPs and a storage services provider.[52]

The Haifa District Court granted an interlocutory injunction shutting down the P2P network operators' websites. The judge urged the parties to reach a comprehensive settlement that would enable the websites to operate legitimate businesses. The website proprietors settled, which enabled renewed access to their sites. They acknowledged that providing links to files containing copyright works constitutes copyright infringement even when the works are stored only on users' computers, and undertook to pay the equivalent of statutory damages for each such link that would appear on their websites in the future.

The terms of settlement entitle the plaintiffs to monitor the traffic on the defendants' websites, but enjoin them from using information of illegal activity thus obtained against the websites' users. The provider of storage services to the websites refused to settle, and the plaintiffs eventually withdrew their case against him.

Undeterred by this case, file sharing networks continue to thrive in Israel. There are occasional reports of settlements between website proprietors and copyright owners in the press. A private bill dealing with the phenomenon has been tabled twice, but has not had a first reading.[53] The bill proposes the prohibition of unauthorised uploading and downloading of works, and related acts, and prescribes in detail the potential liability of end users, website proprietors, and the providers of access, hosting, and temporary storage service.

Beyond the scope of existing copyright protection, and solutions

6-208   There are limits to the applicability of the Copyright Act 1911 to the internet. Exclusive rental and leasing rights apply only to the distribution of physical media on which visual or audio works are fixed (such as DVDs or CDs).[54] There was a bold but unsuccessful attempt to claim that in addition to infringing the right of reproduction, posting song lyrics on a website constitutes an infringement of the right to make a contrivance for mechanically delivering a work.[55]

There is no general right of public distribution under Israeli law, except in the case of an unpublished work.[56] In *Eisenman v Qimron* (Dead Sea Scrolls dispute), the Supreme Court held on appeal that the respondent's

---

[52] *NMC Music Ltd v Hirsch*, Haifa District Court Civil Files, primarily 915/05, 12647/05, 14391/05, 18204/05 and 8193/06, decision granting interlocutory judgment dated 11/9/05.

[53] Intellectual Property Law (Digital Media) Bill 2005.

[54] Copyright Ordinance, ss.3B and 3F (1996 amendment).

[55] *Rotblitt v Barmag Life Ltd*, Kfar Saba Magistrates Court Civil File 2445/04, decision dated August 14, 2005.

[56] Copyright Act 1911, s.1(2).

right of first publication had been infringed by the distribution within Israel of three copies of an infringing book, each of which had been purchased from one of the US based appellants via mail order.[57] Following this decision, where a work is previously unpublished in Israel, a website proprietor may be liable in respect of e-commerce sales of an infringing copyright work to customers based in Israel.

ISPs, bulletin boards, or news groups may claim the defence of innocent infringer, on the ground that the alleged copying occurred automatically.[58] Under Israeli copyright law an innocent infringer may be exempted from liability to pay damages and the plaintiff will be restricted to injunctive relief. An innocent infringer must establish that he was unaware of the existence of the copyright and had no reasonable ground for suspecting that copyright subsisted in the work.[59] Israeli courts tend to interpret this exemption broadly in internet cases. In 2005, the government published a Memorandum for a proposed electronic commerce bill. The bill would exempt internet intermediaries that provide access, hosting and storage services, from liability for unintentional infringement.[59a]

Articles 11 and 12 of the 1996 WIPO Copyright Treaty (WCT) oblige contracting states to provide protection and remedies for digital rights management (DRM), namely against circumvention of technological protection measures, and tampering with electronic rights management information. Israel has signed but not ratified the Treaty. The government intends to introduce DRM legislation, and in February 2007, it published a discussion paper that called for public submissions on the issue.

The copyright owners lobby favours enacting a law that protects DRM, and argues that the current law does not adequately address these issues. However, the applicability of the Computer Law 1995 to these activities has not been tested. Depending on the method used, a person who is circumventing or tampering may commit an offence under any or all of the following: s.2 by erasing software or data, altering it, distorting it, or interfering with its use; s.4 by unlawfully accessing software or data in a computer, or s.5 by unlawfully accessing software or data in a computer in order to commit an offence under another law (such as copyright infringement).[60]

In summary, it is probable that Arts. 11 and 12 of the WCT will ultimately find expression in the Israeli Copyright Act. More difficult to predict is whether both before and after this likely event, copyright owners will continue to all but ignore the potential of the Computer Law.

---

[57] *Eisenman v Qimron*, fn.1.
[58] Copyright Act 1911, s.1(2).
[59] *ibid.*, s.8.
[59a] See, for instance, *"On the Table" Gastronomical Centre Ltd v Ort Israel*, Tel Aviv Magistrates Court Civil File 64045/04, decision dated May 10, 2007.
[60] Computer Law 1995, ss.2, 4, and 5.

Jurisdictional and international issues

6–209 There is very little case law on conflict of laws and jurisdiction in Israeli copyright law. Although copyright is considered a property right under Israeli law, copyright infringement is a tort. Accordingly, to establish a legal claim under Israeli law it would be necessary for the alleged infringement to take place in Israel.

As noted above, the Supreme Court held in the *Eisenman v Qimron* appeal that mail order distribution of three books from abroad constituted infringement in Israel. Moreover, because the Supreme Court determined that an infringement had occurred in Israel, it did not overrule the District Court's decision that the defendant was liable for copyright infringement even though that court had determined that the infringements had occurred in the US.

The District Court had decided that US copyright law governed the dispute, but applied Israeli law under the doctrine of equivalence, whereby Israeli copyright law and American copyright law are considered equivalent for the purpose of using the law of the jurisdiction where the case is being heard.[61] Both the District Court and the Supreme Court decisions have been subjected to considerable academic criticism. Nonetheless, they are highly pertinent to any current discussion of the possible outcomes of an internet copyright dispute.

The issue of where copyright infringement occurs was addressed by the Jerusalem District Court in a local internet case involving the display on a website of photographic works, which had been downloaded from another website without the owner's permission. In *Reut Electronics and Components Ltd v Mirrors Image Ltd*,[62] the court dismissed any notion that the location of the server was critical in determining where the infringement occurred, and ruled that the infringement occurred in all jurisdictions. The judge approved the decision of the Magistrates' Court of Kiryat Gat in *Landau v Hasson*. That court was the first in Israel to modernise the Roman Law rule to fit the internet era, by holding that a defendant who is a website proprietor is "located" wherever his website is accessible, that is, everywhere.

Reut Electronics and Components Ltd v Mirrors Image Ltd has been used as a precedent for local internet jurisdiction cases since 2003, and the courts determining the jurisdictional issue for copyright proceedings involving foreign defendants may be influenced by the approach taken by the Jerusalem District Court.

A magistrates' court recently held that where infringing works illustrating goods are posted on a website, the copyright infringement occurs

---

[61] *Eisenman v Qimron*, fn.1. *Qimron v Shanks*, District Court Reports, Vol.1993(3), p.10, at 21.
[62] fn.10. *Landau v Hasson*, fn.27.

wherever the goods are intended to be for sale.[63] The higher courts have not yet had an opportunity to consider this decision.

6.14.6 Trade marks

Registered trade marks are protected in Israel under the Trade Marks Ordinance. The proprietor of a registered trade mark has the exclusive right to use the trade mark "upon, and in every matter relating to, the goods in respect of which it is registered."[64] It is well established that this right includes use of an internet domain name which is the same or similar to the trade mark.[65]

6–210

Every unauthorised use (excluding parallel importation) in Israel may constitute trade mark infringement. Evidence of confusion is not always required,[66] nor is proof that the defendant intended to cause confusion.[67] For example, a website proprietor using a trade name or trade mark, in order to either sell or promote his goods or services in Israel, and to the world in general, may be liable to the proprietor of the same or similar trade mark or trade name that is registered in Israel with respect to those goods or services.[68]

The Israel Trade Mark Ordinance reflects Israel's obligations under the Agreement on Trade-Related Aspects of Intellectual Property Rights (the TRIPS Agreement), by extending protection to "well-known" or "famous" marks.

A well-known mark is infringed by use of an identical or similar mark in a manner that may lead to confusion with the goods to which the well-known mark refers or with goods of a similar type.[69] The legislation distinguishes between the scope of protection afforded to well-known marks that are registered in Israel and to those that are not registered in Israel. The owner of a well-known mark that is *not registered* in Israel is entitled to the exclusive right to use the mark in conjunction with goods for which the mark is well known, or goods of the same description. However, the rights afforded the owner of a well-known *registered* mark in Israel extend to use

---

[63] *Levy v Steinberg*, Jerusalem Magistrates' Court Civil File 8033/06, decision dated April 15, 2007.

[64] Trade Marks Ordinance (New Version) 1972, s.46. An exception is made in the case of genuine use by a person of his own name, of the name of his or his predecessor's place of business, or of a genuine description of his goods (s.47).

[65] For example, *Israel Bar Association v Yair Ben David*, fn.11, followed in many instances.

[66] *A Elionel Ltd v MacDonald*, Supreme Court Reports Vol.58(4), p.314 (2005).

[67] *Frou Frou Biscuits (Kfar Saba) Ltd v Froumine & Sons Ltd*, Supreme Court Reports, Vol.23(2), p.43 (1969).

[68] *Dead Sea Laboratories v Leshno Felix.*, Tel Aviv District Court Civil Files, 2176/04, 18216/04 20936/04, Interlocutory Decision, dated January 4, 2005, enjoining use of the domain name "Ahavashop" on a site selling genuine Ahava products, in proceedings brought by the owner of the registered trade mark "Ahava". However, in a later decision, *Matim Li Fashion Chain for Large Sizes Ltd v Crazy Line Ltd*, the Tel Aviv District Court sanctioned a company's use of metatags that were similar to a competitor's registered trade marks. Tel Aviv District Court Civil File 506/06, decision dated July 31, 2006.

[69] Trade Marks Ordinance (New Version) 1972, ss.1(3), 1(4), 46A(a) and 46A(b).

of the mark in conjunction with non-identical goods, provided that use of the mark by an unauthorised third party is likely to create an association with the goods sold under the well-known registered mark and that the proprietor of the registered mark is likely to be injured as a result of such use.

Unregistered trade marks, trade names and trade dress are protected under a number of other statutes.[70] These statutes, which provide causes of action for passing off, unjust enrichment, trespass on incorporeal property, and unfair intervention may be available even where a website proprietor is using the trade mark or trade name in connection with different goods or services. However, the existence of confusion or damage to the owner of the unregistered mark, the fame of the mark, and a lack of good faith by the alleged infringer, are generally required by the court in order to protect such unregistered marks in these cases. Website use of his own trade mark by a genuine trade mark owner in another country is likely to be allowed.

Jurisdictional and International Issues

6–211   In *Ahava USA Inc v J Dablin Jay Ltd,*[71] the Jerusalem District Court enforced an injunction and damages granted by a US court for trade mark infringement that arose from e-commerce conducted between the owner of an Israeli website and purchasers in the US. The court stated unequivocally that in a *reverse case*, where a website owner located in the US sells to purchasers in Israel, the Israeli courts can assume jurisdiction over the US website owner in a suit for infringement of an Israeli trade mark.

There is no case law on the use of unregistered Israeli marks on foreign websites.

The Tel Aviv District Court has assumed extraterritorial jurisdiction in domain name disputes. In *Israel Bar Association v Yair Ben David,*[72] the court approved its earlier decision in *Cellcom Israel Ltd v TM Aquanet Computer Communications Ltd.*[73] It held that the top level domain .com and the second level domain .co.il are insufficiently distinct to prevent a likelihood of confusion between identical third level domain names. The judge ordered the transfer of both "hapraklit.com" and "hapraklit.co.il" to the Israeli trade mark owner, despite the fact that .com domains are administered in the US.

---

[70] See Commercial Torts Law 1999, s.1; Unjust Enrichment Law 1981, s.1; Property Law 1969, s.17 read together with Chattels Law 1971, s.8, and Commercial Torts Law 1999, s.3.

[71] fn.2. In both *Ahava USA Inc v J Dablin Jay Ltd,* and in *Dead Sea Laboratories v Leshno Felix, supra,* the disputed trade mark was "Ahava", a well-known brand for skin care products.

[72] fn.408 above.

[73] District Court Reports Vol.33 (3) p.424 (1999).

6.14.7 Website notices

Notices specifying territorial limitations

There is no Israeli case law on the legal effect of notices purporting to limit **6–212** liability of the website proprietor in one way or another. Under contract law, a notice stating that the site is not intended for reading in Israel may be viewed as an offer attempting to subject the end-user to a contractual relationship. The offer will bind the end-user only upon acceptance. The notice itself may then be treated as an attempted disclaimer.

It is more difficult to establish the validity of a disclaimer in Israel than in most common law countries. As a matter of public policy, contract law severely restricts the validity of disclaimers.[74] Indeed, it is unlikely that use of a notice alone, if it does not form part of a contract between the website proprietor and a user, will limit the website proprietor's liability in any area of law.

Enforcement of notices through restricted access

A website proprietor might combine the use of a notice on its website with **6–213** technical measures to prevent Israeli end-users from accessing the material on the site. In this way (if it is practical), the website proprietor may be able to avoid liability for incorrect information published on the site, both under torts and consumer protection legislation. It can demonstrate that it is taking steps to perform its duty of care towards Israeli end-users. A similar strategy may also assist a website proprietor in avoiding liability for trade mark infringement on the ground that it is not using the trade mark in Israel.[75]

6.15 CROSS-BORDER LIABILITY—ITALY

6.15.1 Governing law and jurisdiction for foreign websites

Jurisdiction in civil matters

In Italian civil law for the competent judge to be identified, the provisions to **6–214** be taken into account are Arts. 18–20 of the Civil Procedure Code.

When individuals are bringing an action, the local judge has the authority to rule over a case in the place where the defendant is domiciled or habitually resident. If the defendant does not live or is not resident within the

---

[74] Contracts (General Parts) Law 1973, s.30 and Standard Terms Contracts Law 1982, ss.3 and 4(1).

[75] See the arguments in *City Central Ltd v Chanel (French Societe Anonyme)* District Court Reports Vol.26(5), p.351 (1995).

Italian Republic then the applicable jurisdiction is the place where the plaintiff resides.[76]

As for undertakings, the generally applicable rule is that the judicial authority of the place where an undertaking has its administrative head-quarters is competent to decide the matter. The competent jurisdiction can also be located where the undertaking owns a subsidiary and has appointed an authorised legal representative.[77]

A further provision, Art.20, sets out an alternative *forum* of competence to the aforementioned Arts. 18–19. Article 20 permits the competent judge to be located not where the defendant is domiciled, but to establish judicial competence in the place where the obligation causing the dispute arises or where such obligation has to be fulfilled.

The case law regarding the circumstances where an Italian judge can be deemed to have jurisdiction over a foreign website, in relation to unlawful acts carried out on the internet, is founded upon the principles set out in Council Regulation (EC) No., 44/2001[78] and Law 218/1995 on the reform of the Italian system of Private International Law.

First and foremost, a distinction must be drawn among contractual liability, tortious infringements and criminal liability.

(1) **Contracts** A judge could assert his jurisdiction in the following main instances:

  (a) the defendant is domiciled or resident in Italy or has an authorised legal representative within the country[79];
  (b) the parties to the contract in question have agreed that the contract would be governed and construed according to Italian Law[80];
  (c) the foreign defendant has not objected to the trial being held in the country[81];
  (d) the contractual obligation to be fulfilled must be complied within the country[82];
  (e) a interim measure is to be enforced within the country[83];
  (f) a consumer, who has suffered an injury of any kind caused by a producer, is domiciled in Italy whereby the coming into force of the agreement for the supply of goods or services was the result of a specific offer or advertisement launched in Italy.[84]

---

[76] Civil Procedure Code, Art.18.

[77] Civil Procedure code, Art.19.

[78] Paolo Cerina "Il problema della legge applicabile e della giurisdizione" in E Tosi "*I Problemi giuridici di internet*" Giuffrè Editore (1999) p.367 onwards.

[79] Art.77 of the Civil Procedure Code.

[80] Art.4 of Law 218/1995 on the reform of the Italian system of International Private Law and Art.23, Council Regulation (EC) No. 44/2001.

[81] Art.4 of Law 218/1995.

[82] Art.5.1(a) Council Regulation No. 44/2001.

[83] Art.10 Law 218/1995 and Art.31 Council Regulation (EC) No. 44/2001.

[84] Art.33(2)(u) Legislative Decree. 6.9.2005, n. 206 also called Consumers Code and Art.15, Council Regulation (EC) No. 44/2001.

(2) **Tort** The competent judge can be established according to the place where the defendant is domiciled or, alternatively, to the place where the tortious event has come into existence.[85] Article 20 of the Civil Procedure Code establishes that territorial competence is given to the place where the obligation arises or where it has to be fulfilled. The so called *forum commissi delicti* is based upon the close link existing between the source of the obligation with the place where the breach occurs. Case law proves that the application of such provision ranges from trade mark infringement and unfair competition to defamation cases, concerning the use of the internet, as we shall see below.

(3) **Criminal matters** Article 6 of the Penal Code provides that anyone who commits a crime or an omission within the territory of the State shall be punished according to Italian Law. A crime is deemed to have been committed within the State when, be it an act or an omission, it has partially or totally occurred within it, that is to say an event which is the consequence of the act or omission has occurred.

Furthermore, Art.10 of the Penal Code sets forth that a foreigner committing a crime from abroad, causing damage to the State, the EU or a citizen thereof, shall be punished in compliance with Italian law, if he is to be found within the territory.

Additionally, Art.8(1) of the Penal Procedure Code sets forth, on a general level, that territorial competence is determined according to where the crime was committed. If competence cannot be derived from the provisions in Art.8, then the territorial competence shall refer to the judicial authority of the last place where the act or omission was committed.[86] If such place cannot be tracked, the competence shall pertain to the judicial authority corresponding to the domicile or residency of the defendant. And lastly, if it is still impossible to determine competence, this shall vest in the judge of the place where the prosecutor first filed the crime in the relevant register.

In the sections below we provide an overview of the substantive law as well as providing an account of the approach adopted by the Italian courts where there has been an unlawful conduct pursued on the web by a foreign website.

6.15.2 Defamation

The law on defamation is ruled by Art.595 of the Italian Penal Code which   **6–215** establishes that anyone who injures the reputation of another, by spreading

---

[85] Art.3(2) Law 218/1995 and Art.5(3), Council Regulation (EC) No. 44/2001.
[86] See Art.9 of the Penal Code.

defamatory information to third parties, shall be subjected to either detention or to an administrative penalty.[87] In Italy, defamation is governed by the Penal Code, despite being afforded relief also under the Civil Code,[88] as opposed to (for instance) the UK where it falls under tort law.

In the event of a defamatory statement being uploaded on a website, the place where the harmful event occurs gives rise to several interpretations: it could refer to the place where the website owner and defamer resides; also, it could be the place where the server is to be found; or, finally, each and every place where the defamatory statement was spread and where the plaintiff has suffered actual injury.[89]

However, a more reasonable and efficient application of the law seems to admit that the plaintiff ought to sue the defendant in the place where the latter habitually resides, with a view to recovering the damages suffered all in the same place.

The case law demonstrates that the issue relating to what jurisdiction may be relevant has been faced in a practical fashion by the courts. An Italian judge has jurisdiction on internet defamation when the two following conditions arise: (1) the material activity of uploading the defamatory statement on a website occurs within the country; and/or (2) the unlawful act is carried out in the Italian territory, that is to say, the social context which witnesses a harm to the reputation of the complainant can be located within the national borders.[90] Nevertheless, it is immaterial to know where the server is based, for the Italian judge shall have jurisdictional competence, inter alia, to forbid any further publication of the defamation and request removal of the defamatory material from the web.[91]

6.15.3 Content liability

6–216   The Italian legislation on the responsibility of content providers has implemented the E-Commerce Directive[92] following the enactment of the Legislative Decree April 9, 2003, n.70.

The role of the service provider is central to most discussions on internet liability. The general rule enforced does not recognise the service provider as accountable for the content of a website hosted on its server, unless the provider is aware that the unlawful conducts are being put in place and does not take any reasonable steps to prevent this from persisting.[93]

Usually, disclaimers are formulated to limit such responsibility; they aim

---

[87]   Penal Code, Art.595.
[88]   Art.2043 Italian Civil Code.
[89]   *Shevill v Press Alliance*, 68/3, ECJ.
[90]   Cassazione Penale, sez. V, December 27, 2000, n.4741; also see Luigi Iannicelli, Tribunale di Oristano, sentenza 25–05–2000.
[91]   Tribunal of Teramo 11–12–1997.
[92]   Directive 2000/31/CE.
[93]   Legislative Decree April 9, 2003, n°70 on E-Commerce; Tribunal of Milan, March 18, 2004, Foro Ambrosiano, 2004, 181.

at warning website users that no one is accountable for the information provided and prove very useful tools in this sense. However, Art.1229 of the Civil Code restricts the range of application of disclaimers: no one, in fact, can exclude his/her liability for any intentional unlawful act or negligent act.[94]

The objective of disclaimers is also to limit geographically the communication or the offer for the supply of goods and services available to web users, which often specify that the message may be, i.e. addressed to Italian or EU citizens only.

As far as incorrect or denigratory information is concerned, the issue regarding jurisdiction was faced by the court in a case where denigratory commercial information was published on the internet through a server based in the UK. The damages suffered abroad by the claimant—an Italian undertaking, namely, Candy Elettrodomestici—were the object of the dispute. It was held that there was lack of jurisdiction on the part of the Italian judge who was prevented from awarding Candy compensatory damages.

The ruling suggested that what confers jurisdiction to a particular territory is the persistence of direct consequences of the initial harmful act in a specific place. Indeed, it would seem unreasonable to summon the tortfeasor to a judgement in a country which he/she has not had any effective contact with.[95]

6.15.4 Misleading advertising

By law, advertising has to be truthful, clear and correct. Misleading   6–217
advertising, on the contrary, is defined as information addressed to consumers which is likely to influence their economic behaviour and consequently, likely to injure the reputation of a competitor. The regulatory body is to be identified with the authority on competition and market. For civil matters, the competent jurisdiction is to be found—without any derogation—in the place where the consumer is resident or domiciled, if it is within the State.[96]

6.15.5 Infringement of intellectual property rights

In Italy, lawsuits grounded on IP protection, where a title of ownership has   6–218
been licensed or assigned in Italy, can be brought before the Italian judge regardless of the nationality or domicile of the parties.[97] Article 120 of the Industrial Property Code, which came into force in 2005, also sets forth that the relevant competence shall vest in the judicial authority of the place where the defendant is domiciled or resides; and, in the absence of such

---

[94] Emilio Tosi "Le responsabilità civili" in Emilio Tosi "*I Problemi giuridici di internet*" Giuffrè Editore (1999) p.245 onwards.
[95] Tribunal of Monza, May 20, 2002, Soc. *Candy Elettrodomestici c Dyson Ltd.*
[96] Legislative Decree, September 6, 2005, aka Consumers Code, Art.20(b) and Art.63.
[97] Art.120, Industrial Property Code.

information, the competence shall pertain to the place where the plaintiff is domiciled or resides.

When the defendant is not resident or domiciled within the State, proceedings can be brought before the judicial authority of the place where the plaintiff is resident or domiciled. Failing that, the judicial authority in Rome acquires competence over the case.

It is worth mentioning that territorial competence within the State is detailed in Art.4 of the Legislative Decree 168/2003.

Lawsuits arising out of infringements carried on against the plaintiff's rights can also be brought before the judicial authority linked to the place where the unlawful acts have been committed.

Trade marks

6–219 The *Soc. Carpoint c. Microsoft Corp* case affirmed that an Italian judge obtains jurisdiction any time the claimant contends the infringement of a trade mark, for which protection is afforded in Italy, on a website registered abroad.[98] This case dealt with a website located on a foreign server, owned by a foreign subject domiciled abroad and accessible from anywhere in the world, including Italy, which infringed the rights of an Italian trade mark holder.

The obstacle the court attempted to overcome was to understand how one can assess whether the harmful conduct linked to the abuse of a trade mark over the internet has had harmful effects within one specific country.

Two opposite standpoints were considered. The first one argued that mere visibility of the website in one state is sufficient for the harmful event to be regarded as having an impact in that country. On the other side of the spectrum, the second and opposite theory held that mere visibility of the sign cannot suffice. There needs to be commercial activities associated with the use of the trade mark in the country in question. The court adhered to the second approach.[99]

Thus, for an infringement of a trade mark to take place on the internet, it is irrelevant that the product bearing the mark on the web page be imported into the country. Yet, there needs to be an offer to supply the goods or services thereof within Italy, such as the launch of an advertisement campaign within the state and/or the existence of a contract for the supply of the goods and services or any related services as encompassed by the trade mark registration.

In this instance, the judge declined to have jurisdiction on the grounds that the defendant was not, at the time, engaging in any promotional activity.[1] This said, the lack of jurisdiction of the domestic judge was stressed in view of the fact that the mark was solely visible on a web page which could be uploaded in Italy. As a matter of fact, any type of com-

---

[98] Tribunal of Rome, March 9, 2000.

[99] Cesare Galli "L'allargamento della tutela del marchio e I problemi di internet", in Riv.-dir.ind. 2002, 3,103

[1] *Soc. Carpoint c. Microsoft*, Tribunal of Rome February 2, 2000.

mercial activity in relation to the product in question was exclusively addressed to an audience not resident in Italy.

Unfair competition

A case on unfair competition highlights, again, on what basis an Italian judge is competent. By acquiring the name of another with a view to registering a domain name, a trade mark infringement is brought about. Submitting an application to the US authority requesting registration does not entail that the American judge shall enjoy jurisdiction to decide over the case. Conversely, the domestic judge shall be in charge where the undertakings involved, both plaintiff and defendant, are headquartered in Italy and where the unlawful acts have been put into being there.[2]

6–220

6.15.6 Conclusion

The plaintiff can elect between two routes to follow when bringing an action: proceedings could either be commenced in the place where the defendant resides according to the aforementioned Arts. 18–19 of the Civil Procedure Code or by invoking Art.20 of the same Code, therefore bringing the action in the place where the obligation has arisen.[3]

6–221

In the light of the above, it must be pointed out that the Supreme Court has consistently been inclined to construe Art.20 according to the view that territorial competence shall vest in the judge of the place where the plaintiff resides, in consideration of the fact that the latter's major interests are negatively affected by the unlawful conduct carried out over the internet in that place more than anywhere else.[4]

6.16 CROSS-BORDER LIABILITY—JAPAN

6.16.1 Enforcement

General

As pointed out in section 6.1, it is a practical question "how substantive rights can be enforced." In Japan, as in the UK, practitioners have had to address some fundamental issues anew for the purposes of rights enforcement on the internet, such as who can be sued and where the infringing act is committed. In this section we focus mainly on two issues. The first issue is how to identify the defendant, and the second issue is jurisdiction and applicable law.

6–222

---

[2] Tribunal of Lecco, 31.5.2000.
[3] Francesco Ciompo "Ancora sulla competenza territoriale ex Art.20 c.p.c. in caso di illecito commesso via internet" in Diritto dell'Internet – 2007 n.2 (IPSOA).
[4] Corte di Cassazione (Supreme Court), ordinanza May 8, 2002, n. 6591(1).

The "Law on Restrictions on the Liability for Damages of Specified Telecommunications Service Providers and the Right to Demand Disclosure of Identity Information of the Sender (Law No. 137 of 2001)" (hereinafter "Provider Liability Restriction Law") has been enacted and includes legal measures to identify the defendant. The purpose and the interpretation of the law are discussed in detail below.

In an infringement case involving international elements many legal points have to be considered under the conflicts law of Japan. Such issues are analysed from two aspects, "Judicial jurisdiction" and "the choice of law".

Whether or not the Japanese court can hear the case should be considered under the heading of "Judicial jurisdiction". Once the court has decided that it can hear the case, the next problem is "the choice of law". In the intellectual property field, we also have to take into account the nature of intellectual property, that the right is protected within the territory of the country where the protection is claimed.

6.16.2 Identifying the defendant

6–223 To identify an infringer can be very difficult. If the infringer uses an anonymous remailer or proxy server, it is very difficult for the plaintiff to identify the infringer. In contrast with English law, it is a principal rule that an ISP that merely stores materials that infringe the copyright or defamatory materials is not liable for copyright infringement or defamation in Japan.

The "Provider Liability Restriction Law"[5] sets out restrictions on the liability of ISPs. According to Art.3, s.1:

> "When circulation of information via Specific Telecommunication results in infringement of rights of the other person, Specific Telecommunication Service Provider using Specific Telecommunication Facility for the use of such Specific Telecommunication (hereafter defined as "Related Service Provider" in this paragraph) is not liable for damages unless it can technically apply measures by which transmission of such information resulting in the infringement of rights is prevented and where either of the following items apply, provided that the foregoing shall not apply if such Related Service Provider is Sender of such information resulting in the infringement of rights:
>
> (i) where such Related Service Provider knows that such other person's rights are infringed by circulation of information via such Specific Telecommunication, or

---

[5] A tentative English translation of the "Provider Liability Restriction Law" is located at *www.isc.meiji.ac.jp/~sumwel_h/doc/codeJ/provider-e.htm*.

(ii) where such Related Service Provider knows circulation of information via such Specific Telecommunication and there is an appropriate reason, which is enough to determine that it should have been able to know that such other person's rights are infringed by the circulation of information via such Specific Telecommunication."

So a plaintiff has no basis on which to file a suit against a provider that only provides communication service. Therefore, the plaintiff cannot use litigation against the provider as a measure to collect information about the infringer and it is necessary to identify the infringer as a basic step.

The "Provider Liability Restriction Law" also provides a means to obtain disclosure of the sender information from the ISP. According to Art.4, s.1:

"(1) A person, who alleges that its rights are infringed by circulation of information via Specific Telecommunication, has a right to require Specific Telecommunication Service Provider using Specific Telecommunication Facility for the use of such Specific Telecommunication (hereafter defined as 'Disclosure Related Service Provider') to disclose Sender Information related to such alleged infringement of rights (name, address, or other information useful to specify Sender of Infringing Information to be stipulated in the applicable ministerial ordinance of the Ministry of Public Management, Home Affairs, Posts and Telecommunications) in the possession of such Disclosure Related Service Provider if all of the following items are satisfied:

(i) it is obvious that rights of such person requesting for disclosure of Sender Information are infringed by Infringing Information, and

(ii) such Sender Information is necessary for such person requesting for disclosure of Sender Information to claim damages, or such person has otherwise justifiable reason to require the disclosure of Sender Information."

6.16.3 Who is the wrongdoer?

As discussed above, the plaintiff has no grounds on which to file a suit **6–224** against a provider which only provides a communication service according to the Provider Liability Restriction Law, Art.3.

However, case law has developed in two areas in Japan. One is a defamation case involving an anonymous BBS called "2 channel". The other is a copyright infringement case involving a P2P service provider called "File Rogue". In both cases, courts held that both providers were liable for defamation postings and copyright infringement.

There are many legal defamation cases relating to "2 channel".

"2 channel"[6] is one of most popular BBS in Japan. It used to state that the administrator did not record traffic logs at all. Even now, the administrator states that their BBS is anonymous.

The "Provider Liability Restriction Law" was enacted on May 27, 2002. After enactment, the court held that "2 channel" is liable for defamatory posts by an anonymous third party. In the *female professional majyang player v 2 channel* case,[7] according to the judgment,

> "as the defendant can technically apply measures by which transmission of such information resulting in the infringement of rights is prevented, the defendant has a duty to apply measures to prevent such transmission by deleting it immediately when a defamatory post are uploaded to BBS which the defendant provides and invites third parties to transmit their postings."

The court held "2 channel" liable and ruled that it should pay damages.

The *File Rogue* case is similar to the US *Napster* case. "File Rogue" is the name of the P2P service which MMO Japan Company provided. The service used a client-server structure for some tasks (e.g. searching) and a peer-to-peer structure for others.

Many internet users converted musical compact discs into files such as MP3 files and used this website.

JASRAC (The Japanese Society for Rights of Authors, Composers and Publishers) applied for a provisional injunction to the Tokyo District Court seeking to halt the service. The application was made jointly with 19 companies under the Recording Industry Association of Japan, owner of neighboring rights.

On the application for a provisional injunction by JASRAC in January 2002, the Tokyo District Court made an order against MMO Japan Ltd on April 11, 2002, not to transmit to users information of musical works administered by JASRAC.

According to the "interim ruling" judgment[8] made on February 28, 2002, against MMO Japan Ltd, the court held that MMO Japan is liable to pay damages for copyright infringement. The points of the judgment are as follows: the File Rogue service has the characteristics of a service enabling users to make MP3 files available for transmission. The files are automatically transmitted to the public and made transmittable under the administration of MMO Japan Ltd, and from this, the company gains business profit. Therefore, MMO Japan Ltd is the main subject of the infringement of automatic public transmission rights and the right of making transmittable.

On December 17, 2003, the Tokyo District Court made a judgment ordering MMO Japan to suspend transmission of music files and pay

---

[6] *www.2ch.net.*
[7] Tokyo District Court judgment, June 25, 2003.
[8] *http://www.jasrac.or.jp/ejhp/release/2003/0129.html.*

compensation money to JASRAC.[9] The Tokyo appeal court upheld[10] the judgment.

Regardless of the statute's limitation of ISP liability, providers that invite third party defamatory postings or illegal exchange of music files may be regarded as a wrongdoer and liable for defamation or copyright infringement.

6.16.3 Judicial jurisdiction

If a harmful event takes place which has some international elements, can the Japanese court hear the case?   6–225

This has to be considered as a problem of "judicial jurisdiction". It is said that state jurisdiction consists of legislative jurisdiction, judicial jurisdiction and enforcement jurisdiction. Usually judicial jurisdiction is called simply "jurisdiction" in Japan. There is no distinction between *in personam, in rem* and *quasi in rem* actions in Japan. Therefore, the only question to be considered is whether the Japanese court has jurisdiction over the case or not.

The leading case on jurisdiction is the *Malaysia Air Lines* case.[11] In 1977, a Malaysia Air Lines aircraft crashed on the way from Penang to Kuala Lumpur. All the passengers died. The family of one of the victims who was Japanese commenced litigation against Malaysia Air Lines at Nagoya District Court. Malaysia Air Lines had a business branch in Tokyo. However, the passenger bought his ticket for the plane in Malaysia. The Supreme Court said about international judicial jurisdiction:

> "It is reasonable to decide according to fairness to the parties and the ideal of fairness and early resolution of the judicial procedure. Reviewing the articles of domestic jurisdiction, when one of the elements, eg domicile of the defendant (Article 2 of the Civil Procedure Law (CPL)), the place where duty should be done (Article 5 of CPL), the place of the property of the defendant (Article 8 of CPL), the place of the tort (Article 15 of CPL) or the other [sic] which are described regarding the venue exists in Japan, it is reasonable that the defendant should be submitted under the judicial jurisdiction of our country."

In that case, as a branch of the defendant existed in Japan, jurisdiction was found.

After this judgment, lower courts have shown more flexible solutions. According to some judgments, in some exceptional situations, the court has a discretion to dismiss the case because of lack of jurisdiction.

---

[9] *http://www.jasrac.or.jp/ejhp/release/2003/1217.html.*
[10] *http://www.jasrac.or.jp/ejhp/release/2005/0330.html.*
[11] (Supreme Court, Showa56 (1981) October 16, Minshu 35, Vol.7, p.1224).

An example is the *Taiwan Ento Air Lines* case[12] The court dismissed the case on the basis that it was an "exceptional situation". The situations which the court mentioned are as follows. Regarding the evidence: "There is no official relationship between Taiwan and our country. We cannot use this evidence by the way of international co-operation".[13] Therefore, "it can be said that it is very difficult for our court to do justice based on the evidence." According to the expert examiner, the Taiwan court had jurisdiction over the case. The plaintiff alleged that he could not afford to proceed in Taiwan. But the court did not accept this assertion.

If the proprietor of a website lives in Japan or has a branch in Japan, then Japanese courts will have the jurisdiction over the case which is generally based on "domicile of the defendant". If the proprietor of the website has property in Japan, then the Japanese court would admit jurisdiction over the defendant.

In the case of a harmful event having a connection with Japan, the matter will be considered as a tort case. In a tort case, it is said that if the "place of tort" is in Japan, the Japanese court will have judicial jurisdiction. The "place of tort" is construed to include not only "the place of harmful activity" but also "the place in which the result occurred". However, it is severely disputed whether such "result" should be limited to direct or physical harm or not. The Japanese courts have not made a definite decision about this issue. The majority opinion is that harm is not limited to direct result.

In any event, in cases concerning trade mark and copyright infringement, reliance on content and defamation, where the person is suffering from the harmful activity and lives in Japan, it is likely that that would be recognised as the direct result of the harmful activity. In that case the Japanese court should hear the case filed by such a person generally as long as there are no exceptional circumstances.

6.16.4 Choice of law

General

6–226　If the court has judicial jurisdiction, we move into the stage of "choice of law". At this stage, we first have to decide the "nature of the problem". If the problem is recognised as one of procedure, the law of the place of the court is applied. If the problem is a substantive problem, it is governed by the choice of the law provided by the conflicts of laws rules of Japan.

The choice of law is provided by "*Hou no tekiyou ni kansuru Tsusoku Hou*" (General Law concerning the Application of Laws) (hereafter GLAL).

---

[12] Tokyo District Court, Showa61 (1986) June 20, Hanrei Jiho Vol. 1196, p. 87.

[13] Owing to the "two China problem" there is no diplomatic relationship between Taiwan and Japan. Therefore, Japanese courts cannot use the international co-operation system of collecting evidence through diplomatic channels.

Formerly, the law was called Horei (law concerning the application of laws in general), but has been amended totally.

If the problem is recognised as a substantive problem, distinctions should be made between contract, tort, title of property, and so on. For example, if the case is recognised as a title of property, the law of the location of the property is applied (Art.3 of GLAL). If the problem is recognised as a problem of tort, "the law of the place where the result occurred" shall be applied (Art.17) as to the existence and the effect of the tort.

If the problem is recognised as infringement of intellectual property, the territorial nature of intellectual property influences the choice of law. There are some disputes about this. But the majority opinion recognises that there is no need to confront the problem of "choice of law" in the case of intellectual property.

Tort

Questions of defamation and liability for reliance on content would be   6–227
discussed as problems of tort under the conflicts of laws of Japan. However, Art.19 of GLAL sets out that "the law of the domicile of the harmed person (or if the harmed person is a legal person, the law of the location of the main business)" shall be applied as to the existence and the effect of the defamation instead of Art.17.

The aggrieved person can file a suit in Japan as long as he proves he has suffered substantial damage. Once the court decides there is jurisdiction over the case, the court may apply the law of his domicile.

In a defamation case, if the court applied the law of the domicile of the damaged person, compensatory damage would be ordered. An injunction against an overseas website proprietor would be a problem. In Japan, it is not necessary that the defamatory statement is regarded as being published in Japan to found a tort action.

As for reliance on incorrect information, content liability rules in Japan are little developed. But comments similar to those about defamation can be applied to this problem.

Intellectual property

When it appears that copyright is infringed by international action, what   6–228
law is applied? In the majority opinion, the law of the country in which the protection would be claimed is applied (Art.5 of the Berne Convention). However, the Supreme Court's opinion in the card reader case (described below) may suggest that the above rule of tort may be applied in a copyright infringement case.

The extra-territorial application of the Japanese Copyright Law is ambiguous. If unauthorised Disney video tapes are about to be imported from the US, the copyright law of Japan is claimed to protect Disney's right and the court will order the injunction of the import. No one doubts that Japanese laws will protect the intellectual property in such a case. However, when the infringing activity occurs abroad but the harm results in Japan, it is difficult to know whether the Japanese Copyright Law applies.

First, if the copyright law of Japan is applied to the action of the infringer, the Copyright Law of Japan admits a right of wire transmission in Art.23 which states: "The author shall have the exclusive rights to broadcast and to transmit by wire his work". Therefore the protection of the author's right is clear.

Next, whether the Copyright Law of Japan can be applied or not is unclear. This is a problem of legislative jurisdiction. It is recognised in Japan that temporary loading into RAM or viewing a work on the screen are not infringements of copyright. However, if the question of infringement were to depend on whether the infringement affected the Japanese market, then there could be infringement of Japanese copyright.

A Besides copyright infringemen disputes, the Supreme Court made a remarkable judgment[14] in a patent case. The case is called the "card reader case". In this case, the plaintiff was a company located in Japan and has a US patent for an "FM signal recovery device". However, the plaintiff did not have such patent in Japan. The defendant was located in Japan and had produced the card reader in Japan. Its subsidiary US company imported the products into the US. The plaintiff asserted that the defendant was liable for infringement of the plaintiff's US patent based on Art.271(b) of US patent law.

The court held that the court should decide the choice of law based on *Horei*[15] (law concerning the application of laws in general). On that basis the case was regarded as concerning a tort, so that Art.11, s.1 of Horei, the laws of where the facts of the cause of action occur, should be applied to the existence and the effect of the tort. Therefore, US patent law should be applied in the case. However, s.2 of the article that "when the facts would not be illegal if they happened in Japan, section 1 does not apply to the event" should also be applied. Japanese patent law does not have extraterritorial effect as US law Art.271(b) has. The defendant's activities were not "illegal if they happened in Japan". The Supreme Court therefore held that the plaintiff's claim had no grounds.

6.16.5 Cases

6–229 Some cases show that consideration of choice of law can affect judicial jurisdiction.

A case decided by the Tokyo District Court on January 28, 1999, concerned jurisdiction over a copyright claim. The plaintiff was a company located in Japan, whose business was to produce movie films and television films. The defendant was a natural person living in Thailand. The plaintiff

---

[14] Supreme Court judgment, September 26, 2002.
[15] GLAL was enacted on January 1. The case occurred before amendment. The court applied *Horei*.

filed a suit in the Tokyo District Court on the following causes of actions, following which the plaintiff filed a suit in Thailand.

The causes of action were:

(1) based on copyright:

    (a) to request the court to declare that the contract was void as regards the defendant being the exclusive licensee in the countries other than Japan;

    (b) to request the court to declare that the plaintiff was the legitimate holder of the copyright in the work in Thailand;

    (c) to request the court to declare that the defendant had no licence in the work.

(2) based on the unfair competition prevention law:

    (a) an injunction against the defendant to insist that the plaintiff had the exclusive right in countries other than Japan.

(3) Tort

    (a) compensation damage for 10,000,000 Yen.

The court denied jurisdiction based on the following reasons:

(1) The main issue was whether the defendant had the exclusive right or not in countries other than Japan.

(2) The plaintiff's legal agent in Hong Kong sent letters from Hong Kong to Hong Kong, Bangkok and the branch offices located in East Asia. The court said that the main activities occurred outside Japan.

(3) Even if the work was authored in Japan, the laws of the countries where the work was exploited were disputed. The court could not say that the right is located in Japan.

(4) The defendant was a natural person and had no business base in Japan. Therefore, if the court admitted jurisdiction in Japan, it would be a serious burden for the defendant.

Two defamation cases are also of interest. The first was a Tokyo District Court case decided on August 28, 1989. The publisher of a magazine filed a suit which requested the court to declare that the magazine did not harm the defendant, who was a Japanese living in California. The Japanese court declined jurisdiction because the defendant insisted that the magazine issued in Japan was not itself the tort, but that the distribution in California was a tort.

The second was a Tokyo District Court case decided on September 30, 1992. The plaintiff was a Japanese horse jockey who was successful in Malaysia and Singapore. He filed a suit complaining that newspaper companies had defamed him. The court admitted the defamation and ordered the defendants to pay the damage for 3,000,000 Yen. Whether the compensation damage was limited merely to Japan or not was not disputed in the judgment. The judge found that the plaintiff had a hope to be successful all over the world including Japan, Malaysia and Singapore.

6.16.6 Territory notices

6–230   As mentioned above, the contents of web pages may infringe someone else's right in another country. In Japan, some people advise that the site should contain a notice that it is intended for specified countries. There is no definite discussion on the effectiveness of the notices. But in intellectual property litigation, not only is the existence of illegality important but the degree of infringement is also important. Such notices may weaken the degree of infringement.

6.17 THE NETHERLANDS

6.17.1 Jurisdiction

6–231   The jurisdiction of the Dutch courts is governed by European Community law for Community trade marks, Community design rights and for defendants domiciled in the EU. Community trade marks constitute an ever growing part of the trade marks valid for the Netherlands.

The Community Trade Mark Regulation and Community Design Right Regulation provide their own exclusive jurisdiction rules, regardless of the nationality of the infringer. The home court of the defendant has jurisdiction to grant cross-border injunctions for the whole EU. In addition, the court of the place where infringement occurs has jurisdiction to grant injunctions with a national effect. The determination of the place of infringement is subject to national law. Within the Netherlands, the District Court in the Hague has exclusive jurisdiction in Community trade mark and Community design right cases.

For infringements of other intellectual property rights and for tort claims against defendants domiciled in the EU, jurisdiction is determined by the Brussels Regulation. The main rule is that the home court of the defendant has jurisdiction. This jurisdiction is cross-border and Dutch courts indeed are willing to grant cross-border injunctions. In its 1989 judgment in *Lincoln v Interlas*, the Dutch Supreme Court confirmed that courts can grant cross-border injunctions.[16]

In a recent judgment in *Roche v Primus & Goldenberg*, the Supreme Court confirmed that the courts should assume the validity of foreign intellectual property rights as long as these have not been challenged.[17]

---

[16] Supreme Court 24–11–1989, NJ 1992/404.
[17] Supreme Court 19–12–2003, BIE 2005/78.

However, the European Court of Justice ruled in *GAT v LuK* that if the validity of a foreign registered intellectual property right is challenged, this puts an end to cross-border jurisdiction, as long as the validity issue has not been decided by the court of the country of registration.[18]

However, in three more recent judgments, the District Court in The Hague ruled that the *GAT v LuK* limitation does not apply to injunctions on infringements in preliminary injunction proceedings (the so-called *kort geding*) or to interim injunctions on infringement granted in full proceedings, since in such cases only a first evaluation of the validity of the registered intellectual property right is made and the issue is not really decided.[19]

If a Dutch court has jurisdiction over a defendant, co-defendants can be sued in the same court, regardless of their domicile. This option has been used since 1989 to bring several companies from one group of companies before the same court, especially where the group contains sales companies per EU Member State. This option has now been limited by the European Court of Justice in *Roche v Primus & Goldenberg*[20] for intellectual property rights that have to be seen as a bundle of rights, such as patents. It may still be an option for unitary intellectual property rights, such as community trade marks, but this still has to be decided by the courts.

6–232

With regard to non-EU-based defendants in cases that involve other intellectual property rights than Community rights or in cases based on tort, jurisdiction is decided by national procedural law. The rules are basically the same as for the Brussels Regulation, but the case can also be brought before a Dutch court if it would be unacceptable to require the plaintiff to bring the case before a foreign court.

The District Court of The Hague hinted that this rule might be applied in intellectual property cases in *Angiotech v Sahajanand*, but found that the plaintiff had presented insufficient circumstances to assume jurisdiction on that ground.[21] In a recent case *SBM v Bluewater*, the court held that this might apply if otherwise a due process as meant in Art.6 of the European Human Rights Treaty would not be guaranteed, for instance if no court would take the case.[22] This approach still requires further exploration.

Since a change in the law in 2002, jurisdiction can no longer be based on the mere fact that the plaintiff is Dutch.

If a foreign website is, inter alia, directed at The Netherlands but the defendant is not domiciled in The Netherlands, the courts may assume that an infringement is committed in The Netherlands or that there is a real threat that an infringement will be committed, and assume jurisdiction on that basis. The plaintiff has to show circumstances that the website is, inter

---

[18] ECJ 13–07–2006, C–4/03.

[19] District Court The Hague 21–09–2006, BIE 2006/91, *Bettecare v H3 Products*, District Court The Hague 19–10–2006, 272529 / KG ZA 06–1082, *Van Kempen v Kuipers* and District Court The Hague 07–03–2007, *Fleuren v Ruvo*, see *www.boek9.nl*.

[20] ECJ 13–07–2006, C–539/03.

[21] District Court The Hague 31–08–2005, IER 2005/91.

[22] District Court The Hague 11–04–2007, see *www.boek9.nl*.

alia, specifically directed at The Netherlands.[23] The website needs to be accessible from The Netherlands, but there need to be additional circumstances, such as use of the Dutch language, use of a .nl domain name, use of Dutch phone numbers, etc.

6.17.2 Applicable law

6–233   The applicable law for infringement of intellectual property rights is determined by Dutch private international law.[24] The main rule is the *lex loci protectionis*, meaning that the applicable substantive law is the law of the country for which the right has been granted and where protection is sought under that right.[25] This law rules the establishment and scope of infringement, proof of infringement, and the applicable sanctions.

So, if jurisdiction is based on the domicile of the defendant, Dutch law will normally apply in as far as relief is sought for The Netherlands, but the courts may have to apply foreign substantive law in as far as cross-border relief is sought. Under Dutch procedural law, the courts in principle will have to establish the content of foreign substantive law *ex officio*, but in practice there is a rule that the party that wants relief under foreign substantive law should inform the court on its content, although a high level overview may be sufficient, dependent on the remedies required.

Many intellectual property laws have been harmonised throughout Europe to some extent and therefore the court may assume that the issue should be decided on the basis of the same test as under Dutch law, in which case the defendant will have the option to prove otherwise. That of course does not apply to substantive law of non-European countries.

Copyright

6–234   Publication of works subject to copyright, and therefore also copyright infringements that occur in The Netherlands, are subject to Dutch law under Art.5, s.2 of the Berne Convention. Whether publication on a website is a publication in The Netherlands will be decided by the same test as for jurisdiction.

---

[23] District Court The Hague 8–2–2005, BIE 2005/99, *Vitra Collection v Classic Design International*; District Court The Hague 25–08–2005, IER 2005/87, *Allergan v Basic Research* and District Court The Hague 6–12–2006, 219109 HA ZA 04–1201, *Phonenames Ltd v 1-800-flowers.com, Inc*, see *www.boek9.nl*.

[24] We do not deal here with the substantive law governing other issues, such as ownership. For those issues, see Th.C.J.A. van Engelen, Intellectuele eigendom en internationaal privaatrecht, Den Haag, Boom Juridische Uitgevers, 2007.

[25] Supreme Court 27–01–1995, NJ 1995/669, *Bigott-Batco v Doucal* and Court of Appeal The Hague 23–03–1988, BIE 1988/85, *Butter Ghee*. See also the Dutch national report on AIPPI Q174, questions I.3.1 and I.3.2 at *www.aippi.org*.

Trade marks, design rights and trade names

Infringements of Community Trade Marks and Community Design Rights 6–235
anywhere within the European Union are governed by the substantive law
provided by the Community Trade Marks Regulation and Community
Design Rights Regulation. However, some of the relief, such as damages, is
subject to the national law of the country for which protection is requested.

Infringements of national trade marks and design rights in the Netherlands, Belgium and Luxemburg are governed by the mutual substantive law
contained in the Benelux Treaty on Intellectual Property (*Beneluxverdrag
inzake de Intellectuele Eigendom*). This replaced the Uniform Benelux
Trade Mark Law and the Uniform Benelux Design Right Law on September
1, 2006, insofar as it provides such substantive law and for the remainder
by the national law of the country for which protection is requested.

The use of a company name on a website, *inter alia*, directed at The
Netherlands may constitute an infringement on the trade name rights of a
Dutch plaintiff. Under Dutch law, trade names are protected as intellectual
property rights. This right confers protection to the trade name that a
company actually uses in the normal course of business. A company may
have more than one trade name.

An internet domain name may both infringe a third party's trade mark
rights and trade name rights, as courts have found quite often.[26]

Tort

Under Dutch private international law, the substantive law for torts is the
lex loci delicti, the law of the country where the tort took place. So, if a
website is, inter alia, directed at The Netherlands, the courts will apply
Dutch substantive law to a tort claim based on that.

If for instance an offer for sale on an internet site that is not specifically
directed at The Netherlands is followed by an actual sale to a customer in
The Netherlands or other act in The Netherlands which constitutes a tort,
Dutch law will also be applied. An example is District Court Arnhem
January 27, 2003, IER 2003/36, *Sporttotalisator v Ladbrokes*, where
Ladbrokes was ordered to stop offering illegal lotteries in The Netherlands
through the internet.

In its Green Paper on Copyright and Related Rights in the Information
Society, the European Commission indicated that on matters relating to the
publication of tortious information on the internet, the law of the "country
of origin" must be applied. This view has not been followed by the Dutch
courts.

---

[26] For an overview of relevant case law, see *http://www.domjur.nl/engine.php?
Cmd=see&P_site=5&P_self=2362&Fresh=1&PSkip=0&PMax=1&Format=domjur%2
Fjurisprudentie.php&Push=652387395&skoop=%28577%2C2108%29.*

6.18 CROSS-BORDER LIABILITY—NEW ZEALAND

6.18.1 Defamation

6-236   Defamation is the branch of law which protects a person's reputation against unjustifiable attack.[27] Under New Zealand law, defamation occurs upon the publication, to one or more people, of an untrue imputation against the reputation of another.

The law of defamation in New Zealand is a combination of statute, under the Defamation Act 1992, and common law.[28] To succeed in an action of defamation, the plaintiff must establish that:

- A defamatory statement was made;
- The statement was about the plaintiff; and
- The statement was published by the defendant.

The legal position in New Zealand concerning defamation on the internet can be understood by considering how the existing law of defamation can be applied to electronic publications. It is unlikely that the internet, as a new medium for publication, will require any extension or modification of defamation law. Instead, the main issue may be considering how traditional elements of defamation will apply to the new technology.

Defamatory statements can be published on the internet in several ways; the most common methods including web pages, email, and news and discussion groups. Some of the most important characteristics of internet publications, as opposed to traditional paper publications, are the potential speed and scope of dissemination. The internet is a tool allowing mass communication, free of any practical geographic limitation, and at practically no cost to publishers.

Few New Zealand cases have considered the publication of defamatory statements on the internet. One of the leading cases so far is the District Court case of *O'Brien v Brown*.[29] That case involved statements published by a member of the Internet Society of New Zealand Incorporated (ISOCNZ) on the ISOCNZ website defaming the then CEO of Domainz, the central domain name registry for the. nz country code. The defendant argued, among other things, that the culture of the internet included the robust exchange of ideas and views, and the promotion of healthy discussion. On this point, the learned judge said[30]:

> "I must say I know of no forum in which an individual citizen has the freedom to say what he likes and in any manner he wishes,

---

[27] John Burrows "Defamation" in Todd et al. (ed). *The Law of Torts in New Zealand* (4th ed., Brookers, Wellington, 2005) 649–742 at 651.

[28] "Defamation" is not defined in any statute.

[29] [2001] D.C.R. 1065.

[30] *ibid.*, para: 32.

about another individual citizen with immunity from suit for all consequences. Merely because the publication is being made to cyberspace does not alter this. I am not aware of any precedent for internet-type material deriving protection from action in the tort of defamation. There can be no question that publication on the internet counts as publication for defamation purposes."

In another New Zealand case,[31] it was held that even a statement in the media—such as an article in a magazine—referring to a website with defamatory content might itself be a publication for the purposes of defamation.

6–237

A more recent New Zealand decision relating to defamation and the internet is the High Court case of *University of Newlands Ltd v Nationwide News Pty Ltd*.[32] Although the proceedings were ultimately dismissed at the interlocutory stage, on appeal, for there being no arguable case, the High Court made findings relating to publication that did not appear to have been disturbed in either the Court of Appeal or the Supreme Court.[33]

The New Zealand company made a claim for defamation against the Australian company, alleging that it was defamed in New Zealand by publication of a statement on an Australian news website accessible in New Zealand. One of the issues considered in the High Court was whether the plaintiff had established that the defendant had done an act in New Zealand. The High Court found that the act of publishing the material took place in New Zealand when it was downloaded in New Zealand from the defendant's website.

The finding in the High Court suggests that, at least for the purposes of New Zealand defamation law, the publication of material on the internet occurs in the place where the information is downloaded. The judge considered that if defendants choose to upload information on the internet, then they assume the associated risks, including the risk of being sued for defamation. The judge also considered that if it were held that publication occurred at the place of uploading, defendants could potentially defame with impunity by uploading information in countries with relaxed, or no, defamation laws.

This finding is consistent with the leading decision of the High Court of Australia in *Dow Jones v Gutnick*,[34] also adopted in the UK in *King v Lewis*.[35]

On appeal to the Court of Appeal, the court considered whether there was an arguable case on the merits. The court considered that whereas publication by mass media generally rendered it unnecessary for a plaintiff to establish publication, the issue of whether the present case naturally fell

6–238

---

[31] *International Telephone Link Pty Ltd v IDG Communications Ltd* (unreported, HC Auckland, CP 344/97, February 20, 1998, Master Kennedy-Grant).
[32] (2004) 17 P.R.N.Z. 206 (HC).
[33] [2006] B.C.L. 203 (CA); (2006) 18 P.R.N.Z. 70 (SC).
[34] [2002] 194 A.L.R. 433.
[35] [2004] EWHC 168 (QB).

within the mass media principle was debatable. The court noted that there was a lack of evidence regarding whether the allegedly defamatory statement had in fact been downloaded in New Zealand, and that further there was a lack of proper evidence as a basis to predicate the likelihood of economic loss. The court concluded that the plaintiffs had not shown the existence of an arguable case and therefore it was not appropriate for the New Zealand courts to assume jurisdiction over the overseas appellant in the particular circumstances of the case. The Court of Appeal decision was upheld in the Supreme Court.

An important issue arises over whether an internet service provider (ISP) can be liable for the publication of defamatory material. Traditionally, anyone who has a role in publishing defamatory material may be liable. There are various ways in which material may be published on the internet and all of the parties who take part in the process of publication of defamatory material on the internet theoretically face potential liability. In practice, however, there will often be a defence available to those who are only secondarily involved as processors and distributors, where they have innocently distributed defamatory material.

Under s.21 of the Defamation Act 1992, the defence of innocent dissemination is available to any person who has published defamatory material solely in the capacity of a processor or distributor, or employee or agent of a processor or distributor. In order to make out the defence, the processor or distributor must have been unaware that the relevant information contained or was likely to contain defamatory material.[36]

In New Zealand, the s.21 defence of innocent dissemination applies only to a "processor" or a "distributor". "Distributor" is not exhaustively defined (it is only defined as including booksellers and librarians). "Processor" is defined in the Act as meaning "a person who prints or reproduces, or plays a role in printing or reproducing, any matter".

In order for a host or owner of a bulletin board or network to be entitled to rely on this defence in New Zealand, it will need to show that it is a "processor" or "distributor" and establish the requisite lack of knowledge and negligence. It is not immediately clear that a host or owner of a bulletin board or network will fall within either of these definitions, although such a defence ought to apply where they acted merely as an innocent conduit for defamatory material.

6–239   However, it is likely that a host or owner of a bulletin board or network that holds itself out as exercising some form of editorial control, or who refuses to remove a defamatory publication after being made aware of its existence, will not be able to benefit from this defence.[37]

A party outside New Zealand may be sued in New Zealand for pub-

---

[36] It is likely that the English case of *Godfrey v Demon Internet Ltd* [1999] 4 All E.R. 342 (no defence of innocent dissemination where there is knowledge of defamatory publication) will be applied in New Zealand. That case was referred to in *O'Brien v Brown* (see fn.29) though the particular issue did not arise there.

[37] For example, see *Godfrey v Demon Internet Ltd* [1999] 4 All E.R. 342, *per* Morland J.

lication of defamatory material within New Zealand.[38] Likewise, a foreign plaintiff cannot be stopped from suing in New Zealand in relation to a publication occurring abroad, provided that the conduct is actionable both here and in the place where it occurred.[39] However, in order to sue in New Zealand, it is necessary for the plaintiff to show damage to his or her reputation in New Zealand. Proceedings issued in New Zealand need to be served on the defendant overseas.

The New Zealand Law Commission, in its report entitled *Electronic Commerce Part Two: A Basic Legal Framework*,[40] recommended that the Defamation Act 1992 be amended to include ISPs in the definition of "distributor" so as to limit the liability of ISPs where they have acted merely as an innocent conduit for defamatory material. These proposed changes have not been implemented at the time of writing.

6.18.2. Content Liability

The Fair Trading Act 1986 regulates conduct and practices by persons in trade in New Zealand, including representations made about products or services. The Fair Trading Act prohibits conduct in trade that is, or is likely to be, misleading or deceptive; it also prohibits making various false and misleading representations in trade.   6–240

The Fair Trading Act's provisions are capable of extending to activities undertaken overseas through the internet. Section 3 of the Fair Trading Act states:

> "This Act extends to the engaging in conduct outside New Zeal-
> and by any person resident or carrying on business in New
> Zealand to the extent that such conduct relates to the supply of
> goods or services, or the granting of interests in land, within New
> Zealand."

It is not settled whether a person who sells goods or services on the internet to New Zealanders is "carrying on business in New Zealand" although it is arguable that a person who advertises in New Zealand through the internet and delivers goods and services to New Zealand does in ordinary usage "carry on business in New Zealand", even if they are not physically present in New Zealand.[41] Misleading information relating to those goods and

---

[38] *Eyre v Nationwide News Pty Ltd* [1967] N.Z.L.R. 851.
[39] *Cooper v Independent News Auckland Ltd* (unreported, DC, Auckland, NP 552/96, April 21, 1997, Judge Joyce Q.C.).
[40] New Zealand Law Commission *Electronic Commerce Part Two: A Basic Legal Framework* (NZLC Report 58, Wellington, 1999).
[41] For example, see *Churchill Group Holdings Ltd v Aral Property Holdings Ltd* [2003] B.C.L. 983.

services could be classified as "conduct relating to the supply of goods or services within New Zealand".[42]

The Fair Trading Act imposes both criminal and civil liability. It is not possible to contractually exclude the liability that a person may face for breaches of the Fair Trading Act.[43] A New Zealand court may therefore apply the Fair Trading Act notwithstanding any disclaimers or disclosures incorporated into, or any express choice of foreign law governing, a website.

The Consumer Guarantees Act 1993 deems certain guarantees to be given where goods or services are supplied to a consumer and provides rights of redress against suppliers, manufacturers and others in respect of any failure by goods or services to comply with those guarantees.

The Consumer Guarantees Act provides that a consumer is a person who acquires from a supplier goods or services of a kind ordinarily acquired for personal, domestic or household use or consumption. The Consumer Guarantees Act is therefore likely to apply to goods or services supplied through the internet, unless the particular securities or services are not of a kind ordinarily acquired for personal, domestic or household use or consumption.

There are limited rights to contract out of the Consumer Guarantees Act. A New Zealand court is likely to apply the Consumer Guarantees Act notwithstanding any disclaimers incorporated into, or any express choice of foreign law governing, a website unless the disclaimers comply with the limited statutory rights to contract out. Conversely, for New Zealand suppliers of overseas consumers, a contractual term providing for the contract of supply to be governed by New Zealand law may be overridden by consumer protection legislation in the consumer's jurisdiction.

It is not settled in New Zealand law whether a website proprietor owes a duty of care, actionable in negligence, if there is a breach in relation to the provision of inaccurate or misleading information over the internet. Parties to a contract may agree that if a duty of care exists between them, the liability of one party to the other may be limited by agreement. In principle therefore, where the website proprietor expressly disclaims liability in the website, it should be difficult to successfully sue the proprietor in negligence.

6.18.3 Copyright infringement

6-241   The Copyright Act 1994 offers protection for original works including: literary, dramatic, musical or artistic works; sound recordings; films; broadcasts; and cable programmes. The works are broadly defined, with computer programs included in the definition of literary work. Copyright

---

[42] Kate Tokeley "Shopping on the Net: Legal Protection for Consumers" (1997) 9(1) *Otago Law Review* 51–70 at 65.
[43] *Smythe v Bayleys Real Estate Ltd* (1993) 5 T.C.L.R. 454 at 472.

does not require registration and will effectively exist from the time the work is recorded, whether this is in writing or otherwise.

Once copyright exists, the owner has exclusive rights in New Zealand to copy the work, issue copies of the work to the public, broadcast the work or make an adaptation of the work.

Many things which reside on the internet could fall within the types of work protected by copyright. The requirement that they be recorded in writing or otherwise could be met by their residing on the internet. As a result, pictures, articles and layouts of home pages are likely to be afforded copyright protection as literary or artistic works (provided that they are also original and of some substance).

Material on a website can also be a cable programme service. The definition of a cable programme service is essentially a service for transmission of images, sound or other information for reception at two or more places, either simultaneously or at different times, in response to requests by different users.

As a restricted act is an act that the owner of copyright has an exclusive right to do in New Zealand, the High Court of New Zealand will only be able to assume jurisdiction if the particular restricted act takes place in New Zealand.

It is unlikely that copyright would reside in an internet address, since small combinations of words are not generally regarded as literary works. For example, earlier cases have held that titles such as "Opportunity Knocks" are either not substantial enough or not sufficiently original to qualify as a copyright work.[44]

The unauthorised uploading of the whole or a substantial part of a copyright work onto a website in New Zealand will constitute infringement. A question of jurisdiction will arise where a copyright work is uploaded to a website overseas. New Zealand courts will likely assume jurisdiction where the defendant is resident in New Zealand and where the infringing material is accessible by a computer in New Zealand.[45]

When a person views a website, a copy of what is viewed is downloaded onto the viewer's computer's RAM. Therefore, it is arguable that viewing this material without permission for possible later use breaches the Copyright Act in New Zealand (unless any of the fair dealing exceptions apply). It is, however, equally arguable that there is an implied licence to make such "copies", as the making of a copy in viewing or holding a transient copy is a necessary part of operating on the internet. To resolve this dispute, it may be necessary for the industry and legislature to formalise acceptance.

On the other hand, the copying of a New Zealand copyright work by viewing it on, or downloading it from, an overseas computer would be outside the scope of the Copyright Act, and not an infringing act in New Zealand.

The question of copyright infringement becomes complicated in relation **6–242**

---

[44] *Green v Broadcasting Corp of New Zealand* [1988] 2 N.Z.L.R. 490.
[45] *New Zealand Post Ltd v Leng* [1998] 3 N.Z.L.R. 219.

to hyperlinking. If an overseas website accessible in New Zealand has a hyperlink to the copyright work on a New Zealand-based site, and that link is unwanted by or undesirable to the copyright owner, the copyright owner may have a cause of action in New Zealand.

If the hyperlink involves the inclusion of a "cable programme" (being the work) in a "cable programme service" provided by the hyperlinker, this also may infringe copyright. Infringement may be found if the hyperlinking is "embedded" and shortcuts the copyright owner's home page or results in the "framing" of the copyright owner's web page.

As the law in this area develops, copyright owners may find they will not be able to prevent hyperlinking under the Copyright Act, except for the more blatant forms that justify a finding of infringement such as embedded links and framing.

Some hyperlinking simply will not amount to an infringing act in breach of the Copyright Act. Further, it may be held in many situations that third parties have an implied licence to link to another website (unless the copyright owner expressly prohibits linking). This may be claimed due to the fact that hyperlinking is arguably an integral part of the internet and has generally been an accepted commercial practice.

Given the rapid changes in digital technology since the Copyright Act came into force, the government recently undertook a review to assess the applicability, adequacy and operation of the Copyright Act in the face of this technological change and the development and adoption of new technologies.

In December 2006, the Copyright (New Technologies and Performers' Rights) Amendment Bill was introduced into Parliament. The Bill seeks to amend the Copyright Act to clarify the application of existing rights and exceptions in a digital environment and to take account of international developments. It also seeks to create a more technology-neutral framework for the Copyright Act. It is not intended to change the balance between protection and access already established in the Copyright Act, but to ensure that the balance continues to operate in the face of new technologies.

The Bill aims to give effect to the government's decisions to:

- Provide a limited exception to the reproduction right for transient copying;
- Amend various matters relating to broadcasting and cable programme services;
- Limit the potential liability of ISPs for certain types of copyright infringement;
- Amend various matters relating to technological protection measures, including the introduction of a new criminal offence for commercial dealing in devices, services, or information designed to circumvent technological protection measures;
- Provide for various matters relating to the protection for electronic rights management information that identifies content protected by copyright and the terms and conditions of use, including the

introduction of a criminal offence for commercial dealing in works where the electronic rights management information has been removed or altered;

- Clarify and amend the exceptions to copyright owners' exclusive rights, particularly in relation to fair dealing, library, archival, and educational use, and time shifting; and
- Introduce new exceptions for format-shifting of sound recordings for private and domestic use, and for decompilation and error correction of software.

6.18.4 Trade mark infringement

Well-established principles relating to infringement embodied in the Trade Marks Act 2002 can be comfortably applied to unauthorised use of marks on the internet, particularly where that use is to advertise and offer goods for sale or to promote and provide certain services.   **6–243**

Infringing activity will, however, require conduct by the infringing party directed at New Zealand internet users. In other words, use of an infringing mark on an overseas registered or hosted website, in relation to a product or service, should be directed towards New Zealanders when they access the site and be likely to cause harm in New Zealand.

This was the approach adopted by the High Court in the *Leng* decision.[46] This case involved the US registered domain name "nzpost.com" and the defendant's website using that domain name. The High Court considered that it had jurisdiction to issue an injunction against the defendant, who was resident in New Zealand, as he had registered a domain name containing New Zealand Post's trade mark which does business in New Zealand.

The *Leng* case was an interlocutory decision and an injunction was granted on the basis of there being an arguable case of passing off and breach of the Fair Trading Act, with the balance of convenience favouring the plaintiff. However, the defendant later consented to a permanent injunction and transfer of the domain name to the plaintiff, so the substantive issues were not taken to trial.

Under the Trade Marks Act, the owner of a registered trade mark has the exclusive right to use the trade mark in relation to the goods or services for which it is registered. The Act only applies to trade marks registered in New Zealand, so this exclusive right is limited to New Zealand.

The exclusive right shall be deemed to be infringed by use by another person of a "sign" (i.e. a trade mark), which is identical or confusingly similar to the trade mark, on or in relation to the goods or services for which the trade mark is registered or "similar" goods or services.   **6–244**

That use by another person would have to take place in New Zealand for

---

[46] *ibid.*

the High Court to hear claims of infringement. This issue of jurisdiction was contemplated by the court in the *Leng* case.

The High Court in the *Leng* case held that it had jurisdiction to hear the passing off and unfair trading claims, as the nature of the medium (the internet) in which the conduct complained of occurs does not alter the nature of the conduct and can still amount to passing off; that despite the defendant's "nzpost.com" domain name being attached to a US host computer, the conduct was directed at New Zealand (as New Zealanders could access the US-based site); and that there was a real likelihood of confusion occurring resulting in harm to New Zealand Post.

Another case in which jurisdiction was considered was *Hirepool Auckland Ltd v Uren*.[47] Here, the plaintiff was successful in obtaining an interim injunction restraining the defendant from using the word "Hirepool" or the domain name "hirepool.com". The High Court held that, although it was not clear that the plaintiff had established a reputation in other jurisdictions, the New Zealand market was encompassed in the broader international market and therefore the plaintiff's New Zealand reputation in its name "Hirepool" was relevant. Additionally, the defendant had not provided sufficient information to establish that "hirepool.com" would be used only outside New Zealand.

Having regard to the decisions in the *Leng* and *Hirepool* cases (despite them not having been trade mark infringement claims), it appears that New Zealand courts will be willing to assume jurisdiction on the basis that the infringing use is directed at New Zealand computers and their users, and that the New Zealand trade mark owner may be harmed by the use.

In a substantive action for trade mark infringement, the court has to be satisfied that the mark (whether a domain name or a trade mark used on the website) is being used "in the course of trade" in relation to the goods or services for which the mark is registered, and that the ability to access the website and view the trade mark on a computer in New Zealand in fact amounts to use of the mark in the course of trade in New Zealand.

6.18.5 Electronic Transactions Act 2002

6–245   The New Zealand legislature has addressed the uncertainty regarding the use of electronic technology in the law by passing legislation that provides that certain paper-based legal requirements may be met by using electronic technology that is functionally equivalent to those legal requirements.

The Electronic Transaction Act 2002 also clarifies the legal effect of information that is in electronic form or that is communicated by electronic means, and the time and place of dispatch and receipt of electronic communications.

---

[47] Unreported, HC Auckland, CP29/00, September 11, 2000, Cartwright J.

6.18.6 Unsolicited Electronic Messages Bill

The Unsolicited Electronic Messages Bill is currently before Parliament, **6–246** having undergone its second reading on December 5, 2006.

The Unsolicited Electronic Messages Bill implements the government's decisions on the regulation of unsolicited electronic messages, commonly known as "spam". The purposes of the Bill are, currently, to:

(a) prohibit unsolicited commercial electronic messages with a New Zealand link from being sent, in order to—

    (i) promote a safer and more secure environment for the use of information and communications technologies in New Zealand; and

    (ii) reduce impediments to the uptake and effective use of information and communications technologies by businesses and the wider community in New Zealand; and

    (iii) reduce the costs to businesses and the wider community that arise from unsolicited commercial electronic messages; and

(b) require commercial electronic messages to include accurate information about the person who authorised the sending of the message and a functional unsubscribe facility in order to enable the recipient to instruct the sender that no further messages are to be sent to the recipient; and

(c) prohibit address-harvesting software or a harvested-address list from being used in connection with sending unsolicited commercial electronic messages in contravention of this Act; and

(d) deter people from using information and communications technologies inappropriately.

The Bill, as currently drafted, provides for a number of matters relating to enforcement, including:

- By an enforcement department: formal warnings, civil infringement notices and enforceable undertakings;
- By the courts: injunctions, pecuniary penalties, compensation, and damages; and
- Provisions relating to search and seizure.

6.19 CROSS-BORDER LIABILITY—SINGAPORE

6.19.1 Jurisdiction

Any matter may be brought before the Singapore courts. Whether or not **6–247** the court would have jurisdiction to hear the matter would be for the parties to present to the court. In any event, the plaintiff must be in a position to serve the writ, summons or motion on the defendant. This is usually possible if the defendant is physically present in Singapore or if the defendant has appointed a local agent to accept service of process. However, in situations where the defendant is located out of jurisdiction, an application would have to be made to the court for service out of jurisdiction. Therefore, even if a website is located out of Singapore, legal process could be commenced in Singapore if there are sufficient interests in Singapore to protect.

6.19.2 Defamation

6–248   A defamatory statement may either be made verbally or in some other recorded form. Such a statement would be one which lowered the target (i.e. the subject of the statement) in the mind of right-thinking members of society. A defamatory statement may either be slanderous or libellous. In the context of websites, blogs, newsgroup postings or just simple email, the cause of action would most probably be libel because such statements may be considered to have been published in recorded form; that is to say, that the statements have been stored in a computer system somewhere in permanent or quasi-permanent form.

One essential element of the tort of defamation is that the allegedly damaging statement must have been published to a third party. If the statement was merely made to, or made known only to, the plaintiff and no other party, the plaintiff would not have been defamed. In the context of the internet, the issue is therefore whether a defamatory statement has been published in the jurisdiction where the action is brought or whether publication per se of the statement in a manner which could be accessed in any part of the world would be sufficient to found a cause of action.

Given that a website could be accessed from any part of the world, action could be brought in Singapore if the plaintiff could show that computer users in Singapore could have access to the statement and that somebody in Singapore had read the damaging statement. This would be so even if the site or blog has been protected by passwords and access to it is restricted.

Alternatively, the plaintiff could show that users in another country have read the statement and that his esteem among the people in that other country has been lowered; the reason why an action was brought in Singapore and not in the other country being left to be argued during any contest as the Singapore court's jurisdiction to hear the matter and/or when there is a question of conflict of laws (cf. Philips v Eyre). In any event, the plaintiff would have to present evidence to show publication and this would normally be in the form of putting a witness on the stand to prove that the defamatory statement has been so published to the witness by the defendant.

With the proliferation of the internet as a forum to communicate or make one's views known, the inherent characteristics of the medium has brought a whole new aspect to ascertaining liability under the law of defamation in

Singapore. The anonymity, or rather perceived anonymity of the internet lulls users into thinking that they can get away with nameless, faceless comments, resulting in people tending to be somewhat less circumspect with their words and opinions expressed.

With the widespread use of electronic personalities and pseudonyms and **6–249** the existence of "anonymous remailer" sites that are able to strip the author's identity from an email or web posting, plaintiffs commonly face problems in finding and proving the identities of authors. The corresponding ease of running a domain name search to conclusively ascertain the identity of the ISP and the deeper pockets such ISPs have (as compared to individual authors) has therefore exposed ISPs to potentially inordinate liability for on-line defamation. ISPs' liability may rest on the supposition that they too were publishers of the damaging statement.

Recent developments have, however, unearthed the fallacy of this reasoning. Individuals who make defamatory remarks over the internet are not protected by their ISPs or forum owners as legal counsels of plaintiffs may obtain court orders obliging these internet intermediaries to reveal the identities of the individuals concerned.

In any case, the current practice of ISPs in Singapore is to expressly incorporate terms of disclosure into contracts between themselves and their customers with the implicit objective of promoting responsible internet usage. With such a framework in place to trace, identify and apprehend the authors of defamatory statements over the internet, it is unlikely that ISPs will end up liable for defamation in Singapore.

Under s.10 of the Electronic Transactions Act (Cap 88), ISPs are protected from all civil and criminal liability under any rule of law in respect of third party material in the form of electronic records to which it merely provided access. This protection extends to liability for the making, publication, dissemination or distribution of such materials and emphasises the reasoning that ISPs typically have little or no editorial control over the data containing the defamatory statements.

Consequentially, it has been suggested that ISPs should be protected to the extent that they have exercised reasonable care in relation to the provision of internet service. ISPs cannot possibly be expected to review and scrutinise every remark posted on the internet and there should, therefore, be no liability unless there is actual knowledge of defamatory material or at least special circumstances that give the ISP reason to be aware of the defamatory material.

In the particular context of internet defamation, the courts do not take a favourable view of attempts by authors to assert their intention to limit circulation of a defamatory email or forum posting to a specific number of recipients or members as it would be naïve for the author to expect the privileged communication clause or restricted nature of the forum to effectively prevent further dissemination when it is clearly foreseeable that such emails and postings are easily and frequently re-published and circulated.[48]

---

[48] *T J Systems (S) Pte Ltd v Ngow Kheong Shen* [2003] S.G.H.C. 73 (*obiter*).

As such, an author of a defamatory statement published on the internet is largely restricted to existing common law defences of libel and slander, such as limitation, unintentional defamation and innocent dissemination, depending on his status (if he was the person who made the statement, or merely the publisher of the statement or had just unintentionally distributed the statement).

6.19.3 Inaccurate information

6–250   An action of the sort contemplated in this question would only arise if the plaintiff had relied on the information provided by the defendant and acted on such statement to the plaintiff's detriment. This sort of action would normally only result if:

>   (a) a contractual relationship between the plaintiff and defendant came about only because of the false statement made by the defendant to the plaintiff (an action for misrepresentation usually claiming avoidance of a contract as a relief); or
>   (b) there is some other relationship between the plaintiff and the defendant which may not amount to a direct contractual relationship but nonetheless, the plaintiff has suffered some damage as a result of the statement made by the defendant (negligent misstatement variety).

In both cases above, it would be necessary to ascertain the nature of the relationship between the parties. It is also understood that publication would have occurred in Singapore even if the website was physically situated outside of Singapore but that the information contained therein was available to the Singapore user.

In the first type of case, there would be the additional need to determine the law governing the contract which had been made between the parties. If the contract was governed by Singapore law, rescission of the contract by reason of misrepresentation would be available. Otherwise, it falls to be determined whether the governing law of the contract allows for rescission in the first place and specifically, rescission by reason of misrepresentation.

In the second type of case, again, it would be necessary to determine where the tort was committed so that the right law might be applied.

6.19.4 Copyright

6–251   In general, the Singapore Copyright Act provides that it would be an infringement of an author's rights if his work was reproduced without permission. There is no statement in the Copyright Act which requires that the reproduction be in more than transient form. The Copyright Act provides that:

(a) software is a type of literary work;

(b) reproduction of a work shall include references to the storage of that work or adaptation thereof in a computer; and

(c) the copyright in the work would be infringed if the work was reproduced without the consent of the copyright owner.

In the light of these provisions, the very act of loading a computer program into the computer's RAM would infringe the copyright in the program since the software has been reproduced in the computer's (transient) RAM memory. However, the Copyright Act provides, at s.39(3) that:

"Notwithstanding section 31, it is not an infringement for the owner of a copy of a computer program or of a compilation within the meaning of section 7A in an electronic form to make or authorise the making of another copy or adaptation of that computer program or compilation provided that such a new copy or adaptation is created as an essential step in the utilisation of the computer program or compilation in conjunction with a machine and that it is used in no other manner."

This section therefore makes it legal for the owner (perhaps the term licensee might be more accurate in most cases) of a computer program to make a transient copy of the computer program if such transient copy is an essential step in the utilisation of the software (it usually is).

However, if the software itself is an infringing copy, the likelihood of this 6–252 exception applying is virtually nil since it would otherwise not make sense. Therefore, if the website contains infringing software, all further copies of that infringing software would not be legitimate copies.

The Copyright Act has undergone several amendments, the latest of which seek to further clarify the existing law with regards to the digital age and the internet.

The Copyright Act provides that incidental copies such as caching do not constitute an infringement of copyright when made for the purpose of allowing a user to view, listen or utilise materials from the internet. However, infringing acts such as the manufacture, distribution or sale of infringing articles have now been extended to apply to non-commercial infringements and situations where there is no distribution or profit motive. There are now criminal penalties (fine or imprisonment) against significant wilful infringement on a commercial scale which has a substantial pre-judicial impact on the copyright owner, regardless of whether the infringement is done in the course of trade.

As such, distribution of infringing articles via the internet and significant infringement by companies using infringing software may now be regarded as criminal offences. It is therefore important for all businesses to put in place policies and processes to ensure that common wilful infringing acts such as the use of unlicensed software are not carried out in their organisations.

In addition, the latest amendments provide legal incentives for ISPs to co-operate with copyright owners in deterring unauthorised storage and transmission of copyright materials. The provisions map out a framework for both sides to work together to ensure a balanced and fair system for all parties alike—ISPs, rights holders and content owners. Under the new regime, copyright owners need only lodge a prescribed notification with the ISPs to remove or disable access to material where the ISP has knowledge of infringement.

In addition, the content provider whose content has been taken down can lodge a counter-notification requesting restoration of the content, unless the one who requested the takedown institutes a civil action against the content provider. Limits are now placed on the liability (for monetary and court ordered relief) of ISPs as long as they comply with a right holder's request to take down infringing material (supported by a Statutory Declaration from the copyright proprietor stating that the web page contains material which infringes his copyright) when notified. The limits on liability are conditional on certain criteria and apply in relation to transmitting, routing or providing connections to on-line material, automatic caching processes, storage of material at the direction of a user, and referring or linking users to on-line locations.

Section 139 of the Copyright Act also provides that it shall be an offence to publish or cause to be published in Singapore an advertisement offering to supply in Singapore infringing copies of computer software even if the publication was made from outside of Singapore. Further, for the purposes of that section, supply shall be deemed to have been made if the transmission of the computer program when received and recorded resulted in the creation of a copy of the computer program. Therefore, if a website contains such infringing programs and the website proprietor knew that the programs contained at the site were infringing software, an offence would have been committed, the only issue being whether the law in Singapore could be effectively enforced against a foreign website proprietor who is out of jurisdiction.

It is worth noting that some software houses have in the past proceeded against bulletin board operators in Singapore under this provision when it was found that infringing software was being up/downloaded onto or from the bulletin board. In principle, there is little to distinguish a website from a bulletin board in this respect.

6.19.5 Trade marks

6–253   The new Trade Marks Act which came into force on January 15, 1999, has undergone extensive revisions since, the latest of which were in July 2005. Under the Trade Marks Act, the following are considered use of a trade mark:

(a) applying the trade mark to goods or the packaging thereof;
(b) offering or exposing goods for sale, putting them on the market or

stocking them for those purposes under the trade mark, or offering or supplying services under the trade mark;

(c) importing or exporting goods under the trade mark;

(d) using the trade mark on an invoice, wine list, catalogue, business letter, business paper, price list or other commercial document; or

(e) using the trade mark in advertising.

Where the owner of a website has offered his goods or services via the web under a trade mark, such use would be considered use in the trade mark sense. Similarly, advertising on the web ought not to be treated differently from other forms of advertising since all the ingredients are present, namely, there is a trade mark, by which the goods or services are distinguished from those offered by other traders and that the mark has been used in the course of trade.

It is therefore thought that an owner of a registered Singapore trade mark may have a cause of action against a trader who utilised a mark that is identical or similar to his registered mark on goods or services for which the mark has been registered when such use is via the World Wide Web.

6.19.6 SPAM measures

Often described as the bane of the 21st century, one of the most significant **6–254** and rampant problems enabled by widespread use of the internet is spam, also known as unsolicited commercial email messages. In recent years, what started as a minor annoyance to internet users has now developed into a major global economic and social problem. According to a recent survey by the Infocomm Development Authority of Singapore (IDA) in 2003, spam accounts for one out of every three emails received in Singapore, costing end-users more than S$20 million a year in lost productivity. Spam clogs the wheels of commerce not only by forcing people to spend precious time deleting junk email, but also using up email box storage quotas and blocking wanted mail from getting through.

Recognising the international dimensions and magnitude of the spam problem, Singapore has stepped up efforts in a bid to do her part to counter the complex and multi-faceted global threat. To this end, IDA has worked closely with key stakeholders to develop a multi-pronged approach to curb email spam in Singapore, comprising of public education, industry self-regulation, proposing appropriate legislation, and international co-operation. This multi-pronged approach represents a concerted effort by both the public and private sectors to stamp out email spam.

Public education

End-user measures are essentially the first and foremost line of defence **6–255** against email spam, especially given the fact that almost 80 per cent of email spam received in Singapore originates from overseas-based sources.

Public education of measures available to end-users to combat email spam is effected through the establishment of a national anti-spam repository website known as the Singapore Anti-Spam Resource Centre (*www.antispam. org.sg*). Together with initiatives by the Consumer Association of Singapore and Singapore Business Federation, they seek to educate the public and business organisations with general information about spam, available resources, anti-spam measures and the proposed legislative framework to curb its proliferation. In addition, IDA and the Singapore Infocomm Technology Federation have also introduced anti-spam initiatives in the form of awareness drives and promotions to increase public awareness of the impact of spam and protection against it. Education on the proper rules of marketing via email and free trials of anti-spam software are just some of the measures offered by these authorities.

Industry self-regulation

6–256   The three major internet service providers (ISPs) in Singapore have jointly established anti-spam guidelines which serve as guiding principles to be adopted jointly by the three ISPs to reduce email spam for their subscribers. Furthermore, the Direct Marketing Association of Singapore has launched an E-Mail Marketing Code of Practice for its members as well as a Consumer Communications Preference Programme allowing users to register their preference not to receive email spam.

Proposed legislation

6–257   IDA and the Attorney-General's Chambers have issued a joint consultation paper on a proposed legislative framework to control email spam in Singapore. The new law seeks to strike a balance between the legitimate commercial interests of businesses using emails to conduct their advertising and the interests of email users not to be deluged with unwanted email solicitations. Apart from clarifying the rules applicable to local marketers and prescribing civil offences for those who fail to comply, the proposed legislation seeks to give ISPs, which are the main victims of spam and in the best position to enforce the law, a right of legal recourse against spammers even in the absence of any existing contractual relationship between the parties.

This would be a significant advancement in the law, as spamming per se is not actionable under current laws, which also do not provide for recovery of pure economic loss which is not directly connected to physical damage. The consultation paper discussed at some length the following points:

(i)   Any proposed spam control legislation only applies to spamming activities carried out in Singapore, enabling legal action to be taken against spammers (both individuals and the businesses commissioning the spamming activities) based in Singapore, whether they send spam to local or foreign mail servers.

Whilst it is widely recognised that the preponderance of spam in

Singapore originates overseas where enforcement of any Singapore legislation would be difficult if not impossible, it is submitted that such measures would at least minimise the risk of Singapore being used as a base for spamming activities. As with every global crisis, it is up to each country to initiate its own territorial laws to curb the problem—if other countries were to institute similar spam control legislation, spamming activities would inevitably be significantly impeded worldwide.

The proposed legislation with limited extra-territorial application therefore represents a step forward for Singapore, putting her in a ready position to co-operate with other like-minded countries in presenting a united international front against spam.

(ii) Unsolicited commercial email must comply with the minimum standards of an opt-out regime. This scheme seeks to legitimise unsolicited commercial email by prescribing certain minimum requirements, such as:

1. the inclusion of a valid return email address to which the recipient may send an opt-out request, or an internet location address at which the recipient may effect the opt-out request;

2. instructions for opting-out of future unsolicited commercial email must be clearly provided in the internationally-recognised English language;

3. the opt-out mechanism must be genuine and functional, and not a deceitful facility used by the spammer to confirm the validity and "live" status of email addresses;

4. opt-out requests must be honoured within a specified time frame, and the sender is not to transfer the recipient's email address to other parties, enabling them to send unsolicited commercial email; and

5. labelling requirements, requiring that the subject title of unsolicited commercial email messages be accurately indicated and contain the characters [ADV] such that recipients are not misled as to their content; email messages should also contain genuine originating email addresses and valid postal addresses.

(iii) Where it is established that spam was sent "blindly" through the use of a dictionary attack or automated spamming tool, ISPs will be allowed to commence legal action against the spammer without having to prove that the unsolicited commercial emails fail to comply with the above-mentioned minimum requirements. Apart from damages for economic loss, courts will also be empowered to grant statutory damages, costs and expenses, and injunctions in favour of the ISPs.

As the concept at the heart of the spam control regime, the opt-out model is **6–258** not without its detractors. Rather than permitting senders to distribute unsolicited commercial email until they are asked by recipients to stop doing so, an opt-in regime forbids senders from sending any such unsolicited commercial email until such time that the recipient indicates that he is willing to receive them.

While there is no doubt that the opt-out regime is more business friendly, many have criticised it as too easily hijacked by unscrupulous spammers who abuse such a system by using it as a means to detect active email addresses so that even more unsolicited emails can be sent to those addresses, thereby encouraging the proliferation of spam. On the other hand, while an opt-in regime threatens to make it more difficult for new and innovative businesses to break into the market and compete, the reality is that it does not completely eradicate the problem of unwanted commercial email as businesses are still entitled to send opt-in marketing emails enticing consumers to consent to receiving further commercial emails from them.

In the delicate balance between arguments for and against both regimes, the key factor that appears to tilt the balance in favour of an opt-out regime in Singapore is the fact that a significant majority of spam originates from foreign sources, especially from jurisdictions that either have an opt-out regime or no spam control legislation at all. Given the worldwide nature of this problem, it would simply be more practical to control spam by prescribing the basic regulation requiring that all requests to opt-out of mailing lists are honoured.

This arguably strikes the most practical compromise in that businesses are not unduly precluded from using the internet as a medium through which commercial advertisements may be circulated via email, but at the same time providing consumers—even those residing in jurisdictions adhering to the opt-in regime—sufficient protection by ensuring that any requests to stop receiving such commercial emails will be respected.

International co-operation

6–259   In the final analysis, all of the above-mentioned measures will only be as effective as the resolve of other countries around the world to control spam. Singapore recognises this inherent limitation and the reality that no single country can fight this global battle alone. To this end, the IDA has participated in the "Operation Secure Your Server" campaign organised by the US Federal Trade Commission, encouraging worldwide organisations to protect their servers and computer systems from misuse. In addition, Singapore actively participates in initiatives and forums with other countries and international organisations to do its part in addressing the spam problem.

It is still too early to predict the success of Singapore's multi-pronged approach, but it is hoped that it at least represents a concerted effort by the government, industries, public, and the internet community, sending a clear signal that Singapore is prepared to fulfil her responsibility firstly by eradicating spam originating within her borders, before aiding other countries to do likewise. Only when every country does its individual part to internally control spam in its own jurisdiction can the spam problem truly be collectively eliminated on a global scale.

6.19.7 Territory disclaimers

It is questionable if such restrictions would be completely effective in shielding the website owner from liability. Unless technical measures are put in place to bar any Singapore user from having access to the web, Singapore users would be able to receive information from that site unimpeded regardless of the (legal) restrictions imposed by the website owner. However, if litigation was to ensue, the restrictions might operate to lessen culpability or as mitigating factors. **6–260**

6.19.8 General

The Singapore Media Development Authority (MDA) has established an internet regulatory framework to promote and facilitate the growth of the internet. By adopting a balanced and light-touch approach, MDA ensures minimum standards are set to promote the responsible use of the internet. The MDA also receives feedback from the National Internet Advisory Committee (NIAC) in formulating its policies governing the regulation and development of the internet industry. **6–261**

MDA recognises that there are inherent limits to the efficacy of domestic legislation in regulating a global and borderless medium like the internet. MDA therefore adopts a three-pronged approach comprising joint government and industry initiatives as well as public involvement to encourage a balanced and judicious approach to the use of the internet. The approach comprises the following aspects.

Regulatory framework

All internet access service providers, localised and non-localised internet service resellers providing computer on-line service; political parties registered in Singapore providing any content on the World Wide Web through the internet; individuals, groups, organisations and corporations engaged in providing any programme for the propagation, promotion or discussion of political or religious issues relating to Singapore on the World Wide Web through the internet; and internet content providers who are in the business of providing through the internet an on-line newspaper for a subscription fee, or other consideration, are required to register for an Internet Class Licence. **6–262**

Under the Class Licence Scheme instituted by virtue of the Broadcasting (Class Licence) Notification 2001, internet content providers and ISPs are deemed automatically licensed and are required to observe and comply with the Class Licence Conditions and the Internet Code of Practice, which stipulates what is considered offensive or harmful to Singapore's racial and religious harmony.

The Internet Code of Practice require ISPs to refrain from subscribing to internet newsgroups containing prohibited material, deny access to contributions to forums hosted on its service containing prohibited material and block access to sites which contain prohibited material. Prohibited material is material that is objectionable on the grounds of public interest, public morality, public order, public security, national harmony or otherwise prohibited by the laws of Singapore, and generally includes pornography and material which glorifies, incites, promotes, endorses or otherwise provokes racial or religious hatred, intolerance or strife. While MDA does not specify the means which must be employed to block access to these sites, the service providers here have used proxy servers to achieve this objective.

Industry self-regulation

6–263 MDA encourages content providers in Singapore to label their sites and to develop Industry Codes of Practice which can be used to promote greater industry self-regulation and complement existing internet content regulations. By enabling the industry to proactively set its own standards, MDA seeks to ensure a high level of credibility and quality for internet services, cultivating greater confidence in and encouraging wider use of the internet in Singapore.

Public education

6–264 MDA also seeks to promote on-line safety awareness by educating the public on the advantageous as well as the dangerous aspects of use of the internet. The Parents Advisory Group for the internet (PAGi) aims to develop and sustain a long-term programme to educate the public on their role in teaching those in their care to be more discerning and responsible when using the internet. MDA also supports initiatives to provide parents with tools such as the Family Access Networks that help them better manage their children's use of the internet.

6.20 CROSS-BORDER LIABILITY—SPAIN

6.20.1 Criteria followed by the Spanish courts

6–265 The criteria for international jurisdiction, applicable where a defendant is not domiciled in a Member State (Art.4.1 of EU Council Regulation 44/2001) are regulated in Spanish law in Art.21 *et seq.* of the Organic Act of the Judiciary Branch (Ley Orgánica del Poder Judicial, Spanish acronym

"LOPJ"). More specifically, the general rule of choice of law is established in Art.21, whereby:

> "Spanish Courts and Tribunals shall hear proceedings instituted in Spanish territory between Spanish nationals, between foreigners and between Spanish nationals and foreigners pursuant to the provisions of this Act and the Treaties and international conventions to which Spain may be a signatory."

In turn, Art.22, LOPJ determines the choice of law criteria in relative matters, for instance, in contractual obligations, extra-contractual obligations, or consumer agreements. Thus, on the issue of contractual obligations, Art.22–3 establishes that the Spanish courts and tribunals shall have jurisdiction to hear these cases where said obligations have arisen or must be fulfilled in Spain.

On the issue of extra-contractual obligations, such as infringement on intellectual property rights, jurisdiction shall depend on whether the fact from which the extra-contractual obligation derives has occurred in Spanish territory or not (*lex loci delicti*) or whether the party causing the damage or the victim have their usual habitual common residence in Spain or not.

Also, in the criminal field, Art.23, LOPJ establishes that Spanish courts and tribunals shall have jurisdiction when felonies or misdemeanors have been committed in Spanish territory.

As can be inferred from the foregoing, the Spanish legislator wanted to determine the jurisdiction of the Spanish courts and tribunals based on the principle of territoriality. However, this principle which impregnates different Spanish jurisdictional hierarchies collides frontally with the characteristics of the internet, among which are its lack of territoriality or international and decentralised nature.

Not many decisions have been entered in Spain up to date on the issue of **6–266** infringement of rights via the internet. However, from the decisions issued until now, as well as from the principles set forth in Act 34/2002, on Information Society Services and Electronic Commerce, we can extract the following criteria:

Ties with Spain. The main factor which Spanish courts and tribunals consider when assuming jurisdiction to hear a proceeding concerning the internet are the ties that said proceedings may have with Spain. Thus, insofar as the internet website by means of which the infringement is taking place is available in Spanish, that the server where the infringing contents are hosted is located in Spanish territory or that the process of uploading the information on-line has been carried out in Spain, it is probable that the Spanish courts and tribunals will declare that they have jurisdiction to hear the case submitted before them.

However, not all the elements concerning ties with Spain need to be met. Thus, it is possible for the website through which said trade mark rights are being infringed to be hosted in a foreign server, or for the person responsible for the contents to also be a foreigner.

An example of the foregoing is the case *"elvinoyeljamon.com"*, decided by the Criminal Court of Barcelona in its Order of May 5, 2003 (ARP 2003\430). In this case, the defendant had created two websites through which they provided means to suppress or neutralise the technical measures used to protect computer software and other works. The said websites had been created in Spain by Spanish nationals. The introduction, management and administration of unlawful contents was also carried out from Spain, more specifically from Madrid. However, the authors of said pages had subsequently moved abroad to continue developing their activities through a free server named "Isla Tortuga" (Turtle Island) in the US.

Given that the proceeding was instituted before the Criminal Court of Barcelona, the defendants alleged that this court did not have jurisdiction neither based on the activity theory (the facts had been initiated in Madrid, not in Barcelona), nor based on the result theory (the infringement had been consummated in the United States of America, and not in Spain). However, the Court of Barcelona considered that it had jurisdiction to hear these facts, and, to support its decision, it argued as follows:

> "there is no doubt that the following data and circumstances shall be taken into account (...) Defendants are Spanish nationals, and the evidence of the purported crime prepared by them have also been found in national territory; Defendant's main clients are also Spaniards, and therefore the purported crimes committed by them have full effect in national territory; likewise, the crime was discovered in Spain, place where, as mentioned earlier, it has full effect and causes harm".

6–267   The *"GEOCITIES"* case follows a similar line. In this case, the facts denounced consisted of the publication and distribution online, more specifically through the address "geocities.com/gasolus", of the literary works of a Spanish author, the publication rights of whom had been assigned to the Spanish publisher Editorial Planeta, SA. The user "gasolus", creator of the website *http://geocities.yahoo.com/gasolus* belonged to Yahoo!, US.

The judge who tried the case in the District Court considered that the conduct had to be understood as carried out in the US—since it was there where the domain name through which a number of persons could access the works included at said address could be found—and that the uploading carried out by the owner of the domain name from Spain was merely a preparatory act.

However, the Provincial Court of Barcelona, through its decision of April 25, 2002 (ARP 2002\484) held that said uploading acts could not be deemed as unpunished preparatory acts since they also jeopardised the protected copyrights, as the intervention of the charged party allowed the protected works to be stored in a server to which a plurality of persons had access. Consequently, the Provincial Court of Barcelona held that Spanish courts had jurisdiction as the first act infringing on the protected works had been carried out in Spain.

From the foregoing we can, therefore, infer that the courts take into account the criterion of having ties with Spain—however weak they may be—to declare whether they have jurisdiction or not to hear internet related matters.

6.20.2 Conditions for liability of information society service providers

On occasion the actions for on-line infringement of third party rights are brought against information society providers as opposed against those who have actually carried out said infringement given the difficulties involved in their identification. **6–268**

Act 34/2002, on Information Society Services and Electronic Commerce establishes the requisites that must be met in order for a service provider to be held liable for the unlawful actions carried out by a third party.

Generally speaking, a service provider shall not be liable if:

— he does not have actual knowledge of the actions carried out through the server or the contents stored therein;
— being aware of the unlawful character of the conduct or contents, he acts diligently to procure the cessation thereof or the withdrawal or the contents.

In this regard, the service provider is deemed to have actual knowledge of the unlawful action if a competent administrative or judicial body has declared the unlawfulness of the conduct or issued an injunction, and the service provider was aware of this holding.

There are cases where the actual knowledge of the illegality is presumed. An example is the case *"PUTASGAE.ORG"* (Provincial Court of Madrid, February 6, 2006; AC 2006\188).

In this case, the defendant owned a website and an internet server, through which the website "putasgae.org" could be accessed; this site included offensive content which violated the honour of the plaintiff, the management entity Sociedad General de Autores y Editores (General Society of Authors and Editors—Spanish acronym "SGAE").

Given that said page "putasgae.org" was owned by a third party, and that the defendant had only acted as the intermediary of such third party, the defendant raised the argument that it had only acted as a "mirror" of the contents prepared by the owner of the domain name, and that it had only made in Spain an internet server available for others to post their own contents, opinions and information (hosting agreement), without any possibility to exercise any control thereon. The defendant further argued that the theory of the "neutral report" had to be applied.

None of these arguments were admitted by the District Court or by the Higher Court, which affirmed that the defendant could not be discharged from liability on the basis that it had no control on the information, and that the theory of the neutral report was not applicable since the defamatory nature resulting from the domain name itself could not be ignored.

In the more recent judgment of December 20, 2005 (AC 2006\233) the Higher Court of Madrid declared, more favorably to internet traffic, that the defendant service provider was not bound to withdraw or prevent access to those contents hosted in its server which may violate the plaintiff's honour rights, since this would be tantamount to forcing it to become a censoring body. Thus, the High Court considered that the service provider had acted diligently as, when required by the plaintiff to withdraw the unlawful contents, it immediately notified the owner of said contents, even when they were not withdrawn.

In conclusion, cross-border liability issues in Spain are in an incipient state. Thus, the decisions of the courts do not yet apply uniform criteria concerning the liability of service providers or when Spanish courts are the jurisdiction to hear such cases. In any event, the lack of precedents shows the reluctance of Spanish courts to assume an expansive interpretation of the jurisdiction on this issue.

6.21 CROSS-BORDER LIABILITY—SWEDEN

6–269　Swedish laws on jurisdiction and choice of law are often very old and based on geographical/territorial/connection and not yet fully adapted to the internet. However, they are existing law and must therefore be applied.

6.21.1 General principles of penal jurisdiction

6–270　Swedish law is naturally applicable in respect of crimes committed in Sweden. According to the Swedish Penal Code, a crime is considered to have been committed both where the criminal act *occurred* as well as where the crime was *completed* (i.e. where the criminal "effect" occurred).

This means, for example, that if someone in Sweden makes a defamatory statement about someone in France, or if a person from England illegally intrudes into a computer in Sweden, both situations may be punished in Sweden according to Swedish law. The foregoing shall also apply when it is uncertain where the crime was committed but grounds exist for assuming that it was committed within Sweden. Furthermore, the same provision provides that an attempt to commit a crime is committed either where the act of attempt was committed or where the crime would have been completed.

As for crimes committed outside Sweden, the Swedish Penal Code establishes jurisdiction for Swedish courts according to the personality principal which states that Swedish courts have jurisdiction and that Swedish law shall apply if the crime was committed by (i) a Swedish citizen or a foreigner who is domiciled in Sweden, (ii) a foreigner not domiciled in Sweden, but who has become a Swedish citizen or has become domiciled in Sweden after the crime was committed or who is a Danish, Finnish, Icelandic or Norwegian citizen who is present in Sweden, or (iii) any other foreigner who is within Swedish territory and the crime in question is punishable according to Swedish law by imprisonment for more than six months and the crime was equally punishable in the country where the crime was committed.

6.21.2 General principles of civil jurisdiction

The main bodies for establishing jurisdiction in Europe are the Brussels and Lugano Conventions, and the Brussels I and II Regulations. These documents are implemented in Sweden and are therefore applicable if the parties to the conflict are domiciled in the EU or the EES. The Brussels Convention has been replaced by the Brussels I Regulation, but the Convention is still applicable in cases that have been brought before a court before March 1, 2002. The Convention is also applicable to the Member States that have ratified the Convention but have not ratified the Brussels I Regulation.   6–271

The general rule of the Conventions and the Brussels I Regulation is that a defendant shall be sued in the Contracting State where he is domiciled. Special grounds for jurisdiction are applicable alternatively with the general rule. Furthermore, in contractual matters, a person domiciled in a Contracting State may be sued in Sweden if the place of performance of the obligations in question is within Sweden.

However, matters of tort, delict and quasi-delict are outside the scope of the Brussels Regulation. (Non contractual obligations are dealt with in the forthcoming EU Rome II Regulation.) At the time of writing, Swedish courts accept jurisdiction if the act or harmful event occurred in Sweden or if the matter regards a crime and Swedish courts have assumed jurisdiction over the accused

It should also be noted that besides the aforementioned conventions and regulations there are further specific EC and domestic legislation concerning certain branches of jurisprudence which are not dealt within this context.

Sweden—as well as most other countries—faces problems when it comes to applying its traditional approaches to the internet realities. Difficulties appear when assessing where (and when) an act has been "committed", where and when a contractual obligation has been "performed". Regarding e-commerce activities in the EU, the creation of the "co-ordinated field" (providing for the use of the "country of origin" principle concerning regulatory matters) resolves some of these issues, but since there is no such understanding with a global reach, the difficulties will continue for the foreseeable future. Also, it remains to be seen if courts will rely on the mere accessibility in Sweden of a particular website as sufficient basis for accepting jurisdiction.

Concerning jurisdiction over civil matters regarding a defendant domiciled in a Non-Contracting State (i.e. outside the EU or the EES) the courts apply by analogy the venue rules of the Swedish Code of Judicial Procedure. For example, the venue rule establishing that a tort claim may be heard in the court of the judicial district within which a tortuous act or injury has occurred (*forum delicti*) will support Swedish jurisdiction over the claim, if there is a Swedish court competent to hear the case under that rule.

Such analogous application is based on the premise that if a dispute is so closely connected to the judicial district of a given Swedish court as to render that court competent under existing venue rules, then the dispute is likely to have as sufficiently close connection to Sweden as to justify Swedish jurisdiction in that matter.

Venue rules will not however form the basis of jurisdiction where this would cause unreasonable results in cases of an international character. On the other hand, even where the venue rules do not indicate any particular judicial district, the courts have displayed a willingness to find jurisdiction where the case in question has had a sufficiently close and relevant connection to Sweden.

It should be noted that certain Swedish venue rules may provide for Swedish jurisdiction in cases not recognised within the framework of Lugano/Brussels. For example, a claimant may bring an action concerning debt obligations at the place where the property belonging to the defendant is located. There is also a special venue rule according to which a Swedish court would have jurisdiction if the dispute concerns a dispute over property and the property which the dispute concerns is situated in Sweden.

6–272 A legal entity may be sued in Sweden if it has sufficient connection to Sweden. A legal entity may for example be sued in Sweden if it is registered there and/or if its board has its permanent seat there. Where a legal entity lacks a permanent seat for its board or where there is no such board, suit may still be brought in Sweden if the legal entity carries out its administration there. Where the Lugano/Brussels framework is not applicable, a Swedish court could also have jurisdiction under certain Swedish venue rules, see examples above.

Swedish courts will, as a rule, hear a case when the defendant appears in the proceedings without raising any objection to jurisdiction. But neither a silent appearance nor an agreement between the parties is necessarily sufficient to establish jurisdiction if the case lacks any connection to Sweden.

6.21.3 Server location

6–273 In Sweden it has been a widespread opinion that the geographical location of a server should be of significant importance to issues of jurisdiction and choice of law. Today it is quite clear that such an opinion is wrong, which, inter alia, follows from the above-mentioned general principles. Instead, it is of importance where certain kinds of actions occur or are completed, where the parties are domiciled or where the place of performance of contractual obligations is carried out.

This is not to say that the location of the server is of no interest. Its location may, together with other circumstances, contribute to establish enough connection to Sweden in order for Swedish courts to assume jurisdiction. However, the location of the server is in itself very seldom decisive and the fact that a server is located in, for example, the USA may not stop Swedish courts from assuming Swedish jurisdiction and applying Swedish law in relation to any act on the internet that has a relevant connection to Sweden. However, there is substantial uncertainty due to lack of precedents. It is not likely that the courts will rely on the "effects principle" in all situations.

6.21.4 Defamation

If a person makes a defamatory statement regarding another person; the crime is completed and thus committed when the statement reaches a third party. As mentioned above, if a crime is completed in Sweden, the Swedish Penal Code would apply and Swedish courts would have jurisdiction. If a defamatory (criminal) statement is made on an overseas website and the statement (crime) is considered to have been committed in Sweden (by reaching a third party), Swedish courts would have jurisdiction.   **6–274**

The mere fact that someone posts a defamatory statement on a website and that the statement thereafter is read by someone in Sweden is however, not necessarily sufficient to establish Swedish jurisdiction. It normally requires a more obvious connection to Sweden, such as that the perpetrator (sender) has knowledge of the fact that the website is directed towards Sweden and that he has an intention to cause the victim harm in Sweden or that the perpetrator and/or the victim are Swedish citizens and/or domiciled in Sweden.

A Swedish Court of Appeal has sentenced a person for grave defamation when an obscene personal ad in the perpetrator's former girlfriend's name was posted by him on an overseas Bulletin Board System (BBS). The ad, which was written in English, led to the former girlfriend receiving offensive telephone calls and email messages. The court's decision to assume jurisdiction and apply Swedish law was based on several circumstances such as the fact that the victim, as well as the perpetrator, were Swedish citizens domiciled in Sweden and that the posting of the ad and the effect thereof took place in Sweden.

6.21.5 Content liability

In content liability matters, Swedish courts may assume jurisdiction based on the above-mentioned general principles. Since the internet reflects a very large number of different cultures, values and legal systems, a strict appli-   **6–275** cation of Swedish general principles of penal and civil jurisdiction would lead to an unreasonable number of cases were Swedish courts should or could interfere. In order for the Swedish legal system to work efficiently and maintain its international reputation it is required that it limits the reach of the Swedish legal system to situations that have a direct connection to Sweden and Swedish interest.

This means that the Swedish legal system in general accepts websites that are legal according to their "home country", provided that the content of such websites is not directly intended for the Swedish market or otherwise directed towards Sweden. By home country it means the country where the person/entity that has the factual control over the content of the web page is domiciled. If, however, an overseas web page is directed towards Sweden, its content also needs to be in accordance with Swedish law.

6.21.6 Copyright law generally

6-276 Most countries of some importance to international trade and international relations, including Sweden, have adopted international conventions on copyright regulations, such as the Bern Convention (1886) and the World Convention (1952), the TRIPS agreement, and the WIPO copyright Treaty (1996). This means that copyright legislation in most democratic states is very similar and that foreign copyright protected work often has the same protection as Swedish work. The aforementioned Conventions imply that Sweden shall provide the same protection for foreign works as it provides to domestic works.

The Conventions do not directly treat issues on how cross border use of copyright protected work shall be dealt with. They assume that protection is available for the use of a copyright work in a given territory. In the internet world, it can be expected that a closer determination of when and where the "use" of the work occurs, will be required. However, matters dealing with jurisdiction and choice of law still have to be dealt with in accordance with the above-mentioned general principles. When it comes to infringement and considering the significant similarities between the major legal systems, choice of law matters is often of minor interest. The same applies to jurisdiction. Therefore, it is normally recommended to initiate legal action in the jurisdiction of the defendant or where the infringement occurs in order to avoid any problems with enforcement.

6.21.7 Copyright infringement

6-277 Only the creator of a work may reproduce the work and make it available in public. When someone else makes a copyright protected work available to the public, without the consent of the creator, he violates the exclusive right for the creator which would most certainly qualify as a copyright infringement. Intentional or grossly negligent copyright infringement is penalised and may result in imprisonment for up to two years.

The same copyright laws apply to the internet as to any other media in society. When a work has been published it is normally permissible to make copies of the work for private use. Naturally a person is allowed to surf the internet and to view pictures, read text, look at films or listen to music, etc. However, it cannot be taken for granted that the person is allowed to store the copyright protected work in question on a computer (at least not the server of your employer) or to take a printout copy of the work.

Any such use (reproduction) is dependent on (i) the limits of private use, and (ii) what it reasonably can be taken for granted that the copyright owner has consented to by making the work available on the internet. Private use is normally defined as use within close family and a small circle of friends. To upload protected work to a BBS or website is not considered to be private use.

Amendments to the Swedish Copyright Act which entered into force July 1, 2005, have narrowed the expression "Private use" further. The numbers of copies allowed to be reproduced has been reduced (it has been made clear that only one or a very few copies are allowed), the possibility to make a copy of a whole book has been strongly diminished and it has also been made clear that a work which is reproduced for private use must have been legally published with the right holders' consent in the first place for the private use exception to apply (there previously having been an ongoing debate in Sweden whether this had to be the case).

The exception for private use does not cover computer programs or digital databases.

6.21.8 Trade mark infringement

Trade marks can be protected by registration at the Swedish Patent and Registration Office or by established knowledge of the trade mark by working up the recognition of it.   6–278

Trade marks that are protected by registration in Sweden must be renewed every 10 years to remain in effect. Unlike other industrial and intellectual property rights, the basic rule regarding the durability of protection is that trade marks in principle can last forever. Intentional or gross negligent trade mark infringement is penalised and may result in imprisonment for up to two years.

As is the case with copyright legislation, Swedish trade mark legislation is based on international conventions and therefore bears many similarities with trade mark legislation in most western countries. It should however be kept in mind that a trade mark protected in Sweden—through registration or use—only receives such protection nationally, i.e. within Sweden.

Generally, Swedish courts would have jurisdiction in a trade mark infringement case concerning a Swedish trade mark and Swedish law could be applied if (i) the trade mark in question is protected in Sweden, and (ii) the infringement is occurring in Sweden. Thus, if someone is displaying a trade mark on an overseas website and such display could be a possible infringement of a trade mark protected in Sweden, the main question would be to decide if the infringement is occurring in Sweden.

Facts supporting that the website is "used" in or directed at Sweden, and that a possible infringement therefore is occurring in Sweden, could be that it is in Swedish or deals with information, products or advertising of specific interest to people within Sweden or that it states prices in Swedish currency or otherwise makes references that could be considered connected to Sweden.

A notice on a website stating that the site is not intended to be read in Sweden does not automatically mean that any facts supporting a connection between the site and Sweden are of no importance. In fact, such notice would probably only be of significance if there are no other, or only very weak, connections to Sweden.

The use of trade marks through links to foreign websites has been considered in a recent judgment by a Swedish Court of Appeal (the judgement was, however, later overturned by the Swedish Supreme Court which judged the case on formal grounds and therefore never got into the statements that were put forward by the Court of Appeal). A Swedish company had put links on its website to foreign websites belonging to companies that were not under the control of the Swedish company but was part of the same company group as the Swedish company. On the foreign companies' websites a trade mark registered in Sweden had been used without approval from the registered holder in Sweden since these were considered not to be directed towards the Swedish market.

The court however considered the action by the Swedish company, to put a link on its website, to be use of the claimant's trade mark in Sweden and create a responsibility for such use, and thus claimed jurisdiction.

6.22 SWITZERLAND

6.22.1 International jurisdiction of Swiss courts—general comments

6–279   Swiss courts generally only have jurisdiction if there is an adequate connection with Switzerland in the facts of the case. A connection of this kind could, for instance, exist if a certain action is performed in Switzerland, or the effect of a particular course of conduct takes place in Switzerland, or effects are identifiable on the Swiss market, or if the habitual residence of the injured party is Switzerland.

The criteria according to which jurisdiction is determined in each individual case are governed by the type of subject-matter involved in the case. For criminal law, the law of civil torts, unfair competition law and in the case of infringements of trade marks and copyrights, similar but not entirely identical principles apply where international jurisdiction is concerned.

However, generally speaking it can be said that the simple fact that the owner of a website and the server on which this is maintained are located in a foreign country does not in itself mean that the jurisdiction of the Swiss courts is excluded.

The fundamental principles for determining international jurisdiction of Swiss courts are regulated by law. This means that the courts do not have the option of refusing the jurisdiction which is determined by legal principles because they are of the opinion that, in a specific individual case, Swiss jurisdiction would not be appropriate. Swiss law does not recognise the doctrine of *forum non conveniens*.

However, as the internet is creating new sets of circumstances and as yet no fixed judicial practice exists for interpreting legal provisions relating to international jurisdiction in connection with the internet, the courts currently still have a great amount of flexibility in judging whether they should deem the legally defined criteria for international jurisdiction in a specific case to have been fulfilled or not.

6.22.2 Defamation

Under Swiss law, defamatory statements may be of legal relevance from three points of view. Defamation is a criminal offence. At the same time, defamation is also a civil law offence in relation to which the defamed person may apply for an injunction or enforce claims for redress and compensation. Finally, in the case of defamatory or disparaging statements against business companies, there is also an infringement of the Law against Unfair Competition.   6–280

Different principles apply in determining the jurisdiction of the Swiss courts in the case of a defamatory website, depending on whether it is judged from the point of view of the criminal law, the law of civil torts or the law against unfair competition.

Criminal law

The Swiss criminal courts have jurisdiction if the criminal act is committed in Switzerland or if the effect of a criminal act takes place in Switzerland. In the case of websites with defamatory content located on servers in a foreign country, the relevant actions usually are committed in that foreign country. There is an exception to this, of course, in cases where the content is uploaded from Switzerland onto a server in a foreign country.   6–281

Thus, generally speaking, where websites on foreign servers are concerned, it is a question of determining whether any effect of a defamatory action took place in Switzerland. The effect of defamatory statements is considered to be the cognisance thereof by the defamed party itself or by a third party. In the case of websites with defamatory content, therefore,

Swiss jurisdiction will, in principle, always exist, as websites are accessible all over the world from Switzerland, and note can be taken of their content.

However, in the case of websites which are produced in a language which is not usual in Switzerland (e.g. Chinese) and which contain defamatory material directed against persons who are completely unknown in Switzerland, it cannot be said that any effect has actually taken place in Switzerland. It can therefore be assumed that the Swiss criminal courts would not have jurisdiction in these circumstances.

On the other hand, it is of no help to a website operator to include a notice stating that its website is not directed at internet users in Switzerland if it contains defamatory material directed against persons who are well-known in Switzerland, such as internationally famous politicians, artists, entrepreneurs, etc., even if these individuals are not themselves domiciled in Switzerland.

The principles set out above regarding the effect of defamatory actions in Switzerland are also relevant if the content is uploaded by a perpetrator in a foreign country onto a server located in Switzerland. However, a recent decision handed down by the Swiss Federal Court has resulted in some confusion in this respect. In the case in point, the court assumed that a perpetrator supplying pornographic material by email to a recipient in Switzerland produces a copy of the material in question in the place where it is received and therefore carries out an action in Switzerland.

This decision has been criticised by various commentators. But if the Supreme Court adheres to its view, then Swiss penal jurisdiction would possibly also have to be affirmed when defamatory content is uploaded from a foreign country onto a server located in Switzerland because the perpetrator in Switzerland produces a copy of the content and is thus taking action in Switzerland. It would then no longer be of relevance whether or not the defamatory content in question has a relevant effect in Switzerland. It remains to be seen how the courts will decide in such cases in future.

The law of civil torts

6–282   Defamatory and slanderous statements constitute a violation of the personality of the person concerned and thus a civil tort. In the case of civil torts, even if the violating party is not domiciled in Switzerland and has acted outside Switzerland, international jurisdiction will lie in Switzerland provided that the effect took place in Switzerland. Thus, similar principles apply as in the case of international jurisdiction in relation to criminal offences. Swiss courts will have jurisdiction if either the place where the act occurs or the place of effect is located in Switzerland.

In Switzerland a defamed person may therefore take action against the operator of a foreign website which contains defamatory material. The action instigated may seek redress (e.g. publication of a correction of false statements), an injunction, and the reimbursement of possible losses incurred.

Even if, according to the principles mentioned, it is found that international jurisdiction for a claim exists in Switzerland, the question of whether a Swiss judgment can be enforced abroad needs to be investigated in each case. However, this is a matter for the plaintiff and not for the Swiss courts. The latter may not refuse jurisdiction because they consider the chances of enforcing the judgment against the defaming party abroad to be slight.

Unfair competition

Under Swiss law, disparagement of the good reputation of a company or its products through the dissemination of false, misleading or unnecessarily offending statements constitutes a typical example of unfair competition. If the offending party has neither domicile nor habitual residence in Switzerland, the international jurisdiction of Swiss courts in the event of unfair competition is governed by the same principles as are applied in the case of civil torts. Swiss courts will have jurisdiction if either the place where the act occurs or the place of effect is located in Switzerland. There is a presumption that acts of unfair competition have an effect in Switzerland if they have an effect on the Swiss market.

6–283

In the case of disparaging comments, an effect on the Swiss market is deemed to exist if the defamed company is active on the Swiss market and offers its services there. This is because in these circumstances the disparagement can affect sales prospects in Switzerland. It is enough that the goods or services provided by the defamed company are imported into Switzerland or provided to customers in Switzerland. The defamed company therefore does not need to have a headoffice in Switzerland nor any subsidiary of its own.

Provided that the requirement of an effect on the market in Switzerland is fulfilled, it is irrelevant where the defamed statement has been issued or where the defaming party is based. Swiss jurisdiction is thus uncontested even for websites with defamatory content if the operator of the website and the server on which they are maintained are located abroad.

In the case of defamatory statements it is also irrelevant whether they originate from a competitor of the defamed party or from a third party. Thus newspapers were, for instance, found guilty of unfair competition because articles published by them contained false or unnecessarily defamatory statements about a company.

6.22.3 Content liability

Under Swiss law, liability for the content of websites is significant from the point of view of both criminal law and the law of civil torts.

6–284

Websites which contain pornographic or racist material or which depict violence may be subject to prosecution under criminal law. As already mentioned, the Swiss criminal courts have jurisdiction if the criminal act is committed in Switzerland or if the effect of the criminal act takes place in Switzerland.

In the case of pornography, racism and depictions of violence, the offences are not ones which require an identifiable effect. In these cases the criminal circumstances are constituted by the committal of the act which is designated criminal. If this takes place abroad, the Swiss courts will therefore, in principle, not have jurisdiction.

However, where illegal content is concerned, the law describes the criminal conduct in very broad terms. In the case of hardcore pornography (sexual acts involving children or animals, bodily excretions, or acts of violence), for instance, the production, import, storage, marketing, recommendation, exhibiting, offering, display, assignment, making available, acquisition, procurement using electronic means, and possession of material or objects of a pornographic nature are all liable to prosecution.

6–285　　In the case of websites which are operated by foreign owners on servers located abroad, some Swiss jurisprudence assumes, in the case of those above-mentioned offences described in broad terms (such as making available, recommending or offering), that an act has taken place in Switzerland by means of telecommunications channels. Others hold the view that the risk that people in Switzerland might be able to take note of content of this kind constitutes a relevant effect, allowing the application of Swiss penal jurisdiction.

Taking either of these viewpoints, it would not be enough for the website operator to put a notice on the website stating that it is not intended for users in Switzerland in order to avoid criminal liability. The only circumstances in which Swiss courts would have no jurisdiction would be if an effective control system were set up preventing access to the illegal content of a website by users in Switzerland. It is only on websites of this type that the content will not be offered, recommended or made accessible in Switzerland.

However, it is increasingly thought that in the case of illegal content such as pornography, racism, and acts of violence uploaded by perpetrators living abroad onto servers that are also located abroad, there is no Swiss penal jurisdiction. If this were not the case, then competence would have to be imputed on the part of Swiss courts for all disseminated internet content deemed illegal under Swiss law, which would not be sensible.

Taking this view, it is assumed that the perpetrator is acting exclusively abroad. The fact that the perpetrator makes use of the global internet does not mean that part of the action can be regarded as having taken place in Switzerland. Moreover, the possibility that the content in question could be viewed or downloaded in Switzerland would not constitute an effect distinct from the action performed by the perpetrator that would justify the establishment of penal jurisdiction, precisely because the legal circumscription of the elements of the offences at issue does not stipulate any effect of the respective action.

It remains to be seen which attitude the courts will adopt.

In terms of current legislative developments in Switzerland on illegal internet content, attention is drawn to the current on-going revision of the Criminal Code concerning cybercrime. The main aim of the revision is to adapt Swiss criminal law on the liability of internet service providers for criminal acts committed on the internet to the current legal framework outside Switzerland, particularly that in the EU.

For example, access providers, who only provide customers with internet access will be excluded from criminal liability. In addition, hosting providers, who make storage space available on their servers to customers for website publication or input of other data on the internet, will only have criminal liability if they were aware that one of their customers was distributing illegal content using their infrastructure and took no action against that customer (despite the fact that this is technically possible and reasonable for them), or if they fail to report to the criminal prosecution authorities references to illegal content passed on to them by third parties.

This regulation of hosting providers' liability was criticised by various parties in the course of the consultation procedure completed in April 2005. It has not yet been announced when the government will present the draft bill to Parliament for debate.

If someone relies on the content of a website and suffers loss or damage as a result, for example because he or she follows incorrect medical advice given on the website concerned, this will lie within the jurisdiction of the Swiss courts. As mentioned previously, where civil law offences are concerned, international jurisdiction in Switzerland is contingent upon Switzerland being the location of the action or the location of the effect of the damaging conduct. The effect indisputably occurs in Switzerland if someone suffers loss or damage in Switzerland as a result of incorrect website content.

6.22.4 Copyright infringement

Where copyright law is concerned, the jurisdiction of Swiss courts is con-   6–286
tingent upon either the infringing party being domiciled in Switzerland, or
the act of infringement taking place in Switzerland.

Where copyright infringements on the internet are concerned, therefore, websites operated by persons domiciled abroad on servers which are located abroad are of particular interest from a Swiss point of view if Swiss website visitors are offered the possibility of downloading unauthorised copies of protected works. Where these circumstances prevail, it can be assumed that the work concerned is distributed in Switzerland. However, the right of distribution is one which is exclusively reserved for the copyright holder.

The inclusion of a notice stating that the website concerned is not intended for persons in Switzerland cannot exclude the jurisdiction of the Swiss courts. The possibility of downloading by website users in Switzerland must be prevented through an effective control system. Only when this is guaranteed can the website owner successfully prove that the works concerned are not distributed in Switzerland.

Work is currently in progress to revise the Swiss Copyright Law of 1993. The draft bill is currently being debated in Parliament. The main aim of the revision is to implement the so-called WIPO Treaties concluded in December 1996. However, it should be noted that the current definition of the exclusive rights of the originator under existing copyright law in Switzerland means that the use of protected works on the internet is already largely covered.

At the focal point of the debate about the revision of copyright law is, on the one hand the planned criminal law protection against avoidance of anti-copying measures, and on the other, the issue of whether or not down-loading illegal copies of protected works for personal use should be declared a punishable offence. However, it is expected that no steps will be taken to alter the fact that offering illegal copies on the internet is a punishable offence.

6.22.5 Trade mark infringement

6–287   As is the case with copyright infringements, in the case of trade mark infringements, if the infringing party is not domiciled in Switzerland, the Swiss courts will have jurisdiction if an act of infringement takes place in Switzerland. This is only the case if there is some kind of connection between the act in question and the territory of Switzerland.

The fact that goods or services are offered on a website under a trade mark which is protected in Switzerland is not enough to constitute an infringement of Swiss trade mark law. A further condition is that it must be assumed, on the basis of the actual circumstances, that the goods or services offered on the website concerned are also supplied to Switzerland, and thus to customers in Switzerland.

If the operator places a notice on his website stating that his offer is not intended for customers in Switzerland, this constitutes an indication that no trade mark infringement will occur in Switzerland. However, if it can be proved that, despite this notice, goods are supplied to Switzerland, trade mark infringement in Switzerland would exist and the Swiss courts would have jurisdiction. Any website operator wishing to avoid Swiss jurisdiction must therefore ensure that no goods are in fact delivered to Switzerland and that no services are supplied to customers in Switzerland.

6.23 CROSS-BORDER LIABILITY—USA

6.23.1 US jurisdictional analysis

6–288   Determining whether personal jurisdiction exists over foreign defendants when the allegedly wrongful acts have all been committed outside the US can be a difficult legal challenge for US courts.[49] When the alleged acts are

---

[49] See, e.g. *Klinghoffer v SNC Achille Lauro*, 937 F. 2d 44 (2d Cir 1991).

purely electronic in nature and the defendant has no physical presence in the US, the challenge is especially formidable.

Although numerous US courts have ruled on whether and when personal jurisdiction exists over parties engaged in internet activities, relatively few of these cases have involved non-resident international defendants. However, the jurisdictional analysis is virtually the same for non-resident international defendants as that employed to determine whether a court of one US state (e.g. New York) has jurisdiction over a defendant resident in a "foreign" state (such as New Jersey).[50] Thus, US cases involving jurisdiction over non-resident *international* defendants should be examined in the broader context of cases involving jurisdiction over out-of-state US defendants.

A US court may exercise personal jurisdiction over a non-resident defendant based on either general or specific activities within the forum state. General jurisdiction is premised on defendant's "continuous and systematic" activities in the forum state, and may be established regardless of whether the particular cause of action arises from such forum-related activities.[51] On the other hand, even in the absence of general jurisdiction, specific jurisdiction may be established where a plaintiff's cause of action is deemed to arise out of or relate to a defendant's activities in the forum state.[52] The threshold for the required contacts under general jurisdiction ("continuous and systematic") is higher than it is for specific jurisdiction ("purposeful availment").

Although it can be challenging for a court to rule on whether a defendant's conduct in the forum state is sufficiently "continuous and systematic" to subject him or her to the general jurisdiction of the court, it is often quite difficult for the court to determine whether a defendant's particular forum-related activities are sufficient to establish "specific" jurisdiction in connection with a particular claim. Indeed, the court is required to engage in a highly fact-intensive analysis of a defendant's conduct and different courts reach different results based on seemingly similar facts.

US courts traditionally apply a two-part test to determine whether to **6–289**

---

[50] One need only compare the jurisdictional analysis conducted by the US Supreme Court in *Burger King Corp v Rudzewicz*, 471 US 462 (1985) (upholding jurisdiction over Michigan franchisee sued in Florida) to that used in *Asahi Metal Industry Co Ltd v Superior Court of California, Solano County*, 480 US 102 (1987) (reversing grant of jurisdiction over Japanese manufacturer sued in California) to see that the underlying "minimum contacts" and "fair play" analysis is virtually the same for interstate and international disputes.

[51] See, e.g. *Helicopteros Nacionales de Colombia SA v Hall*, 466 US 408 (1984) (Colombian corporation's contacts with Texas, consisting of one trip to Texas by corporation's CEO for purpose of negotiating service contract, acceptance of cheques drawn on Texas bank, and helicopter and equipment purchases from Texas manufacturer, were insufficient to allow Texas court to assert general personal jurisdiction over corporation in wrongful death action which occurred in Peru).

[52] *International Shoe Co v Washington*, 326 US 310, 316 (1945) (citation omitted).

exercise specific personal jurisdiction over a non-resident defendant.[53] First, the court must determine whether the defendant's actions satisfy the forum state's particular "long-arm statute" (i.e. the state's guidelines for determining whether personal jurisdiction may be established in the forum state).[54] Secondly, the court must determine whether exercising jurisdiction over the defendant violates the Due Process Clause of the Fourteenth Amendment of the US Constitution.[55] The Due Process Clause establishes the outer boundary of a state court's power to exercise personal jurisdiction. Thus, even if jurisdiction were proper under a particular state's long-arm statute, jurisdiction could not be established where doing so would violate the Due Process guaranteed by the US Constitution.

The Due Process Clause requires that a non-resident defendant have "minimum contacts" with the forum state and that the exercise of jurisdiction over the defendant does not offend "traditional notions of fair play and substantial justice."[56] Moreover, as one court put it, "jurisdiction is only appropriate in circumstances where defendant has purposely directed his activities at residents of the forum, resulting in litigation that emanates from alleged injuries arising out of or relating to those activities."[57] Certain activities (in and of themselves) are not sufficient to establish minimum contacts. For example, merely placing a product into the "stream of commerce" without purposefully directing that product towards the forum state is not sufficient to constitute minimum contacts.[58] Whether personal jurisdiction exists in any given case involves a highly fact-intensive inquiry by the court.[59] For example, in New York, where the long-arm statute is somewhat more restrictive than the permissible limits under the US Constitution,[60] a court would begin with an analysis of the applicable state jurisdictional law before launching into the constitutional

---

[53] The constitutional and policy framework employed by courts to analyse whether or not it may exercise personal jurisdiction over a defendant is derived from *International Shoe Co v Washington*, 326 US 310 (1945) and its progeny: *Burger King Corp v Rudzewicz*, 471 US 462, 471–78 (1985) (setting forth the two-part Due Process test for analysing defendant's litigation-related connections with the forum, and the fairness of exercising jurisdiction over a non-resident defendant); *Asahi Metal Industry Co Ltd v Superior Court of California, Solano County*, 480 US 102, 113–16 (1987) (applying multi-factor test to determine fairness and reasonableness of exercising personal jurisdiction over non-resident, foreign defendant); *World-Wide Volkswagen Corp v Woodson*, 444 US 286, 294 (1980) (suggesting that geographically distant defendants must sometimes be protected from inconvenient litigation).

[54] See, e.g. N.Y. C.P.L.R. 302 (Consol. 2006) (enumerating those categories of contacts, including committing a tortious act within the forum, which suffice to confer jurisdiction); 42 Pa. Cons. Stat. § 5322 (2001).

[55] See US Const amend. XIV.

[56] *International Shoe Co v Washington*, 326 US 310, 316 (1945).

[57] *Alitalia-Linee Aeree Italiane SpA v Casinoalitalia.com*, 128 F. Supp. 2d 340, 348–49 (E.D. Va. 2001) (citing *Burger King Corp v Rudzewicz*, 471 US 462, 462 (1985).

[58] See, e.g. *Asahi Metal Industry Co Ltd v Superior Court of California, Solano County*, 480 US 102 (1987) (holding that a Taiwanese company that manufactured and sold its products in Taiwan was not subject to personal jurisdiction in California merely because its products eventually made their way into California through the "stream of commerce").

[59] See, e.g. *Burger King Corp v Rudzewicz*, 471 US 462, 471–78 (1985).

[60] See N.Y. C.P.L.R. 302(a) (Consol. 2006).

analysis set forth by the leading US Supreme Court cases.[61] On the other hand, in a jurisdiction such as California, where the applicable long-arm statute confers jurisdiction to the full extent of the limits set by the federal Due Process Clause, a court would begin (and end) its jurisdictional analysis with a constitutional review.[62]

6.23.2 Internet jurisdiction analysis

For at least the past decade, US courts, both state and federal, have been wrestling with the thorny issue of personal jurisdiction in the context of internet-related activities. In deciding these cases, US courts have been reluctant to view the mere general availability of a website as a "minimum contact" sufficient to establish specific personal jurisdiction over a non-resident defendant, at least in the absence of other contacts with the forum state. As one US judge opined, conferring jurisdiction on the basis of a website alone:

6–290

> "would be tantamount to a declaration that this Court, and every other court throughout the world, may assert [personal] jurisdiction over all information providers on the global World Wide Web."[63]

Another court stated in dicta that it had no power to shut down a foreign website "merely because the site is accessible from within one country in which its product is banned."[64] To do so, reasoned the court, "would have

---

[61] See, e.g. *Bensusan Restaurant Corp v King*, 126 F. 3d 25, 27 (2d Cir. 1997) (stating that "in diversity or federal question cases the court must look first to the long-arm statute of the forum state ... [i]f the exercise of jurisdiction is appropriate under that statute, the court then must decide whether such exercise comports with the requisites of due process" of the constitution).

[62] See Cal. Civ. Proc. Code § 410.10 (Deering 2006) (providing that California courts "may exercise jurisdiction on any basis not inconsistent with the Constitution of this State or of the United States") (enacted 1969).

[63] *Hearst Corp v Goldberger*, 1997 US Dist LEXIS 2065, *55 (S.D.N.Y. Feb 26, 1997). In *Hearst*, the magistrate judge found that the New Jersey defendant's only contact with the New York forum was via electronic "visits" from New York residents, plus a few email messages sent to New-York based newspapers after commencement of the litigation.

[64] *Playboy Enters Inc v Chuckleberry Publ'g Inc*, 939 F. Supp. 1032, 1039 (S.D.N.Y. 1996) (dicta). Playboy was one of the earliest cases to touch (though not rule directly) upon personal jurisdiction in the internet age. In *Playboy*, a federal judge in New York found no constitutional or other impediment to exercising personal jurisdiction over an Italian website owner who had been enjoined by the same court from publishing or distributing its magazine in the US in traditional print form. The court held that it retained personal jurisdiction over the defendant for the purposes of enforcing the existing injunction and that although the existing injunction did not specifically mention the internet, the injunction would still be applicable to this new media. See also *Jeri-Jo Knitwear v Club Italia*, 94 F. Supp. 2d 457 (S.D.N.Y. 2000) (ordering an Italian company to remove website hyperlinks deemed to violate prior injunction against advertising or promoting trade mark-infringing apparel in the US).

a devastating impact on those who use" the internet.[65] As the US Court of Appeals for the District of Columbia Circuit commented in rejecting the "mere accessibility" of a website as a basis for jurisdiction, "[w]e do not believe that the advent of advanced technology, say, as with the internet, should vitiate long-held and inviolate principles of federal court jurisdiction."[66] This principle has been reiterated by several other US federal courts,[67] including in *Minge v Cohen*, where the court declined to exercise jurisdiction over a Canadian corporation in a securities case where defendant's only contact with the US was the maintenance of a Canadian website accessible in the US.[68]

6–291   Proceeding from the broad principle stated above, that mere accessibility of a website within the forum state, without more, is not sufficient to justify the exercise of specific jurisdiction, courts have developed two general lines of analysis in determining whether jurisdiction can be exercised in cases involving internet activity.

---

[65] *Playboy Enters Inc v Chuckleberry Publ'g Inc*, 939 F. Supp. 1032,1039–40 (S.D.N.Y. 1996).

[66] *GTE New Media Servs Inc v Bellsouth Corp*, 199 F. 3d 1343 (D.C. Cir. 2000).

[67] See, e.g. *Toys "R" Us Inc v Step Two*, S.A., 318 F. 3d 446, 453 (3d Cir. 2003) (stating "there must be 'something more [beyond the mere posting of a passive web site] to indicate that the defendant purposefully (albeit electronically) directed his activity in a substantial way to the forum state,'" (quoting *Cybersell Inc v Cybersell Inc*, 130 F. 3d 414, 418 (9th Cir. 1997)); *Remick v Manfredy*, 238 F. 3d 248, 259 n.3 (3d Cir. 2001) (stating "the mere posting of information or advertisements on an internet website does not confer nationwide personal jurisdiction"); *Bensusan Restaurant Corp v King*, 126 F. 3d 25, 27 (2d Cir. 1997) (approving the application of "well-established doctrines of personal jurisdiction law" to an internet-related case); *ICP Solar Techs v TAB Consulting Inc*, 413 F. Supp. 2d 12, 18 (D.N.H. 2006) (stating "the mere fact that an entity operates a commercial, interactive website does not, without more, subject that entity to jurisdiction anywhere in the world"); *Dagesse v Plant Hotel NV*, 113 F. Supp. 2d 211, 221 (D. N.H. 2000) (noting that "to hold that the mere existence of an internet website establishes general jurisdiction would render any individual or entity that created such a website subject to personal jurisdiction in every state"); *ESAB Group Inc v Centricut LLC*, 34 F. Supp. 2d 323, 331 (D.S.C. 1999) ("something more" than a mere internet presence is required to assert personal jurisdiction); *McDonough v Fallon McElligot Inc*, 1996 US Dist LEXIS 15139, *7, 40 U.S.P.Q.2D 1826 (S.D. Cal Aug. 6, 1996), (merely operating a website used by forum residents not sufficient to establish jurisdiction). See also the following cases where jurisdiction was found lacking: *Burleson v Toback*, 391 F. Supp. 2d 401 (D. N.C. 2005) (dismissing claims for libel, harassment, tortious interference with contract, and various intellectual property claims against defendants for lack of personal jurisdiction where websites were passive sites that merely displayed information and nothing more); *Barrett v Catacombs Press*, 44 F. Supp. 2d 717 (E D. Pa. 1999) (declining to find personal jurisdiction over defendant in a defamation action where defendant posted messages to listserves and USENET discussion groups because statements were not directed toward forum); *Millennium Entm't v Millennium Music LP*, 33 F Supp 2d 907 (D. Or. 1999) (declining to exercise personal jurisdiction over defendant in a trade mark infringement action where defendants merely published information on a website); *Rannoch Inc v Rannoch Corp* 52 F. Supp. 2d 681 (E.D. Va. 1999) (declining to find personal jurisdiction where defendant's posting of website satisfied state long-arm statute, but failed constitutional prong of jurisdictional test).

[68] *Minge v Cohen*, 2000 US Dist LEXIS 403 (E.D. La. Jan. 19, 2000) ("maintaining a website on the internet ... cannot without more satisfy the 'purposefully availing' element")); see also *ICP Solar Techs v TAB Consulting Inc*, 413 F. Supp. 2d 12, 18 (D.N.H. 2006) (declining to exercise personal jurisdiction where the defendant advertised allegedly infringing products on its website, but there were no sales made over the internet to forum state citizens, nor was there any evidence that residents of the forum state actually visited defendant's website).

The first, a "sliding scale" approach, seeks to classify the "nature and quality" of the commercial activity, if any, that the defendant conducts over the internet. The second analysis seeks to determine to what extent a defendant's intentional conduct outside the forum state, e.g. the posting of defamatory statements on a website, is calculated to cause injury to a plaintiff within the forum state, i.e. an "effects test." These two approaches have been widely applied by the courts (albeit with disparate and inconsistent results) in internet-related personal jurisdiction inquiries, and courts often employ both lines of analysis in determining whether specific jurisdiction exists.[69] The two approaches are discussed more fully below.

The "sliding scale" approach to analysing on-line contacts is perhaps most formulaically stated in *Zippo Manufacturing Co v Zippo Dot Com Inc.*[70] At one end of the spectrum are strictly "passive" websites that only display information to users. Absent other contact with the forum state, the mere availability of these sites in the forum would generally not result in the exercise of jurisdiction.

At the other end of the spectrum are sites where a defendant "clearly" conducts business over the internet, e.g. where the "defendant enters into contracts with residents of a foreign jurisdiction that involve the knowing and repeated transmission of computer files over the internet."[71] A defendant conducting business in a US state via such a site would generally be subject to personal jurisdiction in the courts of that state.

In the middle are sites that the *Zippo* court classified as "interactive [w]eb sites where a user can exchange information with the host computer."[72] In order to determine whether the operator of such an interactive site is subject to personal jurisdiction, the *Zippo* court explained that a court must review the "level of interactivity and commercial nature of the exchange of information" on the site.[73]

Consistent with the general rule stated above, under *Zippo*, merely making **6–292** a passive website available, without additional conduct directed toward the forum state by the website operator, will not generally be sufficient to

---

[69] See *Revell v Lidov*, 317 F. 3d 467 (5th Cir. 2002) (analysing the defendant's website and the interactivity on that site under both the "sliding scale" and "effects" tests and affirming the district court's order dismissing defamation claims for lack of personal jurisdiction); *Qwest Communs Int'l v Sonny Corp*, 2006 US Dist. LEXIS 29832 (W.D. Wash., May 15, 2006) (finding personal jurisdiction and discussing that defendant's conduct meets the requirement under both the "sliding scale" test and the "effects test"); *Amway Corp v P&G*, 2000 US Dist LEXIS 372 (W.D. Mich. January 6, 2000), *aff'd*, 346 F. 3d 180 (6th Cir. 2003)

[70] *Zippo Manufacturing Co v Zippo Dot Com Inc*, 952 F. Supp. 1119 (W.D. Pa. 1997). In *Zippo*, an out-of-state defendant was using the plaintiff's registered trade mark "Zippo" as part of a website domain name accessible in Pennsylvania. Some 140,000 subscribers around the world—not all of them in Pennsylvania— had registered and paid for Dot Com's internet news service. In holding that personal jurisdiction over the defendant existed in Pennsylvania, the US District Court for the Western District of Pennsylvania determined that "Dot Com's conducting of electronic commerce with Pennsylvania residents constitutes the purposeful availment of doing business in Pennsylvania."

[71] *Ibid.*, at 1124.

[72] *Ibid.*

[73] *Ibid.*

establish personal jurisdiction over the site operator.[74] For example, in *Virtuality LLC v Bata Ltd*, a US District Court held in a domain name dispute that a passive website maintained by a Canadian corporation, on which it neither sold products nor conducted any other commercial activity for profit, did not provide a basis for the exercise of personal jurisdiction in the US.[75] In *Dawson v Pepin*, a US District Court found that the website of a Canadian resident, which contained an 800 number for US orders and a list of dealers located within the forum state, was nevertheless a passive website which did not give rise to personal jurisdiction in the forum state.[76]

At the other end of the *Zippo* sliding scale are websites on which business is conducted. In general, a website that is sufficiently interactive so as to fall into the *Zippo* category of "clearly conducting business" will be subject to the exercise of jurisdiction. For example, in *Alitalia-Linee Aeree Italiane SpA v Casinoalitalia.com*,[77] a US District Court found that an Italian company could obtain jurisdiction in Virginia in a domain name dispute over an on-line gambling enterprise located in the Dominican Republic. The court reasoned that a website on which interactive casino-like gambling was conducted around the clock engaged in repeated and ongoing business

---

[74] See, e.g. *American Girl LLC v Nameview Inc*, 381 F. Supp. 2d 876 (D. Wis. 2005) (finding that plaintiff failed to establish personal jurisdiction where the defendant's website constituted a passive website and "the record did not indicate that the registrar ever purposefully availed itself of Wisconsin's laws by accepting a domain name registration from anyone in the state"); *Harbuck v Aramco Inc*, 1999 US Dist LEXIS 16892 (E.D. Pa. October 22, 1999) (holding that subjecting Saudi Arabian defendant to jurisdiction in Pennsylvania for having a "passive" website would be unreasonable); *Smith v Hobby Lobby Stores Inc*, 968 F. Supp 1356, 1364–65 (W.D. Ark. 1997) (Hong Kong fireworks manufacturer's advertisement in internet trade publication constituted insufficient contact for Arkansas court to exercise personal jurisdiction in products liability action, where manufacturer did not contract to sell goods and services to citizens of Arkansas over the internet).

[75] *Virtuality LLC v Bata Ltd*, 138 F. Supp. 2d 677 (D. Md. 2001). The defendant had been the successful complainant in a domain name dispute conducted under the Uniform Domain Name Dispute Resolution Policy, and the plaintiff had filed suit in the US court in order to challenge the decision in the UDRP proceeding, as permitted under the UDRP (see Ch.3). The court also found that the defendant's consent to the jurisdiction of the court pursuant to the provisions of the UDRP did not constitute consent to the jurisdiction of the court with respect to other claims asserted by the plaintiff.

[76] *Dawson v Pepin*, 2001 US Dist LEXIS 10074 (W.D. Mich. March 29, 2001); see also *ALS Scan v Digital Serv Consultants Inc*, 293 F. 3d 707 (4th Cir. 2002) (refusing to find jurisdiction when a website was a clearly passive website); *Mink v AAAA Dev*, 190 F.3d 333 (5th Cir. 1999) (finding a website to be no more than a passive website where the site provided a printable mail-in order form, a toll-free number and mail and email addresses, but did not take orders); but see *Inset Systems Inc v Instruction Set Inc*, 937 F. Supp. 161 (D. Conn. 1996) (domain name trade mark infringement action; jurisdiction established by website accessible to Connecticut internet users that solicited US residents generally by providing a toll-free number).

[77] *Alitalia-Linee Aeree Italiane SpA v Casinoalitalia.com*. 128 F. Supp. 2d 340 (E.D. Va. 2001). As the court noted, "the product is an inherently interactive activity ... and necessarily requires [defendant] to enter into contacts with member, who must purchase 'credits' in order to play individual names." *ibid.*, at 350 (citing *Millennium Entm't Inc v Millennium Music LP*, 33 F. Supp. 2d 907, 916 (D. Or. 1999)).

transactions on-line with Virginia residents, which put it on notice that it could be haled into a court in Virginia.[78]

Similarly, in *Quokka Sports Inc v Cup Int'l Ltd*,[79] a US District Court found that a website which targeted US customers and which permitted customers to fill out on-line order forms, enter credit card information and complete orders on-line was sufficiently interactive to support the court's exercise of personal jurisdiction over the website operator in a domain name dispute.[80]

Between the "passive" and "doing business" extremes of the *Zippo* sliding scale are cases involving "interactive" websites, such as those through which a consumer can exchange email messages with the site operator or download information or products. Some courts have held that the mere existence of an interactive site is enough to subject an out-of-state defendant to personal jurisdiction,[81] while other courts require evidence that someone in the forum state actually interacted with the site.[82]

For example, in *Ty Inc v Clark*, a US District Court declined to exercise personal jurisdiction over a private corporation headquartered in England on the basis of its website.[83] Although the website was "interactive" in that it permitted customers to email questions about products and to receive information about orders, no transactions were conducted online, and the

---

[78] *Alitalia-Linee Aeree Italiane SpA*, 937 F. Supp. at 351; see also *US v Cohen*, 260 F.3d 68 (2d Cir. 2001) (upholding conviction under federal Wire Wager Act for activities involving an on-line gambling website located outside the US); *People v World Interactive Gaming Corp*, 185 Misc. 2d 852 (N.Y. Sup. Ct. 1999) (exercising jurisdiction in criminal prosecution over defendant who maintained gambling website using servers located outside US).

[79] See *Quokka Sports Inc v Cup Int'l Ltd*, 99 F. Supp. 2d 1105 (N.D. Cal. 1999) (citing *Zippo* and finding that "this type of interactive commercial activity, aimed at US consumers [is] evidence of purposeful availment").

[80] *Quokka Sports Inc v Cup Int'l Ltd*, 99 F. Supp. 2d 1105, at 1112 (N.D. Cal. 1999); see also *Kollmorgen Corp v Yaskawa Electric Corp*, 169 F. Supp. 2d 530 (W.D. Va. 1999) (finding that a Japanese parent corporation was subject to jurisdiction in Virginia based on subsidiary's website and sales in Virginia from orders taken over the internet). cf. *Inset Systems Inc v Instruction Set Inc*, 937 F. Supp. 161 (D. Conn. 1996) (early internet-related case exercising personal jurisdiction over non-resident defendant based on defendant posting an advertisement including a toll-free 800 number on its website). But see *Mink v AAAA Dev*, 190 F.3d 333, 336 (5th Cir. 1999) ("the presence of an electronic mail access, a printable order form, and a toll-free phone number on a website, without more, is insufficient to establish personal jurisdiction").

[81] See e.g. *3DO Co v Poptop Software Inc*, 1998 US Dist LEXIS 21281, 49 U.S.P.Q.2D 1469 (N.D. Cal. October 27, 1998) (exercising personal jurisdiction where non-resident defendants' website "encourage[d] and facilitate[d]'" people in the forum state and elsewhere to download allegedly copyright infringing software).

[82] See, e.g. *Millennium Entm't Inc v Millennium Music LP*, 33 F. Supp. 2d at 923 ("Until transactions with Oregon residents are consummated through defendants' website, defendants cannot reasonably anticipate that they will be brought before this court, simply because they advertise their products through a global medium which provides the capability of engaging in commercial transactions."); *Advanced Software, Inc v Datapharm Inc*, 1998 US Dist LEXIS 22091, *12 (C.D. Cal. November. 9, 1998) (finding that, absent a showing that anyone in the forum state utilised defendant's website, "the fact that it has interactive potential is irrelevant").

[83] *Ty Inc v Clark*, 2000 US Dist LEXIS 383 (N.D Ill. January 14, 2000) (noting that the defendants "do not clearly do business on their website, for they do not take orders nor enter into contracts over the website").

court found that the defendant company had done nothing to direct its activity particularly to the forum state.[84]

Similarly, in *LaSalle National Bank v Vitro Sociedad Anonima*,[85] a US District Court found that a website operated by a Mexican corporation, which had "a minimal level of 'interactivity,'" including email buttons to obtain information about the company and access to an on-line product catalog, was still a passive website under the "sliding scale" test, and declined to exercise jurisdiction. As in *Ty v Clark*, the court in *LaSalle* found that there was no showing that the defendant's website targeted residents of the forum state.[86] More recently, in *Toys "R" Us Inc v Step Two SA*,[87] the Fourth Circuit declined to find personal jurisdiction where a website based in Spain, was entirely in Spanish, its merchandise prices were in foreign currency, and none of the interactive portions on the website could accommodate addresses in the US. The court found that the foregoing facts combined with other minor contacts were insufficient to find personal jurisdiction because the defendant did not target its website to New Jersey residents.[88]

By contrast, in *Batzel v Smith*, a website operated from The Netherlands by a Netherlands resident provided a sufficient basis for establishing jurisdiction in a defamation action where the operation of the website was coupled with the defendant's actions in emailing newsletters and invitations to view the website to residents of the forum state.[89]

6–293 In summary, cases following the *Zippo* sliding scale analysis are highly fact-sensitive and have led to disparate results. However, as a general proposition, it still appears to be the case that the mere general availability of a website will not—without other contacts—subject site owners to jurisdiction in every jurisdiction in which the site is available.

In addition to the "sliding scale" analysis propounded by the *Zippo* court, some US courts have cited the pre-internet "effects test" set forth by the US Supreme Court in *Calder v Jones*[90] in support of finding personal jurisdiction based on on-line activity. Under the "effects test," jurisdiction can be premised on the intentional conduct of the defendants outside the forum state that is calculated to cause injury to the plaintiffs within the forum state.

The "effects test" was applied in the context of internet-related activities in *Panavision Int'l v Toeppen*,[91] a case involving a non-resident US defendant who registered the plaintiff's trade mark as a domain name and

---

[84] *ibid.*, at *9–*11.
[85] *LaSalle Nat'l Bank v Vitro Sociedad Anonima*, 85 F. Supp. 2d 857 (N.D. Ill. 2000) (declining to exercise personal jurisdiction over a Mexican corporation).
[86] *ibid.*
[87] *Toys "R" Us Inc v Step Two SA*, 318 F.3d 446 (3d Cir. 2003).
[88] *ibid.*, at 454.
[89] *Batzel v Smith*, 2001 US Dist LEXIS 8929 (C.D. Cal. June 5, 2001). See also *3M Co v Icuiti Corp*, 2006 US Dist. LEXIS 35706 (D. Minn. 2006) (finding personal jurisdiction over non-resident proper due to the inclusion of the forum state in its advertising, shipping destination and payment collection).
[90] *Calder v Jones*, 465 US 783 (1984) (holding that personal jurisdiction over non-resident defendants in a libel case involving a print publication was properly applied where the publication of defendants' libelous statements was calculated to cause injury to plaintiff in the forum state).
[91] *Panavision Int'l v Toeppen*, 141 F.3d 1316 (9th Cir 1998).

then sought to extort money from the plaintiff in return for relinquishing the domain name (i.e. a classic "cybersquatting" case). The court concluded that the non-resident defendant's actions satisfied the "purposeful availment" requirement because the defendant knew that his conduct would have the effect of injuring the plaintiff in the forum state, where the plaintiff corporation had its principal place of business.[92]

Courts are more likely to consider or apply the *Calder* "effects test" in cases involving defamation[93] or some other alleged tortious act on the part of the defendant.[94] For example, the use of a plaintiff's trade marks as metatags on the defendant's website was treated as a tort under the New York State long-arm statute in *Roberts-Gordon LLC v Superior Radiant Products Ltd.*[95] The court applied the *Calder* effects test in exercising jurisdiction over a Canadian corporation (which was not engaged in a "continuous and systematic course of doing business" in New York), concluding that the harm from the defendant's trade mark infringement on its website was cognisable at the plaintiff's place of business in New York and was sufficient to support a finding that the defendant had "purposely availed itself of New York law."

In a more recent internet-related application of the effects test, the court in *Yahoo! Inc v La Ligue Contre Le Racisme*[96] concluded that jurisdiction

---

[92] *Panavision Int'l v Toeppen*, 141 F.3d 1316, 1323 (9th Cir 1998); see also *Macconnell v Schwamm*, 2000 US Dist LEXIS 13850 (S.D. Cal. July 25, 2000). (Court exercised jurisdiction in a domain name dispute where the defendant, a resident of Japan, contacted the plaintiff in the forum state and offered to sell the infringing domain name to the plaintiff. The defendant had registered a domain name that had been previously registered by the plaintiff but lost due to the bankruptcy of the domain name registrar. Although the defendant claimed that he intended to use the domain name to market products in Asia, he contacted the plaintiff and offered to sell the domain name to the plaintiff. The court concluded that the there was no evidence of a legitimate business operation on the part of the plaintiff, thereby suggesting "the type of tort-like purposeful behavior" involved in *Panavision*.) Compare these decisions with the earlier decision of the Ninth Circuit Court of Appeals in *Cybersell Inc v Cybersell Inc*, 130 F.3d 414 (9th Cir 1997) (considering the *Calder* effects test; declining to exercise jurisdiction in domain name dispute where there was no "express aiming" at the forum state).

[93] See discussion of defamation cases *infra* and see, e.g. *Revell v Lidov*, 317 F.3d 467 (5th Cir. 2002) (declining to exercise personal jurisdiction in defamation case); *Lofton v Turbine Design Inc.* 100 F. Supp. 2d 404 (N.D. Miss. 2000) (same); *Barrett v Catacombs Press*, 44 F. Supp. 2d 717 (E.D. Pa. 1999) (same); *EDIAS Software Int'l LLC v Basis Int'l Ltd*, 947 F. Supp. 413 (D. Ariz. 1996) (holding that jurisdiction was established in a defamation case).

[94] See, e.g. *Bancroft & Masters Inc v Augusta Nat'l Inc*, 223 F.3d 1082 (9th Cir. 2000) (in a trade mark dispute over domain name, defendant's letter to the domain name registrar asking that domain name be put on hold was conduct individually targeting plaintiff, whom defendant knew to be resident of forum state and which had effects felt primarily in forum state); *Intercon Inc v Bell Atlantic Internet Solutions Inc*, 205 F.3d 1244 (10th Cir. 2000) (exercising personal jurisdiction where defendant's transmissions through plaintiff's mail server constituted conduct purposefully directed at the forum state that caused plaintiff's harm); *American Information Corp v American Infometrics Inc*, 139 F. Supp. 2d 696 (D. Md. 2001) (use of a service mark as a website address without evidence of entry into forum state, deliberate targeting of plaintiff, or concentration of harmful effects in forum state, does not satisfy effects test).

[95] *Roberts-Gordon LLC v Superior Radiant Products LTD*, 85 F. Supp. 2d 202 (W.D.N.Y. 2000).

[96] *Yahoo! Inc v La Ligue Contre Le Racisme*, 433 F.3d 1199 (9th Cir. 2006), *cert denied* 126 S.Ct. 2332 (2006).

could be exercised in California over French civil rights groups for acts committed by them in France, because the effects of their acts were experienced by a corporation in California. The effects justifying the exercise of jurisdiction resulted from an action brought against Yahoo! in a French court by French civil rights groups under French anti-hate laws.[97] The French court ordered Yahoo! to block access by French citizens to auctions of Nazi items and threatened to impose large fines if Yahoo! failed to comply. Although it complied, Yahoo! subsequently initiated a federal court action in the US seeking a declaration that the French court order was not enforceable against Yahoo! in US courts.

In refusing to dismiss the action for lack of jurisdiction, the court pointed to the effects that the action had on Yahoo! in California and stated that, while the institution of the action may have been proper under French law, "such an act nonetheless may be 'wrongful' from the standpoint of a court in the US if its primary purpose or intended effect is to deprive a US resident of its constitutional rights."[98]

6–294   The cases discussed above demonstrate that a foreign internet entrepreneur, although lacking "continuous and systematic" contacts with any US forum state sufficient to subject him or her to general jurisdiction, may nonetheless be subject to personal jurisdiction in the US based on two broad theories of "specific" personal jurisdiction.

Under the *Zippo* "sliding scale" analysis, a US court will classify the "nature and quality" of any commercial activity that the defendant conducts over the internet and place it on a continuum ranging from "passive," where no business is conducted, to "clearly conducting business." The closer the internet activities are to "clearly conducting business," the more likely that a US court will exercise personal jurisdiction.

Courts may also apply the *Calder* "effects test" to determine whether the defendant's intentional conduct was calculated to cause harm to a plaintiff within the forum state. Where a defendant "purposefully directs" his activities at the jurisdiction, he may be liable to suit for any injury relating to or arising from those activities. On the other hand, "mere awareness" of the ability of US residents to access a website will probably not subject a foreign website owner to personal jurisdiction in the US.

Thus, non-US citizens should not conduct their internet activities with disregard for US laws in the belief that operating outside US borders will allow them to avoid personal jurisdiction. In the substantive areas of intellectual property, commercial relations, fair trade, obscenity, and other tortious or criminal conduct, US courts are likely to subject foreign website owners to a jurisdictional analysis that is virtually the same as that afforded domestic defendants.

---

[97] See *Ligue Contre le Racisme et L'Antisemitisme v Yahoo! Inc*, No RG:00/05308 (TGI Paris, November 20, 2000) available at *http://www.juriscom.net/txt/jurisfr/cti/tgiparis 20001120.pdf*.

[98] *ibid.*

6.23.3 Some additional practitioner notes

The non-US legal practitioner who seeks to advise foreign clients about the   **6–295**
scope of liability for internet-related activities would do well to heed the
cautionary tales established by US website cases in the discrete substantive
areas discussed below, as well as to keep abreast of recent US legislative
developments which may result in increased risk of liability for non-US-
website owners. A sampling of recent legal developments in some of these
more substantive areas follows.[99]

Online copyright infringement

In many cases of on-line copyright infringement,[1] rights holders seek to   **6–296**
hold liable the internet service provider (ISP), website operator, or bulletin
board service (BBS) operator as well as the individual who uploaded or
downloaded infringing material.[2] Title II of the Digital Millennium Copyright Act of 1998 (DMCA), the on-line Copyright Infringement Liability

---

[99] The foreign practitioner should bear in mind that common and statutory law in any given
area is not necessarily uniform from state to state. Particularly in the realm of internet law,
legal standards are evolving at different rates as US courts and state legislatures continue to
grapple with the implications of the internet. Retention of local counsel may be essential to
timely addressing a given issue.

[1] The three primary theories of copyright infringement—direct infringement, contributory
liability and vicarious liability—have been articulated in the context of on-line activities.
For a leading pre-DMCA example see *Religious Technology Center v Netcom On-Line
Communications Services Inc*, 907 F. Supp. 1361 (N.D. Cal. 1995) (analysing all three
theories in relation to the liability of an ISP). See also *Religious Technology Center v Lerma*,
1996 US Dist. LEXIS 15454 (E.D. Va. October 4, 1996) (direct infringement); *Playboy
Enters Inc v Frena*, 839 F. Supp. 1552 (M.D. Fla. 1993) (direct infringement); *Sega Enters
Ltd v MAPHIA*, 948 F. Supp. 923 (N.D. Cal. 1996) (contributory liability); *Sega Enters Ltd
v Sabella*, 1996 US Dist. LEXIS 20470 (N.D. Cal. December 18, 1996) (contributory
liability); *Playboy Enters v Webbworld Inc*, 991 F. Supp. 543 (N.D. Tex. 1997) (vicarious
liability). For a more complete discussion of copyright issues related to the internet, see
Julian S Millstein, Jeffrey D Neuburger, Jeffrey P Weingart, *Doing Business on the Internet:
Forms & Analysis* (Law Journal Press, 1997–2001).

[2] See, e.g. *Metro-Goldwyn-Mayer Studios Inc v Grokster Ltd*, 545 US 913 (2005) (holding
that one who distributes a device with the object of promoting its use to infringe copyright,
as shown by clear expression or other affirmative steps taken to foster infringement, is liable
for the resulting acts of infringement by third parties); *A&M Records v Napster Inc*, 239
F.3d 1004 (9th Cir 2001) (upholding the federal district court's issuance of a preliminary
injunction directing Napster to prevent infringing music files from being distributed through
its online, peer-to-peer music file-sharing system); *UMG Recordings Inc v MP3.com Inc*, 92
F. Supp. 2d 349 (S.D.N.Y. 2000) (holding that defendant infringed plaintiffs' copyrights
and denying defendant's "fair use" defense where defendant copied plaintiffs' recordings
onto its computer servers and replayed the recordings for its subscribers). In another music
piracy case, several record labels filed suit against Aimster, a service allowing users to trade
files using America Online's Instant Messenger software, alleging contributory and vicarious copyright infringement and unfair competition. See also *In re Aimster Copyright
Litigation*, 334 F.3d 643 (7th Cir. 2003), *cert. denied, Deep v Recording Indus Ass'n of Am
Inc*, 540 US 1107 (2004) (finding, among other things that Aimster was likely to be found
liable for copyright infringement where Aimster allowed the sharing of music files, provided
a tutorial regarding how to share files on how to share files, and failed to provided sufficient
evidence that its services had ever been used for a non-infringing use).

Limitation Act (the "Act")[3] clarifies some of these issues by providing certain exemptions to "service providers"[4] from copyright infringement liability in certain circumstances.

Specifically, the Act provides certain exemptions or "safe harbors" from liability for claims of copyright infringement that arise out of the following service provider activities: (1) routing[5]; (2) caching[6]; (3) storage[7]; and (4) linking.[8] According to the Act, these safe harbors are additions to, rather than substitutes for, the defenses that service providers already possess under law.[9]

To be eligible for these safe harbors, service providers must meet minimum eligibility criteria, including adopting, reasonably implementing, and informing its subscribers and account holders of its policy providing for the termination of subscribers and account holders who repeatedly display or transmit infringing material.[10] In addition, to benefit from some of the limitations on liability, a service provider must designate an agent to receive notifications of alleged infringement.[11] The designated agent's contact

---

[3] Online Copyright Infringement Liability Limitation Act, 17 USC § 512 (2006) [hereinafter OCILLA].

[4] See 17 USC § 512(k)(1) (defining "service provider"). OCILLA defines "service provider" in two different ways, depending on the activity in which the entity is engaged. When an entity transmits, routes, or provides connections for third party material within the meaning of the safe harbor in 17 USC § 512(a), a "service provider" is defined as "an entity offering the transmission, routing or providing of connections for digital on-line communications, between or among points specified by a user, of material of the user's choosing, without modification to the content of the materials as sent or received." OCILLA, § 202 (new § 512 (k)(1)(A) (defining the term "service provider" for purposes of the safe harbor in 17 USC 512(a)). This definition is based on the definition of "telecommunications" in the Communications Act of 1934 and, according to the legislative history of the OCILLA, is intended to focus on providers of conduit functionality. H. Rep. No. 105–551, pt. 2, at 63 (1998). The legislative history further provides that "hosting a website" does not fall within the definition, while the "mere" provision of connectivity to a website does. *ibid.*, at 63–64. A university intranet is specifically envisioned as qualifying for the exemption. OCILLA, § 202 (new § 512(e)). For all other on-line activities addressed in the remaining safe harbor provisions of OCILLA, in 17 USC §§ 512(b), (c) & (d), the term "service provider" is expanded to include "providers of on-line services or network access or the providers of facilities therefor." OCILLA § 202 (new § 512(k)(1)(B)). The legislative history states that the definition includes, for example, "providing internet access, email, chat room and web page hosting services." H. Rep. No. 105–551, pt. 2, at 64 (1998). It is unclear whether the provider of a website that does not include such functionality is a "service provider" under this definition. In this regard, the frequent use of the terms "subscriber" and "account holder" suggests that OCILLA may not have been intended to apply generally to all websites, but only to those in which a "subscriber" or "account holder" relationship exists.

[5] See 17 USC § 512(a).

[6] See 17 USC § 512(b).

[7] See 17 USC § 512(c).

[8] See 17 USC § 512(d).

[9] See 17 USC § 512(l).

[10] See 17 USC § 512(i).

[11] While the DMCA requires that a copyright owner provide notice of alleged infringement to the ISP in a detailed manner, at least one court has held that such notice need not "perfectly" comply with the format described in the act. Rather, in order to take advantage of the DMCA's safe harbor provision, an ISP must remove or disable access to allegedly infringing material upon receiving a notice from the copyright owner that "substantially" complies with the notification requirement. *ALS Scan Inc v RemarQ Communities Inc*, 239 F.3d 619, 625 (4th Cir. 2001).

information must be made available through (a) the service provider's service, including the service provider's website in a location "accessible to the public", and (b) registration of the designated agent's contact information with the Copyright Office.[12]

In one case decided under the DMCA, *Corbis Corp v Amazon.com*,[13] the defendant company sued Amazon and others for copyright infringement, unfair competition, dilution of trade mark and other various claims. Amazon argued that it was immune to infringement claims under the DMCA.[14] The court found that Amazon qualified as a service provider by meeting all of the requirements for protection under the DMCA's safe harbor provision by adopting a user policy to suspend or terminate service for copyright infringers, communicating this policy to users, and reasonably implementing this policy.[15]

Likewise, in *Perfect 10 v CCBill*,[16] the court found that the defendant IBill was entitled to protection under the safe harbor provisions of the DMCA, and in its analysis reasoned that the defendant met the threshold requirements by adopting a policy that "states that [IBill] will terminate or disable the accounts of IBill clients who are accused of infringing third-party copyrights," and that IBill implemented this repeat infringer policy.[17]

The DMCA also makes it a crime to "circumvent a technological measure that effectively controls access to" a copyrighted work[18] or to sell or distribute to the public a technology that is designed to do so.[19] This circumvention provision has been the subject of several high-profile cases,[20] including one in which a federal district court enjoined the posting of computer code that circumvents a copy protection scheme,[21] and a criminal case in which a Russian computer programmer was charged with offering

6-297

---

[12] On November 3, 1998, the Copyright Office issued Interim Regulations that explain how service providers can properly register a designated agent for purposes of the Act. See 37 CFR § 201.38 (2006).

[13] *Corbis Corp v Amazon.com*, 351 F. Supp. 2d 1090 (W.D. Wash. 2004).

[14] *ibid.*, at 1098.

[15] *ibid.*, at 1100–02.

[16] *Perfect 10 v CCBill*, LLC, 340 F. Supp. 2d 1077 (D. Cal. 2004).

[17] *ibid.*, at 1087–90.

[18] 17 USC § 1201(a)(1)(A).

[19] 17 USC § 1201(b)(1)(A).

[20] See, e.g. *Real Networks Inc v Streambox Inc*, 2000 US Dist. LEXIS 1889 (W.D. Wash, January 18, 2000) (holding that plaintiff, a developer of products that enable users to access streaming audio and video content over the internet, had demonstrated a reasonable likelihood of success on its claims that defendant's software violated the DMCA because at least a part of defendant's product was "primarily, if not exclusively, designed to circumvent the access control and copy protection measures that RealNetworks affords copyright owners").

[21] See *Universal City Studios Inc v Reimerdes* 82 F. Supp. 2d 211 (S.D.N.Y. 2000) (enjoining website from posting or linking to a program capable of circumventing the copy protection of digital versatile disks (DVDs)). See also *Davidson & Assocs v Jung*, 422 F.3d 630 (8th Cir. 2005) (finding that appellants violated the anti-circumvention and anti-trafficking provisions of the Digital Millennium Copyright Act (DMCA) where appellants bought appellees game and thereby accepted an end user license agreement (EULA) and terms of use (TOU), which both banned reverse engineering and then used reverse engineering to allow anyone to play the games or pirated versions online).

for sale a software product allowing users to defeat the copy protection on electronic documents encoded in certain proprietary formats.[22]

Linking, framing and crawling

6-298 Although, as a general proposition, one cannot be held liable for simply linking[23] (or hosting a link) to another website, the act of linking to another website may in some circumstances be enjoined or otherwise lead to legal liability in the US. For example, a hyperlink may point to a website that incorporates textual or graphical materials protected by copyright and/or trade mark law.[24] In addition, hyperlinks may be used improperly to engage in a host of unfair trade practices including passing off and mis-appropriation of goods and services, as well as false advertising.

In one case, a Federal District Court enjoined a non-resident international defendant from using hyperlinks on its US-oriented website that directed users to its Italian-oriented website which contained infringing products. The company had previously been enjoined from advertising infringing products in the US.[25]

Hyperlinks that bypass the home page and advertising of a website (deep links) in a commercial setting have also been the subject of litigation. In *Ticketmaster v Tickets.com*, a US District Court judge refused to dismiss an action for multiple claims including tortious interference with business

---

[22] See *US v Sklyarov*, No 5–01–257 (ND Cal filed July 7, 2001) available at *http://www.eff.org/IP/DMCA/US_v_Elcomsoft/20010707_complaint.html* (criminal complaint alleging that a product offered for sale by a Russian company allowing users to defeat the copy protection on electronic documents encoded in certain proprietary formats violates the DMCA).

[23] Hyperlinks, also known as links, are points in web documents through which users may "branch" to other bodies of information. Web pages may contain any number of hyperlinks, each of which may point to files or documents on different machines in different locations. The power of linking lies in the fact that the links themselves can be embedded in content, thus allowing users of the web to easily locate information and seamlessly follow relationships between documents. As a general rule, materials published on the web may be viewed by all internet users unless affirmative steps are taken to limit access. As a result, websites are widely linked without prior consent from website owners.

[24] See, e.g. *Intellectual Reserve Inc v Utah Lighthouse Ministry Inc*, 75 F. Supp. 2d 1290 (C.D. Utah 1999) (preliminarily enjoining the defendant from linking to copyright-protected material on third-party websites); *Universal City Studios Inc v Reimerdes*, 273 F.3d 429 (2d Cir. 2001) (enjoining, under the anti-circumvention provision of the Digital Millennium Copyright Act, the posting of source code, as well as linking to the source code, of a computer program that decrypts the copyright protection scheme for DVDs). See also *Live Nation Motor Sports Inc v Davis*, 2006 US Dist. LEXIS 89552 (N.D. Tex. December 20, 2006) (holding that a live internet broadcast (webcast) is copyrightable material and the owner of the webcast has the right to prevent others from maintaining an unauthorised link to the webcast).

[25] *Jeri-Jo Knitwear Inc v Club Italia Inc*, 94 F. Supp. 2d 457 (S.D.N.Y. 2000). The defendant, an Italian clothing manufacturer, was accused of violating a prior injunction against "advertising or promoting" apparel bearing the plaintiff's trade mark in the US. The defendant operated two websites that were intended to market its non-infringing products to US consumers and another website, intended for consumers in Italy, where apparel bearing the plaintiff's trade marks was displayed. The two US websites contained links to the Italian website. The court found that the presence of these links on the US websites violated the injunction, and ordered the defendant to immediately "de-link" its Italian site from the others.

advantage, false advertising, unfair competition, reverse passing off and copyright infringement against Tickets.com for its deep links to information on Ticketmaster's site.[26]

The practice of using frames to incorporate third-party content into websites (i.e. framing), is also a source of controversy.[27]

"Web crawling" or "spidering," which allows internet users to search for merchandise or other information across many websites at once, can also lead to legal liability. In *Register.com v Verio Inc*, a federal judge in New York granted a preliminary injunction against Verio Inc, a provider of web hosting, high-speed internet access, and e-commerce products, ruling that Verio cannot use software robots to "crawl" the domain name registrar Register.com's computer system, including the "WHOIS" domain registration database, for mass marketing purposes.[28] Similarly, in *eBay v Bidder's Edge*, a federal court judge preliminarily enjoined an "auction aggregation" website from using web crawlers to access eBay's computer systems.[29] The court based its decision on the arcane theory of trespass to chattels, finding that the generation of 80,000 to 100,000 requests to eBay's computers each day was a "load on eBay's computer system [that] would qualify as a substantial impairment of condition or value."

Defamation

It is not clear to what extent US courts will be satisfied that jurisdiction exists in a defamation case where the only harmful event which occurs in a   **6–299**

---

[26] *Ticketmaster Corp v Tickets.com Inc*, 2000 US Dist. LEXIS 4553, 54 U.S.P.Q.2D 1344 (C.D. Cal. March 27, 2000) (denying preliminary injunction) and 2000 US Dist. LEXIS 12987 (August 11, 2000) (denying preliminary injunction), aff'd, 2001 US App. LEXIS 1454, 2 Fed. Appx. 741 (9th Cir January 22, 2001) (summarily affirming denial of preliminary injunction). In its opinion denying in part and granting in part defendant's motion to dismiss the plaintiff's complaint, the court found that "hyperlinking does not itself involve a violation of the Copyright Act ... since no copying is involved," and that there was no deception involved in Tickets's links, comparing them to "using a library's card index to get reference to particular items, albeit faster and more efficiently." *Ticketmaster Corp v Tickets.com Inc*, 2000 US Dist. LEXIS 4553 at *6, *9 (C.D. Cal. March 27, 2000). The court also dismissed Ticketmaster's breach of contract claim, holding that the agreement on Ticketmaster's home page setting forth terms and conditions of use—including no deep linking to its pages and no commercial use of the information—did not create an enforceable contract, and dismissing the claim with leave for Ticketmaster to amend to show that Tickets.com had knowledge of and agreed to those terms. *ibid.*, at *8. However, the decision explicitly let stand the claim that Tickets.com's links tortuously interfered with Ticketmaster's business advantage by disrupting income that would have been derived from its home page banner ads. *ibid.*, at *11–*12. The court also denied the motion to dismiss several other of Ticketmaster's claims, including false advertising, unfair competition, reverse passing off, and even the copyright infringement claim, on grounds separate from the linking. *ibid.*, at *9. The court refused, however, to grant the preliminary relief sought by the plaintiff. 2001 US Dist LEXIS 12987.

[27] See, e.g. *Hard Rock Café Int'l Inc v Morton*, 1999 US Dist. LEXIS 13760 (S.D.N.Y. September 9, 1999) (amending prior judgment prohibiting defendant from framing a third party website). See also *Shetland Times Ltd v Wills Scot. Sess.* Cas (10/24/96) 1 E.I.P.L.R. 723 (11/1/96) (temporary judgment requiring defendant to remove all links to the pages of the plaintiff's website). The case settled November 11, 1997.

[28] *Register.com v Verio Inc*, 126 F. Supp. 2d 239 (S.D.N.Y. 2000), aff'd, 356 F.3d 393 (2d Cir. 2004).

[29] *eBay Inc v Bidder's Edge Inc*, 100 F. Supp. 2d 1058 (N.D. Cal. 2000).

given forum is the actual damage suffered by a plaintiff.[30] Although a defamatory statement on an overseas website may well be regarded as having been "published" in the US,[31] a significant jurisdictional issue would still remain as to whether the "publisher" has purposefully availed himself of any US forum so as to allow a court to exercise personal jurisdiction over him.

Allegations of jurisdictional "minimum contacts" have been found to be sufficient in internet defamation cases by courts applying the *Calder* "effects" test,[32] although a number of others have held that mere allegations that a plaintiff feels harm in the forum state as a result of defamatory statements made on the internet are not enough to satisfy the "express aiming" required by *Calder*.[33]

However, in *Batzel v Smith*, a federal district court based a finding of sufficient contacts for the exercise of jurisdiction over an overseas defendant in a defamation case on the basis of both the highly interactive nature of the website and the defendant's purposeful activities in emailing news-

---

[30] There is much controversy surrounding federal and state law regarding the elements of defamation and, in particular, relating to on line defamation. For a more complete discussion of defamation issues related to the internet, see Julian S Millstein, Jeffrey D Neuburger, Jeffrey P Weingart, *Doing Business on the Internet: Forms and Analysis* (Law Journal Press, 1997–2001).

[31] See *American Civil Liberties Union v Reno*, 929 F. Supp. 824, 837 (E.D. Pa. 1996) aff'd, 521 US 844 (1997) (characterising as publishers those who post information on a website). While not a defamation case, *ACLU v Reno* has been cited by at least one US court for its definition of what it means to "publish" via the World Wide Web. See *Hearst Corp v Goldberger*, 1997 US Dist. LEXIS 2065 (S.D.N.Y. February 26, 1997).

[32] See para.6–294, see also *Northwest Healthcare Alliance Inc v Healthgrades.com Inc*, 50 Fed. Appx. 339, 341 (9th Cir. 2002) (finding that district court's jurisdiction was constitutional where the effects of "defendant's out-of-state conduct were felt in Washington, plaintiff's claims arise from that out-of-state conduct, and defendant could reasonably expect to be called to account for its conduct in the forum."); *EIAS Software Int'l LLC v Basis Int'l Ltd*, 947 F. Supp. 413, 420 (D. Ariz. 1996) (jurisdiction established by New Mexico defendant's posting on website of allegedly defamatory press release, which had "effects" in Arizona) and discussion *infra*. See also *Bochan v La Fontaine*, 68 F. Supp. 2d 692 (E.D. Va. 1999) (jurisdiction established by defendants' using their AOL account to post to Usenet newsgroup). In *Bochan*, the alleged defamatory statement was transmitted to AOL's Usenet server hardware located in Virginia, was temporarily stored on the server, and was then transmitted to other Usenet servers around the world. The court explained that because publication is a required element of defamation and because a "prima facie showing has been made that the use of Usenet server in Virginia was integral to that publication, there is a sufficient act in Virginia" to satisfy the state's long-arm statute.

[33] See *Revell v Lidov*, 2001 US Dist LEXIS 3133 (N.D. Tex. March 20, 2001) aff'd, 317 F.3d 467 (5th Cir. 2002) (applying effects test in declining to exercise personal jurisdiction in defamation case); *Lofton v Turbine Design Inc*, 100 F. Supp. 2d 404 (N.D. Miss. 2000) (applying effects test in declining to exercise personal jurisdiction in defamation case); *Bailey v Turbine Design Inc*, 86 F. Supp. 2d 790 (W.D. Tenn. 2000) (holding that posting of defamatory statements concerning the plaintiff on a passive website is not sufficient to support jurisdiction in Tennessee, the plaintiff's home state, because the plaintiff "was not attacked as a Tennessee businessman"); *Barrett v Catacombs Press*, 44 F. Supp. 2d 717 (E.D. Pa. 1999) (holding that the effects test of *Calder* was not satisfied because the defamatory statements were not expressly aimed at Pennsylvania: "If anything, the defamatory statements concern the plaintiff's non-Pennsylvania activities and impugn his professionalism as a nationally-recognised consumer health advocate").

letters and invitations to view the website to residents of the forum state, without analysing the *Calder*-type "effects" in the forum state.[34]

Right of publicity

The unauthorised commercial use of an individual's name or likeness on a   **6–300**
website can lead to liability under the laws of many US states.[35] For
example, in *Cuccioli v Jekyll & Hyde Neue Metropol Bremen Theater
Production GMBH & Co*,[36] a federal court recognised that the plaintiff
actor had a right of publicity in his image used on the cover of a CD
recording of the German production of a Broadway musical in which he
appeared. However, the court held that the offering for sale of the German
language CD on a German language internet website, created and maintained in Germany in connection with the German production of the show,
did not constitute a use within the state of New York as required by the
relevant New York statute.

Misrepresentation

A foreign website owner or operator might find itself subject to personal   **6–301**
jurisdiction in the US based on the posting of incorrect or misleading
information on an overseas internet site. Someone in the US who has relied
to his detriment upon such information might successfully claim that the
information was "published in" or "purposefully directed" at the US.

    For example, in *Cody v Ward*,[37] a Connecticut stock market investor
alleged that a combination of materially false computerised bulletin board
postings, email messages, and telephone calls, all from an out-of-state
defendant, led him to purchase securities in a company that was actually in
poor financial health. Focusing on the various telephone calls and email
messages directed by the California defendant toward the Connecticut

---

[34] *Batzel v Smith*, 2001 US Dist. LEXIS 8929 (C.D. Cal. June 5, 2001) (holding that the
emails, the republication of California newspaper articles on the defendant's website, and a
trip to California and sponsorship of the website by a California company "demonstrate
that the Defendants purposefully availed themselves of numerous opportunities to conduct
significant activities in the state").

[35] See, e.g. *Gridiron.com Inc v National Football League*, 106 F. Supp. 2d 1309 (S.D. Fla. July
11, 2000) (construing a contract with National Football League players concerning their
rights of publicity in connection with an internet website); *Suze Randall Photography v
Reactor Inc*, 2000 US Dist. LEXIS 6576 (N.D. Ill. May 12, 2000) (awarding damages under
federal copyright law and the Illinois Right of Publicity Statute for posting of photographs
on internet website).

[36] *Cuccioli v Jekyll & Hyde Neue Metropol Bremen Theater Production GMBH & Co*, 2001
US Dist. LEXIS 8699 (S.D.N.Y. June 28, 2001).

[37] *Cody v Ward*, 954 F. Supp. 43 (D. Conn. 1997).

plaintiff, the court refused to dismiss the case for want of personal jurisdiction.[38]

Similarly, the court in *Fowler v Broussard* held that it could exercise personal jurisdiction over numerous claims (including misrepresentation) relating to a dispute over the ownership and operations of a corporation, on the basis of the email and telephone communications that the non-resident defendants had with the plaintiff.[39]

In another case, a Maryland state court considered the jurisdictional impact of alleged misrepresentations made by email and fax in connection with the sale of a business. The court stated that when a party "knowingly sends into a state a false statement, intending that it should there be relied upon to the injury of a resident of that state, he has, for jurisdictional purposes, acted within that state" and the exercise of jurisdiction is therefore constitutionally permissible.[40]

6.23.4 Disclaimer defence?

6–302   A foreign website operator may not avoid liability in the US relating to the content of its website simply by posting a disclaimer notice on the site. For example, in *Euromarket Designs Inc v Crate & Barrel Ltd*,[41] the defendant's website contained the disclaimer, "Goods Sold Only in Republic of Ireland" and the Irish defendant asserted that it was not conducting commerce in the forum state. The court found the defendant's claim unpersuasive in light of the fact that the website allowed users to select US as part of both their shipping and billing addresses, the fields in which users entered their shipping and billing addresses were organised for a US-format address, i.e. city, state, zip code, and there was evidence that the company sold to at least one person in the forum state through its website.

To the extent that a unilateral notice limiting geographic access to a foreign site is accompanied by something more, e.g. a blocking mechanism or a choice of forum agreement, foreign website operators may be able to limit their liability.[42] In *Tech Heads Inc v Desktop Service Center Inc*, a

---

[38] The court held that defendant Ward's four telephone calls and 15 email transmissions to Cody rendered Ward liable to suit in Connecticut, where Ward's transmissions contained fraudulent misrepresentations made for the purpose of inducing Cody to buy and hold securities. *Cody v Ward*, 954 F. Supp. 43, 44 (D. Conn. 1997). Thus, under the "purposeful availment requirement of *Burger King*, the court's exercise of personal jurisdiction over Ward would not violate due process." *ibid.*, at 46–47.

[39] *Fowler v Broussard*, 2001 US Dist. LEXIS 573 (N.D. Tex. January 22, 2001).

[40] *Christian Book Distributors Inc v Great Christian Books Inc*, 137 Md App 367 (Ct. App. 2001) (upholding the exercise of jurisdiction) (quoting prior Massachusetts opinions, in a case involving the enforcement of a Massachusetts judgment).

[41] *Euromarket Designs Inc v Crate & Barrel Ltd*, 96 F. Supp. 2d 824 (N.D. Ill. May 16, 2000).

[42] *cf. Ligue Contre le Racisme et L'Antisemitisme v Yahoo! Inc*, No RG:00/05308 (TGI Paris, November 20, 2000) available at *http://www.juriscom.net/txt/jurisfr/cti/tgiparis20001120.pdf* (ordering a US website operator to block access by French citizens to auctions of Nazi items).

federal court found that it could exercise jurisdiction over a non-resident defendant on the basis of the defendant's "highly interactive" commercial website, because it encouraged interactivity and the exchange of information with users in other states as well as globally.[43]

However, the court commented in dicta that enterprises conducting business over the internet might be able to limit the jurisdictions to which they could be subject by adopting "(1) a disclaimer that they will not sell products or provide services outside a certain geographic area; and (2) an interactive agreement that includes a choice of venue clause to which a consumer or client must agree before purchasing any products or receiving any service."[44]

---

[43] *Tech Heads Inc v Desktop Service Center Inc*, 105 F. Supp. 2d 1142 (D. Or. July 11, 2000).
[44] *ibid.*, at 1152.

CHAPTER 7

Data Protection

7.1 WHY DATA PROTECTION IS RELEVANT TO THE INTERNET

7-001 The use of the internet for handling information may raise data protection issues in the following main areas, which we address in turn: publishing personal data, holding material on an internal system with internet connectivity, sending information by email, and acquiring data from a visitor to a website or similar resource.

7.1.1 Publishing personal data

7-002 Broadly, publishing personal data concerns publishing any information relating to an identifiable living individual on a website. This raises some issues which differ from publication in a hard copy medium:

- Publication on a website renders the material, by default, immediately available for transfer to a user in any country in the world. Although publication locally in hard copy may result in the material being taken to another jurisdiction, publication on a website may, depending on the way the material is hosted, have different consequences regarding, for instance, restrictions on transborder data flows.
- Publication on a website may, due to its greater reach, be regarded as different in kind from publication in a hard copy medium. For instance, personal data might be volunteered for publication in a small circulation magazine having a defined audience with a common interest.
- Publishing the same magazine on the web, even if primarily for the benefit of the same audience, exposes the personal data to a vastly wider readership than that which may have been

contemplated by those who submitted personal data for publication.[1] The fact that a website is a computerised medium also brings the publication firmly within the scope of data protection legislation.

- Publication on a website will give rise to issues concerning the security of the computer system driving the website and the ease or difficulty with which the system may be hacked and material altered or damaged.

- The internet has thrown up some novel forms of publication. For instance, public webcams are now common. These are cameras, connected to a website, pointed at views of offices, streets, beaches, ski slopes, townscape and landscape views or almost anything. They typically refresh every few minutes, or in some cases deliver live video. Their output can be viewed by anyone visiting the website. In some cases the visitor to the website can take control of the camera and pan and zoom it.[2]

7.1.2 Holding material on an internal database or computer system with internet connectivity

Most internal corporate computer systems have internet connectivity, for 7–003 instance to allow staff to access the internet or to allow third parties to access parts of the system (e.g. members of a closed "extranet" user group accessing their customer or supplier relationship data, or public access to a self-hosted website).

As soon as internet connectivity is made available, security concerns will arise from the fact that the internal computer system is now connected to the public network. These concerns will extend both to the protections built in to ensure that unauthorised third parties do not enter the private parts of the system and to whether the data are encrypted so as to be useless to a hacker who does breach the system's defences.

Issues will also arise within an international corporation as to cross-border data flows, for instance when customer and supplier staff (or indeed the corporation's own staff) are able to access the system from wherever in the world they may be.

Where personal data are incorporated into material held on an internet site available for public access or for access by members of a closed user

---

[1] In Belgium the Flemish regional government was ordered by the Belgian constitutional court to remove from its public website a list of sportsmen suspended for doping offences. The court held that publication on the website was a disproportionate interference with the right of privacy. However, circulation of lists by less intrusive means was still permitted. (Belgian Court of Arbitration Judgment 16/2005 of January 19, 2005.)

[2] It is reported that in 2002 the Danish Data Protection Agency ruled that a pub owner who broadcast live video of his customers on the internet required their consent in order to do so, since the pictures constituted personal data. (World eBusiness Law Report, October 2, 2002.)

group, different considerations apply. Unless access is restricted to a closed user group and is coupled with encryption and/or a firewall, any person with access to the internet can visit the site and extract information held on it. Such wide dissemination exposes data subjects to the risk that information relating to them may be acquired by strangers in other countries and used for unregulated purposes which were not in contemplation when the information in question was originally obtained from the data subjects concerned.

7.1.3 Sending information by internet email

7–004 This chapter is concerned primarily with the data protection implications of exposing personal data to public access through websites, but emails incorporating personal data, if addressed to users outside the UK or if unprotected by encryption, could carry less obvious risks of contravening EU or UK data protection law.

Internet email raises security issues as to whether the information can be intercepted during transmission, or at any of the points at which the email may be stored, and the significance of the country of location of such storage (e.g. an English resident who uses a US ISP for his dial-up internet access, so that his mail is held on a server in the US).

Again, the use of encryption may be relevant to the security concerns. Any internet transmission, not just email, may be routed through a number of different countries and may potentially be "sniffed" during transmission.

E-mail differs in often being stored in mailboxes hosted by intermediaries pending being accessed by the recipient, whereas a web or file download session is conducted in real time between the server and the user's PC. This also raises issues as to the obligations on intermediaries to comply with data protection principles.

The use of internet email may occasionally carry unexpected publication consequences. An example is the famous Clare Swire email incident, in which personal data of a salacious character was forwarded to a small local group of email recipients and within hours had found its way onto computer screens around the world.

When this effect is achieved intentionally, to promote a product or service, it goes under the name "viral marketing"; taking its name from the behaviour of email viruses that multiply as they are forwarded from one address list to the next.

7.1.4 Acquisition of data from a person visiting an internet resource such as a website

7–005 It is common for website operators, or banner advertisement companies and others, to acquire data about visitors to websites. Such acquisition may be overt, through the visitor completing a form, or may be invisible to the user (e.g. a "cookie" which tracks the user's path through the site and can be used to personalise the site for the individual visitor).

All these areas raise questions about the degree to which any activity falls within the territorial scope of EU or UK data protection legislation. Particular problems may be encountered in ascertaining where and by whom "processing" is taking place in a distributed network environment such as the internet.

The internet is an open environment which exists to publicise information and which encourages browsing. It presents unrivalled opportunities for the widespread dissemination of personal data. The scope for breach, whether through inadvertence or deliberate abuse, of the data protection principles is enormous.

For these reasons, it is important to take data protection considerations into account, and in doing so to consider the provisions of EU and UK data protection legislation, before allowing any personal data to be transmitted through the internet, or adding personal data to any website or internet accessible database.

7.2 EU DIRECTIVE ON DATA PROTECTION

7.2.1 General

On October 24, 1995, the European Union adopted Directive 95/46.[3] The   7–006
UK was required to enact the Directive's provisions not later than October 24, 1998, and did so on July 16, 1998 when the Royal Assent was given to the Data Protection Act 1998 (the "1998 Act"). The 1998 Act was brought into effect on March 1, 2000, when it repealed the 1984 Act in its entirety.

The objectives of Directive 95/46[4] are stated as being to protect the fundamental rights and freedoms of natural persons, and in particular their right to privacy with respect to the processing of personal data, and to prevent the restriction or prohibition of the free flow of personal data between Member States for privacy reasons (Art. 1).

The scope of Directive 95/46[5] is stated to extend to the processing of personal data wholly or partly by automatic means, and to the processing otherwise than by automatic means of personal data which form part of a filing system or are intended to form part of a filing system. These references to filing systems relate to the Directive's extension of the European Community's data protection regime to manual personal data held in structured sets which are accessible according to specific criteria (Art. 2(c)).

---

[3] Directive on the processing of personal data (Data Protection Directive).
[4] See fn.3 above.
[5] See fn.3 above.

The Directive is concerned primarily with the control of the purposes and methods of processing of personal data, and persons exercising such control, either alone or jointly or in common with others, are described by the Directive as "controllers".

The Data Protection Directive:

- Sets out principles relating to data quality;
- Provides that personal data may only be processed if specific criteria are met;
- Requires Member States to balance data protection with freedom of expression;
- Sets out rights for individuals—being

  - The right to be informed that their information is being processed;
  - The right to access their information and the right to object to certain types of processing.

These rights and obligations are subject to a number of exceptions.

In addition, the Directive:

- Sets out principles in relation to confidentiality and security;
- Requires Member States to establish notification schemes, whereby data controllers processing personal data must register with the local supervisory authority;
- Requires Member States to ensure that there are judicial remedies for breach of data protection legislation and that individuals who have suffered damage as a result can obtain compensation;
- Provides that transfers of personal data to countries outside the European Economic Area are to be prohibited unless such countries ensure "an adequate level of protection";
- Requires that Member States must establish public authorities responsible for monitoring data protection; and
- Finally, establishes a working party at European level (known as the Article 29 Working Party) with a remit to advise on all matters relating to data protection within the EU.

7.2.2 Applicable national law

7–007   Each Member State is to apply its national data protection law to processing of personal data which is carried out in the context of the activity of an establishment of the controller in that Member State.

Where a controller is established in the territory of several Member States, the controller must take the necessary measures to ensure that each of these establishments complies with the obligations laid down by each of these applicable national laws.

Where a controller is not established within any EEA territory, but makes use of equipment situated in a Member State for the purpose of processing personal data (otherwise than only for the purposes of transit through EEA territory), the controller must comply with the law of the Member State in which the equipment is situated and must designate a representative established in that territory (Art. 4).

On a strict reading of the Directive, a controller established outside the EAA who plants a cookie containing personal data on a user's hard drive located in an EEA state will be making use of that user's equipment and so must comply with the data protection law of that EEA state. In May 2002 the Article 29 Working Party established under the Data Protection Directive issued a Working Document on the international application of EU data protection law to personal data processing on the internet by non-EU based websites. The Working Party expressed the opinion that the Directive applies to cookies planted by data controllers outside the EU on computers located within the EU, the applicable national law being that of the country in which the computer is situated. The rationale for this view was that by means of a cookie the data controller exercised a degree of control over the user's equipment: "the controller determines which data are collected, stored, transferred, altered, etc., in which way and for what purpose".

The Working Document was issued before the adoption of the Directive on Privacy and Electronic Communications.[6] The question of the degree of control exercised by a data controller over the user's equipment now has to be viewed in light of Art. 5.3 of the Directive, which requires that the user be offered the right to refuse processing consisting of storing or gaining access to information stored in the user's equipment. The Directive was implemented in the UK by the Privacy and Electronic Communications (EC Directive) Regulations 2003,[7] which came into force on December 11, 2003. See discussion at para.7–012 below.

7.2.3 Cross-border data transfers to non-EEA countries

Controversially, Directive 95/46 requires Member States to provide that   7–008 the transfer to a non-EEA country or territory ("third country") of personal data which are undergoing processing or which are intended for processing after transfer, may take place only if the third country ensures an adequate level of protection. For this purpose, adequacy is to be assessed in the light of all the circumstances surrounding a data transfer operation, with particular consideration to be given to the nature of the data, the country of origin, the country of final destination, and the laws of that country (Art. 25).

Subject to the domestic laws of Member States governing particular

---

[6] 2002/58/EC of the European Parliament and of the Council of July 12, 2002.
[7] SI 2003/2426.

cases, transfers to third countries which do not ensure an adequate level of protection may take place only when:

- The data subject has given his consent unambiguously to the proposed transfer; or
- The transfer is necessary for the performance of a contract between the data subject and the controller or the implementation of pre-contractual measures taken in response to the data subject's request; or
- The transfer is necessary for the conclusion or performance of a contract concluded in the interest of the data subject between the controller and a third party; or
- The transfer is necessary or legally required on important public interest grounds, or for the establishment, exercise or defence of legal claims; or
- The transfer is necessary in order to protect the vital interests of the data subject; or
- The transfer is made from a register which, according to laws or regulations, is intended to provide information to the public and which is open to consultation either by the public in general or by any person who can demonstrate legitimate interest, to the extent that the conditions laid down in law for consultation are fulfilled in the particular case (Art. 26 (1)).

7–009   In addition to the derogations from Art. 25 listed above, there are also mechanisms under Directive 95/46 for certain third countries or certain types of transfer to be acknowledged as "adequate". In particular, the following options are available:

- To allow transfer to third countries which do ensure an adequate level of protection. Adequacy has been considered by the Working Party established by the Commission under Art. 29 of Directive 95/46[8] whose Working Document adopted in July 1998 sets out the Working Party's views on:
    - What constitutes "adequate protection";
    - The role of contractual provisions; and
    - Procedural issues and examples.

    A limited number of countries have been assessed as adequate—either in full, or in respect of certain data transfers only;
- To subject transfers to standard contractual clauses authorised by the European Commission, which are then imposed upon transferees (Art. 26(2)):

    — In June 2001 the Commission approved standard contractual

---

[8] See fn.3 above.

clauses for controller–controller transfers ensuring adequate safeguards for personal data transferred from countries within the EU to countries outside the EU;

— In December 2001, the Commission approved standard contractual clauses for controller–processor transfers;

— In December 2004, the Commission approved an alternative set of standard contractual clauses for controller–controller transfers which had been submitted by a number of business associations and which are generally accepted to offer more flexibility than the original standard contractual clauses for data controllers.

In *Lindqvist v Kammaraklagaren*[9] the European Court of Justice held that an individual in a Member State who loads personal data onto a website hosted by a person established in that State or another Member State, thereby making those data accessible to anyone who connects to the internet, including in a non-EU country, does not thereby transfer data to a third country. The court held that it was unnecessary to investigate whether the hosting provider's servers were physically located in a third country. 7–010

The reasoning of the court was that for a person to be held to have transferred data to a third country, that person has to have sent the data to that country. In the circumstances outlined above, the website proprietor who uploads personal data only sends the data to the person, established within the EU, who hosts the site. That allows the subsequent transmission of the data, by the hosting provider, to anyone who connects to the internet and seeks access to the data.

The court observed that if the Directive were interpreted to mean that there is a transfer of data to a third country every time that personal data are loaded onto an internet page, that transfer would necessarily be a transfer to all the third countries where there are the technical means needed to access the internet. The special regime provided by Ch. IV of the Directive would thus necessarily become a regime of general application, as regards operations on the internet. Even if one third country did not ensure adequate protection, the Member States would be obliged to prevent any personal data being placed on the internet.

The court stressed that the question referred to it concerned only activities of the individual uploading the data to the website, and not those of hosting providers. The logic of the court's decision puts hosts squarely in the frame, since it is the host that performs the act of transmission in response to a request received from a third country.

It should also be noted that the protection afforded by the hosting liability provisions of the Electronic Commerce Directive does not extend to data protection, since that is excluded from the scope for the Directive (see

---

[9] ECJ Case C–101/01, November 6, 2003.

reg.3(1)(b) of the Electronic Commerce (EC Directive) Regulations 2002[10]).

There are two further factual situations in which the *Lindqvist* decision would not be of assistance to a website proprietor. The first is where an individual makes use of a hosting provider established outside the EU. In that situation the act of uploading the data to the site would be a cross-border transfer. The second is where the website is self-hosted, rather than being outsourced to an independent host. In that situation the website proprietor would not only upload the data to the site, but would also send out data in response to requests from third countries. The latter would constitute a cross-border transfer.

7.3 DIRECTIVE ON PRIVACY AND ELECTRONIC COMMUNICATIONS

7.3.1 General

7–011   In 1997, the European Union adopted a directive relating to privacy in the telecommunications sector.[11] Almost as soon as this directive was adopted, it became apparent that it was out of date, as it was far from clear how—if at all—it would apply to the internet and other developing technology.

Widespread concern about the potential threats to privacy posed by the internet (for example through the use of cookies, spyware and similar) prompted the European Union to adopt a replacement directive—the Directive on Privacy and Electronic Communications.[12] This directive restates provisions relevant to telecommunications companies (for example relating to itemised billing and directories of subscribers and call forwarding provisions) but, in addition, it broadens the previous directive so as to apply it to new technologies.

Some provisions in the Privacy and Electronic Communications Directive only apply to service providers such as telecommunication companies and ISPs—for example obligations to ensure security of services and restrictions on use of traffic and location data.

However, in addition to the service provider specific obligations, the Privacy and Electronic Communications Directive also contains provisions of relevance to anybody who maintains a website or who uses email for the distribution of marketing material.

---

[10] SI 2002/2013.
[11] Directive 97/66/EC.
[12] 2002/58/EC of the European Parliament and of the Council of July 12, 2002.

7.3.2 Cookies and similar technology

Article 5 prohibits the use of technology such as cookies which allows   7–012
information to be stored or obtained from users unless the users have been
given "clear and comprehensive" information in advance about the purposes of the processing. In addition, users must be offered the right to refuse
this processing. The net effect of this is that an organisation wishing to use
cookies on its website must provide visitors to the website with a cookie
notice, which should either allow visitors to reject the planting of cookies or
should explain to them how they may configure their browser so as to do
this.

7.3.3 Unsolicited emails

Article 13 restricts the distribution of unsolicited direct marketing material   7–013
by electronic means. The article applies to automatic calling machines, fax
and email. In relation to email, unsolicited direct marketing is only allowed
in respect of individual subscribers who have given prior consent. Member
States have the option as to whether or not to extend this to corporate
subscribers.

There is an exception from this prohibition where the person sending the
marketing has obtained contact details from its customers in the context of
sale of a product or service and where it then wishes to use the contact
details to market its own similar products and services. For an organisation
to take advantage of this exemption, it must have offered an opt-out when
it first obtained the customer's details and it must repeat this opt-out on
each subsequent contact with the individual.

The net effect of Art.13 is to set up a prior consent (i.e. opt-in) regime
within the EU for direct marketing by email to individual subscribers. The
exemption which allows for direct marketing on an opt-out basis is quite
limited as it only covers an organisation's marketing of its own similar
products and services and does not apply at all where an organisation buys
in an email mailing list.

In addition, Art.13 requires organisations sending emails to ensure that
all marketing emails contain a valid address for unsubscribe requests.
Direct marketing which disguises or conceals the identity of the sender is
prohibited.

In the UK, the Directive is implemented by the Privacy & Electronic
Communications (EC Directive) Regulations 2003[13] and the Privacy &
Electronic Communications (EC Directive) (Amendment) Regulations
2004.[14]

---

[13] SI 2003/2426; see Ch.12.8 for further discussion of the UK implementation of the anti-spam
provisions of the Directive and the first UK case under the 2003 Regulations, *Microsoft
Corp v McDonald* (Lawtel, Lewison J., December 12, 2006).
[14] SI 2004/1039.

7.4 THE DATA PROTECTION ACT 1998—DEFINITIONS

7–014   Directive 95/46[15] was required to be implemented in each EEA state, including each of the EU Member States before October 24, 1998. The UK enacted the Data Protection Act 1998 (the "1998 Act"). The 1998 Act received Royal Assent on July 16, 1998, and was brought into effect on March 1, 2000. It repealed and replaced the Data Protection Act 1984 (the "1984 Act").

In an internet context, the most important definitions are of "data", "personal data", "processing", "data controller", and "data processor".

7.4.1 "Data"

7–015   "Data" under the 1998 Act means information which:

(a) is being processed by means of equipment operating automatically in response to instructions given for that purpose;

(b) is recorded with the intention that it should be processed by means of such equipment;

(c) is recorded as part of a relevant filing system, as defined by the 1998 Act, or with the intention that it should form part of a relevant filing system. The case of *Durant v Financial Services Authority*, considered further at para.7–023 below, adopts a restrictive interpretation of the term "relevant filing system". As this term relates to non-computerised—i.e. paper records—it is unlikely to be of relevance to organisations concerned with the processing of personal data in the context of the internet.

(d) does not fall within para.(a), (b) or (c) but forms part of an accessible record as defined by s.68 of 1998 Act (1998 Act, s.1(1)). (Broadly, an accessible record is defined by s.68 as a health record, local authority or special school record, local authority housing record or local authority social services record, in each case whether or not processed automatically); or

(e) is recorded information held by a public authority and does not fall within any of paras (a) to (d).

7.4.2 "Personal data"

7–016   "Personal data" under the 1998 Act means data which relate to a living individual who can be identified from those data or from those data and other information which is in the possession of, or is likely to come into the possession of, the data controller, and includes any expression of opinion

---

[15] See fn.3 above.

about the individual and any indication of the intentions of the data controller or any other person in respect of the individual.

Under the 1998 Act it is not essential that the data subject be immediately identifiable from the data held, or from those data and other information in the possession of the data controller, if other information identifying the data subject is likely to come into the possession of the data controller at some future time.

It follows that encrypted or otherwise anonymised data relating to an individual whose identity is hidden by the anonymisation will nevertheless be personal data if there is a likelihood of future identification, or capability of future identification, by the data controller either by decryption or by discovery by, or disclosure to, the data controller of other identifying information. "Likelihood" in this context is to be distinguished from probability on the one hand, and possibility on the other, and is presumably to be judged from current circumstances and not from hindsight.

In 2000 the Information Commissioner issued a guidance note[16] setting out his views on the meaning of "personal data" under the 1998 Act. This includes discussion of some specific internet issues.

As to email addresses, the Commissioner suggested that many email addresses are personal data, where the email address clearly identifies a particular individual. This might suggest that email addresses that do not identify a particular individual are not personal data. However, that would be too simplistic an approach. It is a question of fact in each case whether data relate to a particular individual.

The Commissioner suggested that data can relate to more than one individual and still be personal data about each of them, such as individuals who use the same email address. However, the individual must still be capable of being identified from the data or from other data in the possession of, or likely to come into the possession of, the data controller. The Commissioner's view was that it is sufficient if the data are capable of being processed by the data controller in such a way as to enable the data controller to distinguish the data subject from any other individual. So an email address that does not clearly identify an individual, but in combination with other data in the possession of the data controller can identify an individual, would be personal data.[17]

The Commissioner also took the view that information compiled about a   7–017
particular web user, even if there is no intention to link it to a name and
address or to an email address, is still personal data:

> "In the context of the on-line world the information that identifies
> an individual is that which uniquely locates him in that world, by
> distinguishing him from others."

[16] Personal Data Definition, Guidance Note, December 14, 2000.
[17] See also "E-mail Addresses—are they personal data? An assessment of the potential implications for Web site owners" P Carey [2000] Ent. L.R. 11 and "Data Protection and E-mail Addresses Revisited; is the DPA Workable?" J Harrington [2000] Ent. L.R. 141.

In this context the unique number and other information implanted in a cookie would be personal data.

However, an IP address alone, at least in the context of the public internet, would in most cases be unlikely to be personal data.[18] This is because, as used in the public internet, an IP address does not uniquely locate a user in the on-line world. Although a computer may be permanently associated with one IP address (a static IP address), many users of the internet do not have static IP addresses. They may be allocated a different IP address by their ISP each time they dial up to the internet (a dynamic IP address), or they may access through an anonymiser, or they may access through a corporate network, in which case the IP address visible to the outside world will often (for all users on the network) be that of a network proxy server. Conversely, in a private network that uses static IP addresses the data controller could identify at least the computer associated with the IP address, in which case the IP address could well be regarded as personal data relating to the regular user or users of that computer.

In *Durant v Financial Services Authority*[19] the Court of Appeal considered the breadth of the concept of personal data. The court adopted a narrow interpretation of "personal data". Auld L.J., with whom the other members of the court agreed, said:

> "not all information retrieved from a computer search against an individual's name or unique identifier is personal data within the Act. Mere mention of the data subject in a document held by a data controller does not necessarily amount to his personal data. Whether it does so in any particular instance depends on where it falls in a continuum of relevance or proximity to the data subject as distinct, say, from transactions or matters in which he may have been involved to a greater or lesser degree."

His Lordship went on to identify notions that might be of assistance. The first was whether the information was biographical in a significant sense, that is:

> "going beyond the recording of the putative data subject's involvement in a matter or an event that has no personal connotations, a life event in respect of which his privacy could not be said to be compromised".

The second was one of focus. The information should have the putative data subject as its focus rather than some other person with whom he may

---

[18] The Article 29 Data Protection Working Party established under the Data Protection Directive does not appear to share this view. See "Working document on data protection issues related to intellectual property rights", January 18, 2005.

[19] [2003] EWCA 1746.

have been involved or some transaction of event in which he may have figured or had an interest. "In short", said his Lordship,

> "it is information that affects his privacy, whether in his personal or family life, business or professional capacity."

This meaning of personal data is narrower than that previously adopted by the Information Commissioner. The Commissioner has subsequently issued specific guidance on the effect of *Durant*.[20]

7.4.3 "Processing"

The term "processing" is defined by the 1998 Act in such wide terms that it is difficult to imagine any activity in relation to information which is not included, from obtaining to destruction and including retrieval, disclosure, dissemination, alteration and combination. The addition of information to, or the alteration or deletion of information on or from, a website will be processing, as will the obtaining of information with a view to its addition to a website database or collection of pages.   **7–018**

7.4.4 "Data controller"

The term "data controller" means a person who, either alone or jointly or in common with other persons, determines the purposes for which and the manner in which any personal data are, or are to be, processed. This definition is subject to an exception where personal data are processed only for statutory purposes, in which case the person on whom the statutory obligation to process is imposed is the data controller.   **7–019**

7.4.5 "Data processor"

The 1998 Act's "data processor" is defined in relation to personal data as any person (other than an employee of a data controller who processes the data on behalf of the data controller) (1998 Act, s.1(1)). This definition appears effectively to exclude from the definition of data controller persons who process personal data solely on a data controller's behalf and replaces the 1984 Act's references to computer bureaux.   **7–020**

---

[20] "The Durant Guidance and its impact on the interpretation of the Data Protection Act 1998" (*www.ico.gov.uk/upload/documents/library/data_protection/detailed_specialist_guides/the_durant_case_and_its_impact_on_the_interpretation_of_the_data_protection_act.pdf*).

7.4.6 "Obtaining", "recording", "using" and "disclosing"

7–021　The terms "obtaining" and "recording" in relation to personal data include obtaining and recording information to be contained in personal data, and "using" and "disclosing" in relation to personal data include using and disclosing the information contained in personal data (1998 Act, s.1(2)). This appears to extend the concept of processing personal data to include obtaining, recording, using and disclosing information to be contained in, or contained in, or extracted from, personal data even though that information may not itself be personal data having, for example, been anonymised.

Whether this extends to anonymised so-called metadata, or meta-information, deduced from personal data remains to be seen. The first instance decision in *R v Department of Health, Source Informatics Ltd*[21] suggested that a UK court may construe confidence, and so the 1998 Act's control over unlawful processing, as extending to personal medical information even after the information had been anonymised, though the first instance finding of a breach of confidence was reversed on appeal.[22]

7.4.7 Notification

7–022　One of the key principles underlying data protection is the need for transparency—i.e. that there should be an easy way for individuals to find out which organisations are processing personal data about them. In order to promote this aim, the Data Protection Directive requires each Member State to set up a register of organisations that process personal data. In the UK, this register is maintained by the Information Commissioner. It is a public document and can be inspected on-line at the Commissioner's website.

Section 17 of the 1998 Act provides that a data controller may not process personal data unless he is included in this register—although secondary legislation has introduced a number of exemptions from this principle. Failure to notify, unless exempt, can result in criminal charges. In addition to the specific exemptions from notification introduced by secondary legislation, certain of the general exemptions in the provisions of the Act also mean that an organisation may not need to notify (see paras 7.6 *et. seq.*). For example, an individual who processes personal data purely for social and domestic purposes does not need to notify this processing with the Information Commissioner.

The obligation to notify also only covers records processed automatically. There is, therefore, no need to notify the fact that an organisation processes paper or other manual records—although this exemption is unlikely to be of assistance in the context of the internet.

---

[21] Queen's Bench Division. Judgment given May 28, 1999.
[22] [2001] 1 All E.R. 788.

If an organisation does have to notify, then this can either be done by telephone (current registration line is 01625 545740) or via the Commissioner's website. In fact, notification is a fairly straightforward process with guidance and template forms available online.

In April 1997 the Data Protection Registrar (as she then was) issued guidance on registration for internet users under the 1984 Act. This followed general guidance on data protection and the internet published in June 1995 as Appendix 6 to the Registrar's Eleventh Annual Report. The Appendix stressed the purpose of the internet as facilitating the exchange of information, and that protecting information runs counter to its culture: any proposal to use the internet to provide access to personal data or to communicate personal data from one user to another therefore needed to be regarded with caution. The whole tenor of the Appendix was to warn against the risks to privacy inherent in the use of personal data in a way which allowed access to or from the internet.

In the Notification Handbook issued under the 1998 Act the Commissioner points out that data controllers must indicate in their notifications (the term used in the 1998 Act and the Directive for registration) whether personal data are, or are to be, transferred outside the EEA: "transfer" in this context is not defined, but the ordinary meaning of the word is transmission from one place or person to another and this will include posting information on a website which can be accessed from overseas. In these circumstances the Commissioner states it is appropriate to indicate that worldwide transfers may be made.

7.5 THE 1998 ACT'S DATA PROTECTION PRINCIPLES

The 1998 Act includes, in Sch. 1, a set of eight data protection principles. 7–023
These are summarised as follows:

7.5.1 First principle (fair and lawful obtaining and processing)

Fair processing requires that the source of the information not be misled 7–024
and be made aware of the identity of the data controller acquiring the information and the purposes for which the information is to be used or disclosed.

In the context of internet use, potential disclosure and redisclosure is unlimited and almost any conceivable use by a third party may result from disclosure. It follows that it would be unfair to obtain personal data from an individual for publication on the internet without making this clear to the individual at the outset.

Informing the data subject about non-obvious purposes

7-025 Under the 1984 Act the Data Protection Tribunal supported the Registrar's view that personal information was not fairly obtained unless, before the information was obtained, the individual was informed of any non-obvious purpose for which the information was required (*Innovations (Mail Order) Ltd v Data Protection Registrar*[23]).

Again, if the data controller intends to include personal data on a database which will be publicly accessible over the internet, that fact should be made clear to the data subject to whom the data relate before the data controller obtains the relevant information from the data subject. Alternatively, the data controller should obtain the data subject's express positive consent before making the data publicly accessible over the internet.

The same principle applies to making personal data accessible to a closed user group, as opposed to making the data publicly accessible, though the consequences may be less serious in the former case. The Commissioner takes the view that disclosure by one company in a group of its customers' names and addresses to another company in the same group may be unfair unless either the intention to disclose was made clear to data subjects before their information was obtained, or data subjects' express consent to disclosure is given before disclosure is made.

Information obtained other than from the data subject

7-026 Where information is obtained from a source other than the data subject to which the information relates, consideration should be given to the position of the data subject. The Data Protection Registrar's Guidelines under the 1984 Act gave as an example a marketing company obtaining information from a secretary about his or her boss's lifestyle (Registrar's Guidelines (Fourth Series, September 1997), at p. 55).

The same principle applies to the 1998 Act. Personal data including information obtained from a source which had itself obtained the information for a limited purpose could be unfairly processed if the result of the processing were to make such personal data available over the internet, either publicly or to a closed user group.

Information obtained from a website

7-027 Where information is obtained by an internet user from a website, the user obtaining the information will usually be doing so at the implied invitation of the information provider controlling the site. Since one of the main purposes of such sites is to disseminate information to site visitors, a visitor could hardly be said to be unfairly obtaining any of the information offered.

However, if the information offered was of a kind which manifestly should not have been made available without the consent of the relevant

---

[23] Case DA/92 31/49/1.

data subjects, and was in fact made available without their consent, there may be unfair obtaining, and so unfair processing, of those data by site visitors: alternatively or additionally making the information available may be unfair processing by the data controller controlling the site.

Further conditions under the 1998 Act

Under the 1998 Act the first principle is elaborated with conditions which must be satisfied in relation to the processing of all personal data (Sch. 2) and further conditions which must additionally be satisfied in relation to the processing of sensitive personal data (Sch. 3). The term "sensitive personal data" means personal data consisting of information as to: **7–028**

- The racial or ethnic origin of the data subject;
- His political opinions;
- His religious beliefs or other beliefs of a similar nature;
- Whether he is a member of a trade union;
- His physical or mental health condition; or
- His sexual life;
- The commission or alleged commission by him of any offence; or
- Any proceedings for any offence committed or alleged to have been committed by him, the disposal of such proceedings or the sentence of any court in such proceedings (1998 Act, s.2).

Information to be provided to the data subject

A fair processing code is imposed (Sch.1, Pt II, paras 1–4) to regulate the obtaining of all forms of personal data, and requires that the following information be provided or made readily available to the data subject: **7–029**

- The identity of the data controller;
- The identity of any representative nominated by a data controller (when established outside the EU);
- The purposes for which the data are to be processed; and
- Any further information which is necessary, having regard to the specific circumstances in which the data are or are to be processed, to enable processing in respect of the data subject to be fair.

So far as is practicable, this information is to be provided to the data subject, or made readily available to him, whether the personal data are obtained either directly from him or from a third party.

Where the personal data are obtained otherwise than directly from the data subject, the required information is to be provided or to be made available when the data controller first processes the data, or before disclosure of the data to a third party. Where the personal data are obtained from a third party, providing the required information to the data subject is excused where its provision would involve a disproportionate effort, or where the recording or disclosing of the personal data is necessary for compliance by the data controller with a legal obligation other than an obligation imposed by contract.

Collecting information about website users

7–030   If site controllers collect information about their visitors, fair obtaining notices should be displayed at the site. A fair obtaining notice should state succinctly that the data are being collected, the identity of the controller of the site collecting the information or for whom the collection is being made, and any non-obvious purposes for which the collected information will be used.

If the site is maintained by a host or service provider for the site's controller, that controller will usually be the data controller in relation to the site and the service provider will be a processor for the 1998 Act's purposes.

However, the Commissioner recognises that a person may decide the purposes for which personal data are to be processed but delegate to another person responsibility for the way in which those data are to be processed: in such circumstances determination of the purpose for which personal data are to be processed is paramount in deciding whether or not a person is a data controller.

If both the service provider and the controller contribute to the control of the purposes and manner in which personal data are processed, each will be a data controller in the 1998 Act's terms.

In deciding whether any particular processing was fair for the purposes of the 1984 Act's first principle, the Data Protection Tribunal has held that first and paramount consideration must be given to the data subject, and that processing must be carried out in accordance with the principles laid down by the 1984 Act (*CCN v Data Protection Registrar*).[24]

7–031   The same principle applies to the 1998 Act. It follows that the exposure of any item of personal information on the internet is at risk of being held to be unfair processing if that item includes information relating to an identifiable individual who provided it for a limited purpose, was not then aware of a risk of its virtually worldwide exposure, and who had not subsequently given express and informed consent to disclosure of the data through the internet, whether publicly or to a closed user group or by email.

In the context of EU Directive 95/46,[25] the Article 29 Working Party has considered these issues. On February 23, 1999, it adopted a working document on the processing of personal data on the internet and its recommendation 1/99 on invisible and automatic processing of personal data on the internet performed by software and hardware. The working document criticises the secret collection of personal data and makes recommendations against such practices.

This working document has been succeeded by a number of other

---

[24] Case DA/90 25/49/9, at [52].
[25] See fn.3 above

documents, adopted by the same Working Party, considering data protection and the internet:

WP 100—opinion on proposals for a more consistent EU-wide approach to implementing the Data Protection Directive on the provision of information to data subjects (November 25, 2004).

WP 86—Working document on Trusted Computing Platforms and in particular on the work done by the Trusted Computing Group (TCG group) (January 23, 2004).

WP 76—Opinion 2/2003 on the application of the data protection principles to the Whois directories (June 13, 2003).

WP 60—Working document—First orientations of the Article 29 Working Party concerning on-line authentication services (July 2, 2002).

WP 56—Working document on determining the international application of EU data protection law to personal data processing on the internet by non-EU based websites (May 30, 2002).

WP 43—Recommendation 2/2001 on certain minimum requirements for collecting personal data on-line in the European Union (May 17, 2001).

WP 37—Working document "Privacy on the Internet"—An integrated EU Approach to On-line Data Protection (November 21, 2000).

WP 28—Opinion 1/2000 on certain data protection aspects of electronic commerce (February 3, 2000).

Cookies

The use of cookies (whether or not they make use of personal data) is now   7–032
governed by reg.6 of the Privacy and Electronic Communications (EC Directive) Regulations 2003 (SI 2003/2426), which came into force on December 11, 2003. These Regulations implement the Directive on Privacy and Electronic Communications.[26]

Regulation 6(1) lays down the general principle that a person shall not use an electronic communications network to store information, or to gain access to information stored, in the terminal equipment of a subscriber or user (i.e. to plant a cookie) unless the subscriber or user of that terminal equipment:

(a) is provided with clear and comprehensive information about the purposes of the storage of, or access to, that information; and

(b) is given the opportunity to refuse the storage of or access to that information.

Regulation 6(3) provides that where an electronic communications network is used by the same person to store or access information in the terminal

---

[26] 2002/58/EC of the European Parliament and of the Council of July 12, 2002.

equipment of a subscriber or user on more than one occasion, it is sufficient that the requirements set out above are met in respect of the initial use.

Under reg. 6(4), the principle set out in reg.6(1) does not apply to the technical storage of, or access to, information:

(a) for the sole purpose of carrying out or facilitating the transmission of a communication over an electronic communications network; or

(b) where such storage or access is strictly necessary for the provision of an information society service requested by the subscriber or user.

The requirements of the Regulations are in addition to, and do not detract from, the requirements of the 1998 Act in relation to processing of personal data (reg.4).

7.5.2 Second principle (specified and lawful purposes)

7–033   The second principle requires that personal data shall be obtained only for one or more specified and lawful purposes, and shall not be further processed in any manner incompatible with that purpose or those purposes.

The data controller may, in particular, specify the purposes for which personal data are obtained either in a notice to the data subject, or in a notification to the Commissioner under the notification provisions of Pt III of the Act (Sch.1, Pt II, para.5).

In determining whether any disclosure of personal data is compatible with the purposes for which the data were obtained, regard is to be had to the purposes for which the personal data are intended to be processed by any person to whom they are disclosed (Sch.1, Pt II, para.6). In the context of disclosure through the internet without the data subject's consent, the lack of any means of controlling the purposes for which the data may be used by persons to whom they are disclosed is likely to result in contravention of the second principle.

7.5.3 Third, fourth and fifth principles (adequacy, relevance, up-to-dateness and period of retention)

7–034   Data retention is becoming an increasingly contentious issue. The fifth principle provides that personal data processed for any purpose or purposes shall not be kept for longer than is necessary for that purpose or purposes. This principle is highly relevant to the data retention practices of internet service providers and others involved in the transmission of data through the internet.

Article 15 of the Directive on Privacy and Electronic Communications[27]

---

[27] 2002/58/EC of the European Parliament and of the Council of July 12, 2002.

permits Member States to adopt legislative measures providing for the retention of data for a limited period. Such measures must be necessary, appropriate and proportionate and must be to safeguard national security (i.e. State security), defence, and public security, for the prevention, investigation, detection and prosecution of criminal offences or of unauthorised use of an electronic communication system.

Section 102 of the Anti-terrorism, Crime and Security Act 2001 requires the Secretary of State to issue a code of practice relating to the retention by communications providers of communications data obtained by or held by them. The code of practice may contain such provision as appears to the Secretary of State to be necessary for the purpose of safeguarding national security; or for the purposes of prevention or detection of crime or the prosecution of offenders which may relate directly or indirectly to national security.

The status of the code of practice issued under this section is unclear, in particular as regards the extent to which it may affect a communication provider's obligations under the Data Protection Act 1998 not to keep personal data longer than necessary.

It is specifically provided that a failure to comply with a code of practice shall not of itself render the person liable to criminal or civil proceedings. A code of practice under the section is, however, admissible in evidence in any proceedings in which the question arises whether the retention of any communications data is justified on the grounds that failure to retain the data would be likely to prejudice national security; the prevention or detection of crime; or the prosecution of offenders.

The Foreword to the code of practice issued under the Act (as to which, see below) suggests that although individual communications providers must satisfy themselves that processing is "necessary", in doing so they are "entitled to rely heavily on the Secretary of State's assurance that the retention of communications data for the periods specified in the Code is necessary for the government's function of safeguarding national security, and on the fact that the Code has been approved by Parliament."

7–035

A Code of Practice (the "Voluntary Retention of Communications Data under Part 11: Anti-terrorism, Crime and Security Act 2001—Voluntary Code of Practice"), setting out a variety of retention periods for different types of communications data, was laid before Parliament on September 11, 2003. An Order (the Retention of Communications Data (Code of Practice) Order 2003[28]) bringing the code of practice into force was made on December 5, 2003.

Section 104 of the Anti-terrorism, Crime and Security Act enables the Secretary of State to make an order authorising the giving of mandatory directions to communications providers about the retention of communications data, and specifying the maximum period for which a direction may require a communications provider to retain communications data. Such an order is subject to approval by a resolution of each House. An

---

[28] SI 2003/3175.

order can only be made if the Secretary of State regards it as necessary to do so, after having reviewed the operation of the voluntary code of practice required to be issued under s.102.

Section 104 is subject to a "sunset" provision. Under this provision the power to make an order lapses after an initial period of two years from the passing of the Act, unless extended by a statutory instrument approved by a resolution of each House. On December 5, 2005 the Retention of Communications Data (Further Extension of Initial Period) Order 2005[29] came into force, extending the initial period for a second time until December 14, 2007.

Part 1, Ch. II of the Regulation of Investigatory Powers Act 2000, concerning access to communications data by government agencies, was brought into force on January 5, 2004. Details of the wide range of government agencies (in addition to those specified in the Act itself) and the individuals within them authorised to issue notices requiring the disclosure of communications data, for which of the purposes specified in s.22(2) of the Act and subject to what restrictions, are contained in the Regulation of Investigatory Powers (Communications Data) Order 2003.[30]

Information Tribunal decision on adequacy, relevance, and period of retention

7–036   On October 12, 2005, the Information Tribunal considered the application of the third and fifth principles to the police's practice of retaining "old" conviction data relating to individuals long after the individuals concerned had been convicted of the relevant offences and when there had been no subsequent convictions. The Tribunal Decision itself is very specific to facts of the particular cases and to policing requirements. Nonetheless, it shows the difficulty that organisations face generally in determining appropriate retention periods and the tension between the interests of law enforcement agencies and privacy and data protection concerns.

These tensions have been the subject of great controversy at a European level. A political commitment to a European legal instrument mandating that electronic communications service providers maintain certain types of data resulted in the adoption on March 15, 2006, of the Data Retention Directive.[31] This lays down mandatory data retention periods, applicable to providers of publicly available electronic communications services and public communications networks, in relation to specified traffic and location data and the related data necessary to identify the subscriber or registered user.

The Directive has to be implemented in Member States no later than

---

[29] SI 2005/3335.
[30] SI 2003/3172.
[31] Directive 2006/24/EC of the European Parliament and of the Council of March 15, 2006, on the retention of data generated or processed in connection with the provision of publicly available electronic communications services or of public communications networks and amending Directive 2002/58/EC.

September 15, 2007. However, Member States who have made a declaration to that effect may postpone implementation until March 15, 2009, in relation to internet access, internet telephony and internet email. The UK has made such a declaration. Member States are required to ensure that the categories of data specified in the Directive are retained for periods of not less than six months and not more than two years from the date of the communication.

7.5.4 Sixth principle (rights of data subjects)

The sixth principle requires that personal data shall be processed in accordance with certain of the rights granted to individuals by the Act—i.e. of access and to object to certain kinds of processing. Individuals may object to processing for direct marketing purposes and processing involving "automated decision taking" techniques (credit scoring being a good example of this). There is also a right to object to processing causing substantial damage or distress which is unwarranted. However, the detailed conditions relating to this right (at s.10 of the 1998 Act) mean that it is quite limited in practice. 7–037

7.5.5 Seventh principle (security)

The seventh principle requires that appropriate technical and organisational measures shall be taken against unauthorised or unlawful processing of personal data and against accidental loss or destruction of, or damage to, personal data. In the context of the internet and its known lack of security, storage of personal data on a database underlying a website without either firewall or other protection may be a breach of the seventh principle. 7–038

It is suggested in the Information Commissioner's Employment Code of Practice (Pt 1: Recruitment and Selection) that it is good practice, where an employer accepts job applications electronically (e.g. through a website), for the employer to provide a secure method of transmission. This is justified by reference to the seventh principle. It would extend the application of the seventh principle beyond the data controller's own IT systems or those of persons acting on his behalf, since the secure method would apply to the transmission over a public network of a message sent by a member of the public to the data controller's system.

Where any processing, including disclosure of personal data on a website, is undertaken by a data processor on behalf of a data controller, the 1998 Act includes express provisions for compliance with the seventh principle which require that:

- The data controller must choose a data processor providing sufficient guarantees in respect of the technical and organisational security measures governing the processing to be carried out; and

- Take reasonable steps to ensure compliance with those measures (1998 Act, Sch. 1, Pt II, para. 11).

Additionally, the processing must be carried out under a contract which is made or evidenced in writing and under which the data processor is to act only on instructions from the data controller, and the contract must require the data processor to comply with obligations equivalent to those imposed on a data controller by the seventh principle (Sch. 1, Pt II, para. 12 to the 1998 Act).

Since control of the purposes for which personal data are processed on a website is usually retained by the person promoting the website, it is likely that that person will be the data controller in relation to that processing and, even though the processing is undertaken or managed by an ISP, host or other third party, the third party is likely in this context to be a processor only. A written contract between the website promoter and the ISP will then be required to comply with the seventh principle.

7.5.6 Eighth principle (transborder data flows)

7–039   The eighth principle under the 1998 Act requires that personal data shall not be transferred to a country or territory outside the EEA unless that country or territory ensures an adequate level of protection for the rights and freedoms of data subjects in relation to the processing of personal data.

An adequate level of protection is one which is adequate in all the circumstances, having regard in particular to:

- The nature of the personal data;
- The country or territory of origin of the information contained in the data;
- The country or territory of final destination of that information;
- The purposes for which, and period during which, the data are intended to be processed;
- The law in force in the country or territory in question;
- The international obligations of that country or territory;
- Any relevant codes of conduct or other rules which are enforceable in that country or territory (whether generally or by arrangement in particular cases); and
- Any security measures taken in respect of the data in that country or territory (Sch. 1, Pt II, para. 13 to the 1998 Act).

7–040   This principle is subject to express exceptions in cases where the eighth principle does not apply, namely where:

- The data subject has given his consent to the transfer;
- The transfer is necessary for the performance of a contract between the data subject and the data controller, or for the taking of steps at

the request of the data subject with a view to his entering into a contract with the data controller;

- The transfer is necessary for the conclusion of a contract between the data controller and a person other than the data subject which is entered into at the request of the data subject or is in the interest of the data subject, or for the performance of such a contract;
- The transfer is necessary for reasons of substantial public interest; or
- The transfer is necessary for the purpose of, or in connection with, legal proceedings, obtaining legal advice, or otherwise for establishing, exercising or defending legal rights; or
- The transfer is necessary to protect the vital interests of the data subject; or
- The transfer is part of the personal data on a public register and any conditions subject to which the register is open to inspection are complied with by any person to whom the data are or may be disclosed after the transfer; or
- The transfer is made on terms which are of a kind approved by the Commissioner as ensuring adequate safeguards for the rights and freedoms of data subjects; or
- The transfer has been authorised by the Commissioner as being made in such a manner as to ensure adequate safeguards for the rights and freedoms of data subjects (the Commissioner has not, in practice, authorised specific transfer in this way) (Sch. 4 to the 1998 Act).

The application of this principle to the publication of personal data on the internet has been considered by the European Court of Justice and is discussed further at para.7–014.

7.6 THE 1998 ACT'S EXEMPTIONS

The 1998 Act provides for a number of exemptions which are of varying   7–041
scope and effect. In relation to the internet, many of these exemptions are only likely to be relevant to personal data transmitted by email to specified addressees and most of them are unlikely to apply to personal data exposed to the internet on a website: however, for completeness, a summarised list of the 1998 Act's exemptions is set out below.

Some of these exemptions are expressed in s.27 to be from:

- the 1998 Act's subject information provisions: these are, broadly, that part of the fair processing code under the first data protection principle (Sch.1, Pt II, para.2) which requires information to be provided to the data subject, together with subject access right (ss.7 and 8); and/or in the alternative from:
- the 1998 Act's non-disclosure provisions: these are broadly the first data protection principle, except Schs. 2 and 3 imposing conditions

on the processing of all personal data and of sensitive personal data respectively, the second, third, fourth and fifth data protection principles, the right to prevent processing likely to cause damage or distress (s.10) and the rights to rectification, blocking, erasure and destruction (s.14(1)–(3)).

The subject information provisions may broadly be characterised as provisions of the 1998 Act which entitle data subjects to be given information about personal data relating to them, and the non-disclosure provisions may broadly be characterised as provisions of the 1998 Act which protect data subjects in certain circumstances from the adverse consequences of disclosure and certain other processing of personal data relating to them.

The 1998 Act's exemptions have been classified by the Commissioner as primary and miscellaneous respectively: the primary exemptions are set out in Pt IV of the 1998 Act, and the miscellaneous exemptions are set out in Sch. 7.

7.6.1 Primary exemptions

7–042   The primary exemptions may be summarised as follows:

National security (s.28)

Personal data are exempt from:

- The data protection principles;
- Pt II (rights of data subjects);
- Pt III (notification and registration);
- Pt V (enforcement); and
- Section 55 (unlawful obtaining and sale of personal data)

if the exemption is required for the purpose of safeguarding national security. The exemption is by certificate given by a Minister of the Crown.

In *Norman Baker MP v Secretary of State for the Home Department*,[32] the Information Tribunal held that even the wide terms of this provision did not allow the Home Secretary to issue a blanket certificate exempting the Security Service from complying with a subject access request under s.7(1)(a) of the 1988 Act.

Crime and taxation (s.29)

7–043   Personal data processed for the purposes of:

- Prevention or detection of crime;
- Apprehension or prosecution of offenders; or

---

[32] Information Tribunal, October 1, 2001.

- Assessment or collection of taxes

are exempt from the subject information provisions (see above) in any case to the extent that the application of those provisions would be likely to prejudice those purposes. The inclusion of the words "in any case", which do not appear in s.29 (national security), avoid the use of claims to exemption in general terms without consideration of particular facts;

Health, education and social work (s.30)

The Secretary of State may (and has) by order, exempt information from   7–044
the subject information provisions (see above) where the information relates to:

- The physical or mental health of a data subject;
- Present or former pupils of a school; or
- Social work;

Regulatory activity (s.31)

Personal data processed for certain specified regulatory activities (e.g.   7–045
financial services, charities and health and safety at work) are exempt from the subject information provisions (see above) in any case to the extent that their application would be likely to compromise the proper discharge of those regulatory functions;

Journalism, literature and art (ss.3 and 32)

Personal data processed for journalistic, artistic or literary purposes (the   7–046
"special purposes") are exempted from:

- The data protection principles, except the seventh (security);
- Subject access (ss.7 and 8);
- The right to prevent processing likely to cause damage or distress (s.10);
- Rights in relation to automated decision-taking (s.12); and
- Certain of the rights to rectification, blocking, erasure or destruction (s.14(1)–(3)).

These special purposes exemptions are only available if the processing is undertaken with a view to publication of journalistic, literary or artistic material and the data controller reasonably believes that, having regard in particular to the special importance of the public interest in freedom of expression, publication will be in the public interest and that, in all the circumstances, compliance with the provision exempted is incompatible with the special purposes.

While directed primarily at protecting the freedom of the media, and in particular the press, the special purposes exemption is in broad terms and may have a wider effect than is immediately apparent. The terms "journalism", "artistic" and "literary" are not defined, and in the context of the internet any person may claim to be a journalist or engaged in literary or artistic expression.

There is a requirement (s.32(4)(b)) that, when proceedings are brought against a data controller under certain provisions of the 1998 Act, the court shall stay the proceedings if it appears to the court that any personal data to which the proceedings relate are being processed only for the special purposes and with a view to publication by any person of any journalistic, literary or artistic material which, at the time 24 hours immediately before the court's consideration, had not previously been published by the data controller. Prior publication by another person is not relevant.

There is a separate requirement under s.12 of the Human Rights Act 1998 which applies if a court is considering whether to grant any relief which may affect the rights of freedom of expression under Art. 10 of the European Convention on Human Rights, to which the UK is a party. Apparently aimed at preventing applications to the court to restrain publication on privacy grounds, these provisions may be difficult to apply if publication occurs on or through the internet.

The provisions of s.32 of the Data Protection Act 1998 were considered both at first instance[33] and then by the Court of Appeal in *Campbell v Mirror Group Newspapers Ltd.*[34] At first instance, Morland J. held that the s.32 exemptions only applied pre-publication; once material was published, newspapers would have to comply with the 1998 Act. The Court of Appeal held: (1) that publication of hard copies that reproduce data previously processed by means of automatic equipment forms part of processing and falls within the scope of the Act, (2) that the protection of ss.32(1)–(3) of the Act applied both before and after publication, and (3) that the protection of s.32 applied to publication as well as to prior processing.

The House of Lords' judgment[35] upheld Ms Campbell's appeal and reinstated the award of damages made at first instance. However, as none of the Law Lords considered s.32, its application remains unclear.

The Swedish Supreme Court in the *Ramsbro* case[36] considered the scope of the journalism exemption in the Data Protection Directive and concluded that the data controller need not be a professional journalist. It was sufficient that the personal data published contributed to a debate on issues of general interest.

Research, history and statistics (s.33)

7–047 Personal data processed only for research purposes are, subject to detailed and complex conditions, exempted from:

---

[33] [2002] EMLR 30: [2002] HRLK 28: *The Times*, March 29, 2002.
[34] [2002] EWCA Civ 1373.
[35] [2004] 2 A.C. 457.
[36] June 12, 2001.

- The second principle (processing to be compatible with specified and lawful purposes), to the extent that the processing for research purposes may be said to be incompatible with the purposes for which the personal data were obtained;
- The fifth data protection principle (personal data not to be kept longer than necessary); and
- Subject access (s.7).

Information statutorily available to the public (s.34)

Personal data consisting of such information are exempt from: 7–048

- The subject information provisions;
- The fourth data protection principle (accuracy and up-to-dateness);
- Certain of the rights to rectification, blocking, erasure or destruction (s.14(1)–(3)); and
- The non-disclosure provisions.

Disclosures required by law or made in connection with legal proceedings (s.35)

Personal data are exempt from the non-disclosure provisions where the   7–049
disclosure is required by or under any enactment, by any rule of law or by
order of a court (s.35(1)), or where the disclosure is necessary for the
purpose of or in connection with any legal proceedings (including prospective legal proceedings) or for the purpose of obtaining legal advice or
otherwise for the purposes of establishing, exercising or defending legal
rights (s.35(2)).

In *Totalise Plc v The Motley Fool Ltd*[37] Owen J. held that the exemption
under s.35(2) was not limited to legal proceedings brought by the data
controller or to legal advice obtained by the data controller. So s.35(2) did
not restrict the jurisdiction of the court under *Norwich Pharmacal* principles[38] to order the proprietor of a website discussion board to disclose the
identity of someone who had made defamatory postings to the discussion
board. Certain aspects of Owen J.'s judgment were overturned on appeal,[39]
however, this element of his judgment was not.

Domestic purposes (s.36)

Personal data processed by an individual only for the purposes of that   7–050
individual's personal, family or household affairs (including recreational
purposes) are exempt from the data protection principles and the provisions
of Pt II (rights of data subjects) and Pt III (notification and registration). In
the *Lindqvist* case (considered at para.7–010) the ECJ held that the

---

[37] Unreported, February 19, 2001, QBD.
[38] See Ch. 6.
[39] [2002] 1 W.L.R. 1233: [2003] 2 All E.R. 872: [2002] E.M.L.R. 20: FSR 50: *The Times*, January 10, 2002: *The Independent*, February 25, 2002.

exemption only covers "activities which are carried out in the course of private or family life of individuals which is clearly not the case with the processing of personal data consisting in the publication on the internet so that those data are made accessible to an indefinite number of people".

7.6.2 Miscellaneous exemptions

7–051 The miscellaneous exemptions are set out in Sch.7 and in summary comprise:

Confidential references (para.1)

7–052 References given or to be given by a data controller in confidence for the purposes of education, employment or appointment of the data subject, or for the purpose of the provision by the data subject of any service, are exempted from subject access (s.7).

Armed forces (para.2)

7–053 Personal data are exempt from the subject information provisions in any case to the extent to which the application of those provisions would be likely to prejudice the combat effectiveness of any of the armed forces of the Crown.

Judicial appointments and honours (para.3)

7–054 Personal data processed for the purposes of assessing any person's suitability for judicial office or the office of Queen's Counsel, or the conferring by the Crown of any honour, are exempt from the subject information provisions.

Crown employment and Crown or ministerial appointments (para.4)

7–055 The Secretary of State may by order exempt from the subject information provisions personal data processed for the purposes of assessing any person's suitability for employment or appointment by the Crown.

Management forecasts (para.5)

7–056 Personal data processed for the purposes of management forecasting or management planning to assist the data controller in the conduct of any business or other activity are exempt from the subject information provisions in any case to the extent to which the application of those provisions would be likely to prejudice the conduct of that business or other activity.

Corporate finance (para.6)

7–057 Where personal data are processed for the purposes of or in connection with a corporate finance service the data are exempt from the subject information provisions to the extent that the data controller reasonably believes that the application of those provisions to the data could affect the price of a financial instrument, or if the exemption is required for the purpose of safeguarding an important economic or financial interest of the UK.

Negotiations (para.7)

Personal data which consist of records of the intentions of the data controller in relation to any negotiations with the data subject are exempt from the subject information provisions in any case to the extent to which the application of those provisions would be likely to prejudice those negotiations.

7–058

Examination marks (para.8)

Personal data consisting of marks or other information processed by a data controller for the purpose of determining the results of an academic, professional or other examination are subject to an exemption from subject access (s.7) under detailed provisions intended to suspend subject access for a period of time until and after the announcement of the results of the examination.

7–059

Examination scripts (para.9)

Personal data consisting of information recorded by candidates during an examination are exempt from subject access (s.7).

7–060

Legal professional privilege (para.10)

Personal data are exempt from the subject information provisions if the data consist of information in respect of which a claim to legal professional privilege, or in Scotland to confidentiality as between client and professional legal adviser, could be maintained in legal proceedings.

7–061

Self-incrimination (para.11)

A person need not comply with a subject access request to the extent that compliance would, by revealing evidence of the commission of any offence other than an offence under the 1998 Act, expose him to proceedings for that offence, and information disclosed by any person in compliance with a subject access request is not to be admissible against him in proceedings for an offence under the 1998 Act.

7–062

7.7 OFFENCES UNDER THE 1998 ACT

The following is a summary of offences under the 1998 Act, any of which may relate to processing in connection with the inclusion of personal data

7–063

on a website openly accessible from the internet or the transmission of personal data by email over the internet:

- Ss.17 and 21: processing without notification;
- Ss.20 and 21: failure to notify changes to registrable particulars;
- S.22: in the case of processing designated by a Secretary of State's order as "assessable processing", undertaking processing of that kind before expiry of the 28 days' period allowed for assessment by the Commissioner, or before expiry of that period and any extension of up to a further 14 days notified by the Commissioner. No assessable processing order has been made to date;
- S.24: failure to comply within 21 days with a written request for relevant particulars which a data controller has elected not to notify to the Commissioner in respect of manual data in relevant filing systems;
- S.47(1): failure to comply with a Commissioner's supervisory notice;
- S.47(2): knowingly or recklessly making a false statement in response to an information notice;
- S.50 and Sch.9: intentional obstruction of, or failure to give reasonable assistance in, execution of a warrant of entry and inspection granted to the Commissioner by a circuit judge; and
- S.55: knowingly or recklessly, without the consent of the data controller, obtaining or disclosing personal data or the information contained in personal data, or procuring the disclosure to another person of the information contained in personal data; or selling data obtained by the seller in contravention of the foregoing provisions.

In July 2006 the Department of Constitutional Affairs (DCA) issued a Consultation Paper on increasing penalties for deliberate and wilful misuse of personal data. The DCA proposes to increase the penalties under s.55 of the Act to imprisonment for up to two years on indictment and up to six months on summary conviction. This followed a report to Parliament by the Information Commissioner "What Price Privacy? The unlawful trade in confidential personal information".

7.8 ENFORCEMENT AND REMEDIES UNDER THE 1998 ACT

7.8.1 Enforcement notices (ss.40 and 41)

7–064 The Commissioner may serve an enforcement notice on a data controller if the Commissioner is satisfied that the data controller has contravened or is contravening any of the data protection principles. The Commissioner may not serve enforcement notices on data processors and others: this is a weakness in the Act.

In deciding whether to serve an enforcement notice, the Commissioner is required to consider whether the contravention has caused or is likely to cause any person damage or distress, but it is not necessary for the issue of an enforcement notice that any such damage or distress should in fact have been caused.

An enforcement notice is obliged to require the person on whom the notice is served to take such steps as are specified in the notice for complying with the principle or principles contravened.

The 1998 Act also contains provisions in relation to inaccurate data and the rectification, blocking, erasure or destruction of data containing expressions of opinion based on inaccurate data.

The power to issue enforcement notices under the 1998 Act is substantially restricted in relation to processing for the special purposes (journalism etc.: see para.7–046 above). There is power for the Commissioner to cancel or vary an enforcement notice.

7.8.2 Request for assessment (s.42)

Any person who is, or who believes himself to be, directly affected by any processing of personal data may request the Commissioner for an assessment as to whether it is likely or unlikely that the processing in question has been or is being carried out in compliance with the 1998 Act. **7–065**

The person making the request need not be a data subject and may, for example, be a competitor of a data controller whose alleged non-compliance directly affects the person making the request.

The Commissioner must make the assessment requested, but may determine the manner of its making and is not required to take further action beyond informing the person making the request as to whether the assessment has been made and, to the extent that the Commissioner considers it appropriate, any view formed or action taken as a result of the request.

7.8.3 Information notices (ss.43 and 44)

The Commissioner is given power under the 1998 Act (ss.43 and 44) to serve a notice on a data controller requiring the provision by the data controller of information as specified in the notice. An information notice may be served either: **7–066**

- Following a request for assessment under s.42 (see above); or
- In order to determine compliance by the data controller with any of the data protection principles.

There is a right of appeal from an information notice, and there are urgency provisions.

An information notice may not require:

- Any breach of legal professional privilege; or
- The provision of information which may reveal the commission of offences other than offences under the 1998 Act.

The Commissioner is given power to cancel an information notice.

The Commissioner's information notice powers in relation to processing for the special purposes (journalism, etc.: see para.7–046 above) are restricted to a limited "special information notice" (s.44), but the Commissioner is given power to determine that personal data are not being processed only for the special purposes or are not being processed with a view to publication by any person of journalistic, literary or artistic material which has not previously been published by the data controller.

Such a determination is subject to a right of appeal, but is not to take effect until the end of the period within which an appeal can be brought and, where an appeal is brought, pending the determination or withdrawal of the appeal.

Failure to comply with an information notice or a special information notice is an offence (s.47(1)).

Points to be considered in connection with information notices include the following.

An information notice may only be served on a data controller. Accordingly, an information notice may not be served on:

- A person who processes only data which are not personal data; or
- A person who processes personal data but only does so as a "data processor" as defined by the 1998 Act, who is not otherwise a data controller and who processes personal data only on behalf of data controllers. Except in respect of data controllers, the Commissioner appears to be as powerless under the 1998 Act as the Registrar under the 1984 Act to obtain information, including information as to whether or not a person is a data controller.

7.8.4 Powers of entry and inspection (s.50 and Sch.9)

7–067   Powers of entry and inspection exercisable under a warrant issued by a circuit judge are provided (s.50 and Sch.9 to the 1998 Act).

Under the 1998 Act a judge may issue a warrant even though entry into premises is granted if the occupier then unreasonably refuses to comply with a request by the Commissioner to permit searching, inspection, examination, operation and testing of equipment or inspection or seizure of documents and other materials.

A judge may not issue a warrant unless the Commissioner has given seven days' notice in writing to the occupier of the premises demanding access and access and searching has been unreasonably refused, but this provision is not to apply if the judge is satisfied that the case is urgent and that compliance with the notice requirement will defeat the object of the entry.

The powers of entry and seizure conferred by a warrant are not exercisable in respect of personal data:

- Exempted by virtue of s.28 (national security); or
- Protected by legal professional privilege.

7.8.5 Individuals' rights

Subject access (ss.7 and 8)

Under ss.7 and 8 an individual is entitled to be told whether a data con-   7–068
troller processes personal data in relation to him and to be given a copy of such information in permanent form, together with certain supplemental information. The following detailed points should be noted:

- The 40 day period allowed for response to a subject access request does not start to run until the data controller has received the required fee and any information reasonably requested by the data controller in order to satisfy himself as to the identity of the person making the request and to locate the information sought;
- The data controller must tell the individual the purposes for which the relevant personal data are being processed and to whom they are or may be disclosed;
- The individual's personal data must be supplied in permanent form by way of a copy, except where the supply of a copy is not possible or would involve disproportionate effort;
- The data controller must provide any information available as to the source of the data, except where the source is an individual who may be identified and who has not consented to the disclosure (in this case, the Act requires the data controller to balance the rights of the two individuals); and
- Where processing by automatic means is used to evaluate matters relating to the subject access applicant, such as, for example, his performance at work, his creditworthiness, his reliability or his conduct, and has constituted or is likely to constitute the sole basis for any decision significantly affecting him, the applicant is entitled to be informed of the logic involved in that decision-taking, if he requests this information and unless it amounts to a trade secret.

Where a subject access request is made to a credit reference agency the request will be deemed to be limited to personal data relevant to the individual's financial standing unless the request shows a contrary intention.

Right to prevent processing likely to cause damage or distress (s.10)

7–069 An individual is entitled by written notice to a data controller to require the data controller to cease or not to begin processing personal data relating to that individual where such processing is causing or is likely to cause unwarranted substantial damage or substantial distress, either to the data subject or to another individual. This right is subject to exceptions where the data subject has consented to the processing or where the processing is necessary:

- For the performance of a contract to which the data subject is a party, or for taking steps at the request of the data subject with a view to entering into such contract;
- For compliance with any legal obligation to which the data controller is subject, other than an obligation imposed by contract; or
- To protect the vital interests of the data subject.

The data controller has 21 days to respond to the data subject's notice to prevent processing: the response is to be by written notice to the data subject stating that the data controller has complied or intends to comply, or alternatively setting out reasons for regarding the data subject's notice as unjustified.

Where the data subject considers that the data controller has not complied with the request to prevent processing the data subject can seek a court order, and the court may order the data controller to take such steps as are necessary to comply with the notice. In practice, a data subject may be reluctant to incur the expense of applying to a court, and may look to other remedies by way of complaint to the Commissioner and by request assessment under s.42.

The right to prevent processing is required to be exercised by written notice to the data controller. Failure to give notice would not necessarily deprive a data subject of the right to claim compensation for unfair processing in contravention of the first principle.

The right to prevent processing may be of particular relevance if defamatory material is posted on websites, such as anonymously on a website discussion forum. However, the journalism exemptions may also be relevant.

Right to prevent processing for direct marketing (s.11)

7–070 An individual is entitled by written notice to a data controller to require the data controller to cease, or not to begin, processing personal data relating to the applicant for purposes of direct marketing. "Direct marketing" means the communication (by whatever means) of any advertising or marketing material which is directed to particular individuals, and there is a right to apply to the court if a data controller fails to comply with the data subject's notice. The court may order the data controller to take such steps to comply with the notice as the court thinks fit: alternatively, the data subject may request assessment by the Commissioner under s.42.

Rights in relation to automated decision-taking (s.12)

In addition to the extended right of subject access under s.7 in relation to automated assessment and decision-taking (see above), an individual is entitled by notice in writing to a data controller to require the data controller to ensure that no decision taken by or on behalf of the data controller which significantly affects the individual is based solely on processing by automatic means of personal data relating to the individual, where the processing is for the purpose of evaluating matters relating to the individual as, for example, his performance at work, his credit worthiness, his reliability, or his conduct.

7–071

Where no such notice has effect and a decision which significantly affects an individual is based solely on processing by automatic means of personal data relating to that individual, the data controller must, as soon as is practicable, notify the individual that the decision was taken on that basis and the individual is entitled, within 21 days of receiving the notification, by notice in writing to require the data controller to reconsider the decision.

These provisions have no effect in relation to "exempt decisions". These are defined as decisions taken in the course of steps taken:

- For the purpose of considering whether to enter into a contract with the data subject; or
- With a view to entering into or in the course of performing such a contract; or
- Which are authorised or required by or under any enactment; or
- If the effect of the decision is to grant a request of the data subject; or
- If steps have been taken to safeguard the legitimate interests of the data subject, for example by allowing him to make representations.

An individual may apply for relief to the court, but the court's power is limited to ordering the person responsible for the decision to re-consider it or to take a new decision not based solely on automated processing.

As for the rights to prevent processing under ss.10 and 11, this right must be exercised by written notice to the data controller, but failure to give written notice would not necessarily deprive the data subject of the right to claim compensation for unfair processing in contravention of the first principle.

The provision that this right relates only to decisions based solely on automatic processing of personal data will presumably exclude decisions which are in any respect based on any other factors, and the remedy available, namely application to the court, is limited. It may be possible alternatively to apply to the Commissioner for assessment under s.42.

Compensation (s.13)

7–072   An individual who suffers damage by reason of any contravention by a data controller of any of the requirements of the 1998 Act is entitled to compensation from the data controller for that damage, and for associated distress. It is a defence to a claim for compensation to prove that the data controller has taken such care as in all the circumstances was reasonably required to comply with the requirement concerned.

Rectification, blocking, erasure and destruction (s.14)

7–073   If a court is satisfied on the application of a data subject that personal data of which the applicant is the subject are inaccurate, the court may order the data controller to rectify, block, erase or destroy those data and any other personal data in respect of which he is the data controller, and which contain an expression of opinion which appears to the court to be based on inaccurate data.

Where the court makes an order and is satisfied that personal data which have been rectified, blocked, erased or destroyed were inaccurate, the court may also, where it considers it reasonably practicable, order the data controller to notify third parties to whom the data have been disclosed of the rectification, blocking, erasure of destruction ordered by the court. In determining whether it is reasonably practicable to require such notification the court is to have regard, in particular, to the number of persons who would have to be notified.

If a website were to contain inaccurate personal data which a court were to order to be deleted from the site, it would be open to the court to order the data controller to trace visitors to the site and to inform them of the deletion, to the extent that it was reasonably practicable to do so.

CHAPTER 8

Communications and Broadcasting Regulation

8.1 INTRODUCTION

This Chapter explains how current UK and EU communications and broadcasting regulations apply to the internet, and to services provided by means of the internet. **8–001**

When considering regulation in this context, it is important to ask who is doing what. A communications operator that owns and operates the communications infrastructure which makes up the internet is performing a different function from an internet service provider (ISP), that provides internet access and web hosting services to its customers across the communications operator's infrastructure, or an Application Service Provider (ASP) that provides on-line applications across the internet to its customers.

Considerable progress has been made over recent years towards adapting the communications regulatory framework to the activities of ISPs and ASPs. This has resulted in some curious paradoxes. The internet has become an open environment through the effectiveness of the self-regulation and non-discrimination in which it has its origins. Despite this, now that it is established as a competitive industry, communications-style regulation is becoming increasingly relevant.

The Communications Act 2003 introduced some significant changes to the regulation of communications and broadcasting in the UK, most notably through the implementation of the EU Electronic Communications Directives of 2002 and the introduction of a new converged[1] regulator, the Office of Communications (OFCOM). The focus of communications regulation is now on electronic communications networks and electronic communications services instead of *"telecommunications systems"* as under the old regime.

---

[1] OFCOM replaced the previous Office of Telecommunications, Independent Television Commission and Radio Authority.

Convergence

8–002 Despite the geographical and technical neutrality of the internet making regulation difficult to apply, a desire to promote convergence has prompted regulators to try to extend existing communications regulatory principles to include the internet, rather than rolling back communications regulation to avoid it. This may be a short term trend: if current proposals prove unenforceable or appear to constrain rather than promote competition, regulation may be rapidly scaled down, if not eliminated altogether. The regulatory framework which affects the internet for the time being is discussed below.

As we discuss later in this Chapter, there may be potential for existing broadcasting regulations to impact on some internet activities. In practice to date, broadcast regulators in the UK have, for the most part, not attempted to assert any significant regulatory authority over internet content.

The rapid speed at which the internet has evolved has demonstrated that established regulations and procedures appear outmoded and in some cases inappropriate. The internet has been a contributing factor to the increasing breakdown of the distinction between broadcasting and communications.

Communications regulation seeks to control the provision and operation of the underlying physical network and access to that network through imposition of service supply obligations on operators with market power, promotion of competition, sophisticated interconnection rules, and non-discriminatory tariffing policies.

In contrast, broadcast regulation has tended to focus on preventing a concentration of media ownership and the imposition of controls on content, such as requiring a balanced and impartial range of programme content and minimum quotas for local and/or independent content.

8–003 As we explain in this Chapter, technical and commercial convergence between communications and broadcasting service provision is making it increasingly nonsensical to maintain distinct regulatory structures, designed for separate activities with differing aims in mind.

The task becomes impossible where a single dynamic new technology is involved. For instance, any regulatory structure which seeks to regulate according to content, e.g. distinguishing between voice and data traffic or regulating video graphics as opposed to text, is fraught with problems. The convergence of the broadcasting, communications and IT industries has allowed text, data, video, audio, and images to be reduced to binary code before transmission to the end-user, often rendering it impossible to know what type of content is being transmitted. This is particularly the case with the internet where, generally,[2] data is reduced to uniform packets transmitted using the TCP/IP protocol.

---

[2] Some specialised protocols do exist within the general internet protocol structure. For instance, UDP (Uniform Datagram Protocol) can be used instead of TCP (Transmission Control Protocol). Because of its particular characteristics UDP is more suitable for real-time applications such as voice or video. However, that does not mean that the type of content contained within a UDP packet can reliably be deduced from the use of UDP.

Technical and commercial convergence have, in turn, brought about pressure for regulatory convergence, which have led to the replacement of the existing separate communications and broadcast regulatory structures with a single regulatory framework. This has been achieved in the UK by the Communications Act 2003, which introduced a single regulator, OFCOM.

Whether the type of content regulation that has been thought appropriate for broadcast media has any place in relation to interactive content, has been, and remains, a hotly debated topic. Much content on the internet has its roots in print media or individual speech (which are largely unregulated) rather than in television (which is heavily regulated). These issues are discussed further in Ch.12.

8.1.1 Regulatory background

Communications regulation

The communications sector is a regulated industry. In common with water,   8–004 gas, electricity and rail, telecommunications services were, for many years, provided by a government owned utility company with monopoly rights. The UK monopolist, British Telecommunications Plc (BT) was privatised in 1984, by the Telecommunications Act (the T. Act) to make way for a competitive market. However, BT's historical monopoly gave it market power in practically every services market which other operators might wish to enter.

The situation was, and is, complicated by the "networked" nature of the telecommunications industry, which means that BT's new competitors were reliant on BT for essential inputs into their services, the most important of which is BT's national and international network infrastructure, particularly its access lines into end-user premises.

A sectoral regulator was appointed to ensure competition and to protect consumers of communications services. In practice, at the time of privatisation, the regulator's job was to impose constraints on BT, so that other operators might offer competing services on something like a level competitive playing field. Until this could happen, the regulator had to ensure that consumers' rights did not take second place to shareholders interests through the imposition of retail price controls.

The original telecommunications regulator was the Director General of   8–005 Telecommunications, whose Office of Telecommunications was generally known as "OFTEL". Whereas OFTEL's primary function at the time of privatisation was regulation of BT's retail prices for voice services, technological change, and in particular the commercialisation of the internet, brought about a sea-change in OFTEL and now OFCOM's remit.

OFTEL's regulatory functions in the electronic communications sector were transferred to OFCOM at the end of 2003. At the beginning of the 21st century, the principal focus of communications regulation is to remove barriers to a flourishing IP and internet based electronic communications industry.

Broadcast regulation

8–006   Broadcast regulation has a completely different genesis from communications regulation. Broadcast regulation has historically been justified mainly on the basis of spectrum scarcity—that broadcast airwaves being limited in what they can carry, broadcast programming should be subjected to a degree of control that does not apply to traditional media such as newsprint.

Spectrum scarcity does not exist on the internet. Some may argue that other justifications for broadcast regulation, such as intrusiveness or pervasiveness, can apply to some types of internet content. However, the internet has developed fundamentally as a user-selectable medium, in contrast to the programmed, simultaneous, "push" environments characteristic of traditional broadcasting.

8.2 TELECOMMUNICATIONS LICENSING AND REGULATION

8.2.1 Licensing

8–007   The Communications Act 2003 abolished the previous system of telecommunications licences and introduced a new general authorisation scheme whereby, as a general rule, providers of electronic communications networks and electronic communications services are authorised to operate subject only to complying with certain "General Conditions of Entitlement".

Under the Communications Act 2003 anyone who provides an electronic communications service (ECS), electronic communications network (ECN) or associated facilities,[3] is subject to the General Conditions of Entitlement. Collectively, these operators are known as communications providers. Not every condition applies to every communications provider. The Communications Act 2003 gives OFCOM the power to decide which, if any, services must be pre-notified to OFCOM. Operators can only be prohibited from providing services which have been made subject to such a process. OFCOM has not yet required any services to be pre-notified to it.

Further conditions are imposed on those operators with "Significant Market Power" (SMP) (see para.8–008 below) and "universal service conditions" are imposed on designated universal service operators, BT and Kingston Communications (Hull) Plc.

---

[3] An Associated Facility is neither an ECN or an ECS, but supports the provision of either: for example, conditional access facilities are associated facilities.

In addition, whether or not SMP has been identified, OFCOM is authorised generally to apply specified types of access related conditions (in particular relating to conditional access systems in relation to broadcasting) and to apply privileged supplier conditions in relation to operator(s) holding special or exclusive rights in non-communications markets.

Individual conditions may also be imposed where an individual licence is granted to use a radio spectrum allocation or where numbers are designated for an operator's use. Individual orders can also be made by OFCOM, which impose consumer protection obligations on specified operators, particularly requiring membership of a dispute resolution body such as Otelo (the Office of Telecommunications Ombudsman). OFCOM also determines which operators are to be given powers to apply the Electronic Communications Code facilitating the location of their facilities on roads or private land.

Significant market power conditions

Before imposing SMP conditions, OFCOM must first identify which operators have SMP in a given market based on prior analysis of that market. In defining the relevant markets for this purpose and in considering whether to make a determination of SMP, OFCOM must take account of the European Commission's Recommendation on Relevant Product and Service Markets within the Electronic Communications Sector and the Commission's accompanying Guidelines, pursuant to the EU Framework Directive.

The existence of SMP is to be determined on the basis of whether or not the network or services provider in question has a dominant position in the relevant market[4] (i.e. a position of economic strength affording it the power to behave, to an appreciable extent, independently of competitors, customers and ultimately consumers). Two or more operators may be treated as jointly dominant and therefore jointly to have SMP.[5] One or more operators can also be taken to enjoy a dominant position in a market by reason of his or their position in a closely related market, where the links between the two markets allow the market power held in the closely related market to be used in a way that influences the other market so as to strengthen the position of such operator(s) in that other market.

Where OFCOM has made a determination that the operator(s) in

8–008

---

[4] Construed in accordance with Art.14 of the EU Framework Directive.
[5] Two or more undertakings can be found to be in a position of joint dominance therefore jointly to have SMP if, even in the absence of structural or other links between them, they operate in a market the structure of which is likely to give rise to co-ordination between such undertakings. Criteria such as a mature market, similar cost structures, similar market shares and absence of excess capacity are some of those used to determine whether or not two undertakings have joint dominance in the context of the Access Directive.

question holds SMP in an identified market,[6] it is authorised to impose the following types of SMP conditions: on network access; concerning carrier pre-selection and pre-selection; regulating services for end-users, concerning the supply of electronic communications equipment and conditions concerning leased lines.

Any SMP conditions imposed must be: objectively justifiable in relation to the networks, services, facilities, apparatus or directories in question; not unduly discriminatory between persons or classes of persons; and proportionate and transparent to what is intended to be achieved.

OFCOM is required to publish in advance its proposed decisions identifying a market for these purposes, making any SMP determination and imposing SMP conditions.[7]

8.2.2 Interconnection and access

8–009   Whereas retail service is increasingly open to intense competition, regulation at the network level still underpins relationships between all providers of communications networks and services. The internet has raised a host of new issues, for example, unmetered access.

Interconnection is the connection of different communications systems. This is essential so that end-users on one network can be connected to end-users on another network. It also enables end-users to access services and content which are hosted by a service provider other than the operator used to obtain access to "the network".

8–010   The Communications Act 2003, in implementing the EU Access and Interconnection Directive 2002/19 (the "Access Directive") sets out the basic rules for interconnection rights and obligations. The basic principle under the new regime is that interconnection of, and access to, networks should be agreed on the basis of commercial negotiations and it is only

---

[6] Member States are required to carry out analysis of relevant markets to determine whether the particular market is sufficiently competitive. OFTEL (prior to the transfer of powers to OFCOM in December 2003) concluded that, in relation to fixed geographic call termination markets, each operator of a fixed public electronic communications network has SMP in respect of a distinct market for fixed call termination on its network. This conclusion applies to each of BT, Kingston Communications (Hull) Plc and 52 named network providers listed in an annex to OFTEL's Notification. Under the old regime, only BT and (for the Hull area) Kingston were designated as SMP operators.

[7] A copy of such notifications must be sent to the European Commission and to the national regulatory authorities ("NRA") of all other Member States where, in OFCOM's view, trade between EC Member States would be affected. If the European Commission informs OFCOM within a month that it has serious doubts about as to the compatibility of the proposed measure with EU requirements, then OFCOM may not implement the proposal for a further two months. If the Commission vetoes the proposal during this two month period OFCOM must withdraw it.

when this is not achieved that regulation should intervene. Therefore, all providers of Public Electronic Communications Networks[8] now have rights and obligations to negotiate interconnection (previously this was restricted to Annex II operators[9]).

All Electronic Communications Services are now subject to interconnection obligations (previously these were restricted to network services, i.e. basic conveyancing, excluding value added services). Equally, all providers of Electronic Communications Services can now require "Access" whether or not they have their own systems. One fundamental aspect of the regime that has not changed[10] is that additional obligations (to supply interconnection and access to meet reasonable standards) are imposed on those communications providers with SMP.

Although generally more relaxed in its approach, the Access Directive fixes a considerable degree of responsibility on fixed operators determined to have SMP,[11] to allow access to their networks, not to discriminate or show preferential treatment between their own downstream activities and those of other operators, to publish standard terms and conditions for service supply and to offer cost-orientated interconnection and access charges. These operators must also publish separate accounts to prevent anti-competitive cross subsidies. As before, mobile operators with SMP remain subject to a lesser set of obligations.

While the Access Directive establishes clear criteria for the obligation to supply access, the ultimate decision as to which particular obligations are imposed is placed with the national regulator. The Access Directive defines who should be granted interconnection rights in general terms to be interpreted and given practical effect by national regulatory authorities. Under the old system, OFTEL took an inclusive approach to granting these rights, extending what was historically known as "Relevant Connectable System" (RCS) status to internet service providers for the first time.

8–011

Disputes relating to network access can be referred to OFCOM by either party and OFCOM must handle that dispute unless it considers an alternative means of resolution more appropriate (s.185, Communications Act 2003). OFCOM then has four months from the date of referral to resolve

---

[8] Rights to negotiate interconnection rights will be granted, by virtue of the General Conditions of Entitlement, to those who can show they provide an ECN which is provided wholly or mainly for the purpose of making ECS available to members of the public. See OFTEL draft Interconnection Guidelines which can be found on the OFCOM website (*www.ofcom.org.uk/static/archive/Oftel/publications/eu_directives/2002/intg0902.htm*).

[9] Annex II to the old Interconnection Directive (97/33/EC).

[10] Although clearly the definition of SMP has itself changed.

[11] Under the old regime, operators with more than a 25 per cent share in specified markets such as fixed, mobile and leased lines were deemed to have SMP. The new definition of SMP is more in line with the traditional competition law concept of dominance which is generally considered to be somewhere above a 40 per cent market share. OFTEL concluded that, in relation to fixed geographic call termination markets, each operator of a fixed public electronic communications network has SMP in respect of a distinct market for fixed call termination on its network. This conclusion applies to each of BT, Kingston Communications (Hull) Plc and 52 named network providers listed in an annex to OFTEL's Notification. Under the old regime, only BT and (for the Hull area) Kingston were designated as SMP operators.

the dispute. In this context, OFCOM may make a declaration as to the rights and obligations of the parties to the dispute and may even fix the terms of future transactions between the parties, including the imposition of new obligations on each. In particular, within these powers, OFCOM is entitled to direct a party to make payments to the other to adjust over-payment or underpayment.

8.2.3 Competition rules

8–012 In addition to regulatory obligations in significant market power condi-tions, general conditions of entitlement and universal service conditions, general competition law applies to the electronic communications sector.

The Competition Act 1998, introduced into UK legislation in 2000, adopts established EU concepts, such as the prohibitions against abuse of a dominant position and anti-competitive agreements or concerted practices.

The Communications Act 2003 also gives general competition law powers to OFCOM under the Competition Act and the Enterprise Act 2002. In particular, OFCOM is given concurrent jurisdiction with the Office of Fair Trading with regard to the electronic communications sector, under the provisions of the Competition Act concerning restrictive agree-ments (and concerted practices) and abuse of a dominant position.[12]

Internet Service Providers, whose activities are frequently dependent on services provided by third party operators with established market power, may need to have recourse to competition remedies. These are dealt with in detail in Ch.14.

8.2.4 Regulation of the internet and ISPs

8–013 The internet is not, in itself, the subject of communications style regulation. This is because, as the platform for a commercial industry, it has grown organically from a situation of commercial parity, rather than out of a monopoly. Service diversification and technological innovation have pro-moted competition, making regulation unnecessary.

Nevertheless, convergence between traditional circuit switched commu-nications networks and modern infrastructure which uses Internet Protocol (IP) routing, as well as erosion in the distinction between internet service providers and communications service providers means that some com-munications regulation now maps directly onto the internet industry. It can be both a risk factor and a strategic tool. How communications regulation directly affects the internet and the businesses which provide its constituent networks and services, is discussed in the next section.

---

[12] OFCOM also has concurrent powers with regard to market investigation references to the Competition Commission under Pt 4 of the Enterprise Act 2002.

8.3 LICENSING INTERNET SERVICE PROVISION

The focus of communications regulation is now on ECNs and electronic **8–014** communications services instead of *"telecommunications systems"* as under the old regime. Electronic communications networks are wider in scope than "systems" in that they include satellite broadcasting networks, the internet, cable TV networks, and radio broadcasting networks as well as traditional circuit switched communications networks. ECNs also include software and stored data associated with a transmission network. An ECS involves a service of conveying signals by means of any such network, but excludes the provision of content.

A broadcast transmission service which distributes a television or radio channel is thus an ECS although the channel itself is not—so the network or platform provider is a service provider, but the company which creates the channel is not a service provider (unless of course they are one and the same).

PECS and PATS

The General Conditions of Entitlement impose a small set of obligations on **8–015** all service providers whose activities it authorises. Within these rules, a distinction is drawn between those who provide Public Electronic Communications Services (PECS) and those who provide electronic communications services which cannot be treated as being provided to the public, for example, services provided by means of a private network or to certain closed user groups only.

Within the class of providers of PECS, there is a further sub-class of providers of Publicly Available Telephone Services (PATS) and these are usually confined to originating and terminating operators (i.e. those controlling access and excluding transit or trunk operators and resellers).

The General Conditions of Entitlement also impose certain consumer protection obligations on providers of PECS and providers of PATS. Providers of PATS must make access to emergency services available, give customers the opportunity to be included in directories and the right to have such information withheld and generally provide access to a directory enquires service and operator assistance. They are also required to give priority service restoration to public bodies, at the request of OFCOM, in times of civil emergency or disaster. Any provider of PATS must also publish certain information relating to its services. They are also subject to additional responsibilities to customers with disabilities. Suppliers of PATS must offer number portability to any of their subscribers on request by the subscriber or by another communications provider. Suppliers of PATS with revenues over a certain threshold set by OFCOM must also seek approval of their metering and billing systems.

All PECS providers must make available an out of court scheme to settle disputes with customers (e.g. Otelo), publish a consumer Code of Practice which OFCOM must approve,[13] and offer contracts covering certain specified matters.

8.3.1 Licensing internet systems and services

8–016   Providers of internet network infrastructure—Tiers 1 to 3 backbone providers, for example, offering international routing and conveyance—will generally have to build or take a long term lease in international cables. These providers generally no longer require individual licences: they operate under the General Conditions of Entitlement.

8.3.2 Voice and data

8–017   The previous regulatory distinctions between voice and data services are no longer relevant. Under the old regime, EU rules on licensing treated voice and data differently. Voice service providers were subject to individual licensing procedures, whereas data service providers generally were not, although they were subject to general authorisations or class licences. The UK licensing framework was designed for systems, rather than services, and most systems do not distinguish between voice and data. The UK solution was to move to a system of class licensing for most types of system, irrespective of whether it is used for voice or data services.

8–018   The systems run by internet access providers typically consist of routers, switches and private circuits leased from public telecommunications operators and used to provide data international simple resale services between the UK and all countries in the world. This is now permissible under the General Conditions of Entitlement.[14]

Previously, an operator wishing to provide voice international simple resale services was required to register its activities with the Department of Trade and Industry ("DTI") under the ISVR class licence. Again, this is now permissible under the General Conditions of Entitlement.

8.3.3 Internet voice telephony services

What is VoIP?

8–019   It is possible, using internet protocols and packet-switching techniques, to provide voice telephony services over the internet and other data networks (VoIP). Voice calls are conveyed as data packets, using internet protocol as a routing and transmission technology, over the public internet and also over private, point to point networks.

---

[13] There is a standard industry template.
[14] Under the previous regime many operated under the Telecommunications Services Class Licence.

VoIP may be used with a broad spectrum of existing technologies, such as ATM or SDH and increasingly MPLS. VoIP is increasingly the technology of choice for the international backbone networks of ISPs who use their own infrastructure to convey PSTN traffic nationally and internationally and to support the public internet.

What are the advantages of VoIP?

This service can be a substitute for traditional circuit switched voice telephony, even though it is a data-based technology. Over recent years the quality of voice calls over the internet has increased dramatically towards the standards to which users are now accustomed from traditional circuit switched technology. This has facilitated a mass commercialisation of these services. 8–020

VoIP is fundamentally re-shaping the economics of the voice telephony market because packet switching permits much more efficient use of network capacity than circuit switching. The increasing take up of domestic broadband[15] is a key enabler, together with features like "always-on internet" and fixed monthly charges for access. The latter can reduce the incremental costs of VoIP calls to nothing.

Flavours of VoIP?

VoIP originally only enabled voice messages to be transmitted between personal computers logged on to the internet. Video-conferencing applications were also developed which enabled voice and visual messages to be transmitted over the internet. 8–021

Before flat rate internet access became widespread, internet voice telephony services were marketed as a means of making international and/or long distance calls for the price of a local telephone call. The caller would typically need a multimedia computer with an internet connection, a modem capable of transmitting voice and a soundcard allowing the computer to record sounds and play them back. A commercially available software package would allow international calls to be made at local call rates by sending calls from the user's home via the PSTN to the nearest internet access provider's server. The calls were then routed over private circuits to the country of destination and then via the PSTN to an internet user in that country. The set up is simple for the user and the only charge the caller pays is for the internet call, which may even be free if the caller is on a flat monthly charge. The disadvantages include the caller being limited to calling people using the same software, and only being able to speak to the intended recipient of the call if their computer is switched on.

Many operators now also offer a connection from the VoIP service to the public telephone network, enabling callers to use the internet to call anyone with a phone. This requires an IP phone or an analogue to digital converter. A service provider node is used to access the internet and a service provider

---

[15] Broadband as a consumer product in the UK has grown from 0 to 10 million in just seven years. Industry estimates suggest that there are now 500,000 active VoIP users in the UK.

gateway to interconnect with the PSTN for onward access to PC and telephone terminals. It is possible to combine DSL or cable networks for initial access, linked through a node to a private IP network and then through a gateway to the PSTN.

There are as many flavours of VoIP pricing as there are flavours of VoIP itself. Not all services are free to the caller. Some operators offer a flat rate for a fixed number of minutes each month, others charge per minute for long distance calls outside the caller's calling area. One facility that can be significant for some callers is the ability to choose an area code different from the area in which the caller lives. There are many people living in India with Californian calling area codes!

The use of the internet for internal calls within an organisation is also becoming increasingly prevalent. Typically, corporate VoIP involves an access from IP phones via an IP-PBX to a private IP network and then through a gateway to the PSTN or through an IP-PBX to IP phones. One advantage of this corporate VoIP is that there is no need for a separate IT infrastructure and telephone system.

VoIP used in this way can also facilitate the implementation of integrated corporate management and information systems, for example, integrating fax, email, telephony, mobile, text messaging and presence management systems. The reality is that VoIP is now just another data application over an IP network.

Communications providers themselves have also been making use of VoIP within their internal networks for many years, for example, to avoid high cost international charging regimes. The use of these data networks can also facilitate enhanced network management systems and a higher level of service to the outer limits of the network.

Regulatory

8–022 The starting point is whether VoIP services should be regulated at all. If so, to what extent? If something looks and feels like a standard telephony service should it not be regulated as such? Do end-users need the same legal and regulatory rights? Would imposing these rights result in the stagnation of a new and emerging market, the development of which has significant economic benefits?

EU and UK regulators are grappling with striking the right balance between facilitating these new and exciting services and in ensuring that the new VoIP operators do not get an unfair advantage over traditional networks for which the current rules were designed. The debates have focused around issues such as access to the emergency services and the ability of law enforcement agencies to monitor VoIP calls as well as the interaction between social policy objectives achieved through regulation.

An example of the latter is where certain operators with certain licences must contribute to a universal service fund, but operators providing competing services over alternative technologies do not and can reduce retail prices accordingly.

OFCOM's philosophy on these issues was succinctly summarised by Stephen Carter, its then Chief Executive, in September 2004: "Broadband voice services are a new and emerging market. Our first task as regulator is to keep out of the way". Before we see whether the UK has lived up to these laudable aims it is perhaps interesting to look at how these issues have played out in the US and the European background.

Historically, the Federal Communications Commission (FCC) has also been reluctant to regulate the internet and services provided over it, an entirely internet-based VoIP service being considered to be an information service rather than a regulated communications service.

The FCC has largely won its battles with those States that have sought to impose regulation of VoIP. That said, VoIP providers in the US are now required to pay the same levies as traditional communications providers to support emergency services and access to all. However, VoIP providers are not required to pay inter- and intra-state access charges to the incumbent local carriers but pay the cheaper reciprocal compensation fees instead.

The issue of the possibility of criminals being able to use VoIP to avoid wiretaps has also caused significant concern for a number of law enforcement bodies. The FCC has stated that any VoIP providers deemed to be providing telecommunications services should be subject to common carrier regulations, but that it is premature to issue a definitive pronouncement on the regulatory status of phone-to-phone VoIP.

Prior to the adoption of the new EU regulatory package, the European Commission reviewed the regulatory status of VoIP services available in 1998 and concluded that such services should not be considered to be voice telephony services for three reasons. First, VoIP was not generally available. Secondly, internet users could not generally reach any user of the public switched network. Thirdly, the transmission quality of internet telephony was not generally equivalent to traditional voice transmission services. These findings were confirmed in 2000.

As discussed above, the new EU regulatory regime applies according to   8–023
whether a person is providing an ECN or an ECS regardless of the technology used, for example, circuit switched or packet switched/IP network. Additional rights and obligations attach to those operators who provide PATS and to those that have universal service obligations.

So are providers of VoIP services providing an ECN or an ECS? Are they PATS providers? In June 2004 the European Commission published "The Treatment of VOIP under the EU regulatory framework—an information and consultation document". Unfortunately this did not provide all of the clarity that had been hoped for.

Let us start with something that is clear: if a VoIP service comprises the mere provision of a product, e.g. the software to be run on a personal computer with no ongoing service provision, the provision of this product does not of itself entail an ECS. This applies even if the VoIP offering allows for voice communications between users who have purchased the product.

What about a corporate provider network that is used for VoIP services? These are within the scope of the new EU regulatory framework in that they are covered by the Authorisation Directive, but there are no specific obligations addressed to private networks. There are no conditions or restrictions on the use of VoIP services within a company, for the sole use of that company.

The same goes for VoIP technologies used within a public operator's core network that do not impinge on the retail services offered to customers nor on the quality of those services.

Publicly available VoIP services, where there is access to and from E164 telephone numbers do potentially fall more squarely within the EU regime. There are, however, many flavours in publicly available VoIP services and the regulatory treatment of each depends on the nature of the service being offered. Any classification of those flavours is unlikely to be stable, given the pace of technological and market driver change.

Turning to the UK position under the Communications Act 2003, a VoIP operator that is a provider of ECS would not need to make any prior notification to OFCOM. The operator would need to comply with all applicable compulsory standards and specifications and would be subject to certain consumer protection requirements but would be allowed to obtain and assign telephone numbers in the UK plan, and may also utilise non-geographic numbers.

8–024   OFCOM's informal guidance of November 2003 confirms that a VoIP operator is considered to be a provider of PATS if: (i) the VoIP provider markets its services as a substitute for traditional telephone services; or (ii) if the services appear to the customer to be a substitute for a traditional telephony service with which they would expect to access the emergency service or directory assistance; or (iii) the service provides the customer's sole means of access to the circuit switched telephone network. Clearly the latter would not apply where a VoIP service is being provided as an adjunct to a traditional telephone service or a secondary service.

The debate has moved on, at least in part, with regard to access to the emergency services with OFCOM making it clear that a consumer's decision to purchase a phone must be made on the basis of an awareness of whether that phone can or cannot be used to access the emergency services if this is the case. Further, such phones should be labelled to ensure that all those using the phone are aware that access to the emergency services is not available.

OFCOM has published a further consultation[16] on VoIP and at the time of publication proposed to issue a full statement later in 2006. This consultation represents the first significant landmark since September 2004 when OFCOM took the interim position not to take action against any VoIP operators which entered the market without complying with all the PATS regulatory requirements. OFCOM's provisional conclusions set out in the consultation propose new requirements on VoIP providers. The essential requirements of a PATS provider are the provision of an origi-

---

[16] Regulation of VoIP Services—Statement and further consultation, OFCOM, February 22, 2006.

nating and receiving voice call service to the public and the provision of call access to emergency services. Further PATS obligations are set out in the General Conditions of Entitlement and these concern the provision of uninterrupted access to emergency services, maintenance of network integrity (for providers of services at fixed locations) and the requirement to provide number portability to its subscribers and in response to requests from other service providers.

With regard to the provision of network integrity, emergency services access, and caller location information for emergency calls, OFCOM is proposing to issue a binding Code of Practice on the steps to be taken by e-comms service providers, including VoIP providers. The net effect, as per the consultation approach, will be on the one hand a limited concession to VoIP providers regarding the provision of uninterrupted access to emergency services, but on the other hand, a range of new obligations on VoIP providers regarding the giving of notices and warnings to domestic and small business customers regarding the services provided.

The key features of the consultation, in addition to the withdrawal of OFCOM's interim forbearance policy, are as follows: 8–025

> All VoIP services which fulfil the definition of PATS will be subject to and able to benefit from number portability even if they are a calls-receive only service. In a new definition of PATS for this purpose, a distinction is drawn between VoIP services for making and receiving calls, in respect of which providers are required to comply with the above general PATS obligations, and the VoIP services for receiving calls only, where the provider is not required so to comply. Thus, calls-receive only VoIP services will benefit from number portability (with the reciprocal obligation to provide number portability) whilst two-way VoIP services must comply with the general PATS obligations in order so to benefit.
>
> As regards the PATS obligations applicable to VoIP services, a distinction is drawn between VoIP service providers at fixed locations and nomadic VoIP services. In particular, general condition 3 requires a provider of PATS (or a public telephone network) at a fixed location to maintain network integrity (the proper and effective functioning of the network) at all times. This will not apply to nomadic voice services, insofar as these are not provided at a fixed location. However, the OFCOM consultation document proposes the issuing of a set of guidelines on the steps which VoIP service providers should be required or expected to take regarding network integrity or steps which they would be required to take to support nomadic users with regard to network integrity. It could be argued by VoIP providers that these additional guidelines purport to introduce new rules going beyond the actual regulatory requirements of the General Conditions of entitlement and are therefore not justified.
>
> With regard to the required availability of access to emergency

organisations (using call numbers "112" and "999" at no charge) this will apply to all providers of incoming and receiving VoIP services which are PATS. Under the proposed OFCOM Code, any service provider would be required to give appropriate warnings to domestic and small business users where the service does not enable access to emergency services, and where appropriate, a service provider must give appropriate reliability warnings of the possible loss of the ability to make emergency calls in the event of a network failure (network integrity being an obligation which applies only to providers of PATS at a fixed location).

Proposed OFCOM guidelines state that whilst the provision of uninterrupted caller access to emergency services is an obligation for providers of PATS (for incoming and outgoing calls) whether at a fixed location or nomadic, the service provider may, in respect of nomadic services, not be expected to have sufficient control over the underlying network so as to be able to ensure the ability to make such calls in all situations. On these points however, there is scope for further debate.

8–026   As regards the obligation on network providers to make available call location information for emergency services calls, OFCOM's proposed Code of Practice requires service providers to require users to provide location information whether the service is used principally at a single fixed location or from several locations and the consequences of not providing such information, and also requires a service provider that does not provide emergency location information to give notice of this to its domestic and small business customers.

The Code will further require service providers, including VoIP operators, to provide information to domestic and small business customers if certain facilities are not provided, including the following: directory enquiry services, operator assistance services, calling line identification, and provision of a directory on request.

More generally, the proposed Code sets out a general requirement for a warning to be given by VoIP service providers to its domestic and small business customers, that the service is provided over a data network and as such, service availability is not guaranteed but is subject to interruptions in the underlying broadband connection or other power failures outside the service provider's control.

Whilst the regulatory position continues to evolve, there is no doubt that VoIP is here and real and of huge commercial significance. VoIP services represent a significant opportunity for some new operators and a significant threat (and opportunity) for some of the more traditional operators. Already the advent of VoIP is becoming established as a very low cost alternative to traditional telephony, and requiring a shaking-up of fixed and mobile operators' approaches to pricing and interconnection. The regulatory balance that is struck on interconnection and other issues such as consumer protection and social obligations will have a significant impact. Other potentially disruptive technologies such as WiFi and WiMax will also strongly influence how the markets develop.

WiMAX

Another new technology, WiMAX (worldwide interoperability for micro-wave access) is emerging which is also enabling wide area wireless communication via computers, in effect mobile or fixed access to broadband. It is also mobilising VoIP because VoIP works on any broadband connection, whether cable, DSL or wireless. WiMAX and VoIP together, therefore, are facilitating a total convergence of internet, voice telephony, data and multimedia communications via a single device, whether mobile or fixed. WiMAX operates on the same principles as WiFi in transmitting data between computers via radio signals. WiMAX technology, however, enables metropolitan area networks, allowing areas the size of an entire city to be connected with wireless access. Whereas WiFi covers a local area network (LAN) with a maximum reach of approximately 100 metres, a WiMAX transmitter can cover an area with a radius of up to 30 miles.

8–027

A WiMAX system consists of a WiMAX tower linked to a base station and WiMAX receivers and antennae which can be built into individual laptops, phones and PDAs. A WiMAX tower station can connect directly to the internet using a high bandwidth wired connection. It can also connect to other WiMAX towers by microwave link (the backhaul connection). WiMAX systems could, it seems, provide nationwide coverage on an interconnected basis.

One of the key issues surrounding WiMAX in the present climate is the identification of spectrum bands where the service can be deployed. It is currently envisaged that WiMAX will rely mainly on spectrum in the 2 to 11 GHz range and to this end increasing amounts of spectrum are being made available as a result of OFCOM's spectrum liberalisation programme.[17] The frequency levels are important as they will have a direct effect on the technical capability of a WiMAX system and the geographic reach of the transmitter: higher frequencies could allow higher data speeds and capacity but would cover smaller geographic areas. The allocation of spectrum frequencies will be a key issue in the future and success of WiMAX. Where possible, OFCOM is committed to issuing technologically neutral licences.[18]

VoIP and WiMAX look likely, therefore, to seriously threaten existing voice services and together they raise important questions about the scope,

---

[17] See for example "Ofcom and CoReg announce joint spectrum awards" (*www.ofcom.org.uk/media/news/2006/12/nr_20061214*); "Ofcom announces proposals for the UK's largest spectrum auction (*www.ofcom.org.uk/media/news/2006/12/nr_20061211*) and Spectrum licences for broadband, wireless communications and mobile multimedia services (*www.ofcom.org.uk/media/news/2006/03/nr_20060331a*).

[18] See for example "Ofcom awards 12 licences following spectrum auction" (*www.ofcom.org.uk/media/news/2006/05/nr_20060503*).

operation and regulation of the universal service in telecommunications, as regulation struggles to keep up with technology.

Spectrum liberalisation and trading

8–028 Spectrum liberalisation and trading has been high on OFCOM's agenda ever since its creation and great progress has been made in the area.

Trading of spectrum rights was made possible as from December 23, 2004, by the Wireless Telegraphy (Spectrum Trading) Regulations (SI 2004/3154), in respect of public mobile operations (data), private business radio, fixed wireless access, point to point fixed links and scanning telemetry.

OFCOM issued a Statement on Spectrum Liberalisation (January 26, 2005) revealing its plans to deal with liberalisation by both varying individual Wireless Telegraphy Act licences (to reduce or remove restrictions that prevent the use of spectrum for mobile services other than 3G) and also by bringing about generic changes to licences to make them less usage and technology specific (e.g. changes of use from non–2G services to 3G services after 2007).

After issuing various consultation papers during the course of 2003 and 2004, OFCOM announced in July 2005 its proposal to award a number of low power Wireless Telegraphy Act licences via spectrum auction in early 2006. It is also understood to be intending to release further spectrum, in the 2.6GHz band, for 3G use, as from 2008. There is some concern amongst 3G operators that if OFCOM does allow changes of use under existing licences in favour of 3G operations, this would involve inconsistent and discriminatory treatment on the terms of market entry as between those operators who have entered the market pursuant to the auction process in 2000 and operators entering the market pursuant to a change of use.

The digital switchover programme currently underway in the UK provides another means by which spectrum is to be released, the resulting available spectrum being labelled the "digital dividend". Such a dividend in terms of spectrum creates a number of opportunities for wireless innovation which, in turn, opens up the possibility for launch of a wide range of different services.

There are, however, among various industry groups, concerns that the wider use of spectrum will require to a certain extent, the co-operation of various partners, both in Europe and potentially further afield: airwaves do not respect national borders. In addition, the regulatory landscape/backdrop to all of this is still unclear but OFCOM have stated its intention to withdraw from harmonisation activities in this area and to leave the potentially problematic issues of interoperability and enforcement to private arrangements between the operators.

8.4 ACCESS RIGHTS AND NETWORK SERVICES

8–029 A minority of Internet Service Providers control their own network infrastructure. The majority depend on access and conveyance being provided by network operators, with whom they, in many cases, compete, or whose business it is to maximise revenues according to a business model whose economics are inconsistent with how the internet works. Put simply, broadband infrastructure maximises the potential of the internet and can make internet services economically and commercially viable, but traditional narrowband charging approaches to broadband capacity can make its use prohibitively expensive.

Securing access to third party facilities on commercially viable terms is fundamental to being able to provide internet services. This section explains how regulation is being used to achieve this.

8.4.1 Interconnection and peering

Networks which carry internet traffic may require both interconnection and peering. In very simple terms, interconnection is the process of making a physical or logical connection at a geographic boundary between one set of infrastructure and another over which various types of electronic communications traffic may be exchanged. Peering is based on a similar principle but involves technical processes which are exclusive to IP traffic. Peering is essentially a relationship established between two or more ISPs allowing traffic to be exchanged directly rather than through an internet backbone provider. Peering may take place at the physical interconnection boundary or somewhere else entirely.   8–030

Interconnection

Interconnection is firmly regulated in most liberalised national jurisdictions by national regulatory authorities (NRAs): the fixed telecommunications market in most Member States is dominated by one ex-incumbent operator so regulation of interconnection is considered essential to ensure the ex-incumbent does not inhibit competition within the market. As we have already seen, this is achieved in the UK and throughout the EU by the imposition of access and interconnection conditions on those operators that are found to have SMP in the relevant market.   8–031

As discussed above, the rules by which operators are entitled to interconnection rights were changed in the UK as a result of the Communications Act 2003, itself implementing the EU Regulatory Framework 2002, more specifically the Access Directive (which applies to all forms of communications networks carrying publicly-available communication services whether used for voice or data).

As mentioned earlier, under the Access Directive, OFCOM has the power to impose additional obligations on those operators determined to have SMP. In this context, regulation of interconnection covers three main areas: obligations to provide cost-based interconnection charges; obligations to publish interconnection prices and apply them on a non-discriminatory basis, and obligations to offer new interconnection services. Each of these is considered in more detail below.

Regulatory controls on interconnection charges

8–032   In the UK, all network operators are required by the General Conditions of Entitlement to negotiate interconnection. The Competition Appeal Tribunal has interpreted this obligation as inferring a duty to negotiate and agree terms which are fair and reasonable.[19] Further, OFCOM's dispute resolution obligations apply to such interconnection negotiations.

Further charge controls in relation to interconnection can only be imposed by OFCOM in respect of operators designated as having SMP in a relevant market. OFTEL, acting on behalf of OFCOM under the transitional provisions of the Communications Act 2003 concluded however, that the market for internet termination services is competitive and that no operator has SMP in that market.[20]

As regards the provision of narrowband wholesale exchange line, conveyance and transit services and fixed network termination services, BT has in each case been designated as having SMP and is required to limit its charges to a level that reflects its long run incremental costs, and is at the same time subject to limits on the level of increases in charges that can be made each year.[21]

Further, as regards call termination on fixed networks, OFTEL (acting as above on behalf of OFCOM) has also determined that certain other providers of public electronic communications networks (PECNs) have SMP for the termination of calls on their networks (without having to commit to cost-based interconnection charges) and has imposed SMP obligations on them to provide fixed geographical call termination services on fair and reasonable terms, conditions and charges and on such terms, conditions and charges as OFCOM may determine.[22]

Publication of prices and non-discriminatory application

8–033   In all markets where BT has SMP, OFCOM has determined that it must publish a reference offer (RO) which contains the prices charged and BT is not allowed to depart from such published prices.

New services

8–034   In order to allow new entrants to the market, OFCOM has the power under

---

[19] *Hutchison 3G (UK) Ltd v The Office of Communications supported by British Telecommunications Plc*, (Case No. 1047/3/3/04) judgment of November 29, 2005.

[20] Wholesale unmetered narrowband internet termination services—UK excluding Hull area market—Final Explanatory Statement and Notification, OFTEL, November 28, 2003.

[21] Review of the fixed narrowband wholesale exchange line, call organisation, conveyance and transit markets—Final Explanatory Statement and Notification, OFTEL, November 28, 2003.

[22] Review of fixed geographic call termination markets—Final Explanatory Statement and Notification, OFTEL, November 28, 2003.

the Access Directive to impose an obligation on operators to offer new interconnection services when requested to do so by a new entrant. OFCOM has stated its belief that the precise nature of such new services should be left to commercial negotiation between the parties on the basis that the parties, as opposed to the regulator, are better placed to define products. Nevertheless, in some markets where BT has SMP it is required to follow a specified process when dealing with requests for new wholesale services.

Peering and transit

Every ISP requires access to the public internet. This is achieved through commercial agreements for either peering or transit.   8–035

Peering may be defined as a reciprocal business agreement between network operators who are ISPs to accept, at no charge,[23] all traffic originating from the other's network.

Transit, on the other hand, may be defined as a business relationship where one ISP pays another ISP for routing its internet traffic to and from all destinations. In effect one ISP becomes the customer of the other.

Since peering requires no outflow of payments, it is generally considered commercially preferable to paying for transit. At present, ISPs have no legal or regulatory obligations to offer peering to other ISPs, but are likely to do so if the balance of traffic between them is comparable. Peering may be refused to smaller ISPs, forcing them into paying for transit instead.

Because the public internet generally, and peering in particular, are not regulated, an ISP's licensing status in a particular jurisdiction is not an indicator of the terms on which it may gain access to the public internet. That said, an ISP which owns it own network facilities, is more likely to be the sort of ISP which offers and is offered peering. The ISPs who use peering rather than transit are a self-selecting group. Larger ISPs may however, take a commercial decision to offer peering to smaller ISPs.

Peering may take place at either public or private "peering points".   8–036
Historically, public peering locations were officially sanctioned locations known as NAPs (Network Access Points) and were limited in number. The growth of the internet, with its increased traffic flow has raised the demand for such exchange points offering more capacity at a reduced cost.

Today, there are a number of public peering points for public peering amongst ISPs in the UK, including for example, LINX,[24] LoNaP and MANAP. LINX (London Internet Exchange Ltd), which is a non-profit making organisation, is currently the second largest and most successful internet exchange point in Europe (the largest being AMS-IX in Amsterdam). ISPs who meet the criteria in the LINX Memorandum of

---

[23] Whilst historically this was true, the issue of charging has begun to raise its head in this context.
[24] LINX's commercial membership terms and conditions are available on its website at: *www.linx.net*, under the section entitled "Join LINX".

Understanding, most of which are based on technical systems compatibility, may apply to join, whether UK or overseas based.

Some of the most common criteria that are at the heart of any sort of peering arrangement include: the likely traffic flows, the overall traffic volumes, the traffic exchange ratios, backbone capacity, geographic location, and the desirability of a provider as a peering partner, with capacity, number of websites and location being key.

Public peering, by its nature, allows networks interested in peering to interconnect with many other networks through a single port and is consequently considered to offer "less capacity" than private peering. Nevertheless, public peering offers advantages to smaller networks or networks "starting to peer" by providing them with the environment in which to "meet" and interconnect with other networks, perhaps with a view to developing a peering arrangement.

By the same token, larger networks remain interested in public peering locations as a means of attracting smaller networks as potential peer partners. They may also see the reward in "using" the exchange point as a location for "trial peering" at a low cost (i.e. without entering a more expensive private peering arrangement).

8–037   The alternative to joining a public peering point is to arrange private peering. Major ISPs, such as MCI and Level 3 publish their guidelines for ISP's wishing to peer with them. The perceived advantage of using private peering is the opportunity for guaranteed service levels and higher speed connections, and avoiding bottlenecks which can be experienced at public exchange points because of the sheer number of networks peering through the single port.

The disadvantage, at least for the bigger players, is growing regulatory scrutiny of peering arrangements[25] and the risk of introduction of telecommunications interconnection-style tariff regulation. This could happen as a result of discussion at international level or through a competition complaint, possibly in the EU or the UK.

8.4.2 Access to end-users

8–038   It is one thing to secure access to the public internet, and another to secure access to end-users. Whereas dial-up internet access has been widely possible for some time, key issues for the Regulator have been the provision of high bandwidth infrastructure and unmetered internet access for the mass

---

[25] At the ITU World Telecommunications Standards Assembly (WTSA) held in Autumn 2000, a proposal was considered for regulating exchange of internet traffic, known as ICAIS, or International Charging Arrangements for Internet Service. The proposal was to replace commercially negotiated peering and transit with a regulated international settlements system similar to the one followed by national incumbent telecommunications operators. Charges would be based on fixed, per minute fees for call termination. The proposal was generally supported in smaller countries with net inflows and resisted in countries with net outflows, such as the USA.

market, both of which were seen as key to promoting widespread retail use of the internet.

Because BT controls the access lines into the majority of UK households, use of high bandwidth infrastructure is still largely dependent on investment by BT. BT is continuing to make very significant investments in introducing its 21st century network. BT offers a range of high bandwidth access products, which all ISPs have rights to purchase.[26] Alternatively, BT is required to unbundle individual local loops at the request of operators, who may then co-locate their facilities in BT's local exchanges and install high bandwidth equipment, such as ADSL modems. The terms, conditions and charges for local loop unbundling (LLU) are regulated by OFCOM.[27] 8–039

The second review of the Telecoms Adjudication Scheme for LLU was launched in June 2004 and OFCOM published its conclusions in October 2005. The findings revealed that while considerable progress had been made, there remain a number of outstanding challenges and it was thought that the anticipated winding-up of the scheme at the end of 2005 would be premature. OFCOM are of the view that the on-going presence of the scheme is required in order to maintain pressure on BT to deliver strategic systems implementation in accordance with the scheme.

As for unmetered internet access, OFTEL ordered BT to offer flat rate internet access call origination (FRIACO), an unmetered call origination interconnection service, to all operators. This meant that operators pay a non-discriminatory, regulated charge to use BT's local access network for internet access and are not charged on a per minute basis. This made it economically viable for ISPs to offer unmetered internet services over BT's network to end customers. It should be noted that OFCOM stated in March 2006[28] a desire to remove significant market power regulation where appropriate, especially as regards retail markets, including in relation to narrowband internet access and in particular FRIACO, as markets become more competitive.

In October 2005 and after a year of detailed consultation involving the whole industry, OFCOM accepted legally binding undertakings from BT to effect a substantial degree of organisational (but not structural) separation of its access services operations and further organisational separation between its wholesale and retail divisions, as well as undertakings to offer equivalence of inputs as between BT's downstream divisions and its downstream competitors regarding various products, principally local access products.[29] These create a new regulatory approach to the access

---

[26] Examples include Videostream, IPStream and Datastream.

[27] For details of local loop unbundling, see *www.ofcom.org.uk/media/news/2005/02/nr_20050208_2*.

[28] Next Generation Networks: Developing the regulatory framework, OFCOM, March 7, 2006.

[29] See OFCOM News Release of September 22, 2005.

infrastructure operated by BT in the UK.[30] At the same time, BT announced the establishment of its new access services business—Openreach.

A further key enabler is Wholesale Line Rental (WLR). This allows alternative suppliers to rent access lines on wholesale terms from BT and resell the lines to customers, providing a single bill that covers both line rental and telephone calls, thus enabling increased competition in the area.

In August 2002, OFTEL modified BT's licence to make the provision of WLR product a regulatory obligation. Following changes to the prices of such WLR products, in the latest review of market issued in December 2005,[31] OFCOM concluded that the WLR product offered by BT met almost all agreed product criteria. BT gave written commitments to resolve the small number of outstanding issues during the first half of 2006.

As a result of such progress, OFCOM relaxed the current retail price controls for BT.[32] OFCOM has recently proposed to further deregulate and remove the retail price controls on BT line rental and calls.[33] As part of BT's voluntary undertakings, Openreach is committed to delivering further improvements on the WLR product by mid 2007 to give BT's competitors access to a WLR product which is exactly equivalent to the product available to BT's retain business.

8.5 BROADCASTING REGULATION

8.5.1 Background

8-040   Broadcasting regulation in the UK as in many other regimes, is concerned with the licensing of services and in particular the content of broadcast material. At first glance, it might seem odd that broadcasting regulation can apply to services provided over the internet, as mainstream broadcasting normally involves the transmission of programmes for simultaneous reception by a group of persons. In contrast, services over the internet are generally made available in response to a request by users who dial-up a service provider. However, there is some potential for licensing requirements under the Communications Act 2003 to be applied to internet services as we discuss below.

---

[30] BT originally proposed the undertakings as an alternative to a full scale investigation by the Competition Commission which could potentially have resulted in more far-reaching separation of BT businesses (structural separation is allowed for as a remedy under the legislation).

[31] OFCOM announced further price cuts for WLR products offered by BT on November 9, 2005.

[32] See OFCOM News Release, December 15, 2005.

[33] See OFCOM News Release, March 21, 2006.

EU—TV Without Frontiers

The Television Without Frontiers Directive 1989 (TWFD)[34] as amended[35]   **8–041**
provides the framework for the mutual recognition and harmonisation of
television broadcasting: throughout the EU Member States are required not
to restrict the reception or retransmission in their territory of lawful
broadcasts transmitted from other Member States. The following national
rules are harmonised: the time reserved for "European" works; the proportion of material produced by independent producers that must be
broadcast; the rules concerning the separation of advertising and sponsorship from programming; the types of television advertising that may be
included in programming; and the total advertising time. Further measures
relate to, for example, the protection of minors and a right of reply.

The broadcasting market throughout the EU remains diverse despite
these measures. In addition to the different cultures and languages, Member
States remain free to lay down more onerous requirements in the harmonised areas and several have done so. The 1997 amendments also
introduced, amongst other things, further derogations from the obligations
not to restrict retransmission; the concept that certain "listed events"
should be available to the public on free television; additional restrictions
on advertisement; and requirements on Member States to ensure that
broadcasts do not include any incitement of hatred on grounds of race, sex,
religion or nationality.

The European Commission is currently preparing further amendments to
the 1989 TWFD (last amended in 1997). The amending Directive as originally proposed would expand the concept of broadcasting to include any
"audiovisual media service", i.e. any service whose principal purpose is the
provision of moving images (to inform, entertain or educate) to the general
public by means of electronic communication services.

This covers all audio visual mass media services, whether scheduled or on
demand, and could also cover the audiovisual content of websites, aggregator services for material provided as website content, and also services to
be provided on 3G mobile phones.

Further current debate within the EU centres on achieving the correct
balance between citizens' rights (democratic, social and cultural) and
commercial interests, and is focused on the following key issues: scope of
the Directive (as to what services are included), general access to major
events (such as sports), cultural diversity and programming content quotas,
advertising rules, product placement and the right to short reporting. The
EU aims to achieve a balance between citizens' rights (democratic, social
and cultural) and commercial interests.

The Council of Ministers adopted, on November 13, 2006,[36] a general
approach with a narrower scope of application, limited to broadcast and
on-demand services.

---

[34] Council Directive 89/552/EEC.
[35] Council Directive 97/36/EC.
[36] *http://ec.europa.eu/prelex/detail_dossier_real.cfm?CL=en&DosId=193682.*

UK

8–042 The regulation of broadcasting in the UK was contained primarily in the Broadcasting Acts 1990 and 1996 (the 1990 Act or the 1996 Act as applicable). The principal aim of the 1996 Act was to put in place the necessary legislative framework for digital terrestrial broadcasting. These Acts have now been significantly amended by, and much of the broadcasting regulation is now also contained in, the Communications Act 2003.

The Communications Act 2003 introduced significant regulatory changes in relation to media and broadcasting. These included the relaxation of many of the licensing requirements on broadcasting in order to achieve consistency with the new regime for the regulation of electronic communications networks and services. The Act also introduced a new regulatory structure for television and radio services and wide ranging content related requirements.

Under the Communications Act 2003, OFCOM largely took over the functions of the Independent Television Commission, the Radio Authority and Broadcasting Standards Council with regard to broadcasting.

In carrying out its s.3 duties, OFCOM is required to secure: the availability throughout the UK of a wide range of television and radio services which (taken as a whole) are both of high quality and calculated to appeal to a variety of tastes and interests; the maintenance of a sufficient plurality of providers of different television and radio services; the application of standards that provide adequate protection to members of the public from the inclusion of offensive and harmful material in such services; and the application, in the case of television and radio services, of standards that provide adequate protection to members of the public and other persons from both unfair treatment and unwarranted infringements of privacy.[37]

OFCOM is also required to have regard to such of the following matters that appear to it to be relevant in the circumstances: the desirability of promoting the fulfilment of the purposes of public service television broadcasting in the UK; the need to balance obligations to provide protection against offensive and harmful material with "an appropriate level of freedom of expression"; the vulnerability of children and others whose circumstances appear to OFCOM to put them in need of special protection; and the desirability of preventing crime and discord.[38]

OFCOM is required to regulate with a light touch.[39] In reviewing the burdens it imposes and maintains, OFCOM must have regard to the extent to which its objectives are already furthered or secured by effective self-regulation and must remove or reduce regulatory burdens where appropriate.[40] OFCOM's functions relating to content are delegated to its Content Board.

---

[37] S.3(2), Communications Act 2003.
[38] S.3(3), Communications Act 2003.
[39] S.6, Communications Act 2003.
[40] S.6(2), Communications Act 2003.

Digital switchover

In accordance with its obligations under the Communications Act 2003,   **8–043**
OFCOM offered digital replacement licences (DLRs) to the current
Channel 3 analogue licensees, Channel 5 and Public Teletext, to replace the
current analogue licences. Channel 4 was treated slightly differently but
was also offered a new licence.

On December 28, 2004, new digital licences came into force for all of the
commercial public service broadcasters in the UK (Channel 3 (ITV),
Channel 4, Channel 5 and Teletext). The new licences include an obligation
on these broadcasters to end the transmission of their services in analogue
terrestrial form by December 31, 2012, the anticipated date for the completion of the process of digital switchover.

OFCOM has, together with its planning partners (ntl Broadcast, Crown
Castle and the BBC) and broadcasters, undertaken an engineering-led
analysis of how the switchover might be achieved. This project has effectively superseded the switchover plan originally developed in 2002/03 by
the Spectrum Planning Group as part of the Digital Television Action Plan.
More recently, the planners have initiated co-operation with the SwitchCo
Working Group whose aim is, during the course of 2005–06, to set up
SwitchCo, an organisation to take responsibility for the development, co-
ordination and implementation of the range of technical requirements of
the switchover programme.

8.5.2 Broadcasting licensing in the UK

Television licensable content services

The key concept at the heart of television broadcasting regulation in the UK   **8–044**
is that a licence is required in respect of *"television licensable content
services"*, namely the provision of television services (or electronic programme guides) by means of an electronic communications network or by
satellite, but excluding interactive services.

Before we consider what a television licensable content service is we must
first consider what a television programme is. A "television programme" is
defined as:

> "any programme (with or without sounds) which:
>
> (a) is produced wholly or partly to be seen on television; and
> (b) consists of moving or still images or of legible text or of a
>   combination of those things."

Neither the phrase "intended to be seen on television" or indeed the word   **8–045**
"television", are themselves further defined and it is consequently unclear
whether it means broadcast to the home or transmitted over an alternative
type of ECN. The line between computer screens and traditional televisions

might be considered to be becoming increasingly blurred.[41] A television licensable content service is defined as:

> "[S.232(1)] ... (subject to section 233) any service falling within sub-section (2) insofar as it is provided with a view to its availability for reception by members of the public being secured by one or both of the following means:
>
> (a) the broadcasting of a service (whether by the person providing it or another) from a satellite; or
> (b) the distribution of the service (whether by that person or another) by any means involving the use of an electronic communications network.
>
> S232(2) ... a service falls within this sub-section if it:
>
> (a) is provided (whether in digital form or in analogue form) as a service that is to be made available by members of the public[42]; and
> (b) consists of television programmes or electronic programme guides or both."

Section 233 sets out a number of important exceptions (e.g. for two way services such as video conferencing). However, perhaps the most interesting and important exception for present purposes is subs.3:

> "S233(3) A service is not a television licensable content service to the extent that it is provided by means of an electronic communications service if:
>
> (a) it forms part only of a service provided by means of that electronic communications service or is one of a number of services access to which is made available by means of a service so provided; and
> (b) the service of which it forms a part, or by which it may be accessed, is provided for purposes that do not consist wholly or mainly in making available television programmes or radio programmes (or both) for reception by members of the public."

---

[41] One example of this blurring is the question of whether a television licence is required for a personal computer when it is used to watch television programmes. The position of the TV Licensing Authority used to be that a licence is necessary only if the computer is equipped with a TV broadcast card (*http://web.archive.org/web/20060417180826/http://www.tvlicensing.co.uk/information/index.jsp*). However, in June 2006, TV Licensing suggested that a licence would be required if a personal computer was used to view live World Cup broadcasts via a broadband connection. (*http://news.bbc.co.uk/1/hi/entertainment/5081350.stm*). That is now reflected in the revised guidance on TV Licensing's website (*www.tvlicensing.co.uk/information/index.jsp*).

[42] "Members of the public" are defined in s.361, Communications Act 2003.

Internet access itself is clearly an electronic communications service. To the extent that for example the webcasts provided by an ISP form "part only" of the overall service provided by the ISP and do not consist "wholly or mainly in making available television programmes or radio programmes (or both) for reception by members of the public" then a television licensable content service licence is not required.

This is consistent with the aim behind these provisions which was, broadly speaking, to maintain licensing obligations in respect of services which are or equate to broadcasting while excluding internet services, such as websites or web-casting, from OFCOM's regulatory powers. The effect of subs.3 is to exclude not only any website material provided as part of another service (for example a website which is accessed via an ISP which also provides its own in house content) but also material provided from a stand alone site, whether it be text, web-cast or video images.[43]

Section 234 provides some flexibility by permitting the Secretary of State to amend ss.232 or 233 having regard to one or more of the following:

"(a) the protection which, taking account of the means by which the programmes and services are received or may be accessed, is expected by members of the public as respect the contents of television programmes;

(b) the extent to which members of the public are also, before television programmes are watched or accessed, able to make use of facilities for exercising control, by reference to the contents of the programmes, over what is watched or accessed;

(c) the practicability of applying different levels of regulation in relation to different services;

(d) the financial impact for providers of particular services or any modification of the provision of that service; and

(e) technological developments that have occurred or are likely to occur."

Whilst this might be considered to provide some useful flexibility to support the overall policy objectives, the inclusion of these powers was a controversial issue as the Communications Bill passed through Parliament (see also the discussion in Ch.12).

The previous separate licence requirements for satellite television services and licensable programme service licences have been replaced by the television licensable content services licence.[44] Wireless telegraphy licenses are also required for television multiplex services as they use radio frequency (for which a radio frequency licence is required).

Where a licence is required for a television licensable content service,[45]

---

[43] See Explanatory Notes to s.233 of the Communications Act 2003.
[44] S.240, Communications Act 2003.
[45] S.235, Communications Act 2003.

OFCOM may only refuse an application for such licence where the applicant is not a fit and proper person; or is a disqualified person (which includes, amongst other things, bodies of a political nature, local authorities and certain religious bodies) or on the basis of likely contravention of certain OFCOM codes of practice. A discussion of the "must offer" and "must provide" obligations is beyond the scope of this Chapter.

Broadcasting regulation/OFCOM Codes

8–046   Broadcasting licences generally include obligations to observe the OFCOM Codes of Conduct, for example the Programme Code which sets out constraints on programming freedom relating to taste and decency, strong language and sexual portrayal, violence, privacy, impartiality, charitable appeals, religious programmes, undue prominence for commercial products, and protection of children. Many of these would in practice be difficult for internet-based content providers to comply with.

The Programme Code is written with broadcast programming schedules for a single time zone in mind. It includes watershed requirements and rules on advertising breaks. It requires certain types of programme material which are not suitable for children to be scheduled for transmission at particular times. This requires the holders of licences to restrict access to adult material to late evening and night-time slots.

However, special rules apply to subscription channels and Pay Per View services. Where the viewer has elected to take a specialist service, it is considered to take a greater share of responsibility for protecting children from the channel's content and the watershed is consequently an hour earlier than for generally available channels. Likewise, where security mechanisms such as PIN numbers restrict access to programming, watershed rules may be waived altogether, although other restrictions in the Programme Code are not necessarily affected.

The rules regarding advertising are contained in OFCOM's Programme Code and Rules on Amount and Scheduling of Advertising which a licensee is required to comply with. These rules, which generally allow a maximum of nine minutes advertising in any hour and prescribe the minimum time periods between advertisements, are disapplied to home shopping programming and dedicated tele-shopping channels and other similar services which consist purely of advertising. The concept of an advertising break is, in any event, meaningless in the context of most internet services and indeed any service which is not based around sequential scheduling.

Interestingly, although the internet is not subject to licensing rules, the websites of licensed broadcasters are treated as programme related services and are subject to the Programme Code and all provisions relating to editorial responsibility, advertising content and promotion which apply to licensed broadcast services. In order not to fall foul of the advertising rules, internet addresses which appear on screen must be limited to the name of the licensee or the title of the programme concerned.

Conversely, websites which are not controlled by the licensee or which are not directly related to the licensed programme service are considered by the ITC to be commercial products and must comply with the rules on advertising for such products.

Interactive services

Interactive services are currently governed by the rules contained in the Guidance to Broadcasters on the Regulation of Interactive Television Services (published unamended from the text issued by the former ITC in February 2001 and agreed with by OFCOM in November 2004)[46] which should be read alongside the Broadcast Committee of Advertising (BCAP) Television Advertising Standards Code.

8–047

Since November 1, 2004, the Code and the Guidance have been the responsibility of BCAP, under contract from OFCOM. The purpose of the Guidance is principally to ensure that advertising and editorial content are clearly distinguished in those cases where interactivity is designed to permit cross-selling of products or services.

For example, where the licensee provides interactive access to a commercial website, it must ensure that the viewer is aware of this before any advertising is shown. Such connections are not permitted from services which are prohibited from carrying advertising in the first place, e.g. programmes for schools. In any event, advertising which is directly accessed from the licensable programme service must comply with OFCOM's Advertising Codes.

In short, OFCOM has continued the ITC's approach that it would not be appropriate to develop any new regulations for interactive services but they wish to ensure that viewers are clear about the kind of environment they are in, and that programme integrity is effectively maintained.

The Guidance and the Codes distinguish between "dedicated interactive services" and "enhanced programme services". Dedicated interactive services are services accessed in their own right such as electronic shopping malls and entertainment services such as betting and gaming, the content of which is not normally linked to specific programmes. OFCOM requires that any content must conform to OFCOM content rules where broadcasters provide content of their own, for example as part of a portal to an electronic high street.

Enhanced programme services provide for interaction with a linear programme so the viewer may well regard the interactivity as an extension of the programme. There are concerns as to the possible impact of interactive services on the integrity of linear programmes if the commercial content is unchecked. Licensees are therefore required to ensure that the material they transmit complies with OFCOM's Programme and Advertising Codes.

---

[46] The full text is available at *www.asa.org.uk/asa/codes/tv_code/Interactive/BCAP+Guidance+to+Broadcasters+on+the+Regulation+of+Interactive+ Television+Services.htm.*

OFCOM distinguishes between web content which is moderated or selected by a licensed broadcaster and internet via TV services which provide unrestricted access to the public internet and the World Wide Web. These latter services simply treat the TV as a PC and are treated as falling outside the scope of the rules on interactive services. Presumably, because OFCOM does not have powers to enforce these rules on internet content providers, it places an expectation on licensees to ensure observation of the rules (contained in the Guidance and Codes) through commercial arrangements. It is not clear how such an expectation can be enforced or indeed whether it would constitute a breach of the Broadcasting Act licence should compliance not be secured.

Licensable sound programme services

8–048 The Communications Act 2003 also regulates "radio licensable content services",[47] which consist of the provision of "sound programmes" as a service to be made available for reception by members of the public by means of the broadcasting of the service by satellite or the distribution of the service by any means involving the use of an electronic communications network. The content of such programmes is regulated by OFCOM.

Internet radio services

8–049 Internet radio services typically consist of a website which allows the user to access radio stations via the internet which would normally be accessed by traditional radio apparatus. These radio stations will probably be licensed as radio licensable content services, or they could be foreign radio stations not so licensed.

As the provider of the internet site which allows access to these stations is merely providing access to radio programmes provided by others, he cannot be said to be providing sound programmes and should not need to be licensed.[48] If, on the other hand, specific audio/radio based services which do not merely involve the provision of access to existing radio station programming (whether or not such services are intended to be received simultaneously by two or more persons) become available on the internet, a licence under s.113 of the 1990 Act would, in principle, almost certainly be needed by the providers of such services.

In any event, when examining the licensing position in any particular case, the relationship (if any) of the website proprietor to the audio content would have to be carefully considered. It is notable that the policy of the Radio Authority (now part of OFCOM) was that internet radio services do

[47] S.250, Communications Act 2003.
[48] It should also be noted that s.112(2) of the 1990 Act expressly excludes from the definition of licensable sound programme services "a service which the programmes are provided for transmission in the course of the provision of a sound broadcasting service ...". The term "in the course of" is not defined but could have the effect of excluding services which involve merely the provision of access to sound broadcasting services (i.e. existing radio stations).

not require to be regulated. Indeed, in its 1998 response to the government Green Paper *Regulating Communications: Approaching Convergence in the Information Age*, the Radio Authority stated:

> "Existing legislation should not be used to introduce the regulation of new, interactive services by the back door. The Broadcasting Acts were never intended to cover such services, and their growth will be better served by self-regulation (under whatever co-ordinating 'umbrella' is appropriate) and by the application of general law than through the uncomfortable enforcement of inappropriate broadcasting-specific legislation".[49]

More recent statements from OFCOM, including those made in its review of the Communications Market 2005, have remained true to these laudable aims.

---

[49] Radio Authority Response, pp.28–29.

CHAPTER 9

Contracts between Internet Service Providers, Content Owners and Others

9.1 INTRODUCTION

9–001　This chapter examines some of the legal issues surrounding three of the most important commercial contracts relating to use of the internet: the contract for the creation of a website; the contract for the placing of advertising or sponsorship on a website; and the contract for the provision of internet access. Contracts with and between the providers of internet access services themselves are considered briefly. Contracts formed in connection with websites for the sale or supply of goods and services are dealt with separately in Ch.10.

　　In this chapter the term "site owner" refers to the party on whose behalf a website is created or hosted. "User" refers to a person accessing the website.

9.2 CONTRACTS FOR THE PROVISION OF A WEBSITE

9–002　Before goods and services can be marketed or sold, the site owner will need to establish a website as its shop window to the world. Both the design of the site and its establishment on the internet are typically contracted out to a third party. This section looks at the legal issues involved.

9.2.1 The contract with the website designer

9–003　If the site owner intends to use an agency to design its website, his first concern is to ensure that he selects a designer who understands how the internet works and the way in which visitors to the website are likely to access it.

Many issues can arise. For instance, for visitors to the website using narrowband dial-up, large graphics may not download on a timescale which users will find acceptable. Users behind corporate firewalls may be able to download faster, but may have difficulty in accessing streaming audio and video or Java applets if they are barred by the firewall. The web utilises a limited palette of colours and has limited resolution, both of which place limits on the type of design that is suitable for use on the web. Usability and ease of navigation are difficult to achieve and, legally, not easy to define. The range of browsers (including different versions of the same browser) with which the site is to be compatible has to be decided.

Is the site to include a content management system for the site owner to allow direct updating of the content? If so, what facilities should it provide and to what level of user (business user, IT expert, etc.)? Will the content management system allow the site owner merely to add content, or to create additional instances of existing content types, or to create new content types and sections of the site? What level of skill will be required to use these facilities?

The contract with the design agency will primarily address the question of ownership of the intellectual property rights in the design of the website and in any content or code that is specially written or created by the agency. Essentially, this will be a question of copyright and database right.[1]

The design agency will be the first owner of the copyright in any works created by its employees under the Copyright, Designs and Patents Act 1988. As noted in Ch.2, under s.90 of the 1988 Act copyright can only be assigned if the assignment is signed by or on behalf of the assignor and in writing.[2] Therefore the site owner will need to ensure, if it is to own all the rights in the site, that its contract with the design agency includes a present assignment of the future copyright in the designs created by the agency.[3] In practice, the question of the extent to which the agency can re-use work done for other customers, which work the agency retains from one project to the next, and the extent to which it can in the future re-use work done for this project, are likely to be the subject of negotiation.[4]

The site owner wishing to have the rights assigned to it should require

---

[1] As to the subsistence of database right in websites, see discussion in Ch.2.

[2] Note, however, that the definition of "writing" in s.178 of the 1988 Act is relatively broad and is apt to cover electronic form. The requirement that the assignment be signed should, by necessary implication, extend to include signatures in electronic form. Such signatures are admissible in evidence by virtue of s.7 of the Electronic Communications Act 2000, if they satisfy the definition of signatures for the purposes of the section. However, since there was no real doubt about the admissibility of signatures in electronic form anyway, it may be that such signatures remain admissible as evidence even if they do not fall within the definition of the section. See further, Ch.10.

[3] Under reg.23 of the Copyright and Rights in Databases Regulation 1997, s.90 of the 1988 Act is applied to database right as it applies in relation to copyright and copyright works. Although the definition of "writing" in s.178 is not specifically applied, it must be implicit that "writing" should be construed in the same way when the section is applied to database right.

[4] For the default position in the absence of specific provision, see *Clearsprings Management Ltd v Businesslinx Ltd* [2005] EWHC 1487 (Ch).

contractually binding undertakings from the agency that the design work for the website will be undertaken by persons employed by it. The site owner will want undertakings that the works produced by those employees will be original works and will not infringe any third party copyright. The contract between the site owner and the design agency should also impose a requirement on the agency to obtain waivers from those employees which undertake the design work of their moral rights in that work since otherwise the site owner will need to credit those employees as the authors of the works if they choose to assert their moral rights.

The contract will also address the need for compliance with a variety of legislation to be designed in. These will include information to be provided, how it is to be provided and at what point in the process, and requirements such as adjustment to the needs of disabled users. Accordingly, it is appropriate to specify in a web design contract that the web designer will either ensure, or at least use its reasonable endeavours to ensure, that the website will comply with the relevant legislation. Alternatively, it may be appropriate to refer to a set of guidelines which would imply compliance with, for instance, the Disability Discrimination Act 1995. These requirements are discussed in Ch.10.

As no intellectual property rights are likely to exist in the ideas underlying the design of the website (as opposed to the design itself),[5] the site owner will need to place a contractual restriction on the agency designing a similar site for a rival organisation, if it wishes to secure a measure of exclusivity in respect of these ideas. It is beyond the scope of this chapter to consider the possible UK or EU competition law aspects of such restrictions.

Whilst the intellectual property issues are key to the design contract, the site owner will also want to ensure that the design contract covers the more mundane but nonetheless important issues of the deadline for the creation and delivery of the design and the fee for the design work. Liability for the cost of materials should also be addressed.

9.2.2 The contract for building the website

9–004　The contract for building the website will be akin in many ways to a software development agreement, being typically divided into phases with milestones for delivery of work product and payment.

Specification and initial design

9–005　From the website owner's perspective, the key to a contract for the creation of a website is to include a detailed design specification and to provide for acceptance testing of work product before fees are paid to the designer. In many cases the creation of the specification will be the first work under-

---

[5] Inventions can of course be protected by patents. Ideas can be the subject of protection by confidential information but that protection will cease to exist, insofar as the ideas are then ascertainable, once the site goes live.

taken by the designer and it is only once this is agreed that the remainder of the contract for the creation of the website will come into place.

The specification for the website will usually consist of a description of the website and/or storyboards for the appearance of various sections of the site and details of how the site will be navigated by users. It will set out the operating system on which the site is to run, and any necessary third party software such as database managers and web servers. It will also set out whether certain sections of the site are to have restricted access. It will specify with which browsers the site must work and whether, for example, the site should work both with and without frames, or whether there should be a text-only version. It may address any number of the issues outlined above.

The site owner will wish to build in requirements for minimum response times in use. The designer is likely to resist this, especially if the designer is not also providing the platform on which the site will be hosted. Even if he is, he will be unwilling to be tied down to response times when the site is accessed over the public internet, which introduces its own delays. The specification may also address security standards, especially if the site holds financial or personal data.

The specification will usually be based around text, graphics and other materials provided by the site owner. The designer will wish to specify the format in which these are to be provided or provide for the costs of conversion into a suitable format.

Creation and testing

The designer will code the text, graphics and other material provided by the **9–006** site owner, and/or create any necessary database(s) and create the website. Depending on the timescales and complexity of the site, the contract may subdivide this process into further stages.

The contract may allow for periodic inspection of the work by the site owner or for the site owner to monitor progress through the provision of remote access to the work. The site owner should, in any event, ensure that the designer is required to keep him regularly updated of progress and problems in order that he can identify and deal with potential delays that might impact on the launch of his website as soon as possible. If there are serious delays to the agreed timetable the site owner will want the right to bring in additional resources to perform particular tasks at the cost of the designer or the right to move the work elsewhere.

Whether the designer is being paid on a fixed fee or a time and materials basis, payments should be linked to the achievement of key milestones and thought should be given to using variable payments (that increase or decrease depending on the achievement or otherwise of specified tasks) to provide an incentive to the designer to meet or exceed delivery deadlines.[6]

---

[6] Care must obviously be taken to avoid imposing an illegal penalty on the designer for failure to meet a deadline.

The site owner will usually conduct acceptance tests on the site once the designer has completed his own internal tests. These may be carried out in a variety of ways but typically the designer will create a prototype site on a closed system which the site owner will test as to functionality, compliance with specification, and reliability. There may then be further live testing on the internet but with the site hidden under a dummy name until it is ready to be made public.

The site owner will want to ensure that the site runs acceptably fast, that multiple end-users can access the site simultaneously and that the site works with all major browsers. For e-commerce sites, where the number of possible multiple users may be extremely large, the site owner may want to provide for "stress-testing" of the site, to simulate the effect of large numbers of users. Testing of the site's security may also be provided for, at least if the design agency is to perform the hosting function. If the site is to be transferred to a third party host on completion, careful thought will need to be given as to whether testing in the live environment is required, and if so how the agency and the third party host are to co-operate to achieve that. The contract should address how any dispute as to whether an acceptance test has been passed should be resolved.

Ownership of intellectual property rights

9–007   The issue of ownership of the intellectual property rights in the site is another key issue which needs to be addressed and one which is frequently overlooked. Before considering the strict legal position, it is important to understand the parties' commercial needs. The site owner will be concerned about website portability: that is, its ability to move the site to another service provider should it wish to do so, with the minimum delay. Given the nature of the internet, the site owner will not wish to countenance a period during which the site ceases to be available while it is recreated by another provider but instead will wish to take whatever material is necessary from the existing provider to enable a seamless transfer to take place. The designer, however, will not wish to grant rights in its underlying proprietary software to the site owner and still less to see a competitor taking advantage of it.

9–008   **Static content and code**   It is also important to understand the nature of the components that go to make up a website. In the early days of the web, websites were almost always constructed as "flat HTML" sites. These were relatively simple sites in which the web pages themselves were stored on the server and uploaded to the user's browser on request. More complex interactivity was typically provided by program scripts stored on the web server.

HTML itself is nothing more than a text mark-up language, controlling the format of the pages. It has no facilities to, for instance, change the formatting or content of pages dynamically according to the existence or absence of pre-set criteria. So, for instance, if a site owner wanted to offer the user a choice of languages by selecting from a list, the program to achieve this would be separate from the web pages and would be stored on the server. The web pages themselves would be duplicated in separate language versions, each stored discretely on the server.

At this time, therefore, there was generally a reasonably clear distinction between programming and content, although even then the HTML code could be relatively complex and look remarkably like a computer program.[7] Nonetheless, it was generally possible to look at a web page in a browser and identify a corresponding HTML file or files stored on the website server. Both the content and the HTML code were static. This made the task of the contract draftsman, tasked with allocating rights as between the parties, relatively simple.

Dynamic content and code   Since then things have become much more   9–009
complicated. A number of changes have taken place which significantly blur the distinction between programming and content. First, the introduction of client-side programming facilities such as Javascript and Dynamic HTML means that some of the programming that previously was executed on the server can now be written into the web pages themselves, so that it is executed by the user's PC when the pages are uploaded.

This means that the uploaded web page, instead of corresponding reasonably well to the page as viewed by the user, may now contain a vast amount of programming and also contain content only some of which is selected for viewing in a particular format by a particular user. The selection of content and format presented to the user is created "on the fly" at the user's PC, in response to the programming built into the web page. However, although the content is dynamic, the code that generates the content is still static, embedded in the pages stored on the server.

When allocating rights in content and format, it is necessary to allocate rights in all possible combinations of form and content resulting from the operation of the client-side programming. It is no longer enough (assuming that it might once have been) to define the content by, for instance, annexing a copy of the set of web pages to the contract. The possible permutations and combinations render such an approach unrealistic.

The next level of complexity is brought about by the increasing use of databases to manage website content. In this case no web pages may be stored on the web server at all,[8] but the components (text, graphic elements, forms, controls, etc.) are stored separately in the database and combined "on the fly" to generate pages in response to a request from the user's browser. Since the user's browser still needs to receive the pages in HTML (or similar compatible language such as Javascript), the database has to generate the pages in HTML or Javascript code. So whereas in the case of

---

[7] See discussion in Ch.2 regarding whether web pages qualify as computer programs for the purposes of copyright protection.

[8] In practice, in order to provide acceptable response times most databases store ("cache") temporary copies of recently or frequently requested pages, rather than generating them from scratch in response to each request.

plain Javascript/DHTML the code is static, in the case of database-driven sites not only content, but also the HTML or similar program code itself may be dynamically generated.

Additionally, sites may contain numerous other types of content: downloadable programs (screensavers and games), downloadable video files, streaming audio and video, real-time animations, and so on.

9–010   **Allocating intellectual property rights**   As regards ownership of copyright, to the extent that the dynamically generated content, format or program code represents a computer-generated work, attention needs to be paid to the provisions of the 1988 Act regarding the authorship of such works.[9]

In practice, there is likely to be little dispute over the material originally provided by the site owner and over the "look and feel" of the site. Clearly the designer does not own the site owner-supplied material and, at least in the case of static HTML, will have little interest in the coded version of that material.

If the site owner has agreed that the designer can use proprietary software in the creation of the site, the site owner will have no legitimate claim to the ownership of that proprietary software or to the underlying server operating software. The site owner will, however, need to seek a licence to use this proprietary software in order to operate the website and will want to put escrow arrangements in place to ensure it has continued access to this software if the designer becomes insolvent.

Where the designer has written software or other routines specifically for the site, as noted above, copyright will vest in the designer. The site owner may wish to specify that copyright is assigned to it. If the designer wishes to use that software for other clients—and if the site owner is prepared to agree to this—the site owner may be satisfied with a licence to use that software. Where database design or dynamically generated content and/or code are involved, considerable care will need to be taken to ensure that the contract achieves an appropriate and acceptable division of rights.

9–011   **Proprietary software**   In some cases, the site owner will not wish the designer to use proprietary software in the creation of the website as it will not wish to run the risk of losing its licence to use that software in the future through, for example, an inadvertent breach of the terms of the licence.

The site owner may also wish to ensure that the designer is prevented from using the software for its rivals and (in addition to any competition law issues) may be unhappy about relying on a contractual undertaking from the designer not to do so.

In this case the site owner may wish to insist that all software and routines used in the creation of the site are written specifically for it and that the designer assigns the intellectual property rights in that software to the site owner. If the site owner wishes to take this approach he will need to

---

[9] 1988 Act, s.9(3). The author is taken to be the person by whom the arrangements necessary for the creation of the work are undertaken.

make it clear in the specification for the website[10] and will need to have budgeted for the consequential increase in the cost of the creation of the site.

Physical materials   Ownership of intellectual property rights in a work   9–012
does not itself entitle the owner to have physical possession of the work (although in some circumstances a term to that effect may be implied). So although the site owner who owns the copyright/database right can prevent the web designer or any third party from infringing, that does not necessarily entitle him to demand that the designer provides him with a copy of the site materials.

The contract should therefore provide for delivery to the site owner of copies of the site (preferably at regular intervals throughout the initial development and, if the designer is hosting the finished site, beyond). It should also provide for the form in which the copies are provided and for provision of any ancillary materials or information required to render the materials usable and understandable. For instance, if the site has been built using a particular web development tool, the site owner may need to know what tool was used in order to make proper use of the materials.

Third party software   Where the website runs on third party software   9–013
(such as operating systems, database management systems or content management systems), careful thought will be required as to the licensing of such software especially if, on completion of development, the site is to be transferred to a third party host, or taken in-house onto the site owner's system. While the agency will have a licence to run such software on its development servers, what is the position for the live and back-up servers?

The site owner should require the designer to identify to it at the outset any third party software that it intends to use in the creation of the site so that the site owner can identify whether there are any particularly onerous terms attached to the licence of that software and whether the software has one unique source or whether equivalent software is available from other suppliers.

Domain name

If a domain name for the website is to be registered by the agency, provision   9–014
should be made for this. It may be necessary to consider carefully who is to be notified to the domain name registry as the administrative contact, since changes (such as re-delegating the domain name to a different server) are made on the instructions of that person.

If the agency is named as the contact, then in the event of a dispute, the agency may effectively be able to prevent the site being transferred elsewhere. As a result of such incidents, the internet service providers Association (ISPA) Code of Conduct now mandates ISPA members to

---

[10] See fn.4 above.

provide, in some circumstances, a degree of protection for their customers in such situations. Similarly, thought should be given as to whom is to be nominated as the billing contact.

9.2.3 The contract for website hosting

9–015 Once the website has been accepted, the role of the agency (if it is to undertake the role) becomes that of host and maintainer. The contract will be similar to other information technology services contracts. Specifically, however, it needs to address two key issues, reflecting the two key roles of the host's server. First, the server is the storage device on which all the information constituting the website is kept. Secondly, it connects with the internet and provides a conduit through which visitors to the website access that information.

Storage of the website data

9–016 As regards storage, the contract needs to set out not only how much capacity on the server will initially be made available but also the basis on which this is varied. In particular, the basis of calculating any difference in the charges should be set out.

A website is not static: the site owner will want to retain its immediacy by regular updates. The contract should set out how updates to the site are to be made, the frequency with which they can be made, the time it will take for the host to implement an update, and the cost of doing so. The site owner may want the ability to update its own site remotely by using an editing address and a password.

The contract may also deal with security issues, such as whether the server data is mirrored on another server for safety and whether particular security or encryption protocols are supported. If (as will almost inevitably be the case) the host is processing personal data on behalf of the site owner, the site owner will need to satisfy himself that the host offers the guarantees required by para.11 of Sch.1 of the Data Protection Act 1998 concerning security, and ensure that the contract is made or evidenced in writing and otherwise complies with the requirements of para.12 of Sch.1.

Since "writing" is not defined in the 1988 Act, it should be construed in accordance with the definition in the Interpretation Act 1978. Although it may perhaps be open to doubt whether every variety of contract in electronic form would necessarily satisfy the requirement that the contract be made in writing, in most case electronic form will suffice.[11] The alternative requirement that it be evidenced in writing would appear to permit a printout of the relevant electronic documents to be adduced in evidence.

---

[11] See discussion of requirements of form in Ch.10.

Access to the site

The capacity (bandwidth) of the host's connection to the rest of the internet will be of vital importance to both the host and its customers. The host will not want to pay for unused bandwidth; the site owner will not want its site to be unavailable to potential clients due to bandwidth congestion. **9–017**

The contract should specify the obligations of the host to manage peaks and troughs in bandwidth requirement effectively, so as to ensure that the site is reliably available but that this is balanced against the host's concern to avoid carrying excess bandwidth. It is becoming increasingly the case that hosts can buy variable bandwidth on demand. More hosting permutations have become available, such as locating the site owner's servers at a third party server farm with high internet connectivity, with varying allocations of responsibilities between the site owner and the operator of the server farm.

Other performance indicators and service levels should also be set out in the contract, including the availability of the site (i.e. whether and when down time is permitted). Defining "availability" in information technology contracts is notoriously difficult. The parties should aim to tie it specifically to clearly measured criteria and set out how it is to be monitored and reported.

The contract should also specify what responsibility the host may have to provide alternative or back up server capacity if the main system is down or there is a problem with a particular communications link. These obligations need to reflect the global nature of the internet marketplace and therefore the time zones which are important to the site owner.

Of course, in specifying service levels the parties need to take into account that quality of access will depend on a number of factors outside the host's control, such as quality of the provider through which each end-user is accessing the site and the level of traffic on the internet as a whole.

Information and reports

If a website allows for the sending of emails or the collecting of other information, the contract with the host should specify how and at what frequency this information is passed to the user. Even for a relatively passive site, the owner will normally require meaningful statistical information about the number of visitors not only to measure the success of the website but to provide to potential advertisers and sponsors. For e-commerce and advertising-driven sites, the owner may require extremely detailed information about usage patterns, page impressions and so on. These may need to be capable of being audited by third parties. **9–018**

As technology moves on, so previously accepted measurement methods may become redundant. For instance, so-called Ajax (Asynchronous Java and XML) web programming allows the user to interact with the site while remaining within a single web page frame. This seriously affects the utility of page impressions as a measure of volume. It has been suggested that page views as a measure of volume will be close to disappearing by the end of 2007.[12]

Where the site contains forms allowing for the requesting of information or for the sending of contractual messages (see Ch.10) the user will wish to ensure that the data in forms submitted by potential customers is passed through immediately, that any appropriate automatic response is generated and that appropriate records of the transactions are kept for compliance and evidential purposes.

The contract should contain provisions dealing with ownership of this data and requiring the host to comply with the provisions of the Data Protection Act 1998 if it processes this data on behalf of the site owner.

The host's concerns

9–019   The host will be anxious to avoid liability for any defamatory, infringing or obscene material which may appear on a page on its server. To this end, it will seek to impose an obligation on the site owner to exercise appropriate control over content and to indemnify the ISP should there be a claim. Such an indemnity will usually stand outside any limitations on liability that are agreed in the contract and, since like any indemnity its value will depend on the ability of the indemnifying party to pay up, hosts should consider requiring the site owner to obtain insurance to cover third party claims or do so themselves.

Where the host is hosting material supplied in final form by the site owner or which can be updated by the site owner online, the contract should set out guidelines as to taste and decency which must be observed and give the host the right to remove material which it believes could give rise to liability. For pornographic material, there is the risk that, as it is effectively being published to the world at large, including children, it will be held to be obscene. See Ch.5 for a discussion of the liability of the host in such event.

To reduce this risk, the host may insist on a standard warning screen being implemented or the use of an age verification system. In any event, the host will wish to ensure that it is free to remove materials in compliance with a request received from bodies such as the Internet Watch Foundation. (Similarly, where the site owner does not have the ability to update its own site remotely, it will want the right to require the host to promptly remove any material that is discoverd to be defamatory, infringing or obscene.)

However, the host must be careful, from the point of view of defamation liability, not to assume too great a degree of control over the content provided by the site owner. If a third party were to argue that the host had assumed editorial responsibility for the purposes of the Defamation Act 1996, then the allocation of responsibilities under the contract would be strong evidence of what responsibilities the host had assumed. On the other

---

[12] "Rise of Ajax sites set to phase out UK reliance on page views" New Media Age February 22, 2007.

hand (as discussed in Ch.4), it is unlikely that reserving the right to delete unlawful material would be regarded as assuming editorial responsibility.

Similarly, the hosting protection of Art.14 of the Electronic Commerce Directive (see Ch.5) is lost if the site owner is acting under the authority or control of the host (Art.14.2).

Sharing of risk

Where the website is being used for commercial purposes, the site owner may wish to specify financial remedies for failures to provide services, for example if the server goes down or access is impossible to compensate him. The host will wish to exclude liability for lost business, which may in any event be impossible to quantify. **9–020**

9.3 SPONSORSHIP AND ADVERTISING AGREEMENTS

A significant development in the commercialisation of the internet has been the placing of advertising within, and commercial sponsorship of websites. The advertiser or sponsor pays the owner of the site in return for the display of a logo or other advertising material on that site and, typically, a hypertext link to the website of the advertiser or sponsor. A number of specific content based sites exist purely to generate revenue from advertisers and sponsors who are interested in promoting themselves to users of that site who, because they are interested in the subject-matter of the site, believe they will also be interested in the advertisers/sponsor's goods or services. **9–021**

As websites, which have email capabilities, offer a cheap way of communicating with individual consumers, site owners and advertisers are increasingly seeking ways to capture and utilise "rich" data from website users to obtain the holy grail of advertising—the ability to target advertising at individual users.

If a content provider has a valuable site, such as in relation to a major sporting event, it will be concerned to maximise its revenue from advertising and/or site sponsorship. This involves analysing the package or packages of rights which it can most effectively sell. For example, it may sell all the rights to insert graphic logos and hypertext links to one advertiser or it may divide the rights among a number of advertisers. It may distinguish between a "sponsor", who is entitled to a more prominent place on the site, and other advertisers who will receive lesser billing.

On the other hand the advertiser or sponsor will be concerned about how much prominence its brand will have on the website and where it sits in the "hierarchy." It may want to ensure that none of its rivals will be permitted to display their branding or advertising on the website.

Both parties will want to make the advertising or sponsorship work for them. The site owner will want to ensure that the advertising placed on its site and the sponsors with which it is associated are in keeping with the content and purpose of the site. The advertiser or sponsor will want to ensure that the website is a suitable medium to carry its advertising and that it fits with its overall advertising and marketing strategy.

With this in mind, a contract for advertising on a website should address the issues discussed below.

9.3.1 The rights being granted in respect of the website

9–022 As regards the site itself, is the advertiser to have exclusive or non-exclusive rights? Are there categories of advertising within which the advertiser will have exclusivity, e.g. that it will be the only food retailer on the site?

If the site is established in connection with a prestigious event or a high profile product (such as a rock group), is the advertiser to be granted a designation which it can use in other advertising, such as "Official Sponsor of the XYZ Web Page"?

9.3.2 Positioning and size

9–023 The advertiser will wish to specify where on the website its advertisement will appear, in what form and at what size relative to other text and graphics. Unlike with a paper-based campaign where sizes are constant, this will involve a consideration of the working of the hypertext mark-up language and the operation of the web browsers (discussed in Ch.1) which are likely to be used to access the site. The advertiser may want to specify the technical details of how, in particular, its logo is created so as to ensure that it both downloads at an acceptable speed and is attractive. This of course also involves an analysis of the likely market: if the website is aimed at students, who may have "free" access, download time may not be so much of an issue. However, students accessing via a mainframe may use different browsers from home users so this will also need to be taken into account.

The advertiser may also want some contractual assurance that the web page itself will be changed over time to keep up with new versions or releases of relevant browsers or, conversely, that it will remain usable with older versions. Whether this is a concern will depend very much on whether the site and advertising are relatively static or are relevant only for a campaign of short duration, such as in connection with a specific event.

9.3.3 Obligations in relation to promotion of the website

9–024 Where the site relates to a campaign by the owner in other media, advertisers may also wish to have assurances about the promotion of the website within that campaign, such as by the inclusion of the website's URL (Uniform Resource Locator) on posters and other forms of advertising. Conversely, and particularly where there is one major sponsor, the owner may wish to oblige that sponsor to promote the site as part of the sponsor's own advertising.

9.3.4 Hypertext links

Both parties will have concerns relating to the hypertext links from the **9–025** advertisement to the advertiser's own web page. The advertiser will want to ensure that the link is correctly created and that the site owner is obliged to update it correctly should there be a change in the URL of the advertiser's website. The advertiser will also no doubt want to ensure that the link can be triggered either from a text message or a graphic.

The owner of the site will want to ensure that the link to the advertiser's website will not give rise to any liability to third parties for defamation (see Ch.4) or otherwise and that the advertiser will advise him promptly of changes: a non-functioning link will detract from the original website.

Both parties will want to ensure that they are not linked to or associated with inappropriate material.

9.3.5 Intellectual property

The advertiser will wish to specify the extent of the right of the owner of the **9–026** website to use any trade or service marks on the site and to ensure that the owner applies the marks consistently with any standard guidelines. The form of the advertising in general will be of concern to the advertiser and he will wish to have prior approval of relevant copy.

The owner of the site will seek an indemnity in respect of third party claims arising out of the use of the advertiser's marks on the World Wide Web, particularly bearing in mind the global nature of the internet (see Ch.3).

9.3.6 Use of information about visitors to the site

Both parties will be interested in information about who visits the site: the **9–027** owner so as to justify its rate card for advertising and the advertiser to judge whether the site is an appropriate place to advertise. Both parties will need to be aware of the distortion of these figures which "hits" to a cached version of the site will cause.

Where specific information about the identity of particular visitors to the site and those who visit the advertiser's site via the hypertext link is collected, the parties will need to ensure that this is dealt with in compliance with applicable data protection regulations (see Ch.7).

9.4 INTERNET ACCESS AGREEMENTS

9–028   These are the agreements under which the end-users of the internet are provided with access to the internet via an ISP.

There will be a distinction between the terms which are offered to a domestic as opposed to a corporate user, reflecting the different methods of access and the importance of the service.

Domestic users

9–029   Typically there will be a flat monthly fee for unlimited access (excluding telephone charges, if any) and the internet will be reached by dial-up or broadband access. Alternatively, some ISPs offer a combination of a lower fee for a certain number of hours access with a usage charge above that threshold. Some offer non-subscription services, for which the user pays only the network provider's telephone charges if any—some services provide access through a free telephone number, and any extra charges, for instance for support. Such extra charges may be levied indirectly, for instance by providing telephone support through a premium rate telephone number.

It is unlikely that the contract will contain any specific pledges as to availability or quality of service, although the ISP should bear in mind that any exclusions of liability or attempts to limit its responsibility will be subject to reasonableness criteria (see Ch.10). The ISP will seek to impose contractual restrictions on the ability of the user to access unlawful information and may spell out guidelines for use designed to minimise the risk that the ISP will carry infringing, defamatory or obscene material.

As regards any software provided by the ISP, the contract should make clear the terms on which it may be used, especially if third party software, such as a browser, is being provided. The ISP may provide that the user must register use of the software directly with the copyright owner.

ISPs commonly provide a range of services in addition to internet access: free or chargeable web space, domain name registration and maintenance, chat room and instant messaging facilities, overseas roaming access, and others. The contract will clearly need to address the full range of services of which user may make use.

Further, if the ISP software makes any unexpected changes to the user's computer configuration (especially any that may hinder the use of other ISPs), or collects any information about the user or his computer usage, then the contract may need to address these. If the "click-wrap" approach to contract formation is adopted, care may need to be taken to ensure that no potentially contentious system changes or data collection take place before the user has had the opportunity to review and accept the contract terms.[13]

---

[13] Note the US case of *Williams v America Online Inc*, Mass. Super. Ct., No 00–0962, February 8, 2001 (ECLR Vol.6 No.10 p.242).

It should not be assumed that ISP contracts can be regarded as mere small print which will lie unnoticed. It only takes one user to notice an unusual or apparently unfair term and to raise the issue on the internet, for it to snowball into a very public controversy.

Corporate users

Increasingly, corporate users are demanding service contracts akin to other telecommunications contracts, with statements as to service quality and remedies such as service credits for default. The issue for the ISP in such circumstances is to ensure that it only accepts responsibility for matters within its control. Those ISPs which own substantial infrastructure will be able to offer greater guarantees of service quality than those which are more dependent on third party infrastructure.

9–030

As with other IT services contracts, there will be a tension between the ISP's desire to define the service by way of end result and the desire of the user to set out the means by which this result is to be obtained. For example, the ISP may simply wish to state that the service is available for a certain percentage of the time; the user may wish to specify that the ISP safeguards service provision by using mirrored servers or alternative leased lines to an information exchange.

The contract will also need to address issues of the type of material which is accessed using the ISP's system and to require indemnities from the user should the ISP be liable for the transmission of obscene, defamatory or infringing material.

Allocation of resources: anti "spamming" clauses

With any user, the ISP may wish to prohibit the posting of emails to multiple newsgroups for advertising purposes ("spamming") to avoid the danger of the ISP's mail server being clogged up with multiple responses or "flaming". The ISP may also wish to restrict the use of bandwidth-hungry applications such as video-conferencing.

9–031

Internet telephony and other specialist traffic

As explored in Ch.8, ISPs may fall foul of telecommunications regulation if they carry some types of internet telephony service without complying with relevant authorisations, if any. The ISP may therefore also wish to prohibit the use of some internet telephony services over its network. In any event, some ISPs, for technical reasons, impose restrictions on certain types of traffic that can cause congestion on their networks.

9–032

9.5 PEERING AGREEMENTS

These are the internet equivalent of telecommunications interconnect agreements and set out the basis on which ISPs exchange traffic. This

9–033

exchange can be either via direct bilateral links or via traffic exchanges which act as central multilateral clearing houses.

Initially, these agreements amounted to little more than an informal agreement to exchange traffic without payment. However, the growth in internet traffic and the increasing investment in infrastructure has led to some similarities with interconnect agreements being introduced. For example, there may be volume-related payments between ISPs and statements as to service quality. Most recently the question of whether it is appropriate to apply different treatment to varying types of content transmitted over public internet capacity has become a political issue, at least in the US, under the banner of Net Neutrality.

CHAPTER 10

Electronic Contracts and Transactions

10.1 INTRODUCTION

The internet has evolved from an academic and military resource to the   10–001
platform for a global marketplace. The essence of a marketplace is that it is
the forum for exchanging goods and services for money or other value.
Underpinning such buying and selling are commercial contracts between
the parties. This chapter considers these contracts in the context of the
internet.

In so doing, basic principles of contract law will be examined in the light
of the types of contracts being formed over the internet and the means of
formation. However, this chapter is not intended to be a treatise on contract law but to consider the application of that law to contracts made over
the internet. For further detail on the underlying legal principles, the
standard texts on the subject should therefore be consulted.

In order to set the scene, the chapter begins with a brief comparison with
the principles of law relating to electronic data interchange then a consideration of the types of contracts typically formed over the internet, the
methods by which such contracts are formed and the impact of EU legislation concerning online contracts. The chapter also considers
developments in the law applicable to electronic signatures and other
aspects of conducting transactions electronically. We also consider the
evidential aspects of proving electronic transactions.

10.1.1 Comparison with the law relating to electronic data interchange

Forming online contracts by communication between computers was car-   10–002
ried out prior to the advent of the internet. For some time, commercial
concerns have been using electronic data interchange (EDI). EDI is the
exchange by computers of business information in a standard format. It

pre-supposes that both parties to the communication use a standard format and, in most cases, that they have pre-agreed what this format will be. It is often used where companies exchange similar information on a frequent basis and where the process can readily be mechanised. One example of this is "just in time" stocking systems used by supermarkets where the tills automatically record purchases, which updates an inventory system which in turn automatically orders new stock from suppliers. EDI is also much used in the vehicle manufacturing industry and by airlines.

A body of law and regulation has built up around EDI and it has been suggested that useful comparisons can be drawn between contracting over the internet and EDI. However, there are some vital distinctions between EDI, as defined above, and trading over the internet (at least in the "B2C" (business to consumer) sector).

EDI assumes that the computers involved use a highly structured form of messaging with pre-defined fields and contents: contracting over the internet usually involves free-form communications.

EDI assumes an on-going relationship and, usually, that the parties have signed an "interchange agreement" setting out the basis of exchange: internet trading is likely to involve a casual buying of goods or services with little or no prior contact between the parties and no necessity for a continuing relationship.

EDI frequently has no direct human involvement as the communicating computers may exchange information automatically: as yet, trading over the internet usually involves the conscious act of the buyer, at least, in ordering the goods and services.

EDI is likely to be carried out over a value added network with guarantees of service quality and certainty as to the identity of the carriers: the internet cannot as yet provide either.

The trading partners in an EDI relationship are likely to be substantial commercial concerns: with the internet, in a B2C transaction the commercial organisation will be selling to an individual. The internet can also enable consumers to contract directly with each other.

10–003 It is therefore suggested that, although many of the legal principles which have been considered in the context of EDI will be common to internet trading, the application of these principles, the balance of convenience between the parties, and the solutions to problems are likely to be different.

Having said that, it should be noted that B2C is only one aspect of internet trading. B2B (business to business) constitutes a significant element of internet activity, especially when transactions are measured by value rather than by volume. For B2B, some aspects of existing EDI knowhow may usefully be applied. Indeed there has been a move, with some success, to promote "Internet EDI" as a trading concept.[1]

---

[1] See for instance Internet Engineering Task Force EDIINT Working Group Internet Draft "Requirements for Inter-operable Internet EDI" (*www.ietf.org/html.charters/OLD/ediint-charter.html*). For a general discussion of the concepts see *http://www.ediiseasy.com/*.

10.1.2 Current means of forming contracts in relation to the internet

Before considering the application of contract law to contracts formed in **10–004**
relation to the internet, it may be helpful to put the methods of contract
formation in context. Broadly, these divide into two main methods: (i)
forming contracts by the exchange of electronic messages, and (ii) the
formation of contracts "off-line", by telephone, facsimile or post. This
chapter considers largely only the former method, save where the internet
adds a new factor to the existing law relating to contract formation in the
latter ways and where the voice telephony service is over the internet itself.

Looking more closely at electronic contract formation, it is apparent that
there are many ways that this can be achieved. Examples include the direct
exchange of emails, an email response to a web page, other agreements
formed directly via a web page (for example where a traditional trader
utilises an "online storefront" to sell its goods), agreeing the sale of an item
using an online auction web page, and the exchange of messages over a
Usenet group or other discussion forum.

This last method, involving the publication of messages in an open
forum, is least likely to be utilised in commercial practice as it necessarily
involves the public disclosure of what may be a bi-partite agreement and
because the ethos of these groups largely precludes their use for commercial
purposes. In practice therefore the most likely scenarios for the conclusion
of contracts over the internet are via email or in connection with a web
page.

10.1.3 The typical subject matter of contracts currently formed over the internet

This breaks down into three broad categories: **10–005**

-   *Contracts for the sale of physical goods.* Typically, these arise
    where a web page is being used in conjunction with more tradi-
    tional advertising as an alternative shop window, e.g. for the sale
    of alcohol, books or compact disks. Although the contract is
    formed over the internet, the performance by the supplier is con-
    stituted by the despatch of the goods to the purchaser.
-   *Contracts for the supply of digitised products.* These contracts
    involve the online supply of data, such as software, text, music,
    video or multimedia products, often together with the granting of
    a licence of any copyright material comprised within the products.
-   *Contracts for the supply of services and facilities.* This would
    include online banking and other financial services, the giving of
    professional advice over the internet and, increasingly, the provi-
    sion of voice telephony and potentially video-conferencing.

At present the majority of contracts are formed between businesses and consumers, rather than between businesses themselves or directly between consumers. Nevertheless, the bulk of high value or high complexity electronic contracts are created using EDI rather than the internet.

As the internet increases in reliability and security, the distinction between B2B internet contracting and EDI is becoming less valid. Also, with the advent of online auctions and seller rating systems, the potential for small traders to access worldwide markets and to gain online reputations has increased dramatically.

However, the assumption underlying this chapter is that the majority of contracts created over the internet at present are of relatively low value between parties which do not have an existing or continuing business relationship.

10.1.4 Content of contracts

10–006 As discussed below (for example in para.10–050), there can be a tension between the desire to ensure that all relevant contractual terms are incorporated into a contract and the limitations of screen size and the need to use the medium attractively. In respect of contracts to be formed over or in relation to the internet, the parties will need to consider, as with any contract, the appropriate extent and content of the contractual terms. This section considers additional points to be borne in mind in relation to contracts to be formed electronically and draws together some of the points already made.

- *Contract formation*. The contract terms should state the method and procedure for accepting the offer and the duration of, or conditions relating to, the offer, and the parties must be sufficiently aware of such terms to ensure that they are adequately incorporated into the contract.
- *Delivery*. The method and timing of delivery of the relevant goods should be spelled out and whether these vary depending on method of payment, availability of stock or jurisdiction of the recipient.
- *Risk and insurance*. Where physical goods are to be despatched, the question of risk of damage or loss and the responsibility for insurance should be stated: again, this may vary with jurisdiction.
- *Price, currency and payment*. The contract should state clearly the price (including any applicable taxes and insurance) and the currency and acceptable means of payment. Where payment is to be made by physical means, such as the sending of a money order, the offeror will no doubt wish to have the right to delay delivery until this is received.
- *Subject matter*. This is particularly relevant where there is a grant

of rights in digitised material, where the extent of the licence should be clearly spelled out.

– *Geographical limitations.* Where goods or services are available only in certain countries, or advice can only be given in or in respect of certain jurisdictions, this should be stated.

– *Limitations and exclusions of liability.* To the extent permitted by the relevant legal systems, the supplier will wish to limit its liability and to exclude implied terms. See also section 10.2 below.

– *Governing law.* See section 10.3 below.

Some of these points are now the subject of specific requirements under the transparency provisions of the Distance Selling Directive and the Electronic Commerce Directive. These are implemented in the UK by the Consumer Protection (Distance Selling) Regulation 2000 (the "Distance Selling Regulations") and the Electronic Commerce (EC Directive) Regulations 2002 ("E-Commerce Regulations") respectively. They are discussed in detail below.

10.2 EXCLUSIONS, LIMITATIONS AND COMPLIANCE MEASURES

In respect of contracts made within England and Wales, and in particular in respect of contracts made with consumers, the supplier of goods or services will need to take into account the provisions of various pieces of legislation. In brief, these include: 10–007

The Consumer Credit Act 1974

This regulates the content of agreements for the provision of credit, sets out various procedures which must be followed to protect consumers and establishes a regime for licensing businesses which provide consumer credit or consumer hire.   10–008

The Unfair Contract Terms Act 1977

Among other things, this prohibits a supplier from excluding or restricting its liability for death or personal injury caused by negligence (s.2); or circumscribes the limitation of liability in respect of certain implied terms in relation to goods or services (ss.3, 6 and 11).   10–009

The Consumer Protection Act 1987

This imposes in certain circumstances strict liability on the manufacturer and other members of the distribution chain of defective goods which cause death or personal injury or loss of or damage to property.   10–010

The Unfair Contract Terms Directive 1993 (93/13)

10–011 The Unfair Contract Terms Directive applies to standard contracts entered into between the sellers or suppliers of goods or services to consumers. It introduces a general concept of "unfairness" and terms which are found to be unfair will be unenforceable as against the consumer.

It was originally implemented in the UK by the Unfair Terms in Consumer Contracts Regulations 1994 (the 1994 Regulations). These were replaced by the Unfair Terms in Consumer Contracts Regulations 1999,[2] which came into force on October 1, 1999, and aligned the substance of the UK Regulations more closely to the wording of the Directive.

These include a general provision that all consumer contractual terms must be fair. Similarly, if there is any doubt as to the meaning of a term in a consumer contract, then it will be given the meaning most beneficial to the consumer.

The Distance Selling Directive (97/7)

10–012 The Distance Selling Directive (97/7) has been implemented by the Consumer Protection (Distance Selling) Regulations 2000,[3] which came into force on October 31, 2000. These have since been amended by the Consumer Protection (Distance Selling) (Amendment) Regulations 2005, which came into force on April 6, 2006. The Distance Selling Regulations are discussed below.

The Consumer Goods and Associated Guarantees Directive (1999/44/EC)

10–013 The Consumer Goods and Associated Guarantees Directive was implemented in the UK by the Sale and Supply of Goods to Consumers Regulations 2002,[4] which came into force on March 31, 2003. These Regulations made various amendments to the Sale of Goods Act 1979, the Supply of Goods and Services Act 1982, the Supply of Goods (Implied Terms) Act 1973, and the Unfair Contract Terms Act 1977.

Regulation 14 may be of relevance to e-commerce. It amends the exclusion of auctions from the 1977 Act, so that the Act applies where an individual purchases goods at an auction which he does not have the opportunity of attending in person. Arguably, this could apply to online auctions—although the term "auction" is not defined in the legislation (see discussion at para.10–025 and section 10.4.9).

The Regulations also make provisions for consumer guarantees, including that on request the guarantee shall be made available to the consumer "in writing or in another durable medium available and accessible to him".

10–014 The online trader will also have to take into account requirements of consumer protection legislation which, while not directly affecting the

---

[2] SI 1999/2083.
[3] SI 2000/2334.
[4] SI 2002/3045.

contract with the consumer, will affect the trader's dealings generally with the consumer. These include:

The Control of Misleading Advertisements Regulations 1988

These regulate misleading advertisements and contain provisions regarding the use of comparative advertising.

10–015

The Disability Discrimination Act 1995

This Act came into force in various stages and arguably means that the owners of websites must make reasonable adjustments to ensure that their sites are "accessible" to those with disabilities.[5]

10–016

The Electronic Commerce Directive (2000/31)

The Electronic Commerce Directive has been implemented generally in the UK by the Electronic Commerce (EC Directive) Regulations 2002,[6] which (with the exception of reg.16, which came into force on October 23, 2002) came into force on August 21, 2002. The E-Commerce Regulations are discussed extensively below.

10–017

The Privacy and Electronic Communications Directive (2002/58/EC)

The Directive on Privacy and Electronic Communication was implemented in the UK by the Privacy and Electronic Communications (EC Directive) Regulations 2003,[7] which came into force on December 11, 2003. A discussion of these Regulations to the extent that they may affect online communications and marketing is set out below.

10–018

The Trade Descriptions Act 1968

This Act makes it an offence for a trader to apply a false description to any goods or to supply any goods with a false description. It is also an offence under the Act for a trader to knowingly or recklessly make a false statement about a service.

10–019

The Unfair Commercial Practices Directive (2005/29/EC)

This Directive is due to be implemented by December 12, 2007. It seeks to provide a comprehensive code of business to consumer commercial practices that are prohibited because they are unfair, particularly those that are misleading or aggressive.

10–020

---

[5] See the discussion below at section 10.2.4.
[6] SI 2002/2013.
[7] SI 2003/2426.

10.2.1 The Distance Selling Directive

10–021 EC Directive 97/7 of the European Parliament and of the Council on the protection of consumers in respect of distance contracts was adopted on May 20, 1997. It has been implemented in the UK by the Consumer Protection (Distance Selling) Regulations 2000,[8] which came into force on October 31, 2000 and by the Consumer Protection (Distance Selling) (Amendment) Regulations 2005 which came into force on April 6, 2005.

The Department of Trade and Industry (DTI) and the Office of Fair Trading (OFT) have produced guidance in relation to distance selling—both individually and, more recently, jointly.[9] While the guidance does not have the force of law, in view of the central enforcement role played by the OFT it is useful in assessing what activities the OFT is likely to regard as breaching the Regulations.

The joint Guide for Business on Distance Selling[10] was issued in September 2006, following a consultation draft in August 2005.[11] The guide includes discussion of both the Distance Selling Regulations and the E-Commerce Regulations (discussed below).

10–022 The Regulations apply to certain "distance contracts". This means "any contract concerning goods or services concluded between a supplier and a consumer under an organised distance sales or service provision scheme run by the supplier who, for the purpose of the contract, makes exclusive use of one or more means of distance communication up to and including the moment at which the contract is concluded".

"Means of distance communication" means "any means which, without the simultaneous physical presence of the supplier and the consumer, may be used for the conclusion of a contract between those parties".

An indicative list of such means is contained in Sch.1 to the Regulations. Insofar as it may include electronic or similar communications, the list includes: catalogue; telephone with human intervention; telephone without human intervention (automatic calling machine, audiotext); radio; video-phone (telephone with screen); videotext (microcomputer and television screen) with keyboard or touch screen; electronic mail; facsimile machine (fax); television (teleshopping).

"Supplier" means any person who, in contracts to which the Regulations apply, is acting in his commercial or professional capacity.

"Consumer" means any natural person who, in contracts to which the Regulations apply, is acting for purposes which are outside his business (which includes a trade or profession).

10–023 Although not specifically named in the indicative list, sales through websites and other electronic means such as text messaging are clearly covered by the

---

[8] SI 2000/2334.
[9] See, in general, *www.oft.gov.uk/advice_and_resources/resource_base/legal/distance-selling-regulations/.*
[10] *www.oft.gov.uk/shared_oft/business_leaflets/general/oft698.pdf.*
[11] *www.oft.gov.uk/.*

Regulations. Although the Regulations have their origins in traditional mail-order and telephone sales transactions, they (and the underlying Directive) have been drafted so as to include internet transactions. It may be that thought rules devised for mail order do not translate well into the interactive e-commerce environment.

Certain types of contract are excepted from the Regulations under reg.5(1). These are any contract: **10–024**

(a) for the sale or other disposition of an interest in land except for a rental agreement (the Regulations contain further provisions regarding what constitutes a rental agreement);

(b) for the construction of a building where the contract also provides for a sale or other disposition of an interest in land on which the building is constructed, except for a rental agreement;

(c) relating to financial services (a non-exhaustive list of which is contained in Sch.2 to the Regulations);

(d) concluded by means of an automated vending machine or automated commercial premises;

(e) concluded with a telecommunications operator through the use of a public payphone;

(f) concluded at an auction.

There is no definition of "auction" in the Regulations.[12] Nor is there a   **10–025**
generally applicable definition in UK statute law.

The OFT/DTI Guidance considers whether an item purchased from a business using an online auction website would be covered by the Regulations. The typical online auction site differs from the traditional auction model in that the sales and purchases are made directly between the buyers and sellers, rather than through an auctioneer acting as the seller's agent. Ultimately, the only firm guidance given by the OFT and DTI is that where the item is purchased for a fixed, predetermined price using a 'buy it now" facility, this definitely would not fall within the exception.

Germany's highest civil court has decided that a purchase from a commercial seller using an online auction platform, in this case eBay, did not fall within the exception granted by the German law implementing the Distance Selling Directive.[13] The court appears to have held that a sale on eBay was not an auction under German law due to the way that the parties concluded the contract.[14] That is, the contract was not formed by an auctioneer's acceptance of the highest bid—rather the seller simply accepted the buyer's offer by virtue of the fact that it was the highest bid for the item.

Ultimately, whether an online auction falls within the exception in the

---

[12] Similarly, there is no definition of "auction" in the Sale of Goods Act 1979, despite there being provisions relating to auctions—i.e. s.57.

[13] Ruling November 3, [2004] Bundesgerichtshof (Case No.VIII ZR 375/03)—available (in German) at *http://www.bundesgerichtshof.de*.

[14] see "EU Right to Revoke Distance Purchase Extends to Commercial eBay 'Auctions'"—ECLR Vol.9 No.43 p.923.

Regulations is a matter for the courts. Assuming that "auction" has an autonomous meaning under the Directive, it would be for the European Court of Justice to determine the scope of the exception. If it were a matter for each Member State's national law, it seems marginally more likely that the UK courts would follow the German approach if only because given that the purpose of the Regulations is consumer protection, it is likely that the court would construe any exception narrowly.

The question would be whether the absence of an auctioneer is fatal, or whether the open competitive bidding provides sufficient of the character of an auction without the need for an auctioneer. Although the term "auction" is not generally defined in legislation, s.57(2) of the Sale of Goods Act 1979 states that an auction "is complete when the auctioneer announces its completion by the fall of the hammer, or in other customary manner". While the reference to an auctioneer envisages the input of a third party, the section does allow for other possibilities.

10–026　　The bulk of the Regulations (reg.7–20) do not apply to timeshare agreements within the meaning of the Timeshare Act 1992. Similarly, regs 7–19(1) (relating to information to be provided to the consumer before and after the formation of the contract, the right to cancel during the "cooling-off period" and the timescale for performance—discussed in depth below) do not apply to:

(a) contracts for the supply of food, beverages or other goods intended for everyday consumption supplied to the consumer's residence or to his workplace by regular roundsmen; or

(b) contracts for the provision of accommodation, transport, catering or leisure services, where the supplier undertakes, when the contract is concluded, to provide these services on a specific date or within a specific period.

10–027　　The case of *easyCar (UK) v Office of Fair Trading* was the European Court of Jutice's first ruling on the Distance Selling Directive.[15] On a reference from the English High Court the ECJ decided that car rental services fell within the exemption granted to "transport services" and hence parties that hired cars online were not entitled to cancel the hire contract during the "cooling-off" period.

In the High Court the OFT had argued that easyCar's cancellation terms did not comply with the obligation to provide a consumer with a "cooling-off period" following a booking. This position was supported by French and Spanish Governments, the European Commission and the ECJ's own Advocate General.

Nevertheless, the ECJ held that car rental was, indeed a "transport service" for the purposes of the Directive when the phrase was given its usual meaning using "everyday language" and that transport included the mode

---

[15] (C–336/03)—see *http://europa.eu.int/eur-lex/lex/LexUriServ/LexUriServ.do?uri=CELEX: 62003J0336:EN:HTML.*

of transport, not simply the action of moving persons or goods from one place to another.

The court further held that the purpose of the exception was to prevent suppliers from suffering "disproportionate consequences" as a result of the cancellation. It must be presumed that such hardship would be suffered by car rental companies that could otherwise be left with a number of cars that it could not hire out at short notice following a cancellation.

Regulations 19(2)–(8) and 20 (relating to rights of the consumer where the supplier is unable to perform the contract when goods or services are not available and the effect of non-performance on related credit agreements) do not apply to a contract for a package within the meaning of the Package Travel, Package Holidays and Package Tours Regulations 1992 which is sold or offered for sale in the territory of the Member States. **10–028**

There are also exceptions from individual regulations which are noted below.

The Regulations provide various rights for the benefit of consumers: transparency rights (i.e. the right to be provided with information), cancellation rights and rights as to the period within which the contract must be performed. These, to an extent, interconnect. We shall concentrate in this discussion on aspects of particular relevance to the internet. Reference may be made to the Regulations for full details of the rights in question, and of associated rights such as cancellation of related credit agreements. **10–029**

Transparency

Under reg.7(1), the supplier must, in good time prior to the conclusion of the contract: **10–030**

    (a) provide to the consumer the following information—

        (i) the identity of the supplier and, where the contract requires payment in advance, the supplier's address;

        (ii) a description of the main characteristics of the goods or services;

        (iii) the price of the goods or services including all taxes;

        (iv) delivery costs where appropriate;

        (v) the arrangements for payment, delivery or performance;

        (vi) the existence of a right of cancellation (except where reg.13 excludes the right to cancel);

        (vii) the cost of using the means of distance communication where it is calculated other than at the basic rate;

        (viii) the period for which the offer or the price remains valid; and

        (ix) where appropriate, the minimum duration of the contract, in the case of contracts for the supply of goods or services to be performed permanently or recurrently;

    (b) inform the consumer if he proposes, in the event of the goods or services ordered by the consumer being unavailable, to provide substitute goods or services (as the case may be) of equivalent quality and price; and

  (c) inform the consumer that the cost of returning any such substitute goods to the supplier in the event of cancellation by the consumer would be met by the supplier.

Under reg.7(2) the supplier must ensure that the information required by para.(1) is "provided in a clear and comprehensible manner appropriate to the means of distance communication used, with due regard in particular to the principles of good faith in commercial transactions and the principles governing the protection of those who are unable to give their consent such as minors".

Under reg.7(3) the supplier must ensure that his commercial purpose is made clear when providing the information required by para.(1).

10–031   Failure to observe these requirements of reg.7 does not appear to affect the validity of any contract between the supplier and the consumer (although under reg.19(7) the ability of the supplier to provide substitute goods or services depends upon the contract providing for this and upon the information about this having been provided under reg.7). (Regulation 25 provides that a term in a contract to which the Regulations apply is void if and to the extent that it is inconsistent with a provision for the protection of the consumer contained in the Regulations.)

The provisions may, however, be enforced by injunction by an appropriate enforcement authority under regs. 26 and 27 or by a private sector consumer protection body designated under the Enterprise Act 2002 (discussed below).

10–032   A German court has applied the transparency requirements of the Distance Selling Directive in the case *OLG Karlsruhe*.[16] The defendant was an internet portal which provided a lottery form for users to fill in. The portal then forwarded the data from the completed form to the company running the lottery. The claimant, a competitor, alleged three breaches of the transparency requirements of the Directive. The court upheld all three complaints.

First, the court held that providing information about the defendant's identity and address behind a "contact" link was insufficient. The information had to be provided in such a way that the consumer would receive it automatically.

Secondly, the court found that the defendant had not made clear that it was not itself providing lottery services, but was only acting as an agent for the collection of the data and its transmission to the lottery service provider. It had therefore failed to provide information about the essential characteristics of its service.

Thirdly, because it was not itself running a lottery service but only collecting and forwarding data, the defendant could not rely on the lottery's exemption from the cancellation right.

---

[16] Case No. U 200/01, March 27, 2002, EBL December 2002, p.14.

Confirmatory and other information

The Regulations further provide in reg.8 for the consumer to receive certain   **10–033**
confirmatory and related information. The information to be provided
where there is a supply of services was amended by the Consumer Protection (Distance Selling) (Amendment) Regulations 2005.

The supplier must provide to the consumer in writing, or in "another
durable medium which is available and accessible to the consumer", the
information referred to in reg.8(2), either:

(a) prior to the conclusion of the contract, or
(b) thereafter, in good time and in any event—

  (i) during the performance of the contract, in the case of services;
       and
  (ii) at the latest at the time of delivery where goods not for
        delivery to third parties are concerned.

Under reg.8(2) the information required to be provided by para.(1) is—   **10–034**

(a) the information set out in paras. (i)–(vi) of reg.7(1)(a) (see above);
(b) information about the conditions and procedures for exercising the
     right to cancel under reg.10, including—

  (i) where a term of the contract requires (or the supplier intends
       that it will require) that the consumer shall return the goods to
       the supplier in the event of cancellation, notification of that
       requirement;
  (ii) information as to whether the consumer or the supplier would
        be responsible under these Regulations for the cost of
        returning any goods to the supplier, or the cost of his reco-
        vering them, if the consumer cancels the contract under
        reg.10; and
  (iii) in the case of a contract for the supply of services, information
         as to how the right to cancel may be affected by the consumer
         agreeing to performance of the services beginning before the
         end of the seven working day period referred to in reg.12.

(c) the geographical address of the place of business of the supplier to
     which the consumer may address any complaints;
(d) information about any after-sales services and guarantees; and
(e) the conditions for exercising any contractual right to cancel the
     contract, where the contract is of an unspecified duration or a
     duration exceeding one year.

The Regulations do not define what is meant by "in writing or in another   **10–035**
durable medium which is available and accessible to the consumer." The
question arises whether this requires e-commerce providers to send out
information in hard copy (or on another physical medium such as disk), or

whether provision of the information by email or on the provider's website is sufficient.

The Directive on which the Regulations are based does not make this clear. The OFT and DTI have stated, in their joint Guide for Business to Distance Selling, that in their view a "durable medium" is one on which the information can be retained and reproduced, but not edited—such as an email that can be printed or a letter that can be kept for future reference. However, they go on to say:

> "We do not consider that information on a website is durable as it can be changed at any time after the consumer has accessed it. Technological advances may change what we regard as durable in the future."

10–036 The OFT/DTI view of what constitutes a durable medium may prove to be unduly narrow, and certainly lacks logic—concentrating as it does on the durability of the information, not on the durability of the medium as required by the Regulations and the Directive. The fact that a medium is erasable does not mean that it is not durable. Further, the joint view contradicts the previously published view of the DTI as to how the contract process information provisions of the E-Commerce Regulations can be satisfied in the case of a contract concluded by SMS message (see discussion, para.10–050 below).

An alternative view would be that provision of information on a website does satisfy this requirement since the information is stored on the hard disk of the website server, that this is a durable medium and that that medium is available and accessible to the user, albeit at a distance through the internet.

Conceptually, a user opening the document on the website is in no different a position from the user opening the document on a floppy disk in his possession, or for that matter opening an email using a web email account.

For an email, if and when the consumer downloads the email to his computer, it ultimately resides on the consumer's own hard disk (or other memory medium, in the case of, e.g. PDAs). That would appear to satisfy the requirement, since nothing in the Regulations apparently requires the durable medium to be one provided by the supplier. A problem would only appear to arise if the provisions do in fact mean that the user must be provided with the durable medium, or with control over the durable medium, as well as with the information contained in it. If so, that would rule out providing the information on a website. But that would also rule out email, which the DTI/OFT regard as satisfying the requirement.

The requirement of accessibility does not on the face of it mandate the provision of the medium itself to the consumer. The requirement that the medium be "available" to the consumer is perhaps more problematic, since if it is not mere surplusage it presumably means something more than "accessible".

That could suggest that the consumer has to have, or have the right to have, possession of or control over a physical medium. However, neither the Directive nor the Regulations spell out such a requirement. The better view is that there is no requirement to provide a durable medium to the consumer. It follows that, contrary to the OFT/DTI view, if the end-user is able to print off the information or download it from the website, that should satisfy the requirement of the Regulations just as much as sending an email.

For email, it should also be noted that a similar formulation is used in reg.10 (discussed below), governing notices sent by a consumer to the supplier. Regulation 10(d) provides for the place of sending a notice sent by email.   **10–037**

This provision would be nonsensical if email did not comply with the underlying requirement for the notice to be in a durable medium. That would suggest (assuming that the meaning is the same in both regulations) that email would satisfy the requirements of reg.8. However, the Directive itself contains no provisions regarding how the consumer is to give notice, so that reg.10(d) has no equivalent in the Directive and is of no assistance in construing the meaning of the requirement for a durable medium in the Directive.

Finally on the topic of what constitutes a durable medium, it is of interest to note that the Consumer Credit (Disclosure of Information) Regulations 2004 do include a definition of durable medium, as follows:

> "'durable medium' means any instrument which enables the debtor or hirer to store information addressed personally to him in a way accessible for future reference for a period of time adequate for the purposes of the information and which allows the unchanged reproduction of the information stored."

While these Regulations have no connection with the Distance Selling Directive, this definition clearly relates to the durability of the medium, not the information. The medium merely has to "allow" unchanged reproduction. It does not have to render alteration impossible. The Regulations address the question of remotely available durable media separately, by requiring that certain information be provided to the debtor or hirer in a document which:

> "...
>
>   (iv) is on paper or on another durable medium which is available and accessible to the debtor or hirer; and
>
>   (v) is of a nature that enables the debtor or hirer to remove it from the place where it is disclosed to him."

The formulation of these Regulations, we suggest, emphasises the contrast with the Distance Selling Directive and Regulations, in which there is no requirement either that the information itself be durable or that a durable medium be provided to the consumer.

10–038   Under reg.9 of the Distance Selling Regulations, reg.8 does not apply to a contract for the supply of services which are performed through the use of a means of distance communication, where those services are supplied on only one occasion and are invoiced by the operator of the means of distance communication. However, the supplier must take all necessary steps to ensure that a consumer who is a party to such a contract is able to obtain the supplier's geographical address and the place of business to which the consumer may address any complaints.

Cancellation right

10–039   Regulation 10 provides for the consumer's right to cancel within a certain period. Where the consumer gives notice of cancellation, reg.10(2) sets out that the contract shall be treated as if the contract had not been made. Regulation 14 states that the supplier shall reimburse any sum paid by or on behalf of the consumer in relation to the contract free of charge, less any charge for returning the goods permitted under sub-para.5 of reg.14 (i.e. where the customer is obliged to return the goods under the contract and fails to do so, and such charge does not exceed the direct costs of returning the goods).

Difficulties arise, however, with the determination of the amount of the refund that online retailers have to give to consumers who exercise their right of cancellation under the Distance Selling Regulations. For example, there is potential for dispute over whether the retailer is obliged to refund delivery charges, and if so, how they are to be calculated, especially if more than one product or order has been aggregated by the retailer and sent to the customer in one delivery.

The consumer must, according to the Guidance, have all moneys returned to it, including the costs of postage and packaging. In May 2002 the OFT announced that Amazon.co.uk and BOL.com had agreed to follow the OFT interpretation of the regulations.

10–040   There is no provision in the Regulations that obliges the consumer to return any goods following cancellation. However, the Guidance confirms that a supplier can oblige the customer to do so in the relevant terms and conditions.

Of course, it should be remembered that any such term must be reasonable under the Unfair Terms in Consumer Contracts Regulations. The Directive, in general, is not concerned with the suppliers' inability to re-sell an item returned by a consumer, although one should note the exception in reg.13 in relation to items made to the consumer's specifications.

10–041   The cancellation period may be affected by whether the supplier has complied with the information provision requirements of reg.8 and when the notice to the consumer regarding its cancellation rights has been provided. The cancellation period also varies depending on whether the contract is for the supply of goods or services.

A contract for the downloading of electronic media (such as a software download) is likely to be a contract for services as it does not involve the supply of goods. However, the supply of software on a tangible medium such as a CD-ROM would be a supply of goods. That follows from the English case law on the nature of software[17] and is also the view of the OFT and DTI in the Guidance.

Under reg.13 certain contracts are excluded, unless the parties have agreed otherwise, from the cancellation provisions. Those are contracts: **10–042**

(a) for the supply of services if the performance of the contract has begun with the consumer's agreement—

    (i) before the end of the cancellation period applicable under reg.12(2); and

    (ii) after the supplier has provided the information referred to in reg.8(2).

(b) for the supply of goods or services the price of which is dependent on fluctuations in the financial market which cannot be controlled by the supplier;

(c) for the supply of goods made to the consumer's specifications or clearly personalised or which by reason of their nature cannot be returned or are liable to deteriorate or expire rapidly;

(d) for the supply of audio or video recordings or computer software if they are unsealed by the consumer;

(e) for the supply of newspapers, periodicals or magazines; or

(f) for gaming, betting or lottery services.

The German Federal Court of Justice has held that the exception from the Distance Selling Directive for goods made to the customer's specifications did not apply where the manufacturer could easily disassemble and re-sell the product components.[18] In this case the customer had ordered a notebook computer from a mail order computer company, specifying the configuration of standard parts and additional components. The court held that the customer had a right to cancel. **10–043**

The Scottish Court of Session has considered the legal effect of the cancellation right where goods are purchased online in the context of a case regarding when a supply was made to consumers for VAT purposes.[19] Here, on appeal by Customs and Excise, it was held that when the order was accepted an outright contract of sale was created, and the Regulations only affected this "to the extent of conferring on the purchaser an unqualified right of cancellation of the sale". Accordingly, the online retailer was not entitled to retain VAT moneys for the duration of the cooling-off period

---

[17] See in particular the comments of Glidewell L.J. in *St Albans City and DC v International Computers Ltd* [1996] 4 All E.R. 481, CA.

[18] *BGH*, Case No.VIII ZR 295/01, February 4, 2003, E.C.L.R. Vol. 8 No. 18, p.460.

[19] *Customs and Excise v Robertsons Electrical Ltd* [2005] ScotCS CSIH_75.

in case the consumer cancelled the contract. The practical impact of this for businesses is potentially significant—especially where the cancellation could occur in a different accounting period than when the goods were paid for.

10–044   The consumer's notice to cancel has to be given within the relevant cancellation period and comply with the requirements of reg.10. Under reg.10(3) a notice of cancellation is a notice in writing or in another durable medium (see the commentary in para.10–035 to 10–037 regarding what can constitute a durable medium) available and accessible to the supplier (or, if the supplier has notified another person to receive cancellation notices, that other person) which, however expressed, indicates the intention of the consumer to cancel the contract.

This is a "home-grown" provision which has no equivalent in the Directive. Nor does reg.10(4), which states circumstances in which a notice of cancellation given by a consumer to a supplier or other person is to be treated as having been properly given. These include the following, of particular relevance to electronic transactions:

-   if the consumer sends it by facsimile to the business facsimile number last known to the consumer (in which case it is to be taken to have been given on the day on which it is sent); or
-   if the consumer sends it by electronic mail, to the business electronic mail address last known to the consumer (in which case it is to be taken to have been given on the day on which it is sent).

The cancellation periods are set out in regs. 11 and 12, for goods and services respectively. The calculation of the cancellation period is complex, and depends on the extent to which and when the supplier has complied with the information provision requirements of reg.8, in particular reg.8(2) concerning information about the right to cancel.

10–045   The Consumer Protection (Distance Selling) (Amendment) Regulations 2005 amended the cancellation rights of a consumer in relation to the supply of services. Regulations 12 and 13 were amended in relation to the "cooling-off" period (i.e. the timescale where the consumer can cancel the contract) that a consumer has in contracts for the provision of services. The net effect is that:

(a)   where the supplier provides the information required by reg.8 before beginning of the services, and the consumer agrees to the performance commencing before the end of the "cooling-off" period, then there is no right to cancel; and

(b)   where the information required by reg.8 is provided during the performance of the services, the cancellation period runs from when the consumer received the information for seven working days or whenever performance is completed (whichever is the sooner).

Regulation 25(5) provides that the regulations shall apply notwithstanding any contract term which applies or purports to apply the law of a non-Member State if the contract has a close connection with the territory of a Member State.

10.2.2 The Electronic Commerce Directive

Directive 2000/31 of the European Parliament and Council on "certain legal aspects of information society services, in particular electronic commerce, in the Internal Market (Directive on electronic commerce)" was adopted on June 8, 2000. The Directive has been implemented generally in the UK by the Electronic Commerce (EC Directive) Regulations 2002 (SI 2002/2013).[20]

10–046

The Directive, and therefore the Regulations, covers a broad range of issues. The "country of origin" aspects of the Directive are discussed in Ch.6 and the liability of intermediaries provisions in Ch.5. Here we shall concentrate on the consumer protection aspects of the Regulations, in particular the transparency provisions. These overlap with those of the Distance Selling Directive that we have already discussed. However, although there is a degree of overlap, the requirements under the two directives are not identical. Indeed, it should be remembered that a supplier is required to comply with both sets of Regulations.

The Regulations apply to "information society services". These are defined as services within the meaning of Art.2(a) of the Directive, which in turn refers to the definition in Art.1(2) of a previous Directive, the so-called Transparency Directive.[21]

10–047

The definition is set out in detail in Ch.6. In essence an information society service is any service normally provided for remuneration, at a distance, by means of electronic equipment for the processing (including digital compression) and storage of data, and at the individual request of a recipient of the service.

---

[20] Following the implementation of the Regulations, the UK Government has embarked upon a series of extending regulations, applying the original regulations to selected new legislation and statutory instruments. So far the series consists of the Electronic Commerce (EC Directive) (Extension) Regulations 2003 (SI 2003/115), and the Electronic Commerce (EC Directive) (Extension) (No.2) Regulations 2003 (SI 2003/2500). The former, which came into force on February 14, 2003, extended the original Regulations to the Copyright (Visually Impaired Persons) Act 2002 and to the Tobacco Advertising and Promotion Act 2002. The latter, which came into force on October 31, 2003, extended the original Regulations to a series of existing copyright statutes and instruments, as amended by the Copyright and Related Rights Regulations 2003, and to two new copyright instruments. Further the Electronic Commerce (EC Directive) (Extension) Regulations 2004 came into force on May 14, 2004, to ensure that the E-Commerce Regulations apply to the Sexual Offences Act 2003. Parallel provisions have also been implemented in relation to areas regulated by the Advertising Standards Authority under the Financial Services and Markets Act 2000. At the date of writing, these are the Electronic Commerce Directive (Financial Services and Markets) Regulations 2002 (SI 2002/1775), the Financial Services and Markets Act 2000 (Regulated Activities) (Amendment) (No. 2) Order 2002 (SI 2002/1776), the Electronic Commerce Directive (Financial Services and Markets) (Amendment) Regulations 2002 (SI 2002/2015), and the Financial Services and Markets Act 2000 (Financial Promotion) (Amendment) (Electronic Commerce Directive) Order 2002.

[21] Directive 98/34 as amended by Directive 98/48.

The Regulations define a "service provider" as any person providing an "information society service". A "recipient of the service" is defined as "any person who, for professional ends or otherwise, uses an information society service, in particular for the purposes of seeking information or making it accessible". It should therefore be noted that the Regulations do not only apply to consumers as is the case in the Distance Selling Regulations, but also to persons acting in a professional capacity.

The Transparency Directive provides an indicative list of information society services. However, Recital (17) of the Electronic Commerce Directive states that those services contained in the list that do not imply data processing and storage are not covered by the definition. Recital (18) of the Electronic Commerce Directive provides a list of services that do and do not constitute information society services.

The range of e-commerce services to which the E-Commerce Regulations may relate is very wide. Indeed, it is reported that the Austrian Supreme Court has held that the Directive is applicable to an interactive pornography webcam service.[22]

10–048   Different aspects of the same transaction may fall both within and outside the scope of the Regulations. So concluding an online contract for the sale of a book may be within the scope of the Regulations, but the fulfilment of the contract by delivery of a physical book would not be. If the book were to be downloaded in electronic form from the supplier's website, however, the whole transaction would fall within the scope of the Directive.

Some matters are excluded from the scope of the Regulations: taxation, data protection, questions relating to agreements or practices governed by cartel law, certain activities of notaries or equivalent professions, the representation of a client and defence of his interests before the courts and certain gambling activities.

Recital (58) of the Directive states that the Directive should not apply to services supplied by service providers established in a third country. This limitation has probably not been transposed into the Regulations (see Ch.5 for a discussion of this).

Transparency requirements—general

10–049   Regulation 6 provides that a person providing an information society service shall make available to the recipient of the service and any relevant enforcement authority, in a form and manner which is easily, directly and permanently accessible, the following information:

    (a) the name of the service provider;
    (b) the geographic address at which the service provider is established;
    (c) the details of the service provider, including his electronic mail address, which allow him to be contacted rapidly and communicated with in a direct and effective manner;

---

[22] Supreme Court Case 4 (Ob 219/03).

(d) where the service provider is registered in a trade or similar public register, the trade register in which the service provider is entered and his registration number, or equivalent means of identification in that register;

(e) where the provision of the service is subject to an authorisation scheme, the particulars of the relevant supervisory authority;

(f) where the service provider exercises a regulated profession (as defined in the Regulations):

 – the details of any professional body or similar institution with which the service provider is registered,

 – his professional title and where that title has been granted,

 – a reference to the professional rules in the Member State of establishment and the means to access them; and

(g) where the service provider undertakes an activity that is subject to VAT, the VAT identification number.

A provider of an information society service who fails to comply with reg.6 is, under reg.13, liable to any recipient of the service for damages for breach of statutory duty.

The requirement that information must be provided "in a form and manner which is easily, directly and permanently accessible" may be contrasted with the requirements under the Distance Selling Regulations to have information supplied to a consumer in a "durable medium available and accessible to him".

The requirement can give rise to practical issues. For example, there could be problems of compliance for those providing mobile phone SMS-based services, since SMS messages are restricted to 160 characters.   **10–050**

The Department of Trade and Industry Guide for Business, published in 2002,[23] suggests that the relevant information for text messages may be provided on an associated website.

To satisfy the requirement of permanence the Department of Trade and Industry (DTI) suggests that evidence be retained of the information that recipients had at the relevant time. It is also stated in the guidance that "the Government also envisages that temporary interruptions to the availability of the information that are essential (e.g. to maintain a website or the integrity of a network) or unavoidable (e.g. in the event of force majeure) will not count against its being permanently accessible. However, the onus is on the service provider to make the information accessible for as long as it may be necessary to do so."

The requirement that the information be "easily, directly and permanently accessible" would suggest that the address of the relevant web page (not merely the home page) ought to be stated in the text message.

It will be noted that the DTI Guide predates the subsequent Guidance

---

[23] http://web.archive.org/web/20030623113340/http://www.dti.gov.uk/industry_files/pdf/businessguidance.pdf.

issued jointly by the OFT and DTI, where in the context of the slightly different requirements in relation to the Distance Selling Regulations they suggested that information provided on a website is not "durable" if it can be amended at will by the supplier (see discussion at paras 10–035–10–037).

10–051   Regulation 6(2) sets out that where "a person providing an information society service refers to prices, these shall be indicated clearly and unambiguously and, in particular, shall indicate whether they are inclusive of tax and delivery costs". This requirement is different from reg.7(1) of the Distance Selling Regulations whereby a price must be given as inclusive of all taxes. The difference is explained by the fact that the E-Commerce Regulations cover all types of transaction, not just consumer transactions.

This provision, if it were to bite on the accuracy of the pricing as well as on its presentation, would fall to be compared with s.39 of the Consumer Protection Act 1987 (misleading price indications). That contains a due diligence defence, which on at least one occasion[24] has saved a vendor from the consequences of a computer error. However, the provisions of the Regulations contain no due diligence defence.

The Department of Trade and Industry Guide for Business[25] appears to support the view that the Regulations bite only on presentation, not on accuracy. It states: "The accuracy of prices (as opposed to their presentation) continues to be subject to the provisions of Part III of the Consumer Protection Act 1987".

In relation to the 1987 Act, in March 2003 the DTI issued a consultation paper on proposals for a revised Code of Practice for Traders on Price Indications. A response to this was issued in October 2005.[26] The code does not have mandatory force. Non-compliance with the Code is not, of itself, an offence, although it may be taken into account in establishing whether an offence has been committed under the 1987 Act.

It should also be noted that as from January 1, 2007, the Companies (Registrar, Languages and Trading Disclosures) Regulations 2006 (SI 2006/3429) implemented amendments to the Companies Act 1985 that specify information that has to be disclosed in a company or limited liability partnership's electronic documents and website.

Under ss.349 and 351 of the Companies Act 1985 companies have an obligation to give certain information about themselves in their documentation. Section 349 requires the company's name to appear in all business letters, notices, other official publications, bills of exchange, promissory notes, endorsements, cheques, orders for money or goods, invoices, receipts and letters of credit. Similarly, s.351 of the 1985 Act requires every company to state in all business letters and order forms the company's place of registration, company number and registered office.

Previously there was uncertainty as to whether these requirements related

---

[24] *Berkshire CC v Olympic Holidays* [1994] Crim L.R. 277, DC.
[25] See fn.23 above.
[26] *http://web.archive.org/web/20060422202703/http://www.dti.gov.uk/ccp/consultpdf/pricecodeconresponse.pdf.*

solely to paper documentation. However, the amendments inserted subs s.349(5) and 351(6), which state that the provisions extend to documents "in hard copy, electronic or any other form." As a result, companies are now required to state the relevant information on any of the above documents sent by fax, email or other electronic communication, or indeed if contained on a physical medium in electronic form.

Sections 349(1) and 351(1) are also amended, so as to require the company's name, place of registration, company number and registered office to be stated on all the company's websites.

These provisions apply to limited liability partnerships as well as to companies. They will be replaced by regulations to be made under s.82 of the Companies Act 2006 when that comes into force.

Website pricing errors

There has been a regular flow of news reports worldwide of website pricing errors, wherein by human or software error, an article or service has been advertised at an extremely low price. These errors have proven to be potentially expensive for the retailer, since word can spread extremely quickly, resulting in thousands of orders being placed at the mistaken price in a very short space of time. **10–052**

Examples of such cases include the £2.99 television from Argos (should have been £299), the £7.32 iPaq Pocket PC from Amazon UK (should have been £300), the £100 camera from Kodak (should have been £329) and the £55 London to Bangkok first class return air fare from Thai Airways (should have been £6,000). None of these cases were taken to court.

In Sweden, the National Board for Consumer Complaints (non-binding consumer arbitration body) held that Telia were not bound to honour a price of SEK297 (without subscription) for a mobile phone advertised on its website, the correct price being SEK2,997.

In Seattle, USA, a small claims court held that Amazon.com were not bound by a price of $99.99 for a 36-inch television, the correct price being $849.99. Amazon.com were able to rely on their terms and conditions, which contained specific provisions about pricing errors and also successfully argued that the contract was not complete until the buyer's credit card was charged.[27]

A court in Cologne, Germany, however, has held that an automatically generated order confirmation email stating that the order would be processed immediately bound the retailer to a mistaken price 50 per cent less than the true retail price. The court held that the mistake was not so obvious that fulfilment of the contract would be contrary to principles of good faith.[28]

In a Singapore case, IT products distributor Digiland International successfully defended a case against six customers who had sued the company

---

[27] *Seattle Times*, January 29, 2003.
[28] *World eBusiness Law Report*, June 17, 2003.

as it had failed to sell goods at the price advertised on its web page.[29] Here, the six buyers had placed more than 1600 orders for laser printers that were mistakenly advertised at $66 each. The correct price was $3,854. If Digiland had honoured the orders, the customers would have paid $106,000 rather than $6.1 million. Ultimately, the plaintiffs failed, the judge noting that they had clearly intended to take advantage of the seller's mistake.

Cases such as these can sometimes place online retailers in a difficult position. If the price is so low as to be an obvious mistake, then even if a contract is notionally formed it is likely to be void for mistake. However, whether that applies in a particular case will depend on the size of the mistake and on the discounting practice in the retail sector in question.

Retailers may wish to structure their online purchasing process and terms and conditions so that the formation of a contract, or the commitment to deliver, is deferred until the last possible moment. A common example is to state that the submission of an "order" by a proposed buyer is legally an offer that "may" be accepted by the seller—for example when payment is processed. However, retailers have to take care that the terms comply with consumer protection legislation such as the Unfair Contract Terms Act 1977 and the Unfair Terms in Consumer Contracts Regulations 1999; and that the process complies with the Electronic Commerce Regulations, especially the requirement to acknowledge an order.

Since manual checking of the price on each order is unlikely to be cost effective, a retailer may wish to consider resorting to more sophisticated techniques such as software designed to detect unusual purchasing patterns.

Transparency requirements—commercial communications

10–053   Regulation 7 contains further transparency provisions for commercial communications. A "commercial communication" is defined as:

> "a communication, in any form, designed to promote, directly or indirectly, the goods, services or image of a any person pursuing a commercial, industrial or craft activity or exercising a regulated profession, other than a communication–
>
> > consisting only of information allowing direct access to the activity of that person, including a geographic address, a domain name or an electronic mail address; or
> > relating to the goods, services or image of that person provided that the communication has been prepared independently of the person making it (and for this purpose, a communication prepared without financial consideration is to be taken to have been prepared independently unless the contrary is shown)".

10–054   Regulation 7 states that commercial communications which:

---

[29] *Chwee Kin Keong v Digilandmall.com Pte Ltd* [2005] SGCA—see also *www.singapore law.sg/rss/judy/46654.html.*

"constitutes or forms part of an information society service shall:

(a) be clearly identifiable as a commercial communication;

(b) clearly identify the person on whose behalf the commercial communication is made;

(c) clearly identify as such any promotional offer (including any discount, premium or gift) and ensure that any conditions which must be met to qualify for it are easily accessible, and presented clearly and unambiguously; and;

(d) clearly identify as such any promotional competition or game and ensure that any conditions for participation are easily accessible and presented clearly and unambiguously."

The provider of an information society service, who fails to comply with reg.7 is, under reg.13, liable to any recipient of the service for damages for breach of statutory duty.

These transparency requirements are wide-ranging and do not simply apply to information to be provided as part of a contractual relationship, but also, for example in the course of carrying out promotional activity. A "commercial communication" could be constituted in a number of ways. For example, as well as internet communications and emails, the definition also extends to text messages. Again, the Department of Trade and Industry Guide for Business suggests that the relevant information in relation to text messages may be provided on an associated website (see the analysis above at para.10–050).

Unsolicited commercial communications

The Regulations also impose certain transparency requirements on service providers that send unsolicited commercial communications. It should be noted that the legality of such communications must also be considered in light of the Privacy and Electronic Communications (EC Directive) Regulations 2003, the main provisions of which are discussed below (at section 10.2.3).

10–055

Regulation 8 provides that the "service provider shall ensure that any unsolicited commercial communication sent by him by electronic mail is clearly and unambiguously identifiable as such as soon as it is received".

Significantly, reg.8 is limited to "commercial communications sent by 'electronic mail' "—i.e. not all commercial communications. In this case, it seems that the intention is for the term "electronic mail" to be construed narrowly. Indeed, the Department of Trade and Industry Guide for Business takes the view that SMS text messages do not fall within the scope of reg.8. However, it should be noted that the sender of unsolicited SMS messages still has to comply with the provisions of the Privacy and Electronic Communications (EC Directive) Regulations 2003.

The provider of an information society service, who fails to comply with reg.8 is, under reg.13, liable to any recipient of the service for damages for breach of statutory duty.

Conclusion of contract—technical and transparency requirements

10–056 The Regulations set out further transparency requirements where contracts are concluded by "electronic means". "Electronic means" is not defined in the Directive or the Regulations, but presumably should apply widely to cover all forms of electronic communication, including SMS, internet and website contracts. Regulation 9(1) states that except when otherwise agreed by parties who are not consumers,

> "where a contract is to be concluded by electronic means a service provider shall prior to the order being placed by the recipient of a service, provide to the recipient in a clear, comprehensive and unambiguous manner . . .:
>
> (a) the different technical steps to follow to conclude the contract;
> (b) whether or not the concluded contract will be filed by the service provider and whether it will be accessible;
> (c) the technical means for identifying and correcting input errors prior to the placing of the order;
> (d) the languages offered for the conclusion of the contract."

In addition, reg.9(2) sets out that except when otherwise agreed by parties who are not consumers, the service provider must indicate any relevant codes of conduct to which he subscribes and information on how those codes can be consulted electronically.

Regulation 9(3) states that where the service provider provides contract terms and general conditions to the recipient, these must be made available in a way that allows the recipient to store and reproduce them. Again, this should be contrasted with the requirements that such terms and conditions be provided in a "durable medium" under the Distance Selling Regulations (see discussion at paras 10–053–10–055). A recipient of the service may enforce this requirement in reg.9(3) by seeking a court order against the service provider to require compliance (reg.14).

It should be noted that reg.9(4) sets out that the requirements under regs. 9(1) and 9(2) do not apply to "contracts concluded exclusively by exchange of electronic mail or by equivalent individual communications".

Regulation 9 presupposes that the recipient of the service places an "order", and requires the mandated information to be provided prior to the order being placed. It is suggested, therefore, that the regulation does not apply to general terms and conditions intended to govern the non-chargeable use of a website, as opposed to those applicable to an online purchase. The regulation would apply where the purchase is of material available within the website.

Indeed, the Austrian Supreme Court is reported[30] to have held that Art.11 of the Austrian E-Commerce Act (equivalent to reg.9(3) of the UK Electronic Commerce Regulations) did not apply to a website used only for advertising purposes and applied only to websites on which it was possible to conclude a contract.

Regulation 11 lays down certain technical requirements with which the online ordering process must comply. Accordingly, reg.11(1) provides that except when otherwise agreed by parties who are not consumers,   10–057

> "where the recipient of the service places his order through technological means, a service provider shall:
>
> — acknowledge the receipt of the recipient's order without undue delay and by electronic means,
> — make available to the recipient of the service appropriate, effective and accessible technical means allowing him to identify and correct input errors prior to the placing of the order."

Regulation 11(2) goes on to state that for the purposes of reg.11(1):

> "the order and the acknowledgement of receipt will be deemed to be received when the parties to whom they are addressed are able to access them; and
> the acknowledgement of receipt may take the form of the provision of the service paid for where that service is an information society service."

Where a service provider fails to comply with reg.11(1)(b) the customer is entitled to rescind the contract unless any court having jurisdiction in relation to the contract in question orders otherwise on the application of the service provider (reg.15). This is the only provision of the regulations breach of which gives rise to a right to rescind the contract.

It should be noted that, again, reg.11(3) states that reg.11(1) does not apply to "contracts concluded exclusively by exchange of electronic mail or by equivalent individual communications".

Regulation 12 sets out that for the purposes of regs. 11 and 12 "order"   10–058 may be, but need not be, the contractual offer. This is subject to the exception that in regs. 11(1)(b) and 9(1)(c) the order shall mean the "contractual offer". Regulations 11(1)(b) and 9(1)(c) relate to the technical means for identifying and correcting input errors, and information about those technical means, both of which have to be provided prior to the placing of the order.

So the effect of reg.12 is that the technical means and the information must be provided "prior to the placing of the order, which shall be the

---

[30] *World eBusiness Law Report* (October 21, 2003).

contractual offer". This could be interpreted as mandating a particular purchase process, in which the placing of the order must constitute the contractual offer to be accepted by the seller.

This may suit some, but not all, online purchasing models. Since there is no basis in the Directive for mandating a particular process of contract formation, the better interpretation of the regulation may be that the technical means and the information must be provided prior to both the contractual offer and the placing of the order.

Stop Now/Enforcement Orders

10–059   Regulation 16 states that regs. 6, 7, 8, 9 and 11 are enforceable by orders under the Stop Now Orders (EC Directive) Regulations 2001, which implement the Injunctions Directive.[31] These Regulations have now been replaced by Pt 8 of the Enterprise Act 2002.

Part 8 of the Enterprise Act 2002 enables certain specified bodies (including the OFT and every weights and measures authority in Great Britain) to apply to a court for an "enforcement order" (which is very similar to a "Stop Now" order under the old regime). Such an order may be granted where a trader "has engaged or is engaging in conduct which constitutes a domestic or a Community infringement ... or is likely to engage in conduct which constitutes a Community infringement".

"Domestic infringements" are defined in s.211 of the Act as an act or omission which—

"(a) is done or made by a person in the course of a business,
 (b) falls within subsection (2), and
 (c) harms the collective interests of consumers in the United Kingdom."

Subsection 2 describes various acts and omissions which may be specified by the Secretary of State by order to be "domestic infringements" such as "an act or omission by which a person supplying or seeking to supply goods or services purports or attempts to exercise a right or remedy relating to the supply in circumstances where the exercise of the right or remedy is restricted or excluded under or by virtue of an enactment" and "an act done or omission made in breach of contract".

"Community infringements" (as detailed in s.212 of the Act) are breaches of specified legislation, including certain provisions of the E-Commerce Regulations and the entire Distance Selling Regulations, which "harms the collective interests of consumers". If the enforcement order is granted, the court may order a trader to cease doing a particular activity that is in contravention of the specified legislation. The courts may also order offending traders to publish corrective statements with regard to

---

[31] Directive 98/27/EC of the European Parliament and of the Council of May 19, 1998, on injunctions for the protection of consumers' interests.

prior infringements. Failure to comply with an enforcement order would constitute contempt of court.

Enforcement orders are in addition and supplemental to existing regulations and sanctions that traders must comply with.

The Enterprise Act permits, in addition to public sector bodies such as the Office of Fair Trading, private sector bodies to be designated as enforcers under the Act. So far only the Consumers' Association has been designated. At the time of writing it has not made use of these powers since its appointment on April 22, 2005.

10.2.3 The Privacy and Electronic Communications (EC Directive) Regulations 2003

A prominent issue since the internet became a popular medium has been the rise in unsolicited bulk email, also known as 'spam". The EU instituted a common legal framework with the passing of the Directive on privacy and electronic communications.[32] One of the Directive's stated aims (in Recital (40)) is that:

10–060

> "safeguards should be provided for subscribers against intrusion of their privacy by unsolicited communications for direct marketing purposes in particular by means of automated calling machines, telefaxes, and emails, including SMS messages. These forms of unsolicited commercial communications may on the one hand be relatively easy and cheap to send and on the other may impose a burden and/or cost on the recipient".

The Directive was implemented in the UK by the Privacy and Electronic Communications (EC Directive) Regulations 2003,[33] which came into force on December 11, 2003. Enforcement of the Regulations is the responsibility of the Information Commissioner, who has produced detailed guidance on the regulations[34].

10–061

The scheme of the Regulations is as follows:

For unsolicited direct marketing emails to living individuals (including sole traders and partnerships): the recipient must opt-in (reg.22(1) and (2)). This is subject to the "soft opt-in" exception for existing customers set out in reg.22(3) (discussed below).

10–062

Unsolicited direct marketing emails to anyone else are permitted, subject to satisfying the "opt-out" provisions of reg.23.

Regulation 22 is stated to apply to the transmission of unsolicited communications by means of electronic mail to individual subscribers (reg.

---

[32] 2002/58/EC of the European Parliament and of the Council of July 12, 2002.

[33] SI 2003/2426.

[34] *http://www.ico.gov.uk/Home/what_we_cover/privacy_and_electronic_communications/ guidance.aspx.*

22(1)). Despite the breadth of this provision (which would include emails sent for any purpose, not just direct marketing) the operative provisions of the regulation, contained in reg.22(2), relate only to communications sent for the purposes of direct marketing. Communications sent for other purposes are not subject to any restriction under reg.22.

A "subscriber" is "a person who is party to a contract with a provider of public electronic communications services for the supply of such services".

An "individual" means "a living individual and includes an unincorporated body of such individuals".

"Electronic mail" means "any text, voice, sound or image message sent over a public electronic communications network which can be stored in the network or in the recipient's terminal equipment until it is collected by the recipient and includes messages sent using a short message service".

Regulation 22(2) provides that (subject to the "soft opt-in" exception—described below): "a person shall neither transmit, nor instigate the transmission of, unsolicited communications for the purposes of direct marketing by means of electronic mail unless the recipient of the electronic mail has previously notified the sender that he consents, for the time being, to such communications being sent by, or at the instigation of, the sender".

10–063   The recipient of the electronic mail is not necessarily the subscriber. However, under the Regulations it is the recipient, not the subscriber, from whom consent must be obtained. This differs from the Directive, which in Art.13.1 refers to "subscribers who have given their prior consent". The difference is significant, since the wording of the Directive would enable an individual subscriber (such as the partners in a partnership) to consent to the sending of mail to all individual potential recipients within the organisation.

The Information Commissioner's Guidance suggests (p.30) that, whilst the sender must obtain the individual's consent, the individual should remember that the wishes of the partnership may ultimately prevail over their individual choices. Presumably the Information Commissioner has in mind that the partnership employer is entitled to require individuals to consent to receiving certain types of emails as a matter of office policy.

10–064   Under reg.22(2) the recipient's prior consent must be notified to the sender. That does not appear in the Directive (which places no limitation on the person to whom the consent may be provided). The Information Commissioner's Guidance (p.24) suggests that consent may be provided to the sender via a third party (such as a list broker).

Under reg.22(4) a subscriber must not permit his line to be used in contravention of reg.22(2). The interpretation section of the Regulations states that the word "line" is to "be construed as including a reference to anything that performs the function of a line".

10–065   The sanction for breach of this prohibition is two-fold. Under reg.30 a person who suffers damage by reason of any contravention of any of the requirements of the regulations by any other person shall be entitled to bring proceedings for compensation from that other person for that damage. It is a defence to prove that the person had taken such care as was in all the circumstances reasonably required to comply with the relevant requirement.

There is no provision enabling a recipient of electronic mail prohibited by the regulations to apply for an injunction. Enforcement of that nature is the domain of the Information Commissioner. Regulation 31 extends, with some modifications, his enforcement functions under the Data Protection Act 1998 to these Regulations.

The introduction of a statutory regime may affect the willingness of the courts to grant remedies against unsolicited electronic mail based on common law rights (see discussion in Ch.12, para.12–126), at least in cases within the field covered by the Regulations.   **10–066**

Regulation 22(3) provides for the "soft opt-in" exception to the prohibition set out in reg.22(2). A person may send, or instigate the sending of, electronic mail for direct marketing purposes where: **10–067**

(a) that person has obtained the contact details of the recipient of that electronic mail in the course of the sale or negotiations for the sale of a product or service to that recipient;

(b) the direct marketing is in respect of that person's similar products and services only; and

(c) the recipient has been given a simple means of refusing (free of charge except for the costs of the transmission of the refusal) the use of his contact details for the purposes of such direct marketing, at the time that the details were initially collected, and, where he did not initially refuse the use of the details, at the time of each subsequent communication.

Several features of this exception are noteworthy.

It only applies to commercial activities. So, for instance, a charity that solicited a donation but did not sell a product or service would be unable to take advantage of the exception. This is anomalous (as is recognised in the Information Commissioner's Guidance, p.32), but is what the Directive requires.

The only person permitted to take advantage of the "soft opt-in" is the person who obtained the contact details in the first place. It cannot be used to market products or services of, for instance, subsidiary or related companies.

What constitutes "similar" goods or services is not defined. The Information Commissioner's Guidance states that he will take a purposive approach, having regard to what an individual would reasonably expect to receive. For the time being the Information Commissioner's resources will be focused on failures to comply with opt-out requests.

No limit is specified on the period for which a "soft opt-in" can be relied upon. However, general data protection principles may place a limit on the period for which personal data may be retained and used.

Regulation 23 lays down requirements applicable to all direct marketing electronic mail, whether solicited or unsolicited and whether sent to individual or corporate recipients.   **10–068**

It provides that a person shall neither transmit, nor instigate the transmission of, a communication for the purposes of direct marketing by means of electronic mail:

(a) where the identity of the person on whose behalf the communication has been sent has been disguised or concealed; or
(b) where a valid address to which the recipient of the communication may send a request that such communications cease has not been provided.

Requirement (b) will affect legitimate marketers, since it requires all direct marketing emails, SMS messages and similar communications to contain a valid "suppression address". This creates particular difficulties with mobile messaging, SMS messages being limited for technical reasons to 160 characters. The Information Commissioner's Guidance (pp.22 and 23) contains suggestions as to how mobile marketers may comply with the suppression address requirement and with the requirement to provide a simple opt-out means in order to make use of the "soft opt-in" exemption.

10.2.4 Disability discrimination

10–069 Legislative requirements for websites to cater for disabled users first arose as an issue in relation to the 2000 Sydney Olympics website. A complaint was made to the Australian Human Rights and Equal Opportunity Commission under the Australian Disability Discrimination Act 1992 that the site did not cater for disabled users in three respects, including lack of alternate text for images that would enable blind users to use text to speech converters. The complaint was upheld.[35]

In the UK the accessibility of the website for disabled users arises as an issue under the Disability Discrimination Act 1995 (DDA). Arguably, both the website owner and website developer have obligations under the DDA in relation to making the website content "accessible" for disabled users. Given that the developer will normally be building the website, the contracts tend to place obligations on the developer to ensure that adequate standards are reached.

Whilst it is widely accepted that websites need to be considered in light of the DDA, there is no reported UK case law on the matter.[36] This is despite

---

[35] *Bruce Maguire v Sydney Organising Committee for the Olympic Games*, HREOC No: H99/115 (August 24, 2000). Here a court ultimately held that the website for the Sydney Olympic games contravened the Australian Discrimination Act 1992 due to its inaccessibility to Mr Maguire, who is blind. The court awarded Mr Maguire $20,000 AUD, including damages for his hurt, humiliation and rejection as a result of certain statements by the Committee following the initial hearing.

[36] This is despite the parts of the relevant sections of the DDA being in force since April 1999, with the remainder in force since October 1999.

various surveys indicating that figures of around to 80 per cent of UK websites do not comply with the DDA.[37]

Section 19 of the DDA sets out a number of ways in which it is unlawful for a provider of services to discriminate against a disabled person when providing services. Discrimination is defined in s.20, in effect, as treating the disabled person less favourably due to their disability. The most relevant instance for website providers is likely to be a failure to make 'reasonable adjustments' to the service (as required by s.21).[38]

Although the Act does not explicitly state that s.19 applies to websites, the Act does say that the "services" includes "access to and use of means of communication" and "access to and use of information services". This is likely to include all website content. In addition, it does not matter that the service is provided for free—meaning that even "brochure" type websites would be caught by the requirements.

The duty on the website owner is akin to a tortious duty. Under s.25 of the DDA, in England, any party that considers that they have been discriminated against can commence civil proceedings in the county court "in the same way as any other claim in tort". Any damages awarded can include compensation for injury to feelings.

One issue is that website pages can be designed to enable visually impaired users to use a "screen-reader" browser to access the content (i.e. where a virtual voice reads out the contents of the web page). Images can be made compatible by adding "alt text" to that image to enable the screen-reader to describe the image to the user. The argument, therefore, is that failure to make a website compatible with screen-reader software means that the visually impaired person is discriminated against as they are unable to use the "service" provided by that website. Similar arguments exist in relation to using colour schemes which cannot be interpreted by users with colour blindness and websites where the text size cannot be increased in the user's browser.[39]

Although the most attention in relation to accessible website standards has been focused on blind users, other types of disability (such as deafness, regarding the provision of sound) may have to be considered.

---

[37] See for example the research carried out by the Royal National Institute for the Blind (RNIB) from August 2000, and the report from 2004 from the Disability Rights Commission.

[38] S.21(1) states "Where a provider of services has a practice, policy or procedure which makes it impossible or unreasonably difficult for disabled persons to make use of a service which he provides, or is prepared to provide, to other members of the public, it is his duty to take such steps as is reasonable, in all the circumstances of the case, for him to take in order to change that practice, policy or procedure so that it no longer has that effect."

[39] In *Latif v Project Management Institute* (October 19, 2006) (*www.drc.org.uk/the_law/transcripts_of_key_judgments/latif_v_project_management_ins.aspx*) the defendant was found to have discriminated against the claimant, who was blind in failing to make reasonable adjustments in relation to examination arrangements. The claimant successfully argued that it would have been reasonable for the defendant to have made available certain examination materials in a form that could be read by her "JAWS" text to speech software, and have arranged for her to take the examination on a standalone computer on which that software was installed.

There are various guidelines which give examples of accessibility standards, which if complied with, will presumably go some way to influencing a court as to whether a website complies with the DDA. The most famous international standard is the W3C guidelines from the "World Wide Web Consortium"[40]—where compliant websites are rated from "A" to "AAA", with an A rating generally considered to be the minimum threshold for DDA compliance.

10–070 The UK Disability Rights Commission in 2002 issued a Code of Practice on Rights of Access for Goods, Facilities, Services and Premises[41] which sets out a detailed analysis of the various obligations under the DDA. Indeed, there is an obligation under the DDA for courts to take into account any part of the Code that appears to them relevant to any question arising in those proceedings.

Although the Code did not set out specific things that must be included in a website to ensure compliance, it did refer to website compliance and gave an example of an airline booking site, thus bringing the question of website compliance to public notice.

More specific guidance is found in the British Standards Institution (BSI) "Publicly Available Specification 78" (PAS 78).[42] The Royal National Institute for the Blind has a section on its website devoted to accessibility.[43] Ultimately, however, none of these guidelines have the force of law, and it is up to the courts to decide whether a website is DDA compliant.

One final point of note is that s.57 of the DDA states that "a person who knowingly aids another person to do an [unlawful act] is to be treated for the purposes of this Act as himself doing the same kind of unlawful act". Accordingly, a website designer that knowingly fails to comply with the DDA could also be exposed under the DDA as well as the website owner.

The owners of new and existing websites alike would be wise to bear in mind the obligations under the DDA even though the obligations to make "reasonable adjustments" have been in force since 1999 and, despite there being various reports about the proportion of non-compliant websites, there have been no reported cases of any claims brought by a disabled person.

10.3 INTERNATIONAL CONTRACTS

10–071 Many contracts made on the internet will be made between parties located or resident in different countries. This brings into play the rules on choice of governing law and jurisdiction. These rules are addressed in detail in Ch.6.

---

[40] *www.w3.org/TR/WAI-WEBCONTENT/.* It should be noted that there are proposals to update the W3C standards—see *www.w3.org/TR/WCAG20/.*

[41] *www.drc-gb.org/pdf/DRC_Rights_of_Access_Part_3.pdf.*

[42] *http://www.bsi-global.com/en/standards-and-publications/industry-sectors/services/services-products/PAS-78.*

[43] *http://www.rnib.org.uk/xpedio/groups/public/documents/code/public_rnib008789.hcsp.*

Here we outline their impact on the practical aspects of contract drafting. In particular we focus on the differences between situations where the parties are commercial entities negotiating at arm's length over a non-standard form of contract and those which involve contracts (almost always in standard form) with consumers.

Applicable law and jurisdiction

The contract should specify a governing law. If it does not do so there will be even more room than usual to argue over which country's law governs the terms of the contract and its operation. Where no governing law is referred to in a contract, a court in England and Wales will decide on what law should be applied according to the provisions of the Contracts (Applicable Law) Act 1990 which implements the 1980 Rome Convention on the Law Applicable to Contractual Obligations. Under the Act the applicable law is that with which the transaction has the closest connection.   **10–072**

However, in consumer contracts, in some circumstances a choice of law expressed in the contract will be overridden by the mandatory rules of the country in which the consumer has his habitual residence.[44,45] Those circumstances could certainly cover a consumer in one country responding to an advertisement on a website based in another country, at least if it is targeted at the consumer's home country.[46] It would also cover situations where a consumer purchases online, if such contract was preceded by "a specific invitation" addressed to the consumer.

If courts in other countries are seized with a dispute under the contract they may apply different rules for deciding what is the governing law, such as the law of the place of contracting or the law of the place of performance.[47] The risk, therefore, to a seller offering its goods for sale online—even where these are offered in the seller's standard "click-wrap" terms, is that the laws of a country other than that specified in the contract may be applied to the contract by operation of law, notwithstanding that the seller has no connection with that legal system and is unaware of the consumer protection laws in that country.

---

[44] Contracts (Applicable Law) Act 1990, Sch.1, Art.5.

[45] The circumstances are:
   "1 If in that country the conclusion of the contract was preceded by a specific invitation addressed to him or by advertising, and he had taken in that country all the steps necessary on his part for the conclusion of the contract; or
   2 If the other party or his agent received the consumer's order in that country; or
   3 [omitted]."
   The provisions do not apply to a contract of carriage, or to a contract for the supply of services where the services are to be supplied to the consumer exclusively in a country other than that in which he has his habitual residence. However, they do apply to a contract which, for an inclusive price, provides for a combination of travel and accommodation (Contracts (Applicable Law) Act 1990, Sch.1, Art.5).

[46] See the discussion in Ch.6 concerning the extent to which the advertising limb requires positive conduct on the part of the supplier, as opposed to passive availability of the website.

[47] But a country which is a signatory to the Rome Convention, discussed below, will operate the same rule.

10–073   When it comes to choosing a governing law the obvious choice will be the law with which the persons preparing the contract are most familiar. However, at the time of specifying a governing law of any contract it is normal to also specify in the courts of which country it is at least preferred that any dispute is dealt with, and it is clearly going to be easier for those courts and the conduct of any dispute if the governing law of the contract is that of the court dealing with the matter.

In choosing the preferred courts (the jurisdiction) some consideration needs to be given to enforceability of the judgment of any such court against the parties. If a person has a place of business in the same country as the court giving the judgment there is no problem. But if this is not the case then one has to look to the availability of reciprocal enforcement treaties between the country in which the court is situated and the country in which the person against whom the judgment is given is based.

As between countries in the EU there is not such a problem with reciprocity of enforcement because of the arrangements between most Member States dealing with this (the Judgments Regulation which came into force on March 1, 2002, and replaced the Brussels Convention in most Member States—see discussion in Ch.6).

Some companies may try to deal with this sort of problem by making it clear that certain products they are offering over the internet are only available for order online from certain countries where they know that they will not experience problems with enforcement and refuse to accept such orders online from individuals in other countries.

10–074   However, over the internet there can be real problems in knowing from which jurisdiction the purchaser is in fact accessing the site.

The seller may be tempted to specify the law of its own country in order to simplify matters and achieve some certainty. However, a choice of law or jurisdiction clause may be affected by consumer protection legislation in the country of the purchaser.

For instance the Unfair Terms in Consumer Contracts Regulations 1999 specify that they "shall apply notwithstanding any contract term which applies or purports to apply the law of a non-Member State, if the contract has a close connection with the territory of the Member States". The Distance Selling Regulations (see above) contain a similar provision.

As we have seen the Contracts (Applicable Law) Act 1990 provides that a choice of law clause shall not, in some circumstances, deprive a consumer of the protection of the mandatory rules of his country of habitual residence. There are similar provisions in the Brussels Regulation regarding choice of jurisdiction clauses (see Ch.6). "Mandatory rules" in this context are those which cannot be derogated from by contract.

The European Court of Justice has held that a clause conferring exclusive jurisdiction on the court of a city in which the seller had its principal place of business but the consumer was not domiciled, and which was not individually negotiated, must be regarded as unfair within the meaning of Art.3 of the Unfair Contract Terms Directive insofar as it causes, contrary to the requirement of good faith, a significant imbalance in the parties' rights and obligations arising under the contract, to the detriment of the consumer.[48]

There is also a problem when it comes to making contracts with con- **10–075** sumers in terms of exclusions or limitations of liability and warranties. Different countries have different rules about what is acceptable. One way of attempting to deal with this is the way in which, for example, this issue is dealt with in software licensing, by providing separate country-specific clauses of the contract for individual countries.

We discuss in Ch.6 the potential application of the "country of origin" rules of the Electronic Commerce Directive, and related Regulations. We also discuss in Ch.6 the proposed conversion of the 1980 Rome Convention into an EU Regulation, which as currently drafted would make significant changes to the consumer protection provisions.

10.4 FORMING ELECTRONIC CONTRACTS

10.4.1 Introduction: the formation of a contract

At its most basic, a contract is an agreement between or among two or **10–076** more parties which the law recognises and which can be enforced in the courts. For simplicity, this chapter will assume that contracts are being formed between two parties but the principles apply equally to multi-partite agreements.

A contract is formed when one party makes an offer which is accepted in unequivocal terms by the other party and that acceptance is communicated to the offeror. In addition, under English law, consideration needs to flow between the parties and there has to be the intent to create legal relations. Each of these requirements will be considered in turn in the context of the internet.

10.4.2 Pre-contractual information

Although this chapter is concerned primarily with the exchange of messages **10–077** to form a contract, there may be other information imparted by either party prior to the contract which may have legal consequences for one or other of them.

Advertising and other regulation

In the context of goods and services the advertising of which is regulated in **10–078** other media, the advertiser will need to be aware of the extent to which the

---

[48] *Océano Grupo Editorial SA v Rocío Murciano Quintero* (Case C240/98) June 27, 2000, ECJ.

relevant regulations or restrictions will apply to web pages or to goods or services offered via email.

The most common restrictions or regulations relate to: the identity or some other feature of the recipient (for example age restrictions on the advertising of alcohol or tobacco); or the information which must be imparted (such as in connection with the advertising of financial services, credit or shares); or the accuracy of that information (such as the provisions of the Trade Descriptions Act 1968).

Such requirements have a direct impact on how a seller may advertise its products and on the design of the website. For example, the Consumer Credit (Advertisements) Regulations 2004 (SI 2004/1484) which came into force on October 31, 2004 (replacing the Consumer Credit (Advertisements) Regulations 1989 (SI 1989/1125)) place certain requirements on businesses that advertise credit services. In general, the cost of borrowing money (including the APR rate) must be displayed prominently in any advert to enable consumers to understand to what they are committing to. Such information must also be displayed in a form that is "easily legible". Failure to do so is a criminal offence under s.167(2) of the Consumer Credit Act 1974. Accordingly, this does not simply affect the text to be contained in the website, but also the font and background colour to ensure that the consumer is given adequate notice.

See also the discussion of the transparency requirements of the Distance Selling and Electronic Commerce Regulations, above.

Misrepresentation

10–079 Irrespective of their incorporation into the final contract, certain statements of either party made prior to the formation of a contract may constitute representations which, if untrue, can give rise to a right to damages and/or rescission by the party to whom the representation is made. A representation is a statement of fact (and not, generally, opinion) which induces the recipient to enter into the contract concerned.

Thus, untrue statements made in a web page or in an email about the quality of goods or services, may amount to misrepresentations. The state of mind of the maker of the statement is relevant to determine the remedy of the recipient of the misrepresentation who has relied on that representation, in entering into a subsequent contract.

In outline, if the maker of the misrepresentation has acted fraudulently the recipient will be entitled to damages and/or to rescind the contract. Rescission results in the parties being treated as if the contract had never come into being. If he has been negligent or has made the misrepresentation innocently, the recipient will generally not have an absolute right to either remedy. The common law relating to misrepresentation was clarified and, to some extent, modified by the Misrepresentation Act 1967.

Collateral contracts

A collateral contract is one which may underpin or supplement another contract—for example a credit agreement that enables a buyer to enter the main contract to purchase goods. Typically, such a contract is entered into in order to induce one party to enter into the other contract either with the other party to the collateral contract or with a third party. In practice, a court will determine whether a statement made amounts to a representation or whether the elements necessary to constitute a contract are also present and that the representation therefore has contractual effect. If this is the case, it may have the effect of allowing a contract claim to be brought even where the representation has not been incorporated into the main contract.

10–080

10.4.3 Offer/invitation to treat

An offer is made when one party offers to do or to supply something on the basis that it will be legally bound by the acceptance of that offer by the offeree. The intention can either be stated or can be apparent from the circumstances. The terms of the offer must be certain: for example, if the subject-matter of the offer or the price are not stated, there may be too great a degree of uncertainty for the courts to give effect to the contract. There are, however, important qualifications to this principle: for example, s.8(2) of the Sale of Goods Act 1979 gives the court the ability to determine a "reasonable price" and the courts may also imply the terms in certain circumstances.

10–081

There can also be uncertainty over whether a particular action or statement constitutes an offer or merely an "invitation to treat" which is intended to provoke an offer from another party. Depending on the proper construction of the action or statement, a response by the other party may either constitute acceptance of an offer or the making of an offer which itself may be accepted.

The most common example given of an invitation to treat is the display of goods in a shop window or on supermarket shelves. The picking up of the goods by the shopper and their presentation at the checkout amounts to the offer which is accepted by the cashier. By analogy, the description of goods in a web page advertisement may also be regarded as being an invitation to treat. The analogy is aided by the presentation of some web pages as "virtual shops" within the internet version of a shopping mall.

However, the test is essentially one of the intention of the person putting the information on the web page: did he intend to be bound by a response (in which case he has made an offer) or did he intend that he would need to acknowledge the response by word or action, such as despatching the goods (in which case the web page constitutes an invitation to treat)?

The importance of the distinction in the context of the internet is likely to arise in two circumstances: where the web page owner has only a limited stock of goods to despatch or where it is prepared only to sell to a limited class of persons.

10–082

In the former case, it will not wish to find itself in breach of a binding obligation to supply goods where it has underestimated the demand. Similarly, the web page owner will not wish to be contractually bound by mistakes made in its online advertising—see the discussion at para.10–052 (above) regarding cases where online retailers have set the wrong price for goods advertised for sale online.

The fact that, by the very nature of a campaign mounted on the internet, it will not be able to assess in advance the success of such a campaign makes it unlikely that it will want to make an unqualified offer to supply tangible goods in material form to all applicants or rely on an implied term that the offer lapses with the exhaustion of his stock. In the latter case, the web page owner may wish to reserve the right not to supply goods or services to certain jurisdictions, to applicants under a certain age or to exercise other forms of discretion, such as requiring payment to be received prior to despatch. In these cases, therefore, the information contained in the web page or preliminary email will be intended to constitute an invitation to treat

The test of the offeror's intention is essentially an objective one, in the absence of express statement or actual knowledge by the recipient that the maker does not intend to be bound. There is unlikely to be any prior dealing between the parties or any interchange agreement, and in the absence of any established recognised market practice as regards offers made via the internet, there is therefore the risk of uncertainty as to whether a web page statement or preliminary email should be treated as an offer or not. In this context, the practical approach must be to state expressly the procedure to be followed for a binding contract to come into existence.

10.4.4 Acceptance and communication of acceptance

10–083 The second element for the creation of a contract is that the offer is accepted by the offeree and that the acceptance is communicated to the offeror. The offer must be accepted unequivocally: any suggested variation or qualification of the terms of the offer is likely to constitute a counter-offer.

It is unlikely in the context of contracts formed over the internet that the "battle of the forms" (where the parties exchange incompatible sets of standard terms) will arise. The nature of the methods of contract formation outlined above and the likely classes of offeree suggest that a relatively informal response will be made or that, alternatively, the format of the response to a web page will be pre-determined by the offeror as part of the implementation of the page itself. Clearly this is something which should be taken into account in the design of the page.

Acceptance need not be express and can be inferred from the conduct of the offeree. However, again in the context of the internet where the parties' only knowledge of each other is via that medium, it is most likely that some positive action, such as the sending of an email or the filling in of an automated response form, will be the means of acceptance. Electronic acceptance could be relevant where the web page states that it can or should be used, or where (although this is unlikely in the context of the web) it is silent or where it is otherwise reasonable for electronic communication to be used.

Conceivably, where a web page provides for the completion of a standard form but does not state that it is mandatory, the sending of a separate email by the offeree could also constitute acceptance, as could the sending of a message via a general feedback hypertext link (even though the recipient of the message may be a separate organisation which maintains the page on behalf of the apparent owner). Conversely, the sending of a response by post or facsimile could also be appropriate.

The key therefore must be for the offeror to state expressly how acceptance should be made and that other methods of communication will not be valid. In addition, however, it should be noted that formation of the contract may be subject to the process and transparency requirements of the Consumer Protection (Distance Selling) Regulations 2000 and the Electronic Commerce (EC Directive) Regulations 2002 described above.

Even where the method of communication of acceptance has been stated, **10–084** there may still be uncertainty as to when or if that communication is deemed to be effective and to bind the offeror. The time that the contract comes into force and the place where it is formed may be crucial to crystallise its terms, to determine the priority of two parties wishing to accept an offer where there is insufficient stock to satisfy them both and to determine the legal system which will govern certain aspects of the contract.

Where the method of communication is stated to be by telephone or by post, the normal rules will apply. In essence, in respect of a domestic as opposed to an international contract, acceptance by telephone is deemed to happen at the place and at the time it is heard by the offeror. This is logical because instantaneous communication, such as over a working telephone line, is unlikely to lead to any dispute between the offeror and the offeree about whether there has been communication of the acceptance. Conversely, acceptance by post is deemed to be effective when the letter is posted, not when it is received.

Similar rules have been held to apply to telex. The basic rule is that the **10–085** telex is deemed to be received effectively by the intended recipient at the time of despatch because this is also the time of receipt. However, in the case of *Schelde Delta Shipping BV v Astarte Shipping Ltd (The Pamela)*,[49] the court took a pragmatic approach to a telex received at 19 minutes to midnight on a Friday.

The court held that receipt was not effective until opening of business on the following Monday morning. Although this still amounted to deeming receipt to occur at that time (whether or not a human being had actually read the telex), the result suggests that the time when the sender could reasonably expect the telex to be read was more important rather than the

---

[49] [1995] 2 Lloyd's Rep. 249.

actual time of receipt. It was clear that during business hours this would still be the time of dispatch. Strictly, the case did not deal with a telex which amounted to the acceptance of an offer to form a contract, but the principle should be equally applicable in such circumstances.

The problem with electronic contracting over the internet is to determine whether the rule as regards instantaneous communication should apply (so that receipt or deemed receipt by the offeror is the key) or whether the postal rule is the more appropriate analogy (so that despatch of the accepting email or response form is effective).

Before considering this, it is important to explore in this context what "receipt", "despatch" and "instantaneous" could mean and whether the offeree will have knowledge either of whether his message has been received or of whether it has been received in the form it was sent. This analysis is subject to the applicability provisions regarding deemed receipt of an order and acknowledgment of receipt in reg.11 of the E-Commerce Regulations (see the discussion at para.10–057).

Receipt of electronic communication

10–086   Depending on the means by which the offeror has established its presence on the internet, there are a number of points at which it could be considered to have "received" an electronic message. If (as is frequently the case) its email capability is operated on the server of a third party service provider, it could be said that an email is received when it arrives on that server.

However, it could be argued that it would be fairer to the offeror that receipt should be when the email is received in the local mailbox of the offeror. It could also be argued that actual knowledge either of the email's arrival or even of its content should be the point of communication, i.e. when the offeror is notified that the email has arrived or reads it. A similar series of arguments could apply to a website which is hosted on a remote server: receipt of a response could be deemed to take place on its arrival on the remote server or at the local server of the offeror.

10–087   There are additional complications. Should it make a difference whether the offeror's system has an open line to a remote server or periodic dial-up access? Should whether data transfer is initiated by the remote or the local server affect the position? Should ownership of the remote server by a third party affect acceptance? What if the remote server is in a different jurisdiction from the local one?

Some guidance is given by reg.11(2) of the E-Commerce Regulations where, for the purposes of reg.11(1) (which can include a contractual offer) it is stated "the order and the acknowledgement of receipt will be deemed to be received when the parties to whom they are addressed are able to access them" (see full discussion at para.10–057). Unfortunately, there is no further guidance on what "able to access them" means. Does this mean that where an acknowledgement is sent to a work email address whilst the worker is on holiday, it is not deemed to be received until the recipient is back in the office?

Another complication arises when firewalls and spam filters are taken **10–088** into account. For example, a seller may do everything in its power to attempt to send an acknowledgement or confirmation to a customer, only for this to be blocked en route. In such circumstances, is it fair to consider that the contract was never formed because there was never a valid acceptance?

These are questions which are difficult to answer, and which in the final analysis are likely to be addressed only by the courts if and when disputes of this nature arise.

Questions such as these were given extensive consideration by a working group of the United Nations Commission on International Trade Law (UNCITRAL).[50] This has resulted in the Convention on the use of electronic communications in international contracts, adopted by the General Assembly on November 23, 2005.[51] The draft Convention "aims to enhance legal certainty and commercial predictability where electronic communications are used in relation to international contracts"—although it does not apply to "contracts concluded for personal, family or household purposes"—i.e. consumer contracts.

The Convention perhaps has taken into account the possibility of spam filters and firewalls and states that:

> "The time of receipt of an electronic communication is the time when it becomes capable of being retrieved by the addressee at an electronic address designated by the addressee ... An electronic communication is presumed to be capable of being retrieved by the addressee when it reaches the addressee's electronic address."

The Convention is open for signature by all States at the United Nations until January 18, 2008. It should, of course, be noted that the Convention is not at present, and there is no guarantee that it will ever become, part of UK law. At the time of writing, the signatories were the Central African Republic, Lebanon, Senegal, China, Singapore, Sri Lanka, Madagascar, and Sierra Leone.

Despatch of acceptance

A similar series of arguments can be applied to the offeree, especially (as is **10–089** likely) when his emails are routed via an internet access provider. Does sending the email from the offeree's system entitle him to assume that the acceptance is effective?

The answer is likely to turn to some extent on what the offeree is able,

---

[50] Meeting in Vienna October 11–22, 2004. See report at *http://www.uncitral.org/uncitral/en/ commission/sessions/38th.html*—especially para.149 of the report and the draft text itself. This is also reported in ECLR Vol.9 No.41 p.868. For further debate of principles at ECLR Vol.10 No.14 p.349.

[51] *http://www.uncitral.org/uncitral/en/uncitral_texts/electronic_commerce/ 2005Convention.html*.

and can reasonably be expected, to check. The offeree's system may or may not notify a successful transfer to the access provider or via, for example, a gateway from another protocol (such as X400) to the internet. The system may or may not confirm that an attachment has been successfully delivered along with the basic email. The offeree may be entitled to have greater confidence in the safe despatch of a pre-formatted response to a web page rather than a free-form email.

Is the internet instantaneous?

10–090   Can one assume that the gap between deemed despatch and deemed receipt is as narrow as possible? This could be the case if neither the offeree nor the offeror uses remote servers or intermediaries or because despatch is deemed to take place only at the departure of the message from the offeree's internet access provider's server and receipt is deemed to be at the remote server of the offeror. It is still the case that there is as yet no guarantee when or if an email will arrive. However, there is no certainty over the route of the email or even that all of the email will take the same route over the packet-switched network.

Therefore, if the present internet cannot be regarded as being analogous to the telephone or telex systems, the rules on instantaneous communication should not apply. However, the alternative postal rule depends on there being a single reliable organisation responsible for the postal service, which it is reasonable for the offeree to trust. This again is not the case with the internet.

It would seem therefore that neither the rules on instantaneous communication nor postal acceptance can slavishly be applied to the internet.

Application of the normal rules to the Internet

10–091   It is important to bear in mind that the rules evolved to deal with other forms of communication were intended to meet the need for certainty and the fair allocation of risk, as between offeror and offeree, of a problem in communication. A similar approach should be taken in considering the position with internet communication.

It is suggested that, in the context of a system primarily used by commercial offerors to elicit acceptance from individuals, the balance of convenience would tend to render most of the questions as to receipt irrelevant. The offeree will not know, or have any means of knowing the answers.

Some of the risks, such as the breakdown of communication between the offeror and the host of a remote server, can be covered in the service contract between those parties. The question ought therefore to be as to when the offeree is entitled to believe that its response has been reliably despatched. The test of this will be a matter of fact but must depend on the information available to the offeree as to the progress of the email. This approach is consistent with that taken in *The Pamela*, discussed above, in which it was the time at which the message could be *expected* to have been read that was the key.

However, harsh as this may seem to the offeror, there are balancing factors. Given the current status of the internet, neither party is likely to place absolute reliance on it and both are likely to be aware of the risk that an email will be mis-routed. Where the service to be provided is the delivery of on-line material, the customer will know quickly if there is a problem and will simply request that the offeror resends the material. This may in fact take place automatically.

10–092

If physical goods are not received, the customer is again likely to query the situation (this should be distinguished from the question of risk in goods which have been despatched, which is a matter for the contract). Where payment is also made electronically, depending on the exact means, the customer is unlikely to lose money if the message to the offeror is not delivered as the offeror will not act, for example, to debit a credit card account.

Minimising the risks of uncertainty

Given that it is not possible to be certain about the communication of acceptance of an offer over the internet, the offeror should take steps to avoid the issue becoming a problem, subject, of course, to rules on deemed delivery in reg.11 of the E-Commerce Regulations if they apply. The first question must be to assess, in the light of the continuing development of the internet, whether it is appropriate to sell particular goods or services over the internet at all. This will depend on the value of the transactions and the importance of incorporating particular contract terms, such as the extent of a licence or the limitation of liability. The potential offeror must then incorporate terms in its web page (or preliminary emails) as to the acceptable methods of communication; the time of despatch of goods; when the contract is formed and how the offeree should raise queries in the event of problems.

10–093

Communication over internet voice link

A final issue is where the telephone is used to communicate acceptance but the telephone service used is over the internet itself rather than over the public switched telephone network. It is suggested that, where the service is full duplex (i.e. both parties can speak without cutting the other off) and in real-time, the position should not differ from that where a more traditional telephone service is used.

10–094

Electronic agents

The use of electronic agents introduces some uncertainty into the process of contract formation. An electronic agent is software programmed to conclude contracts with other persons or electronic agents according to predetermined criteria. The agent will search for offers that match the

10–095

criteria and (without any intervention from the person on whose behalf the agent is contracting) conclude the contract.

For instance, an electronic agent could be programmed to purchase supplies within a particular range of prices if the proprietor's stocks fall below a set level. It is quite possible that an electronic agent could conclude the contract on each side of the transaction. The lack of human involvement in the contract has led to concerns as to whether there is a true offer and acceptance in this situation.

It has long been accepted in English law that a contract can be formed without the intervention of a human being at the time of formation of the contract, such as when a driver enters an automatic car park.[52] However, in that case a human being has (by displaying prices and terms and conditions) made a specific offer capable of acceptance by the person who enters the car park.

The electronic agent takes the process further, by effectively allowing the agent to negotiate terms within a range of authority programmed into the agent. In principle, there seems to be no reason why English law should not embrace this development and find that a binding contract has been formed.

10–096   Some jurisdictions (not the UK as yet) have thought it necessary to legislate for the validity of transactions conducted through electronic agents. The Bermuda Electronic Transactions Act 1999, for instance, in implementing provisions concerned with the attribution of messages to a person, referred to the action of a person acting, inter alia, through his "electronic agent device" (defined as "a program, or other electronic or automated means configured and enabled by a person that is used to initiate or respond to electronic records or performance in whole or in part without review by an individual").

The US Uniform Electronic Transactions Act (UETA) (a model law which is reported to be adopted in at least 28 states) also provides that a contract may be formed by the interaction of electronic agents "even if no individual was aware of or reviewed the electronic agents' actions or the resulting terms and agreements" and between an electronic agent and an individual. The US Federal E-SIGN Act also provides, albeit slightly differently from UETA, for the enforceability of contracts via electronic agents.

In one reported case from the US, similar principles seem to have been applied in relation to "spider" programs—although not, it seems, by reference to the UETA or E-SIGN. Spider programs are pieces of software

---

[52] *Thornton v Shoe Lane Parking Ltd* [1971] 2 Q.B. 163. Lord Denning M.R.: "... the offer is made when the proprietor of the machine holds it out as being ready to receive the money. The acceptance takes place when the customer puts his money in the slot. ... In the present case the offer was contained in the notice at the entrance giving the charges for garaging. ... The offer was accepted when Mr Thornton drove up to the entrance and, by the movement of his car, turned the light from red to green, and the ticket was thrust at him. The contract was then concluded ..." Although Lord Denning distinguished the old "ticket" cases on the basis that the customer could not refuse the ticket once he had put his money in the machine, he did (if he was wrong in that) consider the position if the machine was "a booking clerk in disguise" (pp.169–170).

that trawl through data on websites, subject to pre-defined parameters set by the spider's operator. In *Cairo Inc v Crossmedia Services Inc*,[53] decided on April 1, 2005, in the US District Court for the Northern District of California, it was held that that the use of a spider program can render the program's operator bound by the terms of use of the websites scoured, notwithstanding that the owner had never had sight of such terms. Here, the court held that it was proper to impute knowledge of the terms of use because of the repeated access to the site.

10.4.5 Revocation and lapsing of offer

An offer can be revoked at any time before it is accepted (or deemed to be accepted) and it can also lapse after a specified time or on a specified event. As with acceptance, communication of revocation is required. In the context of a web page where the offeree is required to respond directly, merely amending the page to end the offer and remove any electronic order form is likely to suffice. **10–097**

Where an offer by email has been sent, revocation may not be effective unless another email is sent (and possibly received) prior to acceptance or revocation is communicated in some other way. Again, it would be prudent, where there is a risk of the offeror being bound by an unwanted contract, to specify in the initial offer how it can be revoked. This may also be the case where there could be a risk of a delay between an alteration to a web page and its availability to all users, such as where certain access providers cache pages.

As noted above, if there is a risk of the supply of goods not meeting demand, it would also be prudent to have an express statement that the offer is subject to the availability of the goods, or to expressly state that an order by a customer is itself an offer and that the contract will only be formed when the seller confirms that the order has been accepted, rather than to rely on an implied term or the assumption that there is merely an invitation to treat.

10.4.6 Consideration and intention to create legal relations

The two remaining required elements for the creation of a binding contract are less likely to be problematic in the context of internet contracts. Consideration (that is the passing of benefit between the parties) is likely to be clear: the offeror offers to supply goods and/or services and the offeree agrees to pay for them. The necessary intention to create a binding contract is likely to be able to be readily inferred from the circumstances. **10–098**

---

[53] ND Cal No. C 04–04852 JW 4/1/05—reported in ECLR Vol.10 No.14 p.382.

10.4.7 Incorporation of terms

10–099 The terms of the contract will comprise those expressly agreed by the parties and any which are implied, either by the courts or by the general law (to the extent that they are not successfully excluded). Where there has been an exchange of emails which contain the full terms of the agreement and there has been acceptance of an offer incorporating those terms, there is no more likely to be a dispute about those terms than with other forms of contracting (although see section 10.9 below as to the evidencing of those terms).

The most likely issue to arise in the context of the internet is where a party attempts to incorporate standard terms into a contract formed via a web page. The basic rule is that, for him to be bound, the other party must have sufficient notice of the terms and that they must be brought to his attention prior to the contract being formed (see also section 10.4.4 above).

One option is to ensure that no one can place an order via the web page until he has signed a separate contract exchanged by post.

Another is for the terms and conditions to be set out in full as part of the web page so that the reader must scroll through them and specifically acknowledge them by clicking a hypertext link to that effect before he can proceed to order the goods or services (this is an example of "click-wrap" and discussed below).

Yet another is to have a hypertext link to the terms and conditions so that they can be accessed from the web page (this can be known as either "browse-wrap" or "web-wrap" depending on the circumstances and also discussed below). The simplest option is to refer to standard terms which are not set out on the internet at all. There are a number of variations on each option.

The appropriateness and adequacy of each of these methods will depend on the importance of the terms themselves, which in turn may depend on the value of the goods or services and whether certain terms must be incorporated to protect the supplier, such as the extent of a copyright licence, or issues of liability or the means of communication of acceptance.

It is a general principle also that the more onerous or unusual the terms, the more that must be done to bring them to the attention of the person to be bound by them. The options above are given in decreasing order of "safety".

Online retailers should also take account of the transparency requirements contained in the Distance Selling and E-Commerce Regulations, particularly in relation to the information that must be provided to parties prior to the formation of the contract. See discussions above at para.10–057.

10.4.8 Incorporating terms by click-wrap, browse-wrap and web-wrap

Where a business seeks to form a contract online, it will normally try to incorporate its standard terms and conditions into the relevant contract. There are various ways that have been used in an attempt to incorporate such terms—with varying degrees of success. As discussed above (in para.10–099) the incorporation of such general terms and conditions is subject to the general principles of contract law.

10–100

The various methods used can broadly be divided into three categories known as "browse-wrap", "click-wrap" and "web-wrap"—although the distinctions between these forms may not be particularly clear-cut in practice. While the terminology is not completely settled, a useful taxonomy is as follows. "Click-wrap" means that positive assent to the displayed terms (e.g. by an "I agree" button) is required. "Browse-wrap" means that the terms are accessible via a hypertext link. "web-wrap" denotes a notice attempting to make entry into and further use of the website conditional on posted terms and conditions.

The validity of the incorporation of terms and conditions via a web page has been the subject of a number of cases in various jurisdictions where the validity of all the various ways has been enforced. However, it seems that the conclusions of the various courts has depended greatly on the specific factual circumstances, rather than laying down any particular rules. Nevertheless, although there are not yet any reported UK cases on the subject,[54] it is useful to consider how other jurisdictions have treated the incorporation of online terms and conditions into contracts formed entirely online.

10–101

Click-wrap

In relation to Click-wrap formation in the case of *Moore v Microsoft Corporation*[55]—it was held that a prominent display of terms before installation of software and requirement to click on "I agree" button before downloading could create legal obligations.

10–102

In *Williams v America Online Inc*,[56] the plaintiff alleged that installation of the defendant's software had caused unauthorised changes to his computer. The defendant sought to rely on a jurisdiction clause contained in its terms of service agreement. The plaintiff adduced expert evidence to show that the changes to the computer were made at the beginning of the installation process, before he had the opportunity to agree to the terms of

---

[54] In *Midasplayer.Com Ltd v Watkins* [2006] All E.R. (D) 98 (Jun) the defendant was found liable on the basis of terms and conditions that he had to have assented to when registering as a member in order to play games for prizes on a website. However, the defendant did not appear and was not represented and the case report gives no details of the method by which members of the site assented to the terms.

[55] N.Y. Sup. Ct., App. Div., 2d Dept., April 15, 2002.

[56] 2001 WL 135825 (Mass. Super., February 8, 2001).

service. The evidence also showed that they were not reversed even if the user declined to agree to the terms and cancelled the installation process. The court found that the plaintiff did not have notice of the jurisdiction clause before the changes were made to his computer.

Browse-wrap

10–103   In relation to "browse-wrap", in *Net2Phone Inc v Los Angeles County Superior Court*,[57] it was held that a user had positively accepted terms accessible by hypertext link before downloading software.

Again, in *DeJohn v TV Corporation International*[58] there was held to be positive acceptance by the user of terms accessible by hypertext link before submitting application to register a domain name. The fact that the user did not read those terms was held to be irrelevant.

Similarly, in the case of *Hubbert v Dell Corporation*,[59] the court used the analogy that a hyperlink was merely a way for a contracting party to view all the terms of a contract, in the same way that a party to a written contract could page-turn through all the written terms or simply sign the final page. In both cases, all "pages" formed part of the contract, regardless of whether the parties had actually viewed those terms.

However, in *Specht v Netscape Communications*[60] the US Court of Appeals of the Second Circuit declined to enforce a browse-wrap agreement. In this case the user clicked on a "Download" button in order to download the defendant's "SmartDownload" software.

At no time was the user required positively to assent to contractual terms. If the user had scrolled down to the next screen, below the fold, he would have seen an invitation to "review and agree to the terms of the Netscape SmartDownload software license agreement before downloading and using the software".

Clicking on a link would take the user to a page containing links to a number of Netscape licence agreements stating that the user must read and agree to the licence terms before downloading the software. Clicking on the link to the SmartDownload licence agreement would display the text of that agreement.

The court saw no reason to assume that users would scroll down to the next screen, nor that if they knew there was another screen they should reasonably have concluded that it contained licence terms. The court held the terms were not incorporated.

In the Dutch case of *Curry v Audax Publishing B V*[61] the District Court of Amsterdam held that certain photographs posted to the Flickr.com website were subject to the Creative Commons licence where the words "some rights reserved" were visible with the photographs, clicking on the link led

---

[57] Cal. Ct. App., 2d Dist., June 9, 2003.
[58] N.D. Ill., January 16, 2003.
[59] Ill App. Ct., 5th Dist., No.02-L–786 8/12/05).
[60] (No. 01- 7860 (L) (2d Cir., October 1, 2002).
[61] Case 334492/KG 06–176 SR, March 9, 2006.

to a short summary of the licence, and a further link leading to the complete text of the licence, which opened with the words "By exercising any rights to the work provided here, you accept and agree to be bound by the terms of this license".

Web-wrap

Regarding "web-wrap", in *Ticketmaster Corp v Tickets.com Inc*[62] it was held that a contract was capable of being formed where a prominent notice on the home page stated that further use of the website was subject to terms of use published on the site.

    Similarly, in it was held that a contract for use of information on *Pollstar v Gigmania Ltd*,[63] website was arguably binding where terms were linked from a homepage notice "use is subject to licence agreement", notwithstanding that the notice was in small grey text on grey background with no underlining to indicate that it was a hyperlink.

    In *Register.com Inc v Verio Inc*,[64] the US Court of Appeals for the Second Circuit held that a contract was formed and enforceable where the defendant repeatedly visited the site to gather WHOIS data after becoming aware of terms of use, even though the terms of use were provided to the defendant after each receipt of data.

    A Dutch court has also upheld a web-wrap agreement in *Netwise v NTS*,[65] where a home page button marked "general terms and conditions" was sufficient to create a binding contract with a business user governing its use of the rest of the website.

    However, it may be that the supplier does not want the terms set out in its website to be binding. For example, *in Re JetBlue Airways Corp Privacy Litigation*,[66] the court decided that the airline's privacy policy, which was viewable via a hyperlink, formed part of the contract for sale of an airline ticket, even though the airline had argued that it was not intended to do so.

    Finally, some caution should be noted from a German case where it was decided that web-wrap terms are not enforceable if these are not sufficiently brought to the users' attention. In *Case No 3 U 168/00*[67] a German court stated that terms and conditions must be attached to an offer, or be clearly indicated at a point that every user must encounter. The court stated that the law is not complied with if the customer must search out the terms and conditions.

    A close analogy may be drawn with the practice adopted in respect of shrinkwrapped software. As with web pages, there are limitations of space and considerations of attractive presentation. With such software, the practice is to state clearly on the packaging that the software is subject to a

10–104

10–105

---

[62] C.D. Cal., March 7, 2003.
[63] U.S.D.C., E.D. Cal., October 17, 2000.
[64] 2d Cir., 00- 9596, January 31, 2004.
[65] Court of Rotterdam, December 5, 2002.
[66] EDNY No 04-MD–1587 (CBA) 8/2/05.
[67] Oberlandesgericht Hamburg, June 13, 2002.

licence and that by breaking the plastic wrapping the user is bound by the terms of that licence. The user may decline to proceed and return the software unopened and obtain a refund. It is generally assumed that shrink-wrap licences are efficacious as contracts, but this is not certain.[68]

However, it should be noted that the analogy is not exact. Shrink-wrapped software is generally sold as a package by a retailer or bundled by a third party hardware manufacturer. There is therefore no direct contact between the copyright owner and the ultimate user. Many copyright owners therefore seek additional acknowledgement of terms by offering an inducement (such as ongoing support) if the licensee completes and returns a guarantee card. In the case of a web page, there will be direct communication between the parties (unless the web page is operated by a distributor) and less need for such devices.

10–106   One other point to note is that a licence of copyright material must be distinguished from a contract. A licence is simply a permission to do something which would otherwise be forbidden: in the case of software, it sets out the basis on which the user can make use of the program. In theory, therefore, all a software licence need do is describe the permitted use of the software. If the user goes beyond what is permitted, this will infringe copyright and the licensor will have a right of action against him. The main concern would be the necessity of setting out clearly the terms of the licence in such a way as to ensure that the user could not claim that he was unaware of the restrictions. This could be done by an on-screen notice without the need for a contract.

However, the breadth of types of material which can be supplied on-line over the internet would tend to make this a less attractive approach in practice. Even where there is an on-line publication of material which is also available in hard copy, the normal copyright notice may not offer sufficient protection. This is because material supplied in digital form is inherently easier to copy. In addition, unlike with, for example, books, the copyright owner cannot rely on a general understanding of recipients of what is and is not permitted. Taking this with the frequent need to incorporate other terms suggests that most providers of copyright material over the internet will prefer to rely on a binding contract rather than purely on copyright.

10.4.8 Certainty of identity of parties

10–107   There may be certain circumstances where the identity or some other quality of one of the contracting parties may be of particular concern. This may be, for example, where certain goods can only be sold to persons over a certain age or cannot legally be sold in certain jurisdictions. The nature of

---

[68] Some support for the enforceability of shrink-wrap licences can be gained from the Scottish case *Beta Computers (Europe) Ltd v Adobe Systems (Europe) Ltd* [1996] F.S.R. 367.

services may also be relevant: an on-line bank will wish to ensure that it minimises the risk of fraud by the impersonation of one of its customers.

In such cases, the precautions to be taken will vary but it would be usual to incorporate in any contract a declaration by the other party that he or she meets certain criteria, or to enter into a preliminary written contract accompanied by appropriate evidence of age or other qualification.

The question of proving the identity of a party to an online contract arose in a German decision, *Case No. 19 U 16/02.*[69] In this case a watch was offered for sale on an internet auction site. An offer of €9,000 was made from the defendant's password-protected email account. The auction host informed the seller of the defendant's contact details. When the seller asked for payment, the defendant denied having made the offer and said it had been made by an unauthorised third party. In fact at the time of the auction he knew that his email password had been intercepted and his ISP had blocked his email account for this reason.

The Higher Regional Court of Cologne held that use of the email account was not in itself sufficient to discharge the burden on the plaintiff to show that the defendant had made the offer. It commented that the use of an electronic signature (by which the court must be assumed to mean some type of digital signature) may establish prima facie evidence that the sender was the signatory and reverse the burden of proof. The court granted permission to appeal to the German Federal Supreme Court.

In a more recent German case on almost identical facts, the Regional Court of Konstanz came to the same conclusion (*Case No. 2 O 141/01*). (For discussion of transfer of risk to the user of a digital signature under English law, see paras. 10–113–10–118 below.)

In January 2003 the UK Government issued a policy document setting out its "Minimum Requirements for the Verification of the Identity of Organisations"[70], for use as part of the process of issuing a digital certificate or a PIN or password for use with e-government services.

10.4.9 Online auction analysis—contract formation

In recent years, the popularity of online auction websites has been significant. Such sites have added a new dimension to how contracts are formed on-line—by both introducing the concept of an "auction", and also by allowing consumers to contract directly with each other. 10–108

We have noted at para.10–025 how the Department of Trade and Industry and the Office of Fair Trading view such sites for the purposes of the Distance Selling and E-Commerce Regulations and also how such sites may be regarded by the courts.

---

[69] Oberlandesgericht Köln, September 6, 2002.
[70] *www.cabinetoffice.gov.uk/csia/documents/pdf/HMG_reqmnt_veri_ID_org.pdf.* Similar guidance is given in relation to the identification of individuals at *www.cabinetoffice.gov.uk/csia/documents/pdf/HMG_reqmnt_veri_ID_individual.pdf.*

10–109   Does bidding on an item legally oblige the buyer to buy that item? It is submitted that this is not so, as the bid is simply an offer to buy that item for the stated price. Accordingly, legal obligations will only arise when that offer is accepted—i.e. the online auction comes to an end and the highest bidder is obliged to purchase the item—and the buyer can in principle withdraw its offer until the offer is accepted (see the discussion above generally about the status of offers—especially para.10–144).

The buyer may perhaps be restricted in withdrawing its offer by the "terms of use" of the website. However, this agreement is normally between the buyer and the website owner. Even though both the buyer and seller may have signed up to the same terms of use with the website owner, there is no contract directly between the buyer and seller until a sale is completed.

Unless the relevant section of the terms of use can be enforced by the seller under the Contracts (Rights of Third Parties) Act 1999, the seller will not be able to enforce the restriction and will have to rely upon the website owner taking action against the buyer.

The ability to withdraw a bid is in practice more likely to be conditioned by the technical means available on the site and the site's policies, including as regards sanctions against future misconduct. One final point to note is that if an online auction were considered to be an "auction" in the legal sense, s.57 of the Sale of Goods Act 1979 permits a bidder to retract his bid at any time prior to acceptance.

10.5 FORMALITIES OF CONTRACTING

10–110   Under the laws of England and Wales, most contracts can be concluded without formality and need not be in writing. As a matter of practice, all but the simplest contracts of course tend to be evidenced in writing to aid certainty. This is considered further in section 10.10 below.

However, certain contracts do need to be in writing or to be signed in order to be effective, and failure to comply with such requirements may render the contract void or unenforceable or difficult to enforce. The most obvious examples are certain contracts transferring title to land or otherwise falling within s.2 of the Law of Property (Miscellaneous Provisions) Act 1989. Guarantees and certain contracts relating to the giving of credit and contracts effecting the transfer of shares must also be in writing.

10–111   The question of what is "writing" has received some attention. The question is essentially whether writing in electronic or digital form, as opposed to handwritten writing on paper, complies with any relevant requirement of writing under English law.

Some statutes, such as the Copyright Designs and Patents Act 1988, contain their own autonomous definitions of writing. So an assignment of copyright complies with the requirements of that Act if it is in writing as defined in that Act: "any form of notation or code, whether by hand or otherwise and regardless of the method by which, all medium in or on which, it is recorded". The Arbitration Act 1996 also contains an autonomous definition of writing: "References in this Part to anything being written or in writing include its being recorded by any means". That definition effectively equates the concept of writing with that of a document.

Many statutes that impose requirements of writing do not contain autonomous definitions. They are likely to be governed by the Interpretation Act 1978. "Writing" under the 1978 Act "includes typing, printing, lithography, photography and other modes of representing or reproducing words in a visible form".[71]

This definition includes a requirement for something to be in visible form. By this analysis, writing in digital form (at least when called up on screen) is sufficiently visible to fall within the definition. However, although the courts may be expected to construe the Act so as to take account of technological advances,[72] the requirement of visibility has nonetheless led to academic debate about whether the requirement would in all circumstances be satisfied.

Essentially, the debate turns on the question of whether the fact that something may be rendered into visible form is sufficient to satisfy a requirement that the thing be *in* writing, when the transaction may take place without anything in fact appearing on a screen or being rendered visible at all. All the examples of writing listed in the Interpretation Act inevitably result in the creation of something which, if it is to be used for communication, is rendered visible (even if the process that leads up to it, such as photography, includes a stage where the material is not visible).

The same is not true of electronic communications, using which (for instance through communications between electronic agents) a transaction can be concluded without anything being rendered visible. Take for example, an exchange of voicemail messages. These are undoubtedly recorded, so that they would fall within a broad definition of "document".[73] However are they "writing" within the meaning of the Interpretation Act, when voicemail is not normally contemplated as being rendered visible? What about voice attachments to emails?

Examples such as these suggest that although in many cases electronic form will satisfy the Interpretation Act definition of writing, there may be some instances where it does not do so even though the electronic form in question has a sufficient element of recordal to qualify as a document for, for instance, the purpose of disclosure in litigation.

The Law Commission in its advice *Electronic Commerce: Formal*

---

[71] Interpretation Act 1978, Sch.1.

[72] For examples see Bennion, *Statutory Interpretation* (4th ed Butterworths), pp.775 *et seq.*; and see *Victor Chandler International Ltd v Customs & Excise Commissioners* [2000] 1 W.L.R. 1296.

[73] See e.g. *Derby v Weldon (No.9)* [1991] 1 W.L.R. 652; and note the comments of the Vice-Chancellor in *Victor Chandler*: "VCI's computers, Teletext's central editing system and the remote databases, each of which held the relevant information, can be regarded as documents. Each of them possesses the essential characteristic of a document, namely containing recorded information".

Requirements in Commercial Transactions, published in December 2001, reached similar conclusions to those stated above about the ability of an electronic document or communication to satisfy a requirement of writing under the Interpretation Act 1978.

10–112   Similar arguments in other contexts, such as that computer data were not a photograph,[74] have usually failed—at least where to hold otherwise would deprive the statute of its effectiveness. However, the definition of "writing" in the Interpretation Act is presumably there as a form of protection for the unwary, so that the court, when considering the mischief of the statute, may consider (within the constraints of the wording of the statute) whether the medium that is argued to fall within it offers equivalent protection to those media that undoubtedly do so.[75]

In relation to particular types of contract, and those which may need to be enforced in other jurisdictions with stricter requirements, the parties will need to analyse the specific requirement for "writing", both to ensure that the contract is legally effective and in relation to its use in evidence.

It should also be borne in mind that even if there is no direct statutory requirement of writing, there may be other requirements that render the statute incapable of being complied with electronically.

For instance, under the Consumer Credit Act 1974 there is no requirement in the Act that the statutory forms be in writing. However, some of the Regulations made under the Act, until amended in 2004[76], referred to paper. Another example was s.3 of the Unsolicited Goods and Services Act 1971, which (until amended in August 2001) referred to a customer's order being placed by means of "an order form or other stationery belonging to the person".

10.6 ELECTRONIC SIGNATURES

10.6.1 General law on signatures

Validity of electronic signatures

10–113   In the absence of a specific statutory requirement, there is no requirement in English law for any document to be signed in order to be legally valid or effective. So even for a class of contract required to be in writing or evidenced in writing, that does not require a signature unless the legislation so specifies.

However, there are many statutory requirements for signature, usually in

---

[74] *R. v Fellows, R. v Arnold* [1997] 2 All E.R. 548.

[75] As to whether requirements of form in fact achieve the desired protection, and as regards the unreliability of traditional media such as paper, see the discussion in section 10.7.5.

[76] The Regulations were modernised by the Consumer Credit (Disclosure of Information) Regulations 2004, which now allow information to be provided on paper or another durable medium which is available and accessible to the debtor or hirer. See para.10–055 for the full text of these provisions.

combination with one or more other requirements such as that the document be in writing (however defined). While it is very rare (if any exists at all) for a statute to define what amounts to a signature, accompanying requirements may restrict in practice the mode of signature. If a requirement of writing mandates signed paper, that would preclude signature by most (but not necessarily all[77]) forms of electronic signature. If, on the other hand, a writing requirement is broadly defined so as to encompass a document in electronic form, that would suggest that an accompanying signature requirement can be satisfied by signing the document electronically.

English law has traditionally taken a liberal view of what satisfies a legislative requirement for a signature. Indeed, there is no English case in which a signature has been held not to satisfy a legislative requirement for a signature merely because it is not in the correct form.

Signatures have been disqualified because they were applied by an agent when the particular statute on its true construction requires a personal signature (i.e. one applied by the signatory)[78]; or because the name that was alleged to be a signature simply was not a signature[79]; or because the signature was mass-produced and pre-printed on a document, when the particular statute (on its true construction) required a signature to be applied individually to each form.[80] In the few cases in which the form of signature has been in issue, the court has each time permitted the signature to stand.

Jenkins v Gaisford, Re Jenkins (decd)'s goods[81] concerned both form of   **10–114**

---

[77] The US E-SIGN legislation specifically contemplates the possibility of a non-electronic document being signed electronically.

[78] E.g. *Re Prince Blucher, Ex p. Debtor* [1931] 2 Ch. D. 70.

[79] E.g. *Firstpost Homes v Johnson* [1995] 4 All E.R. 355. The Court of Appeal, interpreting s.2 of the Law of Property (Miscellaneous Provisions) Act 1989, rejected the previous "generous" interpretations of the Statute of Frauds and s.40 of the Law of Property Act 1925 as inapplicable to the 1989 Act. They held that the printing or typing of the name of an addressee of a letter, when the addressee had printed or typed the document, was not the signature of the addressee. However, this was not on the grounds that the "signature" was printed or typed, but on the grounds that inserting the name of an addressee of a letter did not amount to signing the document. Peter Gibson L.J. stated: "This decision is of course limited to a case where the party whose signature is said to appear on the contract is only named as the addressee of a letter prepared by him. No doubt other considerations will apply in other circumstances." The decision focused not on the form of the signature, but on the fact that the name was typed as the addressee of the letter, leaving open the possibility that in other circumstances a typed signature would suffice. Although not expressly stated, on the logic of the reasoning the same result would have been reached if the addressee had written out the letter by hand.

[80] *R. v Cowper* [1890] 24 Q.B.D. 533. This case was concerned not with the form of signature, but with the mode of its application. The Divisional Court held that a pre-prepared lithographed version of a solicitor's name did not comply with the particular requirement for signature. The two-judge Court of Appeal disagreed, so the Divisional Court decision stood. Fry L.J., who agreed with the court below, made clear that this was not because the signature was a facsimile, but because of the lack of cognisance of the individual document inherent in a mass-produced pre-prepared facsimile (and see the explanation of the decision in *France v Dutton* [1891] 2 Q.B. 208). The case did not suggest that the solicitor could not sign by, for instance, inscribing his name in block capitals, or typing his name individually on each form that came before him.

[81] (1863) 3 Sw. & Tr. 93, 164 E.R. 1208.

signature and whether signature by an agent was permitted. Section 9 of the Wills Act 1837 required a will or codicil to be signed at the end by the testator. The testator became infirm and had difficulty writing or signing his name. He had an engraving of his signature made and this was used under his direction by a person acting as his agent, including to sign the codicil in issue. The court held that the codicil was duly executed:

> "It has been decided that a testator sufficiently signs by making his mark, and I think it was rightly contended that the word 'signed' in that section must have the same meaning whether the signature is made by the testator himself, or by some other person in his presence or by his direction, and therefore a mark made by some other person under such circumstances must suffice. Now, whether the mark is made by pen or by some other instrument cannot make any difference, neither can it in reason make a difference that a facsimile of the whole name was impressed on the will instead of a mere mark or X. The mark made by the instrument or stamp used was intended to stand for and represent the signature of the testator. In the case where it was held that sealing was not signing, the seals were not affixed by way of signature."

It can be seen that, insofar as this case related to the form of signature, it placed no restriction on the form of signature but turned on the intent of the signatory.

10–115   *Goodman v J Eban Ltd*[82] addressed both form of signature and the mode of its application. A rubber stamp facsimile signature was individually applied and held to comply with the statutory requirement. Evershed M.R. stated:

> "It follows, I think, that the essential requirement of signing is the affixing, either by writing with a pen or pencil or by otherwise impressing on the document one's name or 'signature' so as personally to authenticate the document."

The question whether a rubber stamp consisting of a typed or printed representation, as opposed to a facsimile of the signature, would have sufficed was expressly left open by the majority of the Court of Appeal.[83]

---

[82] [1954] 1 All E.R. 763.

[83] Denning L.J. (as he then was), in his dissenting judgment, stated: "Suppose he were to type his name or to use a rubber stamp with his name printed on it in block letters, no-one would then suggest that he had signed the document". However, Evershed M.R. left this question open: "It is unnecessary for the purposes of this case to express any view whether or not the same result would follow if the 'signature' impressed by the stamp was not a facsimile representation of the solicitor's handwriting, but a mere typed or printed representation of his name or the name of his firm." Romer L.J. agreed with the judgment of Evershed M.R and expressed no view on this point. See also *Brydges v Dix* (1891) 7 T.L.R. 215, in which (distinguishing *R. v Cowper*) a printed signature was held sufficient to satisfy the relevant statutory requirement for a signature.

Another case to consider the form of a signature was *Re a debtor* **10–116** *(No.2021 of 1995)*.[84] This concerned a proxy form for a creditors' meeting under s.257 of the Insolvency Act 1986. The proxy form was faxed to the chairman of the meeting. The question was whether the form was signed within the meaning of r.8.2(3) of the Insolvency Rules 1986, which provided that a proxy form "shall be signed by the principal, or by some person authorised by him".

It was common ground in the case that signing "could not be restricted to the narrow concept of marking a substrate manually by direct use of a pen or similar writing instrument. It was conceded that a proxy form could be 'signed' by use . . . of a stamp". Similarly, it was conceded that if a form had a signature impressed on it by a printing machine in the way that share dividend cheques frequently are signed by company secretaries,[85] the form can be said to be "signed".

Laddie J. held that the proxy was signed within the meaning of the rule. In his view the concession as to stamping and printing was correct. After pointing out that even if the rule required direct manual marking of the form, the authentication is not perfect, he went on to say:

> "It seems to me that the function of a signature is to indicate, but not necessarily prove, that the document has been considered personally by the creditor and is approved of by him. . . . Once it is accepted that the close physical linkage of hand, pen and paper is not necessary for the form to be signed, it is difficult to see why some forms of non-human agency for impressing the mark on the paper should be acceptable while others are not.
>
> For example, it is possible to instruct a printing machine to print a signature by electronic signal sent over a network or via a modem. Similarly, it is now possible with standard personal computer equipment and readily available popular word processing software to compose, say, a letter on a computer screen, incorporate within it the author's signature which has been scanned into the computer and is stored in electronic form, and to send the whole document including the signature by fax modem to a remote fax. The fax received at the remote station may well be the only hard copy of the document. It seems to me that such a document has been 'signed' by the author."

Finding that the proxy form was signed for the purposes of r.8.2(3) if it bore upon it some "distinctive or personal marking which has been placed there by, or with the authority of the creditor", Laddie J. also commented:

---

[84] [1996] 2 All E.R. 345.

[85] As to cheques, see the comments of Professor Goode in *Commercial Law* (2nd edn Butterworths), p.582: "The cheque must carry the drawer's signature, but despite doubts that have been expressed [e.g. by Denning J. in *Goodman v J Eban Ltd*], it would seem that this need not be handwritten and that a stamped facsimile suffices. The same would appear to be true even of a pre-printed facsimile. . ."

"If it is legitimate to send by post a proxy form signed with a rubber stamp, why should it not be at least as authentic to send the form by fax?"

10–117 An Australian decision has assumed that a printed name sent by telex is sufficient.[86] In *Clipper Maritime Ltd v Shirlstar Container Transport Ltd (The "Anemone")*[87] Staughton J. (as he then was) said (*obiter*) in relation to s.4 of the Statute of Frauds 1677:

> "I reached a provisional conclusion in the course of the argument that the answerback of the sender of a telex would constitute a signature, whilst that of the receiver would not since it only authenticates the document and does not convey approval of the contents."

If that was correct, the form of the signatures (telex answerbacks) was of no significance, whereas the purposes for which the two signatures were affixed was significant in relation to the particular statute under consideration, namely a signature requirement in relation to an agreement. Hence the distinction drawn between the effect of the two "signatures", each in identical form.

In *Good Challenger Navegante SA v Metalexportimport SA*,[88] the Court of Appeal held that typing a name at the end of a telex with the inferred intent of approving its contents constituted a signature for the purposes of s.30 of the Limitation Act 1980. That section provides that to be effective for the purposes of re-starting a limitation period pursuant to s.29 of the Act, an acknowledgment of a debt or other liquidated pecuniary claim "must be in writing and signed by the person making it".

Most recently, in *Mehta v J Pereira Fernandes SA*,[89] H.H. Judge Pelling Q.C. (sitting as a judge of the High Court) ruled that the appearance of the sender's email address at the top of an email was not a signature for the purposes of s.4 of the Statute of Frauds, because it had not been included with the intention of giving authenticity.

The judge held that the email was capable of being a sufficient written note or memorandum for the purpose of s.4 of the Statute, but that it did not contain a signature, within the meaning of that section, of either Mr Mehta or his authorised agent.

The judge went on to give detailed consideration to the issue of whether the automatic insertion of the sender's email address was capable of constituting a signature. He relied in particular on a 19th century case, *Caton v Caton*,[90] in which the House of Lords distinguished between signatures

---

[86] *Torrac Investments Pty Ltd v Australian National Airline Commission* (1985) ANZ Conv. R. 82, cited by the Australian Electronic Commerce Expert Group at para.2.7.32 of their Report to the Attorney General.

[87] [1987] 1 Lloyd's Rep. 546.

[88] [2004] 1 Lloyd's Rep. 67.

[89] [2006] EWHC 813 (Ch).

[90] (1867) L.R. 2 H.L. 127.

giving authentication to a whole document and those appearing incidentally or in relation to only part.

In the absence of evidence to the contrary, the judge held that the automatic insertion of a person's email address by the sending and/or receiving ISP after the email was transmitted was clearly in the "incidental" category. It could not be deemed to be intended as a signature for the purposes of s.4. In the judge's view, to conclude otherwise would undermine or potentially undermine the Statute's purpose and have widespread and wholly unintended legal and commercial effects.

The judge noted that if the respondent's arguments were applied to a fax communication it could result in the automatically generated name and fax number of the sender, on a faxed document that is otherwise a s.4 note or memorandum, constituting a signature for the purposes of the Statute.

The judge accepted that a party could sign a document for the purposes of s.4 by using his name or initials, and possibly by using a pseudonym or a combination of letters and numbers, providing always that whatever was used was inserted into the document in order to give, and with the intention of giving, authenticity to it. Its inclusion must have been intended as a signature for these purposes.

In summary, therefore, the English cases on compliance with statutory requirements for signature place little or no emphasis on the form of the signature as such. The emphasis is on whether the statute requires the personal and individual application of the name, mark or signature to the document and the purpose for which it is applied, not on the form of the name, mark or signature. When we come to consider the implementation of the EU Electronic Signatures Directive, the fact that English law therefore attaches little or no significance to the existence of, in particular, a handwritten signature will assume some importance.

These cases suggest that under existing English law any electronic signature regardless of inherent reliability (such as typing the sender's name at the end of an email), would be capable of satisfying a generally expressed requirement of signature, so long as the requisite intention was present and (if necessary) some extrinsic evidence such as oral testimony could be adduced to identify the person who signed.[91]

10–118

It is easy to be diverted from the simplicity of this broad facilitative approach by considering first, the provisions of s.7 of the Electronic Communications Act 2000; and secondly, the EU Electronic Signatures Directive. These are discussed below. However, they do not in fact affect the above analysis. Ultimately they are superfluous pieces of legislation which, for practical purposes, can largely be ignored as far as English law is concerned.

---

[91] For a similar view of pre-existing US signature law, see "The Verdict on Plaintext Signatures: They're Legal", Benjamin Wright, [1994] 10 C.L.S.R. 311.

Allocating risk in the use of electronic signatures

10–119   A separate question from whether an electronic signature satisfies a legislative requirement for a signature is that of who bears the risk of a forged signature, or one affixed without authority. This is of especial concern with electronic signatures since it is less easy to detect forgery or impersonation than with manuscript signatures where (at least at leisure after the event if not in the heat of the transaction) a forensic handwriting expert can provide expert evidence to the court).

The basic rule regarding ordinary signatures in English law is that a forged signature is a nullity. That, taken in isolation, would tend to place any risk of forgery firmly on the recipient. However, that risk allocation can be modified to suit the surrounding circumstances by application of, for instance, the rules of mistake, estoppel and representation.

We have discussed at para.10–107 a German case touching on the question of risk allocation in the use of electronic signatures.

10–120   Further, the nature of the underlying risk depends on what is being signed, since the legal significance of a signature may vary widely. Forgery of a signature may render the instrument a nullity. Thus, for a cheque, "... a forged cheque is of course in law not a cheque or negotiable instrument but a mere sham piece of paper".[92]

Where the validity of the legal instrument does not depend on it having been signed, then an allegation that a signature is forged is likely to be an evidential matter as to what conclusions can be drawn from the document; for example whether the person who is alleged to have signed it was aware of the contents of the document.

In the case of a signed contract, the outcome of a dispute over a signature may be determinative of the question whether a contract was concluded, or was void for mistake or was voidable for fraud—not because the contract is invalid without a signature, but because proof of forgery may demonstrate, if the identity of the opposing party to the contract be material (which in many cases it is not), that there was in fact no offer and acceptance between the apparent parties.[93]

There is also a practical risk that a person who did in fact sign a document later repudiates the signature. With handwritten signatures the resolution of this dispute will turn largely on forensic evidence. A commonly expressed concern with electronic signatures is that, since the

---

[92] Kerr J. in *National Westminster Bank Ltd v Barclays Bank International Ltd* [1975] Q.B. 654 at 656.

[93] See *Chitty on Contracts* (29th ed., Sweet & Maxwell) paras. 5–076 *et seq.* for a full discussion of the effect of mistaken identity. Of course the party whose signature is established to have been forged could not be bound by the alleged contract. The complexities arise when considering the effect of the forgery on the other party to the contract, or on third parties whose title to goods sold under the contract derives from the fraudster.

characteristics of handwritten signatures that underlie traditional forensic examination are lacking, the evidential risk of repudiation (either of the signature, or of the document alleged to have been signed) is correspondingly increased.[94] This has led to the development of technologies that seek to reduce or eliminate the risk of repudiation.[95]

The examples that we have discussed all concern ordinary signatures, where there is no attempt to put in place special procedures to authenticate the signature. Where such procedures are put in place, then even where (such as in the case of negotiable instruments) the forged signature renders the instrument a nullity, application of estoppel and representation rules can result in the risk being shifted away from the recipient. This, as we have mentioned, is of especial significance given the emphasis in the electronic environment in devising digital signatures certified by third parties, intended to offer the recipient (among other things) a guarantee of certainty as to the identity of the signatory and the ability to prevent the signatory denying that the signature was his.

In England there has been one case concerning reliance on a fraudulently issued digital signature, albeit of a primitive nature. The case, *Standard Bank London Ltd v The Bank of Tokyo Ltd*[96] concerned a "tested telex", which is a telex authenticated by a secret code known only to the sender and the recipient. The recipient bank relied upon the tested telex received from the sending bank as confirming the authenticity of a documentary letter of credit. The documentary credit was in fact forged and the fraudsters had dishonestly procured the issue of the tested telex by the sending bank. **10–121**

The court held that the recipient of the tested telex would be able to rely on it unless the recipient was on notice of dishonesty, or of facts that should put it on inquiry as to dishonesty, or if it had been wilfully blind. The sending bank was therefore liable for the loss suffered by the recipient bank. The decision was in the context of evidence that the banking system relies on tested telexes and that they are intended to avoid arguments about authority.

The decision placed the responsibility for keeping keys secure fairly and squarely on the person using the key to authenticate a message. It absolves the recipient from any duty to enquire into the authenticity of the message unless he is on notice of dishonesty. **10–122**

That appears to be an efficient economic result in the particular commercial circumstances of the case. It reduces the individual transaction

---

[94] It should be appreciated that although traditional forensic handwriting examination may be impossible, there is a new and growing body of experts with forensic expertise in the digital environment. However, acquisition and use of such evidence to establish identity is complex and costly. See, for example, *Takenaka (UK) Ltd v Frankl* (Alliott J.) October 11, 2000, QBD (upheld on appeal [2001] EWCA Civ 348).

[95] The converse risk is that, due to the ease of impersonating someone electronically, a person may wrongly be bound to a contract that he or she did not make. For a discussion of the ease with which email addresses can be spoofed, see "I never sent that…", Barry Fox, *New Scientist* March 28, 1998.

[96] [1996] 1 C.T.L.R. T-17.

costs, and gives senders an incentive to take security precautions. Whether this allocation of risk would be appropriate in the consumer context, where unsophisticated individuals may use digital signature keys, is another matter.

10–123   Electronic signature technologies vary widely in their purposes and methodologies. Some technologies are intended, as with the "tested telex" in the *Standard Bank* case, to allow the sender to offer the recipient in an online environment a higher than normal degree of confidence that the sender is who he claims to be. Other technologies provide an electronic substitute for written signatures in the paper environment, capturing the handwritten signature electronically and storing its characteristics for later comparison if necessary.

It does not follow that the legal consequences of using such technologies should always be the same, nor that the legal consequences should depend only (or at all) upon the technology being used. The legal consequences may, as we have seen, depend on a variety of commercial and societal factors, including any contractual relationship with the other parties to the transaction.

10–124   The use of a digital signature, especially one verified by a third party certifying authority, to offer reassurance to the recipient is in some ways akin to the use of a cheque guarantee card. The bank (= certifying authority) issues the card (= certificate) to its customer, and by means of the customer's presentation of the card (= certificate) makes a unilateral offer to the payee (= signature recipient) that, on fulfilment of certain conditions, it will honour the cheque (= use of the signature) up to a specified limit.

The question arose in *First Sport Ltd v Barclays Bank Plc*[97] whether the bank was bound to honour a cheque where a retailer accepted the cheque from an imposter in possession of a cheque card and where the signature on the cheque, although it corresponded with that on the cheque card, was forged. The Court of Appeal held that the terms of the unilateral contractual offer made by the bank, as reflected in the terms printed on the cheque card, were such that the bank assumed the risk of forgery. The Court of Appeal made clear that the terms could have been written so as to place the risk of theft and forgery on the retailer accepting the cheque and card.

The issuance of a card (which will often function as a cash withdrawal card as well as a cheque guarantee card) is itself governed by a contract between the bank and the customer, which will seek to allocate risk as between the bank and the customer for unauthorised use of the card and accompanying PIN number.

Thus, a certifying authority could in principle govern its relationship with its own customer by contract and could (so long as it could bring the relevant terms to the notice of the person relying on its certificate, and subject to the constraints of consumer protection legislation) specify its degree of liability to third parties relying on the certificate (both in terms of

---

[97] [1993] 3 All E.R. 789.

a unilateral contractual offer and also in terms of seeking to limit any liability in tort).

However, as we shall see in the discussion of the EU Electronic Signatures Directive, the liability of certain types of certifying authorities to third parties is provided for by legislation as a result of the Directive having been implemented in UK law.

10.6.2 EU Electronic Signatures Directive

Directive 1999/93 of the European Parliament and Council on a Community Framework for Electronic Signatures[98] was adopted on December 13, 1999. It was implemented in the UK, to the extent that s.7 of the Electronic Communications Act 2000 had not already done so, by the Electronic Signatures Regulations 2002.[99]

10–125

The Directive addresses a number of topics surrounding electronic signatures, including: the legal effects of ordinary and "advanced" electronic signatures, certain standard-setting issues, the application of internal market principles to the circulation of signature products and services within the Community, the liability of certain certification service providers, recognition of certain certificates from non-Community countries, and certain data protection issues.

The Directive defines an electronic signature relatively broadly: "data in electronic form which are attached to or logically associated with other electronic data and which serve as a method of authentication" (Art.2.1). It may be observed, however, that this would not include data in electronic form attached to or associated with non-electronic data.[1] Nor does it include signatures used other than as an authentication method. It does not specify that the signature must be used to authenticate the data to which it is attached or logically associated.

So, for instance, would a sample scan of a handwritten signature provided by a customer to a third party for record purposes fall within the definition? It is clearly not an authentication method for the document to which it is attached, but could be used to authenticate other signatures received by the third party in the future. It could also be argued that in some circumstances the purpose of signing a contract is not (or not only) to authenticate the document but to indicate acceptance of its terms.[2] However, it is to be expected that the definition will be broadly interpreted, since the expressed purpose of the Directive is to facilitate the use of electronic signatures and to contribute to their legal recognition (Art.1).

---

[98] O.J. 2000 L13/12.
[99] SI 2002/318.
[1] Compare the definition in the US E-SIGN legislation, which does include such cross-media signatures.
[2] See *Clipper Maritime Ltd v Shirlstar Container Transport Ltd (The "Anemone")* (para.10–111, above), in which Staughton J. (as he then was) made, albeit *obiter*, precisely this distinction in relation to the sender's and receiver's telex answerback.

Neither the Directive nor the implementing Regulations define "electronic". This may give rise to uncertainty as to whether signatures attached to documents whose life-cycle goes through both electronic and paper phases are within the Directive. On the other hand, the wide variety of definitions in other electronic transactions legislation suggests that the task of definition is far from easy and may be better not attempted.

Electronic signatures

10–126   As to electronic signatures, Art.5.2 of the Directive provides that a Member State shall ensure that an electronic signature is not denied legal effectiveness and admissibility solely on the grounds that it is:

— in electronic form, or
— not based upon a qualified certificate, or
— not based upon a qualified certificate issued by an accredited certification-service-provider, or
— not created by a secure-signature-creation device.

We discuss below the concepts of qualified certificate, accredited certification-service-provider (CSP) and secure-signature-creation device (SSCD). Suffice it to say that this provision is intended broadly to facilitate the use of electronic signatures, while Art.5.1 permits a special status for advanced signatures created by an SSCD and supported by a qualified certificate.

The Regulations make no provision in relation to Art.5.2 of the Directive. The UK Government has taken the view that s.7 of the Electronic Communications Act 2000 adequately implements Art.5.2.[3]

10–127   The UK has already implemented, in s.7 of the Electronic Communications Act 2000, a provision broadly similar to Art.5.1 concerning electronic signatures generally. Section 7 provides:

"(1) In any legal proceedings—

(a) an electronic signature incorporated into or logically associated with a particular electronic communication or particular electronic data, and
(b) the certification by any person of such a signature, shall each be admissible in evidence in relation to any question as to the authenticity of the communication or data or as to the integrity of the communication or data.

(2) For the purposes of this section an electronic signature is so much of anything in electronic form as—

(a) is incorporated into or otherwise logically associated with any electronic communication or electronic data; and

---

[3] See the Department of Trade and Industry Discussion Document on Electronic Signatures Directive Implementing Regulations, January 25, 2002, comments on Question 5.

    (b) purports to be so incorporated or associated for the purpose of being used in establishing the authenticity of the communication or data, the integrity of the communication or data, or both.

(3) For the purposes of this section an electronic signature incorporated into or associated with a particular electronic communication or particular electronic data is certified by any person if that person (whether before or after the making of the communication) has made a statement confirming that—

    (a) the signature,
    (b) a means of producing, communicating or verifying the signature, or
    (c) a procedure applied to the signature,

is (either alone or in combination with other factors) a valid means of establishing the authenticity of the communication or data, the integrity of the communication or data, or both."

10–128 "Electronic communication" is defined (as amended by the Communications Act 2003) as meaning a communication transmitted (whether from one person to another, from one device to another or from a person to a device or vice versa):

    (a) by means of an electronic communications network; or
    (b) by other means but while in an electronic form.

"Communication" includes a communication comprising sounds or images or both and a communication effecting a payment.

References to the authenticity of any communication or data are stated to be references to any one or more of the following—

    (i)   whether the communication or data comes from a particular person or other source;
    (ii) whether it is accurately timed and dated;
    (iii) whether it is intended to have legal effect;

and references to the integrity of any communication or data are stated to be references to whether there has been any tampering with or other modification of the communication or data.

There is no definition of "electronic".

The view of the government is that these provisions meet the obligation to implement Art.5.2 of the Directive.[4] However, s.7 is not a straight transposition of Art.5.2. It is considerably more detailed and on the face of it differs in certain respects from the Directive, for instance:

---

[4] DTI Consultation on the Directive, March 2001, para.36; and see fn.3, para.10–021 above.

— it introduces a definition of authenticity which does not appear in the Directive;

— it requires that a signature be "incorporated into", rather than "attached to";

— it omits any reference to "legal effectiveness", restricting itself to admissibility;

— it places a restriction on the purposes for which the electronic signature is stated to be admissible which does not appear in the Directive.

There are also other provisions (references to integrity, admissibility of certificates) which are not expressly included in the Directive.

10–129 However, none of this matters at all if, as is likely, s.7 should be regarded as purely permissive and not intended to restrict the admissibility of signatures and certificates under the general evidential rules regarding documentary evidence. Certainly there is nothing in the Act that purports to restrict the admissibility of other electronic signatures and certificates and the Act does not include any express amendments to other evidence legislation.

In both civil and criminal proceedings a signature (whether on paper or electronic) would, we suggest, be likely to constitute "real" evidence (see discussion of evidential issues below) and therefore admissible with appropriate founding testimony. If that is correct, then no further legislative provision was ever required to secure the admissibility of electronic signatures of any nature in English proceedings. It would be most unfortunate if s.7 were to be regarded as having introduced, by implication, a restriction on such admissibility.

Advanced electronic signatures

10–130 The Directive, by Art.5.1, permits Member States to accord a special status to advanced electronic signatures which are based on a qualified certificate and which are created by a secure-signature-creation device. Member States are required to ensure that such signatures (which may perhaps be described as "qualified signatures"[5]) "satisfy the legal requirements of a signature in relation to data in electronic form in the same manner as a handwritten signature satisfies those requirements in relation to paper-based data; and are admissible as evidence in legal proceedings."

Notably, the Directive does not require Member States to ensure that only qualified signatures satisfy those requirements. It is therefore open to a Member State to permit ordinary electronic signatures also to satisfy the

---

[5] An example of descriptions adopted by some Member States to distinguish signatures that meet all the stated requirements from mere advanced signatures (see DTI Consultation Paper, para.23 (fn.4)).

requirements. That approach would be the closest to the existing English law, which (as we have noted) takes a liberal view of signature requirements in the off-line environment.[6] On that basis, under existing English law no legislation is required to implement this aspect of the Directive, since such signatures would be within the broader class of signatures that (as a matter of pure form) are already capable of satisfying English signature requirements.

Originally the Department of Trade and Industry took the view that legislation was required to implement this aspect of the Directive.[7] However, it later adopted the view suggested above that under existing English law a signature requirement in relation to data in electronic form is already capable of being satisfied by any electronic signature, including a qualified electronic signature.

English law therefore continues to make no distinction between different types of electronic or digital signature. This is an enlightened approach to implementation of the Directive. The views of the government in this respect were bolstered by an Advice to Government published by the Law Commission in December 2001, "Electronic Commerce: Formal Requirements in Commercial Transactions". The Law Commission concluded[8] that:

> "digital signatures, scanned manuscript signatures, typing one's name (or initials) and clicking on a website button are, in our view, all methods of signature which are generally capable of satisfying a statutory signature requirement. We say that on the basis that it is function, rather than form, which is determinative of the validity of a signature. These methods are all capable of satisfying the principal function: namely, demonstrating an authenticating intention."

We discuss below the requirements for an advanced electronic signature. These bring to mind, but are not limited to, the use of public key cryptography (see Ch.12 for a discussion of this), to enable the sender of a message to "sign" it with an encrypted identifier, which the recipient can decrypt using the sender's public key.

It should be borne in mind, however, that the use of advanced or qualified signatures as defined in the Directive has been miniscule and is likely to remain so. The main stimulant for any growth that may occur is likely to be government itself. The European Commission Report on the operation of the Directive,[9] published in March 2006, concluded:

---

[6] This contrasts with the position of Member States which have a tradition of requiring written contracts and accord a special status to handwritten signatures. See, for instance, "Digital Signature Legislation in Europe", Vincenzo Sinisi I.B.L. 2000, 28(11), 487–493.

[7] DTI Consultation Paper, paras. 36–38.

[8] Para.3.39.

[9] Report on the operation of Directive 1999/93/EC on a Community framework for electronic signatures, COM(2006) 120 final March 15, 2006.

"The use of qualified electronic signatures has been much less than expected and the market is not very well developed today. ... The main reason for the slow take-off of the market is economic: service providers have little incentive to develop multi-application electronic signature and prefer to offer solutions for their own services, for instance, solutions developed by the banking sector. This slows down the process of developing interoperable solutions. The lack of applications, such as comprehensive solutions for electronic archives, might also prevent the development of a multi-purpose e-signature, which requires reaching a critical mass of users and usage.

A number of applications in the future might however trigger market growth. The use of signatures in e-government services has already reached a certain volume and will probably be an important driver in the future. ... The need for secure electronic means of identification to access and use public services is essential for citizens and businesses and will promote the use of electronic signatures. Different forms of eID will be emerging and will require some degree of interoperability..."

10–131 An "advanced electronic signature" is an electronic signature that meets the following requirements:

— it is uniquely linked to the signatory;
— it is capable of identifying the signatory;
— it is created using means that the signatory can maintain under his sole control; and
— it is linked to the data to which it relates in such a manner that any subsequent change of the data is detectable.

A "qualified certificate" means a certificate which meets the requirements laid down in Annex I of the Directive and is provided by a CSP who fulfils the requirements laid down in Annex II of the Directive. A "certificate" means an electronic attestation which links signature-verification-data to a person and confirms the identity of that person. "Signature-verification-data" means data, such as codes or public cryptographic keys, which are used for the purpose of verifying an electronic signature.

10–132 An SSCD (secure-signature-creation device) means a signature-creation device which meets the requirements laid down in Annex III of the Directive. A signature-creation device means configured software or hardware used to implement the signature-creation data. "Signature-creation data" means unique data, such as codes or private cryptographic keys, which are used by the signatory to create an electronic signature.

Annexes I, II and III of the Directive contain detailed terms with which the certificate, CSP, or signature-creation device must comply if they are to qualify as a qualified certificate, CSP for the purpose of issuing a qualified certificate, or SSCD respectively.

These criteria are also of relevance to the supervision and internal market **10–133** aspects of the Directive. As to supervision, the Directive establishes the general principle that certification services (i.e. certificates or other services in relation to electronic signatures) are not to be subject to prior authorisation. So State licensing of providers would be contrary to the Directive. However, Member States may introduce voluntary accreditation schemes aiming at enhanced levels of certification-service provision.

Although Pt 1 of the Electronic Communications Act 2000 empowered the government to introduce a statutory (but still voluntary) accreditation scheme, the government gave undertakings during the passage of the Bill as to the limited circumstances in which it would consider doing this. The provisions were also subject to a "sunset" clause under which the provisions would lapse if they had not been brought into force after five years.[10] The provisions duly lapsed on May 25, 2005.

The Directive also requires Member States to introduce a system allowing for the supervision of CSPs established on its territory that issue qualified certificates to the public (Art.3.3). The DTI proposed to operate *de minimis* supervision by observation, recording and publicity, conducted by the DTI with assistance from the private sector T-Scheme.

The *de minimis* principle is reflected in the Regulations. Regulation 3(1) provides that the Secretary of State shall keep under review the carrying on of activities of certification-service-providers ("CSPs") who are established in the UK and who issue qualified certificates to the public and the persons by whom they are carried on with the view to her becoming aware of the identity of those persons and the circumstances relating to the carrying on of those activities.

Regulation 3(2) requires the Secretary of State to establish and maintain a register of CSPs who are established in the UK and who issue qualified certificates to the public. The Secretary of State is required to record in the register the names and addresses of those CSPs of whom she is aware who are established in the UK and who issue qualified certificates to the public. The register may be published in such manner as the Secretary of State considers appropriate.

Finally, the Secretary of State is required to have regard to evidence becoming available to her with respect to any course of conduct of a CSP established in the UK who issues qualified certificates to the public and which appears to her to be conduct detrimental to the interests of those persons who use or rely on those certificates with a view to making any of this evidence as she considers expedient available to the public in such manner as she considers appropriate.

It should be noted that there is no requirement that a CSP be recorded on the register. This is consistent with the prohibition in the Directive on subjecting certification services to prior authorisation. Nor is there any mechanism for removing a CSP from the register.

The internal market provisions have the effect that (other than under the

---

[10] Electronic Communications Act 2000, s.16(4).

public sector exceptions noted below) a Member State cannot impose stricter requirements for valid electronic signatures than are represented by an advanced signature based on a qualifying signature and created by an SSCD.

Liability of certain certification service providers

10–134   As to liability, we have discussed above the likely liability position of third parties who verify electronic signatures and issue certificates to persons who rely upon them. This would involve the certificate issuer in strict liability, rather than the negligence standard of a tortious duty to take reasonable care.

The Directive requires Member States to make special provision for the liability of CSPs who issue qualified certificates to the public. Article 6.1 provides that, as a minimum, Member States must ensure that by issuing a certificate as a qualified certificate to the public or by guaranteeing such a certificate to the public a certification-service-provider is liable for damage caused to any entity or legal or natural person who reasonably relies on that certificate:

(a) as regards the accuracy at the time of issuance of all information contained in the qualified certificate and as regards the fact that the certificate contains all the details prescribed for a qualified certificate;

(b) for assurance that at the time of the issuance of the certificate, the signatory identified in the qualified certificate held the signature-creation-data corresponding to the signature-verification data given or identified in the certificate;

(c) for assurance that the signature-creation data and the signature-verification-data can be used in a complementary manner in cases where the certification-service-provider generates them both

unless the certification-service-provider proves that he has not acted negligently.

Regulation 4 implements these provisions. Regulation 4(1) concerns the situation where a CSP issues a certificate as a qualified certificate to the public, or guarantees a qualified certificate to the public, and a person reasonably relies on that certificate for any of the following matters:

1. the accuracy of any of the information contained in the qualified certificate at the time of the issue;

2. the inclusion in the qualified certificate of all the details referred to in Sch.1 of the Regulations (equivalent to Annex 1 to the Directive);

3. the holding by the signatory identified in the qualified certificate at the time of its issue of the signature-creation-data corresponding to the signature-verification-data given or identified in the certificate; or

4.   the ability of the signature-creation-data and the signature-ver-
     ification-data to be used in a complementary manner in cases
     where the CSP generates them both.

If that person suffers loss as a result of such reliance, and if the CSP would
be liable in damages in respect of any extent of the loss had a duty of care
existed between him and the person relying on the certificate, and had the
CSP been negligent, then the CSP is made liable to the same extent notwithstanding that there is no proof that the CSP was negligent, unless the
CSP proves that he was not negligent.

Regulation 4(2) provides that there shall be a duty of care between the
CSP and the person relying on the certificate.

The effect of these provisions is two-fold: first, to impose a statutory duty
of care; and secondly, to reverse the normal burden of proof so that the
burden is on the CSP to prove lack of negligence once a person has
established reasonable reliance on the certificate and loss as a result of such
reliance.

Further, under Art.6.2 as a minimum, Member States shall ensure that a   **10–135**
certification-service-provider who has issued a certificate as a qualified
certificate to the public is liable for damage caused to any entity or legal or
natural person who reasonably relies on the certificate for failure to register
revocation of the certificate unless the certification-service-provider proves
that he has not acted negligently.

This requirement is implemented by reg.4(3). Member States must, under
Art.6.3, ensure that a certification-service-provider may indicate in a qualified certificate limitations on the use of that certificate (provided that the
limitations are recognisable to third parties), and that the certification-
service-provider shall not be liable for damage arising from use of a qualified certificate which exceeds the limitations placed on it.

The government's view[11] is that no specific provision to implement this
was necessary since certification service providers can already exclude liability, subject to the applicable laws on the exclusion or limitation of
liability.

Similarly, Member States must, under Art.6.4, ensure that a certification-   **10–136**
service-provider may indicate in the qualified certificate a limit on the value
of transactions for which the certificate can be used, provided that the limit
is recognisable to third parties and that the certification-service-provider
shall not be liable for damage resulting from this maximum limit being
exceeded. Again, the government's view is that no implementing legislation
was necessary to achieve this.

All the provisions of Art.6 regarding liability are stated to be without
prejudice to the Unfair Contract Terms Directive.[12]

It should noted that these liability provisions apply only to CSPs who

---

[11] Transposition Note, *www.dti.gov.uk/sectors/infosec/electronicsig/Note/page10057.html.*
[12] Council Directive 93/13 of April 5, 1993, implemented in the UK by the Unfair Terms in
Consumer Contracts Regulations 1999.

issue qualified certificates within the meaning of the Directive. Since one of the requirements for a qualified certificate is that the certificate should contain an indication that it is issued as a qualified certificate,[13] it appears that a CSP who issues certificates that in all other respects comply with the requirements of the Directive for qualified certificates would avoid the Directive's liability regime if he made no claim in the certificate that it was a qualified certificate.[14]

Data protection

10–137   The Directive places especially strict data protection obligations on certification-service-providers who issue certificates to the public. Unlike the liability provisions of the Directive, these obligations apply to all CSPs who issue certificates to the public, not just to those who issue qualified certificates.

Under Art.8.2 Member States must ensure that a certification-service-provider which issues certificates to the public may collect personal data only directly from the data subject, or after the explicit consent of the data subject, and only insofar as it is necessary for the purposes of issuing and maintaining the certificate. The data may not be collected or processed for any other purposes without the explicit consent of the data subject.

The requirements for explicit consent are analogous to those under the Data Protection Act 1998 for the processing of sensitive personal data, as to which see Ch.7.

CSPs must be permitted in a certificate to indicate a pseudonym instead of the signatory's name (Art.8.3).

Regulation 5 implements these data protection provisions.

Regulation 5(1) provides that a CSP established in the UK who issues a certificate to the public, in respect of personal data processed in the context of that establishment, shall not obtain personal data for the purpose of issuing or maintaining that certificate otherwise than directly from the data subject or after the specific consent of the data subject.

Such a CSP shall not process that personal data to a greater extent than is necessary for the purpose of issuing or maintaining that certificate, or to a greater extent than is necessary for any other purpose to which the data subject has explicitly consented, unless the processing is necessary for compliance with any legal obligation to which this CSP is subject, other than an obligation imposed by contract.

The obligation described is a duty owed to any data subject who may be affected by contravention of the provisions. A breach of that duty which causes that data subject to sustain loss or damage is actionable by him. Compliance is also enforceable by civil proceedings by the Crown for an injunction or any other appropriate relief or remedy.

---

[13] Annex I, para.(a).

[14] This assumes that the relevant Member State does not, as it is permitted to do under the Directive, apply the same liability scheme to CSPs who issue certificates of any description.

Third country qualified certificates

Article 7 of the Directive provides for the recognition of qualified certifi-   **10–138**
cates issued by non-EU CSPs. Member States must treat them as legally
equivalent to certificates issued by an EU CSP if:

— the CSP fulfils the requirements laid down under the Directive and
has been accredited under a voluntary accreditation scheme
established in a Member State; or
— the certificate is guaranteed by a CSP established within the
Community which complies with the Directive's requirements; or
— the certificate or CSP is recognised under a bilateral or multilateral
Community agreement.

The government's view is that specific provision to implement these provisions was not necessary since the definition of qualified certificate in the
Regulations does not depend on where the certification service provider
who issues the certificate is established.

Public sector

Under Art.3.7, Member States may make the use of electronic signatures in   **10–139**
the public sector subject to possible additional requirements. Such
requirements must be objective, transparent, proportionate and non-discriminatory and must relate only to the specific characteristics of the
application concerned. Such requirements may not constitute an obstacle to
cross-border services for citizens.

Under Art.11.1(a), the Member State must notify any such additional
requirements to the Commission and other Member States. Thus, any order
made under s.8(4) of the Electronic Communications Act 2000, which
enables conditions to be imposed for the use of electronic communications
and storage, would (insofar as it affects the use of electronic signatures in
the public sector) have to respect these principles.

Use of signatures in the public sector must also take account of the
internal market principle enunciated in Art.4, notably that Member States
may not restrict the provision of certification-services originating in another
Member State in the fields covered by the Directive; and that Member
States must ensure that electronic-signature products which comply with
this Directive are permitted to circulate freely in the internal market.

Thus, although government may specify the use of advanced electronic
signatures for certain transactions with government, it may not specify the
use of particular service providers or of service providers based in a particular EU country. Even if it wishes to specify additional requirements, again
those cannot specify particular service providers.

However, Recital (6) of the Directive should be noted, since it provides
that the Directive does not harmonise the provision of services with respect
to the confidentiality of information where they are covered by national
provisions concerned with public policy or public security.

Exclusions

10–140   Under Art.1, the Directive is stated not to cover aspects related to the conclusion and validity of contracts or other legal obligations where there are requirements as regards form prescribed by national or Community law, nor does it affect rules and limits, contained in national or Community law, governing the use of documents.

Recital (16) also states that the Directive is not intended to affect national law governing private agreements regulating electronic transactions between the parties, such as EDI agreements:

> "a regulatory framework is not needed for electronic signatures exclusively used within systems, which are based on voluntary agreements under private law between a specified number of participants; the freedom of parties to agree among themselves the terms and conditions under which they accept electronically signed data should be respected to the extent allowed by national law".

Further, Recital (17) states that the Directive does not seek to harmonise national rules concerning contract law, particularly the formation and performance of contracts, or other formalities of a non-contractual nature concerning signatures; and that for this reason the provisions concerning the legal effect of electronic signatures should be without prejudice to requirements regarding form laid down in national law with regard to the conclusion of contracts or the rules determining where a contract is concluded.

10.7 ELECTRONIC TRANSACTIONS LEGISLATION—A DISCUSSION

10.7.1 Background

10–141   Many countries have legislated specifically for electronic commerce and electronic transactions. Early adopters included the UK, US, Australia, Bermuda, Guernsey, Hong Kong, Ireland, Jersey, the Isle of Man, and Singapore. Many more have joined the fray since. Some of this legislation is based, to a greater or lesser degree, on the UNCITRAL Model Law on Electronic Commerce. Some EU legislation addresses e-commerce in the broadest sense, some of it (for instance parts of the Electronic Commerce Directive) specifically addressing facilitation of electronic transactions.

10.7.2 Removing obstacles to electronic transactions

The most compelling reason to legislate for electronic commerce is to 10–142
reform any existing laws that create obstacles to e-commerce. Such obstacles usually consist of laws laying down requirements of form as
preconditions to legal effectiveness. Such laws expressly or impliedly stipulate a particular medium (e.g. paper) in which information must be
contained. These laws may clearly exclude electronic form, or may create
uncertainty as to whether electronic form satisfies the requirements.

A primary objective of electronic commerce legislation is therefore to
remove such obstacles and create clarity, certainty and equality of treatment between media. Further, for those areas in which there are no
requirements of form in the existing off-line environment, the law should
naturally permit similar activities to take place online.

It is also important, and may be regarded as an aspect of equality of
treatment between media, that while electronic commerce legislation
should facilitate electronic transactions, it should not require or prescribe
their use. This is, however, as we discuss below, easier to state than to
achieve.

We also suggest that electronic commerce legislation should create, so far 10–143
as possible, a single medium-neutral legal environment governing paper and
non-paper transactions, rather than to create separate parallel regimes for
paper and electronic form. As far as possible an electronic commerce actor
should not be subjected to a two-stage process of deciding whether his
transaction is in paper or electronic form, then complying with the rules
that govern that particular form. That is not only unnecessarily burdensome, but is also predicated on an increasingly unmaintainable distinction
between paper and electronic form.

For instance, a hard copy may be scanned as a digital image, attached to
an email and sent to a mailbox equipped with text-to-voice conversion that
enables the recipient to listen to emails. The mailbox also forwards the
email and attachment via a fax conversion service to a fax machine which
stores the incoming fax on disk and prints it out on demand. What starts
and finishes as paper goes through a number of different electronic communication stages.

Similarly, is there any real difference between sending a fax to a memory-
resident fax machine, and sending an email to someone who has his email
client set to print out the email? In each case it is almost impossible to say
whether the transaction is paper or electronic; and whether a paper record
is created depends entirely on how the recipient configures his machine.

10.7.3 Achieving certainty

A second reason for legislating may be to create confidence in the legal 10–144
environment among laypersons and industry. This may involve legislating,

849

even when the majority of lawyers are agreed that the existing legal environment accommodates electronic transactions. The argument in support of the proposition that it is necessary to legislate so as to eliminate even wrongly perceived uncertainties in the legal environment[15] was well expressed, in relation to electronic signatures, by the Minister introducing the Second Reading of the UK Electronic Communications Bill[16]:

"Lawyers argue about whether electronic signatures would be recognised as valid by the courts, but we cannot afford to wait while lawyers argue and the courts decide. Instead, clause 7 will allow businesses and consumers to have confidence in electronic signatures, because it puts beyond doubt that a court can admit evidence of an electronic signature and a certificate in support of that signature not only to establish from whom the communication came, but to establish the date and time at which it was sent and whether it was intended to have legal effect."

10–145   The Chair of the US Uniform Electronic Transactions Act drafting committee also stated:

"Legal uncertainty about the enforceability and admissibility of electronic communications and records is inefficient, creates barriers to electronic commerce, and imposes unnecessary costs on participants in legitimate electronic commerce."[17]

10.7.4 Traps to be avoided when legislating for electronic commerce

10–146   It is easy to fall into error when legislating for electronic transactions. Common pitfalls encountered in such legislation include:

— it prescribes and requires, rather than facilitates, the use of electronic communications and form;
— it deliberately or inadvertently, and without sufficient justification, sets minimum standards that exclude some categories of electronic information from being legally effective;
— it is explicitly or implicitly biased towards a particular technology or assumed business model;

---

[15] A similar situation occurred in the early 1980s regarding the copyright protection of computer programs as literary works. There was no doubt among lawyers expert in the field that computer programs were protected. However, the software industry was not content until the copyright legislation was amended to make this clear.
[16] *Hansard*, November 29, 1999, Col.46.
[17] Professor Patricia Blumfeld Fry, "Impressions on California's Changes to the Uniform Electronic Transactions Act" *Electronic Commerce and Law Report*, December 22, 1999.

— it carries unacceptably high risks of unintended and undesirable consequences;

— it creates the potential for unnecessary disputes over compliance with new electronic requirements of form;

— it creates inefficient rules for which it is costly to determine the outcome;

— it seeks to intervene or regulate in inappropriate ways.

10.7.5 Facilitation versus prescription

Extreme caution should be exercised when proposing legislation that lays down new prescriptive rules for electronic commerce, as opposed to removing obstacles and uncertainties. Since electronic commerce is a fast-evolving field, the risk of unintended and undesirable consequences as a result of implementing new prescriptive rules is very high.   10–147

Caution also has to be exercised even when attempting to legislate only to facilitate electronic commerce by removing obstacles and uncertainty. When legislating to achieve facilitation it is possible by, for instance, laying down minimum standards of reliability and permanence with which the relevant records or communications must comply, inadvertently to introduce new electronic requirements of form. Legislatures have sometimes found the temptation to legislate for the reliability of electronic records to be overwhelming. We suggest that this temptation should be resisted.

The imposition of more restrictive requirements on-line than off-line is generally undesirable. To specify minimum standards of reliability and permanence in order to conclude a contract electronically, or to adduce electronic evidence of it, would be anomalous in jurisdictions such as the UK which permit the making of oral contracts. Although an oral contract may be regarded colloquially as being "not worth the paper it is written on" (reflecting the inherent unreliability of oral testimony), a court is still able to find that an oral contract has been concluded. A legal system that permits that should logically also permit electronic contracts to be made using informal means, notwithstanding concerns about unreliability and impermanence of some electronic records.   10–148

Even where existing law does set minimum standards in the off-line world by legislating for "writing", "signature" and so on there is a risk, when legislating for equivalent minimum standards for electronic communications, of in fact setting higher standards than for paper compliance.

In English law, for instance, a pencil cross on a piece of paper can qualify as a signature notwithstanding its impermanence and inherent unreliability. Paper is not an inherently reliable medium. To regard it as inherently reliable when legislating for electronic equivalence can result in the creation of a class of electronic communications outlawed as unreliable, but whose unreliable paper siblings still benefit from being within the law.

Legislation such as that of Singapore, whose avowed purpose is "to facilitate electronic communications by means of *reliable* electronic

851

records" (emphasis added),[18] is unlikely to achieve true equivalence between on-line and off-line transactions.

10–149   These risks were noted by the Australian Electronic Commerce Expert Group in its Report to the Attorney-General[19]:

> "There is always the temptation, in dealing with the law as it relates to unfamiliar and new technologies, to set the standards required of a new technology higher than those which currently apply to paper and to overlook the weaknesses that we know to inhere in the familiar."

Such "minimum standards" provisions lead to considerable difficulties of definition. They also run the risk of being over technology-specific, since the standards are inevitably drawn with today's technology and communications structures in mind.

10–150   Further, the more restrictive and the more widely applicable are such "minimum standards", the greater the risk that a jurisdiction will re-introduce the injustices associated with widespread legal requirements of form. In the UK in 1937 the Sixth Interim Report of the Law Revision Committee[20] set out a number of reasons why most of s.4 of the Statute of Frauds 1677 and s.4 of the Sale of Goods Act 1893[21] should be repealed (as they subsequently were in 1954). Amongst the many criticisms noted, the following was especially powerful:

> " 'The Act', in the words of Lord Campbell ... 'promotes more frauds than it prevents'. True, it shuts out perjury; but it also and more frequently shuts out the truth. It strikes impartially at the perjurer and at the honest man who has omitted a precaution, sealing the lips of both. Mr Justice FitzJames Stephen ... went so far as to assert that 'in the vast majority of cases its operation is simply to enable a man to break a promise with impunity, because he did not write it down with sufficient formality'."

10–151   The temptation to legislate for minimum acceptable standards of electronic form should, we suggest, be tempered by the risk of doing injustice by denying a person his rights through failure to comply with a required form. That risk is compounded in a new environment in which sophisticated technical knowledge may be required on the part of the user to determine what complies with the electronic requirement of form, such as to identify an appropriately reliable identification method for an electronic

---

[18] Electronic Transactions Bill 1998, s.3(a).
[19] *Electronic Commerce: Building the Legal Framework*, March 31, 1998. See also the comments of Laddie J. in *Re a debtor (No.2021 of 1995)* [1996] 2 All E.R. 345, at 351b.
[20] May 1937, Cmnd 5449.
[21] Which laid down, *inter alia*, a requirement of writing as a condition of the enforceability of contracts for the sale of goods of the value of £10 or upwards.

signature (as required by Art.7 of the UNCITRAL Model Electronic Commerce Law).

Electronic commerce legislation, if it is to remove uncertainty, should be clear. The EU Distance Selling Directive illustrates the problems that can be caused by lack of clarity in legislating for e-commerce. Article 5 of the Directive specifies information that the consumer must receive by way of confirmation of the transaction. The consumer must receive "written confirmation or confirmation in another durable medium available and accessible to him" of the relevant information. However, as discussed above (section 10.2.1), this is not defined so as to make clear which electronic forms would comply with this.

To leave a point of such significance open to serious doubt in legislation promulgated with e-commerce specifically in mind is most undesirable.

10.7.6 The evolution of electronic transactions legislation

Electronic transactions legislation typically allows and legislates for electronic versions of traditional legal concepts such as contract, document, record, notice, instrument, signature, attestation, sealing, and notarisation. Such legislation typically also seeks to translate into the electronic environment traditional legislative requirements of form and process such as writing, record and document retention requirements, requirements to produce documents, service and delivery of documents and aspects of sending and receipt of documents such as time and place of sending and receipt.   **10–152**

Legislation may also address issues such as the liability of electronic intermediaries, the ability to use encryption and the use of electronic agents.

Early legislation in, for instance, the field of electronic signatures, was highly technology specific. Typically it legislated for the use of digital signatures based on public key encryption. Such legislation was criticised on the basis not only that it sought to enshrine particular, unproven, technologies in legislation, but also that it sought to legislate for particular assumed business models that would not evolve naturally in the marketplace.[22] Such legislation was highly prescriptive, tending to legislate for high levels of reliability and security.[23]   **10–153**

Such legislation was also medium-specific, in that it effectively established separate regimes for electronic and non-electronic transactions. As we have noted above, the increasing convergence of electronic and non-

---

[22] See, for instance, C Bradford Biddle, "Legislating Market Winners" *World Wide Web Journal* Vol. II Issue 3, Summer 1997 (*http://web.archive.org/web/20030418022758, http://www.w3j.com/7/s3.biddle.wrap.html*).

[23] For surveys of US and international digital and electronic signature legislation from 1997 onwards refer to the Internet Law and Policy Forum Electronic Authentication Working Group (*www.ilpf.org/groups/index.html#authentication*).

electronic transactions means that the attempt to distinguish between the two is already relatively meaningless.[24]

There is now increasing acceptance that the early approach was erroneous. The 1995 Utah Digital Signature Act, the first US state digital signatures legislation, was a fine example of the prescriptive public key model. It was repealed in May 2006, 11 years to the day after it came into force.

10–154   Following the criticism of earlier electronic transactions and signature legislation, more recent legislation has tended to be more technology neutral and more facilitative. Thus, legislation such as the EU Electronic Signatures Directive recognises the legal effectiveness and admissibility in evidence of all forms of electronic signature (including, for instance, typing one's name at the end of an email). Similarly, the UNCITRAL Model Law on Electronic Commerce does not seek to enshrine a particular technology for electronic signatures.

Nonetheless, legislation such as these still tend to lean in favour of enshrining minimum standards. This is reflected in the favourable treatment given in the EU Electronic Signatures Directive to "advanced" electronic signatures (which are somewhat akin to the old public key digital signature model).

Article 7 of the UNCITRAL Model Law provides that where the law requires a signature of a person, that requirement is met if (*inter alia*) the method used to identify the person and indicate the person's approval of the information is "as reliable as was appropriate for the purpose for which the message was generated or communicated in the light of all the circumstances including any relevant agreement".

Thus, although not enshrining any particular technology, this provision contemplates a hierarchy of electronic signatures of differing reliability, some of which will not satisfy legal requirements in relation to some types of transaction. The same criticism can be made of the UNCITRAL Model Law on Electronic Signatures, which adopts the same terminology. Much of this draft Model Law is also predicated on the existence of business and technology models based on certifying reliable signatures. Since as yet it is not known whether these models will prove to embody an appropriate balance of cost, benefit and ease of use, the assumption may or may not turn out to be justified.

10–155   Some of the most recent legislation takes a further step forward by being wholly technology neutral, more medium neutral and highly facilitative. Legislation of this type contains, for instance, broad electronic signature definitions with no minimum standards.

This can be seen in, for instance, the US Uniform Electronic Transactions

---

[24] It should be noted, for instance, that the most recent definition of an electronic signature (in the US UETA and E-SIGN legislation), encompasses electronic signature of a non-electronic document. This differs from the definitions in the EU Electronic Signatures Directive and the UK Electronic Communications Act 2000, which only encompass electronic signature of an electronic document.

Act (UETA) and the US Federal "E-SIGN" legislation.[25] The definition of "electronic signature" used in s.7 of the UK Electronic Communications Act 2000 is also broadly facilitative, although slightly more restrictive than that used in the US legislation.

The differing approaches to electronic commerce legislation are explained not only by evolving views about what such legislation should aim to achieve, but also the variety of legal systems with differing requirements of form in the off-line environment. **10–156**

Jurisdictions that place great store by formal requirements of notarisation, sealing and so on to validate traditional transactions[26] are likely to be naturally inclined towards replicating such systems in the electronic environment. Those jurisdictions such as the UK, on the other hand, that traditionally impose few requirements of form in the off-line environment are likely to be more open to the view that electronic transactions legislation should be broadly facilitative and not prescriptive.

We have noted above that one of the objections to the prescriptive approach is that the imposition of minimum standards creates new electronic requirements of form and that such requirements can be used by the unscrupulous to evade what would otherwise be binding legal obligations. The UNCITRAL Model Law on Electronic Commerce has been influential and certain of its electronic requirements of form have been widely reproduced in legislation.

For instance, the US E-SIGN legislation (which on the question of signatures is extremely facilitative) defines "writing" as involving an "electronic record ... in a form which is capable of being retained and accurately reproduced for later reference ...". This is similar to the UNCITRAL provision, that where the law requires information to be in writing, that requirement is met by a data message if "the information contained therein is accessible so as to be useable for subsequent reference".

However, these types of provision will inevitably lead to debate, uncertainty and costly court arguments about whether any particular electronic record satisfies the requirement. For instance, a document saved in a common word processing format may appear differently, even using the same word processor software, depending on what fonts are installed on the software and how it is configured. **10–157**

We suggest that formal requirements of this sort are unhelpful. A useful comparison may be drawn with s.178 of the UK Copyright Designs and Patents Act 1988 which defines writing for the purposes of Pt 1 of that Act as including "any form of notation or code, whether by hand or otherwise and regardless of the method by which, all medium in or on which, it is recorded".

We have already mentioned the the reliability requirement in the elec-

---

[25] Electronic Signatures in Global and National Commerce Act, Pub. L. No.106–229.
[26] See, for instance, the presentations at the Joint Keidanren/Internet Law and Policy Forum Workshop on Electronic Signatures and Authentication held in Tokyo in November 1999, especially those describing the Japanese "Inkan" seal system (*www.ilpf.org/events/keidanren/*).

tronic signature provisions of the UNCITRAL Model Laws on Electronic Commerce and Electronic Signatures. Such a requirement will inevitably engender immense uncertainty as to the type of signature that is appropriate for a particular type of transaction. It also suffers from the problem that it requires the user to assess the reliability of the proposed type of signature and therefore to be familiar with electronic and digital signature technologies. This is wholly unrealistic. Few IT experts understand these technologies, let alone non-expert users.

It is noteworthy that the latest emanation from UNCITRAL, the Convention on the Use of Electronic Communications in International Contracts, has stepped back from the reliability requirement of the Model Laws on Electronic Commerce and Electronic Signatures. The Convention (which is open for signature until 2008) provides that:

> "Where the law requires that a communication or a contract should be signed by a party, or provides consequences for the absence of a signature, that requirement is met in relation to an electronic communication if:
>
> (a) A method is used to identify the party and to indicate that party's intention in respect of the information contained in the electronic communication; and
> (b) The method used is either:
>
>   (i) As reliable as appropriate for the purpose for which the electronic communication was generated or communicated, in the light of all the circumstances, including any relevant agreement; or
>   (ii) Proven in fact to have fulfilled the functions described in subparagraph (a) above, by itself or together with further evidence."

The significant difference compared with previous texts is in the inclusion of sub-para.(b)(ii) as an alternative to (b)(i).

10.7.7 Efficient and inefficient rules

10–158 We have referred to some difficulties with technology-specific approaches. There is also danger in creating rules that require technological investigation to determine the outcome of the rule. This investigation is inevitably costly and results in an inefficient rule.

A good example of such a rule is the UNCITRAL Model Law provisions regarding time of receipt of an electronic message. For an information system which has not been designated by the recipient, UNCITRAL, Art.15 provides that the message is deemed received "when the data message enters an information system of the addressee".

Such a rule may be practicable where two large companies with IT departments are communicating electronically with each other on a pre-agreed basis. If necessary, the two companies can keep gateway logs that can be examined to determine when the relevant event occurred. However, a rule such as this is wholly unrealistic for a home PC user.

A rule that requires IT experts to be employed to determine (if it can be done at all) the deemed time of receipt of a message is, we suggest, inappropriate, costly and inefficient.

In the off-line world, rules about service and delivery of documents tend   **10–159** to provide for a presumption of service or delivery after the expiry of a conventional period after, for instance, posting, and do not investigate when the post office actually delivered the item. Such a factual investigation tends to take place only if the alleged recipient wishes to challenge actual receipt, if at all.[27]

The Australian Electronic Transactions Act 1999 provides for receipt "when the electronic communication comes to the attention of the addressee".[28] Again, conventional rules of service tend to focus on an easily ascertainable event, such as posting or delivery, to establish a presumption of service, and not to enquire except perhaps in the case of a challenge to the presumption when the individual actually became aware of it.

When considering appropriate rules of delivery and receipt for electronic communications, as with off-line provisions, both the efficiency of the rule and justice to the recipient have to be taken into account and an appropriate balance achieved.

A recent example of a conventional rule to determine service of an email   **10–160** notice is contained in reg.10 of the Consumer Protection (Distance Selling) Regulations 2000. This provides that a cancellation notice given by a consumer is to be treated as properly given if the consumer "sends it by electronic mail, to the business electronic mail address last known to the consumer (in which case it is to be taken to have been given on the day on which it is sent)".

An attempt to replicate the traditional concept of the last known business address, coupled with an attempt to avoid the need for technical (although not all factual) enquiries can be seen here. However, it may be commented that the notion of when an email is "sent" is by no means as simple as may first appear. What if the sender presses the send button, but the email remains in the outbox for some period until the system is ready to forward it through a gateway to the outside world? What if the sender presses the send button, but sets a time delay?

Considerations such as these have led to UNCITRAL-style formulations such as when the message enters or leaves a person's information system. But as we have pointed out, these have their own problems. It will probably only be with experience of applying early attempts at rules that the appropriate balance can be achieved.

---

[27] See e.g. *Godwin v Swindon BC* CA, *The Independent*, October 19, 2001, and *WX Investments Ltd v Begg* [2002] 1 W.L.R. 2849.
[28] S.14.

A more recent example of balancing modernisation with justice to the recipient is contained in the amendments to the Consumer Credit Act 1974 made in 2004. These deal with, amongst other things, the circumstances in which notices may be given electronically and when such notices are deemed to be given.

So, for a notice of cancellation sent electronically by the debtor or hirer, the notice is deemed to be served at the time of transmission.[29] However any other electronically transmitted notice is, unless the contrary is proved, treated as having been delivered on the working day immediately following the day on which it is transmitted.[30]

A case that raised some eyebrows, and should certainly have organisations rushing to check their email inboxes, was *Bernuth Lines Ltd v High Seas Shipping Ltd*.[31] It could be said that with this case email has come of age as a recognised means of business and official communication.

The case concerned the validity of service of arbitration proceedings concerning a shipping dispute at the applicant's email address at "info@-bernuth.com". The email address appeared on the applicant's website and in the Lloyds Maritime Directory. The applicant's solicitors sent the initiating documentation by email to that address. There followed a series of eight further emails from the defendant's solicitors and the arbitrator as the arbitration proceeded. The emails from the defendants' solicitors generated confirmation receipts. Finally, the arbitrator issued his final award, which he sent to the applicant by email at the same address and by post. At that point, for the first time, solicitors appeared for the applicant, saying that their client had been unaware of the award.

10–161   Under the Arbitration Act 1996, arbitration proceedings are commenced by notice to the other party. In the absence of agreement as to the manner of service, under s.76(3) of the Act, "A notice or other document may be served by any effective means."

The applicant applied to set aside the award on the ground that the arbitration was purportedly commenced by email but not effectively served. The applicant's evidence was that the emails were ignored as "spam". "The Customer Service Representative took the view that no serious legal matter would be sent to the Applicant using that address" and "that the email was not serious and that serious legal correspondence would go through appropriate channels."

The judge held that the notice commencing the arbitration proceedings had been validly served. He was influenced by the fact that arbitrations are usually conducted by businessmen represented by, or with ready access to, lawyers. He went on to say:

---

[29] Consumer Credit Act 2004, s.69(7), as substituted by the Consumer Credit Act 1974 (Electronic Communications) Order 2004 (SI 2004/3236).
[30] Consumer Credit Act 2004, s.176A(2).
[31] [2005] EWHC 3020 (Comm).

"Section 76(3), when providing that a notice could be served on a person by any effective means was, in my judgment, purposely wide. It contemplates that any means of service will suffice provided that it is a recognised means of communication effective to deliver the document to the party to whom it is sent at his address for the purpose of that means of communication (e.g. post, fax or email). There is no reason why, in this context, delivery of a document by email—a method habitually used by businessmen, lawyers and civil servants—should be regarded as essentially different from communication by post, fax or telex.

29. That is not to say that clicking on the 'send' icon automatically amounts to good service. The email must, of course, be despatched to what is, in fact, the email address of the intended recipient. It must not be rejected by the system. If the sender does not require confirmation of receipt he may not be able to show that receipt has occurred. There may be circumstances where, for instance, there are several email addresses for a number of different divisions of the same company, possibly in different countries, where despatch to a particular email address is not effective service.

30. But in the present case none of those difficulties arise. The email of 5th May 2005 and, so it would appear, all subsequent emails, were received at an email address that was held out to the world as the, and so far as the evidence shows, the only email address of Bernuth. Someone looked at the emails on receipt and, apparently, decided that they could be ignored, without making any contact with the sender. The position is, to my mind, no different to the receipt at a company's office of a letter or telex which, for whatever reason, someone at the company decides to discard. In both cases service has effectively been made, and the document received will, in the first instance, be dealt with by a clerical officer. . . .

34. In short I do not regard service of the 5th May notice by email as ineffective because, when it was received, a particular employee did not think that a serious legal matter would be sent to that address. That email and those that followed it, are plain and straightforward in their terms. They bear none of the hallmarks of 'spam'. On the contrary they called for serious attention. The email of 5th May was sent with High Importance. It referred to a vessel which Bernuth had in fact chartered by the charterparty mentioned in it. It identified Swinnerton Moore as High Seas' London solicitors, which they were, and referred to an outstanding hire claim which had been the subject of earlier correspondence. It purported to initiate arbitration proceedings by calling for agreement as to an arbitrator. I should be surprised if much junk email purports to do that or to emanate, as later emails did, from an LMAA arbitrator. If the emails never reached the

relevant managerial and legal staff, that is an internal failing which does not affect the validity of service and for which Bernuth has only itself to blame. Having put info@bernuth.com into the current Lloyd's Maritime Directory as their only email address, they can scarcely be surprised to find that an email inviting them to agree to the appointment of an arbitrator in a maritime matter was sent to that address.

35. I do not accept that, in an arbitration context, in order for service to be effective it is essential that the email address at which service is purportedly made has been notified to the serving party as an address to be used in the context of the relevant dispute. Section 76 does not say as much and there is no basis upon which that can be implied.''

A book on internet law is not the place to explore further, in the light of this judgment, precisely when arbitration proceedings can and cannot be validly served at a given email address. Rather, this case illustrates nicely the issues that can arise as the internet matures into an acceptable means of formal communication.

10.7.8 Facilitating without requiring the use of electronic transactions

10–162 While the facilitative approach to electronic transactions has been gaining ground, that approach is not free of difficulties. The main problem is how to facilitate use of electronic form, while avoiding legislation that compels the use of electronic form or means. In the case of a bilateral transaction, one party's facilitation is the other party's compulsion.

While, as enacted in some jurisdictions, it is possible to provide that use of electronic form in bilateral transactions requires the other party's consent, that substantially reduces the utility of the legislation from the point of view of the party who wishes to use electronic form. But the alternative amounts to compelling the other party to use electronic form.

The problem is especially acute where the document or communication has direct legal consequences, such as service of proceedings, statutory notices and so on. Take, for example, the case of a company receiving notices under companies legislation. Should a company be entitled to insist on receiving hard copy notices? If so, does that apply whether or not the company has electronic facilities such as an email address? If it is prepared to accept electronic notices, should it be entitled to specify particular rules and processes for receipt of such notices, including its own rules as to when they will be deemed received?

These questions do raise extremely difficult issues which have only recently been seriously addressed.[32]

In the modernised Consumer Credit Act regime mentioned above, the use of electronic communications requires the agreement of the recipient to the document being transmitted to a particular electronic address in a particular electronic form.[33] Some types of communication (default, enforcement and termination notices) are excluded from the electronic communication regime completely.

The reason for this is explained in the Explanatory Memorandum[34] accompanying the legislation:

"Default, enforcement and termination notices have been singled-out as a special case because they are issued to borrowers who have breached the regulated agreement (e.g. fallen behind with their repayments) or where the creditor or owner wishes to terminate the regulated agreement for reasons other than a breach. The effect of default action or termination will have a significant impact on the rights of the debtor or hirer. The likelihood that default is a result of financial hardship, and that individuals who are experiencing such financial difficulties may no longer have access to the equipment or network access that enabled them to contract by electronic communications in the first place, makes an insistence on paper communication by post an essential safeguard."

There are also often questions about whether facilitation should apply to transactions with government in the same way as for transactions between private persons.　　　　　　　　　　　　　　　　　　　　　　　　　**10–163**

These difficulties have led to two widely differing approaches. First there is the "macro" approach of the US UETA and E-SIGN legislation, which is to legislate, as an overlay over existing legislation, a broad and wide-ranging facilitation of electronic form and means. This has been done in the knowledge that it may lead to potential anomalies. As the Chair of the Drafting Committee for the US Uniform Electronic Transactions Act Law (UETA) put it:

"... UETA preserves the requirements concerning the manner of sending, posting, displaying, formatting, etc. contained in other State law. If other State law requires information to be furnished in a conspicuous manner, UETA § 8 states that you can furnish the

---

[32] The US E-SIGN legislation contains the most comprehensive attempt so far to address the issues. In the UK, some of the difficulties involved in facilitating electronic transactions can be seen from the fact that legislation addressing one area alone (communication with shareholders and filing returns at Companies House), the Companies Act 1985 (Electronic Communications) Order 2000, runs to 32 sections and two Schedules.

[33] Consumer Credit Act 1974, s.176A(1)(a).

[34] *www.opsi.gov.uk/SI/em2004/uksiem_20043236_en.pdf.*

information electronically, but must do so in a conspicuous manner. If other State law requires the information to appear in purple ink sprinkled with glitter, you can furnish the information electronically only if you can assure that it appear to the recipient in purple sprinkled with glitter.[35]"

The alternative, "micro" approach is that adopted by the UK in s.8 of the Electronic Communications Act 2000. This provides a rule-making power whereby existing legislation can be amended to provide for electronic form and means on a case by case basis (such as the amendments to the Consumer Credit Act discussed above). This allows for the elimination of anomalies and unintended consequences. However, it suffers from the disadvantage of potential institutional inertia, bearing in mind the massive amount of legislation that may have to be amended on a case by case basis.[36]

10–164 Typical examples of exclusions from the "macro" approach are areas such as real property, wills and testamentary instruments, trusts, negotiable instruments, documents of title and powers of attorney. The E-SIGN legislation carries the exclusions into other fields such as proximity requirements concerning warnings and notices, notices of cancellation or termination of utility services, notice of default, foreclosure, eviction, etc. in relation to an individual's primary residence, notice of cancellation or termination of health or life assurance, notice of product recall and any document required to accompany transportation or handling of hazardous materials and the like.

The E-SIGN provisions for consumer consent to use of electronic records state that a consumer may consent to the use of an electronic record where a statute requires information to be provided or made available to a consumer in writing. The writing requirement is satisfied if the consumer has affirmatively consented and not withdrawn that consent and, prior to consenting, a clear and conspicuous statement has been provided satisfying a lengthy list of statutory requirements.

10–165 In summary, it is suggested that electronic transactions legislation should be facilitative and technology neutral. It should also be medium neutral, avoiding the creation of new electronic requirements of form and avoiding the temptation to legislate for reliability. However, such legislation has to respect the rights of recipients of electronic records and communications and reconcile the inherent conflict between sender and recipient's rights.

Legislation should seek efficient and just solutions to the problems raised by the facilitating electronic form and means. That may require a very different approach to electronic transactions legislation than has been common in many countries to date.

---

[35] Professor Patricia Blumfeld Fry, "A Preliminary Analysis of Federal and State Electronic Commerce Laws", *Electronic Commerce and Law Report*, Vol.5 No.7, July 12, 2000.
[36] At the time of writing 24 UK and 4 Scottish orders have been made.

10.8 EVIDENCE—PROVING THE TRANSACTION

As with other contracts, there may be occasions on which the existence and/ **10–166**
or terms of a contract formed over the internet must be established in court.
The most likely scenario for this is where there is a dispute as to its terms
and whether they have been complied with, or even where a party denies
that he was the person who made the contract. Problems of identity are of
particular relevance with regard to the internet, given that the parties are
unlikely to have any other form of personal contact.

There are two main considerations in this context: what evidence of the
contract will be admissible and what weight will that evidence carry in
court?

10.8.1 Which law of evidence?

The first point to note is that matters of evidence and procedure are gen- **10–167**
erally a matter for the law of the forum in which the case is tried. So if a
cross-border contract dispute were heard in an English court, English rules
of evidence would apply even if the substantive law of the contract were
that of some other jurisdiction.

Under the Convention on the Law Applicable to Contractual Obligations
1980 (the Rome Convention), enacted in the UK by the Contracts
(Applicable Law) Act 1990, the following principles generally apply to
cross-border contract disputes tried in England:

— As regards matters of form, a contract is valid if it satisfies the laws
of any of the following three countries: the country of the
applicable law, or either of the countries in which the parties were
when the contract was concluded (Art.9(2)).
— A contract can be proved by a method recognised by the law of the
forum or of any of the laws mentioned in Art.9 under which the
contract is formally valid, provided that such method of proof can
be administered by the forum (Art.14(2)).
— The applicable law applies on matters of presumptions of law or
burden of proof (Art.14(1)).

The dividing line between form and evidence is not always clear. Even **10–168**
where it is clear, foreign formal requirements can be relevant.

Assuming (as is the case) that English requirements of form (such as
writing) are relatively few, it might be thought that someone setting up a
website in England should not be too concerned about the possibility of
formal requirements affecting the validity of on-line contracts in countries
from which the site can be accessed, so long as the dispute is litigated in
England. While that may be true of commercial contracts, if the contract is
a consumer contract concluded in circumstances in which the applicable

law is that of the consumer's habitual residence (as to which see above, para.10–072), then the formal requirements of that country will apply.[37]

10.8.2 Proving the transaction

10–169 On the assumption that the contract has been formed by the exchange of emails or the response by the offeree to a web page, the contract may be recorded in a number of different ways. The offeror may have made an electronic record of the exchange of electronic messages. The offeree may have such a record. Either party may have printed out a hard copy of the exchange. Each party may have a record of part of the exchange.

Problems are likely to arise only where there is a disagreement between the parties to the exchange of messages, either as to their content or their timing, and there is conflicting oral evidence. In such event, the court is likely to be requested to look at the electronic or hard copy records of the transaction to resolve the issue.

Until relatively recently, in civil litigation, the admissibility of electronic records in evidence was bedevilled by technical rules which applied to computer-produced documents, combined with restrictions on hearsay evidence (including documentary evidence).

10–170 However, the Civil Evidence Act 1995, which came into force on January 31, 1997, abolished the computer evidence rules and introduced a relaxed scheme for admission into evidence of hearsay. It also includes a provision that a document which is shown to form part of the records of a business or public authority may be received in evidence in civil proceedings without further proof. There are provisions for certificates to be provided as to the status of the documents as business records. "Documents" include electronic documents.

Notwithstanding the relaxation of the rules about admissibility of evidence, the judge is given a wide discretion as the weight he will attach to the evidence before him. It is of little use the judge reading the document if he does not believe it. So a party must pay careful attention to ensure that its procedures and record-keeping will enable it to satisfy the court as to what occurred when, who the parties were, what the contents of the electronic documents were, and so on.

Bearing in mind that these matters may have to be proved years after the event, it is sensible either to generate hard copies at the time and keep them safe, or to put in place tamper-proof electronic archiving systems (e.g. on CD-ROM, DVD or a secure online system) operated by persons who can give evidence to the court of the way in which the information was recorded (to show that it was a true record at the time) and of the way in which it has been preserved since. Issues such as the source and reliability of date and time-stamping and other information contained in the record should be carefully considered.

---

[37] Contracts (Applicable Law) Act 1990, Sch.1, Art.9(5).

Consideration must be given to the subject-matter, value and significance of the contract, the likelihood of disputes arising and the purposes for which the evidence will be needed.

We now discuss in more detail the rules of evidence. For completeness we have included criminal, as well as civil, proceedings.

Admissibility and weight of evidence

If a document is admissible the court is able to look at it. It is not excluded **10–171** from the court's consideration. There remains, however, the question of the weight that the court will attach to an admissible document. How much reliance will the court place on the document? How useful will the document be? This is nowadays a much more important question than admissibility.

The modern trend of the English courts is to admit the evidence and leave the judge to gauge its weight, rather than become embroiled in technical disputes about whether the judge should look at the document at all. For instance, under the Civil Evidence Act 1995 the general prohibition on admitting hearsay evidence (including hearsay in documentary form) has been abolished. This trend can be expected to apply as much to electronic records as to any other form of documentary evidence.

However, an electronic record will be of little use if the judge will not accept it as a reliable guide to what actually happened. Procedures to be adopted in relation to electronic records should be directed as much at maximising the court's confidence in the record as to overcoming any perceived obstacles to admissibility as such.

What are electronic records?

Electronic records are a form of documentary evidence and, subject to any **10–172** specific requirements applicable to computer evidence, their evidential status will be assessed as such. The application of the rules of documentary evidence to electronic records is discussed in detail below. At the risk of oversimplifying a complex topic, an electronic record is potentially inadmissible only if:

(1) it constitutes real evidence and admissible evidence to establish its provenance is not available[38]; or
(2) it is hearsay evidence that is otherwise admissible but cannot be authenticated in a manner approved by the court.[39]

An electronic record may also be accorded no weight (which is tantamount **10–173** to being held inadmissible) if (in the absence of special circumstances) it is a

---

[38] See e.g. *R. v Cochrane* [1993] Crim.L.R. 48, CA, for an example of a case in which insufficient evidence of the workings of a building society ATM system was adduced. Compare with *R. v. Shephard* [1993] A.C. 380.
[39] See s.8, Civil Evidence Act 1995 and s.133, Criminal Justice Act 2003.

copy of another document and the original document is readily available and withheld.[40] A copy may be admissible under s.8 of the Civil Evidence Act 1995 ("CEA") (for civil proceedings) or s.133 Criminal Justice Act 2003 (for criminal proceedings).

If it is a copy of a copy and is not admissible by virtue of those statutory provisions, then it may still be a requirement of admissibility that evidence be available to authenticate each copy in the chain, although the modern practice is to approach these matters as a question of weight of evidence, allowing the judge discretion whether to admit evidence and how much weight to place on it rather than laying down absolute prohibitions on admissibility.[41]

Otherwise an electronic record ought to be admissible to the same extent as any other documentary evidence.

Documentary evidence can, for present purposes, be divided into three categories: hearsay evidence, real evidence, and copies. The basis on which each is admissible in evidence may differ.

Hearsay evidence

10–174 This is a record that embodies information emanating from a human being—e.g. a note made by a scientist recording his observation or opinion. Hearsay is admissible as evidence in criminal proceedings if it falls within an exception to the hearsay rule (see below) and is now generally admissible in civil proceedings. A computer record or output may constitute hearsay evidence, but does not necessarily do so (see below).

Real evidence

10–175 Real evidence generally refers to physical objects such as smoking guns or bloody knives. Someone gives evidence that the item was found at the scene, describes how it was preserved for the trial and the item is then admitted in evidence. As extended to documents, real evidence means a non-human statement in a document. For instance, a recording made by an unattended radar scanner or an automatic camera would be real evidence, the trace or film representing an observation made entirely by the machine. There would need to be founding testimony establishing that the trace or film was in fact produced by the machine.[42]

Evidence for this purpose would be, for instance, evidence from someone who was responsible for the machine and could give evidence of the trace or film having been removed, logged and stored, thereby establishing the authenticity of the document.

Some computer records may constitute real evidence, not hearsay. In *R. v*

---

[40] This situation is now to be approached as a matter of weight of evidence, rather than admissibility. The old "best evidence" rule has finally expired. *Masquerade Music Ltd v Springsteen* [2001] 4 E.M.L.R. 654.

[41] *ibid.*

[42] *Statue of Liberty* [1968] 2 All E.R. 195.

Governor of Brixton Prison, Ex *p. Levin*[43] the House of Lords held that computer printouts recording transfers of funds were not hearsay and therefore were not inadmissible as hearsay. The printouts recorded the transfers themselves, created by the interaction between whoever purported to request the transfers and the computer. The evidential status of the printouts was no different from that of a photocopy of a forged cheque.

In *R.* v *Coventry Magistrates Court*[44] printouts from a web server database recording accesses to websites and corresponding name, physical address, email address and credit card number were held admissible as real evidence.

Another form of real evidence is a document which contains no relevant assertive statements. An example of this is a disputed contract. The issue may be whether or not the defendant signed it. In that case the document is real evidence on the basis of which a forensic document examiner will give expert evidence. If the dispute is about the interpretation of the contract, the document is real evidence because it evidences the legal obligations entered into, not statements by the author of the document asserting some fact on which someone wants to rely. This applies to documents in electronic form as much as to paper documents. **10–176**

Similarly a signature (whether manuscript or electronic) ought to be regarded as real evidence. However, a certificate authenticating a digital signature would be a hearsay record of a statement made by the issuer of the certificate.[45]

The boundary between real evidence and hearsay is sometimes blurred, particularly if the interaction between human being and machine is such that it is not clear whether the document has recorded information observed only by machine—for instance, where a human being is operating the machine.[46]

---

[43] [1997] A.C. 741.

[44] [2004] EWHC 905 (Admin).

[45] Note the comment to this effect at para.42 of the Digital Signature Guidelines, July 2000, published by the Judicial Studies Board (*www.jsboard.co.uk*). Although the Guidelines suggest that in criminal proceedings the admissibility of the certificate would have to be considered under s.24, Criminal Justice Act 1988 (now s.117, Criminal Justice Act 2003), that would only appear to be necessary if the certificate were to be used for a purpose outside the scope of the "deemed admissibility" provisions of s.7 of the Electronic Communications Act 2000.

[46] See the case of *R.* v *Pettigrew* (1980) 71 Cr. App. R. 39 for an example of this confusion. The case involved a printout from a Bank of England computer which listed the first and last numbers of a consignment of checked banknotes. The operator of the checking machine entered the first number of the sequence. The computer calculated the last number taking into account any notes rejected and also calculated the numbers of the rejected notes. The court rejected the printout as inadmissible as a business record under the Criminal Evidence Act 1965. It has been suggested that the court could have admitted the record on the basis that it was real evidence (even though the counter was set initially by a human being), the basis of the court's decision having been that the information on the printout contained no human knowledge. That appears to have been the approach of the House of Lords in *R.* v *Governor of Brixton Prison,* Ex *p. Levin* (above).

Direct versus hearsay evidence

10–177 Because documents so often constitute hearsay evidence, it is impossible to consider the admission of documentary evidence (including electronic records) without taking into account the rules about hearsay evidence. In civil proceedings the distinction is far less important than it used to be, since hearsay is now generally admissible in civil proceedings. The distinction still retains considerable importance in criminal proceedings.

The courts have always been suspicious of hearsay evidence and have in the past excluded it unless it falls within special exceptions permitting admissibility. Unfortunately the subject of hearsay evidence is complex and confusing, so much so that Lord Reid said in 1964 that it was "difficult to make any general statement about the law of hearsay evidence which is entirely accurate",[47] and went on to comment that even so concise an author as Professor Cross took over 100 closely packed pages to explain hearsay evidence. We shall attempt it in a few paragraphs.

10–178 The core of a trial is that human witnesses in person tell the court what they themselves *did* and *saw*. That is direct evidence. What the witness *heard* is also direct evidence of events such as bangs, crashes, screams and gunshots.

But if Client A says that he heard Trainee Z saying "I saw Lawyer X drunk on the street", that could be either direct evidence or hearsay evidence, depending on what is to be proved.

If Lawyer X is complaining that he was defamed by Trainee Z's statement, then Client A is giving direct evidence that he heard Trainee Z make the statement.

If Lawyer X is prosecuted for drunkenness, then Client A would be giving hearsay evidence of what Trainee Z saw. That would be first-hand hearsay (i.e. evidence at one remove). If Trainee Z wrote on a board "I saw Lawyer X drunk in the street", then the board would be first-hand hearsay evidence of what she saw.

In a libel action by Lawyer X against Trainee Z the board would be real evidence, not hearsay, because the relevant facts to be proved would be the existence and publication of the statement on the board. But Lawyer X would still have to prove that the inscription on the board originated from Trainee Z.

Civil evidence—hearsay

10–179 Under the Civil Evidence Act 1995, hearsay is generally admissible in civil proceedings. This is subject to procedural safeguards—notice has to be given that hearsay evidence will be adduced, and the person whose statement has been tendered as hearsay can be called. Further, guidelines (discussed further below) are given as to the weight a court should place on hearsay statements.

---

[47] *Myers v DPP* [1964] 2 All E.R. 881.

Criminal evidence—hearsay

The rules about documents constituting "real" evidence are the same in   **10–180**
criminal proceedings as in civil proceedings. In fact most of the law concerning this has been made in criminal cases, where the rules as to evidence
tend to be more strictly observed than in civil proceedings.

As to hearsay statements in documents, the relevant provisions governing
admissibility are in the Criminal Justice Act 2003. The most relevant of
these are as follows.

(1) Under s.116 of the 2003 Act a statement not made in oral evidence
in the proceedings is admissible as evidence of any matter stated if
the witness:

— is dead;
— is unfit to be a witness because of his bodily or mental
condition;
— is outside the UK and it is not reasonably practicable to secure
his attendance;
— cannot be found although such steps as it is reasonably practicable to take to find him have been taken;
— through fear does not give oral evidence and the court gives
leave for the statement to be given in evidence.

(2) Business records. For the purposes of s.117 of the 2003 Act an
admissible business record is a document created or received by a
person in the course of a trade, business, profession or other
occupation, or as the holder of a paid or unpaid office; and the
information contained in the document was supplied by a person
(whether or not the maker of the statement) who had, or may
reasonably be supposed to have had, personal knowledge of the
matters dealt with.
This applies whether the information contained in the document
was supplied directly or indirectly but, if it was supplied indirectly,
only if each person through whom it was supplied received it in the
course of a trade, business, profession or other occupation; or as
the holder of a paid or unpaid office.

Under s.117 the judge still retains a discretion not to admit the document,   **10–181**
and may make a direction to that effect if satisfied that the statement's
reliability as evidence for the purpose for which it is tendered is doubtful in
view of: its contents, the source of the information contained in it, the way
in which or the circumstances in which the information was supplied or
received, or the way in which or the circumstances in which the document
concerned was created or received.

It may be necessary to produce a witness who can testify as to the origin
of the documents, so as to demonstrate that they fall within the scope of
s.117. However, it is open to the court to infer from the documents

themselves and the method or route by which they are produced to the court that they fall within the section, although often oral evidence as to their origin may be desirable.[48]

Copies

10–1828 We have mentioned above the modern approach of the courts to the admissibility of secondary evidence of documents, including copies.

The historic rules restricting admissibility of copies (to the small extent, if any, that they are still relevant) are becoming increasingly difficult to apply when the very concept of an "original" document is vanishing in the electronic environment in which temporary and transient copies are common, and a digital copy is a 100 per cent bit for bit reproduction of its predecessor.

Even if an "original" can be identified and is relevant, what constitutes an original depends on what is sought to be proved. For the purpose of establishing a hacking offence, an electronic document on the system may be regarded as an original document. But for the purpose of proving the contents of a letter sent from the organisation, the same electronic document is only a copy of the original document sent out.

While from a technical point of view it is valid to describe one document as a copy of another, for evidential purposes it is conceptually impossible to categorise any document (including an electronic document) as an original or a copy without knowing what is to be proved with it.

Civil evidence—current law

10–183 Section 8 of the Civil Evidence Act 1995 provides that where a statement contained in a document is admissible in civil proceedings, it may be proved by production of the document or (whether or not that document is still in existence) by the production of a copy of that document authenticated in such manner as the court may approve; and it is immaterial how many removes there are between a copy and an original.

In the light of the apparent demise of the best evidence rule as a rule of admissibility, this provision may now be regarded as merely governing the fashion in which copies are to be proved, rather than rendering copies admissible.

Criminal evidence

10–184 Under s.133 of the Criminal Justice Act 1988, where a statement contained in a document is admissible in criminal proceedings, it may be proved by production of the document or (whether or not the document still exists) by the production of a copy of that document authenticated in whatever way the court may approve.

---

[48] *R. v Foxley* [1995] 2 Cr. App. R. 523.

Copies of copies

As noted above, the old rule was that copies of copies were not admissible **10–185** unless it could be proved by admissible evidence that each copy in the chain was a true copy of the previous one, back to the original. Whether that is still the case in the light of the demise of the best evidence rule and the modern approach to admissibility may be doubtful.

We have noted that in both criminal and civil proceedings there are provisions that where a statement contained in a document is admissible, it may be proved by production of a copy of the document, authenticated in such manner as the court may approve. In the case of civil proceedings it is stated that the copy is admissible irrespective of how many removes there are from the original. Under s.134 of the Criminal Justice Act 2003 "copy" is defined to include both direct and indirect copies.

However, neither provision appears necessarily to apply where the **10–186** document is not being produced for the purpose of evidencing a statement whose truth is asserted. If it is produced merely as evidence that the statement was made or to evidence a legal obligation (e.g. a contract) then if the rule against copies of copies survives it could still be relevant. On the other hand, it would appear artificial that a multiple copy may be admitted to prove the truth of a statement made in the document, but not to prove the mere fact that the statement was made.

The rule (if it still exists) against copies of copies becomes extremely difficult to apply when, as is increasingly the case with computer systems and word processors, it is not at all clear what (if anything) constitutes the "original" and the vast majority of electronic documents can be characterised as copies of predecessor documents.

10.8.3 Factors affecting weight of evidence

Statutory provisions

Under the Civil Evidence Act 1995, the court, when estimating the weight **10–187** to be given to hearsay evidence in civil proceedings, shall have regard to any circumstances from which any inference can reasonably be drawn as to the reliability or otherwise of the evidence.

The Act provides a list of particular matters to which the court may have regard. They are:

— whether it would have been reasonable and practicable for the party by whom the evidence was adduced to have produced the maker of the original statement as a witness;
— whether the original statement was made contemporaneously with the occurrence or existence of the matters stated;
— whether the evidence involves multiple hearsay;
— whether any person involved had any motive to conceal or misrepresent matters;

— whether the original statement was an edited account, or was made in collaboration with another for a particular purpose; and

— whether the circumstances in which the evidence is adduced as hearsay are such as to suggest an attempt to prevent proper evaluation of its weight.

These factors should heavily influence the way in which companies who wish their computer records to carry weight in court and be accepted as authentic, design and implement their systems and procedures.

10.8.4 Electronic records procedures

10–188 In the quest to allay concerns from industry that their electronic records and document images may not stand up in court, the British Standards Institution has produced a number of relevant publications. The original BS7768:1994, "Recommendations for management of optical disk (WORM) systems for the recording of documents that may be required as evidence" has now been withdrawn. Currently it publishes three Codes of Practice: BIP 0008 "Code of practice for legal admissibility and evidential weight of information stored electronically", BIP 0008–2 "Code of Practice for Legal Admissibility and Evidential Weight: Electronic Communications", and BIP 0008–3 "Code of Practice for Legal Admissibility and Evidential Weight: Linking Electronic Identity to Documents".

The purpose of these publications is to suggest procedures which will maximise the authenticity, weight and usefulness of information (including source electronic data).

For electronic records derived from source electronic data, such as records of electronic transactions, the objective of the recording process must be to create a record that can be demonstrated to have captured complete and accurate information about the relevant events at the time the record was created and to have been preserved without alteration since the events took place.

10–189 The factor that usually causes most immediate concern with stored electronic records, due to the ease with which alterations can be made to an electronic record, is convincing the court that the document has not been tampered with and so is authentic. This is, in principle, easily dealt with by implementing proper procedures. The principle is similar to that of microfilm: put in place procedures which create an audit trail upon which you can rely to show that the original was correctly stored, and that there has been no possibility of tampering with the stored copy.

If the court thinks that the stored copy may have been altered, it will attach little or no weight to it (and may decide that it is not admissible at all). So if there is a risk that the copy document may be challenged it is crucial that suitable procedures are put in place to satisfy the court that no alteration has taken place. Documents such as the Codes of Practice should assist greatly with this.

872

However, it should not be thought that a court will always require complete and positive proof of lack of alteration of an electronic document in order to attach weight to it. It will approach the matter pragmatically. Indeed, for the vast majority of electronic documents and communications (such as emails) that already pass through the courts every day there is no challenge to their authenticity and their inclusion in evidence passes without comment or special proof, even where no special steps have been taken to capture and preserve them securely.

Useful as Codes of Practice may be in enhancing the weight to be **10–190** attached to stored electronic records, it would be a mistake to reverse the process and imagine that it would be desirable to exclude from evidence electronic data whose preservation did not comply with a Code. This would be wrong in principle, since it would revert to the old practice of creating bars to admissibility rather than leaving the judge to assess weight.

It would also be undesirable in practice, since it would impose costs on business and in practice exclude most data stored on home computers. Worst of all, it would constitute a malefactor's charter if incriminating electronic records could be objected to simply because they had not been stored in accordance with a Code.[49]

While assessing the reliability of electronic records undoubtedly presents challenges for the courts,[50] those challenges need to be met in a way that recognises the ubiquity of informally generated and stored electronic data and that, as with informal paper documents, their reliability should be approached as a matter of weight, not admissibility.

---

[49] There may well be room for a code of practice governing the collection and storage of electronic evidence by officials such as the police. However, that is an entirely different matter from excluding evidence because the data were not stored in a particular way for everyday use.

[50] See, for instance, *Takenaka (UK) Ltd v Frankl* (above, fn.94).

CHAPTER 11

Payment Mechanisms for Internet Commerce

11.1 INTRODUCTION

11–001 Internet commerce has been thriving for many years across the world and is still growing rapidly. Commerce requires effective mechanisms for payment and transactions are being settled by a variety of means—credit cards, debit cards, prepayment debits, specialist payment provider transfers to name but a few. However, no one payment mechanism of those currently used is suitable for all types of payment and, importantly, there are still areas which are not fully covered.

For example, there is no widely accepted system for handling very small payments (so called "micropayments") at a transaction cost which makes the provision of services in return for such payments a viable business proposition. Equally, there is no universally accepted way of making very quick and low cost person-to-person transfers. It is worth spending a little time considering what the characteristics of an ideal internet payment mechanism would be. We can then evaluate how the mechanisms currently available measure up against this yardstick.

11.2 THE IDEAL INTERNET PAYMENT MECHANISM

11–002 The ideal internet payment mechanism would have the following key characteristics:

- **User-friendly:** it would be easy to use on a fully online basis (and, at the payee end, on a purely automated basis);
- **All payment party types:** it would be available for use by all potential sellers and buyers (so both businesses and individuals could use it to make and receive payments);
- **Low cost:** the cost of making or receiving payments would be low;
- **No minimum or maximum transaction size:** the ideal mechanism

would be capable of being applied equally to substantial payments (such as for the supply of a major item of software) and also to very small ones (such as the few pence that might be charged for access to a particular page of a database);

- **Free from the risk of fraud:** it would not expose the payer, the recipient or the mechanism provider to the risk of loss as a result of fraud or other loss of value;
- **No credit risk for end user:** it would not involve any of the end users taking a credit risk on the provider of the system;
- **Universal acceptance:** it would be capable of being used to make all purchases, not just within its country of origin but also internationally;
- **Immediate settlement:** it should result in immediate settlement of the payment obligation, that is, there should be no delay before the recipient of the payment knows that it has been made and the goods or services ordered can be supplied;
- **Bridging the trust gap:** an ideal mechanism should bridge the "trust gap" which potentially exists in any internet transaction. This gap arises from the fact that the buyer and the seller will often not be known to each other and so will not trust the other to perform their side of the bargain. In particular, a buyer will not want to pay until it knows that its purchases have been despatched and match their description, while the seller will not want to despatch goods ordered until it has received payment; and
- **Anonymity/traceability:** there are conflicting views as to whether the ideal payment mechanism would allow the payer to remain anonymous. Some argue that payer anonymity is critical to the protection of civil liberties. Others fear that anonymous electronic payment systems facilitate money laundering, tax evasion and the making of purchases on the internet of an illegal nature. This issue is considered briefly at the end of this chapter.

11.3 TYPES OF PAYMENT MECHANISM

A number of payment mechanisms either are currently available for use on the internet or have been proposed for internet use. They can be divided into the following principal categories:

11–003

- **Credit and charge cards:** these are clearly a very widely used mechanism in internet commerce;
- **Debit cards—account-linked:** cards which are linked to a normal banking account of the payer—similar in operation to credit cards and also very popular;
- **Named prepaid debit cards:** cards "onto" which value is loaded (and can then be used to make payments) and which are linked to a named cardholder;

- **Anonymous prepaid debit cards:** cards "onto" which value is loaded (and can then be used to make payments) but which are not linked to a named cardholder;
- **Single-operator "account-based" systems:** systems in which the system operator takes real world payments in return for the crediting of electronic value to centrally-recorded electronic accounts of system users. Payments are then made by users giving electronic instructions to the system operator to transfer electronic value from the payer's electronic account to the electronic account of the payee within the same system;
- **Electronic "true cash" equivalents:** systems in which electronic value is loaded onto the cards of users (or their hard drives) and can be transferred between cards (or hard drives) without being centrally accounted—the best known example of this category being the *Mondex* system.

There are, of course, variations on the above categories. For example, there are systems which provide for "electronic cheques" and which are essentially variations of the account-linked debit card category but without a payment card ever being in existence.

A further variation would be a major telephone company allowing its customers to add the cost of small-value purchases to their monthly telephone bill—so providing a single operator account-based system but with the variation of not requiring pre-funding of the user's account. At the time of writing, a system called "Click & Buy" offers a facility similar to this under which purchases made during one month are accrued intra-month and then paid for either by credit/debit card, or by being added to a user's telephone bill, at the end of the month.

Another variation of the single operator account-based scheme is that run by E-gold under which the electronic value issued is denominated by reference to a weight of gold—this being a variation of the single operator account-based system. Finally, a variation which has been introduced to the prepaid debit card is a card which can be reloaded by the purchase of vouchers from participating retailers—similar to the way in which vouchers can be used to buy airtime on prepay mobiles.

11.4 THE CURRENT PREDOMINANT MECHANISMS

11–004   Credit cards and debit cards hold a very strong position in relation to internet payments at the time of writing. As will be seen below, their success is undoubtedly due in large part to the fact that they satisfy many of the criteria for an ideal internet payment mechanism. However, they are far from perfect and thus have left the door open for the creation of alternative payment mechanisms. In particular, their cost per transaction is such that they are not always suitable for micropayments. Equally, they cannot be used to enable non-business users to receive payments.

A key alternative mechanism which has seen significant growth during the last few years is *PayPal*. This is essentially a single operator account-based system under which electronic value can be purchased using a credit or debit card and is credited to the user's *PayPal* account. From that account, stored value can then be used to make purchases with *PayPal*-enabled retailers or transferred to the account of another *PayPal* user.

To be successful, a single-operator scheme must overcome a "critical mass" problem. To persuade any retailer to invest in setting itself up to accept a payment mechanism, the system operator must justify the set-up cost by showing that there are sufficient potential customers of that retailer out there who will want to use it. But members of the public will only take up a payment mechanism if they know it can be widely used. *PayPal* is unusual in having been able to overcome this problem and build up a very substantial customer base—its success being derived in part from its long association with, and its role as payment provider for, the auction website *eBay* (of which *PayPal* became a subsidiary in 2003).

A number of mobile phone companies have also created, or are trialling, single operator account-based systems using mobile phones as the equivalent of a card onto which purchased value can be loaded. Transfers are made by sending a special form of secure text message to the mobile phone company operator to instruct it to move value from the value account of the payer to that of the payee. A key advantage of such systems is that they can be used for transfers between individuals (known in the industry as "peer-to-peer transfers") and that transfers can be made wherever there is mobile phone reception.

An interesting development also in the area of single operator account-based systems is the expansion of schemes originally created for a narrow range of payments to a single supplier. In Hong Kong, for example, the *Octopus* card was created as a prepaid card onto which value could be loaded to pay electronically for public transport services. It is now, however, accepted as a form of payment by vendors of other services and goods—such as newsagents and fast food chains. London has a similar type of card (the *Oyster* card) which is currently only used for mass transit payments (it can be used on buses, underground trains and certain suburban trains) but may well follow the *Octopus* example in due course, subject to overcoming the regulatory issues that this would pose.

Single operator account-based systems can, in principle, either be named or anonymous. For example, the *Oyster* card can be purchased at an underground train ticket office without any identity disclosure but can, at the option of the user, be registered to his or her particular name. An advantage of this to the user is the ability to cancel value on the card in the event that it is stolen.

11.5 THE MICROPAYMENT GAP

11–005 There is one area of internet payments which is not particularly well served by the principal current mechanisms and this is micropayments. The key issue is transaction cost. Suppose that a music website wants to give listeners the chance to listen to songs without downloading them permanently (that is, without "buying" them) and therefore wants to charge a few pence per song on a "pay as you listen" basis. The current reality is that the per-transaction cost of presently available payment mechanisms is a barrier to charging on this basis.

Of course, businesses often get around this problem by operating a subscription model (for example, the customer pays initially for, say, £20 of songs and tops up his or her account when that balance has been exhausted) but the time involved in the creation and funding of such an account, and the fact that some funds must remain tied up in it, mean that this solution is sub-optimal. In theory, for any payment system which works on the basis of the transmission of electronic impulses, the marginal cost of each transaction is negligible and should make it possible for micropayments to be handled cost effectively. However, the reality is that payment systems can be expensive to operate and the fixed costs have to be spread between all the transactions which they handle. If a micropayment transfer is charged at only a few pence, it will effectively be cross-subsidised by other larger payments.

Single operator account-based systems are those best placed to overcome this problem, since all transfers are handled within the operator's own computer system and are virtually cost free. In particular, no transaction needs to be settled through a "clearing" process with other banks or payment providers (by contrast to account-linked debit cards where the bank of the payer may not be the same as the bank of the retailer). Although any such operator must obviously also cover its fixed costs, it may accept the cross-subsidisation of micropayments as a cost of running the system, provided that sufficient larger transactions will also be handled. This may, however, mean that it is difficult to be a payment provider which focuses just on enabling micropayments. With systems such as *Octopus*, a large part of the fixed costs of running the system is met by its use as a payment method for mass transit payments, meaning that the system can afford to be flexible in its approach to unrelated micropayments.

Payment mechanisms in more detail

11–006 The various payment mechanisms referred to above are now considered in more detail, with a particular focus on which of the ideal payment mechanism criteria they both meet and fail to meet. Some legal issues with the different mechanisms will then be considered.

11.6 CREDIT AND CHARGE CARDS

Credit and charge cards have, in a relatively short period of time, achieved a **11–007** very high degree of popularity as internet payment mechanisms. Where payment in a transaction is made by credit or charge card, that payment is made by the buyer giving an instruction to the issuer of the relevant card to make payment to the retailer on the buyer's behalf. It is a term of the contract between the card issuer and the buyer that the card issuer is entitled to debit the buyer's account with the amount of those payments which it is validly instructed to make. For a credit card, the resulting debit balance on the account will be required to be paid off in accordance with the terms of that contract. For a charge card the balance must be discharged in full by a set date following the monthly statement date.

In an internet context, the instruction to the card issuer is given by filling in the relevant payment boxes on the retailer's website checkout and the retailer will generally obtain "authorisation" of the instruction (that is, the credit card issuer's confirmation that it will honour the instruction—which will generally be given if the transaction is within the cardholder's credit limit and the card is not suspected to be stolen)—while the customer is still online to the checkout page.

11.7 CREDIT AND CHARGE CARD ADVANTAGES

Credit and charge cards have many advantages and do indeed meet many of **11–008** the criteria for an ideal internet payment mechanism. In particular:

(a) **Easy to use:** from a purchaser point of view all that is required to make an internet payment using a credit or charge card is the transmission of the card details. From the retailer's point of view, the process is capable of being completely automated.

(b) **Safe from fraud:** this may at first seem a strange statement, because credit card fraud is, of course, a major problem which costs the providers of credit and charge cards hundreds of millions of pounds every year. Many credit card holders are sufficiently concerned about the risk of fraud with their cards to be cautious about making online purchases. However, the key point is that the loss from credit card fraud is rarely passed on to the card holder and is generally borne by the card issuer (or in certain cases the retailer). The legal background to this is considered further below. Of course, the fact that card issuers pick up most of the risk of fraud is reflected in the cost of running credit card systems and contributes to one of their disadvantages mentioned below—transaction cost.

(c) **No credit risk for end user:** credit/charge cards involve no prepayment by the customer. The card issuer takes a credit risk on the persons to whom it issues cards, but those customers never bear any credit risk on the card issuer because the card issuer never owes them any money (other than, of course, in unusual circumstances involving refunds of the purchase moneys of reversed transactions).

(d) **Universal acceptance:** credit/charge cards operated by the major players such as Visa, MasterCard and American Express have achieved a degree of universal acceptance which is striking. It is possible to use the same card to make purchases from retailers in countries all around the world, normally with no additional formality or cost when contracting with a retailer outside the country in which the card was issued.

The key to this acceptability is the role of the international card organisation concerned. A retailer in, for example Sydney, Australia which accepts a Visa card payment from a UK buyer is unlikely even to have heard the name of the card's issuing bank. However, it will be relying on the international card organisation and the local bank which acts as the retailer's interface to the card scheme (normally the retailer's current account bank) to effect settlement of duly authorised claims, thus enabling it (and, indeed, requiring it) to accept all card payments made under the umbrella of the card organisation.

(e) **Immediate settlement:** the immediate clearance of charge/credit cards is a critical factor behind the development of internet commerce, enabling the virtually instantaneous supply of services where internet delivery is possible and meaning that other transactions do not become delayed or fail because a supplied form of payment does not work—since the failure will immediately be reported to the customer through the online "checkout" facility, the customer can then solve the problem (for example, an incorrectly keyed number) or supply an alternative payment method (for example, if his/her card is declined as having a credit limit which is insufficient to cover the transaction concerned).

(f) **Bridging the "trust gap":** as noted above, the "trust gap" is the problem which arises from the fact that the buyer and the seller in an internet transaction will often not be known to each other. It is not uncommon to make large-value purchases from internet suppliers one has never heard of and whom one has no reason to trust to supply the goods ordered. This can happen because credit cards are particularly good at bridging the trust gap by virtue of the "chargeback" mechanism. This is explained in more detail below.

The chargeback mechanism works as follows. In order to participate in the payment schemes of the major credit card organisations, a retailer must sign up to their terms and conditions and must form a relationship with a bank (called the "merchant acquirer" of the retailer) which will (1) put all the retailer's payments-received into the system for clearance and (2) pay the retailer in respect of those receivables (less a discount), recouping such payment from each card issuing bank through the system. If a customer who has used a credit card for payment does not receive the goods/services purchased with his or her card or they are otherwise defective, he/she complains to the card company which will then refund the payment. It passes this refund back through the card system so that the merchant acquirer of the retailer ultimately passes it back to the retailer as a debit. If the retailer continues to assert that the customer is liable there are then certain further steps provided for by the card system rules which operate as a kind of rudimentary dispute resolution mechanism.

For credit cards (but not, it seems, charge cards or debit cards) issued in the UK, the chargeback scheme operated by the major card companies is supplemented by a statutory provision. An individual (but not a corporate) credit card holder has the benefit of ss.56 and 75 of the Consumer Credit Act 1974 in respect of purchases made using the card—although for s.75 to apply and for s.56 to be available without a specific representation having been made by the merchant, the cash price of the item purchased must fall within the relevant statutory limits (currently a minimum of £100 and a maximum of £30,000) and the amount of credit provided must not be more than £25,000.

This means that the credit card issuer will be co-liable with the retailer in respect of misrepresentations or breaches of contract by the retailer and is called "connected lender liability". It is of particular comfort to a buyer purchasing from a retailer of whose commercial standing he or she is unaware.

There used to be uncertainty as to whether the sections applied in relation to purchases from suppliers outside the UK but it has recently been determined that they do by a decision of the Court of Appeal in *Office of Fair Trading v Lloyds TSB Bank Plc, Tesco Personal Finance and American Express Services Ltd.*[1]

(g) **Time to pay:** There is a final benefit provided to buyers by the use of credit cards, and this is that they give the buyer time to pay. Generally speaking, there is an interest-free period during which no interest is charged and thereafter interest is charged (at a rate which is normally some way above a typical overdraft rate). A large number of users of credit cards utilise this facility simply on a short-term basis (and discharge their balances in full before the stipulated day after which interest is charged) but others use it to provide them with extended credit on a revolving basis. For charge cards, there is a short interest-free credit period, but all transactions must be settled by a stipulated date in the month in which they were incurred and longer-term credit is not permitted.

---

[1] [2006] 3 W.L.R. 452, [2007] Q.B. 1.

11.8 WEAKNESSES OF CREDIT/CHARGE CARDS

11–009   So the credit/charge card is currently very widely used for internet payment, but it is not without its problems as an internet payment mechanism. The principal problems are:

- Limitation of users;
- Transaction costs;
- Fraud concerns; and
- Privacy.

11.8.1 Limitation of users

11–010   It is obvious that, in order to use a credit or charge card, a buyer must have had such a card issued to him or her. Although the market penetration of such cards in developed countries is substantial, there is nonetheless a vast number of people using the internet who will not be in this position.

Particular problems arise in relation to the uncreditworthy and the young. The issue of a credit card requires that the issuing bank be prepared to take a credit risk on the cardholder and, for the young, there are statutory restrictions on making credit available to young people (added to which, contracts involving credit provided to minors may be void on common law principles).

Even more significant is the position in relation to sellers. In order to receive payment by means of a credit or charge card, the retailer must join the system operated by the relevant card organisation. For a small retailer this may not prove economic. Furthermore, an individual, such as a hobbyist software writer, might wish to sell products from time to time on the internet and yet not really be running a business. Obviously such a person would not want to have to become a credit card acceptor simply in order to be able to receive occasional small payments for their work.

11.8.2 Transaction costs

11–011   By their very nature, credit and charge card payments require central processing. The major card schemes also involve complex arrangements between a number of players (the card issuing banks, the merchant acquirer banks, the card organisation itself, the retailer, the cardholders) and each debit passed through the system will need to be settled.

These systems are not inexpensive to operate and the considerable cost is only partially offset by the economies of scale which result from the enormous volume of transactions handled. There are also additional hidden costs. For example, a card issuer bears a "bad-debt risk", namely the risk that the cardholder will not ultimately discharge the debit balance resulting from a transaction.

There is also the fact that the loss resulting from fraudulent use of cards issued will often fall on the card issuer rather than the cardholder and that chargeback liabilities can fall on the merchant acquirer where the retailer has, for example, become insolvent. All of these costs are reflected in charges for the payment transactions handled.

The norm in the UK is for such costs to be passed on to the retailer by way of transaction commissions. It is also conventional in the UK for the retailer not to pass on such costs to the customer by way of a higher charge for credit card payments. The rules of the major card schemes generally prohibit such differential charging and, although the Credit Cards (Price Discrimination) Order 1990 (SI 1999/2159) invalidates any such contractual term for UK retailers, it is now well-established market practice in the UK that the use of credit cards is generally free as far as the customer is concerned.

The charge made by the credit card companies is generally calculated as a percentage of the amount of the transaction financed. However, since much of the processing of a particular payment will be (and therefore will cost) the same whether the payment is for £100 or 50p, minimum transaction charges are often applied and this can make credit, charge and debit cards uneconomic for micropayments.

11.8.3 Fraud concerns

Some explanation is obviously required of the fact that "Safe from fraud" should appear in the list of advantages for credit/charge cards above and yet "Fraud concerns" should appear in the list of their disadvantages. As noted above, the majority of situations where fraud is committed involving a credit/charge card result in a loss to the credit card issuer (or in some cases the retailer) and not to the cardholder. The legal basis for this is considered further below. However, cardholders remain concerned in relation to the disclosure of their card details through the internet and some may be so concerned that they eschew internet purchases as a result. Their concerns are not entirely without foundation.

11–012

The first point to note is that the disclosure of credit card details across the internet will involve the possibility of their being transmitted to a fraudster. The use of secure connection channels within the "checkout" section of commercial websites does reduce the interception possibilities and the card providers are working on improving security further in this regard, particularly on systems which will enable the sending of card details in an encrypted form which is unlocked only by the card organisation systems. However, fraudsters are nothing if not innovative and any new security measure is often very rapidly met with a claim that the measure has been defeated.

A further danger is the collection of credit card details by means of "phishing" sites—sites which purport to be genuine sites of well-known entities but are in fact merely fronts for the collection of personal details of unsuspecting members of the public. So, a replica site for a major online retailer might collect hundreds of credit card details from people believing that they were making payment for genuine items on the site.

Even when disclosed to a genuine retailer, credit card details may be at risk. There have been a number of reported cases where retailers have stored credit card details on insufficiently secure servers leaving the details free to be plundered by talented hackers. In one case, a hacker stole thousands of details and then blackmailed the retailer with the threat of posting those details on the internet if not paid a substantial ransom.

Clearly one answer to this problem is to ensure that the card authorisation process does not involve disclosure of a card's details to the retailer taking it in payment, but instead involves a direct link being opened up between the customer and the card organisation network.

The second point is that, if one's card details are misused, one will have to prove that the use was not authorised. For a person who has a long-established relationship with the bank issuer of his or her card, this may not be too difficult, particularly when the unauthorised debits are completely outside his or her normal scope of spending. For people with a less well-developed, or possibly a difficult, relationship with their card issuer, matters may not always be so straightforward.

Thirdly, since many people do not check their credit card statements on a regular basis, there is always a risk that a fraudster who is prepared to play a longer game will use card details to effect small payments on a restricted number of occasions without being detected for some time.

Finally, while the terms and conditions of credit card use and/or the legal framework for such use, generally remove liability for fraudulent transaction from the cardholder (see further below), this may not always apply where the cardholder has been "grossly negligent". The concept of negligence is a failure to take reasonable care but there is no clear definition of how serious the failure to take care must be for the negligence to be "gross". It is entirely natural that a card holder should be concerned that it could face significant liability (at least up to the amount of his or her credit limit) on this basis. After all, if a card holder gives card details on a phishing site which is a poor fake of the real website of a major retailer, how poor does the fake have to be before the card holder can be said to be "grossly negligent"?

11.8.4 Privacy

11–013   Because all transactions using a credit or charge card require central processing, they also involve a complete record being maintained by the card issuer of the spending patterns of all its cardholders. Useful though this may be for home accounting purposes, many people are concerned that this entails an unacceptable invasion of their privacy and would prefer a payment mechanism where their spending could be entirely anonymous and untraceable. Others will point out that a number of internet users visiting websites supplying illegal material have been traced by virtue of their use of credit cards to make payment and that anything which enables such conduct to be monitored and controlled is a good thing.

11.9 DEBIT CARDS ACCOUNT-LINKED

From the perspective of a cardholder making an internet payment, debit **11–014** cards linked to an account and credit/charge cards produce a very similar payment experience. Payment is made by disclosing the card details and providing an authority to debit "the card". The retailer obtains authorisation for the transaction and payment "goes through". The legal background to what happens behind the scenes is, however, different. With an account-linked debit card, the cardholder maintains an account with the card-issuing bank and payment is effected by the cardholder instructing the bank holding that account to pay the retailer by a debit from the account. If the relevant account has a positive balance, there is no credit involved in the transaction (as there is with credit or charge cards). In many ways, the transaction is an electronic version of payment by cheque, with the important difference that settlement can take place immediately, leaving no possibility of the "cheque" bouncing.

Behind the scenes, the retailer will have a "merchant acquirer" bank for debit card payments in just the same way as it does for credit/charge card payments (indeed it will often be the same bank) and this bank will pass the payment instructions through the system of the debit card scheme operator back to the account holding bank.

Although the legal background is different, the benefits and weaknesses of account-linked debit cards are very similar to those of credit cards. It is, however, worth mentioning a few key points of difference:

- **No interest-free period or extended credit possibility:** because debit card payments of this kind are immediately debited to the linked bank account of the cardholder, there is no interest-free period provided and no automatic ability to pay on a longer-term credit basis.
- **Credit risk on the account bank:** there must be an account to which the card is linked and this will generally need to be in credit of an amount sufficient to discharge the requested payment (unless there is a sufficiently large agreed overdraft facility on the account). This means that the cardholder will take a credit risk on the issuing bank but, given that most such issuers are generally large banks, this is not something which normally concerns the typical cardholder.
- **Wider availability as no credit risk on cardholder:** since the card issuer does not have to take a credit risk on the cardholder with a

debit card of this type (it can permit payments only within the balance available on the cardholder's account), this increases the range of people who can use this payment mechanism to include, for example, those who are not creditworthy.

- **Acceptance:** in relation to universal acceptance, debit cards of this kind do not have the same acceptance level as is enjoyed by credit cards issued under the umbrella of the major card organisations. They do, however, very often have virtually the same level of (almost universal) acceptance in their "own" country (that is, the country in which they were created) and steps are being taken by many operators of such schemes to increase their international recognition and acceptance. A number of such schemes now operate under the umbrella of the major credit card schemes such as Visa and MasterCard which means that they can often benefit from the same level of acceptance as credit cards.

- **No purchaser protection:** connected lender liability (see references to s.75 of the Consumer Credit Act 1974 above) does not apply to situations where a debit card linked to a current account of a cardholder is used to make a purchase (s.187(3A) of the Consumer Credit Act 1974—and this applies even if the current account goes into debit as a result of the purchase and so some element of "credit" is provided). Accordingly, the card issuer is not jointly liable with the retailer under the supply contract as it is with many transactions settled with a UK credit card (see above). This means that well-advised card holders will use a credit card in preference to a debit card for larger-value internet purchases.

- **Fraud risk:** the risk of fraudulent transactions being carried out using a debit card number is similar to the risk in relation to credit cards. However, some customers may be concerned that fraudulent use of an account-linked debit card may enable a fraudster to drain all their current account resources, rather than being limited to the amount of the credit limit on a credit/charge card.

- **Transaction charges:** because the issuing bank takes no credit risk in relation to account-linked debit card payments and because it also does not face connected lender liability, the transaction charges for the processing of debit card payments tend to be significantly lower than those for credit cards. However, even small transaction charges still represent a significant percentage of the amount of a micro-payment which is made with a debit card.

11.10 NAMED PREPAID DEBIT CARDS

11–015   As noted above, credit cards linked to the major card organisations provide the cardholder with the ability to pay a wide range of retailers all around the world. However, because they involve the holder being given credit by the card issuer, not everyone can be issued with one. Debit cards linked to the major card organisations can offer similar functionality, but even they require that the cardholder should have a current bank account to which the card can be linked.

The function of a prepaid debit card is to make available the benefits of holding a debit card to the holder but on the basis that the card holder will prepay for the value that is spent on the card. Effectively, the card issuer maintains an account linked to the card which is not a current account but is an account which can be accessed and drawn upon only by the use of the card.

The account can be funded in a number of ways, including by the payment in of cash at a participating outlet (such as a post office), cheque or the use of a credit card. One current scheme envisages that the card can be funded by the purchase of vouchers from retailers which contain a unique identifier and represent a certain amount of value that can be loaded "onto" the card.

The benefits and weaknesses of prepaid debit cards are very similar to those of the debit cards from which they are derived, but a few points of difference can be mentioned:

- Prepaid debit cards are open to a wider range of users than account-linked debit cards, because they do not require the holding of a bank account. Minors and those with poor credit histories are a particular focus of the providers of such cards.
- From the point of view of the cardholder, a debit card is normally provided (in the UK at least) as a free part of the service of a current account bank. Such banks will generally work on the basis that the costs of providing such a facility are cross-subsidised by the revenue which the bank earns from other aspects of the customer relationship. This will not apply to prepaid debit cards and such cards often carry monthly, and other, charges. These charges are in addition to the amount which the card issuer is paid each time that the card is used which, in the UK at least, is borne by the retailer as the transaction fee.
- The risk of fraudulent debits being made to prepaid debit cards is much the same as it is in the case of account-linked debit cards. However, a potentially important difference is that the amount that can be stolen in this way is limited to the prepaid value loaded onto the card.
- Since it is not necessary for a prepaid debit card to be linked to a current account, it is in principle possible for them to be issued by non-banks. However, as will be discussed below, the taking of the prepayments is treated by the laws of the EU States as a form of banking business meaning that card issuers must generally be authorised either as banks or as "E-money issuers".

11.11 PREPAID DEBIT CARDS—ANONYMOUS

11–016 From a technical point of view, there is no reason why prepaid debit cards should not be capable of being issued on an anonymous basis. Indeed, it would even be possible to issue disposable cards which came pre-loaded with value and were sold by distribution outlets for their face value in the same way that prepaid phone cards are sold.

This would meet the concern that is expressed by many that a payment mechanism should exist for internet commerce which does not automatically reveal (and leave a record of) the identity of the payer. As noted above, there are those who take the opposite view that accountability in respect of all spending is a good thing (or at least that its benefits outweigh its disadvantages).

Any card issuer providing a card on this basis would need to take account of the rules which have been adopted across all EU States for the prevention of money laundering. These rules require the identification of customers with whom a payment service provider is entering into a business relationship.

The advantages and disadvantages of an anonymous prepaid debit would otherwise be similar to those for a named card. However, there would be a difference if the card was lost. With an anonymous card, there would be no way in which the value loaded on a lost card could be cancelled, because it would be impossible for the card issuer to know whether a cancellation instruction came from the true holder (its having no record of who the true holder actually was). Additionally, whereas with a named card, there may be an argument that the issuer should be liable in respect of unauthorised debits (see below), it seems less likely that this argument would apply in relation to an anonymous card.

11.12 SINGLE OPERATOR ACCOUNT BASED SCHEMES

11–017 The prepaid debit cards referred to above work on the basis that transactions will be settled through one of the major card organisation systems. It is not, therefore, necessary for the retailer who accepts any card also to hold an account with the card issuer—the link between retailer and card issuer can be made by the card organisation system. The past decade has, however, also seen the successful growth of a number of schemes which have the following characteristics:

(a) all persons who wish to use the scheme to make or receive payments ("system participants") must open up an account with a single scheme operator;

(b) system participants can credit their scheme accounts by making payments to the scheme operator in "real money"—for example, payments by credit or debit card. System value is denominated in a "real world" currency. The amounts standing to the credit of the accounts of the system participants can be thought of as "system value";

(c) system participants can also convert their system value back into real money (for example, by directing the operator to make a transfer in the amount of such system value to the participant's bank account). This convertibility or "redeemability" makes system value a surrogate for real money (provided, of course, that the system terms and conditions and the credit standing of the operator are such that the redeemability can be relied upon);

(d) since system value can be a surrogate for real money, transfers of system value can be used to effect payments;

(e) system value transfers take effect by means of an instruction being given to the system operator to transfer system value from the system participant who is the payer to the one who is the payee. Clearly the system operator must set the system up so that, so far as possible, only instructions which are actually authorised by the payer will be acted upon. This will involve encryption and authorisation coding of payment instructions.

The *PayPal* payment system is an example of this sort of scheme. This is also a type of scheme which can be operated by mobile phone companies using encrypted and passworded texts as the transfer messages.

11.13 ADVANTAGES OF SINGLE OPERATOR ACCOUNT-BASED SCHEMES

The key advantages of a system of this kind over credit or debit cards are: **11–018**

- **A wide range of user types:** schemes of this type generally do not allow any user to go into debit on any account. So there is no reason in principle why they should not be made available to persons who have poor credit standing or are minors.
- **Non-commercial payees:** these systems allow the receipt of payments by system participants who are non-commercial parties—the payee does not have to be a merchant with a link to the system of a major card organisation through its merchant acquirer bank.
- **Fraud risk:** in the case of fraudulent access to a system participant's account, the most that is at risk is the amount standing to the credit of that account; by contrast, a debit card linked to a current account puts at risk both whatever amount is in that account and an amount up to any agreed overdraft facility (although see further below).
- **Potentially low per transaction cost:** payment transactions involve an electronic instruction to the system operator which is acted upon automatically by the electronic infrastructure set up by the system

operator. The whole of the system is within the ownership and control of the system operator and no third party is involved. This contrasts with credit/charge cards and debit cards where links are made through the major card organisations.

The marginal cost of an individual transaction on a single operator account-based system is therefore virtually zero—involving no more than the cost of the electricity involved in transfer messages. Obviously, there are system costs which have to be passed on to system participants, but the system operator has a broad discretion as to how it apportions such costs between transactions and it is open to it to charge on a basis (such as a percentage basis), which means that micropayments remain cost-effective.

11.14 DISADVANTAGES OF SINGLE OPERATOR ACCOUNT-BASED SCHEMES

11–019   Key disadvantages of such a scheme are as follows:

- **Payments only between scheme participants:** since transfers are made by the transfer of system value between system accounts, any transfer can generally only take place between parties who have signed up to the system. Consumers will only want to be participants in a limited number of such systems, yet for any system to be appealing it must achieve a high level of acceptance (put simply, there is no point in enduring the hassle of signing up to a payment system unless you can use it to make lots of the payments you want to make in life).

  As noted above, the system operated by *PayPal* seems to have managed to overcome this "critical mass" problem, and a system operated by a major mobile operator would also be able to do this because it would have a readily recruitable customer base. For other potential operators, the critical mass issue would be a significant barrier to entry.

- **"Bridging the gap" protection:** protection under s.75 of the Consumer Credit Act 1974 (see above) is only provided where the payment system operator provides "credit" and most single operator account-based systems operate on the basis that the system accounts must always have positive balances. It is, of course, open to system operators to agree to provide an element of purchaser protection as part of the terms and conditions of the scheme, and *PayPal* is an example of an operator which has decided to do this as part of its service offering. However, the very strong level of protection provided by the Consumer Credit Act is not automatically available as it is for credit cards.

- **Credit risk on operator:** as noted above, schemes of this kind involve the system accounts of participants being credited with system value in return for real money. In a sense, the participants "buy" system value. However, if the system operator were to become insolvent, it might not be able to redeem system value for real value. Any participant in the system therefore takes a credit risk on the operator. For this reason, the provision of such a system in the EU States is generally restricted to operators who are either duly authorised credit institutions (for example, banks) or a particular type of organisation authorised as an electronic money issuer—see further below.

11.15 ELECTRONIC "TRUE CASH" EQUIVALENTS

The past two decades have seen the emergence, and in some cases the subsequent collapse, of a number of payment mechanisms marketed as "electronic cash"—often with names involving some combination of "e-", or another typically "e-commerce" word, and a word related to money—for example, "e-cash", "digicash", "cyberbucks", etc. Many initiatives have been limited to the US market, but several European countries can point to schemes falling under an "electronic cash" banner. However, many such schemes are simply implementations of the types of system referred to above and are based on instructions being given to a central system operator to transfer value between accounts. This is, of course, not how real cash works.

11–020

When we think of "cash" in the conventional sense, we think of a note or a coin which can circulate between holders without any need for it to be returned to, and processed by, a bank each time it is used to effect payment. And the virtual world has seen the creation of some types of system which seek to replicate this feature of conventional cash. This type of system will therefore be referred to in this chapter as a "true" electronic cash system.

The basic concept of a true electronic cash scheme is that consumers will buy electronic value from the issuing system. The electronic value so purchased is represented by electronic data held either on a personal computer hard drive or on an integrated circuit or "microchip" on a smart card which consumers can carry around with them.

The most well-known system of this kind is that created under the *Mondex* banner. Originally a joint venture between Midland/HSBC Bank Plc and National Westminster Bank Plc, *Mondex* is now a wholly owned subsidiary of MasterCard International. *Mondex* has always attributed considerable importance to the potential for its system to be used for internet payments. However, at the time of writing it is fair to say that its development has not progressed at the pace originally anticipated, and this is partly due to the strength of the competing payment systems.

The operation of a true electronic cash system is most easily understood by reference to the *Mondex* example. Figure 11.1 below depicts, in a simplified form, the operation of the *Mondex* system in a typical jurisdiction (the model would need to be adapted in each jurisdiction to take account of any local regulatory or legal constraints).

Fig 11.1

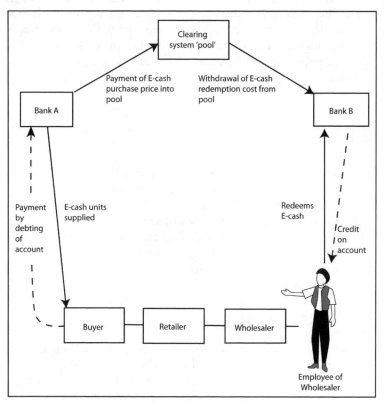

Our buyer in this example is a customer of Bank A. In anticipation of her making payments using *Mondex* money, she has been issued with a smart card onto which can be loaded electronic impulses which will be treated by the system as representing monetary value. To load her smart card with money, she goes to a cashpoint at Bank A and inserts her card into the automated teller machine. Her card is loaded with the relevant units and her account is debited immediately with the "purchase price" of the units.

In order to make a purchase with her electronic money, the buyer transfers the necessary value of the electronic impulses on her own card to the retailer's *Mondex* terminal. However, the retailer need not simply redeem those impulses by cashing them at Bank A (as in an EFTPOS-type system). Instead it can, for example, transfer them to its wholesaler by way of payment for stock (provided, of course, that the wholesaler has its own *Mondex* facility).

In the example represented by Fig.11.1, it is assumed that the wholesaler proceeds to use electronic impulses received by it from the retailer to pay the wages of one of its employees. It is also assumed that it is only when the relevant electronic impulses reach the wholesaler's employee that they are "redeemed" by being transferred to a participating bank in the system. On redemption, the employee's bank credits his account with the value of the electronic impulses surrendered.

To complete the picture above, both Bank A and Bank B is in a clearing system. Essentially, in order to provide our buyer with the electronic impulses which she loads at the cashpoint, Bank A buys those impulses from a value issuer in the clearing system. When Bank B receives those impulses back from the employee of the wholesaler, it sells them back to the value issuer in the clearing system and thus receives the funds to reimburse it for the credit it has made to the employee's account.

For completeness, it should be mentioned that, in practice, business recipients of impulses are likely to redeem them promptly following receipt (indeed, it is understood that where *Mondex*'s system has been implemented, it has generally worked on the basis that retailers' terminals automatically retire value received from consumers as and when received). Doing this will enable them to receive interest on the payments received (or reduce their overdraft) and will avoid the potential security risks of holding a large quantity of potentially spendable cash—the same reasons for which retailers return real world surplus cash to their bank each day.

However, the important point to note is that it is not an intrinsic element of the operation of a true electronic cash system that impulses must always be redeemed when received. It is the defining feature of any such system that impulses can circulate and pass through many hands to effect payments before being redeemed. Importantly, transactions can still be carried out even when both payer and payee are off-line.

11.16 ADVANTAGES AND DISADVANTAGES OF TRUE ELECTRONIC CASH AS AN INTERNET PAYMENT MECHANISM

The similarity of true electronic cash to real cash is striking. In particular, it **11–021** can be transferred instantly and without cost to either the payer or the recipient (although it is likely that standing charges would be made for hardware needed to use the system). Most importantly, once received, it can be immediately re-used by the recipient to make further payments.

From the point of view of making payments over the internet, this type of electronic cash has a great deal to commend it. In particular:

- Because it consists of electronic impulses, it is, in principle, capable of being transferred over the internet;
- In principle, it can be used by a very wide range of buyers and sellers, requiring only possession of the necessary smartcard hardware. Because the providers of electronic cash facilities do not take a

credit risk on its holders, there should be no creditworthiness barrier to being able to use this form of payment;

- Because transfers of it are effectively free from transaction charges, it can be used to make very small payments in a cost-effective way; it also has a significant advantage over real cash in that it can also be used for large payments;
- When transferring it across the internet, even if there were a risk of it being intercepted and re-routed, at least that risk would be limited to the value of the payment sent (there would not, for example, be the risk that arises where the disclosure of a credit card number enables multiple fraudulent debits to be made at some stage in the future);
- In principle, it can be issued in any currency and thus be used for making payment in any country in the world; and
- Systems could be arranged to ensure that transfers of it would leave no "audit trail" of the kind that exists when payments are made through bank accounts or on credit/debit cards (this would satisfy the requirements of those who want their internet dealings to be confidential, although it also has other implications which are discussed below).

It is, however, not perfect. There remains a risk of the interception of payment messages in internet transmission and, perhaps more significantly, payment using electronic cash does not offer any protection in respect of goods or services which are inadequate or maybe not supplied at all. It is obvious that it also does not offer the "time-to-pay" feature that a credit card provides.

11.17 ACCEPTANCE OF TRUE ELECTRONIC CASH SYSTEMS

11–022 It is suggested that there are a number of features that any true electronic cash system will need to possess if it is to gain general acceptance. Features of particular importance are discussed below.

11.17.1 Convertibility

11–023 Users of electronic cash will be unwilling to treat it as having value unless it is capable of being converted more or less instantly into real cash or a bank account credit with a bank acceptable to the recipient of the cash. This means that a recipient will have either to be a participant in the scheme himself or herself or be able to use the services of another participant (for example, his or her own bank) who will redeem electronic cash on his or her behalf.

11.17.2 Good credit backing

It is clear that electronic cash impulses are only as good as the credit   11–024
standing of the entities which underwrite their conversion into conventional
cash. Thus, for example, electronic cash issued by an unknown bank in a
foreign jurisdiction will not be appealing to a retailer in the UK. To achieve
general international acceptance, an electronic cash system would probably
need to be underwritten by parties of internationally recognised standing or
to be underwritten in each jurisdiction by major local banks.

11.17.3 Low vulnerability to fraud

Any provider of an electronic cash product will need to be able to show that   11–025
its system is sufficiently safe from the risk of counterfeiting and this is
considered further below at section 11.19.2. Historical experience in the
sphere of physical cash has shown that successful counterfeiting of a currency may rapidly destroy the value which is attributed to it in the market
place.

Legal issues with internet payment systems

Considered above are those payments systems that are either currently   11–026
available for internet payments or have been developed with internet capability, but are not yet widely available. There are legal issues which arise in
relation to every payment system and these are considered further below.

11.18 FRAUD INVOLVING ABUSE OF CREDIT/CHARGE/ DEBIT CARDS AND OTHER "INSTRUCTIONS BASED" SYSTEMS

Where a payment system operates through the debiting of an account of the   11–027
buyer on the basis of instructions given by him or her, there is obviously
scope for fraud to occur where instructions are fraudulently given, or
validly given instructions are fraudulently altered, so as to effect payment to
an unintended recipient. Where the resulting loss lies in these circumstances
will primarily be a matter to be determined in accordance with the terms of
the contracts between the relevant parties, that is, the bank or credit card
issuer making payment, the payment's recipient (for example, the retailer)
and the person whose account has been fraudulently drawn upon. Some
general principles of English law do, however, remain significant.

11.18.1 The basic principle

11–028   On the principle established in the case of *Orr v Union Bank of Scotland*[2] (as confirmed by the more recent case of *Tai Hing Cotton Mills*[3] and the even more recent case of *Price Meats Ltd v Barclays Bank Plc*[4]), it is generally considered that a bank is not entitled to debit a customer's account in respect of a forged cheque, even though the forgery may have been undetectable and there may have been no negligence on the part of the bank.

Although this case is decided in relation to the paper instrument of a cheque, there is no obvious reason why it would not be applied to an unauthorised payment instruction given electronically. The case did, however, relate to a situation where the instruction was given to an account holding bank and the decision was based on the reasoning that the implied terms of the bank's mandate authorised it only to act on validly given instructions. It is possible that a court would not apply the same logic to a situation where the "bank" was replaced by a system operator effecting transfers of value in respect of, say, a prepaid anonymous debit card where there is no clear banker/customer relationship.

11.18.2 Exceptions to the basic principle

11–029   The principle in *Orr* is, however, subject to certain exceptions, in particular:

- Where the fraudster has apparent authority (for example, from the terms of the bank mandate) to draw a cheque which is in fact drawn outside the scope of his actual authority. This exception could be relevant where, for example, a company allowed an employee authority to operate an electronic payment system on its behalf but the employee overstepped internal limits applicable to him/her, but not imparted to, and accepted by, the system operator; and/or
- Where the relevant forgery has been facilitated by negligence on the part of the customer in the drawing of cheques (see *London Joint Stock Bank v Macmillan*[5] although note that the *Tai Hing* case established some limitations to this principle).

Again, it is thought likely that these exceptions would be applied by analogy to payment instructions given by electronic means.

---

[2] [1854] Macq. H.L. Cas. 512.
[3] *Tai Hing Cotton Mill Ltd v Chang Hing Bank Ltd* [1986] A.C. 80, [1985] 3 W.L.R. 317, PC.
[4] [2000] 2 All E.R. (Comm) 346.
[5] [1918] A.C. 777.

11.18.3 Alteration of the basic principle by express contract terms

The principle in *Orr* is capable of variation by the express terms of the 11–030
contract between a bank and its customer, but the scope of UK banks and
credit card issuers to impose such variations is limited by the "The Good
Banking Code" (a voluntary code of conduct drawn up by the British
Bankers Association), the Consumer Credit Act 1974 and the Payment
Services Directive when it is implemented into UK law (such implementation being due to occur by November 1, 2009). The Good Banking Code
essentially provides that the loss suffered by bank customers as a result of
fraudulent debits should be limited to a fairly small monetary amount (at
the time of writing, £50 unless the customer has been guilty of gross negligence). It should, however, be noted that this is a voluntary code and does
not apply to any bank or payment service provider which has not signed up
to it.

Section 84(3A) of the Consumer Credit Act 1974 implements Art.8 of the
Distance Selling Directive (Directive 97/7) which requires Member States to
ensure that appropriate measures exist to allow a consumer: (1) to request
cancellation of a payment where fraudulent use has been made of his
payment card in connection with distance contracts covered by the Directive; and (2) in the event of fraudulent use, to be recredited with the sums
paid or have them returned. The Directive is implemented into UK law by
the Consumer Protection (Distance Selling) Regulations 2000 (SI 2000/
2334). It is noteworthy that there is no exclusion of this protection simply
because the consumer has been negligent.

At the time of writing, a proposed new EU Directive commonly known as
"the Payment Services Directive" is not yet in final form but is expected to
be finalised shortly. On the basis of the form approved by the European
Parliament it is expected that this Directive will, when implemented into
UK law, create further limitations on the ability of a payment service
provider to transfer the risk of fraudulent transactions onto the end user.
Current indications are that the liability of customers will be limited to a
relatively small amount other than where those customers have been grossly
negligent or fraudulent or have failed to inform the service provider that
relevant transactions are not authorised by them within a reasonable time
(and in any event within 13 months).

The effectiveness of any variations to the *Orr* principle which are sought
to be imposed by contract may also be subject to challenge under the Unfair
Contract Terms Act 1977 and (in the case of contracts with consumers), the
Unfair Terms in Consumer Contracts Regulations 1999 (SI 1999/2083).
The success of any such challenge will depend on whether the system
operator can show that the variation was "reasonable" in all the
circumstances.

11.18.4 Retailer risk where fraudulent payment innocently received

11–031 For retailers who accept payment from a fraudster using a stolen card or, in an internet context, stolen card details, the key question will be whether the card issuer is still obliged to honour payment under the transaction as if the card use had been genuine.

The case of *First Sport Ltd v Barclays Bank Plc*[6] (which involved the fraudulent use of a cheque and guarantee card) makes it clear that this will depend on the exact terms of the contract under which the retailer is claiming payment. A critical issue is likely to be whether the retailer has complied with the authentication procedures it is required to perform in relation to card payments of the relevant kind.

11.19 FRAUD INVOLVING TRUE ELECTRONIC CASH

11–032 True electronic cash of the *Mondex* kind raises some substantially novel legal issues where fraud is concerned. Two crucial civil law questions which it seems will ultimately need to be answered are:

- Where such electronic cash is stolen, can a later innocent recipient get good title to it?
- Where digital money is counterfeited, who will bear the loss?

11.19.1 Stolen Electronic cash

11–033 If a car is stolen, then, even after its sale through a chain of entirely innocent purchasers, it remains the property of the original owner (subject to certain limited exceptions). The same is not true of cash. If a thief steals £5 and with it buys a bottle of wine, then the £5 in the cash till of the wine merchant belongs to the wine merchant, even though the thief had no title to it.

The reason for the distinction is that the £5 note is what is termed a "negotiable instrument" under the Bills of Exchange Act 1882 and, by virtue of that Act, a person acquiring such a note for value and in good faith acquires good title to the instrument irrespective of any defect in the title of the person from whom it was acquired. Can a wine merchant who accepts £5 of stolen "true cash" money be sure that he is as safe as he would be accepting a £5 note?

As it is currently drafted, the Bills of Exchange Act 1882 is unlikely to assist since it is confined to instruments in writing. It is, however, possible for an instrument which does not comply with the Act to acquire negotiable

---

[6] [1993] 1 W.L.R. 1229.

status by "mercantile usage", provided that such usage is "notorious", "certain", "reasonable" and "general". It remains to be seen whether general use of electronic money would enable it to meet these tests. For electronic cash which fails to meet the requirement of negotiability, the danger to the holder of it is that a defect in title anywhere along the chain of ownership leading to the current holder may leave the current holder out of pocket.

11.19.2 Counterfeit money

It is not surprising that those marketing electronic cash products are insistent that their product cannot be counterfeited. In this connection it is interesting to note that one of the driving forces behind the Finnish *AVANT* electronic purse scheme was a concern that the general availability of sophisticated printing devices was making conventional bank notes too easy to forge—the assumption presumably being that electronic cash is a much harder target.

11–034

To be incapable of being counterfeited, the codes used in the creation of electronic cash must be incapable of being broken. Yet, given the huge potential reward for the successful counterfeiter, it is likely that considerable resources may be mobilised to such a task. Indeed, it is generally recognised that there is no such thing as a perfectly secure system, and that the key is constantly updating security devices to keep at least one step ahead of the criminal fraternity. If the unthinkable should happen and perfect, or near perfect, counterfeit electronic cash should be created, where would the loss fall?

By analogy with the position in relation to counterfeit conventional cash, it seems likely that payment with counterfeit cash would be ineffective. Thus in theory the loss could be forced back down its chain of ownership. However, since earlier holders may be difficult to identify or locate, in most cases the loss is, for practical purposes, likely to fall on the person holding the cash at the time when it is discovered to be a forgery.

One possibility is, however, that counterfeit electronic cash will be undetectable as a forgery while circulating but will be detectable as such when it is sought to be redeemed (for example, because it is only at this point that the existence of multiple units with the same serial number is revealed). In this situation, it may be the party who seeks to redeem forged electronic cash rather than simply transferring it on who will bear the loss.

Another possibility is that, where forged electronic cash is created by the perfect digital copying of genuine electronic cash, it may be undetectable even when redeemed. Furthermore, if the only means whereby a forgery can be detected is when the issuing system detects that the same serial number unit is being redeemed twice, then the issuing system may nonetheless have to honour both units—even though one is known to be a forgery—for the simple reason that it is not known which is the genuine one. It is far from clear how this situation would be treated under English law.

If banks operating an electronic cash system end up honouring counterfeit electronic cash redemptions (either accidentally or because they are legally obliged to do so) then this will be a matter of concern to bank regulators, since the introduction of substantial sums of counterfeit cash into a system could then threaten the ability of the underwriting banks to meet their obligations to their depositors.

Another risk area which should not be overlooked is the danger that a concern that counterfeit money is in circulation may suddenly and dramatically reduce public confidence in the use of an electronic cash product, meaning that the issuing system is immediately required to redeem the great majority of the units in issue.

11.20 WHO CAN ISSUE ELECTRONIC CASH? THE FSMA 2000 AND THE EMI DIRECTIVE

11.20.1 Account-based and cash-based systems

11–035   It was noted earlier that, where a payment mechanism involves prepayment for the "value" issued under it, the system participants have a credit risk on the system operator in relation to the conversion back of system value into real money. Many electronic cash systems are intended to be used by individuals (and not just businesses) and it is a key function of regulation to protect consumers in respect of risks of this kind.

A key regulatory question for any electronic cash system is, therefore, whether the person who issues value under it, in return for payments in "real money" requires any form of authorisation to perform this role. It has been noted above that there are essentially two types of electronic cash system at present. The first is the type in which "accounts" are held for participants in the system which are credited and debited according to the transfers made between participants (this will be referred to as an "account-based system"). The second is the type where electronic value is issued on a non-accounted basis and may circulate between system participants before finally being redeemed (this will be referred to as a "cash based system").

11.20.2 The deposit taking restriction

11–036   There was, for some time in the UK, a debate as to whether either or both types of system required that the value issuer should be authorised to "take deposits". As will be seen below, the context of this debate has been altered for the UK by the implementation of Directive 2000/46, commonly known as the "Electronic Money Institutions Directive" or "EMI Directive". It is nonetheless worth rehearsing the issues briefly for reasons which will be explained below.

The activity of "taking deposits" is limited to authorised persons (for example, banks) by the Financial Services and Markets Act 2000 (the "FSMA") and the Financial Services and Markets Act 2000 (Regulated Activities) Order 2001 (the "Regulated Activities Order"). Section 19 of the FSMA stipulates that no person may carry on a regulated activity in the UK, or purport to do so, unless he is an authorised or exempt person. Article 5 of the Regulated Activities Order stipulates a form of regulated activity as being the taking of "deposits" in the course of a business where either:

(a) money received by way of deposit is lent to others; or
(b) any other activity of the person accepting the deposit is financed wholly, or to a material extent, out of the capital of or interest on money received by way of deposit.

A "deposit" is defined by Art.5(2) of the Regulated Activities Order as being an amount of money which is paid on terms under which it will be repaid, with or without interest or premium, and either on demand or at a time or in circumstances agreed by or on behalf of the person making the payment and the person receiving it.

There is an exclusion from the definition of any amount which is "referable to the provision of property (other than currency) or services or the giving of security"—this exclusion being intended to cover such things as advance payment deposits and rent deposits. There is also an exclusion (in Art.9 of the Regulated Activities Order) for any moneys accepted in return for the issue of "debt securities"—an expression which (subject itself to certain exceptions) includes any debentures, loan stock, bonds, certificates of deposit and any other "instrument creating or acknowledging indebtedness".

11.20.3 Deposit-taking and account-based systems

The above provisions would appear to raise some issues for a non-bank entity operating an account-based payment system. Under that system, the entity will be taking money in from the system users and crediting an account for them from which payments can be made. Since the money so taken will normally be repayable to the system users at any time, there seems to be a strong argument that the system operator would, unless authorised, find itself in breach of the FSMA restriction on deposit-taking, and thus committing a criminal offence. **11–037**

One possible qualification to this conclusion relates to what the operator does with the float of money which derives from the deposits made by its customers. In particular, that there will only be a breach of the FSMA under Art.5 of the Regulated Activities Order if that float is either lent to others or any other activity of the business is financed wholly or to a material extent out of the capital of, or interest on, the float.

The difficulty with this is that most system operators will look to interest on the float as an important source of income to make their business plan work. Additionally, there is no clear delineation of what "to a material extent" actually means. Finally, it is not clear whether "lent to others" would include placing the relevant moneys on deposit with a bank.

For a non-UK entity operating overseas but from time to time issuing value to UK customers, a critical question will be whether any deposits which it is taking are taken "in the United Kingdom". This is because the FSMA limits its territorial reach to deposit-taking actually occurring in the UK. The use of agents in the UK to accept deposits from UK persons can be problematic in this respect.

As noted above, however, this analysis now has to be looked at in the context of the implementation of the EMI Directive.

11.20.4 Deposit-taking and cash-based systems

11–038 The deposit-taking position of the value issuer under a cash-based system is somewhat less clear. There are some commentators who take the view that the issuer of value under a cash-based system is not really taking deposits—that is, they are not accepting sums of money on terms that those sums will be repaid, even if the value issued is redeemable at any time. Instead they argue that what is occurring is a "sale" of the electronic value acquired by the system's customers.

It could even be argued that such sales of value can benefit from the exclusion in Art.9 of the Regulated Activities Order for monies accepted in return for the issue of debt securities, on the grounds that the electronic value issued is an electronic form of acknowledgement of indebtedness. However, this might not be a wise argument for an electronic value issuer to run since, although it might save them from the application of the deposit-taking regime, it would place them right in the middle of the FSMA's regime relating to the issue of, and all types of dealing with, investments in the nature of securities.

Other commentators observe that, if accepting money from the public on the basis of a promise to repay it constitutes deposit-taking, there is no reason why it should cease to constitute deposit-taking simply because it is accompanied by the issue of electronic tokens which can be used by the customer when they, or an assignee of the customer to whom those electronic tokens have been transferred, want to demand repayment. There is no case law authority to resolve this debate but this debate is largely overtaken, for the UK and the other EU Member States at least, by the implementation of the EMI Directive. This is discussed in the following paragraphs.

11.20.5 The Electronic Money Institutions Directive

11–039 The regulatory framework concerning electronic money in the UK and elsewhere in the EU has undergone significant change by virtue of the implementation into the domestic law of the UK and the other Member States of Directive 2000/46 on the taking up, pursuit of and prudential supervision of the business of electronic money institutions (the "EMI Directive") which was required to be implemented in the UK (and all other EU Member States) by the end of April 2002.

The primary purpose of the EMI Directive is to create an authorisation and regulation structure for the issue of electronic money. The idea is that this structure will give non-bank institutions a clear right to be issuers (in place of the previously existing legal uncertainty) but only provided that they meet the necessary authorisation criteria and comply with certain rules in relation to the operation of their business. This Directive needs to be read in conjunction with the parallel Directive 2000/28 which adds electronic money institutions to the definition of "credit institutions" for certain (but not all) purposes.

11.20.6 What is an EMI and what is "electronic money"?

The EMI Directive introduces a new concept of an "electronic money institution" which is defined as "an undertaking or any other legal person which issues a means of payment in the form of electronic money". The concept of electronic money is defined as: 11–040

"monetary value as represented by a claim on the issuer which is:

(a) stored on an electronic device;
(b) issued on receipt of funds of an amount not less in value than the monetary value issued;
(c) accepted as means of payment by undertakings other than the issuer."

One of the recitals to the Directive describes electronic money as "a surrogate for coins and notes". Being only a recital, this description does not form part of the definition, but it is instructive. At a first look, this seems to be a wide ranging definition which should catch all the types of scheme currently thought of as electronic cash. However, on a closer look it becomes apparent that value issued under a purely account-based system may not necessarily be caught within the definition of "electronic money".

An account-based system does not have to issue monetary tokens so there is in fact no need for any "value" to be "stored on an electronic device". Even the wording of the recital may not help since account-based systems are not really "a surrogate for coins or notes", given that they do not involve the free circulation of negotiable instruments; they are rather more of a surrogate for debit card transfers or cheques.

In the UK, the Financial Services Authority (the "FSA"), as the financial services regulator, seems to have taken the view that account-based systems should be treated as falling within the scope of the EMI Directive, it is believed on the basis that funds are "stored on an electronic device" by virtue of being held on a centralised computer of the system operator. There are, however, two points to note:

(i) it seems that not all EU Member State regulators have taken the same view so, for some states, account-based systems may still be caught by laws related to "deposit-taking"; and

(ii) the FSA's position, although undoubtedly practical, does not decide the law on this issue and it therefore remains possible that the operator of an account-based system is taking deposits.

At the time of writing, a second EMI Directive is in prospect and it is expected that this will resolve issues of this kind. For the time being, however, it should be noted by any potential issuer of money planning to rely on the EMI Directive (and so avoid being subject to the more rigorous regime on deposit-taking), that it may be important to structure its product in such a way as to make it fit as closely as possible within the definition of "electronic money".

For example, a primarily account-based system may, in some jurisdictions, be well advised to structure its technical solution so as to ensure that its customers appear to hold "money" on their hard drive or a smartcard rather than just having account balances.

An electronic money institution which is duly authorised to operate in any EU Member State will have a "passport" to provide the same product in other Member States.

11.20.7 Waivers

11–041 The EMI Directive envisages that Member States are allowed to grant waivers from the application of the EMI Directive to certain types of scheme, provided that they operate only within the national boundaries of the Member State concerned. For the UK, the FSA has implemented most of the possible waivers, although it does require that any person wishing to rely on the waivers must register with it. Some other EU Member States have decided to largely ignore, or have imposed additional restrictions on entities relying on, the waiver provisions. The waivers envisaged by the EMI Directive are:

(a) **Small schemes:** schemes where the total issued value does not normally exceed €5 million and never exceeds €6 million;

(b) **Only same-group acceptors of value:** schemes where the acceptance in payment of the value issued is restricted to persons in the same corporate group as the issuer (schemes where value is accepted in payment only by the issuer itself are outside the scope of the Directive altogether because they do not involve any "money" in the first place; they may, however, still involve deposit taking); and

(c) **Limited acceptors of value:** schemes where the acceptance in payment of the value issued is restricted to a limited number of undertakings which can be clearly distinguished by:

(i) their location in the same premises or other limited local area; or

(ii) a close financial or business relationship with the issuer such as a common marketing or distribution scheme.

The idea behind the waiver provisions was to enable certain small or localised acceptance schemes to be set up and operate without the burdensome weight of regulation on them. After all, students who load £25 onto a smartcard to enable them to make small electronic payments around their University campus may not need the full protection of the FSA in relation to the possibility that the system operator collapses into insolvency.

11.20.8 Supervision of EMIs and requirements for authorisation

If an issuer of electronic value decides to obtain authorisation as an EMI, it should be noted that the EMI Directive imposes a number of restrictions on the initial authorisation of EMIs and the way in which they subsequently carry on business. In particular: **11–042**

(a) **Business restriction:** An EMI cannot carry on any business other than running the relevant scheme and other ancillary business. There is a specific prohibition on the provision of credit (on the basis that this is a particularly risky form of business).

(b) **Minimum capital:** an EMI must have a minimum of own capital equal to the greater of:

(i) €1 million; and

(ii) between 2 and 5 per cent of the amount of its electronic money liabilities (see below).

(c) **Investment of the float:** an EMI is subject to restrictions on what it can do with the float of money yielded by selling electronic value. It is limited to highly liquid and very safe investments. There are two classes of these, called 0 per cent-weighted and 20 per cent-weighted. The 20 per cent-weighted assets are generally more risky than those that are 0 per cent-weighted and once more than 40 per cent of the float is invested in 20 per cent-weighted assets, the own capital requirement increases from 2 per cent of electronic money liabilities on a straight line basis until it is 5 per cent if all such investment is in 20 per cent-weighted assets.

(d) **Supervision:** EMIs are subject to supervision by the FSA, but such supervision is with a "lighter touch" than that applied to banks. Such supervision covers such things as the resistance of the value issuer's system to fraud, technological collapse, money laundering, its compliance with such things as data protection laws and an element of verification of the suitability of persons controlling the EMI to run it (covering both competence and integrity issues).

11.20.9 Criticism of the EMI Directive

11–043   A key purpose of the EMI Directive was to open up the field for competition in the electronic cash domain. In particular, it was a response to the argument that running a payment system which involved prepayment for value also involved "deposit-taking", an argument which effectively meant that the operators of such systems either had to be banks or to partner with a bank as the issuer of electronic value. It was hoped that the new entity of an electronic money institution would be easier to set up than a bank, while nonetheless not exposing consumers to undue risk. Unfortunately, at the time of writing at least, the extent to which this has increased competition has not been impressive and some argue that the burden of regulation is still too great.

11.21 SHOULD TRUE ELECTRONIC MONEY OFFER PAYMENT ANONYMITY?

11–044   In the banking world as it stands at the moment, most medium-scale and large-scale fund movements will depend on the alteration of entries in the books of trusted third parties, notably banks and credit card companies. As a result, each such transaction will therefore leave an audit trail. Considerable efforts are necessary to obscure or erase any such trail. On the other hand, the transfer of electronic value under a true electronic cash system needs no book entries with third parties and can thus be structured so that no audit trail is left as the value is moved around. Essentially, an audit trail feature would need to be built into a true electronic cash scheme rather than being an intrinsic feature of it.

It is clear that the widespread acceptance of true electronic cash (which for these purposes can be treated as including any other anonymous electronic payment mechanism such as prepaid anonymous debit cards) may, therefore, have considerable significance for those who wish to conceal the movement of funds for unlawful purposes—and for those who are charged with the duty of trying to control them. To give just two examples:

- If money requiring laundering could be converted into electronic cash, it might thereafter become extremely difficult if not impossible to trace. It could be moved between jurisdictions in potentially unlimited amounts or in a series of very small amounts at the touch of a button.

- In countries such as the UK, the fact that the vast majority of payments leave a clear audit trail is a significant obstacle to tax evasion. If the advent of electronic cash means that it becomes possible to make many more payments on a cash basis, it seems likely seriously to undermine the ability of tax authorities to keep track of payments and levy the taxes which ought to be due. Essentially, the black economy could become easier to operate.

System operators are alive to these issues and have incorporated in their system safeguards such as a restriction on the maximum amount that can be held on any card. There are those who argue that such steps are not enough and that more steps must be taken to build safeguards into any true electronic cash system which is allowed to operate in the UK. The next obvious step is to build into electronic cash systems devices which remove or limit the anonymity that such systems can in principle offer to both payers and payees. This can be done at least in part by ensuring that the devices which hold electronic value identify their owner whenever they effect a payment transaction and that such devices also keep a record of past inward and outward transactions which they have effected, including the identity of the counterparty. A *Mondex* smart card issued to an identified account holder was said to keep a record of the last ten transactions it has effected. It is understood, however, that such cards could be configured to hold records of considerably more transactions than ten and even to download their transaction information each time that they were linked to the issuer's system, for example, when reloaded at an automated teller machine or over the telephone.

Criminals have shown themselves to be a resourceful and highly adaptable breed when it comes to new technology and there is every reason to think that they will be quick to find ways to add the abuse of a new payment system to their armoury of criminal devices. Against this background there might at first seem to be strong arguments for minimising the payee/payer anonymity that electronic cash payments can offer to the greatest extent possible.

On the other hand, respected commentators have identified significant potential civil liberties risks in such an approach.[7] They start by stressing the obvious but important point that if we cannot pay for anything anonymously, then we cease to be able to buy anything anonymously. From this, they construct a disturbing picture in three stages.

First, they point out that with virtually all retailing moving in the direction of automation, retailers are starting to have the ability to create

---

[7] For an excellent analysis of the arguments on this issue, see A Michael Froomkin's article "Flood Control on the Information Ocean: Living With Anonymity, Digital Cash and Distributed Databases" in the Spring 1996 edition of the *University of Pittsburgh Journal of Law and Commerce*, Vol.15, Issue 2.

and store a complete record of all the sales they make, including the name of the buyer. Buyer anonymity is obviously not possible when payment is made using such devices as credit cards. If traditional cash ceases to exist and electronic cash replaces it, buyer anonymity will be impossible unless electronic cash itself offers such a possibility.

This in turn gives rise to the possibility that it would, in principle, be possible to construct a complete record of a person's spending by consulting the databases of the retailers with whom he or she has spent money. Although this may sound like a difficult and time consuming task, it is pointed out that "data mining" techniques, together with the linking of all retailer systems through networks such as the internet, mean that this could actually become a very easy and virtually instantaneous task. The increasing use of store loyalty cards is evidence of the value that retailers attribute to such information.

The final piece of the jigsaw is the fact that access to written information is becoming less hardcopy and more online based. So, in the future we may no longer buy a newspaper but instead download articles which we think will be of interest from the newspaper's online server. As we will pay-as-we-read, the consumer profiling that "data mining" will permit may able to extend beyond what we buy to what we are reading, and, by inference, what we may be thinking.

An argument that appropriate data protection legislation can deal with such concerns is not entirely convincing. The consumer may justifiably be concerned that such legislation will contain exceptions that permit access to relevant data by government bodies. They may also be sceptical as to whether such legislation will always be complied with by information gatherers and processors. True protection, it could be said, lies in the information not being collected in the first place rather than its use being restricted once it is in existence.

So what emerges is a conflict between the needs of law enforcement and the protection of the privacy of the individual. It is not a technical issue or one which ought to be left simply to the regulators of electronic money to resolve: it is an issue which requires a well informed public debate.

11.22 CONCLUSION

11–045   The area of payment on the internet is one of potentially rapid change. It is likely that credit, charge and debit cards will retain their current dominance for some time to come. They have considerable appeal for medium-to-large value purchases made both on and off the internet. The use of such things as subscription-based charging models or account pre-funding can sometimes be used to circumvent the micropayments problem. However, they cannot easily be made to work for consumer-to-consumer transfers.

True electronic cash remains a real threat of competition to credit and debit cards for the future, but it is disappointing that it has not developed more rapidly over the past decade than it has. For example, although the *Mondex* system originally promised much, neither it, nor any other similar "true cash" system, has been rolled out to a mass market as seemed likely to happen when the first edition of this book was published nearly a decade ago. This is particularly unfortunate given that systems like this would appear particularly well suited to low value payments on the internet.

So far as legal status of true electronic cash is concerned, issues such as the effect of the use of such cash by a thief do give rise to some thorny problems. It seems possible that legislation will be necessary to give the new cash the same protections as have been afforded for centuries to its physical counterpart. From a regulatory point of view, there are some difficult and highly political questions to be tackled in relation to whether payment anonymity should be permitted.

There has been growth in the field of single operator account-based schemes such as that operated by *PayPal* and there is likely to be further growth in this area, quite probably from mobile phone companies creating their own schemes (and, in due course, possibly even schemes that link to the schemes of the other operators).

For those setting out to provide alternative cash systems, the current dominance of conventional payment cards is a concern. However, there are needs which they do not fulfil and in these areas we can expect to see alternative models continuing to exist or develop to satisfy end-user demand.

CHAPTER 12

Prohibited and Regulated Activities

12.1 INTRODUCTION

12–001 In this Chapter we examine various fields in which the internet has presented particular challenges to law enforcement agencies and to the overseers of regulated industries. We encompass traditional media laws such as obscenity and contempt of court, and industries such as gambling, pharmaceuticals and financial services. We also address encryption—a topic that the internet has thrust into the limelight—and touch on advertising regulation.

We start, however, with a discussion of the ways in which governments and others have responded, ought to respond and ought not to respond to the cross-border nature of the internet. This section complements Ch.6, in which we discussed jurisdiction and applicable law in civil matters. Here we describe the consequences, especially for freedom of speech and international movement of information and services, of different rule-making approaches to the cross-border internet.

We shall see that while the internet does not necessarily change everything, some legal rules that have worked well in the off-line environment have completely different consequences in the on-line world, thus demanding re-examination from first principles.

12.2 CROSS-BORDER CONTENT

12–002 Originally a barely visible minority medium, the internet has now entered the consciousness of governments, non-governmental organisations and law enforcement agencies around the world. They have made many attempts to enforce national laws against content transmitted across borders by the internet. The relationship between national laws and the international nature of the internet has become increasingly strained.

As a result, attention has turned to the international legal framework within which communication takes place on the internet. Traditionally this meant private international law. Private international law has, however, had to compete with the rise of supranational regimes such as the internal market elements of the EC Treaty.

Some have suggested that the internet requires nothing less than an international convention to govern its cross-border aspects. It is easily forgotten that those who would have to agree to such a convention include the very governments who so enthusiastically seek to apply their domestic laws to internet activity in other countries.[1]

In this section we look at the differing principles and policies that might in theory underlie an international framework to govern the flow of content on the internet. We also examine the varieties of national laws and regulations that could inspire international action and its possible implications for freedom of speech and cross-border trade on the internet.

12.2.1 Why international action?

Pressure for an international framework to govern the internet emanates   **12–003**
from a variety of constituencies. These have different, often conflicting, motivations and self-interest. So even if all are agreed on the need for an international framework, that masks fundamental disagreement on what that framework should seek to achieve and what it should contain. Here are five factors that underpin different constituencies' desire for an international framework.

Uncertainty and cost

The task of content-clearing a website in every jurisdiction from which it   **12–004**
can be accessed is extremely expensive and may, due to the wide variety of national laws, in fact be impossible.

If it were simply a matter of complying with the most restrictive standard for each type of potential liability the task could theoretically be achieved, even if the resulting content were so bland as to be commercially useless.

But in some areas (especially in highly regulated industries) national regimes impose conflicting requirements, so that there is no lowest denominator of content common to all. Compliance with all regimes is then impossible, and the publisher has to resort to devices of uncertain legal efficacy—territory disclaimers, entry screens and so on—to minimise the risk of civil or criminal sanctions in a country in which he may have no commercial interest.

Commercial users of the internet have a clear interest in action which

---

[1] *Cf* the comments of Professor Eli Noam in "A First Amendment for the Internet", *Financial Times* November 16, 2005: "... it is important that any international internet regulation be based in advance on constitution-like principles. What is needed is a strong rule against governmental restrictiveness on the international flows of information over the internet, such as the First Amendment of the US constitution, which protects free speech and press in America. Such a rule must be clear and unambiguous. Anything less will be undermined since it will be easy to find an international majority to support various qualifications."

would reduce the cost and risks of publishing on the internet. An effective international framework would have the potential to deliver that.

Uncertain risk of cross-border liability is the enemy of cross-border availability. The temptation is to put up the shutters and deal only with visitors who can be positively identified as originating from a few known countries. This results in undesirable discrimination among users of different nationalities or countries of origin and deprives consumers of a broader choice of on-line services.

However, the benefits of legal certainty can be exaggerated. Faced with a choice between the certainty of liability in every country in the world and an uncertain argument for more limited exposure, what on-line actor would opt for certainty?

Extra-territorial effect

12–005   Incidents in which national authorities have exercised dominion over foreign content on the internet, such as the German *CompuServe* and *Radikal* cases in 1995 and 1996 respectively and the French *Yahoo!* case in 2000, give rise to concern over extra-territoriality as the effects of such actions spill out across the internet without regard for national borders.

Some have believed that national action to prohibit content can never be effective because, as expressed by John Gilmore (a co-founder of the Electronic Frontier Foundation), the internet interprets censorship as damage and routes around it.

While that may be to some extent true of the content itself, it is not true of the human originators, publishers and distributors of the content. These people and companies exist in the real world, not in cyberspace. In practice they (and their directors and employees) may be subject to the criminal laws of the jurisdictions in which they reside or have assets, to which they travel[2] or to which they can be extradited; and may be subject to the civil laws of countries whose judgments can be enforced against their persons and assets.

Extra-territoriality is, therefore, a real concern, at least to those who do not wish to spend their remaining days confined within the borders of some content haven from which they cannot be extradited.

If an international framework could be devised which created rules for cyberspace independent of national regimes, then content on the internet and its human progenitors could both be insulated from extra-territorial effects. Such a scheme would be attractive to those (a sadly dwindling band) who regard cyberspace as a domain which ought to be subject only to its own liberal rules.

---

[2] At the time of writing the directors of some British on-line gaming companies have become rudely aware of the potential for being arrested at American airports. Note also the English prosecution and conviction under English obscenity laws of the French director of a US company operating a US-hosted adult website that could be accessed in England (*R v Perrin* [2002] EWCA Crim 747). Note also the German *Toben* case, involving the prosecution and conviction under the German Holocaust-denial laws of the Australian (although German-born) proprietor of an Australian website. The defendant was originally arrested while travelling in Germany.

On the other hand, there can be no guarantee that an international framework—certainly one taking the form of a multilateral convention arrived at by negotiation among national governments—would take a liberal form.

As we discuss below, a cross-border liability rule is not value-neutral as to content standards. It must either embody its own content standards or have the effect of preferring some national laws over others. Even a convention that addresses only jurisdiction, purporting to have nothing to say about substantive law, will have different practical consequences for substantive law, depending on how the jurisdiction rules are written.[3]

Since, realistically, a formal convention could only emerge from a top-down inter-governmental process,[4] a convention setting up cyberspace as an independent dominion would not necessarily embody rules and values any more liberal than those of the many restrictive national regimes who would participate in such discussions.

Fear of a foreign flood

If enlightened users of the internet fear extra-territoriality, governments fear the opposite: that the internet will render their domestic laws impotent as citizens gain access to material originating outside the jurisdiction which local laws cannot reach.

12–006

Such concerns arise acutely in matters of culture (especially collectivised attitudes to alcohol, gambling, exposure of bare flesh and protection of language) and political and religious dissent. Much of the pressure for international rules to govern the internet originates from governments anxious to preserve the efficacy of their local laws.

The urge to regulate

Previous forms of new media such as television and radio have been subjected to controls of a fundamentally different type from those applying to old media such as the printing press.

12–007

It has for many years been regarded as acceptable to require new media to operate under licence from the state, under the immediate control of a

---

[3] This was apparent in the negotiations over the proposed Hague Convention on International Jurisdiction and Foreign Judgments in Civil and Commercial Matters (*www.hcch.net*). For cross-border information torts, an "effects" based jurisdiction rule makes it very easy for a court to take jurisdiction and then to apply its home law to the conduct complained about. If the jurisdiction rule is more limited, then the court may have to decline jurisdiction and will not get the opportunity to apply its home law. If a jurisdiction rules allows a consumer to sue in his home country then, then the court will have the opportunity to apply the mandatory rules (e.g. consumer protection laws) of the home country. So even pure jurisdiction rules have consequences for the substantive law applied to internet content. See also the Report of the American Bar Association Jurisdiction in Cyberspace Project (*http://meetings.abanet.org/webupload/commupload/CL320000/relatedresources/Jurisdiction_Paper.pdf*).

[4] See, however, the ABA Jurisdiction Project recommendation that a "multinational Global on-line Standards Commission ('GOSC') should be empanelled to study jurisdiction issues and develop uniform principles and global protocol standards by a specific sunset date, working in conjunction with other international bodies considering similar issues" (Report, para.1.4).

regulatory body (such as the former Independent Television Commission or Radio Authority, now combined in the Office of Communications (OFCOM)) empowered with a wide degree of discretion to devise detailed codes of practice to achieve general objectives laid out in the relevant legislation. Those objectives have often been highly restrictive, for instance in their requirements of political impartiality.[5]

Such a regulatory regime, backed up by the sanction of withdrawal of licence, contrasts with the freedom traditionally accorded to the print media, who can set up and operate without licence[6] and are in the main subject only to general laws applied and interpreted by an independent judiciary.[7]

12–008   The licensing and regulatory model has also been used in the telecommunications industry to govern provision of telecommunication services. So widespread have such regulatory schemes become that there is sometimes almost an unspoken assumption that a regulatory scheme is necessary and appropriate for any new medium of communication.

Historically, existing new media regulators have frequently become involved in the debate about appropriate laws for the internet, and occasionally their existing areas of authority touched upon internet issues. That certainly occurred in the broadcast area. There was significant debate during the passage of the Communications Act 2003 about whether the content jurisdiction of the new Office of Communications (OFCOM) should extend to the internet.

In the result, for the most part internet content was excluded from

---

[5] For instance, if the requirements of political impartiality for television and radio services under s.320 of the Communications Act 2003 were to be applied to the internet, web versions of print newspapers would have to be rewritten to remove the political partisanship characteristic of the print press. A partisan editorial line would be impermissible. See also *R v Radio Authority, Ex p Bull* [1997] E.M.L.R. 201 in which the Court of Appeal upheld a decision by the Radio Authority to prohibit radio advertising by Amnesty International (British Section) on the ground that the organisation's objects were wholly or mainly of a political nature, contrary to s.92(2)(a) of the then Broadcasting Act 1990. Far from there being a case for extending broadcast regulation to the internet, with satellite and cable television channels now numbering in the hundreds and the looming prospect of all-digital terrestrial television, the ban on politically partisan television appears increasingly anachronistic. However, in *R v Secretary of State for Culture Media and Sport, Ex p. Animal Defenders International* [2006] EWHC 3069 (Admin) the Divisional Court held that the prohibition on radio and television political advertising under the 2003 Act was not incompatible with Art.10 of the European Convention on Human Rights.

[6] As long ago as 1644 John Milton's *Areopagitica* famously criticised Cromwell's practice of licensing books and periodicals: "Truth and understanding are not such wares as to be monopolised and traded in by tickets and statutes and standards. We must not think to make a staple commodity of all the knowledge in the land, to mark and licence it like our broadcloth and our woolpacks." In contrast, the licensing of broadcast media has flourished without serious opposition. The continuing lack of protest against broadcast regulation is all the more surprising considering that the original justifications based on spectrum scarcity have long since withered away.

[7] Recent years have seen an increase in the importance of self-regulatory bodies such as the Press Complaints Commission, in response to heavy criticism of some activities of the print press, especially in the area of privacy. For the first time, with the enactment of s.12(4) of the Human Rights Act, linkage has been established between private codes of practice and statutory rules.

OFCOM's jurisdiction. However, the debate about the boundary between broadcast and non-broadcast services has now reignited with the proposed revision of the TV Without Frontiers Directive, which we discuss below at para.12–015.

Before the advent of the Communications Act 2003 the then Independent Television Commission issued guidelines for websites operated by regulated broadcasters. The current OFCOM Programme Code similarly applies to the websites of licensed broadcasters, as being programme related services.[8]

The question of whether the scope of then Broadcasting Act 1990 could extend to some types of internet content occasionally caused anxiety.[9]

There was also an alarming precedent set by OFTEL, the then tele-communications regulator (whose brief under s.3 of the Telecommunications Act 1984 made no explicit reference to content carried by telecommunication systems, restricting itself to the "prices charged for, and the quality and variety of, telecommunication services"), involving itself in approving rules about content.

This occurred in the area of premium rate telephone services, in which through a telecommunications licence amendment following a Monopolies and Mergers Commission report OFTEL took powers to approve codes of practice for the provision of chatline services. The approved codes of practice (submitted for approval by ICSTIS, the Independent Committee for the supervision of Standards of Telephone Information Services) included relatively restrictive content rules.[10] OFTEL justified its involvement in this area as reducing the "impairment of quality of service" associated with chatlines, which had been identified by the MMC as being to the detriment of the public interest.[11] ICSTIS has since been lauded by the government as a prime example of "self-regulation".[12]

Certainly the predominance of the regulatory model has subverted the language, so that the concept of content being "regulated" has gained ascendancy, obscuring the crucial distinction between general laws and discretionary regulation.

---

[8] See Ch.8, para.8–046.

[9] Before the advent of the Communications Act 2003 the ITC claimed that its powers under the Broadcasting Act 1990 extended to television programmes on the internet and to advertisements which contained still or moving pictures but that it was "not seeking to apply these powers at present".

[10] Chatline Services Code of Practice recognised by Director-General of Telecommunications December 7, 1989, para.2.3.2 (recognition was subsequently withdrawn in 1992). Under s.120 to 124 of the Communications Act 2003 ICTSIS's codes of practice are now under OFCOM's jurisdiction. The Act provides for recognition of ICSTIS's codes by OFCOM and affords OFCOM a last-resort power to intervene. This has the potential to impact on some internet services where charges are paid through the customer's telephone bill, although before the passage of the 2003 Act OFTEL and ICSTIS disclaimed any intention to regulate the internet in this regard (Statement by Director-General of Telecommunications, July 24, 2001). See also J. Edwards and A. Sylvester, "A Law by Any Other Name—ICSTIS" [1997] 4 C.T.L.R. 157.

[11] Statement from the Director General of Telecommunications July 27, 1989.

[12] Communications White Paper (fn.13 below), p.83. The White Paper described the proposal to bring all of ICSTIS's codes of practice under the jurisdiction of the communications regulator as "licence changes to help make ICSTIS even more effective".

The debate about the laws that should govern content on the internet is usually conducted as a discussion of the appropriate form of "content regulation". The UK government, in the Communications White Paper of December 2000,[13] even referred to general content laws as "tier zero" or "negative" "content regulation".

Phrases such as these obscure the important distinction between, on the one hand, a regulatory regime founded on licensing or similar principles, and, on the other, the freedom to publish without prior permission from a government body, subject only to general laws adjudicated upon by independent courts and applicable to anyone who chooses to publish.

12–009   Concepts such as co-regulation are similarly of concern when applied to the content field. Co-regulation was defined by the government in "*e-commerce@its.best.uk*" as follows:

> "Government defines the public policy objectives that need to be secured, but tasks industry to design and operate self-regulatory solutions and stands behind industry ready to take statutory action if necessary."[14]

So the idea here is that individual citizens and companies, spurred on by the threat of statutory action, are there to act as the servants of government in achieving its policy objectives. It is difficult to imagine anything further removed from the proper function of content laws in a liberal society.

The distinction between self-regulation and co-regulation can be hard to fathom where self-regulation is backed up with statutory powers, as with the new ICSTIS scheme noted above.

The distinction between the internet and television was taken up very early in the US. As long ago as 1996 the Citizens Internet Empowerment Coalition, one of the parties challenging certain sections of the Communications Decency Act (CDA) in Philadelphia,[15] based its challenge on the proposition that "the internet is newspaper, not TV".

The *CDA* case was considered both at first instance and on appeal by the US Supreme Court. The distinction between newspaper and television was taken up in the judgment of District Judge Dalzell (one of three judgments of the first instance court), who in a section of his judgment dealt with "medium-specific analysis" of the constitutionality of the CDA.

He commented that the government's argument relying on the *Pacifica*[16] decision assumed that "what is good for broadcasting is good for the internet". He pointed out that in *Turner Broadcasting System Inc v FCC*[17] the Supreme Court declined to adopt the broadcast rationale for the medium of cable television, citing the fundamental technical differences between broadcast and cable transmission. This, said the judge, meant that

---

[13] *A new future for Communications* (Cm. 5010) December 12, 2000.
[14] *e-commerce@its.best.uk*, para.5.6.
[15] *ACLU v Reno*, 929 F. Supp. 824 (DC EPa 1996).
[16] *FCC v Pacifica Foundation*, 438 US 726 (1978).
[17] 114 S. Ct 2445 (1994).

the justification for the constitutionality of the broadcast rules arose out of scarcity of the medium, not the end product that the viewer watches. Therefore, the question had to be addressed whether the government had the power to regulate protected speech at all, not just whether the CDA was a constitutional exercise of that power.

The judge commented that far from justifying broadcast-style regulation, **12–010** his examination of the special characteristics of internet communication led him to conclude that:

> "The internet deserves the broadest possible protection from government-imposed, content-based regulation. If 'the First Amendment erects a virtually insurmountable barrier between government and the print media', *Tornillo*, 418 US at 259 (White J. concurring), even though the print medium fails to achieve the hoped-for diversity in the marketplace of ideas, then that 'insurmountable barrier' must also exist for a medium that succeeds in achieving that diversity."

District Judge Dalzell concluded his judgment thus:

> "As the most participatory form of mass speech yet developed, the internet deserves the highest protection from governmental intrusion ... The absence of governmental regulation of internet content has unquestionably produced a kind of chaos, but as one of the plaintiffs' experts put it with such resonance at the hearing: 'what achieved success was the very chaos that the internet is. The strength of the internet is that chaos'. Just as the strength of the internet is chaos, so the strength of our liberty depends upon the chaos and cacophony of the unfettered speech the First Amendment protects."

The Supreme Court, holding that the challenged parts of the CDA were unconstitutional, also engaged in a medium-specific analysis. The Supreme Court pointed out that the "vast democratic fora" of the internet had not been subject to the type of government supervision and regulation that had attended the broadcast industry, and that the internet was not as "invasive" as radio or television.

The court also pointed out that "unlike the conditions that prevailed when Congress first authorised regulation of the broadcast spectrum, the internet can hardly be considered a 'scarce' expressive commodity." The court went on to state:

> "This dynamic, multi-faceted category of communication includes not only traditional print and news services, but also audio, video and still images, as well as interactive, real-time dialogue. Through the use of chat rooms, any person with a phone line can become a town crier with a voice that resonates farther than it

could from any soapbox. Through the use of web pages, mail exploders, and newsgroups, the same individual can become a pamphleteer. As the District Court found, 'the content on the internet is as diverse as human thought' ... We agree with its conclusion that our cases provide no basis for qualifying the level of First Amendment scrutiny that should be applied to this medium."

The Supreme Court at the very least put down a marker challenging any assumption that the internet should be subject to broadcast-style licensing and regulation.

The findings put in question whether the US would be constitutionally capable of adhering to an international internet convention based on licensing and regulation. They are also of more domestic relevance now that the UK has incorporated the European Convention on Human Rights (albeit that is a considerably weaker instrument than the US Bill of Rights) into its domestic law.

12–011   There has been some recognition in the UK of the fact that internet is not a broadcast medium. In its 1998 report *The Multi-media Revolution*[18] the House of Commons Culture Media and Sport Select Committee remarked:

"The internet will increasingly become a platform for audio—visual content barely distinguishable from broadcast content. This does not mean it can be subject to regulation comparable to broadcasting. Self-regulation through service providers is in its early stages and should be encouraged. We are far from persuaded that any particular legislative provision for regulation for internet content (as opposed to legislation to clarify the application of the current general law to the internet) is viable."

The Committee repeated this position in its Second Report of 2001, *The Communications White Paper*[19]:

"Although the internet is being used and will be used increasingly as a medium for audio and video material, the internet is fundamentally different to traditional broadcast media. Whereas there is closely controlled and licensed access to broadcast media, there is no spectrum scarcity on the internet and no tradition of licensing. The internet has flourished with a minimum of regulation, partly because the internet first developed in the United States, a country that provides specific constitutional protection for freedom of speech. We have noted previously that, due to the almost infinite scale and international character of the internet, content

---

[18] Session 1997–98, Fourth Report, May 6, 1998.
[19] Session 2000–01, Second Report, March 15, 2001.

regulation of the traditional kind is not viable for the internet."[20]

This position was reflected in the almost complete exclusion of the internet from the content jurisdiction of OFCOM under the Communications Act 2003.

More recently the UK government has adopted a commendably robust stance in opposing the European Commission's proposed extension[21] of the TV Without Frontiers Directive to "non-linear" on-demand audio-visual content on the internet.[22]

That stance, which has achieved some success in reducing the scope of the proposed Directive,[23] has been supported by the House of Lords European Union Committee, which in its January 2007 report "Television without Frontiers?"[24] commented:

"The Council text seeks to identify and propose the regulation of 'television-like' services but proposes to regulate them differently. As we note above, if they are to be included at all we agree that they must be regulated differently, but the wording and definitions in the latest versions of the text may encourage the idea that they can and should be regulated in the same way as television. We would consider such a move now or in the future to be a grave error.

There may also be a second problem with extending the draft Directive into non-television services, such as the internet and other new media services. It might be taken as an encouragement that it is desirable to extend regulation into these services more widely and eventually to go beyond 'television-like' services into other parts of the internet and new media.

Given the practical difficulties in defining, regulating and enforcing a Directive based on 'television-like' services, we believe that any further incursion into the internet and other new media services will be fraught with even greater difficulties and, as we

---

[20] Para.112.

[21] Proposal for a Directive of the European Parliament and of the Council Amending Council Directive 89/552/EEC (COM (2005) 646 final December 13, 2005) (Draft Audiovisual Media Services Directive).

[22] "In the UK's view, extending regulation to internet content is not an appropriate course of action." (UK government response to the European Commission's Public Consultation for the review of the Television without Frontiers Directive *http://ec.europa.eu/comm/avpolicy/ docs/reg/modernisation/issue_papers/contributions/ip1-uk.pdf.*) See also speech by the Secretary of State for Culture, Media & Sport to the Royal Television Society on September 14, 2006: "... we think it is a mistake to include non-linear services in the new Television Without Frontiers Directive. But if any of them must be included, they have to be restricted to video-on-demand."

[23] Education, Youth and Culture Council text of November 13, 2006; European Parliament plenary text adopted in First Reading, December 2006.

[24] "Television without Frontiers?" Report of the House of Lords European Union Committee, 3rd Report of Session 2006–07, January 31, 2007, HL Paper 27 at paras 83 to 85.

have indicated above, is unnecessary in order to secure a single internal market."

Order and chaos

12–012 The last of our five factors that create pressure for an international framework is the natural human tendency, especially prevalent in lawyers, to want to tidy up chaos and replace it with order.

The internet is undoubtedly chaotic—that is how it grew up—and has minimal centrally imposed authority. When faced with this chaos, there may be a desire to create structures designed to impose order in a top-down fashion. Whether or not that is wise, the tendency exists and can be expected to contribute to calls for an international framework to bring order to the internet.

But as we have observed above, of those whose interests would have to be accommodated in order to reach agreement on such a framework, a great many are unlikely to have the interests of a free internet at heart—as can be seen from the section on national actions that follows.

While the temptation to try to impose top-down order on the internet continues to attract some, others are more sanguine about the prospects of succeeding in such an endeavour. Although, as we have noted, the adage that the internet routes around censorship tends to ignore the fact that laws can be enforced against people and assets, in a very real sense the internet is able to route around bad laws. A local dispute can, as in the *Nottinghamshire County Council (JET Report)*[25] and *Radikal*[26] cases, suddenly become a worldwide and insoluble problem as internet sites mirror the content under threat.

Even if a conviction or judgment is obtained initially, the resulting outcry (especially over attempts to enforce local laws in ways that have extra-territorial effect in countries in which the content is legal) is often enough to stimulate a change in the law in due course.[27]

It may well be thought that the causes of freedom of speech and unimpeded cross-border flow of information and services on the internet are better served by continuing chaos, imperfect as it may be, than by any currently achievable form of international framework.

As a matter of pragmatic politics, the potential ignominy of being associated with futile laws may be expected to act as a brake on some of the more ill-considered proposals to legislate for (or against) the internet. For instance, the House of Commons Culture Media and Sport Select Committee remarked in its 1998 MultiMedia Revolution report:

---

[25] See Ch.6.

[26] Discussed below, under Germany.

[27] For instance, in the German prosecution of Felix Somm over the CompuServe newsgroups in 1995, not only was the initial conviction reversed on appeal, but new legislation (the German Multimedia Act) had by then been introduced which gave on-line service providers a measure of protection in respect of third party content that they carried.

"The potential of the internet as an engine of economic growth and social progress is enormous; it would be an act of self-indulgence to purport to jeopardise this unique opportunity by means of a virtually unenforceable law."[28]

Illustrations of the effects of some of the five factors outlined above can be found in the following examples of national enforcement and legislation.

12.2.2 National action—the urge to regulate

Australia

Australia is an example of a country that, in the teeth of controversy,[29] has 12–013 gone down the discretionary content regulation route. Its Commonwealth (i.e. federal) legislation[30] is less draconian than, for instance, the Singapore model discussed below, since it does not implement a full licensing model. However, the legislation does, as well as putting in place a complex content-rating system, permit the Australian Broadcasting Authority in certain circumstances to impose content standards on internet service providers and content hosts, backed up by criminal sanctions.

European Union and Council of Europe

The European Commission has an inglorious history of proposals to reg- 12–014 ulate internet content.

On December 3, 1997, the Commission published a Green Paper entitled "Convergence of the Telecommunications, Media and Information Technology Sectors, and the Implications for Regulation. Towards an Information Society Approach".[31]

The Green Paper raised a series of wide-ranging questions, largely stemming from the challenge to existing regulatory structures (in the regulated industries of telecommunications and broadcasting) posed by the cutting of traditional ties between content and delivery channels. It could no longer be assumed, for instance, that voice telephony is restricted to the public switched telephone network, or that video is restricted to traditional broadcast and cable channels.

The Green Paper and speeches by the then Commissioner Martin Bangemann floated the possibility of a European Communications Act and a single regulator, possibly at a European level, which would include content in their scope. Commissioner Bangemann also suggested an International Charter for global communications, in particular the internet. The proposed content of such a Charter was unclear.

---

[28] Para.114.
[29] For a collection of critical articles see *www.libertus.net*.
[30] The Broadcasting Services Amendment (Online Services) Act 1999.
[31] *http://europa.eu.int/ISPO/convergencegp/*.

On February 4, 1998, the Commission in its Communication on the Need for Strengthened International Co-ordination[32] suggested that an International Charter would be a "multi-lateral understanding on a method of co-ordination to remove obstacles for the global electronic market-place". It would not define the key issues to be solved as such, but contain an "understanding on how a process of strengthened international co-ordination should be organised, with as wide as possible a participation of the international community". The Commission suggested that a Charter could be agreed by or in the course of 1999. This did not occur and the proposed Charter has never reappeared.

In March 2002 the EU adopted a Directive on a common regulatory framework for electronic communications networks and services.[33] Admirably, the Directive excludes content from the definition of "electronic communications service".[34]

12–015 The original 1997 Convergence Green Paper saw as a "risk" for the Internal Market the greater possibility for divergent approaches in developing self-regulation, unless co-ordinated to some degree at Community level.

The most detailed proposals for the content of codes of conduct are contained in the Council Recommendation of September 24, 1998 on the protection of minors and human dignity.[35] This followed the Commission Communication of November 18, 1997 on the follow-up to the Green Paper on the Protection of Minors and Human Dignity in Audiovisual and Information Services.[36]

The Recommendation, while purporting to take into account the voluntary nature of self-regulation, distinguished between legal content which is liable to harm minors by impairing their physical, mental or moral development, and illegal content which is offensive to human dignity. It set out detailed "indicative guidelines" for national self-regulatory frameworks including the content of codes of conduct.

This included, in relation to both types of content, matters such as information for users, conditions of supply of filtering tools, complaint handling by hotlines and (in the case of illegal content offensive to human dignity) co-operation with police and judicial authorities.

For content that may be harmful to minors the guidelines also suggested that codes of practice should address the conditions when protection

---

[32] COM(98)50, *http://europa.eu/scadplus/leg/en/lvb/l24193.htm.*

[33] Directive 2002/21/EC of the European Parliament and of the Council of March 7, 2002 on a Common Regulatory Framework for Electronic Communications Networks and Services (Framework Directive).

[34] The definition of "electronic communications service" in Art.2(c) excludes "services providing, or exercising editorial control over, content transmitted using electronic communications networks and services". Recital (5) states that it is "necessary to separate the regulation of transmission from the regulation of content".

[35] Council Recommendation of September 24, 1998 on the development of the competitiveness of the European audiovisual and information services industry by promoting national frameworks aimed at achieving a comparable and effective level of protection of minors and human dignity (No. 98/560, [1998] O.J. L270/48).

[36] COM (97) 5, *http://europa.eu/scadplus/leg/en/lvb/l24030.htm.*

measures should be put in place, such as a warning page, visual or sound signal; descriptive labeling and/or classification of contents; and systems to check the age of users.

The distinction between illegal and legal but potentially harmful content has been carried through into the measures such as the 1999 Action Plan on promoting safer use of the internet.[37] This focused on the development of guidelines at European level for self-regulatory codes of conduct, through building of consensus. The Action Plan also emphasised the development of hotlines for reporting illegal content and of filtering and rating systems.

The Action Plan was extended to the end of 2004, then replaced by the Safer Internet Plus programme[38], which will last until the end of 2008. Equipped with a tax-funded budget of €45 million, it has a similar focus to the original Safer Internet programme.

In May 2003 the Committee of Ministers of the Council of Europe (not, of course, an EU institution) adopted a Declaration on Freedom of Communication on the Internet. As far as content rules are concerned, the Declaration is something of a curate's egg.

Principle 1 states that "Member states should not subject content on the internet to restrictions which go further than those applied to other means of content delivery". However, this does not address the critical point, which is whether the baseline for comparison should be broadcast, the press, or individual speech.[39]

Principle 3 sets out the laudable goal that "public authorities should not, through general blocking or filtering measures, deny access by the public to information and other communication on the internet, regardless of frontiers". However, it goes on to qualify this for filtering for the protection of minors and for the removal or blockage of access to "clearly identifiable internet content" if the competent national authorities have taken a provisional or final decision on its illegality, provided that Art.10(2) of the European Convention on Human Rights is respected.

This latter proviso fits well with the liability of intermediary provisions of the Electronic Commerce Directive (see Ch.5 para.5-030 above), which while providing certain on-line intermediaries with exemptions from criminal and civil pecuniary liability, allow for the possibility of administrative and civil orders requiring an infringement to be prevented or terminated. **12–016**

In December 2004 the Council of Europe Committee of Ministers adopted a further Recommendation, this time on the Right of Reply in the New Media Environment. This attempted to mirror the Council's 1974 recommendation for off-line media, by providing for a right of reply in

---

[37] Decision No. 276/1999 of the European Parliament and of the Council of January 25, 1999 adopting a multiannual Community action plan on promoting safer use of the Internet by combating illegal and harmful content on global networks ([1999] O.J. L33/1).

[38] Decision No 854/2005/EC of the European Parliament and of the Council of May 11, 2005 establishing a multiannual Community Programme on promoting safer use of the Internet and new on-line technologies.

[39] See discussion at 12–007 above.

relation to information appearing in "any means of communication for the periodic dissemination to the public of edited information, whether on-line or off-line, such as newspapers, periodicals, radio, television and ITC web-based news services".

The spectre of broadcast-style regulation of internet content raised its head once again with the European Commission's proposals, issued in 2005, for revision of the TV Without Frontiers Directive.

The existing Directive applies only to broadcast content. The European Commission proposed to broaden its compass to include internet audio-visual content, but drawing a distinction between "linear" and "non-linear" services. Whereas the full panoply of broadcast regulation would apply to linear services, non-linear services would be subject to a smaller selection of minimum requirements.

The extension of the Directive to non-linear services provoked fierce opposition in the UK, including from the UK government, amid concerns that the revised Directive could apply to, for instance, amateur bloggers.[40]

At the time of writing this opposition appears to have borne some fruit, with the Council of Ministers having adopted on November 13, 2006[41] a general approach with a narrower scope of application, limited to broadcast and on-demand services.

The introduction of the European Arrest Warrant has caused concern as to the potential for automatic extradition between EU Member States if a website established in one Member State is illegal in another.[42]

Germany

12–017   The German Multimedia Act of August 1, 1997 provides that "teleservices" falling within it shall not be subject to any licensing requirement. However, the Act may permit Broadcasting Authorities deriving power from the German states to assume broadcast regulatory jurisdiction over a potentially wide range of material.

United Kingdom

12–018   In December 2000 the government issued a White Paper, *A New Future for Communications* (commonly known as the "Communications White Paper"). This primarily addressed the challenges to the regulatory structure in broadcasting and telecommunications brought about by convergence. It proposed the creation of a new statutory regulatory body, OFCOM to replace OFTEL (the Office of Telecommunications), the ITC (the Inde-

---

[40] Speech to the Foreign Policy Centre on January 26, 2006 by James Purnell, MP, Parliamentary Under-Secretary (Media and Tourism), Department for Culture, Media & Sport; UK Government Briefing to Members of the European Parliament, September 13, 2006 (*www.mediawatchuk.org/newsbriefs/UK amendments mep brief 13 9 06.doc*); Speech by Rt. Hon. Tessa Jowell, MP, Secretary of State for Culture Media & Sport to Royal Television Society Conference, September 14, 2006.

[41] *http://ec.europa.eu/prelex/detail_dossier_real.cfm?CL=en&DosId=193682.*

[42] See further: "E-Commerce and the European Arrest Warrant" by Simon Chalton, *Communications Law*, Vol.8, No.4, 2003.

pendent Television Commission), and some other existing regulatory bodies. OFCOM would be responsible for all aspects of regulation, ranging from competition to content.

The proposal was implemented in the Communications Act 2003. The White Paper was vague as to whether OFCOM would have no jurisdiction over internet content, or whether it would have jurisdiction but would be expected to exercise it sparingly.

The Commons Select Committee on Culture, Media and Sport, in its Second Report of the 1999–2000 Session,[43] criticised the parts of the White Paper that could be interpreted as going beyond the principle that the general law should apply on-line as off-line. It recommended that OFCOM be explicitly excluded by statute from imposing regulatory obligations relating to internet content and recommended that the government should clarify that it does not envisage any form of co-regulation of the internet.

In the event the 2003 Act restricted OFCOM's jurisdiction to television services properly so called, leaving internet content to be governed by the general law of the land. This follows from ss.232 and 233 of the Act, defining services that are and are not television licensable content services. However, s.234 of the Act empowers the Secretary of State to modify, by order, s.232 or 233 if he considers it appropriate having regard to certain factors set out in the section. No order relevant to the internet has yet been made under s.234.

In June 2006 the TV Licensing Authority suggested that watching live broadcasts of the World Cup on a computer with an internet connection required a television licence.[44]

The British Board of Film Classification, the body responsible for censoring films, video, DVDs and video games, has raised the possibility that the Video Recordings Act 1984 could be extended to cover DVD-like downloads.[45]

12.2.3 National action—illegality, language, culture, political and religious expression

Governments of some countries, anxious to preserve the cultural identity of their citizenry, legislate for matters such as language. Or they may legislate against content that is especially sensitive, often for historical reasons. Others have simply been prepared to enforce local laws against overseas internet content, regardless of the consequences for other countries with more liberal laws.   **12–019**

Governments of other countries have attempted to restrict access to content that they deem politically unacceptable or subversive, or as

---

[43] Second Report, paras 112 to 118, "The limits of Internet regulation".
[44] http://news.bbc.co.uk/1/hi/entertainment/5081350.stm.
[45] Evidence to Culture, Media and Sport Select Committee Inquiry on New Media and the Creative Industries, November 7, 2006.

undermining official cultural values. Generally, details of such actions can be found at the websites of organisations such as Amnesty International,[46] Human Rights Watch,[47] the Freedom Forum,[48] Reporters sans Frontieres,[49] the Committee to Protect Journalists[50] and the OpenNet Initiative.[51]

Some examples follow of all the types of activity mentioned. These are by no means exhaustive. Other countries whose governments are reported to have embraced, in particular, the filtering and blocking of websites include the United Arab Emirates, Iran, Vietnam, South Korea, Thailand and Tunisia. India also gained brief notoriety in December 2004 when the local manager of a local eBay subsidiary company was arrested and detained for four days after a user sold a pornographic video through its website.

Burma (Myanmar)

12–020   On September 21, 1996 a Computer Science Development Law was announced. It provided that anyone who wished to import, keep in his possession or utilise a computer for purposes other than teaching or transacting business must obtain prior permission from the Ministry of Communications, Posts and Telegraphs. Further, anyone who wished to set up a computer network or connect a link inside the computer network must also obtain permission. Contraventions were punishable by from seven to 15 years' imprisonment and a fine. Full details of the legislation are contained in the Amnesty International Country Report for Myanmar, September–December 1996.[52]

The OpenNet Initiative Country Study for Burma 2005[53] records a bewildering variety of subsequent restrictions, including sweeping prohibitions on the content that can be posted on the internet. It also found that the Burmese government employs filtering technology to block access to objectionable internet sites and content.

China

12–021   China is never far from the news when it comes to internet censorship. The Great Firewall of China may not be visible from space, but is still a massive hindrance to Chinese citizens seeking information emanating from outside the borders of their country.

By 2001 China was reputed to have issued more than 60 sets of regulations governing internet content since 1995.[54] These included in February 1996 a requirement for service providers and users to register with

---

[46] www.amnesty.org.
[47] http://hrw.org/doc/?t=internet.
[48] www.freedomforum.org.
[49] www.rsf.fr.
[50] www.cpj.org.
[51] www.opennetinitiative.net.
[52] http://web.amnesty.org/library/Index/ENGASA160011997?open&of=ENG-MMR.
[53] www.opennetinitiative.net/burma/øc2c.
[54] Human Rights Watch Backgrounder "Freedom of Expression and the Internet in China" (http://www.hrw.org/backgrounder/asia/china-bck–0701.htm).

public security departments. In December 1997 the China Ministry of Public Security promulgated new Computer Information Network and Internet Security, Protection and Management Regulations. The regulations provided, among other things, that connecting network units, entry point units and corporations that use computer information networks and the internet should, within 30 days of opening the network connection, register with a unit designated by the local Public Security organisation.

Subsequent activities have included closing down over 2,000 cyber-cafes and various arrests. Visitors to website chatrooms may be warned that if Chinese nationals break the local content laws within the chatroom the website proprietor is obliged to report them to the Public Security Bureau. Websites, search engines, even *Wikipedia* and the *BBC World* website have found themselves blocked.

In September 2005 the Chinese government issued new regulations, designed to ensure that on-line news service units "serve the people, uphold the correct leadership of public opinion, and protect the interests of the nation and public. ... the state encourages on-line news service units to transmit healthy and civilized news ...".[55]

Most recently, the roles of some well known US internet companies have come under public scrutiny as a result of their co-operation with Chinese government requirements, such as to filter search results.

A study by Harvard Law School researchers in 2002[56] found 19,032 websites that were inaccessible within China. A later report by the Open-Net Initiative[57] concluded that "China operates the most extensive, technologically sophisticated, and broad-reaching system of internet filtering in the world".

Cuba

For an account of the Cuban government's attempts to restrict internet access by Cuban citizens, see *Wired* magazine, Issue 6.02 February 1998.   **12–022**

A study in 2001 observed that Cuba's attempts to control internet use were mainly by restricting the means of access to the internet, largely banning private internet connections, rather than by content filtering.[58]

A similar picture appears from a BBC news report in May 2006,[59] but which also reports that some websites are blocked, and from an October 2006 report by Reporters Sans Frontieres which additionally notes evidence of email surveillance.[60]

---

[55] "Beijing pledges 'healthy' on-line news" *Times*, September 27, 2005.
[56] "Empirical Analysis of Internet Filtering in China" by Jonathan Zittrain and Benjamin Edelman (*http://cyber.law.harvard.edu/filtering/china*).
[57] "Internet Filtering in China in 2004–2005: A Country Study" (*www.opennetinitiative.net/studies/china/*).
[58] "Internet and State Control in Authoritarian Regimes: China, Cuba, and the Counter-revolution" by Shanthi Kalathil and Taylor Boas Carnegie Paper No. 21, July 2001.
[59] "Web censorship: Correspondent reports" May 29, 2006 (*http://news.bbc.co.uk/1/hi/technology/5024874.stm*).
[60] "Going on-line in Cuba – Internet under surveillance" by Claire Voeux (*http://www.rsf.org/article.php3?id_article=19335*).

France

12–023 France has well-known legislation, the Loi Toubon, designed to preserve the use of the French language in public places. Two pressure groups, Defence of the French Language and Future of the French language, sued the French branch of a US college, the Georgia Tech Lorraine International School, because its website was written only in English. In 1997 the action was dismissed on a technicality.

The French government has been active in lobbying the European Commission to ensure that cultural issues are fully reflected in European multimedia policy. The problem of culturally based content quotas was raised as a potential barrier to the free flow of information in the NIIT Global Electronic Commerce Framework paper.[61]

The EU Electronic Commerce Directive (Art.1.6) includes language designed to preserve respect for cultural issues: "This Directive does not affect measures taken at Community or national level, in the respect of Community law, in order to promote cultural and linguistic diversity and to ensure the defence of pluralism."

In 2000 a French court, in the case of *League against Racism and Anti-Semitism and Union of French Jewish Students v Yahoo! Inc,*[62] assumed jurisdiction over the US company Yahoo! Inc and ordered it to prevent access to Nazi memorabilia offered for sale by individuals on its yahoo.com on-line auction site, contrary to French law. Yahoo! contended that the court had no jurisdiction and that compliance with the order was impossible since it could not reliably exclude access to the site from France.

The French court found that it had jurisdiction on several bases: first, that the mere display of the items offended against French law; second, that although (as Yahoo! argued) some aspects of the auction site could be regarded as aimed at the US, that was not true of Nazi memorabilia, which would be of interest to anyone (including French people); third, there was obvious harm to the particular plaintiffs; and fourth, that the yahoo.com site was in any event targeting France, since it used geographical IP address filtering to serve up French language banner advertisements to users who appeared to be from France. This latter factor was doubly damaging to Yahoo!, since the court relied heavily upon it when assessing Yahoo!'s ability to comply with the order by filtering out users coming from France.

12–024 As to compliance, a three man panel of technical experts was empanelled and asked to consider whether it was technically possible for Yahoo! to comply with the order, and if not to what extent could compliance be achieved.

---

[61] See below, fn.74.

[62] English translations of the decision of May 22, 2000 and November 20, 2000 are available at *www.juriscom.net/txt/jurisfr/cti/yauctions20000522.htm* and *www.cdt.org/speech/001120yahoofrance.pdf* respectively. The two decisions, together with the expert reports, are available in French on *www.legalis.net/cgi-iddn/french/affiche-jnet.cgi?droite=internet_illicites.htm.*

The panel reported that Yahoo! could exclude about 70 per cent of users emanating from France.[63]

It could not achieve 100 per cent for three reasons: first, a number of large ISPs (of which AoL was the best-known example) allocated IP addresses to their users from their bank of US addresses, so that a French AoL user would appear to be accessing Yahoo! from Virginia, US; second, users of multinational corporate networks similarly would often appear to be accessing from a country other than that in which they were located; thirdly, users could readily make use of anonymising services, which hide the IP address of the user and replace it with another one. Indeed one of the empanelled experts, Mr Ben Laurie, in a personal statement[64] after the judgment, commented that the "rather flakey guess at nationality, using IP address or domain name" could be "trivially circumvented".

The majority of the expert panel (Vinton Cerf dissenting on the feasibility of geographical filtering) suggested that the filtering effectiveness could be increased to about 90 per cent by requiring a statement of nationality (which the court interpreted to mean geographical origin) in cases of ambiguous IP addresses.

The expert panel also examined the question of how Yahoo! should identify the material to which French users were to be denied access, such as filtering on the item descriptions and on users' search keywords.

On compliance, the court decided that geographical localisation was possible and, in dismissing Yahoo!'s objections that this was a crude tool, relied heavily on Yahoo!'s own use of the technique to serve up banner advertisements to users whom it thought came from France, and on the representations that the court assumed Yahoo! must have made to its advertisers about the effectiveness of that service.

The court also suggested that Yahoo! could rely on delivery addresses for **12–025** items (although it is not clear how that is relevant, when the mere display of items on the auction site was held to violate French law) and identify the language version of the user's browser. Finally, the court found that Yahoo! had not demonstrated that it would consume significant resources to implement geographical filtering.

The court also suggested that if Yahoo! were, at little cost, to prohibit the sale of symbols of Nazism on its site that would have the merit of "satisfying a requirement of ethics and morals which are shared by all democratic societies" and that Yahoo! could implement filtering "if only for the sake of elementary public morals".

However, that accords no respect to the fact that the US (Yahoo!'s home country) places a greater moral value on protecting freedom of expression than it does on obliterating the insignia of Nazism. It suggests that the French court regarded French law as embodying a higher morality than

---

[63] The panel report occasionally seems to use French nationality and French location interchangeably. In context, the panel must be taken to be referring to French location, at least in the case of IP address filtering.

[64] Ben Laurie, *An Expert's Apology*, November 21, 2000; *www.apache-ssl.org/apology.html*.

different laws elsewhere in the world and was content for the consequences of its ruling to be visited on the citizens of other countries which do not share the same laws.

The dispute then crossed the Atlantic, with Yahoo! in December 2000 launching US proceedings requesting a declaration that the French judgment was unenforceable in the US. This was ultimately unsuccessful, with a majority of the Ninth Circuit Court of Appeals in January 2006 combining to dismiss the suit, in the view of some of the judges because the US court had no jurisdiction, and in the view of others because the suit was premature. The US Supreme Court in May 2006 declined to review the case.

Meanwhile, in January 2001, Yahoo! had voluntarily removed Nazi memorabilia from its US auction site.

In October 2001 separate criminal proceedings were launched in France against Yahoo! and its former chief executive, Timothy Koogle. In February 2002 the Paris Criminal Court ruled that it was competent to hear the charges. The defendants were then acquitted in February 2003, which decision was affirmed by an appeals court in April 2005.

Germany

12–026   The German authorities have taken action to prevent access to a Dutch website hosting a copy of a political magazine. In September 1996, German authorities requested German ISPs to block access to a Dutch service provider's site in the Netherlands, which hosted copies of a magazine, *Radikal*. The German authorities considered that issue 154 of this magazine contained material justifying a preliminary suspicion of promoting a terrorist organisation and other offences under the German Criminal Code. The German Public Prosecutor General informed the ICTF (Internet Content Task Force, an association of German on-line providers) that German ISPs could be subject to criminal prosecution for aiding and abetting criminal activities if they continued to allow the pages to be called up via their access points and network nodes.

After an exchange of correspondence the ICTF agreed to recommend its members to block access to Access for All (XS4ALL), the Dutch service provider which hosted *Radikal* and thousands of other unrelated pages. The proprietor of Access for All publicly expressed his fear that he could be in danger of arrest if he travelled to Germany.

It is understood that the issue of the magazine in question has been removed from Access for All by the user, but that the pages have been mirrored (duplicated) on about 50 other sites around the world. The German authorities also unsuccessfully prosecuted the German MP Angela Marquardt over a web link to the *Radikal* website. The prosecution were unable to show that the offending material was present on the target site when Ms Marquardt created the link to it.

As a postscript, in April 2002 Deutsche Bahn[65] obtained an interim order

---

[65] The interest of Deutsche Bahn was that the offending articles were alleged to contain material about ways of disrupting railways.

in the Netherlands against XS4ALL, requiring it to remove direct and indirect links to the *Radikal* material. Deutsche Bahn then brought a similar action in the Netherlands against Indymedia NL, obtaining an order in June 2002. The Amsterdam Court of Appeal in November 2002 dismissed XS4ALL's appeal against the April 2002 order.

Germany was also the location for the notorious *CompuServe/Felix Somm* case. Felix Somm was the local CompuServe manager in Germany. A Munich prosecutor charged him in 1997 with offences under German obscenity legislation, arising out of the accessibility via CompuServe's system in Germany of nearly 300 Usenet newsgroups. The newsgroups were hosted by CompuServe in the US and were not tailored to different countries.

In December 1995 CompuServe had, in response to the police action in raiding CompuServe's office, decided to suspend, temporarily, access to the newsgroups. The effect of that action was to suspend access to the newsgroups worldwide through CompuServe's internet news facilities. Mr Somm's subsequent conviction was overturned on appeal.

In March 2005 the Cologne Administrative Court upheld a Dusseldorf district government order requiring a local ISP to block access to to US based websites that promoted Nazi propaganda.[66]

In December 2000 the German Federal Court of Justice upheld the criminal conviction of Frederick Toben over a holocaust denial website. He objected that the website was produced in Australia, where he was also resident. However, the court held that the accessibility of the site to German users was sufficient for German law to apply.

Saudi Arabia

The *San Jose Mercury* on November 4, 1997 reported that Saudi Arabia **12–027** was planning to introduce internet access in a way which would prevent "objectionable material that goes against the country's religious and moral values" from being accessible. Local ISPs are routed through a government proxy server. However, as in any country with international telephone facilities, government proxy servers can be bypassed (at a price) by dialling up on an international call to a foreign ISP.

The filtering policy is publicly available on the website of the King Abdulaziz City for Science & Technology (KACST) Internet Services Unit.[67] The overall policy is stated as follows:

> "Pursuant to the Council of Ministers' decree concerning the regulation of use of the internet in Saudi Arabia, all sites that contain content in violation of Islamic tradition or national regulations shall be blocked.
>
> A security committee chaired by the Ministry of Interior was

---

[66] Electronic Commerce and Law Report, April 6, 2005, Vol. 10 No. 14 p. 363.
[67] *www.isu.net.sa/index.htm.*

formulated. One of the tasks assigned to this committee is the selection of sites to be blocked and the oversight of this process. However, due to the wide-spread and diverse nature of porno-graphic sites, KACST was commissioned to directly block these types of sites.

Other non-pornographic sites are only blocked based upon direct requests from the security bodies within the government. KACST has no authority in the selection of such sites and it's role is limited to carrying out the directions of these security bodies."

In July 2002 a Harvard Law School report found over 2,000 blocked pages.[68] A further report in 2004, under the auspices of the OpenNet Initiative, found that the filtering focused on pornography, drugs, gambling, religious conversion and sites with tools to circumvent filters.[69]

Singapore

12–028   The Singapore authorities introduced in July 1996 a licensing scheme for internet activities,[70] closely based on a broadcast model. The scheme introduced a class licence governing internet activities and required all ISPs to register with the then Singapore Broadcasting Authority (SBA), now replaced by the Media Development Authority (MDA). Certain internet content providers (i.e. anyone providing information on the web, including web publishers and server administrators) were (and are still) also required to register, namely:

- Political parties registered in Singapore who provide web pages;
- Groups of persons engaged in political or religious discussions related to Singapore on the web;
- Individuals providing web pages for political or religious purposes and who are notified by the SBA to register; and
- On-line newspapers targeting sales in Singapore through the inter-net and which are notified by the SBA to register.

The SBA stressed that registration "serves to reinforce responsible use of the medium and ensure that discussions are conducted in a mature fashion without harmful intent" and that "political and religious organisations are free to conduct discussions provided they guard against breaking the law or disrupting social harmony".

Under Clause 13 of the Class Licence a licensee is required to use its best efforts to ensure that its service complies with the Code of Practice and is not used for any purpose, and does not contain any programme, that is against the public interest, public order or national harmony, or offends

---

[68] "Documentation of Internet Filtering in Saudi Arabia" by Jonathan Zittrain and Benjamin Edelman (*http://cyber.law.harvard.edu/filtering/saudiarabia*).

[69] "Internet Filtering in Saudi Arabia in 2004" (*www.opennetinitiative.net/studies/saudi*).

[70] The scheme can be found at *www.mda.gov.sg/wms.www/devnpolicies.aspx?sid=161#1*.

against good taste or decency. Under Clause 14 a licensee has an obligation in relation to web pages to which other persons are invited to contribute or post content to use its best efforts to ensure that they comply with the Code of Practice. Under Clause 16 a licensee shall remove material included in its service if the MDA informs it that the material is in breach of the conditions in Clause 13.

The Singapore authorities have also introduced a proxy server system with major ISPs, with the object of preventing access by technical means to blacklisted websites, and require re-sellers to connect to those servers. A report by the OpenNet Initiative in 2005[71] suggests that in practice little filtering is done.

12.2.4 Responses to national action

Reconciling international co-operation with freedom of expression

What is the appropriate response to inter-jurisdiction problems, especially where foreign content is regarded as criminal in the state receiving the content?   **12–029**

In this context inter-jurisdictional rules are not value neutral, since the rules will necessarily favour more or less liberal content regimes. So is international co-operation to result in indiscriminate mutual enforcement of criminal content laws? If so, the result will be multilateral export to liberal countries of the most restrictive domestic content regimes.

The opposite solution, that governments agree to respect the domestic laws of more liberal regimes, is unlikely to be acceptable to governments anxious to prevent foreign material reaching their citizens for political, religious or cultural reasons.

Papers such as the EU paper on Illegal and Harmful Content on the Internet (see below) tend to suggest that common minimum standards can be agreed and enforced only in limited areas, such as child pornography, trafficking in human beings, racial hatred, terrorism and fraud. Even in these areas there is less consensus than might be expected.

On October 16, 1996 the European Commission published a Communication to the European Parliament and other EU institutions discussing the question of Illegal and Harmful Content on the Internet.[72]

This document, and a subsequent working party report,[73] recognised the difficulties of taking an international approach without compromising freedom of speech. The Communication drew a line between illegal content (for which greater international co-operation was recommended) and content which might be harmful but not illegal (for which voluntary

---

[71] "Internet Filtering in Singapore in 2004–2005: A Country Study" (*www.opennetinitiative.net/studies/singapore/#toc2e*).
[72] COM (96) 487.
[73] Welcomed by the Telecommunications Council on November 28, 1996.

adoption of rating systems was suggested). The communication commented that:

> "Some third countries have introduced wide-ranging legislation to block all direct access to internet via access providers by introducing a requirement for 'proxy servers' similar to those used by large organisations for security reasons, combined with centralised blacklisting of documents, for reasons which go far beyond the limited category of illegal content as defined in this communication. Such a restrictive regime is inconceivable for Europe as it would severely interfere with the freedom of the individual and its political traditions."

The subsequent working party report suggested that information on the internet should be allowed the same free flow as paper-based information, and that any restrictions should respect fundamental rights such as freedom of expression and the right to privacy. It says that any international agreement should be in conformity with fundamental rights and European traditions of free expression.

12–030 The paper "A Framework for Global Electronic Commerce"[74] published in July 1997 by the US Information Infrastructure Task Force (NIIT) also touched on the subject. The "Content" section suggested that the US Administration would pursue negotiations to ensure that measures, policies and regulations that limit the ability of content providers to communicate through the internet are promulgated only when necessary and implemented in a manner that minimises trade distortion.

The paper identified five priority areas of concern: foreign content quotas, regulation of advertising, regulation of content, regulation to prevent fraud, and differences in defining "seditious" material.

The difficulties of reconciling international governmental co-operation with freedom of expression have again become apparent with the Cybercrime Convention (discussed in section 12.9.6 below).

Content blocking

12–031 Another possible response, alluded to in the Communication on Illegal and Harmful Content mentioned above, is the retrograde, and technically difficult, solution of governments or other national authorities seeking to impose technical methods of blocking content at their virtual borders (i.e. at their domestic ISPs). We have cited above (para.12–019) several examples of the lengthening list of countries whose governments have attempted this, the most notorious being China's Great Firewall project.

As well as direct blocking action by governments, over-enthusiastic enforcement of local laws against foreign services can incentivise private actors to introduce geographically based content filtering and blocking.

---

[74] www.technology.gov/digeconomy/framewrk.htm.

Outcomes such as that of the French *Yahoo!* court case, discussed above, provide a clear economic incentive for content providers to choose between complying with the international most restrictive common denominator, or incurring the cost of content filtering and blocking on a nation by nation basis.

Rating and filtering

The last response is to rely on a rating-enabling system such as PICS **12–032** (Platform for Internet Content Selection)[75] or RDF (a more generalised model expressed in XML).

PICS allows for the voluntary adoption of multiple criteria upon which to select viewable content. It does not specify the content of rating systems, but defines a technical platform upon which content labeling schemes can be built. The labeling schemes can be built and made available by content providers, access providers, hosts, or even independent third parties such as campaigning organisations who wish to label content according to their own sets of values.

PICS, while likely to be acceptable in many countries as a way of dealing with a diversity of views as to what constitutes "harmful" content, is perhaps unlikely to satisfy governments nervous that the voluntary nature of PICS-based rating systems would still permit their citizens to choose to access foreign content regarded as illegal domestically.

On the other hand, such a system if widely adopted could perhaps make the third option of compulsory content blocking at virtual borders easier for so minded governments to impose. The potential use of PICS and other rating systems by governments for such purposes is controversial.

At least one country, Argentina, has passed legislation requiring internet service providers to provide their customers with filtering software.[76]

In December 1997 the World Wide Web Consortium (W3C) published PICSRules Version 1.1,[77] a W3C Recommendation which defines a language for writing filtering rules which allow or block access to URLs based on PICS labels that describe those URLs. Such filtering rules are known as "profiles". The PICSRules also allow filtering by URL, independently of PICS labeling. A PICSRule profile could rely on the content provider's own rating, or specify the use of one or more third party PICS rating services, and one or more PICS label bureaus to query for labels.

In the UK the Internet Watch Foundation, founded in 1996, had as part of its brief the development of a rating and labelling system. It has since withdrawn from that role, leaving it to the Internet Content Rating Association. ICRA's labels use RDF, alongside a simplified version compatible with PICS-based filters.

As we have mentioned above, the British Board of Film Classification has

---

[75] For a description of PICS see *www.w3.org/pub/WWW/PICS/*.
[76] *World eBusiness Law Report*, February 27, 2003.
[77] *www.w3.org/TR/REC-PICSRules*.

ventilated the possibility that the Video Recordings Act 1984 could be amended to extend its film classification powers to DVD-like downloads.

12.2.5 Differing approaches to an international solution

12–033 A useful way of characterising a cross-border liability rule, whether in the context of traditional private international law rules or of a supranational regime such as the EC Treaty, is to consider where it sits in the spectrum between country of origin and country of destination.

A country of origin regime is one which favours the home law and jurisdiction of the actor—by permitting an unfettered choice of law and jurisdiction, by specifying the actor's home law and jurisdiction as the default, or both. In the context of the internet the actor is the proprietor of an internet site, the publisher of internet content, or the supplier of goods or services sold over the internet.

A country of receipt (or country of destination) regime favours the home law and jurisdiction of the alleged victim. In the context of the internet this means the reader of an internet site, the owner of reputation, goodwill, intellectual property or other rights alleged to be damaged by internet content, or the purchaser of goods or services sold over the internet.

The choice between country of origin, country of destination, or a formulation somewhere between the two, is politically highly charged. The country of origin clause in the proposed Services Directive sparked trade union demonstrations in Brussels during the European Parliament debates.

A country of origin approach is very difficult to achieve politically unless all participating countries have relatively uniform laws. The concern is that on-line businesses will move their operations to countries with least restrictive laws and the lightest regulatory burden, thereby nullifying the domestic laws of other countries.

This is a concern for governments, keen to preserve the efficacy of their domestic laws. It is shared by the consumer protection community, which fears that a country of origin regime would strip consumers of the legal protection to which they are accustomed in their home countries when they purchase on-line from foreign e-businesses. Country of origin regimes are, however, the most encouraging to the free flow of trade and information.

The country of destination approach can manifest itself in many guises, ranging from an explicitly stated rule of applicable law or jurisdiction[78] through to being the consequence of some apparently innocuous substantive legal principle.[79]

Country of destination regimes are criticised, mainly for enabling overrestrictive governments unilaterally to export their domestic laws to more

---

[78] Article 5(3) of the Brussels Judgments Regulation, permitting jurisdiction based upon the place of occurrence of a harmful event or the arising of damage, is a country of destination rule.

[79] The rule in defamation that publication takes place where a statement it is read and comprehended translates, in a cross border context, into a country of destination rule.

liberal and enlightened countries. This is particularly an issue when (as is often the case in such countries) domestic courts and authorities are keen to apply their local laws to foreign internet sites on the sole ground that they can be read in their country.

Country of destination rules have the potential to create worldwide exposure to liability based on nothing more than the accessibility of a website, encouraging on-line actors to erect electronic walls around their sites and restrict their information and services to their home countries.

So there is an impasse. Country of destination rules are seen as protecting the interest of the alleged victims in their own countries, but do not pay sufficient regard to the injustice of exposing the proprietor of a website to automatic worldwide liability. Country of origin rules, on the other hand, are criticised as paying insufficient regard to the interest of the alleged victim in his own country.

The policy challenges of devising cross-border legal structures that are good for the internet are compounded by the instability of the juris-prudential foundation on which they have to be erected.

Two factions with different backgrounds, the adherents of traditional private international law and the economic proponents of the EU internal market, vie for precedence. Legislation such as the Electronic Commerce Directive,[80] promoted by the European Commission's Internal Market and Services Directorate and designed to foster the free flow of on-line services within the EU, rides roughshod over the myriad subtleties of traditional private international law.

Private international law measures such as Rome I and II,[81] promulgated by the European Commission's Justice, Freedom and Security Directorate, are grounded not in economic analysis but in received legal wisdom devised in an age when cross-border activity was the exception rather than the norm.

Internal market measures tend to favour the home law and jurisdiction of the internet actor, whereas private international law measures have historically tended to favour that of the consumer or alleged victim. The interaction between the two types of measure is itself often obscure.

This distracting battle for precedence between internal market and private international law measures tends to obscure the need for informed consideration of the economic and social consequences of cross-border on-line liability rules, whatever the legal foundation on which the rules are built.

The rise of the internet, an inherently cross-border medium, has turned the spotlight on the rules governing cross-border liability. What used to be a minority interest is, or should now be, the concern of everyone who publishes or trades on the internet.

---

[80] The internal market provisions of the Electronic Commerce Directive are discussed in Ch.6.
[81] Rome I and II are proposals for EU Regulations on the law applicable to contractual and non-contractual obligations respectively. They are discussed in detail in Ch.6.

937

Country of origin

12–034 The country of origin principle is to a limited extent embodied in the internal market provisions of the EC Treaty. Achieving an internal market within Europe demands that Member States should not use their national laws to restrict the free flow of goods and services from other Member States. The converse is that Member States should enforce their home laws over anyone established in their territories. However, this principle is subject to severe qualifications, reflecting the political reality that no national government will lightly give up the right to enforce its country's domestic laws against incoming goods and services.

Until the Electronic Commerce Directive was adopted in 2000, the closest to a pure country of origin regime in Europe was that governing satellite broadcasting within Europe.[82] Essentially, broadcast content cannot be restricted in the country of reception if it is legal in the country of establishment of the broadcaster. However, even in such a tightly licensed and regulated area as broadcasting, Member States were still permitted under the terms of the Directive some residual, closely circumscribed, powers to suspend broadcasting if (for instance) there was perceived to be a serious threat to minors. The balance between home and destination country control embodied in the Directive has been at the heart of several cases that have come before the European Court of Justice.

Most internet liability issues revolve around content laws, the area in which differences in national law are perhaps most jealously guarded. If in the tightly regulated area of broadcasting, in the relatively homogenous zone of Europe, pure country of origin could not be achieved, what chance then of achieving it in the unregulated area of individual and press speech, on a worldwide basis?

It is difficult to see the more restrictive governments accepting internationally harmonised liberal standards. Having taken the trouble to, for instance, create a licensing regime with the specific objective of preventing access to objectionable material on the internet, would a restrictive country's government accede easily to the suggestion that it should permit access to any foreign website which was legal in its country of origin? The recipient country would almost certainly wish to retain wide residual power to block unacceptable content, negating the point of a country of origin solution. It is predictable that there would be a long list of permissible national derogations from an international country of origin regime.

The converse, a restrictive harmonised standard, would require acceptance by liberal states of restrictions on freedom of expression within their own borders. While multilateral agreement might be possible in a field (such as broadcasting) in which it is traditionally accepted that regulatory content restrictions are justifiable, it is difficult to see how such agreement could be reached in the case of the internet without sacrificing the high

---

[82] The Television without Frontiers Directive (89/552, amended by Directive 97/36).

degree of speech protection accorded to non-broadcast speech in liberal democracies, and so far jealously defended on the internet.

The Electronic Commerce Directive has provided a laboratory for such an attempt within Europe. Unsurprisingly, given the broader scope of the Directive, in its final form it contains many more exceptions and derogations for countries of receipt than does the satellite broadcasting regime.

Additionally, the powers granted to the European Commission, in the event of a Member State notifying to the Commission a measure to restrict a given incoming information society service which the Commission decides are incompatible with Community law, are limited to requesting that the Member State refrain from taking or urgently put an end to the measure.[83] These powers were considerably diluted from the Commission's original proposal.

Where is the country of origin?

What would constitute the country of origin in an internet convention? **12–035** Some internet afficionados may say that on the internet content has no location. However, while content on the internet may be everywhere it is not nowhere.

To the user the storage location of the content is irrelevant. Pages can be switched from a server on one side of the world to the other without affecting the user's browsing experience and without substantially affecting the cost of access. And, of course, that user may access the content from anywhere in the world.

However, that does not mean that the content is nowhere. While some liabilities on the internet essentially revolve around the place of reception (e.g. publication for purposes of defamation), others depend upon storage (copying of copyright works, possession of obscene materials and so on).

To an ISP faced with a visit by the local police carrying a warrant to seize his hard disks, the idea that content is "nowhere" on the internet may seem a little far-fetched. It is true that, at least in theory, the service provider could site its servers out of the jurisdiction and continue to provide its service. However, in practice that would not be a trivial or cost-free decision. Location still matters.

Nor is it beyond the wit of legislators to devise a rule to define country of origin of content. Within the European Community the Electronic Commerce Directive has adopted the concept, well known in European Community law, of place of establishment of the service provider. The outcome of this rule, where virtual enterprises split their operations among different locations and instantaneously switch among servers located in different countries, may be unpredictable. However, that has not deterred the legislators from adopting it.

---

[83] Electronic Commerce Directive, Art.3.6.

Country of receipt

12–036 With the significant exception of the law applicable to business to business contracts, the rules of private international law, at least in Europe, tend to be receipt-oriented. For non-contractual liability, in many cases they permit jurisdiction to be taken, or local law to be applied, where the effects of the wrongdoing are felt. For contractual liability they lean towards enabling consumers to sue in their home countries and to have the protection at least of their local consumer protection laws.

Receipt-oriented rules have a disproportionately burdensome effect on on-line actors. By default a website is available throughout the world. The website proprietor who wishes to trade only with certain jurisdictions must take positive steps to prevent transactions occurring with customers in other jurisdictions. This is the reverse of the position that obtained in the off-line world when the old rules were written. Then trade was domestic by default and a supplier would generally have to take positive steps in order address an overseas market. The advent of cheap cross-border on-line trade has put into question the appropriateness of the old rules.

A comprehensive international country of receipt regime would imply greater international co-operation between governments leading to enforcement by prosecution across borders. Such a regime would seem to imply the wholesale import of restrictive standards, reinforcing the notion of an international "most conservative common denominator" system.

Competing national laws

12–037 The status quo is neither consistently country of origin nor country of receipt. National laws compete on the basis of existing applicable law and jurisdiction rules. These can produce a variety of outcomes. Governments in countries of receipt may try to put up barriers and enforce content blocking at their virtual borders. As we have seen, national courts from time to time make orders (as in the French *Yahoo!* case) that have the practical effect of requiring the service provider either to ensure that its personnel and assets never venture out of its home country, or to remove the content completely and deny it to users worldwide, or to attempt some form of geographic filtering, blocking and verification.[84]

Directing and targeting

12–038 An approach that is more enlightened than country of receipt and more achievable than country of origin is directing and targeting. According to this mid-way position a website is not to be regarded, through its mere availability in the country of receipt, as susceptible to that country's juris-

---

[84] Another example is a decision of the Italian Corte de Cassazione on December 27, 2000, assuming criminal jurisdiction in a libel case over non-Italians who made postings about an Italian citizen to a website located outside Italy. Libel is a criminal offence in Italy. The court held that the effects of the postings were perceived inside Italy and that was sufficient to assume jurisdiction. *World Internet Law Report* May 1, 2001 p.16.

diction or as infringing its laws. However, if it targets that country or directs activities towards it, then it is so susceptible. As discussed in Ch.6, in some areas there is significant movement towards such a test.

The usual criticism of a targeting test is that it lacks certainty. It is true that the general concept of targeting is sufficiently flexible that there is room to interpret it in either a receipt-oriented or origin-oriented manner. It is important therefore to have as much clarity as possible about what does and does not amount to targeting.

For instance, can a site be regarded as directed to a country simply because it does not take positive steps to prevent access to the site from that country? If so, then the targeting test would effectively be a country of receipt test.[85] The cost of maintaining a matrix of all countries' content rules and taking positive steps to filter access for each country could well be so great[86] that in practice providers would take the least cost route of adopting the most restrictive common content denominator across the board on their sites.

We suggest that, on the contrary, one characteristic of a true targeting test is that an on-line actor can only be found to have targeted a country if he has engaged in positive conduct towards it. This would be consistent with what Waller L.J. had to say in *Rayner v Davies*,[87] commenting on the Guiliano/Lagarde Report on Art.15 of the 1968 Brussels Jurisdiction Convention:

> " 'specific invitation' is coupled with 'advertising' preceding the conclusion of the contract. That seems to contemplate some positive conduct on the part of the seller of goods or services preceding the contract, and (I would suggest normally) preceding the involvement of the consumer."

A true targeting test would mean that, for instance, the court in the French *Yahoo!* case could not have found that the mere display of Nazi memorabilia was sufficient to violate French law, without some element of targeting or direction at France. Nor would it have been open to it to find jurisdiction, as it did, on the basis that because Nazi memorabilia were of interest to all, the areas containing those items were directed at all countries simultaneously including France.

However, it might still have been be possible for a court to find that Yahoo!'s serving up of French banner advertisements to French IP addresses would satisfy a "directed at" test. While it is doubtful whether the use of a particular language alone ought to suffice, this was not a mere use of language. It was an attempt to serve up French language advertisements to users coming to the site from French territory.

---

[85] For a discussion of the contents of targeting tests generally, see "Directing and Targeting—the Answer to the Internet's Jurisdiction Problems?", G.J.H. Smith, *Computer Law Review International* 5/2004 p.145.

[86] See Ben Laurie, *An Expert's Apology* (fn.64 above).

[87] [2002] EWCA Civ 1880 (C.A.), at para.24.

12–039   A true targeting test would also require governments to accept that when their citizens go on-line and access sites that are not targeted at their home country, they are effectively travelling out of the country.[88]

A true targeting test would also mean that an English court could not, as it can according to the present state of English defamation law when applied to internet publication (see discussion in Ch.4), assume libel jurisdiction over a foreign website based on mere publication. The meaning of responsibility for publication would have to be restricted to connote an element of targeting. We have in Ch.6 suggested that this could be achieved within the existing framework of causation.

In the context of libel the contrasting policy arguments for country of receipt and country of origin were extensively canvassed in the Australian case of *Gutnick v Dow Jones & Co. Inc*,[89] decided in August 2001 at first instance and in 2002 on appeal.

The court rejected the policy argument that liability for cyberspace defamation should be determined by the jurisdiction of the website. The defendant had argued that applying a country of download (i.e. receipt) approach to the internet would result in a serious "chilling effect" on free speech and would have the likely effect of diminishing the amount of information made available on the internet.

The judge at first instance made some revealing comments about the policy considerations underlying the judgment:

> "The defendant's argument really is that liability for cyber-space defamation must be determined by the jurisdiction of the website. It was virtually admitted that the reason for this is the claimed policy of the law to assist free speech, apparently including defamatory free speech ... To say that the country where the article is written, edited and uploaded and where the publisher does its business, must be the forum is an invitation to entrench the United States, the primary home of much of internet publishing, as the forum. The applicant's argument that it would be unfair for the publisher to have to litigate in the multitude of jurisdictions in which its statements are downloaded and read, must be balanced against the world-wide inconvenience caused to litigants, from Outer Mongolia to the Outer Barcoo, frequently not of notable means, who would at enormous expense and inconvenience have to embark upon the formidable task of suing in the USA, with its different fee and costs structures and where the libel laws are, in many respects, tilted in favour of defendants, or, if you will, in favour of the constitutional free speech concepts and rights developed in the USA which originated in the liberal construction by the courts of the First Amendment."

---

[88] *Cf.* the remarks of Jacob J. in the *Crate & Barrel* case discussed in Ch.6: "Indeed the very language of the internet conveys the idea of the user going to the site—"visit" is the word".

[89] [2001] V.S.C. 305.

The judge also said:

> "...I am also of the view that [the conclusion that publication took place in Victoria and that the defendant caused it] is a correct and just law, and that the arguments advanced against it are primarily policy-driven, by which I mean policies which are in the interests of the defendant and, in a less business-centric vein, perhaps, by a belief in the superiority of the United States concept of the freedom of speech over the management of freedom of speech in other places and lands."

These comments neatly highlight the inescapable truth that differing conflicts of law rules do embody inherent values favouring or inhibiting the free flow of information and trade across borders.

The judge's adverse reaction to suggestions that, for the sake of freedom **12–040** of speech on the internet, the court should forgo jurisdiction in favour of the US was perhaps understandable in that particular case, given that the defendant had freely accepted paid subscriptions from the State of Victoria. One might think that if the policy issues had been debated in the context of a freely available rather than a subscription website the arguments against country of receipt could not be so easily dismissed.

However, on appeal the High Court of Australia expressed itself in even broader terms, applicable to both free and subscription sites, so that now according to the *Gutnick* approach anyone who chooses to publish on the internet is apparently taken to know the global reach of the medium, and to take the consequences in terms of potential worldwide liability.

As we have discussed above, in an environment in which the website proprietor cannot restrict availability on a country by country basis, or would find it uneconomic to do so, the practical effect of a country of receipt rule is to give extra-territorial effect to the law of the most restrictive country of receipt: a result which is every bit as undesirable, or more so, than Hedigan J. considered the international entrenchment of US freedom of speech rules to be.

The detailed findings in the *Gutnick* case are discussed in Ch.6.

International regimes

An alternative to approaches seeking to arbitrate between national laws is **12–041** to create an international regulatory regime, based not on arbitrating among existing national laws, but on creating a new supra-national code, possibly enforced by an internationally accepted body.

Such a regime has the disadvantage that it would particularly lend itself to being based on the broadcast, premium rate telephone services or advertising regulation models, which so far have successfully been prevented from encroaching on most areas of the internet. It would be most likely to find acceptance if there were consensus among governments that the internet should be a restricted form of communication.

Even then such a proposal would not find support outside the corridors of government. It is also difficult to see how such an international regulatory regime could be consistent with, for instance, the approach to internet content protection promulgated by District Judge Dalzell in *ACLU v Reno*.

The American Bar Association, in its report on jurisdiction in cyberspace,[90] suggested the formation of a Global on-line Standards Commission, which would seek to achieve global consensus on matters of jurisdiction in the on-line environment. While not explicitly setting content standards, jurisdiction rules do (as we noted at the outset) have consequences for substantive laws in a cross-border environment.

A market in virtual legal regimes?

12–042 Another possibility is international, but may require no international convention. It is based on the premise that the internet transcends national boundaries and creates a new domain, cyberspace, which is effectively independent of national laws. The consequence is that the diverse proprietors of multiple networks can set different content and behaviour rules within their virtual boundaries, so that a market in quasi-legal regimes arises which is independent of national boundaries.[91] This solution, while attractive, would be regarded as deeply subversive by many governments.

It is currently fashionable to decry the early cyber-libertarians for the Utopianism of the idea that the internet is inherently wired for freedom. There is now sympathy in some circles with the notion that not only is there evidence of numerous attempts to re-erect national borders in cyberspace, but to do that is a good thing.[92] While the first proposition may be undeniable (as evidenced by a goodly chunk of this chapter), the second is highly contentious.

12.3 GAMBLING

12.3.1 Overview

12–043 Gambling on the internet has grown exponentially in the last decade to become a multi-billion dollar industry. The pace of change in the gambling industry had not been matched by changes in gambling legislation until the UK Government responded to the need to legislate for gambling over new technologies with the introduction of the Gambling Act 2005 (the "2005 Act"), which is scheduled to be fully implemented by September 2007.

---

[90] fn.3 above.

[91] David G Post, "Anarchy, State, and the Internet: An Essay on Law-Making in Cyberspace," 1995 *J. on-line L.* art.3 (*www.wm.edu/law/publications/jol/articles/post.shtml*).

[92] See for instance the book "Who Controls the Internet?: Illusions of a Borderless World" by Jack Goldsmith and Tim Wu (Oxford University Press). Also "Damn the Constitution: Europe must take back the Web" by Bill Thompson, *The Register*, August 13, 2002.

In the UK lotteries, prize competitions, betting and gaming (the activities which are generally considered to fall under the umbrella term of "gambling") are currently governed by complex and frequently confusing rules principally under the Betting, Gaming and Lotteries Act 1963 (the "1963 Act"), the Gaming Act 1968 (the "1968 Act"), Lotteries and Amusements Act 1976 (the "1976 Act") and the Betting and Gaming Duties Act 1981 (the "1981 Act").

The existing legislative framework is anachronistic and unsuited to regulating gambling services that are provided through means of technology that was not envisaged at the time the relevant statutes were enacted. For example the 1968 Act contemplated face-to-face gambling whereby gamblers would congregate in a regulated location such as a bookmaker's shop or a racecourse. Modern technology allows gamblers to bet in isolation via the internet, on their mobile phones and through interactive services via their television.

The 2005 Act will repeal all existing legislation and replace it with one codified Act. A new enforcement body (the "Gambling Commission") has also been established to regulate compliance with gambling laws.

12.3.2 The Current Law

Lotteries

The term "lottery" is not defined by statute. Instead, one must look to case **12–044** law to establish what it means. According to Lord Widgery C.J. in the case of *Reader's Digest Association Ltd v Williams*[93] a lottery has three features: Firstly, there must be the distribution of prizes. Second, such distribution should be dependent upon "chance" and thirdly, there must be some actual contribution made by the participants in return for them obtaining a chance to take part in the lottery.

With a few exceptions (notably the National Lottery) it is unlawful to operate a lottery in the UK. It is also an offence to "print, publish or distribute advertisements" for a lottery in the UK even though the lottery is conducted outside the UK.

There is clear judicial authority that a prize need not be a sum of money but can be "anything that can be sold, or indeed anything which can be said to be of value".[94]

It is also clear that a scheme will not be a lottery if the prizes are distributed according to skill or effort, even though the skill or effort involved may be small as this would still remove the pure element of chance which is central to the idea of a lottery. (A scheme involving the distribution of prizes on the basis of little skill or effort may, however, fall foul of the rules on unfair prize competitions which are considered below).

---

[93] *Reader's Digest Association Ltd v Williams* [1976] 3 All E.R. 737 (CA).
[94] *DPP v Bradfute* [1967] 1 All E.R. 112 (QB FC), Lord Parker C.J. at 115.

Much of the case law in this area, therefore, examines attempts by promoters to argue that their schemes were not lotteries because entry to the scheme did not require the payment of a contribution. This is not the place to consider these cases in detail. However, it is worth noting that on the basis of current case law it is key that at least part of the contribution must flow to the promoter/organiser of the scheme for the scheme to be a lottery. Hence the usual fees paid to an ISP for the provision of internet access would not constitute a "contribution" for these purposes. On the other hand, the requirement to pay to subscribe to an internet based service or product as a condition of entry to a scheme would constitute a contribution under current case law if any part of the subscription fee is paid to the promoter/organiser of the lottery.

Prize Competitions

12–045   The current law on prize competitions is contained in s.14 of the 1976 Act. Section 14 states that three types of competition are prohibited:

- Competitions in which prizes are offered for forecasts of the result of a future event;
- Competitions in which prizes are offered for forecasts of the result of a past event, the result of which is not yet ascertained or not yet generally known; and
- Any other competition in which success does not depend to a substantial degree on the exercise of skill.

The first two types of scheme are prohibited as they are seen as types of activities which, if they involve the payment of a sum of money as a condition of entry, are generally considered to constitute "betting" and are hence regulated as such.

However, not only does the Act not define "competition", it fails also to define "forecast," "result" or "event". This has led to some fairly tortured arguments made by counsel when prosecutions under s.14 have been attempted. For example, must an "event" be something as prominent as a football match or a horserace, or can it be something as unnoticed and fleeting as the unobserved last kick or other last touch of a football before a photograph was taken—when that photograph ends up being used in a "Spot the Ball" competition?

The third prohibition was introduced to prevent persons circumventing the rules prohibiting lotteries by providing schemes which involve little skill or effort. Again the 1976 Act gives no guidance as to what level of skill is required for the purposes of s.14. The lack of prosecutions in this area would suggest that the bar is set fairly low, although there is a grey area surrounding multiple-choice questions which are so simple as to be ineffective in eliminating any of the entrants.

Betting

Prior to the 2005 Act neither the term "bet" or "betting" was defined by statute. The most frequently adopted definition was that used by the Royal Commission on Lotteries and Betting in 1933 which described a "bet" as a "promise to give money or monies worth upon the determination of an uncertain or unascertained event in a particular way". **12–046**

It is permissible to carry on a betting business via an internet or other remote service based in the UK provided the operator of the business holds a bookmaker's or betting agency permit from the local licensing magistrates. In this regard remote betting services are treated no differently from bricks and mortar operations.

A number of other jurisdictions permit remote betting services and have done so under more favourable tax regimes than that which exists in the UK to encourage new businesses to set up in their jurisdictions.

It is worth noting however that s.9 of the 1981 Act prohibits the issue or distribution of advertisements relating to overseas based betting services in the UK. The question of how this applied to electronic media came before the Court of Appeal in *Victor Chandler International v Customs and Excise Commissioners*.[95] The court ruled that if an overseas bookmaker placed advertisements on Teletext, that would amount to circulating or distributing an advertisement or other document in the UK for the purposes of s.9(1)(b) of the 1981 Act. The court held that provision, which was for the protection of the revenue and to protect domestic bookmakers from unfair offshore competition, should be given an "always speaking" construction to take account of technological developments since the provision was first enacted in the Finance Act 1952.

Gaming

The 1968 Act defines "gaming" as the playing of a game of chance for winnings in money or money's worth, whether any person playing the game is at risk of losing any money or money's worth or not. **12–047**

It is currently illegal to carry on an on-line gaming operation from the UK. The 1968 Act only permits gaming to be carried out on licensed bricks and mortar premises at which participants are physically present.

Section 42 of the 1968 Act also makes it illegal to issue advertising within the UK that invites members of the public to subscribe money for use in gaming or to apply for information about doing so. This applies regardless of whether the relevant gaming services are provided in or outside the UK. The prohibition is obviously important for the operators of remote gaming services that are provided legally from another jurisdiction. There is little judicial guidance as to what is meant by the phrase "inviting the public to subscribe money ... to be used in gaming". Guidance issued by the Department of Culture, Media and Sport (DCMS) indicates that DCMS

---

[95] [2000] 2 All E.R. 315.

consider that anything more than providing factual details about the name and address of a gaming operator would breach s.42.

Given the total prohibition on the provision of remote gaming services within the UK many operators have sought to exploit the current lack of clarity as to what distinguishes betting and gaming by setting up services providing casino style games structured as fixed odds betting services provided under bookmakers' licences. Such services have been the subject of largely confidential investigations by the Gambling Commission and its predecessor the Gaming Board and the validity of each has turned on its particular facts.

12.3.3 Reform and Codification under the Gambling Act 2005

12–048　When it comes into full effect in September 2007, the 2005 Act will govern all forms of gambling with the exception of the National Lottery (which is governed by the National Lottery Act) and spread betting (which must be advertised as an investment activity and is subject to financial services legislation). Gambling will be illegal unless permitted by the 2005 Act, the National Lottery etc. Act 1993 or pursuant to the Financial Services and Markets Act 2000.

Whilst most countries have responded to the rise in on-line gaming by imposing new restrictions, the 2005 Act will make the UK the first major jurisdiction to seek to regulate on-line and other forms of remote gambling rather than restrict it. The new UK model is based on three tenets designed to safeguard the public:

- Ensuring gambling is done in a fair and open way;
- Protecting children; and
- Preventing gambling from being associated with crime.

In contrast to the current legislative framework, the 2005 Act contains definitions of what will constitute gambling, being

- Gaming;
- Betting; and
- Participation in a lottery

and seeks to address the position where an activity might legitimately be caught by one or more of the above categories.

Participation in a Lottery

12–049　Lotteries will fall into two categories: simple and complex. The essential definition of a "simple" lottery will not change: entrants must pay a contribution to enter a scheme in which prizes are distributed wholly on chance. However, the 2005 Act provides further guidance as to what constitutes "wholly on chance", which includes situations where a question or process does not prevent a significant proportion of people from receiving a prize or discourage a significant proportion of people from entering.

Complex lotteries will be schemes in which prizes are allocated by a series of processes, the first of which relies wholly on chance. If more than three such processes are involved before a prize can be won, the scheme will cease to be a lottery and instead will be classed as gaming (s.17(2)).

Lotteries will remain unlawful unless carried out under a lottery operating licence. Such licences will only be available to non-commercial societies, local authorities and persons proposing to act as external lottery managers on behalf of a non-commercial society or local authority.

The advertising of overseas remote lotteries will be caught by the provisions relating to advertising of remote gambling services generally which are considered below.

Prize Competitions

Section 339 of the 2005 Act abolishes the restrictions on prize competitions **12–050** contained in the 1976 Act. Prize competitions will be legal if they do not constitute gaming, betting, or participating in a lottery.

One consequence of this is that the provision of a contribution towards entry will be essential in order for an offence to be committed. (Guidance on what constitutes a contribution is contained in the first and second Schedules to the 2005 Act). If a charge is made for entry, operators will need to ensure that the level of skill required to participate eliminates a significant proportion of people to prevent the competition being deemed a simple lottery. It is unlikely that overly-simplistic multiple-choice questions will satisfy this requirement.

Betting

The 2005 Act defines betting as "making or accepting a bet on: **12–051**

  (a) the outcome of a race, competition or other event or process;
  (b) the likelihood of anything occurring or not occurring, or
  (c) whether anything is or is not true."

The term "bet" is not defined, however. Hence the definition adopted by the Royal Commission (see above) will presumably continue to apply. All forms of betting will be illegal unless carried out under one of the forms of licence that are available under the 2005 Act.

Gaming

The 2005 Act defines gaming as "playing a game of chance for a prize". **12–052** "Game of chance" is in turn defined as including:

"a game that involves an element of chance and an element of skill, a game that includes an element of chance that can be eliminated by superlative skill and a game that is presented as involving an element of chance. It does not include a sport".

For the purposes of the 2005 Act a person can be involved in a game of chance even if there are no other players and whether or not he risks losing. As with lotteries and betting, all forms of gaming will be illegal unless carried out under one of the forms of licence that are available under the 2005 Act.

Remote Gambling

12–053 The 2005 Act will introduce a system which permits remote gambling (whether gaming, betting or participating in a lottery). Gambling "remotely" encompasses use of the internet, telephone, television, radio and any other type of electronic communications technology that might be developed in the future; the Secretary of State will be able to determine whether any new form of communication system falls under the auspices of the 2005 Act.

The regulatory structure of the 2005 Act is underpinned by s.33, which creates the fundamental offence of providing facilities for gambling. That is further elucidated by s.36, which sets out the territorial application of the Act:

"(1) For the purposes of section 33 it is immaterial whether facilities are provided–

(a) wholly or partly by means of remote communication;
(b) subject to subsections (2) and (3), inside the United Kingdom, outside the United Kingdom, or partly inside and partly outside.

(2) Section 33 applies to the provision of facilities for non-remote gambling only if anything done in the course of the provision of the facilities is done in Great Britain.

(3) Section 33 applies to the provision of facilities for remote gambling only if at least one piece of remote gambling equipment used in the provision of the facilities is situated in Great Britain (but whether or not the facilities are provided for use wholly or partly in the United Kingdom).

(4) In this Act 'remote gambling equipment' means, subject to subsection (5), electronic or other equipment used by or on behalf of a person providing facilities for remote gambling–

(a) to store information relating to a person's participation in the gambling,
(b) to present, to persons who are participating or may participate in the gambling, a virtual game, virtual race or other

> virtual event or process by reference to which the gambling is conducted,
>
> (c) to determine all or part of a result or of the effect of a result, or
>
> (d) to store information relating to a result.
>
> (5) In this Act 'remote gambling equipment' does not include equipment which–
>
> (a) is used by a person to take advantage of remote gambling facilities provided by another person, and
>
> (b) is not provided by that other person."

Remote gambling operators seeking to run their services from UK-based servers will therefore need to obtain the relevant type of remote gambling licence. Existing offshore operators should note the provision of subs.(3), that if any one piece of remote gambling equipment is situated in the UK, the 2005 Act will apply.

It should also be noted that under s.44 it will be an offence if a person does anything in Great Britain, or uses remote gambling equipment situated in Great Britain, for the purpose of inviting or enabling a person in a "prohibited territory" to participate in remote gambling. A "prohibited territory" means a country or place designated for the purpose of this section by order made by the Secretary of State.

The Explanatory Notes to the 2005 Act state that the Secretary of State's decision whether or not to exercise the power to designate a prohibited territory could depend on matters such as: the development of the global gambling market; the laws which other countries establish to permit, constrain or prohibit the use of remote gambling; the practical measures employed by those countries to secure compliance with such laws; and the extent to which it is possible to reach international agreements about the cross-border use of the internet for gambling.

The Gambling Commission

The 2005 Act has already established the Gambling Commission—a new regulatory body to supervise all forms of gambling in the UK.   **12–054**

The most important function of the Commission will be to grant licences for gambling operators. It will be possible to be awarded one licence for multiple forms of gambling activity—for example only one licence will be necessary to run a casino and a lottery—but operators will need separate licences for carrying on remote and traditional "physical" gambling activities (s.67).

The Commission has issued a new Code of Conduct[96] (the "Code") with which all gambling operators will have to comply. If the Commission believes that any individual or company is not complying with the Code it

---

[96] "Licence Conditions and Codes of Practice", The Gambling Commission, November 2006.

may impose a financial penalty, attach restrictions to a licence or revoke it entirely.

The licensing structure

12–055   The new licensing regime will be wider ranging than the previous one: for example, anyone who manufactures, supplies, installs or adapts gambling software will commit an offence unless they have an appropriate licence (s.41). It will also be necessary for individuals holding specified management offices within a company to hold personal licences. The Gambling Commission has published the specific conditions that will attach to the licences of various different types.[97]

Children, young persons and other vulnerable users

12–056   Operators will be obliged to take steps to protect the vulnerable. The 2005 Act creates a new criminal offence of inviting, causing or permitting a child or young person to gamble (s.46). The penalty for this offence can carry a jail term of up to 51 weeks. However, there is a defence that a person took all reasonable steps to determine a user's age and reasonably believed that the user was not a child or a young person (s.63).

As a general requirement under the Code, remote operators will also have to use the best publicly available information for age verification purposes from whichever country a potential customer is resident in. To promote socially responsible gambling operators must also provide a mechanism whereby an individual may "self-exclude" themselves from accessing an operator's gambling facilities for a period of at least six months. Operators must take all reasonable steps to refuse service to anyone who has entered such a period.

12.3.4 Advertisement of Remote Gambling

12–057   Under the current legislation it is not permissible to advertise gambling facilities on TV and radio (except for advertisements for the National Lottery, bingo events or pool betting). The 2005 Act will relax these restrictions and there will be more scope for the advertisement of gambling services in broadcast and non-broadcast media from September 2007.

The Committee of Advertising Practice (CAP) has published new rules that will regulate both broadcast and non-broadcast advertising of gambling services from September 2007. The Gambling Commission's Code of Practice will require compliance with the CAP Codes. The CAP Codes will prohibit any advertising of gambling services that:

- Portrays, condones or encourages gambling behaviour that is

---

[97] "Licence Conditions and Codes of Practice", fn.5 above.

socially irresponsible or could lead to financial, social or emotional harm;

- Exploits the susceptibilities, aspirations, credulity, inexperience or lack of knowledge of children, young persons or other vulnerable persons;
- Suggest that gambling can be a solution to financial concerns;
- Links gambling to seduction, sexual success or enhanced attractiveness; or
- Is likely to be of particular appeal to children or young persons, especially by reflecting or being associated with youth culture.

Section 328 of the 2005 Act also makes provision enabling the Secretary of State to issue regulations controlling the advertising of gambling. However, these are reserve powers which are unlikely to be invoked unless the CAP Codes are thought to have proved ineffective.

Under the Act it will be an offence to advertise any unlawful gambling (s.330). Advertising gambling includes knowingly participating in or facilitating a relevant activity (s.327(1)(c)).

Section 330(6) provides a defence to this offence which may be compared **12–058** with the defences for conduits and hosts in the EU E-Commerce Directive (which does not apply to most gambling activities[98]). Section 330(6) provides that:

"A person does not commit an offence under subsection (1) by reason only of delivering, transmitting or broadcasting a communication or making data available if–

    (a) he acts in the course of a business of delivering, transmitting or broadcasting communications (in whatever form or by whatever means) or making data available, and

    (b) the nature of the business is such that persons undertaking it have no control over the nature or content of the communications or data."

It is notable that this exception applies not only to "mere conduits", i.e. those who transmit data, but also to those who "make data available". It, therefore, has potential application to those who host third party data and also to search engines and the like for general search results.

However, the precise application of this exception will remain to be worked out. For example, where an ISP contracts to provide hosting facilities for a customer that it knows is a gambling site, does it still have no control over the nature of content of the data? It may be unlikely that a search engine provider could avail itself of this exception if it had actively chosen to maintain a sponsored hyperlink or advert for unlawful gambling

---

[98] Defined as "gambling activities which involve wagering a stake with monetary value in games of chance, including lotteries and betting transactions" (Art.1.5(d)).

on its site. Until the scope of the advertising offences is determined, it is advisable for any party wishing to provide participate in or facilitate the provision of gambling advertisements to determine what licences the gambling operator holds.

There are complex provisions governing the territorial scope of the advertising prohibitions. Any physical advertising within the UK will be directly within the scope of the prohibitions and regulations. Section 333 contains provisions clarifying the circumstances in which remote advertising (i.e. advertising by remote communications) will contravene UK law. These are broadly intended to follow the internal market provisions of the Electronic Commerce Directive.

Thus the prohibition on advertising unlawful gambling under s.330 will bite on remote advertising contained within an information society service (e.g. on a website) only if:

(a) the advertising is targeted at the UK in one of the ways provided for in s.333(4); and

(b) the service provider is:

   (i) established within the UK; or
   (ii) established in a non-EEA state; or
   (iii) established in an EEA state other than the UK and has been notified of a derogation under Art.3(4) of the Directive;

   and

(c) the gambling to which the advertising relates either, in the case of non-remote gambling is to take place in Great Britain or, in the case of remote gambling, is gambling for which at least one piece of remote gambling equipment will be situate in Great Britain.

12–059   The condition that at least one piece of remote gambling equipment be situate in Great Britain is the requirement that triggers the application of the Act to remote gambling in the first place (*cf.* s.33(3) above) and thus distinguishes domestic from foreign gambling. The remainder of the provisions reflect (a) the E-Commerce Directive approach that regulatory control is to be exercised by the Member State in which the operator is established, and that information society services incoming from another Member State can only be restricted on a case by case basis and in exceptional circumstances; and (b) the overall policy that the UK should not seek to apply its laws to foreign websites on the basis that they are merely available in this country.

It is also an offence to advertise foreign (i.e. outside the EEA or Gibraltar) gambling other than a lottery (s.331). However, for remote advertising of foreign gambling to contravene s.331 the advertisements would have to be targeted towards the UK in one of the ways specified in s.333(4).

Finally, it is notable that s.335 of the 2005 Act, overturns the centuries-old rule that gambling contracts in the UK are unenforceable.

This change epitomises the shift in the UK's attitude to gambling: from restrictive to liberal. By adopting the most facilitative rules towards gambling of any of the EU States, the UK is hoping to become the legitimate home of the on-line gambling industry. Individual persons who wish to gamble on-line commit no offence under UK law if they use websites based in other jurisdictions, but the existence of a regulated system closer to home where any claims can be legally enforced more conveniently may make gamblers feel more comfortable when handing over their credit card details. However, only time will tell whether these reforms will provide sufficient temptation to lure operators away from the tax benefits of the offshore havens.

Meanwhile, it should noted that legality within the UK does not insulate the operator of an on-line gambling service from exposure to the laws of other countries. At the time of writing the US is continuing with its campaign against UK on-line gaming operators, which has resulted in the arrest of several company directors while visiting the US. Executives from an Austrian on-line gambling site were arrested in France in September 2006.

12.4 PORNOGRAPHY AND SEXUAL OFFENCES

A great deal of concern has from time to time been expressed in the press **12–060** and elsewhere about the spread of computer pornography, in particular, how it is readily available to children and young teenagers. Access by children to "top shelf" magazines and adult films and videos can be controlled by parents and by newsagents and cinemas. However, parents may not be aware of what can be accessed from their own home, and are likely to be less computer literate than their offspring.

This concern, together with pressure from government and the police, led during 1996, first, to the adoption of a Code of Practice by the internet service providers Association[99] (ISPA), then to the formation of the Internet Watch Foundation,[1] a more widely supported independent body which acts as a focus for the identification and removal of illegal material from UK ISPs' servers and encourages the classification of legal material in the internet.

In summer 2004, BT introduced content filtering at source for child pornography with its CleanFeed system, based on a database of child pornography sites held by the IWF. This has since been adopted by some other UK ISPs. According to an answer to a Parliamentary Question given by the Secretary of State for the Home Department on May 15, 2006 the providers of 90 per cent of domestic UK broadband connections were either already blocking or had plans to do so by the end of 2006. The Minister went on to say:

---

[99] ISPA (an organisation representing a number of UK service providers) can be found at *www.ispa.org.uk*.
[1] The Internet Watch Foundation can be found at *www.internetwatch.org.uk*.

"...we are setting a target that by the end of 2007, all ISPs offering broadband internet connectivity to the UK general public put in place technical measures that prevent their customers accessing websites containing illegal images of child abuse identified by the IWF. For new ISPs or services, we would expect them to put in place measures within nine months of offering the service to the public. If it appears that we are not going to meet our target through co-operation, we will review the options for stopping UK residents accessing websites on the IWF list."

On October 25, 2006 the Minister stated, in another Parliamentary Answer, that the government was working with the industry to publish and maintain the full list of ISPs blocking these websites.

12.4.1 Obscenity

12–061   The Obscene Publications Act 1959 covers material which has the effect such as to tend to deprave and corrupt. There has been a great deal of case law on what constitutes obscenity. A major factor in determining whether accused material is obscene is whether it would, taken as a whole, tend to deprave and corrupt the type of persons who may get hold of the material. Children are regarded as particularly at risk.

In *R v Perrin*[2] (discussed in detail below, para.12.063) the Court of Appeal drew a distinction between website preview material available to anybody and material available only to persons who took out a subscription to the service. The Court of Appeal found that where the publication relied upon was "the making available of preview material to any viewer who might choose to access it (including of course vulnerable young people)", in such a situation the prosecution was entitled to invite the jury to look beyond the police constable whose evidence of publication to himself was relied upon and to consider whether any person or persons were likely to see the published material, and if so whether the effect of the published material, taken as a whole, was such as to tend to deprave and corrupt the person or persons who were likely, having regard to all relevant circumstances, to see the matter contained or embodied in it.

The Court of Appeal emphasised that s.1(1) of the 1959 Act only required the jury to be satisfied that there was a likelihood of vulnerable persons seeing the material. The prosecution did not have to show that any such person actually saw it or would have seen it in the future. The defendant was convicted at trial on the basis of the preview material, but acquitted in relation to the subscription material. The conviction was upheld on appeal.

Criminal liability for obscenity is an area in which it is especially important to bear in mind the differing activities which persons involved in

---

[2] [2002] EWCA. Crim 747.

providing internet services undertake. There are two main routes to liability: having an obscene article (e.g. of a disk containing obscene material) for publication for gain; and publication. An "article" means any description of article containing or embodying matter to be read or looked at or both, any sound record, and any film or other record of a picture or pictures (s.1(2)). The 1959 Act was amended by the Criminal Justice and Public Order Act 1994 (the "1994 Act") to include the transmission of electronically stored data (see s.1(3)(b), discussed next).

Publication

A person "publishes" an article who: 12–062

- Distributes, circulates, sells, lets on hire, gives, or lends it, or who offers it for sale or for letting on hire (s.1(3)(a));
- Or in the case of an article containing or embodying matter to be looked at or a record,

    – shows, plays or projects it,
    – or, where the matter is data stored electronically, transmits that data (s.1(3)(b)).

A person also publishes an article to the extent that any matter recorded on it is included by him in a programme included in a programme service (as to which see below) (s.1(4)).

It is an open question whether "shows" requires active conduct on the part of the defendant. In *R. v Fellows, R. v Arnold*[3] one of the defendants to charges under both the Obscene Publications Act 1959 and the Protection of Children Act 1978 (see below) argued that giving certain others password access to his archive of indecent pictures on his employer's computer did not amount to "showing" the pictures as contended by the prosecution. The defendant argued that "distributes" and "shows" were active rather than passive, and that he did nothing more than permit others to have access to his archive.

As to "shows", the Court of Appeal accepted, for the purposes of the case, that active conduct on the defendant's part was required. Even so Evans L.J. said:

"... it seems to us that there is ample evidence of such conduct on his part. He took whatever steps were necessary not merely to store the data on his computer but also to make it available worldwide to other computers via the internet. He corresponded by email with those who sought to have access to it and he imposed certain conditions before they were permitted to do so. He gave permission by giving them the password. He did all this with the

---

[3] [1997] 2 All E.R. 548, CA.

sole object of allowing others, as well as himself, to view exact reproductions of the photographs stored in his archive."

The court expressed no view on whether the conduct amounted to distribution.

An offence is committed under s.2(1) of the 1959 Act if the defendant publishes an obscene article, even if not for gain. There is no requirement under the Obscene Publications Act that the defendant must have actually have had an intent to deprave or corrupt.

12–063 As to cases with an overseas element, in *R. v Waddon*[4] His Honour Judge Hardy ruled at first instance that where the defendant uploaded obscene materials from England to a web server in America, and an English police constable accessed that website from England and downloaded the material here, the defendant had published the materials in England for the purposes of the 1959 Act notwithstanding the intermediate elements that took place outside the jurisdiction. He said:

"I have no difficulty in finding in this case that an act of publication took place when the data was transmitted by the defendant or his agent to the service provider and that the publication was in effect still taking place when PC Ysart acting on instructions originating from the defendant received the data into his computer. Since both the sending and the receiving took place within the jurisdiction, in my view, it matters not, that the transmission in between times may have left the jurisdiction."

The conclusion that there was a publication in England was endorsed on appeal to the Court of Appeal.[5] The defendant conceded in the Court of Appeal that the defendant was himself, or through his agents, involved both in the transmission of material to the website and its transmission back again to England. In the light of that concession and the electronic transmission provisions of s.1(3) of the 1959 Act the Defendant could not and did not contend that publication did not take place in the England.

While the Court of Appeal commented that the concession was correctly made, it took a significantly different view from the court below of what constituted publication:

"As it seems to us, the fallacy in the submission advanced before the lower court was that there could only be a single publication. As it seems to us, there can be publication on a website abroad, when images are there uploaded; and there can be further publication when those images are downloaded elsewhere. That approach is, as it seems to us, underlined by the provisions of

---

[4] [1999] Masons C.L.R. 396.
[5] [2000] All E.R. (D) 502.

section 1(3)(b), as to what is capable of giving rise to publication where matter has been electronically transmitted."

This analysis appears to have been heavily influenced by the transmission provisions of s.1(3)(b), which extend the notion of publication to include mere transmission, without the need to show that anyone can read the material at the receiving end. That interpretation must follow from the Court of Appeal's observation that the mere upload to a website can amount to publication, and was confirmed in *R v Perrin* (discussed below). So it would appear that uploading from the UK to a foreign website amounts to publication within the UK, as does serving up content from abroad to the UK in response to a user request—in both cases because at least some part of the transmission occurs within the UK.

The Court of Appeal in *Waddon* declined to rule upon what the position might be in relation to jurisdiction if a person storing material on a website outside England intended that no transmission of that material should take place back to this country. The court commented that the issues would no doubt depend upon questions of intention and causation in relation to where publication should take place. It is unclear whether the court intended by this comment to refer to the situation whether the upload to the foreign website originated from within the UK, or from outside the UK, or to both situations.

The applicability of the 1959 Act to overseas websites was considered again by the Court of Appeal in *R v Perrin*.[6] In that case the defendant was a director and/or majority shareholder of one or more US companies involved in operating a website from the US. At trial a formal admission was made on behalf of the defendant as follows: "It is agreed and accepted by the defendant that he was legally responsible for the publication of the articles referred to in counts 1, 2 and 3 on the indictment".

Count 1 of the indictment related to a trailer or preview page, which was available free of charge to anyone with access to the internet. Counts 2 and 3 related to material available through a link marked "subscription to our best filthy sites", to access which the user had to provide name, address and credit card details.

At trial the defendant was convicted on count 1 (the preview page) but acquitted on counts 2 and 3, relating to the subscription material.

The evidence of publication was that the relevant pages had been visited **12–064** by PC Ysart, an officer with the Obscene Publications Unit, in the course of his duties. The defendant did not give or adduce evidence.

One of the grounds of appeal was that the conviction offended against Art.10 of the European Convention on Human Rights, concerning the right of freedom of expression. The right is qualified by Art.10(2), which provides that:

"...since it carries with it duties and responsibilities may be

---

[6] [2002] EWCA Crim 747.

> subject to such formalities, conditions, restrictions or penalties as
> are prescribed by law and are necessary in a democratic society . . .
> for the prevention of disorder or crime, for the protection of
> health or morals."

The appellant submitted that to satisfy the requirement in Art.10(2) of "prescribed by law" the law had to be formulated with sufficient precision to enable the citizen to regulate his conduct and to foresee, to a degree that is reasonable in the circumstances, the consequences which a given action may entail. Because of the worldwide nature of the internet it was difficult for publishers to comply with the statutory requirements of individual states, and if they were obliged to do so the most restrictive laws would prevail (*cf.* generally the discussion of this issue in section 12.2 above).

The appellant, therefore, submitted that the jury should have been instructed to consider first where the major steps in relation to publication took place, and only to convict if satisfied that those steps took place within the jurisdiction of the court. This submission was made against the background that there was no evidence to rebut the defendant's statements in interview that the material published was lawful in the US where the major steps involved in publishing the web page took place.

The appellant submitted that in Europe the problems are the same as those which have been experienced in the US regarding conflicting community standards. Community standards as to what tends to deprave and corrupt are not Europe-wide, and the Court should look at the problem from the point of view of the publisher who is prepared to comply with the law. The publisher could not attach a condition that there will be no access to his material in a given country, although a service provider could operate such a limitation.

The appellant accepted that under Convention law regulation of morals is normally regarded as a matter for individual states, but submitted that a more stringent view should be taken in relation to the internet because of the difficulty of knowing where it would be viewed. If inhibition were necessary it could be achieved more effectively in ways such as industry self regulation, blockage by service providers and steps taken in the home.

The respondent submitted, and the court accepted, that the protection to be afforded to freedom of expression under Art.10 of the Convention varied to some extent with the subject matter. Responsible exchange of political ideas attracted more protection than projection of pornography for gain.

12–065 The court accepted that the restriction in the 1959 Act was prescribed by law for a legitimate purpose. As to whether the restriction was necessary in a democratic society, the Court found that the infringement of the appellant's freedom was limited, as could be seen by reference to the acquittal on counts 2 and 3, and although the protection to vulnerable people afforded by the 1959 Act might be limited, there was no reason why a responsible government should abandon that protection in favour of other limited remedies already available to parents and others.

The court found that the US authorities were of limited value because of the protection given to free speech in the US constitution and the different inter-relationship between the states.

The court rejected the suggestion that it is necessary for the Crown to show where the major steps in relation to publication were taken. It implicitly accepted the prosecution's argument that to accept that submission would lead to publishers taking their major steps in countries with the most relaxed laws, but such countries might also have little interest in prosecuting, especially if the offensive material were targeted elsewhere.

This approach has similarities to the rejection by the Australian courts in *Gutnick v Dow Jones & Co. Inc.* of a "country of origin" rule for publication of defamatory content contained in a subscription website, discussed above at para.12–039. However, it should be cautioned that as a result of the transmission provisions of s.1(3)(b), the concept of publication in the law of obscenity has diverged markedly from that in defamation.

The court relied upon *R v Waddon* (see above) in determining that there was publication when anyone accessed the preview page of the website, and that a mere transmission of data constitutes publication.[7] It held that the publication shown by the evidence was sufficient to give jurisdiction to the court. The evidence of the police constable presumably was regarded as proving not so much that he had read the page, but that the page had been transmitted from abroad into the UK—which according to *Waddon* and *Perrin* is sufficient for the purposes of the Act. Since Perrin had admitted responsibility for publication there was no need in this case for further evidence to link the download to him.[8]

If a defendant has stored the material himself and he can be proved to have transmitted it to others, then prosecution for publication will be a clear option. A physical disk can be seized and presented to the court as evidence of what was published. Thus, subject to the defences available to him (which are discussed below), an ISP may be potentially at risk of committing publication offences in respect of material contained on its own disks, such as Usenet newsgroups and material on websites which it hosts. However, proving the elements of transmission-based offences in relation to material not stored by the defendant, although possible in principle, may be potentially more difficult, especially given the requirement to prove that what was transmitted originated from an article, in other words that the original matter was electronically stored.

Broadcasting and programme services

Another route to liability for transmitting obscene material across the internet may be provided by the Broadcasting Act 1990. The 1990 Act made amendments to the 1959 Act designed to apply its obscenity provisions to recorded and live "programme services". **12–066**

---

[7] *Perrin*, para.18.
[8] For a different perspective on *Perrin* see U. Kohl, "Who has the right to govern on-line activity? A criminal and civil point of view", *International Review of Law, Computers & Technology*, Vol.18, No.3/November 2004, p.387.

A programme service under s.201 of the 1990 Act (as amended by the Communications Act 2003) includes, as well as programme services within the meaning of the 2003 Act:

"...any other service which consists in the sending, by means of an electronic communications network (within the meaning of the Communications Act 2003), of sounds or visual images or both ... for reception at two or more places in the United Kingdom (whether they are so sent for simultaneous reception or at different times in response to requests made by different users of the service)".

This does not apply, *inter alia*, to two-way services, as defined under the 2003 Act.

The provisions are specifically not restricted to programme services that require to be licensed under the 2003 Act. They would appear to apply to activities on the internet.

Section 1(4) of the 1959 Act, as amended, provides that a person publishes an article to the extent that any matter recorded on it is included by him in a programme included in a programme service. A programme includes any item included in that service.[9] Section 1(5) contains provisions applying the Act to live as well as recorded material.

Under Sch.15, para.4 of the Broadcasting Act 1990, proceedings for offences under s.2 of the Obscene Publications Act 1959—either for publishing an obscene article or for having an obscene article for gain—shall not be instituted without the consent of the Director of Public Prosecutions in cases where the relevant publication, or the only other publication which followed from the relevant publication, took place in the course of the inclusion of a programme in a programme service.

This would appear to mean, given the wide definition of "programme service", that the consent of the DPP is required to institute a prosecution under the Act in respect of material on the internet where the content of the "service" consists of sounds or visual images or both.

Possession

12–067 An offence is also committed if the defendant has an obscene article for publication for gain (whether gain for himself or gain for another). A person is deemed to have an article for publication for gain if with a view to such publication he has the article in his ownership, possession or control. References to publication for gain apply to any publication with a view to gain, whether the gain is to accrue by way of consideration for the publication or in any other way.

These provisions provide the basis for an argument that a commercial ISP who acts a host, by providing in return for a subscription fee access to

---

[9] Obscene Publications Act 1959, s.1(6); Broadcasting Act 1990, s.202(1).

(among other things) materials which it stores on its disks, has the disks for publication for gain. An ISP who acts merely as a "pass through" or "conduit" access provider and who does not host anything itself ought to be in a strong position as regards these possession-based provisions of the Act.

In relation to possession offences, the provisions of Sch.15, para.3 of the Broadcasting Act 1990 should also be noted. These provide that where a person has an obscene article in his ownership, possession or control with a view to the matter recorded on it being included in a relevant programme, the article shall be taken to be an obscene article had or kept by that person for publication for gain.

Defences and ISPs

The specific defences provided in the 1959 Act are now of less importance   **12–068** in the light of the broad protection from civil and criminal liability provided for ISPs by the Electronic Commerce Directive, implemented in the UK by the Electronic Commerce (EC Directive) Regulations 2002. These defences, which co-exist with those under the 1959 Act, are discussed in detail in Ch.5.

Under the 1959 Act it is a defence to both the publication and possession based offences for the defendant to prove both that he had not examined the article and that he had no reasonable cause to suspect that it was of such a nature that its publication, or his having it (as appropriate), would constitute an offence under the Obscene Publications Act.[10] For inclusion in a programme, the defendant must show that he did not know and had no reason to suspect that the programme would include matter rendering him liable to be convicted.[11]

As both elements of these defences must be proved, it would not be enough for an ISP to simply shut its eyes to material which it stores or transmits; it must have no reasonable cause to suspect. Under the 1959 Act an ISP could be liable in respect of material on a website which it hosts for a customer, if it was aware of facts which should have put it on inquiry as to the nature of the material on the website.

This contrasts with the position as regards hosting liability under the Electronic Commerce Directive and Regulations. For a host to be fixed with criminal liability, it must have actual knowledge of unlawful activity or information. For criminal liability, awareness of facts or circumstances from which it would have been apparent to the service provider that the activity or information was unlawful is insufficient.[12] So an ISP that might otherwise be liable under the 1959 Act could still have a defence under the Electronic Commerce Regulations.

There might also be potential liability under the 1959 Act for publishing obscene material not hosted by the ISP, because of the transmission pro-

---

[10] Obscene Publications Act 1959, s.1(5).
[11] Broadcasting Act 1990, Sch.15, para.5(1).
[12] The Electronic Commerce (EC Directive) Regulations 2002 (SI 2002/2013), reg.19(a)(i).

visions of s.1(3)(b).[13] If liability were a possibility, then in this case the prosecuting authority would have a far more difficult task in resisting the ISP's innocence defence under the Act. The ISP would also most likely benefit from the conduit defence under the Electronic Commerce Directive and Regulations, which provides blanket immunity regardless of knowledge.

12.4.2 Child pornography

12–069   There are distinct offences relating to child pornography. The Protection of Children Act 1978 (as amended by the 1994 Act) makes it an offence to take, make, permit to be taken (s.1(1)(a)); distribute or show (s.1(1)(b)); or possess with a view to their being distributed or shown (by the defendant or others) (s.1(1)(c)); any indecent photograph or indecent pseudo-photograph of a child. Section 1(1)(d) creates an offence in relation to the publication of advertisements.

The 1994 Act amended the definition of photograph in s.7 of the 1978 Act to include "data stored on computer disk or by other electronic means which is capable of conversion into a photograph." References to an indecent photograph include a copy of an indecent photograph.

The term "pseudo-photograph" was introduced by the 1994 Act. "Pseudo-photograph" means an image, whether made by computer-graphics or otherwise, which appears to be a photograph. Further, if the impression conveyed by the pseudo-photograph is one which is difficult to classify as either an adult or a child, but the predominant impression is that the person shown is a child, then it shall be treated as such. This is intended to cover computer-generated and manipulated images.

A child was originally a person under 16. The age was raised to 18 by the Sexual Offences Act 2003.

Both a person and a company may be charged with an offence under this Act. The material covered by the 1978 Act must be "indecent", which is different from obscene. Indecency occurs at a lower threshold than obscenity, particularly where children are involved. Most people would consider indecent photographs of children which imitated the widely accepted "Page 3" photographs of adult women.

There are two potential defences to offences under s.1(1)(b) and (c). The first defence is similar to that under the 1959 Act—that the defendant did not see the image and had no knowledge or suspicion that it was indecent. It is also a defence that there was a legitimate reason for possessing or distributing the image.

The Sexual Offences Act 2003 added two further defences. One is for

---

[13] However, it must be strongly arguable that the transmission provisions are aimed at the person who is responsible for the particular transmission taking place (as in *Waddon* and *Perrin*, discussed above), rather than at someone who merely facilitates it by providing the medium through which the transmission is carried.

persons married to or living with a child aged between 16 and 18. Of more interest to us is the second defence, concerning criminal investigations.

There had been concern that police officers who made copies of indecent photographs or downloaded them from the internet for evidential purposes were technically committing an offence, as would a civilian (such as a member of an IT department) who made a copy to pass on to the authorities (see section 12–070 below). On May 1, 2004 a new s.1B of the 1978 Act was introduced. This includes a provision that a defendant is not guilty of an offence under s.1(1)(a) of the Act if he proves that it was necessary for him to make the photograph or pseudo-photograph for the purposes of the prevention, detection or investigation of crime, or for the purposes of criminal proceedings, in any part of the world.

The Association of Chief Police Officers and the Crown Prosecution Service have published a Memorandum[14] setting out the major factors that the police and the CPS consider would be relevant to a decision on how to proceed in a particular case.

The Criminal Justice Act 1988 s.160 also covers the area of child pornography, providing a summary offence of possession of an indecent photo of a child. The 1994 Act has amended this Act in a similar way to the amendments to the Protection of Children Act. The original defences under the 1978 Act are available, as well as the marriage defence (but not the criminal investigations defence). A further possible defence is that the image was not requested and was not kept for an unreasonable length of time after receipt.

"Making" and downloading

We have referred above to the meaning of "show" in both the 1959 Act and the 1978 Act. The meaning of "makes" under s.1(1)(a) of the 1978 Act and "possession" under the 1988 Act have also been judicially considered in relation to the internet.   **12–070**

In *R. v Bowden*[15] the Court of Appeal considered the meaning of "makes" under the 1978 Act. The defendant had taken his computer hard drive for repair, and while examining the computer the repairer found indecent material on the hard drive. The defendant had downloaded images from the internet and either printed them out himself or stored them on his hard disk. The images were all for his own use. The Court of Appeal held that "makes" applied not only to original photographs but (by virtue of s.7) also to copies of photographs and to data stored on computer disk. The court accepted the submissions of counsel for the Crown, that:

> "A person who either downloads images on to disc or who prints them off is making them. The Act is not only concerned with the

---

[14] Memorandum of Understanding Between Crown Prosecution Service and the Association of Chief Police Officers concerning Section 46 Sexual Offences Act 2003, October 2004 (*www.iwf.org.uk/police/page.22.213.htm*).
[15] [2000] 2 All E.R. 418, CA.

original creation of images, but also their proliferation. Photographs or pseudo-photographs found on the internet may have originated from outside the United Kingdom; to download or print within the jurisdiction is to create new material which hitherto may not have existed therein".

This point was considered again in *Atkins v DPP*,[16] in which it was argued that the application of "making" to acts of copying and storage, as opposed to an act of creation, could lead to injustice since the Act provided no defence to offences under s.1(1)(a). People engaged in innocent activity (such as making copies for the purpose of collecting of evidence) could be caught by an absolute offence. However, although the force of the argument was recognised (and the interpretation to include copies described as "problematic"), the court concluded that it was bound by *Bowden* and should not regard it as wrongly decided. The defendant should have been convicted by the magistrate in respect of images downloaded and stored in a directory on his computer hard drive.

Bowden and *Atkins* were applied, in *R v Smith and Jayson*,[17] to the opening of an email attachment and to the viewing of indecent images on screen.

In the case of *Smith*, the appellant had opened an email attachment containing an indecent image of a child. The appellant did not delete the image, which remained as part of the email in the appellant's Inbox. As regards the *actus reus* of the offence, it was not suggested that the actual opening of the attachment was not capable of being an act of making the image that appeared on the attachment (either by merely opening the attachment, or by causing the computer by opening the attachment automatically to store the data in the computer's memory). The argument in the Court of Appeal, therefore, concerned the necessary *mens rea* required to constitute the offence.

The court commented that if the appellant had not known that the attachment contained or was likely to contain indecent photographs or pseudo-photographs of a child, he could not be guilty of the offence of making those photographs or pseudo-photographs when he opened the email and its attachments. Nor could he have been guilty of making the photographs by the automatic storing of them in the cache if he was unaware of the existence of the cache.

However, on the facts proved by the prosecution this was not a case where the appellant simply opened an unsolicited email and attachments, not knowing what the attachments were likely to contain. On the facts, the jury would have been entitled to find that when he received the email, he must have known that the attachment contained or was likely to contain indecent images of the child. Moreover, he had not deleted any of the images. They remained in his Inbox.

---

[16] [2000] 2 All E.R. 425, QBD, Divisional Court.
[17] [2002] EWCA Crim 683.

The unsuccessful argument of the appellant in *Atkins* for a narrow construction of s.1(1)(a) of the 1978 Act, based on the lack of a statutory defence to that section, was again rejected in *R v Smith and Jayson*.

As noted above (para.12–069), the Sexual Offences Act 2003 has now amended the 1978 Act so as to provide a statutory defence to s.1(1))(a) in the case of criminal investigations.

Cache copies

Atkins also decided a point that was not in issue in *Bowden*, namely   **12–071** whether "making" under the 1978 Act extended to copies made unknowingly.[18] Some of the images found on the defendant's computer were stored in the cache created automatically by the defendant's internet browser. The magistrate had stated that he could not be sure that the defendant knew of the operation of the cache, "knew in other words that the computer would automatically retain upon its hard disk information sent to it at the user's request." The Divisional Court held that "making" did not extend to unintentional copying.

The defendant in *Atkins* was also charged with possession under the 1988 Act, in relation to the cache copies. The question arose whether knowledge (in the sense of knowledge of the existence and effect of the cache, as opposed to knowledge of its contents[19]) was an element of possession. The Divisional Court held that it was, so that in this case the defendant could not be convicted.

Screen images

It was common ground in *Atkins* that the defendant would have had no   **12–072** defence (subject to the prosecution being able to establish that the offence had occurred within the time limit for prosecution) to a prosecution under the 1988 Act for possession based on the "transient downloading of the image onto the screen". As a technical statement this is inaccurate, conflating two entirely distinct events: the temporary storage of a copy of the image in the computer's volatile memory (RAM); and the transient appearance of the image on the computer screen as a result of cathode rays energising the phosphor dots on the screen.

It has been argued, in relation to copyright, that the image displayed on the screen is not a copy because it is not stored, by contrast with the RAM copy which, while admittedly transient, is stored.[20] On the other hand, it was held in *Bookmakers' Afternoon Greyhound Racing Services v Wilf Gilbert (Staffordshire) Ltd*,[21] a case under the now superseded Copyright

---

[18] See also Angus Hamilton, "Caught Looking" and "Caught Looking Revisited" *Computers and Law*, August/September and October/November 1998.

[19] Ignorance of the indecent nature of the contents of the cache would fall to be considered under the defence provided by s.160(2)(b) of the 1988 Act.

[20] Laddie Prescott and Vitoria, *Modern Law of Copyright*, 3rd edn (2000), para.14.12.

[21] [1994] F.S.R. 723.

Act 1956, that a screen display did amount to reproduction in a material form.

If a distinction were to be drawn between the RAM copy and the screen display, it could lead to a conundrum: the image displayed in screen is so evanescent as not to amount either to a copy or to stored data under the definitions of indecent photograph in s.7 of the 1988 Act; yet the copy held in RAM, while probably "stored" within the meaning of the s.7 definitions, may not be known to the user to exist and so is subject to the same objection as the browser cache copies. The firmness of the common ground in *Atkins* may be questionable.

In any event, whether one is considering browser cache copies or (even more so) transient RAM copies, it does seem curious that the commission of an offence should depend on the degree of technical knowledge that the user happens to possess of the inner workings of the computer and its software.

Whether viewing on screen would also amount to "making" under the 1978 Act was not specifically discussed in either *Atkins* or *Bowden*. Would creating the temporary copy in RAM, or creating the transient image on the computer screen, amount to "making" as well as (apparently) possession? If it does, that would create the situation described in *Atkins* as a "striking oddity", that the self-same set of facts would involve the commission of two quite distinct offences, no additional proof being required for the more serious offence of "making" under the 1978 Act.

This question has now been addressed by the Court of Appeal in *R. v Smith and Jayson* (see above, para.12–070).

In the *Jayson* appeal, the appellant's home was searched and his computer seized. The hard drive was analysed by an expert who recovered a number of pornographic images including some relating to children. It was common ground that these images had not been stored on to the appellant's hard drive. They had been stored by the computer because of an automatic function of Internet Explorer. This had automatically stored on to a temporary cache any material viewed on the screen by the operator while browsing. All the images had been automatically emptied from the cache before the computer was seized by the police. The images were retrieved by a special process undertaken by the prosecution computer expert.

12–073   The prosecution put its case in two ways:

1. that searching the worldwide web and selecting images to appear on the computer monitor was sufficient to amount to "making" and
2. that the automatic storage of the images in the temporary cache amounted to making an indecent photograph of a child.

As to the first submission, the prosecution argued that the positive action of causing the photograph to be downloaded from the web page onto the screen involves the making of a photograph and that it is analogous to copying in that it replicates the image from the web.

The defence relied on s.7(4)(b) of the 1978 Act, in particular the reference in the definition of photograph to data being "stored", which the defence argued connoted a requirement that electronic data be retained for future use and in order to enable subsequent retrieval.

The court held:

> "In our view, the act of voluntarily downloading an indecent image from a web page on to a computer screen is an act of making a photograph or pseudo-photograph. We reach that conclusion as a matter of the ordinary use of language, and giving to the word 'make' its ordinary and natural meaning, as did this court in *Bowden*. By downloading the image, the operator is creating or causing the image to exist on the computer screen. The image may remain on the screen for a second or for a much longer period. Whether its creation amounts to an act of making cannot be determined by the length of time that the image remains on the screen."

The court rejected the suggestion that the question of retrieval was relevant to this question, commenting that the definition in s.7(4) of the 1978 Act was part of the definition of photograph and had nothing to do with the quite separate question of what constitutes the act of making a photograph.

The court also commented that s.7(4)(b) requires that:

> "... data stored on a computer disk or by other electronic means 'should be capable of conversion into a photograph'. It is not a requirement that the data should be retrievable. It is not suggested that an image downloaded on to a computer screen is not capable of conversion into a photograph. It plainly is".

As to the prosecution's second submission, the prosecution argued that it would be iniquitous for a knowledgeable operator to evade liability by using the temporary cache in a similar fashion to a designated file in order to store revisitable and viewable material. Neither the destination of the images, nor the fact that they were held in a temporary location for a finite period, was (it was argued) relevant.

The second submission is consistent with the decision in *Bowden*. The **12–074** defence did not contest the *actus reus* aspect of the second submission, but made unsuccessful submissions on *mens rea*. As to *mens rea*, the court held that the *mens rea* was that the act of making should be a deliberate and intentional act with knowledge that the image made is, or is likely to be an indecent photograph or pseudo-photograph of a child.

We observe that (whatever its merits otherwise) the finding that viewing on screen amounts to making a photograph may avoid the increasing probability of the courts sinking into a technical morass if they focus on the operation of computer caches, in particular if the question of when the cache copies come into existence is considered carefully. Consider the factual difference in the aspects of the two appeals concerning copies of images created automatically on the computer's disk. The *Smith* appeal concerned email attachments that were opened and not deleted from the Inbox. *Jayson* concerned the creation of a copy of the image in the browser cache, which subsequently was automatically deleted.

A copy of the attachment is created on the user's hard disk as soon as the email is received.[22] With a network connection the user may have done nothing to create that copy other than configure his computer to receive emails as and when they are routed to him. With a dial-up connection the user will have caused his computer to download a batch of emails, which will be stored on its disk. In the *Smith* case there was evidence that the appellant had solicited the emails. In the case of unsolicited emails, it could be argued (at least with a network, rather than a dial-up connection), that the recipient did not himself cause the copy on his hard disk to be created. Even if he did cause the copy to be created, in the case of unsolicited email the necessary *mens rea* may well not be present at that point, but only become so subsequently when he examines the email before deciding whether to open it. However, by the time the *mens rea* is formed, has the act of "making" already been completed? If so, how can an offence be committed in relation to that copy, unless "making" connotes some continuing act of storage?

The judge at first instance in *Smith* suggested that the defendant "has sought to 'make' photographs, in effect by proliferating them rather than taking the option, which was otherwise available to him, which was to delete them altogether". But what can be the relevance of deletion to the offence, unless "making" connotes a continuing act of storage? Is it then an offence to leave the email on disk without either opening or deleting it, once its nature has become apparent? If (as stated in *Smith*), it is not an offence to open an email in ignorance of its likely contents, is it an offence subsequently to leave the email undeleted once the contents have become apparent?

For these to be offences, "making" would have to encompass continued storage of an already created copy. But that would seem to go beyond the *Bowden* meaning of making: "cause to exist; to produce by action, to bring about", *a fortiori* if the email was not originally downloaded to the user's computer by a positive action of the user. Although the definition of "photograph" in s.7 includes the word "stored", the Court of Appeal in *R. v Smith and Jayson* held that that had nothing to do with the question of what constitutes the act of making a photograph.

12–075   The receipt of an email differs from the usual process of opening a web page, where normally the creation of a browser cache copy will occur only when the user opens the page in question. However, some browser speed-

---

[22] This assumes that the user's email program is configured to receive the entire text and attachments when emails arrive into his local Inbox or are downloaded from his email provider, as opposed to receiving only the subject matter or text of the email, leaving the attachment to be downloaded at the user's option.

up programs guess which pages the user may open next, and download those pages before the user has opened them. That is more analogous to the email situation.

If "making" does connote continuing storage, then if deletion before opening an apparently illegal attachment can prevent the offence, how far does the user have to go to delete the image? If the user is sufficiently computer-literate to know that forensically recoverable images still exist on the computer, does the user have to take steps to delete even those? As we have noted, in the *Jayson* appeal the police forensic experts were able to retrieve images from the computer even though they had been deleted from the cache. What if the user knows they may exist, but does not know how to perform such a low-level deletion? While these issues have not been addressed in the context of "making", the Court of Appeal in *R. v Porter*[23] has addressed them in the context of the mental element of "possession" under s.160 of the Criminal Justice Act 1988 (see discussion below), suggesting that the technical knowledge of the defendant may indeed be relevant.

If, as seems to be the preferable construction, "making" does not connote continuing storage, then the various references to failure to delete in the *Smith* appeal may be understood as referring to evidence of the guilty state of mind of the appellant, rather than to any aspect of the act of "making".

These could be important questions for an innocent user who receives unsolicited email, realises that it is likely to contain illegal material and deletes in from the Inbox, but fails to expunge other copies that may have come into existence automatically or to undertake a low-level deletion that would prevent the material being forensically recoverable. Indeed a user who realises the likely content of an email and who deletes it from the Inbox may (depending on how his email software is configured) thereby simply cause the email and attachment to be moved into a Deleted folder, thereby (if he is aware that that is the operation of the Delete command) possibly committing the offence of making any new copy thereby created.[24]

We have seen that "making" under the 1978 Act includes the intentional making of a copy. If the screen image does count as a copy, then in the case of ordinary websites it is perfectly clear to the user (since he is viewing it) that he is creating that copy, so lack of knowledge cannot be an issue. An offence has been committed.   **12–076**

If the screen image does not count as a copy, and the question turns around the making of the RAM copy, then again the offence would seem to turn on the technical knowledge of the user.

In some cases, notably sites which deliberately hide their graphical content by using zero height and width images, it is possible for an image to be automatically stored in the browser cache without ever being displayed on screen. In this way an innocent user can visit what appears to be an

---

[23] [2006] EWCA Crim 560.
[24] It is possible that no new copy is in fact created, and that only the flags in the email database are changed so that the email is displayed in a different folder.

innocuous website, yet end up with a browser cache full of illegal images.[25]

In this situation the lack of knowledge either that he had visited a site containing illegal material, or that it had been downloaded to the cache, ought to give the innocent user a good answer to a prosecution. However, there may also be concern that this would also enable guilty parties to escape prosecution through the difficulty in proving that the guilty party knew that he was visiting an illegal site. Of course, once the user copies the material from the cache to a permanent directory (which would have to be done in order to prevent the copies expiring from the cache) then, as was the case in *Atkins*, the requisite knowledge becomes relatively easy to prove in respect of the manually created permanent copies.

In *Atkins* it was pointed out in argument that before the amendments to the 1978 Act introduced by the 1994 Act, the absolute offence under s.1(1)(a) applied only to the taking of indecent photographs of children, an activity involving the direct exploitation of children in their actual presence for which there could be no defence. Parliament could not, it was argued, have intended when inserting "making" and "pseudo-photographs" into s.1(1)(a), to extend the offence beyond such acts of primary creation. Less morally culpable acts in s.1(1)(b)and(c), it was pointed out, such as distribution, showing, or possession with a view to distribution or showing, were provided with a defence.

These arguments did not hold sway. Yet the consequence of holding that "making" extends to copies would appear to be that the mere act of personal viewing could also amount to "making", a result which does not fit at all into the hierarchy of offences created in s.1; offends against the principle expressed in *Atkins* that the same facts should not amount to two distinct offences of different seriousness; may render the commission of the offence dependent on the degree of technical computer knowledge possessed by the user; and creates a gulf between the criminal consequences of merely viewing a hard copy photograph and merely viewing an image on a computer screen.

As to the relevance of the user's technical knowledge, in *R. v Smith and Jayson* the appellant Jayson told the police at his interview that he was computer literate, having had 30 years experience with computers. It was the prosecution's case that he must have been aware of the fact that images called up on to his screen would be automatically downloaded into the temporary cache. Indeed, it was conceded on behalf of the appellant on appeal that he was aware of how the temporary internet cache operated.

Linking

12–077   In January 1998 a student pleaded guilty at Preston Crown Court to offences under the 1959 Act and the 1978 Act. He had been charged with publishing obscene articles on the internet contrary to the 1959 Act and with making indecent photographs of children contrary to the 1978 Act. He

---

[25] See Clive Grace, "Unseen, obscene and dangerous," *The Guardian*, November 18, 1999.

created a UK based website for the purpose of providing links to other websites, including a website of his own hosted in the US, which contained what the police described as "extreme adult pornography". A search of his home also found "extreme child pornography" downloaded from the internet. As the prosecution was not contested, the case sets no legal precedent. However, the police commented that "any attempt by a person in this country to escape prosecution by lodging material elsewhere will fail".

Clearly the case involved more activities by the defendant than simply creating hypertext web links to overseas pornography sites. However, it does raise the question whether creating a link to material, the publication of which is illegal under the 1959 Act or the 1978 Act, is an offence.

The prosecution would have to establish, under the 1959 Act, that the person responsible for creating the web link thereby published the obscene article in one of the following ways (omitting those of no apparent relevance):

- Showed, played or projected it; or
- Where the matter embodied in the article was data stored electronically, transmitted the data; or
- Included the matter in a programme included in a programme service.

Under the 1978 Act the prosecution would have to establish that the defendant did one of the following acts in relation to an indecent photograph or pseudo-photograph of a child:

- Distributed or showed it; or
- Published or caused to be published an advertisement likely to be understood as conveying that the advertiser distributed or showed indecent photographs of a child, or intended to do so

Under s.1(2) of the 1978 Act, a person is to be regarded as "distributing" if he parts with possession to, or exposes or offers for acquisition to, another person.

A number of difficult issues arise in relation to web links. **12–078**

If the link is to a site on which the offending material is available, but not displayed on the top level, does that constitute an offence? If so, how many links removed does the material have to be before no offence is committed? Or is an offence only committed (if at all) if clicking on the link causes the offending material to be displayed on the user's screen?

Does providing a hypertext link constitute "showing"? On the basis of *R. v Fellows*, the fact that a defendant does not "push" the material to the user's screen does not appear to be determinative. If providing a link is "showing", would providing the URL of the material without coding it as an active hypertext link also amount to "showing"? If so, that is tantamount to finding that merely to publish information about where obscene material may be found is an offence.

Can the person who includes a link to another site be said to transmit the data from that site for the purposes of s.1(3)(b) of the 1959 Act? This seems far-fetched. No transmission occurs until the user executes the link. The data is then transmitted from the target site, not that of the defendant. At the most the defendant provides the user with means to cause the target site to transmit the data to the user (see also the discussion of copyright infringement by web linking, section 2.6.3).

If the target site is also operated by the defendant, then the defendant's position is likely to be more difficult. Even if the defendant's own target site is abroad, at least part of the transmission path to an English user will be through the English jurisdiction (but note comments on *R. v Waddon* above).

Does providing a link to obscene material amount to including the matter in a programme included in a programme service under s.1(4) of the 1959 Act? A "programme" includes an advertisement and, in relation to any service, any item included in that service. The Act provides no guidance as to the meaning of "include". On a broad construction of the word, a court might be prepared to find that linked material was "included" in the service. However, that still suffers from the difficulty of distinguishing sensibly, in the context of the web, between including the material itself and including information about where to find the material.

How are the requirements for a conviction affected by the possibility that the content on the target site may change, or that the precise matter regarded as illegal may not have been present when the link was created? It is notable that the German prosecution of Angela Marquardt over a web link to the *Radikal* website (see section 12.2.3) failed on this point. The prosecution were unable to show that the offending material was present on the target site when Ms Marquardt created the link to it.

Could a link in some circumstances be regarded as an "advertisement" under s.1(1)(d) of the 1978 Act? Or if a web page creator links to material which is itself clearly an advertisement, could the person creating the link be regarded as "causing" the advertisement to be published? Does the fact that the user has to execute the link break any chain of causation?

Distribution under the 1978 Act

12–079 In *R v P*[26] the Court of Appeal held that s.1(1)(b) of the 1978 Act created an offence of strict liability, so that a defendant's claim that he did not know that a CD he had passed on to a third party contained indecent images was irrelevant. Knowledge was relevant only to the statutory defences.

Possession with a view to distribution under the 1978 Act

12–080 Under s.1(1)(c) of the 1978 Act it is an offence for a person to have in his possession indecent photographs or pseudo-photographs of a child with a view to their being distributed or shown by himself or others.

---

[26] [2006] All E.R. (D) 238 (Oct).

The meaning of "with a view" was considered by the Court of Appeal in *R v Dooley*.[27] In this case a police raid discovered thousands of images on the defendant's computer, six of which were in the "My Shared Folder" directory created by the Kazaa file-sharing programme. The defendant's case was that it was his specific intention to move these out of the public shared directory to a private area of his computer. However, at the time of the police raid the six images had been in the shared folder for some 10 days and were available to be accessed by other Kazaa users during this period. Although the Kazaa software had a facility to make the shared folder private, the defendant was unaware of that.

The judge had ruled that "with a view" meant that the prosecution had to prove that the participant downloaded a particular photograph or image in the knowledge that it was likely to be seen by other participants with access to the same folder into which the image went. In the light of that ruling the defendant pleaded guilty, then appealed on the basis that the judge's ruling was incorrect.

The Court of Appeal held that whilst the defendant's knowledge might be very important, nonetheless the question that the jury would have to resolve would be whether at least one of the reasons why the defendant left the images in the public shared folder was so that others could have access to images within it. The ability to foresee that doing an act was likely have a particular result did not mean that the act was done with a view to that result.

Possession under the 1988 Act

As we have noted above, when discussing cache copies, the Court of Appeal in *Atkins* held that under s.160 of the Criminal Justice Act 1988 "possession" connoted a mental element.

12–081

This was explored further in *R v Porter*.[28] The issue in this case was whether the defendant could be said to "possess" images which he had deleted from his computer hard drive, but which could be retrieved with the aid of specialist forensic software which he did not have. The Court of Appeal reaffirmed *Atkins* and held that this did not amount to possession. The Court of Appeal did not shrink from the consequences that we have discussed above in relation to "making", that liability can depend on the technical knowledge of the defendant:

> "Suppose that a person receives unsolicited images of child pornography as an attachment to an email. He is shocked by what he sees and immediately deletes the attachment and deletes it from the recycle bin. Suppose further that he knows that the images are retrievable from the hard disk drive, but he believes that they can only be retrieved and removed by specialists who have software

---

[27] [2005] EWCA Crim 3093.
[28] [2006] EWCA Crim 560.

and equipment which he does not have. It does not occur to him to seek to acquire the software or engage a specialist for this purpose. So far as he is concerned, he has no intention of ever seeking to retrieve the images and he has done all that is reasonably necessary to make them irretrievable. We think that it would be surprising if Parliament had intended that such a person should be guilty of an offence under section 160(1) of the 1988 Act....

In the special case of deleted computer images, if a person cannot retrieve or gain access to an image, in our view he no longer has custody or control of it. He has put it beyond his reach just as does a person who destroys or otherwise gets rid of a hard copy photograph. For this reason, it is not appropriate to say that a person who cannot retrieve an image from the hard disk drive is in possession of the image because he is in possession of the hard disk drive and the computer....

[T]he first question for the jury is whether the defendant in a case of this kind has possession of the image at the relevant time, in the sense of custody or control of the image at that time. If at the alleged time of possession the image is beyond his control, then for the reasons given earlier he will not possess it. If, however, at that time the image is within his control, for example, because he has the ability to produce it on his screen, to make a hard copy of it, or to send it to someone else, then he will possess it. It will be a matter for the jury to decide whether images are beyond the control of the defendant having regard to all the factors in the case, including his knowledge and particular circumstances. Thus, images which have been emptied from the recycle bin may be considered to be within the control of a defendant who is skilled in the use of computers and in fact owns the software necessary to retrieve such images; whereas such images may be considered not to be within the control of a defendant who does not possess these skills and does not own such software....

It will, therefore, be a matter for the jury to decide whether images on a hard disk drive are within the control of the defendant, and to do so having regard to all the circumstances of the case. Such is the speed at which computer technology is developing that what a jury may consider not to be within a defendant's control today may be considered by a jury to be within a defendant's control in the near future. Further, in the course of time more and more people will become skilled in the use of computers. This too will be a relevant factor for the jury to take into account."

12.4.3 On-line harassment and offensive electronic communications

Under s.127 of the Communications Act 2003 it is a summary offence to **12–082** send by means of a public electronic communications network a message or other matter that is grossly offensive or of an indecent, obscene or menacing character; or to cause any such message or matter to be so sent.

It is also an offence if a person, for the purpose of causing annoyance, inconvenience or needless anxiety to another, sends by means of a public electronic communications network a message that he knows to be false, causes such a message to be sent; or persistently makes use of a public electronic communications network for that purpose.

This extends to data transmitted by a public communications network and therefore catches the use of the internet. However, it does not apply to anything done in the course of providing a programme service within the meaning of the Broadcasting Act 1990 (as to which, see above para.12–066).

The ambit of the Act catches the originator of the material rather than the person distributing it. Therefore, it is unlikely that the internet service provider will be caught by this provision in the Act (who in any event would most likely have the protection of the conduit defence under the Electronic Commerce (EC Directive) Regulations 2002) but the originator of the material will be caught.

The House of Lords in *DPP v Collins*[29] has considered the meaning of s.127. It held that the purpose of s.127 was to protect the integrity of the public telecommunications system. The offence under s.127 is complete when the message is sent, regardless of whether it was received at all or whether the particular recipient was offended. The yardstick of gross offensiveness is the application of reasonably enlightened, but not perfectionist, contemporary standards to the particular message sent in its particular context. The test is whether a message is couched in terms liable to cause gross offence to those to whom it relates.

As to the mental element, a culpable state of mind will ordinarily be found where a message is couched in terms showing an intention to insult those to whom the message relates or giving rise to the inference that a risk of doing so must have been recognised by the sender. The same will be true where facts known to the sender of a message about an intended recipient render the message peculiarly offensive to that recipient, or likely to be so, whether or not the message in fact reaches the recipient. Lord Brown observed that where these conclusions left telephone chatlines, the very essence of which might be thought to involve the sending of indecent or obscene messages, was not explored and could be left for another day.

From May 1, 2001 the Malicious Communications Act 1988 was **12–083** extended to include electronic communications.[30] It is, therefore, a sum-

---

[29] [2006] UKHL 40.
[30] Criminal Justice and Police Act 2001, s.43.

mary offence, under s.1(1) of the Act, for a person to send (a) a letter, electronic communication or article of any description which conveys a message which is indecent or grossly offensive; a threat; or information which is false and known or believed to be false by the sender; or (b) any other article or electronic communication which is, in whole or in part, of an indecent or grossly offensive nature, if the purpose, or one of the purposes, of the person in sending it is that it should cause distress or anxiety to the recipient or to any other person to whom he intends that it or its contents or nature should be communicated. An electronic communication is defined as "any oral or other communication by means of an electronic communications network; and any communication (however sent) that is in electronic form".

There is a specific defence to the offence concerning threats.

In contrast to s.127 of the Communications Act 2003, for an offence to be committed under s.1 of the Malicious Communications Act 1988 the sender of the grossly offensive message must intend it to cause distress or anxiety to its immediate or eventual recipient.[31]

The Protection from Harassment Act 1997, although enacted to deal with stalkers, applies to a much broader category of conduct. It is capable of applying to on-line harassment. Section 1 provides that a person must not pursue a course of conduct which amounts to harassment of another and which he knows or ought to know amounts to harassment of the other. A course of conduct must involve conduct on at least two occasions (s.7(3)). A person ought to know, if a reasonable person in possession of the same information would think the course of conduct amounted to harassment of the other.

There are various defences. A breach of the prohibition on harassment is both a summary offence and may also be the subject of civil proceedings by an actual or apprehended victim of harassment for damages (including for anxiety and financial loss) and an injunction. There is also a more serious offence of putting people in fear of violence. A course of conduct consisting of sending two letters four and a half months apart was capable of amounting to harassment,[32] as were two articles published in a newspaper.[33]

In *R v Debnath*[34] the Court of Appeal after considering the exceptional circumstances of the defendant's course of conduct which included setting up a website containing a fake newspaper article about the complainant, signing him up to an internet database of people with sexually transmitted diseases seeking sexual liaisons, arranging for a group of hackers to sabotage his emails and numerous other activities, upheld a restraining order couched in the following terms:

---

[31] *DPP v Collins, ibid, per* Lord Brown.
[32] *Baron v Crown Prosecution Service* June 13, 2000 (DC, unreported).
[33] *Thomas v News Group Newspapers Ltd* July 25, 2001, CA, TLR.
[34] [2005] EWCA Crim 3472.

"...the Defendant is prohibited from (1) contacting directly or indirectly A, H and other persons named, and (2) publishing any information concerning A and H whether true or not."

In *Cray v Hancock*[35] the claimant was a partner in a firm of solicitors who had represented the defendant's wife in a building dispute. The defendant sent a letter and faxes alleging that the claimant was greedy, incompetent and had overcharged the defendant's wife. The claimant subsequently received numerous emails and became aware of internet forum postings and spoof websites repeating the allegations. The claimant sued for libel and harassment and was awarded £19,000 damages.

12.4.4 Public display of indecent matter

Section 1(1) of the Indecent Displays (Control) Act 1981 makes a person guilty of an offence if he publicly displays indecent matter. Those caught are the person making the display, and any person causing or permitting the display. The prime aim of the Act is to control displays in places which people can physically enter.   **12–084**

Under s.1(2) matter displayed in or so as to be visible from any public place is deemed to be publicly displayed; this would include for example, internet terminals in public libraries, "cyber-cafes", etc. Section 1(3) makes it clear that payment of a fee to access a place to view the material where the fee includes payment for the display has the effect of making that place not a public place for the purposes of s.1(2), so long as persons under 18 are barred.

However, the general provisions of s.1(1) (which could possibly apply directly to the provider of a website accessible to the public, as opposed to a person locating the screen in public premises), contains no such qualifications. Once again, bodies corporate may face liability as well as individuals. Nothing in the Act applies to a television programme service within the meaning of the Broadcasting Act 1990.

12.4.5 Sex tourism

The Sexual Offences (Conspiracy and Incitement) Act 1996 became law on October 1, 1996. The Act is directed mainly at child sex tourism, and aims to make triable in England and Wales acts of conspiracy and incitement to commit certain sexual offences abroad. Section 2(3) of the Act provides that any act of incitement by means of a message (however communicated) is to be treated as done in England and Wales if the message is sent or received in England and Wales. That would clearly apply to internet emails. It should   **12–085**

---

[35] [2005] All E.R. (D) 66 (Nov) QBD.

also cover advertising on websites, whose contents can easily be characterised as messages received by the viewer of the site.

12.4.6 Cross-border content standards

12–086 Public concern about internet pornography in the US caused Congress to pass, by an overwhelming majority, the Communications Decency Act 1996. Aspects of the legislation were strongly opposed by internet providers and civil liberties groups, and some parts of it were declared unconstitutional by Philadelphia and New York courts in the light of the First Amendment and subsequently by the US Supreme Court.

Because of the First Amendment, the US has probably the world's most highly developed case law on what constitutes obscenity. One factor that must be considered in determining whether something amounts to obscenity and therefore unprotected speech is local community standards. What might be considered utterly shocking and depraved in rural Arkansas may be merely titillating in Los Angeles.

This sensible test was undermined by a successful prosecution for obscenity in Tennessee of a bulletin board operator based in California, for material that very likely would not have been considered obscene by a California jury.

The possibility of being prosecuted in a jurisdiction with very strict standards (such as Saudi Arabia) for material which would probably not offend in its place of origin must be a great concern to the major service providers. The decision of CompuServe in December 1995 to suspend, temporarily, access to about 200 Usenet newsgroups in response to action by a German prosecutor is a good example of this. CompuServe stated that it was investigating ways in which it could restrict user access to selected newsgroups by geographical location. In the meantime the effect of the action was to suspend access to the newsgroups worldwide through CompuServe's internet news facilities. For further discussion of these cross-border issues see section 12.2 above.

12.4.7 Chat rooms

12–087 Following the 2001 election a Task Force on Child Protection on the Internet made recommendations to the Home Secretary for a new criminal offence relating to meeting with a child with intent to commit a sex offence; and for a new civil order to protect children from an adult making contact with them for a harmful or unlawful sexual purpose, which would include contact through email or internet chat rooms.

The so-called "grooming" offence was enacted in s.15 of the Sexual Offences Act 2003, entitled "Meeting a child following sexual grooming etc". Grooming itself is not defined, nor is any on-line behaviour in itself criminalised, but the necessary precondition to the offence "having met or communicated with another person on at least two earlier occasions" is broad enough to cover both on-line and off-line behaviour.

12.5 CONTEMPT OF COURT

The term "contempt of court" covers a wide range of conduct which in **12–088** some way interferes with the administration of justice. The types of conduct relevant to the internet are those that relate to publishing matter which could prejudice the fair trial of a civil or criminal case and those concerning breach of a court injunction. The law of contempt of court has been developed through the common law since early times, although most of the types of contempt applicable to internet activities are now covered by the Contempt of Court Act 1981. There are two types of contempt, civil and criminal. Civil contempt concerns disobedience to court orders such as injunctions. That is of little direct relevance to the internet, although as we shall see a third party who seeks to undermine the effects of an injunction pending trial, for instance by publishing injuncted material, may find that he is accused of contempt.

12.5.1 Criminal contempt

The 1981 Act makes it an offence of strict liability to publish to the public **12–089** at large or any section of the public, while proceedings are active, anything which "creates a substantial risk that the course of justice in the proceedings in question will be seriously impeded or prejudiced." "Strict liability" means that it is an offence even if the person making the publication did not intend to interfere in the course of justice. "Publication" is defined to include any speech, writing, broadcast or "other communication in whatever form", so Usenet newsgroup messages and publications through websites would be covered. Other contempts of court remain governed by the common law rules.

A publication relating to a case will only be an offence if it occurs while the proceedings are *sub judice*. At common law this certainly covers the period from the commencement of the proceedings, which would include the arrest in a criminal case, to their final determination. However, anyone knowing or having good reason to believe that proceedings are imminent when they publish matter likely to prejudice a fair trial is also liable to be charged with contempt.

Because of the uncertainty caused by the common law rules, the 1981 Act sought to define more exactly the commencement and ending of the period in which the proceedings are "active", within which the strict liability rule would apply. It is possible that publications outside this period which would otherwise come under the 1981 Act could be common law contempt.

Charges of contempt are nowadays more often brought with respect to **12–090** criminal than to civil proceedings. This is because it is felt that jurors are more likely to be prejudiced than a judge, and almost all civil trials in this country are tried by a judge alone.

Publications which have been held to be in contempt of court fall into a number of categories. A common cause for contempt is that the publication prejudges the merits of the case, in particular assuming that the accused in a criminal trial is guilty of the crime charged. There have been few modern cases of an express imputation of guilt, but a tacit assumption can be just as prejudicial.

For example, immediately after Peter Sutcliffe was arrested, almost every newspaper reported the fact under headlines referring to the Yorkshire Ripper, clearly implying that he was guilty of the series of horrific murders of women.

Even without any assumption of guilt, emotive or disparaging remarks may carry a serious risk or prejudice, in particular when they amount to guilt by association. For example, one newspaper insinuated that the man who broke into Buckingham Palace and was found in the Queen's bedroom was linked to the Queen's personal police officer who had just resigned after the revelation that he had had a homosexual affair with a male prostitute.

It is also a contempt to publish matter which is likely to be inadmissible in evidence at the trial. For example, the prejudicial nature of previous convictions is recognised by the law which provides that they may only be put in evidence under certain circumstances; publishing them so that they become known to the jury where those circumstances have not occurred would be a contempt. The same is true of confessions, admissions and improperly obtained evidence. The publication of a photograph may also be prejudicial, for example where identification will be an issue at trial.

12–091   The trial of Rose West raised serious concerns about the publication of interviews with witnesses, particularly when the witnesses had been paid large sums of money for those interviews. This could be contempt if the interview were published before that witness gave evidence, or if the payment caused the witness to "embellish" their evidence at the trial. It could also be contempt to attempt to prevent a witness from testifying by subjecting them to abuse or threats.

Although most judicial proceedings take place in public, where they do not it may be a contempt to publish an account of those proceedings. For example, in this country jury deliberations are kept secret, so disclosing jury deliberations is contempt under the 1981 Act.

That Act also made it an offence to record legal proceedings without the consent of the court and to publish any recording of legal proceedings. It is a serious contempt to publish an account of proceedings which are closed to the public for the protection of one of the parties, usually a child or a mental patient, or to protect commercially valuable confidential information, or where there is an issue of national security.

There are also occasions where it is a contempt to publish matters relating to proceedings held in open court, such as most details of committal proceedings in the magistrates' court unless the reporting restrictions are lifted.

There are specific legislative provisions prohibiting the publication of information identifying children involved in proceedings or rape victims. A court also has power to order that reports of the proceedings be postponed where a contemporaneous report poses a serious risk of prejudice. It is notorious that transcripts of the Rose West committal hearing were available on the internet notwithstanding that reporting restrictions in England were not lifted.

The 1981 Act provides three specified defences to the strict liability offence, which had developed as common law defences.

12–092

It is a defence that the publisher, acting with all due care, did not know and had no reason to know that proceedings were active, and the distributor of such publication will not be liable if, again having taken reasonable care, he did not know and had no reason to suspect that the material contains matter giving rise to the offence.

The other statutory defences are that the publication was a fair and accurate report of the proceedings where there was no reporting restriction in effect, and that it was part of a discussion in good faith of matters of general public interest and any prejudice was merely incidental to the discussion. The balancing of the right of free speech and a free press against the right to a fair trial is never an easy one.

At common law a superior court could commit a person found guilty of criminal contempt to prison for a fixed but unlimited period, or could impose a fine of unlimited amount. Lower courts only have power to punish contempts which are acts committed in the court itself. For contempts under the 1981 Act, the penalties available to a superior court are committal to prison for a fixed term not exceeding two years or an unlimited fine, inferior courts may imprison for up to one month and fine up to £1,000.

12.5.2 International aspects of contempt

The international nature of the internet poses challenges to the system of protecting judicial proceedings. A foreign national could publish prejudicial matter, or could attend a hearing subject to reporting restrictions and publish a report on his return home. The *Spycatcher* case showed the difficulties even without the internet; although publication was banned in the UK, the book was on sale in the US and it was not difficult for individuals to obtain copies.

12–093

In these circumstances, the authorities could seek to proceed against any UK-based ISP through whose service the contempt is published. The law relating to the liability of parties to an offending publication in the print medium is well established, that relating to broadcast media less so.

With the implementation of the intermediary liability provisions of the Electronic Commerce Directive (see Ch.5), ISPs have a measure of protection for both civil (pecuniary) and criminal liability, but not from injunctions.

The *New York Times* at the end of August 2006 took steps to prevent access from the UK to an article on its website, out of concern for possible breach of UK contempt laws.

12.5.3 Third parties and injunctions

12–094   Civil contempt concerns breach of a court order. The situation with which we are particularly concerned is where a court grants an injunction against a person and someone else does an act which would breach the injunction if it had been granted against him. So if a court grants an interim injunction against a national newspaper restraining publication of certain material pending trial and the grant of the injunction is widely publicised, is it a contempt of court for someone else to publish the material, for instance if an individual were to post it on a website?

This question has received some attention from the courts. A third party who aids and abets the defendant in a breach of the injunction is guilty of contempt. Further, where an interim injunction has been granted, for instance prohibiting disclosure of information, a third party who wilfully interfered with the administration of justice by thwarting the achievement of the court's purpose in granting the interlocutory injunction (namely that pending a decision by the court on the claims in the proceedings, the restrained act should not be done) would be guilty of contempt. It is also necessary, for there to be contempt of this type, that there be some significant and adverse effect on the administration of justice.[36] A third party who acts independently may not, however, be bound by a final injunction restraining breach of confidence.[37]

A different situation may arise where an injunction is granted against the whole world. The jurisdiction to do so is extremely limited, for instance in wardship proceedings.[38] An example was the case of the murder by two ten year old boys of the two year old child James Bulger. The case caused widespread public revulsion. When the time came for the boys' release from detention at age 18, the question arose whether they should be able to preserve the confidentiality of the new identities with which they would be provided on their release and other information about themselves.

In *Venables v News Group Newspapers Ltd*[39] the judge, consciously departing from authority of 200 years' standing that "you cannot have an injunction except against a party to the suit",[40] granted injunctions *contra mundem* (against the world) restraining publication in various media of

---

[36] *Attorney-General v Punch Ltd* [2002] UKHL 50.

[37] *The Jockey Club v Buffham* [2002] EWHC 1866 (QB). Although decided partly in reliance on the Court of Appeal decision in *A-G v Punch*, which was subsequently overturned by the House of Lords, the distinction between interlocutory and final injunctions still appears to be valid in the light of the House of Lords decision.

[38] *X County Council v A* [1985] 1 All E.R. 53 (the *Mary Bell* case).

[39] [2001] 1 All E.R. 908.

[40] *Iveson v Harris* (1802) 7 Ves. 251, 32 E.R. 102, *per* Lord Eldon.

various information about the claimants. The subsequent amendment of the injunction at the behest of an ISP, and other similar injunctions, are discussed in Ch.5. The judge did make the following observations about the enforceability of the order in relation to the internet:

> "I am, of course, aware that injunctions may not be fully effective to protect the claimants from acts committed outside England and Wales resulting in information about them being placed on the internet. The injunctions can, however, prevent wider circulation of that information through the newspapers or television and radio. To that end, therefore, I would be disposed to add, in relation to information in the public domain, a further proviso, suitably limited, which would protect the special quality of the new identity, appearance and address of the claimants or information leading to that identification, even after that information had entered the public domain to the extent that it had been published on the internet or elsewhere such as outside the UK."

The order provided an exception in the injunction for information in the public domain at the time of the original order of January 8, 2001, but provided that that should not permit publication of certain of the material merely on the ground that material had at any time been published on the internet and/or outside England and Wales.

12.6 FINANCIAL SERVICES

12.6.1 Regulated activities and financial promotion

Some of the most innovative and sophisticated sites on the World Wide Web are those that provide financial information and services. In many ways financial services are an ideal product for internet commerce. In particular, effective selling of them requires the provision of large volumes of tailored financial information (an easy task for a smart website) and fulfilment of orders does not require any physical product delivery. However, the provision of financial services is highly regulated in many jurisdictions, the UK being no exception.   **12–095**

12.6.2 Two key areas of concern

There are two key areas of concern in the context of financial services provided through the internet: **12–096**

    (a) anyone providing an internet-based product from an establishment in the UK (whether to persons in the UK or another state in the

European Economic Area ("EEA")) must ensure that no element of the product involves the unlawful carrying on of regulated financial services activity. If it fails to do this and a breach of UK financial services law is committed then, in addition to criminal sanctions, the product provider may find that all customer contracts are unenforceable; and

(b) anyone providing a financial services product from an establishment outside the UK will want to ensure that it does not, through a website available in the UK, either contract with, or market its products to, persons in the UK in breach of UK financial services law. If it does so, once again, in addition to potential criminal sanctions, any contracts with UK customers may be void.

For duly authorised persons providing financial services in the UK, there are additional issues related to ensuring that the provision of their services in a virtual manner complies not only with applicable financial services law but also with the various financial service codes of conduct and other regulatory requirements which cover them. Consideration of these latter issues is, however, outside the scope of this discussion.

12.6.3 The Financial Services and Markets Act 2000

12–097   A defining issue for both of the above key areas of concern is the exact scope of UK financial services regulation. The main source of such regulation is the Financial Services and Markets Act 2000 (the "FSMA") and the various detailed rules and regulations created under it. The approach of the FSMA in relation to the conduct of financial service business is to create a general prohibition on the carrying on of "regulated activities" in the UK by way of business, other than by persons who are duly authorised to carry them on. It does, however, provide for exclusions from that general prohibition which may be available in certain cases.

12.6.4 The General Prohibition

12–098   Under s.19 of the FSMA, no person may carry on a regulated activity in the UK, or purport to do so, unless such person is an "authorised person" or an "exempt person" (this is referred to in the FSMA, and will be referred to in this Chapter, as the "General Prohibition"). It is an offence punishable by up to two years imprisonment, a fine or both to breach this prohibition.

Under s.26 of the FSMA, any agreement made by an unauthorised person in breach of the General Prohibition will be unenforceable and the counterparty to that agreement is entitled to recover both (1) any money paid under it and (2) compensation.

Authorisation can be obtained in the UK by applying to the Financial Services Authority (the statutory regulator under the FSMA) for author-

986

isation to carry out the particular intended regulated activity or activities. The applicant will need to be able to satisfy the Financial Services Authority of its suitability for authorisation with regard to such things as its business plan and procedures, compliance systems, expertise, capital adequacy and controlling persons (in particular, their fitness to be involved in regulated business etc.). Authorisation also involves compliance with a rigorous ongoing supervision regime which will include complying with "Conduct of Business Rules" promulgated by the Financial Services Authority (different rules applying to different regulated activities).

Under what is known as the "Investment Services Directive",[41] a firm authorised to carry on investment business in another EEA Member State can, subject to certain formalities, carry on the same business in the UK without requiring a separate UK authorisation (referred to as "passporting"). It will, however, generally have to comply with UK Conduct of Business Rules in relation to its activities here unless it is carrying on business in the UK only by means of providing "Information Society Services"—see further below.

At the time of writing, these provisions of the Investment Services Directive are shortly to be replaced by parallel provisions of the Market in Financial Investments Directive (known as "MiFID").[42] This is due to be implemented by November 1, 2007, although there is some evidence that a number of Member States will not achieve this deadline. MiFID is designed to cure a number of perceived defects in the Investment Services Directive. First of all, it allows for the passporting of a wider range of investment business, including the provision of standalone investment advice. Secondly, it seeks to provide for a harmonised set of conduct of business rules, so that providers are not faced with markedly different sets of rules in each jurisdiction.

In a similar development and in order to promote a single market for financial services across the EEA, the UK (in line with all EEA Member States) has taken steps to:

(a) remove from the scope of UK regulation the provision of any financial service which constitutes an "information society service" (ISS) and which is provided from an establishment in another EEA member state; and

(b) apply UK regulation to the provision of any financial service constituting an ISS from an establishment in the UK to another EEA member state.

---

[41] Council Directive 93/22/EEC of May 10, 1993 on investment services in the securities field.
[42] Directive 2004/39/EC of the European Parliament and of the Council of April 21, 2004 on markets in financial instruments amending Council Directives 85/611/EEC and 93/6/EEC and Directive 2000/12/EC of the European Parliament and of the Council and repealing Council Directive 93/22/EEC.

This is an implementation of what is called the "country of origin" principle underlying the E-Commerce Directive.[43] The key concept is that each EEA member state will be responsible for determining whether any establishment operating within its jurisdiction is conducting regulated financial services business, applying its own law to this question. If it is found that regulated business is being conducted, then it will be for the EEA member state concerned to grant the necessary authorisation and conduct the required ongoing supervision (or, of course, if the relevant provider is not suitable for authorisation, to take proceedings to prevent the continuation of the relevant business). It will also be for that EEA member state to impose any rules in relation to the way in which the relevant business is carried on (the so-called "conduct of business rules") but, as noted above, conduct of business rules will themselves be the subject of a MiFID harmonisation process.

Importantly, it will not then be open to a regulator in another EEA jurisdiction to impose a further authorisation requirement related to that jurisdiction or to require adherence to that other jurisdiction's conduct of business rules, provided that the services provided to persons in that other EEA jurisdiction are limited to Information Society Services. Once again, this is in some respects an illustration of the "passporting" approach, under which the home State Supervisor is responsible for the supervision of service providers established within its jurisdiction.

12.6.5. Regulated Activities

12–099   An activity is a regulated activity for the purposes of the FSMA if it is (a) specified as such in any statutory instrument made under that Act and (b) carried on by way of business.

At the time of writing, the primary statutory instrument is the Financial Services and Markets Act 2000 (Regulated Activities) Order 2001[44] (the "Regulated Activities Order"). The approach of using statutory instruments to define the scope of regulated activity was adopted (rather than setting out all classes of regulated activity in the FSMA itself) to facilitate the easy and rapid addition of new classes of regulated activity by UK regulators. Indeed, several amendment orders have been issued over the years varying the Regulated Activities Order for these purposes.

A non-exhaustive list of the activities classified as regulated activities by the Regulated Activities Order includes:

- Activities relating to "investments", including: dealing in (i.e. buying/selling) investments as principal or as agent (although many

---

[43] Directive 2000/31/EC of the European Parliament and of the Council of June 8, 2000 on certain legal aspects of information society services, in particular electronic commerce, in the Internal Market ("Directive on electronic commerce"). See Ch.6 for a general discussion of the country of origin aspects of the Directive.

[44] SI 2001/544.

dealings as principal are subsequently excepted or excluded); arranging deals in investments; managing investments; safeguarding and administering investments; providing advice on the purchase, sale and exercise of rights under investments; sending dematerialised instructions; establishing, operating or winding up collective investment schemes; and agreeing to carry on any of these activities. The definition of "investments" is widely cast to include virtually all types of security (whether debt or equity) as well as rights derived from securities or, indeed, derivative rights in respect of assets which are not themselves securities or investments;

- Taking "deposits", defined as sums of money accepted on terms that they will be repaid (with or without interest);
- Issuing "electronic money" (see Ch.11 for further information on this subject)
- Effecting and carrying out contracts of insurance;
- Operating or winding up a stakeholder pension scheme;
- Certain activities relating to the Lloyd's insurance market; providing funeral plan contracts; and
- Lending under, or administering, regulated mortgage contracts— essentially mortgages on property which is to be used (or a substantial part of which is to be used) for domestic purposes by the borrower.

If an internet service proposed to be offered includes any activity within the above list, it is necessary for the person providing the service to consider whether an authorisation is needed or whether an exclusion is available.

Similarly, an overseas financial service provider who may be intending to undertake any of the above activities with a customer base which may include people in the UK will need to consider its regulatory position carefully and in particular: (1) what, if any, of its activities with those customers will actually be carried on in the UK; and (2) whether their service may constitute an ISS (in which case, no UK authorisation will be required if the service is provided from an establishment in another EEA State).

12.6.6 Exclusions

An activity which would otherwise be a regulated activity can be carried on **12–100** by a person who is not authorised provided that such person's conduct of that activity falls within one of the exclusions allowed by the FSMA. Such exclusions as exist at the time of writing are set out in the Regulated Activities Order, as amended. Once again, the approach of including exclusions in a statutory order simplifies the addition of new exclusions where considered necessary by the UK regulator and this is an important element of flexibility built into the UK legislation.

Different activities have different exclusions. So, for example there is an exclusion from the regulated activity of "insurance" for breakdown insurance which satisfies certain conditions. Similarly, an exclusion from the activity of "deposit-taking" exists for "deposits" taken by companies issuing commercial paper on certain terms.

There is a wide range of exclusions for various activities related to dealings with, and arrangements concerning, securities. For example, one key exclusion permits a person who is not FSMA–authorised to deal in securities for its own account in most circumstances, provided that such person is not generally holding itself out to the public as being willing to buy or sell the relevant type of investments.

A detailed analysis of the various exclusions available is beyond the scope of this Chapter. However, there are two types of exclusion which are of particular interest in the context of the key areas of concern mentioned earlier in this chapter and these are discussed in the succeeding paragraphs. It is worth noting, however, that persons providing any financial service to persons in the UK from an establishment in another EEA state will not need to fall within the terms of the exclusions referred to in this paragraph to the extent that they are providing an "information society service"—see section 12.6.4 above.

12.6.7 Financial Information Websites

12–101   Good independent financial advice is a much sought after commodity. Furthermore, with the growing (one may even say, bewildering) diversity of investment options now available, well-informed and unbiased advice becomes ever more important for the ordinary investing member of the public. The need for such advice is something which is addressed in the UK by "independent financial advisers" or "IFAs" as they are commonly known. To be permitted to give the investment advice they provide, IFAs are required to be authorised under the FSMA.

Newspapers have, right from their beginnings, used the provision of financial information and advice as a way of selling more copies and most UK papers have a section concerning personal money matters and/or a "tipster" section where the likely future movement of key stock prices is considered. Furthermore, in more recent times, many specialist journals have been created with a focus on investing (e.g. *Investors Chronicle* to name but one).

The provision of financial advice of a general kind and which is not related to particular investments (e.g. "technology stocks look strong at present") is not a regulated activity. However, newspapers and specialist journals will often provide advice in relation to particular investments which, on the face it, is a type of advice which should only be provided by a person duly authorised under the FSMA. The UK regulatory position has always sought to draw a distinction between persons providing such advice as a profession on the one hand and, on the other, newspapers or journals providing it for the general entertainment of their readership without an

990

overlay of professional responsibility or professed specialist knowledge or expertise. This distinction is continued under the FSMA by the provision of an exclusion from the regulated activity of providing investment advice if the advice (1) is contained in a newspaper, journal, magazine, or other periodical publication, or (2) is given by way of a service comprising regularly updated news or information.

However, there is an important limitation to this exclusion. In order to benefit from it, the principal purpose of the relevant publication or service, taken as a whole and including any advertisements or other promotional material contained in it, must be neither (1) to provide investment advice related to particular securities nor (2) to lead or enable persons to buy, sell or subscribe for securities or contractually based investments nor (3) to enter into regulated mortgage contracts or certain other arrangements regarding the purchase of property which are intended to release value in that property or to enable the acquisition of that property to be made over time.

For a website which sets out to provide financial information and is published by persons who are not authorised to provide financial advice in the UK, this exclusion is very useful. But it is clear that there is a dividing line between an essentially "journalistic" site where some investment advice is incidental to the main purpose of the site and a site which has, as its main purpose, providing investment advice. Whether a site crosses this line may not always be easy to determine and it should be noted that the publication has to be looked at as a whole, including any advertisements, etc. on it. An area of concern might, for example, be a site which contained certain pages of advice related to buying or selling particular shares and, on each relevant page, also set out an advertisement for a share dealing service. A further area of concern would be if the site providers received commission in respect of sales of investments referred to on the site.

12.6.8 Overseas Financial Service Providers

In certain areas, the way in which the internet opens up the possibility of cross-border contracting is a significant benefit. In the field of financial services, however, it can raise some difficult issues. In particular, a financial services provider which is not authorised to provide financial services in the UK but contracts with UK persons through its website may commit a criminal offence in the UK and may also find that the contracts it has made are unenforceable. There are, however, three key potential sources of comfort for such an overseas financial services provider in this respect:

12–102

(a) The General Prohibition only applies to regulated activity which is carried on by an overseas provider "in the UK". So, if the activities of an overseas financial service provider, although conducted with UK persons, do not involve the conduct of regulated activity "in the UK", then there will be no breach of the General Prohibition.

However, the usefulness of this geographic delimitation of the General Prohibition to an overseas financial services provider is restricted by the difficulty that exists in determining what "in the UK" actually means. In traditional tests of whether a business is being carried on in the UK, a key issue has always been the degree of physical presence maintained by the business in the UK. For overseas persons who do have such a physical presence, it should be noted that s.418 stipulates that activity carried on from any establishment in the UK will be deemed to be carried on "in the UK".

For persons without a physical establishment in the UK, the position is less clear. In an internet world, it would seem illogical to focus only on a bricks-and-mortar test and it may be expected that, in future, the English courts will adopt a more purposive approach—looking at such factors as the degree to which a business is actively soliciting, and contracting with, customers in the UK.

(b) As noted above, a person who provides a financial service which falls within the definition of an ISS from an establishment outside the UK but within the EEA will not be treated as carrying on a regulated activity in the UK.

(c) There are certain additional exclusions provided by the Regulated Activities Order which are available to persons who, although they are carrying on regulated activities in the UK (and those activities are not ISS provided from an establishment in an EEA State), do not carry on such activities from a permanent place of business in the UK (any such person being defined as an "overseas person").

There are, in particular, exclusions for overseas persons dealing in securities (as agent or principal), arranging deals in securities and providing advice in relation to securities. However, an important point to note is that, for a number of these exclusions to apply to dealings between the overseas person and persons in the UK, those contracts must not have derived from any form of promotional approach from the overseas person which has breached the UK law on financial promotions described below.

12.6.9 Financial Promotions Restriction

12-103   The FSMA (like the Financial Services Act 1986 before it) does not only restrict the carrying on of regulated activity in the UK. It also restricts the issue of promotional material inviting or seeking to induce members of the public to enter into agreements relating to certain types of investments.

The restriction (the "Financial Promotion Restriction") is set out in s.21 of the FSMA and creates an offence for any person who, in the course of business, communicates an invitation or inducement to engage in investment activity unless that person is either an authorised person or the content of the communication is approved by an authorised person. The detail of the Financial Promotion Restriction is set out in a statutory instrument called the Financial Services and Markets Act 2000 (Financial Promotion) Order 2001[45] (the "Financial Promotion Order").

There are three important points to note in relation to the Financial Promotion Restriction:

(a) The words "invitation" and "inducement" are not defined but are likely to be construed broadly. It is clear that they can include material disseminated through a website, and can also include communications by email.

(b) An invitation or inducement to enter into investment activity can constitute an offence even if, were that investment activity actually to be entered into by the issuer of the invitation or inducement, there would be no "regulated activity" by virtue of the existence of an exclusion applying. So, a business which advertises to sell shares it holds in another company without procuring the approval of the advertisement by an authorised person will be committing an offence even though the actual sale of those shares may not constitute regulated activity on the part of that business because it would be a "dealing as principal".

(c) By virtue of s.30 of the FSMA, a contract which is entered into with a financial service provider may be rendered unenforceable if entry into that contract was induced by a promotion issued in breach of the Financial Promotion Restriction (although the English courts have a discretion to permit enforcement of the contract if this is considered just and equitable in all the circumstances). The effect of a breach can therefore be draconian.

The Financial Promotion Restriction will create problems for any person who seeks to advertise an investment scheme through the internet or even by email communications to a selected potential investor base. However, the Financial Promotion Order does contain some exemptions which may be available in certain cases of this kind—for example, where the target audience on the investment promotion consists of investment professionals or sophisticated high net worth individuals. There are also other exclusions available under the Order and different types of advertised product have different exemptions. For some exemptions a distinction is drawn between real time (e.g. personal meetings and telephone calls) and non-real time communications (including emails) and between solicited (initiated by the customer or expressly invited by them) and unsolicited communications.

---

[45] SI 2001/1335.

12.6.10 The Financial Promotion Restriction and Overseas Financial Service Providers

12–104   The Financial Promotion Restriction also needs to be borne in mind by overseas financial service providers. Because the restriction operates independently from the General Prohibition, it is possible for such a financial service provider to breach the Financial Promotion Restriction even though it is not actually carrying on any regulated activity in the UK.

This raises an issue for overseas financial service providers who advertise their services or products on their websites. It is currently difficult for any such provider to impose an effective barrier on access to its site to people located in the UK. Accordingly, their websites and promotional material on them will be available in the UK and thus potentially breach the Financial Promotion Restriction. However, recognising that this may sometimes be an unfair result, Art.12 of the Financial Promotion Order Restriction stipulates that, with certain exceptions, the Financial Promotion Restriction will not apply to any communication which is "directed (whether from inside or outside the United Kingdom) only at persons outside the United Kingdom" (Art.12(1)(b)).

The Financial Promotion Order sets out the conditions to be met for a communication to be regarded as "directed only at persons outside the UK" (Art.12(4)). These conditions are:

- the communication is accompanied by an indication that it is directed only at persons outside the UK;
- the communication is accompanied by an indication that it must not be acted upon by persons in the UK;
- the communication is not referred to in, or directly accessible from, any other communication which is made to a person, or directed at persons, in the UK by or on behalf of the same person;
- there are in place proper systems and procedures to prevent recipients in the UK (other than those to whom the communication might otherwise have lawfully been made) engaging in the investment activity to which the communication relates with the person directing the communication, a close relative of his or a member of the same group; and
- the communication is included in a website, newspaper journal, magazine or periodical publication which is principally accessed in or intended for a market outside the UK or a radio or television broadcast or teletext service transmitted principally for reception outside the UK.

Furthermore, in some cases, the Financial Promotion Restriction will not apply if the person despatching the communication is an "information society service" provider and is based in another EU Member State: see para.12.6.4 above.

12.6.11 Exclusion from Financial Promotion Restriction for hosts and access providers

Because the Financial Promotion Restriction renders it an offence to "communicate" an invitation or inducement to engage in investment activity, on the face of things it could pose a problem for website hosts or access providers who may be said to be "communicating" infringing material on websites for which they act as a host or provide access services. However, Art.18 of the Financial Promotion Order provides an exemption for persons whose role in any restricted communication is that of a "mere conduit". A person acts as a mere conduit for a communication if:

12–105

- that person communicates it in the course of business carried on by him, the principal purpose of which is transmitting or receiving material provided to him by others;
- the content of the communication is wholly devised by another person; and
- the nature of the service provided by that person in relation to the communication is such that the person does not select, modify or otherwise exercise control over its content prior to its transmission or receipt.

It is important to note that a person does not select, modify or otherwise exercise control over the content of a communication merely by removing or having the power to remove material:

- which is, or is alleged to be, illegal, defamatory or in breach of copyright;
- in response to a request of a body which is empowered by or under any enactment to make such a request; or
- when otherwise required to do so by law.

12.6.12 Content of Distance Promotions

Under the Financial Services (Distance Marketing) Regulations 2004 (implementing a corresponding European Directive) certain content requirements are imposed on distance advertisements of financial services. In particular, the customer must be allowed a "cooling off" period in many cases. However, in parallel with the "country of origin" principle, those UK regulations will not normally apply to communications emanating from another EU Member State. In such cases, the UK recipient would rely on the corresponding rules laid down under the laws of the country of origin.

12–106

12.7 PHARMACEUTICALS

12–107   The specific issues which face the pharmaceutical industry so far as the internet is concerned are the restrictions on advertising of pharmaceutical products and data protection. Data protection is dealt with elsewhere in detail in Ch.7, but it is worth noting that in addition to the greater protection afforded to health data under the Data Protection Directive, a number of jurisdictions have further specific restrictions concerning the use and dissemination of health related data.

The advertising of pharmaceutical products is regulated in many countries. However, the nature and extent of the regulation varies enormously. New Zealand and the US permit direct to consumer advertising of prescription only products. In the EU, the advertising of medicinal products is governed by Council Directive 92/28 which prohibits the advertising to the general public of prescription only medicines or medicinal products containing psychotropic or narcotic substances. The advertising of medicines available "over the counter" is permitted by the Directive, subject to restrictions on the mentioning of certain types of indications.

The bare framework set out in the Directive is fleshed out by the various self-regulatory codes which the pharmaceutical industry follow, which include the IFPMA[46] code, the EFPIA[47] code and the ABPI[48] code. The codes attempt to deal with the problems faced by the internet. Detailed information which may be legally provided to the consumers in one country can be accessed by a consumer in another country where such promotion would be contrary to the law or codes of practice of that country.

The ABPI code of practice governs websites which are operated by UK companies or by their affiliates where information concerning the use or availability of a product in the UK is mentioned. The ABPI code provides that open access sites must not include promotional material relating to prescription only medicines, but the summary of product characteristics, patient information leaflet and European public assessment report relating to medicinal products can be published. Sites which are restricted to members of the medical profession can contain promotional material, although the MHRA[49] has advised that each page should be labeled "intended for health professionals".

Recent proposals by the European Commission sought to amend Directive 92/28 to permit Member States, on an initial five year trial basis, to allow the dissemination to the public of products authorised for the treatment of AIDS, asthma and chronic broncopulmonary disease and diabetes. Despite backing from the ABPI this proposal was considered extremely controversial and was dropped early on in the review.

---

[46] The International Federation of Pharmaceutical Manufacturers Associations (*www.ifpma.org*).
[47] The European Federation of Pharmaceutical Industries and Associations (*www.efpia.org*).
[48] The Association of the British Pharmaceutical Industry (*www.abpi.org*).
[49] The Medicines and Healthcare Products Regulatory Agency.

In addition to the restrictions on advertising, the rules relating to the sale **12–108** of pharmaceuticals vary between countries. Following the case of *Deutscher Apothekerverband v DocMorris NV and Jacques Waterval*,[50] however, all European countries other than Germany, the UK and the Netherlands (whose laws were already compliant) were forced to change their laws to allow non-prescription drugs to be bought by mail order.

In this case the German pharmacists' trade association brought proceedings against a Dutch on-line pharmacy which was supplying medicines into Germany. Germany at the time had a law prohibiting mail order pharmacies and the association was granted injunctions preventing the pharmacy from selling medicines over the internet. The injunction was challenged on the basis of restriction of the free movement of goods and the Frankfurt court referred to the ECJ for guidance.

The judgment of the ECJ aimed to strike a balance between the protection of human health and the internal market, and offered guidance as to where the line between the two should be drawn. The decision in the case was that it is justifiable for Member States to prohibit mail order sales of prescription drugs, where confusion over language or labeling could lead to "harmful consequences". However, according to the ECJ a ban on non-prescription drugs would be a violation of EU law and Member States should amend their domestic laws accordingly.

12.8 ADVERTISING AND PROMOTIONAL ACTIVITIES ON THE INTERNET

Advertising is generally regulated in the UK by voluntary codes, although **12–109** there are a large number of statutes which may affect advertising. In particular, there are a number of offences relating to misleading advertising. Some sectors, such as advertising of alcoholic drinks, medicines and financial products and services, are subject to more stringent regulation. Further, the content of commercial websites and promotional materials are now subject to the provisions of the Electronic Commerce Directive and the Distance Selling Directive (both discussed in Ch.10).

The main voluntary code in the UK is the British Code of Advertising, Sales Promotion and Direct Marketing (11th edn), which came into force on March 4, 2003. The Code is drawn up by the Committee of Advertising Practice, which includes representatives of the advertising, sales promotion and media businesses. Compliance is monitored by the Advertising Standards Authority (ASA), an independent body. The Code sets out the rules for what is acceptable in advertisements, sales promotions and direct marketing.

There are special rules in addition to the general Code, for Children, Motoring, Environmental Claims, Health & Beauty Products and Thera-

---

[50] C–322/01.

pies, Weight Control, Employment Business Opportunities, Financial Products, Betting Gaming, Tobacco,[51] Rolling Papers Filters and Alcoholic Drinks. The Code covers advertising in all non-broadcast media. Broadcast commercials are addressed under separate Codes for TV and radio, maintained and administered under a co-regulatory regime involving OFCOM, the Broadcast Committee of Advertising Practice and the ASA.[52]

ASA has focused on UK-originated websites, but if it is faced with a foreign site it may be able to refer the complaint to an equivalent regulatory body in the foreign jurisdiction, for instance, via the European Advertising Standards Alliance. ASA's remit for the internet includes advertisements in paid-for space, such as banner and pop-up advertisements, on-line sales promotion and commercial emails. It does not extend to general product information on home pages.

In April 2003 the ASA released the results of a survey showing that only 1 per cent of banner ads contravened the Codes on Advertising and Sales Promotion. More recently, the ASA has been critical of claims made for telephone and internet broadband packages, particularly the use of the word "free".

The use of premium rate telephone services in relation to websites or the internet will bring into account the ICSTIS[53] Code of Practice, the Eleventh edition of which came into force on January 4, 2007.

12–110   In general, advertising regulations impose stricter standards for justification of claims than are required by the general law, such as defamation, for editorial content. The combination of advertising and broadcasting standards has especial potential to be restrictive.

On the internet, problems may arise with the distinction between advertising/promotional material and editorial on websites, especially given the seamless linking of pages on the web which renders it difficult to separate the two. This could result in the inadvertent extension of advertising content restrictions to editorial content.

In one case ASA upheld a complaint against a cinema advertising campaign run by Friends of the Earth (FoE). FoE placed the same material on its campaigning website. ASA felt powerless in practice to pursue the matter because FoE was hosting the site on its own server, so that there was no media owner to turn to. If ASA had pursued the matter, the question could well have arisen whether the material on the website was still advertising or promotional material at all, or whether it was in fact editorial material.

Such an issue arose in a case in Ireland under regulations equivalent to the UK Control of Misleading Advertisements Regulations 1988.[54] A trade union representing the plaintiff's workforce placed an advertisement in the

---

[51] The Tobacco Advertising and Promotion Act 2002 prohibits the advertising of tobacco products, other than certain tobacco advertising at the point of sale. It does not cover advertisements for rolling papers or filters.

[52] For further discussion of the broadcast Codes see Ch.8, para.8–038.

[53] Independent Committee for the Supervision of Standards of the Telephone Information Services (ICSTIS) (*www.icstis.org*).

[54] *Dunnes Stores Ltd v Mandate* [1996] 2 C.M.L.R. 120.

national press seeking to justify strike action by the union's members over Christmas pay. The Irish Supreme Court held that the trade union's advertisement had nothing to do with the promotion of a supply of goods or services, and so was not "advertising" within the meaning of the Directive from which the regulations were derived.

If an advertisement breaks the Code's rules, ASA will ask the advertiser to withdraw or amend it.[55] Other sanctions include adverse publicity, the refusal of further space, removal of trade incentives and finally legal proceedings via a referral from ASA to the Office of Fair Trading (OFT) under the Control of Misleading Advertisements Regulations 1988.

The OFT has the power to obtain an injunction against advertisers to prevent them from repeating the same or similar claims in future advertisements. In a cross-border case the EU Consumer Protection Co-Operation Regulation, which came into force on December 29, 2006, will enable enforcement authorities within the EU to exchange information and co-operate in a variety of cases.[56] The OFT is the UK designated enforcement authority under the Regulation.

Certain professional or trade bodies may control advertising by their members. For example, advertising by solicitors is governed by the Solicitors' Publicity Code promulgated by the Law Society.

Advertising may also be unlawful because the advertisement is in breach of other legal rules, such as being defamatory or infringing another's copyright or trade mark, matters that are dealt with elsewhere in this book.

In the UK there are also various statutory regulations which if breached can amount to a criminal offence with penalties such as fines and even imprisonment attached. For example, there are the various offences of applying a false trade description to goods under the Trade Descriptions Act 1986. And there are particular offences relating to unfair pricing such as very specific rules about advertising prices in a sale.

Junk email

Blatant commercial exploitation in traditional areas of the internet such as Usenet and email was originally resented by internet users because it was only recently that the internet had been used for commercial purposes. In the early days two US attorneys famously used the internet to advertise their services in connection with US immigration to every newsgroup. This was a breach of the unwritten rules of internet etiquette, but the attorneys refused to apologise. Internet users retaliated by clogging the attorneys' electronic mailbox with enormously long messages, which caused their service provider's system to become unusable, so the provider terminated service to the offenders.

12–111

---

[55] Under the UK internet service providers Association Code of Practice, members of the Association must comply with the Codes of Practice supervised by ASA (cl. 3.1.2).

[56] Regulation (EC) No 2006/2004 of the European Parliament and of the Council of October 27, 2004 on co-operation between national authorities responsible for the enforcement of consumer protection laws (the Regulation on consumer protection cooperation).

Although the use of much of the internet for commercial purposes is now accepted, junk email and spam continue to be regarded as something that needs to be controlled. It has provoked series of lawsuits in the US, in which ISPs have successfully invoked trespass laws against spammers.[57] This is reminiscent of the reportedly successful use of trespass laws in England against junk faxes.[58] Microsoft are also reported to have pursued civil proceedings in the UK against a UK spammer alleging (among other things) trespass to goods, resulting in a settlement of £45,000.[59]

Specific legislation, actual and proposed, on unsolicited email was for some time in disarray. The Telecommunications Data Protection Directive permitted Member States to adopt either an opt-in or an opt-out policy. The Department of Trade and Industry encountered widely differing views on the merits of these and chose to defer any steps to implement Art.12 of the Directive.[60] It was, in any event, doubtful whether that aspect of the Directive applied to email.

The Electronic Commerce Directive also contained provisions about unsolicited commercial communications, but other than encouraging the use of opt-out registers left the matter to national law.

12–112   The legitimacy of unsolicited email is now addressed by the Privacy and Electronic Communications Directive,[61] which requires opt-in or "soft opt-in" for many types of communications, but permits opt-out for others. The Directive was implemented in the UK by the Privacy and Electronic Communications (EC Directive) Regulations 2003.

Regulation 30 provides that a person who suffers damage by reason of any contravention of any requirement of the Regulations by any other person is entitled to bring proceedings for compensation. In *Microsoft Corporation v McDonald*[62] Microsoft operated a web-based email service (MSN Hotmail) and had received complaints from its customers about unsolicited emails received from purchasers of database lists supplied by the defendant. Microsoft argued that it had suffered loss through damage to its goodwill, the expense of fighting spam and the cost of buying additional servers to cope with the volume of spam transmitted.

The court held that the defendant had instigated unsolicited email within the meaning of reg.22 and that Microsoft fell within the class of persons for whom the benefit of the requirements were imposed. Microsoft had a cause of action and was entitled to compensation under reg.30. The court in the

---

[57] See discussion of "spidering" in Ch.2. See also *School of Visual Arts v Kuprewitz* (Supreme Court of State of New York, December 22, 2003), holding arguable a claim of trespass to chattels in respect of large volumes of unwanted pornographic emails.

[58] See "Junk faxes" 90/24 *L.S. Gaz.*, June 23, 1993, 9; "Faxamatosis: fresh outbreak" *New Law Journal* February 26, 1993, 278.

[59] *Computing* magazine, September 7, 2006.

[60] See, for instance, "Online sales rules postponed to settle dispute" *Financial Times* June 7, 2000.

[61] Directive 2002/58/EC Of the European Parliament and of the Council of July 12, 2002 concerning the processing of personal data and the protection of privacy in the electronic communications sector (Directive on privacy and electronic communications).

[62] Lawtel, Lewison J., December 12, 2006. The defendant did not appear and was not represented. The claimant obtained summary judgment.

exercise of its inherent jurisdiction was also able to grant an injunction and would do so in this case.

The CAP Code discussed above contains restrictions on sending promotional emails in similar terms to the Directive. The use of personal data for electronic mailing purposes is in any event subject to the constraints of the Data Protection Act 1998 (for more detailed discussion of both Directives, see Ch.7).

The European Commission on November 13, 2006 issued a Communication on Fighting spam, spyware and malicious software. It concludes that further action, including new legislative proposals, is required.

In July 2004 various law enforcement agencies in the UK, US and Australia signed a mutual co-operation pact to co-operate in pursuing cross-border spammers.[63]

12.9 ENCRYPTION

12.9.1 Introduction

Encryption has emerged as one of the potential cornerstones of e-commerce, for a variety of uses. The most widely known use is to enable secure, confidential communications between businesses and their customers, but encryption technologies are also used in several other ways, primarily relating to:

12–113

- The use of digital signatures to establish the identities of the parties to a transaction, and provide evidence of intention to contract;
- Watermarking documents to aid in the enforcement of intellectual property rights (such as the copyright in materials published on or broadcast over the internet);

Encryption is not the only mechanism available to perform these functions,[64] and the extent of the need for them in everyday e-commerce, especially for secure digital signatures, continues to be debatable. For historical reasons the use of encryption has been the subject of more controversy than the potentially competing alternatives. Encryption technology was historically the province of the security services, with the result that governments, in particular the US, viewed its release into civil society with deep suspicion.

The result is that development of the law in this area was initially premised on conflicting agendas: business utility versus government anxiety. It took some considerable time before the discussions as to where the law

---

[63] *Electronic Commerce and Law Review*, Vol.9 No.27, p.614.
[64] For example, Virtual Private Networks using controlled internet pathways offer confidence about the identity of correspondents since only authorised parties are able to communicate through them.

should intervene began to address encryption not as a military technology, but as a potentially important element of e-commerce, the appropriate legal framework for which should be viewed from a primarily civilian perspective.

This is still a changing area in terms of commercial solutions. Many of the predictions originally made about the marketplace for encryption-based products have turned out to be wrong. Solutions proposed today could well be superseded in a few years or even months by alternatives not yet on the drawing board. Thus, legislation ought to be framed as broadly as possible, in an attempt not to incorporate any unnecessary assumptions as to the technical nature, function or usage of materials. However, some areas of uncertainty as to the legal status of particular encryption technologies and services persist.

12.9.2 Technical background

Terminology

12–114 "Cryptography" is the art of writing messages in such ways that they cannot be read by third parties; it was developed in order to ensure the confidentiality of the message. The process of transforming a readable "plaintext" message into an unreadable form or "cipher" or "cryptogram" is encryption. Hundreds of different codes and enciphering techniques have been developed over the centuries.[65] However, the methods of code-breaking ("cryptanalysis" or "decryption"), such as frequency analysis of the appearances of given letters, are well known and tend to be painstaking but mechanical, making them ideally suited for computer attack. Thus, the subtlest encryption techniques developed before the advent of computers, cracking which required enormous skill and patience over many weeks of study, can now be done by an average PC in a matter of hours.

Cryptographic systems

12–115 There are two common forms of cryptography which are in widespread use: private key encryption and public key encryption, otherwise known as symmetric and asymmetric key encryption. In both of these, a complex cryptographic algorithm is applied to the plaintext to produce the crypto-gram. The algorithm in each case calculates the transposition of each letter of the plaintext based upon a number which is called the key.

In private key encryption,[66] both parties use the same key—the system is

---

[65] A thorough discussion of the evolution of cryptography is given in David Kahn's book *The Codebreakers* (Simon & Schuster, 1996 revised edn).

[66] For example, using the Data Encryption Standard (DES) of the US, the International Data Encryption Algorithm (IDEA) from Switzerland, algorithms RC4 and RC5, and so on. DES has been the most commonly used private key algorithm for some time, but the search is underway to produce a replacement, tentatively known as AES—Advanced Encryption System.

symmetric from either side. The disadvantages of this are that it is necessary for both sides to know and agree the key in advance, and to keep it completely secret thereafter. Thus, there is a need for a "key exchange mechanism" before the encrypted transmissions can start, and two possible attack points for any third party trying to obtain the key. The risk of loss of key secrecy can be reduced by using the keys only for one exchange of messages, or "session", but the obvious disadvantage is the need constantly to generate new keys even for communications between the same two parties.

Public key encryption[67] does away with both of these disadvantages. Instead, in public key systems, each party has two keys: a public key, which can harmlessly be published to the world at large, and a private key, which must be kept to oneself at all costs. There is no need for one party to any exchange to know the other's private key. Further, the private key cannot (if the key is sufficiently long) feasibly be deduced from the public key. Instead, each part can use the other's public key to encrypt the message; the message will then only be decryptable by someone holding the right private key. Public key systems are, therefore, in theory stronger than private key systems; the downside is that they are also considerably heavier in terms of computing power needed.

In practice the security of any encryption system depends upon the length of the key used. The "key" is just a number, expressed in binary form. Any encryption problem can therefore be attacked by trying to guess the key, known as the "brute force" attack. A key one "bit" long must be either 0 or 1, so it can take no more than two attempts to guess. It will take a fast PC or two quite a number of hours to run through all of the possibilities for a 40 bit key, but is not impossible. The DES (Data Encryption Standard) private key system is generally used with a 56 bit key—enough to tie up a serious amount of computing power for some time but not beyond the reach of any reasonably sized business or very determined hacker.[68]

Key administration infrastructure

Correct handling of keys is clearly a vital aspect of any cryptographic system. Apart from the initial function of generating keys, there must also be means for: **12–116**

(1) Establishing or verifying the "real world" identity of a particular keyholder, which in commercial terms is likely to be through certification by a neutral party ("certification authority");

(2) Enabling distribution (by publication or secure exchange,

---

[67] The best known public key algorithm is the RSA (Rivest, Shamir, Adelman) now licensed by RSA Data Security in the US. The PGP (Pretty Good Privacy) encryption software, developed and released onto the internet by Phil Zimmerman, uses the RSA algorithm.

[68] Pragmatically, it should be remembered that in reality there are very few problems which warrant the dedication of unlimited time and resources to solve.

depending on the cryptographic system being utilised) of keys to those who need and are entitled to have them;

(3) Revocation and deletion of keys whose security is suspected to have been compromised by any means, and letting those who need to know with certainty of the revocation. In the absence of such systems, the uncertainty and potential incompleteness of changes (some people still using old keys, contractors not sure exactly when a key was revoked) may be a substantial handicap to electronic commerce. Further;

(4) The multitude of keys any one user will need must also be safely stored and indexed for use as required;

(5) In some contexts, it may be necessary to incorporate some system to facilitate retrieval of data without recourse to the key. Most discussion has centred on governments' desire to be able to read communications intercepted in the course of criminal intelligence gathering, but it could be necessary in the private context too: the key management system may break down,[69] or it may be suspected that communications are taking place either between unauthorised persons or for unauthorised purposes. The principal solutions proposed are key escrow[70] and key recovery,[71] but there may be security issues associated with both of these solutions.[72] There has also been controversy over the terms on which police or government should be allowed to obtain access: in particular, whether

---

[69] If an employee who was able to generate keys, or the sole holder of a particular key, leaves without disclosing one, for example.

[70] A system under which legitimate users of encryption will deposit a copy of their private key with an escrow agent. This may be an external "trusted third party", where communication between companies or other organisations is concerned, or within an organisation it may be an additional function of the system administrator in respect of keys for use with corporate data or communications. The Electronic Communications Act 2000, s.14, prohibits the use of powers under the Act to impose key escrow requirements.

[71] In this scenario the Trusted Third Party, a "Key Recovery Centre", has a public key of its own. Compliant encryption users would, in every message sent, include a copy of their own private key, encrypted with the Centre's public key so that only the Centre would be in a position to decrypt it. As long as the Centre has at least one message from each party to the exchange they will have access to all of the relevant keys. Alternatively, the data needed to "recover" the key is included, encrypted, in either a header or appendix to each message. Different agencies would have to be invoked to get access to the different parts of the data. Further, some of the data may be left over to be cryptanalysed, to discourage casual requests for access and reduce the prospect of collusion amongst the recovery agencies.

[72] The disadvantages of key escrow arrangements are:
- The increased vulnerability of having keys held in a single place;
- The increased number of communication paths required for dealings with the archived key;
- The inherent distrust of consumers and users generally for any potential imposed third party;
- Users' loss of control over key management; and
- The high entry cost of setting up such an arrangement in the first place.

In either version of key recovery, no communication with any third party is required in the preparatory stage and no third party holds a key, so reducing the vulnerability of the system compared with a key escrow. The remaining disadvantages still apply.

this should require a warrant to be obtained from the courts, or merely some administrative procedure to be carried out.

A considerable administrative infrastructure is likely to arise, to provide Trusted Third Party[73] ("TTP") services associated with transactions using encryption, at least to support digital signatures. Some service providers originally operating commercially and with some success on an unregulated basis, notably VeriSign in the US. Various other organisations have emerged to offer similar services, either commercially or on an industry basis—for example, banking and insurance TTP schemes have been established.

Digital signatures

Probably the most common application of cryptography in connection with internet transactions, after simple encryption of messages, is the production of digital signatures. These require the use of public key cryptography but are widely promoted as the most effective and workable means of establishing the level of trust required between parties to high value business transactions.
    A digital signature is calculated by taking the message to be signed and applying to it a "Message Digest" or "hash" function. This calculates a data string, analogous to a fingerprint of the message. No two messages will produce the same short string. The sender then encrypts this data string with his or her private key. The resulting data string is the digital signature.
    Subject to concerns over unauthorised access to a signatory's private key, a digital signature can identify with certainty the originator of the message, since it can only be decrypted with that person's public key. A digital signature can also assure the integrity of either a communication or of stored data, and establish the time of creation of a message or document.[74] Further, there should be no issue as to people using copies of other people's signatures by the "cut and paste" method—unless they wish to retransmit the identical message, the signature is incorrect.
    A digital signature does not, as such, make any contribution to the confidentiality of the message: the message itself may be transmitted in plaintext, with only the message digest encrypted to give the signature.
    For complete confidence, the sender can have two private keys, one to be used to produce the signature and another to encrypt the plaintext. Tech-

12–117

---

[73] The term TTP is used for a service provider which carries out functions other than simple certification of identities: keeping directories, effecting and notifying users of changes such as revocation of keys (for example, where their security was believed to have been compromised), time-stamping electronic documents and so on.

[74] Any alteration to the contents of the message or stored data will produce a new fingerprint. Thus, all the recipient has to do is decrypt the signature and calculate the fingerprint of the message/data as received/retrieved. If it matches the fingerprint originally calculated by the sender/archivist, the message/data has not been altered. If it does not match, there has been tampering—although it will not be possible to tell what kind.

nical means exist[75] to signal when keys are being used for functions other than the one for which they were generated. However, where users have more than one key each, it will be important for the sake of certainty in transactions to ensure that each person has only one key per function—that they must use Key A if they are producing a signature which signals "adopting the writing", Key B if they are encrypting for confidentiality and so on. Otherwise, a contracting party might repudiate their signature on the basis that the individual who signed was not authorised to sign for that purpose but did so anyway using an inappropriate key. This will clearly require an unambiguous means of ensuring that the keys being used are those appropriate to the function.

Use of a separate key for digital signature purposes is also advisable in the light of the key disclosure provisions of the Regulation of Investigatory Powers Act 2000, discussed below.

12.9.3 The Legal Environment

12–118 Legislation relating to encryption technology falls into three distinct areas: that governing dealings in encryption goods, such as software packages; that concerning services associated with cryptographic functions, such as certification of keys for digital signatures; and that concerning the circumstances in which state agencies can require the delivery up of encryption keys.

Legislation relating to the former stems principally from the international level and derives from the potential for encryption devices or methods to be used for military, terrorist or criminal as readily as for commercial purposes: they are categorised as "dual use" goods. As a result they fall within the classes of goods subjected to export controls by many countries.

Legislation relating to the second is aimed more at pursuing government policy objectives to ensure secure transactions over the internet and to build up confidence in those, among both businesses and consumers. Governments are increasingly of the view that they need to encourage internet users to be confident in passing confidential information such as credit card numbers: and to encourage technology designed to ensure that internet users are passing the information to the entity they think they are; that it will not be open to detection in the course of the transaction; that the transaction will be legally binding and enforceable.

The extent to which it is appropriate for governments to pursue such policy objectives through legislation, when the technology and business models are in embryonic states, is a matter of great controversy. While there has been a flurry of legislative activity at European as well as national levels, the initial tendency to establish strict regulatory schemes has now largely ebbed away. The situation may well continue to change rapidly over

---

[75] Albeit subject to reservations as to their security.

the next few years while the various schemes which emerge are thoroughly tried and tested.

12.9.4 Dealings in encryption products

International level

The major international instrument is the Wassenaar Arrangement, which came into force on November 1, 1996.[76] The Arrangement is the successor to the cold war COCOM, the Co-ordinating Committee for Multilateral Exports Control; 40 states are party to it. It aims to promote transparency and responsibility with respect to transfers of potentially military technologies, and to enhance co-operation to prevent the acquisition of armaments and sensitive dual-use goods for military end-uses by regions or states which are causing the Participating States concern. The Arrangement applies to both conventional arms and dual-use goods. The provisions of this Arrangement are reflected in the export controls imposed by the EU (discussed below) and the various other signatories.

12–119

The Arrangement was amended in December 1998 to loosen the controls in respect of private key encryption software which uses a key length of less than 64 bits and is generally available to the public through "over the counter" or equivalent channels, as long as the cryptographic function cannot easily be changed by the user. This is likely to include most commercial private key encryption products already in circulation, many of which use keys of this sort of length or less. In addition, cryptographic products designed solely for authentication or digital signatures and products for the protection of copyright-protected data are excluded from the control scheme.

In a more peripheral fashion the two Copyright Treaties which the World Intellectual Property Organisation adopted in December 1996 also affect encryption products. Among other matters, they aim to restrict dealings in and use of devices for circumventing copy-protection devices (including encryption methods). This is an attempt to reinforce the effectiveness of copy protection and the integrity of rights management information incorporated in any digitised copyright work. These Treaties came into force in December 2001 and February 2002 respectively. Many of the countries which recently acceded to the EU had ratified them before accession. The EU Copyright in the Information Society Directive, discussed in Ch.2, implements the WIPO treaties. It was implemented in the UK by the Copyright and Related Rights Regulations 2003.

European Union

A new Regulation (1334/2000) governing the Community-wide regime for

12–120

---

[76] Text available at *http://www.wassenaar.org*; the relevant sections are the General Software Note and related materials.

the control of export of dual-use goods was adopted by the European Council of Ministers on June 22, 2000 and came into force on September 28, 2000. This Regulation was passed to update the Community regime to conform with the revised Wassenaar Arrangement. It extended the meaning of "export" to include the transmission of software or technology by electronic media, fax or telephone to a destination outside the Community. However, oral transmission of technology by telephone is covered only where the technology is contained in a document the relevant part of which is read out over the telephone, or is described over the telephone in such a way as to achieve substantially the same result.[77]

The Dual-Use list in the Regulation, which is updated periodically,[78] agrees broadly with the agreed Dual-Use list from the Wassenaar Arrangement, as it is intended to do. Cryptographic products, including software, are included in Annex IV of the related EC Council Decision 94/942/CFSP[79] and thus (subject to some stated exceptions not relevant to use of encryption by internet users) in principle require a licence for export from the EU. No licences are required for movement of cryptographic goods within the EU.

The only other pieces of European legislation with relevance to encryption products are the European Commission's Conditional Access Directive[80] and the Copyright in the Information Society Directive, mentioned above. The former takes pains to point out that it is not directly concerned with the legal status of encryption technology as such. Rather, it aims to provide a framework for the use of encryption as a mechanism whereby services which depend for their remuneration on limiting access should be able to be certain of achieving effective limitation—that is, ensuring that access to their services is conditional upon meeting the subscription conditions. This is the foundation for providers of on-line services such as digital radio services or video on demand to broadcast commercially over the internet.

The Directive, which was meant to have been implemented by Member States by May 2000, requires Member States to prohibit the commercial sale, installation or use of "illicit devices", that is equipment or software designed or adapted to give access to a protected service in an intelligible form without the authorisation of the service provider.[81] It does not include any express regulation of encrypting mechanisms or devices except to ban Member States from restricting free movement of conditional access devices.[82]

The European Commission's explanatory notes accompanying the adopted Directive hinted that this Directive may form the model for a

---

[77] Art.2.
[78] Most recently by EC Regulation 1504 2004 OJ L 281 August 31, 2004.
[79] As amended by EC Council Decisions 96/613/CFSP, 99/54/CFSP and 99/193/CFSP.
[80] Published in the Official Journal at [1998] O.J. L320/54.
[81] Definition in Art.1; prohibition in Art.3.
[82] Art.2.

broader international instrument on the control of illicit devices, but there has been no further indication of any intention to proceed further.

National

The UK passed a new Export Control Act[83] in 2002 to replace the anti- **12–121** quated Import, Export and Customs Powers (Defence) Act 1939 and consolidate the existing primary and secondary legislation governing the control of exports. It governs the procedures for obtaining export licences for encryption products and software from the UK.

The express intention was to make the decision making procedures in respect of applications for export licences more transparent. The new Act also covers the export of technology through the provision of technical assistance in addition to the straightforward sale of goods; this is intended to permit the implementation of the EU's Joint Action of June 22, 2000[84] concerning the use of technical assistance related to military end-uses.

The principal implementing provisions are contained in the Export of Goods, Transfer of Technology and Provision of Technical Assistance (Control) Order 2003.[85] As far as software is concerned, the Order implements Annex 1 of the EU Regulations. This contains the General Software Note which gives a general exception in respect of software generally available without restriction at retail points and through mail order etc, or otherwise "in the public domain" (by which is meant publicly available, rather than that the term of copyright has expired).

The only category of software which is not included in the exception under the General Software Note is that relating to information security, such as cryptographic software for confidentiality purposes or firewalls, unless the product is accompanying the user for the user's own personal use.

There are, therefore, no restrictions on most "consumer" cryptographic items being transferred to other Member States of the EU. However, the Trade in Goods (Control) Order 2003[86] imposes a requirement for detailed information to be retained about encryption products which are exported to other Member States, including: descriptions of all relevant encryption algorithms and key management schemes, and descriptions of how they are used by the item (for example, which algorithm is used for authentication, which for confidentiality and which for key exchange); and details (for example, source code) of how they are implemented (for example, how keys are generated and distributed; how key length is governed and how the algorithm and keys are called by the software); details of any measures taken to preclude user modification of the encryption algorithm, key management scheme or key length; and details of programming interfaces

---

[83] 2002 Ch.28.
[84] 2000/401/CFSP.
[85] SI 2003/2764, as amended by SI 2004/1050.
[86] SI 2003/2765.

that can be used to gain access to the cryptographic functionality of the item.

If the exporter knows that the ultimate destination of the goods is outside the EU, then a specific licence may be required.

Other specific technologies are also excepted by Annex 1: certain personalised smart cards; equipment for radio broadcasting or pay-TV which includes decryption technology for audio/video or management functions; mobile telephones for civil use; cryptographic equipment specifically designed and limited for banking use or money transactions; and decryption functions to allow the execution of copy-protected software, as long as these are not accessible to the user.

There are also Open General Export Licences in respect of software to be used for cryptographic development and computers meeting certain specifications.[87] An exporter nevertheless needs to register with the DTi's Export Control Organisation to benefit from these.

Since the EU Regulation is directly effective upon all Member States, the remaining Member States of the EU have more or less equivalent restrictions on export for encryption software.

Although the regulations have been updated they remain Byzantine, and it would be prudent to check with the DTI before exporting or uploading any encrypting technology.

Other Wassenaar signatory states will have more or less equivalent restrictions on export for encryption software.

12.9.5 Cryptography services/service providers

International

12–122 No legally binding instruments have yet been signed on this issue at the international level, and there are no proposals for any to be introduced.

European Union

12–123 The Electronic Signature Directive permits certification service providers to limit their liability for third party losses, but expressly prohibits Member States from making this benefit contingent upon the licensing or accreditation of certification service providers. However, Annex II(a) of the Directive does require certification service providers wishing to issue qualified certificates to demonstrate the reliability necessary for providing certification services. "Demonstration" implies some external observer with the authority to confirm or deny that the necessary standard has been achieved. In practice almost all current Member States have established some system of supervision, whether by a government agency or through an industry scheme of self-regulation.

---

[87] See *www.dti.gov.uk/europeandtrade/strategic-export-control/licensing-rating/licences/ogels/ogels-dual-use/index.html.*

National

The regulatory regime in the UK is possibly the most limited in the EU. **12–124**
There is no obligation upon certification service providers to be registered
or approved before beginning operations, whether or not they issue qualified certificates. Nor is there any obligation to notify after beginning
operations, although the Secretary of State for Trade and Industry is
required to keep a register of those certification service providers which
issue qualified certificates to the public, of which he or she is aware.[88]
Where the Secretary of State becomes aware of any conduct of such a
certification service provider which appears detrimental to the interests of
either subscribers or relying parties, he or she may publish evidence of this.
No other state supervision is contemplated.

Part I of the Electronic Communications Act 2000 did provide for the
establishment of a statutory, but voluntary, register of approved providers
of cryptography support services but the power to do so lapsed on May 25,
2005 without having been exercised.

Other Member States have taken a far more active stance. Under the
German Framework Law and Signatures Ordinance, for instance, very
detailed provisions are laid down for the regulation of certification service
providers issuing qualified certificates or time-stamps. Although no
approval is required, only those who can prove that they have the necessary
reliability and specialised knowledge may operate as a certification service
provider.[89] The Regulierungsbehörde, a government agency under the
Economics Ministry, must be notified of beginning operations as a certification service provider, including proof that these criteria are fulfilled.[90]
Thereafter certification service providers must co-operate with the Regulierungsbehörde, including permitting access to premises during normal
operating hours and providing documents for inspection.[91] All certification
service providers must also carry at least €250,000 insurance cover.[92]
Failure to comply with these provisions can lead to the imposition of a fine.

12.9.6 Access to encrypted data

International

No legally binding instruments have yet been signed on this issue at the **12–125**
international level, and there are no proposals for any to be introduced.

On the non-binding level, the most important document is the recommended cryptography policy Guidelines issued on March 27, 1997 by the

---

[88] Regulation 3, Electronic Signatures Regulations 2002.
[89] Section 4(2).
[90] Section 4(3).
[91] Section 20. The right not to incriminate oneself is expressly preserved, however.
[92] Section 12.

OECD (Organisation for Economic Co-operation and Development).[93] This was under prompting from the US, which in 1997 raised the status of its representative to this forum to that of Ambassador, possibly in part to emphasise the seriousness with which it views the issue of widespread availability of strong encryption.[94]

The Guidelines envisage that governments will require lawful access to plaintext or to the cryptographic keys for encrypted data. They, nevertheless, require that the policies implementing such access should respect to the greatest extent possible the other principles set out in the Guidelines. These are: trustworthiness of cryptographic methods; availability to users of a choice of methods; market-driven development; international and national standards for cryptographic methods; respect for privacy; and clear allocation of liability.

The factors the Guidelines propose should be taken into account are: the benefits for public safety, law enforcement and national security; the risks of misuse; the additional expense of the necessary supporting infrastructure; the prospects of technical failure; and other costs. They also lay down that access should only be given where there is a legal right to possession of the plaintext, and that it must only be used for lawful purposes. The access process should also be recorded, to enable judicial review if necessary.

European Union

12–126 A Council of Europe Convention on Cybercrime[95] was adopted in November 2001 and came into force in July 2004. It is intended to address problems of substantive and procedural criminal law connected with information technology, including:

- Criminal computer misuse laws; including unauthorised access to computers, illegal interception of communications, intentional damage to computer data, intentional serious hindering of the functioning of a computer system, and misuse of devices (including software) designed or adapted primarily for committing any of the aforesaid;
- Computer-related offences such as computer-related forgery and computer-related fraud;
- Computer-related offences in relation to child pornography (there

---

[93] Available at *http://www.oecd.org/document/34/0,2340,en_2649_201185_1814690_1_1_1_1,00.html.*

[94] Although since then even the US has taken a slightly more relaxed stance in that in the course of 2000 it successively abandoned the export controls on mass market cryptographic commodities and software with a key length of up to 64 bits, subject to a prior review on a product-by-product basis unless the proposed export is to the EU or certain other designated destinations. Finance specific, 56-bit non-mass market products with a key length between 512 and 1024 bits, network-based applications and other products which are functionally equivalent to retail products are also exempt.

[95] *http://conventions.coe.int/Treaty/en/Treaties/Html/185.htm.*

are significant opt-outs for pseudo-photographs and other aspects of these offences);

- Copyright and related offences; copyright and related rights (but not moral rights) infringement when undertaken wilfully, on a commercial scale and by means of a computer system;
- Measures to enable authortities to order the expeditious pre-servation of specified computer data, including traffic data, for up to 90 days to enable the authorities to seek disclosure; and to ensure that sufficient traffic data is disclosed to enable the service providers and the path through which the communication was transmitted to be identified; production orders; search and seizure of stored computer data; real-time collection of traffic data from service providers; interception of content data from service pro-viders in relation to serious offences;
- Jurisdiction over criminal offences; international co-operation; extradition principles; mutual assistance and provision of spon-taneous information.

A further protocol, on the criminalisation of acts of a racist and xenophobic nature committed through computer systems, was adopted in January 2003 and came into force on March 1, 2006.

The Convention, during its drafting process, drew considerable fire on privacy and civil liberties grounds.

The criminal provisions relating to accessing of computer systems and transmitted data, in each case where the access or interception is "without right", include any measure requiring the breaking of any form of encryption in order to obtain access.

National—the Regulation of Investigatory Powers Act 2000 and access to encrypted material

The Government's requirement for access to encrypted material was ori- **12–127** ginally mooted as part of the proposed Secure Electronic Communications Bill, which became the Electronic Communications Act 2000. The topic was the subject of controversy throughout the consultations leading up to the Bill. A key escrow scheme, as originally proposed, was dropped after stiff opposition from industry, civil liberties groups and the European Commission. The arrangements that replaced it were eventually enacted as Pt III of the Regulation of Investigatory Powers Act 2000 ("RIPA"). This is not yet in force, at the time of writing. However, in June 2007 the Home Office laid before Parliament an order intended to introduce a Code of Practice,[96] preparatory to the Government's stated intention of bringing Pt III into force.

Under Pt III of RIPA, various government agencies will be empowered, if

---

[96] Consultation on the Draft Code of Practice for the Investigation of Protected Electronic Information—Part III of the Regulation of Investigatory Powers Act 2000 (*http://www.homeoffice.gov.uk/documents/cons–2006-ripa-part3/*).

certain threshold conditions are satisfied, to issue disclosure notices requiring the production of the encryption key[97] which will enable them to unlock encrypted material which they have lawfully obtained (for example, under a search warrant).

The recipient of the notice can in most cases comply with the notice providing a copy of the plaintext and so avoid giving up the key.[98] If a "s.51 direction" has been issued, he must disclose the key. If he is not in possession of the protected information, or needs another key to obtain access to it or put it into intelligible form, then he must also disclose the key. There is also a requirement to disclose information that would facilitate obtaining or discovery of a key or putting the information into intelligible form.

Section 50 also sets out the circumstances in which disclosure of one of several keys is sufficient. Knowing failure to comply with the disclosure notice would be a criminal offence. Two defences are provided: one, not having the key; and the other, that it was not reasonably practicable to produce the key in the time allowed but the key was disclosed as soon as reasonably practicable thereafter. A further offence of "tipping off" is introduced: if the notice requires its existence to be kept secret, failure to do so would be an offence. No disclosure can be required of any key intended, and in fact used, for the purpose only of generating electronic signatures (s.49(9)). For that reason it is important to ensure that signatures used for that purpose are used for that purpose alone.

Data retention and access to communications data

12–128   Although they do not concern encryption, this a convenient point at which to mention the provisions of Pt I Ch.II of the Regulation of Investigatory Powers Act 2000, concerning government access to communications data, Pt 11 of the Anti-Terrorism, Crime and Security Act 2001 and the Data Retention Directive.

Part I Ch.II of RIPA came into force on January 5, 2004[99]. It creates a statutory framework within which various arms of government can, by notice, require a postal or telecommunications operator to disclose communications data to the requesting authority. If the operator does not co-operate, the notice is enforceable by civil proceedings for an injunction.[1]

The general thrust of the provisions is that data surrounding the communication (time of sending, the address from which and to which it was sent, and so on) are disclosable, but that the contents of the communication

---

[97] "Key" is in fact defined far more widely than an encryption key. "Protected information" is information that requires a key for access or to render it intelligible. A "key" is any "key, code, password, algorithm or other data".

[98] These are to a limited extent equivalent, in that possession of the plaintext would enable a cryptanalyst to deduce the encryption algorithm and key; but this would still require some effort, and it may be that the security services will not in general have the resources to devote to this degree of cross-checking the information with which they have been provided.

[99] The Regulation of Investigatory Powers Act 2000 (Commencement No. 3) Order 2003 SI 2003/3140.

[1] Regulation of Investigatory Powers Act 2000, s.22(8).

are not. The definition of communications data adopted to achieve this is complex. Account also needs to taken of the Code of Practice[2] (at present in a revised consultation draft) intended at some stage to be issued under s.71 of the Act. The list of government bodies entitled to make use of the RIPA powers, and the authorisation levels for each, are prescribed by statutory instrument and were heavily debated.[3]

Nothing in RIPA specifies any period for which communications data should be retained by a telecommunications or postal operator, or imposes any duty to retain data prior to the giving of a notice.[4]

Part 11 of the Anti-Terrorism, Crime and Security Act 2001 contains provisions for a voluntary communications data retention framework. On December 4, 2003 the Home Office issued[5] a data retention code of practice[6] under s.102 of the Act setting out voluntary retention periods for various types of data. Section 104 of the Act contains provisions enabling the Secretary of State, by statutory instrument, to take powers to direct the retention of communications data. No such instrument has yet been passed. Section 104 lapses after two years if not renewed by statutory instrument. It has so far been renewed twice, until December 14, 2007.

The data retention periods set out in Appendix A of the voluntary Code   **12–129** of Practice are as follows:

Subscriber Information *12 months*

(From end of subscription/last change)

Subscriber details relating to the person

e.g. Name, date of birth, installation and billing address, payment methods, account/credit card details

Contact information (information held about the subscriber but not verified by the CSP)

e.g. Telephone number, email address

Identity of services subscribed to (information determined by the communication service provider)

e.g. Customer reference/account number, list of services subscribed to

---

[2] Consultation on the Revised Statutory Code for Acquisition and Disclosure of Communications Data—Chapter II of Part I of the Regulation of Investigatory Powers Act 2000, June 2006 (*http://www.homeoffice.gov.uk/documents/cons–2006-ripa-part1/*).

[3] For the current status of orders and RIPA-related consultations see the Home Office RIPA website at *http://security.homeoffice.gov.uk/ripa/about-ripa/*.

[4] Note, however, that the Secretary of State can require a communications service provider to maintain a permanent intercept capability, thus facilitating the interception of communications pursuant to a warrant (Regulation of Investigatory Powers Act, ss.12–14).

[5] Retention of Communications Data (Code of Practice) Order 2003, SI 2003/3175.

[6] Retention of Communications Data under Pt 11: Anti-terrorism, Crime and Security Act 2001 Voluntary Code of Practice (*http://security.homeoffice.gov.uk/news-publications/publication-search/general/5b1.pdf?version=1*).

Telephony: telephone number(s), IMEI, IMSI(s)
E-mail: email address(es), IP at registration
Instant messaging: Internet Message Handle, IP at registration
ISP – dial-in: Log-in, CLI at registration (if kept)
ISP – always-on: Unique identifiers, MAC address (if kept), ADSL end points, IP tunnel address

Telephony Data *12 months*

e.g. All numbers (or other identifiers e.g. name@bt) associated with call (e.g. physical/presentational/network assigned CLI, DNI, IMSI, IMEI, exchange/divert numbers)
Date and time of start of call
Duration of call/date and time of end of call
Type of call (if available)
Location data at start and/or end of call, in form of lat/long reference.
Cell site data from time cell ceases to be used.
IMSI/MSISDN/IMEI mappings.
For GPRS & 3G, date and time of connection, IMSI, IP address assigned.
Mobile data exchanged with foreign operators; IMSI & MSISDN, sets of GSM triples, sets of 3G quintuples, global titles of equipment communicating with or about the subscriber.

SMS, EMS and MMS DATA *6 months*

e.g. Calling number, IMEI
Called number, IMEI
Date and time of sending
Delivery receipt – if available
Location data when messages sent and received, in form of latitude/longitude reference.

E-mail Data *6 months*

e.g. Log-on (authentication user name, date and time of log-in/log-off, IP address logged-in from)
Sent email (authentication user name, from/to/cc email addresses, date and time sent)
Received email (authentication user name, from/to email addresses, date and time received)

ISP Data *6 months*

e.g. Log-on (authentication user name, date and time of log-in/log-off, IP address assigned)
Dial-up: CLI and number dialled
Always-on: ADSL end point/MAC address (If available)

Web Activity Logs *4 days*

e.g. Proxy server logs (date/time, IP address used, URL's visited, services)
The data types here will be restricted solely to Communications Data and
exclude content of communication. This will mean that storage under this
code can only take place to the level of *www.homeoffice.gov.uk/*.......

Other Services   *Retention relative to service provided*

e.g. Instant Message Type Services (log-on/off time) If available.

Collateral Data   *Retention relative to data to which it is related*

e.g. Data needed to interpret other communications data. For example:

- the mapping between cellmast identifiers and their location
- translation of dialling (as supported by IN networks)

On March 15, 2006 the EU adopted the Data Retention Directive,[7] which **12–130**
lays down mandatory data retention periods, applicable to providers of
publicly available electronic communications services and public communications networks, in relation to specified traffic and location data and the
related data necessary to identify the subscriber or registered user.

The Directive has to be implemented in Member States no later than
September 15, 2007. However, Member States who have made a declaration to that effect may postpone implementation until March 15, 2009 in
relation to internet access, internet telephony and internet email. The UK
has made such a declaration. Member States are required to ensure that the
categories of data specified in the Directive are retained for periods of not
less than six months and not more than two years from the date of the
communication.

The categories of data that will require to be retained under the Directive
are:

(a) data necessary to trace and identify the source of a
communication:

    (1) concerning fixed network telephony and mobile telephony:

        (i) the calling telephone number;
        (ii) the name and address of the subscriber or registered user;

    (2) concerning internet access, internet email and internet
telephony:

        (i) the user ID(s) allocated;

---

[7] Directive 2006/24/EC of the European Parliament and of the Council of March 15, 2006 on
the retention of data generated or processed in connection with the provision of publicly
available electronic communications services or of public communications networks and
amending Directive 2002/58/EC.

      (ii)   the user ID and telephone number allocated to any communication entering the public telephone network;

     (iii) the name and address of the subscriber or registered user to whom an Internet Protocol (IP) address, user ID or telephone number was allocated at the time of the communication;

(b) data necessary to identify the destination of a communication:

  (1) concerning fixed network telephony and mobile telephony:

      (i)   the number(s) dialled (the telephone number(s) called), and, in cases involving supplementary services such as call forwarding or call transfer, the number or numbers to which the call is routed;

      (ii) the name(s) and address(es) of the subscriber(s) or registered user(s);

  (2) concerning internet email and internet telephony:

      (i)   the user ID or telephone number of the intended recipient(s) of an internet telephony call;

      (ii) the name(s) and address(es) of the subscriber(s) or registered user(s) and user ID of the intended recipient of the communication;

(c) data necessary to identify the date, time and duration of a communication:

  (1) concerning fixed network telephony and mobile telephony, the date and time of the start and end of the communication;

  (2) concerning internet access, internet email and internet telephony:

      (i)   the date and time of the log-in and log-off of the internet access service, based on a certain time zone, together with the IP address, whether dynamic or static, allocated by the Internet access service provider to a communication, and the user ID of the subscriber or registered user;

      (ii) the date and time of the log-in and log-off of the internet email service or internet telephony service, based on a certain time zone;

(d) data necessary to identify the type of communication:

  (1) concerning fixed network telephony and mobile telephony: the telephone service used;

  (2) concerning internet email and internet telephony: the internet service used;

(e) data necessary to identify users' communication equipment or what purports to be their equipment:

(1) concerning fixed network telephony, the calling and called telephone numbers;

(2) concerning mobile telephony:

　(i) the calling and called telephone numbers;

　(ii) the International Mobile Subscriber Identity (IMSI) of the calling party;

　(iii) the International Mobile Equipment Identity (IMEI) of the calling party;

　(iv) the IMSI of the called party;

　(v) the IMEI of the called party;

　(vi) in the case of pre-paid anonymous services, the date and time of the initial activation of the service and the location label (Cell ID) from which the service was activated;

(3) concerning internet access, internet email and internet telephony:

　(i) the calling telephone number for dial-up access;

　(ii) the digital subscriber line (DSL) or other end point of the originator of the communication;

(f) data necessary to identify the location of mobile communication equipment:

(1) the location label (Cell ID) at the start of the communication;

(2) data identifying the geographic location of cells by reference to their location labels (Cell ID) during the period for which communications data are retained.

The Directive does not authorise the retention of data revealing the content of the communication.

12.10 COMPUTER MISUSE

12.10.1 The Computer Misuse Act 1990

The Computer Misuse Act 1990 was introduced in the UK to create specific **12–131** offences in relation to unauthorised access to computer systems. Although aimed mainly at the activities of traditional computer hackers, the Act has caught a wider class of activities, such as the release of viruses.[8]

---

[8] For a survey of prosecutions under the 1990 Act, see R. Battcock, "Prosecutions under the Computer Misuse Act 1990", *Computers and Law* Vol. 6 issue 6, February/March 1996.

Following a media campaign suggesting that the 1990 Act did not adequately address denial of service attacks,[9] and in order to ensure compliance with the CyberCrime Convention,[10] the Act is due to be amended. This will occur when the Police and Justice Act 2006, which received Royal Assent in November 2006, comes into force. In fact, as demonstrated by the Divisional Court decision in *DPP v Lennon*,[11] the existing legislation was adequate for the purpose of dealing with denial of service attacks. We will consider the Act in both its unamended and amended form.

For possible bases of civil liability for hacking, see *Ashton Investments Ltd v OJSC Russian Aluminium*.[12] The claimants alleged that overseas defendants had hacked into their server located in London in order to obtain confidential and privileged information. The claimants obtained permission to serve out of the jurisdiction based on pleas of unlawful interference with business and breach of confidence. The jurisdictional aspects of this case are discussed in Ch.6. Reference should also be made to the discussion in Ch.5 of civil liability for virus dissemination and to the discussion earlier in this chapter of civil liability for junk email.

The 1990 Act creates three separate offences.[13]

Unauthorised access to computer material

12–132   A person is guilty of an offence under s.1 of the Act if he causes a computer to perform any function with intent to secure access to any program or data held in any computer, the access he intends to secure is unauthorised and he knows at the time when he causes the computer to perform the function that that is the case. The section specifically provides that the intent of the person need not be directed at any particular program or data, a program or data of any particular kind or a program or data held in any particular computer. This renders the Act peculiarly suitable for use against activities carried out across networks.

---

[9] A denial of service (DoS) attack consists of the repeated sending of messages to a computer system, in such volumes as to swamp it and prevent it coping with normal traffic. A distributed denial of service (DDoS) is a version of the same thing where the attacker uses hundreds or thousands of other computers (normally commandeered for the purpose by means of a virus) to send the messages.

[10] The Convention on Cybercrime November 23, 2001 (*http://conventions.coe.int/Treaty/EN/Treaties/Html/185.htm*). The main respect in which the UK does not satisfy the Convention requirements is in the lack of an offence in relation to the making, supplying etc of articles for use in computer misuse offences. For general background see the All Party Parliamentary Internet Group Report on the Revision of the Computer Misuse Act, June 2004.

[11] [2006] EWHC 1201 (Admin).

[12] [2006] EWHC 2545 (Comm).

[13] The Act (s.3(6)) also abolished, in cases where there is no impairment of the physical condition of the computer, the previously available possibility of obtaining a conviction for hacking under the Criminal Damage Act 1971. In *R. v Whiteley* [1993] F.S.R. 168 the Court of Appeal upheld a conviction of a hacker under this Act. In order to obtain a conviction the prosecution had to demonstrate that the defendant caused damage to tangible property. The Court of Appeal held that it was sufficient that the particles on the hard disk were altered in such a way as to cause an impairment of the value or usefulness of the disk to the owner.

Under s.17(5) a person's access is unauthorised if: the person is not himself entitled to control access of the kind in question to the program or data; and he does not have consent to access by him of the kind in question to the program or data from any person who is so entitled.

A person secures access to any program or data held in a computer if by causing the computer to perform any function he:

(a) alters or erases the program or data;
(b) copies or moves it to any storage medium other than that in which it is held or to a different location in the storage medium in which it is held;
(c) uses it; or
(d) has it output from the computer in which it is held (whether by having it displayed or in any other manner).

An offence under this section is punishable by imprisonment of up to six months or a fine of up to £5,000 or both.

The prospective substantive amendments to the s.1 offence[14] are relatively small, providing in essence that "securing" access also includes enabling access to be secured.

As regards penalties, the offence will be made indictable, the terms of imprisonment being up to 12 months on summary conviction (6 months in Scotland) and up to two years on indictment. The fines will be up to £5,000 on summary conviction and unlimited on indictment.

Unauthorised access with intent to commit or facilitate commission of further offences

This is, in essence, an aggravated version of the offence under s.1. Under s.2 **12–133** a person is guilty of an offence if he commits an offence under s.1 with intent to commit one of certain further specified offences, or to facilitate the commission of such an offence by himself or any other person. An offence under this section is punishable on summary conviction by the same penalties as under s.1, or on indictment by imprisonment for a term not exceeding five years, or to a fine (unlimited) or to both.

The prospective amendments amend the penalties on summary conviction so as to remain in line with those under s.1. The penalties on indictment will remain unchanged.

Unauthorised modification of computer material

Under s.3 a person is guilty of an offence if he does any act which causes an **12–134** unauthorised modification of the contents of any computer and at the time when he does the act he has "the requisite intent and the requisite knowledge". The requisite intent is an intent to cause a modification of the content of any computer and by so doing:

---

[14] Police and Justice Act 2006, s.35.

(a) to impair the operation of any computer;

(b) to prevent or hinder access to any program or data held in the computer; or

(c) to impair the operation of any such program or the reliability of any such data.

The requisite knowledge is knowledge that any modification he intends to cause is unauthorised. The section provides that intent need not be directed to any particular computer, any particular program or data or a program or data of any particular kind or any particular modification or modification of any particular kind.

12–135 Under s.17(7) a modification of the contents of any computer takes place if, by the operation of any function of the computer concerned or any other computer, any program or data held in the computer concerned is altered or erased; or any program or data is added to its contents.

Under s.17(8) such modification is unauthorised if: the person whose act causes it is not himself entitled to determine whether the modification should be made; and he does not have consent to the modification from any person who is so entitled.

The penalties for an offence under s.3 are the same as under s.2.

Significant changes will be made to s.3. It will now read:

"(1) A person is guilty of an offence if—

    (a) he does any unauthorised act in relation to a computer;

    (b) at the time when he does the act he knows that it is unauthorised; and

    (c) either subsection (2) or subsection (3) below applies.

(2) This subsection applies if the person intends by doing the act—

    (a) to impair the operation of any computer;

    (b) to prevent or hinder access to any program or data held in any computer;

    (c) to impair the operation of any such program or the reliability of any such data; or

    (d) to enable any of the things mentioned in paragraphs (a) to (c) above to be done.

(3) This subsection applies if the person is reckless as to whether the act will do any of the things mentioned in paragraphs (a) to (d) of subsection (2) above.

(4) The intention referred to in subsection (2) above, or the recklessness referred to in subsection (3) above, need not relate to—

    (a) any particular computer;

    (b) any particular program or data; or

    (c) a program or data of any particular kind.

(5) In this section—

    (a) a reference to doing an act includes a reference to causing an act to be done;

    (b) 'act' includes a series of acts;

    (c) a reference to impairing, preventing or hindering something includes a reference to doing so temporarily."

The penalties will now be, on summary conviction imprisonment for up to 12 months (6 months in Scotland) or to a fine not exceeding £5,000 or to both; on indictment, to imprisonment for up to ten years or to an unlimited fine or to both.

The effect of the substantive amendments is to broaden even further the *actus reus* of the offence by removing any requirement to show modification of the contents of the computer, and to specify that intent includes recklessness. Whether the change to the *actus reus* will make any practical difference at all is doubtful, given the extreme width[15] of the previous definition of modification. The difficult area with the 1990 Act has always been what is meant by the concept of "unauthorised".

As we have noted, much of the pressure to amend the Act came because of concern that it did not deal adequately with DoS attacks. Two such cases reached the courts. In the first case the defendant was acquitted by the jury after claiming that the DoS software must have been put on his computer by a surreptitious Trojan Horse.[16] That was a matter of evidence and credibility, which no amount of fiddling with the drafting of the Act will change. In the second case the defendant was acquitted by the youth court, but the acquittal was subsequently reversed following a successful appeal by the prosecution to the Divisional Court.[17] The only point at issue was authorisation.

Making, supplying or obtaining articles for use in computer misuse offences

The prospective amendments to the 1990 Act introduce a new offence of making, supplying or obtaining articles for use in computer misuse offences. The new s.3A offence will be as follows:

12–136

"(1) A person is guilty of an offence if he makes, adapts, supplies or offers to supply any article intending it to be used to commit, or to assist in the commission of, an offence under section 1 or 3.

(2) A person is guilty of an offence if he supplies or offers to

---

[15] Lord Woolf M.R., in *Zezev and Yarimaka v Governor of H.M. Prison Brixton* (QBD Div. Ct. March 20, 2002) commented: "That language is very wide indeed. The consequence is that if a computer is caused to record data, it seems to me that that amounts to a modification for the purposes of section 3 because of the effect upon section 3 of section 17(7)."

[16] "Hacker trial raises issues over evidence gathering" *Computing* October 23, 2003.

[17] *DPP v Lennon* [2006] EWHC 1201 (Admin).

supply any article believing that it is likely to be used to commit, or to assist in the commission of, an offence under section 1 or 3.

(3) A person is guilty of an offence if he obtains any article with a view to its being supplied for use to commit, or to assist in the commission of, an offence under section 1 or 3.

(4) In this section 'article' includes any program or data held in electronic form."

The penalties are on summary conviction, imprisonment for up to 12 months (6 months in Scotland) or to a fine of up to £5,000 or to both; on indictment, imprisonment for up to two years or to an unlimited fine or to both.

This new offence has raised concerns about potential criminal liability of those, particularly researchers, who devise and share tools that can have both innocent and nefarious uses.

It is notable that the tool does not have to be a program. It can be mere data.

It is unclear whether the guilty knowledge required is that an offence is likely, or that a thing is likely to be done which in the event constitutes an offence. To take an extreme example, suppose that someone has been banned from a website and, pretending that he has forgotten his account details, asks a colleague to borrow his user account and password. The colleague foolishly supplies the information and the malefactor enters the website.

The malefactor probably commits an offence under s.1. If the foolish colleague did not know that the malefactor was banned, does he commit an offence under the new s.3A? If knowledge of the purpose for which the user details and password were to be used (i.e. entering the website) suffices, then having supplied the relevant data he is guilty under s.3A whether or not he knew that his colleague was banned. It is to be hoped that that is not sufficient, and that in order to be culpable he has at least to know that what the colleague proposed to do was wrongful.

12.10.2 E-mail viruses, access to websites, denial of service attacks and the 1990 Act

E-mail viruses

12–137 The Act clearly applies to those who release damaging viruses into the wild, even though the person doing so does not have an intent to damage a particular computer.

Some email may not be specifically intended to destroy data or prevent programs from operating, but simply use email directories to propagate themselves around email systems. There could still be the possibility of a conviction. Notwithstanding that email systems are intended to receive emails, nonetheless under s.1 is the use of the recipient's email program to cause the incoming email virus to propagate onwards by means of the email system is access of an unauthorised nature and would the perpetrator therefore be liable to prosecution under s.1? This question turns around questions of implied permission, which we will consider below in the context of authorisation.

Access to websites

Questions may arise as to when, if at all, accessing a website could be an offence under the Act. Clearly, accessing a publicly available website could not be an offence in itself, since there is an implied authorisation for the public to visit the website.   **12–138**

But what, for instance, if part of the website is restricted to persons who are qualified by age, occupation, or some other criteria and someone gains access by making untrue statements? Or if someone has been banned from a discussion forum and re-enters it under an alias?

Denial of service attacks

What about where access is available but abused? Is, for instance, a denial of service attack an offence? Such an attack consists of sending massive quantities of otherwise normal messages or page requests to an internet host. The server is overloaded, cannot deal with legitimate requests and effectively becomes unavailable. If the access could be regarded as unauthorised, there would seem to be both a s.1 offence and (given the effect on the server) a s.3 offence. As we shall see, the decision of the Divisional Court in *Lennon* confirms that, as might be expected, this does indeed constitute an offence.   **12–139**

Unauthorised access

The nature of unauthorised access can cause difficulties. In *DPP v Bignall*[18] two police officers, who were authorised to do so for their work, used the Police National Computer System to obtain information for their personal purposes. The Divisional Court, on appeal, reasoned that the Defendants did have authorised access to the system and so could not be in violation of s.1 of the 1990 Act, notwithstanding that the purpose for which they accessed the system was not a purpose for which they were given access to the system.   **12–140**

Bignell was considered in the House of Lords decision of *R. v Bow Street Stipendiary Magistrate, Ex p. Government of the United States of America*.[19] The House of Lords held (when considering a case involving unauthorised access by an employee) that the pertinent question is whether access to the data in question was authorised; whether the kind of access secured to that data was authorised; and that the question of authorisation

---

[18] (1998) Crim. L.R. 53.
[19] [1999] 4 All E.R. 2.

was a question of entitlement to control access in the sense of having the right to authorise or forbid access—not the physical ability to operate or manipulate the computer.[20] The actual decision in *Bignell* was considered to be probably right, since the defendants were authorised to access the particular data in question, but the broader statements in *Bignell* as to the purpose and interpretation of the 1990 Act were disapproved.

The *Bow Street* decision discusses the provisions of s.17(5) (see above). "[Section 17(5)] makes clear that the authority must relate not simply to the data or program but also to the kind of access secured". An example is given that "Authority to view data may not extend to authority to copy or alter that data."

On the basis of the *Bow Street* criteria for unauthorised access, a banned user entering a website would seem to fall pretty clearly within the parameters of a s.1 offence, but not (given the lack of requisite intent to impair etc) a s.3 offence.

The example given in *Bow Street* concerning a distinction between viewing and copying data raises the surprising possibility that someone who downloads material from a website in contravention of a copyright licence that only permits viewing on screen, may commit an offence under the 1990 Act. Their Lordships may not have fully considered the fact that, in the electronic environment, viewing necessarily involves copying (in the sense of creating a temporary copy in the RAM of the user's computer), so that the distinction between the two is less than might be first thought.

Under the prospective amendments to the 1990 Act made by the Police and Justice Act 2006, the existing definition of unauthorised modification for the purposes of s.3 contained in s.17(8) is replaced by a more general definition of "unauthorised", in the following terms:

"An act done in relation to a computer is unauthorised if the person doing the act (or causing it to be done)—

(a) is not himself a person who has responsibility for the computer and is entitled to determine whether the act may be done; and

(b) does not have consent to the act from any such person.

In this subsection 'act' includes a series of acts."[21]

The new definition follows closely the existing caselaw discussed above.

Unauthorised modification

12–141 As regards s.3, the question is firstly whether an email virus has caused an unauthorised modification of the contents of any computer. Although the

---

[20] This interpretation of "unauthorised" has also been adopted in relation to the offence of unauthorised interception of communications under s.1 of the Regulation of Investigatory Powers Act 2000 (*R v Stanford* [2006] EWCA Crim 258).

[21] Police and Justice Act 2006, Sch.14 para.29.

receiving system is open for receipt of emails and modifications to the contents of that computer as the result of such access are inevitable, by going beyond the intended use of the receiving email system is the actual modification made to be regarded as unauthorised?

Authorisation and publicly available interfaces

The question of authorisation, in the context of messages sent to a publicly available interface (such as an email address) intended to receive messages, was first considered in *Zezev and Yarimaka v Governor of H.M. Prison Brixton.*[22] This was a case under s.3 of the 1990 Act. In the Divisional Court Wright J. considered the question of whether sending an email to a computer constituted an unauthorised modification of the contents of that computer. He commented firstly, in relation to modification:

    12–142

> "Section 17(7) of the 1990 Act provides that any addition of data to the contents of a computer amounts to a modification of those contents, although obviously in the case of legitimate emails such as are invited by the owner of a computer by the publication of his email address, such modification is not a criminal matter, without more, within the meaning of section 3 of the same Act."

He went to say, as regards authorisation:

> "But if an individual, by misusing or bypassing any relevant password, places in the files of the computer a bogus email by pretending that the password holder is the author when he is not, then such an addition to such data is plainly unauthorised, as defined in section 17(8). Intent to modify the contents of the computer as defined in section 3(2) is self-evident and, by so doing, the reliability of the data in the computer is impaired within the meaning of section 3(2)(c)."

This judgment left open for further exploration the question of what would and would not constitute a "legitimate" email, for the purpose of considering whether it was unauthorised. Would any unwanted email count?

Some elucidation was provided by the Divisional Court in *DPP v Lennon.*[23] This was a s.3, unauthorised modification, case. It concerned an ex-employee who downloaded a mail-bombing program from the internet and used it to send about five million emails to his former employer, purporting to come from faked email addresses including the former employer's Human Resources Manager. Reversing the acquittal by the youth court, the Divisional Court considered the question of authorisation. The defendant argued that the function of the servers was to receive emails, so the former

    12–143

---

[22] *Zezev and Yarimaka v Governor of H.M. Prison Brixton* (QBD Div. Ct. March 20, 2002).
[23] [2006] EWHC 1201 (Admin).

employer consented to receiving emails on them, and so authorised potential senders of emails to modify the contents of the server by sending them.

Jack J. said:

> "I agree, and it is not in dispute, that the owner of a computer which is able to receive emails is ordinarily to be taken as consenting to the sending of emails to the computer. His consent is to be implied from his conduct in relation to the computer. Some analogy can be drawn with consent by a householder to members of the public to walk up the path to his door when they have a legitimate reason for doing so, and also with the use of a private letter box. But that implied consent given by a computer owner is not without limit. The point can be illustrated by the same analogies. The householder does not consent to a burglar coming up his path. Nor does he consent to having his letter box choked with rubbish. That second example seems to me to be very much to the point here. I do not think that it is necessary for the decision in this case to try to define the limits of the consent which a computer owner impliedly gives to the sending of emails. It is enough to say that it plainly does not cover emails which are not sent for the purpose of communication with the owner, but are sent for the purpose of interrupting the proper operation and use of his system. That was the plain intent of Mr Lennon in using the Avalanche program. The difference can be demonstrated in this way. If Mr Lennon had telephoned Ms Rhodes and requested consent to send her an email raising a point about the termination of his employment, she would have been puzzled as to why he bothered to ask and said that of course he might. If he had asked if he might send the half million emails he did send, he would have got a quite different answer. In short the purpose of Mr Lennon in sending the half million emails was an unauthorised purpose and the use made of D&G's email facility was an unauthorised use."

The argument that had found favour with the District Judge, namely that each email had to be considered individually and that there was implied consent to each and therefore to all, was rejected. The defendant's conduct had to be considered as a whole.

12–144 It was also argued that the fact that the emails purported to come from someone who was not the sender rendered them unauthorised. As to that, Jack J. said (referring to the second passage quoted above from *Zezev*):

> "I consider that the same analysis is also applicable to the circumstances here because D&G gave no implied consent to the receipt of malicious emails purporting to come from its Human Resources Manager. But I would not necessarily be of the view that in all circumstances an email purporting to come from one

person but coming from another is to be treated as unauthorised. For example such an email might be sent as a joke with no malicious intent, and then it could be argued that it was covered by the implied consent of the computer's owner. The answer would depend upon the circumstances, and I express no view upon it.

Keene L.J. placed a further gloss on the question of implied consent, finding that there can be implied consent to receive a merely unwanted email and introducing factors similar to those considered by the US courts in the trespass to chattels cases discussed in Ch. 2:

"The critical issue is that of "consent" as that word is used in section 17(8) of the Act. I, for my part, see a clear distinction between the receipt of emails which the recipient merely does not want but which do not overwhelm or otherwise harm the server, and the receipt of bulk emails which do overwhelm it. It may be that the recipient is to be taken to have consented to the receipt of the former if he does not configure the server so as to exclude them. But in my judgment he does not consent to receiving emails sent in a quantity and at a speed which are likely to overwhelm the server. Such consent is not to be implied from the fact that the server has an open as opposed to a restricted configuration."

On the basis of *Zezev* and *Lennon* there would be no difficulty in finding that the sending of an email virus was unauthorised.

CHAPTER 13

Tax

13.1 INTRODUCTION

13–001   It has become evident that the worldwide spread of the internet and other factors such as globalisation, have dramatically changed how business is conducted in local, national and multinational environments, creating opportunities and benefits for both businesses and consumers as well as posing new problems and challenges. Through the internet, businesses can now structure their activities cost-effectively and sell to a wider consumer audience without having to establish any local, physical presence near their desired markets.

A video games company, for instance, can now market and distribute its products for sale or rental directly to the public over the internet while having its server located in a low cost jurisdiction. Using web-based systems, core business functions (e.g. order and payment processing, inventory management) may be automated while other functions are outsourced to third parties. This reduces costs for consumers and gives access to new ways of buying products or services and comparing prices.

From a tax perspective, these changes have presented important challenges to the application of traditional tax rules and concepts such as "establishment" and "residence", originally developed for a business environment before the emergence of the internet. Many of these challenges therefore arise from the intangible and global nature of the internet and the greater ability of businesses to trade across borders, combined with the flexibility and potential anonymity the internet affords cross-border transactions. These challenges are compounded by the potential for different implementing legislation in individual countries, creating compliance and revenue risks for the tax regimes of the jurisdictions in which the business is conducted, and greater uncertainties for businesses.

In order for tax to operate within the prevailing business environment, both governments and businesses have recognised that there needs to be a balance between ensuring that tax revenues are fairly secured whilst also providing a clear fiscal environment that does not restrict e-commerce, or e-business,[1] development.

In finding this balance, work programmes on e-commerce tax issues have been actively pursued at the highest international level, particularly by the European Commission (Commission) and the Organisation for Economic Co-operation and Development (OECD—the primary forum for co-operation in matters of international taxation). In recent years, those work programmes have led to the development of a number of legal initiatives, mainly directed towards providing practical solutions for the implementation of the 1998 Ottawa Taxation Framework Conditions; a broad set of tax principles which were formulated to guide governments in their tax treatment of e-commerce. Particular attention has been given to modernising, rather than replacing, existing tax mechanisms, and to creating some degree of international coherence in their application to e-commerce.

This chapter will examine the major tax issues which are of most significance to e-commerce, namely value added tax (VAT), customs duties and particular direct tax issues such as withholding tax and taxable presence. It will also cover developments in internet tax policy in the UK and elsewhere. The chapter will address these issues and developments principally from a UK perspective, and more specifically, in relation to their impact on business conducted over the internet (although they should also be relevant to other jurisdictions, especially other European Union (EU) Member States, and to business conducted via other media such as television sets and radio broadcasts).

13.2 EMERGING TAX POLICY—AN OVERVIEW

History

Tax issues related to e-commerce have been, and continue to be, the subject **13–002** of international discussion and collaboration through the OECD, the EU and the World Customs Organisation, involving input from all levels of the international community—governments, various taxing authorities, tax professionals and the business community itself.

In a Communication in April 1997,[2] the Commission stressed the need to ensure that tax obligations in relation to e-commerce were clear, transparent, predictable and, so that there was no extra burden on e-commerce as opposed to more traditional forms of commerce, neutral. Furthermore,

---

[1] These terms tend to be used interchangeably but it is understood that e-business is the newer, wider term to refer generally to the use of computer networks to facilitate transactions (both internally and externally) and not just e-commerce, i.e. the selling and buying of products and services to customers over the internet. This chapter mainly refers to the term "e-commerce" since this term has been used more substantially within OECD documents.

[2] Communication from the Commission to the European Parliament, the Council, the Economic and Social Committee and the Committee of the Regions: A European Initiative in Electronic Commerce, COM (1997) 157.

the importance of implementing tax rules which did not create market distortions was also emphasised. In the Joint EU-US Statement on Electronic Commerce of December 5, 1997, it was also accepted that the taxation of e-commerce should be "clear, consistent, neutral and non-discriminatory".

The subsequent Commission Communication of June 1998[3] expanded upon the principles laid down in the 1997 Communication and set out the following key guidelines for the way forward:

(i) efforts should be concentrated on adapting existing taxes, and in particular VAT, to the developments of e-commerce: no new or additional taxes should be considered;

(ii) a supply of digitised products via an electronic network should be treated for VAT purposes as a supply of services;

(iii) services, whether supplied by e-commerce or otherwise, which are supplied for consumption within the EU should be subject to VAT within the EU (whatever their origin) and services supplied for consumption outside the EU should not be subject to EU VAT, although VAT on related costs or "inputs" should be eligible for deduction; and

(iv) the VAT regime should ensure that taxation is enforceable on supplies of services received within the EU via e-commerce by both businesses and private individuals.

This Communication had been prepared in anticipation of the OECD Ministerial Conference on Electronic Commerce which took place in Ottawa in October 1998. Pursuant to that conference the Ottawa Taxation Framework Conditions were published by the OECD Committee on Fiscal Affairs addressing four areas: tax treaties, consumption taxes, tax administration, and taxpayer service.

The key conclusions mirrored those reached independently by the EU and US. It was stated that the taxation principles that guide governments in relation to conventional commerce should also guide them in relation to e-commerce. These principles were the principles of neutrality, efficiency, certainty and simplicity, effectiveness and fairness, and flexibility.

Thus, the consequences of taxation should be the same for transactions in goods and services regardless of the mode of commerce used, whether they are purchased from within or from outside the EU and whether delivery is effected on-line or off-line, so that no particular form of commerce is advantaged or disadvantaged.

Compliance costs for taxpayers and administrative costs for tax authorities should be minimised as far as possible. The rules should be clear and

---

[3] Communication from the Commission to the Council, the European Parliament and the Economic and Social Committee: Electronic Commerce and Indirect Taxation, COM (1998) 374 final.

simple to understand so that the taxpayer can anticipate in advance the tax consequences of a transaction. Furthermore, the rules should not result in double or unintentional non-taxation but in the right amount of tax being paid at the right time and in the right country. They should minimise the potential for evasion and avoidance and be flexible and dynamic enough to keep pace with technological and commercial developments.

The Committee believed, at that stage of development of internet commerce, that existing taxation measures could implement these principles. However, new or modified measures were not precluded provided that they assisted in the application of existing principles and were not intended to impose a discriminatory tax treatment of e-commerce or resulted in an unfair distortion of competition which would result from a de facto double taxation or non-taxation of e-commerce vis-à-vis fully taxed traditional commerce.

So, it can be seen that the consensus was that there were to be no new or special e-commerce taxes. Rather, the existing tax structure would be made to work using the above-mentioned guiding principles.

The Framework Conditions established an ambitious timetable to study and decide upon the various implementation options identified in the paper. Key elements of the work programme included how payments for digitised products should be characterised under tax treaties; in what circumstances a website may constitute a permanent establishment giving rise to tax jurisdiction in the country where the server on which it is hosted is located; and, in relation to consumption taxes such as VAT, obtaining a consensus on defining the place of supply and on internationally compatible definitions of services and intangible property.

As will be seen later in this chapter, there are existing taxes which are sufficiently robust to be able to accommodate certain forms of e-commerce (for example, the "email" order of goods which are then delivered by traditional means) but not others, where work was still necessary both at the domestic and international level to agree upon the tools needed to put policy in place.

13.3 RECENT DEVELOPMENTS

Since agreeing the Framework Conditions, both the EU and the OECD, **13–003** through its Committee on Fiscal Affairs and the business/government technical advisory groups established by it to examine e-commerce tax issues, have made considerable progress towards their implementation.

The OECD's review has covered all the main tax areas to be addressed; namely international direct taxes and tax treaties, consumption taxes; and tax administration/taxpayer service, with continued input from businesses and non-OECD governments. Its work programme has involved a detailed analysis of the tax implications of e-commerce activities and has led to a number of important conclusions and recommendations. These are now available on-line in various guidance documents, discussion drafts, progress reports and technical papers.[4] A brief overview of the implementation work is given below, some of which will be detailed later in this chapter.

Direct taxes

13–004　International discussions on the application of the "permanent establishment" concept to website servers and how e-commerce payments may be characterised for tax treaty purposes have resulted in clarifications to the OECD's Commentary on its Model Tax Convention on Income and Capital.[5]

Two other key issues have been the subject of discussion drafts[6] which are well-advanced but these have not yet resulted in changes being incorporated in the OECD's Model Tax Convention. The first of these concerns a refinement of the concept of "place of effective management" in determining which jurisdiction has primary taxing rights given that it is now possible for a company's board of directors to hold meetings (e.g. via video conferencing) simultaneously in different locations. The second is a critical examination of the adequacy of current treaty rules for the taxation of business profits, including transfer pricing,[7] in the context of e-commerce by reference to the Framework Conditions.

Consumption taxes

13–005　Notably, significant attention has been given by the OECD towards achieving an international consensus in the field of VAT. The EU has complemented the OECD's work by focussing its efforts on dealing with shortcomings in EU VAT legislation. Their work programmes have progressed along the same lines: reaffirming the principle of taxation at the place of consumption, and simplifying traders' obligations via effective tax collection mechanisms that do not impose undue burdens on business.

To assist member governments, the OECD has, for instance, published a Consumption Tax Guidance Series (the "Guidance") to develop greater awareness of policy and administrative issues for e-commerce taxation. This Guidance endorsed draft guidelines set out in a draft report from the

---

[4] Please refer to the OECD's website at: *www.oecd.org/taxation* for publications and documents in relation to electronic commerce.

[5] The Convention comprises a set of principles on the taxation of income and capital, and is used by countries, including the UK, when negotiating bilateral agreements to eliminate double taxation. See further at section 13.27.

[6] Namely; "Attribution of Profit to a Permanent Establishment involved in Electronic Commerce Transactions" and "The Impact of the Communications Revolution on the Application of 'Place of Effective Management' as the Tie Breaker Rule", both released in February 2001; "Place of Effective Management Concept: Suggestions for Changes to the OECD Model Tax Convention" released in May 2003; and "Are the Current Treaty Rules for Taxing Business Profits Appropriate for E-Commerce", final report released in December 2005.

[7] See further below at section 13.30.

OECD's Working Party No.9 on Consumption Taxes to the OECD's Committee on Fiscal Affairs in February 2001,[8] and the UK, together with the Commission and other Member States, contributed to the development of this work. The Guidance addresses tax issues such as defining the place of consumption for cross-border supplies of services and intangible property in the context of e-commerce, verifying customer status and location, simplifying VAT registration procedures, and contains recommended approaches to the practical application of the Guidance.

Although not legally binding, OECD member countries are encouraged to review existing national legislation to determine its compatibility with the Guidance and to align such legislation with the objectives of the Guidance (i.e. to remove conflicts, distortions and disincentives to international trade). In the UK for instance, customer verification guidelines on the latest EU developments for VAT generally mirror the OECD's Guidance on verification.

Meanwhile the Commission's work has led to temporary amendments being made to the EU place of supply rules for charging VAT on the supply over electronic networks of software and other digitised products generally in order to re-establish a balance of competition between EU and non-EU suppliers.

Broadly, these measures provide that supplies of "digitised products" will be taxed in the country where the customer resides, i.e. at the place of consumption, which will ensure that such supplies from non-EU operators to private customers inside the EU are chargeable to EU VAT.

Novel tax administrative measures have also been adopted, allowing the option of simplified registration, filing, and payment mechanisms for assisting compliance by non-EU operators. As it was a particular priority of the Commission to deliver solutions capable of implementation in conformity with the Framework Conditions, the new rules are largely consistent with the OECD's Guidance and the EU is reported to be the first tax jurisdiction to tax internet services in line with the Framework Conditions.

Tax administration and taxpayer service

In the area of tax administration and taxpayer service,[9] OECD governments have reached a broad consensus on the main administrative challenges and opportunities facing tax administrations, and on the type of responses they need to consider in improving the application of technology to tax administration and taxpayer service.

13–006

The general assumption is that technological developments will emerge

---

[8] This report is available for review on the OECD's website at: *http://www.oecd.org/ dataoecd/37/19/2673667.pdf.*

[9] The OECD has established a Forum on Tax Administration and various papers can be found at the following link: *http://www.oecd.org/department/0,2688,en_2649_ 33749_1_1_1_1,00.html.* The Tax Administration Guidance Series is available at: *http:// www.oecd.org/dataoecd/25/30/17851138.pdf.*

and create new methods of administering taxes. However, in the interim, it is essential to maintain and simplify current tax systems to ease burdens, costs and encourage compliance. So a range of options have been reviewed: such as the development of technology to allow non-EU suppliers to remit tax for multiple jurisdictions, the electronic availability of consumption tax rates, comparable/common technical and audit standards across jurisdictions, standardised registration and filing requirements, simplified tax returns and automated tax payments, electronic record-keeping and storage.

A key area for discussion has been jurisdictional verification, i.e. how to satisfactorily identify an internet business, and the mechanisms available for tracing inadequately identified websites and other electronic places of business. A detailed "Tax Administration Guidance Series" has also been created as a result of this work, encouraging appropriate standards for internet business identification (including website contact information), appropriate standards for record-keeping, appropriate transaction data for audit purposes, and accountability in electronic payment systems.

Tax administrations are also being encouraged to share practice and experience and develop systems which will provide a supportive environment (e.g. call centres) for e-commerce traders which have to cope with the sum of requirements for compliance across countries. Finally, on-line government functions for reporting, declaring and collecting tax are now more readily available.

Further implementation work

13–007   In its latest progress report[10] on the implementation of the Framework Conditions, the OECD's Committee on Fiscal Affairs confirms that the most frequently quoted principle during its analysis has been that of the neutrality of taxation between electronic commerce and conventional commerce. However, it has also noted that this principle may be breached if the taxation of e-commerce continues to be studied in isolation to international tax issues impacting conventional commerce.

The OECD's Consumption Tax Technical Advisory Group ("TAG") released a report[11] in 2003 on e-commerce implementation issues which considered two further issues high on the political agenda: the potential for double taxation or non-taxation as a result of conflicting place of supply rules, conflicting definitions, conflicting tax results arising from differences in verification requirements between jurisdictions, and incompatible approaches to "bundling" issues, i.e. where an e-commerce supply involves a number of different elements.

That report identified different approaches which have been taken by countries to the taxation of cross-border services and intangibles in national

---

[10] "Implementation of the Ottawa Taxation Framework Conditions", the 2003 Report, which is available for review at: *http://www.oecd.org/dataoecd/45/19/20499630.pdf*.

[11] The 2003 report is entitled "Implementation Issues for Taxation of Electronic Commerce". See: *http://www.oecd.org/dataoecd/38/42/5594899.pdf*.

tax systems. The emerging international view is that such differences have increased the potential for double taxation and unintentional non-taxation, not just for e-commerce, but in the broader context of international trade in services and intangibles where consistency between countries is increasingly essential. Consequently, focussing on e-commerce issues as a separate category of services alone may mean that issues affecting other internationally traded services will be missed or lead to further international conflicts.

The OECD, through its Committee on Fiscal Affairs, is therefore adopting a more "holistic" approach to taxation, rather than on specific aspects such as e-commerce. This is not to say that the Framework Conditions are no longer relevant—although they were designed in the context of e-commerce, the international view is that they will remain valid as they broadly reflect the philosophies and policy goals of existing tax rules in most countries. However, the Framework Conditions and related work on e-commerce, are now being incorporated into the Committee's mainstream work on international commerce issues.

This is illustrated by the Committee's latest project on the application of consumption taxes to international trade in services and intangibles, for which further tax principles and remedies are being developed, and is also consistent with the approach being taken by the Commission to amend the EU VAT place of supply rules on a wider basis and not just affecting internet traders (see further under the heading "The Future" at section 13.24).

Therefore, it would now seem that any further policy work specifically on e-commerce is only likely to arise as a result of the EU and the OECD's monitoring of e-commerce developments and new technologies, where these may significantly challenge the international consensus reflected in the work achieved to date, and which may necessarily require refinements to treaty rules or new taxes to be introduced.

13.4 UK TAX POLICY AND E-COMMERCE

In October 1998, the former UK Inland Revenue and HM Customs and Excise published a joint paper on UK tax policy[12] regarding e-commerce. Not surprisingly, the paper was almost identical in content to that of the Framework Conditions. At about the same time legislation[13] was passed in the United States which imposed a three year moratorium (until October 2001) on new taxes on internet access fees and prohibited "multiple and

13–008

---

[12] Electronic Commerce: UK Policy on Taxation Issues for the OECD Conference in Ottawa, Canada, October 8–9: News Release 25/98 dated October 6, 1998. This paper enlarged on the tax issues identified in the paper entitled "Net Benefit: The Electronic Commerce Agenda for the UK" published by the UK Department of Trade and Industry on the same date.

[13] Internet Tax Freedom Act of 1998.

discriminatory" taxes on e-commerce at either the state or the federal level. It did not, however, prevent a tax authority from imposing a previously existing tax on e-commerce transactions provided that the tax was equally applicable to e-commerce companies and traditional companies. This legislation also created a Congressionally-appointed Commission, whose remit was to determine how e-commerce should be taxed, if at all.

In April 2005 the Inland Revenue and Her Majesty's Customs and Excise merged departments to become "Her Majesty's Revenue & Customs", (hereafter referred to in this chapter as the "UK Revenue"). Following that merger, the UK's 1998 joint paper regarding e-commerce has been withdrawn, but as an active contributor to the development of international tax policy, the UK has continued to support and implement into its own tax regime the approaches taken by the OECD and the EU on the taxation of e-commerce.

So, on a purely domestic level, UK tax policy seeks to promote the Framework Conditions, particularly the principle of neutrality to ensure that UK residents conducting business via the internet in the UK are taxed in the same way as persons running a traditional, physical business.

Meanwhile in the United States, the Congressionally-appointed Commission concluded its study in 2000 making a series of findings and recommendations but without reaching a consensus on the central issues.[14] In November 2001 new legislation was passed to extend the moratorium introduced by the 1998 Internet Tax Freedom Act for a further two years, and in November 2003 the US House of Representatives passed the Internet Tax Non-Discrimination Bill, a piece of legislation designed to permanently extend the moratorium. That Bill was not approved however by the US Senate and a compromise Bill was subsequently passed in December 2004 which has extended the moratorium by four years (retroactively to November 1, 2003) and is due to expire on November 1, 2007. We have yet to see whether the US Government will permanently extend the moratorium in 2007.

13.5 GROWTH OF E-COMMERCE AND VAT

13–009 The application of VAT to the supply of goods and services via the internet is considered first because, as highlighted above, this area has been given significant attention internationally, and its correct application presents the biggest practical problems for businesses operating over the internet, as well as for tax authorities themselves.

The importance to governments of the correct VAT treatment of e-commerce must be appreciated, as consumption taxes are becoming an increasingly important means of raising tax revenues worldwide. It has

---

[14] The Commission's findings are available for review on its website: *http://www.e-commercecommission.org/*.

recently been reported that consumption taxes account for more than 30 per cent of overall taxation in OECD member countries. Perhaps more tellingly, a VAT (or Goods and Services Tax/GST) is now in place in every OECD Member State except the US (although a sales and use tax operates at the sub-federal level).

In the EU, VAT rates currently vary between 15 per cent and 25 per cent and it typically accounts for one-fifth of a country's total tax receipts,[15] and, as an own resource, for around 15 per cent of the Community's budget. It has also been acknowledged that the substantially increased importance of VAT has served to counteract the diminishing share of other specific consumption taxes, such as excise and custom duties (for example on tobacco, alcoholic drinks and fuels).

In the UK, a report investigating the UK Revenue's administration and collection of VAT on e-commerce was published in May 2006 by the National Audit Office ("NAO").[16] According to the NAO's report, around 22 million Britons shopped on-line in 2005 buying a wide range of items such as CDs, electrical goods, food and holidays, and in the period 2005 to 2006, the UK Revenue collected over £1 billion in VAT on e-commerce goods and services. It is also reported that internet sales in the UK alone are expected to rise to £60 billion a year by April 2010 so that the proportion of UK VAT to be collected from internet sales is likely to grow substantially.

13.6 EU HARMONISATION AND SUMMARY OF UK VAT LAW

VAT is a creature of the EU and its primary legislative basis is the Sixth **13–010** Council Directive (77/388) which has been the subject of substantial amendment since its promulgation in 1977. The Directive has been implemented by local legislation in each Member State. In the UK, the current legislation is mainly to be found in the Value Added Tax Act 1994 and the various Orders and Regulations made thereunder.

VAT is intended eventually to be fully harmonised within the EU. If full harmonisation is achieved, VAT will apply across the boundaries of each EU Member State in a way that it does not at present. Under the current system, each Member State charges VAT at its national rate under its own local legislation and special rules have to apply to cross-border supplies within the EU.

Under a fully harmonised system, transactions within the EU should be treated in the same way as transactions are currently treated if made within the boundaries of a Member State: the "international" element only arising where the transaction involves services supplied to or by a person outside

---

[15] See the attached link for details of VAT rates as at September 2006: *http://ec.europa.eu/taxation_customs/taxation/vat/how_vat_works/rates/index_en.htm.*
[16] The NAO's May 2006 report is entitled "HM Revenue & Customs: VAT on e-commerce". See: *http://www.nao.org.uk/publications/nao_reports/05–06/05061051.pdf.*

the EU, or goods are imported from or exported to a jurisdiction outside the EU. Therefore if full harmonisation is ever achieved, some of the difficulties which arise at present within the EU should be simplified. However, the lack of complete VAT harmonisation in the EU means that there are situations where the VAT rules as applied differently by Member States, constitute obstacles for firms wishing to take advantage of the internal market and may lead to double or unintentional non-taxation of cross-border trade.

Factors such as EU enlargement since May 2004, increases in global trade, and the more widespread use of electronic communications by traders and tax administrations, have nonetheless created a fresh momentum towards VAT harmonisation. This has also been encouraged, for instance, by the Commission's "New Strategy for VAT", launched in June 2000 and updated in 2003,[17] which has four main objectives for improving the current EU VAT system for the benefit of EU taxpayers, namely: simplification and modernisation of existing rules, more uniform application of current rules, and closer administrative co-operation between tax administrations in dealing with issues such as VAT carousel fraud, an increasing concern for Member States.

Over the last few years, the Commission has had relative success as several of its proposals have been unanimously adopted by the European Council. Examples of its success include the new Directive on electronic invoicing which has established some common rules for the content and tranmission of VAT invoices. On October 17, 2005, the Council adopted a Regulation[18] that ensures a more uniform application of certain common rules on VAT by giving force of law to a number of approaches in specific areas such as the place of supply of certain services, and the scope of exemptions from VAT, thereby providing some legal certainty both for traders and for tax administrations.

More recently the Council has adopted a new Directive 2006/112/EC which is a recast of the text of the Sixth Council Directive. The provisions of this new Directive came into force on January 1, 2007.[19] This will not materially change current EU and UK VAT legislation: its main objective being to re-organise the Sixth Council Directive, making it more user-friendly and accessible.

There has also been progress on establishing administrative co-operation between Member States, for example, the adoption of a Directive on mutual assistance for the recovery of tax claims in June 2001,[20] and of

---

[17] Communication from the Commission to the Council, the European Parliament and the European Economic and Social Committee: Review and update of VAT strategy priorities, COM (2003) 614, 20.01.2003. See: *http://eur-lex.europa.eu/LexUriServ/site/en/com/2003/com2003_0614en01.pdf*.

[18] Council Regulation (EC) No. 1777/2005 of October 17, 2005. See: *http://eur-lex.europa.eu/LexUriServ/site/en/oj/2005/l_288/l_28820051029en00010009.pdf*.

[19] We have only referred to the provisions of the Sixth Council Directive in this chapter for ease of reference.

[20] Council Directive 2001/22/EC of June 15, 2001.

Regulations[21] aimed at providing a single legal instrument covering administrative co-operation, including the establishment of a common system for the exchange of information between Member States, whereby administrative authorities are to mutually assist each other and co-operate with the Commission in order to ensure the proper application of VAT (and excise duties) on supplies of goods and services, intra-Community acquisition of goods, and importation of goods.

Notably, as part of its New Strategy for VAT, the Commission has presented several key proposals (since 2004) with the objectives of establishing clearer rules for determining the place of taxation for services by both EU and non-EU operators, and minimising regulatory burdens on businesses engaged in cross-border trade.

13–011

These proposals (labelled the "VAT package" by the European Council) are not confined to traders in e-commerce, although dealing with e-commerce is a major initiative. Broadly, these proposals comprise:

(a) two elements of a VAT simplification proposal, the first being the "One Stop Shop" (which aims to allow traders to fulfil their VAT obligations for EU-wide activities via a simplified electronic system for registration and declaration of EU VAT), and the second being simplified rules for the refund of VAT under EU procedures to traders established in another Member State;

(b) a renewal of the "e-commerce VAT Directive", being Council Directive 2002/38/EC (see further below at section 13.14);

(c) changes to general EU VAT rules on the place of supply (and so the taxation) of services for both business to business and business to consumer transactions[22]; and

(d) further initiatives for improved administrative co-operation to combat VAT fraud more efficiently.

Political agreement still needs to be reached on these proposals. Interestingly, however, the Council has recently announced[23] its intention to take forward work on the VAT package as a matter of priority, with a suggested timetable for political agreement by mid-2007. As a result, EU VAT rules, and thus UK VAT rules, may become subject to various changes and improvements in the foreseeable future which will be of particular importance to e-commerce traders.

---

[21] Council Regulation (EC) No. 1798/2003 of October 7, 2003, and Council Regulation (EC) No. 2073/2004 of November 16, 2004.

[22] "Amended Proposal for a Council Directive amending Directive 77/388/EEC as regards the place of supply of services", COM (2005) 334 final of July 20, 2005, and COM (2004) 728 final of October 29, 2004: *http://eur-lex.europa.eu/LexUriServ/site/en/com/2004/com2004_0728en01.pdf.*

[23] Confirmed in the following press release by the Council: *http://www.consilium.europa.eu/ueDocs/cms_Data/docs/pressData/en/ecofin/91899.pdf.*

13.6.1 Basic elements of VAT

13–012 The essential elements of UK VAT, as currently applied to both conventional and e-commerce vendors, are relatively straightforward and may be summarised in the following propositions:

> UK VAT is generally chargeable in three situations:
>
> (i)   on a supply of goods and services made in the UK;
> (ii) on the acquisition in the UK of goods from another EU Member State; and
> (iii) on the importation of goods into the UK from outside the EU.

We consider each in turn below.

13.6.2 Supplies of goods and services in the United Kingdom

13–013 For the charge to UK VAT under (i) above to apply, each of four elements must be satisfied:

> (i)   there must be a supply of goods or services;
> (ii) the supply must be made in the UK;
> (iii) it must be made by a taxable person in the course or furtherance of a business carried on by him; and
> (iv) the supply must be a taxable supply.

In essence, anything "done for a consideration" will be a supply of either goods or services, unless specifically excluded. One example of an excluded supply is the transfer of the assets of a business as part of the transfer of the business as a going concern. Certain types of supply are expressly defined as supplies of goods or services (so that, for example, a lease of an asset is generally a supply of services while the lease of land for more than 21 years is a supply of goods). While a "supply of goods" is not defined on a general basis in the UK legislation, a supply of services is anything "done for a consideration" which is not a supply of goods.

The complex "place of supply" rules determine in which Member State, if any, a supply of goods or services should be taxed. The result is that UK VAT is only chargeable where the place of supply under these rules is the UK. UK VAT is not chargeable if the place of supply is outside the UK, even if made by a taxable person. If the place of supply is another Member State of the EU, that Member State has the jurisdiction to charge its local equivalent of VAT on the supply. If the place of supply is outside the EU, no Member State has the jurisdiction to charge VAT on the supply although value added or sales tax may be chargeable outside the EU.

These "place of supply" rules are complicated further as they differ fundamentally in their approach in relation to supplies of goods and supplies of services. For goods, the rules essentially look to where the goods are dispatched or made available to the customer. For services, the crucial question is normally where the supplier "belongs". A supplier's place of "belonging" also has a particular meaning for VAT purposes and is broadly the place where that person has its business establishment or some other "fixed establishment",[24] or (in the UK at least), if it has more than one business establishment, that which is most directly concerned with the supply of services in question.

13.6.3 Schedule 5 services

However, there are special place of supply rules for certain types of services, **13–014** in particular those services which are listed in Art.9(2)(e) of the Sixth Council Directive, as implemented in the UK by Sch.5 of the Value Added Tax Act 1994 ("Schedule 5 services"—see Table 13.1 below). Schedule 5 services (which are of particular relevance to the internet) include advertising services, data processing and the provision of information, banking, financial and insurance services, and telecommunication services, (and as of July 1, 2003, radio and television broadcasting services, and certain electronically supplied services but these are subject to extra rules—see sections 13.14 and 13.21).

For these services (other than Table 13.1, item 9) the place of supply will normally be the place where the customer "belongs" if the customer either:

(a) belongs outside the EU (irrespective of whether the customer carries on business or is a private individual); or

(b) belongs in a different Member State to that of the provider, is registered for VAT in that Member State and it receives the supply in its business capacity.

Again, the place where the customer "belongs" has a particular meaning for VAT purposes. In all other cases involving a supply of a Schedule 5 service (for example, where the customer is a private individual who does not use the service for business purposes), the general rule for determining the place of supply of services applies and the place of supply will be where the supplier "belongs".

---

[24] See below at para.13–035.

Table 13.1: Schedule 5 services

Schedule 5 paragraph	Services included
1	Transfers and assignments of copyright, patents, licences, trade marks and similar rights
2	Advertising services
3	Services of consultants, engineers, consultancy, bureaux, lawyers, accountants and other similar services; data processing and provision of information (but not any such services relating to land)
4	Acceptance of any obligation to refrain from pursuing or exercising any business activity or any rights within (1) above
5	Banking, financial and insurance services (including reinsurance but not provision of safe deposit facilities)
6	Supply of staff
7	Letting on hire of goods other than a means of transport
7A	Telecommunication services
7B (with effect from July 1, 2003)	Radio and television broadcasting services
7C (with effect from July 1, 2003)	Electronically supplied services, for example • Website supply, web-hosting and distance maintenance of programmes and equipment • Supply of software and the updating of software • Supply of images, text and information and the making available of databases • The supply of music, films and games (including games of chance and gambling games) • Supply of political, cultural, artistic, sporting, scientific and entertainment broadcasts (including broadcasts of events) • The supply of distance teaching But where the supplier of a service and his customer communicate via electronic mail, this shall not of itself mean that the service performed is an electronically supplied service
8	Services rendered by one person to another in procuring for the other any of the services listed above
9	Any service not within (1)–(7) and (8) above when supplied to a UK taxable person (i.e. a customer who is registered for VAT in the UK)

A "taxable person" is essentially a person who makes taxable supplies in the UK in the course or furtherance of a business carried on by him and the aggregate value of the supplies that have been made by him in the previous 12 months or less, or are expected to be made in the forthcoming 12 months (or in the next 30 days alone), exceeds the prevailing registration limit (this is currently £61,000 in the UK for tax year 2006/2007). Businesses may also register voluntarily for VAT.

A "taxable supply" is a supply of goods or services which is of such a kind that is chargeable to UK VAT at 17.5 per cent (the current standard rate), 5 per cent (the current reduced rate) or nil (that is to say, 0 per cent or the zero rate). An example of a supply of goods chargeable at the reduced rate is the supply of fuel for domestic use, and of a zero rated supply is the sale of young children's clothing and footwear.

It should also be noted that there are three other categories of supply which are important for VAT purposes: exempt supplies where no VAT is chargeable and input tax recovery is not possible (for example certain financial services), "outside the scope" supplies and other supplies treated as not involving a supply of goods or services with the result that VAT is not chargeable. An example of an "outside the scope" supply is the supply of certain international services.

The difference between zero rated and exempt supplies is that "input VAT" is recoverable in relation to zero rated supplies but not for exempt supplies, for which recoverability is "blocked" (see section 13.11 below). Importantly, the zero rate applies to certain types of supply (such as books), the export of goods outside the EU and the supply of goods to another Member State where the purchaser is registered for VAT purposes in that Member State.

13.7 ACQUISITIONS OF GOODS IN THE UK FROM OTHER MEMBER STATES

As mentioned above, a charge to UK VAT also arises on the acquisition in the UK of goods from a supplier in another EU Member State. There are special rules relating to "distance selling" of goods into the UK by persons registered for VAT in another EU Member State. **13–015**

Broadly speaking, the distance selling rules cover sales (for instance, mail order sales) to "non-taxable" UK customers where the EU supplier's aggregate supplies exceed the prevailing special registration limit applicable to distance selling (which in the UK is £70,000 for tax year 2006/2007). A "non-taxable" customer will usually be a private individual, but may also be a public body, charity or any business whose supplies do not exceed the current VAT registration threshold or whose activities are totally exempt.

The effect of the distance selling rules is that the non-taxable customer pays UK VAT rather than VAT in the supplier's home state and the EU supplier becomes liable to be registered in the UK. These rules operate in reverse for supplies of goods made by UK suppliers to non-taxable customers in other EU Member States, although registration limits vary between the Member States.[25]

13.8 IMPORTATION OF GOODS INTO THE UNITED KINGDOM FROM OTHER COUNTRIES

13–016 A charge to UK VAT also arises on the importation of goods into the UK from countries outside the EU ("third countries"). Such a supply of goods is chargeable to UK VAT at the standard rate as if it were a customs duty. This treatment applies if the goods have never previously been exported to the third country from one of the EU Member States and is irrespective of whether the customer is a business or private individual and whether or not the customer is registered for UK VAT.

13.9 IMPORTATION OF SERVICES FROM OTHER COUNTRIES

13–017 There are anti-avoidance provisions which are designed to prevent "partially exempt traders" (see further at para.13–019) from buying services from outside the UK (which if the services had been provided by a UK supplier would have involved a VAT cost). These provisions are known as the "reverse charge" and apply to Schedule 5 services. Where the reverse charge applies, the recipient of the services (rather than the supplier of the services) is required to account for VAT at the rate applicable in the Member State in which he belongs to the relevant tax authority. It also gives the right to input tax deduction in respect of purchases related to taxable outputs.

The effect of the reverse charge in the UK is to treat Schedule 5 services brought in from outside the UK in the same way as services that are actually supplied in the UK if the recipient of the services is VAT registered. It is important to note, however, that the reverse charge has no effect on recipients acting in a private capacity.

13.10 EXPORTS

13–018 As stated in section 13.6.2 above, UK VAT is not chargeable if a supply is treated as made outside the UK. This is the case even if the supply is made

---

[25] The annual registration limit is generally €100,000 or €35,000 but the following sets out which countries have different limits: *http://ec.europa.eu/taxation_customs/resources/documents/taxation/vat/traders/vat_community/vat_in_EC_annexI.pdf*.

by a UK taxable person. However, not all exports/supplies of goods and services from an EU Member State escape VAT.

Generally speaking, the supply of goods to private customers in other EU Member States attracts VAT in the Member State of the supplier, except where the supplier is required to register locally for VAT under the so-called "distance selling" rules described above (in which case local VAT will be chargeable instead). The export of goods outside the EU should not attract VAT in any Member State (subject to the relevant conditions for export being met).

Exports of certain services outside the EU will escape VAT (both UK and EU VAT). These include the "Schedule 5 services" referred to above (which mirror the rules on the importation of such services). As outlined above, exports of most types of Schedule 5 services from one Member State of the EU to another are chargeable to VAT in the Member State where the recipient of the services belongs if the recipient is registered for VAT purposes in that other Member State and receives the services for the purposes of its business.

Exports of Schedule 5 services from EU suppliers to EU private customers continue to attract VAT in the Member State of the supplier. Exports of Schedule 5 services to recipients belonging in third countries do not attract UK (or EU) VAT. There are, however, further special rules relating to the supply of telecommunication, radio and television broadcasting and electronically supplied services, for which see below.

13.11 "INPUT" AND "OUTPUT" VAT

The "cost" of VAT is intended to be borne by the end-user but the tax is collected at different stages in the production process (or "chain of supply"). A VAT-registered person who only makes taxable supplies is able to offset the VAT it pays on supplies received by it ("input tax") against the VAT it charges to its customers on supplies made by it ("output tax"). It pays to the UK Revenue (generally on a monthly or quarterly basis) the difference between its output and input tax (or receives a repayment where input tax exceeds output tax). **13–019**

Where a VAT-registered person makes both taxable and non-taxable supplies (i.e. supplies which are exempt from or outside the scope of VAT), only a proportion of his input tax will be able to be offset or "recoverable" against output tax. This is because input tax is generally only recoverable to the extent it is attributable to taxable supplies. In particular, the recovery of input tax attributable to exempt supplies is blocked (the principle being that the irrecoverability of input tax should be built into the price for the supply).

Businesses which make taxable and exempt supplies are generally referred to as "partially exempt traders", typical examples of which are banks and insurance companies. The recovery of input tax attributable to "outside the scope" supplies varies. Suffice in this context to say that recovery is not blocked in the case of exports of services that would be taxable if made in the UK. Overall, this process aims to ensure the "tax neutrality" of VAT, i.e. by ensuring that businesses in a chain of supply do not incur irrecoverable VAT unless there is some legitimate reason for the VAT burden to be placed on them.

13.12 VAT IMPLICATIONS OF E-COMMERCE

13–020 For EU VAT purposes, anything "done for a consideration" will be a supply of either goods or services and therefore within the VAT regime, unless specifically excluded. This means that where the use of the internet is free, VAT issues will not be relevant because no consideration is given. But, where payment or another form of consideration is given for a supply made over the internet, VAT will be relevant.

In accordance with general principles, UK VAT will be an issue for UK e-businesses if they supply goods or services in or from the UK. It will also be an issue for any non-UK e-business to the extent that the supply is treated as taking place in the UK.

As for conventional supplies, internet suppliers will need to ascertain the nature of their supplies (goods or services), the place of supply, and the status and location of their customer to establish the correct liability. They would also need to consider whether they need to register for VAT and if so, how they would account and pay such VAT and at what rate, as well as how to recover any input tax.

These compliance issues present a number of challenges for tax administrations and for e-businesses, such as having to manage different rules applying across multiple jurisdictions in which the business makes supplies, getting appropriate transaction information via the internet in real time, and verifying the status and location of a remote customer in the absence of any face-to-face interaction.

All these issues are further complicated by the fact that users of the internet are afforded a certain degree of anonymity (in terms of identity, location and/or transactions) and the internet itself has no respect for national borders. Moreover, the internet and new technologies have introduced new distribution channels for sales which have raised questions about the nature of the supply and how it should be taxed.

In contrast, there may be many instances where using the internet or other electronic networks makes no difference to the way a supply will be taxed. The nature of a transaction is not changed, for example, where parties simply use the internet to communicate in the course of a business transaction or to facilitate trading (i.e. taking and processing orders or receiving payment).

The position is more complex however in relation to a supply that is completely dependent on the internet in order to be carried out, for example, searching and retrieving information from a database with no human intervention or the supply of "digitised products". Digitised products mean those forms of intangible property (computer software, information, music, text, video) that are able to be accessed and downloaded via the internet directly from the content provider. They are not tangible products when received initially by internet users. A tangible product may be created thereafter (by downloading onto a CD) but that would be a matter of choice.

From the outline of the current system of VAT that operates in the UK and EU (as given above), it will also be apparent that the place of supply rules for services (based on where the supplier belongs) offer scope for tax planning by locating a supplier's business establishment in a tax friendly environment outside the EU, thus avoiding EU VAT. As mentioned above, there are provisions in the legislation designed to prevent such devices and ensure the charging of EU VAT, such as the reverse charge procedure (in relation to Schedule 5 services) and the use and enjoyment principle (for which see section 13.21 below). However questions have arisen as to how effective these existing provisions are and whether, particularly in light of the lack of complete VAT harmonisation in Europe, any distortions of competition, or double taxation or unintentional non-taxation, can be avoided.

Furthermore, the opportunities that the internet has offered to businesses of all sizes cannot be underestimated. Importantly, suppliers of goods and/or services over the internet no longer need a physical presence in the country of their customers, and with the rapid increase in the levels of supplies of services over the internet from outside the EU to EU customers, this has raised concerns about the effects of the place of supply of services rules on competition and the internal market within Europe.

These points can be brought out more clearly by looking in some further detail at the relevance of VAT to business conducted over the internet falling within the following five broad categories of transaction:

(i)   supplies of physical goods to both business and private customers;
(ii)   business to business supplies of "electronically supplied services" and digitised products;
(iii)   business to private customer supplies of "electronically supplied services" and digitised products;
(iv)   supplies of telecommunication services, or radio and television broadcasting services and the application to each (as well as to "electronically supplied services") of the use and enjoyment principle; and
(v)   supplies of "packages" containing a variety of internet related elements.

Before looking at these however, the adoption and implementation in the UK of the e-commerce VAT Directive (as mentioned in para.13–011) needs to be considered.

13.13 PREVIOUS SHORTCOMINGS IN EU VAT PLACE OF SUPPLY OF SERVICES RULES

13–021 In line with the Framework Conditions, a supply of digitised products is a supply of services and not goods and the UK subscribes to this approach. This means that the place of supply rules in relation to the supply of services (and not goods) would determine which country (if any) has the jurisdiction to charge VAT on such products.

Before July 1, 2003, supplies of digitised products were liable to EU VAT based on the general rule, i.e. where the supplier was established. The effect of this however was that non-EU suppliers did not have to charge VAT on these supplies to EU customers (by reason of the supplier belonging outside the EU).

An EU operator, on the other hand, was required to charge VAT at the applicable rate in their Member State on such supplies to all their customers, irrespective of the customer's location. Business customers based outside the EU and customers registered for VAT in another Member State would then need to claim this VAT back under the unwieldy terms of the Eighth or Thirteenth Directives. This situation clearly offended against the principle of neutrality as it had the potential to distort competition and place EU service providers at a competitive disadvantage to non-EU suppliers when selling to EU customers.

An example of the "unequalness of the playing field" in the UK is given in the 2003 case of *R. (on the application of Freeserve.com Plc) v Customs and Excise Commissioners (America On Line Inc. (AOL))*.[26] Freeserve, based in the United Kingdom, sought judicial review proceedings against the Commissioners' decision not to proceed against its US rival, AOL, in respect of VAT on its mixed telecoms supplies to EU customers. While Freeserve was required to account for VAT on comparable supplies, AOL, being classified as an internet services and content (as opposed to predominantly a telecommunications) provider based outside the EU was not required to charge VAT on supplies to UK customers, conferring on AOL the ability to undercut the prices of their UK competitor. That advantage has now disappeared as a result of the changes which are discussed below.

Furthermore, it was recognised that existing provisions did not comprehensively take account of the full range of services which could be delivered electronically, which meant that there was a "lacuna" in the coverage of the Sixth Council Directive caused by technological change and a need to ensure consistent application of the tax.

---

[26] [2003] EWHC 2736.

13.14 THE E-COMMERCE VAT DIRECTIVE—FROM JULY 1, 2003

In June 2000, the Commission proposed[27] a Council Directive to create a **13–022** "level playing field" between EU and non-EU businesses in respect of the VAT treatment of outbound digitised products. This objective would be achieved by ensuring that, when such services were supplied for consumption within the EU, the supplies would be subject to EU VAT, and where such supplies were supplied for consumption outside the EU, no EU VAT would be chargeable, consistent with the Framework Conditions.

These proposals eventually led to the adoption on May 7, 2002, of Council Directive 2002/38/EC,[28] the so-called "e-commerce VAT Directive". This Directive amended the special EU place of supply rules for certain services at Art.9(2)(e) (the legislative basis for Schedule 5 services in the UK) so as to establish two additional categories of services, being "electronically supplied services" (including digitised products and content provision) and "radio and television broadcasting services".

The provisions of this Directive were required to be adopted into the national laws of all Member States on July 1, 2003. They have been implemented into UK national law, via the insertions of paras 7B and 7C to Sch.5 of the Value Added Tax Act 1994[29] with effect for services performed after June 30, 2003. Therefore, in the UK, the new rules operate under the umbrella of "Schedule 5 services" according to the special rules already discussed, but with an additional complexity in the case of electronically supplied services. For these services, the place of supply will be the place where the customer "belongs" if the customer either:-

(a) belongs outside the EU (irrespective of whether the service is used for business and non-business purposes); or

(b) belongs in another Member State to that of the content provider, is registered for VAT in that Member State and receives the supply in its business capacity, in which case the recipient will account for local VAT under the applicable reverse charge procedure; or

(c) (with effect from July 1, 2003), belongs in a different Member State to that of the content provider, is not registered or liable to be registered for VAT in the UK (or the EU) and receives the supply in a non-business or private capacity from a supplier who belongs outside the EU.

---

[27] The Commission's proposals are available for review at the following link: *http://eur-lex.europa.eu/LexUriServ/site/en/com/2000/com2000_0349en01.pdf.*

[28] The Directive is available for review at: *http://eur-lex.europa.eu/LexUriServ/site/en/oj/2002/l_128/l_12820020515en00410044.pdf.*

[29] Implemented at UK level via the VAT (Reverse Charge) (Amendment) Order 2003 (SI 2003/863).

Consequently, a UK supplier of these services will no longer be required to account for VAT on supplies of electronically supplied services to businesses in other EU Member States or to non-EU customers, whilst UK businesses receiving electronically supplied services from non-UK suppliers will have to account for UK VAT using the reverse charge procedure.

Non-EU suppliers will be required to register and account for UK VAT on supplies to UK private customers. In all other cases, the general rule for determining the place of supply will apply and the place of supply will therefore be where the content provider "belongs". A UK supplier will, for example, continue to charge UK VAT on these supplies to UK customers (private or business) or to other EU private customers who receive the service other than for business purposes.

The special measures for non-EU established service providers at (c) above do not apply to radio and television broadcasting services so the rules are more simplistic—they are a Schedule 5 service and the place of supply is determined according to the special rules already discussed for other Schedule 5 services.

However, as distinct from other Schedule 5 services, the place of supply of electronically supplied services, radio and television broadcasting services, and telecommuniction services, may also be determined, in certain circumstances, according to where those services are effectively "used and enjoyed". This extra rule is derived from Art.9(3) of the Sixth Council Directive, allowing countries to deal with place of supply situations where the EU VAT position would otherwise be distortive, and is discussed further at section 13.21 below. Two tables are also provided in this chapter at section 13.21 (paras 13–040 and 13–041) setting out a convenient summary of the new place of supply rules as applied in the UK to such services.

To assist with the interpretation of the definition of "electronically supplied services", the European Council suggested that, when enacting the e-commerce VAT Directive, illustrative examples of these services should be included in an annex to the Directive, and this has led to the production of Annex L, a set of EU Guidelines with the intention of helping businesses decide whether their services fall within the new place of supply rules for electronically supplied services.

The new rules are wide-ranging and cover supplies by internet service providers; providers of on-line content services and databases; sellers of on-line software applications and upgrades, as well as suppliers of websites and web-hosting facilities. To assist taxpayers in applying the new rules, the UK Revenue has also published guidelines in several VAT Information Sheets.[30] These guidelines include helpful flowcharts on the application of the new rules depending on whether the supplier is based in the UK, another Member State, or outside the EU.

---

[30] These Sheets are available on the UK Revenue's website at the following link: *http://customs.hmrc.gov.uk/channelsPortalWebApp/channelsPortalWebApp.portal?_nfpb=true&_pageLabel=pageImport_ShowContent&id=HMCE_CL_001460&propertyType=document.*

13.15 SIMPLIFIED REGISTRATION—THE SPECIAL SCHEME

The changes in the place of supply rules described above are linked to a **13–023** number of facilitation and simplification measures to make VAT compliance as straightforward as possible. This is because concerns had been raised about the various administrative compliance difficulties facing a non-EU supplier now that supplies of electronically supplied services to non-taxable, private customers would be taxable in the recipient's country; particularly, the potential prospect of a non-EU supplier being required, under normal EU VAT rules, to register separately and account for VAT in each and every Member State in which it makes those supplies.

Consequently, to avoid multiple registrations, the e-commerce VAT Directive has introduced a "special scheme" which provides non-EU suppliers an optional, simplified means of registering and accounting electronically for EU VAT on electronically supplied services. Council Regulations[31] have also been adopted alongside the e-commerce VAT Directive concerning the registration of non-EU operators under the special scheme and a framework for the distribution of VAT receipts and exchange of data needed for confirmation purposes to the appropriate Member States where the services are consumed. This scheme does not apply to non-EU businesses supplying broadcasting or other Schedule 5 services.

Broadly, the "special scheme" allows non-EU businesses to register with a single European tax administration of their choice and account for the VAT at the rates applicable in the Member States of consumption on a single quarterly electronic VAT declaration in a standard format showing the details of taxable activities over the different Member States. This is then submitted, together with payment, to that chosen administration. That tax administration would then distribute the VAT to the relevant Member States where the services are consumed, thus avoiding the need to register in every Member State. The aim of the scheme is to put non-EU operators in a comparable position to EU operators dealing with only one tax administration.

UK legislation on the special scheme is set out in s.3A and Sch.3B to the Value Added Tax Act 1994. To put the scheme into operation, the UK Revenue has established the "VAT on e-Services" web service at the dedicated website *http://secure.hmce.gov.uk/ecom/voes* for non-EU suppliers who want to register in the UK. This is a secure site which provides further guidance on the electronic registration process and on completing and submitting electronic VAT returns and paying online. VAT Information Sheets 07/03 and 10/03 also provide helpful guidance to non-EU operators on the operation of this special scheme. Further details of how it operates in the UK are given at section 13.20.1

---

[31] Council Regulation (EC) No. 792/2002 of May 7, 2002, and also Council Regulation (EC) No. 1798/2003 of October 7, 2003.

The measures of the e-commerce VAT Directive were initially limited to a period of three years. When enacted, the above-mentioned facilitation measures allowing non-EU traders to register in a single Member State for VAT compliance purposes were regarded as a significant departure from existing norms of requiring taxpayers to deal directly with each relevant tax administration for VAT purposes. Although limited in coverage to non-established e-commerce service suppliers, their novelty led to a requirement for a review of the Directive before June 30, 2006. That review would either lead to the adoption of revised non-discriminatory measures for charging and collecting VAT on electronically supplied services or an extension of the period beyond its expiry date, July 1, 2006.

Following a report from the Commission to the European Council in May 2006[32] concluding that the Directive was "well-settled" and had met its objectives, the period of its expiry was extended to December 31, 2006, and in late November 2006, the Council approved a renewal of the Directive until the end of 2008, pending further work on the Commission's "VAT package" proposals (see further at section 13.24.1). Without this extension in time, the VAT rules would have reverted back to those prevailing before July 1, 2003, which, in the Commission's view, would have been wholly unwelcome.

13.16 WHAT ARE "ELECTRONICALLY SUPPLIED SERVICES"?

13–024 At the time of writing, there have been no significant court decisions on the meaning of this term. However, Annex L which is a set of EU Guidelines that received unanimous agreement of Member States, including the UK, is an important point of reference as to how "electronically supplied services" may be interpreted within the EU. It is referred to in VAT Information Sheet 04/03, and has been given legal force by Council Regulation EC No.1777/2005 with effect from July 1, 2006.

Annex L gives examples of transactions that are either included or excluded from the definition of "electronically supplied services". There may also be other services which will be relevant to e-commerce but which are not in fact Schedule 5 services and/or are excluded from the definition of "electronically supplied services". For those types of services and for supplies of goods, the normal rules will apply, so that the place of supply will be treated as taking place where the supplier belongs. As intended by the Commission, the illustrations in Annex L are not overly definitive as they should be sufficiently broad to take account of new innovations and e-commerce developments.

---

[32] "Report from the Commission to the Council on Council Directive 2002/38/EC of May 7, 2002", COM (2006) 210 final of May 15, 2006. See: *http://ec.europa.eu/taxation_customs/resources/documents/taxation/vat/*COM(2006)210_en.pdf.

Essentially, an "electronically supplied service" is one which:

(i) in the first instance is delivered over the internet or other electronic network including telecommunications (fixed or mobile), intranets and extranets, whether public or private (i.e. in other words reliant on the internet or similar network for its provision); and

(ii) the nature of the service in question is heavily dependent on information technology for its supply.

Common indicators of an electronically supplied service which is likely to be heavily dependent upon the internet for its provision (i.e. accessing and downloading), are a high degree of automation, often with minimal human intervention and which, in the absence of information technology, has no viability. Accordingly, an electronically supplied service would include:

- Digitised products generally, such as software and changes to or upgrades of software that are intangible and are provided over electronic networks where there is digital, rather than physical, delivery of the product;
- Website supply, web-hosting, web page hosting, and automated, on-line distance maintenance of programmes and equipment;
- Downloaded music, films or games;
- Downloaded images, text or information, including use of search engines and the provision of advertising space;
- Digitised books or other electronic publications;
- Web-based broadcasting of, for example, cultural or sporting events, which is only provided over the internet or similar electronic network and is not simultaneously broadcast over a traditional radio or television network; and
- The supply of distance teaching (for example, workbooks completed on-line and marked automatically, without human intervention).

Electronically supplied services would also include a service which provides or supports a business or personal presence on a website or web page; a service automatically generated from a computer, via the internet or other electronic network, in response to specific data input from the customer; and services other than those listed which are automated and depend on the internet or other electronic network for their provision. Importantly, services which are included within the definition but which are not explicitly listed are:

(i) online auction services (to the extent that they are not already considered to be web-hosting services) that are dependent on automated databases and data input by the customer requiring little or no human intervention (for example, an on-line market place or shopping portal); and

(ii) internet service packages in which the telecommunications component is an ancillary and subordinate part (in other words a package that goes beyond mere internet access comprising various elements, for example, content pages containing news, weather, travel information, games fora, web-hosting, access to chat lines and so on).

Annex L also confirms that these services will be standard-rated within the EU unless an exempting provision in a Member State applies. For example, when considering the supply of gambling, if the supply in the traditional manner is exempt in a Member State, it would also be exempt if it constituted a supply of an electronically supplied service. This treatment does not however apply where a comparable supply is made in the traditional manner and is either zero rated or reduced.[33]

13.16.1 Exclusions

13-025   As indicated above, Annex L lists a number of exclusions that are not regarded as electronically supplied services. For example, supplies where the internet, or other electronic network, is only used as a means of communication to facilitate a supply (i.e. where parties use email, in the same way as telephone or fax, to convey information in the course of a business transaction) should not result in the underlying supply being treated as electronically supplied. The UK subscribes to this approach, which is thus restated at para.7C of Sch.5.

Telecommunications, radio and television broadcasting services are not "electronically supplied services". For UK VAT purposes, telecommunication services are defined as services relating to the transmission, emission or reception of signals, writing, images and sounds or information of any nature by wire, radio, optical or other electromagnetic systems, including the related transfer or assignment of the right to use such capacity for such transmission, emission or reception and the provision of access to global information networks (with effect from July 1, 2003).[34] This definition draws on definitions that were previously adopted at international level and will also include international telephone call routing and termination services, as well as basic access to the internet and the World Wide Web. Radio and television broadcasting services are defined (see VAT Information Sheet 01/03) as including audio and video signals, regardless of the means used such as landline, line of sight or satellite link.

An example of a service covered is a subscription for satellite or cable television. However, the service of transmitting another person's material by electronic means is not a broadcasting service, rather it is a tele-

---

[33] See later at para.13-028.
[34] As a result of Value Added Tax (Reverse Charge) (Amendment) Order 2003 (SI 2003/863), Art.(1), Art.2(2).

communications service[35] (although this distinction should have no practical effect in relation to their VAT treatment).

Importantly the following are also excluded from the definition of electronically supplied services; supplies which rely on substantial human intervention (for example, the physical repair services of computer equipment; advertising services such as in newspapers and on television; telephone helpdesk services; a lawyer advising a client via email; interactive teaching services via remote link) and supplies of goods, such as CDs, DVDs or other goods where the order and processing are conducted electronically (see further under the next heading).

13.17 SUPPLIES OF PHYSICAL GOODS TO BOTH BUSINESS AND PRIVATE CUSTOMERS

An example of the kind of transaction contemplated here is where the internet user visits a website and uses the internet as a means of communication in order to conclude a contract for home delivery of goods with payment, e.g. by way of credit card. The goods so ordered are delivered to the user by traditional means such as the post.

13–026

As already indicated, there is little difference between this type of internet transaction and a conventional mail order sale and, generally speaking, the existing VAT rules are readily applicable to such a situation. The place of supply is also easier to determine for supplies of goods involving physical delivery, since the supplier would normally need to know the source and destination of the goods in order to deliver them. The new rules on "electronically-supplied services", or other Schedule 5 services, are not therefore relevant. However, e-businesses using the internet to facilitate a supply of goods will have to overcome compliance issues, such as verifying on-line the status of its customer during the ordering process.

From a UK perspective, the transaction will either be a "supply" of goods made in the UK, an "acquisition" of goods in the UK from another Member State of the EU, or the "import" of goods into the UK from a territory outside the EU with the following consequences (just as if the customer had purchased the goods from a shop or via mail order):

(i)   If the supplier of the goods and the customer are both in the UK, the supplier must charge UK VAT at the standard rate on the supply (unless the supply is an exempt or zero rated supply for UK

---

[35] The example given by the UK Revenue in VAT Information Sheet 01/03 is that of a company transmitting the programmes of a subscription TV company via satellite. The transmitting company is supplying telecommunications services within para.7A of Sch.5 to the subscription company, whereas that latter company is supplying broadcasting to its subscribers. See: *http://customs.hmrc.gov.uk/channelsPortalWebApp/channelsPortalWeb App.portal?_nfpb=true&_pageLabel=pageImport_ShowContent&id=HMCE_CL_000902 &propertyType=document.*

VAT purposes, such as the supply of books) and account to the UK Revenue for the VAT so charged.

(ii) Goods ordered via the internet and supplied by a UK supplier to private customers in another EU Member State (in effect, all customers who are not registered for VAT in the Member State in which they belong) will generally attract UK VAT at the standard rate, unless the supplier is required to register locally for VAT under the distance selling rules (as outlined in para.13–015). If this is the case, the supplier will be required to register, charge and account for VAT in the customer's Member State at the rate applicable in that state.

(iii) Goods ordered via the internet and supplied by a UK supplier to a VAT-registered customer in another EU Member State who receives the supply for the purposes of a business carried on by him will be zero rated (under certain conditions) in the United Kingdom (or in EU terms "exempt with input tax recovery") and may attract VAT at the rate applicable in the customer's Member State, accountable under a reverse charge procedure.

(iv) Exports of goods ordered via the internet by a UK supplier to customers in third countries will generally be zero rated or outside the scope of UK VAT and may be subject to any relevant sales (or use, turnover or consumption) tax in the third country.

(v) Acquisitions of goods by a UK customer from a supplier based in another EU Member State will attract either VAT in the Member State of the supplier or UK VAT, depending upon the circum-stances. Generally speaking, if the customer is VAT registered, he will be required to pay and account for UK VAT on the supply, whereas, if the customer is a private customer, VAT will be chargeable and accountable in the supplier's Member State.

(vi) Imports of goods into the UK from third countries will attract UK import VAT.

UK import VAT is the liability of the importer and is applied as though it were a duty of customs. The importer may be the supplier or the customer. If the title in the goods passes to the UK customer prior to importation, it is the customer who will be the importer for VAT purposes. The value of the goods for UK import VAT purposes will be their customs value plus, if not already included in the price, all incidental expenses such as commission, packing, transport and insurance costs, and any customs and/or excise duty or levy payable upon importation into the UK.

In the simplest of cases, and assuming that the goods will be sent by post to the UK and that the value of the goods does not exceed £2000, the VAT (and duty) payable is paid by the purchaser to Royal Mail/Parcelforce when the parcel is delivered. This treatment may, however, change if, for example, the third country supplier has an agent in the UK which imports the goods and then uses such stocks to satisfy orders placed with the third country supplier. To assist taxpayers, the UK Revenue has now published guidance on the application of duties and import VAT on common goods such as DVDs bought via the internet into the UK.[36]

There are also a number of reliefs in the UK from the charge to import VAT. Most relevant to the import of goods into the UK ordered via the internet, is that no UK VAT is charged on such import of goods (other than alcoholic beverages, tobacco products, perfumes or toilet waters) not exceeding £18 in value or small occasional non-commercial consignments less than £36 in value consigned by one private individual to another.   **13–027**

This relief has however come under recent scrutiny. In the 2006 Budget, the UK Government announced that it is keeping under close review the way in which some UK businesses have restructured their activities abroad to take advantage of this relief. Some UK mainland businesses have complained that they are losing turnover on low value goods (such as CDs and DVDs) through losing customers to those businesses which are selling directly from places such as the Channel Islands, where postage rates are lower and no local VAT is applied. Those businesses have been able to undercut prices by exporting UK goods to the Channel Islands and mailing them back to the UK free of import VAT using the relief. It is understood however that the States of Jersey Government have recently announced measures to restrain UK traders from establishing themselves in Jersey and supplying such goods to private customers in the UK.

Another significant problem in relation to the supply of goods through e-commerce is that faced by the taxing authorities in ensuring that VAT is properly charged and collected where appropriate, especially where it is a supplier in a third country making a supply to a recipient in the EU. The application of customs duties to such supplies of goods also has its problems (see section 13.25 below).

It is interesting to note in this respect the NAO's report (mentioned in para.13–009 above) on e-commerce risks affecting import VAT. The main risk identified is that some overseas businesses are not correctly describing or valuing the content of commercial packages for import VAT purposes, therefore raising the potential for tax evasion. The report acknowledges however that the UK Revenue has recognised this type of activity, and that it is responding by strengthing border controls and operating checks at the point of dispatch in partnership with overseas organisations to safeguard the collection of import VAT due on such consignments.

A further point to note is that there can be differences between the VAT treatment of a conventional sale of goods and its equivalent transaction on or via the internet. This can be of relevance to the rate of VAT charged and there may be additional issues (for example, related to the place of supply) if the equivalent transaction is a supply of services (and not "goods").   **13–028**

---

[36] This guidance from the UK Revenue: "Shopping on the Internet", is available at: *http:// customs.hmrc.gov.uk/channelsPortalWebApp/channelsPortalWebApp.portal?_nfpb=true &_pageLabel=pageVAT_ShowContent&id=HMCE_CL_001454&propertyType= document.*

Two UK cases before the adoption of the e-commerce VAT Directive illustrate this point. One concerned an "e-meal" facility which involved the ordering of sandwiches, confectionary and drinks from a catering company by electronic mail.[37] The catering company would deliver the food ordered to the client's premises.

Customs and Excise (pre-merger) argued that the treatment of this arrangement differed from a conventional cold food takeaway shop and that the service was standard rated (as a supply of catering services) rather than zero rated (as a supply of food). This argument was, however, rejected by the court who viewed the arrangement as no different from a telephone ordering service (which could be zero rated).

However, in *Forexia (UK) Ltd*,[38] the London VAT and Duties Tribunal upheld a decision that the publication and distribution of a regular news service communicated to most customers by fax, electronic mail or by accessing their website was a supply of services (namely the provision of information) which was standard rated when supplied in the UK. In contrast, a supply of a book or other written material (such as a brochure, pamphlet or newspaper) is treated as a supply of goods which, if supplied in the UK, is zero rated.

The Tribunal reached its decision with the "greatest reluctance". Amongst the reasons given for this reluctance was the fact that such a decision clearly offended against the principle of neutrality (between e-commerce and traditional commerce) and produced distortion of competition.

Unfortunately, these inconsistencies have not been removed by the e-commerce VAT Directive so that, in the case of digital sales of printed matter (e.g. books, newspapers), no zero rating will apply.

When reviewing implementation issues for the taxation of e-commerce, business members of the OECD's Consumption Tax TAG raised concerns about this very subject: namely, that by defining digitised products as services and not goods, differing channels of delivery results in different tax rates and discrimination.

However, this differential treatment has been justified by governments, including the UK Revenue, and by the Commission,[39] on the basis that the supply of digitised information services is not necessarily the direct equivalent of the traditional or hard copy product, as it often provides more functionality (for example, search facilities, hyperlinks, archives, updated information) which, it is argued, can produce a "fundamentally different" product to the point where the tax treatment should be different. As noted by critics however, it is difficult to see how there is a "fundamental difference" which can justify the different tax treatment of, for example,

---

[37] *Emphasis Limited* [1995] V.A.T.D.R. 419 (13759).
[38] VAT and Duties Tribunal Decision No.16041, April 22, 1999.
[39] One of the FAQs on the Commission's website in relation to the e-commerce VAT Directive is *"will the Directive ensure neutrality between traditional and electronic media?"* See further at: *http://ec.europa.eu/taxation_customs/taxation/vat/how_vat_works/e-services/article_1610_en.htm#7neutrality.*

distance learning on-line (standard rated) compared with distance learning via a paper correspondence course (zero rated).

The result is that, while there will be no discrimination between content supplied via traditional media and that supplied electronically if such content is standard rated (since electronically supplied services are also standard rated), where reduced or zero rates apply, for example, to printed material, these inconsistencies will remain. Although not a major issue given the range of e-commerce, this does leave questions concerning neutrality unresolved and will continue to be problematic for businesses in supplying such digitised products.

13.18 IMPORTATION OF COMPUTER SOFTWARE

The VAT treatment of computer software is another example where there is **13–029** a difference between e-commerce transactions and their conventional equivalent. While software downloaded via the internet will be treated as a supply of services, the UK VAT treatment on the importation of tangible software from a country outside the EU will be treated as a supply of goods and/or services depending on whether, at the time of importation, the software is "normalised" (off the shelf) or "specific" (custom made or bespoke).

If the software is "normalised" software, it will be regarded as an importation of goods (made up of the carrier medium) and services (the data and/or the instructions). Examples given by the UK Revenue are home computer software and games packages.

Where the goods and services are not identified separately, the whole importation may be treated as an importation of goods which means that UK VAT at 17.5 per cent must be paid on the goods at the time of importation or under duty deferment arrangements. If, however, the customer is registered for VAT in the United Kingdom, and the value of the goods and services are separately identified, the customer may pay VAT on importation only on the cost or value of the carrier medium and VAT on the supply of the service element may be accounted for by the customer under the reverse charge procedure.

If the software is bespoke software, the importation of such an item is also made up of an importation of goods (the carrier medium) and a supply of services (the data and/or the instructions). However, to simplify import procedures, the carrier medium is treated as an accessory to the data and the importation is treated as a supply of services to the customer. No import VAT is therefore charged on the carrier medium at importation. However, if the customer is registered for VAT in the UK, he may be required to account for VAT at 17.5 per cent on the licence fee under the reverse charge procedure.

13.19 BUSINESS TO BUSINESS SUPPLIES OF ELECTRONICALLY SUPPLIED SERVICES AND DIGITISED PRODUCTS

13–030 Even before the introduction of "electronically supplied services", the application of existing VAT rules to these supplies did not, generally speaking, cause many problems: the VAT treatment of supplies of services between businesses simply delivered via the internet was determined by the actual nature of the services, rather than their means of delivery. The result was that it was necessary to determine the precise nature of the service provided in order to decide the appropriate place of supply rules and thereby the EU Member State (if any) which had the jurisdiction to levy VAT.

Take, for instance, the example of a website owner deriving income from advertisements held on its web page. This could be treated as a supply of advertising services to the advertiser. Advertising services are a Schedule 5 service and so the place of supply (and the place where VAT was chargeable and by whom it would be accounted for to the relevant tax authorities) would be determined by applying the special place of supply rules which relate to Schedule 5 services (given above at section 13.6.3). Invariably, the supply of digitised products would involve the provision of Schedule 5 services, such as the provision of information and/or the grant or transfer of intellectual property rights.

Therefore, the changes to the EU place of supply rules have probably had little practical impact on businesses whose services were already taxed as Schedule 5 services, since they will continue to be treated as such under the new place of supply rules for "electronically supplied services".

However, if, under the previous rules, the service was not within one of the categories of Sch.5, the general place of supply rule would have applied with the result that the place of supply would have been by reference to where the supplier was located. Such services could have included, for example, subscriptions to broadcasting services and internet related services such as website design and website hosting. Thus, where a supplier was based outside of the EU, EU VAT would not have been chargeable on these particular supplies to customers inside the EU, and consequently this would have given rise to a distortion of competition between EU and non-EU service providers as outlined above.

The provisions of the e-commerce VAT Directive, together with Annex L, have now helped to address these issues by clearly identifying a wider range of services delivered over the internet as subject to EU VAT, as well as eliminating the distortion of competition that could have arisen between EU and non-EU operators in cases where such services were not treated as Schedule 5 services.

A further point to note is that, under the previous rules, there were sometimes differences between the VAT treatment of a conventional supply of services and its equivalent transaction on or via the internet. For example, the supply of conventional translation services and educational and training services are generally treated for VAT purposes as supplied where the service is performed. However, where these services are supplied over the internet, the service could not be treated as supplied where performed since the supply did not involve physical performance. Such characterisation issues have generally been resolved as a result of the e-commerce VAT Directive but inconsistencies may remain, especially where other countries do not apply the same place of supply rules to determine the place of consumption.

To encourage consistency among member countries, the OECD's Guidance (mentioned at para.13–005) provides two guidelines on defining the place of consumption in the case of business to business e-commerce transactions where the customer is not resident in the same country as the supplier. **13–031**

First, it recommends that the place of consumption and taxation should be the jurisdiction in which the recipient has located its "business presence". This would be in principle the establishment of the recipient (for example, its headquarters, registered office, or branch of the business) to which the supply is made.

The OECD builds on this in the case of customers with multiple locations. In those cases, normal commercial practices as evidenced in the terms of any contract (for example, invoices, terms of payment, use of intellectual property rights), will be important and should normally provide sufficient indicative evidence to assist businesses and tax authorities in determining the business presence.

Where the application of this test could lead to distortion of competition or tax avoidance opportunities, for example from the routing of services through low tax jurisdictions, the OECD recommends an additional rule, called the "override criterion", which would operate to ensure that VAT accrued where consumption actually took place. This is generally represented by the EU application of the "use and enjoyment" principle as applied in the UK (discussed further at section 13.21).

The question as to how the above-mentioned first guideline should be practically applied for these types of transactions highlights a further problem, especially for VAT authorities, of VAT collection, particularly where Schedule 5 services are supplied to business customers who belong in a different Member State to that in which the supplier of the service belongs.

The OECD's Guidance proposes that the reverse charge procedure be retained as the basis for taxing cross-border e-commerce transactions between businesses, thereby making use of a mechanism with which businesses and administrations would already be familiar. This approach is consistent with the changes now introduced by the e-commerce VAT Directive. The use of the reverse charge mechanism also minimises the impact of the new rules on non-EU businesses, since it is the business customer who accounts for the VAT, not the overseas supplier.

The reverse charge mechanism is therefore applied to ensure that local suppliers are not unfairly disadvantaged (as compared with non-local suppliers), that VAT is accounted for and that the non-local supplier is not required to register for VAT in the customer's home state. The collection of VAT however relies on the business customer voluntarily accounting for VAT in his own Member State, the question begs asking as to how truly efficient this mechanism is for collecting VAT.

In its 2006 review of the e-commerce VAT Directive, the Commission concluded however that the collection of VAT by importing businesses under reverse charge arrangements is well-established and operates in a satisfactory manner by producing the right balance between tax collection and simplified obligations. As a result, in the absence of technological advances on tax collection mechanisms, it is likely that the reverse charge mechanism will continue to be applied in relation to e-commerce transactions between businesses.

Consequently, verifying the status (as well as the location) of a customer will be central to any taxing decision by a supplier in order to be sure that the reverse charge should be applied. The e-commerce VAT Directive does not give any guidance on how operators should make the distinction between business and non-business status, nor on acceptable methods of verifying the location of the customer.

There is however guidance on this from the OECD and, as noted by the NAO, the UK has produced guidance which closely mirrors the OECD's recommendations for suppliers of electronically supplied services on identifying the status and location of customers following the implementation of the e-commerce VAT Directive (see VAT Information Sheet 05/03 "*Electronically supplied services: Evidence of customer location and status*" April 2003).

In the guidance, the UK Revenue generally assumes that, under normal trading practices, suppliers would often know their business customers and where they are located, but that this would be less likely for lower value transactions with business customers with which the supplier does not have an established relationship (and for transactions with private customers). It also recognises that suppliers may already have in place established procedures to identify and verify the country where their customer belongs, and it would therefore seek to rely as far as possible on those procedures to ensure that suppliers are not burdened with unnecessary requirements. Further discussion on verifying the location of a customer is at para.13–035 below.

13–032 Broadly, when determining if customers are in business, suppliers are required by the UK Revenue to obtain commercial evidence from their customer to support any claim that they are in business in the EU. This draws upon existing business practices in e-commerce so as to minimise burdens on business.

The principal evidence required at the time of the transaction would normally be the customer's VAT registration number and country identification code prefix, conforming to the correct country format for the relevant Member State. The absence of a verifiable VAT number will, in most cases, be a prima facie indication that the supplier is not dealing with a business customer. However, examples are also provided as to the kind of reasonable commercial evidence (such as contracts, business letterheads, a commercial website address, etc.) that is acceptable for verification purposes where a VAT number cannot be provided (e.g. by a non-EU business).

Where a relationship has not been established with a business customer, VAT Information Sheet 05/03 specifies that the VAT number should be checked when the VAT involved exceeds £500 on a single transaction, or where the VAT on cumulative transactions with a single customer in a reporting period exceeds £500; and VAT numbers should also be checked where a business has any reason to believe that a VAT number quoted by a customer is false or is being used incorrectly (for instance, businesses which supply downloaded games and music, etc. are expected to challenge VAT numbers quoted by customers due to the particular nature of their supply). VAT should also be charged where verification checks fail to confirm a customer's business status.

To assist businesses with this verification process, the EU has adopted measures giving suppliers on-line access to VAT registration numbers stored in EU government databases, the VAT Information Exchange System (VIES).[40] This will allow traders to establish in real time the VAT status of their customer. Businesses may also contact the UK Revenue to verify names and addresses as well as dates of registration and de-registration where appropriate. However, the VIES cannot be expected to function as a definitive guide to taxable status, and is merely one element of the verification process. Work on the quality and functionality of VIES will continue in response to demands from business.

The UK Revenue has indicated in VAT Information Sheet 05/03 that, where the customer wrongly represents his status, they will not seek to recover the VAT from the supplier provided they are satisfied that the supplier acted in good faith, for instance, where verification had been undertaken, the details provided were believed to be correct, and there was no reasonable information at the relevant time of sale that would indicate that the customer's information was incorrect.

13.20 BUSINESS TO PRIVATE CUSTOMER SUPPLIES OF ELECTRONICALLY SUPPLIED SERVICES AND DIGITISED PRODUCTS

The vast majority of business currently conducted over the internet comprises the two categories of transactions already discussed: supplies of physical goods to business and private customers; and business to business supplies of electronically delivered services and digitised products. However, a third category of transaction—supplies of services and intangible

13–033

---

[40] The VIES can be accessed at *http://europa.eu.int/comm/taxation_customs/vies/en/vieshome.htm.*

property to individuals in their private capacity (that is, to anyone not registered or liable to be registered for VAT)—has offered the greatest opportunities to small and medium-sized businesses and is recognised by most taxing authorities as the greatest test to effective tax administration. This is especially the case where the supply crosses frontiers.

Before the introduction of the e-commerce VAT Directive, generally no VAT was chargeable in relation to transactions between businesses and private customers. However, the volume of business to private consumer transactions in services over the internet has grown significantly in recent years. As reported by the NAO, sales over the internet to such customers almost trebled from 2002 to 2004. The volume and value of these sales is also likely to increase even further as new technological developments continue to facilitate the transfer of data such as software, music, and video at high speeds. Consequently, and in light of the distortion of competition which existed between EU and non-EU businesses in relation to these sales as discussed above, international co-operation was needed to lay down rules to determine the circumstances in which such sales should be held to be consumed in a jurisdiction (and thereby chargeable to VAT), and an efficient mechanism to collect the tax.

Generally, the changes to the place of supply rules by the e-commerce VAT Directive have had little impact on EU providers of these supplies, other than to remove a VAT charge in respect of some supplies to non-EU customers. As far as suppliers who are not established in the EU are concerned, however, the changes are quite significant in relation to their supplies to EU private customers.

For example, a US-based content provider supplying computer software to an individual in a personal capacity via the internet will now need to make itself familiar with the rules of every EU Member State in which it makes supplies and identify and charge the correct rate applicable in the Member State where it makes supplies. An EU-based content provider on the other hand, which would already be familiar with the existing rules applied by its Member State, would only have to levy VAT on supplies to EU non-business customers at its single local VAT rate applied by its Member State.

This may also result in a distortion of competition against non-EU suppliers, since the changes now also mean that non-EU suppliers may be liable to charge a higher rate of VAT (the rate in the customer's Member State) to the rate for which an EU supplier will be liable on identical supplies (EU suppliers can still charge the rate of VAT applicable in the Member State in which it belongs).

By way of an example, where a UK-based content provider supplies computer software to an individual in his private capacity via the internet:

(i) If the customer belongs in Sweden, the place of supply is the UK. This means that the content provider must charge UK VAT at the standard rate of 17.5 per cent, and account for the VAT to the UK Revenue.

(ii) If the customer belongs in a non-EU country, the place of supply is outside the UK, and thus outside the scope of the charge to UK VAT.

Contrast this treatment where a US-based content provider supplies the same computer software to an individual in his private capacity via the internet: **13–034**

(i) If the customer belongs in Sweden, the place of supply will be Sweden and the supply will be chargeable to Swedish VAT at a rate of 25 per cent.

(ii) If the customer belongs in a non-EU country, the place of supply will be outside the EU, and thus outside the scope of the charge to EU VAT.

The measures of the e-commerce VAT Directive have therefore been ambitious in seeking to impose tax burdens across international borders without any effective legal basis of enforcing these rules in non-EU jurisdictions.

Perhaps not surprisingly then, the Directive has met with criticism from non-EU jurisdictions, such as the United States. Where previously US headquarters did not generally have to consider ways of managing EU VAT on these supplies, they are now directly exposed to EU VAT by reason of the e-commerce VAT Directive. So organisations may now need to design and implement a global strategy for the management of VAT that is consistent with its overall business strategy.

It is understood that EU VAT compliance in the US is now recognised as a significant issue and one which needs to be effectively managed especially in the light of increasing compliance requirements in the US. Generally it would also seem that foreign companies are expected to comply with the EU's new regime, despite not having any taxable presence in the EU, as failure to do so may make it difficult for such companies subsequently to establish operations in the EU.

As EU Member States have the primary responsibility for ensuring compliance by non-EU established suppliers with their own VAT obligations, a further approach is being taken to assist Member States in enforcing compliance. As reported by the NAO, administrative arrangements are now in place for co-operation on VAT including a common system for the exchange of information and collaboration with the Commission to ensure the proper application of VAT. To identify and estimate the VAT liability of those non-EU businesses supplying these services to EU customers, the NAO's report recommends that such systems for exchanges of information and co-operation need to be extended with the non-EU countries in which the businesses are based.

It is understood that the UK does not yet have any administrative co-operation agreements covering VAT with third countries. However, the UK Government announced in its 2006 Budget that it will propose legislative changes to make such arrangements possible, including extending the exchange of information provisions in its double tax treaties with non-EU countries to VAT, and ratifying the joint OECD/Council of Europe 1988 Convention on Mutual Administrative Assistance in Tax Matters (which provides a legal basis for the exchange of information on taxpayers between countries on a multi-lateral basis).

Again, as with transactions between businesses, the correct application of UK (and EU) VAT requires that the content provider be able to satisfy itself as to where the customer belongs (i.e. the place of consumption), and the OECD's Guidance makes some recommendations on defining the place of consumption in the case of business to private consumer e-commerce transactions. Broadly, it recommends that the place of consumption should be located by reference to the consumer's "usual jurisdiction of residence". This approach was consistent with the Commission's proposals for the e-commerce VAT Directive. The international view is that this will be the country where the private consumer has his or her permanent address or is usually resident.

13–035   There is, however, an inherent difficulty involved in identifying the customer in internet-based transactions, particularly where the customer is a private consumer. Moreover, the content provider needs to be able to satisfy itself that the customer is downloading the product for his own personal or private use. The difficulty of associating such on-line activities with physically defined locations therefore means that there will be problems for content providers in applying VAT correctly and for the authorities in policing the application of VAT. Further, the electronic record of a transaction will need to contain sufficient evidence to prove that the recipient is established in the country identified as the place where consumption takes place.

The OECD's Guidance has suggested a number of ways as to how verification of location can be made for these types of transactions, including looking at payment/credit card details and invoice addresses within payment information, using tracking software to determine customer location, looking at the nature of the supply to determine who it is made to and what components it consists of (for instance, film downloads of a low value are more likely to be purchased by private rather than business consumers), and looking at digital certificates which provide a unique set of numbers for a business so its authenticity can be checked.

Generally, a supplier's accounting systems and websites will need to be more sophisticated to ascertain such information and apply the appropriate rate of VAT to the transaction, creating extra costs for businesses. However, self-declaration by a customer combined with a reasonable level of verification in line with the OECD's recommendations will generally be acceptable to the UK Revenue (as set out in VAT Information Sheet 05/03).

Effective tax collection in respect of business to private customer cross-border e-commerce transactions presents particular challenges and no single option, of those examined as part of the international debate, is without difficulty.

In its 2001 report, the OECD's Working Party considered five methods of collecting consumption taxes on e-commerce transactions: the reverse charge system, remote registration, tax at source and redistribution (between tax authorities), collection by third parties, and technology-based/facilitated withholding mechanisms.

The reverse charge (as discussed above) and remote registration options were considered to be useful starting points in determining the most appropriate approach. However, taxation at source and subsequent transfer and collection by third parties were seen as involving unfeasible complications. Furthermore, the reverse charge procedure was not regarded as a practical means of tax collection where the customer is a private individual given the serious problems of control and enforcement which would arise if VAT was required to be collected from private individuals in that way.

The preferred option therefore was a simplified remote registration system, and this has now been implemented by the special scheme as a result of the e-commerce VAT Directive (see further below). However, this is not regarded by the OECD as the ultimate solution, since non-EU businesses must still make themselves familiar with a large number of different rules and rates in countries in which they have no physical presence.

More advanced systems will need to be developed so that tax collection on international sales may be automated. Therefore, tax administrations are being encouraged to develop an environment so that new business-driven technological solutions may be created which are also tax compatible, including being able to compute and collect VAT on the basis of the private customer's location. The development of technology-based/facilitated options are therefore seen as the medium to long term solution, and is currently the subject of ongoing research.

Additional work by the OECD to further simplify tax collection in the short term for cross-border business-to-private consumer e-commerce transactions is under way. A report was recently released in February 2005[41] studying various facilitation measures, including the use of intermediaries, the role of certified software, the feasibility of on-line remote auditing, and the environment necessary to allow the development of more advanced or automated tax collection solutions.

The removal of barriers to the use of intermediaries was particularly encouraged since it acknowledged that tax intermediaries acting on behalf of overseas taxpayers may have an increasingly important role to play within the EU (for instance, in assisting in tax calculations, filing, collections and remittances), and the possibility of a "global intermediary" was also mentioned.

Furthermore, to avoid some of the compliance issues mentioned above, and instead of registering under the special scheme, many overseas e-businesses, and other EU operators, have created establishments else-

---

[41] The report is entitled "Facilitating Collection of Consumption Taxes on Business-to-Consumer Cross-Border E-Commerce Transactions", and is available for review at *http://www.oecd.org/dataoecd/51/33/34422641.pdf*.

where in the EU, motivated by the attraction of lower VAT rates in countries like Luxembourg (15 per cent). By doing this, the overseas company could register and charge VAT in accordance with the rules of the Member State of establishment, and thereby operate within the EU on the same basis as an EU operator in relation to private customers.

This trend may be discouraged however by the recent "VAT package" proposals from the Commission as part of its New Strategy for VAT (see further at section 13.24 below).

In relation to establishments, the question has also been raised as to whether a server from which the website is run can constitute a "fixed establishment" of a business so as to determine the place of supply for VAT purposes. The conclusion seems to be, however, that this concept would only apply to a server where the "necessary human and technical resources" are also present, as applied to conventional businesses.[42]

Increasingly, VAT authorities throughout the EU are looking at the question of where a business is effectively controlled and where the activities or functions are carried out. If a business purports to operate from a specific location, the authorities are looking to see whether it has the necessary technical and human resources to do so. As a result, businesses which may try to argue that they are supplying services from an EU establishment will need to ensure that the necessary evidence to support this position is available, otherwise the arrangements could be challenged.

13.20.1 Operation of the special scheme in the United Kingdom

13.036   To indicate how the special scheme generally works in the UK, the UK Revenue gives a basic example[43] of a US business with customers in the UK, Italy, and Spain who registers in the UK for the special scheme. The US business will need to charge UK VAT to its UK customers, Italian VAT to its Italian customers, and Spanish VAT to its Spanish customers.

To do this, it will enter the VAT for each country on the appropriate line of its electronic declaration, and send that declaration with payment to the UK Revenue (in sterling), who will retain the UK VAT and pass on the Italian VAT to the Italian authorities and the Spanish VAT to the Spanish authorities. VAT identification numbers for registration under the special scheme have their own unique format beginning with the prefix "EU", followed by a nine digit number. To assist businesses in completing their electronic VAT returns, the UK Revenue publishes on-line exchange rates for converting leading currencies direct into sterling.

---

[42] See, for instance, the case of *RAL (Channel Islands) Ltd v Commissioners of Customs & Excise (and related appeals)* (Case C–452/03) [2005] S.T.C. 1025, and *Berkholz v Finanzamt Hamburg-Mitte-Altstadt* (Case 168/84) [1985] E.C.R. 2251.

[43] See the UK Revenue's VAT Information Sheet 07/03: *http://customs.hmrc.gov.uk/ channelsPortalWebApp/channelsPortalWebApp.portal?_nfpb=true&_pageLabel=page Import_ShowContent&id=HMCE_ CL_000922&propertyType=document.*

To be eligible for registration under the special scheme, certain conditions need to be satisfied. Put simply, businesses are eligible if they:

(i) supply electronically supplied services to consumers (private individuals and non-business organisations) belonging in the EU;

(ii) are not established within the EU; and

(iii) are not registered for EU VAT under the normal rules in any Member State in relation to any supplies of goods and/or services (such registrations would need to be cancelled).

The scheme is generally a self-policing system, requiring registered businesses to notify the UK Revenue of any changes that would mean they would cease to be eligible for registration. It does not apply to supplies to business customers as they will account for any VAT due using the reverse charge procedure. If the non-EU supplier has both business and non-business customers in the EU, it can still register under the scheme, but only for the services supplied to non-business customers. There is no threshold for registration under the scheme so businesses are also entitled to voluntarily register even if they are not actually making supplies at the time, but intend to do so at a later stage.

While there are no penalties which apply under the scheme, businesses can be excluded from registration if they cease supplies or if they no longer meet (or persistently fail to meet) the necessary conditions, and in that event may be required to register under the normal rules (subject to penalties and registration thresholds).

Businesses will also be required to keep records of supplies covered by the scheme in sufficient detail which will enable the tax administrations in the customers' Member States to determine the accuracy of VAT declarations and payments. These records will need to be kept for a period of 10 years and be made available electronically.

It was assumed by the EU that at the end of the expiry period of the e-commerce VAT Directive, a fully comprehensive electronic system would be in place which would automatically charge, collect and allocate VAT to each Member State. However, this has not yet been forthcoming, so the operation of the special scheme will continue to be reviewed.

One key complaint about the special scheme however, is that it does not allow for recovery of input tax, so a non-EU operator will only be able to reclaim input tax under the time-consuming terms of the thirteenth Directive. EU suppliers on the other hand can generally recover VAT they incur at the same time and on the same tax return as they account for VAT on their outbound supplies in their own jurisdiction.

13.21 SUPPLIES OF TELECOMS, BROADCASTING AND ELECTRONIC SERVICES: THE "USE AND ENJOYMENT" PRINCIPLE

13–037   Under the current UK VAT regime, telecommunications services are a Schedule 5 service for which the place of supply is determined according to the special rules already discussed (at section 13.6.3).

However, as previously mentioned at para.13–022, the place of supply of telecommunication services as determined under these rules is also subject to the application of the "use and enjoyment principle". The UK "use and enjoyment principle" implements the provisions in Art.9(3) of the Sixth Council Directive, which has applied in the UK to telecommunication services supplied on or after March 18, 1998.

Subsequent to the changes to Art.9(3) resulting from the e-commerce VAT Directive, this principle has now been extended with effect from July 1, 2003, in the UK to supplies of radio and television broadcasting services in the same way as for telecommunication services, and to a lesser degree, to electronically supplied services.

The purpose of the principle is to correct instances of distortion which still remain as a result of only considering where the supplier and the customer belong. Basically, the use and enjoyment provisions are applied under UK law[44] to these services as follows:

(a)   where the services would otherwise be treated as supplied in the UK, they will not be treated as supplied in the UK (and VAT will not therefore be charged) to the extent that the effective use and enjoyment of the services takes place outside the EU; and

(b)   where the services would otherwise be treated as supplied in a place outside the EU, they shall be treated as supplied in the United Kingdom (and VAT will therefore be charged) to the extent that the effective use and enjoyment of the services takes place in the UK,

and, in respect of electronically supplied services, the above rules only apply where the services are received by a person for the purposes of a business carried on by him.

13–038   Thus, "effective use and enjoyment" is only a consideration when these services supplied by a UK provider are consumed outside the EU (and not in another EU Member State), or when made by a non-EU provider and consumed in the UK, and in the case of electronically supplied services, only where such services are consumed by businesses and not by private customers. It would be distortive for such services that are actually consumed

---

[44] As set out in the Value Added Tax (Place of Supply of Services) Order (SI 1992/3121), art.17.

outside the EU to be subject to UK VAT, or for there to be no charge to VAT where these services are consumed in the UK.

An example is that of a US business purchasing web hosting services for its international business, including its UK branch. Although the supply may be received in the US, to the extent that it is used in the UK, it will be subject to UK VAT.

The rationale for the limitation of the principle in relation to electronically supplied services is, according to the UK Revenue, because most private customers will use and enjoy electronically supplied services in the same country in which they belong, but it has been noted (e.g. by the OECD) that it would also be very difficult to apply this principle to private consumers receiving such services (due to the mobility of the act of downloading from the internet, for instance).

All Member States are obliged to implement the "effective use and enjoyment" provisions where these services are otherwise treated as supplied outside the EU, or where such services are supplied by persons established outside the EU to private persons established in the EU (save in respect of electronically supplied services).

There is, however, no such requirement to implement the principle where the services are otherwise treated as supplied in the EU but used and enjoyed outside the EU. However, as outlined above, the UK has implemented this principle into its domestic law so that telecommunications, radio and television broadcasting, and electronically supplied services, which are supplied by UK providers but used outside the EU, can be treated as outside the scope of UK VAT.

The term "effective use and enjoyment" is not defined in the UK legislation. However, published guidance by the UK Revenue on its application (see VAT Information Sheet 01/03) states that effective use and enjoyment takes place where the customer actually consumes the services and that, generally, this will be where the services are physically used, irrespective of the place of contract, payment or beneficial interest.

In practice, where only part of a supply is consumed in the United Kingdom, the extent of use and enjoyment will in most cases be difficult to quantify. The UK Revenue has, however, said that, in these cases, it will adopt a pragmatic approach in order to reach a mutually agreeable solution with the supplier. Invariably, the approach adopted will have as its basis, factual data available, such as measured usage, internal company management records showing inter-company recharges, or percentage business transactions at the specific location.

Take, for example, the position in relation to UK branches. A UK VAT registered branch of an international company which is using electronically supplied or broadcasting services that were previously supplied to its US headquarters by a US provider may be required to account for UK VAT, to the extent that the services are used and enjoyed in the UK, by applying the reverse charge at the time the provider is paid.

The UK Revenue recognises that branches may not always know at the relevant point in time the exact amount which relates to its use and enjoyment in the UK (or may even be unaware that a payment has been made). In these circumstances, the UK Revenue will accept agreed provisional figures to be corrected at such time as actual figures become available.

13–039   Similarly, the UK Revenue has also stated that it will adopt a pragmatic approach to the application of the use and enjoyment principle in situations where the place of supply would probably be the same where an e-business supplies a mixture of electronically supplied services, telecommunications and broadcasting services. Consequently, where:

- A UK business supplies electronically supplied services to private individuals or non-business organisations; and
- Existing accounting systems are set up by the UK supplier to tax supplies where they are effectively used and enjoyed;

then the UK supplier may, exceptionally, opt to apply the use and enjoyment rules to their supplies of electronically supplied services to private individuals. This is regarded as a simplification measure which prevents the need for businesses to adjust their accounting systems. However, the UK Revenue will not allow this simplification measure to be used in any case where they consider it leads to abuse.

Tables 13.2 and 13.3 contain summaries of the place of supply rules in relation to telecommunications, radio and television broadcasting services, and electronically supplied services and the impact of the use and enjoyment principle as applied in the UK, including who may have to account for the VAT on such supplies.[45]

13–040   **Table 13.2: Place of supply and VAT treatment of telecommunications and, with effect from July 1, 2003, radio and television broadcasting services**

Supplier belongs	Customer belongs	UK VAT position
In the UK	in another EU Member State and receives the services for non-business purposes, or in the UK (irrespective of whether or not the services are received for business purposes)	services are supplied in the UK and the supplier must charge and account for UK VAT on the supply (subject to the registration threshold); where the customer belongs in the UK, the use and enjoyment provisions may apply with the result that services used outside the EU are outside the scope of UK (and EU) VAT

---

[45] Please also refer to VAT Information Sheet 01/03 and the flowcharts contained therein: *http://customs.hmrc.gov.uk/channelsPortalWebApp/channelsPortalWebApp.portal?_nfpb= true&_pageLabel=pageImport_ShowContent&id=HMCE_CL_000902&propertyType= document.*

Supplier belongs	Customer belongs	UK VAT position
In the UK	in another EU Member State and receives the services for business purposes	services are supplied in the other Member State; UK VAT is not chargeable; however, the customer must charge and account for VAT in the Member State where he belongs
In the UK	outside the EU	services are supplied outside the EU and are outside the scope of UK (and EU) VAT; use and enjoyment provisions, however, may apply with the result that services used in the UK are supplied in the UK and the supplier must charge and account for UK VAT (subject to the registration threshold). Similar rules may apply across the EU
In another EU Member State	in the UK and receives the services for non-business purposes	services are supplied in the supplier's Member State; the supply is therefore outside the scope of UK VAT but the supplier must account for VAT in his Member State subject to any local use and enjoyment rules
In another EU Member State	in another Member State (which is not the UK)	the place of supply will be outside the UK (but not the EU) and therefore outside the scope of the charge to UK VAT (but not EU VAT subject to any local use and enjoyment rules)
In another EU Member State, or outside the EU	in the UK and receives the services for business purposes	services are supplied in the UK and the customer must account for UK VAT under the reverse charge procedure (subject to the registration threshold); use and enjoyment provisions may apply with the result that services used outside the EU are outside the scope of UK (and EU) VAT

Supplier belongs	Customer belongs	UK VAT position
In another EU Member State, or outside the EU	outside the EU	services are supplied outside the EU and are outside the scope of UK (and EU) VAT; use and enjoyment provisions, however, may apply with the result that services used in the UK are supplied in the UK and the supplier must charge and account for UK VAT subject to the registration threshold (unless the customer provides a UK VAT registration number and accounts for UK VAT under the reverse charge procedure). Similar rules may apply across the EU
Outside the EU	in the UK (or another EU Member State) and receives the services for non-business purposes	services are supplied in the supplier's country and are outside the scope of UK (and EU) VAT; use and enjoyment provisions may, however, apply with the result that services used in the UK are supplied in the UK and the supplier must charge and account for UK VAT (subject to the registration threshold). Similar rules may apply across the EU
Outside the EU	in another EU Member State and receives the services for business purposes	services are supplied in the other Member State and are outside the scope of UK VAT (but not EU VAT); use and enjoyment provisions may apply as above

Table 13.3: Place of supply and VAT treatment of electronically supplied   13–041 services (with effect from July 1, 2003)

Supplier belongs	Customer belongs	UK VAT position
In the UK	in another EU Member State or in the UK and receives the services for non-business purposes	services are supplied in the UK and the supplier must charge and account for UK VAT on the supply (subject to the registration threshold); use and enjoyment provisions do not apply to non-business services
In the UK	in the UK and receives the services for business purposes	services are supplied in the UK and the supplier must charge and account for UK VAT on the supply (subject to the registration threshold); use and enjoyment provisions may apply with the result that services used outside the EU are outside the scope of UK (and EU) VAT
In the UK	in another EU Member State and receives the services for business purposes	services are supplied in the other Member State; UK VAT is not chargeable; however, the customer must charge and account for VAT in the Member State where he belongs; UK use and enjoyment provisions do not apply, however similar rules may apply in the other EU Member State

Supplier belongs	Customer belongs	UK VAT position
In the UK	outside the EU	services (whether or not they are received for business purposes) are supplied outside the EU and are outside the scope of UK (and EU) VAT; use and enjoyment provisions, however, may apply where the services are received for business purposes only, with the result that those services used in the UK are supplied in the UK and the supplier must charge and account for UK VAT (subject to the registration threshold). Similar rules may apply across the EU
In another EU Member State, or outside the EU	in the UK and receives the services for business purposes	services are supplied in the UK and the customer must account for UK VAT under the reverse charge procedure (subject to the registration threshold); use and enjoyment provisions may apply with the result that services used outside the EU are outside the scope of UK VAT (and EU VAT depending on use and enjoyment provisions in the supplier's EU Member State)
In another EU Member State	in the UK and receives the services for non-business purposes	services are supplied in the supplier's Member State; the supply is outside the scope of UK VAT but the supplier must account for VAT in his Member State; use and enjoyment provisions do not apply to non-business services
In another EU Member State	in another EU Member State (which is not the UK) and whether or not for business purposes	services are supplied in the other EU Member State; the supply will be outside the scope of UK VAT but may be subject to EU VAT; UK use and enjoyment provisions do not apply, however similar rules may apply in the other EU Member State in the case of business customers

Supplier belongs	Customer belongs	UK VAT position
In another EU Member State, or outside the EU	outside the EU	services (whether or not they are received for business purposes) are supplied outside the EU and are outside the scope of UK (and EU) VAT; use and enjoyment provisions, however, may apply where the services are received for business purposes only, with the result that such services used and enjoyed in the UK are treated as supplied in the UK and chargeable to UK VAT for which the supplier would account subject to the registration threshold (unless the customer provides a UK VAT registration number and accounts for UK VAT under the reverse charge procedure). Services used in another EU Member States are outside the scope of UK VAT but may be within the scope of VAT of that Member State
Outside the EU	in the UK and receives the services for non-business purposes	services are supplied in the UK and the supplier accounts for UK VAT (registration may be possible in the UK under the special scheme); use and enjoyment provisions do not apply to non-business services
Outside the EU	in another EU Member State (which is not the UK), and whether or not for business purposes	services are supplied in the other Member State and are outside the scope of UK VAT (but not EU VAT—depending on local use and enjoyment rules); UK use and enjoyment provisions do not apply (registration in an EU Member State may be possible under the special scheme for non-business customers)

13.22 PACKAGES CONTAINING A VARIETY OF INTERNET RELATED ELEMENTS

13–042   Particular care needs to be taken by e-businesses where a service includes both electronic and other elements. For example, the provision of internet "packages" by service providers is a complicated area. Typically such packages present the user, on log-in, with a specially developed and regulated environment rather than just delivering the user directly into the internet or World Wide Web. They may include, in addition, access to specially prepared information pages (e.g. news, weather, stock market or travel reports), access to on-line shopping facilities, personal web space to create a website and games fora, as well as telephone lines and email addresses.

Before the introduction of the e-commerce Directive, the tax treatment in the UK depended on the classification of the constituent elements of the package being provided. If the package extended only to basic internet access (although it may have included, for example, software, some information and customer support facilities), the package of services normally fell within the rules relating to telecommunications services discussed above. However, where the internet package comprised a variety of related elements, and not just mere access, the tax treatment was less straightforward.

In cases where such a package was provided for a single inclusive price, the UK Revenue had issued guidance to the effect that it would treat the package as a single composite supply for UK VAT purposes which fell within Sch.5, but not within the special use and enjoyment rules for telecommunications services. If the package was not to be treated as a single composite supply of Schedule 5 services, the VAT treatment of each constituent element of the package had to be looked at separately, some of which could be classified as telecommunications services and some as other Schedule 5 (but not telecommunications) services.

Broadly, this treatment meant that ISPs based in the UK supplying these packages would charge UK VAT on all sales to customers belonging in the UK and also to customers belonging in other Member States who did not receive the package for business purposes. They were not required to charge UK VAT on supplies to business customers in other Member States but would need to satisfy themselves that the supply was made for business purposes and retain sufficient evidence to support this decision.

On the other hand, ISPs supplying such packages who were not established in the UK or were established outside the EU were not required to charge UK VAT on their sales to UK customers. It was also understood that some overseas suppliers were including, for a flat fee, the telecommunications element previously supplied by a telecommunications provider direct to the consumer. No VAT was being accounted for on those supplies and this caused a distortion of competition with UK businesses.

13–043   In light of concerns by some UK-based ISPs about the perceived distortion of competition caused by these differences in VAT treatment,[46] and the proposed e-commerce VAT Directive, the UK Revenue was prompted to conduct a review of its policy on the VAT treatment of internet service packages in consultation with major ISPs, based both in the UK and outside the EU.

Following this review, its guidance was withdrawn. This was principally because, with effect from July 1, 2003, all internet service packages were subject to tax in the EU irrespective of the location of the supplier and/or the balance between the constituent elements of the package. Thus, non-EU ISPs were required to account for EU VAT on their services. As stated by the UK Revenue in its 2002 Business Brief on its policy review of the tax treatment of internet service packages, the changes introduced by the e-commerce VAT Directive were a "lasting, fair and clear" approach, ensuring all internet service packages supplied by UK and non-EU ISPs are taxed in a similar way.

However, questions remain as to how bundled or mixed supplies of electronically supplied services and other goods or services should be taxed where different rates apply to conventional as opposed to digitised products.

In its report on implementation issues for the taxation of e-commerce, the OECD's Consumption Taxes TAG recognises that e-commerce will contribute to problems concerning "bundling" of services through its ability to effect the combined delivery of individual products (any mix of goods, services or intangible property) that could be viewed as a number of separate individual supplies.

This is therefore an area which may increase the potential for double taxation or unintentional non-taxation resulting from multiple tax rates and different interpretations of VAT within the EU. A bundle of "e-products" could, for instance, result in different countries having the right to tax different parts of the supply because they have different place of supply rules or divergences in their tax definitions.

An example given in the report is that of a telecommunications company supplying access to telecommunications services on a mobile telephone, while at the same time making available items of content for downloading to customers' phones. Whilst the telecommunications services may be taxed on the basis of "use and enjoyment", the content tends to be taxed on the basis of "usual residence", creating a conflict in the tax treatment of the transaction which usually has to be determined in advance of actual consumption by consumers, making it very difficult for e-commerce suppliers to correctly account for their liabilities.

No clear common rules currently exist however to assist on-line suppliers in determining whether VAT should be charged on the separate elements of a transaction or to the package as a whole. Furthermore, while the harmonisation of VAT rates within the EU has been the subject of much

---

[46] This was also an issue at debate in R. (on the application of Freeserve.com Plc) v Customs and Excise Commissioners (America On Line Inc (AOL), mentioned above at para.13–021.

debate, it has also been acknowledged by both the OECD and the EU that VAT rates will not be harmonised for the time being. Therefore, tax issues arising from "bundled supplies" are likely to continue for the foreseeable future, so further clarity will be required.

In the meantime, these questions have been left open for the courts to determine on a case by case basis, principally in accordance with EU case law principles, in particular those as set out in the *Card Protection Plan*[47] case in relation to single and mixed supplies as referred to by UK courts. That case provides the following guidance and further information on this is provided by the UK Revenue in VAT Information Sheet 02/01:

> "There is a single supply in particular in cases where one or more of the elements are to be regarded as constituting the principal service, whilst one or more elements are to be regarded, by contrast, as ancillary services which share the tax treatment of the principal service. A service must be regarded as ancillary to a principal service if it does not constitute for customers an aim in itself, but a means of better enjoying the principle service supplied".

13.23 INVOICING AND RETURNS

13–044   The EU system of VAT is invoice-based, by which it is meant that a VAT registered supplier must issue a valid VAT invoice for all taxable supplies of goods and services it makes and it must, in order to be able to claim input tax, be in receipt of such a valid VAT invoice in respect of supplies received.

When proposing the e-commerce VAT Directive, the Commission recognised that, subject to uniform EU conditions, fiscal administration should provide for operators conducting business over or via the internet to discharge their fiscal obligations by means of electronic VAT invoices, declarations and accounting. As paperless electronic invoicing was to be a characteristic of e-commerce, it needed to be authorised for VAT purposes for transactions within the EU and a framework of co-operation between the EU and other countries established to ensure that conditions, equivalent to those provided in the EU, were also created for international electronic invoicing. A comprehensive study of all invoicing requirements was undertaken and the EU began the process of introducing a Directive on electronic invoicing in order to harmonise practice throughout its history.

Following this study, Council Directive 2001/115/EC was adopted on December 20, 2001, and was implemented by Member States on January 1, 2004. The Directive has had significant practical benefit for companies operating within the European market as it means they now should only have to deal with one piece of legislation with harmonised rules for VAT

---

[47] [2001] 2 All E.R. 143.

invoicing as opposed to dealing with different rules for every country into which they make supplies, thereby removing some administrative obstacles.

The Directive, amongst other things, requires Member States to recognise the validity of electronic invoicing and allow cross-border electronic invoicing. It has defined the powers that Member States have in relation to such invoicing. It has specified the content required for invoices; detailing 10 different pieces of mandatory information to be included on every invoice and four additional pieces of information required in certain circumstances, and also the manner in which such invoices have to be delivered, stored and retrieved.

The Directive has been implemented into UK law,[48] although electronic invoicing by UK VAT registered businesses had already been permitted prior to such implementation. Subject to certain conditions, a UK supplier is treated as providing his customer with a valid VAT invoice if all the information required for a conventional paper invoice is recorded in a computer and transmitted (and stored) by electronic means directly to his customer's computer, without the delivery of a hard copy. Invoices received in this way are acceptable as evidence for input tax deduction, subject to normal rules.

Under the revised rules in the UK, the supplier no longer needs to give the UK Revenue notice of his intention to provide electronic invoices (as of January 1, 2006). However, conditions for electronic invoicing generally include requiring a business to guarantee the authenticity of the origin and integrity of the invoice data by means of an Advanced Electronic Signature or Electronic Data Interchange or any other system whereby the supplier can impose a satisfactory level of control over the authenticity and integrity of the invoice data.

The UK Revenue also require further internal controls to be put in place to control and protect the authenticity and integrity of invoices, although it has not prescribed the form the control must take, allowing businesses to determine their own controls, so long as they can demonstrate that they have control over, for example, the accuracy and completeness of the invoice data. It has also laid down rules relating to the electronic storage of invoices—for example if invoices are sent electronically they must be stored electronically and for a period of six years (subject to certain exceptions).

The internet-based forms for electronic VAT returns are duplicates of the paper forms but have in-built validation of data. If a business opts to submit returns in this manner then payment of VAT must also be made electronically, the benefit being that the business can receive up to an extra seven calendar days to submit the form and the payment. The UK Revenue is also working with software developers to incorporate internet filing applications for VAT directly from business accounting software and they hope to have this process in place for all businesses in the very near future. The general

---

[48] By the Value Added Tax (Amendment) (No.6) Regulations 2003 (SI 2003/3220). Please also refer to the UK Revenue's "E-Commerce Control Notes" at pp. 34. *et seq.*, as well as their guidance on electronic invoicing in Notice 700/63, both available on its website: *www.hmrc.gov.uk.*

intention is for paper filing of VAT returns to be eventually phased out so that on-line filing becomes the norm.

13.24 THE FUTURE

13–045 Both the OECD and the EU, including the UK, have acknowledged the complexities of the existing EU VAT regime and the practical difficulties it poses for businesses involved in international transactions, both in terms of the lack of certainty in applying the rules and the potential for commercial distortion, as well as there being particular challenges relating to business to private consumer e-commerce transactions compared with business to business e-commerce transactions.

The introduction of the e-commerce VAT Directive has been welcomed by EU-based businesses, since for the first time it has brought supplies of electronic services over the internet made by non-EU-based suppliers within the ambit of the VAT regimes of the EU, so remedying a situation that most had seen as giving non-EU suppliers an unfair advantage. The Directive has nonetheless been controversial in that it has brought non-EU suppliers into the EU's VAT net despite not having any taxable presence in the EU and therefore questions of VAT compliance and enforcement remain significant.

However, it has been reported that the tax receipts of Member States, including that of the United Kingdom, have increased by reference to those registering under the special scheme and by reference to those businesses which have opted for establishment within the EU (even though companies may have opted to set up in the EU for a variety of other commercial reasons).

In the UK, for instance, the UK Revenue estimates that it has collected £59 million more in VAT up to December 2005 from non-EU businesses supplying electronic services to UK customers. The combined effect of these types of factors has led the Commission to conclude that the Directive has delivered on its objectives satisfactorily, and that the special scheme has not given rise to many operational difficulties. Concerns about overly burdensome requirements and non-compliance by non-EU businesses' systems appear to have been "without foundation".

In that connection, the NAO itself has agreed with the assessment by the UK Revenue that the "overall risk to VAT revenue from on-line shopping, or e-commerce, is currently low", and that it is "well positioned" to tackle any specific areas of risk, and that other tax authorities have drawn similar conclusions. The main risk identified is that of businesses failing to register and account for VAT which trade solely on the internet, including those who trade on e-marketplaces such as eBay, but the risks presented are low as, on average, the amount of VAT involved is lower compared with other types of business.

The UK Revenue also has well-established audit procedures for monitoring the risks to revenue of VAT non-compliance and will continue to explore "innovative" methods such as "Web Robot", an advanced search engine being developed to search the web in order to identify e-businesses that may be liable to register for VAT in the UK.

The Commission has however identified a number of areas which have not been addressed by the e-commerce VAT Directive and which will need to be monitored, although they have also been described as relatively minor concerns. For instance, the absence of a registration threshold in the Directive could give rise to VAT exposure on a small business outside the EU from a single transaction in a particular country.

Further, it recognises that distinctions in the definitions of broadcasting, telecommunications and "electronically supplied services" are being increasingly blurred since content can now be accessed in several ways, such as via video-on-demand or 3G networks, such that it will be increasingly difficult to justify differences in the tax treatment between them, which may give rise to further conflicts and competitive imbalances.

13.24.1 Commission's proposals

As indicated previously (and despite any "minor" concerns) the Commission is now seeking to make the provisions of the e-commerce VAT Directive permanent as part of its "VAT package" proposals. In December 2003, the Commission presented proposals to amend the general rules on the place of supply of services between businesses, and then in July 2005, following a public consultation, an amended proposal was submitted with the support of the UK presidency which deals with the place of supply of services rules in relation to private, non-taxable consumers.   **13–046**

For supplies of business to business services, the proposal is to change the general rule to the place where the customer is established (subject to certain exceptions) whereby the customer would pay VAT, increasing the use of the reverse charge procedure.

With respect to business to private consumer supplies of services, the proposal is to maintain the general rule based on the supplier's place of establishment, but for certain types of services, specific rules will apply, including in relation to electronically supplied services, telecommunication services, radio and television broadcasting services, and distance-teaching— i.e. services which can be supplied to non-taxable persons "at a distance". For these services, the Commission proposes that they should be taxable at the place where the customer who receives the service is located, irrespective of whether such services are supplied from a non-EU operator or an EU operator. If adopted, this would require any business supplying electronically supplied services to charge and pay EU VAT in every Member State where it has customers.

For instance, under the current rules, if a UK private customer downloads a piece of music from a business based in Italy, Italian VAT will be due at 20 per cent based on where the supplier "belongs". However, if the Commission proposals are accepted, UK VAT will be charged instead based on where the customer "belongs", thus also removing an incentive on businesses relocating to another Member State with lower VAT rates for supplies based on where the supplier "belongs".

Implementation of these amendments are also connected to the Commission's proposal for a "One Stop Shop" mechanism, the main goal of which is to reduce the extra administrative burdens on businesses operating in the EU. This scheme is similar to the "special scheme" under the e-commerce VAT Directive, but there will be some differences such as in relation to the redistribution of tax payments.

Broadly, the One Stop Shop would enable businesses to meet their EU-wide compliance obligations in the Member State of identification/establishment, using a single VAT number for supplies throughout the EU and declaring their VAT liabilities through a single electronic portal, via a standard set of web-based forms to be transmitted to the different Member States. Consequently, the supplier would pay the VAT directly to the tax authorities of those Member States (unlike the special scheme).

The Commission has also proposed further simplification measures for the application of the reverse charge procedure, for refund procedures under the eighth Directive using a web-based portal, and for EU distance selling arrangements, the latter of which is regarded as a typical area in which the One Stop Shop could bring substantial simplifications for traders established in the EU in terms of registration and monitoring turnover and thresholds.

The adoption by the European Council of these wider proposals on the place of supply of services and on the simplification of VAT obligations should ensure that the e-commerce Directive will be given permanent effect and would effectively absorb the special scheme. While legislative progress has been slower than expected on these proposals, they are likely to be adopted in the near future. The VAT package will therefore have implications for the modernisation of tax administration, implying a need for stronger and deeper co-ordination between the tax administrations of different Member States.

In this connection, it is interesting to note that a system called the "Streamlined Sales Tax Project"[49] has been introduced in the US to provide states and businesses with a simplified system, together with more uniform rules and procedures, on the collection of US sales and use tax on distance sales on a voluntary basis (i.e. from sellers without a physical presence or "nexus" in the customer's state). The features of this system are similar to those of the One Stop Shop (e.g. using a single place of identification).

13.24.2 International VAT/GST Guidelines

13–047   It is notable from the focus given by the EU to VAT in relation to e-commerce that it is of substantially increased importance. This may be of

---

[49] For further details, an executive summary of the scheme dated January 2005, is available at: *http://www.streamlinedsalestax.org/execsum0105.pdf.*

no real surprise given its rapid growth as a source of revenue for governments. However, the growth of cross-border transactions in services and intangibles has also made it necessary to address e-commerce tax issues in the broader context of the tax treatment of services and intangibles in the global economy, and as part of the OECD's more "holistic" approach to e-commerce mentioned previously at para.13–007.

Pursuant to a 2004 OECD report entitled "The Application of Consumption Taxes to the International Trade in Services and Intangibles", the OECD has concluded that, despite similarities in the core features of VAT laws among Member States, there is a lack of international consistency and coherence in how VAT is implemented, such as the way the place of taxation is determined, or the scope of the tax and definitions, and this has had an increasing impact on internationally traded services (and not just e-commerce) by creating uncertainty for business and tax administrations, and greater potential for double taxation, involuntary non-taxation and distortion of competition.

Such obstacles to business activity are regarded as significant enough to justify the design of further principles. In particular, the OECD has also recognised that, unlike its extensive work on tackling avoidance and double taxation aspects of direct taxes through its Model Tax Convention, there are no such "rules of the game" available in the field of consumption taxes.

Consequently, in February 2006, the OECD announced a new project looking into providing "International VAT/GST Guidelines",[50] to help governments and businesses agree various approaches for applying VAT/ GST to cross-border trade in services and intangibles. This will involve input from businesses and non-OECD members and organisations, including those protecting US interests.

It is intended that these guidelines, when completed, should provide sufficient guidance to make international trade more efficient and ultimately to ensure that "transactions are taxed only once and in a single, clearly defined jurisdiction in order to avoid uncertainties, double taxation or involuntary non-taxation". Notably, the OECD's Committee on Fiscal Affairs has already begun work on a set of framework principles, with the aim that they will be implemented in legislation, as follows:

(a) for consumption tax purposes, internationally traded services and intangibles should be taxed according to the rules of the jurisdiction of consumption; and

(b) the burden of value added taxes themselves should not lie on taxable businesses, except where explicitly provided for in legislation, i.e. in cases where countries may legitimately place a VAT burden on them, such as taxpayers who are exempt from charging VAT (e.g. on financial services), or for policy reasons (education, health care).

---

[50] The OECD's paper on these new guidelines is available for review at: *www.oecd.org/dataoecd/16/36/36177871.pdf*.

The shared view of businesses and governments is that the imposition of VAT should be clear and explicit and the "tax neutrality" of VAT should be kept as an objective in the design and implementation of these guidelines. Consequently, further international consensus on circumstances under which supplies are held to be consumed in a jurisdiction will be sought, and a table of contents has been provided which will evolve in light of the input and experience. This currently lists issues to be covered on which the position is particularly unclear, such as the treatment of bundled supplies.

"Specific sector" guidance for e-commerce will be included, as well as for financial services and telecommunications. Businesses are also keen for the development of exchange of information systems between countries especially in relation to double taxation disputes for VAT, and a variety of approaches to address this will be explored, including suggestions such as a separate VAT treaty. The Commission is also looking at mechanisms for eliminating double taxation in individual cases in relation to VAT.

Furthermore, there is recognition that the international trade of goods is becoming more complex for VAT/GST application due to developments in international chain of supply structures. So there may also be a need to simplify and streamline the tax to achieve fair taxation and remove risks of double taxation for such trade. How this would be achieved, however, is not discussed and is an area which may be considered at a later date.

This project is to be welcomed as a first step towards the production of international guidelines for businesses and governments on VAT principles and practice and their development will be significant to e-commerce, given that they are likely to form the framework for future development of policy and legislation on the taxation of e-commerce.

13.25 CUSTOMS DUTIES

13–048 Customs duties are, like VAT, a creature of the EU. They are payable on the importation of goods (but not services) into the EU at the point of entry of the goods into the EU. The duties are charged at rates specified in the Common Customs Tariff which incorporates special rates agreed by treaty with other jurisdictions with goods originating from such jurisdictions.

As customs duties only apply to goods, the main implications for the internet are concerned with computer software (whether in the form of "packages" produced by access providers to enable users to access the internet or software downloaded via the internet) and tangible goods ordered electronically over the internet but in each case delivered by traditional means. In relation to the latter, the only real issue for customs is the anticipated increase in small packages brought about by customers using the internet to buy from abroad.

13.25.1 Computer software

The UK subscribes to the World Trade Organisation's (WTO) declaration on Global Electronic Commerce in which it was stated that it was necessary to distinguish goods ordered electronically, but delivered by traditional means, and direct on-line delivery of digitised products. The former were to continue to attract customs duties at the appropriate rate of duty, while the latter were to constitute a supply of services and, as such, were to be free of import duties. No additional import duties were to be introduced relating to electronic transmissions.

Thus, the extent to which software constitutes goods is assessed by reference to the same considerations which apply to VAT. Software packages provided by access providers which are physically imported into the UK are likely to attract duty (subject to any exemptions such as importation from an EFTA nation). Given that supplies of digitised products are treated as services, the position is that customs duties are not chargeable on the importation of digitised products via the internet. Customs duties will not therefore be chargeable on downloaded software, including audio and visual material.

The WTO, and the World Customs Organisation (WCO) are continuing to pursue work programmes examining trade-related, and customs-related, issues impacted by global e-commerce. The WTO agreed during its Sixth Ministerial Conference in December 2005 that its own work programme would be reinvigorated, including discussions on the trade treatment, inter alia, of electronically delivered software. It also agreed that it would maintain the current practice of not imposing customs duties on electronic transmissions.

Taking into account the WTO's approach, the WCO has formulated a business strategy paper[51] on e-commerce. This paper recognises the opportunities and challenges of e-commerce to the effectiveness of customs trade procedures and services, including the growing volume of low-value consignments of goods ordered over the internet (see further under the next heading), and the responses that may be required to deal with the implications of e-commerce, such as simplifying processes and requirements to achieve greater compliance, and improved international co-operation and exchange of information.

13.25.2 Goods ordered electronically but delivered by traditional means

As with VAT, the customs treatment of goods imported into the UK via traditional means pursuant to a contract concluded over the internet is no

---

[51] "WCO Strategy Paper: Customs and E-Commerce", June 2002. See further at: *http://www.wcoomd.org/ie/En/Topics_Issues/InformationTechnology/WCO%20e-commerce%20strategy_final_e.PDF*.

different from a similar transaction effected outside the internet. In general, therefore, the purchaser of the goods will be the "importer" for customs purposes and, as such, liable to pay duty on the goods imported.

The opportunity for cross-border trade, especially between businesses and private consumers, is greatly increased by the internet. The UK is seeing an ever-increasing use of the internet as a method of ordering goods and this has been paralleled by an increase in the number of small packages imported from outside the EU. This was recently confirmed by the NAO's report which recognised that around £45 million of small commercial consignments are imported by post into the UK every year, and reportedly, around half of these sales are from the Channel Islands.

As briefly mentioned in para.13–027 above, EU reliefs and/or exemptions, which also provide that no customs duty is payable on goods ordered via the internet from outside the EU if the duty is less than £7, or if the item is from the Channel Islands, are increasingly being exploited by UK businesses re-establishing themselves outside the EU (particularly the Channel Islands), leading to a greater loss of revenue on such consignments. There are also concerns about overseas suppliers splitting customer orders or under-declaring values of consignments in order to evade import VAT and customs charges as a result of these reliefs.

As the level of small consignments increase therefore, it may become necessary to modify rules on imports and distance selling to overcome tax avoidance opportunities and ensure the collection of customs duties on small packages. The UK has, for instance, introduced new simplified import procedures to speed the importation of consignments from third countries, prompted by the increase in the number of goods ordered over the internet.

As noted by the NAO,[52] the UK entered into revised agreements in 2005 with the States of Jersey, the States of Guernsey, and with Hong Kong (for certain types of goods valued between £18 and £100), requiring the authorities to follow certain procedures on allowing businesses to charge, collect, and pay import VAT on consignments at the time of purchase rather than on importation into the UK; on examining consignments; and on auditing businesses including ensuring that businesses pay the correct amount of import VAT.

The UK Revenue has also said that it will continue to monitor and review the revenue and commercial implications of the *de minimis* limits, presumably in order to assess and minimise any distortion of competition that may result against local suppliers as well as reduce the burdens of compliance.

It should also be borne in mind that the EU is a customs union so that the EU Member States have no customs duty barriers between them but all have a common customs duty tariff against goods arriving from outside the EU. Goods which are free from customs duty in one part of the EU, because they originate there or because any duty on them has already been paid, are

---

[52] See Part 3 of the NAO's report: *http://www.nao.org.uk/publications/nao_reports/05–06/ 05061051.pdf.*

free to circulate within the rest of the EU without any liability to pay further customs charges when they move from one Member State to another.

The EU's common external tariff ensures that goods imported from non-EU countries are subject to the same customs duties wherever they enter the EU. Overall, these arrangements prevent distortion of competition since a private consumer cannot "shop around" the EU for the lowest rate of duty.

13.26 DIRECT TAXES

The issue for income and corporation taxes has been how to apply direct tax rules to international e-commerce bearing in mind that, typically, such rules were not designed to cope with e-commerce. As highlighted in para.13–004, the rules which have been causing e-commerce businesses the most concern are those relating to: **13–051**

  (i)   where internet traders are taxed on their profits (i.e. "taxable presence" issues);

 (ii)   withholding tax and the characterisation of e-commerce payments; and

(iii)   computation of business profits, including transfer pricing.

13.27 TAXABLE PRESENCE ISSUES

An important tax question related to the internet, which perhaps reflects most obviously the tension between advances in technology and current tax rules, arises from the fact that an e-commerce business can provide goods or services to internet users located in a country without necessarily having any significant physical presence in that country and no personnel active in the business in that country. This raises the question of the extent, if any, to which the provider is taxable on its income in that country and the treatment of any such tax liability in its home territory. This question has received considerable attention from the OECD and the UK.   **13–052**

13.27.1 UK law

The UK, like most other jurisdictions, determines "taxability" by reference to the concepts of residency, the source of the income, and "permanent establishment". Each concept evolved in relation to traditional forms of commerce and is based largely on requirements related to physical presence. Broadly, a company will be treated as resident in the UK for tax purposes if it is either incorporated in the UK (with certain exceptions) or the central management and control of a company's business is based in the UK. Such a company is subject to UK corporation tax on its worldwide income and   **13–053** gains. Conversely, a UK company may be treated as tax resident under the domestic laws of another country. If the UK has concluded a double tax treaty with that country, a "tie-breaker" rule may apply to determine the tax residence of the company (for which see section 13.28 below).

A non-UK resident company trading "in" the UK through a UK "permanent establishment" will be chargeable to UK corporation tax on income (whenever arising) and chargeable gains (arising within the UK) which are attributable to that permanent establishment. This "permanent establishment" concept replaces the broadly equivalent term, "branch or agency", which applied to companies subject to UK corporation tax before the Finance Act 2003. That latter term is now only relevant to non-resident persons that are not companies liable to UK tax from a trade, profession or vocation carried on in the UK.

This basic position may be modified where a trader is resident in a country with which the UK has concluded a double tax treaty. However, given that the UK double tax treaty network is generally based on the OECD's Model Tax Convention, the normal corporation tax position should be as stated above; a non-resident trader will only be taxed in the UK on such worldwide income and UK gains as are attributable to its "permanent establishment" trading in the UK. A non-resident company may also be subject to a charge to UK tax if it is trading in the UK even when it has no permanent establishment. However, this would be unusual and the UK does not generally have enforcement procedures in such circumstances. Moreover, treaty protection would make it clear that there should be no income tax liabilities.

A "permanent establishment" has been defined in the UK along very similar lines as that in the OECD's Model Tax Convention, and is broadly a "fixed place of business through which the business of the [non-resident] company is wholly or partly carried on".[53] Examples of such places of business are given in the legislation and include a branch, office, factory or place of management. The definition also extends to agents acting on behalf of the company which have, and habitually exercise in the UK, authority to do business on behalf of the company. This means that, as well as taxing a genuine branch operation, the UK may also tax trading operations conducted through a third party selling agent, but not agents of independent status acting in the ordinary course of their business.

The OECD has produced a Commentary on its Model Tax Convention to which the UK has contributed. The Commentary contains a discussion of the "fixed place of business" concept from which it is clear that some form of permanent physical presence is required to constitute a permanent establishment, normally including personnel but which can, in appropriate

---

[53] As defined in s.148 of the UK Finance Act 2003. See also the UK Revenue's International Manual INTM 260000 (onwards) in relation to non-residents trading in the UK and on permanent establishments: *http://www.hmrc.gov.uk/manuals/intmanual/intm260000.htm*.

cases, be constituted by the mere presence of equipment (for example, in the context of a vending machine business). Fixed places of business are, however, generally excluded from constituting permanent establishments where the activities carried out there are of a preparatory or auxiliary nature to the non-resident's business, for example advertising or the storage of stocks of goods (where this is the only activity carried out).

Due to the similarities in the "permanent establishment" concept under UK law and under Art.5 of the OECD Model Tax Convention, the OECD's Commentary on the interpretation of this concept is, according to the UK Revenue, "substantially applicable" to the UK permanent establishment.

As far as trading "in" the UK by non-residents is concerned, the test for determining this is derived from UK case law and generally seeks to identify whether a non-resident's profits arise in substance from operations in the UK. This would depend on what the essential profit-making operations might be. Where, for instance, such operations are the buying and selling of goods, the trade is normally exercised at the place where the contracts for sale are concluded or accepted.

This is not always the decisive factor however, especially in the case of the provision of services. So a trade may still be treated as exercised in the UK where contracts are formally concluded abroad if there is significant economic activity in the UK contributing to the profit-producing activities. It will, however, be difficult to apply this test to a non-resident business trading globally through a UK sited server, especially in determining where and when contracts have been concluded in the absence of human intervention. Moreover, even where profits do derive from a UK trade, the UK will have limited taxing powers unless the activities of the e-business in the UK constitute a permanent establishment in the UK (or branch or agency, where applicable).

13.27.2 Applying the rules to e-commerce

It is not generally clear as to what constitutes a permanent establishment in the context of e-commerce (or e-business). Where a non-resident trader has no physical presence in the UK at all, it is difficult to see how a permanent establishment could be constituted. It also seems unlikely that traders hosting a web page on a server in another jurisdiction, in order to sell their own products or services, can be treated as having set up a permanent establishment. More debatable, however, is the position where, for example, an ISP has leased lines from a UK telephone company or is selling the use of its server. With respect to the former, whether a permanent establishment is constituted may depend on the terms of the lease (for example, whether only capacity or an identifiable network is being leased). As regards the latter, it may depend upon the scope and functionality of the server and the extent of the supporting human resources.

In January 2001 the OECD published the outcome of discussions on the

13–054

concept of permanent establishment in the context of e-commerce[54] and this has led to amendments being published in its January 2003 update to the OECD's Commentary on Art.5, clarifying the circumstances when the use of automated computer equipment might constitute a permanent establishment. The broad consensus is as follows:

1. a website (which is regarded as a combination of software and electronic data) cannot, of itself, constitute a permanent establishment because it is not tangible and has no physical location (involving premises, machinery, or equipment) that can constitute a "place of business";

2. a website hosting arrangement typically does not constitute a permanent establishment for the enterprise which trades through that medium (since the hosting server is typically not going to be at the disposal of that enterprise, which is a "place of business" requirement);

3. an ISP will not, except in very unusual circumstances, be a dependent agent of another business such as to constitute a permanent establishment of that business;

4. a place where computer equipment, such as a server, is located may constitute a permanent establishment of a business. However, for this proposition to apply, it is required that the functions performed at that place be significant as well as an essential or core part of the business activity of the enterprise. Human intervention is not however necessary and examples can include concluding orders from on-line customers, processing credit card details, automated delivery, i.e. functions which are beyond what is preparatory or auxiliary to the business for the proposition to apply.

With regard to the fourth point above, the UK Revenue has adopted a more simplistic approach. As published in a press release in April 2000,[55] the UK holds the view that, in no circumstances do servers, of themselves or together with websites, constitute permanent establishments in the UK for the purposes of enterprises engaged in e-commerce. This view is held regardless of whether the server is owned, rented or otherwise at the disposal of the business.

In taking this view, the UK Revenue has described the OECD's stance as too restrictive for businesses, and that corporate taxes should generally be due only where companies are registered/established and not where they house their servers. Therefore, a non-UK resident would not have a taxable presence in the UK by virtue of simply owning or otherwise having available a server in the UK through which it carried out its e-commerce business

---

[54] See the report entitled "Clarification on the Application of the Permanent Establishment Definition in E-Commerce: Changes to the Commentary on the Model Tax Convention on Article 5", December 22, 2000, available at *http://www.oecd.org/dataoecd/46/32/ 1923380.pdf.*
[55] UK Revenue's Press Release 84/2000, April 11, 2000.

activities. The UK Revenue has since confirmed that it continues to hold this view in its International Manual on non-residents trading in the UK.[56] Applying the UK's position to servers on a network, it may also be unlikely that ownership of a network done in the UK would constitute a permanent establishment as there is no other establishment of the business in the UK. However, the position is not free from doubt. By way of an example (although not a UK case) in the so-called "*Pipeline*" case[57], a network of underground pipes owned by a Dutch company running through Germany was considered to constitute a permanent establishment in Germany, even though no Dutch employees were present in Germany.

Other OECD member countries (including Australia, the United States, Japan and Norway) do not appear to have departed from the OECD's view on the fourth point above, although Greece, Spain and Portugal have expressed some doubts. **13–055**

The broad view of other members is that a server, as distinct from mere websites which cannot be permanent establishments, can constitute a permanent establishment where the equipment is fixed, i.e. it is located at a specific location and is not moved for a sufficient period of time to become fixed (and what is relevant is not the possibility of the server being moved, but whether in fact it is moved).

This means that if an enterprise carrying on business through a website has the server at its own disposal and operates the server on which the website is stored and used, the place where that server is located could constitute a permanent establishment of the enterprise if the other requirements are met, i.e. it is fixed, the business is wholly or partly carried on through it, and the e-commerce operations carried on through it are not restricted to preparatory or auxiliary activities.

E-commerce activities that do not usually amount to a permanent establishment (because they are preparatory or auxiliary activities)[58] fall within the following categories:

1. providing a communications link between suppliers and customers;
2. advertising of goods and services (for example, displaying a catalogue of products);
3. relaying information through a mirror server for security and efficiency purposes;
4. gathering market data for the business; and
5. supplying information.

Where, however, these activities form in themselves an essential and significant part of the business as a whole, or other core functions of the

---

[56] At INTM p.266100 of the International Manual, dated November 2004: *http://www.hmrc.gov.uk/manuals/intmanual/INTM266100.htm.*
[57] BFH/German Federal Tax Court decision of October 30, 1996, 11 R 1Z/92.
[58] As listed in para.42.7 of the OECD's Commentary on Art.5 of the Model Tax Convention in relation to e-commerce.

business are carried on through the equipment, and are more than preparatory or auxiliary, they may result in a permanent establishment if the relevant equipment is fixed. What constitutes core functions for a particular business depends on the nature of the business carried on generally by the enterprise, and whether the activities performed through the equipment are more than merely preparatory or auxiliary in light of such business carried on by the enterprise. Although these statements are not relevant as to whether or not there is a permanent establishment in the UK (assuming the UK maintains its current policy), they would affect UK resident companies trading in overseas jurisdictions.

Furthermore, according to the OECD's Commentary, it is only in very unusual circumstances that, where a business has a website hosted on the server of an ISP, the ISP will constitute a permanent establishment for that other business (for instance, a more pro-active service is provided by the ISP). If the ISP were to be regarded as a dependent agent for the other business, the ISP would need to have and regularly exercise the right to enter into contracts on behalf of the other business before it would be regarded as a permanent establishment of that other business.

The OECD is continuing its review of the general appropriateness of the permanent establishment concept as a requirement for taxing the profits of non-residents, and not just for those involved in e-commerce. This is in light of how the business environment has changed and, for instance, the increase in the use of servers based in favourable tax havens, and the need for greater consistency to prevent risks of double taxation. The OECD e-commerce analysis of this topic has however already concluded (as at December 2005) that there has not been any "significant decrease to the tax revenues of capital importing companies"[59] caused by internet usage, contrary to early predictions. As a result, it appears that this concept will not be altered for the time being and will remain significant to the taxation of e-commerce for the foreseeable future.

The UK Revenue has also expressed the view that, although the permanent establishment concept may become less appropriate as the threshold for taxation in the long term, it is a long standing concept and one which is widely supported. In light of this and the absence of any clearly better alternative (for which see section 13.30 below), it considers there is at present no compelling reason to depart from it.

13.28 PLACE OF EFFECTIVE MANAGEMENT

13–056   Another tax residency concept which has concerned governments and businesses in the context of e-commerce is that of the "place of effective management" concept as a tie-breaker rule in double tax treaties to determine tax residence (for treaty purposes) of persons or entities that

---

[59] See further at para.13–061 below.

under the domestic legislation of the contracting states are then resident in both states. Such tie-breaker rules determine which treaty country should have the primary taxing rights in relation to an individual or company based on various residence indicia of personal attachment for individuals, and on the "place of effective management" for companies. The latter is usually the place where the key management and commercial decisions that are necessary for the conduct of a company's business are in substance made. Normally this lies with the directors, i.e. those persons exercising the strategic (i.e. the key management and commercial) decisions and powers of the company's business.

Where senior managers operate from a single location, such as a head office, the determination of the place where key management and commercial decisions are made is not too difficult and normally coincides with where the company has its registered office and where the directors reside. However, e-commerce has fundamentally changed the way people run their business, making it very difficult to determine an exact geographical location for decision making.

One obvious example is that of senior managers or directors of various locations/countries who conduct meetings by way of video conferencing or via the internet. It can be difficult to point to one particular location as being pre-eminent and a place of effective management could exist simultaneously in multiple jurisdictions, without any single jurisdiction being dominant. Therefore, the emerging international view has been that modern technology and rapid e-commerce growth have made these types of tests all the more difficult to apply and could also mean that the "place of effective management" concept could become an ineffective and unfair way of determining the single tax residency of a company. The overall conclusion has been that more guidance on determining tax residence is required.

The OECD has considered this issue leading to suggestions (in May 2003) for changes to the OECD's Commentary[60] to clarify the interpretation of the "place of effective management" test. The OECD also considered other tie-break options, including tests based on economic nexus or the place of incorporation, as well as an alternative of denying dual resident companies treaty benefits altogether, but these were not regarded as sufficiently definitive or necessarily producing the right result.

The favoured approach is therefore to refine rather than replace the existing tie-breaker. The suggested changes seek to expand the Commentary to make it clear that the country of residence would be the place where key business decisions are actually considered and substantially made (either by management or a controlling shareholder), rather than routinely approved.

An additional proposal has also been put forward, being the introduction

---

[60] The discussion paper "The Impact of the Communications Revolution on the Application of the 'Place of Effective Management' as a Tie Breaker Rule" is available at *http://www.oecd.org/dataoecd/46/27/1923328.pdf*; and the suggested changes to paras. 21–24 of the OECD's Commentary specifically for Art.4 of the Model Tax Convention are set out in a discussion draft available at: *http://www.oecd.org/dataoecd/24/17/2956428.pdf*.

of a new "hierarchy of tests" as an alternative version of the "tie-breaker" rule for what would otherwise be dual-resident companies. The hierarchy of tests gives a weighting to various factors based on where business functions are carried out, closest economic links, decision-making by senior executives, place of incorporation, or otherwise the tie-breaker would be settled by mutual agreement (although this last test may be somewhat hollow as many treaties contain no provision to deal with the failure of the contracting states to reach agreement). These suggestions are still under review and have not yet been published in the Commentary.

13.29 CHARACTERISATION OF E-COMMERCE PAYMENTS AND WITHHOLDING TAXES

13.29.1 UK law

13–057   In the UK, withholding taxes are only applicable to particular types of income: there is no general obligation to withhold tax at source from payments made to non-UK residents. Of most relevance in the context of the internet is that tax (at the rate currently set at 22 per cent for the tax year 2006/2007) must be withheld from payments of royalties or sums paid periodically in respect of a copyright by a UK resident to a non-UK resident. In the UK, computer software is protected by copyright under the Copyright, Designs and Patents Act 1988 and this treatment flows through for tax purposes. Therefore, the UK withholding tax machinery will apply where a copyright owner, not resident in the UK for tax purposes, is paid royalties and/or licence fees by a UK resident for the use of computer software.

Excluded from the UK withholding obligation are royalties paid in respect of cinematograph films or video recordings and their soundtracks, provided that the soundtrack is not exploited separately. Double tax treaties (at least those based on the OECD Model Tax Convention) also generally exempt film and video royalties, sometimes more expansively than the basic UK rules. If excluded under the terms of a double tax treaty, royalties and fees may be paid gross if an appropriate direction is obtained in advance from the UK Revenue. Alternatively, the tax can be reclaimed from the UK Revenue by the non-resident payee. Note that the withholding obligation is not generally excluded if the licensor is licensing through a permanent establishment in the UK (see section 13.27.2 above).

13.29.2 The problem

13–058   As discussed above, certain products may be transmitted electronically rather than in physical form. Examples already given include written material (such as books, newspapers, and reference material) and computer software. Further examples include audio and visual material such as music, video, and photographs. Digital delivery is now commonplace and the internet is likely to become (if not already) the principal music and film market of the future, where "goods" (music CDs, video tapes, stereos, compact disc players) are being replaced with "services" bought directly through the internet on a "pay per performance basis".

The internet customer may have to pay a fee before being allowed to sample or view the product and will, in any event, usually have to pay a fee before being able to download the product. An underlying licence entitling the customer to use the product often accompanies the purchase and is concluded online. Under that licence, he may be allowed to modify the downloaded product or incorporate it into other products which he develops himself, either for his own use or to sell to others.

The issue which arises is whether payments to sample and/or download such items for these various purposes are, in whole or in part, payments for the right to use a copyright (that is to say, they are a "royalty" which may be subject to withholding tax) or payments for the purchase of goods or services not involving the use of copyright (and therefore not subject to withholding tax).

For tax treaty purposes, this characterisation issue is fundamental to the treaty distinction between payments which constitute royalties and those which are payments for the provisions of services or goods taxable as business profits. Again, practical problems arise for businesses supplying digitised products via the internet because the rules which distinguish between such payments were developed in relation to physical products, so strictly speaking, neither the general exclusion from withholding obligations in the UK which applies to royalties paid in respect of cinematograph films or video recordings, nor any double tax treaty provision, may apply to digitised products.

13.29.3 Current position

As previously noted at para.13–004 above, the OECD had been looking at this problem[61] and the UK had been participating in the discussions. The OECD has now expanded its Commentary to the Model Tax Convention (specifically on Art.12[62]) clarifying how the concepts of royalties, business profits, and provision of services apply to typical e-commerce payments and, in particular, to digitised products obtained from the internet.

The revised Commentary confirms that the primary question to be addressed is "the identification of the consideration for the payment" and

13–059

---

[61] See the February 2001 report to Working Party No.1 of the OECD Committee on Fiscal Affairs, entitled "Tax Treaty Characterisation Issues Arising from E-Commerce", by the TAG on Treaty Characterisation of Electronic Commerce Payments: *http://www.oecd.org/dataoecd/46/34/1923396.pdf*.

[62] Please refer to paras 11–17 of the OECD's revised Commentary on Art.12 as amended in April 2000 and in January 2003.

this will normally depend on what the copyright licence will allow the customer to do with the product which has been downloaded and purchased. A payment will not normally be characterised as a royalty where the copyright licence only exists to enable a customer to use a product (for example, to copy a program onto a computer hard drive), but it will be a royalty where the customer has paid for and is granted rights to use the product in a way that would infringe the copyright without such a licence (for example, to distribute or modify the computer program). Therefore in relation to computer software at least, the OECD takes the view that withholding taxes should only apply in relation to the commercial exploitation of software, rather than its personal use.

The UK Revenue subscribes to this approach as is apparent from its International Manual guidance on when payments for computer software may be treated as royalties.[63] This means, therefore, that where a content provider supplies software via the internet, accompanied by a licence, to a customer for the customer's personal use, the provider and customer do not need concern themselves with the need to withhold UK tax from any payment(s) made. Such an approach avoids the significant problems of enforcement which would otherwise arise.

The approach to computer software has also been adopted for digitised products. Therefore, withholding tax questions should not arise for customers (home-users and enterprises) who order digitised products for their own use and enjoyment. In such cases, the payment is unlikely to be in the nature of a royalty as it is not made for the use or right to use a copyright—rather, it is made "to acquire data transmitted in the form of a digital signal", and, typically, nor would any sum be paid periodically.

Under this approach, the manner of the delivery of the product itself, whether on tangible media or electronically, should not be relevant to the characterisation of the payment, thereby ensuring the principle of neutrality. Additionally, the fact that the customer in such cases may incidentally acquire limited rights to the copyright in the digitised product in order to download, store or operate the product on their computer or copy it onto the computer hard drive or onto a CD will not affect the analysis.

Even if withholding were to apply, it is also difficult to see how the UK Revenue could enforce the withholding obligations. So the main withholding tax issues are likely to arise in relation to the commercial arrangements entered into by content providers, where, for instance, a purchaser has acquired a right of reproduction to make several copies as a way of exploiting the software or product.

The Commentary also gives some practical guidance to deal with the difficulties of distinguishing between payments as royalties or business profits where (increasingly) software, technical assistance and know-how are bundled and sold as a package to customers, and how such payments should be apportioned according to what is provided.

Broadly, it recommends treating as business profits payments made for

---

[63] See further at: *http://www.hmrc.gov.uk/manuals/intmanual/INTM342630.htm.*

advice provided electronically, for electronic communication with technicians or for accessing, through computer networks, a trouble-shooting database such as a database that provides users with non-confidential information in response to frequently asked questions or common problems that arise frequently. To tax the consideration for mixed contracts, it recommends that payments be broken down based on information contained in the contract or reasonably apportioned, unless one element of the total consideration is predominant and the others are only of an ancillary and unimportant character, in which case the total consideration should be taxed according to the treatment applicable to the principal part.

A relatively recent e-commerce case in India has considered these concepts in relation to a UK company. In *Re ABC Ltd UK; Re XYZ Ltd UK*,[64] a UK-based taxpayer company supplied electronic credit-rating reports which could be acquired by customers in India via a (related) Indian company. The reports were retained in a database on a server outside of India. Questions arose as to whether payments for the reports were royalties or business profits and whether there was a permanent establishment in India. On the facts, the reports were standardised products which compiled publicly available factual information. They were accessible by any subscriber on payment with regular internet access for which no particular software or hardware was required. Copyright in the reports was also retained by the taxpayer on each sale.

The taxpayer argued that the sale of a report equated to the sale of a book, which did not involve any transfer of an intellectual property right. The court agreed, so the payments were business profits, not royalties. It was also held that there was no permanent establishment in India. The court recognised that, for e-commerce, it is not necessary to maintain a physical stock or inventory but that on-line access to information might be sufficient to be equated with the maintenance of stock. The Indian company did not however habitually maintain the stock of reports on the website and deliver them on behalf of the taxpayer. Instead, it had to approach the taxpayer and give details of the information required before being permitted access to the server. The taxpayer simply allowed the Indian company to take a report from the website maintained by it (and not the Indian company). Again, this was akin to a sale rather than the delegation of agency functions to the Indian company.

13.30 QUANTIFYING BUSINESS PROFITS AND TRANSFER PRICING

From the preceding discussion, it can be appreciated that a company conducting business over the internet such as an ISP will need to consider the

13–060

---

[64] 8 I.T.L.R. 802, October 26, 2005, decision at the Authority for Advance Rulings (Income Tax), New Delhi.

difficult question of whether it has sufficient presence in a country to constitute a permanent establishment there. If it does, the separate but related question arises of what proportion of the total profits of the company is to be properly attributed to the permanent establishment (over which the country in which the permanent establishment exists will have primary taxing rights). Moreover, where "related" enterprises resident in different countries each have some participation in e-commerce transactions, a further separate but connected issue which may also require consideration is "transfer pricing".

Transfer pricing is the term used to describe the process whereby prices that are set by related enterprises in respect of, inter alia, sales or transfers of goods and the provision of services, including finance, between them may be adjusted for tax purposes to prevent the manipulation of taxable profits by virtue of the prices actually charged being higher or lower (as appropriate) than the market value. Obviously, the "transfer prices" may affect more than one tax jurisdiction and if both jurisdictions do not agree on the appropriate transfer prices (and thus the share of taxing rights), there is the risk of double taxation or of less than single taxation.

This risk is at its greatest if the relevant double tax treaty contains no means of resolving any deadlock between the two domestic tax authorities under the normal "mutual agreement" article—but even if there is, the process is likely to be lengthy and expensive and beyond the resources of many taxpayers.

An example of where this issue may arise is where connected companies are involved in, say, website hosting outside the UK and on-the-ground activities (for example, website design) in the UK, if the UK tax authorities maintain that the fees charged for the website design are too low, but the authorities for the state where the host is located refuse to allow a tax deduction greater than the actual fee paid.

The UK transfer pricing rules were amended in 1998 and 2003 (for domestic UK to UK transactions), bringing them into line with the international consensus reached by the OECD as reflected in the OECD's 1995 transfer pricing guidance.[65] By these rules an "arm's length principle" is to be used to determine transfer prices for tax purposes. This states that the transfer prices for dealings between related enterprises are to be those which would have been agreed between them, for comparable transactions in comparable circumstances, had they been entirely distinct and separate entities dealing on an arm's length basis.

The increased speed and mobility of business activities and cross-border transactions resulting from internet usage has had particular implications for applying transfer pricing methods and for taxing business profits, but the present international consensus appears to be that e-commerce poses no new fundamental problems.

However, governments recognise that some of the factors relevant to its

---

[65] Transfer Pricing Guidelines for Multinational Enterprises and Tax Administrations (OECD July 1995).

practical application may be more difficult to take into account (for example, finding comparable transactions between independents by reference to which the principle can be applied) and that, as e-commerce opens up cross-border trade, transfer pricing issues may occur more frequently for a much wider range of companies, including small- and medium-sized enterprises. E-commerce also gives rise to increasing integration and co-operation in trading activities, and together with increased use of intangible assets, this will inevitably add to the complexities of transfer pricing, both for business and the tax administrations.

Some of these issues have been the subject of consideration by the OECD to which the UK has contributed. An OECD report on the attribution of profits to permanent establishments in the context of "e-tailing" was released in February 2001.[66] This concluded that a transfer pricing analysis to a server permanent establishment where only automated equipment is used would generally reveal that only limited functions would be performed, limited assets used, and restricted business risks assumed in the performance of those functions, given the lack of human intervention/significant "people functions" and their automated nature, and any such risks or assets would only be likely to be those directly associated with the server hardware.

So for example, in e-tailing, a permanent establishment comprising only of a server performing low-level automated functions at a location without supporting personnel would be similar to that of a service provider providing low-value services for a head office, the bulk of profits being attributable to the latter. Consequently, it is likely that little or no profits would be attributable to the server.

Another report examining how appropriate the OECD's transfer pricing guidance is to the issues raised by e-commerce in the context of four other specific business models (automated electronic transactions; on-line auctions for customer to customer and business to business sales; subsidiary to parent web hosting arrangements; and computerised transactions for airline reservations) led to similar conclusions.

The overall consensus therefore is, given the likely low levels of profit attribution, presently no new or pressing issues exist in relation to the transfer pricing aspects of e-commerce. Furthermore, even though the internet has introduced more complex business models in cross-border trade which will be difficult to measure, the OECD's approach has been one of acknowledging that the current guidance presently remains transferable to such models and functions, although this will continue to be monitored.

Following public consultation, the OECD's Business Profits TAG, whose **13–061** general mandate was to consider whether existing double tax treaty rules for taxing business profits are adequate for e-commerce, released a final report in December 2005.[67] That report refers to new e-business models

---

[66] See the discussion paper "Attribution of Profit to a Permanent Establishment Involved in Electronic Commerce Transactions" at: *http://www.oecd.org/dataoecd/46/25/1923312.pdf*.
[67] "Are the Current Treaty Rules for Taxing Business Profits Appropriate for E-Commerce", Final Report. See *http://www.oecd.org/dataoecd/58/53/35869032.pdf*.

and functions as background for their analysis of whether such current treaty rules are capable of dealing with the new reality of e-commerce in a fair and effective manner, applying the Framework Conditions as the criteria for evaluation, and considering whether it could be possible to find better solutions.

The report contains an interesting debate on whether the current "permanent establishment" definition as a primary nexus rule is or will become redundant in the future in light of e-commerce developments, as well as a discussion on a new nexus; an (electronic) virtual permanent establishment based on business carried on via a website.

The report concluded that there are no "clearly superior" methods to justify any fundamental changes to existing treaty rules. Contrary to early predictions, the internet has not caused any significant decrease to tax revenues such that existing rules are sufficient for protecting and sharing tax revenues at the present time, subject to further future developments being identified which take into account their impact on all types of business activities, and not just e-commerce. It also states that the arms' length principle is currently flexible enough for fairly measuring profits in the context of e-commerce.

That report does however identify that there is a need to continue to monitor how tax revenues are affected by changes to business models resulting from evolving technologies so that refinements to the definition of "permanent establishment" may be required from time to time, such as making all the existing exceptions from the definition of "permanent establishment" subject to the overall condition that all the relevant activities be of a "preparatory or auxiliary" character, or excluding functions performed with the use of servers and software. Further "supplementary" nexus rules may be adopted for taxing profits arising from the provision of services based on performance in a country for a certain period of time but this will depend on the outcome of the OECD's general review of the application of tax treaties to services.[68]

The OECD's work programme has also involved a detailed study of how the same considerations that underlie the application of the arm's length principle to transfer pricing should apply in addressing the process of attribution of profits to permanent establishments generally. This has been a long-running project aimed at achieving a greater consensus on the manner of attributing profits to permanent establishments and avoiding double taxation. The so-called "functionally separate entity approach" appears to be the preferred approach by OECD members when attributing profits, which mirrors the type of analysis that would be undertaken if the permanent establishment were a legally distinct and separate enterprise.

While the study does not expressly deal with e-commerce, it recognises that the growth of e-commerce is one of the reasons why a consensus on the

---

[68] Public Discussion Draft, "The Tax Treaty Treatment of Services: Proposed Commentary Changes", December 8, 2006. See further at: *http://www.oecd.org/dataoecd/2/20/37811491.pdf*.

taxation of permanent establishments is increasingly important. The OECD has recently released updated versions of its studies and work is underway to draft the necessary language to implement its conclusions, including a new version of Art.7 (Business Profits) in its Model Tax Convention, together with accompanying Commentary, to be used in the negotiation of future treaties and amendments to existing treaties. Meanwhile, a revised Commentary will also be prepared to improve the interpretation of the current rules. The OECD's Committee on Fiscal Affairs intends to release both parts of this implementation package in draft form for public comment during 2007.

13.31 OTHER POINTS

We have highlighted briefly three direct tax issues (withholding tax, taxable presence, and quantification of business profits) that are of relevance to the internet. Clearly, this only deals with some of the many tax issues that may be pertinent to a business which has trading operations in the UK or is contemplating whether to set up trading operations in the UK. For example, if significant development expenditure is to be incurred by, say, a content provider, it will need to investigate the extent to which tax relief is available (under the capital allowance legislation or the special tax regime applicable to films or on R&D relief). For a multinational, such considerations may be relevant factors in determining whether to site trading operations in the UK or in a more favourable jurisdiction. **13–062**

Other existing taxes have also been affected by technological developments. In the consultation paper on modernising the stamp duty regime, the main impetus for change was the introduction of an electronic conveyancing system allowing for the electronic transfer of land and buildings. The UK stamp duty regime depended on the existence of paper documents (rather than transactions), so it had become outdated. The result was the introduction in December 2003 of Stamp Duty Land Tax based on land transactions rather than the documents executed to effect them.

Advances in technology have also facilitated the provision of betting and gaming services electronically, and as noted by the Commission, on-line gambling, gaming and betting services has been a significant area of e-commerce growth. In response to the growth of offshore betting assisted by e-commerce opportunities, UK General Betting Duty was abolished in 2001 and replaced with a new duty system in a bid to bring offshore betting operations back to the UK, and to allow UK bookmakers the opportunity to strengthen their position in the global telephone and internet betting market. The Gambling Act 2005 is currently being implemented (by September 1, 2007) to consolidate and regulate the entire betting and gaming industry and this has also led to some clarification of the VAT treatment of gaming machines. On-line gaming can now take place and be provided from within the UK, although the UK Government is planning to introduce rules restricting the marketing of, and/or access to, gaming sites that are not adequately regulated, and also a new "remote gaming" duty in relation to the provision of on-line gaming in the UK.

There has also been significant coverage in the media about the amount of tax lost as a result of "carousel" fraud, now more commonly referred to as "MTIC" (Missing Trader Intra Community) fraud, which has been compounded by the internet. The UK therefore sought (and has been given) derogation from the Sixth Council Directive to introduce reverse charge accounting for the supply by businesses of certain (mainly electronic) goods, such as mobile phones, computer chips, and games consoles, with effect from December 2006. It will be the responsibility of the purchaser, rather than the seller, to account for VAT on such supplies.

As a final point, the internet provides many new opportunities for improving taxpayer service and the OECD, in its 1998 Ottawa Taxation Framework Conditions, identified a number of options as to how it saw this could be achieved. In general, the UK Revenue has actively taken advantage of internet technology as a means of communication, processing of returns and tax collection in line with the OECD's recommendations.

CHAPTER 14

Competition Law and the Internet

This chapter looks at the application of EC and UK competition law to the **14–001** Internet and e-commerce.

In terms of EC competition law, this means analysis of:

- The EC Merger Regulation;
- The application of the rules on restrictive agreements under Art.81 of the EC Treaty; and
- The application of the rules on abuse of dominance under Art.82 of the EC Treaty.

The section on UK competition law at the end of the chapter looks at UK merger provisions contained in the Enterprise Act 2002, and the provisions of the Competition Act 1998, which contains rules prohibiting restrictive agreements and the abuse of market dominance which mirror those applying under Art.81 and Art.82 of the EC Treaty. It also considers other provisions of the Enterprise Act, which introduce the disqualification of directors for breaches of UK and EC competition law and the criminalisation of cartel behaviour.

This chapter does not examine the rules on restrictive agreements (Art.53) or abuse of dominance (Art.54) contained in the European Economic Area Agreement. Those rules mirror Arts. 81 and 82 of the EC Treaty, and the territory that they affect covers the States of the European Economic Area ("EEA") which include the 27 EU States, in addition to Norway, Iceland and Liechtenstein. Nor does it cover any other national competition rules other than those of the UK.

14.1 RELEVANT MARKETS

Before looking at the substance of these rules, it is useful to look at the **14–002** question of what are the relevant markets for competition purposes. Such an exercise is essential for nearly all applications of the competition rules. Defining relevant markets is fundamental to the analysis applied under the rules on abuse of a dominant market position, and the rules on merger control. The market power of the parties to an agreement may also determine whether the agreement is seen as having a sufficiently appreciable effect to come within the rules on restrictive agreements.

There are market share thresholds for the application of the EC block exemptions under Art.81, as will be seen below. In addition, market shares may be relevant in deciding whether an agreement can obtain exemption under Art.81(3) (or the UK equivalent).

In this section, we look at some of the markets which have been defined by the European Commission, mostly in merger cases, but occasionally under Art.81.

14.1.1 Access markets

Access infrastructure

14–003   The communications infrastructure "access" market may potentially comprise all types of infrastructure that can be used for the provision of a given service. For instance, in *Nortel/Norweb*,[1] the Commission recognised that electricity networks using "Digital Power Line" technology could provide an alternative to existing traditional local telecommunications access loop, commenting that[2]:

> "in assessing the possible market dominance by the joint venture it should be taken into account that in enabling the existing electricity distribution network to act as a local loop, DPL technology provides an alternative to the existing traditional local telecommunications access loop and that there are still several other alternative solutions available. The findings of the Commission also suggest that the alternative access technologies mentioned above such as fast modem, cable modem, ADSL, HDSL and wireless should provide strong alternatives to DPL technology."

In that case, the Commission did not have to decide, however, whether DPL technology was in the same market as these other forms of access.

There are of course a number of other access technologies for the internet that exist or are in the process of being developed, including ADSL (asymmetric digital subscriber line), HDSL (hierarchical digital subscriber line) on existing copper telephone wire, cable modems which allow the use of a cable TV network as the access loop, and wireless broadband technologies via satellite or stationary ground stations.

---

[1] Case IV/M.1113, *Nortel/Norweb*, March 18, 1998.
[2] *ibid.*, [29].

In its guidelines on market analysis and calculation of market power under the new telecoms regime,[3] the Commission comments that:

> "whether the market for network infrastructures should be divided into as many separate submarkets as there are existing categories of network infrastructure, depends clearly on the degree of substitutability among such (alternative) networks. This exercise should be carried out in relation to the class of users to which access to the network is provided. A distinction should, therefore, be made between provision of infrastructure to other operators (wholesale level) and provision to end-users (retail level). At the retail level, a further segmentation may take place between business and residential customers."

The Commission considers that at the retail level, when the service to be provided concerns only end-users subscribed to a particular network, access to the termination points of that network may well constitute the relevant product market. This will not be the case if it can be established that the same services may be offered to the same class of consumers by means of alternative, easily accessible competing networks.

For example, in its Communication on unbundling the local loop, the Commission stated that although alternatives to the PSTN for providing high speed communications services to residential consumers exist (fibre optic networks, wireless local loops, or upgradable TV networks), none of these alternatives may be considered as a substitute to the fixed local loop infrastructure. This was because:

> "[f]iber optics are currently competitive only on upstream transmission markets whereas wireless local loops which are still to be deployed will target mainly professionals and individuals with particular communications needs. With the exception of certain national markets, existing cable TV networks need costly upgrades to support two ways broadband communications, and, compared with xDLS technologies, they do not offer a guaranteed bandwidth since customers share the same cable channel."

However, "future innovative and technological changes may, however, justify different conclusions."[4]

In the eventually unsuccessful *Telia/Telenor*[5] merger, the Commission found that there was a market for "connection to the local loop" for new entrants:

---

[3] Guidelines on market analysis and the assessment of significant market power under the Community regulatory framework for electronic communications networks and services, O.J. 2002 C165/6, July 11, 2002, para.67.

[4] *ibid.*, [68]. See also Case IV/JV.11, *@Home Benelux BV*, September 15, 1998.

[5] Case COMP/M.1439, *Telia/Telenor*, October 13, 1999, [76].

"Before he or she can access any higher level telephone services, a subscriber has to be physically connected to the PSTN, which is usually done by allocating him or her a twisted copper pair to his nearest local exchange. There is accordingly a demand on the part of subscribers and telecom entrants for connection to the local loop."

The market for top level or universal internet connectivity/wholesale ISP services

14–004   In *Worldcom/MCI*[6] and subsequently in *MCI Worldcom/Sprint*,[7] the Commission described a vertical hierarchical view of the provision of "internet connectivity". Internet service providers must offer their customers universal connectivity on the internet, and must be able to deliver traffic from their customers to other ISPs' networks either through direct connection or via intermediate connection.

One option is a bilateral peering agreement where an agreement is reached with another ISP to reciprocally terminate traffic from each other, traditionally on a no-charge basis, but not including traffic coming from other ISPs through peering agreements.

Another option for an ISP is to enter into a "transit" agreement, and to pay another ISP to acquire the right for its traffic to be treated as traffic from that other ISP which can then be transferred across that ISP's peering interfaces for delivery on other networks, under the other party's peering agreements, or through its transit agreements. Such transit traffic spends much of its time ascending or descending through successive hierarchies, linked to one another by such vertical customer/provider relationships, with a horizontal movement across a peering interface usually only happening once on the journey.

The "top level" networks or ISPs are the only organisations capable of delivering complete internet connectivity entirely on their own account, and this connectivity is referred to as "top level" or "universal" connectivity. Top level ISPs deliver their traffic, and that of their dependent "transit" customer ISPs through peering arrangements with other ISPs, and do not have to rely on any paid interconnection such as transit.

"Secondary peering" ISPs may be able to deliver some of their own peering-based connectivity, but have to supplement it through bought "transit" agreements. Resellers operate totally on the basis of transit agreements, and can only supply resold connectivity, although depending on who they bought it from, it might be a combination of first and second tier connectivity.

For an ISP to have a peering agreement with a top level ISP is dependent on factors influencing traffic flows, such as the number of customers and

---

[6] Case IV/M.1069, *Worldcom/MCI*, July 8, 1998.
[7] Case COMP/M.1741, *MCI Worldcom/Sprint*, June 28, 2000.

websites hosted, capacity of the ISP network and geography, as well as historical legacy.

The products offered by the top level networks are differentiated in that the connectivity is supplied entirely by peering arrangements between these top level ISPs. Neither secondary peering ISPs nor resellers are able to constrain the behaviour of these top level networks and prevent them from acting independently.

If the top level networks increased the price of their internet connectivity by 5 per cent, the cost base of the resellers would be increased by this amount, and this would have to be passed on to the customer. Secondary peering ISPs could not avoid continuing to buy some transit from the top level networks, and therefore, according to the Commission, they would not be capable of providing an adequate service in response to the price increases.

The ISPs outside of the top level group could still provide a competitive constraint, to the extent that they were able to use their peering arrangements with the top level networks to avoid the increase in transit charges. However, if faced with such a challenge to their price increase strategy, the top level networks could react by charging for all internet interconnection, whether described as peering or transit. In that event, the unequal bargaining power of the secondary peering ISPs would not permit them to offer an effective competitive response.

The Commission therefore defined a market for "top level" or "universal" internet connectivity, comprised of top level, or first tier, providers rather than a market which included all ISPs with backbone capacity. In *MCI Worldcom/Sprint*, decided two years later, the parties argued that the structure of the market had changed, due to new techniques, including controlled content distribution, mirroring, caching and multihoming, but the Commission was not convinced and persisted with basically the same view of the market definition.

In the eventually unsuccessful *Telia/Telenor*[8] merger, the Commission discussed the market in wholesale ISP services, stating:

> "Wholesale ISP services comprise the resale of transit in Internet terms, which involves an obligation by the offering ISP to provide connectivity to the whole of the Internet to its customer ISP. This market is global. The information supplied by the parties show that neither of the merging parties would have fitted the definition of a top level network as applied in Commission Decision 1999/287 (WorldCom/MCI) and they are in part resellers of transit obtained from such networks. Moreover, as will be described below in the internet section of the competitive assessment Telenor's business as an internet transit provider is marginal; Telia is stronger at a European level, but still small on a global basis."

---

[8] Case COMP/M.1439, *Telia/Telenor*, October 13, 1999, [106].

Consumer internet access

Internet dial-up access distinguished from dedicated access (narrowband
14–005 **access)** In the *Telia/Telenor*[9] merger decision, the Commission identified a
demand for the supply of internet access services, and distinguished
between dial-up and dedicated access. These were considered to be two
separate product markets, on the basis that dial-up access is targeted at
residential and small- and medium-sized businesses, whereas dedicated
access was requested mainly by large corporate customers.

In *BT/ESAT*[10] it emerged in the course of the market investigation that
within dial-up access, it could be possible to distinguish between residential
and business (large companies) dial-up access, the latter being provided on
the basis of more sophisticated dial-up mechanisms. However, the Commission has so far found it unnecessary to establish whether residential and
business dial-up constitute two separate relevant product markets.

14–006 **Broadband internet access** In the course of its inquiry in *AOL/Time
Warner*,[11] the Commission found evidence of the existence of a developing
demand for the provision of residential broadband internet access. This was
considered to include high-speed internet access delivering greater audio
and visual functionality than dial-up (narrowband) access, including
streaming video and audio, video email, interactive advertising and video
conferencing, none of which can be delivered effectively over traditional
narrowband lines.

The Commission noted that broadband access was not yet widely
available in Europe and was generally more expensive than dial-up access.
It discussed Digital Subscriber Line (DSL) access and cable modems as
being broadband alternatives. However, for the purposes of the assessment
in that case, it was not necessary to conclude whether there existed a
separate broadband internet access market, or whether DSL, cable and
other forms of fast internet access belong to the same relevant product
market, since the conclusion was reached that the transaction did not give
rise to the creation of a dominant position in this area.

14.1.2 Internet/e-commerce-specific markets

Internet browsers

14–007 The Commission started a competition investigation against Microsoft in
respect of the terms under which Microsoft made available its Internet
Explorer browser to European Internet Service Providers. However, the
case was settled informally, and there is no indication as to whether the

---

[9] *ibid.*
[10] Case COMP/M.1838, *BT/ESAT*, March 27, 2000.
[11] Case COMP/M.1845, *AOL/Time Warner*, October 11, 2000.

Commission considered that browsers could constitute a relevant market, or on what basis the Commission was putting its case (see below).

Search engines

As regards other software needed to access the web, the Commission looked at search engines in the *WSI Webseek* case, which involved a joint venture between Deutsche Telekom, Springer, Holzbank and Infoseek to provide search and navigation services for German-speaking internet users.[12] The Commission concluded that since the search engine would be offered free of charge to internet users, the services provided could not constitute a relevant market in themselves. On the other hand, the internet advertising market, the paid-for content market and the internet access market did represent relevant markets.

14–008

Websites, portals and gateways

It is implicit in the early market definitions which had been accepted by the Commission that the provision of portals or gateways cannot be regarded as a market as such if they are accessible without any subscription or charge, although to the extent that such portals or gateways earn money from advertising, the internet advertising market will be a relevant market.

14–009

This was confirmed in the case of *Telia/Telenor/Schibsted*[13] where the parties were intending to provide gateway services, through which users could have access to a range of services, including financial information, games, business and financial information, shopping, travel, and ticket sales. Revenues would be generated by advertising, commission on transactions generated and subscriptions to other services accessed through the gateway.

The Commission considered that gateway services could not constitute a market in themselves. The Commission in this case considered that the service was essentially a kind of website hosting several different services or groups of services, some or all of which would be provided by third parties. They were generally financed through advertising rather than subscription income and most were supplied free of charge to subscribers by ISPs as part of the access package. The Commission did not consider that such gateway services constituted a market in themselves, but considered that the relevant markets were those for internet advertising and paid-for content.

In the "Vizzavi"[14] joint venture between Vodafone, Vivendi and Canal+ and in *Vivendi/Canal+/Seagram*[15] the Commission, however, identified developing national markets for TV-based internet portals and developing national and pan-European markets for horizontal portals offering WAP-based internet access. The existence of a distinct market for horizontal

---

[12] Case IV/JV.8, *Telekom/Springer/Holtzbrink/Infoseek/Webseek*, September 28, 1998.

[13] Case IV/JV.1, *Telia/Telenor/Schibsted*, May 27, 1998.

[14] Case COMP/JV.48, *Vodafone/Vivendi/Canal+*, July 20, 2000, see Commission press release IP 00/821.

[15] Case COMP/M.2050, *Vivendi/Canal+/Seagram*, October 13, 2000.

portals has been confirmed by the Commission in the *UGC/Liberty Media* case.[16]

Internet advertising

14–010   The Commission has in a number of cases considered that internet advertising was a relevant market.[17] Implicit within this definition is the suggestion that internet advertising is a market on its own, which is not part of a broader advertising market based on different media (in a similar way to that in which the Commission has recognised that there are separate markets in TV advertising).

The Commission has not considered whether there might be any further breakdown of internet advertising into separate markets. However, the UK case of *Network Multimedia Television Ltd v Jobserve*[18] considered below, could point towards a much narrower market definition in certain circumstances (although that case settled before final judgment). This involved a site which acted as a notice board for recruitment agencies to advertise job vacancies which was considered by recruiting agencies to be a site which they would need to use in order to obtain access to responses from good quality IT personnel.

Website production and related services

14–011   There may be a separate market for the production of websites. The parties to the *Telia/Telenor/Schibsted*[19] joint venture considered that production demands design and computer skills, which implied that the service constituted a separate market. The Commission did not have to decide the issue in this case, but suggested that website production might be sufficiently technical and specialised to justify a separate market definition.

14.1.3 Busines-to-Consumer (B2C) products and services sold over the internet

14–012   A fundamental question in the definition of e-commerce markets is whether on-line sales of a particular product or service are to be considered to be in the same market as off-line sales. Are traditional and the on-line distribution channels merely two different channels of distribution in the same market, or do the distribution channels define different markets?

Where sales of traditional goods or services are concerned, the Commission may often[20] consider the following questions as being relevant to this issue:

---

[16] Case COMP/M.2222, *UGC/Liberty Media*, April 24, 2001.
[17] See, for example, Case IV/M.1439, *Telia/Telenor*, October 13, 1999.
[18] [2001] UKCLR 814, April 5, 2001.
[19] Case IV/JV.1, *Telia/Telenor/Schibsted*, May 27, 1998.
[20] Commission contribution to OECD round table, "Competition issues in Electronic commerce", DAFFE/CLP(2000)32.

- Does the on-line sale of the product have characteristics different from the off-line sale (availability of off-line goods, range of goods available, product search, product delivery)?
- Is it possible to price discriminate between off-line and on-line users of the goods (bearing in mind that price discrimination here is being used for market definition, and is not an indication of anti-competitive activity)?

The Commission has had to consider this point in a number of cases.

On-line sales/distant sales of books

In a number of cases involving Bertelsmann, relating to the establishment of joint ventures for the sale of books on-line,[21] the Commission has had to consider whether the relevant market was that for all retail sales of books, or a smaller market for "distant sales" of books (including book clubs and mail order, as well as internet), or whether the on-line sales of books through the internet could be considered as a market in itself. The Commission never had to resolve this question, since in the cases it had to consider, there were no competitive concerns under the EC Merger Regulation on any of the plausible market definitions. However, it did seem to shift from considering that a market for all retail books could be the relevant market,[22] to considering that it is at least as narrow as "distant sales", and possibly as narrow as internet sales.[23]   **14–013**

Online travel agencies

In *T-Online/TUI/C&N Touristic*,[24] which involved the creation of a joint venture to establish an on-line travel agency, offering package tours, last minute trips, and flights, the Commission's preliminary investigation identified on-line travel agency services as a product market in its own right, distinct from traditional "bricks and mortar" travel agencies.   **14–014**

It found that both demand- and supply-side elements supported such a conclusion: on-line consumers can search and book trips any time, i.e. including outside regular shopping hours, and without leaving their home, while, on the other hand, on-line suppliers face lower distribution costs. The Commission had concerns that because of the strength of the parent companies, the joint venture might achieve such a strong position in on-line travel that it could progressively foreclose this still emerging market. The merger was eventually abandoned.

---

[21] Case IV/M.1459, *Bertelsmann/Havas/BOL*, May 6, 1999; Case JV.24, *Bertelsmann/Planeta/BOL Spain*, December 3, 1999; Case JV.45, *Bertelsmann/Kooperativa Förbundet/BOL Nordic*, May 12, 2000; Case COMP/JV.51, *Bertelsmann/Mondadori/BOL Italia*, September 1, 2000.

[22] Case IV/M.1459, *Bertelsmann/Havas/BOL*, May 6, 1999.

[23] Case COMP/JV.51, *Bertelsmann/Mondadori/BOL Italia*, September 1, 2000.

[24] Case COMP/M.2149, *T-Online International/TUI/C&N Touristic*, see Commission press release IP/01/670, May 8, 2001.

In *Telefonica Terra/Amadeus*,[25] another case involving the creation of an on-line travel agency, the Commission also found that the travel agency market is split into two segments: physical and on-line travel agencies.

On-line music

14–015 The above cases relate to situations in which traditional goods or services are distributed through the internet, but where they could be distributed through channels other than the internet. Another situation which has been distinguished by the European Commission is where there are on-line sales which have no exact off-line equivalents, such as where the internet itself is the delivery mechanism for the services.

In the *AOL/Time Warner*[26] merger, the Commission concluded that there was a market for on-line music, which it described as a form of narrowband content, distinguishing this from a separate market for broadband content. The Commission included within this description downloadable music files, as well as audio streaming services.

In respect of downloadable music, the parties to the merger did not consider that downloadable music constituted a separate market, but were of the opinion that it formed part of the larger market for recorded music. They claimed that downloadable music was substitutable for music distributed on physical carriers.

The Commission commented that there were a number of significant differences which make downloadable music an entirely different business model, and a separate market:

> "For example, from the demand side, consumers can access or buy and receive music immediately (instead of e-commerce, where they have to wait for the CD that they have ordered) from any computer with internet access, without having to visit a store, no matter the time and the location. They can download individual tracks, instead of buying the entire album or a single, and create customised compilations. They also need, beside the hardware, special software to play the music that they have downloaded. From the supply side, the structure of on-line distribution of downloadable music is completely different from the physical distribution of music (both in bricks and mortar shops and in e-commerce). Music downloading does not involve manufacturing, warehousing, physical sales and distribution. These differences make downloads and physical CDs two completely separate product markets. In addition, downloads and CDs have different pricing structures and the price and volume of CDs have not decreased as a result of the offering of music downloads. In the present case, the parties have provided no empirical evidence

---

[25] Case COMP/M.1812, *Telefonica Terra/Amadeus*, April 27, 2000.
[26] Case COMP/M.1845, *AOL/Time Warner* October 11, 2000.

showing that the pricing of music distributed on physical carriers is restrained by the pricing of downloading or that the pricing of physical CDs has gone down as a result of the offering of music downloads. It is, therefore, concluded that there is an emergent, but separate, market for downloadable music."[27]

The Commission did not fully discuss the implications of the fact that the vast majority of music downloaded from the internet at that time was downloaded for free, in terms of its effect on market definition. In respect of audio streaming services, however, it noted that:

"streaming is at present generally given free of charge and is financed out of internet advertising revenues. However, it can reasonably be expected that users will be charged for streaming in the near future. It can be mentioned in this context that following its licensing agreement with Time Warner and Bertelsmann, the Internet music company MP3 has announced plans to launch a subscription music service over the internet that is a system based on subscription fees to be paid by users for lockers."[28]

The Commission concluded that there was an emerging market for on-line music delivery. For the purpose of its assessment in that case, though, it was unnecessary to decide whether music downloads and streaming constituted one or two separate product markets as the transaction would in any event lead to the creation of a dominant position as originally proposed.

These market definitions were later upheld in *Sony/BMG*.[29] In this case, the Commission also found there was an emerging wholesale market for the granting of licences for on-line music by record companies to providers of on-line music services. These on-line music service providers need to obtain licences from the relevant record labels in order to offer music on-line. These licences will differ depending on whether the music is for downloading or streaming. For the latter, the service provider only needs the right for the communication of the music to the public. For downloading, in addition the right to copy the sound recordings is also required.

However, as with the *AOL/Time Warner* merger, the Commission did not reach a final conclusion as to whether the wholesale market for licences for on-line music should be sub-divided into downloading and streaming.

In *Vivendi/Canal+/Seagram*[30] the Commission had to consider the further question as to whether there was a separate, emerging market for on-line music delivery to mobile telephone customers. It concluded that this would be premature, since it was not possible to receive downloadable or streaming music over a standard GSM telephone, during the first phase of

---

[27] *ibid.*, [21].
[28] *ibid.*, [23].
[29] Case COMP/M.3333, *Sony/BMG*, July 19, 2004.
[30] Case COMP/M.2050, *Vivendi/Canal+/Seagram*, October 13, 2000.

the service under GPRS the service was likely to be poor, and consumer demand was unclear. Ultimately, however, it was unnecessary to decide the issue.

On-line medical services

14–016 A joint venture by Bertelsmann, Burda and Springer, to be called the Health On-line Service (HOS), was intended to provide a closed on-line medical service for professional users only.[31] This was to include offers for office management, office equipment and help with billing systems for doctors and pharmacists. In addition, it would offer articles especially produced for HOS. The service would mainly be financed by user fees, but there would also be some subject-specific advertisement. The parties suggested that there was a special market for closed medical on-line services for professional users, and the Commission agreed with that market distinction. It pointed out that from the users' point of view, other sources of information like specialist journals or conferences were not a sufficient alternative to the complete offer of an on-line service.

This can be contrasted with another case, decided on the same day, September 15, 1997, involving a joint venture between two of the same parties, Bertelsmann and Burda.[32] The joint venture service, Lifeline, was to offer consumer-orientated on-line health, beauty, food and fitness information called Bodyline, Fitnessline, Foodline, Psycholine and Beautyline. The service was at no charge to consumers, and was financed by advertising. The Commission considered that the relevant market was that for internet advertising. More significantly, however, the Commission refused to decide if health care information distributed at no charge could be a relevant market in itself.

On-line computer games

14–017 In another case, the Commission had to consider games played on-line. The case involved a joint venture between Bertelsmann and Viag, which would offer on-line games, the possibility for players to be linked up with each other in playing computer games, and editorial content. The service would initially be provided for free, but later on charges would be introduced.[33]

The Commission stated clearly that games playing provided for free could not be a relevant market. However, paid-for on-line games services could be taken into account in defining the relevant market. The parties suggested that the relevant market was for off-line and on-line electronic games, on the basis that the borderline between the two was not clear, and on-line games were often offered in conjunction with CD-ROM games. The Commission pointed out that in previous decisions, it had defined the relevant market as that for paid-for content in general. However, it con-

---

[31] Case IV/M.972, *Bertelsmann/Burda/Springer—HOS MM*, September 15, 1997.
[32] Case IV/M.973, *Bertelsmann/Burda—HOS Lifeline*, September 15, 1997.
[33] Case IV/JV.16, *Bertelsmann/Viag/Gamechannel*, May 5, 1999.

sidered that it did not have to resolve the issue as to whether the market was one of games, or whether the relevant market was the broader market for paid-for internet content in this case.

Broadband content

The Commission defined a market for paid-for content in *Telia/Telenor/Schibsted*.[34] In the course of its investigation in *AOL/Time Warner*,[35] it found evidence of the existence of an emerging demand for the one-stop integrated supply of broadband content via the internet. This demand was for bundled audio/video content (such as film, plus sporting contests, plus pop music concerts) via the internet and as such appeared to be separate from the demand for films and TV programmes supplied through more traditional distribution channels (such as pay-per-view, video on demand or DVD/video rental). The different broadband contents would not be substitutes, according to the Commission, but complementary goods. An ISP able to offer such a range of content could be compared to a supermarket offering a wide range of complementary products in a single place.

14–018

Audio player software

In the *AOL/Time Warner*[36] case, the Commission also considered that there was a separate market for player software such as Realplayer, Winamp, Quicktime and MusicMatch Jukebox.

14–019

The Commission noted that most of these software products are normally given free over the internet but that for some others there was a price to pay. It suggested that MusicMatch Jukebox was one of the players for which there was a price to pay (although in fact at the time it was only a higher functionality version of MusicMatch which had to be paid for). Once again, the decision did not deal with the impact on market definition that most of these players were given away for free. It concluded that there was already a market for the supply of player software. This could be seen as a contrast to earlier cases, in which the Commission suggested, in areas where the majority of the services are given away for free, that there may be a future market for such services, even if one does not exist at the time of the decision.

Broadcasting of football events via new media

In its *UEFA Champions League* decision,[37] the Commission found there was an emerging market for the broadcasting of football events via the internet at the wholesale level (i.e. the market for the acquisition of these rights) and at the retail level (i.e. to consumers). These market definitions

14–020

---

[34] Case IV/JV.1, *Telia/Telenor/Schibsted*, May 27, 1998.
[35] Case COMP/M.1845, *AOL/Time Warner*, October 11, 2000.
[36] *Ibid.*
[37] Case COMP/C.2–37.398, *Joint selling of the commercial rights of the UEFA Champions League*, July 24, 2003.

were later confirmed by the Commission in its *Bundesliga* and *FA Premier League* decisions.[38] However, the Commission did not state whether or not these markets had progressed past the stage of emerging.[39]

14.1.4 B2B Markets

14–021   The Commission has considered a number of business-to-business ("B2B") exchanges under both the EC Merger Regulation and Art.81.

The Commission considers that it might appear that in many cases, the question as to whether e-commerce creates an additional sales channel would be less pertinent than for B2C distribution, because in industrial supply arrangements, customers are often served directly by the suppliers, or there are mixed forms of vertical delivery chains where bigger customers are served directly and smaller customers via wholesalers.[40]

The question will therefore be whether electronic market places compete with normal bilateral sales or whether they constitute a separate, narrower product market. The former may be more likely if the parties used electronic market places only as an additional sales channel, the latter if the exchange offered additional services which clearly differentiated it from other sales forms.

This issue was discussed by the European Commission in a case involving the *MyAircraft.com* exchange,[41] a B2B exchange for aerospace parts and services and supply chain management services. The Commission considered whether the exchange was part of the wider market for airline equipment or whether it constituted part of a narrower market for exchanges, such as that for exchanges involving aircraft equipment.

The parties suggested that the relevant market was the market for aerospace parts and services and that e-commerce should be considered as one segment among the many means by which companies transact business. This was on the basis that customers, including airlines and service providers, remained free to decide how they wanted to conduct business with UTC, Honeywell or other suppliers, through MyAircraft.com, email, fax, telephone, etc. The parties explained that MyAircraft.com would increase the efficiency of communications between aerospace industry participants without changing the way transactions are conducted in the aerospace

---

[38] Case COMP/C.2–37.214, *Joint selling of the media rights to the German Bundesliga*, January 19, 2005. Case COMP/C.2–38.173 *Joint selling of the media rights to the FA Premier League*, March 22, 2006.

[39] In its Concluding Report on the Sector Inquiry into provision of sports content over 3G mobile networks, (September 21, 2005), the Commission considered mobile and TV sports services to be in different markets whilst acknowledging that competition constraints could change with emerging alternative technologies, e.g. by allowing mobile access to the internet.

[40] See Competition Issues in Electronic Commerce, OECD Roundtable on Competition, DAFFE/CLP(2000)32, contribution from the European Commission, p.117.

[41] Case M.1969, *UTC/Honeywell/i2/MyAircraft.com*, August 4, 2000.

industry and without having an impact on the definition of underlying markets of aerospace parts and services.

The Commission undertook a market investigation which revealed that third parties in general considered B2B exchanges as one among many methods by which they transact business. Some of these third parties seemed to believe that it would not be relevant to distinguish between the general sector of e-commerce and the sub-segment of B2B e-commerce. In any case, third parties considered it premature to draw distinctions between B2B e-commerce in different industry segments.

The services offered by MyAircraft.com to its customers included supply chain management tools and e-procurement. To a large extent, these services formed an integrated part of the services offered by MyAircraft.com in order to enable customers of the site to use MyAircraft.com as a purchasing or selling tool. However, some elements of the supply chain management service might, according to the Commission, have seemed to go beyond what was normally required by a user of MyAircraft.com in order to use the site to do business. This applied in particular to the inventory planning tools and forecasting tools. However, the market investigation revealed that a majority of third parties considered that these services were distinct components that might be offered separately or in combination but third parties did not at the time consider that they formed a distinct market.

The Commission considered that the results of the investigation suggested that the B2B market place formed part of a wider market. However, in the *MyAircraft.com* case itself, the Commission did not have to decide the question. The precise relevant market definition could be left open since irrespective of the market definition chosen, the proposed concentration did not give rise to the creation or strengthening of a dominant position.

In fact, none of the B2B cases which have been considered by the Commission under the EC Merger Regulation have resulted in a decision giving a precise definition of the relevant market. On the other hand, the cases demonstrate the variety of different ways of looking at B2B markets, through the submissions made by the parties as to what the relevant market was.

14–022

In *Chemplorer*[42] the market place was to fulfil the needs of the chemical and pharmaceutical industry, in the procurement of technical and administrative goods and services (known as MRO goods), as well as packaging materials. The parties submitted that the relevant market was the market for the operation of electronic marketplaces for bringing together supply and demand for MRO products, packaging materials, and related services. They had not therefore limited the market to the chemical or pharmaceutical industry, which was the target of the exchange. Whether or not the market should be defined more narrowly as solely applying in the chemical and pharmaceutical sector, or whether it included further participants, such as traditional suppliers or distributors of MRO products, could be left open in this case.

---

[42] Case COMP/M.2096, *Bayer/Deutsche Telekom/Infraserv/JV*, October 6, 2000.

In *ec4ec*[43] (e-commerce for engineered components), the market place related to plant and machine construction and was initially set to cover the US and European markets. The parties proposed that the relevant market in which the exchange would be active would be IT services for e-commerce. They did not suggest any narrower definition relating to the products being traded. The parties considered that the various markets for plant construction and the production of components were neither upstream, downstream, or neighbouring markets to the market for IT services for e-commerce, since the electronic market place was only a means of communication which connected the individual market participants.

Emaro[44] concerned a B2B trading platform, which would provide an IT infrastructure via which third parties would be able to carry out e-commerce transactions in the office equipment sector. According to the view of the parties, the joint venture created a platform in the market for IT services for B2B e-commerce. The relevant market would therefore include all such products and services which enable undertakings to electronically procure products and to enable other undertakings to distribute products.

Date[45] involved a B2B marketplace for procurement of "non-strategic" office supplies, i.e. stationary equipment and consumables such as pencils, pens, paper, hardware, cell phones, office accessories, and flowers. After a start-up period, Date would also provide supplementary services such as payment, financing and shipment. None of the parent companies were active in the same markets as Date. The notifying parties stated that the relevant product market was the procurement media or the procurement channels for "non-strategic" products such as stationary equipment and consumables to the corporate market. For the purpose of this notification, the parties submitted that the relevant geographical market was Norway and that the notified concentration could be assessed on this basis. However, it was not necessary for the Commission to resolve the question in this case.

It is interesting to contrast the Commission discussions on relevant markets in B2B cases with the discussions of the US Federal Trade Commission (FTC).

An FTC Staff Paper[46] was published in November 2000. In addition to discussing the possible competitive concerns in the markets for goods traded on B2B platforms, it also discussed the emerging competition for the provision of B2B services. The staff report points out that just as competition issues can arise in connection with other business-support activities, such as commercial telephone services or commercial internet access,

---

[43] See Case COMP/M.2172, *Babcock Borsig/MG Technologies/SAP Markets/ec4ec*, November 7, 2000; Case COMP/M.2270, *Babcock Borsig/MG Technologies/SAP Markets/ Deutsche Bank/VA TECH/ec4ec*, January 22, 2001.

[44] Case COMP/M.2027, *Deutsche Bank/SAP/JV*, July 13, 2000.

[45] Case COMP/M.2374, *Telenor/ErgoGroup/DNB/Accenture*, May 2, 2001.

[46] *Entering the 21st Century: Competition Policy in the world of B2B electronic marketplaces*, a report by the Federal Trade Commission Staff, October 2000, Part 3, Antitrust Analysis of B2Bs, pp.22–24.

competition in the market for marketplaces raises its own set of antitrust concerns. In this respect, it suggested that the "market for market places" was not intended to suggest that the relevant antitrust market was necessarily limited to B2B e-marketplaces. In theory, more traditional alternatives, such as electronic data interchange (EDI) connections, which allow the exchange of business information between trading partners, could remain competitive restraints.[47]

The issue of EDI connections was recently considered by the UK's Competition Commission, in relation to the acquisition by Francisco Partners LP of G International Inc.[48] Each party provided EDI value added networks (VANs), which is a form of B2B communications which combine a physical communications and computing infrastructure with data management processes, allowing the handling and transmitting of messages that relate to supply chain transactions, such as ordering and invoicing between partners. The Competition Commission concluded that the relevant market is that for the transmission of EDI messages from one business to another. This included traditional EDI VANs and point-to-point EDIs using leased lines, as well as traditional EDI VANs accessed via the internet, internet EDI VANs, web EDI and point-to-point internet EDI, as substitution between each of these products is technically feasible and economically viable.

14.1.4 Geographic Market

For infrastructure access markets, the geographic market will in many cases continue to be national. For internet dial-up access, the geographic market was considered to be essentially national, based on the need for a local loop service. In *Telia/Telenor*[49] the Commission concluded that this characteristic limits the extent to which existing markets could be wider than national.   **14–023**

For B2C markets, the internet enables customers to search much more widely for goods and services, and therefore will tend to broaden geographic markets. The markets may still be limited by whether or not services can be provided at a distance, and the costs and time taken for the transport of goods, as well as cross-border payments and exchange rates. The need to physically deliver traditional products even when bought on-line may therefore be a significant constraining factor to geographic market definition. Where these factors do not limit markets, then it may still be expected that other issues, such as language, or access through particular national gateways, may tend to limit the geographic scope of the search for goods.

---

[47] *ibid.*
[48] Competition Commission *Report on the acquisition of Francisco Partners LP of G International, Inc.*, dated September 2, 2005.
[49] Case COMP/M.1439, *Telia/Telenor*, October 13, 1999.

In relation to the wholesale market for on-line distribution of music, the Commission found in *Sony/BMG*[50] that this market is national in scope. Due to the national scope of licences for on-line music distribution, such services were only offered on a national basis (each licence required the licensee to only offer music to residents of the licensed country). Even if the service provider covered several different Member States, the licensing agreements focused on the national licences, which differed in their content, in terms of pricing and usage rules. The geographic market for on-line music distribution was therefore national.

The Commission also came to the same conclusion as regards the retail market for on-line music distribution, given the national scope of the licences. Even where a licensee had licences for different Member States, it operated a separate website for each of these countries (each licence required the licensee to warrant that its customers were resident in the relevant country). However, for both markets, the Commission did note that the geographic market may change in the future, particularly if cross-border contractual arrangements for licensing develop.

14–024 In the *BOL* cases referred to above concerning the formation of joint ventures to supply books on-line in various countries, the issue was ultimately left open. In some of these cases the parties suggested that the market was national, or broader, encompassing for example the "Spanish speaking world" or the "Italian speaking world", and the issue never had to be decided. In one of the very early cases, *Bertelsmann/Havas/BOL*,[51] the parties submitted that the geographic market for the publishing and the retail sales might be national, but that for internet sales it was worldwide. The sales by internet have a wider scope than traditional book club or mail order sales because of the international accessibility of the internet.

The Commission considered, "on the one hand, that for the reason given by the parties, the market may indeed be wider than France. On the other hand, the first experiences show that sales in France represent the large majority (70 to 80 per cent) of total sales via the internet, which would indicate the existence of a national market." Although the definition of the geographic market was left open in that case, the decision suggests that even the market for on-line sales of books is national.

The Commission has also pointed out[52] that in the case of *BOL Nordic*,[53] sales were done via national subsidiaries necessary both for purchasing and for distribution because the on-line sales needed a national logistic system of storage and next-day delivery. Even for books written in English the geographical market seems to remain national, because there is as yet only limited trade between countries. This may be due to longer terms of delivery and higher costs for the consumer in relation to cross-border payments and exchange rates. The need to physically deliver traditional

---

[50] Case COMP/M.3333, *Sony/BMG*, July 19, 2004.
[51] Case IV/M.1459, *Bertelsmann/Havas/BOL*, May 6, 1999.
[52] Competition Issues in Electronic Commerce, OECD Roundtable on Competition, DAFFE/CLP(2000)32, contribution from the European Commission, p.123.
[53] Case COMP/JV.45, *Bertelsmann/Kooperativa Förbundet/Bol Nordic*, May 12, 2000.

products even when bought on-line may therefore be a significant constraining factor to geographic market definition.

As the European Commission comments,[54] the above considerations of transport costs and similar factors should be irrelevant:

> "where purely electronic products or services are being provided (given that, under current charging arrangements, use of the Internet is not distance-sensitive). More generally, however, concern over cross border trade, consumer protection and complaints mechanisms may dissuade consumers from trading cross border, leaving market definitions national. The relative strengths of these concerns compared to the fundamentally international nature of the internet will require careful analysis in each case."

When looking at the definition of the relevant geographic market for B2B exchanges, the relevant question is likely to be the question whether the geographic market will be widened as geographic location becomes less important for the interaction between buyers and sellers. It is to be expected that such a widening of the geographic market will be brought about by many B2B electronic market places. In many instances, such as the *MyAircraft.com* case, however, this question may be largely irrelevant, as even the "traditional" market is likely to be worldwide.[55]

14.1.6 Characteristics of Internet and E-commerce Markets

Low marginal production costs

Like many new economy industries, a large number of e-commerce businesses are characterised by low marginal production costs. Once the initial investment is made, which can in some cases be substantial, it is cheap to create additional units. Electronic distribution of software, for example, can be done at low cost, and it doesn't cost much to add a new subscriber to the AOL network. Production may therefore exhibit increasing returns. This may result in more concentrated markets.   **14–025**

"Soft durable goods"

Many e-commerce undertakings produce "soft durable goods". This is particularly true of downloaded software, games, and content such as music. The services of these goods can be enjoyed for a long period of time, since they can be used and reused without limit. In practice however, the useful lifetime of these products may be more limited.   **14–026**

---

[54] Competition Issues in Electronic Commerce, OECD Roundtable on Competition, DAFFE/CLP(2000)32, contribution from the European Commission, p.123.
[55] *ibid.*, p.117.

Competition races and leapfrogging

14–027 In many areas of e-commerce, competition may consist of a series of races. Initially, firms invest heavily to develop a product that creates a new category, such as AOL Instant Messenger or the Napster MP3 search engine. Winners obtain very significant market shares initially, but that may be no guarantee of continued success. Subsequently, other firms may invest heavily and develop new innovations which leapfrog the leader's technology. The information economy is sometimes described as being a sector of "fragile monopolies" where today's top seller is at constant risk of being displaced by a new entrant with superior technology or other advantages.

Dynamic competition

14–028 Markets may therefore be in a state of dynamic competition, where, in contrast to static competition which takes place in the market, with each participant trying to produce goods with improved features at lower costs within that market, competition takes place for the market, with each participant trying to come up with significantly new innovations and technology which will displace the old market. Fragile monopolists may only be able to retain their position if they continue to be ahead of the game in innovation. First mover advantages, scale economies in production and/or network effects may ensure that, for a time, there is a single leading firm with a large share of the market. Many firms may invest and fail. Successful innovators may seek to charge high prices to compensate for their significant investment and high risk, although such high prices may not be sustainable in the long term.

Network effects

14–029 Many new economy industries are active in markets which exhibit network effects. Their products and services will be more valuable to each user if more people use them. For example, an instant chat service is more valuable the more users are subscribed to it.

Tippy markets

14–030 A slightly different effect, which may or may not be connected with network effects, is the notion of "tippy" markets. This notion relates to the fact that, once an undertaking achieves more than a certain critical mass in terms of absolute or comparative market power, or ownership of key assets, or number of users, then there may be factors in the market which will tend to further increase the market power of that undertaking, to the exclusion of, or at the expense of, other market participants.

An example can be seen in the *MCI/Worldcom*[56] case, where the Commission suggested that while the system of top level interconnectivity was at the time in a state of some equilibrium, once one network became overly

---

[56] Case IV/M.1069, *Worldcom/MCI*, July 8, 1999.

powerful, it could prevent potential competitors from assuming the status of top level networks by making sure that the prices at which it supplied transit were high enough to prevent the new entrant from building sufficient market share, or preventing competitors from granting a new entrant peering rights by exercising the threat of disconnection or degradation against them. The merger might well create a snowball effect, making the combined entity better placed than any of its competitors to capture future growth through new customers, because of the attractions for any new customer of direct interconnection with the largest network, and the lack of attractiveness of competitors' offerings due to the threat of disconnection or degradation of peering.

14.2 THE EC MERGER REGULATION

The current EC Merger Regulation[57] (hereafter the "Merger Regulation") **14–031** came into force on May 1, 2004. The Merger Regulation applies to "concentrations", which have a "community dimension", meaning that certain turnover thresholds described below are satisfied. A concentration arises where (i) two or more previously independent undertakings merge, or (ii) one or more undertakings acquire, whether by purchase of securities or assets, contract or other means, direct or indirect control of the whole or parts of another undertaking.[58] An undertaking controls another if, as a matter of fact or law, it has the ability to exercise a decisive influence over it. This covers most forms of merger or acquisition. It also covers many joint ventures.

While the possible application of the Merger Regulation to mergers and acquisitions is something which may be easily understandable, it is likely to strike the future shareholders in many e-commerce joint ventures, such as a joint venture establishing a B2B exchange/site, as strange that the possible application of the Merger Regulation needs to be considered. A joint venture to form a start-up internet venture might not appear to be a merger in the normal meaning of the word. However, the Merger Regulation can also apply to joint ventures between separate companies, even where they involve "start-up" or "greenfield" operations, including the formation of internet portals or other website operations.

The Merger Regulation will apply to a joint venture if all of the following are fulfilled:

- The parents acquire "joint control" over the joint venture;
- The joint venture is "full function"; and

---

[57] Council Regulation No.139/2004 of January 20, 2004, on the control of concentrations between undertakings. This replaced the previous Merger Regulation, Council Regulation No.4064/89 of December 21, 1989, as amended by Council Regulation 1310/97 of June 30, 1997.

[58] Merger Regulation, Art.3(1).

- The parents satisfy the turnover thresholds applying under the Merger Regulation.

These elements are explained in more detail below.

14.2.1 The Thresholds

14–032 A concentration will have a community dimension where the turnovers of the undertakings concerned meet one of the threshold tests set out in the Merger Regulation. The Merger Regulation contains two, alternative, threshold tests, which are referred to here as the first tier test and the second tier test, although these descriptions are neither used in the Merger Regulation, nor are they terms of art. A concentration meeting either the first tier test or the second tier test will fall under the Merger Regulation.

First tier test

14–033 A concentration will have a community dimension under the first tier test (and the Merger Regulation will therefore apply) if and only if all of the following three thresholds are satisfied for the preceding financial year[59]:

(i)   the combined aggregate worldwide turnover of all the undertakings concerned is more than €5,000 million;

(ii) the aggregate turnover within the European Community ("Community-wide turnover") of each of at least two of the undertakings concerned separately is more than €250 million; and

(iii) it is not the case that each of the undertakings concerned achieves more than two-thirds of their individual Community-wide turnovers in one and the same Member State.

As to the meaning of the "undertakings concerned", for acquisitions, this means roughly the acquirer group plus the part of the target being acquired; for joint ventures this means roughly the groups of the parent companies which have joint control over the joint venture, as well as the joint venture company itself, if it already exists.

Second tier test

14–034 A merger will be regarded as having a community dimension under the second tier test if and only if all of the following five thresholds are satisfied for the preceding financial year[60]:

---

[59] *ibid.*, Art.1(2).
[60] *ibid.*, Art.1(3).

(i)   the combined aggregate worldwide turnover of all the undertakings concerned is more than €2,500 million;

(ii)   the aggregate Community-wide turnover of each of at least two of the undertakings concerned separately is more than €100 million;

(iii)   within each of at least three Member States, the combined aggregate national turnover of all of the undertakings concerned is more than €100 million;

(iv)   within each of at least three Member States for which condition (iii) above is satisfied, the aggregate national turnover of each of at least two of the undertakings concerned is more than €25 million; and

(v)   it is not the case that each of the undertakings concerned achieves more than two thirds of their individual Community-wide turnovers in the same Member State.

14.2.2 Control and Joint Control

Individual control will arise where ownership or other rights, contracts or other means, having regard to the elements of fact or law involved, confer the possibility of exercising decisive influence over another undertaking.[61]
    14–035

Joint control exists when two or more undertakings have the possibility of exercising decisive influence over a joint venture. This normally means the power to block actions which determine the strategic commercial behaviour of an undertaking. The essential feature of joint control is the possibility of deadlock arising from the power of two or more parent companies to veto proposed strategic decisions, which effectively requires them to reach a common understanding in determining the commercial policy of the joint venture.[62]

The most basic example of joint control is where there are two participants with equal voting rights in the joint venture, such as where they both hold 50 per cent of the shares in the company and the shares have the same voting rights attached, or where they each have the power to appoint 50 per cent of the board with no provision for a casting vote. In this situation, each participant exercises decisive influence over the joint venture, as the consent of both is required for any decisions to be taken.[63]

However, there are also many other situations in which minority shareholders may be deemed to be in joint control. Normally, it is sufficient for a finding of joint control that there are unanimity requirements or negative veto rights for two or more individual parent shareholders over one or more of the following[64]:

---

[61] *ibid.*, Art.3(2).
[62] Commission notice on the concept of concentration under Council Regulation 4064/89, paras. 18 and 19.
[63] *ibid.*, para.20.
[64] *ibid.*, paras. 21–29.

- The appointment of management;
- Major investments;
- The business plan;
- Other market-specific rights; and
- The budget.

In the *MyAircraft.com*[65] decision involving a B2B exchange notified under the Merger Regulation, each of the shareholders was able to veto strategic decisions of MyAircraft.com relating to the annual business plan, acquisitions, and hiring and terminating the CEO's contract. This was sufficient to give joint control.

Where such veto rights or unanimity requirements are only given for a short period, of say, less than three years, there may be an absence of joint control.[66]

Even without veto rights, or unanimity requirements, it is still possible that there could in some circumstances be joint control, where decisive influence is acquired by some other means. The legal means to ensure the joint exercise of voting rights could include the formation of a holding company, to which the minority shareholders transfer their rights, or a legally binding agreement by which they undertake to act in the same way.

Very exceptionally, even in the absence of such veto rights or unanimity requirements for minority shareholders, *de facto* joint control may be found to exist where there are strong common interests between the minority shareholders so that one would not act against the interests of the others. However, normally joint control will not exist where there is a possibility of changing coalitions between minority shareholders.[67]

14.2.3 Full Function

14–036   A joint venture will only fall under the Merger Regulation if it is "full function", that is to say it is capable of "performing on a lasting basis all the functions of an autonomous economc entity".[68] The question here is really whether the joint venture business could stand on its own in the long run, in the same way as other businesses performing the same function.

In respect of portals or other sites, these may not only be providing these products or services against payment, but may also charge for participation, as well as charging for advertising in one form or another, and for individual transactions. It must be remembered that there are many websites which have operated in the market on the basis that they are providing information, and basing their business model on making money out of advertising, with little likelihood of making a profit in the short, or even

---

[65] Case COMP/M.1969, *UTC/Honeywell/i2/MyAircraft.com*, August 4, 2000.
[66] Commission notice on the concept of concentration under Council Regulation 4064/89, para.38.
[67] *ibid.*, paras. 30–37.
[68] Merger Regulation, Art.3(4).

medium term. The degree to which the joint venture depends on finance from the parents on an ongoing basis could be relevant in showing that it is not full function, but may not ultimately be conclusive.

In the *MyAircraft.com* case,[69] the Commission considered that the joint venture was full function because it would have its own premises and its own staff and its own sales and marketing force, as well as initial cash contributions from the parents, who would also provide the necessary software.

14.3 NOTIFICATION REQUIREMENT UNDER THE MERGER REGULATION

If the Merger Regulation applies, then the transaction including any **14–037** shareholders' agreement and other agreements which are essential to the transaction have to be notified on the basis of "Form CO" following the conclusion of the agreement or where the undertakings can demonstrate a "good faith intention" to conclude an agreement.[70]

Notification is obligatory under the Merger Regulation and implementing the agreement without notifying can make the parties subject to potential fines of up to 10 per cent of aggregate turnover.[71]

The European Commission normally has to clear the merger within 25 working days of a valid notification (although this period can be increased to 35 working days if the parties have submitted commitments for consideration to remedy any identified competition concerns),[72] and the merger or joint venture cannot be implemented until clearance has been given.

If the Commission has serious doubts about the merger or joint venture then it may decide to initiate an in-depth investigation, which could last a further 90 working days. This period will automatically be extended by 15 working days if the parties offer commitments for consideration on or after the 55th working day from the opening of the in-depth investigation. The 90 or 105 working day period (as appropriate) may also be further extended by an additional 20 working days at the parties' request or by the Commission, with the agreement of the parties.[73]

14.3.1 Assessment by the European Commission

The substantive test under the Merger Regulation is whether or not the **14–038** merger or joint venture significantly impedes effective competition, in

---

[69] Case COMP/M.1969, *UTC/Honeywell/i2/MyAircraft.com*, August 4, 2000.
[70] *ibid.*, Art.4(1). Under the previous Merger Regulation, notifications had to be made no more than one week after the conclusion of the agreement.
[71] *ibid.*, Art.14(2).
[72] *ibid.*, Art.10(1).
[73] *ibid.*, Art.10(3).

particular as a result of the creation or strengthening of a dominant position.[74] Under the previous Merger Regulation, this test was whether the merger or joint venture created or strengthened a dominant position. Although the test under the current Merger Regulation is slightly different, it is not so different that cases decided under the previous Merger Regulation are not considered as useful precedents. Where the parties are competitors in markets related to the joint venture, the Commission also has to consider whether the joint venture may result in co-ordinated or collusive behaviour in those markets.

Nearly all e-commerce mergers or joint ventures which have fallen under the Merger Regulation or its predecessor have been cleared, as they have not been found to significantly impede competition or raise concerns in respect of the creation or strengthening of a dominant position. The following section contains examples, however, of some of the cases which have raised issues.

14.3.2 Decisions in Merger Cases Relating to E-commerce and the Internet

Strengthening of dominance in the local loop

14–039   In the eventually abandoned *Telia/Telenor* merger, the Commission found that the proposed operation would strengthen the dominant position already enjoyed by the two incumbent operators in their respective domestic markets for the provision of local loop infrastructure in each country.

In order to obtain clearance, the parties gave a commitment that they would unbundle the local loop:

> "that they would allow competitors access to their respective local access networks in order to provide any technically feasible services on non-discriminatory terms. The undertaking will enable competitors to establish a sole customer relationship with telecommunications customers."

This commitment to provide unbundled local loop access was to take effect within three months from the date of the Commission's decision.

Dominance in top level internet connectivity

14–040   In the *MCI/Worldcom* case,[75] the Commission had to assess whether the merger would result in the formation of a dominant position in the market for top level internet connectivity. As regards their combined market shares,

---

[74] *ibid.*, Arts 2(2)–2(3).
[75] See fn.6 above.

the parties originally submitted that they did not have more than 20 per cent of the backbone market, based on the premise that any ISP with its own cable facilities was a backbone provider. However, the Commission had difficulty in accepting this definition, which made no distinction between a small locally based ISP with local clients, and the large multi-national top level networks.

No convincing existing measure for the Commission's purposes was available, so the Commission developed a measure of the top level network market based on the notion that any top level network would necessarily have to peer, at minimum, with all of the top four ISPs (at the time—Worldcom, MCI, Sprint, GTE/BBN), which were capable of supplying universal interconnectivity without recourse to transit. On this basis there was little doubt that the combined entity would hold over 50 per cent of the market, however widely defined, and would be significantly larger than the nearest competitor, Sprint.

The Commission considered that a network of such absolute and relative size would be created that the combined entity would achieve market dominance, and would be able to pursue various strategies to reinforce its market position. It could control market entry by denial of new peering requests, foreclosure or the threat of foreclosure. It could raise rivals' costs and decrease the quality of their service offerings, and the threat of such actions could give the combined entity the opportunity to dictate to whom its competitors could grant transit or peering, and on what terms.

Further, the combined entity could degrade the offering of competitors by deciding not to upgrade capacity. The originally proposed combined entity's chances of implementing such a strategy might well be improved by picking off customers and competitors one by one. As it grew larger, it could change the nature of its interconnection arrangements with competitors, or threaten to do so, oblige them to pay for access to its network, either paid peering or transit, whilst offering no payment in reverse, and influencing their cost position by charging prices which made their prices less competitive.

Once it had obtained dominance, the less likely the new entity would be to be challenged, since the more it grew, the less need it would have to interconnect with competitors and the more need they would have to interconnect with it. The larger it became, the greater its ability to control the costs of new entrants, by denying the opportunity to peer.

The Commission suggested that once one network became overly powerful, it could prevent potential competitors from assuming the status of top level networks by making sure that the prices at which it supplied transit were high enough to prevent the new entrant from building sufficient market share, or by preventing competitors from granting a new entrant peering rights though the exercise of the threat of disconnection or degradation against them. The merger might well create a snowball effect, making the combined entity better placed than any of its competitors to capture future growth through new customers, because of the attractions for any new customer of direct interconnection with the largest network, and the lack of attractiveness of competitors' offerings due to the threat of disconnection or degradation of peering.

In order to allow the merger to go ahead, the parties were therefore forced to agree to divest MCI's internet business as a whole, including its wholesale dedicated access business, retail dedicated access business, consumer and business dial-up businesses, web hosting, broadcast network services, and managed firewall services. This included all the equipment, routers, services, switches, etc., wholesale and retail customer contracts, so far as possible, peering arrangements, including those with Worldcom (which Worldcom would not terminate for at least five years), and all necessary employees. MCI would also provide basic transmission and international leased capacity for the contracts being transferred.

Dominance in on-line music and player software

14–041 In *AOL/Time Warner*,[76] the Commission was concerned that the possible combination of AOL with the Time Warner music catalogue, bearing in mind an existing relationship between AOL and Bertelsmann, which also had a strong music catalogue, could give the combined entity a dominant position in the market for on-line music, and that the combined entity would become dominant in the market for music player software. The Commission looked at whether the new entity would be able to play a gatekeeper role and dictate the technical standards for on-line music distribution over the internet, and also whether AOL would be able to impose Winamp, its software-based music player, as the dominant software player.

AOL and Bertelsmann had been partners since the beginning of the commercialisation of the internet. In 1995 they established the 50:50 joint venture AOL Europe, which permitted AOL's expansion in Europe. In addition, AOL and Bertelsmann, together with Vivendi, had a joint venture in France. In March 2000 AOL and Bertelsmann entered into a joint promotion, distribution and sales agreement. Bertelsmann and Time Warner each had 10 to 20 per cent of the music publishing rights for mechanical and performance rights in the EEA, giving a combined 30 to 40 per cent share of rights.

The deal was only cleared after the parties put in place a mechanism whereby Bertelsmann would progressively exit from AOL Europe and AOL CompuServe France, and AOL would forego certain rights under its marketing agreement with Bertelsmann. In particular, AOL would not exercise its rights to reformat Bertelsmann music content to make it compatible with AOL's music player in a manner which would promote or favour a format which was not available by licence to third parties on reasonable commercial terms. Further, AOL would not enforce any provision in the marketing agreement which prohibited Bertelsmann from promoting third party ISPs.

---

[76] Case COMP/M.1845, *AOL/Time Warner*, October 11, 2000.

Online travel agency services

In *T-Online/TUI/C&N Touristic*[77] the Commission was concerned that the venture, which was to be an on-line travel agency, would have privileged access to the content of TUI and Neckermann, the leading tour operators in Germany, as well as to T-Online's very large internet customer base. Competing on-line agents had submitted that they depended on TUI and Neckermann's product offering and brands and they feared that the new company would end up dominating the on-line segment. They were also concerned about potential discriminatory measures with regard to access to essential content.

14–042

To address these concerns, TUI and Neckermann offered to conclude supply contracts with any other on-line agents. But according to the Commission, a number of conditions were attached to this general commitment which would have provided numerous opportunities for circumvention and *de facto* discrimination. The Commission therefore concluded that the commitments offered did not fully and clearly remove the competition concerns and decided to enter into an in-depth ("second-phase") inquiry. The venture was eventually abandoned after no satisfactory solution could be found. The Commission raised similar concerns under Art.81 in another case related to the creation of an on-line travel agency, *Opodo*.[78]

Dominance in portals

In the "Vizzavi"[79] joint venture between Vodafone, Vivendi and Canal+, the Commission was only able to clear the joint venture under the Merger Regulation after the parties gave commitments regarding access to the mobile telephone and TV portals which would be created.

14–043

Vizzavi was to develop, market, maintain and provide a branded multi-access internet portal throughout Europe, providing customers with a seamless environment for web-based interactive services, across a variety of platforms, such as fixed and mobile telephony networks, PCs and palm-tops, as well as television sets. The Commission's investigation concluded that the joint venture would have led to competitive concerns in the developing national markets for TV-based internet portals and developing national and pan-European markets for mobile phone-based internet portals.

In order to address these competitive concerns identified by the Commission, the parties provided undertakings to ensure that the default portal could be changed, should the consumer so wish. The undertakings would allow consumers to access third party portals, to change the default portal

---

[77] Case COMP/M.2149, *T-Online/TUI/C&N Touristic*, see Commission press release IP/01/1670.

[78] Case COMP/38.006, *Online Travel Portal Ltd (OPODO)*, December 18, 2002, discussed in section 14.4.11.

[79] Case COMP/JV.48, *Vodafone/Vivendi/Canal+*, see Commission press release IP/00/821.

themselves, or to authorise a third party portal operator to change the default setting for them.

In *Vivendi/Canal+/Seagram*,[80] the Commission was concerned about the effect on the emerging pan-European market for portals and the emerging market for on-line music due to the acquisition of Universal's music libraries. Vivendi eventually gave a commitment to give non-discriminatory access to third parties regarding terms and conditions. The commitment provided for an arbitration procedure in case of a dispute concerning the access conditions. The commitment was limited to five years, with a possibility for review after three years.

Ancillary restrictions

14–044   A clearance under the Merger Regulation shall be deemed to also cover "ancillary restrictions" which are directly related to and necessary for the implementation of the concentration.[81]

For example, in the *MyAircraft.com*[82] decision, the following clauses were found to be necessary to ensure that the joint venture was established on a solid base, but were only cleared under the Merger Regulation for certain limited periods:

- Restrictions on the parties from engaging in activities relating to competing internet platforms in the aerospace sector;
- The requirement not to use the services of any competitor internet platform for the purchase and sale of the relevant product and services for a certain period from the formation date;
- The requirement not to make any of their consulting resources or services available to competing internet platforms for a certain period from the formation of the joint venture;
- The requirement not to promote any competitor internet platform for a certain period from the formation date;
- The restriction on acquiring an equity interest in any competitor platform for a certain period after they have reduced their shareholding below x per cent; and
- An obligation on the site provider for a certain period from the formation date not to sell or license to a competitor or certain identified businesses any of the software to be made available to the internet platform.

Further guidance on what types of ancillary restrictions in mergers are acceptable and for what periods of time can be found in the Commission's notice on ancillary restraints.[83] In particular, in relation to joint ventures, a

---

[80] Case COMP/M.2050, *Vivendi/Canal+/Seagram*, October 13, 2000.
[81] Merger Regulation, Arts 6(1)(b) and 8(1) and (2).
[82] Case M.1969, *BTC/Honeywell/i2/MyAircraft.com*, August 4, 2000.
[83] Commission's Notice on restrictions directly related and necessary to concentrations, O.J. 2005 C 56/24 March 5, 2005.

non-compete obligation between the parent companies and the joint venture itself is permitted for the lifetime of the joint venture.[84]

14.4 APPLICATION OF ART.81 OF THE EC TREATY

14.4.1 The Scope of Art.81

Article 81(1) of the EC Treaty prohibits agreements between undertakings, decisions by associations of undertakings and concerted practices that, to an appreciable extent, affect trade between Member States and have as their object or effect the prevention, restriction or distortion of competition within the EU. As a result, in determining whether Art.81(1) applies it is necessary to consider whether: **14–045**

- (i)   an agreement or concerted practice exists between undertakings;
- (ii)   which prevents, distorts or restricts competition within the EU;
- (iii) which affects trade between Member States; and
- (iv)   which has an appreciable effect on competition.

Agreements and concerted practices

Most forms of co-ordination or agreements between undertakings are covered by the terms "agreement" and "concerted practice". There is no requirement that a legally binding contract exist between the parties, or that there be any agreement in writing; a so-called "gentlemen's agreement" is sufficient.[85] Similarly, several separate contracts may be found, together, to form a single agreement.[86] It is sufficient to constitute a "concerted practice" that undertakings co-ordinate their behaviour in a way that "knowingly substitutes practical cooperation between them for the risks of competition".[87]   **14–046**

Between undertakings

The term "undertaking" is defined broadly and covers virtually any entity, regardless of its legal status, engaged in economic or commercial activity.[88] Limited companies, partnerships and individuals may all be undertakings. State-owned companies will also be covered by the term if they engage in commercial or economic activity.[89] The fact that an entity is non-profit making will not prevent it being an undertaking.[90]   **14–047**

---

[84] *ibid.*, para.36.
[85] Cases 209/78 etc., *Van Landewyck v Commission* [1980] E.C.R. 3125, [85]–[91].
[86] *BP Kem*, [1979] O.J. L 286/32.
[87] *ICI Ltd v Commission* (Case 48/69) [1972] E.C.R. 619, [64].
[88] See, e.g. *Höfner and Elser v Macrotron* [1991] E.C.R. I–1979, [21].
[89] *Sacchi* (Case 155/73) [1974] E.C.R. 409; *Aluminium Imports from Eastern Europe*, O.J. 1985 L 92/1, March 30, 1985, at para.37.
[90] *GVL*, O.J. 1981 L370/49, December 28, 1981.

To be caught by Art.81(1), an agreement or concerted practice must exist between at least two undertakings. A parent company and its wholly controlled subsidiaries are usually considered to form a "single economic entity" and, as a result, are treated as a single undertaking for this purpose.[91] Consequently, many intra-group transactions will fall outside Art.81(1).

Effect on trade between Member States

14–048   Again, the concept of effect on trade between Member States is broad. It is sufficient that an agreement "may have an influence direct or indirect, actual or potential, on the pattern of trade between Member States, such as might prejudice the aim of a single market."[92] In practice, an effect on trade will generally be found where an agreement includes terms which relate to imports or exports, extends to more than one Member State or covers the whole of the territory of a single Member State (since this may have the effect of partitioning that State from the rest of the EC market).[93] For these purposes, most if not all economic activity will qualify as "trade". Since e-commerce and internet agreements are usually at least national, if not worldwide, this test will very often be satisfied.

The European Commission has issued guidelines on what constitutes an effect on trade.[94] Under these guidelines, there is unlikely to be an effect on trade between Member States where the combined market share of the parties in the relevant market does not exceed 5 per cent and:

- For horizontal agreements, the combined turnover of the parties does not exceed €40 million;
- For vertical agreements, the turnover of the supplier does not exceed €40 million; and
- For licence agreements, the combined turnover of the licensees and the licensor in products incorporating the licensed technology does not exceed €40 million.

However, if the agreement is by its nature capable of affecting trade between Member States, for example, because it concerns imports or exports or covers several Member States, there is a rebuttable presumption that the effects on trade are appreciable if the above thresholds are exceeded.

Preventing, restricting or distorting competition in the EU

14–049   In principle, any agreement that may lead to reduced competition between the parties or restrict the ability of third parties to compete may be caught

---

[91] *Viho Europe v Commission* (Case C–73/95) [1996] E.C.R. I–5457.
[92] *Remia v Commission* (Case 42/84) [1985] E.C.R. 2545, para.22.
[93] *Cementhandelaren v Commission* (Case 8/72) [1972] E.C.R. 977.
[94] Commission Notice—Guidelines on the effect of trade concept contained in Arts. 81 and 82 of the Treaty, O.J. 2004 C101/07, April 27, 2004.

by Art.81(1), and there is no particular significance in the distinction between "preventing", "restricting" and "distorting" competition.

Particular types of agreements and clauses which may amount to restrictions of competition are described below. It should be pointed out, in respect of the relationship of Art.81 to joint ventures, that Art.81 can apply to the formation of a joint venture or other collaboration which does not fall under the Merger Regulation because it lacks the necessary elements of being "full function" or of the parties having joint control. In addition, even if a joint venture does fall under the Merger Regulation, Art.81 may still apply to other existing or future agreements that relate to the joint venture which have not been cleared under the Merger Regulation.

Among the factors that will be considered in determining whether an agreement leads to a restriction of competition, the most important is likely to be the size of the parties' combined share of the relevant market (the concept of "relevant market" is discussed below in the section dealing with Art.82).

Appreciable effect on competition

The European Court of Justice has established in *Völk v Vervaecke* that an agreement will not be caught by Art.81(1) if it has no appreciable effect on competition.[95] The scope of this exception has never been precisely defined by the court, but it applies when the parties' relevant market shares are extremely small, for example 0.25 per cent as in *Völk v Vervaecke*.

14–050

Separately, the European Commission has issued a notice[96] setting out certain criteria by which an agreement can in its view be treated as not subject to Art.81(1) by reason of its limited impact. This notice states that:

(i)   agreements between parties that are actual or potential competitors ("agreements between competitors") will not be considered appreciable where the parties have a combined market share of 10 per cent or less on the relevant market;

(ii)   agreements between parties that are not actual or potential competitors ("agreements between non-competitors") will not be considered appreciable where the parties have a combined market share of 15 per cent or less on the relevant market[97]; and

(iii)   where competition is restricted by a parallel network of agreements, established by several suppliers or distributors, agreements (whether between competitors or non-competitors) will not be considered appreciable where the parties have a combined market share of five per cent or less on the relevant market. Agreements

---

[95] See, e.g. *Völk v Vervaecke* (Cases 19 & 20/74) [1969] E.C.R. 295.

[96] Commission notice on agreements of minor importance which do not appreciably restrict competition under Art.81(1) of the Treaty establishing the European Community, O.J. 2001 C 368/13, December 22, 2001, para.7(a).

[97] *ibid.*, para.7(b).

which do not exceed this limit are not taken to contribute significantly to any cumulative foreclosure effect.[98]

In cases where it is difficult to say whether or not the parties are competitors, the 10 per cent threshold is the relevant one.[99] Agreements will also be seen as not having an appreciable effect where any of the above thresholds are exceeded by no more than 2 per cent during two successive calendar years.[1] Furthermore, the Commission acknowledges that agreements between small- and medium-sized undertakings are rarely capable of appreciably affecting trade between Member States.[2]

14–051   The presumptions in the notice of lack of appreciable effect on competition do not apply where the agreement contains certain types of "hardcore" restrictive clauses. For horizontal agreements between competitors, i.e. between those operating at the same level of the production or distribution chain, the hardcore clauses include price fixing, limitation of output or sales, and the allocation of markets or customers.[3] For vertical agreements between undertakings operating at different levels of the production or distribution chain for the purposes of the agreement, the forbidden clauses are the hardcore restrictions set out in the Vertical Agreements Block Exemption described below.

These restrictions include[4]:

- Minimum or fixed resale pricing restrictions on the buyer;
- Restrictions of the territory into which, or the customers to whom, the buyer can sell the contract goods or services except:

    - A restriction of active sales into the exclusive territory or an exclusive customer group reserved to the supplier or another buyer;
    - A restriction of sales to end-users by a buyer operating at the wholesale level of trade;
    - A restriction of sales to unauthorised distributors by the members of a selective distribution system;
    - A restriction of a buyer's ability to sell components supplied for incorporation to customers who would use them to manufacture the same type of goods as those produced by the supplier;

- Restrictions of active or passive sales to end-users by members of a selective distribution system operating at the retail level of trade;

---

[98] *ibid.*, para.8.
[99] *ibid.*, para.7.
[1] *ibid.*, para.9.
[2] *ibid.*, Recital 4. Small- and medium-sized undertakings are defined in the Annex to Commission Recommendation 96/280/EC as undertakings which have fewer than 250 employees and have either an annual turnover not exceeding €40 million or an annual balance sheet total not exceeding €27 million.
[3] *ibid.*, para.11(1).
[4] *ibid.*, para.11(2).

- Restrictions of cross supplies between distributors within a selective distribution system; and
- Restrictions agreed between a supplier of components and a buyer who incorporates those components, which limits the supplier's ability to sell the components as spare parts to end-users or to repairers or other service providers not entrusted by the buyer with the repair or servicing of its goods (see below for fuller analysis of all of these clauses).

14.4.2 The Effect of Falling Within Art.81(1)

Several consequences may follow if an agreement falls within Art.81(1) and it does not qualify for exemption under Art.81(3) (discussed below).   **14–052**

First, under Art.81(2), the anti-competitive aspects of an agreement that falls within Art.81(1) are void and will not be enforced by national courts in the EU. This may, depending on the relevant national legal provisions, result in the whole of the agreement becoming unenforceable. Nor will EU courts enforce judgments of foreign courts based on aspects of an agreement which are contrary to Art.81(1).

Secondly, the Commission has powers to impose fines of up to 10 per cent of worldwide turnover on undertakings involved in a breach of Art.81(1).[5] Fines are, however, typically imposed only in the most serious cases.

Thirdly, the Commission may, by decision, order infringing undertakings to take such action as is necessary to terminate the infringement.[6]

Fourthly, the Commission has the power to accept legally binding commitments from undertakings to modify their behaviour in a defined way to overcome identified competition concerns, allowing the Commission to close the file without adopting an infringement decision.[7]

Finally, it is possible for third parties injured as a result of a breach of Art.81(1) to sue the offending undertakings for damages, although the circumstances under which such a remedy is available are governed by the relevant national law. Under English law, it has been confirmed that such damages are available.[8]

14.4.3 Exemption from Art.81(1)

Exemption from Art.81(1) may be obtained under Art.81(3). Two routes are available to undertakings wishing to obtain an Art.81(3) exemption: (i) compliance with one of the Commission's so-called "block exemption"   **14–053**

---

[5] Article 23(2), Regulation 1/2003, O.J. 2003 C 1/1, January 4, 2003.
[6] *ibid.*, Art.7.
[7] *ibid.*, Art.9.
[8] *Crehan v Inntrepreneur Pub Company CPC*, [2004] EWCA 637, judgment of May 21, 2004.

regulations, in which case the exemption is automatic, and (ii) individual exemption, which requires the parties to assess for themselves whether the criteria set out in Art.81(3) are met by a particular agreement. Complying with a block exemption regulation ensures immunity from fines, legal enforceability of the agreement, and protection from damages actions under Art.81.

14.4.4 Individual Exemption

14–054   Prior to May 1, 2004, it was possible for parties to notify an agreement to the European Commission for an individual exemption, confirming that the agreement in question benefited from exemption under Art.81(3). In practice, this system was very slow and inefficient, with only a very small number of exemption decisions (as opposed to administrative comfort letters) being issued each year. This led to the system of prior notification being abolished as of May 1, 2004. Since that date, Art.81(3) applies automatically to agreements that satisfy its requirements, and so these agreements will be valid from the outset, without the need for a decision from the Commission.

It was also possible to apply to the Commission for a formal declaration that an agreement fell outside the scope of Art.81(1), a so-called "negative clearance". This practice has also been discontinued since May 1, 2004. However, the Commission has stated that it will provide guidance (which will be published) in limited circumstances where the agreement raises novel or unresolved questions of law. This is likely to be used infrequently in practice.

14.4.5 Block Exemption Regulations

14–055   The European Commission has enacted block exemption regulations in relation to various categories of agreement.

Existing block exemption regulations include the Technology Transfer Block Exemption[9] and the Vertical Agreements Block Exemption.[10] These two block exemptions will be analysed in some detail in the following sections.

Another block exemption, the Research and Development Block Exemption[11] which applies to joint research and/or development agree-

---

[9] Commission Regulation No.772/2004 of April 27, 2004 on the application of Art.81(3) of the Treaty to categories of technology transfer agreements, O.J. 2004 L 123/11, April 27, 2004.

[10] Commission Regulation No.2790/99 of December 22, 1999, on the application of Art.81(3) to categories of vertical agreements and concerted practices, O.J. 1999 L336/21, December 29,1999.

[11] Commission Regulation No.2659/2000 of November 29, 2000, on the application of Art.81(3) of the Treaty to categories of research and development agreements, O.J. 2000 L 304/7, December 5, 2000.

ments, may also be relevant in some cases, but is not discussed in this chapter.

14.4.6 The Technology Transfer Block Exemption

The Technology Transfer block exemption (hereafter the "Block Exemp- **14–056**
tion") has been in force (in its present form) since May 1, 2004.[12] The Block
Exemption is accompanied by guidelines issued by the European Commission (the "Guidelines"), which explain the interpretation of the Block
Exemption and give a competition analysis of technology transfer agreements which fall outside of the Block Exemption because they are above the
market share thresholds.[13]

Meaning of "technology transfer agreements"

The Block Exemption applies to technology transfer agreements. These are **14–057**
defined in the Block Exemption as patent licences, know-how licences,
software copyright licences and any combination of these. It also covers
patent, know-how and software copyright licences which include terms
relating to additional intellectual property rights, such as trade marks,
provided these are not the primary object of the agreement and are directly
related to the production of the products or services being produced under
the agreement. This means that those provisions would only be covered to
the extent that they are contained in a licence of patent, software copyright
and/or know-how rights and they serve to enable the licensee to better
exploit the licensed technology.[14]

Know-how is defined for the purposes of the Block Exemption as a
package of non-patented practical information, resulting from experience
and testing, which is secret, substantial and identified.[15] This means that,
for a know-how licence to come within the Block Exemption it must cover
know-how that is:

(i) secret, in the sense of not generally known or easily accessible[16]
(this may require that it is confidential and supplied under an
obligation of confidentiality);

(ii) substantial, in the sense that it is significant and useful for the
production of the products or services covered by the licence or
the application of the process covered by the licence.[17] In other

---

[12] Commission Regulation No.772/2004 on the application of Art.81(3) of the Treaty to
   categories of technology transfer agreements, [2004] O.J.L 123/11. This replaced the previous block exemption for technology transfer agreements, Regulation No.240/96.
[13] Guidelines on the application of Art.81 of the EC Treaty to technology transfer agreements,
   O.J. C 101/02, April 27, 2004.
[14] The Guidelines, para.50.
[15] The Technology Transfer Block Exemption, Art.1(1)(i).
[16] *ibid.*, Art.1(1)(i)(i).
[17] *ibid.*, Art.1(1)(i)(ii).

words, the information must significantly contribute to or facilitate the production of the contract products. Where the licence relates to process technologies, the know-how should be useful in the sense that it can reasonably be expected at the date of conclusion of the agreement to be capable of significantly improving the competitive position of the licensee, for example by reducing his production costs[18]; and

(iii) identified, in that the know-how must be described in a sufficiently comprehensive manner so as to make it possible to verify the fulfilment of the two criteria above.[19]

Patents are defined as patents, patent applications, utility models, applications for registration of utility models, designs, topographies of semiconductor products, supplementary protection certificates for medicinal products or other products for which such supplementary protection certificates may be obtained and plant breeder's certificates.[20]

Further, assignments of patents, know-how, software copyright or a combination of these rights come within the scope of the Block Exemption where part of the risk associated with the exploitation of the technology remains with the assignor, in particular where the sum payable in consideration of the assignment is dependent on the turnover obtained by the assignee in respect of products made using the assigned technology, the quantity of such products produced or the number of operations carried out using the technology.[21]

Scope and inclusions

14–058   The Block Exemption only applies to agreements "between two parties".[22] However, the Guidelines state that the Commission will apply the principles set out in the Block Exemption by analogy to agreements between more than two undertakings.[23] The concept of an agreement under Art.81 is not necessarily limited to one contract, and a number of different contracts or licences may be deemed to form part of one agreement. On the other hand, where several companies within a group, which constitute a single economic entity for the purposes of Art.81, are all parties to an agreement, they should be treated as one party for the purposes of the Block Exemption.

There is also a good argument that "connected undertakings" as defined in the Block Exemption[24] should also be seen as a single undertaking for the purpose of the counting of heads, even where there might be some question as to whether the single economic entity doctrine applies, as the Block Exemption states that the licensor and the licensee shall include their

---

[18] The Guidelines, para.47.
[19] The Technology Transfer Block Exemption, Art.1(1)(i)(iii).
[20] *ibid.*, Art.1(1)(h).
[21] *ibid.*, Art.1(1)(b).
[22] *ibid.*, Art.2.
[23] The Guidelines, para.40.
[24] The Technology Transfer Block Exemption, Art.1(2).

respective connected undertakings.[25] "Connected undertakings" are basically undertakings in a relationship defined by ownership of more than half of the capital or business assets, having the power to exercise more than half the voting rights; to appoint more than half the members of the supervisory board, board of directors, or other representative body; or to manage the affairs of the undertaking.

The Block Exemption only applies where the licensee is actually manufacturing a product under the licence using the licensed technology, or is providing the licensed service.[26] It applies to agreements where the licensee has to carry out further development work before obtaining a product or process that can be commercially exploited, provided that an end product has been identified.[27] It also applies to agreements whereby the licensor licenses technology to the licensee who undertakes to produce certain products on the basis of the licensed technology exclusively for the licensor.[28] Further, the Block Exemption covers obligations on the licensee to impose restrictions on its resellers, provided these are compatible with the EC's block exemption Regulation No.2790/1999 on vertical agreements.[29]

Duration of the exemption

Provided the terms of the Block Exemption are met, the exemption will apply for the lifetime of the patent or software copyright (i.e. until it has lapsed, expired or been declared invalid) or, in the case of know-how, for as long as the know-how remains secret (unless the know-how becomes public due to the licensee's actions, in which case the exemption will last for the duration of the agreement). **14–059**

Exclusions

Certain types of patent, software copyright and know-how licences are specifically excluded from the application of the Block Exemption: **14–060**

Pure sales licences As noted above, the Block Exemption only applies where the licensee is actually manufacturing a product under the licence, or is providing the licensed service.[30] It does not apply to pure sales licences. **14–061**

Licences of other intellectual property rights which are not ancillary The Block Exemption does not apply where the licence contains provisions relating to the exploitation of intellectual property rights other than patents, software copyright or know-how which are the primary object of the agreement or are not directly related to the production of the products **14–062**

---

[25] *ibid.*, Art.1(2).
[26] *ibid.*, Art.2.
[27] *ibid.*, Recital 7 and The Guidelines, para.45.
[28] The Guidelines, para.44.
[29] The Technology Transfer Block Exemption, Recital 19.
[30] The Technology Transfer Block Exemption, Art.2.

or services under the licence agreement.[31] However, the Guidelines state that the licensing of copyright for the purpose of reproduction and distribution of the protected work (i.e. the production of copies for resale) is considered similar to technology licensing, and that the principles of the Block Exemption and the Guidelines can therefore be applied by analogy to such licences of copyright.[32]

14–063 **Technology pools**   A technology pool is where the owners of different intellectual property rights pool these rights for the purpose of licensing the created package of technology to third parties. The application of the Block Exemption is excluded in relation to agreements between members to set up a technology pool.[33]

14–064 **Pure sub-licensing agreements**   The Block Exemption does not apply to agreements that have sub-licensing as their primary object. However, it does apply to agreements under which the licensee is permitted to sub-license the technology in question to third parties, provided that the production of products or the provision of services using the licensed technology is the primary object of the agreement. Nevertheless, the Guidelines state that the Commission will apply the principles set out in the Block Exemption by analogy to such a "master licensing" agreement.[34]

14–065 **Research and development**   The Block Exemption does not apply to licensing agreements for the sub-contracting of research and development. In this case, the primary object of the agreement is the provision of research and development services, not the production of goods or services using the licensed technology.[35]

Distinction between competitors and non-competitors

14–066 The Block Exemption makes a distinction between agreements that are entered into by competitors and those that are between non-competitors. Competitors are defined as competitors on the relevant technology market and/or on the relevant product market.[36] The relevant product market includes the products incorporating the technology licensed under the agreement and their substitutes. The relevant technology market comprises the technology licensed under the agreement and its substitutes.

The parties will be competitors on the relevant technology market if they currently license out competing technologies to third parties. They will be competitors on the relevant product market if they currently sell competing products (actual competitors) or would realistically make the necessary

---

[31] *ibid.*, Art.1(1)(b).
[32] The Guidelines, para.51.
[33] *ibid.*, Recital 7.
[34] The Guidelines, para.42.
[35] The Technology Transfer Block Exemption, Recital 7 and the Guidelines, para.45.
[36] The Technology Transfer Block Exemption, Art.1(1)(j).

additional investments to enter the market within a year or two if there was a small but permanent increase in price of the relevant products (potential competitors). In other words, if the parties are actual competitors on the relevant technology market and/or actual or potential competitors on the relevant product market, they will be considered as competitors for the purposes of the Block Exemption.

When deciding whether or not the parties are competitors, it is necessary to consider the situation before the agreement is entered into, i.e. would the parties be considered as competitors in the absence of the agreement? The licensee is not considered to be a competitor of the licensor simply because it is being granted a licence by the licensor. Where the licensor and licensee become competitors *after* the conclusion of the licence agreement, the agreement will still be treated as an agreement between non-competitors unless the agreement is materially amended.[37]

In relation to agreements between competitors, the Block Exemption makes a further distinction between reciprocal and non-reciprocal agreements. A reciprocal agreement is a cross-licensing arrangement where the technologies licensed by each party are competing technologies or can be used for the production of competing products. Even if these licences are entered into as two separate agreements, this will still be considered as a reciprocal licence.[38] Conversely, a non-reciprocal agreement is one where only one party is licensing any technology or, in the case of cross-licensing, the different technologies being licensed do not compete with each other and cannot be used to produce competing products.[39]

Market share cap

There is a different market share test for agreements between competitors and agreements between non-competitors. Market shares will need to be calculated for the relevant product market and the relevant technology market. For agreements between competitors, the combined market share of the parties must not exceed 20 per cent of the relevant technology and/or product market(s). For agreements between non-competitors, the market share of each party must not exceed 30 per cent of any relevant technology and product markets. If the relevant market share is above the applicable threshold, the agreement cannot benefit from the Block Exemption. This does not mean that it is invalid but that the agreement must be considered under the general principles of Art.81 (and Art.82 if either party to the agreement has a dominant position in the market).

If a party's or the parties' individual or combined market share exceed the relevant 20 per cent or 30 per cent threshold (whichever is applicable)

14–067

---

[37] *ibid.*, Art.4(3). Note also that where the parties appear to be competitors at the outset but the licensee's technology or products incorporating it are subsequently shown to be obsolete or uncompetitive in relation to the licensor's, the classification of the relationship between the parties will change into one of non-competitors, for purposes of the Block Exemption: the Guidelines, para.33.

[38] *ibid.*, Art.1(1)(c).

[39] *ibid.*, Art.1(1)(d).

after entering into a licence agreement, the agreement in question continues to benefit from the Block Exemption for a further two calendar years following the year in which the threshold was first exceeded.[40]

Calculating market share

14–068 In order to calculate market shares, the market must first be defined, under the general principles of market definition. It is necessary to define both the relevant product market and the relevant technology market (discussed above). Market shares are then calculated on the basis of market sales value data (or best estimates, including sales of volume data, if this information is not available).[41]

In relation to the technology market, this is measured in terms of the presence of the licensed technology on the relevant product market using figures for the sales of products incorporating the relevant technology. For licensors, their market share is the combined market share on the product market on the basis of the sales of the products incorporating the licensed technology produced by the licensor and all of its licensees.[42]

In the case of product markets, the licensee's market share is calculated on the basis of the licensee's sales of products incorporating the licensor's technology and sales of competing products, in other words the total sales of the licensee on the product market in question. If the licensor also supplies the products itself, its market share is calculated on the basis of its sales. However, in this case, sales by its licensees are not taken into account.[43]

Hardcore restrictions

14–069 The Block Exemption specifies "hardcore" restrictions that, if included in a licence agreement, will prevent the Block Exemption applying to the entire agreement. There is a different list of hardcore restrictions for agreements between competitors and agreements between non-competitors.

Hardcore restrictions in agreements between competitors[44]:

> (i)   restrictions on a party's ability to determine its sale price;
>
> (ii) limitations of output (except those on the licensee in a non-reciprocal agreement or only imposed on one licensee in a reciprocal agreement);
>
> (iii) the allocation of markets or customers apart from:
>
> — obligations on the licensee(s) to produce using the licensed

---

[40] *ibid.*, Art.8(2).
[41] *ibid.*, Art.8(1).
[42] *ibid.*, Art.3(3). Where the parties are competitors on the technology market, sales of products incorporating the licensee's own technology must be combined with the sales of the products incorporating the licensed technology, the Guidelines, para.70.
[43] The Guidelines, para.71.
[44] The Technology Transfer Block Exemption, Art.4(1).

technology only within one or more technical fields of use or product markets;
— obligations on the licensor and/or the licensee, in a non-reciprocal agreement, not to produce with the licensed technology within (i) one or more technical fields of use; or (ii) one or more product markets; or (iii) one or more exclusive territories reserved for the other party;
— obligations on the licensor not to license the technology to another licensee in a particular territory;
— restrictions, in a non-reciprocal agreement, on the licensee and/or the licensor making active sales and/or passive sales into the exclusive territory or exclusive customer group reserved for the other party;
— restrictions, in a non-reciprocal agreement, on the licensee making active sales into the exclusive territory or exclusive customer group allocated by the licensor to another licensee (provided the other licensee was not a competitor of the licensor at the time of the conclusion of its own licence);
— obligations on the licensee to produce the licensed products only for its own use, provided that the licensee can sell the licensed products actively and passively as spare parts for its own products;
— obligations on the licensee, in a non-reciprocal agreement, to produce the licensed products only for a particular customer (provided that the licence was granted in order to create an alternative source of supply for that customer);

(iv) restrictions on the licensee's ability to exploit its own technology or restrictions on either party's ability to carry out independent research and development, unless such a restriction is indispensable to prevent the disclosure of the licensed know-how to third parties.

Hardcore restrictions in agreements between non-competitors[45]: **14–070**

(i) restrictions on a party's ability to determine its sale price, with the exception of recommended resale prices and maximum resale price obligations (provided these do not amount to fixed or minimum resale prices as a result of pressure from or incentives offered by any of the parties);
(ii) restrictions of the territory into which, or the customers to whom, the licensee may sell the contract products or services apart from:

— restrictions on passive sales to territories or customer groups that the supplier has exclusively reserved to itself;
— restrictions on passive sales to territories or customer groups

---

[45] *ibid.*, Art.4(2).

that the supplier has exclusively allocated to another licensee during the first two years that this other licensee is selling the licensed products or services in that territory or to that customer group;

— obligations on the licensee to produce the licensed products or services only for its own use (provided that the licensee is not restricted in selling the licensed products actively and passively as spare parts for its own products);

— obligations on the licensee to produce the licensed products only for a particular customer (provided that the licence was granted in order to create an alternative source of supply for that customer);

— restrictions on sales to end-users by licensees operating at wholesale level;

— restrictions on resale to unauthorised distributors by members of a selective distribution network;

(iii) the restriction of active or passive sales to end-users by members of a selective distribution system operating at the retail level of trade, without prejudice to the possibility of prohibiting a member of the system from operating out of an unauthorised place of establishment.

14–071   The following table summarises the position in relation to common types of restrictions and whether they are acceptable, up to the market share thresholds set out in the Block Exemption (20 per cent for competitors, 30 per cent for non-competitors). If these types of restrictions are included in a licence agreement but the parties exceed the relevant market share threshold, the Guidelines give further guidance on the issues to take into account when considering whether the agreement benefits from exemption under Art.81(3).

Restriction	Reciprocal agreement between competitors	Non-reciprocal agreement between competitors	Agreement between non-competitors
Recommended or maximum prices	No	No	Yes
Output limitations	No (unless only on one licensee)	Yes (as regards contract products only)	Yes
Field of use restrictions on Licensee	Yes	Yes	Yes
Field of use restrictions on Licensor	No	Yes	Yes

Restriction	Reciprocal agreement between competitors	Non-reciprocal agreement between competitors	Agreement between non-competitors
Sole licence	Yes	Yes	Yes
Exclusive licence	No	Yes	Yes
Restriction of active sales into exclusive territory/ customer group reserved to the other party	No	Yes	Yes
Restriction of passive sales into exclusive territory/ customer group reserved to the other party	No	Yes	Yes
Restriction of active sales into exclusive territory/ customer group allocated to another licensee	No	Yes (provided the protected licensee was not a competitor of the licensor at the time of the conclusion of its licence)	Yes
Restriction of passive sales into exclusive territory/ customer group allocated to another licensee	No	No	Yes (for the first two years the protected licensee sells the licensed products in that territory/customer group)
Restriction of active/passive sales into non-exclusive territory/ customer group	No	No	No
Restrictions on the licensee dealing in or producing competing products	Yes (provided the licensee is not restricted from exploiting its own technology or carrying out R&D)	Yes (provided the licensee is not restricted from exploiting its own technology or carrying out R&D)	Yes (provided the licensee is not restricted from exploiting its own technology or carrying out R&D)

Restriction	Reciprocal agreement between competitors	Non-reciprocal agreement between competitors	Agreement between non-competitors
Captive use restriction	Yes (provided the licensed product can be sold as spare parts)	Yes (provided the licensed product can be sold as spare parts)	Yes (provided the licensed product can be sold as spare parts)
Particular customer restriction	Yes (where to create an alternative source of supply)	Yes (where to create an alternative source of supply)	Yes (where to create an alternative source of supply)

The hardcore restrictions (and the exceptions to these hardcore restrictions) are now discussed in more detail.

Price restrictions

14–072 It is a hardcore restriction, in an agreement between competitors, to place any restrictions on a party's ability to determine its sales price when selling products to third parties.[46] Price fixing is also a hardcore restriction in agreements between non-competitors.[47]

However, by contrast, as between non-competitors (but not as between competitors) the Block Exemption permits the parties to recommend resale prices and impose maximum price obligations, provided these recommended and maximum prices do not amount to fixed or minimum resale prices as a result of pressure from or incentives offered by the other party.

The Guidelines make it clear[48] that not only direct price fixing but also indirect price fixing is forbidden. Thus, obligations fixing margins or the maximum level of discount the licensee can grant, or linking the required price to the prices of competitors, are black-listed restrictions. Further, threats, intimidation, warnings, penalties or contract terminations in relation to observance of a given price level are all prohibited.

Prohibited indirect means of price fixing can also include the implementation of a price monitoring system, or the obligation on licensees to report price deviations. Price fixing can also be implemented indirectly by applying disincentives to reduce prices, for example by providing that the royalty rate will increase if product prices are reduced below a certain level.[49]

Cross-licensing between competitors which contain disproportionately high reciprocal royalty obligations can be used to co-ordinate prices in downstream markets. In this case, the arrangement will be regarded by the

---

[46] *ibid.*, Art.4(1)(a).
[47] *ibid.*, Art.4(2)(a).
[48] The Guidelines, para.97.
[49] See also the Guidelines, para.79.

Commission as having no valid business justification and will be treated in the same way as a cartel.[50]

Hardcore pricing restrictions also include the situation where royalties are calculated on the basis of all product sales, whether or not the licensed technology is used (whether the agreement is reciprocal or not). This type of arrangement restricts competition by raising the cost of using the licensee's own competing technology. Such a royalty obligation may only benefit from exemption in exceptional circumstances, such as where it is not possible to calculate whether the licensed technology has been used in a product, as it leaves no visible trace on the final product, and there are no alternative monitoring methods.[51]

Output restrictions

Reciprocal output restrictions (i.e. limitations on how much a party may produce and sell) are prohibited under the Block Exemption in agreements between competitors.[52] Output restrictions imposed on the licensor in respect of its own technology are also not permitted. However, between competitors, such restrictions are permitted (up to the 20 per cent market share threshold) in reciprocal agreements where the restriction is only imposed on one of the licensees and in non-reciprocal agreements. Output restrictions in agreements between non-competitors are exempted up to the 30 per cent market share threshold.

14–073

Field of use restrictions

A field of use restriction is where the licensee is limited to using the licensed technology within one or more technical fields of application or one or more product markets. Although the allocation of markets or customers is a hardcore restriction in agreements between competitors,[53] field of use restrictions on the licensee are permitted, up to the market share threshold of 20 per cent, whether or not the agreement is reciprocal.[54] However, the restriction cannot go beyond the scope of the licensed technology and it cannot restrict the licensee's use of his own technology.[55] However, in reciprocal agreements between competitors, field of use restrictions on the licensor are not permitted.[56] Field of use restrictions are exempted in agreements between non-competitors up to the 30 per cent market share threshold.

14–074

Sole and exclusive licence terms

The grant of a sole or exclusive licence will often be contrary to Art.81(1).

14–075

---

[50] The Technology Transfer Block Exemption, Art.4(1)(c)(ii).
[51] The Guidelines, para.81.
[52] The Technology Transfer Block Exemption, Art.4(1)(b).
[53] *ibid.*, Art.4(1)(c).
[54] *ibid.*, Art.4(1)(c)(i).
[55] The Guidelines, paras 90–91.
[56] *ibid.*, para.80.

The two types of licence are distinguished by the fact that under an exclusive, as opposed to sole, licence, the licensor is itself excluded from supplying the relevant products, as well as being excluded from allowing other licensees to do so. A sole or exclusive licence is exempted under the Block Exemption in agreements between non-competitors up to the 30 per cent market share threshold. The Guidelines state that exclusive licensing between non-competitors may benefit from exemption under Art.81(3), even above this threshold.[57]

For agreements between competitors, reciprocal exclusive licensing is a hardcore restriction. Sole licensing and non-reciprocal exclusive licensing are permitted, up to the 20 per cent market share threshold.[58] This applies irrespective of the territory. Exclusive or sole licensing can also be combined with field of use restrictions (insofar as field of use restrictions are themselves permitted as explained above) up to the relevant market share thresholds.

Territorial/customer restrictions

14–076 Whilst sole and exclusive licences relate to where products can be produced using the licensed technology, sales restrictions restrict the sale of these products to certain customers or into certain territories. A distinction is made between active selling and passive selling: active sales include soliciting orders, direct visits to customers, targeted advertising or establishing a warehouse in the prohibited territory, for example, whereas passive selling occurs where the licensee responds to an unsolicited order from outside his territory or customer group. Internet selling counts as passive selling.

It is a hardcore restriction in agreements between competitors to allocate markets or customers and in agreements between non-competitors to restrict the territory into which, or the customers to whom, the licensee may sell the licensed products.[59] This covers not just direct sales restrictions, such as a straightforward contractual ban on selling in a particular territory, but also any indirect market partitioning by territory or by customer.[60] That would include the obligation to refer orders from customers to other licensees, for example. It also covers indirect measures aimed at encouraging the licensee not to make sales into a particular customer group or territory, such as financial incentives, the implementation of a monitoring policy and quantity restrictions in certain cases.

It is permitted under the Block Exemption in agreements between competitors (up to the 20 per cent market share threshold) to restrict active and/or passive sales by the parties into the exclusive territory or customer group reserved to the other party. However, this is only the case in respect of non-

[57] *ibid.*, para.165.
[58] The Technology Transfer Block Exemption, Arts 4(1)(c)(ii) and (iii).
[59] *ibid.*, Arts 4(1)(c) and 4(2)(b).
[60] The Guidelines, para.98.

reciprocal agreements; similar restrictions in reciprocal agreements are not permitted.[61] It is also permitted in non-reciprocal agreements to restrict active (but not passive) sales by a licensee into a territory or customer group allocated exclusively by the licensor to another licensee, provided however that the protected licensee was not a competitor of the licensor at the time its licence agreement was granted.[62]

In agreements between non-competitors, the restriction of active sales by the licensee into a territory or customer group, whether or not exclusively reserved to the licensor or allocated to another licensee, is permitted up to the 30 per cent market share threshold (subject to what is said below in relation to captive use restrictions and restrictions on members of a selective distribution system acting at the retail level). The same is true of all sales restrictions on the licensor up to the 30 per cent threshold.[63]   14–077

Passive sales can only be restricted in agreements between non-competitors (up to the market share threshold) but only in relation to territories or customer groups that the licensor has exclusively reserved to itself[64] or allocated exclusively to another licensee, and only during the first two years that the protected licensee sells the licensed products in that territory or to that customer group.[65] After this two year period, such a restriction becomes a hardcore restriction.

A territory or customer group will be taken to be exclusively allocated to a licensee when the licensor agrees to license the relevant technology only to one licensee within a particular territory or to a particular customer group and that exclusive licensee is protected against active selling into his territory or to his customer group by the licensor and all the other licensees of the licensor inside the Community. For a territory or customer group to be reserved to the licensor, it is not necessary for the licensor to be actively producing in that territory or for that customer group; a territory or customer group can be reserved for later exploitation.[66]

Captive use/particular customer restrictions

In both non-reciprocal agreements between competitors and agreements between non-competitors, the licensee can be obliged (up to the relevant market share thresholds) to limit his production of the licensed product only for his own use. Where the licensed product is a component in a final product, the licensee can therefore be limited to producing the quantities he requires in manufacturing his own products and to sell the licensed product only as an integral part of or as a spare part for his own products.[67]   14–078

In other words, the licensee can be prevented from selling the components to other producers. However, he must be able to sell the components

---

[61] The Technology Transfer Block Exemption, Art.4(1)(c)(iv).
[62] *ibid.*, Art.4(1)(c)(v).
[63] The Guidelines, para.98.
[64] The Technology Transfer Block Exemption, Art.4(2)(b)(i).
[65] *ibid.*, Art.4(2)(b)(ii).
[66] The Guidelines, para.100.
[67] The Technology Transfer Block Exemption, Arts 4(1)(c)(vi) and 4(2)(b)(iii).

as spare parts for his own products and be able to supply these components to third parties who provide after sales services for the final product.

A licensee can also be obliged (in agreements between non-competitors and in non-reciprocal agreements between competitors, up to the relevant market share thresholds) to limit his production to supplying the licensed product only to a particular customer, provided that the licensee has been appointed so that the customer could have a second source of supply within the licensed territory.[68] The customer may himself assume these second source supply obligations, in which case he may be subject to the same restrictions.

Other exceptions to the hardcore prohibition on territorial/customer restrictions

14–079 Apart from the possibility of sales restrictions outlined above, in agreements between non-competitors, there are a further two exceptions to the hardcore exclusion of restrictions on the territories or customers to which the licensee can sell.[69] A licensee who is a wholesaler can be prevented from selling to end-users (and so can be required to only sell to retailers)[70] and members of a selective distribution network can be restricted from selling to unauthorised distributors.[71]

However, in the latter case, the licensees must be able to sell actively and passively to end-users (unless the licensee is a wholesaler). This is because it is a hardcore restriction in agreements between non-competitors to restrict active and passive sales by members of a selective distribution system operating at the retail level to end-users. It is possible, though, to impose a location clause on a licensee in a selective distribution system, preventing him from running his business from any location other than the one specified or from opening new premises.[72]

Restrictions on exploitation of own technology

14–080 Restricting the licensee's ability to exploit his own technology and/or from carrying out research and development, is a hardcore restriction in agreements between competitors (except as regards such a restriction on research and development, where this is indispensable to prevent the disclosure of the licensed know-how to third parties).[73]

For example, it is not permitted to include a clause limiting where the licensee may sell products produced using his own technology or prohibiting the licensee from licensing his own technology to third parties, as this limits the exploitation of his own technology.

Furthermore, the licensee cannot be required to pay royalties on products

---

[68] *ibid.*, Arts 4(1)(c)(vii) and 4(2)(b)(iv).
[69] *ibid.*, Art.4(2)(b).
[70] *ibid.*, Art.4(2)(b)(v).
[71] *ibid.*, Art.4(2)(b)(vi).
[72] *ibid.*, Art.4(2)(c).
[73] *ibid.*, Art.4(1)(d).

produced using his own technology. In the case of agreements between non-competitors, this is an excluded restriction (discussed below), i.e. the Block Exemption can apply to the rest of the agreement excluding such a restriction provided that is severable. In all cases, any non-compete obligation on the licensee should be limited in scope accordingly, in order to comply with the Block Exemption; see para.14–085 below.

Restrictions on ability to carry out R&D

In agreements between competitors, it is a hardcore restriction to limit either party's ability to carry out independent research and development, unless such a restriction is indispensable to prevent the disclosure of the licensed know-how to third parties.[74] In this case, the restrictions imposed to protect this know-how must be necessary and proportionate, for example by preventing certain employees who have had access to the know-how from carrying out research and development with third parties. In the case of agreements between non-competitors, this is an excluded restriction (discussed below).

14–081

Excluded restrictions

In addition to the list of hardcore restrictions, the Block Exemption also contains a list of excluded restrictions.[75] Unlike hardcore restrictions, these restrictions can be severed from the agreement (if possible under the law of the contract) so the inclusion of such an obligation means that the benefit of the Block Exemption is only lost in relation to the provision in question and the remainder of the agreement continues to benefit from exemption, provided all the other conditions are met (and provided that the restriction can be severed as a matter of contractual law).

14–082

Any direct or indirect obligation on the licensee to assign or grant an exclusive licence to the licensor to use the licensee's own severable improvements or his own new applications of the licensed technology will not benefit from exemption. Severable improvements are those that can be exploited without utilising the licensed technology. Non-exclusive licences of severable improvements or new applications (including those that are not reciprocal) are permitted.

Furthermore, any restriction on the licensee challenging the validity of intellectual property rights which the licensor holds is also an excluded restriction. However, it is permissible to include a provision allowing for the termination of the licence agreement by the licensor if the licensee challenges the validity of the licensed technology.

In addition, where the parties are not competitors, any obligation limiting the licensee's ability to exploit his own technology or limiting either party's ability to carry out independent research and development will not benefit from the Block Exemption (except, as regards such a restriction on

---

[74] *ibid.*, Art.4(1)(d).
[75] *ibid.*, Art.5.

research and development, where this is indispensable to prevent the disclosure of the licensed know-how to third parties). (All such obligations are blacklisted in agreements between competitors, as explained above.) As an example, requiring the licensee to pay royalties on the basis of products he produces using only his own technology will limit the licensee's ability to exploit his own technology.

14.4.7 The Technology Transfer Block Exemption—Other Specific Clauses

14–083   While the hardcore restrictions (and their exceptions) have been discussed separately above, the following section considers other clauses that are commonly found in technology licence agreements, based on the analysis provided in the Guidelines.

The Guidelines list the following types of common obligations that generally do not restrict competition and so do not fall under Art.81(1), whether the agreement is between competitors or non-competitors:

- Confidentiality obligations;
- Obligations on licensees not to sub-license;
- Obligations not to use the licensed technology after the expiry of the agreement, provided that the licensed technology remains valid and in force;
- Obligations to assist the licensor in enforcing the licensed intellectual property rights;
- Obligations to pay minimum royalties or to produce a minimum quantity of products incorporating the licensed technology; and
- Obligations to use the licensor's trade mark or indicate the name of the licensor on the product.[76]

Other common provisions are permitted up to the market share thresholds (in addition to those discussed in the previous section).

Tying and bundling

14–084   Tying is where the licensor makes the licensing of one technology conditional upon the licensee taking a licence for another technology or purchasing a product from the licensor. Bundling is where two technologies or a technology and a product are bundled together and are not sold separately. Tying and bundling are permitted in agreements between competitors and non-competitors, up to the relevant market share threshold.[77]

---

[76] The Guidelines, para.135.
[77] *ibid.*, para.192.

Non-competition clauses

Non-compete obligations (i.e. an obligation on the licensee not to use third party technologies which compete with the licensed technology) are permitted up to the market share thresholds, provided the non-compete obligation does not limit the licensee's ability to exploit his own technology or his ability to carry out independent research and development (unless such latter type of restriction is indispensable to prevent the disclosure of the licensed know-how to third parties).[78] Therefore, in order to comply with the Block Exemption, any non-compete obligation on the licensee should generally be drafted so as to allow the licensee to exploit his own technology and to carry out research and development.

14–085

Royalties

The parties to a licence agreement are generally free to agree the royalties payable, without infringing Art.81. A requirement to pay a minimum royalty, for example, will not generally be restrictive of competition. In addition, an obligation to continue to pay royalties for a period going beyond the duration of the licensed intellectual property rights will not generally infringe Art.81. On the other hand, the setting of royalty rates in order to achieve one of the blacklisted restrictions, such as an obligation, in an agreement between competitors making royalties payable on products that do not incorporate the licensed technology, will result in the Block Exemption ceasing to apply.

14–086

14.4.8 The Vertical Agreements Block Exemption

The Vertical Agreements Block Exemption[79] (hereafter the "Block Exemption") has been applicable since June 1, 2000. It replaced three existing block exemptions: the exclusive distribution, exclusive purchasing and franchising block exemptions. The new approach was not only intended to unify the provisions relating to vertical agreements contained in these block exemptions, but also to widen the scope of the Block Exemption further, and respond to some of the criticisms of the previous block exemptions.

14–087

The Commission also published a set of explanatory guidelines (the "Guidelines"),[80] which not only explain the interpretation of the Block Exemption, but also give a competition analysis of vertical agreements which fall outside of the Block Exemption because they are above the market share thresholds.

---

[78] *ibid.*, para.197.

[79] Commission Regulation No.2790/1999 of December 22, 1999, on the application of Art.81(3) of the Treaty to categories of vertical agreements and concerted practices, O.J. L 336/21, December 29, 1999.

[80] Guidelines on Vertical Restraints, O.J. C 291/1, October 10, 2000.

Meaning of "vertical agreements"

14–088   Vertical agreements are defined in the Block Exemption as agreements or concerted practices "between two or more undertakings each of which operates, for the purposes of the agreement, at a different level of the production or distribution chain, and relating to the conditions under which the parties may purchase, sell or resell certain goods or services".[81]

There are a number of points to notice about this definition. First, the Block Exemption can apply to agreements between more than two parties. This is an advance on the previous block exemptions, which only applied where there were no more than two parties to the agreement. On the other hand, for the purposes of this Block Exemption, each of the parties to the agreement must operate at a different level of the production or distribution chain. So, for example, an agreement between a manufacturer, a wholesaler and a retailer could come under the Block Exemption, but not one which included the manufacturer and more than one wholesaler, or more than one retailer.

The definition also indicates that the parties need only operate at a different level of the market "for the purposes of the agreement". So the fact that two parties actually operate at the same level of the market for other purposes—for example they manufacture competing products—would not exclude them automatically from the Block Exemption, provided that for the purposes of the relevant agreement they were acting at different levels of the market—for example as manufacturer for one party, and as distributor for another party.

That is not to say that all agreements between competitors come within the Block Exemption, however (see below). The definition is deliberately broad enough to include intermediate sales, where one party to the agreement is buying products to be used as an input into a production process. It also applies to the purchase, sale or resale of services.

This is in contrast with the previous block exemptions (or at least the exclusive distribution and exclusive purchasing block exemptions) which applied only to the resale of goods, and did not apply to the sale of services, or to any transaction where the goods purchased by the distributor were to undergo any substantial change in their nature which would amount to more than "resale".

Exclusion of agreements between competing companies

14–089   The Block Exemption will not apply to vertical agreements between actual or potential competitors, even if they operate at different levels of the production/ distribution chain for the purposes of the agreement, unless the agreement is non-reciprocal and either:

    (i)   the buyer's annual turnover does not exceed €100 million; or
    (ii) the supplier is a manufacturer and a distributor of goods, while

---

[81] The Vertical Agreements Block Exemption, Art.2(1).

the buyer is a distributor and does not manufacture goods or services that compete with the contract goods or services; or

(iii)   the supplier is a provider of services at several different levels of trade, while the buyer does not provide competing services at the level of trade where it purchases the contract services.[82]

Competing undertakings are undertakings that are actual or potential suppliers of the contract goods or services or goods or services that are substitutes for the contract goods or services.[83] A potential supplier is an undertaking that does not actually produce the goods or services supplied by the supplier or a competing product or service but could and would be likely to do so in the absence of the agreement in response to a small and permanent increase in relative prices. This applies where the undertaking would be able to undertake the necessary additional investments and supply the market within one year.[84] This assessment has to be based on realistic grounds; the mere theoretical possibility of entering a market is not sufficient.

The exceptional circumstances where agreements between competitors may come under the Block Exemption are intended to cover (i) situations in which the buyer is a relatively small undertaking, and (ii) situations in which the supplier distributes the contract goods directly to certain customers or territories as well as appointing distributors. In other words, if a supplier competes with its distributor by selling the contract goods to end-users itself, the Block Exemption is not excluded provided the distributor does not operate at the level at which it purchased the goods or services (i.e. it is not a competing manufacturer).

Exclusion of intellectual property agreements and agreements coming under other block exemptions

As regards intellectual property agreements and licences, the Block Exemption states[85] that: 14–090

"the exemption ... shall apply to vertical agreements containing provisions which relate to the assignment to the buyer or use by the buyer of intellectual property rights, provided that those provisions do not constitute the primary object of such agreements and are directly related to the use, sale or resale of goods or services by the buyer or its customers."

The Guidelines suggest[86] that the Block Exemption applies to vertical

---

[82] *ibid.*, Art.4.

[83] *ibid.*, Art.1(a).

[84] The Guidelines, para.26.

[85] The Vertical Agreements Block Exemption, Art.2(3). Recital 3 states in this respect that the agreements falling within the Block Exemption "include certain ancillary agreements on the assignment or use of intellectual property rights."

[86] The Guidelines, para.30.

agreements containing intellectual property rights (IPR) provisions when five conditions are fulfilled:

(1) The IPR provisions must be part of a vertical agreement, i.e. an agreement with conditions under which the parties may purchase, sell or resell certain goods or services.

This means that agreements where one party provides another with a master copy and licenses the other to produce and distribute copies will not come under the Block Exemption, nor will trade mark licensing agreements for the purpose of merchandising, sponsorship contracts or copyright licenses such as broadcasting contracts concerning the right to record and/or broadcast (or presumably webcast) an event.

(2) The IPRs must be assigned to, or for use by, the buyer.

Consequently, the Block Exemption does not apply to agreements where IPRs are provided by the buyer to the supplier. This means in particular that subcontracting involving the transfer of know-how to a subcontractor to enable the subcontractor to manufacture products does not fall within the scope of application of the Block Exemption. However, vertical agreements under which the buyer provides only specifications to the supplier which describe the goods or services to be supplied are exempted.

(3) The IPR provisions must not constitute the primary object of the agreement.

According to the Guidelines, this means that the primary object of the agreement must not be the assignment or licensing of IPRs but the purchase or distribution of goods or services and the IPR provisions must serve the implementation of that vertical agreement.

(4) The IPR provisions must be directly related to the use, sale or resale of goods or services by the buyer or his customers.

According to the Guidelines, the goods or services for use or resale are usually supplied by the licensor but may also be purchased by the licensee from a third party supplier. The IPR provisions will normally concern the marketing of goods or services. This is for instance the case in a franchise agreement where the franchisor sells to the franchisee goods for resale and in addition licenses the franchisee to use its trade mark and know-how to market the goods. In the case of franchising where marketing forms the object of the exploitation of the IPRs, the goods or services are distributed by the master franchisee or the franchisees.

(5) The IPR provisions, in relation to the contract goods or services, must not contain restrictions of competition having the same object or effect as vertical restraints which are not exempted under the Block Exemption.

This means that they cannot include any of the forbidden hardcore restrictions (see below) or the various non-compete provisions excluded from the Block Exemption.

The Block Exemption further states that it "does not apply to vertical agreements the subject matter of which is regulated by other block exemption regulations".[87] The Guidelines explain in this respect that the Block Exemption does not apply to vertical agreements "covered by" the Technology Transfer Block Exemption, the Research and Development Block Exemption or the Specialisation Block Exemption.

It may be that as a result of this, any agreement which includes a licence of patent rights, know-how and/or software copyright and which allows manufacturing using these rights may not come within the scope of the Block Exemption, because it comes within the Technology Transfer Block Exemption. However, this may have some unintended consequences. Giving the purchaser of any products or services any technical information concerning its manufacture of a further product could mean losing the benefit of the Block Exemption, as might even an implied patent licence.

Trade marks

In respect of trade marks, the Guidelines[88] comment that a trade mark licence to a distributor may be related to the distribution of the licensor's products in a particular territory. If it is an exclusive licence, the agreement amounts to exclusive distribution.

14–091

Copyright and software

The Guidelines[89] indicate that agreements under which hard copies of software are supplied for resale and where the reseller does not acquire a licence to any rights over the software but only has the right to resell the hard copies are to be regarded as agreements for the supply of goods for resale for the purposes of the Block Exemption. Under this form of distribution, the licence of the software only takes place between the copyright owner and the user of software. This may take the form of a shrink-wrap licence, i.e. a set of conditions included in the package of the hard copy which the end-user is deemed to accept by opening the package. Buyers of hardware incorporating software protected by copyright may be obliged by the copyright holder not to infringe the copyright, for example not to make copies and resell the software or not to make copies and use the software in combination with other hardware, and these restrictions will be covered by the Block Exemption.

14–092

The market share cap

The Block Exemption is subject to a 30 per cent market share threshold, above which the Block Exemption no longer applies.[90] The relevant market share is that of the supplier, except in the case of exclusive supply

14–093

---

[87] The Vertical Agreements Block Exemption, Art.2(5).
[88] The Guidelines, para.38.
[89] The Guidelines, para.40.
[90] The Vertical Agreements Block Exemption, Art.3(1).

arrangements where the relevant market share is that of the buyer.[91] An "exclusive supply obligation" is defined as "any direct or indirect obligation causing the supplier to sell the goods or services specified in the agreement only to one buyer inside the Community for the purposes of a specific use or for resale."[92]

Market shares should then be calculated on the basis of the sales value of the contract goods or services for the proceeding calendar year.[93] If value figures are not available, estimates based on market data, including data on sales volumes, may be used.

After the market share breaks through the 30 per cent barrier, the exemption can continue to apply for a period of two years so long as the market share is less than 35 per cent.[94] Once the market share breaks through the 35 per cent barrier the exemption can only apply for a further period of one year.[95] These two extensions cannot be combined, so that the exemption can only continue to apply for a maximum of two years if the market share threshold is exceeded.[96]

Calculating the market share

14–094 The usual rules of market definition under EC competition law must be applied, in addition to which the Guidelines deal with certain specific issues. The relevant product market comprises goods and services which are regarded by the supplier as interchangeable. The relevant geographic market is the area in which the undertakings concerned are involved in the supply and demand of relevant goods or services, in which the conditions of competition are sufficiently homogenous.

In calculating the market share in the supplier's market, the market share is that of the supplier in the market in which it sells to buyers. This market depends first on substitutability from the buyer's perspective. Where the supplier's product is used as an input to produce other products and is not generally recognisable in the final product, the product market is normally defined by the direct buyer's preferences, since customers will normally not have a strong preference concerning the inputs used by the buyers.

However, in the case of distribution of final products, what are substitutes for the direct buyer will normally be influenced or determined by the preferences of the final consumer when it purchases final goods. In a case where there are three parties, the market share cap must be satisfied for each supplier. For example, where there is a manufacturer, wholesaler and retailer, the market share cap must be satisfied for both the manufacturer and the wholesaler.

---

[91] *ibid.*, Art.3(2).
[92] *ibid.*, Art.1(c).
[93] *ibid.*, Art.9(2)(a).
[94] *ibid.*, Art.9(2)(c).
[95] *ibid.*, Art.9(2)(d).
[96] *ibid.*, Art.9(2)(e).

In the case of exclusive supply, the market share of the buyer is its share of all purchases on the market in which it purchases the goods and services.

The problem with the market share cap, as with all market share tests is that, especially in relation to intermediate markets, market share data may often be unavailable or unreliable, creating uncertainty in the application of the exemption.

Hardcore restrictions

The Block Exemption contains a list of "hardcore" restrictions that, if included in an agreement, will prevent the Block Exemption from applying[97]:   **14–095**

(i) restrictions on the buyer's ability to determine its sale price, with the exception of recommended resale prices and maximum resale price obligations (provided that these do not amount to fixed or minimum resale prices as a result of pressure from or incentives offered by the supplier);

(ii) restrictions of the territory into which, or the customers to whom, the buyer may sell the contract goods or services apart from:

— restrictions on active sales to territories or customer groups that the supplier has exclusively reserved to itself or allocated exclusively to another buyer;
— restrictions on sales to end-users by wholesalers;
— restrictions on resale to unauthorised distributors by members of a selective distribution network; and
— restrictions of the buyer's ability to sell components, supplied for the purposes of incorporation, to customers who would use them to manufacture the same type of goods as those produced by the supplier;

(iii) restrictions of active or passive sales to end-users by members of a selective distribution system operating at the retail level of trade, without prejudice to the possibility of prohibiting a member of the system from operating out of an unauthorised place of establishment;

(iv) restrictions on cross-supplies between members of a selective distribution system; and

(v) restrictions preventing a supplier of spare parts that are used by the buyer for incorporation into its own product from selling them to as spare parts to end-users or to independent repairers or service providers.

The restrictions in the hardcore list are clearly now the central guidance as

---

[97] *ibid.*, Art.4.

to what clauses may be permitted in vertical agreements, and merit close examination.

Resale prices

14-096   Resale price maintenance is the first of the hardcore list.[98] There can be no restriction on the buyer's ability to freely determine its resale prices, with the exception of the possibility of recommended resale prices and maximum resale price obligations. However, these recommended and maximum prices must not amount to fixed or minimum resale prices as a result of pressure from or incentives offered by the supplier.

The Guidelines[99] make it clear that it is not only direct resale price maintenance, but also indirect price maintenance which is forbidden. Thus, the fixing of distribution margins, or the maximum level of discount the distributor can grant, making the grant of rebates or reimbursement of promotional costs by the supplier subject to the observance of a given price level, linking the prescribed resale price to the resale prices of competitors, threats, intimidation, warnings, penalties, delay or suspension of deliveries or contract terminations in relation to observance of a given price level are all prohibited.

A number of activities are described in the Guidelines as measures which can make direct or indirect means of price fixing more effective, but are not blacklisted in themselves. These include monitoring systems, requirements on retailers to report other retailers who deviate from the standard price, printing a recommended resale price on the product or the supplier obliging the buyer to apply a most-favoured-customer clause. On the other hand, if they are used to make recommended prices or maximum prices function as fixed or minimum resale prices, then the recommended price or maximum price may be blacklisted.[1]

Restrictions on territories or customers to whom the buyer can sell

14-097   Restrictions on the territories into which the buyer can sell, or the customers to whom he can sell are blacklisted[2] with certain exceptions.

Before turning to the exceptions, it is important to note that it is not just a straight contractual ban on selling in particular territories or customers which is aimed at, but anything which brings about market partitioning by territory or by customer.[3] That would include the obligation to refer orders from customers to other distributors, for example.

It would also include refusal or reduction of bonuses or discounts, refusal to supply, reduction of supplied volumes or limitation of supplied volumes to the demand within the allocated territory or customer group, threat of contract termination or profit pass-over obligations and the supplier not

---

[98] *ibid.*, Art.4(a).
[99] The Guidelines, para.47.
[1] The Guidelines, para.47.
[2] The Vertical Agreements Block Exemption, Art.4(b).
[3] The Guidelines, para.49.

providing a Community-wide guarantee service, whereby all distributors are required to provide guarantee services and are reimbursed by the supplier, even where the product was sold by other distributors into the territory.

These measures are more likely to be viewed as a restriction of the buyer's ability to sell to such territories or customers where they are combined with monitoring systems, such as the use of differentiated labels or serial numbers. However, a prohibition imposed on all distributors from selling to certain end-users is not a hardcore restriction if there is an objective justification related to the product, such as a ban on selling dangerous substances to certain customers for reasons of health or safety. Obligations relating to the display of the supplier's brand name are also not classified as hardcore.[4]

The first exception to the hardcore prohibition on sales restrictions concerns restrictions on active sales by the buyer. The distinction in EC competition law between active and passive sales is a well-established one. Active sales are those in which customers are approached by active marketing and promotions, such as advertising, in the media or other promotions specifically targeted at a particular customer group or territory, as well as direct mail or visits, or establishing a warehouse or distribution outlet in another distributor's territory. Passive sales, on the other hand, are sales to customers who have made an unsolicited request for a product or service.

In this case, it would also be a restriction on passive sales if distributors were prevented, not from selling, but from delivering the goods or services to such customers.[5] The distinction is significant because the general principle in the past has been that in distribution arrangements, while there might be a ban on active sales, a ban on passive sales into another territory, such as would be implied by a complete ban on exports into that other territory by the distributor, was not permitted and raised a high risk of fines. The new rules are slightly different however, in that only certain restrictions on active sales are allowed.

Only restrictions on active sales by direct buyers to territories or customer groups that the supplier has exclusively reserved to itself or allocated exclusively to another buyer are permitted.[6] A territory or customer group will be taken to be exclusively allocated when the supplier agrees to sell his product only to one distributor for distribution within a particular territory or to a particular customer group and that exclusive distributor is protected against active selling into his territory or to his customer group by the supplier and all the other buyers of the supplier inside the Community.

The allocation of exclusive territories and customer groups can be combined, so that an exclusive distributor can be appointed for a customer group within a particular territory. On the other hand, it is only a

---

[4] The Guidelines, para.49.
[5] The Guidelines, para.50.
[6] The Vertical Agreements Block Exemption, Art.4(b) first indent.

restriction on active sales to such exclusive territories or customer groups which is permitted. A restriction on passive sales to such exclusive groups or territories will never be permitted.[7]

It should be noted that the restrictions on active resale permitted under the Block Exemption are more limited than those permitted under the previous block exemptions, where, for example the exclusive distribution block exemption allowed a prohibition on active resale outside an exclusive contract territory of the distributor, whether or not the other territories were exclusively reserved to another distributor or to the supplier.

Application to sales via the internet

14–098   According to the Guidelines,[8] resale of goods and services via the internet is generally not considered to be a form of active sales, but a form of passive sales. The fact that the internet site may be accessed by customers in other territories results from the fact that the web is accessible from everywhere. If a customer from a territory outside of the buyer's territory visits the website, resulting in a sale, that is considered passive selling, and that is the case whatever the language or languages which may be used on the website.

On the other hand, actions specifically targeted at customers outside of the territory, such as the use of banner advertising or links to pages of providers specifically available to other exclusive territories or customer groups, could be considered to be active sales to those other territories or customer groups, as could unsolicited emails sent to individual customers or customer groups, or use of a ccTLD, such as the use of .de where the distributor is only appointed to the territory of France in the off-line world. On the other hand, the restrictions which may be possible on metatagging in this new scheme of things is not entirely clear. The same rules apply to sales by catalogue.

At the same time, the Guidelines makes it clear that[9] the supplier may require quality standards for the use of the internet site to resell its goods, just as it may impose quality standards for a shop or for advertising and promotion in general.

The Guidelines suggest that this may be relevant in particular for selective distribution. This could include, presumably, on-line equivalents of the type of conditions regarding quality of presentation and service that are applied to the off-line sale of goods, such as the amount of space required to present the product and the quality of presentation of the goods. It might also include the obligation to have sufficient staff available to give advice on-line, which is the equivalent of that supplied during office hours off-line, as well as quality service levels for responses which match those off-line, and requirements relating to the use of help desk and customer service provision. Provisions might also be included regarding payment and cur-

---

[7] The Guidelines, para.50.
[8] The Guidelines, para.51.
[9] The Guidelines, para.51.

rency. Standards and requirements relating to advertising might also be required to match those provided off-line.

Similarly, the equivalent of non-compete provisions might be imposed to prevent sales of competitor products through the site, or perhaps even the mention of competitors' names, or any links to any sites which sell competitor products.

However, any set of restrictions which have the overall effect of making it commercially impossible for distributors to advertise or sell goods on-line and which cannot be properly justified, or which are disproportionate, may be treated as a blanket ban.

In general, the Guidelines make it clear that a blanket ban on sales via the internet will be considered by the Commission to deprive an agreement of the benefit of the Block Exemption, and if it is treated in the same way as restrictions on passive sales have been treated in the past, such a restriction could give rise to a high risk of fines. An outright ban on internet sales would only be permissible where there is an objective justification. In a previous unpublished version of the Guidelines, the Commission indicated that health and safety reasons could justify such a ban. Whatever the case, the supplier cannot reserve to itself sales and/or advertising over the internet.

This does not mean that the supplier is forced to allow all buyers to resell goods over the internet. In a selective distribution system, the supplier can choose only to sell goods to those distributors who have physical sales locations, and to require that no sales be made to distributors who are not appointed to the network. This could also imply limiting the amount of product which can be purchased by end-users in some instances.

The impact of the treatment of internet advertising and sales on distribution is considered below, together with the recent case law of the Commission implementing this policy.

Other exceptions to the hardcore prohibition on customer restrictions

Apart from the possibility of restrictions on active sales by the buyer to **14–099** other exclusive territories or customers, there are three other exceptions to the hardcore exclusion of restrictions on the territories or customers to which the buyer can sell.[10] A buyer who is a wholesaler can be prevented from selling to end-users, members of a selective distribution network can be restricted from selling to unauthorised distributors, in markets where such a system is operated, and there can be a restriction on a buyer's ability to sell components, supplied for the purposes of incorporation, to customers who would use them to manufacture the same type of goods as those produced by the supplier. In the latter case, the term "component" includes any intermediate goods and "incorporation" refers to the use of any input to produce goods.

---

[10] The Vertical Agreements Block Exemption, Art.4(b), second, third and fourth indents.

Restrictions on sales to end-users by selective distributors

14–100 A restriction of active or passive sales to end-users by members of a selective distribution system operating at the retail level of trade is also a hardcore restriction.[11] The Guidelines explain[12] that not only does this mean that dealers in a selective distribution system cannot be restricted in the users to whom they can sell, but it also means that there can be no restriction on selling to purchasing agents acting on behalf of end-users. Selective distributors must also be free to advertise and sell using the internet. According to the Guidelines, selective distribution may be combined with exclusive distribution, provided that active and passive selling is not restricted anywhere. The supplier may therefore commit itself to supplying only one dealer, or a limited number of dealers in a certain territory.

The restriction on sales to end-users by selective distributors is expressed to be without prejudice to the possibility of prohibiting a member of the system from operating out of an unauthorised place of establishment. This means that it is permitted under the Block Exemption to impose a location clause on a selective distributor, preventing them from running their businesses from any location other than that specified, or opening a new outlet.[13]

Restriction on cross-supplies between appointed distributors

14–101 Cross-supplies between appointed distributors within a selective distribution network cannot be restricted under the hardcore list.[14] There must be no direct or indirect restriction on passive or active sales to other selective distributors, operating at the same or at a different level of trade. One consequence is that selective distribution cannot be combined with vertical restraints aimed at forcing distributors to purchase the contract products exclusively from a given source, for instance exclusive purchasing. Another is that there cannot be a restriction on appointed wholesalers selling to appointed retailers.[15]

Restrictions relating to the supply of spare parts

14–102 The final hardcore restriction is:

> "the restriction agreed between a supplier of components and a buyer who incorporates those components, which limits the supplier to selling the components as spare parts to end-users or to repairers or other service providers not entrusted by the buyer with the repair or servicing of its goods."[16]

---

[11] *ibid.*, Art.4(c).
[12] The Guidelines, para.53.
[13] The Guidelines, para.54.
[14] The Vertical Agreements Block Exemption, Art.4(d).
[15] The Guidelines, para.55.
[16] The Vertical Agreements Block Exemption, Art.4(e).

The Guidelines make it clear[17] that the intention is that end-users, independent repairers, and service providers should not be prevented from obtaining spare parts directly from the manufacturer of these spare parts. An agreement between a manufacturer of spare parts and a buyer who incorporates these parts into his own products (OEM) may not, directly or indirectly, prevent or restrict sales by the manufacturer of these spare parts to end-users, independent repairers, or service providers.

Indirect restrictions would include restrictions on the supply of technical information and special equipment which are necessary for the use of spare parts by users, independent repairers or service providers. On the other hand, it is permissible to restrict the supply of spare parts to the repairers or service providers entrusted by the OEM with the repair or servicing of his own goods, and for the OEM to require his own repair and service network to buy the spare parts from him.

Other provisions not exempted

Apart from the hardcore list of prohibited restrictions, there are is also an exclusion for certain types of non-competition provisions that are not allowed under the Block Exemption. However, by contrast with the prohibited hardcore restrictions, whose inclusion will exclude the whole agreement from the application of the exemption, the presence of any of these non-competition restrictions in the agreement only means that those specific clauses are not exempted. It does not prevent the Block Exemption from applying to the remainder of the agreement, according to the Guidelines.[18] These provisions include[19]: **14–103**

- Any "non-compete obligation" as defined by the Block Exemption;
- Post-term restrictions on competition; and
- Restrictions on a selective distributor selling specific competitor brands.

These will now be analysed in more detail.

Non-competes during the term of the agreement

A non-compete obligation is defined as: **14–104**

"any direct or indirect obligation causing the buyer not to manufacture, purchase, sell or resell goods or services which compete with the contract goods or services, or any direct or indirect obligation on the buyer to purchase from the supplier or from another undertaking designated by the supplier more than 80 per cent of the buyer's total purchases of the contract goods or ser-

---

[17] The Guidelines, para.56.
[18] The Guidelines, para.57.
[19] The Vertical Agreements Block Exemption, Art.5.

vices and their substitutes on the relevant market, calculated on the basis of the value of its purchases in the preceding calendar year."[20]

Such restrictions are not covered by the Block Exemption if they are indefinite or exceed five years.[21] A non-compete obligation which is tacitly renewable beyond a period of five years is not allowed,[22] so a provision which provides for continuation of any kind of non-compete arrangement unless one of the parties gives notice of their objection more than a certain period before the end of the term would not comply.

This does not prevent a non-compete clause of this nature from being renewed after the five year period, so long as the parties expressly consent to the extension, i.e. expressly re-negotiate or agree to it. The extension would have to conform to the five year limit, however, in order to benefit from the Block Exemption.

There should also not be any barrier, such as loan arrangements, which hinders the ability of the buyer to effectively terminate at the end of the five year period. The five year limit does not apply, however, where the goods or services are resold by the buyer from premises and land owned by the supplier or leased by the supplier from third parties not connected with the buyer. In these cases the non-compete provision may be of the same duration as the occupancy of the premises by the buyer.[23]

Post-term restrictions

14–105 Any post-term restriction which, directly or indirectly, requires the buyer not to manufacture, purchase, sell or resell goods or services is not covered by the Block Exemption unless it[24]:

- Relates to goods or services which compete with the contract goods or services; and
- Is limited to the premises and land from which the buyer has operated during the contract period; and
- Is indispensable to protect know-how transferred by the supplier to the buyer; and
- The duration of such non-compete obligation is limited to a period of one year after termination of the agreement.

The know-how needs to include information which is indispensable to the buyer for the use, sale or resale of the contact goods or services.

---

[20] *ibid.*, Art.1(b).
[21] *ibid.*, Art.5(a).
[22] *ibid.*, Art.5(a).
[23] *ibid.*, Art.5(a).
[24] *ibid.*, Art.5(b).

Restriction on a selective distributor selling specific brands

The third condition which is not covered by the Block Exemption is any **14–106** direct or indirect obligation causing the members of a selective distribution system not to sell the brands of particular competing suppliers.[25] This would allow the selective distributor to be restricted from selling all competitors' brands but not a restriction only on selling the brands of certain named competitors. The thinking behind this provision was the concern to avoid a situation where a number of suppliers using the same selective distribution outlets prevent one specific competitor or certain specific competitors from using these outlets to distribute their products.[26]

14.4.9 The Implications of Art.81 for the Distribution of Goods and Services Through the Internet

The fact that no distributor or purchaser (apart from perhaps unauthorised **14–107** dealers in the case of selective distribution) can be prevented from making sales of goods or services via the internet under Art.81 (see above) and that the supplier or manufacturer cannot reserve sales by internet to itself has a considerable impact on the distribution of goods and services in the EC, and in many cases has ramifications on the distribution strategy worldwide.

It would be extremely inadvisable to ignore these rules on the basis that the agreement has no appreciable effect (see above) and would not come within Art.81. It would be inadvisable not only because the market share thresholds of ten or 15 per cent are an ongoing condition which are required to be satisfied throughout the course of the agreement, but because a restriction on sales and advertising through the internet, since it is deemed a restriction of passive sales, constitutes a hardcore restriction and the *de minimis* notice (see above) makes it clear that for an agreement to be deemed inappreciable, it could not contain any of the hardcore restrictions set out in the Vertical Agreements Block Exemption.

The Commission is clearly serious about this point. As it states in the Competition Report for the year 2000[27]:

> "... moves by manufacturers to protect their traditional distribution channels from the pro-competitive effects of electronic commerce will be challenged. In this context it can be mentioned that in December the Commission opened formal proceedings against B&W Loudspeakers Ltd as, among other things, this company prohibits its authorised dealers from engaging in distance selling—including sales over the internet—without objective

---

[25] *ibid.*, Art.5(c).
[26] The Guidelines, para.61.
[27] XXXth Report on competition policy 2000 (Published in conjunction with the General Report on the Activities of the European Union—2000) SEC(2001) 694 final, at point 215.

reasons. Such behaviour prevents the benefits of electronic commerce from being fully achieved."

The Commission eventually dropped its objections against B&W Loudspeakers when it agreed to delete the restriction on distance selling from its agreements. Retailers can now request B&W Loudspeakers to do distant selling. B&W Loudspeakers can only refuse such requests in writing and on criteria that concern the need to maintain the brand image and reputation of the products. The criteria must be applied indiscriminately and must be comparable to those for sales from a traditional retail outlet.[28]

14–108   In the case of the Yves Saint Laurent[29] distribution system approved in May 2001, the Commission seems to have convinced Yves Saint Laurent that it had to allow distributors to distribute its luxury perfumes via the internet. The Commission commented, with respect to this point:

> "In ... [the vertical agreements] guidelines the Commission stressed the importance of the internet for the competitiveness of the European economy and encouraged widespread use of this modern means of communication and marketing. In particular it believes that a ban on internet sales, even in a selective distribution system, is a restraint on sales to consumers which could not be covered by the 1999 regulation.
>
>   The YSLP system satisfies the exemption conditions set by this regulation. YSLP has applied selection criteria authorising approved retailers already operating a physical sales point to sell via the Internet as well."

Another case concerned the distribution of books at a fixed price in Germany. The Commission does not object to a system of fixed book prices in a particular territory, as long as it does not appreciably affect trade between Member States.

German publishers and book wholesalers had notified their system of fixed book prices to the Commission for clearance in March 2000. The Commission was minded to grant an exemption, provided the fixed prices did not apply to books that are sold by retailers directly to final consumers in other Members States, i.e. the fixed prices do not apply to direct cross-border sales of books via the internet, including direct cross-border sales of German books from another Member State to German final consumers. The fixed prices can only apply to re-imports into Germany where the sole purpose of the export and re-import is to circumvent the national pricing system.

The Commission had received complaints from internet booksellers located outside Germany, which led the Commission to conclude that direct cross-border sales of books via the internet at a price other than the fixed

---

[28] COMP/37.709 *B&W Loudspeakers*, see Commission press release IP/02/916.
[29] COMP/36.533 *Yves Saint Laurent*, see Commission press release IP/01/713.

price were routinely being seen as a circumvention of the pricing system. It therefore issued a statement of objections in July 2001. The relevant parties then offered commitments guaranteeing the freedom to make cross-border sales of German books to final consumers in Germany, in particular via the internet, and also establishing a definitive list under which the Commission exceptionally accepts that a circumvention of the pricing system occurs. The Commission therefore granted a negative clearance and closed its investigation.[30]

In a more recent case, the Commission fined Yamaha €2.56 million for resale price maintenance and restrictions of trade in Europe.[31] One of these restrictions was a clause in its agreements with distributors which required them to contact Yamaha before exporting musical instruments via the internet. The Commission found that this had the potential to discourage dealers from exporting musical instruments and so reinforced market partitioning. This constituted a hardcore restriction under the Vertical Agreements Block Exemption.

This point, as well as the structure of the Vertical Agreements Block Exemption, especially its rules limiting the circumstances in which distributors, dealers and others can be restricted from making active sales into other territories outside of their own, or to other customers, and those concerning selective distribution and non-compete restrictions means that it is now necessary for suppliers and manufacturers to think about their whole strategy before entering the market, and proceeding in a piecemeal basis in the EC/EEA could result in major problems.

It should be noted that in general the Block Exemption itself is not only important for those transactions which fall within it, but may also be a guide to similar resale-type arrangements which do not fall within its scope.

14.4.10 Application of Art.81 to IPR Licences Other Than Patent, Know-how and Software Copyright Licences

The Technology Transfer Block Exemption will not directly apply to many licensing arrangements relating to e-commerce and the internet, because many of these agreements involve licences of copyright (other than software copyright) and neighbouring rights, database rights and trade marks, which are not ancillary to patent, software copyright and know-how licences, and/or may involve pure sales licences. However, the Technology Transfer Block Exemption, together with the accompanying Guidelines, will be a good guide to the types of restrictions which will be permitted or prohibited in licensing arrangements related to the new economy. **14–109**

This could particularly apply to those arrangements which involve more than just resale of the licensed product, software, database or content, since as was seen above, the Technology Transfer Block Exemption does not

[30] See Commission press release IP/02/461.
[31] COMP/37.975 PO/Yamaha, see Commission press release IP/03/1028, July 16, 2003.

apply to pure sales licences, and requires manufacturing using the licensed technology or the use of licensed processes.

On the other hand, the Vertical Agreements Block Exemption only applies to agreements containing intellectual property licences to the buyer where these are not the primary objective of the agreement, but support other provisions relating to the supply of goods and services. The Vertical Agreements Guidelines concede that sales of packaged software can come under the Block Exemption. The sensible first step in relation to software licences is to assess whether the primary object of the agreement is the licensing of the intellectual property in the software or the supply (and resale) of copies of the software, in order then to assess accordingly whether the Technology Transfer or Vertical Agreements Block Exemptions (and/or the relevant Guidelines in each case) may be applicable.

Where the agreement is primarily for the licensing of copyright other than software, the principles of the Technology Transfer Block Exemption can be applied by analogy where the licence is for the reproduction of the protected work (i.e. the production of copies for resale).[32] Where a licence covers rights in performances or other rights related to copyright, the Technology Transfer Block Exemption and Guidelines will not apply even by analogy. To this extent, there is for some new economy licences no pre-defined set of rules for assessing such agreements and the restrictions they may contain, under Art.81.

14–110   The distinction as to whether the Technology Transfer Block Exemption or the vertical agreements rules should be followed is crucial also, since they differ fundamentally on some very crucial points.

The Technology Transfer Block Exemption allows complete bans on active sales outside the licensee's territory or customer group, and the licensee can be prohibited from even passive sales into the territory or customer group of the licensor or other licensees, although in the latter case, only where this territory or customer group has been exclusively reserved to the licensor or exclusively allotted to another licensee (in this case the restriction can only last for two years from the first marketing of the licensed product in the territory or customer group by the protected licensee).

On the other hand, under the Vertical Agreements Block Exemption, no restriction on passive sales outside of the distributor's territory is possible, and restrictions on active sales are only permissible in respect of the exclusive territories or customer groups of the supplier or other dis-tributors. The list of differences is longer, and careful comparison of the two regimes is necessary in any particular case.

The case law relating to copyright and related rights may provide a useful point of departure in certain situations. In respect of film performance rights, the European Court of Justice has indicated that the grant of exclusive rights to show a film in a particular territory may not in itself

---

[32] See para.14–056 above.

restrict competition,[33] although the court in that case also suggested that an exclusive licence might infringe Art.81(1) where it created artificial and unjustifiable barriers and restricted competition.

In a case concerning film purchases by German television stations,[34] involving exclusive licences to broadcast a large number of films in the MGM/UA film library for a period of 15 years, the Commission found that Art.81 did apply to the exclusivity, and the licensee was obliged to carve out licences which had to be granted in respect of its films to other broadcasting organisations, before the Commission would give an exemption under Art.81(3).

The Commission has also in a number of cases held that a ban on exports of goods produced under copyright licence, such as books, cassettes, tape recordings and records, was contrary to Art.81 and not permissible. It has also found that terms prohibiting the licensee from challenging the validity of copyright are not permissible and that terms requiring the payment of royalties on products which are not protected by the licensed copyright are not permitted. In the light of the changes in approach which have taken place under the Technology Transfer Block Exemption and the Vertical Agreements Block Exemption, many of these points will have to be re-examined.

In any specific case, legal advice should clearly be sought as to the application of Art.81, Art.81(3) and Art.82 (see below).

Licences to end-users

Licences to end-users may in some cases fall within the application of **14–111** Art.81, although the lack of guidance from the European Commission or the European Court of Justice in respect of end-user copyright licences in general means that the rules in this area are to a great extent a matter of conjecture. Limitations restricting the use of copyright material, or a database to a particular physical site, or to a particular computer platform or CPU will arguably fall outside of Art.81 in many cases, as would other restrictions designed to control the number of users of the subject matter of the copyright or database rights.

However, Art.81 might well apply to a restriction which merely limited the use to a particular manufacturer's hardware platform (if, for example, the licensor was thereby attempting to tie the use of his own hardware, without an objective justification). Restrictions on copying or sub-licensing may also arguably fall outside of the scope of Art.81 in many cases. On the other hand, a restriction on the use of competing products, or on the user himself competing with the licensor is likely to fall within the application of Art.81, and it may be very difficult to justify under Art.81(3).

---

[33] *Coditel SA v Cine Vog Films SA (No.2)* [1982] E.C.R. 3381.
[34] Commission Decision 89/536 [1989] O.J. L 284/36.

Contract for development

14–112   A company may hire a developer to develop copyright material or software on its behalf.[35] It may want to require that the developer assign to it all the rights in the material or grant it an exclusive licence, to oblige the developer not to develop similar material for competing companies, or to require the developer not to start competing in the market itself. Clauses attempting to achieve these objectives could potentially fall under Art.81, and legal advice should be sought.

14.4.11 Particular Cases Which Have Been Considered Under Art.81

Internet registry agreements[36]

14–113   The European Commission has investigated the area of internet domain name registries under the competition rules.

   Until the beginning of October 1998, the system for generic Top Level Domains (gTLDs) such as .com, .net, and .org was operated by the Internet Assigned Numbers Authority (IANA) and Network Solutions Inc (NSI), the latter under contract from the US Government, acting as the only registry and registrar of .com, .net, and .org worldwide. The registry functions relate to the operation (e.g. administration, maintenance and up-dating) of the database into which registrants' details as well as the second-level domains' details are registered. The registrar function relates to the registration in the relevant database and allocation of second-level domain names to registrants, as well as all related marketing, billing and other related activities.

   ICANN (Internet Corporation for Assigned Names and Numbers), a private not-for-profit corporation, was incorporated in the US on October 1, 1998, to administer policy for the Internet Name and Address System and succeed IANA. In addition, the gTLD Memorandum of Understanding (MoU) and related agreements foresaw a further substantial modification of the domain name system.

   The Commission appeared to consider that a system for allocating domain names that would be used by companies in the EEA/EU was capable of affecting competition in the EU, founding jurisdiction under the EU/EEA competition rules. It apparently also considered that the agreement by non-governmental organisations to reform the system could fall within Art.81 of the EC Treaty. Its concerns with the gTLD MoU and associated agreements related to the establishment of the governance system for domain name allocation and those relating to the mechanisms for allocating domain names and resolution of disputes.

   In particular, the participants in the domain name system should be a fair

---

[35] A contract for the development of software copyright prior to exploitation of that software copyright by the developer would be covered by the Technology Transfer Block Exemption.
[36] See Commission press release IP/99/596.

representation of interested parties, and membership of all relevant bodies should be based on objective, transparent, and non-discriminatory criteria, a requirement which continues to apply to all consideration of this area. In addition, the operation of the system in practice should not be anti-competitive. Even if competition could not be introduced at every level of the DNS (Domain Name System), it should exist to the maximum extent possible. The Commission was concerned that there should be safeguards to prevent registrars acting, solely or jointly, in an anti-competitive manner. Artificial limits on registrars, such as, for example, giving one registrar allocation rights in respect of a particular gTLD, or limiting the number of registrars without justification, might have been difficult to justify under Art.81.

Under the progressive liberalisation proposed, NSI was required in an **14–114** initial phase to establish a test bed supporting actual registrations in .com, .net, and .org with five registrars to be accredited by ICANN ("Test Bed Registrars") in accordance with ICANN's published accreditation guidelines. Later, an unlimited number of competing registrars could be accredited by ICANN ("Accredited Registrars").

To implement this system and allow for competing registrars, NSI was (directly or indirectly) to develop a protocol and associated software supporting a system permitting multiple registrars to provide registration services for the registry of the existing gTLDs. This was then licensed by NSI to registrars under a standard licensing agreement, the initial version of which was only intended to be valid for the test bed period. These agreements enabled the new registrars to register second-level domain names within the registry of Top Level Domain Names managed by NSI such as .com, .org and .net. The Competition directorate received a number of informal complaints about the test bed standard licensing arrangements, and opened an informal investigation. It identified a number of clauses in that NSI standard registrar licensing agreement that might have raised anti-competitive concerns.

In particular, DG Competition looked into the question of whether the licensing agreements fell within the scope of Art.81(1) of the EC Treaty and of Art.53 of the European Economic Area (EEA) Agreement. It also examined whether certain provisions in the agreements or related actions taken by NSI might also constitute an abuse of NSI's dominant position under Art.82 of the EC Treaty and Art.54 of the EEA Agreement.

It informed the US governmental authorities who were supervising the liberalisation process of concerns related to:

- The lack of safeguards to prevent the NSI registry from discriminating against competing registrars in favour of NSI acting as a registrar;
- The fact that NSI as a registrar was not subject to the conditions and obligations set out in the ICANN accreditation agreements and NSI registrar licensing agreements, since NSI was not required to go through the accreditation procedure by ICANN as a registrar. DG

Competition believed that NSI should be required to get accreditation from ICANN and be subject at least to the same obligations as competing registrars which arose from those accreditation rules;

- certain requirements to enter the market, e.g. a performance bond of US$100,000, which could constitute barriers to market entry; and
- the domain name portability rules and NSI's related policy, which DG Competition believed could act as strong deterrents for TLD holders to transfer their TLD to another competing registrar.

These issues were subsequently resolved to the Competition Directorate's satisfaction, and the Commission closed its investigation into the matter.[37]

However, the Commission continues to be active in a wide range of matters relating to the development of internet organisation and management and the domain name system.[38] For example, Regulation 733/2002 of April 22, 2002, and Regulation 874/2004 of April 28, 2004, lay down the conditions for implementation of the. eu TLD and establish the general policy framework within which the registry will function. In May 2003, the Commission entrusted the operation of the .eu TLD to EURID (European Registry for Internet Domains). The Commission has indicated that it will closely follow developments in this area, to ascertain whether agreements and business registration practices fall under the EC competition rules contained in Arts. 81 and 82 and, where necessary, will take appropriate action under the EC Treaty.

In terms of Art.82, the Commission has previously received a number of complaints against national country code registry bodies (ccTLD) in some Member States, alleging violation of Art.82, and addressed formal requests for information to some to the ccTLD registry bodies.[39]

Microsoft Internet Explorer agreements with ISPs[40]

14-115 In March 1997 DG Competition opened an investigation into the agreements between Microsoft and European ISPs. Under these agreements, Microsoft promoted the ISPs by including them in a list of available services pre-installed on new personal computers which used the Windows operating system. Microsoft also licensed its Internet Explorer software to ISPs who made it available to their subscribers. In return the ISP paid Microsoft a fee for every subscriber gained via this feature and promoted Internet

---

[37] US Internet Governance dispute resolved to EU's satisfaction, see EuroInfoTech Number 0202, October 7, 1999.

[38] See, e.g. Communication from the Commission to the Council and the European Parliament on the Organisation and Management of the Internet International and European Policy Issues 1998–2000 of April 7, 2000, COM(2000)202 and other documents which can be found at *http://europa.eu.int*.

[39] See section 8.2, p.21, Communication from the Commission to the Council and the European Parliament on the Organisation and Management of the Internet International and European Policy Issues 1998–2000 of April 7, 2000, COM(2000)202 which can be found at *http://europa.eu.int*.

[40] See Commission press release IP/99/317.

Explorer products. ISPs could further be granted a licence to customise Microsoft's Internet Explorer software in accordance with specific instructions and use the Internet Explorer logo in conjunction with its use and distribution of the licensed software.

During this inquiry, DG Competition advised Microsoft to re-examine the agreements in the light of the EC competition rules to ensure that they did not contain restrictions that might have the effect of illegally foreclosing the market for internet browser software from Microsoft's competitors and of illegally promoting the use of Microsoft's proprietary technology on the internet.

It appears that the Commission objected to clauses to the effect that:

- The ISPs' failure to attain minimum distribution volumes or percentages of Internet Explorer browser technology would result in termination of their agreements; and
- ISPs were not allowed to promote and advertise competing browser software.

Microsoft then modified the agreements so that the failure to attain minimum volumes or percentages would not result in the termination of the agreement, and ISPs were not prevented from promoting or advertising competing software. It then notified the agreements under Art.81(1) to the Commission. The Commission indicated that the agreements were not contrary to Art.81 by means of an informal comfort letter.

The comfort letter only covered the agreements between Microsoft and ISPs. The Commission did not therefore given any ruling on the global behaviour of Microsoft concerning a possible abuse of dominant position, and the case was different in scope and substance from the later Commission decision concerning abuse of dominance by Microsoft. However, the Commission stressed that it could reopen its investigation into Microsoft's ISP agreements if there were any future change in the factual or legal situation affecting any essential aspect of these agreements.

On-line travel agencies[41]

Opodo is a joint venture created by nine major European airlines to operate **14–116** as an on-line travel agency. It offers airline ticket sales, hotel bookings, car hire, and insurance. The joint venture was notified to the Commission for approval in November 2000. The Commission initially had concerns that, given the strong positions of the shareholders on the air transport market, the joint venture may have allowed these shareholders to exchange commercially sensitive information and to collude in price fixing or market sharing in the air transport market. Another concern was that the shareholder airlines might use their strong market positions to foreclose the travel agency services market, for example by favouring Opodo to the

---

[41] COMP/38.006 *Online Travel Portal Limited+9 (OPODO)*, December 18, 2002.

detriment of other travel agents. To overcome these concerns, the share-holders agreed the following undertakings with the Commission:

- Not to discriminate between Opodo and other travel agents unless this different treatment is objectively justified by reference to the commercial basis on which that shareholder normally deals with travel agents;
- Not to contract with Opodo on an exclusive basis or confer a most favoured nation (MFN) status on Opodo unless objectively justified; and
- Not to disclose commercially sensitive information belonging to travel agents or other third parties to Opodo.

In addition, Opodo gave the following undertakings:

- It is not necessary to be a shareholder to be able to sell inventory as an airline through Opodo;
- Opodo will not discriminate against non-shareholder airlines;
- Exclusive rights or MFN status is not a requirement for share-holders or non-shareholder airlines to be able to sell their inventory through Opodo;
- It will maintain in place various safeguards to ensure that the shareholder airlines cannot exchange commercially sensitive infor-mation, such as separate management at a separate location for Opodo and no access for shareholders to Opodo's IT systems; and
- No commercially sensitive information about the shareholders or non-shareholder airlines will be disclosed to the directors of Opodo.

Following the agreement of these undertakings, the Commission issued an informal comfort letter to the parties, confirming that the arrangements did not infringe Arts. 81 or 82.

Agreements for the licensing of on-line music content

14–117 In April 2001, the Commission received a notification from 16 royalty collecting societies, covering all such societies within the EC (prior to May 1, 2004), excluding the Portuguese society and including the Swiss society. Collecting societies grant licences to users, enforce copyright and collect and distribute royalties on behalf of copyright owners.

The notification for exemption related to standard bilateral agreements between royalty collecting societies within the EEA governing the licensing of the public performance of music on the internet (collectively known as the Santiago Agreement). The arrangements authorise each participating collecting society to grant commercial users a non-exclusive licence for the on-line public performance of musical works of the other parties on a worldwide basis. The licence covers webcasting, on-line music on demand and music included in video transmitted on-line. The licences will generally be granted by the society that operates in the country where either the content provider is located or in the country of the URL of the website used by the content provider (the economic residency clause). The licences granted will be valid in the territories of each of the participating societies. This in effect provides a one-stop shop for copyright licensing.

The Commission believes that the arrangements reduce competition between national collecting societies as the effect of the economic residency clause is to give each collecting society (of which there is one per territory) absolute territorial exclusivity as regards the grant of multi-territorial/ multi-repertoire licences for on-line music rights. This would hinder the development of a single market for copyright marketing services and could result in inefficiencies in the provision of on-line music services, adversely affecting consumers. The exclusivity is reinforced by a Most Favoured Nation (MFN) clause.

The Commission therefore sent each of the parties a statement of objections in May 2004, setting out its objections.[42] Two of the collecting societies (the Dutch and Belgian societies, BUMA and SABAM) responded separately to the statement of objections and offered commitments to remedy the Commission's concerns. They undertook not to be party to any agreement with other copyright management societies on licensing of public performance rights for on-line use which contains an economic residency clause, similar to that contained in the notified Santiago Agreement. As the market for on-line rights is an emerging market which is developing rapidly, the undertakings will remain in effect only for three years. The Commission is satisfied that these commitments remedy its competition concerns and it issued a notice in August 2005 stating that it intends to accept these commitments.[43] Its case against the remaining 14 societies is ongoing.

This is similar to an earlier case where the Commission granted an exemption for the International Federation of the Phonographic Industry (IFPI) simulcasting agreement.[44] This was an agreement for the collective management and licensing of copyright for the purposes of commercial exploitation of musical works on the internet, at the same time as they are broadcast on radio and television. This agreement also provides for a one-stop shop for licences for the whole of the EEA (except Spain and France) but, unlike the Santiago Agreement, the TV and radio broadcaster can obtain a licence from any of the EEA collecting societies. The societies are not therefore granted any territorial exclusivity and so there is competition between the societies to grant multi-territorial licences.

Following these cases, the following principles can be established:

- Owners of IPRs must have a choice in selecting the collecting society that will license their rights;

---

[42] See Commission press release IP/04/586.
[43] Case COMP/C2/39.152, *BUMA* and Case COMP/C2/39.151, *SABAM*, O.J. C 200/12, August 17, 2005, see also Commission press release IP/05/1056.
[44] Case COMP/C2/38.014, *IFPI "Simulcasting"*, [2003] O.J. L 107/58.

- Users of IPRs must have the choice of the one-stop shopping platform when acquiring the licences for the rights for trans-national operation; and
- Territorial restrictions must not be used to prevent the creation of new global and regional one-stop shopping arrangements.

In April 2004, the Commission published a Communication in which it stated that it intends to propose legislation dealing with the collective management and good governance of collecting societies.[45]

14.4.12 Concerns in B2B Marketplaces

14–118 Article 81 can apply to B2B websites for a number of reasons:

- *The mere fact of establishing a joint venture*: even without any of the other effects below, the mere joining together of actual or potential competitors may restrict competition if it results in them doing together an activity which they might have otherwise done separately, and which is a parameter of competition between them;
- *Cartel behaviour*: the arrangement may result in express or tacit price fixing, or fixing of output, even if not intended by the parties;
- *Sharing of information*: the arrangement may result in a sharing of confidential information;
- *Foreclosure of competitors*: the arrangement may exclude competitors of those who are participating in a website from obtaining the benefits of the site, leading to market foreclosure;
- *Exclusion of existing intermediaries*: the arrangement may exclude existing intermediaries in the market for a finished product or service related to the site;
- *Portal exclusivity and exclusion of competing portals*: requiring that participants in the site may not participate in competing websites may result in the exclusion of competing websites from the market, or at least a competitive disadvantage to those websites;
- *Restricting cross-border trade*: if the arrangements restrict the possibility for purchases from other Member States in a way which may limit cross-border trade, this is likely to be considered a significant restriction of competition;
- *Joint sales*: in some cases, where the portal involves parties joining together to jointly sell their products or services, this may have an anti-competitive effect on the market; and
- *Joint purchasing*: in some cases, where the portal involves parties joining together to purchase products or services, this may have an anti-competitive effect on the market.

---

[45] Commission Communication on the Management of Copyright and Related Rights in the Internal Market (COM(2004) 261 final, April 16, 2004.

Simple reduction of competition

In some cases, the fact that competitors join together to enter into an **14–119** activity (i.e. the formation of a joint venture) can, in itself, be seen as a restriction of actual or potential competition, if the parties could have entered into the market and performed the activity independently. Because they have joined together to carry out an activity together which they could have carried out separately, there has been a reduction of competition.

Cartel behaviour

B2B exchanges offer increased risk of a cartel to fix prices or quantities, **14–120** share markets, limit production, or jointly boycott either certain sellers or buyers, activities which are hardly ever exemptable, and often result in significant fines. The parties to a B2B exchange or cooperative B2B site are usually not intending to engage in this type of activity, but care must be taken to avoid the possibility of apparently engaging in such activities. Avoiding the antitrust risks often needs careful thought, and rules, procedures and contractual provisions may have to be put in place.

Exchange of confidential information

The exchange of commercially sensitive business information may be **14–121** contrary to Art.81, and is usually regarded as a serious infringement which can lead to significant fines being imposed on the parties. It is clear that the use of participation in a joint venture as a deliberate method for the parties to exchange commercially sensitive information in a manner which would otherwise infringe the competition rules is unacceptable. However, parties must in any case take care about the information which they exchange in the course of their formation of the portal, and the information that they exchange as part of their ongoing participation. The information which it is risky to discuss could concern prices, output, underlying costs, business strategies or investment plans of the relevant businesses.

There is no set list of information that cannot be exchanged without infringing the competition rules, and specific advice must be obtained which relates to the particular exchange, rather than general advice. However, the following principles may offer some guidance:

- The sharing of sensitive and detailed information in an oligopolistic market (one where there are only a few suppliers) may in itself be a restriction of competition;
- Exchange of data which would normally be considered a business secret or commercially sensitive between companies may well be anti-competitive;
- Exchange of data on prices or sales of individual firms stands a high risk of being considered anti-competitive;
- The sharing of aggregate information which does not allow the identification of particular prices charged by particular firms or

particular quantities sold by particular firms is not generally problematic;

- The publication of historical data is generally less important;
- Collection of sensitive data should not be performed by a market participant; and
- The publication of data which is objectively vital to the achievement of the benefits of the exchange will in many cases be justified, even it could have an effect on competition.

Ultimately, the risks from sharing confidential information can only be assessed by:

- Looking at the individual portal and its functioning;
- Assessing what market information may be produced which would not otherwise be available;
- Assessing which information must be exchanged for the portal to function properly;
- Identifying information which is commercially sensitive, which does not need to be exchanged; and
- Looking at methods of quarantining the information/making Chinese walls/firewalls to prevent the transfer of business sensitive information.

The need to guard against the sharing of confidential information may require competition compliance rules and procedures and the insertion of clauses in employment and other contracts, as well as technical measures and organisational procedures to prevent confidential information from leaking from the portal.

14–122   In one case, *Volbroker*,[46] the parents provided the following assurances to the European Commission to avoid the exchange of commercially sensitive confidential information with parent companies:

- None of the platform's staff or management would have any contractual or other obligation towards any of the parents and vice versa;
- The staff and management would be in a geographically distinct location from that of the parents;
- The representatives of the parents on the platform's Board of Directors would not have access to commercially sensitive information relating to each other or to third parties;
- The parents would not have access to the information technology and communication systems of the platform; and
- The parents would also ensure that the staff and management of all the parties understand and appreciate the importance of maintain-

---

[46] See Commission press release IP/00/896.

ing the confidentiality of sensitive commercial information and that sanctions for breach are spelled out.

Such stringent requirements may not be necessary in every case, and are dependent on the specifics of each market. The case is cited only to show that information sharing may be a significant concern. This issue needs to be considered carefully in each case. However, the adoption of these "Volbroker conditions" may be required in a number of cases. In any case, the adoption of a competition compliance programme will very often be necessary, and in many cases, adherence to strict rules concerning the conduct of meetings will often be required.

Foreclosure of competitors by restricting their participation as users of the portal

In some circumstances, it may be contrary to the competition rules to refuse a competitor access to the portal. This could be the case, for example, where the refusal to allow access to the portal would amount to an agreement between the parents to boycott the relevant party.   **14–123**

This may be contrary to the competition rules if:

- There is not a sufficient number of other portals offering a similar kind of function to the relevant portal;
- Another portal offering a similar function could not be easily established;
- There are strong network effects, which lead to the joint venture portal tending to attract increasing numbers of participants and making it increasingly difficult for other portals to establish; or
- Not participating in the portal would lead to the excluded party having a serious competitive disadvantage, which might eliminate it from a market for any of the goods or services sold through the exchange.

It is undoubtedly easier from a competition perspective to offer open, non-discriminatory access to all interested buyers or sellers who fall within the class of those for whom a B2B marketplace is intended. Otherwise it may be necessary to show that the above factors do not apply. On the other hand, that does not necessarily mean that other competitors must be allowed to participate as founding parties, or that they must be allowed to participate on exactly the same terms as the founding parties. Founding parties are sometimes fully justified in giving a financial incentive to those who are willing to join from the outset, and might, in order to keep the establishment of the joint venture manageable, want to restrict the number of initial parents.

On the other hand, it may be less possible to exclude competitors from accessing the site as suppliers of data to the site or as external users where the above bullet-point factors apply. It is also possible that the parents could be deemed to be entering into an infringing boycott agreement by not making access open to competitors on fair and reasonable terms.

It may also be justified, and in some cases necessary, to apply objective criteria to membership of the site, so that only parties that meet those criteria are accepted as participants on the suppliers' or buyers' side. The necessity may result from the fact that a B2B marketplace will often only be aimed at transactions in certain types of goods or services, or particular types of seller, purchaser or market segment. In addition, however, objectively justified requirements relating to such matters as creditworthiness or ability to meet the rules and requirements of participating in the exchange should be unproblematic. Other criteria which may be objectively justifiable may depend on the specific nature of the exchange.

Exclusion of intermediaries

14–124   In some circumstances, it may be a restriction of competition to prevent intermediaries, who perform a function similar to that of the portal functions, from accessing the portal (and/or the services provided over the portal).

In the *Volbroker* case,[47] the Commission received complaints from a number of "voice broker" sellers who acted as intermediaries, and occasionally as principals, in the sale of foreign currency options, which they did by dealing over the telephone. The voice brokers complained that the exchange, set up by six major market-makers in the industry (Deutsche Bank, UBS, Goldman Sachs, Citibank, JP Morgan, and NatWest) excluded them from participation. The Commission required that the voice brokers, when acting as principal, should be permitted access to the market place, as a condition of issuing a comfort letter under Art.81.

In some cases, where such intermediaries are able to perform their function by being a member of a website, it may be restrictive of competition to exclude them. In other cases, the formation of a portal which may replace existing intermediary functions will simply be part of the inevitable march of progress, and may not be objected to.

Portal exclusivity and foreclosure of competing portals

14–125   It may be restrictive of competition contrary to Art.81 to prohibit the founders of the portal or others from participating in competing portals.

This goes both for those participating as potential suppliers, and for potential purchasers. It is not a universal rule, however, and like the other factors considered here, will depend on the assessment of each individual case. As was seen above in relation to the *MyAircraft.com* case,[48] in certain circumstances, it will not always be viewed as anti-competitive under the EC Merger Regulation to require the founder members not to become actively involved in participating in another site, at least for a certain

---

[47] See Commission press release IP/00/896.
[48] Case M.1969, *UTC/Honeywell/i2/MyAircraft.com*, August 4, 2000.

period. That is especially true where there are a number of other competing portals already in the market, and the restriction on the founders sponsoring competing sites is necessary to allow the portal to become established. That analysis also holds good under Art.81.

On the other hand, in many cases there may be less justification for restricting founders or users from using a competing website, and this could be viewed as a restriction of competition.

That may be particularly true where there are network effects or externalities, or the market is "tippy". This could arise in the case where, once a portal has more than a certain number of members or users, all other vendors or purchasers are going to want to use that portal, and another portal will not be a good substitute. In such a situation, it may become increasingly difficult for other portals to establish themselves. Whether that is a problem or not will depend on the particular facts of each case.

Restrictions on cross-border trade

Restrictions on cross-border trade are some of the most serious infringements of EC competition law, which can often result in a fine. Such restrictions may be found to exist where, for example, there is an attempt to segment national markets, by providing separate portals for each national market, and providing that only purchasers established in the relevant jurisdiction, or who will take delivery within that jurisdiction, may become users of the portal services or otherwise have access to the site.   **14–126**

Specific B2B marketplaces under Art.81: Covisint

The first major B2B exchange to be looked at under Art.81 rather than under the Merger Regulation was Covisint, an electronic marketplace joint venture between DaimlerChrysler, Ford, General Motors, Nissan, Peugeot Citroen, and Renault.[49] The joint venture was intended to provide the automotive industry with procurement, collaborative product development and supply chain management tools, primarily to serve the procurement needs of major car makers and suppliers. Many major component suppliers had indicated that they would use the exchange. Covisint did not constitute a merger under the Merger Regulation, since the companies that created the exchange did not exercise joint or sole control over the new company, and hence it fell to be considered under Art.81.[50]   **14–127**

The Commission noted that such B2B marketplaces potentially have a major impact on the way that companies in certain industries do business, and are in general expected to have pro-competitive effects. They should create more transparency, thereby helping to link more operators and to integrate markets, and they may also create market efficiencies by reducing

---

[49] See Commission press release IP/01/1155.
[50] The German competition authority, the Bundeskartellamt, had already examined the joint venture, however, since it had constituted a merger under German law, due to a provision which deemed control to arise where any party acquired more than 25 per cent of the shares in any company.

search and information costs and improving inventory management, leading ultimately to lower prices for the end consumer.

In certain circumstances, however, the Commission considered that the "negative effects on competition may outweigh market efficiencies. This may in particular be the case where there is discrimination against certain classes of users leading to foreclosure, where it is possible for users to exchange or have access to market-sensitive information, or where buyers or sellers club together to 'bundle' their purchases or sales in a way liable to fall within the scope of Article 81(1) of the Treaty."

The Commission concluded that in this case there were adequate provisions to eliminate the potential competition concerns, and "[i]n particular, the agreements show that Covisint is open to all firms in the industry on a non-discriminatory basis, is based on open standards, allows both shareholders and other users to participate in other B2B exchanges, does not allow joint purchasing between car manufacturers or for automotive-specific products, and provides for adequate data protection, including firewalls and security rules."

The Commission consequently sent the parties a comfort letter indicating that the joint venture would meet the requirements for obtaining a negative clearance under Art.81(1).

14.4.13 Standardisation Agreements

14–128   The approach under Art.81 of the EC Treaty to standardisation agreements is relevant to e-commerce in a number of ways, not only in terms of the high level of internet standards development, governance and management, and the domain name system, but also in terms of more specific standardisation agreements between e-commerce undertakings. This includes standardisation of catalogues and processes which takes place within B2B business sites and agreements between B2B exchanges concerning the adoption of standards. This section discusses the treatment of standards under Art.81, examining the past case law, and concludes with the guidance given in the Commission's horizontal agreements guidelines.

Effects of standards under EC competition law

14–129   From a competition perspective, the mere ownership or establishment of a standard may potentially affect competition on two levels: first, it may restrict competition between the parties establishing or using the standard, and secondly, it may foreclose competition from third parties who wish to have access to the standard.

The foreclosure effect of a standard will depend, in particular, on the following factors:

(i)   the extent to which access to the standard is necessary for participation in the market;

(ii) whether third parties have access to the standard and the standard setting procedure (if any); and

(iii) the conditions attached to such access, in particular, whether access is granted on unreasonable or discriminatory terms.

The extent to which access to a standard is necessary for market participation will in turn depend on a range of factors, including:

(i) the competitive importance of the benefits accruing from access to the standard or the standard setting procedure: this will depend on the market context and, as in the case of a compulsory *de jure* standard, may include the ability to compete in the market at all;

(ii) the availability of alternative standards: in the case of standards permitting interoperability this will be determined by the market share of the parties using the standard; and

(iii) whether there are barriers to establishing a competing standard.

A standard's effects on competition between the parties with access to it **14–130**
will depend, first, on whether the parties are actual or potential competitors. If they are not, the standard can have no restrictive effect on competition between them. If the parties are actual or potential competitors, the standard may reduce the ability of parties using the standard to compete by reducing product diversity and reducing the scope and incentive for innovation. The extent of these restrictive effects will in general depend on:

(i) the market shares of the parties;

(ii) whether the parties agree to use the standard exclusively;

(iii) whether the parties agree to share innovations relating to the standard; and

(iv) the depth of the standard.[51]

In addition, the market power associated with ownership of a standard may enable the owner to impose additional anti-competitive terms and conditions, for example tying, on licensees of the standard.

While seeking to limit these anti-competitive effects that may flow from standardisation, competition law must also take account of the potential advantages of standardisation. In the EU context, these may include the elimination of barriers to trade between Member States. In addition, standardisation may permit private firms to capture the benefits of network effects in marketing, rationalisation of productions, economies of scale, R&D efficiencies and others, while at the same time offering consumers benefits in terms of the interoperability and substitutability of products and known product qualities. Where a standard actually or potentially offers

---

[51] If full design specifications are standardised as opposed to mere functional specifications, product differentiation and further improvements may be foreclosed.

such advantages, these must be set off against any potentially anti-competitive effects.

Multilateral and unilateral standards

14–131   The scope of Art.81(1) may mean that it applies differently to those standards that are jointly owned or jointly established (multilateral standards) and those that are owned and established by a single firm (unilateral standards), although, in principle, the issues raised by multilateral and unilateral standards are the same.

The ownership and often the development of a multilateral standard will be subject to agreements and/or arrangements between undertakings to which Art.81(1) may apply if their effect is exclusive. The Commission has applied Art.81 to require the parties to such agreements to grant access both to the standard itself (as well as any intellectual property included in it) and membership of bodies charged with establishing or developing the standard.[52]

In the case of unilateral standards, the scope for Art.81(1) to apply is more limited. The ownership and development of unilateral marks is not, by definition, subject to any agreement or arrangement between undertakings. However, the situation changes once the standard has been licensed, since at that point there is an agreement on which Art.81(1) may bite.[53] It is clear that the Commission will apply Art.81(1) to terms in the licence of a standard that create obstacles to competition.

The foreclosure effects of standards and standardisation

14–132   Of the two levels of competitive effects a standard may have, the foreclosure effect will depend on the extent to which access to the standard is necessary for participation in the market, whether third parties are allowed access to the standard, and whether such access is allowed on fair and reasonable terms. The treatment of these issues under Art.81 may be illustrated by the contrast between two cases: *IGR Stereo Television* and *X/Open Group*.[54]

The first case, *IGR Stereo Television*, concerned the acquisition, in 1981, of two patents for the production of stereo television sets by IRG, a body whose members included all German TV manufacturers. Following the acquisition, IRG's membership passed a resolution not to license the patents to non-members until 1983, and at that time to license them only for the production of a limited numbers of sets. This effectively excluded

---

[52] See, *IGR Stereo Television*, 1981 Competition Report, point 96, pp.63–64 (access to the standard) and *X/Open Group*, O.J. L 35/36, February 6, 1987 (access to the standards setting group).

[53] Indeed, it may be arguable that, at least where the licence imposes cross-licensing obligations that extend not only to the standard owner but also to other licensees, that the standard has become multilateral as a result of the licence, see, *Video Cassette Recorders*, O.J. L 47/42, February 18, 1978.

[54] *IGR Stereo Television*, 1981 Competition Report, point 96, pp.63–64 (access to the standard) and *X/Open Group*, O.J. L 35/36, February 6, 1987 (access to the standards setting group).

non-German manufacturers of television sets from the market at a time when stereo television was being launched, since it seems that these patents covered a *de facto* standard for stereo television that could not be duplicated or invented around.[55] Following a complaint from a Finnish manufacturer, Salora, the Commission intervened and persuaded IGR to agree to grant licences for the patents free of all restrictions and on reasonable terms to all other manufactures in the Community.

The second case, *X/Open Group*, concerned a collaboration between a number of major computer manufacturers. The objective of the collaboration was to develop an open industry standard for a "stable but evolving common application environment" (CAE) based on AT&T's UNIX operating system. The purpose of the CAE was that programs written in conformity with it would be capable of running on computers using the current version of UNIX, regardless of the identity of the computer manufacturer. The group intended to establish the CAE initially by selecting existing interfaces, and to proceed in due time to the standardisation of selected interfaces by appropriate national and international standards organisations. In order to achieve this, group members agreed to exchange technical and market information.

Membership of the group was however restricted. Applications for membership would be considered only from major manufacturers in the European information technology industry or others with "special attributes" that would significantly contribute to the achievement of the group's objectives. Major manufacturers were understood to be those with revenues from information technology in excess of US$500 million. In addition, applicants would have to obtain the approval of more than half of the existing membership in a vote in order to become members.

The Commission found that, in the context of the relevant market, membership of the group would confer an appreciable competitive advantage. Members would be able to influence the results of the work of the group and would acquire the know-how and technical understanding relating to these results. In addition, members would obtain important advantages of lead time in implementation of the standards due to early knowledge of the final definitions and, potentially, of the direction in which work was going. This advantage in lead time would directly affect the market entry possibilities of those not members of the group.

Consequently, the Commission took the view that the restrictions on membership of the group infringed Art.81(1). In particular, the Commission noted that the ability to admit members with special attributes and the requirement for a majority vote of existing members meant that the restrictions on membership were potentially discriminatory.

However, the Commission concluded that the group arrangements fulfilled the conditions for exemption under Art.81(3). Opening membership

---

[55] J Temple Lang, "European Community Anti-trust Law: Innovation markets and Technology Industries", *Proceedings and Papers of the 23rd Annual Fordham Law Institute*, 519, at 573.

of the group to all would create practical and logistical difficulties so that it was reasonable to impose restrictions that would limit the membership to a manageable size. In addition, the requirement that new members be approved by majority vote could be justified, as this would enable members to prevent the admission of companies that might have an adverse effect on the cooperation and the achievement of the group's objectives. It was appropriate for members of the group to decide on this issue as they were in the best position to assess it.

Moreover, the aim of the group was to publish its work as widely and as quickly as possible, something that the Commission considered to be an "essential element" in allowing exemption. Nonetheless, as a condition of exemption, the Commission required that the group submit an annual report to the Commission on cases where membership was refused and changes in membership, in order to ensure that the conditions for membership were not being applied in an unreasonable manner.

14–133   A number of factors in relation to these two cases should be noted. First, as regards the need for access to the standard, in *IGR Stereo Television*, it seems that access to the standard was absolutely necessary for the supply of stereo television sets to the German market. In *X/Open Group* restrictions on participation in the standard setting group were found to fall within Art.81(1) on the grounds that, in the relevant market, membership constituted an appreciable competitive advantage and that the market entry possibilities of non-members would be affected as a result.[56]

Secondly, as regards the possibility of third party access, in *X/Open Group*, the Commission considered the fact that the standards adopted by the group would be open and available to all as an essential element in its decision to grant exemption. Similarly, in *IGR Stereo Television*, IGR was obliged to agree to license its patent rights to all EC manufacturers.

It is also noteworthy that, although the standard was to be open and widely published, restrictions on membership of the standard setting group in *X/Open Group* were found to be sufficiently important to infringe Art.81(1). Finally, as regards the terms on which access is granted, in *X/Open Group* restrictions on access to the standards setting group were acceptable only to the extent that they were not implemented in an unreasonable manner, and the Commission expressed particular concern that the restrictions were potentially discriminatory.[57]

---

[56] See also, *Philips/Matsushita—D2B*, [1991] O.J. C 220/3, (discussed further below) where one of the factors on which the Commission considered relevant to its finding that the D2B arrangements were capable of exemption under Art.81(3) was the availability of alternative standards.

[57] Note also that in its letter to ETSI in the case *ETSI Interim IPR Policy*, O.J. C 76/5, March 28, 1995 (discussed further below), while rejecting on the facts of the case the allegation of a complainant that ETSI's policy of licensing intellectual property rights included in standards discriminated against persons that were not signatories to ETSI's IPR undertaking, the Commission stated that such discrimination could give rise to action under the competition rules. The Commission's case law with regard to collective refusals to deal may also be relevant in this regard, see, e.g. the cases discussed in Bellamy & Child, *European Community Law of Competition*, (5th ed, and 1st supplement), paras. 4–082 *et seq.*

Restrictions on competition between users of a standard

In addition to foreclosure effects, a standard may also give rise to restrictions on competition between the parties with access to the standard. The importance of these effects will depend on the market share of the parties, whether they agree to use the standard exclusively, whether the parties agree to share future innovations relating to the standard, and the depth of the standard. **14–134**

The treatment of these issues under Art.81 is well illustrated by three cases, *Video Cassette Recorders, Philips/Matsushita—D2B*, and *ETSI Interim IPR Policy*,[58] and by the European Commission's stated position in three subsequent cases, the *3G Patent Partnership* case, *Philips CD-Recordable Disc Patent Licensing*, and *Changes in the ETSI IPR rules*.[59]

Video Cassette Recorders concerned the terms on which Philips licensed the patents covering its VCR standard for video recorders. At the time of the decision, Philips owned the more successful one of only two video system standards available in Europe. Philips licensed its patents to other manufacturers on condition that they manufacture and distribute only video cassette recorders and cassettes observing detailed technical specifications describing the VCR system. No changes could be made to these standards without the consent of Philips and all other licensees. In addition, the licences provided that Philips and the licensee were obliged to grant each other royalty-free cross-licences in respect of patented innovations, where necessary to ensure compatibility and that such cross-licences should extend to all other licensees of the VCR standard. Any party terminating a licence agreement forfeited its right under such cross-licences, while the remaining parties retained theirs. **14–135**

The Commission found that the obligation on licensees to use exclusively the VCR standard and the cross-licensing provisions fell within Art.81(1).[60] The Commission considered these restrictions "particularly marked" in light of Philips' pre-eminent market position: together with its largest competitor, Sony, it accounted for more than 70 per cent of video recorder sales in the EU. Further, the Commission took the view that the licences could not benefit from exemption under Art.81(3), although it recognised that the licences would create interoperability benefits. In its view, the exclusivity requirements could not benefit from exemption as they "led to the exclusion of other, perhaps better, systems", and interoperability benefits could have been achieved through the much less restrictive requirement

---

[58] *Video Cassette Recorders*, O.J. L 47/42, February 18, 1978, *Philips/Matsushita—D2B*, [1991] O.J. C 220/3, and *ETSI Interim IPR Policy*, O.J. C 76/5, March 28, 1995.

[59] Licensing of patents for third generation mobile services, Commission press release IP/02/165, November 12, 2002, *Philips CD-Recordable Disc Patent Licensing*, Commission press release IP/06/139, February 9, 2006, and *Changes in ETSI IPR rules to prevent "patent ambush"*, Commission press release, IP/05/1565 December 12, 2005.

[60] As regards the provision on cross-licensing, the Commission objected in particular (i) to the fact that the cross-licences were not simply bilateral (between Philips and the licensee) but extended to all licenses creating a "horizontal network of licences", and (ii) to the termination provisions.

that licensees observe the VCR standards when manufacturing VCR equipment.

Philips/Matsushita—D2B concerned the establishment of a joint venture by Philips and Matsushita to develop a standard that would allow televisions, VCRs, CDs and other consumer electronics products of different brands to operate together using a common remote control.

Philips and Matsushita agreed to pool their patents covering the D2B system (which had originally been established by Philips but which they had developed together) in the joint venture, which would be controlled by Philips. Licences would be granted to any manufacturer adopting the DB2 standard for ten years, extendable by another 10 years. Licensees would be required to enter into a mutual worldwide non-assertion clause, with the effect that neither the licensor nor the licensee would be able to seek royalties for the use of further patents covering the system for the duration of the licence.

The Commission found that the D2B joint venture arrangements could fall within Art.81(1), but would in any event qualify for exemption pursuant to Art.81(3). The arrangements contributed to technical progress and were not excessive, and competition in the market would remain effective as a number of alternative systems were available.

14–136   *ETSI Interim IPR Policy* concerned the interim intellectual property rights (IPR) policy adopted by ETSI in March 1993. ETSI is a private, non-profit association under French law that was formally recognised as a European standard institute for the telecommunications sector by the EC in 1992. As such, it is charged with establishing common European standards in the telecommunications sector that have an important role under EC law.[61]

According to ETSI's statutes, its membership comprised five groups: (i) national standards organisations and administrations, (ii) public network operators, (iii) manufacturers, (iv) users, and (v) private service providers. The interim IPR policy required its members to sign an IPR undertaking. Broadly, the IPR policy foresaw a system in which members would agree, in advance, to license any of their IPRs deemed "essential" to an ETSI standard, unless they notified ETSI that they did not wish to do so within six months from the relevant draft standard appearing on ETSI's work program. This system was referred to as "licensing by default".

The IPR undertaking set forth conditions under which licences of such IPRs had to be offered to ETSI members. These included: (i) that only monetary consideration could be demanded in return for such a licence, and (ii) that IPR holders should notify a maximum royalty rate to the Director of ETSI. The CBEMA, a trade organisation for computer and business equipment manufacturers, some of which were ETSI members who would be required to sign the IPR undertaking, submitted a complaint to the

---

[61] See, Maurits Dolmans, Restrictions on Innovation: An EU Antitrust Approach, *ABA Antitrust L.J.*, Vol.66, 455, at 478.

Commission claiming that these aspects of ETSI's interim policy infringed Art.81(1).

Although the Commission reached no formal decision on the complaint, it set out its preliminary views on it in a letter to ETSI of February 21, 1994. The Commission took the view that the "license by default" system amounted to a "mutual renunciation of the ability to gain a competitive advantage through technical efforts" and therefore restricted innovation. Nonetheless, it considered that such a system could be legitimate under the competition rules where IPR holders were given a genuine opportunity to withhold a licence. However, due to the amount of information supplied to members by ETSI regarding standards in development, arguably no such genuine opportunity existed within the framework of ETSI's interim IPR policy.

The Commission was also of the view that the prohibition on the holders of IPRs included in ETSI standards requiring non-monetary compensation for licences of those IPRs acted as a restriction on the ability of the IPR holder to negotiate cross-licences and as such fell under Art.81(1), although it considered that the restriction could potentially qualify for exemption under Art.81(3). The Commission, however, regarded the provisions concerning the notification of a maximum royalty rate to be prima facie legitimate.

As a result of the Commission's intervention, ETSI's interim IPR policy was amended to replace the "license by default" system with a system whereby holders of essential IPRs would be requested to give an undertaking in writing of their preparedness to grant irrevocable licences on fair, reasonable and non-discriminatory terms. The provisions as to non-monetary consideration and maximum royalty rates were also removed.

In a press release dated December 12, 2005,[62] the Commission announced it had closed a separate investigation into ETSI, which was prompted by concerns that ETSI's standard-setting rules did not sufficiently protect against so-called "patent ambushing". This is where a company hides the fact that it owns IPRs that are essential for a standard until a standard has been established. This allows the company to gain control over the standard. ETSI therefore adopted changes to its standard-setting rules proposed by the Commission, which strengthen the requirement for early disclosure of IPRs which are essential for the implementation of a particular standard. In the press release, the Competition Commissioner stated:

> "Standards are of increasing importance, particularly in hi-tech sectors of the economy. It is crucial that standard-setting bodies establish rules which ensure fair, transparent procedures and early disclosure of relevant intellectual property."

---

[62] See Commission press release IP/05/1565.

14–137   In the 2003 *Philips/Sony CD licensing programme* case,[63] the European Commission ruled that a series of bilateral agreements between the parties establishing the worldwide Philips/Sony CD disc licensing program were exempt from the provisions of Art.81(1).

Philips Electronics and Sony Corporation have worked together since the 1970s and have produced a number of patent-protected joint inventions. In the 1980s, they produced the CD system standard specifications, which were adopted by music companies and consumer electronic manufacturers. Philips and Sony then established the joint Philips/Sony Licensing Programme, by a number of bilateral agreements. These agreements enabled Philips to offer a joint patent licence to third parties covering both Sony's and Philip's patents, but also enabled each party to offer patent licences in respect of their own patents.

The parties also created a standard joint licence agreement (the 2003 SLA) for third parties in relation to the patents of Philips or Sony which are essential for compliance with the different specifications of the different types of pre-recorded CD discs. Subsequently, the Commission received several complaints from CD disc manufacturers that the bilateral agreements and the 2003 SLA infringed Art.81 and Art.82 and so it began an investigation.

The Commission confirmed in a comfort letter to the parties that the CD Licensing Programme was covered by the then current Technology Transfer Block Exemption and so was exempt from the provisions of Art.81. The Commission also concluded that the 2003 SLA did not appreciably restrict competition and therefore did not fall within Art.81. However, in order for the Commission to be able to reach this conclusion, Sony and Philips had to significantly amend the agreement to make it fully complaint with EC competition rules, the main changes being that:

- The agreement was amended to expressly state that Sony and Philips have the right to license their respective patents separately and to give non-assertion undertakings with regard to jointly-owned patents, whether within or outside the standard specifications of the CD systems;
- The agreement provides for options for each licensee in relation to different types of CD discs and the agreement specifies to patents required to manufacture each type of CD disc;
- Only essential patents (as certified by an independent expert) are included in the agreement, with provisions for the addition of new patents and the removal of any patent which is later deemed not to be essential;
- Licensees are only required to license back their patents that are essential for the type of CD discs they have selected;
- Royalty obligations have been clarified to reflect territorial scope and duration of the licensed patents and licensees will only have to

---

[63] See Commission press release IP/03/1152.

provide Philips with information on the production and sale of royalty-bearing discs produced and sold;

- Conditions of access to the reduced compliance royalty rate have been clarified and made more attractive; and
- Definitive termination dates in respect of the expiry of each essential patent in each EEA country have been set out and the 2003 SLA will terminate at the expiry of the last essential patent.

Any existing licensees could switch to the 2003 SLA free of charge and Philips agreed to inform all licensees of the changes (offering a one-time royalty credit for each EEA licensee). Furthermore, Philips made extensive information available on its website about the changes and the Licensing Programme.

The *3G Patent Platform Partnership* case[64] in November 2002 concerned the licensing of patents for third generation "3G" mobile services. Manufacturers who want to produce 3G equipment need to comply with technical specifications that are set out in the IMT-2000 3G standard. This standard comprises five different technologies, each of which can be used to produce 3G equipment. Manufacturers therefore need to have access to those patents that are indispensable for using a particular technology. An essential patent for using a particular technology can still compete with a patent that is essential for using another technology, provided the two technologies compete. The Commission therefore had to ensure that, when assessing the licensing agreements for 3G equipment, competition between these patents was maintained.

14–138

The notifying parties, who refer to themselves as the 3G Patent Platform Partnership (3G3P), notified a set of agreements which created the rules of operation of a generic scheme designed to deliver licences of "essential patents". These agreements set up procedures to identify whether a patent is essential, to streamline the licensing of those which are deemed essential and to reduce the overall licence fees to be paid for the entire portfolio of essential patents.

In order to gain the Commission's approval for the licensing arrangements, 3G3P agreed to modify the initial structure of the agreements and established five separate sets of arrangements, one for each technology, instead of combining all essential patents in one single platform. In doing this, the revised licensing agreements complied with the requirements that each licensing agreement must be limited to essential patents only, competition will not be foreclosed in related or downstream markets, licensing must be carried out under non-discriminatory terms and there is no exchange of competitively sensitive information. Furthermore, 3G manufacturers should not be forced to pay for patent rights other than those that they really need. The licensing arrangements should also not discourage further R&D and innovation in the mobile communications sector.

In assessing whether competition will be maintained, the Commission

---

[64] See Commission press release IP/02/1651.

also took into account that a number of major 3G essential patent holders (e.g. Ericsson and Nokia) were not party to the notified arrangements, which meant that a significant number of essential patents remain outside of the arrangement. The Commission therefore issued a comfort letter to the parties.

14–139   The Commission closed an investigation in February 2006 into Philips CD-Recordable Disc Licensing system following amendments of the relevant provisions by Philips to facilitate access to the technology. The inquiry was launched in 2003, following a complaint by FIPCOM, an association of European manufacturers of CD-Recordable (CD-R) discs. Previously Philips had offered European manufacturers a joint patent licence which included its own CD-R disc patents as well as those of Sony and Taiyo Yuden, a Japanese technology company. Philips committed to discontinue the joint licence programme in Europe. In addition, Philips had also offered an individual licence limited to its own CD-R patents.

Philips revised the programmes to ensure that all the necessary information concerning the licensed technology was made available and that the programmes are managed in a fair and non-discriminatory way. The most important changes in the new licensing agreement were:

- Making available on its website summary reports of independent experts regarding those Philips patents that are essential to produce CD-R discs;
- Adding the explicit obligation for Philips to address technical problems associated with the management of the CD-R standard;
- Updating the CD-R standard to clarify that discs that do not use Philips' Multi Speed proprietary technology but rather alternative high speed recording technologies still qualify as CD-R discs.

Philips also reduced the level of royalty. The Commission took the opportunity to announce its intention to "continue to closely monitor existing or new technology pools, in particular those that support or establish a *de facto* or a *de jure* industry standard in order to ensure that they comply with Community competition rules".

14–140   A number of factors in relation to these cases are worthy of note. First, the importance attached to the pre-eminence of Philips' market share in the Commission's decision not to grant an exemption in *Video Cassette Recorders* should be contrasted with its reliance on the fact in *Philips/ Matsushita—D2B* that competition in the market would remain effective due to the available alternative systems.

Secondly, the *3G Patent Partnership* case and the *Philips CD-Recordable Disc Patent Licensing* case demonstrate the importance attached by the Commission to independent expert verification of the essentiality of patents included in a standard.

Thirdly, the same two cases show the importance of unbundling of packages of licence rights so that licensees are not required to pay for more technology licences than they actually need or (in the *Philips CD-Record-*

able Disc case) more licences than are objectively and qualitatively necessary to fulfil the essential elements of the standard.

Fourthly, the *Changes in ETSI IPR rules* case demonstrates the importance of structuring standards arrangements so as to require early disclosure of essential patents and thus avoid or reduce the risk of patent ambushes.

Fifthly, the Commission's preliminary view in *ETSI Interim IPR Policy* was that the cross-licensing by default system that it involved restricted innovation but might be compatible with the competition rules. This is reflected in the Commission's view that the bilateral non-enforcement requirement to be imposed on licensees in *Philips/Matsushita—D2B* was found to fulfil the requirements for exemption. Although the multilateral cross-licensing arrangement in relation to innovations in *Video Cassette Recorders* was found to infringe Art.81(1) and not to merit exemption, this may be explained by the harsh conditions imposed on termination.

Finally, the Commission's refusal in *Video Cassette Recorders* to grant exemption to restrictions that went beyond those necessary to achieve the interoperability benefits offered by the standardisation is worthy of note in that it supports the conclusion that multilateral standards that are unnecessarily deep may infringe Art.81(1) and would not qualify for exemption under Art.81(3).[65]

Conditions attached to licences

Certain cases suggest that Art.81(1) may be infringed by clauses in the **14–141** licence of a standard other than those on cross-licensing and exclusivity discussed above. One example arose from a second complaint against IGR, this one concerning the level of royalties charged by IGR for access to the stereo television patents.[66] The Commission again intervened, finding that the royalties constituted a "private tax" on other European television manufacturers, which, in view of the level of royalties, could have an appreciable effect on competition contrary to Art.81(1). As a result of the Commission's intervention, IGR agreed to lower its royalty rate considerably.

---

[65] The conclusion that specifications or depth of standardisation going beyond what is necessary to achieve the objectives of the standard may violate Art.81(1) and may not qualify for exemption is also supported by the Commission's position in *Philips/Matsushita DCC* [1992] O.J. C 333/8, which concerned agreements between Philips and five other companies in relation to the development and exploitation of the digital compact cassette (DCC) system. Under the agreements, the participants pooled their patents relating to DCC systems and Philips was granted the exclusive right to license the relevant patents on their behalf. Philips was to grant ten year licences to third parties on a non-discriminatory, non-exclusive basis. Licences would be subject to a requirement to incorporate a specified piracy protection system in all DCC equipment. The Commission found that the patent pooling and standardisation of specifications resulting from the requirement to include the anti-piracy system could fall within Art.81(1), but that overall, the arrangements would in any event merit exemption under Art.81(3). A second complaint was brought against ETSI by DVSI which concerned, *inter alia*, an allegation that an ETSI standard had involved a level of specification that was unnecessary, however the Commission rejected the complaint. The complaint is discussed in the article by Maurits Dolmans cited above in fn.61, at 481 *et seq.*

[66] *IGR*, 1984 Competition Report, point 92, p.76.

A second example is provided by the agreements the Commission reached with the suppliers of video games consoles Nintendo and Sega regarding the terms under which they license their intellectual property rights to games developers.[67] The Commission required the deletion of licence clauses that:

(i) limited the number of games licensees could release;
(ii) required prior approval from the console supplier for all games before release, regardless of whether the game was sold under a trade mark belonging to the console supplier; and
(iii) required the licensee to have games manufactured by the console supplier or an authorised manufacturer.

Nintendo and Sega were allowed to continue to require prior approval if a licensee wished to attach one of their trademarks and to require limited pre-release testing (bug checking, compatibility testing and to ensure compliance with programming conventions) by an independent tester. Although the press releases issued by the Commission do not specify the reasons why it considered the above terms objectionable, it seems reasonable to speculate that it considered the requirements that only limited numbers of games to be produced and for prior approval to be restrictions on the licensees' ability to compete with the supplier's own video games and that it considered the requirement as to the manufacture of games to be an unjustified tie.

Discussion of standard setting in the Horizontal Agreements Guidelines

14–142 The most recent discussion of the attitude towards standards under Art.81 is contained in the Commission's Guidelines on horizontal co-operation agreements.[68]

These suggest that where participation in standard setting is unrestricted and transparent, standardisation agreements which set no obligation to comply with the standard, or which are part of a wider agreement to ensure compatibility of products, do not restrict competition. Further, there may be no "appreciable" restriction of competition in agreements that standardise aspects such as minor product characteristics, which have an insignificant effect on the main factors affecting competition.[69]

On the other hand, an agreement whereby a group of manufacturers set a standard and put pressure on third parties not to market products that do not comply with the standard almost always fall under Art.81.

Standardisation agreements may be caught by Art.81 if they grant the parties joint control over production and/or innovation, thereby restricting

---

[67] See Commission press releases IP/97/676 and IP/97/757. See also *Sony*, Commission press release, IP/98/ 1069.
[68] Guidelines on the applicability of Art.81 of the EC Treaty to Horizontal Co-operation Agreements, O.J. C 3/2, January 6, 2001, paras 159–175.
[69] *ibid.*, paras 163–164.

their ability to compete on product characteristics, while affecting third parties like suppliers or purchasers of the standardised products.

The existence of a restriction of competition in standardisation agreements depends on the extent to which parties remain free to develop alternative standards or products that do not comply with the standard. Those that entrust certain bodies with the exclusive right to test compliance with the standard go beyond the primary objective of defining the standard and may also restrict competition.

Standards that are not accessible to third parties may discriminate against or foreclose third parties or segment markets according to their geographic scope of application. The assessment as to whether they restrict competition may depend on the extent to which such barriers are likely to be overcome.

As to the likelihood of an exemption being granted under Art.81(3), this depends on the satisfaction of the criteria of exemption, which requires a demonstration that there are economic benefits, that the restriction is indispensable to the achievement of those benefits, and that there is no elimination of competition. As regards the demonstration of economic benefits, the necessary information to apply the standard must be available to those wishing to enter the market, and an appreciable proportion of the industry must be involved in the setting of the standard in a transparent manner. For these purposes, standards should not limit innovation. This will depend primarily on the lifetime of the associated products, in connection with the market development stage. The parties may also have to provide evidence that collective standardisation is efficiency enhancing for the consumer when a new standard may trigger unduly rapid obsolescence of existing products, without objective additional benefits.

As to the requirement of indispensability, the Guidelines suggest that where only one technological solution must be chosen, the standard must be set on a non-discriminatory basis. Standards should ideally be technology neutral or "[i]n any event, it must be justifiable why one standard is chosen over another." All competitors in the market affected by the standard should have the possibility of being involved in the discussions. Consequently, participation in standard setting should be open to all, unless the parties demonstrate important inefficiencies in such participation, or unless recognised procedures are foreseen for the collective representation of interests. Agreements should cover no more than is required to ensure their aims. For example, it may be difficult to justify why an agreement for a standard in an industry where only one competitor offers an alternative should oblige the parties to the agreement to boycott the alternative.

To avoid the elimination of competition, the Commission suggests that access to the standard must be possible for third parties on fair, reasonable and non-discriminatory terms.

Conclusions on Standardisation Agreements

Various conclusions can be drawn from the above decisions. It seems clear that standardisation agreements that exclude third parties from a market   **14–143** are likely to infringe Art.81(1) and the likely remedy in this case is the requirement to license the patents on fair, reasonable and non-discriminatory terms. Some limits on membership of a standards setting organisation may be objectively justified, provided access to the standard is widely available. Multilateral standards that are unnecessarily deep or which extend to future innovations are likely to infringe Art.81(1) and may fall outside Art.81(3). Exemption is more likely to be applicable if alternative technologies are available. Furthermore, standardisation arrangements should only apply to patents which are essential, as independently verified. Any requirements on licensees to grant back licences for improvements to the relevant standard may be acceptable if this is limited to essential patents only.

Arrangements for patent licensing in the context of standardisation agreements should therefore:

- Be based on objective verification as to which patents are essential;
- Not restrict the terms of licences (other than requiring fair, reasonable and non-discriminatory terms);
- Be subject to requirements to ensure licensees are not required to pay for patents they do not need; and
- Not require licensees to ay unreasonably high royalties, at least insofar as this would restrict competition in downstream markets.

14.5 ABUSE OF DOMINANCE AND ART.82 OF THE EC TREATY

14–144 Article 82 prohibits any abuse by one or more undertakings of a dominant position within the EU or a substantial part of it that affects trade between Member States. To determine whether an abuse contrary to Art.82 has occurred, it is, therefore, necessary to consider whether an undertaking:

    (i)   holds a dominant position in a substantial part of the EU;
    (ii) has abused that dominant position; and
    (iii) has, as a result, affected trade between Member States.

The Commission may impose fines on undertakings in breach of Art.82 of up to 10 per cent of their turnover.[70] In addition, it may, by decision, order infringing undertakings to take such action as is necessary to terminate the infringement.[71] Damages or injunctions may also be available to third parties harmed as a result of an infringement of Art.82.

---

[70] Art.23(2), Regulation 1/2003, [2003] O.J. L 1/1.
[71] *ibid.*, Art.7.

14.5.1 Dominance

The European Court of Justice has defined dominance as: "a position of economic strength enjoyed by an undertaking which enables it to hinder the maintenance of effective competition on the relevant market by allowing it to behave to an appreciable extent independently of its competitors and customers and ultimately of consumers".[72]

14–145

To determine whether an undertaking holds a dominant position, it is first necessary to identify the relevant market. This has two aspects: (i) the relevant product market, and (ii) the relevant geographic market.

The relevant product market

The relevant product market will include "all those products and/or services which are regarded as interchangeable or substitutable by the consumer, by reason of the products' characteristics, their prices and their intended use."[73] Non-substitutable products may also come within the relevant product market definition if their producers are able to switch to manufacturing substitutable products in the short term without significant additional costs or risk.[74] To date, the Commission's practice has tended to be to define product markets narrowly, restricting the definition to the relevant products and close substitutes.

14–146

In its communication on the definition of relevant markets, the Commission adopts a test which starts by examining the products directly affected by the agreement, and adding in substitutable products. The Commission suggests that products are sufficiently substitutable to be included within the relevant product market if sufficient customers would switch to them in response to a small but significant non-transitory increase in price of between 5 and 10 per cent of the affected products to make such a price rise unprofitable (the so-called SSNIP test).[75] While this test often proves difficult to apply in terms of obtaining empirical data, it can in fact often provide a useful measure, even in terms of hypothetical examination of the market or the future market.

The approach of EC competition law in focusing on demand side substitutability in market analysis has been criticised, in that it is said to be unresponsive to new economies such as the internet and e-commerce, where the main competitive constraint comes from new, superior products, whose time of introduction, or existence, is uncertain, and where some of the most significant potential competition may come from those who are not present in the market at the time of the analysis.

Nevertheless, the analysis of product markets, even in conventional competition analysis, often has to look at future markets and innovations.

---

[72] *Michelin v Commission* (Case 322/81) [1983] E.C.R. 3461 at 3503.
[73] Commission Notice on the definition of relevant market for the purposes of Community competition law, O.J. C 372/5, December 9, 1997, para.7.
[74] *ibid.*, para.20.
[75] *ibid.*, para.17.

Such market analysis can never be precise, because of the impossibility of predicting the future in innovative markets, but on the other hand it may be the best analysis available. The criticism could also be that of engaging in too much prediction of the future by the competition authorities in some instances.

The relevant geographic market

14–147   The relevant geographic market has been defined as: "the area in which the undertakings concerned are involved in the supply and demand of products or services, in which the conditions of competition are sufficiently homogeneous and which can be distinguished from neighbouring areas because the conditions of competition are appreciably different in those areas".[76] As with the relevant product market, the Commission suggests that an area should be included within the relevant geographic market if sufficient customers would switch their purchases to it in response to a small permanent rise of between 5 and 10 per cent in price in the affected area to make such a price rise unprofitable.

Whether an area constitutes a substantial part of the EU market is a question of fact dependent on the economic significance of the area, as well as its geographic scope. Consequently, ports have been found to be substantial parts of the EU due to their importance for shipping,[77] and it seems that an area as small as Luxembourg (which represents less than 0.25 per cent of the population of the EU) may qualify.[78]

Measuring economic strength on the relevant market

14–148   A firm will usually be regarded as having sufficient economic strength to be dominant where it controls a large share of the relevant market for a significant period, at least provided that other relevant factors point in the same direction. For example, the European Court of Justice has found that a market share in excess of 84 per cent held for three years was proof of dominance.[79] Similarly, a market share of around 50 per cent held for around three years was sufficient, in the absence of counter indications, to raise a presumption of dominance.[80] Conversely, it is unlikely that an undertaking controlling less than 25 per cent of the relevant market would be considered dominant.[81] Dominance may typically be found at levels above 40 per cent.

However, an undertaking's static market share is not the only factor which determines dominance, and a high market share may not be con-

---

[76] *ibid.*, para.8; see also *United Brands v Commission* (Case 27/76) [1978] E.C.R. 207.

[77] *Port of Genoa* (Case 179/90) [1991] I E.C.R. I–5889 and *Sealink/B & I* [1992] 5 C.M.L.R. 255.

[78] Advocate General Warner in *BP v Commission* (Case 77/77) [1978] E.C.R. II–1513.

[79] *Hoffman-La Roche v Commission* (Case 85/76) [1979] E.C.R. 461.

[80] *AKZO v Commission* (C–62/86) [1991] E.C.R. I–3359.

[81] See Recital 32 to Regulation 319/2004, the "Merger Regulation", O.J. L24/29, January 29, 2004.

clusive of dominance where there are other factors which negate it, a point which is particularly significant in e-commerce and new economy areas. Other relevant factors include: the market shares of the other undertakings in the market, the evolution of market shares over time, control of key technology and other barriers to market entry.

The analysis under EC competition law is criticised for being inappropriate for the new economy industries where one entrant typically has a large market share, where competition is often for the market as a whole, and large market shares are under permanent threat from innovating competitors and they are only able to retain their position if they continue to innovate.

However, EC competition law has never focused solely on static analysis, and particularly in the new economy areas, looks at the evolution of market shares over time and all possible factors which could influence market strength in the future. In addition, in many cases there are clearly so many indicators of increasing market power, giving an ability to quash or hijack innovation from other competitors in the market, that clear indications of dominance are provided.

It is often said that a better indicator of market power in this situation is that of contestability. If the market is contestable, a firm with a high market share does not enjoy a position of dominance because potential entry imposes an effective competitive constraint. Contestability analysis often seems to result in the same type of analysis as is engaged in under the more traditional analysis of dominance.

The notion of an essential facility

A doctrine is currently developing under Art.82 in relation to "essential **14–149** facilities" without access to which competitors cannot provide services to their customers in a related market. Those who control essential facilities are under special obligations and may be required to grant access to those facilities, even if they would not be required to do so if they were merely dominant on the conventional assessment suggested above. In addition, they may be required to grant access on terms which are no less favourable than those they grant to themselves as participants in a related market.

An early case concerned a port authority which was operating a ferry service from the port, and which, in its capacity as port authority, was allegedly applying sailing schedules that disadvantaged other ferry operators.[82] The Commission reasoned that a dominant undertaking which both owns or controls and uses an essential facility and which refuses access to that facility or grants access to competitors on terms less favourable than it applies to its own services (thereby placing them at a competitive disadvantage) infringes Art.82 unless it has an objective justification for its actions.

In another case concerning a port controller, the Commission decided

---

[82] *Sea Containers v Stena Sealink*, O.J. L 15/8, January 18, 1994.

that this principle would apply even if the dominant undertaking did not operate a ferry company and so was not active in the relevant market.[83] A refusal of the right to use the port without a valid reason could be an abuse even where the port controller had no economic interest in any of the ferry operators using the port.

The doctrine would be of little interest however if it applied only to ports and it is developing on a more general level. Some decisions which were taken before the doctrine was expressly formulated by the Commission are now being recast as applications of the principle. One example of a case which is claimed to have been an application of the principle is the *London European-Sabena* case.[84] In that case, the Commission decided that the Belgian national airline, Sabena, had infringed Art.82 by refusing to grant another airline, London European, access to its computerised reservation system which would allow its flight schedules and fares to be quoted and reservations to be made.

Clearly the essential facilities doctrine could have important consequences, especially in relation to possible obligations to grant rights to content. However, the doctrine is still in the process of being developed, and many aspects of it are still unclear. In one case, the Commission defined an essential facility as "a facility or infrastructure which is essential for reaching customers and/or enabling competitors to carry on their business, and which cannot be replicated by any reasonable means".[85] However, a much more detailed consideration of this question will be necessary before the issue is fully clarified. The issue is in practice very much intertwined with the consideration of compulsory licensing, and will be considered further below.

Joint or collective dominance

14–150   The European Court of Justice has in a number of cases[86] confirmed that the expression "one or more undertakings" in Art.82 of the EC Treaty implies that a dominant position may be held by two or more economic entities legally independent of each other. That only applies, however, where from an economic point of view they present themselves or act

---

[83] *Irish Continental Group v CCI Morlaix* [1995] 5 C.M.L.R. 77.
[84] *London European—Sabena*, O.J. L 317/47, November 24, 1988.
[85] See the *Notice on the application of the competition rules to access agreements in the telecommunications sector*, O.J. C 265/2, August 22, 1998 at point 68.
[86] *Società Italiana Vetro SpA v Commission* [1992] E.C.R. II–1403; *Almelo v Energiebedijf Ijsselmij* [1994] E.C.R. I–1477; *Centro Servizi Spediporto v Spedizioni Marittima del Golfo* (Case C–96/94) [1995] E.C.R. I–2883, [32] and [33] *DIP v Comune di Bassano del Grappa* (Joined Cases C–140/94, C–141/94 and C–142/94) [1995] E.C.R. I–3257, [26] *Sodemare v Regione Lombardia* (Case C–70/95) [1997] E.C.R. I–3395 [45] and [46]; *SIV*, [358]; *Compagnie Maritime Belge Transports SA v Commission* (Cases T–24–26 and 28/93) [1996] E.C.R. II–1201, [62].

together on a particular market as a collective entity vis-à-vis their competitors, their trading partners and consumers on a particular market.[87]

Establishing the existence of such a collective entity requires examination of whether there are economic links or factors which give rise to a connection between the undertakings concerned, which enable them to act together independently of their competitors, their customers and consumers. This could result from an agreement, decision or concerted practice between them. It may flow from the nature and terms of an agreement, from the way in which it is implemented and, consequently, from the links or factors which give rise to a connection between undertakings which result from it.

The court has stated that the existence of an agreement or of other links in law is not indispensable, and a finding of a collective dominant position under Art.82 may be based on other connecting factors and on an assessment of the structure of the market in question.

However, under Art.82 the court has not yet gone so far as to explicitly follow its pronouncements in the assessment of collective dominance under the Merger Regulation, which suggest that the existence of a "tightly oligopolistic" market structure could in itself found a finding of collective dominance.[88] The criteria of collective dominance under the EC Merger Regulation were established by the court in *Airtours v Commission*.[89] The court held that three conditions were necessary:

(1) there must be sufficient market transparency for all members of the oligopoly to be aware, sufficiently precisely and quickly, of the way in which the other members' market conduct is evolving;

(2) there must be adequate deterrents to ensure that there is a long-term incentive not to depart from the common policy. Retaliation in respect of conduct departing from the common policy is inherent in this condition;

(3) the foreseeable reaction of current and future competitors as well as of consumers, must not jeopardise the results expected from the common policy.

---

[87] *Compagnie Maritime Belge Transports SA v Commission* (Cases T–24–26 and 28/93) [1996] E.C.R. II–1201, appeal dismissed (Cases C–395 & 396/96P) [2000] E.C.R. I–1365, [36].

[88] In *Gencor* (Case T–102/96) [1999] 4 C.M.L.R. 971) the court said:

"there is no reason whatsoever in legal or economic terms to exclude from the notion of economic links the relationship of interdependence existing between the parties to a tight oligopoly within which, in a market with the appropriate characteristics, in particular in terms of market concentration, transparency and product homogeneity, those parties are in a position to anticipate one another's behaviour and are therefore strongly encouraged to align their conduct in the market, in particular in such a way as to maximise their joint profits by restricting production with a view to increasing prices."

[89] *Airtours v Commission* (Case T–342/99) [2002] E.C.R. II–2585.

14.5.2 Abuse

14–151 The following sections list forms of behaviour and contractual requirements which may be considered to be abusive.

Obtaining exclusive rights to content

14–152 In certain circumstances, an operator which is dominant in the market for certain content which formed a market in itself might be committing an abuse if it acquired such a degree of exclusivity regarding the content that competitors were excluded from the market.

Considerations of this type may well have been behind the *Nielsen* case.[90] This concerned retail tracking services (also know as sales or market tracking services), which involve information on product sales, prices, and other market information being obtained electronically from retailers and aggregated, with the aggregated information then being supplied to manufacturers of the relevant products and others.

AC Nielsen Company is the world's leading provider of these services. The second largest provider, IRI, complained to the Commission that the terms of Nielsen's contracts with retailers were preventing it from entering the market. The Commission issued a statement of objections alleging infringement of Art.82. The case never resulted in a formal decision, but was resolved by Nielsen giving undertakings to the Commission, one of which was that in relation to the purchase of data from retailers, Nielsen would not conclude exclusive contracts or contracts including any restriction on the retailers' freedom to supply data to any retail tracking services provider.

Excessive pricing

14–153 A dominant company which charges prices which are unfairly high in comparison to the "economic value" of the products or services being supplied may be committing an abuse. Whether or not this is the case may be assessed by examining prices for comparable goods or services or the costs of production of the relevant goods or services,[91] or even in some circumstances comparing prices in different geographic markets in the absence of other data.[92]

In recent cases, the Commission has also taken into account non-cost related factors, such as the demand for the product or service in question.[93] However, there are considerable difficulties in determining when a price is

---

[90] See Commission press release IP/96/1117.
[91] *United Brands v Commission* (Case 27/76) [1978] E.C.R. 207, [251] *et seq.* (cost of production); *British Leyland v Commission* (Case 226/84) [1986] E.C.R. 3263 (comparisons with equivalent transactions).
[92] *Corinne Bodson v Pompes Funèbres des Regions Liberées SA* (Case 30/87) [1988] E.C.R. 2479.
[93] Case COMP/A.36.568/D3, *Scandlines*, July 23, 2004 and Case COMP/A.36.570/D3, *Sunbusserne*, July 23, 2004.

so high that it constitutes an abuse, with the result that Art.82 has been applied in respect of excessive prices only in very few cases.

On the other hand, it may be that where excessive prices relate to an essential facility (see above) the Commission will be more keen to take action. The case of *ITT/Belgacom* may suggest that prices for access to an essential facility cannot exceed cost plus a reasonable rate of return.[94] The case concerned the prices charged by Belgacom, the incumbent Belgian telecoms operator, to ITT Promedia NV, a provider of alternative telephone directories, for lists of its telephone subscribers and other data (which the Commission may well have seen as an essential facility). ITT complained that the prices were excessive and discriminatory.

The Commission closed its case after Belgacom agreed to reduce such prices to a level that would cover its costs in collecting, compiling and providing such data plus a reasonable profit margin. The new price constituted a reduction of 90 per cent over that originally charged by Belgacom. In other informally settled cases in the telecoms sector, the Commission has determined that interconnection prices set at 100 per cent above those on comparable markets could be regarded as excessive.[95]

The Commission is currently investigating O2 and Vodafone (in the UK) and T-Mobile and Vodafone (in Germany) in relation to alleged abuse of their dominant positions in the provision of international roaming services at wholesale level by charging unfair and excessive prices.[96]

In new economy markets where there is often competition for the market, it is sometimes suggested that very significant profits are justified for those who manage to win the market, since they compensate for the risk undertaken by the winner, and offset the losses suffered by the many losers. However, it is not clear that profits need compensate for the losses suffered by the losers in order to create an efficient market. Consequently, a conventional analysis, which takes into account the cost of developing the product over its lifetime in an analysis of whether or not the price is excessive, does not appear to be an unjustified approach.

Predatory pricing

Predatory pricing, meaning pricing below cost aimed at eliminating a competitor, may be abusive contrary to Art.82. The European Court of Justice has held that pricing below average variable cost is an automatic abuse under Art.82 and that pricing below average total cost may be abusive if it forms part of a plan to eliminate a competitor.[97]

It has been suggested that this test (which is related to the economic analysis applied by Areeda and Turner[98]) of predatory pricing is inap-

14–154

---

[94] *ITT/Belgacom*, see Commission press release IP/97/292.
[95] See Commission press releases IP/96/975 and IP/98/430.
[96] See Commission press releases IP/04/994 and IP/05/161.
[97] *AKZO v Commission* (Case C–62/86) [1991] E.C.R. I–3359.
[98] Philip Areeda and Donald Turner, "Predatory prices and related practices under section 2 of the Sherman Act", Harvard Law Review, Vol.88, No.4. February 1975, pp.697–773.

propriate in the analysis of new economy sectors. In particular, it is suggested that much competition in new economy markets which involve scale economies and network effects will involve firms which engage in significant loss making activities in the early stages of the market, often going beyond merely promotional activities, in order to acquire the whole market for their goods. On the above test, such behaviour, designed to exclude competitors from the market, might be classed as predatory.

However, it is claimed that such loss-making activities in the new economy may not require intervention, because competition takes place in a different form, that of constant innovation, and intervention is likely to slow the innovation race.

While this argument might be justified in some circumstances where the market has not been established, and the low pricing is a necessity in order to establish the market, this argument may mean that these factors should also be taken into consideration in the assessment of abusive behaviour. However, where the market is clearly established or there is no necessity for the low pricing in the market, the existing predatory pricing test may continue to be a valid one.

On December 19, 2003, the Commission announced[99] it had sent a statement of objections to TeliaSonera, a Swedish telecommunications company, alleging that it had abused its dominant position in the markets for the provision of local broadband infrastructure and the provision of high-speed internet access by predatory pricing.

At this time, TeliaSonera owned around 90 per cent of the local infrastructure in Sweden that could be used for the provision of high-speed internet access. The alleged abuse occurred when TeliaSonera submitted a bid for a contract to construct a new fibre-optic network for the provision of broadband services. The contract was later awarded to TeliaSonera. The Commission considered that this bid was intentionally set below cost and TeliaSonera could not reasonably have expected to recover the investments and expenses associated with the contract, thereby constituting predatory pricing. This conclusion was supported by documentary evidence found at TeliaSonera's offices which showed that the losses were incurred intentionally to prevent its competitors from entering the market. This case is still ongoing at the time of writing.

Discriminatory pricing

14–155 Discriminatory pricing may be condemned as an abuse. Art.82 itself lists "applying dissimilar conditions to equivalent transactions with other trading parties, thereby placing them at a competitive disadvantage" as an example of abuse.[1] Does this mean that companies in a dominant position cannot charge different prices for a product in different countries?

One practice which has been condemned is where a dominant company

---

[99] See Commission press release IP/03/1797.
[1] Art.82(c) of the EC Treaty.

charges distributors different prices for particular goods delivered to the same place, according to the country where the distributor is intending to resell them.[2] On the other hand, where the discrimination is less artificial, and there is some objective justification for the difference in price, a price difference may in many cases be permitted. Where discriminatory pricing cannot be justified and has a significant effect on the purchaser's ability to compete in a neighbouring or downstream market on which it competes with the dominant firm, it may however be objectionable. This is discussed further in relation to margin squeezing.

E-commerce has characteristics that might be expected to facilitate price discrimination, both in the B2C and the B2B areas. As the UK Office of Fair Trading commented in its paper to the OECD round table on Competition Issues in Electronic Commerce[3]:

"The direct one-to-one nature of many transactions may enable the seller to more easily price to each individual customer at that customer's maximum willingness to pay. The growing use of auctions and exchanges within on-line marketplaces allows the seller to extract the maximum price offered for a good, without setting a firm price. Third-degree price discrimination may be facilitated by the use of 'cookies' alongside detailed customer databases, which enable companies to tailor their offerings to different categories of customers. The possibility of price discrimination offered by e-commerce might result in smaller or more segmented relevant markets. Although price discrimination can be efficient and beneficial for welfare, it may also both distort competition and facilitate excessive pricing. On-line companies are more easily able to gather and even share sensitive information about customers and their shopping habits. Nevertheless, this should only concern competition authorities when there is market power. Market solutions, such as the ability for individuals to conduct searches, will constrain this behaviour. There is a strong probability that it will be harder to apply competition law on price discrimination to e-commerce. Market segmentation may make the analysis harder, but the main problem is likely to be effective monitoring and market intelligence, and where it facilitates (e.g.) excessive pricing, allocating costs objectively."

This issue arose in relation to the selling by European airlines of air tickets, particularly on the internet. Following a number of complaints, in December 2003, the European Commission asked 18 European airlines whether they charged different prices for identical tickets, depending on the country of residence of the customer. The price differentials were as much as 300 per cent and did not appear to be linked to the date of purchase, the

---

[2] *United Brands v Commission* (Case 27/76) [1978] E.C.R. 207.
[3] OECD round table, CIEC DAFFE/CLP(2000)32, January 23, 2001, p.101.

nature of the ticket (such as whether it could be exchanged) or other features which could have justified charging different prices.

The Commission considered that this price discrimination could constitute an abuse of dominance. In June 2004,[4] the Commission announced that most airlines had declared that they do not have such restrictions in place, although several admitted that there may have been similar restrictions in the past (although now removed). The Commission stated that it would continue to monitor the situation to ensure that such price discrimination based on the country of residence of the purchaser does not happen again.

Margin squeezing

14–156 Margin squeezes are another form of pricing abuse that are closely related to price discrimination. A margin squeeze occurs where a vertically integrated undertaking is dominant in the upstream market for the supply of an input, which is important for supply in the related downstream market, in which it also operates. If the undertaking then sets such a low margin between the price for the input (the wholesale price) and the price it charges on the downstream market (the retail price) that an efficient operator in the downstream market cannot compete effectively, this constitutes a margin squeeze. If this harms competition, it is likely to be abusive.

The Commission has recently investigated an alleged margin squeeze by Deutsche Telekom, the dominant supplier of broadband access in Germany at both the wholesale and retail level. In 2002, the Commission received a complaint from a new market entrant alleging that Deutsche Telekom's tariffs for line sharing were so high that there was little scope for competitors to compete profitably in offering the broadband service at retail level. The Commission found evidence of a margin squeeze as new entrants were unable to compete with Deutsche Telekom in the retail market for ADSL services as a result of there being an insufficient spread between the wholesale access price charged by Deutsche Telekom to these competitors for line sharing and Deutsche Telekom's retail price for ADSL services. Instead of opening formal proceedings, the Commission agreed to accept commitments by Deutsche Telekom to end the margin squeeze from April 1, 2004, by altering its pricing structure to bring the potential abuse to an end.[5] Deutsche Telekom had already been fined €12.6 million by the Commission for abusing its dominant position by imposing a margin squeeze between the wholesale and retail tariffs for full local loop unbundling in relation to fixed voice telephony services.[6]

---

[4] See Commission press release IP/04/720.
[5] See Commission press releases IP/05/1033; IP/04/281. The Commission has also sent a statement of objections to Telefonica in relation to alleged margin squeeze in Spanish broadband internet access markets. See Commission press release MEMO/06/91.
[6] O.J. [2003] L 263/9, October 14, 2003.

Tying

A typical form of abusive tie-in or tying occurs where, as a condition of purchasing one product or service in which an undertaking is dominant, a buyer is forced to purchase another product or service which it could otherwise have bought from a competing supplier, or which it could have self-provided.[7] It is specifically listed in Art.82(d) of the EC Treaty as an example of an abuse.

14–157

However, this is not the only form of tying behaviour that may be considered abusive. If a dominant company gives a reduction in price when products or services are purchased together, compared with the price of purchasing them separately, then that may also be abusive, especially where it forecloses the market because competitors which offer the products or services separately are unable to compete. On the other hand, if the difference in price reflects a reduction in the costs of supplying the bundled package, then it should be permitted.

This is illustrated by a case involving *Digital* which did not reach the stage of a formal decision, and which was resolved by Digital giving undertakings to the Commission.[8] Digital, which was alleged to be dominant in the supply of software and hardware maintenance services for its products, offered a combined package of software maintenance services and hardware maintenance services at a price lower than the combined prices for software and hardware maintenance services if purchased separately.

To avoid action by the Commission under Art.82, Digital had to undertake that the discount in respect of software services which were bundled together would not be greater than 10 per cent compared with the price for purchasing software maintenance services and hardware maintenance services separately. A greater discount would have made it uneconomic for competitors to offer hardware maintenance services alone.

The Commission commented that the 10 per cent discount "allows cost savings and other benefits to be passed on to system users while ensuring the maintenance of effective competition in the supply of hardware services".

In the OFT's investigation into whether BSkyB abused a dominant position by, *inter alia*, practising mixed bundling in the wholesale provision of its premium sports and film channels, it set out the economic test that would indicate in this case (in addition to evidence of foreclosure) whether mixed bundling is abusive behaviour (in the absence of objective justification).[9] The OFT stated that it would not expect under conditions of normal competition bundling to the extent that the incremental avoidable cost per additional subscriber of supplying particular channels exceeds the implied incremental price of such channels when bundled together.

---

[7] *Hilti v Commission* (Case C–53/92P) [1994] E.C.R. I–667.
[8] See Commission press release IP/97/868.
[9] OFT decision No. CA98/20/2002: BSkyB investigation: alleged infringement of the Chapter II prohibition.

Exclusive purchasing requirements and loyalty bonuses

14–158 An obligation imposed by a dominant firm on its customers or distributors requiring them to purchase all or a percentage of their requirements from the dominant firm may be an abuse of a dominant position because it has a foreclosure effect on other suppliers. Pricing practices such as loyalty or fidelity discounts or rebates where a rebate or discount is conditional on a customer purchasing all or a proportion of its requirements from the undertaking offering the discount may also be abusive for the same reason, irrespective whether the quantity of purchases is large or small.[10]

Even discounts or rebates which are based on the purchase of fixed amounts may be contrary to Art.82, where those fixed amounts are in fact calculated for each customer to cover all or a substantial amount of that customer's requirements. Where the reference period for calculating the rebate is relatively long there is likely to be a greater foreclosure effect.

The Court of Justice confirmed in *Michelin I* that individualised, retroactive rebates, selectively applied and calculated over a reference period of a year were abusive.[11] A further key factor in finding abuse in this case was the lack of transparency in applying the rebates since sales thresholds and discounts changed several times and were never confirmed in writing.

However, a rebate system with standardised volume discounts or where rebates are only applied to incremental purchases (as opposed to being applied retrospectively to all purchases) will in general be considered less likely to have a loyalty enhancing effect unless the volume thresholds are well targeted and set at an amount equivalent to purchasers' typical overall requirements.[12]

Refusal to supply and refusal to license

14–159 Refusals to supply, in particular refusals to continue supplies to existing customers, may be abusive. For example, it has been held to be abusive for an undertaking which has previously supplied raw materials to a producer of finished goods to refuse to supply the raw materials to that customer because it wishes to break into the market for finished goods itself.[13] A refusal to supply an existing distributor because it starts to sell the products of a competitor, or starts to compete by itself providing competing products or services could also be an abuse.[14]

---

[10] *Hoffman-La Roche v Commission* (Case 85/76) [1979] E.C.R. 461.
[11] *NV Nederlandsche Banden Industrie Michelin v Commission* (Case 322/81) [1983] E.C.R. 3461.
[12] *Manufacture Française des Pneumatiques Michelin v Commission* (Case T–203/01) [2003] E.C.R. II 4071.
[13] *Commercial Solvents v Commission* (Cases 6 & 7/73) [1974] E.C.R. 223.
[14] *United Brands Co v Commission* (Case 27/76) [1978] E.C.R. 207, *BBI/Boosey and Hawkes* O.J. L 286/36, October 9, 1987.

While refusal to supply a new customer may not in many cases be an abuse, there are some cases where refusal to supply a new customer has been held to be one. These cases are difficult to categorise, but factors involved have included the fact of having a legal monopoly over the service refused, as well as essential facilities considerations.

A special case of a refusal to supply is a refusal to license, an issue which will be of considerable relevance to holders of intellectual property rights in e-commerce. In certain circumstances, a refusal to grant a licence of intellectual property rights may be abusive.

In the *Magill* case, which involved copyright material, the European Court of Justice held that, in exceptional circumstances, the owner of intellectual property rights may be obliged by Art.82 to grant licences to third parties.[15] *Magill* concerned a refusal by a number of television broadcasters in the UK and Ireland to license weekly programme schedules said to be covered by copyright to Magill for inclusion in a weekly television listings magazine. The following were some elements which the court identified as exceptional in that case:

(i) the requested material concerned basic information concerning channel, day, time and title of the programme; and each of the broadcasters was the only possible source of information on its programming schedule. As a result, the refusal to license was preventing the emergence of a new product, namely a comprehensive television guide, for which there was "specific, constant and regular" potential demand;

(ii) by their conduct, the broadcasters reserved to themselves the downstream market for weekly television guides; and

(iii) there was no justification for such a refusal either in the activity of television broadcasting or in that of publishing television programmes.

The scope of the *Magill* judgement has now been interpreted in later cases.

Tiercé Ladbroke[16] concerned the broadcasting of sound and pictures of **14–160** French horse races, the rights to which were controlled by the French horse racing companies, or "sociétés de courses". Ladbroke wanted a right to broadcast the French races in its booking shops in Belgium, but the French horse racing companies refused.

The court in this case found that there was no obligation to license. The *Magill* case could not be relied on because in contrast to *Magill*, in this case the applicant was not only present in but also had the largest share of the main betting market in Belgium, on which the product in question would be offered to consumers, while the French horse racing companies were not present on this market. In the absence of exploitation by those companies of

---

[15] *RTE and ITP v Commission* (Cases C–241/91 P and C–242/91) [1995] E.C.R. I–743.
[16] *Tiercé Ladbroke v Commission* (Case T–504/93) [1997] E.C.R. II–923.

their intellectual property rights in Belgium, their refusal to license could not be regarded as involving any restriction of competition.

Even if the absence of the horse racing companies on the relevant market was not a decisive factor, the refusal to license could not be contrary to Art.82, unless it concerned a product or service which was either essential for the exercise of the activity in question in that there was no real or potential substitute, or it concerned a new product whose introduction might be prevented, despite specific, constant and regular demand on the part of consumers. Sound and pictures were not necessary for taking bets, as shown by Ladbroke's significant position in Belgium for taking bets on French races. Further, broadcasting was not indispensable, because it took place after bets were placed, and therefore did not prevent bookmakers from pursuing their business.

Oscar Bronner[17] was a newspaper publisher which wanted to have its newspapers distributed through Mediaprint's national home delivery system, the only national home delivery network in Austria, and claimed that it was an abuse of Mediaprint's dominant position for it to refuse such access.

The Court of Justice considered the question of whether such a refusal would amount to an abuse, on the ground that it deprived a competitor of a means of distribution judged essential for the sale of the newspapers. It determined that *Magill* could not be relied upon, even if the *Magill* principle on the exercise of an intellectual property right were applicable to the exercise of any property right whatsoever.

In particular, unlike the situation in *Magill*, the refusal of the service would not eliminate all competition in the daily newspaper market. First, there were other methods of distributing papers, such as by post, or through shops and kiosks. Further, there were no technical, legal or even economic obstacles capable of making it impossible, or even unreasonably difficult, for any other publisher of daily newspapers to establish, alone or in cooperation with other publishers, its own daily nationwide home-delivery scheme.

In order to demonstrate that the creation of such a system was not a realistic potential alternative and that access to the existing system was indispensable, it was not enough to argue that it was not viable by reason of the small circulation of the daily newspaper or newspapers to be distributed. It would be necessary to show that it was not economically viable to create a second home-delivery scheme for the distribution of daily newspapers with a circulation comparable to that of the daily newspapers distributed by the existing scheme.

14–161 In *Micro Leader Business*,[18] Micro Leader Business had complained to the European Commission about Microsoft's policy which prevented it

---

[17] *Oscar Bronner GmbH & Co KG v Mediaprint Zeitungs- und Zeitschriftenverlag GmbH & Co KG, Mediaprint Zeitungsvertriebsgesellschaft mbH & Co KG, Mediaprint Anzeigengesellschaft mbH & Co KG* (Case C–7/97) [1998] E.C.R. I–7791.

[18] *Micro Leader Business v Commission* (Case T–198/98) [1999] E.C.R. II–3989.

importing into France for resale French language Microsoft software which was originally marketed in Canada.

The EC rule on the exhaustion of copyright for computer software, as enshrined in Art.4(c) of Directive 91/250 on the legal protection of computer programs, provided that the first sale of a copy of a computer program in the EU would exhaust the distribution right to elsewhere in the EU, but that did not apply where the first sale was in Canada, because of which, Microsoft retained its right to rely on its copyright to prevent distribution in France of such products.

The Commission rejected Micro Leader's complaint, on the basis that the prohibition on importation into Europe fell within the legal enforcement of Microsoft's copyright, and that no evidence had been provided of the wrongful exercise of that right. The Commission had suggested that evidence of such wrongful exercise might be constituted by Microsoft charging lower prices on the Canadian market than on the European market for equivalent transactions, if European prices were, in addition, excessive. The court held that the factual evidence put forward by the applicant constituted, at the very least, an indication that, for equivalent transactions, Microsoft applied lower prices on the Canadian market than on the Community market, and that the Community prices were excessive. It annulled the rejection of Micro Leader's complaint, forcing the Commission to reconsider it.

The significant point about this is that, although not a clear ruling on the point, the tenor of the court's ruling suggested that there might be an argument on the basis of the *Magill* case that a compulsory licence might be imposed, or copyright might not be relied on, where there was a difference in price between France and Canada, the difference in price put the import in competition with the French product because of its significantly lower price, and the price of the French products was excessive.

In *Intel v Via*,[19] the UK Court of Appeal held in a preliminary judgment that there was an arguable case that a refusal to grant a patent licence could constitute abuse of a dominant position. In this case, Intel was itself supplying the relevant products and Via already benefited from a licence in respect of a previous version of the products but was refused a licence for an updated version. Intel had obtained summary judgment against Via for patent infringement and Via successfully appealed on the basis that its defences relating to infringement of Arts. 81 and 82 had a real prospect of success. Via alleged that the patent infringement proceedings were an abuse of Intel's intellectual property rights and Intel's refusal to grant Via a licence was an abuse of its dominant position.

The Court of Appeal in allowing Via's appeal, held that it was not necessary (for there to have been an abuse of a dominant position) for the dominant party's actions to entirely exclude a new product.

The Court of Justice has ruled on two parallel cases involving IMS Health **14–162** (IMS), the world leader in data collection on pharmaceutical sales and

---

[19] *Intel Corp v VIA Technologies Inc* [2002] All E.R.(D) 346.

prescriptions, in relation to its refusal to license its copyright "1860 brick structure".[20] This segments Germany into 1,860 sales areas or "bricks" and the structure had become a national standard in the German pharmaceutical industry. Each brick contains at least four pharmacies as German data protection law prohibits the provision of sales information for individual pharmacies. Regional sales reports are an essential tool for the pharmaceutical industry which uses them to create sales territories, develop incentive schemes for their sales force and to know about their products' market shares and trends in sales over time.

The complainants in these cases, NDC Health and AzyX Geopharma, the subsidiaries of respectively American and Belgian firms, initially attempted to sell their regional sales data in a structure other than the "1860 brick structure". However, discussions with potential customers showed that data presented in another structure would not be marketable, because of the pre-eminent position of the 1860 brick structure within the industry.

In the most recent case, the Frankfurt District Court referred some questions of interpretation of Art.82 in the context of an action by IMS for copyright infringement of its 1860 brick structure before the German courts, against NDC Health. The Court of Justice (in its ruling on April 29, 2004) held that a refusal by a dominant undertaking to grant an intellectual property licence only constitutes an abuse of a dominant position where the product or service at issue is indispensable to an undertaking in order to carry out business in the relevant market (following the *Oscar Bronner* case) and the following conditions are fulfilled:

- The undertaking requesting the licence intends to offer new products or services not offered by the copyright owner and for which there is potential consumer demand (that is, where such undertaking does not intend to limit itself essentially to duplicating the goods or services already offered on the relevant downstream market by the copyright owner);
- The refusal is not justified by objective considerations; and
- The refusal is such as to reserve a downstream market to the copyright owner by eliminating all competition on that market.

The European Commission previously adopted an interim measures decision ordering IMS to grant a licence to NDC Health and another complainant.[21] On appeal, the President of the Court of First Instance found in the *IMS German Brick Structure* "interim measures" judgment that there were serious doubts about the validity of the Commission's interim decision.[22] The Court of First Instance's decision was later upheld by the Court of Justice,[23] which found that the copyrighted system was

---

[20] Case COMP D3/38.044, *IMS Health*, July 3, 2001, see Commission press release IP/01/941.
[21] See Commission press release IP/01/941 (July 3, 2001).
[22] *IMS Health v Commission* (Case T–184/01) [2001] E.C.R. II–3193.
[23] *NDC Health v IMS Health and Commission* (Case C–481–01 PR) [2002] E.C.R. I–3401.

based on freely available information and both IMS and the complainants operated on the same market—there was no downstream market and so the refusal to grant a licence did not prevent the emergence of a new service.

The Commission had considered that IMS's refusal to grant a licence for the use of the brick structure constituted a prima facie abuse of a dominant positionon the basis that: (a) the 1860 brick structure was indispensable for NDC and AzyX to carry on their business, inasmuch as there was no actual or potential substitute for it, and (b) IMS's refusal to license could not be justified objectively and was likely to foreclose the market to potential new entrants and eliminate all prospect of competition in Germany.

The Commission therefore granted interim measures ordering IMS to grant a licence to its current competitors on non-discriminatory, commercially reasonable terms. The royalties to be paid to IMS were to be agreed by IMS and the party requesting a licence, or in case of disagreement, would be determined by independent experts on the basis of transparent and objective criteria. Following IMS's appeal against this decision the Court of First Instance ordered, on October 26, 2001, that the interim measures be suspended pending final judgment on the main action. Following the Court of Justice's decision, the Commission withdrew its interim measures decision on August 14, 2003.[24]

14.5.3 Cases Specifically Related to E-commerce

Obligation to disclose interface information and the IBM System/370 case

Long before the issue of compulsory licences and essential facilities came into the centre stage of European competition law, the European Commission in 1980 alleged in a statement of objections against IBM[25] that IBM had abused its dominant position in the supply of central processing units (CPUs) and basic software for IBM System/370 type mainframe computers, by, amongst other matters, failing to supply other manufacturers in sufficient time with the interface information needed to permit competitive products to be used with IBM System/370 computers.

14–163

A settlement was reached with the Commission, whereby IBM gave extensive undertakings. It agreed to disclose sufficient interface information to allow competing companies in the EU to sell hardware and software products of their own design which could interoperate with IBM System/370 computers. Specifically, it agreed to make all System/370 hardware interface information and all information relating to the System/370 CPUs and software products available within 120 days of the date of the

---

[24] See Commission press release IP/03/1159.
[25] See Fin Lomholt, "The 1984 IBM Undertaking, Commission's monitoring and practical effects," *Competition Policy Newsletter*, 1998 No.3, p.7.

announcement of the product concerned in the EU or at the date of the general availability of the product, if earlier.[26]

For the interface between System/370 software products and competitors' software, IBM undertook to disclose the relevant interface information as soon as the interface was reasonably stable but no later than general availability.[27] Any company which could provide satisfactory evidence that it was doing business in the EU and was developing and manufacturing products of the relevant type was entitled to the relevant information. IBM reserved a right to charge a reasonable royalty to cover its costs and for the supply of proprietary information protected by any right enforceable at law. The undertaking was terminated in 1995.

Microsoft server and Windows 2000 cases

14–164   The Commission fined Microsoft €497 million for abusing its dominant position by leveraging its near monopoly in the market for PC operating systems onto the markets for work group server operating systems and for media players.[28] This is the largest single fine ever imposed on an undertaking to date and is in addition to the remedies also imposed on Microsoft by the Commission.

The Commission found that Microsoft had a near monopoly in the PC operating system market as its operating systems equip more than 95 per cent of the world's PCs. Microsoft had abused its market power by deliberately restricting interoperability between Windows PCs and non-Microsoft work group servers (which was part of a broader strategy intended to exclude competitors from the market for work group server operating systems). It did so by means of discriminatory and selective disclosure of interface information or completely withholding interface information from competing software suppliers. Microsoft was also found to have tied Windows 2000 with other services which resulted in customers having to pay licence fees for unwanted services. It was also found to have tied its Windows Media Player with its ubiquitous Windows operating system.

The Commission found that this illegal conduct had enabled Microsoft to acquire a dominant position in the market for work group server operating systems, which are at the heart of corporate IT networks, and this risked eliminating competition altogether in that market. In addition, Microsoft's conduct had significantly weakened competition on the media player market.

In relation to the refusal to provide interface information, the Commission stated in its press release that "this relegated to a secondary position competition in terms of reliability, security and speed, among other factors, and ensured Microsoft's success on the market". To remedy this abuse, the

---

[26] *ibid.*, p.8.

[27] *ibid.*, p.8.

[28] Case COMP/37.792, *Microsoft/W2000*, March 24, 2004, see Commission press release IP/04/382.

Commission ordered Microsoft to disclose to competitors, within 120 days, complete and accurate interface information required for their products to be able to interoperate fully with the Windows operating system. This will enable competitors to develop products that can compete on a level playing field in the work group server operating system market. To the extent any of this interface information is protected by intellectual property in the EEA, Microsoft can charge a reasonable licence fee.

As regards the tying abuse, according to the press release[29]:

> "The ubiquity which was immediately afforded to Windows Media Player as a result of it being tied with the Windows PC operating system artificially reduces the incentives of music, film and other media companies, as well as software developers and content providers, to develop their offerings to competing media players. As a result, Microsoft's tying of its media player product has the effect of foreclosing the market to competitors, and hence ultimately reducing consumer choice, since competing products are set at a disadvantage which is not related to their price or quality ... Absent intervention from the Commission, the tying of Windows Media Player with Windows is likely to make the market 'tip' definitively in Microsoft's favour. This would allow Microsoft to control related markets in the digital media sector, such as encoding technology, software for broadcasting of music over the Internet and digital rights management etc."

To remedy this abuse, the Commission required Microsoft to offer a version of its Windows operating system without Windows Media Player to PC manufacturers (or when selling directly to end-users) within 90 days. Microsoft is still able to offer a version of its Windows client PC operating system product with Windows Media Player but it cannot use any commercial, technological or contractual terms that would have the effect of rendering the unbundled version of Windows less attractive or less capable in terms of performance. In particular, it must not give PC manufacturers a discount conditional on their buying Windows together with Windows Media Player.

Mario Monti, the Commissioner responsible at that time for competition, is quoted as saying during the course of the investigation:

> "... The Commission ... wants to see undistorted competition in the market for media players. These products will not only revolutionise the way people listen to music or watch videos but will also play an important role with a view to making internet content and electronic commerce more attractive. The Commission is determined to ensure that the Internet remains a

---

[29] *ibid.*

competitive marketplace to the benefit of innovation and consumers alike."[30]

14–165 The case began in December 1998, when the Commission began an investigation into Microsoft, following a complaint from Sun Microsystems (Sun) that Microsoft had refused to provide it with the interface information necessary to enable Sun to develop server products that could operate with Microsoft's Windows PC operating system.

In August 2000, the European Commission issued a statement of objections to Microsoft, alleging that Microsoft had abused its dominant position in the market for personal computer operating systems by using illegal practices to extend its dominant position in the market for personal computer operating systems into the market for low-end server operating systems.

This first statement of objections was followed by a second in August 2001, expanding the investigation to include concerns about the tying of Microsoft's Windows Media Player with Windows 2000, and a third in August 2003, giving Microsoft a final opportunity to comment on the Commission's investigation and to consider a package of possible remedies.

As the Commission and Microsoft were unable to reach a negotiated settlement, the Commission finally issued a decision on March 24, 2004, that Microsoft had abused its dominant position. Microsoft has appealed the Commission's decision to the European Court of First Instance. Microsoft also applied unsuccessfully for an order suspending the remedies imposed by the Commission until the appeal has been heard which was rejected as it failed to show that the implementation of the remedies might cause it serious and irreparable harm.[31]

On July 12, 2006, the Commission fined Microsoft a further €280.5 million for continued non-compliance with certain obligations in the March 2004 infringement decision. In particular, the Commission considered that Microsoft had not yet complied with the obliation to provide complete and accurate interoperability information.[32] Microsoft has appealed this July 2006 decision[33] as well as a decision of the Commission requiring it to disclose certain source code information as part of the interoperability remedy.[34]

Predatory pricing and the *Wanadoo* case

14–166 In July 2003, the Commission fined Wanadoo Interactive (a subsidiary of France Télécom) €10.35 million for abusing its dominant position by

---

[30] See Commission press release IP/01/1232.

[31] *Microsoft v Commission*, (Case T–201/04) December 22, 2004.

[32] See Commission press release IP/06/979. This was based on the Commission's previous decision of November 10, 2005, that it would impose a daily fine of €2 million per day if Microsoft did not comply with its obligation to provide interoperability information by December 15, 2005 (Case Comp/C–3/37.792).

[33] *Microsoft v Commission* (Case T–271/06).

[34] *Microsoft v Commission* (Case T–313/05).

engaging in predatory pricing in ADSL-based internet access services for the general public.[35]

The Commission found that from the end of 1999 to October 2002, Wanadoo marketed its ADSL services at prices that were below their average costs. The prices charged were well below variable costs until August 2001 and then they were approximately equivalent to variable costs, but significantly below total costs.

Since the mass marketing of Wanadoo's ADSL services only began in March 2001, the Commission considered that the abuse only started on that date. During this period, Wanadoo suffered substantial losses up to the end of 2002 as a result of its pricing practices and it was expected at the beginning of 2002 to continue selling at a loss in 2003 and 2004. The Commission therefore considered that this policy was deliberate and part of a plan to eliminate competitors, as Wanadoo was fully aware of the level of losses it was suffering and the legal risks associated it.

From January 2001 to September 2002, Wanadoo's market share rose from 46 per cent to 72 per cent on a market which saw more than a five-fold increase in its size over the same period. The level of losses required in order to compete with Wanadoo had a dissuasive effect on competitors, thereby restricting market entry and development potential for competitors. This is demonstrated by the fact that no competitor held more than 10 per cent of the market, Wanadoo's main competitor had seen its market share decrease significantly and one competitor went out of business.

The Commission is also investigating Wanadoo and France Télécom in relation to the suspected imposition of unfair selling prices in relation to high-speed internet access for residential customers. This investigation is ongoing.[36] The Commission noted in its press release on the predatory pricing case that it considers that practices designed to capture strategic markets such as the high-speed Internet access market call for particular vigilance.

14.6 UK COMPETITION LAW

This section looks at the application of UK competition law to e-commerce. **14–167**
It considers the merger provisions of the Enterprise Act 2002, the Competition Act 1998, and the disqualification of directors and the criminalisation of cartel behaviour under the Enterprise Act 2002.

---

[35] Case COMP/38.233, *Wanadoo*, July 16, 2003, see Commission press release IP/03/1025. Wanadoo is appealing this decision (Case T–340/03).

[36] In May 2004, the Commission issued a decision ordering Wanadoo and France Télécom to submit to an investigation in relation to this investigation. Wanadoo and France Télécom are challenging this investigation before the CFI (Cases T–339/04 and T–340/04).

14.6.1 UK Merger Control Law

14–168 The UK law relating to mergers in the UK is contained in the merger provisions of the Enterprise Act 2002 (the "Enterprise Act"). Under the Enterprise Act a "relevant merger situation" arises if:

- Two or more enterprises cease to be distinct; and either
- As a result, in the UK or a substantial part of it at least 25 per cent of goods or services of any description are supplied by or to the same person or are supplied by or to the persons by whom the relevant enterprises are carried on; or
- The value of the UK turnover of the enterprise acquired or to be acquired exceeds £70 million.[37]

Two enterprises cease to be distinct where one of them ceases to carry on business as a result of an agreement between them or they come under common control or ownership. An enterprise for these purposes includes part of the activities of a business. Some joint ventures may come under the merger provisions on this basis.

The market share test or more accurately the share of supplies test, is satisfied only if:

- Both of the enterprises ceasing to be distinct either supply or purchase goods or services of a particular description in the UK, so that their combination increases a market share of goods or services supplied or purchased; and
- The resulting market share of goods or services purchased or sold is greater than 25 per cent.

In other words, if there is no market share overlap before the enterprises cease to be distinct, then the merger will not qualify for investigation, even if the combined market share is above 25 per cent.

There is no obligation to notify mergers which qualify for investigation. The reason notification is often made is that it results in deadlines (discussed below) within which the Office of Fair Trading ("OFT"), which is the UK competition authority, must either clear the merger, or refer it for a fuller investigation by the Competition Commission. On the other hand, in the absence of notification, a merger may be referred to the Competition Commission up to four months from the date of the completion, or if later, four months from the date on which the merger was made public.

There are no fines for failure to notify, because as stated above, notification is entirely voluntary. The remedy under the Enterprise Act is that if a merger is found to result in a substantial lessening of competition, the

---

[37] Under the merger provisions of the Fair Trading Act 1973, which was replaced by the Enterprise Act, this test was an assets test and was satisfied if the gross assets of the target company exceeded £70 million.

Competition Commission may make an order requiring the parties to modify the arrangement in order to prevent any adverse effects which have been identified by the Competition Commission, and this may include divestiture of assets required through the merger or of overlapping assets already held by the acquirer. The Competition Commission referral process is lengthy, and is used in only a small minority of cases. On the other hand, of the cases which are referred to the Competition Commission, a significant proportion tend to be found to lead to a substantial lessening of competition.

14.6.2 The UK Competition Act 1998

The UK Competition Act 1998 (the "1998 Act") entered into force on   **14–169**
March 1, 2000. It introduced two prohibitions into UK law:

(i)   a prohibition on agreements that restrict competition in the UK (s.2 of the 1998 Act, the "Chapter I prohibition"); and

(ii)   a prohibition of the abuse of a dominant market position in the UK (s.18 of the 1998 Act, the "Chapter II prohibition").

The 1998 Act repealed much of the existing UK competition legislation, including the Restrictive Trade Practices Acts 1976, and 1977, the Resale Prices Act 1976, and the provisions of the Competition Act 1980 concerning anti-competitive practices. The Fair Trading Act 1973, which covered mergers and monopoly situations, was repealed by the Enterprise Act 2002.

One objective of the 1998 Act was to bring UK competition law more closely into line with EC competition law. To this end, the Chapter I and Chapter II prohibitions are closely modelled on, respectively, Arts 81 and 82 of the EC Treaty. In addition, s.60 of the 1998 Act requires that questions arising in relation to the Chapter I and Chapter II prohibitions are, as far as possible and taking into account relevant differences, dealt with in a manner consistent with the treatment of corresponding questions under EC competition law.

In particular, UK courts and the OFT are required to determine such questions with a view to ensuring that there is no inconsistency between, on the one hand, the principles they apply and the decisions they reach under the 1998 Act and, on the other hand, the principles laid down by the EC Treaty and the European Court of Justice in determining corresponding questions under EC competition law. UK courts and the OFT must also "have regard" to relevant statements and decision of the European Commission.

14.6.3 The 1998 Act—The Chapter I Prohibition

14–170   The Chapter I prohibition is contained in s.2(1) of the 1998 Act and applies to "agreements between undertakings, decisions by associations of undertakings or concerted practices" that:

- Have the object or effect of preventing, restricting or distorting competition within the UK; and
- May affect trade within the UK and are implemented in the UK.

Agreements between undertakings, decisions of trade associations and concerted practices

14–171   Most forms of competitive co-ordination between undertakings are potentially caught by the Chapter I prohibition. The term "agreement" covers agreements that are not legally binding and, conversely, several separate binding contracts may be found to form a single agreement. The term "concerted practice" covers all co-ordinated behaviour between undertakings that "knowingly substitutes practical cooperation between them for the risks of competition".

To be caught by the Chapter I prohibition, an agreement or concerted practice must be "between undertakings". A parent company and its wholly controlled subsidiaries are considered to form a "single economic entity" and, as a result, are treated as a single undertaking for this purpose. Consequently, many intra-group transactions will fall outside the Chapter I prohibition.

The meaning of "undertaking"

14–172   The term "undertaking" will be interpreted broadly to cover virtually any entity engaged in economic or commercial activity, regardless of its legal status. Limited companies, partnerships and individuals may all be undertakings. State-owned companies will also be covered if they engage in commercial or economic activity. The fact that an entity is non-profit making will not prevent it being an undertaking.

Object or effect of preventing, restricting or distorting competition in the United Kingdom

14–173   In principle, any agreement that may lead to reduced competition between the parties or restricts the ability of third parties to compete may potentially be caught by the Chapter I prohibition. There is no particular significance in the distinction between preventing, restricting and distorting competition.

Restriction of competition and implementation in the United Kingdom

14–174   An agreement may fall within the Chapter I prohibition if it has the object or effect of restricting competition in the UK and is, or is intended to be, implemented in the UK.[38] The latter requirement is a jurisdictional test which reflects the EC case law under Art.81.[39] An agreement which affects competition in the UK and is implemented in the UK[40] will fall under UK law, and if it also meets the EC requirement of having an actual or potential effect on trade between Member States, it will also fall under Art.81. Article 81 is only infringed where there is an effect on trade between EU Member States. An agreement which has no effect on trade between Member States for the purposes of Art.81 may nevertheless fall under the Chapter I prohibition if it affects trade in the UK.

Appreciable effect

The Chapter I prohibition will not apply to agreements whose effect on trade or competition is not appreciable. This requirement does not appear in the text of the prohibition, but is imported from EC competition law by the s.60 requirement for consistent interpretation.   **14–175**

The OFT has indicated that it will follow the European Commission's notice on agreements of minor importance in relation to an appreciable effect on competition in the UK.[41]

14.6.4 The 1998 Act—the Effect of Falling Within the Chapter I Prohibition

Section 2(4) of the 1998 Act provides that agreements caught by the Chapter I prohibition are void and may not be enforced in UK courts. Such voidness will not necessarily extend to the whole agreement but will be limited to the restrictive aspects of the agreement provided they are severable from the rest of the agreement under the normal rules of contract law. In addition to voidness under s.2(4), agreements caught by the Chapter I prohibition may attract enforcement action including fines and directions to terminate. The Chapter I prohibition is also directly enforceable in the UK courts, by private parties, by actions for an injunction or damages (see section 14.6.11 below).   **14–176**

Agreements may escape these consequences of falling within the Chapter I prohibition if they fall within one of a wide range of exclusions or benefit from an exemption (see sections 14.6.5 and 14.6.6 below).

Directors may also be disqualified if their company is found to have infringed EC or UK competition law and, if an individual has taken part in cartel activity, they can be imprisoned (see section 14.6.8 below).

---

[38] S.2(3) of the 1998 Act provides that the Chapter I prohibition applies only if "the agreement, decision or practice is, or is intended to be, implemented in the UK."

[39] See above.

[40] S.2 of the 1998 Act also includes a requirement that there be an effect on trade in the UK, but this appears to be superfluous in the light of the requirements for an effect on competition in the UK and implementation in the UK.

[41] See para.14–050 above. See OFT guidelines: Agreements and concerted practices (OFT 401) December 2004, para.2:18.

14.6.5 The 1998 Act—Exclusions From The Chapter I Prohibition

Excluded Agreements

14–177   The main category of agreements that are excluded from the Chapter I prohibition is mergers. Mergers as defined under UK merger law (the merger provisions of the Enterprise Act) are excluded from the scope of the Chapter I prohibition,[42] as are agreements giving rise to a concentration falling within the EC Merger Regulation.[43]

There was previously a separate exclusion for vertical agreements in the UK but this was repealed with effect from May 1, 2005, and, from that date, UK vertical agreements must comply with the Vertical Agreements Block Exemption to benefit from exemption from the Chapter I prohibition (see section 14.6.6 below).

14.6.6 The 1998 Act—Exemption From the Chapter I Prohibition

14–178   The 1998 Act gives the OFT powers to exempt agreements from the Chapter I prohibition where they satisfy certain exemption criteria. The relevant criteria mirror those under Art.81(3) of the EC Treaty. Three categories of exemption are provided for:

Parallel exemption if an EC exemption applies

14–179   Agreements that benefit from an exemption granted under EC competition law (pursuant to Art.81(3) of the EC Treaty) are automatically exempt from the Chapter I prohibition.[44] This applies whether the EC exemption was granted on an individual basis (prior to May 1, 2004) or under one of the EC block exemptions. In the 1998 Act, such automatic exemptions are referred to as "parallel exemptions". Parallel exemption is also granted to agreements that meet the conditions for exemption under one of the EC block exemptions but do not affect trade between Member States. In certain circumstances, the OFT may vary or cancel a parallel exemption or impose conditions.

This means, for example, that an agreement that complies with the Vertical Agreements Block Exemption or the Technology Transfer Block Exemption will also benefit from exemption from the Chapter I prohibition.

---

[42] 1998 Act, s.3(1)(a) and Sch.1, para.1(1).
[43] ibid., s.3(1)(a) and Sch.1, para.6.
[44] ibid., s.10.

UK block exemptions

The OFT has the power to adopt block exemptions granting automatic **14–180**
exemption, without the need for notification, to agreements that fall within
the terms of the block exemption.[45] The OFT has so far only issued one
block exemption, for public transport ticketing schemes.[46]

Individual exemption

As in EC law, an agreement will benefit from individual exemption from **14–181**
the Chapter I prohibition if it satisfies the exemption criteria set out in s.9 of
the 1998 Act. These are that the agreement:

(i)   contributes to improving production or distribution, or to pro-
      moting technical or economic progress;
(ii) allows consumers a fair share of the resulting benefits;
(iii) does not impose any unnecessary restrictions; and
(iv) does not afford the possibility of eliminating competition in
      respect of a substantial part of the products in question.

As under EC law, it was possible to notify an agreement to the OFT for
confirmation that the above conditions were met. However, s.9 is directly
applicable as from May 1, 2004, and the parties must now assess for
themselves whether the exemption criteria are met.[47]

Written opinions

As the system for notification of agreements to the OFT for a decision on **14–182**
exemption has been abolished, the OFT has indicated that it may publish a
written opinion, where requested by the parties, as to an agreement's
compatibility with the Chapter I prohibition. Such guidance may include
whether it might qualify for individual, block or parallel exemption.
However, the OFT will only publish such an opinion where:

- the agreement raises novel or unresolved questions about the
  application of the Chapter I prohibition in the UK; or
- the OFT considers that there is an interest in issuing guidance for
  the benefit of a wider audience.[48]

These conditions are only likely to be fulfilled in exceptional circumstances.

---

[45] ibid., s.6.
[46] Competition Act 1998 (Public Transport Ticketing Schemes Block Exemption) Order 2001
(SI 2001/319).
[47] Competition Act 1998 and other Enactments (Amendment) Regulations 2004 (SI 2004/
1261).
[48] See the OFT's guidelines: Agreements and Concerted Practices (OFT 401) December 2004.

14.6.7 The Chapter II Prohibition

14–183 The Chapter II prohibition is contained in s.18(1) of the 1998 Act, which provides that:

> "any conduct on the part of one or more undertakings which amounts to the abuse of a dominant position in a market is prohibited if it may affect trade within the United Kingdom".

For these purposes, a dominant position is defined as "a dominant position within the UK" and the UK is defined as "the UK or any part of it".

It follows that conduct will be caught by the Chapter II prohibition where it:

(i) is carried out by an undertaking holding a dominant position within the UK or a part of it;

(ii) constitutes an abuse of that dominant position; and

(iii) affects trade in the UK.

Dominant position

14–184 The European Court of Justice has defined a dominant position for the purposes of Art.82 of the EC Treaty as:

> "a position of economic strength enjoyed by an undertaking which enables it to prevent effective competition being maintained on the relevant market by affording it the power to behave to an appreciable extent independently of its competitors and customers, and ultimately of consumers".[49]

Pursuant to s.60 of the 1998 Act,[50] this definition will apply in relation to the Chapter II prohibition. The definition involves two key concepts:

(i) the relevant market; and

(ii) a position of economic strength on that market sufficient to allow an appreciable degree of independence from competitive pressures.

It follows that identification of a dominant position is a two stage process. First, it is necessary to identify the relevant market. Secondly, it is necessary to assess the position of the relevant undertaking on that market.

---

[49] *Michelin v Commission* (Case 322/81) [1983] E.C.R. 3401 at 3503.
[50] See para.14–169 above.

Relevant market

In order to identify the relevant market it is necessary to examine two **14–185** issues:

(i) the range of products or services that compete with those of the relevant undertaking, referred to as the "relevant product market"; and

(ii) the geographic extent of the market for such products, referred to as the "relevant geographic market".

As to these, see the discussion above in relation to EC competition law.

The assessment of dominance

An undertaking may be considered dominant if it has a position of strength **14–186** on the relevant market sufficient to allow it to act independently of competitive pressures to a significant degree. The guidelines on the Chapter II prohibition issued by the OFT[51] identify three potential sources of competitive constraints:

(i) existing competitors;
(ii) potential competitors; and
(iii) other constraints.

An important indicator of the strength of existing competitors on the relevant market is the market shares of the undertaking in question, although, according to the guidelines issued by the OFT, market share is not on its own determinative of the issue of dominance.[52] It is also necessary to consider the market shares of competitors in the relevant market.

If an undertaking controls a very high proportion of a relevant market for a significant time, this may indicate that the undertaking holds a dominant position. The European Court of Justice has held that, in the absence of evidence to the contrary, dominance can be presumed if an undertaking has a market share persistently above 50 per cent. The OFT considers that an undertaking is unlikely to be considered individually dominant if its market share is below 40 per cent, although dominance could be established below that figure if other relevant factors (such as the weak position of competitors in the market) provided strong evidence of dominance.[53]

One of the other main issues in assessing the strength of an undertaking's market position is the potential for new competition to arise as a result of new undertakings entering the market. The importance of such potential competitors is dependent on whether there are barriers that prevent new

---

[51] OFT guidelines: Abuse of a Dominant Position (OFT 402) December 2004.
[52] *ibid.*, para.4.17.
[53] *ibid.*, para.4.18.

entry to the relevant market. The lower the entry barriers, the more likely it is that potential competition will prevent undertakings within a market from sustaining prices above competitive levels. The OFT's guidelines on assessment of market power[54] identify six examples of entry barriers:

(i) sunk costs (i.e. costs which cannot be recovered on exiting a particular market);

(ii) poor access to key inputs and distribution outlets;

(iii) regulation, for example limiting the number of undertakings that can operate in a market;

(iv) economies of scale;

(v) network effects (i.e. where the users' perceived value of the network increases the more users join the network); and

(vi) exclusionary behaviour, such as eliminating competitors through predatory pricing (discussed below).

Consideration will also be given to other factors that might constrain an undertaking's ability to act independently on a market. The principle example is strong buyer power, i.e. the ability of large and powerful customers to constrain an undertaking's behaviour by threatening to terminate their purchases, in particular by switching to alternative suppliers.

Abuse

14–187 In general, abuse falls into one of two categories:

(i) behaviour that reduces competition or restricts its development; and

(ii) behaviour that exploits customers or suppliers.

For a full discussion of abusive behaviour, see the sections above on EC competition law. The following discussion follows in particular the guidelines issued by the OFT on assessing abuse of dominance.[55]

Excessively high prices[56]

14–188 Excessively high prices are the classic example of an abuse that exploits customers. Under Art.82, the European Court of Justice has held that prices may be excessive where they have no reasonable relation to the "economic value" of the relevant product and indicated that this may be assessed by examining prices for comparable products or the cost of supplying the relevant products.[57]

---

[54] OFT guidelines: Assessment of Market Power (OFT 415) December 2004.

[55] OFT guidelines: Assessment of Conduct, currently in draft form (OFT 414a) April 2004.

[56] *ibid.*, paras 2.6–2.20.

[57] *United Brands v Commission* (Case 27/76) [1978] E.C.R. 207 [251] *et seq.* (cost of production); *British Leyland v Commission* (Case 226/84) [1986] E.C.R. 3263 (comparison with equivalent transactions).

In the guidelines on the assessment of conduct that may infringe the Chapter II prohibition, the OFT indicates that it would look for evidence that prices are substantially above those that could exist in a competitive market and that there is no effective competitive pressure to bring them down to competitive levels, nor is there likely to be. Evidence includes comparisons with prices of the same product in other markets, with underlying costs or with prices in another more competitive time period and whether the undertaking is making supra-normal profits.

The guidelines go on to state that where a dominant undertaking's profits significantly and consistently exceed its cost of capital, this may indicate excessive prices. However, the guidelines note that prices and profits which at first sight appear excessive are not necessarily abusive, for example where the undertaking is simply more efficient than its competitors.

The OFT held in *Napp Pharmaceutical Holdings Ltd* that Napp had abused its dominant position in the market for sustained release morphine by supplying the drug to patients in the community at excessively high prices, in some cases more than ten times hospital prices and six times export prices.[58] The OFT fined Napp for the infringement and also gave directions to Napp to regulate the price of the drug supplied to the hospital and community segments of the market. The CAT upheld the OFT's decision on Napp's appeal,[59] stating that in order to show that prices are excessive, it must be demonstrated that (i) prices are higher than would be expected in a competitive market, and (ii) there is no effective competitive pressure to bring them down to competitive levels, nor is there likely to be (for example, high profits stimulating successful new entry within a reasonable period).[60]

Excessive prices were also found by the High Court in the context of a constructive refusal to supply in *Attheraces Ltd v British Horseracing Board*.[61]

Price discrimination[62]

Price discrimination arises where different conditions (in particular different prices) are applied in equivalent transactions. Two basic forms exist: first, where different prices are demanded from customers in similar positions in relation to similar products and secondly, where similar prices are charged despite the fact that the cost of supplying certain customers is much less than that of supplying others. In the OFT's guidelines, the OFT indicates that price discrimination raises complex economic issues and does not constitute an automatic abuse. It must therefore be examined on a case-by-case basis. Discrimination can also occur in relation to non-price issues,

14–189

---

[58] OFT Decision; *Napp Pharmaceutical Holdings Ltd*, March 30, 2001.
[59] *Napp Pharmaceutical Holdings Ltd and subsidiaries v DGFT*, Case No. 1001/1/01, January 15, 2002.
[60] *ibid.*, [390], see also [391], [392] and [400]–[403].
[61] [2005] EWHC 3015(Ch), and see para.14–194 below.
[62] OFT Guidelines on Assessment of Conduct, paras. 3.1–3.10.

such as quality of service. As with price discrimination, it is not necessarily abusive, unless it is exploitative or reduces existing or potential competition. The OFT found in *Napp Pharmaceutical Holdings Ltd* that Napp had discriminated between the hospital and community segments of the market for sustained release morphine by offering discounts of up to 90 per cent when tendering for hospital contracts.[63]

Predatory pricing[64]

14–190   Under Art.82, the European Court of Justice has held that below cost pricing aimed at eliminating a competitor may qualify as an abuse, with pricing below variable cost being considered an automatic abuse and pricing below average total cost an abusive if it can be shown to form part of a plan to eliminate a competitor. In its guidelines on the assessment of conduct, the OFT has indicated that its approach will be similar. This will involve an assessment of whether the undertaking is pricing below cost, its intention or otherwise to eliminate a competitor and the feasibility of recouping the losses incurred. The OFT also held in *Napp Pharmaceutical Holdings Ltd* that Napp was targeting competitors by supplying at higher discounts to hospitals where it faced or anticipated competition or higher discounts for dosage strengths of sustained release morphine where it faced competition.[65] The Competition Appeal Tribunal decision confirmed that Napp had discounted to the extent that it was selling below cost and hence its behaviour was predatory.

Discounts[66]

14–191   Discounts are an important form of price competition. However, certain discounts offered by dominant undertakings can be abusive if they have exclusionary or exploitative effects. The OFT's guidelines on assessing the conduct of dominant undertakings highlights three types of discounts that may be abusive: volume discounts (where the customer's discount increases with the size of its order), fidelity rebates or loyalty discounts (i.e. discounts that are conditional not on the size of an order but on the share of the customer's total needs purchased from the supplier) and multi-product discounts (where a discount on one product is given when purchases of another product are made). In each case, an important consideration is whether the discount is commercially rational only because it has the effect (or likely effect) of foreclosing the market to competitors.

Margin squeeze[67]

14–192   A margin squeeze occurs where a vertically integrated undertaking is dominant in the upstream market for the supply of an input, which is

---

[63] *ibid.*, para.14.188.
[64] *ibid.*, paras 4.1–4.27.
[65] *ibid.*, para.14.188.
[66] *ibid.*, paras 5.1–5.13.
[67] *ibid.*, paras 6.1–6.5.

important for supply in the related downstream market, in which it also operates. If the undertaking then sets such a low margin between the price for the input (the wholesale price) and the price it charges on the downstream market (the retail price) that an efficient operator in the downstream market cannot compete effectively, this constitutes a margin squeeze. If this harms competition, it is likely to be abusive.

Vertical restraints[68]

Vertical restraints are restrictions imposed between undertakings operating at different levels of the production and distribution chain. As discussed, vertical restraints may be excluded from the Chapter I prohibition if they satisfy the conditions set out in the Vertical Agreements Block Exemption (see section 14.6.6 above). However, where they are imposed by a dominant undertaking they may potentially constitute abuses contrary to the Chapter II prohibition. Relevant restraints may include: resale price maintenance, exclusive and selective distribution, exclusive purchasing, tie-in sales, bundling and minimum purchase obligations. In assessing whether a vertical restraint constitutes an abuse, the OFT has indicated that it will examine not what form it takes but what effect it has on competition.[69]

14-193

Refusal to supply and essential facilities[70]

The OFT's guidelines identify two situations in which a refusal to supply might constitute an abuse: first, where a dominant undertaking refuses to supply a new or existing customer without an objective justification; and second, where a dominant undertaking controls an "essential facility", i.e. a facility to which access is necessary in order to supply certain goods or services and which is either impossible or extremely difficult to duplicate for physical, geographic or legal reasons. In practice, essential facilities will be rare.

14-194

The British Horse Racing Board (BHB) was held by the High Court (Etherton J.) to have abused its dominant position in refusing to supply pre-race data to Attheraces (who licensed such data from BHB) other than on objectively unreasonable conditions, i.e. a constructive refusal to supply.[71] The court found that BHB had sought to impose unfair terms, in particular prices, for the supply of the pre-race data that Attheraces required for its business, made threats to bring about an end to the supply of such data without which Attheraces would be eliminated from the market and there was no objective justification for BHB's behaviour. The court held that the prices proposed by BHB were unfair and excessive, becuase BHB's charges were significantly in excess of any justifiable allocation of the cost of pro-

---

[68] *ibid.*, paras 7.1–7.12.
[69] OFT Guidelines: Assessment of Conduct, currently in draft form (OFT 414a) April 2004, para.7.12.
[70] *ibid.*, paras 8.1–8.8.
[71] *Attheraces Ltd v The British Horse Racing Board* [2005] EWHC 3015 (Ch), December 21, 2005; see [247] and [279].

duction and a reasonable return (in effect, the competitive price). Further, BHB's data income in the relevant period covered its costs nearly four times over (i.e. a profit margin of 300 per cent of the cost of maintaining the database).[72]

14.6.8 The Cartel Offence and Disqualification of Directors

14–195 Under the Enterprise Act, anybody (not just directors) found guilty of dishonestly taking part in cartel activity faces up to five years in prison and/ or an unlimited fine. Cartel activity includes price fixing, market sharing and bid-rigging.[73] The OFT can issue no-action letters to individuals who whistleblow on cartels. Certain conditions must be met, including being the first to provide information to the OFT, ceasing all involvement in the cartel, full cooperation with the OFT and not having been a ringleader in the cartel.

Directors can also be disqualified from being a director for up to 15 years where their company has breached UK or EC competition law. This can happen where the director knew about the breach, suspected there was a breach but did nothing to prevent it or did not know about the breach but should have done.[74] In other words, the actual knowledge of the director in question is immaterial. This could potentially be used more often than the cartel offence, as it applies to all breaches of competition law, not just cartel activity. It also reinforces the importance for businesses to have competition compliance policies, to ensure that any anti-competitive behaviour is reported and dealt with correctly.

14.6.9 Enforcement Agencies And Responsibilities

The OFT and other industry regulators

14–196 Primary responsibility for enforcing the 1998 Act rests with the OFT. The OFT has powers to investigate potential infringements of the 1998 Act, to determine whether an infringement has occurred and, in such case, direct that the infringement be brought to an end and to impose penalties.

The OFT is also charged with producing a range of guidelines on the application of the 1998 Act. The guidelines and a large amount of information about the 1998 Act and its application can be found on the OFT website.[75]

Regulators in regulated industries such as telecommunications, water, electricity, gas and the railways are able to exercise the same powers as the

[72] *ibid.*, para.305.
[73] Enterprise Act, s.188 and 190.
[74] Company Directors Disqualification Act 1986, s.9A, as amended under the Enterprise Act.
[75] *http://www.oft.gov.uk.*

OFT in the sectors within their responsibility. In contrast with the situation prior to the 1998 Act, these regulators take the leading role in enforcing competition rules in their sectors. This includes carrying out investigations, dealing with complaints from third parties and imposing penalties.

Since May 1, 2004, both the OFT and the industry regulators are also responsible for enforcing EC competition law in the UK.

The Competition Appeal Tribunal

Appeals from decisions of the OFT and industry regulators under the 1998 **14–197** Act are heard by the Competition Appeal Tribunal (CAT), previously the Competition Commission Appeals Tribunal.

On appeal, the CAT has powers to conduct a complete re-examination of the factual and legal basis of the original decision. Decisions of the CAT may in turn be appealed to the Court of Appeal, but only on points of law and the levels of penalties. The CAT also hears third party damages claims where there has been a decision establishing a breach of UK or EC competition law (discussed below).

Powers of investigation

Under the 1998 Act, the OFT (and industry regulators) enjoy much wider **14–198** powers of investigation than under previous UK competition law statutes. These powers of investigation were also strengthened by the Enterprise Act. First, it is considerably easier for the OFT to initiate investigations, as it needs only "reasonable grounds for suspecting" that an infringement has occurred.

The OFT's principal powers of investigation are:

   (i)   to order the production of relevant documents (excluding privileged communications) or the provision of information[76];
   (ii) to enter business premises without a warrant[77]; and
   (iii) to enter and search business and/or domestic premises with a warrant.[78]

In the case of inspections of premises occupied by a person suspected of infringing the 1998 Act, no notice need be give of the inspection, leaving open the possibility of "dawn raids" of the type conducted by officials of the European Commission. In the course of an inspection, officials may require that:

   (i)   documents be produced;
   (ii) the location of documents be disclosed;
   (iii) an explanation of documents be given;

---

[76] 1998 Act, s.26.
[77] *ibid.*, s.27.
[78] *ibid.*, ss.28 and 28A.

(iv) any information which is stored in any electronic format and is accessible from the premises to be produced in a form that can be read and taken away; and

(v) the premises or any part of the premises be sealed for up to 72 hours.

In general, most inspections are carried out with the consent of the occupier. However, the OFT may apply for a warrant permitting its officers to enter and search premises without consent where they have previously been refused permission to conduct an inspection, where the OFT reasonably suspects that requested documents have not been produced, or where the OFT reasonably suspects that documents might be destroyed to conceal evidence.

Deliberate failure to produce documents requested by the OFT, intentionally obstructing its officers in the course of an inspection, deliberately destroying or disposing of requested documents or falsifying or concealing them and deliberately providing false or misleading information all constitute criminal offences that may be punished by fines and, in certain cases, imprisonment.

Interim measures

14–199 The OFT has powers to order interim measures before completing an investigation if it has a reasonable suspicion that an infringement has occurred and considers it necessary to take urgent action to prevent serious irreparable damage to any person or to protect the public interest.[79]

Fines, commitments and directions to terminate

14–200 If, following an investigation, the OFT determines that an infringement has taken place, it may give directions that appropriate action be taken to terminate the infringement, and impose fines on the undertakings involved.[80]

Directions may be enforced by the OFT by seeking a court order where the relevant undertakings fail to comply.[81] Failure to comply with a court order enforcing a direction will constitute contempt of court and may result in fines or imprisonment.

As an alternative to directions, the OFT has the power to accept commitments from the undertakings involved, instead of issuing a formal infringement decision. These commitments are legally binding and can be enforced by the OFT in the courts if the relevant undertakings fail to comply with them.[82]

Fines may of up to a maximum of 10 per cent of the worldwide turnover

---

[79] ibid., s.35.
[80] ibid., ss.32 and 33.
[81] ibid., s.34.
[82] ibid., s.31E.

of the infringing undertaking may be imposed. The OFT has published guidelines[83] setting out a five-stage process for setting fines, as follows:

(i)   first, a percentage rate based on the seriousness of the infringement will be applied to the annual turnover of the undertaking in the relevant market. The most serious infringements will include price fixing, market sharing and other cartel activities, as well as abuses of dominance that are likely to have a significant impact on the competitive process, such as predatory pricing;

(ii) secondly, the basic amount will be increased to take into account the duration of the infringement by multiplying it by a number equal to or less than the number of years for which the infringement took place;

(iii) thirdly, the amount will be adjusted to take account of policy objectives, such as deterrent effect on third parties, the need to prevent the undertakings profiting from an infringement and the size of the market on which the abuse took place;

(iv) fourthly, the amount will be further adjusted to take account of aggravating or mitigating factors relating to the undertaking's behaviour. These may include whether the undertaking played a leading role in a joint infringement, whether there may have been genuine doubt as to whether certain behaviour was infringing and whether the undertaking had implemented an adequate compliance programme; and

(v)   finally, the fine will be adjusted to ensure that it does not exceed the ceiling of 10 per cent of turnover.

In addition, the OFT will impose reduced fines on cartel "whistleblowers". Whistleblowers may even obtain complete immunity from fines if they are the first to bring a cartel to the attention of the OFT before the OFT has begun an investigation in relation to the cartel. Effective cooperation after that stage may also result in reduced fines.

14.6.10 Small Agreements and Conduct of Minor Importance

Undertakings of a size below certain thresholds will be immune from **14–201** financial penalties (but not other penalties) unless they are involved in price fixing. The immunity can be withdrawn in certain circumstances and does not prevent third parties from making a claim for damages. The relevant turnover thresholds and details of how to calculate turnover are set out in the Competition Act 1998 (Small Agreements and Conduct of Minor Significance) Regulations 2000.[84] The thresholds are:

---

[83] OFT Guidance as to the appropriate amount of a penalty (OFT 423) December 2004.
[84] SI 2000/262.

- *Chapter I*: the annual worldwide turnover of the parties to the agreement must not exceed £20 million;
- *Chapter II*: the annual worldwide turnover of the relevant dominant undertaking must not exceed £50 million.

14.6.11 Enforcement by Private Parties

14–202 The 1998 Act gives no express right of action to parties injured as a result of an infringement of the Chapter I and II prohibitions. During the passage of the 1998 Act through the Houses of Parliament, government representatives stated several times that the government's intention was that, pursuant to s.60, private parties would have a right to sue for damages for breach of the 1998 Act equivalent to that existing in relation to Arts. 81 and 82 of the EC Treaty.

The 1998 Act also provides that the UK courts are required to follow the principles of EC law in respect of "the civil liability of an undertaking for harm caused by its infringement of Community law", meaning that the principles relating to the right to damages will develop in line with EC law. The European Court of Justice has held that undertakings are liable in damages to those who have been affected by their infringements of EC competition law[85] and this principle has now been confirmed by the English courts, although the first award of damages for breach of competition law was subsequently overturned by the House of Lords.[86]

In addition, the Enterprise Act added some new provisions into the 1998 Act, which will make it easier for third parties to successfully claim damages for breaches of EC or UK competition law. First, the CAT now has jurisdiction to hear damages claims from third parties, provided there has been a previous finding of infringement. Secondly, where the OFT (or the CAT on appeal from the OFT) has made a decision finding an infringement of Chapters I or II of the 1998 Act or Arts 81 or 82, EC competition law or the European Commission has found an infringement of Arts 81 or 82, that finding of infringement is binding on the courts (including the CAT) when a third party is suing for damages, provided the decision is no longer capable of being overturned on appeal.[87]

---

[85] *Courage v Crehan* (Case C–453/99) [2001] E.C.R. I–6297.
[86] *Inntrepreneur Pub Company CPC v Creham* [2006] UKHL 38 (July 19, 2006), [2004] EWCA 637. Whilst the House of Lords decision did not affect the principle of awarding damages for infringing restrictions of competition law, it reaffirmed the principle that a judge is entitled to conduct a full assessment of the facts in the absence of an EU decision on the same facts. The High Court was not bound to follow a decision of the European Commission assessing the same market, but covering different subject matter.
[87] 1998 Act, ss.47A and 58A.

14.6.12 Transitional Provisions

Most agreements entered into before March 1, 2000, when the 1998 Act   **14–203**
entered into force, were automatically exempt from the Chapter I prohibition for a one-year transitional period. Exceptions include:

- Agreements that were referred to the Restrictive Practices Court
  before the entry into force of the 1998 Act and are found not to
  operate contrary to the public interest benefit from a five-year period of transitional exemption;
- Agreements that before the entry into force of the 1998 Act fell
  within the scope of an exemption under s.14 of the Resale Prices Act
  also benefit from a five-year period of transitional exemption;
- Void agreements under the RTPA or Resale Prices Act, which do not
  benefit from any transitional period; and
- Agreements made during the three months prior to March 1, 2000
  that were notifiable under the RTPA but were not notified before
  that date, will not benefit from any transitional period.

Pre-existing agreements that were notified under the RTPA but were not
referred to the Restrictive Practices Court pursuant to s.21(2) as their
effects were not significant are excluded from the Chapter I prohibition
until May 2007. Transitional immunity (and the exclusion for s.21(2)
agreements) may be withdrawn by the OFT on an individual basis. No
transitional periods apply in relation to abuse of dominance contrary to the
Chapter II prohibition.

14.6.13 Cases Related to E-commerce Under the 1998 Act

Chapter I cases

There have to date been very few cases relating to the Chapter I prohibition   **14–204**
under the 1998 Act. In *BT/BSkyB broadband promotion*,[88] a complaint
was made to the Office of Telecommunications (OFTEL), the predecessor
of the Office of Communications or "OFCOM", that the joint promotion
by BT and BSkyB of broadband infringed the Chapter I prohibition, as it
had the object or effect of restricting competition within the UK by reinforcing BSkyB's position in the retail pay-TV market and BT's position in
the retail DSL enabled broadband market, the latter by foreclosing competition in the retail broadband market. Under the promotion, BSkyB
customers who subscribed to BT broadband services received special offers.
The agreement between BT and BSkyB was non-exclusive, and so other
companies were not prevented from approaching either BT or BSkyB to

---

[88] Decision of May 15, 2003 in relation to a complaint submitted under the Competition Act
1998 by NTL Group Ltd alleging an infringement by BT Plc.

carry out a similar joint promotion. OFTEl concluded that this non-exclusivity, together with an absence of evidence of material foreclosure of competition, meant that the agreement did not infringe the Chapter I prohibition. The Chapter II prohibition was also considered in this case (see below).

Chapter II cases

14–205 There have been several cases relating to alleged abuses of dominance, mostly relating to the provision of broadband Internet services. The main decisions are discussed below.

Network Multimedia Television Ltd v Jobserve Ltd

14–206 In *Network Multimedia Television Ltd v Jobserve Ltd*,[89] the High Court considered, in a decision relating to an interlocutory injunction, that there was a serious issue to be tried as to whether Jobserve had abused its dominant position in the market for on-line advertising of IT vacancies contrary to the Chapter II prohibition.

The company, an internet job board, accepted postings for vacancies from recruitment agencies in the IT sector, amongst other sectors. Network Multimedia Television (NMTV) were starting a competing service, ATS-COjobs.com, but Jobserve had made it clear to IT recruitment agencies that if they placed vacancies on the NMTV site their business would not be accepted by Jobserve. NMTV produced evidence that in that case a large amount of their business would disappear, because recruiters felt that they needed to use Jobserve, due to the large number of quality candidates that used the site. The court considered that there was a serious issue to be tried both in respect of Jobserve's dominance in the relevant service market, and as to whether its behaviour constituted an abuse. This case was settled before the main action came to trial.

BT Surf Together and BT Talk & Surf Together pricing packages

14–207 In its decision of May 4, 2001, in *BT Surf Together and BT Talk & Surf Together pricing packages*,[90] the Director General of Telecommunications investigated under the 1998 Act the pricing of two new tariff packages for residential customers that BT introduced on December 1, 2000: BT Surf Together and BT Talk & Surf Together. The Director was concerned that the "Surf" element of the packages (offering off-peak internet access calls on an unmetered basis) was being provided below cost and that BT was funding the shortfall from profits on local and national residential voice calls in which it appeared to the Director that BT was dominant, or wholesale call origination in which BT is dominant. Such behaviour could be an attempt to leverage market power horizontally (from residential voice

---

[89] [2001] U.K.C.L.R. 814.
[90] Decision of May 4, 2001 in relation to the investigation into the BT SurfTogether and BT Talk and SurfTogether Pricing Packages.

calls) and/or vertically (from wholesale call origination) into either retail internet access or wholesale termination of calls to Internet Service Providers. The Director suspected that this could have materially anti-competitive effects.

In the decision, the Director concluded that there was a retail market for retail internet access which was a national UK market, and that there was a wholesale market for call origination on fixed networks, which might or might not be divided into residential and business markets (it was unnecessary to decide), and which was also national. The Director concluded that BT was dominant in the market for wholesale call origination on fixed telecommunications networks in the UK. BT was also found to be dominant in the markets for local and national retail voice calls by residential customers on fixed telecommunications networks in the UK.

The Director concluded, however, that it was not proven that, at the current prices, BT was pricing or would price "Surf" below cost in the new packages. Furthermore, the Director considered it unlikely that, even if the prices were below cost, a material anti-competitive effect would result on the current prices, because of the presence of competing, sustainable 24/7 retail internet access packages. Consequently, the Director did not consider that BT's pricing of the packages constituted an infringement of the Chapter II prohibition.

BT's wholesale DSL services

The Director has also investigated BT's terms and conditions for wholesale DSL products.[91] The Director was concerned that these terms and conditions (which did not include any service level agreements or service level guarantees) and the levels of service were so unreasonable as to amount to an abuse of a dominant position, in particular because at the time of the investigation, service providers had nowhere else to go for the provision of wholesale xDSL services. BT could therefore force service providers to accept terms and conditions that they might not otherwise have accepted. However, there was insufficient evidence of a material effect on competition as there were other factors which had an effect on service providers, such as BT's capacity and rollout-out capability relative to demand. There was therefore no infringement of the 1998 Act.

The Director has also considered BT's pricing for its wholesale DSL products, in particular whether it involved any predatory pricing.[92] As the provision of telecommunications services is characterised by high levels of capital costs, the Director took the view that the appropriate cost base against which BT's prices should be assessed was the long run incremental cost measure (LRIC). This measure takes into account the total long run capital and operating costs of supplying a specified additional unit of out-

14–208

---

[91] Decision of January 24, 2002 in relation to a complaint under the Competition Act 1998 by the DSL Wholesale Products Industry Group alleging an infringement by BT Plc.

[92] Decision of March 28, 2002 in relation to an investigation to examine whether BT Plc has engaged in anti-competitive pricing in relation to its wholesale DSL products.

put (the increment). The Director did not consider BT had priced its products below LRIC. However, as it is possible for a dominant firm to price above LRIC and still engage in predatory pricing, he had to consider whether there was an intention to eliminate a competitor. In this case, although BT was aware of the threat from its competitors and was keen to ensure its prices were competitive, the Director found no evidence that BT had deliberately priced its products so as to drive this competition out of the market. In particular, some price cuts were aimed at stimulating demand as part of a genuine promotion, and they were offered across a range of products, rather than being limited to a particular product. There was therefore no infringement of the Chapter II prohibition.

The Director also considered whether there was any cross-subsidisation occurring, which can be an abuse of dominance where a dominant entity takes revenues from the market in which it is dominant to subsidise losses in another market. If the revenue generated by a particular service over its lifetime exceeds LRIC, the service is sustainable over the long term and so will not be receiving any cross-subsidy. As the combined revenue of the products in question was not lower than the LRIC of the combination, there was no unfair cross subsidy in operation.

BT's broadband marketing

14–209   Following a complaint by the Internet Service Provider Freeserve.com (now Wanadoo), the Director carried out an investigation into certain pricing policies by BT Openworld (the retail internet business of BT) in relation to its consumer broadband activities.[93] The Director issued his decision on November 20, 2003. Freeserve had alleged that BT was using predatory pricing and unfair cross-subsidisation between BT and BT Openworld. The Director considered these issues in the framework of a margin squeeze (as Freeserve was concerned with BT Openworld's retail price, as compared to BT's upstream wholesale charges) and set out the following questions to be answered:

- Is the firm dominant in the relevant upstream market?
- Is the firm conducting a margin squeeze, i.e. is the margin between downstream and upstream prices insufficient to cover its downstream costs (if it paid the same wholesale charges as its competitors)?
- Is there a material adverse effect on competition in the downstream market?

---

[93] Decision published on December 19, 2003 in relation to an investigation into alleged anti-competitive practices by BT Plc in relation to BT Openworld's consumer broadband products. The Director General had previously issued a decision rejecting Freeserve's complaint in May 2002. Freeserve appealed this decision to the Competition Commission Appeal Tribunal (now the Competition Appeal Tribunal), which set aside the Director General's decision for lack of reasoning in relation to BT Openworld's consumer broadband pricing policies and sent it back to OFTEL for reconsideration.

The Director did not reach a conclusion in relation to the first question, as he found that the margin between BT's residential broadband wholesale and retail prices was sufficient to allow an equally efficient operator to compete effectively with BT Openworld's consumer broadband services, by reference to BT's own costs. He also found that there was no material adverse effect on competition caused by BT Openworld's residential broadband pricing policies, as evidenced by BT Openworld's declining market share, significant market entry and competitors consistently setting prices below those of BT Openworld. There was therefore no infringement of the Chapter II prohibition. Wanadoo is appealing this decision to the Competition Appeal Tribunal.[94]

BT Broadband

Freeserve made a second complaint to the Director in October 2002 that BT **14–210** was leveraging its dominant position in the markets for residential retail voice telephony into the residential retail broadband market. In particular, BT was using customer billing information, which it alone has access to, by virtue of its dominance in the provision of residential local and national voice calls, to specifically target consumers for its internet services. This was achieved by "bundling" promotional material for its BT Broadband product with its "blue bill" retail voice telephony bill. Freeserve also complained that BT was using the "blue bill" to offer joint billing for telephony and Internet services and that it was using its customer service line to market BT Broadband. Freeserve argued that this gave BT an advantage that was unmatchable by any competitor in the broadband market.

The Director set out a three-step test for analysing BT's conduct[95]:

- Is BT dominant in the voice telephony markets? The Director concluded that BT was dominant in the voice telephony markets for local and national calls made by residential customers.
- Is there the ability to leverage from the dominant market into a closely related second market? The Director concluded that there was a sufficiently close relationship between the voice telephony markets and the broadband market (the market on which the abuse occurred) for conduct in the first market to affect competition in the second market.
- Has leveraging occurred? This is assessed by considering whether

---

[94] Following this decision, OFCOM announced on February 18, 2004, that it is resuming its investigation into whether BT's current pricing policies for residential broadband since May 2002 infringe Ch.II by constituting a margin squeeze. The investigation has subsequently been extended to consider a possible breach of Art.82 and to cover all of BT's residential broadband products including one released after the date the investigation began. At the time of writing, OFCOM has sent BT three statements of objections, the third being sent on October 25, 2006.

[95] Decision of July 11, 2003 in relation to an investigation into alleged anti-competitive practices by BT Plc in relation to its BT Broadband products.

the advantages are unmatchable by competitors; whether there is an impact on competition (rather than just competitors); and if so, whether this impact is material and adverse.

The Director concluded that BT's use of its "blue bill" and customer service line for marketing and joint billing did not give it an unmatchable advantage over its competitors, as efficient ISPs should be able to compete with this (based on the conclusion that the appropriate group of customers is narrowband internet users, rather than BT's entire telephony customer base).

Furthermore, as the amount of consumers taking up BT Broadband as a result of the marketing was fairly low, this suggested that competitors could use more effective alternative marketing methods. In relation to the use of BT's customer support number, although competitors could not match the number of consumers calling BT each month, the evidence did not suggest that this resulted in a material adverse effect on competition, given that the take-up figure was sufficiently low for the effect on competition and competitors to be negligible.

Finally, the Director concluded that although the joint billing for retail telephony and broadband services may be attractive to some customers, competitors could offer alternatives which are either substantially the same or which are not perceived by customers to be less satisfactory, and so this did not constitute an unmatchable advantage to BT. Even if the advantages were unmatchable, the Director found no evidence that joint billing had a material adverse effect on customers, as very few customers would be prepared to pay more for this benefit and, in most cases, it was not the reason they had chosen their preferred service. There was therefore no infringement of the Chapter II prohibition.

BT Totalcare

14–211 In October 2002, Energis, a provider of telecoms and internet services, made a complaint to OFTEL against BT regarding its IPStream ASDL broadband product, which it sells to ISPs and corporate customers. BT offered this product on a trial basis with its TotalCare product, which is a form of maintenance programme offered by BT that deals with system faults. Energis participated in this trial. Its package included a target resolution time for faults of 24 hours.

In its complaint, Energis alleged that one of BT's service divisions, BT Ignite Solutions (BTIS), was offering the IPStream product to a retail client on terms which included a guaranteed repair time of five hours for faults. These were better terms than BT was offering to wholesale purchasers of IPStream, where the general contract offered a resolution time of 17 hours. Energis argued that this repair time could only be offered if BTIS was receiving wholesale terms from BT preferential to those it was receiving itself.

The Director was concerned[96] that BT could be leveraging its potentially dominant position in the markets for asymmetric broadband origination and broadband conveyance downstream onto the retail market (where Energis also operates) by acting in a discriminatory way. The Director did not reach any conclusion on whether BT was dominant in the market. However, upon investigation, BT confirmed that BTIS received IPStream from BT Wholesale on the same terms as the standard contract (i.e. with a resolution time of 17 hours). It was found that BTIS had undertaken a risk analysis, in order to access the potential financial exposure which might arise from offering better terms at the retail level than it was receiving at the wholesale level. It was therefore a commercial decision for BTIS to sell the IPStream Totalcare package on better terms than it received from BT Wholesale. This option was also in theory open to Energis and its other competitors. The Director therefore concluded that BT had not infringed the Chapter II prohibition.

BT/BSkyB Broadband Promotion

NTL, a cable operator which provides telephony, broadband internet access and pay-TV services, made a complaint to OFTEL about a joint promotion between BSkyB and BT, where BSkyB customers who subscribed to BT broadband services received special offers. NTL claimed that BT was dominant in the market for residential telephony and it was abusing this dominance by discriminating in favour of those of its subscribers who were prospective customers of BT's competitors. NTL also alleged that BT was leveraging this dominant position in the residential telephony market into retail broadband access services.

14–212

The Director did not reach any definite conclusions on the relevant markets and whether or not BT was dominant in these markets.[97] In relation to the alleged leveraging, the Director found that there was no evidence that BT was offering the broadband services on offer below cost or that it was subsidising its offer in any way that could be seen as abusive cross-subsidisation or predatory pricing.

As regards the alleged discriminatory pricing, the Director did consider that the promotion was aimed at retail customers who may seek substitute suppliers of combined telephone, pay-TV and broadband internet access services. As these customers were able to benefit from the promotion and so receive better terms than were generally available, BT was engaging in price discrimination in favour of those of its customers who were also BSkyB customers. However, there was no evidence that the promotion would have a material effect on competition as the proportion of customers who had

---

[96] Decision of May 28, 2003 in relation to a complaint considered under the Competition Act 1998 by CA Networks Ltd relating to a possible infringement by BT Plc.

[97] Decision of May 15, 2003 in relation to a complaint submitted under the Competition Act 1998 by NTL Group Ltd alleging an infringement by BT Plc relating to BT's broadband promotion in conjunction with BSkyB.

taken up or were predicted to take up the offer was low. There was therefore no infringement of the Chapter II prohibition.

Online property search companies

14–213 The National Land Information Service (NLIS) is an on-line conveyancing service, which provides electronic access to data held by local authorities and other bodies relating to land and property in England and Wales. It was set up by the Local Government Information House (LGIH), who granted a licence to MacDonald Dettwiler (Hub) Ltd (MDHL) to operate as the "hub" of the NLIS system, i.e. to operate at the wholesale level between the local authorities and the channel operators.

Various companies were granted licences by LGIH to act as retail channel operators for NLIS, including MacDonald Dettwiler (Channel) Ltd, trading as Transaction on-line (TOL). TOL and MDHL are both wholly-owned subsidiaries of MacDonald Dettwiler Ltd. The other two channel operators are TM Property and Services Ltd (TM) and the Conveyancing Channel Ltd (trading as Searchflow). The channel operators are required to source all local authority information from MDHL.

TM complained to the OFT, alleging that it was the victim of three abuses:

(1) predatory pricing, in that TOL was pricing a particular land search below average variable cost;
(2) margin squeeze, in that the level of the wholesale price charged by MDHL and TOL's aggressive pricing strategy meant that the other channel operators could not make a reasonable return; and
(3) excessive pricing, in that MDHL was raising its wholesale prices for providing information to retail operators to excessive levels.

In essence, TM alleged that MDHL and TOL together operate as a vertically integrated operator with the intention of forcing TM out of the on-line market for property searches.

As well as NLIS, there are two other property search methods available: official postal searches obtained directly from the relevant local authority and personal search companies, who personally visit the relevant local authority and search the public records to obtain the required information.

After carrying out a qualitative assessment, the OFT concluded[98] that the on-line property search market could not be considered as a separate product market. The alternative search methods are able to replicate the information provided in an NLIS report and, although NLIS offers additional functionality, such as on-line administration and quicker responses, this is currently not sufficient to delineate a separate on-line market (although the OFT did note that this could be the case in the future).

---

[98] OFT decision of August 18, 2004 in relation to TM Property Service Ltd's complaint against MacDonald Dettwiler (Hub) Ltd and MacDonald Dettwiler (Channel) Ltd (trading as Transaction Online).

Consequently, if the property search market was taken as a whole, neither TOL (at the retail level) nor MDHL (at the wholesale level) could be considered as being dominant and therefore there could be no finding of infringement of the Chapter II prohibition.

Despite this, the OFT did still conduct a preliminary assessment of the alleged abusive conduct. With regard to predatory pricing, it found that TOL had been charging below average variable cost for certain searches. However, the OFT considered that this could be objectively justified as TOL had been using these searches as loss leaders to obtain higher revenues from the sale of complementary services. As there was no evidence that this behaviour was intended to eliminate competitors, it was not considered as predatory.

In relation to the margin squeeze, the OFT concluded that TOL would be able to operate profitably on the basis of the wholesale prices charged by MDHL and so there was no evidence of a margin squeeze. Finally, the OFT found no evidence that MDHL had artificially inflated its costs in order to increase its prices to excessive levels.

Although the OFT found no infringement in this case, it did state in its press release that the market required further investigation, as there had been a number of complaints in relation to the workings of the property search market, in particular difficulties in accessing information from the relevant holders of the information.

This investigation was launched by the OFT in December 2004 and **14–214** completed in September 2005.[99] In relation to the NLIS system, the OFT highlighted a number of restrictions that may affect future competition, as electronic searches become more widely used. For example, NLIS is the only source of compiled electronic property searches and local authorities can only provide electronic searches through NLIS. Furthermore, only three retail channel operator licences have been granted and the maximum number of channel operators is set at four.

The OFT therefore recommended that LGIH should remove all exclusivity provisions in the agreements governing the NLIS system and it should remove the limits on the number of hub and channel licences that can be granted and instead set objective criteria to be met by potential licensees. It should also help local authorities and the NLIS hub to set objective criteria necessary to enable new electronic connections with retailers outside the NLIS system to be established. These recommendations were expressly intended to allow for greater consumer choice and competition in this innovative part of the property search market.

Following the OFT's report, the Department of Trade and Industry announced in December 2005 in its response to the report that it was accepting the OFT's recommendations, including those relating to the removal of the exclusivity provisions from the hub and channel licences.

---

[99] OFT Report dated September 2005, Property Searches—A Market Study.

BT: ISP margin squeeze

14–215 In a case opened on July 18, 2003, OFCOM investigated[1] a suspected margin squeeze by BT in relation to the lowering of its retail prices for the 0845 and 0870 number ranges, which were implemented on June 1, 2003.

Some ISPs use these numbers to provide narrowband metered dial-up internet access. To do so, these ISPs purchase number translation services (NTS) call origination services and internet termination services from BT. In providing NTS call origination services, BT retains part of the price of call origination and passes the residual revenue to the terminating provider (called NTS outpayments).

The effect of BT's price reductions was to reduce the NTS outpayments made by BT to itself and other providers for terminating internet dial-up calls using those numbers. As the purchase of termination services by ISPs includes a revenue sharing arrangement with the provider of these services, BT's price reductions resulted in a reduction to the revenue received by ISPs who purchase termination services from BT.

Various ISPs complained to OFCOM that there was insufficient margin after the price change to allow them profitably to provide narrowband metered internet services and that BT was abusing its dominance in the upstream market for call origination with the aim of excluding others from the downstream market of narrowband metered internet access.

BT supplies wholesale inputs (where it is believed to be dominant) to downstream ISPs for the provision of narrowband metered internet access. However, BT also competes in the downstream narrowband metered internet access market as it supplies its own ISP. Due to BT's dominance in the upstream market, OFCOM was concerned that the reductions in NTS outpayments to ISPs might have the effect of imposing a margin squeeze on its competitors in downstream markets, by effectively increasing the cost of the upstream input.

OFCOM concluded, on August 19, 2004, that there was no abuse of any dominant position. To reach this decision, it assessed whether, on the basis of BT's own retail costs, BT would be profitable in the downstream market if it incurred the same upstream input prices as it charged to its downstream competitors, otherwise known as the "equally efficient operator" test. This involved assessing three elements:

(1) the wholesale upstream input prices BT charged to its competitors for narrowband metered Internet terminations (including the wholesale input price charged by BT for call origination on fixed public narrowband networks);

(2) the revenues BT received from the (downstream) supply of narrowband metered Internet access; and

---

[1] OFCOM decision of August 19, 2004 in relation to BT 0845 and 0870 retail price change suspected ISP margin squeeze.

(3) BT's downstream costs of supplying narrowband metered internet access.

OFCOM used return on turnover as a proxy for measuring BT's profitability, rather than return on capital employed (due to the low levels of fixed capital and the fact that many of the input services used by BT were bought-in). OFCOM then compared BT's margins with those of certain other ISPs as shown by their costs data, and found them to be in line with each other.

OFCOM concluded that, during the period of the alleged infringement, BT's narrowband metered internet access business had remained profitable by reference to the comparators used by OFCOM. There was therefore no evidence of a margin squeeze between the wholesale input price that rival ISPs were required to pay and BT's retail prices in the downstream market for narrowband metered internet access.

Technical Glossary

ActiveX	See **Java**
Access provider	A person who provides others with access to the internet.
Address, IP	See **IP address**
ADSL	Asymmetric Digital Subscriber Line. A method of compressing data to provide a high **bandwidth** connection in one direction on ordinary copper telephone lines. The fact that there is only low **bandwidth** in the opposite direction is not a hindrance if that is used for user commands and requests. The family of related technologies is known as **DSL** or xDSL.
Ajax	Asynchronous **Java** and XML. A web programming technique designed to reduce page refreshes and thus minimise the amount of data exchanged between browser and **website**.
Appropriate Use Policy	Some non-commercial or government-funded networks connected to the internet prohibit some types of traffic across their networks. The rules of such a network are its Appropriate Use Policy.
Bandwidth	A term used to describe the capacity of a communications link.
Broadband	High **bandwidth** connection, originally based on optical fibre infrastructure but now also encompassing cable, **DSL**, wireless, mobile telephony and satellite delivery channels, suitable for transmitting video and other such high volume data.
Cache	An electronic store of data copied from elsewhere; also the function of providing a cache. Caches come in many forms. They may be large scale, more or less permanent collections of, typically, **web** pages. These reduce

demands on network communications capacity by providing access to the data locally. Or they may be smaller, ever changing, collections of data maintained for similar reasons and changing in response to user demand. On the smallest scale a **web browser** may cache pages and graphics on the hard disk of the user's personal computer in order to speed up access to **websites.**

CGI Common Gateway Interface. A program standard that enables **HTTP** requests to be executed by internal programs such as databases, and the results to be passed back to the external user.

Client The client, in the context of the internet, is the user's computer (or strictly speaking, the browser or similar software on the user's computer). The client complements the **server,** with which it communicates. Web designers may make design decisions as to whether processing takes place at the client or the **server.** *cf.* **DHTML** and **Ajax.**

Conduit A term used to describe the function of providing telecommunications links. A conduit should be contrasted with, in particular, the function of a **host.**

DHTML Dynamic **HTML.** Use of DHTML allows changes to appear on a Web page, for instance in response to a mouse movement over a menu, processed entirely within the user's computer. This **client**-side approach, rather than processing the changes on the **server,** means that the changes occur without the need for the server to deliver a new page. DHTML is commonly implemented using a language such as **JavaScript,** in combination with ordinary **HTML** and features such as Cascading Style Sheets.

Digital signature A type of **electronic signature** utilising technology designed to ensure that the device generating the signature and the document intended to be signed can reliably and uniquely be identified.

Domain name A name (e.g. twobirds.com) allocated to an entity with an address on a network. On the internet a domain name corresponds to an entity with an **IP address.**

Download The act of retrieving data from a remote site across a communications link to the user's computer. Download is sometimes used to mean retrieving data to the com-

1256

puter's RAM, and sometimes to mean retrieving the data and storing it on the computer's hard disk.

DNS Domain Name Server. A computer which maintains a list of **domain names** and corresponding **IP addresses**. On receipt of a request from another computer it will deliver the **IP address** corresponding to the requested domain name if it has an authoritative list for that domain name. Otherwise it will refer to the request elsewhere in the DNS system until a computer is found which can give an authoritative response.

DSL See ADSL.

EDI Electronic Data Interchange. A generic description applied to systems whereby parties create legal and technical arrangements governing the exchange of electronic data between them. The data is typically structured rather than free form. EDI arrangements are appropriate where parties have a continuing relationship with each other.

Electronic signature A signature in electronic form.

Extranet An **intranet** to which selected outsiders, such as customers or suppliers, are allowed access.

Firewall A device situated at the entry to a computer network, designed to prevent unauthorised data entering the network.

Ftp File transfer protocol. The most common means of transmitting a file (which could be a program or data file) across the internet.

GII Global Information Infrastructure. A term formerly used by American politicians to describe their vision of a worldwide **information superhighway**.

Host In the context of the internet, a host is a computer which stores information in more than transient form and makes it available across the internet. The stored data may vary from **Usenet newsgroups**, to **websites**, to **domain name** databases, to **ftp** resources and many other types. "Host" is often also used to mean the person who owns and operates the computer and who thus carries out the host function. A host should be contrasted, in particular, with a **conduit**.

HTML HyperText Markup Language. A system of additions to plain text which act as instructions to **web browsers** or

1257

other HTML-compliant programs. The **browser** acting on the instructions will convert the marked up text into formatted pages including **hypertext** links.

HTTP　　　　　HyperText Transmission Protocol. The internet protocol which enables the transmission of an **HTML** document across the internet.

Hypertext　　　A hypertext document includes highlighted text which, when clicked upon with a mouse, causes the user to jump to another place in the same document, to another document on the same computer, or (if **HTML** is used on a network with **HTTP**-compliant computers), to a document on another computer altogether. On the internet hypertext links can exist between documents on computers anywhere in the world.

IANA　　　　　The Internet Assigned Numbers Authority (now part of **ICANN**).

ICANN　　　　The Internet Corporation for Assigned Names and Numbers. This is the body now charged with responsibility for co-ordinating policy on internet domain name and number allocation.

Information　　A term formerly used, mainly by politicians, to describe
Superhighway　their vision of a pervasive, probably **broadband**, data network. See also **GII**.

internet service　An internet service provider is a generic term which
provider　　　covers a wide variety of persons providing services relating to the internet. At a minimum an **ISP** will be an **access provider**. It will provide **DNS** services and will probably host **newsgroups** and provide **web** hosting services. It may own or lease its own physical network infrastructure, or it may simply connect up to the network of a larger **ISP**. It may provide **web** design services. Some ISPs, especially those which originated as proprietary on-line services, may source and publicise their own content, making it available as web pages, as e-mail services or as content "pushed" across the network to the subscriber's **web browser** or other internet device.

Intranet　　　An internal network based on internet protocols. An intranet may be geographically dispersed, for instance across different members of a group of companies, but still be insulated by **firewalls** from the outside world.

IP address　　The address of an device on a **TCP/IP** network understood by other computers on the network. The address in its current version (IPv4) takes the form 194.72.244.100, where each component of the IP address is a number below 256. On the internet the ultimate authority for allocating IP address ranges is **IANA**, the Internet Assigned Numbers Authority.

IPv6   The forthcoming new version of **IP addressing** in which each address has a 128 bit form consisting of eight hexadecimal 16 bit blocks with colon separators. An example of an IPv6 address would be 3ffe:ffff:0100:f101:0210:a4ff:fee3:9566.

ISDN   Integrated Services Digital Network. A telephony standard designed to deliver medium **bandwidth** digital voice and data. After a slow start, ISDN became more popular for internet connections where more than the capacity of a dial-up modem connection is required but the expense of a leased line connection cannot be justified. It has now been overtaken by **ADSL** for domestic connections.

ISP   Internet Service Provider

Java   A programming language originating from Sun Microsystems designed to be usable across many different types of computer and operating system. Many **websites** now employ small programs ("applets") written in Java, which are downloaded to the user's computer when he accesses the site. These applets may perform functions such as animating parts of the **website**, or providing more sophisticated user interfaces than can readily be built using **HTML**. Another technology capable of performing similar functions on Windows-based systems is **ActiveX** from Microsoft.

JavaScript   A language in which a **web** page can be written and which a **web browser** will interpret to display the page. It is a sophisticated alternative to **HTML**, but which unlike **Java** does not require the user's computer to download a separate program from the **website**.

Listserver   A **mailing list**

Mailing list   An e-mail based equivalent of a **newsgroup**, in which contributions are sent by e-mail to a central list manager, which forwards them to all subscribers to the mailing list.

Metatag   A keyword within the META section of a **web** page. Although not visible to the user in normal use, metatags may be viewed with a browser in "Source" mode.

Mirror site	A site providing a duplicate of the original site, or part of it. Software companies which provide programs for users to download often arrange for mirror sites around the world, both to reduce the demand on the original site and to reduce the strain on network **bandwidth**. A person whose site is being blocked by the authorities may sometimes respond by asking other sites to mirror the content.
MP3	A compressed file format mainly used for storing music.
Newsgroup	A public discussion forum on the internet, named according to its intended content (e.g. "alt.uk.legal"). Access to newsgroups was originally provided by special news software, but typically the necessary facilities are now included in **web browsers**. Although newsgroups represent only one type of content on the internet (**websites** and **ftp** resources are others), in the early days of the internet they attracted disproportionate publicity. This is because of the explicit names of and notoriety of type of content posted to some newsgroups.
Peering agreement	An agreement between two or more access providers under which they will exchange internet traffic across a connection between their networks. Peering agreements differ from conventional telephony interconnect or transit agreements, which charge for network access on a metered traffic basis. A true peering agreement is on a free exchange basis.
P2P	Peer to peer. A scheme whereby individual users can upload and download files to each other without the need for the files to be stored on a central **server** (hence "filesharing"). Peer to peer protocols come in many flavours. The newest generation coordinate the simultaneous upload/download of file fragments rather than whole files. This results in higher speeds and renders feasible the sharing of video files.
Peer to peer	See P2P.
POP	Point of Presence. A point at which a user can connect to an **ISP**'s network and thereby gain access to the internet.
Post	Send a public message ("article") to a **newsgroup**.
Public key encryption	A cryptographic technique that relies on asymmetric mathematical algorithms. So while one cryptographic key (the public key) can easily be derived from the other

(the private key), the reverse cannot be achieved without unfeasibly large amounts of computing power (so long as the key is sufficiently long). Used to create **digital signatures**.

Router — A specially designed computer which examines incoming **TCP/IP** data packets for destination information and relays the packets to the next appropriate router on the way to the destination. If the link to the next most appropriate router is unavailable, the router will choose another link. This ability was originally a fundamental part of the design of the internet, which was built to withstand damage to components of the network. The same ability now makes it very difficult to isolate parts of the network and gave rise to John Gilmore's aphorism "the internet treats censorship as damage and routes around it".

Search engine — A **website** that indexes other **websites** and allows users to search their contents. A search engine typically creates a full text index of other **websites** and also presents a short contextual abstract of the target page.

Server — Strictly, a server is a piece of software which delivers data from the computer on which it resides across the network in response to requests from elsewhere. Thus a **web** server delivers web pages, a **domain name** server delivers **IP addresses** in response to **domain name** requests, and so on. The term server is often used to denote the computer itself as well as the software.

Spider — A program that visits **websites** in sequence according to a pre-determined algorithm, collecting information from the sites. **Search engines** employ spiders to index **websites**. Also known as **web crawlers**.

TCP — Transmission Control Protocol. See **TCP/IP**.

TCP/IP — Transmission Control Protocol/Internet Protocol. The set of standards that govern how computers communicate with each other across the internet. The Internet Protocol is the lower-level aspect of TCP/IP, setting out how devices on a network recognise each other by means of an **IP address** and communicate and route using data packets. TCP governs how data messages are broken up into IP packets and reassembled and verified at the destination. Although TCP is used to control most messaging across an IP network, alternatives such as **UDP** can also be used.

UDP	User Datagram Protocol.
User Datagram Protocol	An alternative messaging protocol to **TCP**. Because UDP, unlike TCP, does not contain its own verification mechanism it is faster than TCP and thus more suited to the transmission of real-time messages.
Usenet	Usenet is a method of distributing postings to **newsgroups**. It does not in fact require the internet in order to function. Usenet was originally a method of distributing news from one computer to another, whereby each computer periodically dialled up another in the Usenet chain and updated its own **newsgroups** from that computer. The computers did not have to use internet protocols when communicating with each other. Usenet is now mostly distributed by transmissions from computer to computer across the internet, so that that Usenet is now generally perceived to be part of the internet.
URL	Uniform Resource Locator. The address of a **website**, e.g. "*http://www.twobirds.com*", or of a page within a **website**.
VoIP	Voice over IP. The transmission of voice calls over a network utilising internet protocols.
Web	See World Wide Web
Web browser	Client software used to access and read **web** pages. The best known browsers were originally Netscape and Internet Explorer.
Web crawler	See **Spider**.
Website	A cohesive collection of **web** pages, usually maintained by or on behalf one entity (e.g. an individual or a company), stored on a **host**.
World Wide Web	The web is the global collection of **hypertext** linked HTML pages linked which a user equipped with a **web browser** can view and browse.

Index